myeconlab

Get Ahead of the Curve

P9-APJ-573

Problem Solving for Students.

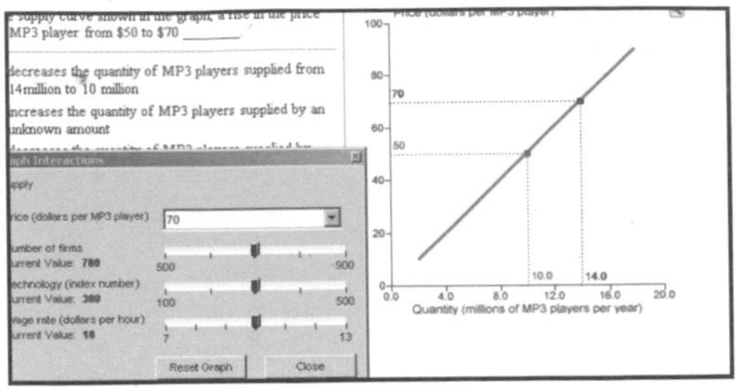

Automatically graded assignments (and the ability to get the highest possible grade by reworking the same assignments with new problems) motivate students to solve a lot more problems.

Instant feedback, including detailed tutorial instruction (complete solutions, step-by-step explanations, links to book material, etc.), provides instant gratification and immediate learning.

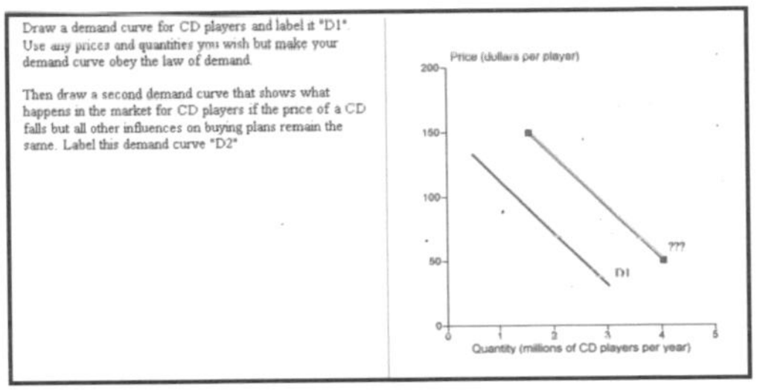

Graphing tools and questions integrated into assignments enable students to manipulate and even draw graphs that are automatically graded.

Solving Problems for Professors.

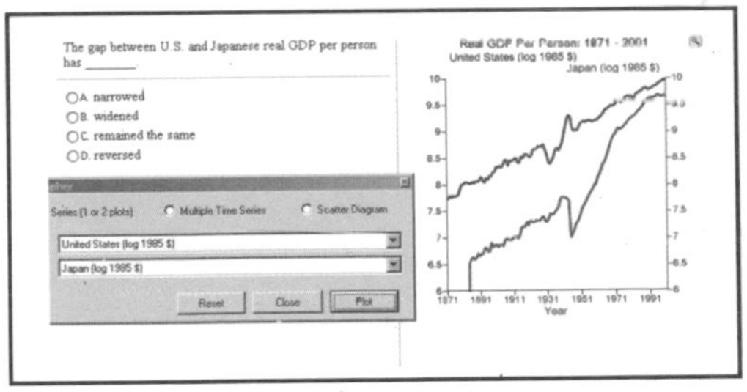

Easily create, assign, and automatically grade homework, quizzes, and tests.

Assign problems and exercises based on the actual end-of-chapter materials in the text book. Many have algorithmic versions for variety and extra practice.

Track students' progress through one easy-to-view, automatically populated grade book.

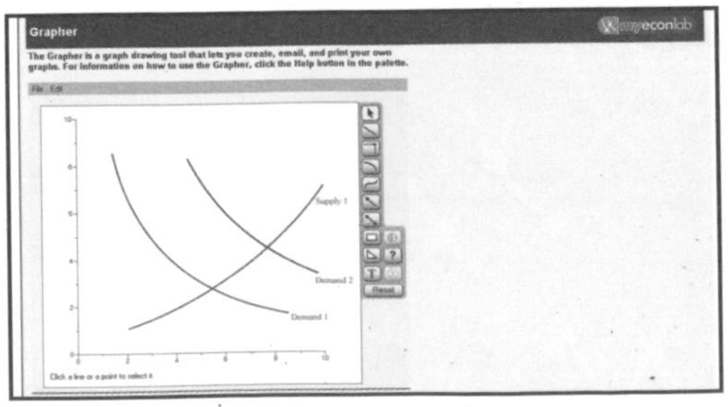

Get supplementary problems and teaching resources (like test banks and lecture slides) all in one place.

These features, plus personalized study plans for students, full etext options, practice tests, eStudy guides, and more, are all available in MyEconLab.

www.myeconlab.com

macroeconomics

R. Glenn Hubbard
Columbia University

Anthony Patrick O'Brien
Lehigh University

PEARSON
Prentice Hall
Upper Saddle River, New Jersey 07458

Library of Congress Cataloging-in-Publication Data

Hubbard, R. Glenn.
Macroeconomics / R. Glenn Hubbard, Anthony Patrick O'Brien.—1st ed.
p. cm.
Includes bibliographical references and index.
ISBN 0-13-034825-2
1. Macroeconomics. I. O'Brien, Anthony Patrick. II. Title.
HB172.5.H86 2006
339—dc22

2005032633

Executive Editor: David Alexander
Developmental Editor: Lena Buonanno
Executive Marketing Manager: Sharon M. Koch
Market Development Manager: Kathleen McLellan
Director, Key Markets: David Theisen
Editorial Director: Jeff Shelstad
Acquisitions Editor: Jon Axelrod
Director of Development: Steve Deitmer
Project Manager, Editorial: Francesca Calogero
Editorial Assistant: Michael Dittamo
Media Project Manager: Peter Snell
Media Product Development Manager: Nancy Welcher
Director of Marketing: Eric Frank
Marketing Assistant: Tina Panagiotou
Director of Market Development: Annie Todd
Associate Director, Production Editorial: Judy Leale
Senior Managing Editor: Cynthia Regan
Production Editor: Michael Reynolds
Permissions Supervisor: Charles Morris
Production Manager, Manufacturing: Arnold Vila
Creative Director: Maria Lange
Art Director: Pat Smythe
Interior Design: Liz Harasymczuk
Cover Design: Pat Smythe
Illustrator, Interior: ElectraGraphics, Inc.
Infographics: Ray Cruz
Director, Image Resource Center: Melinda Reo
Manager, Rights and Permissions: Zina Arabia
Manager: Visual Research: Beth Brenzel
Manager, Cover Visual Research & Permissions: Karen Sanatar
Image Permission Coordinator: Cynthia Vincenti
Photo Researcher: Diane Austin
Manager, Print Production: Christy Mahon
Print Production Liaison: Suzanne Duda
Composition/Full-Service Project Management: Carlisle Publishers Services
Printer/Binder: Courier
Cover Printer: Phoenix Color
Typeface: 10.5/12 Minion

Credits and acknowledgments borrowed from other sources and reproduced, with permission, in this textbook appear on appropriate page C-1.

Pearson Education LTD.
Pearson Education Singapore, Pte. Ltd
Pearson Education, Canada, Ltd
Pearson Education–Japan
Pearson Education Australia PTY, Limited
Pearson Education North Asia Ltd
Pearson Educación de Mexico, S.A. de C.V.
Pearson Education Malaysia, Pte. Ltd

PEARSON Prentice Hall

10 9 8 7 6 5 4 3 2
ISBN 0-13-034825-2

For Constance, Raph, and Will

—R. Glenn Hubbard

To my mother and the memory of my father

—Anthony Patrick O'Brien

Glenn Hubbard policymaker, professor, and researcher. R. Glenn Hubbard is the Dean and Russell L. Carson Professor of Finance and Economics in the Graduate School of Business at Columbia University and Professor of Economics in Columbia's Faculty of Arts and Sciences. He is also a research associate of the National Bureau of Economic Research and a director of Automatic Data Processing, Black Rock Closed-End Funds, R.H. Donnelly, Inc., Duke Realty, KKR Financial Corporation, and Ripplewood Holdings. He received his Ph.D. in economics from Harvard University in 1983. From 2001–2003, he served as Chairman of the White House Council of Economic Advisers, and from 1991–1993, he was Deputy Assistant Secretary of the U.S. Treasury Department. Glenn Hubbard's fields of specialization are public economics, financial markets and institutions, corporate finance, macroeconomics, industrial organization, and public policy. He is the author of more than 90 articles in leading journals, including the *American Economic Review, Journal of Finance, Journal of Financial Economics, Journal of Political Economy, Journal of Public Economics, Quarterly Journal of Economics, RAND Journal of Economics,* and *Review of Economics and Statistics.* His research has been supported by grants from the National Science Foundation, the National Bureau of Economic Research, and numerous private foundations.

Tony O'Brien award-winning professor and researcher. Anthony Patrick O'Brien is a professor of economics at Lehigh University. He received his Ph.D. from the University of California, Berkeley, in 1987. He has taught principles of economics for more than 15 years, in both large sections and small honors classes. He received the Lehigh University Award for Distinguished Teaching. He was formerly the director of the Diamond Center for Economic Education and was named a Dana Foundation Faculty Fellow and Lehigh Class of 1961 Professor of Economics. He has been a visiting professor at the University of California, Santa Barbara, and the Graduate School of Industrial Administration at Carnegie Mellon University. Anthony O'Brien's research has dealt with such issues as the evolution of the U.S. automobile industry, the sources of U.S. economic competitiveness, the development of U.S. trade policy, the causes of the Great Depression, and the causes of black–white income differences. His research has been published in leading journals, including the *American Economic Review,* the *Quarterly Journal of Economics,* the *Journal of Money, Credit, and Banking, Industrial Relations,* and the *Journal of Economic History.* His research has been supported by grants from government agencies and private foundations. In addition to teaching and writing, Anthony O'Brien also serves on the editorial board of the *Journal of Socio-economics.*

CONTEXTUAL LEARNING

Students come to study macroeconomics with a strong interest in understanding events and developments in the economy. We try to capture that interest and develop students' economic intuition and understanding in this text. We present macroeconomics in a way that is modern and based in the real world of business and economic policy. And we believe we achieved this presentation without making the analysis more difficult. We avoid the recent trend of using simplified versions of intermediate models, which are often more detailed and more complex than is necessary to allow students to understand the basic macroeconomic issues. Instead, we use a more realistic version of the familiar aggregate demand-aggregate supply model to analyze short-run fluctuations and monetary and fiscal policy. We also avoid the "dueling schools of thought" approach often used to teach macroeconomics at the principles level. We emphasize the many areas of macroeconomics where most economists agree, which gives students a better context for understanding those issues where disagreements have not yet been resolved. And we present throughout real business and policy situations to develop students' intuition.

A few highlights of our approach:

- *A strong set of introductory chapters.* Our six introductory chapters provide students with a solid foundation in the basics before we move on to explore macroeconomics. We emphasize the key ideas of marginal analysis and economic efficiency. In Chapter 4, "Economic Efficiency, Government Price Setting, and Taxes," we use the concepts of consumer surplus and producer surplus to measure the economic effects of price ceilings and price floors as they relate to the familiar examples of rental properties and the minimum wage. We revisit consumer surplus and producer surplus in Chapter 6, "Comparative Advantage and the Gains from International Trade," where we analyze government policies that affect trade. In Chapter 5, "Firms, the Stock Market, and Corporate Governance" we provide students with a basic understanding of how firms are organized, how they raise funds, and how they provide information to investors. We also illustrate how in a market system entrepreneurs meet consumer wants and efficiently organize production. To explore how government policy affects business, we cover the WorldCom and Enron business scandals and the objectives of the 2002 Sarbanes-Oxley Act. Although the material in Chapter 5 can be skipped without a loss of continuity in the discussion, we believe the chapter provides an important background to macroeconomic issues affecting the financial system.
- *A broader discussion of macro statistics.* Many students pay at least some attention to the financial news and know that the release of stastitics by federal agencies can cause movements in stock and bond prices. A background in macroeconomic statistics helps clarify some of the policy issues encountered in later chapters. In Chapter 7, "GDP: Measuring Total Production and Income," and Chapter 8, "Unemployment and Inflation," we provide students with an understanding of the uses and potential shortcomings of the key macroeconomic statistics, without getting bogged down in the minutiae of how the statistics are constructed. So, for instance, we discuss the important differences between the payroll survey and the household survey for understanding conditions in the labor market. We explain why the financial markets react more strongly to news from the payroll survey.
- *Early coverage of long-run topics.* We place key macroeconomic issues in their long-run context in Chapter 9, "Economic Growth, the Financial System, and Business Cycles," and Chapter 10, "Long-Run Economic Growth: Sources and Policies." Chapter 9 puts the business cycle in the context of underlying long-run growth. In this chapter, we discuss what actually happens during the phases of the business cycle. We believe this material is important if students are to have the understanding of business cycles they will need to interpret economic events, yet this material is

often discussed only briefly or omitted entirely in other books. We know that many instructors prefer to have a short-run orientation to their macro courses, with a strong emphasis on policy. Accordingly, we have structured Chapter 9 so that its discussion of long-run growth would be sufficient for instructors who want to move quickly to short-run analysis. Chapter 10 uses a simple neo-classical growth model to understand important growth issues. We apply the model to topics such as the decline of the Soviet economy, the surprisingly strong growth performance of Botswana, and the failure of many developing countries to sustain high growth rates. And we challenge students with a discussion of "Why Isn't the Whole World Rich?"

- *A dynamic model of aggregate demand and aggregate supply.* We take a fresh approach to the standard aggregate demand-aggregate supply model. We realize there is no good, simple alternative to using the *AD-AS* model when explaining movements in the price level and in real GDP. But we know that more instructors are dissatisfied with the *AD-AS* model than with any other aspect of the macro principles course. The key problem, of course, is that *AD-AS* is a static model that attempts to account for dynamic changes in real GDP and the price level. Our approach retains the basics of the *AD-AS* model, but makes it more accurate and useful by making it more dynamic. We emphasize two points: First, changes in the position of the short-run (upward-sloping) aggregate supply curve depend mainly on the state of expectations of the inflation rate. Second, the existence of growth in the economy means that the long-run (vertical) aggregate supply curve shifts to the right every year. This "dynamic" *AD-AS* model provides students with a more accurate understanding of the causes and consequences of fluctuations in real GDP and the price level. We introduce this model in Chapter 12, "Aggregate Demand and Aggregate Supply Analysis," and use it to discuss monetary policy in Chapter 14, "Monetary Policy," and Chapter 16, "Inflation, Unemployment, and Federal Reserve Policy," as well as fiscal policy in Chapter 15.
- *Extensive coverage of monetary policy.* Because of the central role monetary policy plays in the economy and in students' curiosity about business and financial news, we devote Chapters 14 and 16 to the topic. We emphasize the issues involved in the Fed's choice of monetary policy targets, and we include coverage of the Taylor rule. Our discussion of inflation targeting is particularly pertinent as Ben Bernanke succeeds Alan Greenspan as Fed chair.
- *Coverage of both the demand side and supply side effects of fiscal policy.* Our discussion of fiscal policy carefully distinguishes between automatic stabilizers and discretionary fiscal policy. We also have significant coverage of the supply-side effects of fiscal policy.
- *A self-contained—but thorough—discussion of the Keynesian income-expenditure approach.* The Keynesian income-expenditure approach (the "45°-line diagram" or "Keynesian cross") is a useful way of introducing students to the short-run relationship between spending and production. Many instructors, however, prefer to omit this material. Therefore, we use the income-expenditure approach in only Chapter 11, "Output and Expenditure in the Short Run." The discussion of monetary and fiscal policy in later chapters uses only the *AD-AS* model, making it possible to omit Chapter 11.
- *Extensive international coverage.* We include three chapters devoted to international topics: Chapters 6, 17, and 18. A good understanding of the international trading and financial systems is essential to an understanding of the macroeconomy and to satisfying students' curiosity about the economic world around them. In addition to the material in our three international chapters, we weave international comparisons into the narrative of several chapters, including our discussion of labor market policies and central banking.

When George Lucas was asked why he made *Star Wars,* he replied, "It's the kind of movie I like to see, but no one seemed to be making them. So, I decided to make one." We realized that no one seemed to be writing the kind of textbook we wanted to use in our classes. So, after years of supplementing texts with fresh, lively, real-world examples from newspapers, magazines, and professional journals, we decided to write an economics text that delivered complete economics coverage with many real-world business examples. Our goal was to keep our classes "widget free."

We believe the course is a success if students can apply what they have learned in both personal and business settings, and if they have developed the analytical skills to understand what they read in the media. That's why we explain economic concepts by using many real-world business examples and applications. Here are a few examples:

Which category of unemployment applies to optical engineers at Lucent? (Chapter 8)

How has globalization helped Bangladesh's economy? (Chapter 10)

How do exchange rates affect Caterpillar, Inc.'s sales? (Chapter 12)

Each CHAPTER-OPENING CASE sets a real-world context for learning, sparks students' interest in economics, and gives the chapter a unifying theme.

Each chapter opener covers a real-world situation faced by companies such as Cisco, Ford Motor Company, and the homebuilder Toll Brothers, Inc. The company is integrated in the narrative, graphs, and pedagogical features of the chapter. Many of the chapter openers focus on the role of the entrepreneur in developing new products and bringing them to the market. Here are a few examples of topics we explore:

Why was the Google IPO so successful, and how can we track the stock? (Chapter 5)

How did a tariff on sugar affect candy manufacturers? (Chapter 6)

How did fluctuations in GDP affect hiring at Freightliner, a commercial truck manufacturer based in Portland, Oregon? (Chapter 7)

What role have entrepreneurs played in China's rapid growth? (Chapter 10)

How Hewlett-Packard Manages the Demand for Printers

➤ In early 2005 the board of directors at Hewlett-Packard (H-P) ousted chief executive officer Carly Fiorina and replaced her with Mark Hurd, then the chief executive officer of NCR Corporation. What happened?.

Carly Fiorina had been a business celebrity for many years. In July 1999 she became H-P's chief executive officer, which made her the first woman to head one of the 100 largest firms in the United States. In 2002, she brought about the largest merger of two technology firms in U.S. history when H-P purchased Compaq Computer Corporation. By with Compaq had failed to improve H-P's performance in the personal computer market.

Printers, and not personal computers, are H-P's most successful product. Although printers account for only about 30 percent of the firm's sales, they account for 70 percent of its profits. In fact, as *An Inside Look* at the end of this chapter discusses, to increase the demand for printers the firm is willing to sell its personal computers at low prices.

Hewlett-Packard's success, like that of any firm, depends on its ability

example, Carly Fiorina announced that sales of H-P printers had declined sharply in the first half of that year compared to the first half of 2000. Two events caused this decline: First, many individuals and small businesses unexpectedly decided not to upgrade their existing computers to faster and more powerful machines. Pur are a key part of ers. Second, t moved into rece incomes of ma reducing the pr nesses. Fiorina

POLICY EXAMPLES

AN INSIDE LOOK shows students how to apply the concepts of a chapter to the analysis of a newspaper article.

Reading the newspaper and other periodicals is an important part of understanding the current business climate. At the end of each chapter, a two-page periodical feature consists of an excerpt of an article, analysis of the article, graph(s), and critical thinking questions.

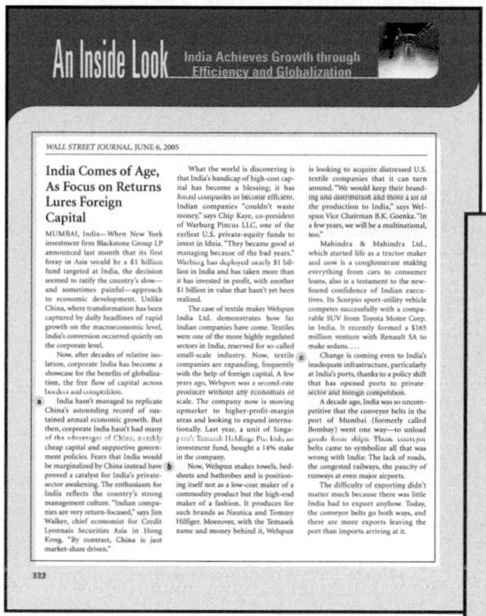

An Inside Look — India Achieves Growth through Efficiency and Globalization

WALL STREET JOURNAL, JUNE 6, 2005

India Comes of Age, As Focus on Returns Lures Foreign Capital

MUMBAI, India—When New York investment firm Blackstone Group LP announced last month that its first foray in Asia would be a $1 billion fund targeted at India, the decision seemed to ratify the country's slow—and sometimes painful—approach to economic development. Unlike China, where transformation has been captured by daily headlines of rapid growth on the macroeconomic level, India's conversion occurred quietly on the corporate level.

Now, after decades of relative isolation, corporate India has become a showcase for the benefits of globalization, the free flow of capital across borders and competition.

a India hasn't managed to replicate China's astounding record of sustained annual economic growth. But then, corporate India hasn't had many of the advantages of China, notably cheap capital and supportive government policies. Fears that India would be marginalized by China instead have proved a catalyst for India's private-sector awakening. The enthusiasm for India reflects the country's strong management culture. "Indian companies are very return-focused," says Jim Walker, chief economist for Credit Lyonnais Securities Asia in Hong Kong. "By contrast, China is just market-share driven."

b What the world is discovering is that India's handicap of high-cost capital has become a blessing; it has forced companies to become efficient. Indian companies "couldn't waste money," says Chip Kaye, co-president of Warburg Pincus LLC, one of the earliest U.S. private-equity funds to invest in Idnia. "They became good at managing because of the bad years." Warburg has deployed nearly $1 billion in India and has taken more than it has invested in profit, with another $1 billion in value that hasn't yet been realized.

The case of textile maker Welspun India Ltd. demonstrates how far Indian companies have come. Textiles were one of the more highly regulated sectors in India, reserved for so-called small-scale industry. Now, textile companies are expanding, frequently with the help of foreign capital. A few years ago, Welspun was a second-rate producer without any economies of scale. The company now is moving upmarket to higher-profit-margin areas and looking to expand internationally. Last year, a unit of Singapore's Temasek Holdings Pte. Ltd.'s investment fund, bought a 14% stake in the company.

Now, Welspun makes towels, bedsheets and bathrobes and is positioning itself not as a low-cost maker of a commodity product but the high-end maker of a fashion. It produces for such brands as Nautica and Tommy Hilfiger. Moreover, with the Temasek name and money behind it, Welspun is looking to acquire distressed U.S. textile companies that it can turn around. "We would keep their branding and distribution and move a lot of the production to India," says Welspun Vice Chairman B.K. Goenka. "In a few years, we will be a multinational, too."

Mahindra & Mahindra Ltd., which started life as a tractor maker and now is a conglomerate making everything from cars to consumer loans, also is a testament to the newfound confidence of Indian executives. Its Scorpio sport-utility vehicle competes successfully with a comparable SUV from Toyota Motor Corp. in India. It recently formed a $165 million venture with Renault SA to make sedans....

c Change is coming even to India's inadequate infrastructure, particularly at India's ports, thanks to a policy shift that has opened ports to private sector and foreign competition.

A decade ago, India was so uncompetitive that the conveyor belts in the port of Mumbai (formerly called Bombay) went one way—to unload goods from ships. Those conveyor belts came to symbolize all that was wrong with India: The lack of roads, the congested railways, the paucity of runways at even major airports.

The difficulty of exporting didn't matter much because there was little India had to export anyhow. Today, the conveyor belts go both ways, and there are more exports leaving the port than imports arriving at it.

322

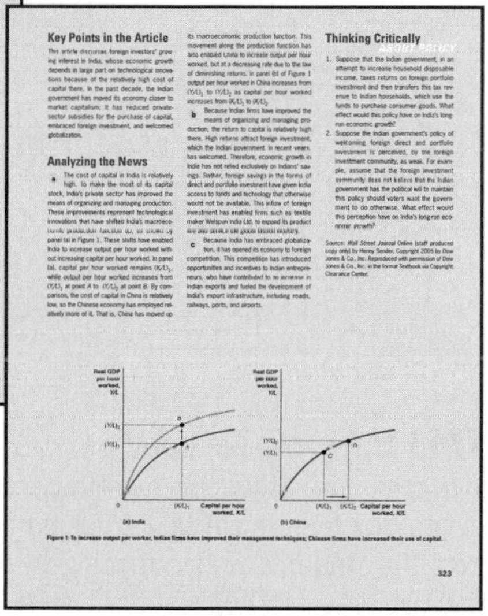

Key Points in the Article

This article discusses foreign investors' growing interest in India, whose economic growth depends in large part on technological innovations because of the relatively high cost of capital there. In the past decade, the Indian government has moved its economy closer to market capitalism: It has reduced private-sector subsidies for the purchase of capital, embraced foreign investment, and welcomed globalization.

Analyzing the News

a The cost of capital in India is relatively high. To make the most of its capital stock, India's private sector has improved the means of organizing and managing production. These improvements represent technological innovations that have shifted India's macroeconomic production function up, as shown by panel (a) in Figure 1. These shifts have enabled India to increase output per hour worked without increasing capital per hour worked. In panel (a), capital per hour worked remains $(K/L)_1$, while output per hour worked increases from $(Y/L)_1$ at point *A* to $(Y/L)_2$ at point *B*. By comparison, the cost of capital in China is relatively low, so the Chinese economy has employed relatively more of it. That is, China has moved up its macroeconomic production function. This movement along the production function has also enabled China to increase output per hour worked, but at a decreasing rate due to the law of diminishing returns. In panel (b) of Figure 1 output per hour worked in China increases from $(Y/L)_1$ to $(Y/L)_2$ as capital per hour worked increases from $(K/L)_1$ to $(K/L)_2$.

b Because Indian firms have improved the means of organizing and managing production, the return to capital is relatively high there. High returns attract foreign investment, which the Indian government in recent years has welcomed. Therefore, economic growth in India has not relied exclusively on Indians' savings. Rather, foreign savings in the forms of direct and portfolio investment have given India access to funds and technology that otherwise would not be available. This inflow of foreign investment has enabled firms such as textile maker Welspun India Ltd. to expand its product line and service the global textile industry.

c Because India has embraced globalization, it has opened its economy to foreign competition. This competition has introduced opportunities and incentives to Indian entrepreneurs, who have contributed to an increase in Indian exports and fueled the development of India's export infrastructure, including roads, railways, ports, and airports.

Thinking Critically ABOUT POLICY

1. Suppose that the Indian government, in an attempt to increase household disposable income, taxes returns on foreign portfolio investment and then transfers this tax revenue to Indian households, which use the funds to purchase consumer goods. What effect would this policy have on India's long-run economic growth?
2. Suppose the Indian government's policy of welcoming foreign direct and portfolio investment is perceived, by the foreign investment community, as weak. For example, assume that the foreign investment community does not believe that the Indian government has the political will to maintain this policy should voters want the government to do otherwise. What effect would this perception have on India's long-run economic growth?

Source: *Wall Street Journal Online* (staff produced copy only) by Henry Sender. Copyright 2005 by Dow Jones & Co., Inc. Reproduced with permission of Dow Jones & Co., Inc. in the format Textbook via Copyright Clearance Center.

Figure 1: To increase output per worker, Indian firms have improved their management techniques; Chinese firms have increased their use of capital.

323

MAKING THE CONNECTION between concepts and the real world.

In each chapter, between two and four "Making the Connection" features present relevant, stimulating, and provocative news stories, primarily about business.

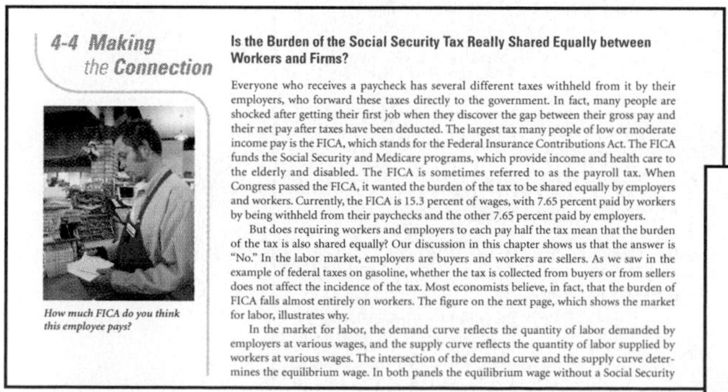

4-4 Making the Connection

Is the Burden of the Social Security Tax Really Shared Equally between Workers and Firms?

How much FICA do you think this employee pays?

Everyone who receives a paycheck has several different taxes withheld from it by their employers, who forward these taxes directly to the government. In fact, many people are shocked after getting their first job when they discover the gap between their gross pay and their net pay after taxes have been deducted. The largest tax many people of low or moderate income pay is the FICA, which stands for the Federal Insurance Contributions Act. The FICA funds the Social Security and Medicare programs, which provide income and health care to the elderly and disabled. The FICA is sometimes referred to as the payroll tax. When Congress passed the FICA, it wanted the burden of the tax to be shared equally by employers and workers. Currently, the FICA is 15.3 percent of wages, with 7.65 percent paid by workers by being withheld from their paychecks and the other 7.65 percent paid by employers.

But does requiring workers and employers to each pay half the tax mean that the burden of the tax is also shared equally? Our discussion in this chapter shows us that the answer is "No." In the labor market, employers are buyers and workers are sellers. As we saw in the example of federal taxes on gasoline, whether the tax is collected from buyers or from sellers does not affect the incidence of the tax. Most economists believe, in fact, that the burden of FICA falls almost entirely on workers. The figure on the next page, which shows the market for labor, illustrates why.

In the market for labor, the demand curve reflects the quantity of labor demanded by employers at various wages, and the supply curve reflects the quantity of labor supplied by workers at various wages. The intersection of the demand curve and the supply curve determines the equilibrium wage. In both panels the equilibrium wage without a Social Security

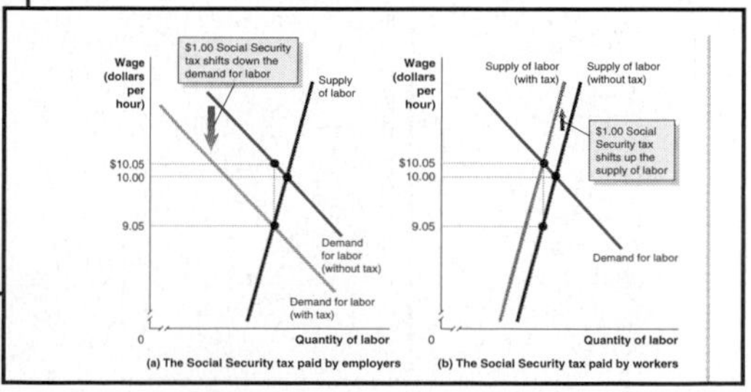

(a) The Social Security tax paid by employers

(b) The Social Security tax paid by workers

SOLVED PROBLEMS offer a hands-on approach to learning.

As we all know, many students have great difficulty handling applied economics problems. We help students overcome this hurdle by including two or three worked-out problems tied to select chapter-opening learning objectives and the associated quantitative information. Our goals are to keep students focused on the main ideas of each chapter and to give students a model of how to solve an economic problem by breaking it down step by step. There are additional exercises in the end-of-chapter materials tied to every Solved Problem.

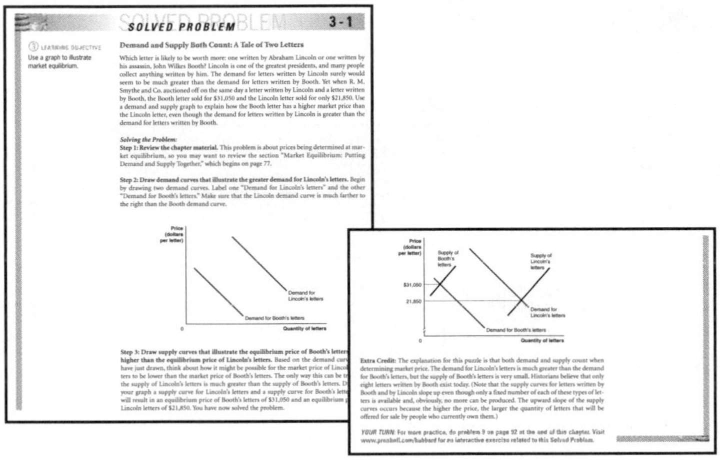

SOLVED PROBLEM 3-1

③ LEARNING OBJECTIVE

Use a graph to illustrate market equilibrium.

Demand and Supply Both Count: A Tale of Two Letters

Which letter is likely to be worth more: one written by Abraham Lincoln or one written by his assassin, John Wilkes Booth? Lincoln is one of the greatest presidents, and many people collect anything written by him. The demand for letters written by Lincoln surely would seem to be much greater than the demand for letters written by Booth. Yet when R. M. Smythe and Co. auctioned off on the same day a letter written by Lincoln and a letter written by Booth, the Booth letter sold for $31,050 and the Lincoln letter sold for only $21,850. Use a demand and supply graph to explain how the Booth letter has a higher market price than the Lincoln letter, even though the demand for letters written by Lincoln is greater than the demand for letters written by Booth.

Solving the Problem:

Step 1: Review the chapter material. This problem is about prices being determined at market equilibrium, so you may want to review the section "Market Equilibrium: Putting Demand and Supply Together," which begins on page 77.

Step 2: Draw demand curves that illustrate the greater demand for Lincoln's letters. Begin by drawing two demand curves. Label one "Demand for Lincoln's letters" and the other "Demand for Booth's letters." Make sure that the Lincoln demand curve is much farther to the right than the Booth demand curve.

Step 3: Draw supply curves that illustrate the equilibrium price of Booth's letter[s] higher than the equilibrium price of Lincoln's letters. Based on the demand cur[ves you] have just drawn, think about how it might be possible for the market price of Linco[ln's let]ters to be lower than the market price of Booth's letters. The only way this can be tr[ue is if] the supply of Lincoln's letters is much greater than the supply of Booth's letters. D[raw on] your graph a supply curve for Lincoln's letters and a supply curve for Booth's lett[ers that] will result in an equilibrium price of Booth's letters of $31,050 and an equilibrium p[rice of] Lincoln letters of $21,850. You have now solved the problem.

Extra Credit: The explanation for this puzzle is that both demand and supply count when determining market price. The demand for Lincoln's letters is much greater than the demand for Booth's letters, but the supply of Booth's letters is very small. Historians believe that only eight letters written by Booth exist today. (Note that the supply curves for letters written by Booth and by Lincoln slope up even though only a fixed number of each of these types of letters is available and, obviously, no more can be produced. The upward slope of the supply curves occurs because the higher the price, the larger the quantity of letters that will be offered for sale by people who currently own them.)

YOUR TURN: For more practice, do problem 9 on page 92 at the end of this chapter. Visit www.prenhall.com/hubbard for an interactive exercise related to this Solved Problem.

Don't Let This Happen To You!

We know from many years of teaching which concepts students find most difficult. Each chapter contains a box feature alerting students to the most common pitfalls in that chapter's material. We test the students' understanding by following up with a related question in the end-of-chapter "Problems and Applications" section.

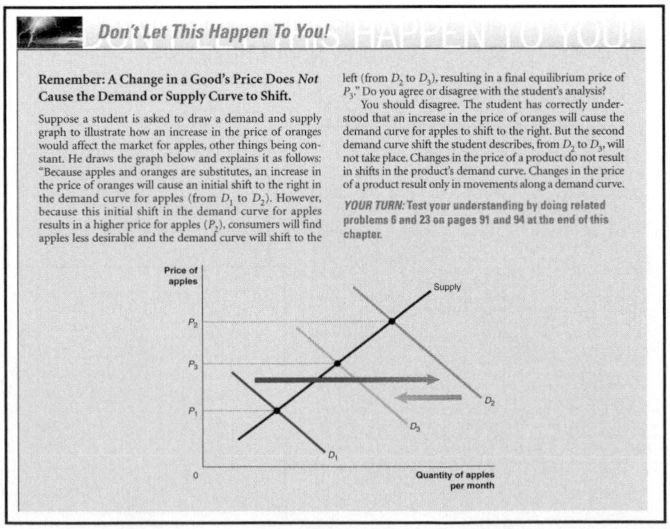

Don't Let This Happen To You!

Remember: A Change in a Good's Price Does *Not* Cause the Demand or Supply Curve to Shift.

Suppose a student is asked to draw a demand and supply graph to illustrate how an increase in the price of oranges would affect the market for apples, other things being constant. He draws the graph below and explains it as follows: "Because apples and oranges are substitutes, an increase in the price of oranges will cause an initial shift to the right in the demand curve for apples (from D_1 to D_2). However, because this initial shift in the demand curve for apples results in a higher price for apples (P_2), consumers will find apples less desirable and the demand curve will shift to the left (from D_2 to D_3), resulting in a final equilibrium price of P_3." Do you agree or disagree with the student's analysis?

You should disagree. The student has correctly understood that an increase in the price of oranges will cause the demand curve for apples to shift to the right. But the second demand curve shift the student describes, from D_2 to D_3, will not take place. Changes in the price of a product do not result in shifts in the product's demand curve. Changes in the price of a product result only in movements along a demand curve.

YOUR TURN: Test your understanding by doing related problems 6 and 23 on pages 91 and 94 at the end of this chapter.

GRAPHS AND SUMMARY TABLES

Graphs

Graphs are an indispensable part of the principles of economics course but are a major stumbling block for many students. Every chapter (except Chapter 1) includes end-of-chapter problems that require students to draw, read, and interpret graphs. Interactive graphing exercises can be found on the book's supporting Web site. We use four devices to help students read and interpret graphs:

1. Captions
2. Boxed Notes
3. Color-Coded Curves

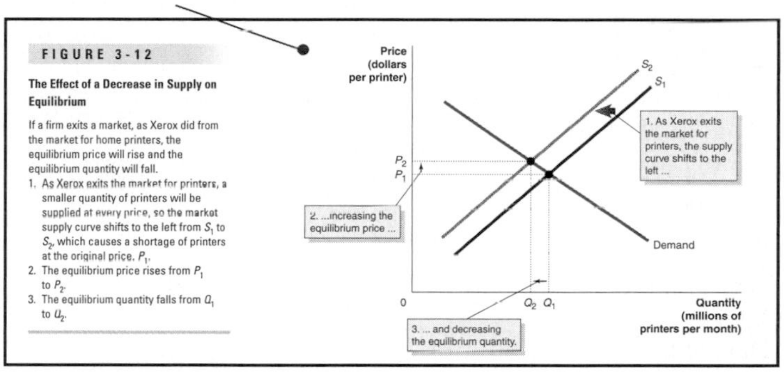
FIGURE 3-12

The Effect of a Decrease in Supply on Equilibrium

If a firm exits a market, as Xerox did from the market for home printers, the equilibrium price will rise and the equilibrium quantity will fall.

1. As Xerox exits the market for printers, a smaller quantity of printers will be supplied at every price, so the market supply curve shifts to the left from S_1 to S_2, which causes a shortage of printers at the original price, P_1.
2. The equilibrium price rises from P_1 to P_2.
3. The equilibrium quantity falls from Q_1 to Q_2.

Price
(dollars
per printer)
S_2
S_1
1. As Xerox exits the market for printers, the supply curve shifts to the left ...
P_2
P_1
2. ...increasing the equilibrium price ...
Demand
0
Q_2 Q_1
Quantity
(millions of
printers per month)
3. ... and decreasing the equilibrium quantity.

4. Summary Tables with Graphs

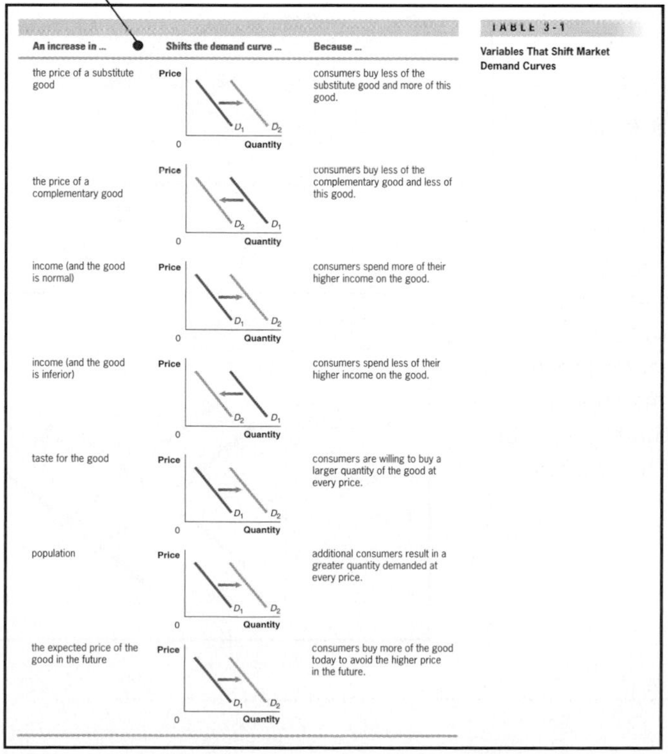
TABLE 3-1

Variables That Shift Market Demand Curves

An increase in ...	Shifts the demand curve ...	Because ...
the price of a substitute good	Price, 0, Quantity, D_1, D_2	consumers buy less of the substitute good and more of this good.
the price of a complementary good	Price, 0, Quantity, D_2, D_1	consumers buy less of the complementary good and less of this good.
income (and the good is normal)	Price, 0, Quantity, D_1, D_2	consumers spend more of their higher income on the good.
income (and the good is inferior)	Price, 0, Quantity, D_2, D_1	consumers spend less of their higher income on the good.
taste for the good	Price, 0, Quantity, D_1, D_2	consumers are willing to buy a larger quantity of the good at every price.
population	Price, 0, Quantity, D_1, D_2	additional consumers result in a greater quantity demanded at every price.
the expected price of the good in the future	Price, 0, Quantity, D_1, D_2	consumers buy more of the good today to avoid the higher price in the future.

INTEGRATED RESOURCES

Integrated Resources

The authors and Prentice Hall have worked together to integrate all text, print, and media resources to make teaching and learning easier.

Integration Benefits Students and Instructors

All textbooks have supporting resources, but not all textbooks have supporting resources that are seamlessly integrated with each other and the text. One of the driving forces behind the development of this resource package is our belief that concepts are grasped more easily in a familiar setting. That's why we decided to integrate the features of the text with the print and media resources for both students and instructors. And we did more than "integrate." We also enhanced the lecture materials by including additional examples in the Instructor's Manual.

Everything works together for a unified, efficient teaching and learning experience. Here's one example:

On this page is a "Solved Problem" that appears in the text. The facing page shows you how we integrate that Solved Problem—as well as the "Don't Let This Happen To You!" feature—in the end-of-chapter problems. Additional Solved Problems appear in the Instructor's Manual and Study Guide. See the pages that follow for more about supplements.

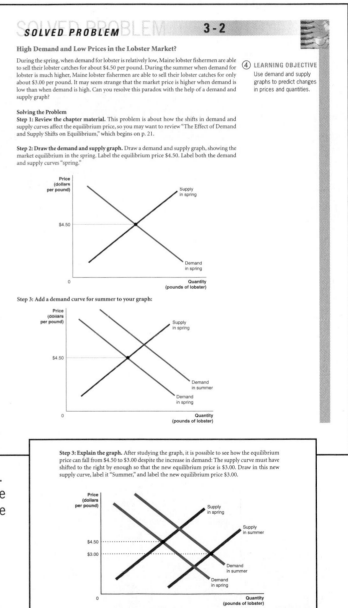

SOLVED PROBLEM 3-2

High Demand and Low Prices in the Lobster Market?

During the spring, when demand for lobster is relatively low, Maine lobster fishermen are able to sell their lobster catches for about $4.50 per pound. During the summer when demand for lobster is much higher, Maine lobster fishermen are able to sell their lobster catches for only about $3.00 per pound. It may seem strange that the market price is higher when demand is low than when demand is high. Can you resolve this paradox with the help of a demand and supply graph?

④ LEARNING OBJECTIVE
Use demand and supply graphs to predict changes in prices and quantities.

Solving the Problem

Step 1: Review the chapter material. This problem is about how the shifts in demand and supply curves affect the equilibrium price, so you may want to review "The Effect of Demand and Supply Shifts on Equilibrium," which begins on p. 21.

Step 2: Draw the demand and supply graph. Draw a demand and supply graph, showing the market equilibrium in the spring. Label the equilibrium price $4.50. Label both the demand and supply curves "spring."

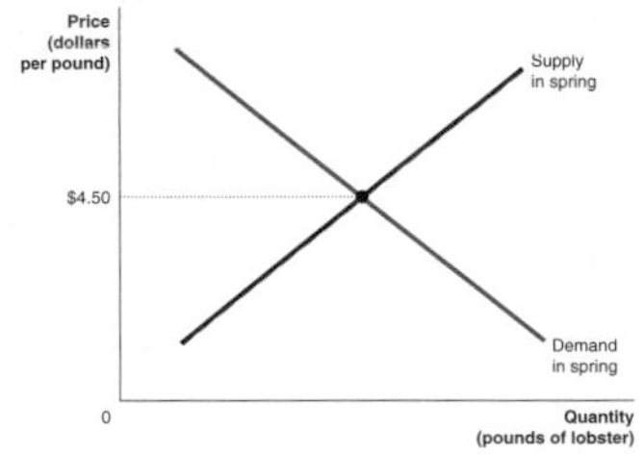

Step 3: Add a demand curve for summer to your graph:

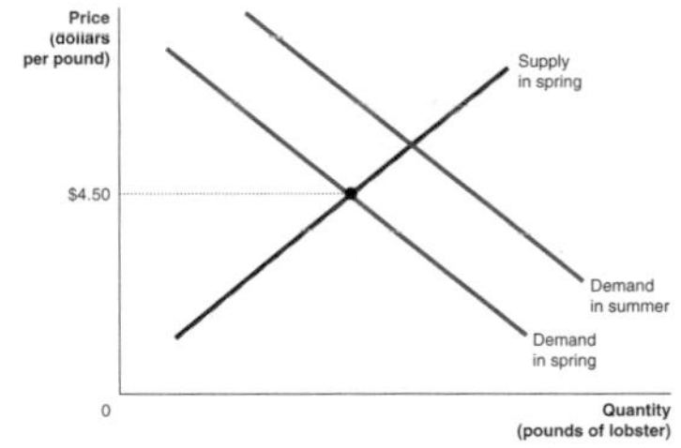

Step 3: Explain the graph. After studying the graph, it is possible to see how the equilibrium price can fall from $4.50 to $3.00 despite the increase in demand: The supply curve must have shifted to the right by enough so that the new equilibrium price is $3.00. Draw in this new supply curve, label it "Summer," and label the new equilibrium price $3.00.

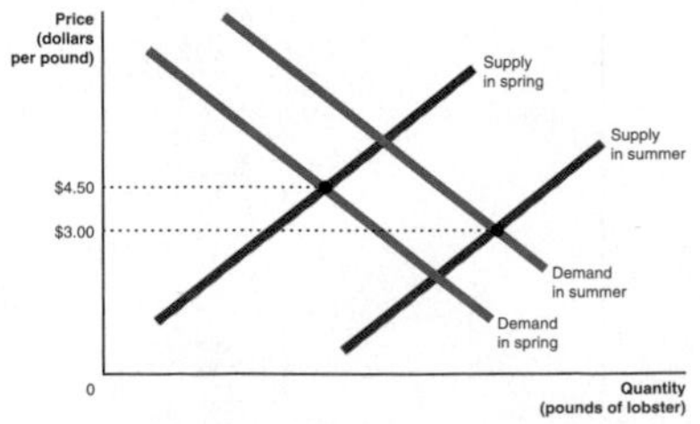

Solved Problems appear in the chapters. Additional Solved Problems appear in following areas:

- ***end-of-chapter Problems and Applications section***
- ***instructor's manual***
- ***PowerPoint slides***
- ***print study guide***
- ***test item file***

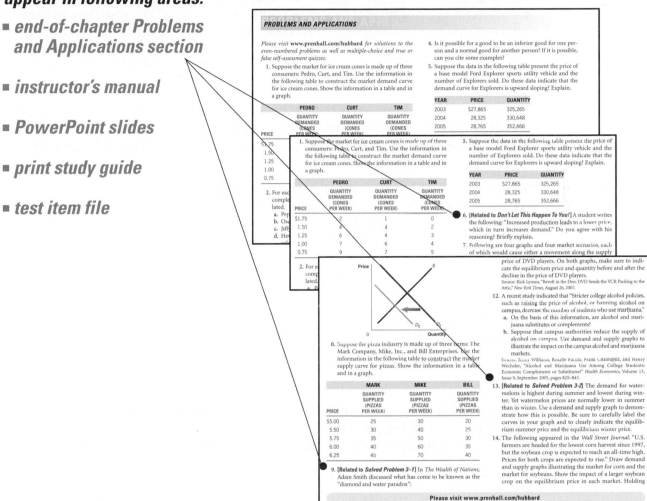

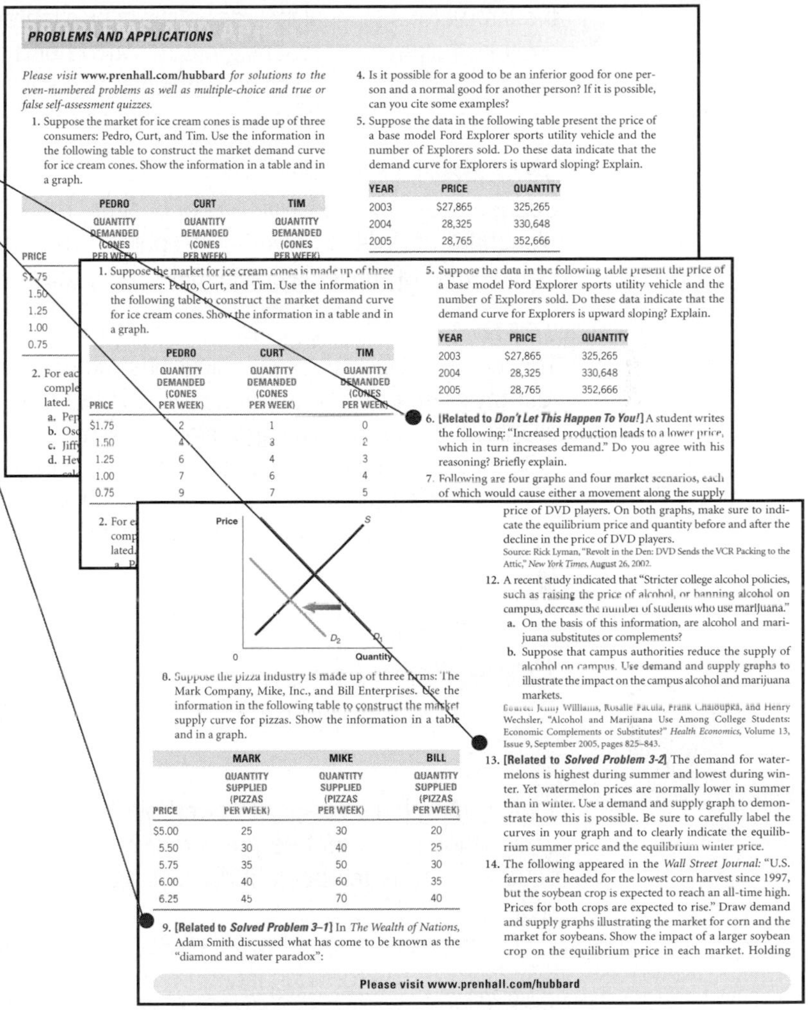

SUPPLEMENTS

Resources for the Instructor

Instructor's Manual

Prepared by Iordanis Petsas of the University of Scranton and Robert Gillette of the University of Kentucky, the Instructor's Manual includes chapter-by-chapter summaries, learning objectives, extended examples and class exercises, teaching outlines incorporating key terms and definitions, teaching tips, topics for class discussion, *new* Solved Problems, and solutions to all review questions and problems in the book. The Instructor's Manual is available in print and for download from the Instructor's Resource Center.

Test Banks

Cathleen Leue of the University of Oregon, Robert Gillette of the University of Kentucky, and Kelly Blanchard of Purdue University prepared two test banks to accompany the text. *Each* test bank includes 1,500 multiple-choice questions, true/false, short answer, and graphing questions.

TestGen

This computerized package allows instructors to customize, save, and generate classroom tests. The test program permits instructors to edit, add, or delete questions from the test banks; edit existing graphics and create new graphics; analyze test results; and organize a database of tests and student results. This software allows for extensive flexibility and ease of use. It provides many options for organizing and displaying tests, along with search and sort features. The software and the test banks can be downloaded from the Instructor's Resource Center (**www.prenhall.com/hubbard**).

Acetates

All figures and tables from the text are reproduced and provided as full-page, four-color acetates.

PowerPoint Lecture Presentation

There are two sets of PowerPoint® slides for professors to use prepared by Fernando and Yvonn Quijano:

1. A comprehensive set of PowerPoint® slides that can be used by instructors for class presentations or by students for lecture preview or review. The presentation includes all the graphs, tables, and equations in the textbook. It displays figures in step-by-step, automated mode, using a single click per slide.
2. A comprehensive set of PowerPoint® slides with CRS (Classroom Response Systems) questions built in so instructors can incorporate CRS "clickers" into their classroom lectures. For more information on Prentice Hall's partnership with CRS systems, see the facing page.

Instructors may download these PowerPoint® presentations from the Instructor's Resource Center (www.prenhall.com/hubbard).

Instructor's Resource CD-ROM

The Instructor's Resource CD-ROM contains all faculty and student resources that support this text. Instructors have the ability to access and edit the Instructor's Manual, Test Banks, and PowerPoint® presentations. By simply clicking on a chapter or searching for a keyword, faculty can access an interactive library of resources. Faculty can pick and choose from the various supplements and export them to their hard drive.

Classroom Response Systems

Classroom Response Systems (CRS) is an exciting new wireless polling technology that makes large and small classrooms even more interactive because it enables instructors to pose questions to their students, record results, and display those results instantly. Students can answer questions easily using compact remote-control transmitters. Prentice Hall has partnerships with leading classroom response systems providers and can show you everything you need to know about setting up and using a CRS system. We'll provide the classroom hardware, text-specific PowerPoint® slides, software, and support, and we'll also show you how your students can benefit! Learn more at **www.prenhall.com/crs.**

Blackboard and WebCT Course Content.

Prentice Hall offers fully customizable course content for the Bb and WebCT Course Management Systems.

Resources for the Student

Study Guide

Prepared by Nicholas Noble of Miami University, the comprehensive study guide reinforces the textbook and provides students with the following:

- Chapter summary
- Discussion of each Learning Objective
- Section-by-section review of the concepts presented
- Helpful study hints
- Additional Solved Problems to supplement those in the text
- Key Terms with definitions
- Self-Test including 40 multiple choice questions, plus a number of Short Answer and True/False questions, with accompanying answers and explanations

Companion Web Site.

This free Web site, **www.prenhall.com/hubbard**, gives students access to select solutions to end-of-chapter problems, an interactive study guide with instant feedback, economics updates, student PowerPoint® slides, and many other resources to promote success in the principles of economics course.

PowerPoint® Slides

For student use as a study aide or note-taking guide, these PowerPoint® slides, prepared by Fernando and Yvonn Quijano, may be downloaded from the companion Web site at **www.prenhall.com/hubbard**. The slides include:

- All graphs, tables, and equations in the text
- Figures in step-by-step, automated mode, using a single click per slide
- End-of-chapter key terms with hyperlinks to relevant slides

SafariX TEXTBOOKS ONLINE

SafariX WebBooks

SafariX WebBooks (online versions of the printed texts) will be available for students to purchase in lieu of a standard print text, without any modifications needed to how the instructor or professor teaches the course.

Learn more at **www.prenhall.com/safariX**.

myeconlab

Get Ahead of the Curve

Problem Solving for Students.

Automatically graded assignments (and the ability to get the highest possible grade by reworking the same assignments with new problems) motivate students to solve a lot more problems.

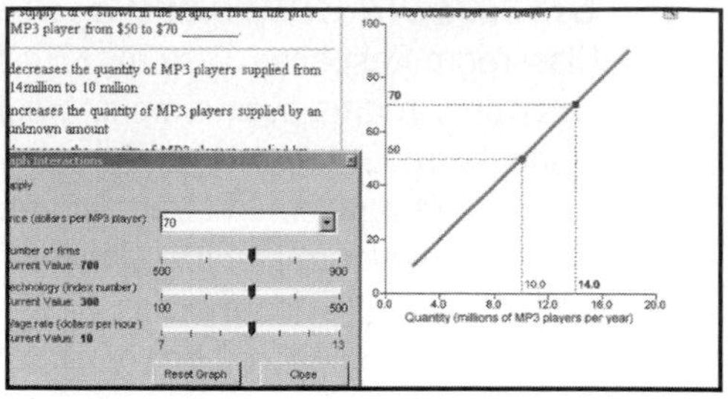

Instant feedback, including detailed tutorial instruction (complete solutions, step-by-step explanations, links to book material, etc.), provides instant gratification and immediate learning.

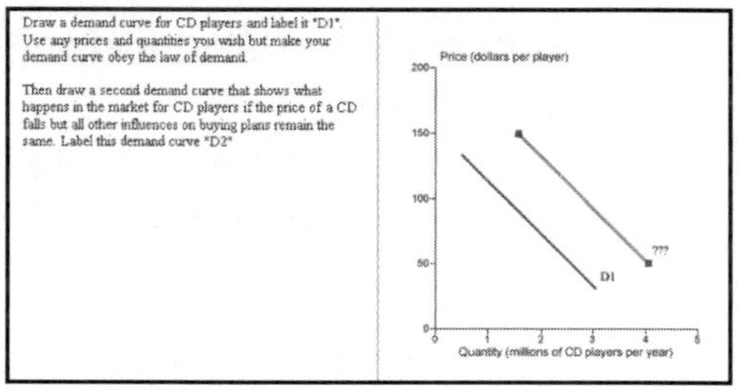

Graphing tools and questions integrated into assignments enable students to manipulate and even draw graphs that are automatically graded.

Solving Problems for Professors.

Easily create, assign, and automatically grade homework, quizzes, and tests.

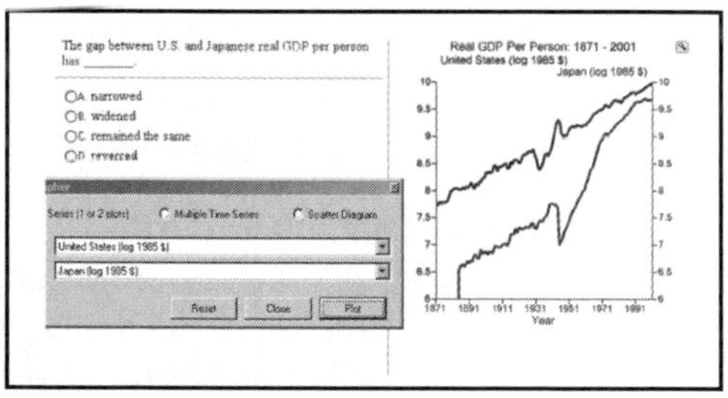

Assign problems and exercises based on the actual end-of-chapter materials in the text book. Many have algorithmic versions for variety and extra practice.

Track students' progress through one easy-to-view, automatically populated grade book.

Get supplementary problems and teaching resources (like test banks and lecture slides) all in one place.

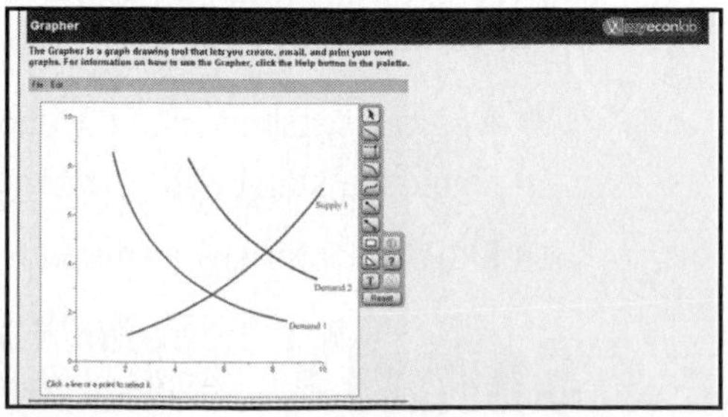

These features, plus personalized study plans for students, full e-text options, practice tests, eStudy guides, and more, are all available in MyEconLab.

CLASS TESTERS, ACCURACY REVIEWERS, AND CONSULTANTS

Class Testers

We are grateful to both the professors who class tested manuscript and their students for providing clear-cut recommendations on how to make chapters interesting, relevant, and comprehensive.

- Charles A. Bennett, Gannon University
- Anne E. Bresnock, University of California–Los Angeles and California State Polytechnic University–Pomona
- John Eastwood, Northern Arizona University
- David Eaton, Murray State University
- Paul Elgatian, St. Ambrose University
- Patricia A. Freeman, Jackson State University
- Robert Godby, University of Wyoming
- Frank Gunter, Lehigh University
- Ahmed Ispahani, University of LaVerne
- Brendan Kennelly, Lehigh University and National University of Ireland–Galway
- Linda Childs-Leatherbury, Lincoln University, Pennsylvania
- Ernest Massie, Franklin University
- Carol McDonough, University of Massachusetts–Lowell
- Shah Mehrabi, Montgomery College
- Sharon Ryan, University of Missouri–Columbia
- Bruce G. Webb, Gordon College
- Madelyn Young, Converse College
- Susan Zumas, Lehigh University

Accuracy Review Board

Our accuracy checkers did a particularly painstaking and thorough job of helping us proof the graphs, equations, and features of the book in page proof stages. We are grateful for their time and commitment to the book and supplements:

- Kelly Hunt Blanchard, Purdue University
- Harold Elder, University of Alabama
- Marc Fusaro, East Carolina University
- Robert Gillette, University of Kentucky
- Bill Goffe, State University of New York–Oswego
- Travis Hayes, University of Tennessee–Chattanooga
- Anisul M. Islam, University of Houston–Downtown
- Faik A. Koray, Louisiana State University
- Tony Lima, California State University–Hayward
- James A. Moreno, Blinn College
- Matthew Rafferty, Quinnipiac University
- Jeff Reynolds, Northern Illinois University
- Brian Rosario, University of California–Davis
- Joseph M. Santos, South Dakota State University
- Edward Scahill, University of Scranton
- Robert Whaples, Wake Forest University

Consultant Board

We received guidance at several critical junctures from a dedicated Consultant Board. We relied on the Board for input on content, figure treatment, and design.

- Susan Dadres, Southern Methodist University
- Harry Ellis, Jr., University of North Texas
- Robert Godby, University of Wyoming
- William L. Goffe, State University of New York–Oswego
- Donn M. Johnson, Quinnipiac College
- Mark Karscig, Central Missouri State University
- Jenny Minier, University of Kentucky
- Nicholas Noble, Miami University
- Matthew Rafferty, Quinnipiac College
- Helen Roberts, University of Illinois–Chicago
- Robert Rosenman, Washington State University
- Joseph M. Santos, South Dakota State University
- Martin C. Spechler, Indiana University–Purdue University–Indianapolis
- Robert Whaples, Wake Forest University

REVIEWERS

Reviewers

The guidance and recommendations of the following professors helped us shape the manuscript over the course of three years. We extend special thanks to Joseph Santos of South Dakota State University for helping prepare some of the Inside Look features, and Robert Gillette of the University of Kentucky, Robert Whaples of Wake Forest University, and Lee Craig of North Carolina State University for reviewing and preparing some of the review questions and problems and applications that appear at the ends of chapters.

ALABAMA Doris Bennett, Jacksonville State University • Harold W. Elder, University of Alabama–Tuscaloosa • James L. Swofford, University of Southern Alabama **ARIZONA** Doug Conway, Mesa Community College • John Eastwood, Northern Arizona University • Price Fishback, University of Arizona **CALIFORNIA** Renatte Adler, San Diego State University • Robert Bise, Orange Coast Community College • Victor Brajer, California State University–Fullerton • Anne E. Bresnock, University of California–Los Angeles and California State Polytechnic University–Pomona • David Brownstone, University of California–Irvine • Maureen Burton, California State Polytechnic University–Pomona • James G. Devine, Loyola Marymount University • Roger Frantz, San Diego State University • Andrew Gill, California State University–Fullerton • Amihai Glazier, Univeristy of California–Irvine • Lisa Grobar, California State University–Long Beach • Steve Hamilton, California Polytechnic State University–San Luis Obispo • Ahmed Ispahani, University of LaVerne • George A. Jouganatos, California State Univeristy–Sacramento • Philip King, San Francisco State University • Don Leet, California State University–Fresno • Rose LeMont, Modesto Junior College • Solina Lindahl, California Polytechnic State University–San Luis Obispo • Kristen Monaco, California State University • W. Douglas Morgan, University of California–Santa Barbara • Joseph M. Pogodzinski, San Jose State University • Michael J. Potepan, San Francisco State University • Ratha Ramoo, Diablo Valley College • Frederica Shockley, California State University–Chico • Mark Siegler, California State Univeristy–Sacramento • Lisa Simon, California Polytechnic State University–San Luis Obispo • Rod Swanson, University of California–Los Angeles • Kristin A. Van Gaasbeck, California State University–Sacramento • Mike Visser, Sonoma State University • Anthony Zambelli, Cuyamaca College **COLORADO** Rhonda Corman, University of Northern Colorado • Dale DeBoer, Univeristy of Colorado–Colorado Springs • Muriat Iyigun, University of Colorado at Boulder • Nancy Jianakoplos, Colorado State University • Jay Kaplan, University of Colorado–Boulder • Stephen Weiler, Colorado State University **CONNECTICUT** Christopher P. Ball, Quinnipiac University • Donn M. Johnson, Quinnipiac College • Judith Mills, Southern Connecticut State University • Matthew Rafferty, Quinnipiac College **DELAWARE** Fatma Abdel-Raouf, Goldey-Beacom College • Andrew T. Hill, University of Delaware **FLORIDA** Herm Baine, Broward Community College–Central • Al DeCook, Broward Community College • Martine Duchatelet, Barry University • Hadley Hartman, Santa Fe Community College • Richard Hawkins, University of West Florida • Barbara Moore, University of Central Florida • Augustine Nelson, University of Miami • Jamie Ortiz, Florida Atlantic University • Robert Pennington, University of Central Florida • Jerry Schwartz, Broward Community College–North • William Stronge, Florida Atlantic University • Nora Underwood, University of Central Florida **IDAHO** Don Holley, Boise State University **IOWA** Terry Alexander, Iowa State University • Paul Elgatian, St. Ambrose University • Jonathan Warner, Dordt College **ILLINOIS** Teshome Abebe, Eastern Illinois University • Ali Akarca, University of Illinois–Chicago • James Bruehler, Eastern Illinois University • Louis Cain, Loyola University Chicago and Northwestern University • Rik Hafer, Southern Illinois University–Edwardsville • Alla Melkumian, Western Illinois Univeristy • Christopher Mushrush, Illinois State University • Jeff Reynolds, Northern Illinois University • Helen Roberts, University of Illinois–Chicago • Eric Schulz, Northwestern University • Charles Sicotte, Rock Valley Community College • Neil T. Skaggs, Illinois State University • Mark Witte, Northwestern University • Laurie Wolff, Southern Illinois University–Carbondale • Paula Worthington, Northwestern University **INDIANA** Cecil Bohanon, Ball State University • Kelly Blanchard, Purdue University • Thomas Gresik, University of Notre Dame • Fred Herschede, Indiana University–South Bend • James K. Self, Indiana University–Bloomington • Esther-Mirjam Sent, University of Notre Dame • Virginia Shingleton, Valparaiso University • Martin C. Spechler, Indiana University–Purdue University–Indianapolis • Geetha Suresh, Purdue University–West Lafayette • Willard

Witte, Indiana Univeristy–Bloomington **KANSAS** Jodi Messer Pelkowski, Wichita State University • Joel Potter, Kansas State University • Josh Rosenbloom, University of Kansas • Bhavneet Walia, Kansas State University **KENTUCKY** Tom Cate, Northern Kentucky University • David Eaton, Murray State University • Robert Gillette, University of Kentucky • Hak Youn Kim, Western Kentucky University • Jenny Minier, University of Kentucky • John Vahaly, University of Louisville **LOUISIANA** Faik Koray, Louisiana State University • Paul Nelson, University of Louisiana–Monroe • Tammy Parker, University of Louisiana–Monroe • Wesley A. Payne, Delgado Community College **MAINE** Michael Enz, Western New England College • Arthur Schiller Casimir, Western New England College **MASSACHUSETTS** William L. Casey, Jr., Babson College • Arthur Schiller Casimir, Western New England College • Michael Enz, Western New England College • Todd Idson, Boston University • Russell Janis, University of Massachusetts–Amherst • Anthony Laramie, Merrimack College • Carol McDonough, University of Massachusetts–Lowell • William O'Brien, Worcester State College • Gregory H. Wassall, Northeastern University • Bruce G. Webb, Gordon College • Gilbert Wolpe, Newbury College **MARYLAND** Carey Borkoski, Anne Arundel Community College • Kathleen A. Carroll, University of Maryland–Baltimore County • Dustin Chambers, Salisbury University • Shah Mehrabi, Montgomery College • David Mitch, University of Maryland–Baltimore County • John Neri, University of Maryland • Henry Terrell, University of Maryland **MICHIGAN** John Nader, Grand Valley State University • Robert J. Rossana, Wayne State University • Mark Wheeler, Western Michigan University **MINNESOTA** Monica Hartman, University of St. Thomas **MISSOURI** Jo Durr, Southwest Missouri State University • Julie H. Gallaway, Southwest Missouri State University • Terrel Galloway, Southwest Missouri State University • Mark Karscig, Central Missouri State University • Steven T. Petty, College of the Ozarks • Sharon Ryan, University of Missouri–Columbia • Ben Young, University of Missouri–Kansas City **MISSISSIPPI** Randall Campbell, Mississippi State Univeristy • Patricia A. Freeman, Jackson State University **NEBRASKA** James Knudsen, Creighton University • Craig MacPhee, University of Nebraska–Lincoln • Mark E. Wohar, University of Nebraska–Omaha **NEW HAMPSHIRE** Evelyn Gick, Dartmouth College • Neil Niman, University of New Hampshire **NEW JERSEY** Len Anyanwu, Union County College • Maharukh Bhiladwalla, Rutgers University–New Brunswick • Gary Gigliotti, Rutgers University–New Brunswick • John Graham, Rutgers University–Newark • Berch Haroian, William Paterson University • Paul Harris, Camden County College **NEW MEXICO** Donald Coes, University of New Mexico **NEW YORK** Erol Balkan, Hamilton College • Ranjit S. Dighe, State University of New York–Oswego • William L. Goffe, State University of New York–Oswego • Wayne A. Grove, LeMoyne College • Christopher Inya, Monroe Community College • Clifford Kern, State University of New York–Binghampton • Mary Lesser, Iona College • Leonie Stone, State University of New York–Geneseo • Ganti Subrahmanyam, University of Buffalo • Jogindar S. Uppal, State University of New York–Albany • Susan Wolcott, Binghamton University **NORTH CAROLINA** Otilia Boldea, North Carolina State University • Robert Burrus, University of North Carolina–Wilmington • Lee A. Craig, North Carolina State University • Kathleen Dorsainvil, Winston-Salem State University • Marc Fusaro, East Carolina University • Salih Hakeem, North Carolina Central University • Haiyong Liu, East Carolina University • Kosmas Marinakis, North Carolina State University • Todd McFall, Wake Forest University • Shahriar Mostashari, Campbell University • Peter Schuhmann, University of North Carolina–Wilmington • Carol Stivender, University of North Carolina–Charlotte • Vera Tabakova, East Carolina University • Robert Whaples, Wake Forest University • Gary W. Zinn, East Carolina University **OHIO** John P. Blair, Wright State University • Kyongwook Choi, Ohio University Main Campus • Darlene DeVera, Miami University • Tim Fuerst, Bowling Green State University • Kenneth Kuttner, Oberlin College • Ernest Massie, Franklin University • Mike Nelson, University of Akron • Nicholas Noble, Miami University • Rochelle Ruffer, Youngstown State University • Kate Sheppard, University of Akron • Melissa Thomasson, Miami University • Yaqin Wang, Youngstown State University • Sourushe Zandvakili, University of Cincinnati **OKLAHOMA** David Hudgins, University of Oklahoma **OREGON** Bill Burrows, Lane Community College • Tom Carroll, Central Oregon Community College • Larry Singell, University of Oregon • Ayca Tekin-Koru, Oregon State University **PENNSYLVANIA** Gustavo Barboza, Mercyhurst College • Charles A. Bennett, Gannon University • Howard Bodenhorn, Lafayette College • Milica Bookman, St. Joseph's University • Robert Brooker, Gannon University • Linda Childs-Leatherbury, Lincoln University • Satyajit Ghosh,

University of Scranton • Mehdi Haririan, Bloomsburg University • James Jozefowicz, Indiana University of Pennsylvania • Nicholas Karatjas, Indiana University of Pennsylvania • Brendan Kennelly, Lehigh University • Iordanis Petsas, University of Scranton • Adam Renhoff, Drexel University • Edward Scahill, University of Scranton • Kosmas Marinakis, North Carolina State University • Rajeev Sooreea, Pennsylvania State University–Altoona • Sandra Trejos, Clarion University • Peter Zaleski, Villanova University **SOUTH CAROLINA** Calvin Blackwell, College of Charleston • Chad Turner, Clemson University • Madelyn Young, Converse College **SOUTH DAKOTA** Joseph M. Santos, South Dakota State University • Jason Zimmerman, South Dakota State University **TENNESSEE** Bichaka Fayissa, Middle Tennessee State University • Travis Hayes, University of Tennessee–Chattanooga • Christopher C. Klein, Middle Tennessee State University • Millicent Sites, Carson–Newman College **TEXAS** Rashid Al-Hmoud, Texas Tech University • Mike Cohick, Collin County Community College • Cesar Corredor, Texas A&M University–Tyler • Susan Dadres, Southern Methodist University • Harry Ellis, Jr., University of North Texas • Paul Emberton, Texas State University • Diego Escobari, Texas A&M University • Nicholas Feltovich, University of Houston–Main • Charles Harold Fifield, Baylor University • Richard Gosselin, Houston Community College–Central • Sheila Amin Gutierrez de Pineres, University of Texas–Dallas • James W. Henderson, Baylor University • Ansul Islam, University of Houston–Downtown • Kathy Kelly, University of Texas–Arlington • Thomas Kemp, Tarrant County College–Northwest • Akbar Marvasti, University of Houston–Downtown •James Mbata, Houston Community College • Carl Montano, Lamar University • James Moreno, Blinn College • John Pisciotta, Baylor University • Sara Saderion, Houston Community College–Southwest • Ivan Tasic, Texas A&M University • Rebecca Thornton, University of Houston • Chris Wreh, North Central Texas **UTAH** Aric Krause, Westminster College • Lowell Glenn, Utah Valley State College • Arden Pope, Brigham Young University **VIRGINIA** Lee Badgett, Virginia Military Institute • Lee A. Coppock, University of Virginia • Carrie Meyer, George Mason University • James Roberts, Tidewater Community College–Virginia Beach • Araine Schauer, Mary Mount College • Sarah Stafford, The College of William & Mary • Michelle Vachris, Christopher Newport University • James Wetzel, Virginia Commonwealth University **WASHINGTON** Robert Rosenman, Washington State University **WASHINGTON, DC** Leon Battista, American Enterprise Institute **WISCONSIN** • Pascal Ngoboka, University of Wisconsin–River Falls • Kevin Quinn, St. Norbert College • John R. Stoll, University of Wisconsin–Green Bay **WYOMING** Robert Godby, University of Wyoming

A Word of Thanks

We benefited greatly from the dedication and professionalism of the Prentice Hall team. Executive Editor David Alexander's energy and support were indispensable. David helped mold the presentation and provided words of encouragement whenever our energy flagged. Developmental Editor Lena Buonanno worked tirelessly to ensure this text was as good as it could be. We are literally astonished at the amount of time, energy, and unfailing good humor she brought to this project. Director of Key Markets David Theisen provided invaluable insight into how best to structure a principles text. His advice helped shape nearly every chapter. Executive Marketing Manager Sharon Koch and Marketing Development Manager Kathleen McLellan helped develop a unique and innovative marketing plan. Steve Deitmer, Director of Development, brought sound judgement to the many decisions required to create this book. Mike Dittamo, Editorial Assistant, was involved in many aspects of the book including the review program and assisting with the supplements. Karen Misler coordinated the extensive supplement package that accompanies the book. Mike Reynolds, Pat Smythe, and Maria Lange turned our manuscript pages into a beautiful published book. Photo researcher Diane Austin located photographs that captured the essence of key concepts.

A good part of the burden of a project of this magnitude is borne by our families. We appreciate the patience, support, and encouragement of our wives and children. We extend special thanks to Constance Hubbard for her diligent reading of page proofs.

BRIEF CONTENTS

Part 1: Introduction

CHAPTER 1: Economics: Foundations and Models 2

CHAPTER 1 APPENDIX: Using Graphs and Formulas 21

CHAPTER 2: Trade-offs, Comparative Advantage, and the Market System 32

CHAPTER 3: Where Prices Come From: The Interaction of Demand and Supply 62

CHAPTER 4: Economic Efficiency, Government Price Setting, and Taxes 96

CHAPTER 4 APPENDIX: Quantitative Demand and Supply Analysis 125

Part 2: Firms in the Domestic and International Economies

CHAPTER 5: Firms, the Stock Market, and Corporate Governance 130

CHAPTER 5 APPENDIX: Tools to Analyze Firms' Financial Information 152

CHAPTER 6: Comparative Advantage and the Gains from International Trade 162

CHAPTER 6 APPENDIX: Multinational Firms 195

Part 3: Macroeconomic Foundations and Long-Run Growth

CHAPTER 7: GDP: Measuring Total Production and Income 202

CHAPTER 8: Unemployment and Inflation 228

CHAPTER 9: Economic Growth, the Financial System, and Business Cycles 260

CHAPTER 10: Long-Run Economic Growth: Sources and Policies 292

Part 4: Short-Run Fluctuations

CHAPTER 11: Output and Expenditure in the Short Run 328

CHAPTER 11 APPENDIX: The Algebra of Macroeconomic Equilibrium 368

CHAPTER 12: Aggregate Demand and Aggregate Supply Analysis 370

CHAPTER 12 APPENDIX: Macroeconomic Schools of Thought 403

CHAPTER 13: Money, Banks, and the Federal Reserve System 406

CHAPTER 14: Monetary Policy 438

CHAPTER 15: Fiscal Policy 472

CHAPTER 15 APPENDIX: A Closer Look at the Multiplier 508

CHAPTER 16: Inflation, Unemployment, and Federal Reserve Policy 514

Part 6: The International Economy

CHAPTER 17: Macroeconomics in an Open Economy 544

CHAPTER 18: The International Financial System 572

CHAPTER 18 APPENDIX: The Gold Standard and the Bretton Woods Systems 596

Glossary G-1

Company Index I-1

Subject Index I-3

Credits C-1

CONTENTS

Preface vi

Acknowledgments xx

Part 1: Introduction

CHAPTER 1: Economics: Foundations and Models **2**

WHAT HAPPENS WHEN U.S. FIRMS MOVE TO CHINA? 2

Building a Foundation: Economics and Individual Decisions 5

People Are Rational 5

People Respond to Economic Incentives 5

Optimal Decisions Are Made at the Margin 5

Solved Problem 1-1: Apple Computer Makes a Decision at the Margin 6

The Economic Problem That Every Society Must Solve 7

What Goods and Services Will Be Produced? 7

How Will the Goods and Services Be Produced? 7

Who Will Receive the Goods and Services Produced? 7

Centrally Planned Economies versus Market Economies 8

The Modern "Mixed" Economy 8

Efficiency and Equity 9

Economic Models 10

The Role of Assumptions in Economic Models 10

Forming and Testing Hypotheses in Economic Models 10

Making the Connection 1-1: When Economists Disagree: A Debate over Outsourcing 11

Normative and Positive Analysis 12

Microeconomics and Macroeconomics 13

"Don't Let This Happen To You!" Don't Confuse Positive Analysis with Normative Analysis 13

A Preview of Important Economic Terms 14

Conclusion 15

AN INSIDE LOOK: How Does Economic Growth in China Affect Other Countries? 16

*Summary 18

*Key Terms 18

*Review Questions 19

*Problems and Applications 19

**End-of-chapter resource materials repeat in all chapters.*

CHAPTER 1 APPENDIX: Using Graphs and Formulas **21**

Graphs of One Variable 22

Graphs of Two Variables 23

Slopes of Lines 23

Taking Into Account More Than Two Variables on a Graph 24

Positive and Negative Relationships 25

Slopes of Nonlinear Curves 25

Formulas 28

Formula for a Percentage Change 28

Formulas for the Areas of a Rectangle and a Triangle 28

Summary of Using Formulas 29

Problems and Applications 29

CHAPTER 2: Trade-offs, Comparative Advantage, and the Market System **32**

MANAGERS MAKING CHOICES AT BMW 32

Production Possibilities Frontiers and Real-World Trade-offs 34

Graphing the Production Possibilities Frontier 34

Solved Problem 2-1: Drawing a Production Possibilities Frontier for Rosie's Boston Bakery 36

Making the Connection 2-1: Trade-offs and Tsunami Relief 38

Increasing Marginal Opportunity Costs 38

Economic Growth 39

Trade 40

Specialization and Gains from Trade 40

Absolute Advantage versus Comparative Advantage 42

"Don't Let This Happen To You!" Don't Confuse Absolute Advantage and Comparative Advantage 44

Comparative Advantage and the Gains from Trade 44

Solved Problem 2-2: Comparative Advantage and the Gains from Trade 44

The Market System 46

The Circular Flow of Income 46

The Gains from Free Markets 48

The Market Mechanism 48

Making the Connection 2-2: Story of the Market System in Action: "I, Pencil" 49

The Role of the Entrepreneur 50

The Legal Basis of a Successful Market System 50

Making the Connection 2-3: Property Rights in Cyberspace: Napster, Kazaa, and iTunes 51

Conclusion 53

AN INSIDE LOOK: Choosing the Production Mix at BMW 54

CHAPTER 3: Where Prices Come From: The Interaction of Demand and Supply 62

HOW HEWLETT-PACKARD MANAGES THE DEMAND FOR PRINTERS 62

The Demand Side of the Market 64

The Demand of an Individual Buyer 64

Demand Schedules and Demand Curves 64

Individual Demand and Market Demand 65

The Law of Demand 66

What Explains the Law of Demand? 66

Holding Everything Else Constant: The *Ceteris Paribus* Condition 67

Variables That Shift Market Demand 68

Making the Connection 3-1: Why Supermarkets Need to Understand Substitutes and Complements 69

Making the Connection 3-2: Companies Respond to a Growing Hispanic Population 70

A Change in Demand versus a Change in Quantity Demanded 72

Making the Connection 3-3: Estimating the Demand for Printers at Hewlett-Packard 72

The Supply Side of the Market 73

Supply Schedules and Supply Curves 73

Individual Supply and Market Supply 74

The Law of Supply 74

Variables That Shift Supply 75

A Change in Supply versus a Change in Quantity Supplied 76

Market Equilibrium: Putting Demand and Supply Together 77

How Markets Eliminate Surpluses and Shortages 78

Demand and Supply Both Count 79

Solved Problem 3-1: Demand and Supply Both Count: A Tale of Two Letters 80

The Effect of Demand and Supply Shifts on Equilibrium 81

The Effect of Shifts in Supply on Equilibrium 81

Making the Connection 3-4: The Falling Price of Large Flat-Screen Televisions 82

The Effect of Shifts in Demand on Equilibrium 83

The Effect of Shifts in Demand and Supply over Time 84

Solved Problem 3-2: High Demand and Low Prices in the Lobster Market? 85

Shifts in a Curve versus Movements along a Curve 86

"Don't Let This Happen To You!" Remember: A Change in a Good's Price Does Not Cause the Demand or Supply Curve to Shift. 87

Conclusion 87

AN INSIDE LOOK: Hewlett-Packard Cuts PC Prices to Sell More Printers 88

CHAPTER 4: Economic Efficiency, Government Price Setting, and Taxes 96

SHOULD THE GOVERNMENT CONTROL APARTMENT RENTS? 96

Consumer Surplus and Producer Surplus 98

Consumer Surplus 99

Making the Connection 4-1: The Consumer Surplus from Satellite Television 100

Producer Surplus 101

What Consumer Surplus and Producer Surplus Measure 101

The Efficiency of Competitive Markets 102

Marginal Benefit Equals Marginal Cost in Competitive Equilibrium 102

Economic Surplus 103

Deadweight Loss 103

Economic Surplus and Economic Efficiency 104

Government Intervention in the Market: Price Floors and Price Ceilings 104

Price Floors: The Example of Agricultural Markets 105

Making the Connection 4-2: Price Floors in Labor Markets: The Minimum Wage 106

Price Ceilings: The Example of Rent Controls 107

"Don't Let This Happen To You!" Don't Confuse "Scarcity" with a "Shortage" 108

Black Markets 109

Solved Problem 4-1: What's the Economic Effect of a "Black Market" for Apartments? 109

Making the Connection 4-3: Does Holiday Gift Giving Have a Deadweight Loss? 110

The Results of Government Intervention: Winners, Losers, and Inefficiency 111

Positive and Normative Analysis of Price Ceilings and Price Floors 111

The Economic Impact of Taxes 112

The Effect of Taxes on Economic Efficiency 112

Tax Incidence: Who Actually Pays a Tax? 112

Solved Problem 4-2: When Do Consumers Pay All of a Sales Tax Increase? 114

Making the Connection 4-4: Is the Burden of the Social Security Tax Really Shared Equally between Workers and Firms? 116

Conclusion 117

AN INSIDE LOOK: Dealing with Rent Control 118

CHAPTER 4 APPENDIX: Quantitative Demand and Supply Analysis 125
Demand and Supply Equations 125
Calculating Consumer Surplus and Producer Surplus 126
Review Questions 128
Problems and Applications 129

Part 2: Firms in the Domestic and International Economies

CHAPTER 5: Firms, the Stock Market, and Corporate Governance 130
GOOGLE: FROM DORM ROOM TO WALL STREET 130
Types of Firms 132
Who Is Liable? Limited and Unlimited Liability 132
Making the Connection 5-1: What's in a "Name"? Lloyd's of London Learns about Unlimited Liability the Hard Way 133
Corporations Earn the Majority of Revenue and Profits 134
The Structure of Corporations and the Principal-Agent Problem 134
Corporate Structure and Corporate Governance 134
Solved Problem 5-1: Does the Principal-Agent Problem Also Apply to the Relationship between Managers and Workers? 135
How Firms Raise Funds 136
Sources of External Funds 136
Stock and Bond Markets Provide Capital—and Information 137
"Don't Let This Happen To You!" When Google Shares Change Hands, Google Doesn't Get the Money 138
Making the Connection 5-2: Following General Electric's Stock and Bond Prices in the Financial Pages 139
Using Financial Statements to Evaluate a Corporation 140
Making the Connection 5-3: A Bull in China's Financial Shop 141
The Income Statement 142
The Balance Sheet 143
Understanding the Business Scandals of 2002 143
Solved Problem 5-2: What Makes a Good Board of Directors? 144
Conclusion 145
AN INSIDE LOOK: Google's Initial Public Offering 146

CHAPTER 5 APPENDIX: Tools to Analyze Firms' Financial Information 152
Using Present Value to Make Investment Decisions 152
Solved Problem 5A-1: How to Receive Your Contest Winnings 154
Using Present Value to Calculate Bond Prices 155
Using Present Value to Calculate Stock Prices 155
A Simple Formula for Calculating Stock Prices 156
Going Deeper into Financial Statements 157
Analyzing Income Statements 157
Analyzing Balance Sheets 158

CHAPTER 6: Comparative Advantage and the Gains from International Trade 162
SUGAR QUOTA DRIVES U.S. CANDY MANUFACTURERS OVERSEAS 162
An Overview of International Trade 164
The Importance of Trade to the U.S. Economy 164
U.S. International Trade in a World Context 165
Making the Connection 6-1: Has Outsourcing Hurt the U.S. Economy? 166
Comparative Advantage: The Basis of All Trade 167
A Brief Review of Comparative Advantage 167
Comparative Advantage in International Trade 167
The Gains from Trade 168
Increasing Consumption through Trade 169
Solved Problem 6-1: The Gains from Trade 170
Why Don't We See Complete Specialization? 172
Does Anyone Lose as a Result of International Trade? 172
"Don't Let This Happen To You!" Remember That Trade Creates Both Winners and Losers 173
Where Does Comparative Advantage Come From? 173
Making the Connection 6-2: Why Is Dalton, Georgia, the Carpet-Making Capital of the World? 174
Comparative Advantage Over Time: The Rise and Fall—and Rise—of the U.S. Consumer Electronics Industry 174
Government Policies That Restrict Trade 175
Tariffs 177
Quotas 178
Measuring the Economic Impact of the Sugar Quota 179
Solved Problem 6-2: Measuring the Economic Effect of a Quota 179
The High Cost of Preserving Jobs with Tariffs and Quotas 181
Gains from Unilateral Elimination of Tariffs and Quotas 181
Other Barriers to Trade 182
The Argument over Trade Policies and Globalization 182
Why Do Some People Oppose the World Trade Organization? 182
Making the Connection 6-3: The Unintended Consequences of Banning Goods Made with Child Labor 183

Making the Connection 6-4: Has NAFTA Helped or Hurt the U.S. Economy? 185
Dumping 186
Positive versus Normative Analysis (Once Again) 187
Conclusion 187
AN INSIDE LOOK: The United States and Australia Reduce Trade Barriers 188

CHAPTER 6 APPENDIX: Multinational Firms 195
Multinational Firms 195
A Brief History of Multinational Enterprises 195
Strategic Factors in Moving from Domestic to Foreign Markets 196
Making the Connection 6A-1: Have Multinational Corporations Reduced Employment and Lowered Wages in the United States? 198
Challenges to U.S. Firms in Foreign Markets 199
Competitive Advantages of U.S. Firms 199

Part 3: Macroeconomic Foundations and Long-Run Growth

CHAPTER 7: GDP: Measuring Total Production and Income 202
INCREASES IN GDP SPUR HIRING AT FREIGHTLINER 202
Gross Domestic Product Measures Total Production 205
Measuring Total Production: Gross Domestic Product 205
Solved Problem 7-1: Calculating GDP 206
Production, Income, and the Circular Flow Diagram 207
Components of GDP 208
"Don't Let This Happen To You!" Remember What Economists Mean by "Investment" 209
Making the Connection 7-1: Spending on Homeland Security 209
An Equation for GDP and Some Actual Values 210
Measuring GDP by the Value Added Method 211
Does GDP Measure What We Want It to Measure? 212
Shortcomings in GDP as a Measure of Total Production 212
Making the Connection 7-2: How the Underground Economy Hurts Developing Countries 213
Shortcomings of GDP as a Measure of Well-Being 214
Making the Connection 7-3: Did World War II Bring Prosperity? 214
Real GDP versus Nominal GDP 215
Calculating Real GDP 215
Solved Problem 7-2: Calculating Real GDP 216
Comparing Real GDP and Nominal GDP 217
Making the Connection 7-4: How Freightliner Uses Forecasts of GDP 218
The GDP Deflator 218
Other Measures of Total Production and Total Income 219
Gross National Product *(GNP)* 219
Net National Product *(NNP)* 220
National Income 220
Personal Income 220
Disposable Personal Income 220
Conclusion 221
AN INSIDE LOOK: Movements in Canadian GDP 222

CHAPTER 8: Unemployment and Inflation 228
LUCENT TECHNOLOGIES DEALS WITH UNEMPLOYMENT AND INFLATION 228
Measuring the Unemployment Rate and the Labor Force Participation Rate 230
The Household Survey 230
Solved Problem 8-1: What Happens If You Include the Military? 232
Problems with Measuring the Unemployment Rate 233
Trends in Labor Force Participation 233
Making the Connection 8-1: What Explains the Increase in "Kramers"? 234
Unemployment Rates for Demographic Groups 235
How Long Are People Usually Unemployed? 235
The Establishment Survey: Another Measure of Employment 236
Job Creation and Job Destruction Over Time 237
Types of Unemployment 237
Frictional Unemployment and Job Search 238
Structural Unemployment 239
Cyclical Unemployment 239
Full Employment 239
Making the Connection 8-2: How Should We Categorize the Unemployment at Lucent Technologies? 240
Explaining Unemployment 240
Government Policies and the Unemployment Rate 240
Labor Unions 242
Efficiency Wages 242
Making the Connection 8-3: Why Did Henry Ford Pay His Workers Twice as Much as Other Car Manufacturers? 243
Measuring Inflation 243
The Consumer Price Index 244
Is the CPI Accurate? 245
"Don't Let This Happen To You!" Don't Miscalculate the Inflation Rate 246

The Producer Price Index 247

Using Price Indexes to Adjust for the Effects of Inflation 247

Solved Problem 8-2: Calculating Real Average Hourly Earnings 248

Falling Real Wages at Lucent 249

Real versus Nominal Interest Rates 249

Does Inflation Impose Costs on the Economy? 251

Inflation Affects the Distribution of Income 251

The Problem with Anticipated Inflation 251

Making the Connection 8-4: Why a Lower Inflation Rate Is Like a Tax Cut for Lucent's Bondholders 252

The Problem with Unanticipated Inflation 253

Conclusion 253

AN INSIDE LOOK: Managers and Workers at Boeing Negotiate Wages 254

CHAPTER 9: Economic Growth, the Financial System, and Business Cycles **260**

GROWTH AND THE BUSINESS CYCLE AT THE FORD MOTOR COMPANY 260

Long-Run Economic Growth Is the Key to Rising Living Standards 262

Making the Connection 9-1: The Connection between Economic Prosperity and Health 264

Calculating Growth Rates and the Rule of 70 265

What Determines the Rate of Long-Run Growth? 266

Solved Problem 9-1: The Role of Technological Change in Growth 267

Making the Connection 9-2: What Explains Rapid Economic Growth in Botswana? 268

Potential Real GDP 269

Saving, Investment, and the Financial System 270

An Overview of the Financial System 270

The Macroeconomics of Saving and Investment 272

The Market for Loanable Funds 273

Making the Connection 9-3: Ebenezer Scrooge: Accidental Promoter of Economic Growth? 274

Solved Problem 9-2: How Would a Consumption Tax Affect Saving, Investment, the Interest Rate, and Economic Growth? 277

The Business Cycle 278

Some Basic Business Cycle Definitions 278

Making the Connection 9-4: Who Decides If the Economy Is in a Recession? 278

What Happens during a Business Cycle? 279

"Don't Let This Happen To You!" Don't Confuse the Price Level and the Inflation Rate 282

Why Is the Economy More Stable? 285

Conclusion 285

AN INSIDE LOOK: Growth and the Chinese Automobile Industry 286

CHAPTER 10: Long-Run Economic Growth: Sources and Policies **292**

THE CHINESE ECONOMIC MIRACLE 292

Economic Growth Over Time and Around the World 294

Economic Growth from 1,000,000 B.C. to the Present 294

Making the Connection 10-1: Why Was England First? 295

Small Differences in Growth Rates Are Important 296

"Don't Let This Happen To You!" Don't Confuse Average Annual Percentage Change with Total Percentage Change 297

Why Do Growth Rates Matter? 297

Making the Connection 10-2: The Benefits of an Earlier Start: Standards of Living in China and Japan 297

"The Rich Get Richer and . . ." 298

What Determines How Fast Economies Grow? 298

The Per-Worker Production Function 300

Which Is More Important for Economic Growth: More Capital or Technological Change? 301

Technological Change: The Key to Sustaining Economic Growth 301

Making the Connection 10-3: Why Did the Soviet Union's Economy Fail? 302

Solved Problem 10-1: Using the Economic Growth Model to Analyze the Failure of the Soviet Union's Economy 303

Endogenous Growth Theory 304

Joseph Schumpeter and Creative Destruction 305

Economic Growth in the United States 306

Economic Growth in the United States Since 1950: Fast, Then Slow, Then Fast Again 306

What Caused the Productivity Slowdown of 1973–1995? 307

The Productivity Boom: Are We in a "New Economy"? 308

Why Has Productivity Growth Been Faster in the United States than in Other Countries? 309

Why Isn't the Whole World Rich? 311

Catch-up: Sometimes, But Not Always 312

Solved Problem 10-2: The Economic Growth Model's Predictions of Catch-up 314

Why Don't More Low-Income Countries Experience Rapid Growth? 315

The Benefits of Globalization 317

Making the Connection 10-4: Globalization and the Spread of Technology in Bangladesh 318

Growth Policies 319

Enhancing Property Rights and the Rule of Law 319

Improving Health and Education 320
Policies with Respect to Technology 320
Policies with Respect to Saving and Investment 320
Is Economic Growth Good or Bad? 321
Conclusion 321
AN INSIDE LOOK: India Achieves Growth through Efficiency and Globalization 322

Part 4: Short-Run Fluctuations

CHAPTER 11: Output and Expenditure in the Short Run 328
DEMAND FORECASTS BACKFIRE AT CISCO SYSTEMS 328
The Aggregate Expenditure Model 330
Aggregate Expenditure 330
The Difference between Planned Investment and Actual Investment 331
Macroeconomic Equilibrium 331
Adjustments to Macroeconomic Equilibrium 332
Determining the Level of Aggregate Expenditure in the Economy 333
Consumption 333
The Relationship between Consumption and National Income 336
Income, Consumption, and Saving 338
Solved Problem 11-1: Calculating the Marginal Propensity to Consume and the Marginal Propensity to Save 339
Planned Investment 340
Making the Connection 11-1: Cisco Rides the Roller Coaster of Information Technology Spending 341
Government Purchases 342
Net Exports 342
Graphing Macroeconomic Equilibrium 344
Showing a Recession on the 45°-Line Diagram 348
The Important Role of Inventories 349
Making the Connection 11-2: Business Attempts to Control Inventories, Then . . . and Now 349
A Numerical Example of Macroeconomic Equilibrium 350
"Don't Let This Happen To You!" Don't Confuse Aggregate Expenditure with Consumption Spendin 351
Solved Problem 11-2: Determining Macroeconomic Equilibrium 351
The Multiplier Effect 352
Making the Connection 11-3: The Multiplier in Reverse: The Great Depression of the 1930s 354
A Formula for the Multiplier 356
Summarizing the Multiplier Effect 357
Solved Problem 11-3: Using the Multiplier Formula 357
The Aggregate Demand Curve 359
Conclusion 360
AN INSIDE LOOK:: Expenditure in Japan Soars, Nudging Up GDP 362

CHAPTER 11 APPENDIX: The Algebra of Macroeconomic Equilibrium 368

CHAPTER 12: Aggregate Demand and Aggregate Supply Analysis 370
CATERPILLAR RECOVERS SLOWLY FROM THE 2001 RECESSION 370
Aggregate Demand 372
Why Is the Aggregate Demand Curve Downward Sloping? 373
Shifts of the Aggregate Demand Curve versus Movements Along It 374
"Don't Let This Happen To You!" Be Clear Why the Aggregate Deman d Curve Is Downward Sloping 374
The Variables that Shift the Aggregate Demand Curve 375
Making the Connection12-1: The Effect of Exchange Rates on Caterpillar's Sales 376
Solved Problem12-1: Movements Along the Aggregate Demand Curve versus Shifts of the Aggregate Demand Curve 377
Aggregate Supply 378
The Long-Run Aggregate Supply Curve 378
The Short-Run Aggregate Supply Curve 380
Shifts of the Short-Run Aggregate Supply Curve versus Movements Along It 381
Variables that Shift the Short-Run Aggregate Supply Curve 382
Macroeconomic Equilibrium in the Long Run and the Short Run 383
Recessions, Expansions, and Supply Shocks 384
A Dynamic Aggregate Demand and Aggregate Supply Model 388
What is the Usual Cause of Inflation? 389
The Slow Recovery from the Recession of 2001 389
Making the Connection 2-2: Does Rising Productivity Growth Reduce Employment? 391
The More Rapid Recovery of 2003–2004 393
Solved Problem 12-2: Showing the Oil Shock of 1974–1975 on a Dynamic Aggregate Demand and Aggregate Supply Graph 394
Conclusion 395
AN INSIDE LOOK: Construction Company Komatsu Benefits from Exports to China 396

CHAPTER 12 APPENDIX: Macroeconomic Schools of Thought 403

The Monetarist Model 403

The New Classical Model 404

The Real Business Cycle Model 404

Making the Connection 12A-1: Karl Marx: Capitalism's Severest Critic 405

Part 5: Monetary and Fiscal Policy

CHAPTER 13: Money, Banks, and the Federal Reserve System 406

MCDONALD'S MONEY PROBLEMS IN ARGENTINA 406

What is Money and Why Do We Need It? 408

Barter and the Invention of Money 408

Making the Connection 13-1: Money in a World War II Prisoner-of-War Camp 409

The Functions of Money 409

What Can Serve as Money? 410

Making the Connection 13-2: Money without a Government? The Strange Case of the Iraqi Dinar 412

How Do We Measure Money Today? 412

M1: The Narrowest Definition of the Money Supply 413

M2: A Broader Definition of Money 414

"Don't Let This Happen To You!" Don't Confuse Money with Income or Wealth 414

Solved Problem 13-1: The Definitions of M1 and M2 415

What About Credit Cards and Debit Cards? 415

How Do Banks Create Money? 415

Bank Balance Sheets 416

"Don't Let This Happen To You!" Know When a Checking Account Is an Asset and When It Is a Liability 416

Using T-Accounts to Show How a Bank Can Create Money 417

The Simple Deposit Multiplier 419

Solved Problem 13-2: Showing How Banks Create Money 420

The Federal Reserve System 423

Making the Connection 13-3: The 2001 Bank Panic in Argentina 423

The Organization of the Federal Reserve System 424

How the Federal Reserve Manages the Money Supply 424

Putting It All Together: Decisions of the Nonbank Public, Banks, nd the Fed 427

The Quantity Theory of Money 427

Connecting Money and Prices: The Quantity Equation 427

The Quantity Theory Explanation of Inflation 428

High Rates of Inflation 429

High Inflation in Argentina 429

Making the Connection 13-4: The German Hyperinflation of the Early 1920s 430

Conclusion 431

AN INSIDE LOOK: Does Using the Dollar Destabalize Latin American Countries? 432

CHAPTER 14: Monetary Policy 438

WHY DID HOMEBUILDER TOLL BROTHERS, INC., PROSPER DURING THE 2001 RECESSION? 438

What Is Monetary Policy? 440

The Goals of Monetary Policy 440

The Money Market and the Fed's Choice of Targets 441

Monetary Policy Targets 442

The Demand for Money 442

Shifts in the Money Demand Curve 443

How the Fed Manages the Money Supply: A Quick Review 444

Equilibrium in the Money Market 444

Solved Problem 14-1: The Relationship between Treasury Bill Prices and Their Interest Rates 446

A Tale of Two Interest Rates 447

Choosing a Monetary Policy Target 447

The Importance of the Federal Funds Rate 448

Monetary Policy and Economic Activity 449

How Interest Rates Affect Aggregate Demand 449

Making the Connection 14-1: Was There a Housing Market "Bubble" in the Early 2000s? 450

The Effects of Monetary Policy on Real GDP and the Price Level 451

Can the Fed Eliminate Recessions? 453

Making the Connection 14-2: The Fed Responds to the Terrorist Attacks of September 11, 2001 452

Making the Connection 14-3: Why Was Monetary Policy Ineffective in Japan? 454

Using Monetary Policy to Fight Inflation 454

Solved Problem 14-2: The Effects of Monetary Policy 456

A Summary of How Monetary Policy Works 457

Making the Connection 14-4: Why Does Wall Street Care about Monetary Policy? 458

"Don't Let This Happen To You!" Remember That with Monetary Policy It's the Interest Rates—Not the Money—That Counts 459

Can the Fed Get the Timing Right? 459

A Closer Look at the Fed's Setting of Monetary Policy Targets 460

Should the Fed Target the Money Supply? 460

Why Doesn't the Fed Target Both the Money Supply and the Interest Rate? 461

The Taylor Rule 461
Should the Fed Target Inflation? 462
Is the Independence of the Federal Reserve a Good Idea? 463
The Case for Fed Independence 464
The Case against Fed Independence 465
Conclusion 465
AN INSIDE LOOK: Monetary Policy Spurs Housing Boom 466

CHAPTER 15: Fiscal Policy 472
A BOON FOR H&R BLOCK 472
Fiscal Policy 474
What Fiscal Policy Is and What It Isn't 474
Automatic Stabilizers versus Discretionary Fiscal Policy 474
An Overview of Government Spending and Taxes 475
Making the Connection 15-1: The Future of Social Security and Medicare 476
Using Fiscal Policy to Influence Aggregate Demand 478
Expansionary Fiscal Policy 478
Contractionary Fiscal Policy 479
A Summary of How Fiscal Policy Affects Aggregate Demand 479
"Don't Let This Happen To You!" Don't Confuse Fiscal Policy and Monetary Policy 480
The Government Purchases and Tax Multipliers 481
The Effect of Changes in Tax Rates 483
Taking Into Account the Effects of Aggregate Supply 483
The Multipliers Work in Both Directions 483
Solved Problem 15-1: Fiscal Policy Multipliers 484
The Limits of Fiscal Policy to Stabalize the Economy 485
Does Government Spending Reduce Private Spending? 487
Crowding Out in the Short Run 487
Crowding Out in the Long Run 488
Making the Connection 15-2: Limits to Fiscal Policy: Japan in the late 1990s 489
Deficits, Surpluses, and Federal Government Debt 490
How the Federal Budget Can Serve as an Automatic Stabilizer 490
Making the Connection 15-3: Did Fiscal Policy Fail During the Great Depression? 492
Solved Problem 15-2: The Effect of Economic Fluctuations on the Budget Deficit 493
Should the Federal Budget Always Be Balanced? 494
The Federal Government Debt 494
Is the Government Debt a Problem? 496
The Effects of Fiscal Policy in the Long Run 496
The Long-Run Effects of Tax Policy 496
Tax Simplification 497
Making the Connection 15-4: Should the United States Adopt the "Flat Tax"? 498
The Economic Effect of Tax Reform 499
How Large Are Supply-Side Effects? 500
Conclusion 501
AN INSIDE LOOK: Tax Receipts Increase in 2005, but Deficit Still Looms Large 502

CHAPTER 15 APPENDIX: A Closer Look at the Multiplier 508
An Expression for Equilibrium Real GDP 508
A Formula for the Government Purchases Multiplier 509
A Formula for the Tax Multiplier 510
The "Balanced Budget" Multiplier 510
The Effects of Changes in Tax Rates on the Multiplier 511
The Multiplier in an Open Economy 511

CHAPTER 16: Inflation, Unemployment, and Federal Reserve Policy 514
WHY DOES WHIRLPOOL CARE ABOUT MONETARY POLICY? 514
The Discovery of the Short-Run Trade-off between Unemployment and Inflation 516
Explaining the Phillips Curve with Aggregate Demand and Aggregate Supply Curves 516
Is the Phillips Curve a Policy Menu? 518
Solved Problem 16-1: The Policy Menu View of the Phillips Curve 519
Is the Short-Run Phillips Curve Stable? 519
The Long-Run Phillips Curve 520
The Role of Expectations of Future Inflation 520
Making the Connection 16-1: Do Workers Understand Inflation? 522
The Short-Run and Long-Run Phillips Curves 522
Shifts in the Short-Run Phillips Curve 523
How Does a Vertical Long-Run Phillips Curve Affect Monetary Policy? 524
Making the Connection 16-2: Does the Natural Rate of Unemployment Ever Change? 525
Solved Problem 16-2: Changing Views of the Phillips Curve 526
Expectations of the Inflation Rate 526
The Effect of Rational Expectations on Monetary Policy 527
Is the Short-Run Phillips Curve Really Vertical? 528
Real Business Cycle Models 529
How the Fed Fights Inflation 530
The Effect of a Supply Shock on the Phillips Curve 530
Paul Volcker and Disinflation 531

"Don't Let This Happen To You!" Don't Confuse Disinflation with Deflation 532
Solved Problem 16-3: Using Monetary Policy to Lower the Inflation Rate 532
Alan Greenspan and the Importance of a Credible Monetary Policy 534
De-emphasizing the Money Supply 534
The Importance of Fed Credibility 535
Monetary Policy Credibility after Greenspan 535
A Failure of Credibility at the Bank of Japan 536
Federal Reserve Policy and Whirlpool's "Pricing Power" 536
Conclusion 537
AN INSIDE LOOK: Wage Rates for Hourly Workers Stagnate 538

Part 6: The International Economy

CHAPTER 17: Macroeconomics in an Open Economy 544
CHINESE TOWELS INVADE JAPAN 544
The Balance of Payments: Linking the United States to the International Economy 546
The Current Account 546
The Financial Account 547
The Capital Account 548
Why Is the Balance of Payments Always Zero? 549
Solved Problem 17-1: Understanding the Arithmetic of Open Economies 549
"Don't Let This Happen To You!" Don't Confuse the Balance of Trade, the Current Account Balance, and the Balance of Payments 550
The Foreign Exchange Market and Exchange Rates 551
Making the Connection 17-1: Exchange Rates in the Financial Pages 551
Equilibrium in the Market for Foreign Exchange 552
"Don't Let This Happen To You!" Don't Confuse What Happens When a Currency Appreciates with What Happens When It Depreciates 553
How Do Shifts in Demand and Supply Affect the Exchange Rate? 553
Some Exchange Rates Are Not Determined by the Market 555
How Movements in the Exchange Rate Affect Exports and Imports 555
Solved Problem 17-2: Effect of Changing Exchange Rates on the Prices of Imports and Exports 556
The Real Exchange Rate 556
The International Sector and National Saving and Investment 557
Net Exports Equal Net Foreign Investment 557
Domestic Saving, Domestic Investment, and Net Foreign Investment 558
Solved Problem 17-3: Arriving at the Saving and Investment Equation 559
The Effect of a Government Budget Deficit on Investment 560
Making the Connection 17-2: Why Is the United States Called the "World's Largest Debtor"? 561
Monetary Policy and Fiscal Policy in an Open Economy 562
Monetary Policy in an Open Economy 562
Fiscal Policy in an Open Economy 563
Conclusion 563
AN INSIDE LOOK: Distorted Price Signals Nurture U.S. Current-Account Deficit 564

CHAPTER 18: The International Financial System 572
FLUCTUATING EXCHANGE RATES PUSH MOLSON BREWERIES TO SELL THE CANADIENS 572
Exchange-Rate Systems 574
"Don't Let This Happen To You!" Remember That Modern Currencies Are Fiat Money 575
The Current Exchange Rate System 575
The Floating Dollar 575
Making the Connection 18-1: The Toronto Blue Jays Gain from the Rising Value of the Canadian Dollar 576
What Determines Exchange Rates in the Long Run? 577
Making the Connection 18-2: The Big Mac Theory of Exchange Rates 578
Solved Problem 18-1: Calculating Purchasing Power Parity Exchange Rates Using Big Macs 579
The Euro 580
Making the Connection 18-3: The Underground Economy in Europe Surfaces 582
Pegging Against the Dollar 582
Making the Connection 18-4: Crisis and Recovery in South Korea 586
Solved Problem 18-2: Coping with Fluctuations in the Value of the U.S. Dollar 587
International Capital Markets 588
Conclusion 589
AN INSIDE LOOK: Strong Euro Slashes Profits at Some EU Firms 590

CHAPTER 18 APPENDIX: THE GOLD STANDARD AND THE BRETTON WOODS SYSTEM 596
The Gold Standard 596
The End of the Gold Standard 596
The Bretton Woods System 597
The Collapse of the Bretton Woods System 598
Glossary G-1
Company Index I-1
Subject Index I-3
Credits C-1

FLEXIBILITY CHART

The following chart helps you organize your syllabus based on your teaching preferences and objectives:

Core

CHAPTER 1: Economics: Foundations and Models
Uses the debate of outsourcing to discuss the role of models in economic analysis.

CHAPTER 2: Trade-offs, Comparative Advantage, and the Market System
Includes coverage of the role of the entrepreneur, property rights, and the legal system in a market system.

CHAPTER 3: Where Prices Come From: The Interaction of Demand and Supply

CHAPTER 7: GDP: Measuring Total Production and Income
Covers how total production is measured and the difference between real and nominal variables.

CHAPTER 8: Unemployment and Inflation
Covers the three types of unemployment, how inflation is measured, and the difference between real and nominal interest rates.

CHAPTER 9: Economic Growth, the Financial System, and Business Cycles
Provides an overview of key macroeconomic issues by discussing the business cycle in the context of long-run growth. Dicusses the roles of entrepreneurship, financial institutions, and policy in economic growth.

CHAPTER 10: Long-Run Growth: Sources and Policies
Highlights the importance of institutions, policies, and technological change for economic growth.

CHAPTER 12: Aggregate Demand and Aggregate Supply Analysis
Carefully develops the AD-AS model and then makes the model dynamic to account better for actual movements in real GDP and the price level.

CHAPTER 13: Money, Banks, and the Federal Reserve System
Explores the role of money in the economy, the money supply process, and the structure of the Federal Reserve.

Policy

CHAPTER 4: Economic Efficiency, Government Price Setting, and Taxes

CHAPTER 14: Monetary Policy
Uses the aggregate demand and aggregate supply model to show the effects of monetary policy on real GDP and the price level. Chapter 14 is a self-contained discussion, so instructors may safely omit the material in Chapter 16.

CHAPTER 15: Fiscal Policy
Uses the aggregate demand and aggregate supply model to show how taxes and government spending affect the economy. Includes significant coverage of the supply-side effects of fiscal policy.

Optional

CHAPTER 1 APPENDIX: Using Graphs and Formulas

CHAPTER 4 APPENDIX: Quantitative Demand and Supply Analysis
Provides a quantitative analysis of rent control.

CHAPTER 5: Firms, the Stock Market, and Corporate Governance
Unique chapter that includes coverage of the Sarbanes-Oxley Act.

CHAPTER 5 APPENDIX: Tools to Analyze Firms' Financial Information
Covers present value and financial statements.

CHAPTER 6: Comparative Advantage and the Gains from International Trade
This chapter may be delayed until after Chapter 16.

CHAPTER 6 APPENDIX: Multinational Firms
Covers the benefits and challenges of operating overseas businesses.

CHAPTER 11: Output and Expenditure in the Short Run
Uses the Keynesian 45°-line aggregate expenditure model to introduce students to the short-run relationship between spending and production. The discussion of monetary and fiscal policy in later chapters uses only the aggregate demand and aggregate supply model, which allows instructors to omit Chapter 11.

CHAPTER 11 APPENDIX: The Algebra of Macroeconomic Equilibrium
Uses equations to represent the aggregate expenditure model described in the chapter.

CHAPTER 12 APPENDIX: Macroeconomic Schools of Thought
overs the monetarist model, the new classical model, and the real business cycle model.

CHAPTER 16: Inflation, Unemployment, and Federal Reserve Policy
Discusses the short-run and long-run Phillips curves. Also covers the roles of expectations formation and central bank credibility in monetary policy.

CHAPTER 17: Macroeconomics in an Open Economy
Explains the linkages among countries at the macroeconomic level and how policymakers in all countries take these linkages into account when conducting monetary and fiscal policy.

CHAPTER 18: The International Financial System
Covers the international financial system and explores the role central banks play in the system.

macroeconomics

chapter one

Economics: Foundations and Models

What Happens When U.S. Firms Move to China?

➤ You have probably seen the words "Made in China" on a variety of the products you own, including running shoes, clothing, towels, and sheets. It may not be surprising that relatively simple products are manufactured in China, where workers receive much lower wages than in the United States. Until recently, though, most people would not have expected sophisticated, high-technology products to be designed and manufactured in China. That is why an announcement by Massachusetts-based 3Com Corporation in late 2004 was so surprising. 3Com is a leading high-technology firm with 2,000 employees and annual sales of $700 million. The firm introduced a new network switch for corporate computer systems that not only was manufactured in China but had been designed by Chinese engineers.

3Com's price for the switch was $183,000. 3Com's even larger rival, Cisco Systems—which is based in San Jose, California, with 34,000 employees and annual sales of more than $30 billion—charged $245,000 for a comparable switch, designed and manufactured in the United States. The difference in price showed that even when producing some high-technology goods, it was cheaper for U.S. firms to operate in China. Because the salaries of engineers are so much lower in China, 3Com was able to use four times as many engineers to design its switch, which it claimed had twice the capacity of Cisco's switch. The cost to manufacture the switch was also much lower in China, where the average factory worker earns only $0.64 per hour, including benefits, compared with about $22.00 per hour earned by the average factory worker in the United States.

Many U.S., Japanese, and European firms have been moving the production of goods and services to other countries. This process of firms producing goods and services outside of their home country is called *outsourcing* (sometimes also referred to as *off-shoring*). U.S. firms have been outsourcing for decades, but some of the recently outsourced jobs require high skill levels, as was true of the jobs 3Com moved from the United States to China. To cite another example that has received much publicity, Dun & Bradstreet (now known as D&B), a

business information firm founded in New York in 1841, has begun purchasing much of its software engineering services from a firm in Bangalore, India, because Indian software engineers typically receive salaries 75 percent lower than do software engineers in the United States.

Articles on outsourcing appear frequently in business magazines and the financial pages of newspapers, and the issue has also been the subject of heated debate among political commentators, policymakers, and presidential candidates. The focus of the debate has been the question: "Has outsourcing been good or bad for the U.S. economy?" This question is one of many that cannot be answered without using economics. In this chapter, and the remainder of this book, we will see how economics helps in answering important questions about outsourcing, as well as many other issues. Economics provides us with tools for understanding why outsourcing has increased, why some firms are more likely to move production to other countries, and what the effects of outsourcing will be on the wages of U.S. workers, the profits of U.S. firms, and the overall ability of the U.S. economy to produce more and better goods and services. *An Inside Look* on page 16 discusses the effects of economic growth in China on jobs and wages in the United States and Europe.

Source: Pete Engardio and Dexter Roberts, "The China Price," *Business Week*, December 6, 2004.

LEARNING OBJECTIVES

After studying this chapter, you should be able to:

① Discuss these three important economic ideas: *People are rational. People respond to incentives. Optimal decisions are made at the margin.*

② Discuss how an economy answers these questions: *What* goods and services will be produced? *How* will the goods and services be produced? *Who* will receive the goods and services?

③ Understand the role of models in economic analysis.

④ Distinguish between microeconomics and macroeconomics.

⑤ Become familiar with important economic terms.

In this book, we use economics to answer questions such as the following:

- How are the prices of goods and services determined?
- How does pollution affect the economy, and how should government policy deal with these effects?
- Why do firms engage in international trade, and how do government policies affect international trade?
- Why does government control the prices of some goods and services, and what are the effects of those controls?

Economists do not always agree on the answers to every question. In fact, as we will see, economists engage in lively debates on some issues. Economics is a dynamic field in which new questions are constantly arising, and new methods of analyzing and answering those questions are being developed.

All the questions we discuss in this book reflect a basic fact of life: People must make choices as they try to attain their goals. The choices reflect the trade-offs people face because we live in a world of **scarcity,** which means that although our wants are unlimited, the resources available to fulfill those wants are limited. You might like to have a 60-inch plasma television in every room of your home, but unless you are a close relative of Bill Gates, you probably lack the money to purchase them. Every day you must make choices about how to spend your limited income on the many goods and services available. The finite amount of time available to you also limits your ability to attain your goals. If you spend an hour studying for your economics midterm, you have one less hour available to study for your history midterm. Firms and the government are in the same situation you are: They have limited resources available to them as they attempt to attain their goals. **Economics** is the study of the choices consumers, business managers, and government officials make to attain their goals, given their scarce resources.

Scarcity The situation in which unlimited wants exceed the limited resources available to fulfill those wants.

Economics The study of the choices people make to attain their goals, given their scarce resources.

We begin this chapter by discussing three important economic ideas that we will return to many times in the book: *People are rational. People respond to incentives. Optimal decisions are made at the margin.* Then we consider the three fundamental questions that any economy must answer: *What* goods and services will be produced? *How* will the goods and services be produced? *Who* will receive the goods and services? Next we consider the role of *economic models* in helping us to analyze the many issues presented throughout this book. **Economic models** are simplified versions of reality used to analyze real-world economic situations. Later in this chapter, we explore why economists use models and how they construct them. Finally, we discuss the difference between microeconomics and macroeconomics, and we preview some important economic terms.

Economic model Simplified versions of reality used to analyze real-world economic situations.

Building a Foundation: Economics and Individual Decisions

1 LEARNING OBJECTIVE

Discuss these three important economic ideas: *People are rational. People respond to incentives. Optimal decisions are made at the margin.*

Market A group of buyers and sellers of a good or service and the institution or arrangement by which they come together to trade

As you try to achieve your goals, whether they are buying a new computer or finding a part-time job, you will interact with other people in *markets.* A **market** is a group of buyers and sellers of a good or service and the institution or arrangement by which they come together to trade. Most of economics involves analyzing what happens in markets. Throughout this book, as we study how people make choices and interact in markets, we will return to three important ideas:

1. People are rational.
2. People respond to economic incentives.
3. Optimal decisions are made at the margin.

People Are Rational

Economists generally assume that people are rational. This assumption does *not* mean that economists believe everyone knows everything or always makes the "best" decision. It does mean that economists assume that consumers and firms use all available information as they act to achieve their goals. Rational individuals weigh the benefits and costs of each action, and they choose an action only if the benefits outweigh the costs. For example, if Microsoft charges a price of $239 for a copy of Windows, economists assume that the managers at Microsoft have estimated that a price of $239 will earn Microsoft the most profit. The managers may be wrong; perhaps a price of $265 would be more profitable, but economists assume that the managers at Microsoft have acted rationally on the basis of the information available to them in choosing the price. Of course, not everyone behaves rationally all the time. Still, the assumption of rational behavior is very useful in explaining most of the choices that people make.

People Respond to Economic Incentives

Human beings act from a variety of motives, including religious belief, envy, and compassion. Economists emphasize that consumers and firms consistently respond to *economic* incentives. This fact may seem obvious, but it is often overlooked. For example, according to an article in the *Wall Street Journal,* the FBI couldn't understand why banks were not taking steps to improve security in the face of an increase in robberies: "FBI officials suggest that banks place uniformed, armed guards outside their doors and install bullet-resistant plastic, known as a 'bandit barrier,' in front of teller windows." FBI officials were surprised that few banks took their advice. But the article also reported that installing bullet-resistant plastic costs $10,000 to $20,000 and a well-trained security guard receives $50,000 per year in salary and benefits. The average loss in a bank robbery is only about $1,200. The economic incentive to banks is clear: It is less costly to put up with bank robberies than to take additional security measures. That banks respond as they do to the threat of robberies may be surprising to the FBI—but not to economists.

Optimal Decisions Are Made at the Margin

Some decisions are "all or nothing": An entrepreneur decides whether or not to open a new restaurant. She either starts the new restaurant or she doesn't. You decide whether to enter graduate school or to take a job. You either enter graduate school or you don't. But most decisions in life are not all or nothing. Instead, most decisions involve doing a little more or a little less. If you are trying to decrease your spending and increase your saving, the decision is not really a choice between saving every dollar you earn or spending it all. The choice is actually between buying a caffè mocha at Starbucks every day or cutting back to three times per week.

Economists use the word *marginal* to mean an extra or additional benefit or cost of a decision. Should you watch another hour of TV or spend that hour studying? The *marginal benefit* (or, in symbols, *MB*) of watching more TV is the additional enjoyment you receive. The *marginal cost* (or *MC*) is the lower grade you receive from having studied a little less. Should Apple Computer produce an additional 300,000 iPods? Firms receive *revenue* from selling goods. Apple's marginal benefit is the additional revenue it receives from selling 300,000 more iPods. Apple's marginal cost is the additional cost—for wages, parts, and so forth—of producing 300,000 more iPods. *Economists reason that the optimal decision is to continue any activity up to the point where the marginal benefit equals the marginal cost—in symbols, where* MB = MC. Often we apply this rule without consciously thinking about it. Usually you will know whether the additional enjoyment from watching a television program is worth the additional cost involved in not spending that hour studying, without giving it a lot of thought. In business situations, however, firms often have to make careful calculations to determine, for example, whether the additional revenue received from increasing production is greater or less than the additional cost of the production. Economists refer to analysis that involves comparing marginal benefits and marginal costs as **marginal analysis.**

Marginal analysis Analysis that involves comparing marginal benefits and marginal costs.

In each chapter of this book, you will see a special feature entitled "Solved Problem." This feature will increase your understanding of the material by leading you through the steps of solving an applied economic problem. After reading the problem, you can test your understanding by working the related problems that appear at the end of the chapter and in the study guide that accompanies this book.

SOLVED PROBLEM 1-1

① LEARNING OBJECTIVE

Discuss these three important economic ideas: *People are rational. People respond to incentives. Optimal decisions are made at the margin.*

Apple Computer Makes a Decision at the Margin

Suppose Apple is currently selling 3,000,000 iPods per year. Managers at Apple are considering whether to raise production to 3,300,000 iPods per year. One manager argues, "Increasing production from 3,000,000 to 3,300,000 is a good idea because we will make a total profit of $100 million if we produce 3,300,000." Do you agree with her reasoning? What, if any, additional information do you need to decide whether Apple should produce the additional 300,000 iPods?

Solving the Problem:

Step 1: Review the chapter material. The problem is about making decisions, so you may want to review the section "Optimal Decisions Are Made at the Margin," which begins on page 5. Remember to think "marginal" whenever you see the word "additional" in economics.

Step 2: Explain whether you agree with the manager's reasoning. We have seen that any activity should be continued to the point where the marginal benefit is equal to the marginal cost. In this case, that involves continuing to produce iPods up to the point where the additional revenue Apple receives from selling more iPods is equal to the marginal cost of producing them. The Apple manager has not done a marginal analysis, so you should not agree with her reasoning. Her statement about the *total* profit of producing 3,300,000 iPods is not relevant to the decision whether or not to produce the last 300,000 iPods.

Step 3: Explain what additional information you need. You will need additional information to make a correct decision. You will need to know the additional revenue Apple would earn from selling 300,000 more iPods and the additional cost of producing them.

YOUR TURN: **For more practice, do related problems 4, 5, and 6 on page 19 at the end of this chapter.**

The Economic Problem That Every Society Must Solve

② LEARNING OBJECTIVE

Discuss how an economy answers these questions: *What* goods and services will be produced? *How* will the goods and services be produced? *Who* will receive the goods and services?

We have already noted the important fact that we live in a world of scarcity. As a result, any society faces the economic problem that it has only a limited amount of economic resources—such as workers, machines, and natural resources—and therefore can produce only a limited amount of goods and services. Therefore, society faces **trade-offs:** Producing more of one good or service means producing less of another good or service. Trade-offs force society to make choices, particularly when answering the following three fundamental questions:

Trade-off The idea that because of scarcity, producing more of one good or service means producing less of another good or service.

1. *What* goods and services will be produced?
2. *How* will the goods and services be produced?
3. *Who* will receive the goods and services produced?

Throughout this book, we will return to these questions many times. For now, we can briefly introduce each question.

What Goods and Services Will Be Produced?

How will society decide whether to produce more economics textbooks or more DVD players? More day care facilities or more football stadiums? Of course, "society" does not make decisions; only individuals make decisions. The answer to the question of what will be produced is determined by the choices made by consumers, firms, and the government. Every day you help to decide which goods and services will be produced when you choose to buy an iPod rather than a DVD player, or a caffè mocha rather than a chai tea. Similarly, Apple must choose whether to devote its scarce resources to making more iPods or more iBook laptop computers. The federal government must also choose whether to spend more of its limited budget on breast cancer research or on homeland security. In each case, consumers, firms, and the government face the problem of scarcity by trading off one good for another.

How Will the Goods and Services Be Produced?

Firms choose how to produce the goods and services they sell. In many cases, firms face a trade-off between using more workers or using more machines. For example, a local service station has to choose whether to provide car repair services using more diagnostic computers and fewer auto mechanics or more auto mechanics and fewer diagnostic computers. Similarly, movie studios have to choose whether to produce animated films using highly skilled animators to draw them by hand or fewer animators and more computers. In deciding whether to move production offshore to China, firms are often choosing between a production method in the United States that uses fewer workers and more machines or a production method in China that uses more workers and fewer machines.

Who Will Receive the Goods and Services Produced?

In the United States, who receives the goods and services produced depends largely on how income is distributed. Those individuals with the highest income have the ability to buy the most goods and services. Often, people are willing to give up some of their income—and, therefore, some of their ability to purchase goods and services—by donating to charities to increase the incomes of poorer people. In 2004, Americans donated $241 billion to charity, or an average donation of $2,100 for each household in the country. An important policy question, however, is whether the government should intervene to make the distribution of income more equal. Such intervention already occurs in the United States, because people with higher incomes pay a larger fraction of their incomes in taxes and because the government makes payments to people with low incomes. There is disagreement over whether the current attempts to redistribute income are sufficient or whether there should be more or less redistribution.

Centrally Planned Economies versus Market Economies

Centrally planned economy An economy in which the government decides how economic resources will be allocated.

Market economy An economy in which the decisions of households and firms interacting in markets allocate economic resources.

Societies organize their economies in two main ways to answer the three questions of what, how, and who. A society can have a **centrally planned economy** in which the government decides how economic resources will be allocated. Or a society can have a **market economy** in which the decisions of households and firms interacting in markets allocate economic resources.

From 1917 to 1991, the most important centrally planned economy in the world was that of the Soviet Union, which was established when V. I. Lenin and his Communist Party staged a revolution and took over the Russian Empire. In the Soviet Union, the government decided what goods to produce, how to produce them, and who would receive them. Government employees managed factories and stores. The objective of these managers was to follow the government's orders, rather than to satisfy the wants of consumers. Centrally planned economies like the Soviet Union have not been successful in producing low-cost, high-quality goods and services. As a result, the standard of living of the average person in a centrally planned economy tends to be quite low. All centrally planned economies have also been political dictatorships. Dissatisfaction with low living standards and political repression finally led to the collapse of the Soviet Union in 1991. Today, only a few small countries, such as Cuba and North Korea, still have completely centrally planned economies.

All the high-income democracies, such as the United States, Canada, Japan, and the countries of Western Europe, are market economies. Market economies rely primarily on privately owned firms to produce goods and services and to decide how to produce them. Markets, rather than the government, determine who receives the goods and services produced. In a market economy, firms must produce goods and services that meet the wants of consumers, or the firms will go out of business. In that sense, it is ultimately consumers who decide what goods and services will be produced. Because firms in a market economy compete to offer the highest-quality products at the lowest price, they are under pressure to use the lowest-cost methods of production. For example, in the past 10 years some U.S. firms, particularly in the electronics and furniture industries, have been under pressure to reduce their costs to meet those of Chinese firms.

In a market economy, the income of an individual is determined by the payments he receives for what he has to sell. If he is a civil engineer and firms are willing to pay a salary of $85,000 per year for engineers with his training and skills, that is the amount of income he will have to purchase goods and services. If the engineer also owns a house that he rents out, his income will be even higher. One of the attractive features of markets is that they reward hard work. Generally, the more extensive the training a person has received and the longer the hours the person works, the higher the person's income will be. Of course, luck—both good and bad—also plays a role here, as elsewhere in life. We can conclude that market economies answer the question "Who receives the goods and services produced?" with the answer "Those who are most willing and able to buy them."

The Modern "Mixed" Economy

In the nineteenth and early twentieth centuries, the U.S. government engaged in relatively little regulation of markets for goods and services. Beginning in the middle of the twentieth century, government intervention in the economy dramatically increased in the United States and other market economies. This increase was primarily caused by the high rates of unemployment and business bankruptcies during the Great Depression of the 1930s. Some government intervention was also intended to raise the incomes of the elderly, the sick, and people with limited skills. For example, in the 1930s, the United States established the Social Security system, which provides government payments to retired and disabled workers, and minimum wage legislation, which sets a floor on the wages employers can pay in many occupations. In more recent years, government intervention in the economy has also expanded to meet such goals as protection of the environment and the promotion of civil rights.

Some economists argue that the extent of government intervention makes it no longer accurate to refer to the U.S., Canadian, Japanese, and Western European economies as market economies. Instead, they should be referred to as *mixed economies*. In a **mixed economy,** most economic decisions result from the interaction of buyers and sellers in markets, but the government plays a significant role in the allocation of resources. As we will see in later chapters, economists continue to debate the role government should play in a market economy.

Mixed economy An economy in which most economic decisions result from the interaction of buyers and sellers in markets, but in which the government plays a significant role in the allocation of resources.

One of the most important developments in the international economy in recent years has been the movement of China from being a centrally planned economy to being a more mixed economy. The Chinese economy had suffered decades of economic stagnation following the takeover of the government by Mao Zedong and the Communist Party in 1949. Although China remains a political dictatorship, production of most goods and services is now determined in the market, rather than by the government. The result has been rapid economic growth that in the near future may lead to total production of goods and services in China surpassing total production in the United States.

Efficiency and Equity

Market economies tend to be more efficient than centrally planned economies. There are two types of efficiency: *productive efficiency* and *allocative efficiency.* **Productive efficiency** occurs when a good or service is produced at the lowest possible cost. **Allocative efficiency** occurs when production reflects consumer preferences. Markets tend to be efficient because they promote competition and facilitate *voluntary exchange.* **Voluntary exchange** refers to the situation in which both the buyer and seller of a product are made better off by the transaction. We know that the buyer and seller are both made better off, because otherwise the buyer would not have agreed to buy the product or the seller would not have agreed to sell it. Productive efficiency is achieved when competition among firms in markets forces the firms to produce goods and services at the lowest cost. Allocative efficiency is achieved when the combination of competition among firms and voluntary exchange between firms and consumers results in firms producing the mix of goods and services that consumers prefer most. Competition will force firms to continue producing and selling goods and services as long as the additional benefit to consumers is greater than the additional cost of production. In this way, the mix of goods and services produced will reflect consumer preferences.

Productive efficiency The situation in which a good or service is produced at the lowest possible cost.

Allocative efficiency A state of the economy in which production reflects consumer preferences; in particular, every good or service is produced up to the point where the last unit provides a marginal benefit to consumers equal to the marginal cost of producing it.

Voluntary exchange The situation that occurs in markets when both the buyer and seller of a product are made better off by the transaction.

Although markets promote efficiency, they don't guarantee it. Inefficiency can arise from various sources. To begin with, it may take some time to achieve an efficient outcome. When DVD players were introduced, for example, productive efficiency was not achieved instantly. It took several years for firms to discover the lowest-cost method of producing this good. As we will discuss in Chapter 4, governments sometimes reduce efficiency by interfering with voluntary exchange in markets. For example, many governments limit the imports of some goods from foreign countries. This limitation reduces efficiency by keeping goods from being produced at the lowest cost. The production of some goods damages the environment. In this case, government intervention can increase efficiency, because without such intervention firms may ignore the costs of environmental damage, and thereby fail to produce the goods at the lowest possible cost.

Just because an economic outcome is efficient does not necessarily mean that society finds it desirable. Many people prefer economic outcomes that they consider fair or equitable, even if these outcomes are less efficient. **Equity** is harder to define than efficiency, but it usually involves a fair distribution of economic benefits. For some people, equity involves a more equal distribution of economic benefits than would result from an emphasis on efficiency alone. For example, some people support taxing people with higher incomes to provide the funds for programs that aid the poor. Although equity may be increased by reducing the incomes of high-income people and increasing the incomes of the poor, efficiency may be reduced. People have less incentive to open new businesses, to supply labor, and to save if the government takes a significant

Equity The fair distribution of economic benefits.

amount of the income they earn from working or saving. The result is that fewer goods and services are produced and less saving takes place. As this example illustrates, *there is often a trade-off between efficiency and equity.* In this case, the total amount of goods and services produced falls, although the distribution of the income to buy those goods and services is made more equal. Government policymakers often confront this trade-off.

③ LEARNING OBJECTIVE

Understand the role of models in economic analysis.

Economic Models

Economists rely on economic theories or *models* (the words "theory" and "model" are used interchangeably) to analyze real-world issues, such as the economic effects of outsourcing. As mentioned earlier, economic models are simplified versions of reality used to analyze real-world economic situations. Economists are certainly not alone in relying on models: An engineer may use a computer model of a bridge to help test whether it will withstand high winds, or a biologist may make a physical model of a nucleic acid to better understand its properties. One purpose of economic models is to make economic ideas sufficiently explicit and concrete to be used for decision making by individuals, firms, or the government. For example, we will see in Chapter 3 that the model of demand and supply is a simplified version of how the prices of products are determined by the interactions among buyers and sellers in markets.

Economists use economic models to answer questions. For example, consider the question from the opening of this chapter: Has outsourcing been good or bad for the U.S. economy? For a complicated question such as the effects of outsourcing, economists often use several models to examine different aspects of the issue. For example, a model of how wages are determined might be used to analyze how outsourcing affects wages in particular industries. A model of international trade might be used to analyze how outsourcing affects income growth in the countries involved. Sometimes economists use an existing model to analyze an issue, but in other cases economists must develop a new model. To develop a model, economists generally follow these steps:

1. Decide on the assumptions to be used in developing the model.
2. Formulate a testable hypothesis.
3. Use economic data to test the hypothesis.
4. Revise the model if it fails to explain well the economic data.
5. Retain the revised model to help answer similar economic questions in the future.

The Role of Assumptions in Economic Models

Any model is based on making assumptions because models have to be simplified to be useful. We cannot analyze an economic issue unless we reduce its complexity. For example, economic models make *behavioral assumptions* about the motives of consumers and firms. Economists assume that consumers will buy those goods and services that will maximize their well-being or their satisfaction. Similarly, economists assume that firms act to maximize their profits. These assumptions are simplifications because they do not describe the motives of every consumer and every firm. How can we know if the assumptions in a model are too simplified or too limiting? We discover this when we form hypotheses based on these assumptions and test these hypotheses using real-world information.

Forming and Testing Hypotheses in Economic Models

Economic variable Something measurable that can have different values, such as the wages of software programmers.

A *hypothesis* in an economic model is a statement that may be either correct or incorrect about an *economic variable.* An **economic variable** is something measurable that can have different values, such as the wages paid to software programmers. An example of a hypothesis in an economic model is the statement that outsourcing by U.S. firms reduces wages paid to software programmers in the United States. An economic hypothesis is usually about a *causal relationship;* in this case, the hypothesis states that outsourcing causes, or leads to, lower wages for software programmers.

Before accepting a hypothesis, we must test it. To test a hypothesis we must analyze statistics on the relevant economic variables. In this case, we must gather statistics on the wages paid to software programmers, and perhaps on other variables as well. Testing a hypothesis can be tricky. For example, showing that the wages paid to software programmers fell at a time when outsourcing was increasing would not be enough to demonstrate that outsourcing *caused* the wage fall. Just because two things are *correlated*—that is, they happen at the same time—does not mean that one caused the other. For example, suppose that the number of workers trained as software engineers greatly increased at the same time that outsourcing was increasing. In that case, the fall in wages paid to software engineers might have been caused by the increased competition among workers for these jobs, rather than by the effects of relocating programming jobs from the United States to India or China. Over a period of time, many economic variables will be changing, which complicates testing hypotheses. In fact, when economists disagree about a hypothesis, such as the effect of outsourcing on wages, it is often because of disagreements over interpreting the statistical analysis used to test the hypothesis.

Note that hypotheses must be statements that could in principle turn out to be incorrect. Statements such as "Outsourcing is good" or "Outsourcing is bad" are value judgments, rather than hypotheses, because it is not possible to disprove them.

Economists accept and use an economic model if it leads to hypotheses that are confirmed by statistical analysis. In many cases, the acceptance is tentative, however, pending the gathering of new data or further statistical analysis. In fact, economists often refer to a hypothesis having been "not rejected," rather than being "accepted," by statistical analysis. But what if statistical analysis clearly rejects a hypothesis? For example, what if the model leads to a hypothesis that outsourcing by U.S. firms lowers wages of U.S. software programmers, but this hypothesis is rejected by the data? In that case, the model must be reconsidered. It may be that an assumption used in the model was too simplified or too limiting. For example, perhaps the model we used to determine the effect of outsourcing on wages paid to software programmers assumed that software programmers in China and India had the same training and experience as software programmers in the United States. If, in fact, U.S. software programmers have more training and experience than Chinese and Indian programmers, this difference may explain why our hypothesis was rejected by the economic statistics.

The process of developing models, testing hypotheses, and revising models occurs not just in economics but also in disciplines such as physics, chemistry, and biology. It is often referred to as the *scientific method.* Economics is a *social science* because it applies the scientific method to the study of the interactions among individuals.

In each chapter, the feature entitled "Making the Connection" discusses a business news story, or other application, related to the chapter material. Read Making the Connection 1-1 for two viewpoints about outsourcing.

When Economists Disagree: A Debate over Outsourcing

1-1 Making the Connection

There is an old saying in the newspaper business that it's not news when a dog bites a man, but it is news when a man bites a dog. In 2004, many newspapers ran a "man bites dog" story concerning economics.

Most economists believe that international trade—including the trade that results when firms move production offshore—increases economic efficiency and raises incomes. It was news, then, when MIT economist Paul Samuelson, a winner of the Nobel Prize in Economics, wrote an article in the *Journal of Economic Perspectives* questioning whether incomes in the United States will be higher as a result of the outsourcing of jobs to India and China. Samuelson presented a model of the effects of outsourcing that can be illustrated with the following hypothetical case: Suppose a bank in New York has been using a company in South Dakota to handle its telephone customer service. It then switches to using a company in Bangalore, India that pays its workers much lower wages. Samuelson argued that even when the workers fired by the

Does outsourcing by U.S. firms raise or lower incomes in the United States?

South Dakota firm eventually find new jobs, these may pay lower wages. If outsourcing becomes widespread enough, Samuelson argued, it may result in a significant decline in U.S. incomes.

Many economists objected to Samuelson's argument. One economist who wrote a rebuttal to Samuelson was Jagdish Bhagwati, a former student of Samuelson's and a professor of economics at Columbia University. Bhagwati argued that in Samuelson's example the wages of South Dakota call center workers were reduced by outsourcing, but the costs to the bank were also reduced, which would allow the bank to reduce the prices it charged its customers. In Bhagwati's model, these gains to consumers from lower prices more than offset the loss to workers from lower wages, so the United States experiences a net gain from outsourcing. Samuelson argued, though, that if the United States exports the product—in this case banking services—to other countries, the lower price hurts the exporting firms. In that case, the United States might still be hurt by outsourcing.

This brief summary does not do full justice to the models of Samuelson and Bhagwati, which are too complicated for us to cover in this chapter. We can, however, discuss the sources of the disagreement between these two economists. We have seen that economists sometimes differ about the assumptions that should be used in building a model. That is not the case here: Samuelson and Bhagwati basically agree on the model and the assumptions to be used. Instead, they disagree over how to interpret the relevant economic statistics. Bhagwati argues that the number of U.S. jobs moving to other countries has been relatively small, amounting to about 1 percent of the jobs created in the U.S. economy each year. He also argues that the jobs lost to outsourcing tend to be low-wage jobs, such as telephone customer service or data entry, and are likely to be replaced by higher-wage jobs. Samuelson argues that the impact of outsourcing is greater than Bhagwati believes, and he is less optimistic that newly created jobs in the United States will pay higher wages than the jobs lost to outsourcing.

The debate between Samuelson and Bhagwati demonstrates that economics is an evolving discipline. New models are continually being introduced, and new hypotheses are being formulated and tested. We can expect the debate over the economic impact of outsourcing to continue to be lively.

Sources: Paul A. Samuelson, "Where Ricardo and Mill Rebut and Confirm Arguments of Mainstream Economists Supporting Globalization," *Journal of Economic Perspectives*, Vol. 18, No. 3, Summer 2004, pp. 135–146; Jagdish Bhagwati, Arvind Panagariya, and T. N. Srinivasan, "The Muddles Over Outsourcing," *Journal of Economic Perspectives*, Vol. 18, No. 4, Fall 2004, pp. 93–114; and Steve Lohr, "An Elder Challenges Outsourcing's Orthodoxy," *New York Times*, September 9, 2004, p. C1.

Normative and Positive Analysis

Throughout this book as we build economic models and use them to answer questions, we need to bear in mind the distinction between *positive analysis* and *normative analysis.*

Positive analysis is concerned with *what is* and **normative analysis** is concerned with *what ought to be.* Economics is about positive analysis, which measures the costs and benefits of different courses of action.

Positive analysis Analysis concerned with what is.

Normative analysis Analysis concerned with what ought to be.

We can use the federal government's minimum wage law to compare positive and normative analysis. In 2005 under this law, it was illegal for an employer to hire a worker at a wage less than $5.15 per hour. Without the minimum wage law, some firms and some workers would voluntarily agree to a lower wage. Because of the minimum wage law, some workers have difficulty finding jobs and some firms end up paying more for labor than they otherwise would have. A positive analysis of the federal minimum wage law uses an economic model to estimate how many workers have lost their jobs because of the law, its impact on the costs and profits of businesses, and the gains to workers receiving the minimum wage. After economists complete this positive analysis, the decision as to whether the minimum wage law is a good idea or a bad idea is a normative one and depends on how people assess the trade-off involved. Supporters of the law believe that the losses to employers and to workers who are unemployed as a result of the law are more than offset by the gains to those workers who receive higher wages than they would have without the law. Opponents of the law believe the losses are greater than the gains. The assessment by any individual would depend, in part, on that person's values and political views. The positive analysis provided by an economist would play a role in the decision but can't by itself decide the issue one way or the other.

In each chapter you will see a "Don't Let This Happen To You!" box like the one below. The goal of these boxes is to alert you to common pitfalls in thinking about economic ideas. After reading the box, test your understanding by working the related problem that appears at the end of the chapter.

④ LEARNING OBJECTIVE

Distinguish between microeconomics and macroeconomics.

Microeconomics and Macroeconomics

Economic models can be used to analyze decision making in many areas. We group some of these areas together as *microeconomics* and others as *macroeconomics.* **Microeconomics** is the study of how households and firms make choices, how they interact in markets, and how the government attempts to influence their choices. Microeconomic issues include explaining how consumers react to changes in product prices and how firms decide what prices to charge. Microeconomics also involves policy issues, such as analyzing the most efficient way to reduce teenage smoking, analyzing the costs and

Microeconomics The study of how households and firms make choices, how they interact in markets, and how the government attempts to influence their choices.

Don't Let This Happen To You!

Don't Confuse Positive Analysis with Normative Analysis

"Economic analysis has shown that the minimum wage law is a bad idea because it causes unemployment." Is this statement accurate? As of 2005, the federal minimum wage law prevents employers from hiring workers at a wage of less than $5.15 per hour. This wage is higher than some employers are willing to pay some workers. If there were no minimum wage law, some workers who currently cannot find any firm willing to hire them at $5.15 per hour would be able to find employment at a lower wage. Therefore, positive economic analysis indicates that the minimum wage law causes unemployment (although economists disagree about how much unemployment is caused by the minimum wage). *But,* those workers who still have jobs benefit from the minimum wage because they are paid a higher wage than they otherwise would be. In other words, the minimum wage law creates both losers (the workers who become unemployed and the firms that have to pay higher wages) and winners (the workers who receive higher wages).

Do the gains to the winners more than offset the losses to the losers? The answer to that question involves normative analysis. Positive economic analysis can only show the consequences of a particular policy; it cannot tell us whether the policy is "good" or "bad." So, the statement at the beginning of this box is inaccurate.

***YOUR TURN:* Test your understanding by doing related problem 16 on page 20 at the end of this chapter.**

benefits of approving the sale of a new prescription drug, and analyzing the most efficient way to reduce air pollution.

Macroeconomics The study of the economy as a whole, including topics such as inflation, unemployment, and economic growth.

Macroeconomics is the study of the economy as a whole, including topics such as inflation, unemployment, and economic growth. Macroeconomic issues include explaining why economies experience periods of recession and increasing unemployment and why over the long run some economies have grown much faster than others. Macroeconomics also involves policy issues, such as whether government intervention is capable of reducing the severity of recessions.

The division between microeconomics and macroeconomics is not hard and fast. Many economic situations have *both* a microeconomic and a macroeconomic aspect. For example, the level of total investment by firms in new machinery and equipment helps to determine how rapidly the economy grows—which is a macroeconomic issue. But to understand how much new machinery and equipment firms decide to purchase, we have to analyze the incentives individual firms face—which is a microeconomic issue.

(5) LEARNING OBJECTIVE

Become familiar with important economic terms.

A Preview of Important Economic Terms

In the following chapters you will encounter certain important terms again and again. Becoming familiar with these terms is a necessary step in learning economics. Here we provide a brief introduction to some of these terms. We will discuss them all in greater depth in later chapters:

- *Entrepreneur.* An entrepreneur is someone who operates a business. In a market system it is entrepreneurs who decide what goods and services to produce and how to produce them. An entrepreneur starting a new business puts his or her own funds at risk. If an entrepreneur is wrong about what consumers want or about the best way to produce goods and services, the entrepreneur's funds can be lost. This is not an unusual occurrence: In the United States, about half of new businesses close within four years. Without entrepreneurs willing to assume the risk of starting and operating businesses, economic progress would be impossible in a market system.
- *Innovation.* There is a distinction between an *invention* and *innovation.* An invention is the development of a new good or a new process for making a good. An innovation is the practical application of an invention. (Innovation also may be used more broadly to refer to any significant improvement in a good or in the means of producing a good.) Much time often passes between the appearance of a new idea and its development to the point where it can be widely used. For example, the Wright Brothers first achieved self-propelled flight at Kitty Hawk, North Carolina, in 1903, but the Wright Brothers' plane was very crude, and it wasn't until the introduction of the DC-3 by Douglas Aircraft in 1936 that regularly scheduled intercity airline flights became common in the United States. Similarly, the first digital electronic computer—the ENIAC—was developed in 1945, but the first IBM personal computer was not introduced until 1981 and widespread use of computers did not have a significant effect on the productivity of American business until the 1990s.
- *Technology.* A firm's technology is the processes it uses to produce goods and services. In the economic sense, a firm's technology depends on many factors, such as the skill of its managers, the training of its workers, and the speed and efficiency of its machinery and equipment.
- *Firm, company, or business.* A firm is an organization that produces a good or service for profit. Economists use the words "firm," "company," and "business" interchangeably.
- *Goods.* Goods are tangible merchandise, such as books, computers, or DVD players.
- *Services.* Services are activities done for others, such as providing haircuts or investment advice.
- *Revenue.* A firm's revenue is the total amount received for selling a good or service. It is calculated by multiplying the price per unit by the number of units sold.

➤ ***Opportunity cost.*** The concept of opportunity cost is one of the most important in economics. The opportunity cost of any activity is the highest-valued alternative that must be given up to engage in that activity. Consider the example of an entrepreneur who could receive a salary of $80,000 per year working as a manager at a firm but opens her own firm instead. In that case, the opportunity cost of her entrepreneurial services to her own firm is $80,000, even though she does not pay herself an explicit salary.

➤ ***Profit.*** A firm's profit is the difference between its revenue and its costs. Economists distinguish between *accounting profit* and *economic profit.* Accounting profit excludes the cost of some economic resources that the firm does not pay for explicitly. Economic profit includes the opportunity cost of all resources used by the firm. When we refer to profit in this book, we mean economic profit. It is important not to confuse *profit* with *revenue.*

➤ ***Household.*** A household consists of all persons occupying a home. Households are suppliers of factors of production—particularly labor—used by firms to make goods and services. Households also demand goods and services produced by firms and governments.

➤ ***Factors of production or economic resources.*** Firms use factors of production to produce goods and services. The main factors of production are labor, capital, human capital, natural resources—including land—and entrepreneurial ability. Households earn income by supplying the factors of production to firms.

➤ ***Capital.*** The word "capital" can refer to *financial capital* or to *physical capital.* Financial capital includes stocks and bonds issued by firms, bank accounts, and holdings of money. In economics, though, "capital" refers to physical capital, which includes manufactured goods that are used to produce other goods and services. Examples of physical capital are computers, factory buildings, machine tools, warehouses, and trucks. The total amount of physical capital available in a country is referred to as the country's *capital stock.*

➤ ***Human capital.*** Human capital refers to the accumulated training and skills that workers possess. For example, workers with a college education generally have more skills and are more productive than workers who have only a high school degree.

Conclusion

The best way to think of economics is as a group of useful ideas about how individuals make choices. Economists have put these ideas into practice by developing economic models. Consumers, business managers, and government officials use these models every day to help them make choices. In this book, we explore many key economic models and give examples of how they can be applied in the real world.

Most students taking an introductory economics course do not major in economics or become professional economists. Whatever your major may be, the economic principles you will learn in this book will improve your ability to make choices in many aspects of your life. These principles will also improve your understanding of how decisions are made in business and government.

Reading the newspaper and other periodicals is an important part of understanding the current business climate and learning how to apply economic concepts to a variety of real-world events. At the end of each chapter, you will see a two-page periodical feature entitled *An Inside Look.* This feature consists of an excerpt of an article that relates to the company we introduced at the start of the chapter and also to the concepts we have discussed throughout the chapter. A summary and analysis and supporting graphs highlight the economic key points of the article. Test your understanding by answering the *Thinking Critically* questions. Read *An Inside Look* on the next page to learn why some economists argue that fears about outsourcing to China are unjustified.

An Inside Look How Does Economic Growth in China Affect Other Countries?

ECONOMIST, SEPTEMBER 30, 2004

The Halo Effect

"WHAT you cannot avoid, welcome," says an old Chinese proverb. The world would be wise to bear that in mind in its dealings with China. The country's global integration will have a bigger impact on the world economy than that of any previous emerging economy. Fortunately, though, it will be mostly a force for good, boosting overall prosperity.

China's ascent will affect the outside world more than Japan's did in its time. . . .

The idea that China may become the world's biggest economy, with an enormous army of cheap workers, fills many in the rich western world with dread. Yet China's combination of rapid growth, vast size and openness could deliver a big boost to incomes outside China as well as at home. Rather like America when it entered the world economy in the late 19th century, China will be giving a huge boost to both global demand and supply. . . .

a Jobs will be lost in manufacturing in the developed world, but new jobs will be created, largely because most of the money that China earns from exports is being spent on imports from rich economies. Sustained growth in income and jobs relies on a continuous shift of resources to higher-value industries. A frozen job market with no hiring or firing would be in nobody's interest.

Individual countries can maximise their gains from Chinese integration and minimise their losses by making their own economies more flexible, increasing mobility between sectors and improving education. A study by the McKinsey Global Institute looked at what happened to workers who lost their jobs because of firms moving their production to low-wage countries such as China or India. McKinsey estimates that in America 70% of them find new work within six months, but in Germany only 40% do, partly because of a generous benefit system as well as strict hiring and firing laws. . . .

b In flexible labour markets, many of the workers who lose their jobs will eventually be re-employed in more productive industries. It is ironic, therefore, that American politicians and businessmen have been complaining most loudly about China stealing their country's jobs. With its flexible economy, America should adjust more easily than Europe. Fears about the threat from China stem from a series of widely held myths.

American business lobbies and trade unions claim that offshoring has cost their country [3 million] manufacturing jobs in the past three years. But most of those job losses were likelier to have been caused by the recession or by labour-saving IT investment. . . .

Moreover, even if outsourcing does export jobs to China, part of the income created there flows back as increased demand for American goods and services. Work by Matthew Slaughter, an economist at the Tuck School of Business at Dartmouth College, finds that outsourcing also creates new jobs back home for engineers, finance and marketing experts to supply services or hi-tech components to foreign affiliates. In a study of 2,500 American multinational firms in the ten years to 2001, Mr. Slaughter found that the number of jobs in their foreign subsidiaries rose by 2.9 [million], but in America itself by as much as 5.5 [million]. Moreover, these firms' domestic employment increased faster than jobs in purely domestic firms. . . .

c Fears that Chinese exports are growing at the expense of other countries are based on a fixed-lump-of-trade fallacy. In fact, trade is a positive-sum game: the more participants there are, the more opportunities arise, allowing countries to produce more with the same amount of labour and to obtain goods and services more cheaply. China's expansion will hugely add to those opportunities.

Key Points in the Article

This article discusses the effect of economic growth in China on jobs and wages in the United States and Europe. The article notes that many people fear that a rapid growth in China will reduce incomes and economic growth in the United States and Europe. The article argues these fears are unjustified. It also provides advice on the types of policies countries should pursue to increase their gains from China's integration into the world economy.

Analyzing the News

a Figure 1 shows that for several countries, including the United States, China has become an increasingly important market for exports. We noted previously in this chapter that markets tend to be efficient because they involve *voluntary exchange*. With voluntary exchange both the buyer and the seller are made better off. This insight applies to international trade between the United States and China as much as to domestic trade within the United States. One strength of a market system is that it facilitates shifting of resources from declining industries to expanding industries, as noted in the article.

b Making the Connection 1-1 presented the debate between economists Paul Samuelson and Jagdish Bhagwati over whether outsourcing has helped or hurt the U.S. economy. One key aspect of the debate concerned whether workers who lose their jobs because of outsourcing are eventually likely to find comparable or better jobs. The article makes the argument that when labor markets are flexible—meaning that there are few restrictions on workers moving between jobs—it is more likely that displaced workers will find good replacement jobs.

c We have seen in this chapter that economists use models to analyze economic issues such as the effects of outsourcing. One advantage of economic models is that they make explicit the assumptions that are being made. Models also generate hypotheses that can be tested against the real world. According to the article, people who fear that an increase in exports from China must come at the expense of other countries also are using a model, but it is a model that is not explicitly stated. The article refers to this model as the "fixed-lump-of-trade fallacy." We know the model is a fallacy because the evidence shows that many countries can increase their exports at the same time.

Thinking Critically

1. The article argues that outsourcing to China will make the global economy and the U.S. economy more prosperous and efficient. What impact does the article suggest outsourcing will have on equity?
2. What evidence from the article suggests that positive analysis of the impact of outsourcing will be difficult, even among people using the same economic model?

Source: "The Halo Effect: How China's Expansion Will Affect Jobs and Growth Elsewhere," *Economist*, September 30, 2004.

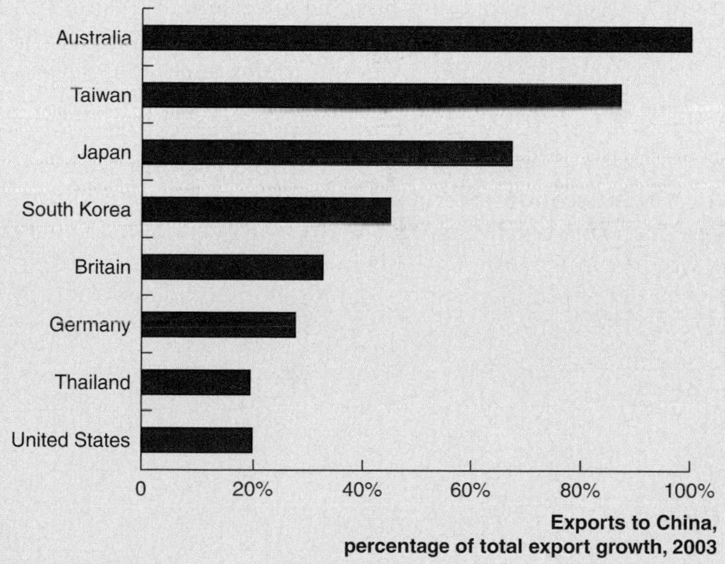

Figure 1: Many countries, including the United States, have experienced rapidly increasing exports to China.

Source: Thomson Datastream: national statistics.

SUMMARY

LEARNING OBJECTIVE ① Discuss these three important economic ideas: People are rational. People respond to incentives. Optimal decisions are made at the margin. Economists assume people are rational in the sense that consumers and firms use all available information as they take actions intended to achieve their goals. Rational individuals weigh the benefits and costs of each action, and choose an action only if the benefits outweigh the costs. Although people act from a variety of motives, ample evidence indicates that they respond to economic incentives. Economists use the word "marginal" to mean extra or additional. The optimal decision is to continue any activity up to the point where the marginal benefit equals the marginal cost.

LEARNING OBJECTIVE ② Discuss how an economy answers these questions: *What* goods and services will be produced? *How* will the goods and services be produced? *Who* will receive the goods and services? The choices of consumers, firms, and governments determine what goods and services will be produced. Firms choose how to produce the goods and services they sell. In the United States, who receives the goods and services produced depends largely on how income is distributed in the marketplace. In a centrally planned economy, most economic decisions are made by the government. In a market economy, most economic decisions are made by consumers and firms. Most economies, including that of the United States, are mixed economies in which most economic decisions are made by consumers and firms, but in which the government also plays a significant role. There are two types of efficiency: *productive efficiency* and *allocative efficiency.* Productive efficiency occurs when a good or service is produced at the lowest possible cost. Allocative efficiency occurs when production reflects consumer preferences. *Equity* is harder to define than efficiency, but it usually involves a fair distribution of economic benefits. Government policymakers often face a trade-off between equity and efficiency.

LEARNING OBJECTIVE ③ Understand the role of models in economic analysis. Economists rely on economic models when they apply economic ideas to real-world problems. *Economic models* are simplified versions of reality used to analyze real-world economic situations. Economists accept and use an economic model if it leads to hypotheses that are confirmed by statistical analysis. In many cases, the acceptance is tentative, however, pending the gathering of new data or further statistical analysis. Economics is a *social science* because it applies the scientific method to the study of the interactions among individuals. Economics is concerned with positive analysis rather than normative analysis. Positive analysis is concerned with what is. Normative analysis is concerned with what ought to be.

LEARNING OBJECTIVE ④ Distinguish between microeconomics and macroeconomics. *Microeconomics* is the study of how households and firms make choices, how they interact in markets, and how the government attempts to influence their choices. *Macroeconomics* is the study of the economy as a whole, including topics such as inflation, unemployment, and economic growth.

LEARNING OBJECTIVE ⑤ Become familiar with important economic terms. Becoming familiar with important terms is a necessary step to learn economics. These important economic terms include capital, entrepreneur, factors of production, firm, goods, household, human capital, innovation, opportunity cost, profit, revenue, and technology.

KEY TERMS

Allocative efficiency 9
Centrally planned economy 8
Economic model 4
Economic variable 10
Economics 4
Equity 9
Macroeconomics 14
Marginal analysis 6
Market 5
Market economy 8
Microeconomics 13
Mixed economy 9
Normative analysis 13
Positive analysis 13
Productive efficiency 9
Scarcity 4
Trade-off 7
Voluntary exchange 9

REVIEW QUESTIONS

1. What is scarcity? Why is scarcity central to the study of economics?
2. Briefly discuss each of the following economic ideas: People are rational. People respond to incentives. Optimal decisions are made at the margin.
3. What are the three economic questions that every society must answer? Briefly discuss the differences in how centrally planned, market, and mixed economies answer these questions.
4. What is the difference between productive efficiency and allocative efficiency?
5. What is the difference between efficiency and equity? Why do government policymakers often face a trade-off between efficiency and equity?
6. Why do economists use models? How are economic data used to test models?
7. Describe the five steps by which economists arrive at a useful economic model.
8. What is the difference between normative analysis and positive analysis? Is economics concerned mainly with normative analysis or mainly with positive analysis? Briefly explain.
9. Briefly discuss the difference between microeconomics and macroeconomics.

PROBLEMS AND APPLICATIONS

Please visit **www.prenhall.com/hubbard** *for solutions to the even-numbered problems as well as multiple-choice and true or false self-assessment quizzes.*

1. In a column in the *Wall Street Journal,* Robert McTeer Jr., former president of the Federal Reserve Bank of Dallas, wrote, "My take on training in economics is that it becomes increasingly valuable as you move up the career ladder. I can't think of a better major for corporate CEO's [chief executive officers], congressmen or American presidents." Why might studying economics be particularly good preparation for being the top manager of a corporation or a leader in government?
   Source: Robert D. McTeer Jr., "The Dismal Science? Hardly!" *Wall Street Journal,* June 4, 2003.
2. Does Bill Gates, the richest person in the world, face scarcity? Does everyone? Are there any exceptions?
3. Do you agree or disagree with the following assertion: "The problem with economics is that it assumes consumers and firms always make the correct decision. But we know everyone's human, and we all make mistakes."
4. **[Related to *Solved Problem 1-1*]** Suppose Dell is currently selling 250,000 Pentium 4 laptops per month. A manager at Dell argues, "The last 10,000 laptops we produced increased our revenue by $8.5 million and our costs by $8.9 million. However, because we are making a substantial total profit of $25 million from producing 250,000 laptops, I think we are producing the optimal number of laptops." Briefly explain whether you agree with the manager's reasoning.
5. **[Related to *Solved Problem 1-1*]** Two students are discussing Solved Problem 1-1.

   Joe: "I think the key additional information you need to know in deciding whether to produce 300,000 more iPods is the amount of profit you currently are making while producing 3,000,000. Then you can compare the profit earned from selling 3,300,000 iPods with the profit earned from selling 3,000,000. This information is more important than the additional revenue and additional cost of the last 300,000 iPods produced."

   Jill: "Actually, Joe, knowing how much profits change when you sell 300,000 more iPods is exactly the same as knowing the additional revenue and the additional cost."

   Briefly evaluate their arguments.
6. **[Related to *Solved Problem 1-1*]** Late in the semester a friend tells you, "I was going to drop my psychology course so I could concentrate on my other courses, but I had already put so much time into the course that I decided not to drop it." What do you think of your friend's reasoning? Would it make a difference to your answer if your friend has to pass the psychology course at some point to graduate? Briefly explain.
7. In the first six months of 2003, branches of Commerce Bank in New York City were robbed 14 times. The New York City Police recommended steps the bank could take to deter robberies, including the installation of plastic barriers called "bandit barriers." The police were surprised the bank did not take their advice. According to a deputy

commissioner of police, "Commerce does very little of what we recommend. They've told our detectives they have no interest in ever putting in the barriers." Wouldn't Commerce Bank have a strong incentive to install bandit barriers to deter robberies? Why, then, wouldn't they do it?
Source: Dan Barry, "Friendly Bank Makes It Easy for Robbers," *New York Times,* July 5, 2003.

8. In 1838, the U.S. Army was given the job of moving the Cherokees, Creeks, Choctaws, and Seminoles from the eastern United States to Oklahoma. Contractors were given $65 per person (about $1,270 in today's money) to provide food and medicine for the Indians during the 1,000-mile forced march. Many of the contractors provided scanty food portions, bad meat, and no medicine. As a result, approximately one-quarter of these Indians perished along the way. How could the incentives have been changed so that the death rates would have been lower?
9. Suppose an economist develops an economic model and finds that "it works great in theory, but it fails in practice." What should the economist do next?
10. Dr. Strangelove's theory is that the price of mushrooms is determined by the activity of subatomic particles that exist in another universe parallel to ours. When the subatomic particles are emitted in profusion, the price of mushrooms is high. When subatomic particle emissions are low, the price of mushrooms also is low. How would you go about testing Dr. Strangelove's theory? Discuss whether or not this theory is useful.
11. Would you expect the new and better machinery and equipment to be adopted more rapidly in a market economy or in a centrally planned economy? Briefly explain.
12. Centrally planned economies have been less efficient than market economies.
    a. Has this happened by chance or is there some underlying reason?
    b. If market economies are more economically efficient than centrally planned economies, would there ever be a reason to prefer having a centrally planned economy rather than a market economy?
13. Thomas Sowell, an economist at the Hoover Institution at Stanford University, has written that "All economic systems not only provide people with goods and services, but also restrict or prevent them from getting as much of these goods and services as they wish."

    Why is it necessary for all economic systems to do this? How does a market system prevent people from getting as many goods and services as they wish?
    Source: Thomas Sowell, *Applied Economics: Thinking Beyond Stage One,* New York: Basic Books, 2004, p. 16.
14. Suppose that your local police department recovers 100 tickets to a big NASCAR race in a drug raid. It decides to distribute these to residents and announces that tickets will be given away at 10 A.M., Monday morning at City Hall.
    a. What groups of people will be most likely to try to get the tickets? Think of specific examples and then generalize.
    b. What is the opportunity cost of distributing the tickets this way?
    c. Productive efficiency occurs when a good or service (such as the distribution of tickets) is produced at the lowest possible cost. Is this an efficient way to distribute the tickets? If possible, think of a more efficient method of distributing the tickets.
    d. Is this an equitable way to distribute the tickets? Explain.
15. Many large firms have begun outsourcing work to China.
    a. Why have they done this?
    b. Is outsourcing work to low-wage Chinese workers a risk-free proposition for large firms?
16. **[Related to *Don't Let This Happen To You!*]** Explain which of the following statements represent positive analysis and which represent normative analysis:
    a. A 50-cent-per-pack tax on cigarettes will reduce smoking by teenagers by 12 percent.
    b. The federal government should spend more on AIDS research.
    c. Rising paper prices will increase textbook prices.
    d. The price of coffee at Starbucks is too high.
17. Briefly explain whether each of the following is primarily a microeconomic issue or a macroeconomic issue:
    a. The effect of higher cigarette taxes on the quantity of cigarettes sold
    b. The effect of higher income taxes on the total amount of consumer spending
    c. The reasons for the economies of East Asian countries growing faster than the economies of sub-Saharan African countries
    d. The reasons for low rates of profit in the airline industry
18. The American Bar Association has proposed a law that would prohibit anyone except lawyers from giving legal advice. Under the proposal, income tax preparers, real estate agents, hospitals, labor unions, and anyone else who offered legal advice would be penalized. One critic of the proposal argued that the proposal would protect attorneys more than it would protect consumers.
    a. How might the proposal protect consumers?
    b. Why did the critic of the proposal argue that it would protect attorneys more than it would protect consumers?
    c. Briefly discuss whether you consider the proposed law to be a good idea.
    Source: Adam Liptak, "U.S. Opposes Proposal to Limit Who May Give Legal Advice," *New York Times,* February 3, 2003.

Using Graphs and Formulas

Appendix

Graphs are used to illustrate key economics ideas. Graphs appear not just in economics textbooks but also in newspaper and magazine articles that discuss business and economic ideas. Why the heavy use of graphs? Because they serve two useful purposes: (1) They simplify economic ideas, and (2) They make the ideas more concrete so they can be applied to real-world problems. Economic and business issues can be complicated, but a graph can help cut through complications and highlight the key relationships needed to understand a business issue. In that sense, a graph can be like a street map.

For example, suppose you take a bus to New York City to see the Empire State Building. After arriving at the Port Authority Bus Terminal, you will probably use a map similar to the one shown below to find your way to the Empire State Building.

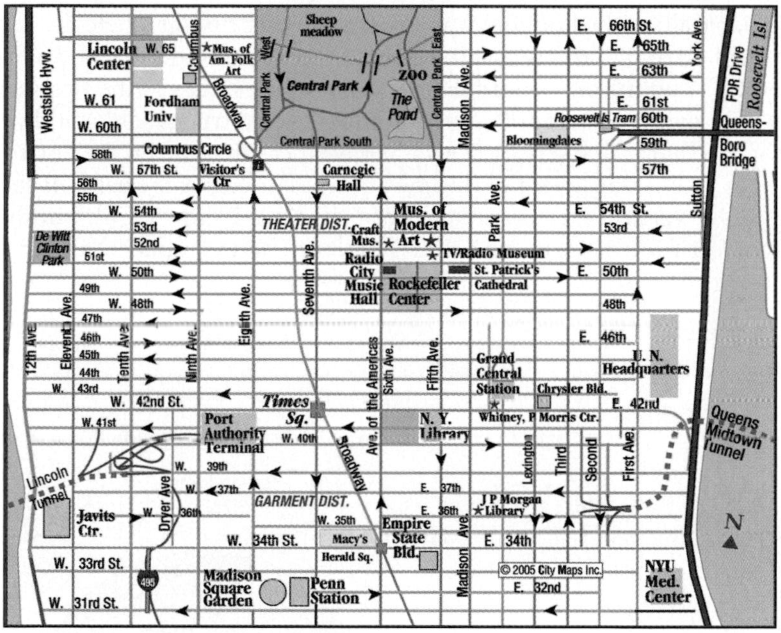

Maps are very familiar to just about everyone, so we don't usually think of them as being simplified versions of reality, but they are. This map does not show much more than the streets in this part of New York City and some of the most important buildings. The names, addresses, and telephone numbers of the people who live and work in the area aren't given. Almost none of the stores and buildings those people work and live in are shown either. It doesn't tell you which streets allow curbside parking and which don't. In fact, the map tells you almost nothing about the messy reality of life in this section of New York City, except how the streets are laid out, which is the essential information you need to get from the Port Authority to the Empire State Building.

Think about someone who says, "I know how to get around in the city, but I just can't figure out how to read a map." It certainly is possible to find your destination in a city without a map, but it's a lot easier with one. The same is true of using graphs in economics. It is possible to arrive at a solution to a real-world problem in economics and business without using graphs, but it is usually a lot easier if you do use them.

Often the difficulty students have with graphs and formulas is just a lack of familiarity. With practice, all the graphs and formulas in this text will become familiar to you. Once you are familiar with them, you will be able to use them to analyze problems that would otherwise seem very difficult. What follows is a brief review of how graphs and formulas are used.

Graphs of One Variable

Figure 1A-1 displays values for *market shares* in the U.S. automobile market using two common types of graphs. Market shares show the percentage of industry sales accounted for by different firms. In this case, the information is for groups of firms: the "Big Three"—Ford, General Motors, and DiamlerChrysler—as well as Japanese firms, European firms, and Korean firms. Panel (a) displays the information on market shares as a *bar graph,* where the market share of each group of firms is represented by the height of its bar. Panel (b) displays the same information as a *pie chart,* with the market share of each group of firms represented by the size of its slice of the pie.

Information on economic variables is also often displayed in *time-series graphs.* Time-series graphs are displayed on a coordinate grid. In a coordinate grid we can measure the value of one variable along the vertical axis (or y-axis), and the value of another variable along the horizontal axis (or x-axis). The point where the vertical axis intersects the horizontal axis is called the *origin.* At the origin the value of both variables is zero. The points on a coordinate grid represent values of the two variables. In Figure 1A-2 we measure the number of automobiles and trucks sold worldwide by the Ford Motor Company on the vertical axis, and we measure time on the horizontal axis. In time-series graphs, the height of the line at each date shows the value of the variable measured on the vertical axis. Both panels of Figure 1A-2 show Ford's worldwide sales during each year from 1999 to 2003. The difference between panel (a) and panel (b)

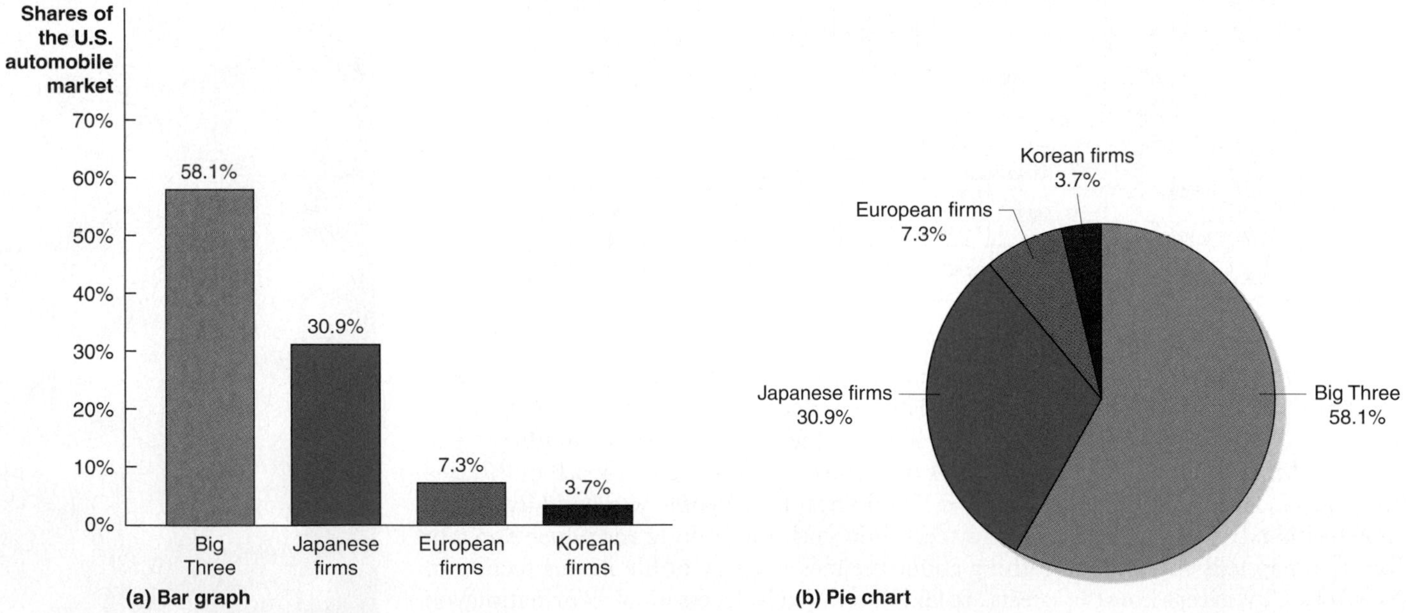

FIGURE 1A-1 Bar Graphs and Pie Charts

Values for an economic variable are often displayed as a bar graph or as a pie chart. In this case, panel (a) shows market share data for the U.S. automobile industry as a *bar graph,* where the market share of each group of firms is represented by the height of its bar. Panel (b) displays the same information as a *pie chart,* with the market share of each group of firms represented by the size of its slice of the pie.

Source: Ann Keeton, "December U.S. Auto Rise; GM's Decline," *Wall Street Journal,* January 5, 2005, p. A2.

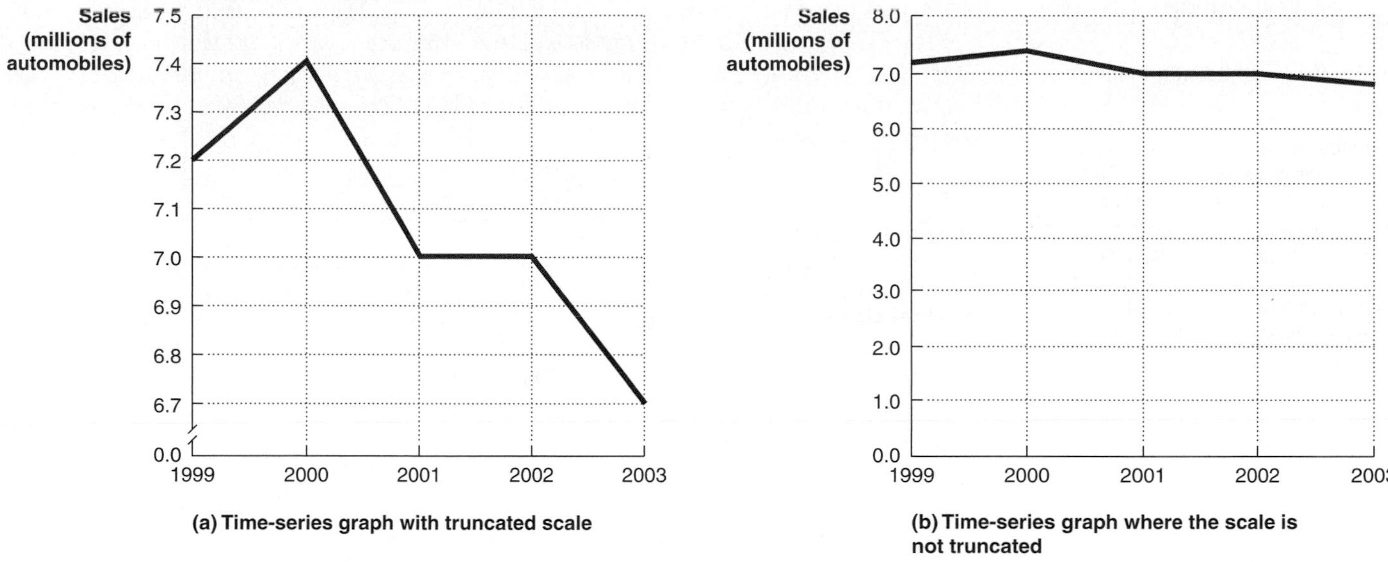

FIGURE 1A-2 Time-Series Graphs

Both panels present time-series graphs of Ford Motor Company's worldwide sales during each year from 1999 to 2003. Panel (a) has a truncated scale on the vertical axis, while panel (b) does not. As a result, the fluctuations in Ford's sales appear smaller in panel (b) than in panel (a).

Source: Ford Motor Company, *Annual Report*, various years.

illustrates the importance of the scale used in a time-series graph. In panel (a), the scale on the vertical axis is truncated, which means that it does not start with zero. The slashes (//) near the bottom of the axis indicate that the scale is truncated. In panel (b), the scale is not truncated. In panel (b) the fluctuations in Ford's sales appear smaller than in panel (a). (Technically, the horizontal axis is also truncated because we start with the year 1999, not the year 0.)

Graphs of Two Variables

We often use graphs to show the relationship between two variables. For example, suppose you are interested in the relationship between the price of a pepperoni pizza and the quantity of pizzas sold per week in the small town of Bryan, Texas. A graph showing the relationship between the price of a good and the quantity of the good demanded at each price is called a *demand curve.* (As we will discuss later, in drawing a demand curve for a good we have to hold constant any variables other than price that might affect the willingness of consumers to buy the good.) Figure 1A-3 shows the data you have collected on price and quantity. The figure shows a two-dimensional grid on which we measure the price of pizza along the *y*-axis and the quantity of pizza sold per week along the *x*-axis. Each point on the grid represents one of the price and quantity combinations listed in the table. We can connect the points to form the demand curve for pizza in Bryan, Texas. Notice that the scales on both axes in the graph are truncated. In this case, truncating the axes allows the graph to illustrate more clearly the relationship between price and quantity by excluding low prices and quantities.

Slopes of Lines

Once you have plotted the data in Figure 1A-3, you may be interested in how much the quantity of pizza sold increases as the price decreases. The *slope* of a line tells us how

FIGURE 1A-3

Plotting Price and Quantity Points in a Graph

The figure shows a two-dimensional grid on which we measure the price of pizza along the vertical axis (or *y*-axis) and the quantity of pizza sold per week along the horizontal axis (or *x*-axis). Each point on the grid represents one of the price and quantity combinations listed in the table. By connecting the points by a line, we can better illustrate the relationship between the two variables.

Price (dollars per pizza)	Quantity (pizzas per week)	Points
$15	50	*A*
14	55	*B*
13	60	*C*
12	65	*D*
11	70	*E*

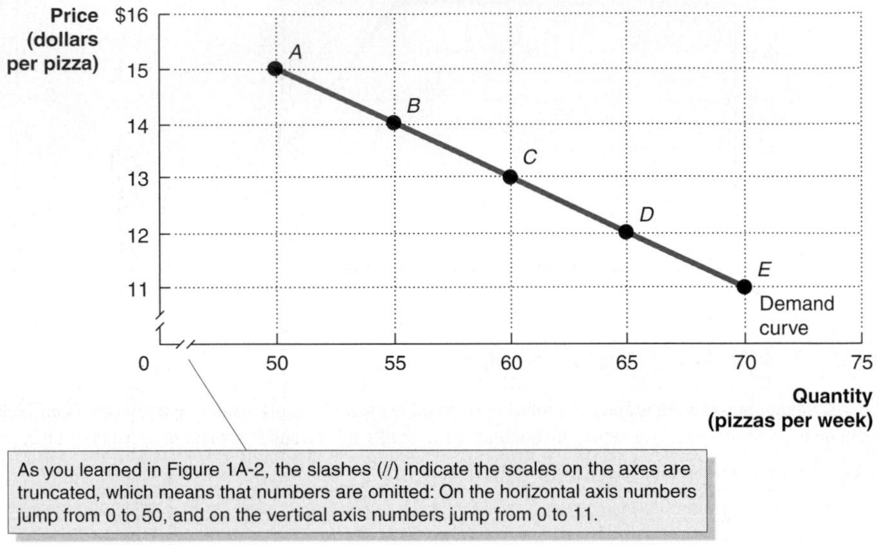

Price (dollars per pizza)
$16
15
14
13
12
11
0
50
55
60
65
70
75
A
B
C
D
E
Demand curve
Quantity (pizzas per week)
As you learned in Figure 1A-2, the slashes (//) indicate the scales on the axes are truncated, which means that numbers are omitted: On the horizontal axis numbers jump from 0 to 50, and on the vertical axis numbers jump from 0 to 11.

much the variable we are measuring on the *y*-axis changes as the variable we are measuring on the *x*-axis changes. We can use the Greek letter delta (Δ) to stand for the change in a variable. The slope is sometimes referred to as the rise over the run. So, we have several ways of expressing slope:

$$\text{Slope} = \frac{\text{Change in value on the vertical axis}}{\text{Change in value on the horizontal axis}} = \frac{\Delta y}{\Delta x} = \frac{\text{Rise}}{\text{Run}}.$$

Figure 1A-4 reproduces the graph from Figure 1A-3. Because the slope of a straight line is the same at any point, we can use any two points in the figure to calculate the slope of the line. For example, when the price of pizza decreases from \$14 to \$12, the quantity of pizza sold increases from 55 per week to 65 per week. Therefore, the slope is:

$$\text{Slope} = \frac{\Delta\text{Price of pizza}}{\Delta\text{Quantity of pizza}} = \frac{(\$12 - \$14)}{(65 - 55)} = \frac{-2}{10} = -0.2.$$

The slope of this line gives us some insight into how responsive consumers in Bryan, Texas are to changes in the price of pizza. The larger the value of the slope (ignoring the negative sign), the steeper the line will be, which indicates that not many additional pizzas are sold when the price falls. The smaller the value of the slope, the flatter the line will be, which indicates a greater increase in pizzas sold when the price falls.

Taking Into Account More Than Two Variables on a Graph

The demand curve graph in Figure 1A-4 shows the relationship between the price of pizza and the quantity of pizza sold, but we know that the quantity of any good sold depends on more than just the price of the good. For example, the quantity of pizza sold in a given week in Bryan, Texas can be affected by such other variables as the price of hamburgers, whether an advertising campaign by local pizza parlors has begun that week, and so on. Allowing the values of any other variables to change will cause the position of the demand curve in the graph to change.

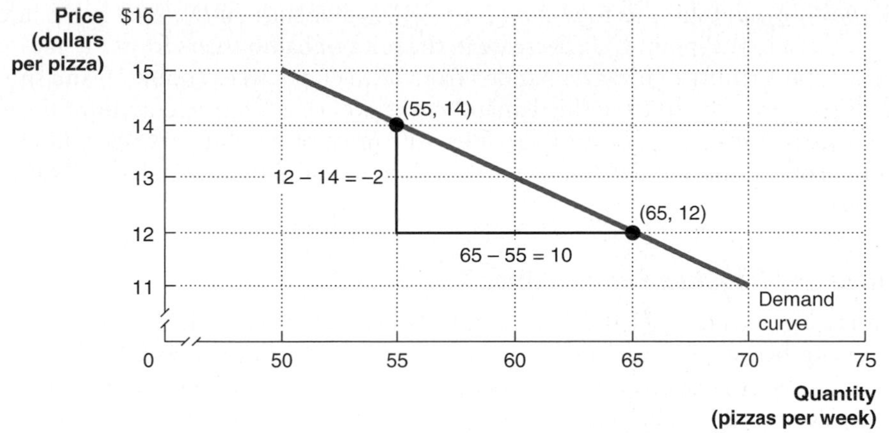

FIGURE 1A-4

Calculating the Slope of a Line

We can calculate the slope of a line as the change in the value of the variable on the *y*-axis divided by the change in the value of the variable on the *x*-axis. Because the slope of a straight line is constant, we can use any two points in the figure to calculate the slope of the line. For example, when the price of pizza decreases from $14 to $12, the quantity of pizza demanded increases from 55 per week to 65 per week. So, the slope of this line equals −2 divided by 10, or −0.2.

Suppose, for example, that the demand curve in Figure 1A-4 was drawn holding the price of hamburgers constant at $1.50. If the price of hamburgers rises to $2.00, then some consumers will switch from buying hamburgers to buying pizza, and more pizzas will be sold at every price. The result on the graph will be to shift the line representing the demand curve to the right. Similarly, if the price of hamburgers falls from $1.50 to $1.00, some consumers will switch from buying pizza to buying hamburgers, and fewer pizzas will be sold at every price. The result on the graph will be to shift the line representing the demand curve to the left.

The table in Figure 1A-5 shows the effect of a change in the price of hamburgers on the quantity of pizza demanded. For example, suppose at first we are on the line labeled *Demand* $curve_1$. If the price of pizza is $14 (point *A*), an increase in the price of hamburgers from $1.50 to $2.00 increases the quantity of pizza demanded from 55 to 60 per

	Quantity (pizzas per week)		
Price (dollars per pizza)	When the Price of Hamburgers = $1.00	When the Price of Hamburgers = $1.50	When the Price of Hamburgers = $2.00
$15	45	50	55
14	50	55	60
13	55	60	65
12	60	65	70
11	65	70	75

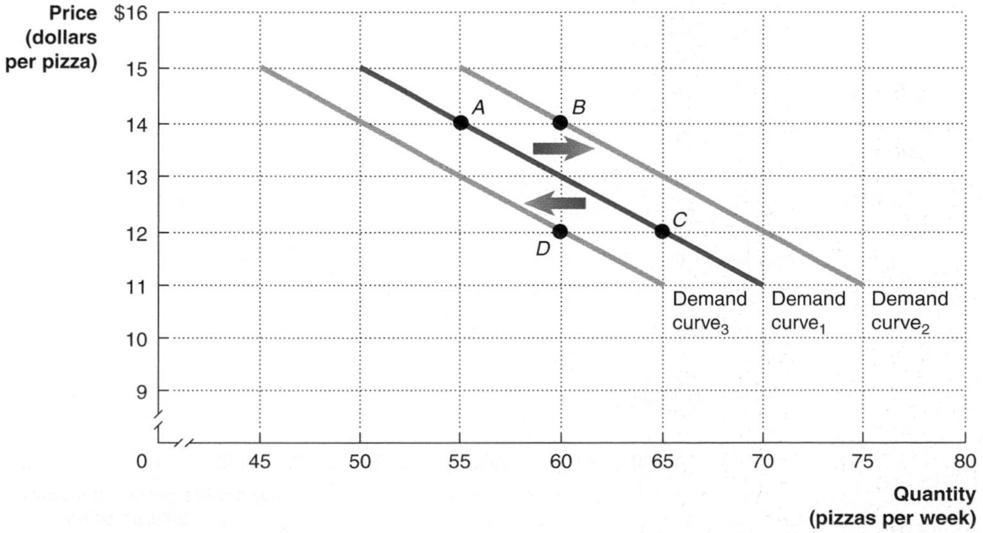

FIGURE 1A-5

Showing Three Variables on a Graph

The demand curve for pizza shows the relationship between the price of pizzas and the quantity of pizza demanded, *holding constant other factors that might affect the willingness of consumers to buy pizza.* If the price of pizza is $14 (point *A*), an increase in the price of hamburgers from $1.50 to $2.00 increases the quantity of pizza demanded from 55 to 60 per week (point *B*) and shifts us to Demand $curve_2$. Or, if we start on Demand $curve_1$ and the price of pizza is $12 (point *C*), a decrease in the price of hamburgers from $1.50 to $1.00 decreases the quantity of pizza demanded from 65 to 60 per week (point *D*), and shifts us to *Demand* $curve_3$.

week (point *B*), and shifts us to *Demand curve*$_2$. Or, if we start on *Demand curve*$_1$ and the price of pizza is $12 (point *C*), a decrease in the price of hamburgers from $1.50 to $1.00 decreases the quantity of pizza demanded from 65 to 60 per week (point *D*) and shifts us to *Demand curve*$_3$. By shifting the demand curve, we have taken into account the effect of changes in the value of a third variable—the price of hamburgers. We will use this technique of shifting curves to allow for the effects of additional variables many times in this book.

Positive and Negative Relationships

We can use graphs to show the relationships between any two variables. Sometimes the relationship between the variables is *negative*, meaning that as one variable increases in value the other variable decreases in value. This was the case with the price of pizza and the quantity of pizza demanded. The relationship between two variables can also be *positive*, meaning that the values of both variables increase together. This positive co-movement is the case, for example, with the level of total income—or *disposable personal income*—received by households in the United States and the level of total *consumption spending*, which is spending by households on all types of goods and services, apart from houses. The table in Figure 1A-6 shows the values for income and consumption spending for the years 2001–2004 (the values are in billions of dollars). The graph plots the data from the table, with national income measured along the horizontal axis and consumption spending measured along the vertical axis. Notice that the four points do not all fall exactly on the line. This is often the case with real-world data. To examine the relationship between two variables, economists often use the straight line that best fits the data.

Slopes of Nonlinear Curves

The relationship between some economic variables cannot be represented accurately by a straight line. For example, panel (a) of Figure 1A-7 shows the hypothetical relationship between Apple's total cost of producing iPods and the quantity of iPods produced. The relationship is curved, rather than linear. In this case, the cost of production is increasing at an increasing rate, which often happens in manufacturing. Put a different way, as we move up the curve, its slope becomes larger. To see this effect, first remember that we calculate the slope of a curve by dividing the change in the variable on the *y*-axis by the

FIGURE 1A-6

Graphing the Positive Relationship between Income and Consumption

In a positive relationship between two economic variables, as one variable increases, the other variable also increases. This figure shows the positive relationship between disposable personal income and consumption spending. As disposable personal income in the United States has increased, so has consumption spending.

Source: U.S. Department of Commerce, Bureau of Economic Analysis.

Year	Disposable Personal Income (billions of dollars)	Consumption Spending (billions of dollars)
2001	$7,486	$7,055
2002	7,827	7,376
2003	8,159	7,760
2004	8,632	8,229

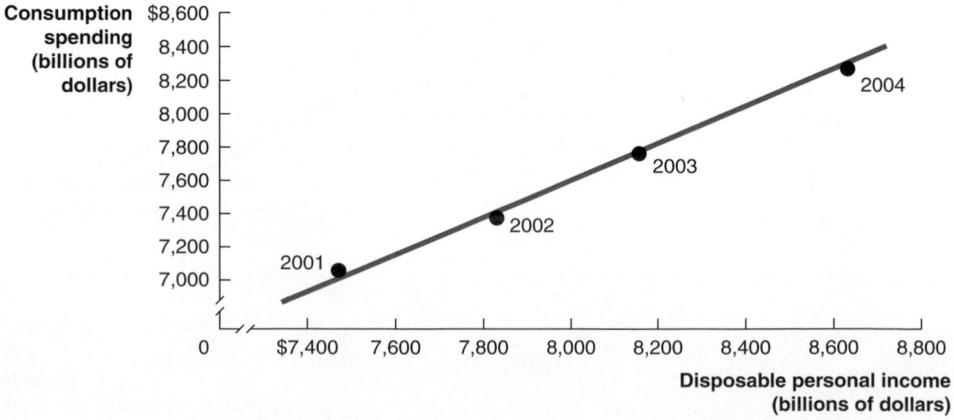

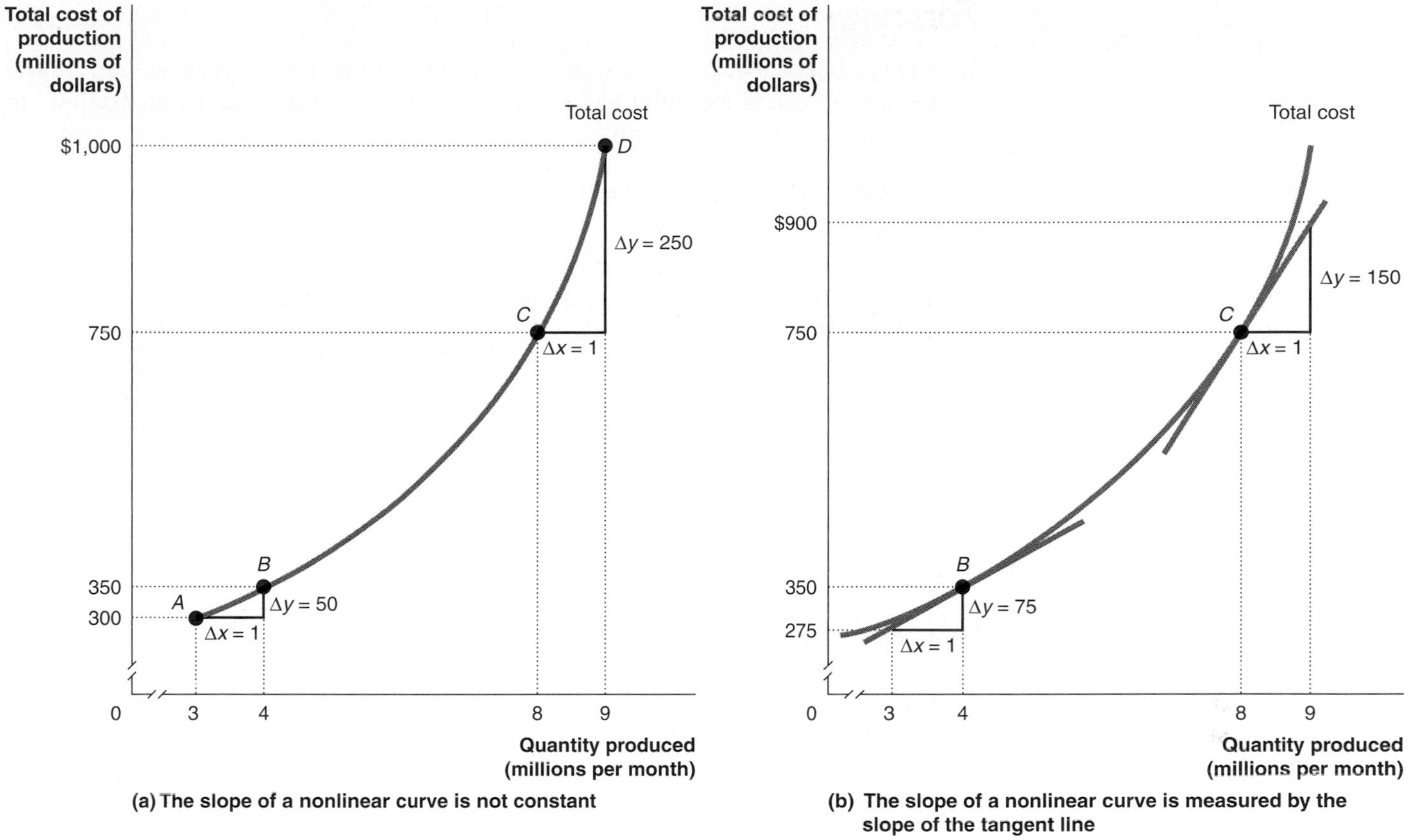

FIGURE 1A-7 The Slope of a Nonlinear Curve

The relationship between the quantity of iPods produced and the total cost of production is curved, rather than linear. In panel (a), in moving from point *A* to point *B*, the quantity produced increases by 1 million iPods, while the total cost of production increases by $50 million. Farther up the curve, as we move from point *C* to point *D*, the change in quantity is the same—1 million iPods—but the change in the total cost of production is now much larger: $250 million. Because the change in the *y* variable has increased, while the change in the *x* variable has remained the same, we know that the slope has increased. In panel (b), we measure the slope of the cuve at a particular point by the slope of the tangent line. The slope of the tangent line at point *B* is 75, and the slope of the tangent line at point *C* is 150.

change in the variable on the *x*-axis. In moving from point *A* to point *B*, the quantity produced increases by 1 million iPods, while the total cost of production increases by $50 million. Farther up the curve, as we move from point *C* to point *D*, the change in quantity is the same—1 million iPods—but the change in the total cost of production is now much larger: $250 million. Because the change in the *y* variable has increased, while the change in the *x* variable has remained the same, we know that the slope has increased.

To measure the slope of a nonlinear curve at a particular point, we must measure the slope of the *tangent line* to the curve at that point. A tangent line will only touch the curve at that point. We can measure the slope of the tangent line just as we would the slope of any straight line. In panel (b), the tangent line at point *B* has a slope equal to

$$\frac{\Delta \text{Cost}}{\Delta \text{Quantity}} = \frac{75}{1} = 75.$$

The tangent line at point *C* has a slope equal to

$$\frac{\Delta \text{Cost}}{\Delta \text{Quantity}} = \frac{150}{1} = 150.$$

Once again we see that the slope of the curve is larger at point *C* than at point *B*.

Formulas

We have just seen that graphs are an important economic tool. In this section, we will review several useful formulas and show how to use them to summarize data and to calculate important relationships.

Formula for a Percentage Change

One important formula is the *percentage change*. The percentage change is the change in some economic variable, usually from one period to the next, expressed as a percentage. An important macroeconomic measure is the real *Gross Domestic Product* or GDP. GDP is the value of all the final goods and services produced in a country during a year. "Real" GDP is corrected for the effects of inflation. When economists say that the U.S. economy grew 4.4 percent during 2004, they mean that real GDP was 4.4 percent higher in 2004 than it was in 2003. The formula for making this calculation is:

$$\left(\frac{GDP_{2004} - GDP_{2003}}{GDP_{2003}}\right) \times 100$$

or, more generally for any two periods:

$$\text{Percentage change} = \left(\frac{\text{Value in the second period} - \text{Value in the first period}}{\text{Value in the first period}}\right) \times 100.$$

In this case, real GDP was \$10,381 billion in 2003 and \$10,842 billion in 2004. So, the growth rate of the U.S. economy during 2004 was:

$$\left(\frac{\$10,842 - \$10,381}{\$10,381}\right) \times 100 = 4.4\%.$$

Notice that it didn't matter that in using the formula we ignored the fact that GDP is measured in billions of dollars. In fact, when calculating percentage changes, *the units don't matter.* The percentage increase from \$10,381 billion to \$10,842 billion is exactly the same as the percentage increase from \$10,381 to \$10,842.

Formulas for the Areas of a Rectangle and a Triangle

Areas that form rectangles and triangles on graphs can have important economic meaning. For example, Figure 1A-8 shows the demand curve for Pepsi. Suppose that the price is currently \$2.00 and that 125,000 bottles of Pepsi are sold at that price. A firm's *total revenue* is equal to the amount it receives from selling its product, or the price times the quantity sold. In this case, total revenue will equal \$2.00 per bottle times 125,000 bottles, or \$250,000.

FIGURE 1A-8

Showing a Firm's Total Revenue on a Graph

The area of a rectangle is equal to its base multiplied by its height. Total revenue is equal to price multiplied by quantity. Here, total revenue is equal to the price of \$2.00 per bottle times 125,000 bottles, or \$250,000. The area of the green-shaded rectangle shows the firm's total revenue.

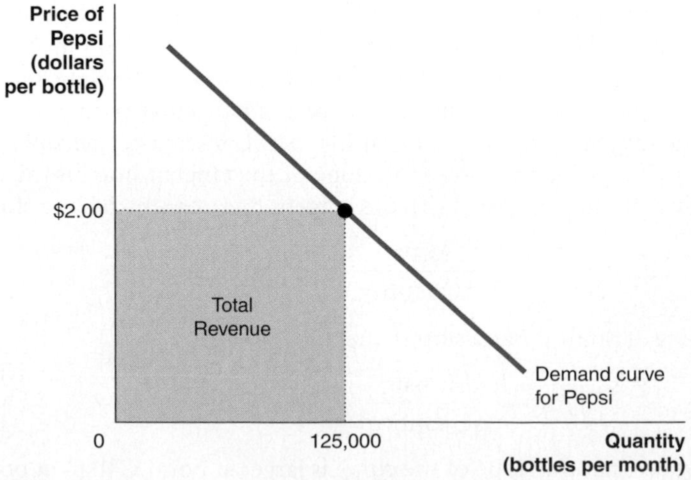

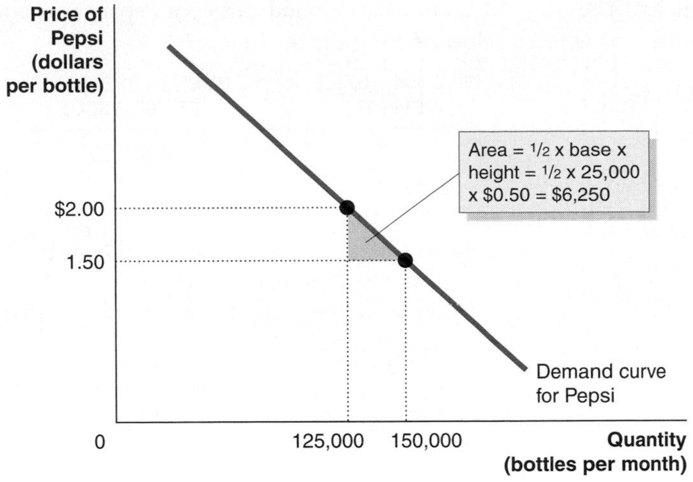

FIGURE 1A-9

The Area of a Triangle

The area of a triangle is equal to ½ multiplied by its base multiplied by its height. The area of the blue-shaded triangle has a base equal to 150,000 − 125,000, or 25,000 and a height equal to \$2.00 − \$1.50, or \$0.50. Therefore, its area equals ½ × 25,000 × \$0.50, or \$6,250.

The formula for the area of a rectangle is:

Area of a rectangle = base × height.

In Figure 1A-8, the green-shaded rectangle also represents the firm's total revenue because its area is given by the base of 125,000 bottles multiplied by the price of \$2.00 per bottle.

We will see in later chapters that areas that are triangles can also have economic significance. The formula for the area of a triangle is:

Area of a triangle = ½ × base × height.

The blue-shaded area in Figure 1A-9 is a triangle. The base equals 150,000 − 125,000, or 25,000. Its height equals \$2.00 − \$1.50, or \$0.50. Therefore its area equals ½ × 25,000 × \$0.50, or \$6,250. Notice that the blue area is only a triangle if the demand curve is a straight line, or linear. Not all demand curves are linear. However, the formula for the area of a triangle will usually still give us a good approximation, even if the demand curve is not linear.

Summary of Using Formulas

You will encounter several other formulas in this book. Whenever you must use a formula, you should follow these steps:

1. Make sure you understand the economic concept that the formula represents.
2. Make sure that you are using the correct formula for the problem you are solving.
3. Make sure that the number you calculate using the formula is economically reasonable. For example, if you are using a formula to calculate a firm's revenue and your answer is a negative number, you know you made a mistake somewhere.

PROBLEMS AND APPLICATIONS

Please visit **www.prenhall.com/hubbard** *for solutions to the even-numbered problems as well as multiple-choice and true or false self-assessment quizzes.*

1. The following table gives the relationship between the price of custard pies and the number of pies Jacob buys per week.

PRICE	QUANTITY OF PIES	WEEK
\$3.00	6	July 2
2.00	7	July 9
5.00	4	July 16
6.00	3	July 23
1.00	8	July 30
4.00	5	August 6

a. Is the relationship between the price of pies and the number of pies Jacob buys a positive relationship or a negative relationship?
b. Plot the data from the table on a graph similar to Figure 1A-3. Draw a straight line that best fits the points.
c. Calculate the slope of the line.

2. The following table gives information on the quantity of lemonade demanded on sunny and overcast days. Plot the data from the table on a graph similar to Figure 1A-5. Draw two straight lines representing the two demand curves—one for sunny days, the other for overcast days.

PRICE (DOLLARS PER GLASS)	QUANTITY (GLASSES OF LEMONADE PER DAY)	WEATHER
$0.80	30	Sunny
0.80	10	Overcast
0.70	40	Sunny
0.70	20	Overcast
0.60	50	Sunny
0.60	30	Overcast
0.50	60	Sunny
0.50	40	Overcast

3. Using the information in Figure 1A-2, calculate the percentage change in auto sales from one year to the next. Between which years did sales fall at the fastest rate?

4. Real GDP in 1981 was $5,292 billion. Real GDP in 1982 was $5,189 billion. What was the percentage change in real GDP from 1981 to 1982? What do economists call the percentage change in real GDP from one year to the next?

5. Assume the demand curve for Pepsi passes through the following two points:

PRICE PER BOTTLE OF PEPSI	NUMBER OF BOTTLES OF PEPSI SOLD
$2.50	100,000
1.25	200,000

a. Draw a graph with a linear demand curve that passes through these two points.
b. Show on the graph the areas representing total revenue at each price. Give the value for total revenue at each price.

6. What is the area of the blue triangle shown in the following figure?

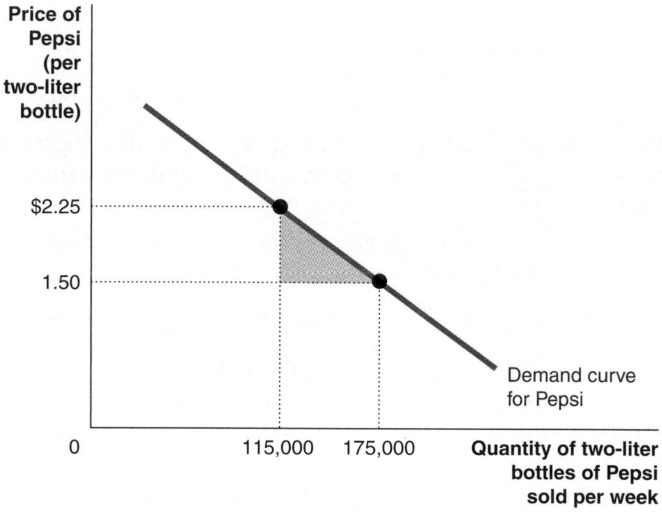

chapter two

Trade-offs, Comparative Advantage, and the Market System

Managers Making Choices at BMW

➤ When you think of cars that combine fine engineering, high performance, and cutting-edge styling, you are likely to think of BMW. The Bayerische Motoren Werke, or Bavarian Motor Works, was founded in Germany in 1916 as a company devoted to manufacturing aircraft engines. In the early 1920s, BMW began to make motorcycles. In 1928 it produced its first car. Today, BMW employs nearly 100,000 workers in 23 factories in 15 countries to produce eight car models. In 2004, it had worldwide sales of about $70 billion.

To compete in the automobile market, the managers of BMW must make many strategic decisions, such as whether to introduce a new car model. In 2004, for example, BMW introduced the 1-Series, a hatchback that is significantly smaller than most other BMW models. Some BMW managers had opposed developing the 1-Series because they believed that it was inconsistent with the company's image of producing more expensive, higher-performance models. But other managers argued that the company needed a model that would appeal to younger drivers and could compete with the Volkswagen Golf and the Audi A3. Another strategic decision faced by BMW's managers is where to focus their advertising. In the late 1990s, for example, some of BMW's managers opposed advertising in China because they were skeptical about the country's sales potential. Other managers, however, argued that rising incomes were rapidly increasing the size of the Chinese market. BMW decided to advertise in China, and by 2004 it had become the company's eighth-largest market.

Over the years, BMW's managers have also faced the strategic decision of whether to concentrate production in factories in Germany or to build new factories in its overseas markets. Keeping production in Germany makes it easier for BMW's managers to supervise production and to employ German workers, who generally have high levels of technical training. Building factories in other countries, however, has two benefits. First, the lower wages paid to workers in other countries reduce the

cost of manufacturing vehicles. Second, BMW can reduce political friction by producing vehicles in the same country in which they sell them. In 2003, BMW opened a plant at Shenyang, in northeast China, to build its 3-Series and 5-Series cars. Previously, in 1995, BMW opened a U.S. factory in Spartanburg, South Carolina, which currently produces the Z4 roadster and X5 sports utility vehicle (SUV).

Managers also face smaller scale—or tactical—business decisions. For instance, for many years, BMW used two workers to attach the gearbox to the engine in each car. In 2002, an alternative method of attaching the gearbox using a robot, rather than workers, was developed. In choosing which method to use, managers at BMW faced a trade-off because the robot method had a higher cost, but installed the gearbox in exactly the correct position, which reduces engine noise when the car is driven. Ultimately, the managers decided to adopt the robot method. A similar type of tactical business decision must be made in scheduling production at BMW's Spartanburg, South Carolina, plant. The plant produces both the Z4 and the X5 models, and a decision must be made each month as to the quantity of each model that should be produced. *An Inside Look* on page 54 discusses a similar decision BMW has to make at its Munich, Germany, plant.

LEARNING OBJECTIVES

After studying this chapter, you should be able to:

① Use a production possibilities frontier to analyze opportunity costs and trade-offs.

② Understand comparative advantage and explain how it is the basis for trade.

③ Explain the basic idea of how a market system works.

Scarcity The situation in which unlimited wants exceed the limited resources available to fulfill those wants.

➤ In a market system, managers at most firms must make decisions like those made by BMW's managers. The decisions managers face reflect the key fact of economic life: ***Scarcity** requires trade-offs.* Scarcity exists because we have unlimited wants but only limited resources available to fulfill those wants. Goods and services are scarce. So, too, are the economic resources, or *factors of production*—workers, capital, natural resources, and entrepreneurial ability—used to make them. Your time is scarce, which means you face trade-offs: If you spend an hour studying for an economics exam, you have one less hour to spend studying for a psychology exam or going to the movies. If your university decides to use some of its scarce budget funds to buy new computers for the computer labs, those funds will not be available to buy new books for the library or to resurface the student parking lot. If BMW decides to devote some of the scarce workers and machinery in its Spartanburg assembly plant to producing more Z4 roadsters, those resources will not be available to produce more X5 SUVs.

Many of the decisions of households and firms are made in markets. One key activity that takes place in markets is trade. By engaging in trade, people can raise their standard of living. Trade involves the decisions of millions of households and firms spread around the world. In this chapter, we provide an overview of how the market system coordinates the independent decisions of these millions of households and firms. We begin our analysis of the economic consequences of scarcity and the working of the market system by introducing an important economic model: the *production possibilities frontier.*

① LEARNING OBJECTIVE

Use a production possibilities frontier to analyze opportunity costs and trade-offs.

Production Possibilities Frontiers and Real-World Trade-offs

As we saw in the opening to this chapter, BMW operates an automobile factory in Spartanburg, South Carolina, where it assembles Z4 roadsters and X5 sports utility vehicles. Because the firm's resources—workers, machinery, materials, and entrepreneurial skills—are limited, BMW faces a trade-off: Resources devoted to producing Z4s are not available for producing X5s, and vice versa. Chapter 1 explained that economic models can be useful in analyzing many questions. We can use a simple model called the *production possibilities frontier* to analyze the trade-offs BMW faces in its Spartanburg plant. A **production possibilities frontier** is a curve showing the maximum attainable combinations of two products that may be produced with available resources. In BMW's case, the two products are Z4 roadsters and X5 sports utility vehicles, and the resources are BMW's workers, materials, robots, and other machinery.

Production possibilities frontier A curve showing the maximum attainable combinations of two products that may be produced with available resources.

Graphing the Production Possibilities Frontier

Figure 2-1 uses a production possibilities frontier to illustrate the trade-offs facing BMW. The numbers from the table are plotted in the graph. The line in the graph is BMW's production possibilities frontier. If BMW uses all its resources to produce roadsters, it can produce 800 per day—point *A* at one end of the production possibilities frontier. If BMW uses all its resources to produce SUVs, it can produce 800 per day—point *E* at the other end of the production possibilities frontier. If BMW devotes resources to producing both vehicles, it could be at a point like *B*, where it produces 600 roadsters and 200 SUVs.

BMW's Production Choices at Its Spartanburg Plant		
Choice	Quantity of Roadsters Produced	Quantity of SUVs Produced
A	800	0
B	600	200
C	400	400
D	200	600
E	0	800

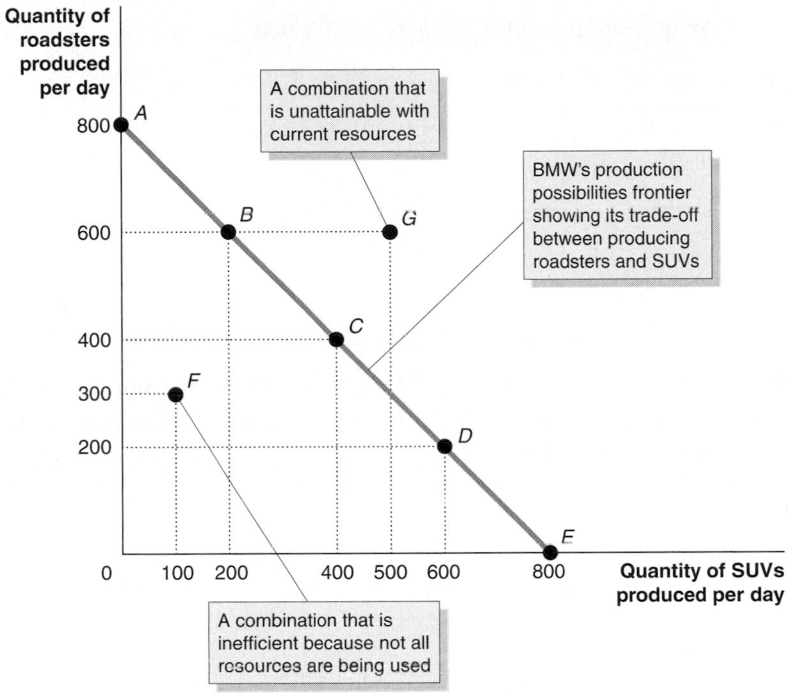

FIGURE 2-1

BMW's Production Possibilities Frontier

BMW faces a trade-off: To build one more roadster, it must build one less SUV. The production possibilities frontier illustrates the trade-off BMW faces. Combinations on the production possibilities frontier—like points *A, B, C, D,* and *E*—are *technically efficient* because the maximum output is being obtained from the available resources. Combinations inside the frontier—like point *F*—are *inefficient* because some resources are not being used. Combinations outside the frontier—like point *G*—are *unattainable* with current resources.

All the combinations either on the frontier—like *A, B, C, D,* and *E*—or inside the frontier—like point *F*—are *attainable* with the resources available. Combinations on the frontier are *efficient* because all available resources are being fully utilized, and the fewest possible resources are being used to produce a given amount of output. Combinations inside the frontier—like point *F*—are *inefficient* because maximum output is not being obtained from the available resources—perhaps because the assembly line is not operating at capacity. BMW might like to be beyond the frontier—at a point like *G* where it would be producing 600 roadsters and 500 SUVs—but points beyond the production possibilities frontier are *unattainable* given the firm's current resources. To produce the combination at *G,* BMW would need more machines or more workers.

Notice that if BMW is producing efficiently and is on the production possibilities frontier, the only way to produce more of one vehicle is to produce less of the other vehicle. Recall from Chapter 1 that the **opportunity cost** of any activity is the highest valued alternative that must be given up to engage in that activity. For BMW, the opportunity cost of producing one SUV is the number of roadsters the company will not be able to produce because it has already devoted those resources to producing SUVs. For example, in moving from point *B* to point *C,* the opportunity cost of producing 200 more SUVs per day is the 200 fewer roadsters that can be produced.

Opportunity cost The highest-valued alternative that must be given up to engage in an activity.

What point on the production possibilities frontier is best? We can't tell without further information. If consumer demand for SUVs is greater than demand for roadsters, the company is likely to choose a point closer to *E.* If demand for roadsters is greater than demand for SUVs, the company is likely to choose a point closer to *A.*

SOLVED PROBLEM 2-1

Drawing a Production Possibilities Frontier for Rosie's Boston Bakery

1 LEARNING OBJECTIVE
Use a production possibilities frontier to analyze opportunity costs and trade-offs.

Rosie's Boston Bakery specializes in cakes and pies. Rosie has 5 hours per day to devote to baking. In 1 hour, Rosie can prepare 2 pies or 1 cake.

a. Use the information given to complete the following table:

	HOURS SPENT MAKING		QUANTITY MADE	
CHOICE	CAKES	PIES	CAKES	PIES
A	5	0		
B	4	1		
C	3	2		
D	2	3		
E	1	4		
F	0	5		

b. Use the data in the table to draw a production possibilities frontier graph illustrating Rosie's trade-offs between making cakes and making pies. Label the vertical axis "Quantity of cakes made." Label the horizontal axis "Quantity of pies made." Make sure to label the values where Rosie's production possibilities frontier intersects the vertical and horizontal axes.

c. Label the points representing choice *D* and choice *E*. If Rosie is at choice *D*, what is her opportunity cost of making more pies?

Solving the Problem:

Step 1: Review the chapter material. This problem is about using production possibilities frontiers to analyze trade-offs, so you may want to review the section "Graphing the Production Possibilities Frontier," which begins on page 34.

Step 2: Answer question (a) by filling in the table. If Rosie can produce 1 cake in 1 hour, then with choice *A* she will make 5 cakes and 0 pies. Because she can produce 2 pies in 1 hour, with choice *B* she will make 4 cakes and 2 pies. By similar reasoning, you can fill in the remaining cells in the following table:

	HOURS SPENT MAKING		QUANTITY MADE	
CHOICE	CAKES	PIES	CAKES	PIES
A	5	0	5	0
B	4	1	4	2
C	3	2	3	4
D	2	3	2	6
E	1	4	1	8
F	0	5	0	10

Step 3: Answer question (b) by drawing the production possibilities frontier graph. Using the data in the table in question (a), you should draw a graph that looks like this:

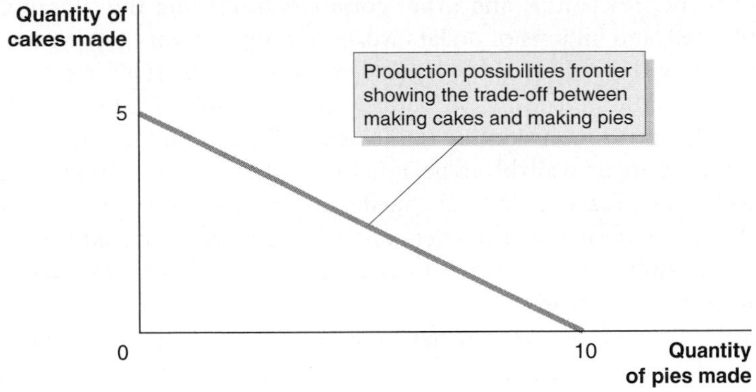

If Rosie devotes all 5 hours to making cakes, she will make 5 cakes. Therefore, her production possibilities frontier will intersect the vertical axis at 5 cakes made. If Rosie devotes all 5 hours to making pies, she will make 10 pies. Therefore, her production possibilities frontier will intersect the horizontal axis at 10 pies made.

Step 4: Answer question (c) by showing choices *D* and *E* on your graph. The points for choices *D* and *E* can be plotted using the information from the table:

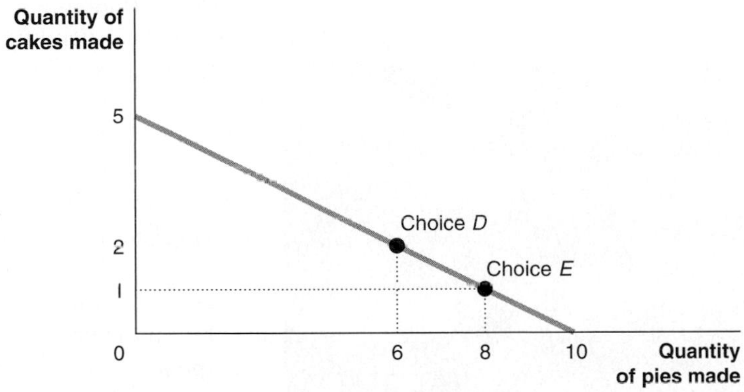

Moving from choice *D* to choice *E* increases Rosie's production of pies by 2 but lowers her production of cakes by 1. Therefore, her opportunity cost of making 2 more pies is making 1 less cake.

YOUR TURN: **For more practice, do related problem 6 on page 58 at the end of this chapter.**

2-1 Making the Connection

Trade-offs and Tsunami Relief

In December 2004, an earthquake caused a tidal wave—or tsunami—to flood coastal areas of Indonesia, Thailand, Sri Lanka, and other countries bordering the Indian Ocean. Over 280,000 people died, and billions of dollars worth of property was destroyed. Governments and individuals around the world moved quickly to donate to relief efforts. The U.S. government donated $950 million, and individual U.S. citizens donated more than an additional $500 million. Both governments and individuals face limited budgets, however, and funds used for one purpose are unavailable to be used for another purpose. Although governments and individuals did increase their total charitable giving following the tsunami disaster, much of the funds spent on tsunami relief appear to have been diverted from other uses. A difficult trade-off resulted: Giving funds to victims of the tsunami meant fewer funds were available to aid other good causes.

For example, some of the funds provided by the U.S. government for reconstruction in the tsunami-devastated areas came from existing aid programs. As a result, spending on other aid projects in the region declined. Similarly, nonprofit organizations in New York City reported sharp declines in donations to the homeless and the poor, as donors gave funds for tsunami relief instead. According to a report in the newspaper *Crain's New York Business*, "Some groups such as Bailey House, which helps homeless people who have AIDS, have even started receiving letters from longtime donors warning that this year's gifts are being redirected to the tsunami relief effort." As one commentator observed, "The milk of human kindness is probably flowing at the usual rate in the United States. It's just getting channeled in different directions."

More funds for tsunami relief meant less funds for other charities.

Governments in the area also faced a trade-off in considering whether to spend funds to install tsunami warning systems, similar to existing systems in the Pacific Ocean. Tsunamis are fairly common in the Pacific Ocean but quite rare in the Indian Ocean. Records dating back to the early 1500s indicate that the tsunami of 2004 was by far the worst in the last 500 years. Funds that governments in poor countries, such as Indonesia, would spend on tsunami warning systems would have to be diverted from spending on health, education, or other programs.

Source: Daniel Gross, "Zero-Sum Charity," *Slate*, January 20, 2005.

Increasing Marginal Opportunity Costs

We can also use the production possibilities frontier to explore issues related to the economy as a whole. For example, suppose we divide all the many goods and services produced in the economy into just two types: military goods and civilian goods. In Figure 2-2, we let tanks represent military goods and automobiles represent civilian goods. If all the country's resources are devoted to producing military goods, 400 tanks can be produced in one year. If all resources are devoted to producing civilian goods, 500 automobiles can be produced in one year. Devoting resources to producing both goods results in the economy being at other points along the production possibilities frontier.

Notice that this production possibilities frontier is bowed outward, rather than being a straight line. Because the curve is bowed out, the opportunity cost of automobiles in terms of tanks depends upon where the economy currently is on the production

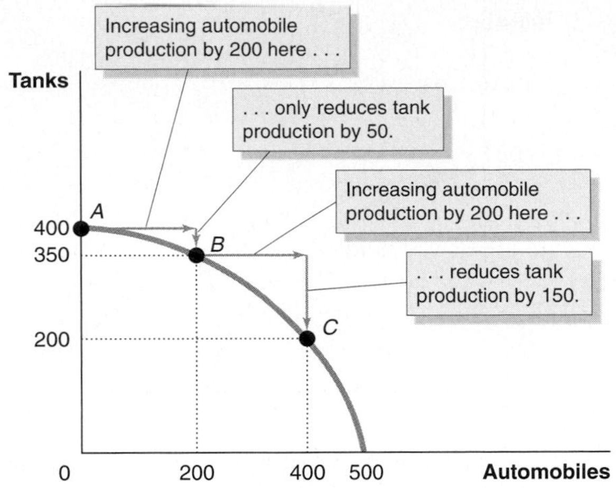

FIGURE 2-2

Increasing Marginal Opportunity Cost

As the economy moves down the production possibilities frontier, it experiences *increasing marginal opportunity costs* because increasing automobile production by a given quantity requires larger and larger decreases in tank production. For example, to increase automobile production from 0 to 200—moving from point *A* to point *B*—the economy only has to give up 50 tanks. But to increase automobile production by another 200 vehicles—moving from point *B* to point *C*—the economy has to give up 150 tanks.

possibilities frontier. For example, to increase automobile production from zero to 200—moving from point *A* to point *B*—the economy only has to give up 50 tanks. But to increase automobile production by another 200 vehicles—moving from point *B* to point *C*—the economy has to give up 150 tanks.

As the economy moves down the production possibilities frontier, it experiences *increasing marginal opportunity costs* because increasing automobile production by a given quantity requires larger and larger decreases in tank production. Increasing marginal opportunity costs occur because some workers, machines, and other resources are better suited to one use than to another. At point *A* some resources that are well suited to producing automobiles are being forced to produce tanks. Shifting these resources into producing automobiles by moving from point *A* to point *B* allows a substantial increase in automobile production, without much loss of tank production. But as the economy moves down the production possibilities frontier, more and more resources that are better suited to tank production are switched into automobile production. As a result, the increases in automobile production become increasingly smaller while the decreases in tank production become increasingly larger. We would expect in most situations that production possibilities frontiers will be bowed outward, rather than linear as in the BMW example we discussed earlier.

The idea of increasing marginal opportunity costs illustrates an important economic concept: *The more resources already devoted to any activity, the smaller the payoff to devoting additional resources to that activity.* The more hours you have already spent studying economics, the smaller the increase in your test grade from each additional hour you spend—and the greater the opportunity cost of using the hour in that way. The more funds a firm has devoted to research and development during a given year, the smaller the amount of useful knowledge it receives from each additional dollar—and the greater the opportunity cost of using the funds in that way. The more funds the federal government spends cleaning up the environment during a given year, the smaller the reduction in pollution from each additional dollar—and, once again, the greater the opportunity cost of using the funds in that way.

Economic Growth

At any given time, the total resources available to any economy are fixed. Therefore, if the United States produces more automobiles, it must produce less of something else—tanks in our example. Over time, though, the resources available to an economy may increase. For example, both the labor force and the capital stock—the amount of physical capital available in the country—may increase. The increase in the available labor force and the capital stock shifts the production possibilities frontier outward for the U.S. economy and makes it possible to produce both more automobiles and more tanks.

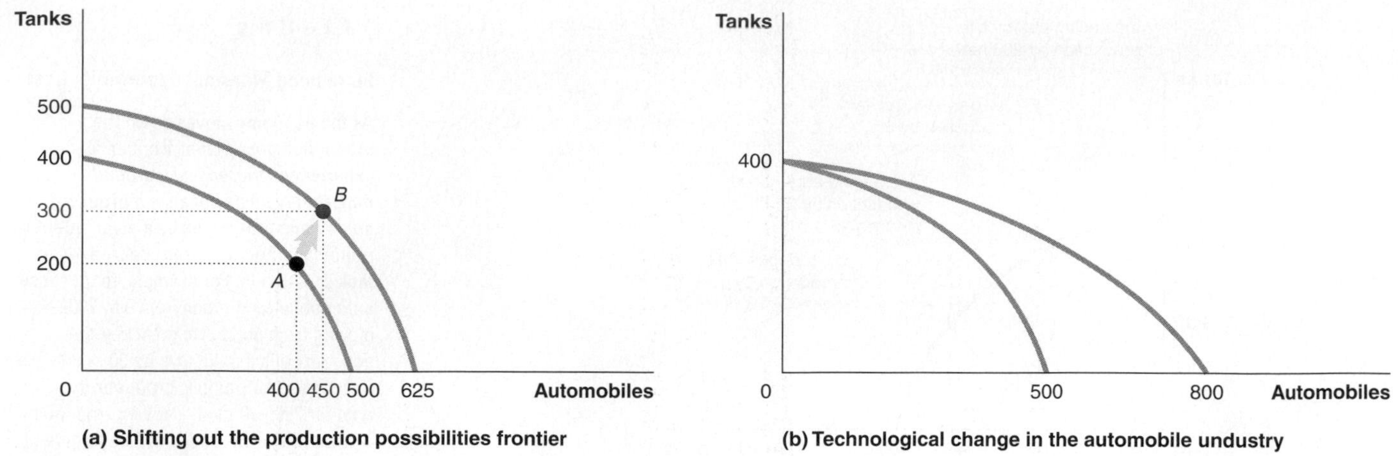

FIGURE 2-3 Economic Growth

Panel (a) shows that as more economic resources become available and technological change occurs, the economy can move from point *A* to point *B*, producing more tanks and more automobiles.

Panel (b) shows the results of technological advance in the automobile industry that increases the quantity of vehicles workers can produce per year, while leaving the maximum quantity of tanks that can be produced unchanged. Shifts in the production possibilities frontier represent *economic growth.*

Panel (a) of Figure 2-3 shows that the economy can move from point *A* to point *B*, producing more tanks and more automobiles.

Similarly, technological advance makes it possible to produce more goods with the same amount of workers and machinery, which also shifts the production possibilities frontier outward. Technological advance need not affect all sectors equally. Panel (b) of Figure 2-3 shows the results of technological advance in the automobile industry that increases the quantity of vehicles workers can produce per year, while leaving unchanged the quantity of tanks that can be produced.

Economic growth The ability of the economy to produce increasing quantities of goods and services.

Shifts in the production possibilities frontier represent **economic growth** because they allow the economy to increase the production of goods and services, which ultimately raises the standard of living. In the United States and other high-income countries, the market system has aided the process of economic growth, which over the past two hundred years has greatly increased the health and well-being of the average person.

② LEARNING OBJECTIVE

Understand comparative advantage and explain how it is the basis for trade.

Trade

Trade The act of buying or selling.

Having discussed the important ideas of production possibilities frontiers and opportunity costs, we can use them to understand the basic economic activity of *trade.* Markets are fundamentally about **trade,** which is the act of buying and selling. Many of the trades in which we engage take place indirectly: We sell our labor services as, say, an accountant, salesperson, or nurse for money, and then use the money to buy goods and services. Ultimately an accountant, salesperson, or nurse is trading his or her services for food, clothing, and other goods and services. One of the great benefits to trade is that it makes it possible for people to become better off by increasing both their production and their consumption.

Specialization and Gains from Trade

Consider the following situation: You and your neighbor both have fruit trees on your property. Initially, suppose that you have only apple trees and your neighbor has only cherry trees. In this situation, if you both like apples and cherries there is an obvious opportunity for both of you to gain from trade: You trade some of your apples for some of your neighbor's cherries, making you both better off. But what if there are apple and

	You		Your Neighbor	
	Apples	Cherries	Apples	Cherries
All time devoted to picking apples	20 pounds	0 pounds	30 pounds	0 pounds
All time devoted to picking cherries	0 pounds	20 pounds	0 pounds	60 pounds

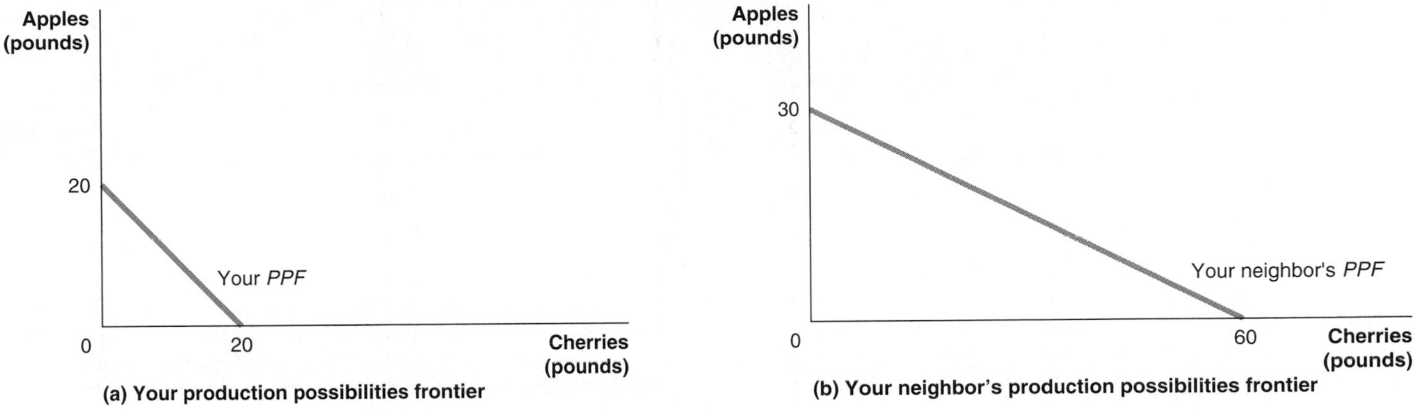

FIGURE 2-4 Production Possibilities for You and Your Neighbor, without Trade

The table in Figure 2-4 shows how many pounds of apples and how many pounds of cherries you and your neighbor can each pick in one month. The graphs in the figure use the data from the table to construct production possibilities frontiers (*PPFs*) for you and your neighbor. Panel (a) shows your *PPF*. If you devote all of your time to picking apples and none of your time to picking cherries, you can pick 20 pounds. If you devote all of your time to picking cherries, you can pick 20 pounds. Panel (b) shows that if your neighbor devotes all of her time to picking apples, she can pick 30 pounds. If she devotes all of her time to picking cherries, she can pick 60 pounds.

cherry trees growing on both of your properties? In that case there can still be gains from trade. For example, your neighbor might be very good at picking apples and you might be very good at picking cherries. In that case, it makes sense that both can benefit if your neighbor concentrates on picking apples and you concentrate on picking cherries. You can then trade some of your cherries for some of your neighbor's apples. But what if your neighbor is actually better at picking both apples and cherries than you are? It might not seem that in this case your neighbor has anything to gain from trading with you, but in fact she does.

We can use production possibilities frontiers (*PPFs*) to show how your neighbor can benefit from trading with you even though she is better than you are at picking both apples and cherries. (For simplicity, and because it will not have any effect on the conclusions we draw, we will assume that the *PPFs* in this example are straight lines.) The table in Figure 2-4 shows how many apples and how many cherries you and your neighbor can pick in one month. The graph in the figure uses the data from the table to construct *PPFs* for you and your neighbor. Panel (a) shows your *PPF*. If you devote all your time to picking apples and none of your time to picking cherries, you can pick 20 pounds of apples per month. If you devote all your time to picking cherries, you can pick 20 pounds per month. Panel (b) shows that if your neighbor devotes all her time to picking apples, she can pick 30 pounds. If she devotes all her time to picking cherries, she can pick 60 pounds.

The production possibilities frontiers in Figure 2-4 show the opportunities you and your neighbor have to consume apples and cherries, *without trade.* Suppose that when you don't trade with your neighbor, you pick and consume 8 pounds of apples and 12 pounds of cherries per month. This combination of apples and cherries is represented by point *A* in panel (a) of Figure 2-5. When she doesn't trade with you, your neighbor picks and consumes 9 pounds of apples and 42 pounds of cherries per

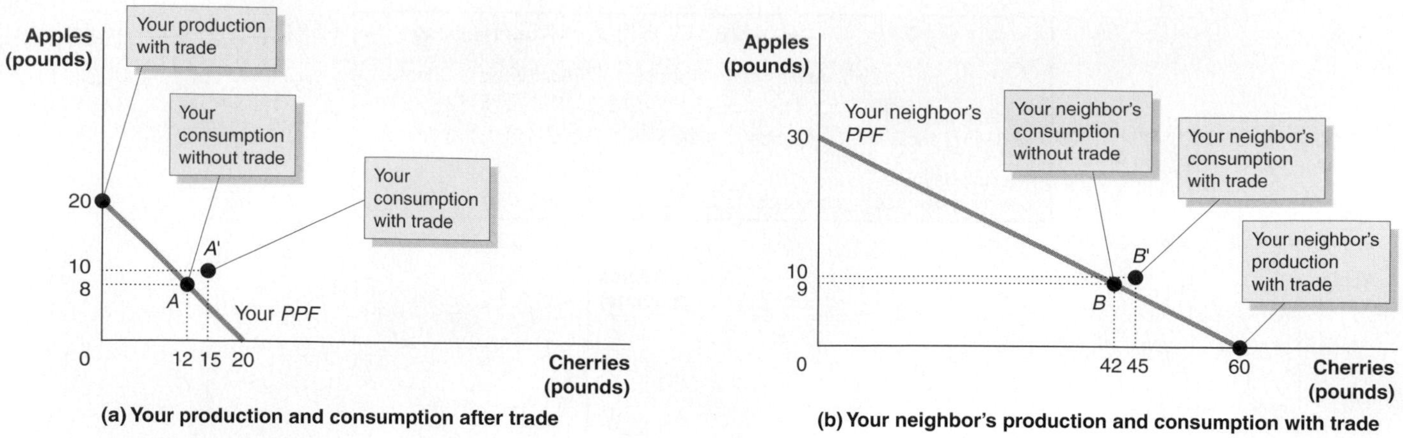

FIGURE 2-5 Gains from Trade

When you don't trade with your neighbor, you pick and consume 8 pounds of apples and 12 pounds of cherries per month—point *A* in panel (a). When your neighbor doesn't trade with you, she picks and consumes 9 pounds of apples and 42 pounds of cherries per month—point *B* in panel (b). If you specialize in picking apples, you can pick 20 pounds. If your neighbor specializes in picking cherries, she can pick 60 pounds. If you trade 10 pounds of your apples for 15 pounds of your neighbor's cherries, you will be able to consume 10 pounds of apples and 15 pounds of cherries—point *A'* in panel (a). Your neighbor can now consume 10 pounds of apples and 45 pounds of cherries—point *B'* in panel (b). You and your neighbor are both better off as a result of trade.

month. This combination of apples and cherries is represented by point *B* in panel (b) of Figure 2-5.

After years of picking and consuming your own apples and cherries, suppose your neighbor comes to you one day with the following proposition: She offers next month to trade you 15 pounds of her cherries for 10 pounds of your apples. Should you accept this offer? You will have more apples and more cherries to consume if you do. To take advantage of her offer, first, rather than splitting your time between picking apples and picking cherries, you should specialize in picking only apples. We know this will allow you to pick 20 pounds of apples. You can trade 10 of those 20 pounds of apples to your neighbor for 15 pounds of her cherries. The result is you will be able to consume 10 pounds of apples and 15 pounds of cherries (point *A'* in panel (a) of Figure 2-5). You are clearly better off as a result of trading with your neighbor: You now can consume 2 more pounds of apples and 3 more pounds of cherries than you were consuming without trading. You have moved beyond your *PPF!*

Your neighbor has also benefited. By specializing in picking only cherries, she can pick 60 pounds. She trades 15 pounds of cherries to you for 10 pounds of apples. The result is she can consume 10 pounds of apples and 45 pounds of cherries (point *B'* in panel (b) of Figure 2-5). This is 1 more pound of apples and 3 more pounds of cherries than she was consuming before trading with you. She also has moved beyond her *PPF.* Table 2-1 summarizes the changes in production and consumption that result from your trade with your neighbor.

Absolute Advantage versus Comparative Advantage

Absolute advantage The ability of an individual, firm, or country to produce more of a good or service than competitors using the same amount of resources.

Perhaps the most remarkable aspect of the preceding example is that your neighbor benefits from trading with you even though she is better at picking both apples and cherries than you are. **Absolute advantage** is the ability to produce more of a good or service than competitors using the same amount of resources. Your neighbor has an absolute advantage over you in producing both apples and cherries because she can pick more of each fruit than you can in the same amount of time. This observation seems to suggest that your neighbor should pick her own apples *and* her own cherries. We have just seen, however, that she is better off if she specializes in cherry picking and leaves the apple picking to you.

TABLE 2-1

A Summary of the Gains from Trade

	YOU		YOUR NEIGHBOR	
	APPLES (IN POUNDS)	CHERRIES (IN POUNDS)	APPLES (IN POUNDS)	CHERRIES (IN POUNDS)
Production *and* consumption *without* trade	8	12	9	42
Production *with* trade	20	0	0	60
Consumption *with* trade	10	15	10	45
Gains from trade (increased consumption)	2	3	1	3

We can consider further why both you and your neighbor benefit from specializing in picking only one fruit. First, think about the opportunity cost to each of you of picking the two fruits. We saw from the *PPF* in Figure 2-4 that if you devoted all your time to picking apples, you would be able to pick 20 pounds of apples per month. As you move down your *PPF* and shift time away from picking apples to picking cherries, you have to give up 1 pound of apples for each pound of cherries you pick (the slope of your *PPF* is −1—for a review of calculating slopes, see the appendix to Chapter 1). Therefore, your opportunity cost of picking 1 pound of cherries is 1 pound of apples. By the same reasoning, your opportunity cost of picking 1 pound of apples is 1 pound of cherries. Your neighbor's *PPF* has a different slope, and so she faces a different trade-off. As she shifts time from picking apples to picking cherries, she has to give up 0.5 pound of apples for every 1 pound of cherries she picks (the slope of your neighbor's *PPF* is −0.5). As she shifts time from picking cherries to picking apples, she gives up 2 pounds of cherries for every 1 pound of apples she picks. Therefore, her opportunity cost of picking 1 pound of apples is 2 pounds of cherries, and her opportunity cost of picking 1 pound of cherries is 0.5 pound of apples.

Table 2-2 summarizes the opportunity costs for you and your neighbor of picking apples and cherries. Note that even though your neighbor can pick more apples in a month than you can, the *opportunity cost* of picking apples is higher for her than for you because when she picks apples she gives up more cherries than you do. So, even though she has an absolute advantage over you in picking apples, it is more costly for her to pick apples than it is for you. The table also shows us that her opportunity cost of picking cherries is lower than your opportunity cost of picking cherries. **Comparative advantage** is the ability of an individual, firm, or country to produce a good or service at a lower opportunity cost than other producers. In apple picking, your neighbor has an *absolute advantage* over you, but you have a *comparative advantage* over her. Your neighbor has both an absolute and a comparative advantage over you in picking cherries. As we have seen, you are better off specializing in picking apples, and your neighbor is better off specializing in picking cherries. Another way of thinking about why it would be costly for your neighbor to spend time picking apples is that even though she can pick 1.5 times as many apples in a month as you can—30 pounds per month for her versus 20 pounds per month for you—she can pick 3 times as many cherries—60 pounds per month for her versus 20 pounds for you. So, by specializing in picking cherries she is spending her time in the activity where her absolute advantage over you is the greatest.

Comparative advantage The ability of an individual, firm, or country to produce a good or service at a lower opportunity cost than other producers.

TABLE 2-2

Opportunity Costs of Picking Apples and Cherries

	OPPORTUNITY COST OF PICKING 1 POUND OF APPLES	OPPORTUNITY COST OF PICKING 1 POUND OF CHERRIES
You	1 pound of cherries	1 pound of apples
Your neighbor	2 pounds of cherries	0.5 pound of apples

Don't Let This Happen To You!

Don't Confuse Absolute Advantage and Comparative Advantage

First, make sure you know the definitions:

- *Absolute advantage:* The ability of an individual, firm, or country to produce more of a good or service than competitors using the same amount of resources. In our example, your neighbor has an absolute advantage over you both in picking apples and in picking cherries.
- *Comparative advantage:* The ability of an individual, firm, or country to produce a good or service at a lower opportunity cost than other producers. In our example, your neighbor has a comparative advantage in picking cherries, but you have a comparative advantage in picking apples.

Keep these two key points in mind:

1. It is possible to have an absolute advantage in producing a good or service without having a comparative advantage. This would be the case with your neighbor picking apples.
2. It is possible to have a comparative advantage in producing a good or service without having an absolute advantage. This would be the case with you picking apples.

YOUR TURN: Test your understanding by doing related problem 14 on page 59 at the end of this chapter.

Comparative Advantage and the Gains from Trade

We have just derived an important economic principle: *The basis for trade is comparative advantage, not absolute advantage.* The fastest apple pickers do not necessarily do much apple picking. If the fastest apple pickers have a comparative advantage in some other activity—picking cherries, playing major league baseball, or being industrial engineers—they are better off specializing in that other activity. Individuals, firms, and countries are better off if they specialize in producing goods and services for which they have a comparative advantage and obtain the other goods and services they need by trading. We will return to the important concept of comparative advantage in Chapter 8, which is devoted to the subject of international trade.

SOLVED PROBLEM 2-2

② LEARNING OBJECTIVE
Understand comparative advantage and explain how it is the basis for trade.

Comparative Advantage and the Gains from Trade

We will see in Chapter 6 the important role that comparative advantage plays in analyzing international trade. For now, consider this simple problem. Suppose that Canada and the United States both produce maple syrup and honey. These are the combinations of the two goods that each country can produce in one day:

CANADA		UNITED STATES	
HONEY (IN TONS)	MAPLE SYRUP (IN TONS)	HONEY (IN TONS)	MAPLE SYRUP (IN TONS)
0	60	0	50
10	45	10	40
20	30	20	30
30	15	30	20
40	0	40	10
		50	0

a. Who has a comparative advantage in producing maple syrup? Who has a comparative advantage in producing honey?

b. Suppose that Canada is currently producing 30 tons of honey and 15 tons of maple syrup and the United States is currently producing 10 tons of honey and 40 tons of maple syrup. Demonstrate that Canada and the United States can both be better off if they specialize in producing only one good and then engage in trade.

c. Illustrate your answer to question (b) by drawing a *PPF* for the United States and a *PPF* for Canada. Show on your *PPF*s the combinations of honey and maple syrup produced and consumed in each country before and after trade.

Solving the Problem:

Step 1: Review the chapter material. This problem concerns comparative advantage, so you may want to review the section "Absolute Advantage versus Comparative Advantage," which begins on page 42.

Step 2: Answer question (a) by calculating who has a comparative advantage in each activity. Remember that a country has a comparative advantage in producing a good if it can produce the good at the lowest opportunity cost. When Canada produces 1 more ton of honey, it produces 1.5 fewer tons of maple syrup. On the one hand, when the United States produces 1 more ton of honey, it produces 1 less ton of maple syrup. Therefore, the United States's opportunity cost of producing honey—1 ton of maple syrup—is lower than Canada's—1.5 tons of maple syrup. On the other hand, when Canada produces 1 more ton of maple syrup, it produces $\frac{2}{3}$ less of a ton of honey. When the United States produces 1 more ton of maple syrup, it produces 1 less ton of honey. Therefore, Canada's opportunity cost of producing maple syrup—$\frac{2}{3}$ of a ton of honey—is lower than that of the United States—1 ton of honey. We can conclude that the United States has a comparative advantage in the production of honey and Canada has a comparative advantage in the production of maple syrup.

Step 3: Answer question (b) by showing that specialization makes Canada and the United States better off. We know that Canada should specialize where it has a comparative advantage and the United States should specialize where it has a comparative advantage. If both countries specialize, Canada will produce 60 tons of maple syrup and 0 tons of honey, and the United States will produce 0 tons of maple syrup and 50 tons of honey. After both countries specialize, the United States could then trade 30 tons of honey to Canada in exchange for 40 tons of maple syrup (other mutually beneficial trades are possible as well). We can summarize the results in a table:

	BEFORE TRADE		AFTER TRADE	
	HONEY (IN TONS)	MAPLE SYRUP (IN TONS)	HONEY (IN TONS)	MAPLE SYRUP (IN TONS)
Canada	30	15	30	20
United States	10	40	20	40

The United States is better off after trade because it can consume the same amount of maple syrup and 10 more tons of honey. Canada is better off after trade because it can consume the same amount of honey and 5 more tons of maple syrup.

Step 4: Answer question (c) by drawing the *PPF*s.

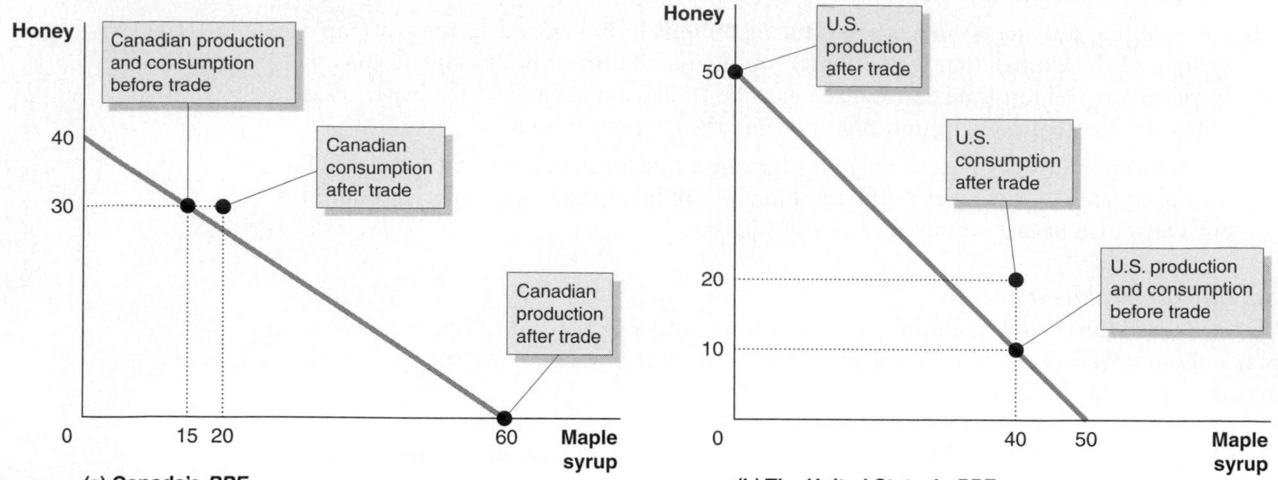

(a) Canada's *PPF* (b) The United States's *PPF*

YOUR TURN: **For more practice, do related problems 12 and 13 on page 59 at the end of this chapter.**

③ LEARNING OBJECTIVE

Explain the basic idea of how a market system works.

The Market System

We have seen that households, firms, and the government face trade-offs and incur opportunity costs because of the scarcity of resources. We have also seen that trade allows people to specialize according to their comparative advantage. By engaging in trade, people can raise their standard of living. Of course, trade in the modern world is much more complex than the examples we have considered so far. Trade today involves the decisions of millions of people spread around the world. But how does an economy make trade possible, and how are the decisions of these millions of people coordinated? In the United States and most other countries, trade is carried out in markets. Markets also determine the answers to the three fundamental questions discussed in Chapter 1: *What* goods and services will be produced? *How* will the goods and services be produced? *Who* will receive the goods and services?

Market A group of buyers and sellers of a good or service and the institution or arrangement by which they come together to trade.

Product markets Markets for goods—such as computers—and services—such as medical treatment.

Factor markets Markets for the factors of production, such as labor, capital, natural resources, and entrepreneurial ability.

Recall that the definition of a **market** is a group of buyers and sellers of a good or service and the institution or arrangement by which they come together to trade. Markets take many forms: They can be physical places, like the local pizza parlor or the New York Stock Exchange, or virtual places, like eBay. In a market, the buyers are demanders of goods or services, and the sellers are suppliers of goods or services. Households and firms interact in two types of markets: *product markets* and *factor markets.* **Product markets** are markets for goods—such as computers—and services—such as medical treatment. In product markets, households are demanders and firms are suppliers. **Factor markets** are markets for the *factors of production,* such as labor, capital, natural resources, and entrepreneurial ability. In factor markets, households are suppliers and firms are demanders. Most people earn most of their income by selling their labor services to firms in the labor market.

The Circular Flow of Income

Two key groups participate in markets:

➤ A *household* consists of all the individuals in a home. Households are suppliers of factors of production—particularly labor—used by firms to make goods and services. Households use the income they receive from selling the factors of production to purchase the goods and services supplied by firms.

➤ *Firms* are suppliers of goods and services. Firms use the funds they receive from selling goods and services to buy the factors of production needed to make the goods and services.

We can use a simple economic model called a **circular-flow diagram** to see how participants in markets are linked. Figure 2-6 shows that in factor markets households supply labor and other factors of production in exchange for wages and other payments from firms. In product markets, households use the payments they earn in factor markets to purchase the goods and services supplied by firms. Firms produce these goods and services using the factors of production supplied by households. In the figure, the

Circular-flow diagram A model that illustrates how participants in markets are linked.

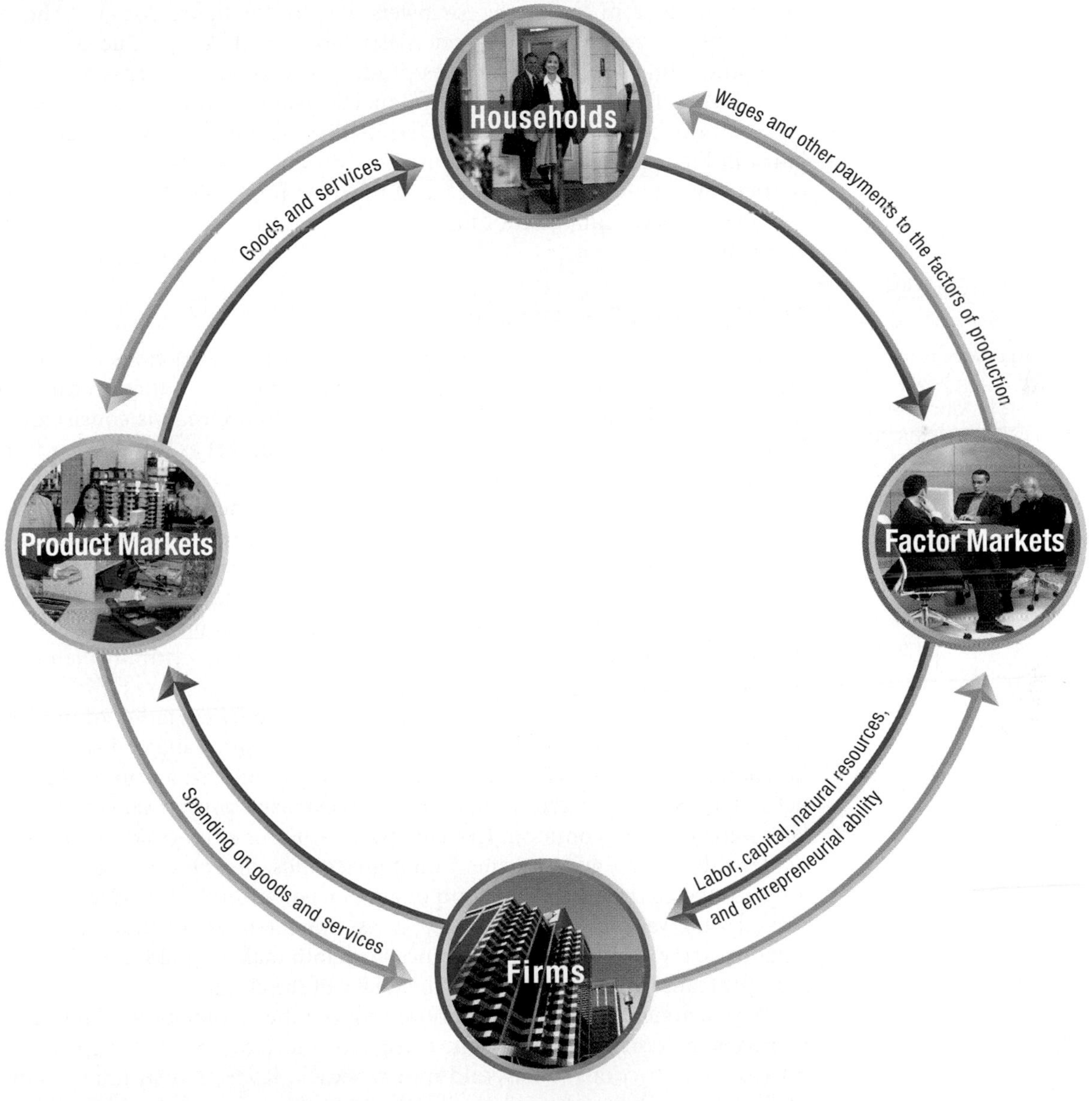

FIGURE 2-6 The Circular-Flow Diagram

Households and firms are linked together in a circular flow of production, income, and spending. The blue arrows show the flow of the factors of production. In factor markets, households supply labor, entrepreneurial ability, and other factors of production to firms. Firms use these factors of production to make goods and services that they supply to households in product markets. The red arrows show the flow of goods and services from firms to households. The green arrows show the flow of funds. In factor markets, households receive wages and other payments from firms in exchange for supplying the factors of production. Households use these wages and other payments to purchase goods and services from firms in product markets. Firms sell goods and services to households in product markets, and they use the funds to purchase the factors of production from households in factor markets.

blue arrows show the flow of factors of production from households through factor markets to firms. The red arrow shows the flow of goods and services from firms through product markets to households. The green arrows show the flow of funds from firms through factor markets to households, and the flow of spending from households through product markets to firms.

Like all economic models, the circular-flow diagram is a simplified version of reality. For example, Figure 2-6 leaves out the important role played by government in buying goods from firms and in making payments, such as Social Security or unemployment insurance payments, to households. The figure also leaves out the role played by banks, the stock and bond markets, and other parts of the *financial system* in aiding the flow of funds from lenders to borrowers. Finally, the figure does not show that some goods and services purchased by domestic households are produced in foreign countries, and some goods and services produced by domestic firms are sold to foreign households. The government, the financial system, and the international sector are explored further in later chapters. Despite these simplifications, the circular-flow diagram in Figure 2-6 is useful in seeing how product markets, factor markets, and their participants are linked together. One of the great mysteries of the market system is that it manages successfully to coordinate the independent activities of so many households and firms.

The Gains from Free Markets

Free market A market with few government restrictions on how a good or service can be produced or sold, or on how a factor of production can be employed.

A **free market** exists when the government places few restrictions on how a good or a service can be produced or sold, or on how a factor of production can be employed. Governments in all modern economies intervene more than is consistent with a fully free market. In that sense, we can think of the free market as being a benchmark against which we can judge actual economies. Relatively few government restrictions are placed on economic activity in the United States, Canada, the countries of Western Europe, Hong Kong, Singapore, and Estonia. So these countries come close to the free market benchmark. In countries such as Cuba and North Korea, the free market system has been rejected in favor of centrally planned economies with extensive government control over product and factor markets. Countries that come closest to the free market benchmark have been more successful than countries with centrally planned economies in providing their people with rising living standards.

The Scottish philosopher Adam Smith is considered the father of modern economics because one of his books, *An Inquiry into the Nature and Causes of the Wealth of Nations,* published in 1776, was an early and very influential argument for the free market system. Smith was writing at a time when extensive government restrictions on markets were still very common. In many parts of Europe the *guild system* still prevailed. Under this system, governments would give guilds, or organizations of producers, the authority to control the production of a good. For example, the shoemakers' guild controlled who was allowed to produce shoes, how many shoes they could produce, and what price they could charge. In France, the cloth makers' guild even dictated the number of threads that were allowed in the weave of the cloth.

Smith argued that such restrictions reduced the income or wealth of a country and its people by restricting the quantity of goods produced. Some people at the time supported the restrictions of the guild system because it was in their financial interest to do so. If you were a member of a guild, the restrictions served to reduce the competition you would face. But other people sincerely believed that the alternative to the guild system was economic chaos. Smith argued that these people were wrong and that a country could enjoy a smoothly functioning economic system if firms were freed from guild restrictions.

The Market Mechanism

In Smith's day, defenders of the guild system worried that if, for instance, the shoemakers' guild did not control shoe production, either too many or too few shoes would be produced. Smith argued that prices would do a better job of coordinating the activities of buyers and sellers than the guilds could. A key to understanding Smith's argument is the assumption that *individuals usually act in a rational, self-interested way.* In particular, individuals take those actions most likely to make themselves better off financially. This assumption of rational, self-interested behavior underlies nearly all economic analysis. In fact, economics can be distinguished from other fields that study human behavior—such as sociology and psychology—by its emphasis on the assumption of self-interested behavior. Adam Smith understood—as economists today understand—that people's motives can be complex. But in analyzing people in the act of buying and selling, the motivation of financial reward usually provides the best explanation for the actions people take.

For example, suppose that a significant number of consumers switch from buying cars to buying SUVs, as in fact happened in the United States during the 1990s. Firms will find that they can charge higher prices for SUVs than they can for cars. The self-interest of these firms will lead them to respond to consumers' wishes by producing more SUVs and fewer cars. Or suppose that consumers decide that they want to eat less bread, pasta, and other foods high in carbohydrates, as many did following the increase in popularity of the Atkins and South Beach diets. Then the prices firms can charge for bread and pasta will fall. The self-interest of firms will lead them to produce less bread and pasta, which in fact is what happened.

In the case where consumers want more of a product, and in the case where they want less of a product, the market system responds without a guild or anyone else giving orders about how much to produce or what price to charge. In a famous phrase, Smith said that firms would be led by the "invisible hand" of the market to provide consumers with what they wanted. Firms would respond to changes in prices by making decisions that ended up satisfying the wants of consumers.

Story of the Market System in Action: "I, Pencil"

2-2 Making the Connection

The pencil seems like a very simple product. In fact, its production requires the coordinated activities of many different people, spread around the world. The economist Leonard Read showed how markets achieve this coordination by writing an "autobiography" of a pencil sold by the Eberhard Faber Pencil Company of California. It is one of the most famous accounts of how the market system works. The pencil writes that:

> My family tree begins with a [cedar] tree that grows in Northern California and Oregon. Now contemplate all the saws and trucks and rope and the countless other gear used in harvesting and carting the cedar logs to the railroad siding. . . .
>
> The logs are shipped to a mill in San Leandro, California. . . . The cedar logs are cut into small, pencil-length slats less than one-fourth of an inch in thickness. . . . Once in the pencil factory . . . each slat is given eight grooves by a complex machine, after which another machine lays leads in every other slat. . . .
>
> My "lead" itself—it contains no lead at all—is complex. The graphite is mined in Ceylon . . . [and] is mixed with clay from Mississippi in which ammonium hydroxide is used in the refining process. . . . To increase their strength and smoothness the leads are then treated with a hot mixture which includes candelilla wax from Mexico, paraffin wax, and hydrogenated natural fats.
>
> My cedar receives six coats of lacquer. Do you know all the ingredients of lacquer? Who would think that the growers of castor beans and the refiners of castor oil are a part of it? They are.
>
> My bit of metal–the ferrule–is brass. Think of all the persons who mine zinc and copper and those who have the skills to make shiny sheet brass from these products of nature.
>
> Then there's my crowning glory . . . the part man uses to erase the errors he makes with me. . . . It is a rubber-like product made by reacting rape-seed oil from the Dutch

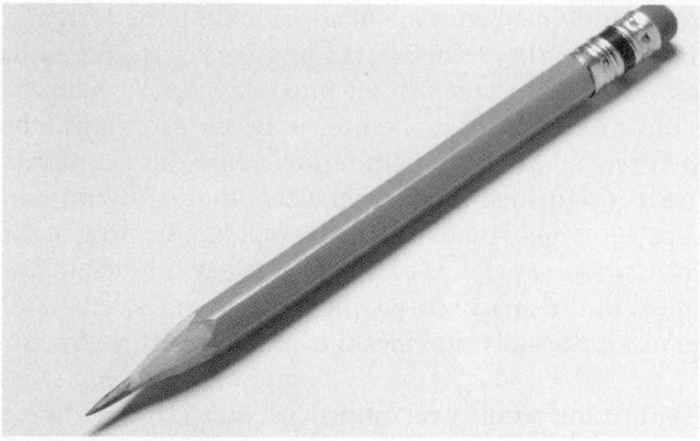

The market coordinates the activities of the many people spread around the world who contribute to the making of a pencil.

East Indies with sulfur chloride. . . . Then, too, there are numerous vulcanizing and accelerating agents. The pumice comes from Italy; and the pigment which gives [the eraser] its color is cadmium sulfide.

[M]illions of human beings have had a hand in my creation, no one of whom even knows more than a very few of the others. . . . There isn't a single person in all these millions, including the president of the pencil company, who contributes more than a tiny, infinitesimal bit of know-how. . . .

There is a fact still more astounding: the absence of a master mind, of anyone dictating or forcibly directing these countless actions which bring me into being. No trace of such a person can be found. Instead, we find the Invisible Hand at work.

Source: Leonard E. Read, *"I, Pencil,"* Irvington-on-Hudson, NY: Foundation for Economic Education, Inc. 1999. Used with permission of Foundation for Economic Education, Inc. Available online at www.econlib.org/library/Essays/rdPncl1.html.

The Role of the Entrepreneur

Entrepreneur Someone who operates a business, bringing together the factors of production—labor, capital, and natural resources—to produce goods and services.

Entrepreneurs are central to the working of the market system. An **entrepreneur** is someone who operates a business. Entrepreneurs must first determine what goods and services they believe consumers want, and then decide how those goods and services might be produced most profitably. Entrepreneurs bring together the factors of production—labor, capital, and natural resources—to produce goods and services. They put their own funds at risk when they start businesses. If they are wrong about what consumers want or about the best way to produce goods and services, they can lose those funds. In fact, it is not unusual for entrepreneurs who eventually achieve great success to fail at first. For instance, early in their careers both Henry Ford and Sakichi Toyoda, whose company eventually became the Toyota Motor Corporation, started companies that quickly failed.

The Legal Basis of a Successful Market System

In a free market, government does not restrict how firms produce and sell goods and services, or how they employ factors of production, but the absence of government intervention is not enough for a market system to work well. Government has to provide secure rights to private property for a market system to work at all. In addition, government can aid the working of the market by enforcing contracts between private individuals through an independent court system. Many economists would also say the government has a role in facilitating the development of an efficient financial system as well as systems of education, transportation, and communication. The protection of private property and the existence of an independent court system to impartially enforce the law provide a *legal environment* that will allow a market system to succeed.

PROTECTION OF PRIVATE PROPERTY For a market system to work well, individuals must be willing to take risks. Someone with $250,000 can be cautious and keep it safely in a bank—or even in cash, if the person doesn't trust the banking system. But the market system won't work unless a significant number of people are willing to risk their funds by investing them in businesses. Investing in businesses is risky in any country. Many businesses fail every year in the United States and other high-income countries. But in the high-income countries, someone who starts a new business or invests in an existing business doesn't have to worry that the government, the military, or criminal gangs might decide to seize the business or demand payments for not destroying the business. Unfortunately, in many poor countries owners of businesses are not well protected from having their businesses seized by the government or from having their profits taken by criminals. Where these problems exist, opening a business can be extremely risky. Cash can be concealed easily, but a business is difficult to conceal and difficult to move.

Property rights refer to the rights individuals or firms have to the exclusive use of their property, including the right to buy or sell it. Property can be tangible, physical property, such as a store or factory. Property can also be intangible, such as the right to an idea.

Property rights The rights individuals or firms have to the exclusive use of their property, including the right to buy or sell it.

Two amendments to the U.S. Constitution guarantee property rights: The 5th Amendment states that the federal government shall not deprive any person "of life, liberty, or property, without due process of law." The 14th Amendment extends this guarantee to the actions of state governments: "No state . . . shall deprive any person of life, liberty, or property, without due process of law." Similar guarantees exist in every high-income country. Unfortunately, in many developing countries such guarantees do not exist or are poorly enforced.

In any modern economy, *intellectual property rights* are very important. Intellectual property includes books, films, software, and ideas for new products or new ways of producing products. To protect intellectual property, the federal government will grant a *patent* that gives an inventor—which is often a firm—the exclusive right to produce and sell a new product for a period of 20 years from the date the product was invented. For instance, because Microsoft has a patent on the Windows operating system, other firms cannot sell their own versions of Windows. The government grants patents to encourage firms to spend money on the research and development necessary to create new products. If other companies could freely copy Windows, Microsoft would not have spent the funds necessary to develop it. Just as a new product or a new method of making a product receives patent protection, books, films, and software receive *copyright* protection. Under U.S. law, the creator of a book, film, or piece of music has the exclusive right to use the creation during the creator's lifetime. The creator's heirs retain this exclusive right for 50 years.

Property Rights in Cyberspace: Napster, Kazaa, and iTunes

2-3 Making the Connection

The development of the Internet has led to new problems in protecting intellectual property rights. Songs, newspaper and magazine articles, and even entire motion pictures can be copied and e-mailed from one computer to another. Controlling unauthorized copying is harder today than it was when "copying" meant making a printed copy. The problem of unauthorized copying of music became particularly severe in 1999 when Napster, a small firm in San Mateo, California, created software that allowed people to download music from the Web without the authorization of the copyright holders. Needless to say, this was not good news for record companies. An article in *Newsweek* quoted a high-school student in Falls Church, Virginia: "I haven't purchased a CD in quite some time." Another student said, "Napster's the best thing ever created. I don't have to spend any money." In fact, a sharp decline in music CD sales occurred in the early 2000s.

The record companies and some artists—including the heavy metal band Metallica—sued Napster for copyright infringement. In spring 2001, a federal court ruled that Napster was violating the copyrights on the songs it allowed to be downloaded and ordered the firm to stop allowing users to swap copyrighted material. Unfortunately for the record companies, a new service called Kazaa quickly replaced Napster. Legal action against Kazaa proved

Metallica sued to stop copyright infringement of their songs on the Internet.

difficult because it was harder to determine the names of people using the service and because the developers of Kazaa live outside the United States and have proved difficult to sue in U.S. courts.

Music companies have attempted to combat free downloads of music by offering inexpensive legal downloads. Some of these legal Web sites, such as Apple's iTunes and Sony's Connect, have been successful. During 2004, legal music downloads increased more than ten times over the previous year. But legal Internet sales still represented only about 1 percent of total music sales worldwide. Not surprisingly, overall music sales were still declining. The failure to give full protection of property rights in music continued to reduce the willingness of music companies to offer as many CDs for sale. The reduction in the quantity of CDs that would be produced if property rights were fully enforced represents a loss of efficiency to the economy.

Sources: Steven Levy, "The Noisy War Over Napster," *Newsweek,* June 5, 2000; "Skype: Catch Us If You Can," *Fortune,* January 26, 2004; Eric Pfanner, "More People Paying for Online Music," *International Herald Tribune,* January 20, 2005.

ENFORCEMENT OF CONTRACTS AND PROPERTY RIGHTS Much business activity involves someone agreeing to carry out some action in the future. For example, you may borrow $20,000 to buy a car and promise the bank—by signing a loan contract—that you will pay back the money over the next five years. Or Microsoft may sign a licensing agreement with a small technology company, agreeing to use that company's technology for a period of several years in return for a fee. Usually these agreements take the form of legal contracts. For a market system to work, businesses and individuals have to rely on these contracts being carried out. If one party to a legal contract does not fulfill its obligations—perhaps the small company had promised Microsoft exclusive use of its technology, but then began licensing it to other companies—the other party can go to court to have the agreement enforced. Similarly, if a property owners in the United States believes that the federal or state government has violated their rights under the 5th or 14th Amendments, they can go to court to have their rights enforced.

But going to court to enforce a contract or private property rights will only be successful if the court system is independent and judges are able to make impartial decisions on the basis of the law. In the United States and other high-income countries, the court systems have enough independence from other parts of the government and enough protection from intimidation by outside forces—such as criminal gangs—that they are able to make their decisions based on the law. In many developing countries, the court systems lack this independence and will not provide a remedy if the government violates private property rights or if a person with powerful political connections decides to violate a business contract.

If property rights are not well enforced, the production of goods and services will be reduced. This reduces economic efficiency, leaving the economy inside its production possibilities frontier.

Conclusion

We have seen that by trading in markets, people are able to specialize and pursue their comparative advantage. Trading on the basis of comparative advantage makes all participants in trade better off. The key role of markets is to facilitate trade. In fact, the market system is a very effective means of coordinating the decisions of millions of consumers, workers, and firms. At the center of the market system is the consumer. To be successful, firms must respond to the desires of consumers. These desires are communicated to firms through prices. To explore how markets work, we must study the behavior of consumers and firms. We continue this exploration of markets in Chapter 3 when we develop the model of demand and supply.

Before moving on to Chapter 3, read *An Inside Look* on the next page to learn how BMW allocates its scarce resources in its Munich plant.

An Inside Look

Choosing the Production Mix at BMW

WALL STREET JOURNAL, MAY 6, 2004

BMW's Net Profit Rises 2.5% As New Models Benefit Sales

Bayerische Motoren Werke AG posted a 2.5% increase in first-quarter net profit, as the launches of the 6-Series coupe and X3 sport-utility vehicle boosted sales.

The luxury-car manufacturer, which sells the BMW, Mini and Rolls-Royce brands, benefited from new products that allowed it to outpace rival Mercedes, a unit of Daimler-Chrysler AG, in terms of vehicle sales in the year's first three months.

BMW's net profit rose to €523 million ($632.3 million) from €510 million a year earlier. Revenue climbed 4.9% to €10.8 billion from €10.3 billion. The rise in revenue outpaced the gain in car sales, which climbed 3.2% to 269,973 vehicles from 261,573.

a The company, based in Munich, got off to a slow start in 2004 as renovation work at its Munich plant through the end of January slowed production of the 3-Series. The second quarter began well, as the company sold 9% more cars in April compared with a year earlier, Chief Executive Helmut Panke said.

That jump in car sales suggests that a stronger earnings rise is in store for the current quarter. Mr. Panke said he expects earnings growth to roughly track a projected rise in car sales.

b The company repeated a forecast for record 2004 earnings, aiming to top 2002's net profit of €2.02 billion. "What's encouraging is that they still expect to achieve record earnings," said Michael Raab, an analyst at Sal. Oppenheim.

BMW's first-quarter performance was enough for the company to overtake Mercedes as the world's leading maker of premium cars—at least for now. BMW's car sales exceeded those of Mercedes, although Mercedes had the upper hand in revenue terms.

"BMW is definitely faring way better than Mercedes, but the two companies are in different stages in their product cycles," said Thomas Ryard, an analyst with forecaster World Markets Research Centre. "I'm not sure it's going to be a long-lasting trend. By 2005, Mercedes should come back."

Last year, BMW launched its flagship 5-Series. This year, it is rolling out the 6-Series, X3, Mini convertible and 1-Series compact. Most of the development expenses for these models have already been booked.

By contrast, Mercedes is at the beginning of the biggest product offensive in its history. It launched a redesigned C-Class in March and is bringing out new versions of its compact A-Class this fall. In 2005, Mercedes expects to introduce two sport-utility vehicles, a redesign of the company's luxury S-Class, and a crossover family, known as the R-Class.

But Mercedes, which produces the Mercedes-Benz, Smart and Maybach brands, won't realize the benefits of these new models until later this year and in 2005.

Mercedes's first-quarter car sales declined 9% to 266,000 vehicles, burdened by the new-model program. But the Mercedes-Benz brand still topped BMW's core brand, selling 246,000 cars during the first quarter, compared with the BMW brand's 222,000.

Key Points in the Article

The article discusses the strong performance of BMW during the first months of 2004. The firm's sales rose sufficiently for it to overtake Mercedes for the lead in production of high-priced, or "premium," cars. The article spotlights the strong sales of the X3 SUV, which along with the Z8 roadster, is assembled at the company's plant in Munich, Germany. Renovations of the Munich plant reduced production of the X3 at the beginning of the year. BMW had been introducing new models and also increasing its capacity to produce existing models.

Analyzing the News

a We can use the economic model of production possibilities frontiers to analyze this news article. First, note that the renovations at the Munich plant meant that initially the company was operating inside its production possibilities frontier at this plant. This is shown in Figure 1, where production in early 2004 is represented by point *A*. Moving to the frontier makes it possible for BMW to produce more roadsters and more SUVs.

b The strong demand for the X3 SUV has caused BMW to allocate more workers and machines to producing this model. Once BMW is on the production possibilities frontier at the Munich plant, its opportunity cost of producing more X3 SUVs is the reduction in the quantity of Z8 roadsters produced. (Actually, we are simplifying a little here, because at various times BMW has produced other models in the Munich plant as well. We could show this by drawing a production possibilities frontier with the quantity of X3 SUVs on the horizontal axis and the quantity of all other models produced in the plant on the vertical axis. But the point would be the same: Once BMW is on the production possibilities frontier for this plant, it can only produce more X3s by producing less of something else.) In Figure 2 the popularity of the X3 causes BMW to move from point *B* to point *C*.

Thinking Critically ABOUT POLICY

1. Launching the 6-Series coupe and the X3 SUV boosted BMW's sales in early 2004. If launching new products boosts sales, should BMW launch a new line of cars *every* year? Every month? Explain.
2. Some BMW's are made in Germany, some in South Carolina, some in other places. Should the U.S. government encourage the domestic production of BMW's by banning imports of BMWs?

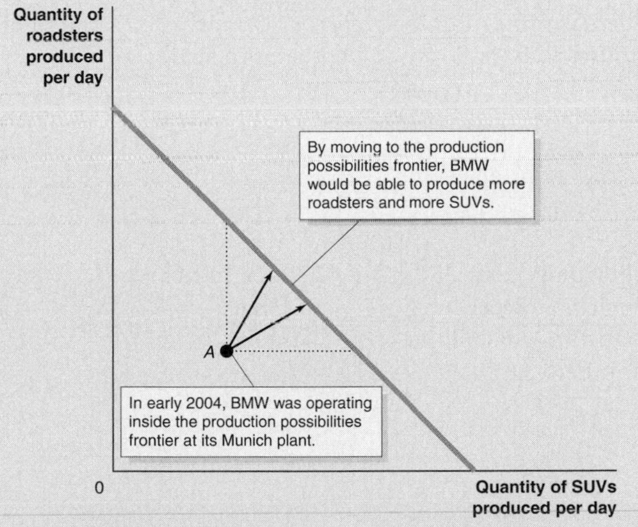

Figure 1: BMW was operating inside the Munich plant's production possibilities frontier in early 2004.

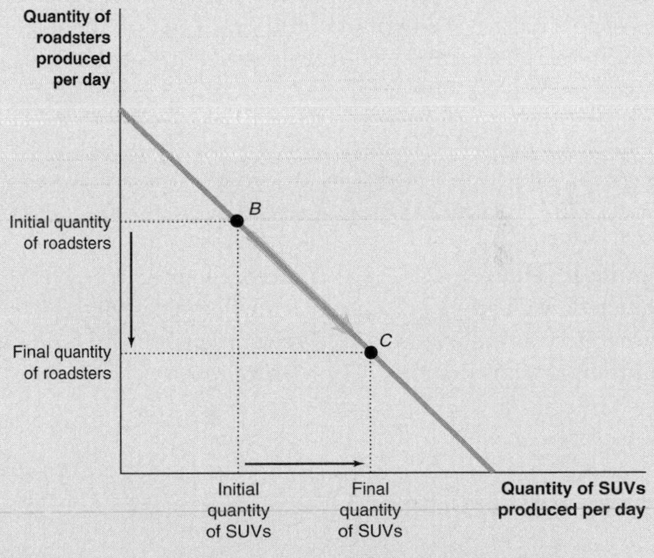

Figure 2: Once BMW is on the production possibilities frontier in its Munich plant, a larger quantity of X3 SUVs produced is only possible if a smaller quantity of Z8 roadsters is produced.

SUMMARY

LEARNING OBJECTIVE ① Use a production possibilities frontier to analyze opportunity costs and trade-offs. The production possibilities frontier is a curve showing the maximum attainable combinations of two products that may be produced with available resources. It is used to illustrate the trade-offs that arise from scarcity. Points on the frontier are technically efficient. Points inside the frontier are inefficient and points outside the frontier are unattainable. Because of increasing marginal opportunity costs, production possibilities frontiers are usually bowed-out, or concave, rather than straight lines. This illustrates the important economic concept that the more resources that are already devoted to any activity, the smaller the payoff to devoting additional resources to that activity is likely to be.

LEARNING OBJECTIVE ② Understand comparative advantage and explain how it is the basis for trade. Fundamentally, markets are about *trade,* which is the act of buying or selling. People trade on the basis of *comparative advantage.* An individual, firm, or country has a comparative advantage in producing a good or service if it can produce the good or service at the lowest opportunity cost. People are usually better off specializing in the activity for which they have a comparative advantage and trading for the other goods and services they need. It is important not to confuse comparative advantage with *absolute advantage.* An individual, firm, or country has an *absolute advantage* in producing a good or service if it can produce more of that good or service from the same amount of resources. It is possible to have an absolute advantage in producing a good or service without having a comparative advantage.

LEARNING OBJECTIVE ③ Explain the basic idea of how a market system works. A *market* is a group of buyers and sellers of a good or service and the institution or arrangement by which they come together to trade. *Product markets* are markets for goods and services, such as computers and medical treatment. *Factor markets* are markets for the factors of production, such as labor, capital, natural resources, and entrepreneurial ability. Adam Smith argued in his 1776 book, *The Wealth of Nations,* that in a free market where the government does not control the production of goods and services, changes in prices lead firms to produce the goods and services most desired by consumers. If consumers demand more of a good, its price will rise. Firms respond to rising prices by increasing production. If consumers demand less of a good, its price will fall. Firms respond to falling prices by producing less of a good. A market system will only work well if there is protection for *property rights,* which are the rights of individuals and firms to use their property.

KEY TERMS

Absolute advantage 42
Circular-flow diagram 47
Comparative advantage 43
Economic growth 40
Entrepreneur 50
Factor markets 46
Free market 48
Market 46
Opportunity cost 35
Product markets 46
Production possibilities frontier 34
Property rights 51
Scarcity 34
Trade 40

REVIEW QUESTIONS

1. What do economists mean by scarcity? Can you think of anything that is not scarce according to the economic definition?
2. What is a production possibilities frontier? How can we show economic efficiency on a production possibilities frontier? How can we show inefficiency? What causes a production possibilities frontier to shift outward?
3. What does increasing marginal opportunity costs mean? What are the implications of this idea for the shape of the production possibilities frontier?
4. What is absolute advantage? What is comparative advantage? Is it possible for a country to have a comparative advantage in producing a good without also having an absolute advantage? Briefly explain.
5. What is the basis for trade? What advantages are there to specialization?
6. What is the circular-flow diagram, and what does it demonstrate?

7. What are the two main categories of participants in markets? Which participants are of greatest importance in determining what goods and services are produced?
8. What is a free market? In what ways does a free market economy differ from a centrally planned economy?
9. What is an entrepreneur? Why do entrepreneurs play a key role in a market system?
10. Under what circumstances are firms likely to produce more of a good or service? Under what circumstances are firms likely to produce less of a good or service?
11. What are private property rights? What role do they play in the working of a market system? Why are independent courts important for a well-functioning economy?

PROBLEMS AND APPLICATIONS

Please visit **www.prenhall.com/hubbard** *for solutions to the even-numbered problems as well as multiple-choice and true or false self-assessment quizzes.*

1. Draw a production possibilities frontier showing the trade-off between the production of cotton and the production of soybeans.
   a. Show the effect that a prolonged drought would have on the initial production possibilities frontier.
   b. Suppose genetic modification makes soybeans resistant to insects, allowing yields to double. Show the effect of this technological change on the initial production possibilities frontier.
2. **[Related to the *Chapter Opener*]** One of the trade-offs faced by BMW is between safety and gas mileage. For example, adding steel to a car makes it safer but also heavier, which results in lower gas mileage. Draw a hypothetical production possibilities frontier facing BMW engineers that shows this trade-off.
3. Suppose you win free tickets to a movie plus all you can eat at the snack bar for free. Would there be a cost to you to attend this movie? Explain.
4. Suppose we can divide all the goods produced by an economy into two types: consumption goods and capital goods. Capital goods, such as machinery, equipment, and computers, are goods used to produce other goods.
   a. Use a production possibilities frontier graph to illustrate the trade-off to an economy between producing consumption goods and producing capital goods. Is it likely that the production possibilities frontier in this situation would be a straight line (as in Figure 2-1) or concave (as in Figure 2-2)? Briefly explain.
   b. Suppose that technological advance occurs that affects the production of capital goods but not consumption goods. Show the effect on the production possibilities frontier.
   c. Suppose that country A and country B currently have identical production possibilities frontiers, but that country A devotes only 5 percent of its resources to producing capital goods over each of the next 10 years, whereas country B devotes 30 percent. Which country is likely to experience more rapid economic growth in the future? Illustrate using a production possibilities frontier graph. Your graph should include production possibilities frontiers for country A today and in 10 years, and for country B today and in 10 years.
5. Use the following production possibilities frontier for a country to answer the questions:

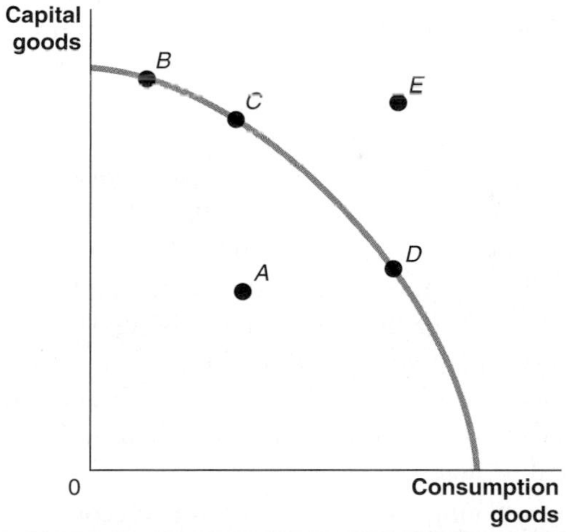

   a. Which point(s) are unattainable? Briefly explain why.
   b. Which point(s) are efficient? Briefly explain why.
   c. Which point(s) are inefficient? Briefly explain why.
   d. At which point is the country's future growth rate likely to be the highest? Briefly explain why.

6. **[Related to *Solved Problem 2-1*]** You have exams in economics and chemistry coming up and 5 hours available for studying. The table shows the trade-offs you face in allocating the time you will spend in studying each subject.

	HOURS SPENT STUDYING		MIDTERM SCORE	
CHOICE	ECONOMICS	CHEMISTRY	ECONOMICS	CHEMISTRY
A	5	0	95	70
B	4	1	93	78
C	3	2	90	84
D	2	3	86	88
E	1	4	81	90
F	0	5	75	91

   a. Use the data in the table to draw a production possibilities frontier graph. Label your vertical axis "Score on economics exam" and label your horizontal axis "Score on chemistry exam." Make sure to label the values where your production possibilities frontier intersects the vertical and horizontal axes.
   b. Label the points representing choice *C* and choice *D*. If you are at choice *C*, what is your opportunity cost of increasing your chemistry score?
   c. Under what circumstances would *A* be a sensible choice?

7. Suppose the president is attempting to decide whether the federal government should spend more on research to find a cure for heart disease. He asks you, one of his economic advisors, to prepare a report discussing the relevant factors he should consider. Discuss the main issues you would deal with in your report.

8. Congress has given the Environmental Protection Agency (EPA) the authority to write regulations to implement the provisions of the Clean Air Act, a law aimed at reducing air pollution. According to the Clean Air Act, the EPA is not to consider the cost of complying with the regulations. Why do you suppose Congress would have constrained the EPA in this way? Do you agree that costs should not be taken into account when drafting environmental regulations?

9. Lawrence Summers was a professor of economics at Harvard and served as Secretary of the Treasury in the Clinton administration before becoming president of Harvard. He has been quoted as giving the following moral defense of the economic approach:

   > There is nothing morally unattractive about saying: We need to analyze which way of spending money on health care will produce more benefit and which less, and using our money as efficiently as we can. I don't think there is anything immoral about seeking to achieve environmental benefits at the lowest possible costs.

   Would it be more moral to reduce pollution without worrying about the cost or by taking the cost into account? Briefly explain.

   Source: David Wessel, "Precepts from Professor Summers," *Wall Street Journal*, October 17, 2002.

10. In *The Wonderful Wizard of Oz* and his other books about the Land of Oz, L. Frank Baum observed that if people's wants were modest enough, most goods would not be scarce. According to Baum, this was the case in Oz:

   > There were no poor people in the Land of Oz, because there was no such thing as money. . . . Each person was given freely by his neighbors whatever he required for his use, which is as much as anyone may reasonably desire. Some tilled the lands and raised great crops of grain, which was divided equally among the whole population, so that all had enough. There were many tailors and dressmakers and shoemakers and the like, who made things that any who desired them might wear. Likewise there were jewelers who made ornaments for the person, which pleased and beautified the people, and these ornaments also were free to those who asked for them. Each man and woman, no matter what he or she produced for the good of the community, was supplied by the neighbors with food and clothing and a house and furniture and ornaments and games. If by chance the supply ever ran short, more was taken from the great storehouses of the Ruler, which were afterward filled up again when there was more of any article than people needed. . . .
   >
   > You will know, by what I have told you here, that the Land of Oz was a remarkable country. I do not suppose such an arrangement would be practical with us.

   Do you agree with Baum that the economic system in Oz wouldn't work in the contemporary United States? Briefly explain why or why not.

   Source: L. Frank Baum, *The Emerald City of Oz*, pp. 30–31. First edition published in 1910.

11. Using the same amount of resources, the United States and Canada can both produce lumberjack shirts and lumberjack boots as shown in the following production possibilities frontiers:

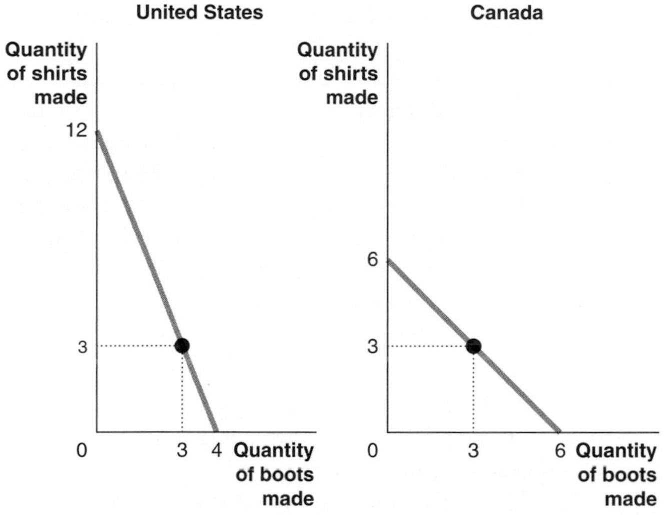

a. Who has a comparative advantage in producing lumberjack boots? Who has a comparative advantage in producing lumberjack shirts? Explain your reasoning.
b. Does either country have an absolute advantage in producing both goods? Explain.
c. Suppose that both countries are currently producing three pairs of boots and three shirts. Show that both can be better off if they specialize in producing one good and then engage in trade.

12. **[Related to *Solved Problem 2-2*]** Suppose Iran and Iraq both produce oil and olive oil. The table shows combinations of both goods that each country can produce in a day, measured in thousands of barrels.

IRAQ		IRAN	
OIL	OLIVE OIL	OIL	OLIVE OIL
0	8	0	4
2	6	1	3
4	4	2	2
6	2	3	1
8	0	4	0

a. Who has the comparative advantage in producing oil? Explain.
b. Can these two countries gain from trading oil and olive oil? Explain.

13. **[Related to *Solved Problem 2-2*]** Suppose that France and Germany both produce schnitzel and wine. The following table shows combinations of the goods that each country can produce in a day:

FRANCE		GERMANY	
WINE (BOTTLES)	SCHNITZEL (POUNDS)	WINE (BOTTLES)	SCHNITZEL (POUNDS)
0	8	0	15
1	6	1	12
2	4	2	9
3	2	3	6
4	0	4	3
		5	0

a. Who has a comparative advantage in producing wine? Who has a comparative advantage in producing schnitzel?
b. Suppose that France is currently producing 1 bottle of wine and 6 pounds of schnitzel and Germany is currently producing 3 bottles of wine and 6 pounds of schnitzel. Demonstrate that France and Germany can both be better off if they specialize in producing only one good and then engage in trade.

14. **[Related to *Don't Let This Happen To You!*]** In the 1950s, the economist Bela Balassa compared 28 manufacturing industries in the United States and Britain. In every one of the 28 industries, Balassa found that the United States had an absolute advantage. In these circumstances, would there have been any gain to the United States from importing any of these products from Britain? Explain.

15. Identify whether each of the following transactions will take place in the factor market or in the product market, and whether households or firms are supplying the good or service, or demanding the good or service:
a. George buys a BMW X5 SUV.
b. BMW increases employment at its Spartanburg plant.
c. George works 20 hours per week at McDonald's.
d. George sells land he owns to McDonald's so it can build a new restaurant.

16. In *The Wealth of Nations,* Adam Smith wrote the following (Book I, Chapter II):

> It is not from the benevolence of the butcher, the brewer, or the baker, that we expect our dinner, but from their regard to their own interest.

Briefly discuss what he meant by this.

17. In a commencement address to economics graduates at the University of Texas, Robert McTeer Jr., who was then the president of the Federal Reserve Bank of Dallas, argued, "For my money, Adam Smith's invisible hand is the most important thing you've learned by studying economics." What's so important about the idea of the invisible hand?
Source: Robert D. McTeer Jr., "The Dismal Science? Hardly!" *Wall Street Journal,* June 4, 2003.

18. Evaluate the following argument: "Adam Smith's analysis is based on a fundamental flaw: He assumes that people are motivated by self-interest. But this isn't true. I'm not selfish, and most people I know aren't selfish."

19. Writing in the *New York Times,* Michael Lewis argued that "a market economy is premised on a system of incentives designed to encourage an ignoble human trait: self-interest." Do you agree that self-interest is an "ignoble human trait"? What incentives does a market system provide to encourage self-interest?
Source: Michael Lewis, "In Defense of the Boom," *New York Times,* October 27, 2002.

20. An editorial in *Business Week* magazine offered this opinion:

> Economies should be judged on a simple measure: their ability to generate a rising standard of living for all members of society, including people at the bottom.

Briefly discuss whether or not you agree.
Source: "Poverty: The Bigger Picture," *Business Week,* October 7, 2002.

21. An estimated 400 million to 600 million people worldwide are squatters who live on land to which they have no legal title, usually on the outskirts of cities in less-developed countries. Economist Hernando de Soto persuaded Peru's government to undertake a program to make it cheap and easy for these squatters to obtain a title to the land they had been occupying. How would this creation of property rights be likely to affect the economic opportunities available to these squatters?
Source: Alan B. Krueger, "A Study Looks at Squatters and Land Title in Peru," *New York Times,* January 9, 2003.

22. In colonial America, the population was spread thinly over a large area and transportation costs were very high because it was difficult to ship products by road for more than short distances. As a result, most of the free population lived on small farms where they not only grew their own food but also usually made their own clothes and very rarely bought or sold anything for money. Explain why the incomes of these farmers were likely to rise as transportation costs fell. Use the concept of comparative advantage in your answer.

23. During the 1928 presidential election campaign, Herbert Hoover, the Republican candidate, argued that the United States should only import those products that could not be produced here. Do you believe that this would be a good policy? Explain.

chapter three

Where Prices Come From: The Interaction of Demand and Supply

How Hewlett-Packard Manages the Demand for Printers

In early 2005 the board of directors at Hewlett-Packard (H-P) ousted chief executive officer Carly Fiorina and replaced her with Mark Hurd, then the chief executive officer of NCR Corporation. What happened?

Carly Fiorina had been a business celebrity for many years. In July 1999 she became H-P's chief executive officer, which made her the first woman to head one of the 100 largest firms in the United States. In 2002, she brought about the largest merger of two technology firms in U.S. history when H-P purchased Compaq Computer Corporation. By 2004, she presided over a firm that employed 150,000 workers and had total sales of $80 billion. Fiorina's ouster in 2005 from H-P reflected the relatively weak performance of the firm during her time as chief executive officer. In particular, the merger with Compaq had failed to improve H-P's performance in the personal computer market.

Printers, and not personal computers, are H-P's most successful product. Although printers account for only about 30 percent of the firm's sales, they account for 70 percent of its profits. In fact, as *An Inside Look* at the end of this chapter discusses, to increase the demand for printers the firm is willing to sell its personal computers at low prices.

Hewlett-Packard's success, like that of any firm, depends on its ability to analyze changes in demand and supply. Because of the importance of printers to H-P, the firm devotes significant resources to monitoring and forecasting consumer demand. Its forecasts of demand, however, are not always successful. In 2001, for example, Carly Fiorina announced that sales of H-P printers had declined sharply in the first half of that year compared to the first half of 2000. Two events caused this decline: First, many individuals and small businesses unexpectedly decided not to upgrade their existing computers to faster and more powerful machines. Purchasers of new PCs are a key part of the market for printers. Second, the U.S. economy moved into recession, lowering the incomes of many consumers and reducing the profits of many businesses. Fiorina admitted she had been taken by surprise by this decline in sales: "Stuff happens that you're not able to see even with a ton of information, and the downturn in the economy was a clear case of that. Everybody had loads of information, and everybody missed it."

H-P did a better job anticipating changes in the types of printers con-

LEARNING OBJECTIVES

After studying this chapter, you should be able to:

① Discuss the variables that influence demand.

② Discuss the variables that influence supply.

③ Use a graph to illustrate market equilibrium.

④ Use demand and supply graphs to predict changes in prices and quantities.

sumers would demand. For example, increasing sales of digital cameras have had an important impact on the market for printers. During 2003, 50 million digital cameras were sold, and many people bought both a camera and a new printer designed to print digital photos. Printers aimed at the digital photo market usually include a slot for memory cards from the cameras, and an LCD (liquid crystal display) screen for previews of photos. Many of these printers are multifunction devices (MFD) that combine printing, scanning, copying, and faxing. These MFDs sell for higher prices—and are more profitable—than basic printers. In 2004, H-P had a 58 percent share of the MFD market in the United States. Lexmark was second but far behind with a 21 percent share.

Unfortunately for Carly Fiorina, H-P's success with MFDs was not matched by success with personal computers. Some members of the firm's board of directors were particularly concerned that H-P had relied too heavily on selling personal computers in retail stores, rather than building up direct sales to consumers through the Internet as Dell Computer had done so successfully. The board gave Mark Hurd, the new chief executive officer, the responsibility of increasing the firm's competitiveness in the personal computer market. *An Inside Look* on page 88 discusses HP's strategy for competing with Dell.

Sources: Olga Kharif, "Printing a Record of Growth," Business Week Online, February 17, 2004; Pui-Wing Tam, "Copy Machine: H-P, Post-Compaq, Looks Like Its Old Self," Wall Street Journal, May 7, 2004; quote from Carly Fiorina: "A Conversation with Carly Fiorina—Forbes 5th Annual CIO Forum," December 2, 2003, Dallas, Texas.

➤ In Chapter 1, we learned how economists use models to predict human behavior. In Chapter 2, we used the model of production possibilities frontiers to analyze scarcity and trade-offs. In this chapter and the next, we explore the model of demand and supply, which is the most powerful tool in economics, and use it to explain how prices are determined. We begin by discussing consumers and the demand side of the market, then we turn to firms and the supply side. As you will see, we will apply the model of demand and supply again and again throughout this book to understand business and the economy.

(1) LEARNING OBJECTIVE
Discuss the variables that influence demand.

The Demand Side of the Market

Chapter 2 explained that in a market system consumers ultimately determine which goods and services will be produced. The most successful businesses are the ones that respond best to consumer demand. But what determines consumer demand for a product? Certainly, many factors influence the willingness of consumers to buy a particular product. For example, consumers who are considering buying a printer will make their decisions based on, among other factors, the income they have available to spend, whether they have recently purchased a personal computer or digital camera, and the effectiveness of the advertising campaigns of the companies that sell printers. The main factor in consumer decisions, though, will be the price of the printers. Thus, it makes sense to begin with price when analyzing the decisions of consumers to buy a product. It is important to note that when we discuss demand, we are considering not what a consumer *wants* to buy, but what the consumer is both willing and *able* to buy.

The Demand of an Individual Buyer

Households, firms, and government agencies all buy printers. Suppose the Prudential Insurance Company intends to purchase printers for a number of its employees. We might determine the relationship between the price of printers and the number of printers the company would be willing to buy during a particular period of time by asking Kate, the company's purchasing manager, "If the price of a printer were $125, how many printers would you be willing to buy over the next month?"

Suppose Kate responds that she would be willing to purchase 5 printers over the next month at a price of $125 each. The amount of a good or a service that a consumer is willing and able to purchase at a particular price is referred to as the **quantity demanded**. Figure 3-1 shows Kate's quantity demanded at a price of $125. On the vertical axis, we measure the price of printers, and on the horizontal axis we measure the number of printers demanded during the next month.

Quantity demanded The amount of a good or service that a consumer is willing and able to purchase at a given price.

Demand Schedules and Demand Curves

We can repeat our question using different prices. The table in Figure 3-2 shows the number of printers Kate would be willing to buy at five different prices. Tables that show the relationship between the price of a product and the quantity of the product demanded are called **demand schedules**. The graph in Figure 3-2 plots the numbers from the table as a **demand curve**, a curve that shows the relationship between the price of a product and the quantity of a product demanded.

Although we have asked Kate only about her willingness to buy printers at five different prices, we can connect the points in Figure 3-2 to form a continuous downward-sloping demand curve. The demand curve slopes downward because Kate

Demand schedule A table showing the relationship between the price of a product and the quantity of the product demanded.

Demand curve A curve that shows the relationship between the price of a product and the quantity of the product demanded.

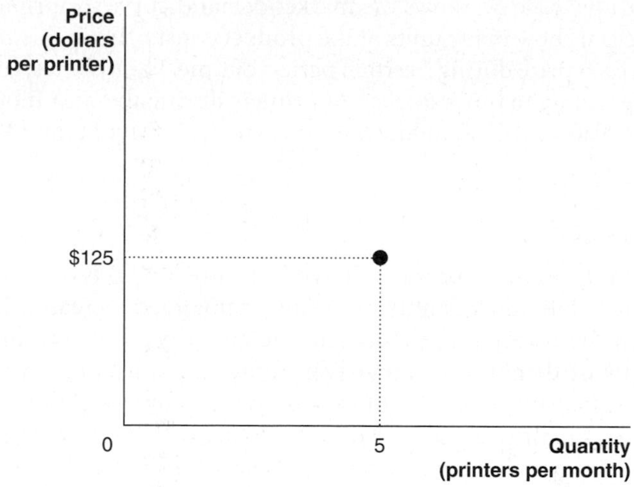

FIGURE 3-1

Plotting a Price–Quantity Combination on a Graph

At a price of $125 per printer, Kate, the purchasing manager for the Prudential Insurance Company, will be willing to buy 5 printers in the next month.

will buy more printers as the price falls. When the price of a printer is $175, Kate buys 3 printers. When the price of a printer falls to $150, Kate buys 4 printers. Buyers demand a larger quantity of a product as the price falls because the product becomes cheaper relative to other products and because they can afford to buy more at a lower price.

Individual Demand and Market Demand

Figure 3-2 shows an individual demand curve. To understand how a market works, however, we need to examine **market demand**, or the demand by all the consumers of a given good or service. We can determine market demand by asking additional consumers how many printers they would purchase at various prices. Ordinarily, the market that we would be interested in would include at least all of the consumers of the product in a city and might include all of the consumers in the world. To keep things simple, let's assume that the market for printers consists of Kate from the Prudential Insurance Company and two individual consumers: Sam and Paul. Figure 3-3 shows that we can find the market demand for printers by adding the number of printers demanded by Kate, Sam, and Paul at each price. The table shows the demand schedules for printers of these three consumers. We plot the numbers from the demand schedule in graphs 3-3(a), 3-3(b), and 3-3(c).

Market demand The demand by all the consumers of a given good or service.

Demand Schedule	
Price (dollars per printer)	Quantity (printers per month)
$175	3
150	4
125	5
100	6
75	7

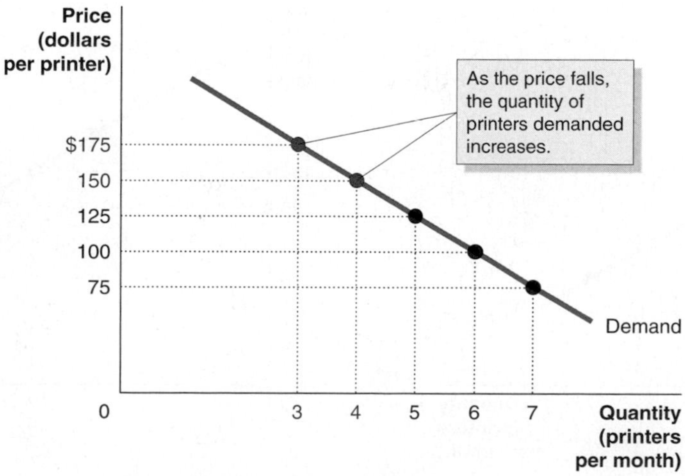

FIGURE 3-2

Kate's Demand Schedule and Demand Curve

As the price changes, Kate changes the quantity of printers she is willing to buy. We can show this as a *demand schedule* in a table, or as a *demand curve* on a graph. The table and graph both show that as the price of printers falls, the quantity demanded rises. When the price of a printer is $175, Kate buys 3 printers. When the price of a printer drops to $150, Kate buys 4 printers. Therefore, Kate's demand curve is downward sloping.

Figure 3-3(d) on page 67 shows the market demand curve for printers. The market demand curve tells us how many units of the product consumers in this market would be willing to buy at each price during a certain period of time. For instance, consumers in this market would be willing to buy a total of 26 printers during the next month at a price of $100 per printer: Kate is willing to buy 6, Sam is willing to buy 11, and Paul is willing to buy 9.

The Law of Demand

Law of demand Holding everything else constant, when the price of a product falls, the quantity demanded of the product will increase, and when the price of a product rises, the quantity demanded of the product will decrease.

The market demand curve for printers shown in Figure 3-3(d) is downward sloping: As the price of printers falls, the quantity of printers demanded increases. The inverse relationship between the price of a product and the quantity of the product demanded is known as the **law of demand**: Holding everything else constant, when the price of a product falls, the quantity demanded of the product will increase, and when the price of a product rises, the quantity demanded of the product will decrease. The law of demand holds for any market demand curve. Economists have never found an exception to it. In fact, Nobel Prize–winning economist Paul Samuelson once remarked that the surest way for an economist to become famous would be to discover a market demand curve that sloped upward rather than downward.

What Explains the Law of Demand?

It makes sense that consumers will buy more of a good when the price falls and less of a good when the price rises, but let's look more closely at why this is true. When the price of printers falls, consumers buy a larger quantity of printers because of the *substitution effect* and the *income effect.*

FIGURE 3-3 Deriving the Market Demand Curve from Individual Demand Curves

The table shows that the total quantity demanded in a market is the sum of the quantities demanded by each buyer at each price. We find the market demand curve by adding horizontally the individual demand curves in parts (a), (b), and (c). At a price of $100, Kate demands 6 printers, Sam demands 11 printers, and Paul demands 9 printers. Therefore, part (d) shows that a price of $100 and a quantity demanded of 26 is a point on the market demand curve.

	Quantity (printers per month)			
Price (dollars per printer)	Kate	Sam	Paul	Market
$175	3	5	6	14
150	4	7	7	18
125	5	9	8	22
100	6	11	9	26
75	7	13	10	30

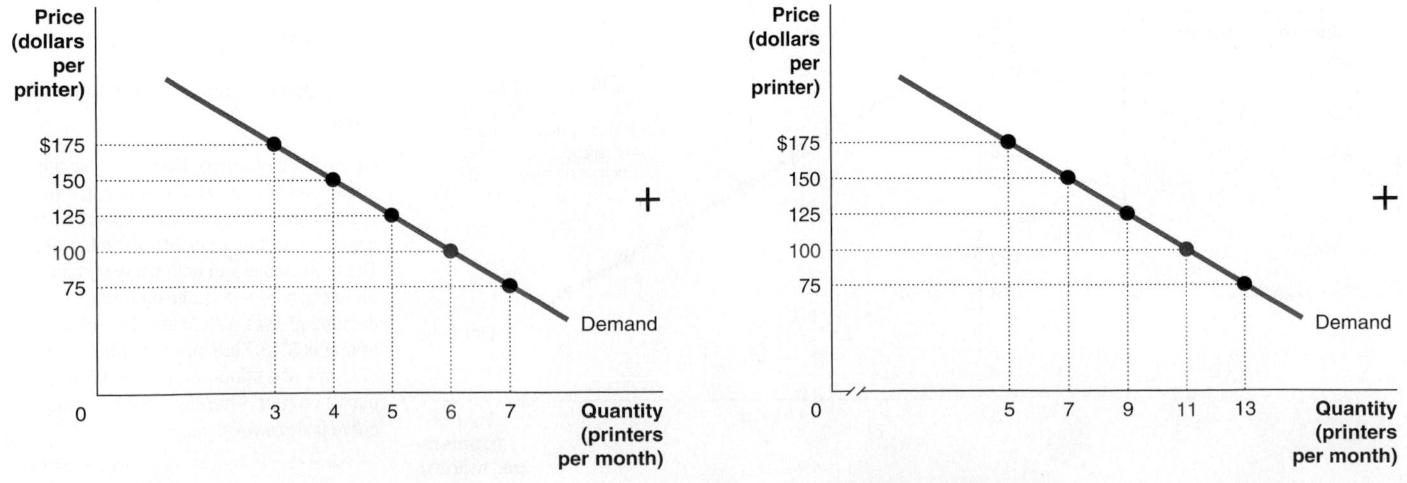

(a) Kate's demand curve

(b) Sam's demand curve

SUBSTITUTION EFFECT The **substitution effect** of a price change refers to the fact that a fall in price makes a good less expensive *relative* to other goods that are *substitutes.* This change leads consumers to buy more of a good when its price falls—or less of a good when its price rises. When the price of printers falls, consumers will substitute buying printers for buying other goods or services. For example, a consumer who has digital camera pictures printed at Wal-Mart might instead buy a printer if the price of printers falls.

Substitution effect The change in the quantity demanded of a good that results from a change in price making the good more or less expensive relative to other goods that are substitutes.

THE INCOME EFFECT The **income effect** of a price change refers to the change in the quantity demanded of a good that results from the effect of a change in the good's price on consumers' purchasing power. Purchasing power refers to the quantity of goods that can be bought with a fixed amount of income. When the price of a good falls, the increased purchasing power of consumers' incomes will usually lead them to purchase a larger quantity of the good. When the price of a good rises, the decreased purchasing power of consumers' incomes will usually lead them to purchase a smaller quantity of the good.

Income effect The change in the quantity demanded of a good that results from the effect of a change in the good's price on consumer purchasing power.

Thus, a fall in the price of printers leads consumers to buy more printers, both because they are now cheaper relative to substitute products and because the purchasing power of the consumers' incomes has increased.

Holding Everything Else Constant: The Ceteris Paribus *Condition*

Notice that the definition of the law of demand contains the phrase "holding everything else constant." In constructing the market demand curve for printers, we focused only on the effect that changes in the price of printers would have on the quantity of printers consumers would be willing and able to buy. We were holding constant other variables that might affect the willingness of consumers to buy printers. Economists refer to the necessity of holding all variables other than price constant in constructing a demand curve as the ***ceteris paribus*** condition—*ceteris paribus* is Latin for "all else equal."

Ceteris paribus ("all else equal") The requirement that when analyzing the relationship between two variables—such as price and quantity demanded—other variables must be held constant.

What would happen if we allowed a variable—other than price—to change that might affect the willingness of consumers to buy printers? Consumers would then change the quantity they demand at each price. We can illustrate this by shifting the market demand curve. A shift of a demand curve is *an increase or decrease in demand.* A movement along a demand curve is *an increase or decrease in the quantity demanded.* As

FIGURE 3-3 continued

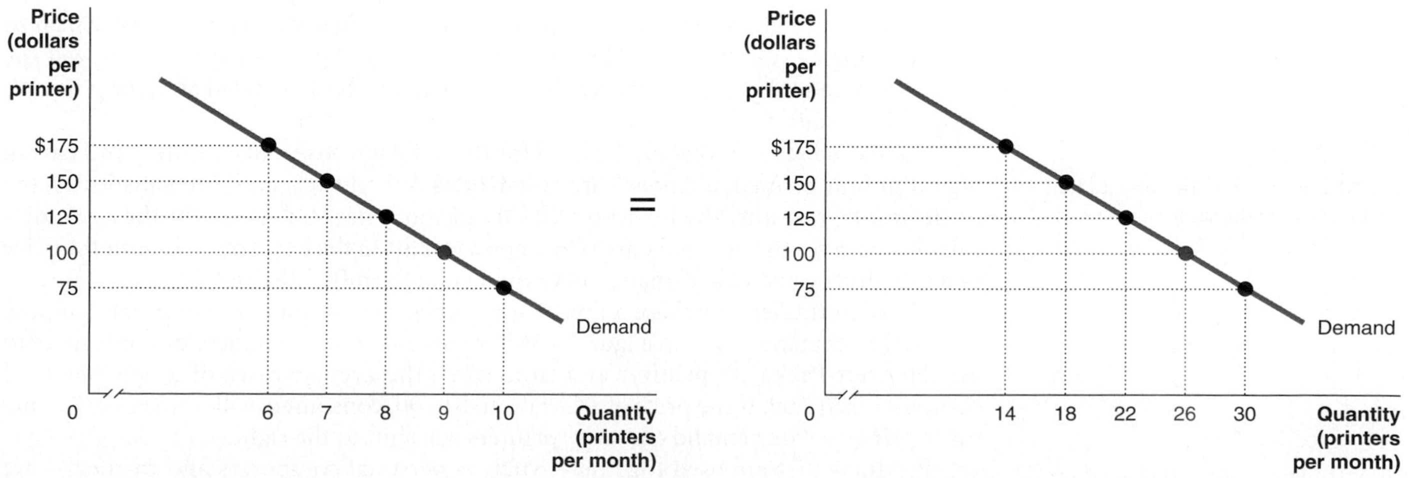

(c) Paul's demand curve

(d) Market demand curve

FIGURE 3-4

Shifting the Demand Curve

When consumers increase the quantity of a product they wish to buy at a given price, the market demand curve shifts to the right from D_1 to D_2. When consumers decrease the quantity of a product they wish to buy at any given price, the demand curve shifts to the left from D_1 to D_3.

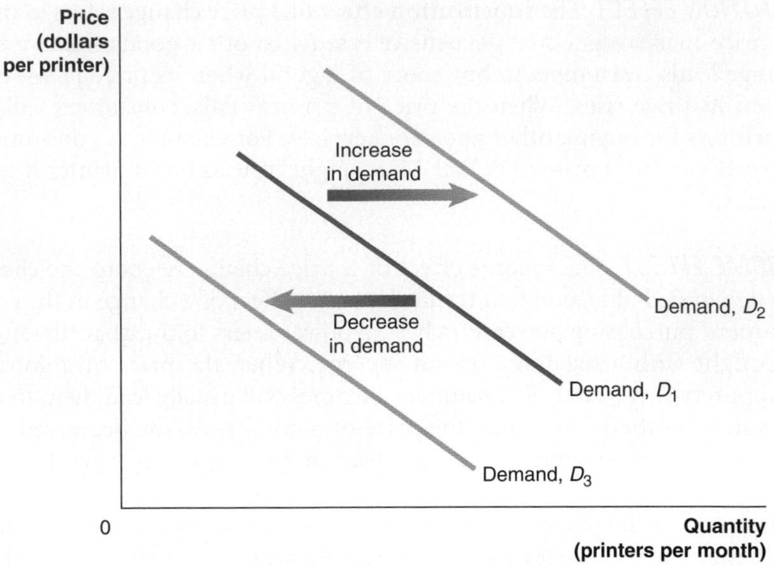

Figure 3-4 shows, we shift the demand curve to the right if consumers decide to buy more of the good at each price, and we shift the demand curve to the left if consumers decide to buy less.

Variables That Shift Market Demand

Many variables other than price can influence market demand. These five are the most important:

- Prices of related goods
- Income
- Tastes
- Population and demographics
- Expected future prices

We can discuss how changes in each of these variables affects the market demand curve for printers.

PRICES OF RELATED GOODS Consider again the market demand curve for printers. Suppose that the market demand curve in Figure 3-3(d) represents the willingness and ability of consumers to buy printers during a period when Wal-Mart charges $0.50 to print one digital photo. If Wal-Mart lowers the price to $0.25 per photo, how will the market demand for printers change? Fewer printers will be demanded at every price. We show this by shifting the demand curve for printers to the left.

Substitutes Goods and services that can be used for the same purpose.

Goods and services that can be used for the same purpose—like printers and having digital photos printed at stores—are **substitutes.** When two goods are substitutes, the more you buy of one, the less you will buy of the other. A decrease in the price of a substitute causes the demand curve for a good to shift to the left. An increase in the price of a substitute causes the demand curve for a good to shift to the right.

Many consumers purchase a new printer when they buy a new computer. Suppose the market demand curve in Figure 3-3(d) represents the willingness of consumers to buy Hewlett-Packard's printers at a time when the average price of a new personal computer is $1,300. If the price of PCs falls to $1,100, consumers will buy more PCs *and* more printers: The demand curve for printers will shift to the right.

Complements Goods that are used together.

Products that are used together—such as personal computers and printers—are **complements.** When two goods are complements, the more you buy of one, the more you will buy of the other. A decrease in the price of a complement causes the demand curve for a good to shift to the right. An increase in the price of a complement causes the demand curve for a good to shift to the left.

3-1 Making the Connection

Why Supermarkets Need to Understand Substitutes and Complements

Supermarkets sell what sometimes seems like a bewildering variety of goods. The first row of the following table shows the varieties of eight products stocked by five Chicago supermarkets.

	COFFEE	FROZEN PIZZA	HOT DOGS	ICE CREAM	POTATO CHIPS	REGULAR CEREAL	SPAGHETTI SAUCE	YOGURT
Varieties in Five Chicago Supermarkets	391	337	128	421	285	242	194	288
Varieties Introduced in a 2-Year Period	113	109	47	129	93	114	70	107
Varieties Removed in a 2-Year Period	135	86	32	118	77	75	36	51

Source: Juin-Kuan Chong, Teck-Hua Ho, and Christopher S. Tang, "A Modeling Framework for Category Assortment Planning," *Manufacturing & Service Operations Management*, 2001, Vol. 3, No. 3, pp. 191–210.

A supermarket shouldn't remove a slow-selling soup from its shelves without researching whether shoppers use that soup as a substitute or a complement for another soup.

Supermarkets are also constantly adding new varieties of goods to their shelves and removing old varieties. The second row of the table shows that these five Chicago supermarkets added 113 new varieties of coffee over a two-year period, while the third row shows they eliminated 135 existing varieties. How do supermarkets decide which varieties to add and which to remove?

Christopher Tang is a professor at the Anderson Graduate School of Management at the University of California, Los Angeles (UCLA). In an interview with the *Baltimore Sun*, Tang argues that supermarkets should not necessarily remove the slowest-selling goods from their shelves but should consider the relationships among the goods. In particular, they should consider whether the goods being removed are substitutes or complements with the remaining goods. A lobster bisque soup, for example, could be a relatively slow seller but might be a complement to other soups because it can be used with them to make a sauce. In that case, removing the lobster bisque would hurt sales of some of the remaining soups. Tang suggests the supermarket would be better off removing a slow-selling soup that is a substitute for another soup. For example, the supermarket might want to remove one of two brands of cream of chicken soup.

Source: Lobster bisque example from Lorraine Mirabella, "Shelf Science in Supermarkets," *Baltimore Sun*, March 17, 2002, p. 16.

INCOME In addition to the prices of other goods, the income that consumers have available to spend also affects their willingness and ability to buy a good. Suppose that the market demand curve in Figure 3-3(d) reflects the willingness of consumers to buy printers when average household income is $43,000. If household income rises to $45,000, the demand for printers will increase, which we show by shifting the demand curve to the right. A good is a **normal good** when demand increases following an increase in income and decreases following a decrease in income. Most goods are normal goods, but the demand for some goods falls when income rises, and rises when income falls. For instance, as your income rises you might buy less canned tuna fish or fewer hot dogs, and buy more prime rib or shrimp. A good is an **inferior good** when demand decreases following an increase in income and increases following a decrease in income. So, hot dogs and tuna fish would be examples of inferior goods, not because they are of low quality, but because you buy less of them as your income increases.

Normal good A good for which the demand increases as income rises and decreases as income falls.

Inferior good A good for which the demand increases as income falls, and decreases as income rises.

TASTES Consumers can also be influenced by an advertising campaign for a product. If Hewlett-Packard and other companies begin to heavily advertise their printers on television and in magazines, consumers are more likely to buy them at every price and the demand curve will shift to the right. An economist would say that the advertising campaign has affected consumers' *taste* for printers. Taste is a catchall category that refers to the many subjective elements that can enter into a consumer's decision to buy a product. A consumer's taste for a product can change for many reasons. Sometimes trends play a substantial role. For example, the popularity of low-carbohydrate diets caused a decline in demand for some goods, such as bread and donuts, and an increase in demand for beef. In general, when consumers' taste for a product increases, the demand curve will shift to the right, and when consumers' taste for a product decreases, the demand curve for the product will shift to the left.

Demographics The characteristics of a population with respect to age, race, and gender.

POPULATION AND DEMOGRAPHICS Population and demographic factors can affect the demand for a product. As the population of the United States increases, so will the number of consumers, and the demand for most products will increase. The **demographics** of a population refers to its characteristics, with respect to age, race, and gender. As the demographics of a country or region change, the demand for particular goods will increase or decrease because different categories of people tend to have different preferences for those goods. For instance, the demand for baby food will be greatest when the fraction of the population under the age of two is the greatest.

3-2 Making the Connection

Firms are responding to the tastes of a growing Hispanic population. Some Home Depot stores, for example, include signs in both English and Spanish.

Companies Respond to a Growing Hispanic Population

In the fall of 2002, Blockbuster Video began stocking more than 1,000 videos and DVDs that had been dubbed in Spanish. Kmart began selling a clothing line named after Thalia, a Mexican singer. The Ford Motor Company hired Mexican actress and singer Salma Hayek to appear in commercials. A used car dealer in Pennsylvania displayed a sign stating "Salga Manejando Hoy Mismo" (or "Drive Out Today" in English). These companies were responding to the rising spending power of Hispanic Americans. The increase in spending by Hispanic households was due partly to increased population growth and partly to rising incomes. By 2020, the Hispanic share of the U.S. consumer market is expected to grow to more than 13 percent—almost twice what it had been in 2000. The Selig Center for Economic Growth at the University of Georgia has forecast that the incomes of Hispanic households will increase more than twice as fast between 2003 and 2007 as the incomes of non-Hispanic households.

As the demand for goods purchased by Hispanic households increases, more can be sold at every price. Not surprisingly, companies have responded by devoting more resources to serving this demographic group.

Source: Eduardo Porter, "Buying Power of Hispanics Is Set to Soar," *Wall Street Journal*, April 18, 2003, p. B1.

EXPECTED FUTURE PRICES Consumers choose not only which products to buy but also when to buy them. On the one hand, if enough consumers become convinced that printers will be selling for lower prices three months from now, the demand for printers will decrease now, as consumers postpone their purchases to wait for the expected price decrease. On the other hand, if enough consumers become convinced that the price of printers will be higher three months from now, the demand for printers will increase now, as consumers try to beat the expected price increase.

Table 3-1 summarizes the most important variables that cause market demand curves to shift. You should note that the table shows the shift in the demand curve that results from an *increase* in each of the variables. A *decrease* in these variables would cause the demand curve to shift in the opposite direction.

TABLE 3-1

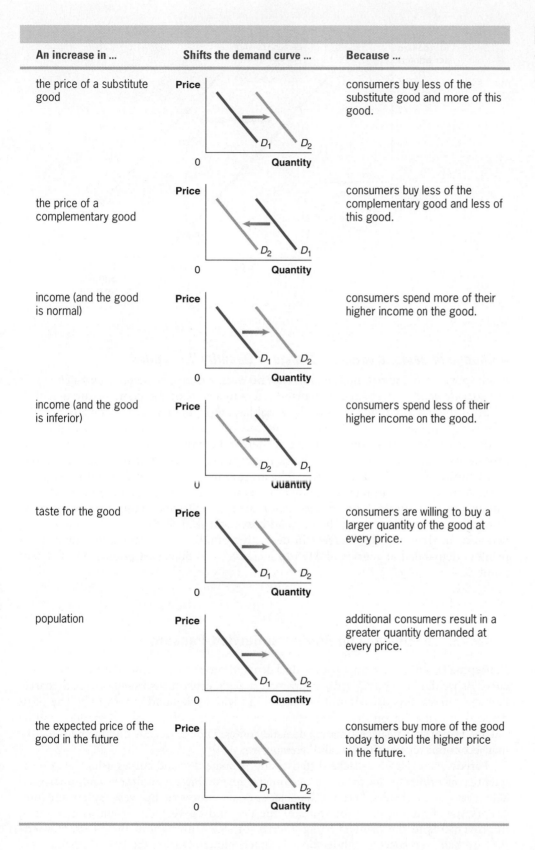

Variables That Shift Market Demand Curves

An increase in ...	Shifts the demand curve ...	Because ...
the price of a substitute good	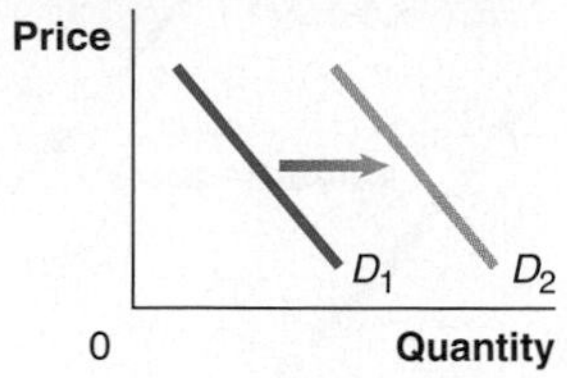	consumers buy less of the substitute good and more of this good.
the price of a complementary good	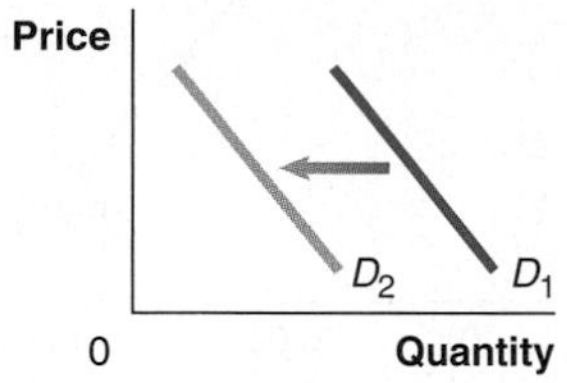	consumers buy less of the complementary good and less of this good.
income (and the good is normal)	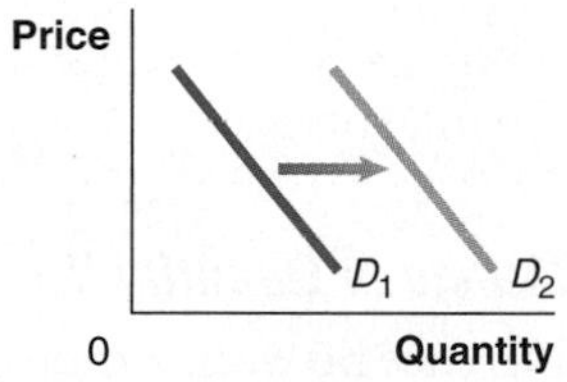	consumers spend more of their higher income on the good.
income (and the good is inferior)	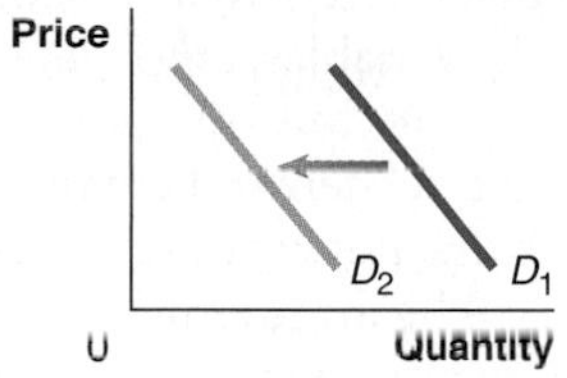	consumers spend less of their higher income on the good.
taste for the good	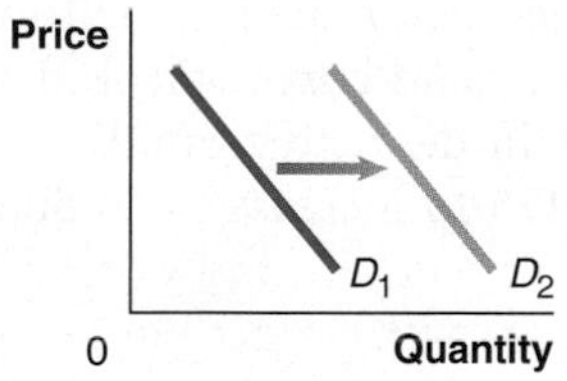	consumers are willing to buy a larger quantity of the good at every price.
population	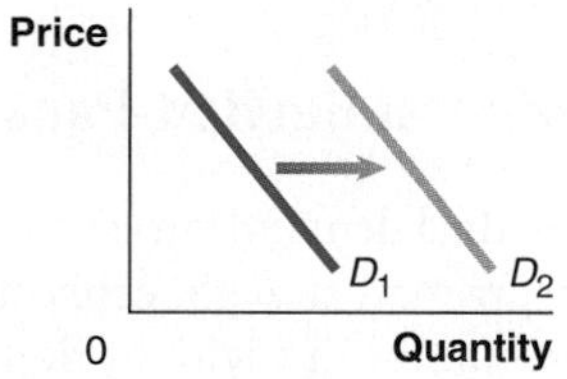	additional consumers result in a greater quantity demanded at every price.
the expected price of the good in the future	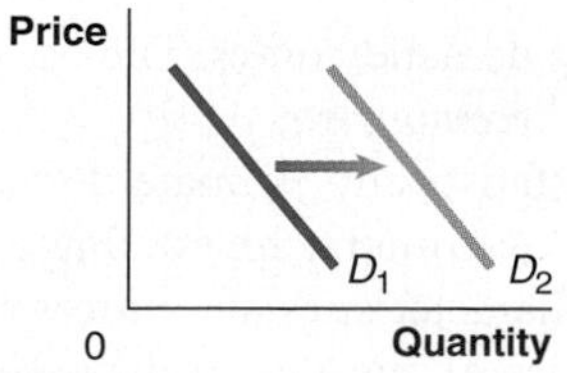	consumers buy more of the good today to avoid the higher price in the future.

FIGURE 3-5

A Change in Demand versus a Change in the Quantity Demanded

If the price of printers falls from \$175 to \$150, the result will be a movement along the demand curve from point *A* to point *B*—an increase in quantity demanded from 50,000 to 60,000. If consumers' income increases, or another factor changes that makes consumers want more of the product at every price, the demand curve will shift to the right—an increase in demand. In this case, the increase in demand from D_1 to D_2 causes the quantity of printers demanded at a price of \$175 to increase from 50,000 at point *A* to 70,000 at point *C*.

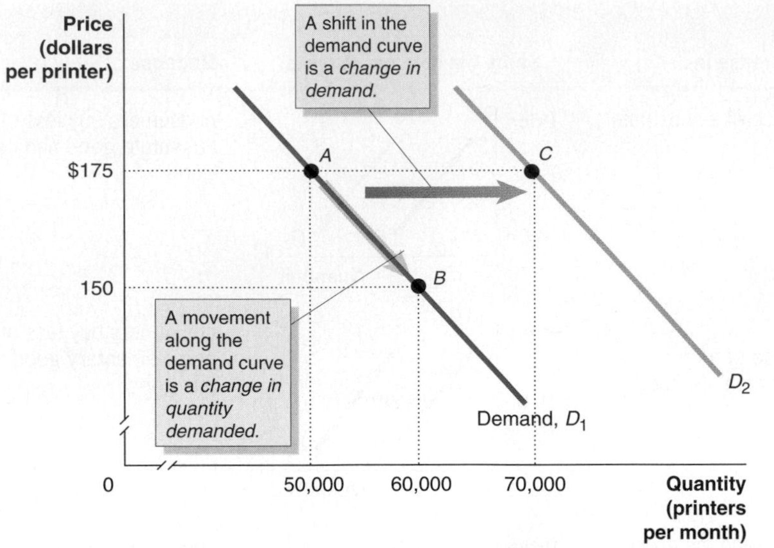

A Change in Demand versus a Change in Quantity Demanded

It is important to understand the difference between a *change in demand* and a *change in quantity demanded*. A change in demand refers to a shift of the demand curve. A shift occurs if there is a change in one of the variables, *other than the price of the product*, that affects the willingness of consumers to buy the product. A change in quantity demanded refers to a movement along the demand curve as a result of a change in the product's price. Figure 3-5 illustrates this important distinction. If the price of printers falls from \$175 to \$150, the result will be a movement along the demand curve from point *A* to point *B*—an increase in quantity demanded from 50,000 to 60,000. If consumers' incomes increase, or another factor changes that makes consumers want more of the product at every price, the demand curve will shift to the right—an increase in demand. In this case, the increase in demand from D_1 to D_2 causes the quantity of printers demanded at a price of \$175 to increase from 50,000 at point *A* to 70,000 at point *C*.

3-3 *Making the Connection*

Estimating the Demand for Printers at Hewlett-Packard

Conceptually, it is easy to sum up individual demand curves to construct the market demand curve, as we did in Figure 3-3(d). In practice, though, economists usually estimate market demand curves directly, without estimating individual demand curves first. The most detailed information on the relationship between price and quantity demanded can be obtained from statistically estimating demand curves. The use of statistical methods to estimate economic relationships is called *econometrics*.

Forecasters at Hewlett-Packard statistically estimate demand curves using data on the quantity of printers sold, the price of printers, advertising expenditures, and other variables that can affect sales. Because characteristics of printers change very rapidly, the forecasters specifically control for shifts of the demand curve to the right as a result of improvements to the printers being offered for sale. Throughout the 1990s, Hewlett-Packard had great success with its forecasting techniques. During the 1999 Christmas season, many companies selling products on the Internet were taken by surprise by the volume of orders they received and disappointed many customers when they couldn't fill their orders. Hewlett-Packard's forecasting system, however, allowed them to avoid this problem.

Unfortunately for Hewlett-Packard, their forecasters were less successful in 2001. During the first half of that year, the demand for printers was much lower than had been forecast and the company was stuck with large numbers of unsold printers. Two events caused the shift to the left of the demand curve for printers in the first half of 2001. The first was the surprising decline in personal computer sales for use in homes and small offices, resulting from the unexpected decisions by many families and small businesses not to upgrade their existing computers. The drop in PC sales caused a drop in printer sales, because printers are a complementary good. The second event was the U.S. economy moving into recession, lowering the incomes of many consumers and reducing the profits of many businesses. As Hewlett-Packard's experiences in 2001 show, forecasting demand can greatly aid the planning of business managers but can never be perfectly accurate.

Sources: Joel Bryant and Kim Jensen, "Forecasting Inkjet Printers at Hewlett-Packard Company," *Journal of Business Forecasting*, Summer 1994; and Scott Culbertson, Jim Burruss, and Lee Buddress, "Control System Approach to E-Commerce Fulfillment: Hewlett-Packard's Experience," *Journal of Business Forecasting*, Winter 2000–2001.

Inaccurate forecasts in 2001 caused Hewlett-Packard to produce more printers than they could sell.

The Supply Side of the Market

Just as many variables influence the willingness and ability of consumers to buy a particular good or service, many variables also influence the willingness and ability of firms to sell a good or service. The most important of these variables is price. The amount of a good or service that a firm is willing and able to supply at a given price is the **quantity supplied.** Holding other variables constant, when the price of a good rises, producing the good is more profitable and the quantity supplied will increase. When the price of a good falls, the good is less profitable and the quantity supplied will decrease.

(2) LEARNING OBJECTIVE

Discuss the variables that influence supply.

Quantity supplied The amount of a good or service that a firm is willing and able to supply at a given price.

Supply Schedules and Supply Curves

A **supply schedule** is a table that shows the relationship between the price of a product and the quantity of the product supplied. The table in Figure 3-6 is a supply schedule showing the quantity of printers that Hewlett-Packard would be willing to supply per month at different prices. The graph in Figure 3-6 plots the numbers from the supply schedule as a *supply curve.* A **supply curve** shows the relationship between the price of a product and the quantity of the product supplied. The supply schedule and supply curve both show that as the price of printers rises, Hewlett-Packard will increase the quantity it supplies. At a price of $150 per printer, H-P will supply 9.5 million printers. At the higher price of $175, it will supply 10 million.

Supply schedule A table that shows the relationship between the price of a product and the quantity of the product supplied.

Supply curve A curve that shows the relationship between the price of a product and the quantity of the product supplied.

Supply Schedule

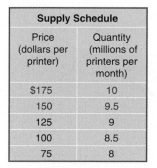

Price (dollars per printer)	Quantity (millions of printers per month)
$175	10
150	9.5
125	9
100	8.5
75	8

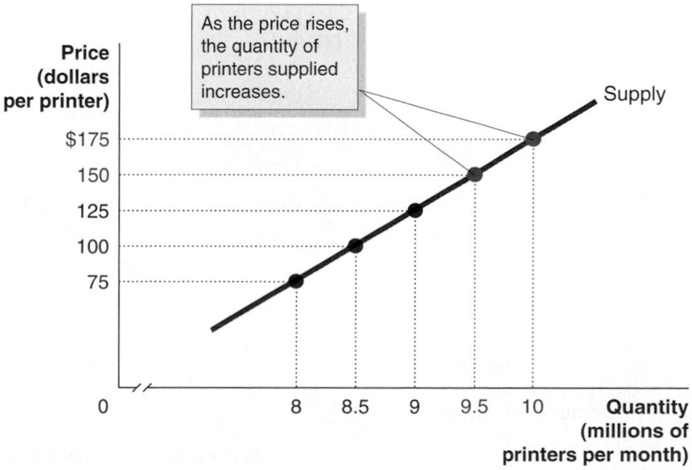

FIGURE 3-6

Hewlett-Packard's Supply Schedule and Supply Curve

As the price changes, Hewlett-Packard changes the quantity of printers it is willing to supply. We can show this as a *supply schedule* in a table, or as a *supply curve* on a graph. The supply schedule and supply curve both show that as the price of printers rises, Hewlett-Packard will increase the quantity it supplies. At a price of $150 per printer, H-P will supply 9.5 million printers. At a price of $175, it will supply 10 million.

Individual Supply and Market Supply

To construct the *market supply curve* for printers, we add the number of printers supplied at each price by each company producing printers. To keep things simple, suppose that Lexmark and Epson are the only other companies producing printers. Figure 3-7 shows that we can find the market supply curve by adding the number of printers supplied by Hewlett-Packard, Lexmark, and Epson at each price. Figure 3-7(d) at the bottom of page 75 shows the market supply curve for printers. For example, at a price of $125, Epson supplies 5 million printers, Lexmark supplies 7.5 million printers, and Hewlett-Packard supplies 9 million printers. Therefore, the quantity supplied in the market at a price of $125 is 21.5 million printers.

The Law of Supply

Law of supply Holding everything else constant, increases in price cause increases in the quantity supplied, and decreases in price cause decreases in the quantity supplied.

The market supply curve in Figure 3-7(d) is upward sloping. This pattern reflects the **law of supply**, which states that, holding everything else constant, increases in price cause increases in the quantity supplied, and decreases in price cause decreases in the quantity supplied. Notice that the definition of the law of supply—like the definition of the law of demand—contains the phrase "holding everything else constant." If only the price of the product changes, there is a movement along the supply curve, which is *an increase or decrease in the quantity supplied*. As Figure 3-8 shows, if any other variable that affects the willingness of firms to supply a good changes, the supply curve will shift, *which is an increase or decrease in supply*. When firms increase the quantity of a product they wish to sell at a given price, the supply curve shifts to the right. The shift from S_1 to S_3 represents an *increase in supply*. When firms decrease the quantity of a product they wish to sell at a given price, the supply curve shifts to the left. The shift from S_1 to S_2 represents a *decrease in supply*.

FIGURE 3-7 Deriving the Market Supply Curve from the Individual Supply Curves

The table shows that the total quantity supplied in a market is the sum of the quantities supplied by each seller. We can find the market supply curve by adding horizontally the individual supply curves. For example, at a price of $125, Epson supplies 5 million printers, Lexmark supplies 7.5 million printers, and Hewlett-Packard supplies 9 million printers. Therefore, the quantity supplied in the market at a price of $125 is 21.5 million printers.

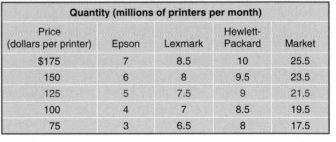

	Quantity (millions of printers per month)			
Price (dollars per printer)	Epson	Lexmark	Hewlett-Packard	Market
$175	7	8.5	10	25.5
150	6	8	9.5	23.5
125	5	7.5	9	21.5
100	4	7	8.5	19.5
75	3	6.5	8	17.5

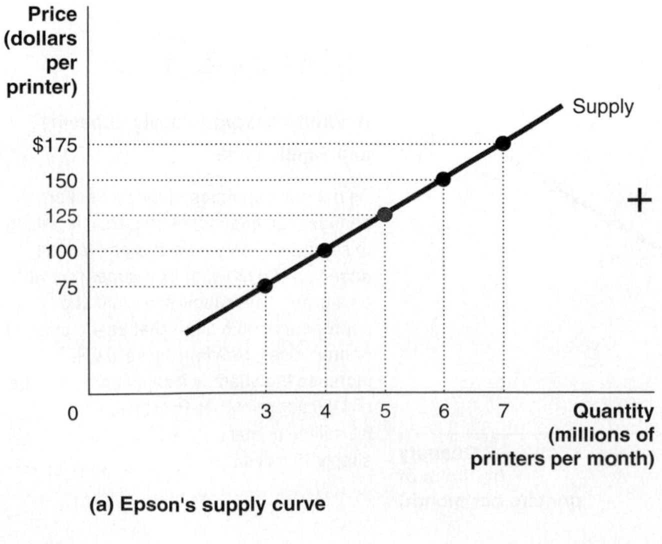

(a) Epson's supply curve

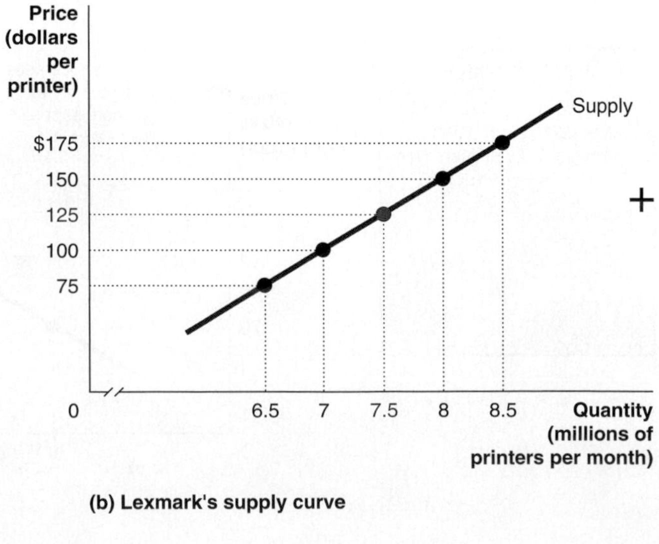

(b) Lexmark's supply curve

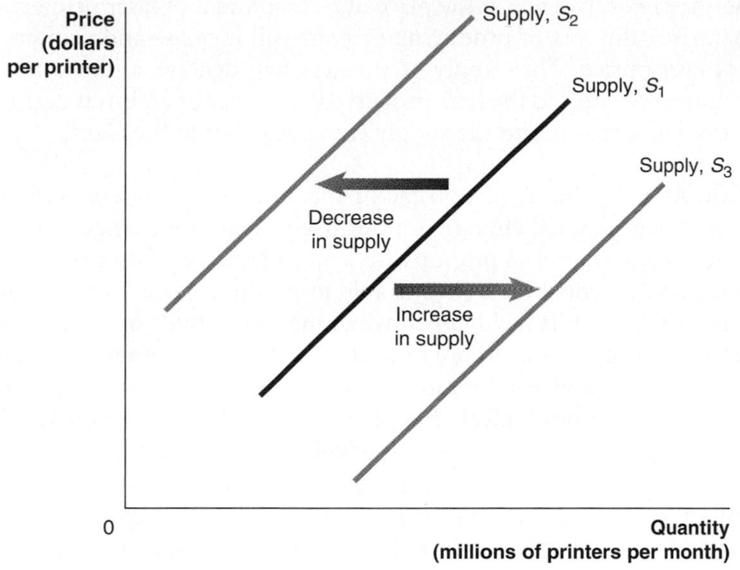

FIGURE 3-8

Shifting the Supply Curve

When firms increase the quantity of a product they wish to sell at a given price, the supply curve shifts to the right. The shift from S_1 to S_3 represents an *increase in supply.* When firms decrease the quantity of a product they wish to sell at a given price, the supply curve shifts to the left. The shift from S_1 to S_2 represents a *decrease in supply.*

Variables That Shift Supply

The following are the most important variables that shift supply:

- Prices of inputs
- Technological change
- Prices of substitutes in production
- Expected future prices
- Number of firms in the market

We can discuss how each of these variables affects the supply of printers.

PRICES OF INPUTS The factor most likely to cause the supply curve for a product to shift is a change in the price of an *input.* (An *input* is anything used in the production of

FIGURE 3-7 continued

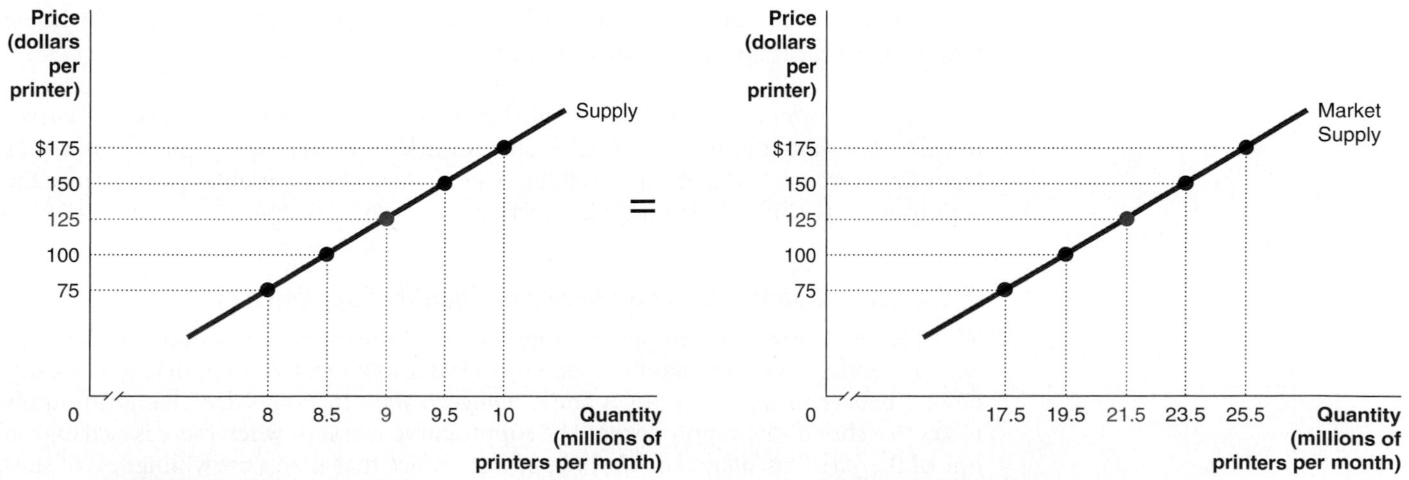

(c) Hewlett-Packard's supply curve

(d) Market supply curve

a good or service.) For instance, if the price of a component of laser printers, such as the laser scanner, rises, the cost of producing printers will increase and printers will be less profitable at every price. The supply of printers will decline, and the market supply curve for printers will shift to the left. Similarly, if the price of an input declines, the supply of printers will increase, and the supply curve will shift to the right.

Technological change A positive or negative change in the ability of a firm to produce a given level of output with a given amount of inputs.

TECHNOLOGICAL CHANGE A second factor that causes a change in supply is *technological change.* **Technological change** is a positive or negative change in the ability of a firm to produce a given level of output with a given amount of inputs. Positive technological change occurs whenever a firm is able to produce more output using the same amount of inputs. This shift will happen when the *productivity* of workers or machines increases. If a firm can produce more output with the same amount of inputs, its costs will be lower and the good will be more profitable to produce at any given price. As a result, when positive technological change occurs, the firm will increase the quantity supplied at every price and its supply curve will shift to the right. Normally, we expect technological change to have a positive impact on a firm's willingness to supply a product. Negative technological change is relatively rare, although it could result from a natural disaster or a war that reduces the ability of a firm to supply as much output with a given amount of inputs. Negative technological change will raise a firm's costs, and the good will be less profitable to produce. Therefore, negative technological change causes a firm's supply curve to shift to the left.

PRICES OF SUBSTITUTES IN PRODUCTION Firms often choose which good or service they will produce. Alternative products that a firm could produce are called *substitutes in production.* For instance, if the price of color printers increases, color printers will become more profitable and Hewlett-Packard, Lexmark, and the other printer companies will shift some of their productive capacity away from black-and-white printers toward color printers. They will offer fewer black-and-white printers for sale at every price, so the supply curve for black-and-white printers will shift to the left.

EXPECTED FUTURE PRICES If a firm expects that the price of its product will be higher in the future than it is today, it has an incentive to decrease supply now and increase it in the future. For instance, if Hewlett-Packard believes that printer prices are temporarily low–perhaps because of a price war among firms making printers—it may store some of its production today to sell tomorrow when it expects prices will be higher.

NUMBER OF FIRMS IN THE MARKET Finally, a change in the number of firms in the market will change supply. When new firms *enter* a market, the supply curve shifts to the right, and when existing firms leave, or *exit,* a market, the supply curve shifts to the left. For instance, when Xerox decided that it would no longer produce printers for home use, the market supply curve shifted to the left.

Table 3-2 summarizes the most important variables that cause market supply curves to shift. You should note that the table shows the shift in the supply curve that results from an *increase* in each of the variables. A *decrease* in these variables would cause the supply curve to shift in the opposite direction.

A Change in Supply versus a Change in Quantity Supplied

We noted earlier that it is important to understand the difference between a change in demand and a change in quantity demanded. It is also important to understand the difference between a *change in supply* and a *change in quantity supplied.* A change in supply refers to a shift of the supply curve. The supply curve will shift when there is a change in one of the variables, *other than the price of the product,* that affects the willingness of suppliers to sell the product. A change in quantity supplied refers to a movement along the

TABLE 3-2

Variables That Shift Market Supply Curves

An increase in ...	Shifts the supply curve ...	Because ...
the price of an input	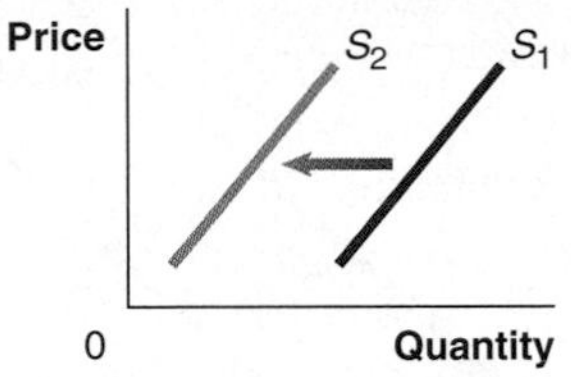	the costs of producing the good rise.
productivity	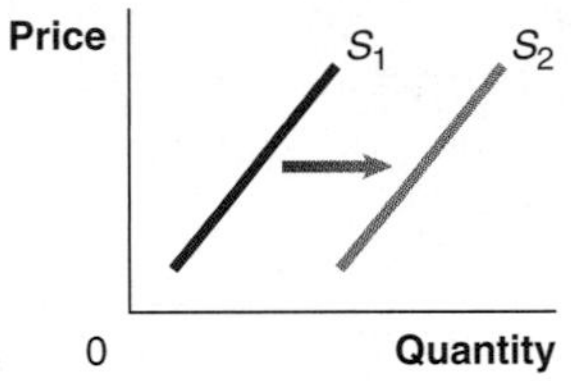	the costs of producing the good fall.
the price of a substitute in production	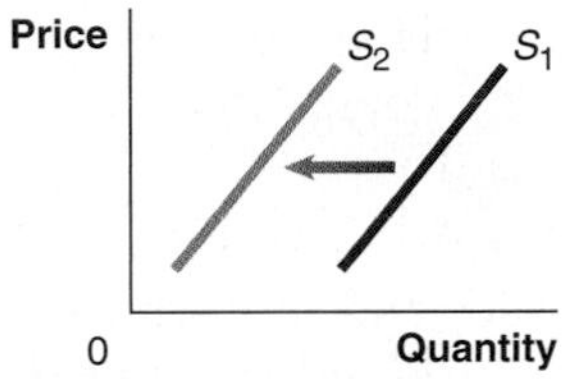	more of the substitute is produced and less of the good is produced.
the expected future price of the product	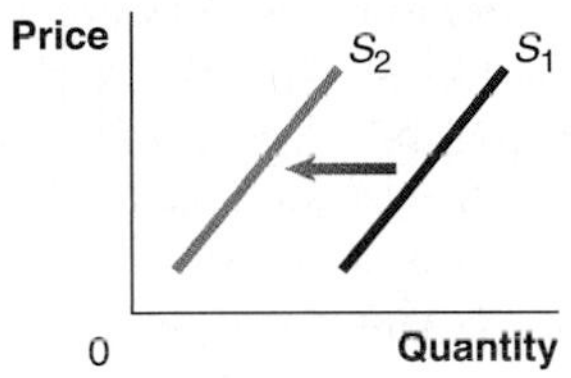	less of the good will be offered for sale today to take advantage of the higher price in the future.
the number of firms in the market	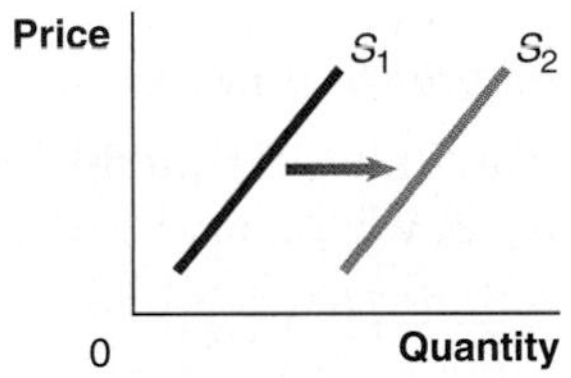	additional firms result in a greater quantity supplied at every price.

supply curve as a result of a change in the product's price. Figure 3-9 illustrates this important distinction. If the price of printers rises from \$125 to \$150, the result will be a movement up the supply curve from point *A* to point *B*—an increase in quantity supplied from 21.5 million to 23.5 million. If the price of an input decreases or another factor makes sellers supply more of the product at every price change, the supply curve will shift to the right—an increase in supply. In this case, the increase in supply from S_1 to S_2 causes the quantity of printers supplied at a price of \$150 to increase from 23.5 million at point *B* to 27.0 million at point *C*.

Market Equilibrium: Putting Demand and Supply Together

③ **LEARNING OBJECTIVE**

Use a graph to illustrate market equilibrium.

The purpose of markets is to bring buyers and sellers together. As we saw in Chapter 2, instead of being chaotic and disorderly, the interaction of buyers and sellers in markets ultimately results in firms being led to produce those goods and services most desired by consumers. To understand how this process happens, we first need to see how markets manage to reconcile the plans of buyers and sellers.

FIGURE 3-9

A Change in Supply versus a Change in the Quantity Supplied

If the price of printers rises from $125 to $150, the result will be a movement up the supply curve from point *A* to point *B*—an increase in quantity supplied from 21.5 million to 23.5 million. If the price of an input decreases or another factor changes that makes sellers supply more of the product at every price, the supply curve will shift to the right—an increase in supply. In this case, the increase in supply from S_1 to S_2 causes the quantity of printers supplied at a price of $150 to increase from 23.5 million at point *B* to 27.0 million at point *C*.

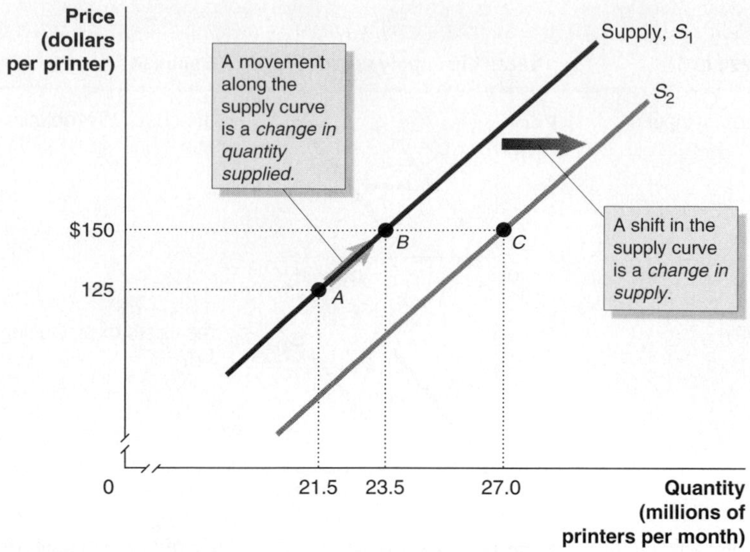

Market equilibrium A situation in which quantity demanded equals quantity supplied.

Competitive market equilibrium A market equilibrium with many buyers and many sellers.

In Figure 3-10, we bring together the market demand curve for printers and the market supply curve. Notice that the demand curve crosses the supply curve at only one point. This point represents a price of $100 and a quantity of 19.5 million printers. Only at this point is the quantity of printers consumers are willing to buy equal to the quantity of printers firms are willing to sell. This is the point of **market equilibrium.** Only at market equilibrium will the quantity demanded equal the quantity supplied. In this case, the *equilibrium price* is $100 and the *equilibrium quantity* is 19.5 million. Markets that have many buyers and many sellers are *competitive markets,* and equilibrium in these markets is a **competitive market equilibrium.**

How Markets Eliminate Surpluses and Shortages

A market that is not in equilibrium moves toward equilibrium. Once a market is in equilibrium, it remains in equilibrium. To see why, consider what happens if a market is not

FIGURE 3-10

Market Equilibrium

Where the demand curve crosses the supply curve determines market equilibrium. In this case, the demand curve for printers crosses the supply curve at a price of $100 and a quantity of 19.5 million. Only at this point is the quantity of printers consumers are willing to buy equal to the quantity of printers firms are willing to sell: The quantity demanded is equal to the quantity supplied.

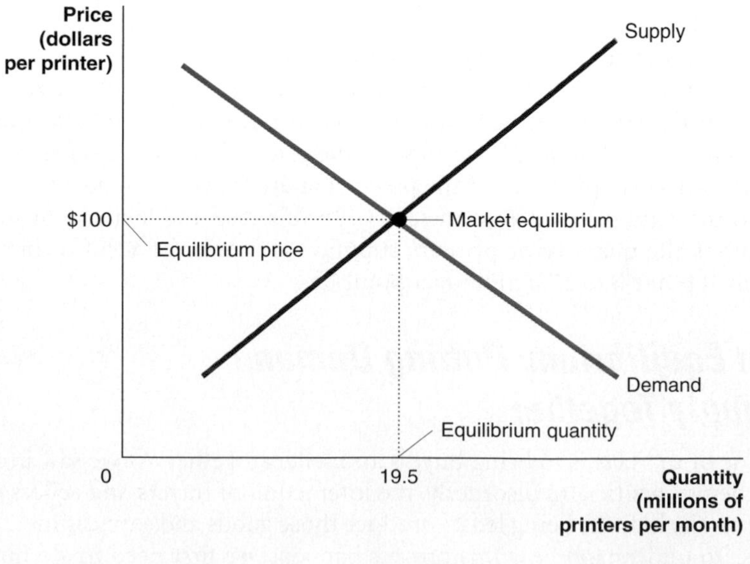

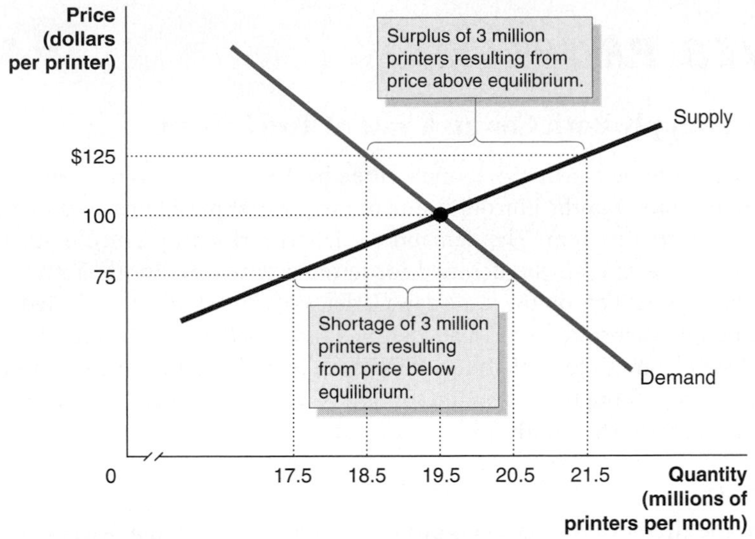

FIGURE 3-11

The Effect of Surpluses and Shortages on the Market Price

When the market price is above equilibrium, there will be a *surplus.* In the figure, a price of $125 for printers results in 21.5 million being supplied, but only 18.5 million being demanded, or a surplus of 3 million. As firms cut the price to dispose of the surplus, the price will fall to the equilibrium of $100. When the market price is below equilibrium, there will be a *shortage.* A price of $75 results in 20.5 million printers being demanded, but only 17.5 million being supplied, or a shortage of 3 million. As consumers who are unable to buy a printer offer to pay higher prices, the price will rise to the equilibrium of $100.

in equilibrium. For instance, suppose that the price in the printer market was $125, rather than the equilibrium price of $100. As Figure 3-11 shows, at a price of $125, the quantity of printers supplied would be 21.5 million and the quantity of printers demanded would be 18.5 million. When the quantity supplied is greater than the quantity demanded, there is a **surplus** in the market. In this case, the surplus is equal to 3 million printers (21.5 million − 18.5 million = 3 million). When there is a surplus, firms have unsold goods piling up, which gives them an incentive to increase their sales by cutting the price. Cutting the price will simultaneously increase the quantity demanded and decrease the quantity supplied. This adjustment will reduce the surplus, but as long as the price is above $100, there will be a surplus and downward pressure on the price will continue. Only when the price has fallen to $100 will the market be in equilibrium.

Surplus A situation in which the quantity supplied is greater than the quantity demanded.

If, however, the price were $75, the quantity supplied would be 17.5 million and the quantity demanded would be 20.5 million, as shown in Figure 3-11. When the quantity demanded is greater than the quantity supplied, there is a **shortage** in the market. In this case, the shortage is equal to 3 million printers (20.5 million − 17.5 million = 3 million). When a shortage occurs, some consumers will be unable to obtain the product and will have an incentive to offer to buy the product at a higher price. A higher price will simultaneously increase the quantity supplied and decrease the quantity demanded. This adjustment will reduce the shortage, but as long as the price is below $100, there will be a shortage and upward pressure on the price will continue. Only when the price has risen to $100 will the market be in equilibrium.

Shortage A situation in which the quantity demanded is greater than the quantity supplied.

At a competitive market equilibrium, all consumers willing to pay the market price will be able to buy as much of the product as they want, and all firms willing to accept the market price will be able to sell as much of the product as they want. As a result, there will be no reason for the price to change unless either the demand curve or the supply curve shifts.

Demand and Supply Both Count

Always keep in mind that it is the interaction of demand and supply that determines the equilibrium price. Neither consumers nor firms can dictate what the equilibrium price will be. No firm can sell anything at any price unless it can find a willing buyer, and no consumer can buy anything at any price without finding a willing seller.

SOLVED PROBLEM 3-1

③ LEARNING OBJECTIVE

Use a graph to illustrate market equilibrium.

Demand and Supply Both Count: A Tale of Two Letters

Which letter is likely to be worth more: one written by Abraham Lincoln or one written by his assassin, John Wilkes Booth? Lincoln is one of the greatest presidents, and many people collect anything written by him. The demand for letters written by Lincoln surely would seem to be much greater than the demand for letters written by Booth. Yet when R. M. Smythe and Co. auctioned off on the same day a letter written by Lincoln and a letter written by Booth, the Booth letter sold for $31,050 and the Lincoln letter sold for only $21,850. Use a demand and supply graph to explain how the Booth letter has a higher market price than the Lincoln letter, even though the demand for letters written by Lincoln is greater than the demand for letters written by Booth.

Solving the Problem:

Step 1: Review the chapter material. This problem is about prices being determined at market equilibrium, so you may want to review the section "Market Equilibrium: Putting Demand and Supply Together," which begins on page 77.

Step 2: Draw demand curves that illustrate the greater demand for Lincoln's letters. Begin by drawing two demand curves. Label one "Demand for Lincoln's letters" and the other "Demand for Booth's letters." Make sure that the Lincoln demand curve is much farther to the right than the Booth demand curve.

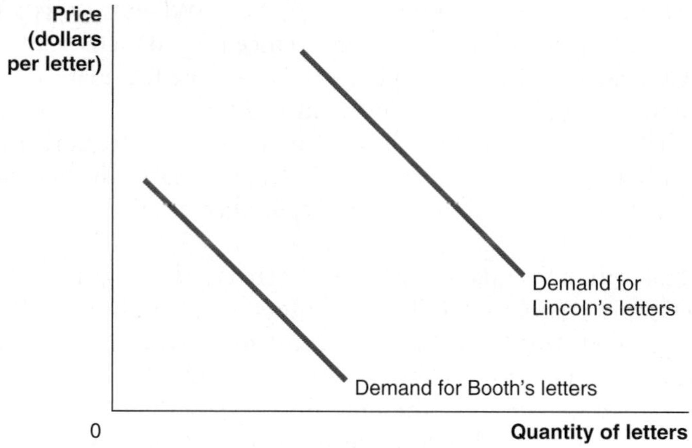

Step 3: Draw supply curves that illustrate the equilibrium price of Booth's letters being higher than the equilibrium price of Lincoln's letters. Based on the demand curves you have just drawn, think about how it might be possible for the market price of Lincoln's letters to be lower than the market price of Booth's letters. The only way this can be true is if the supply of Lincoln's letters is much greater than the supply of Booth's letters. Draw on your graph a supply curve for Lincoln's letters and a supply curve for Booth's letters that will result in an equilibrium price of Booth's letters of $31,050 and an equilibrium price of Lincoln letters of $21,850. You have now solved the problem.

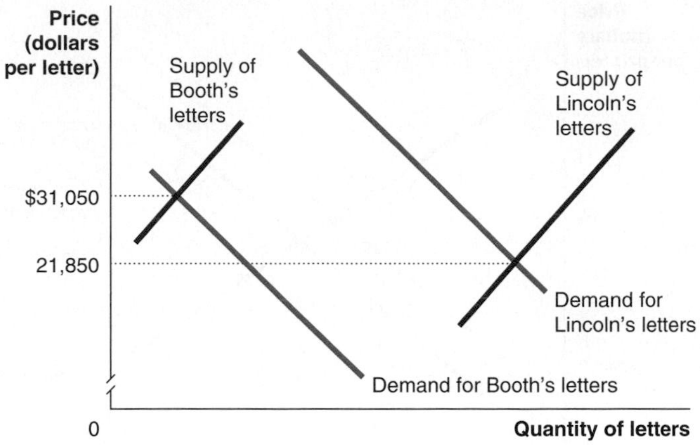

Extra Credit: The explanation for this puzzle is that both demand and supply count when determining market price. The demand for Lincoln's letters is much greater than the demand for Booth's letters, but the supply of Booth's letters is very small. Historians believe that only eight letters written by Booth exist today. (Note that the supply curves for letters written by Booth and by Lincoln slope up even though only a fixed number of each of these types of letters is available and, obviously, no more can be produced. The upward slope of the supply curves occurs because the higher the price, the larger the quantity of letters that will be offered for sale by people who currently own them.)

YOUR TURN: **For more practice, do related problem 9 on page 92 at the end of this chapter.**

The Effect of Demand and Supply Shifts on Equilibrium

(4) LEARNING OBJECTIVE

Use demand and supply graphs to predict changes in prices and quantities.

We have seen that the interaction of demand and supply in markets determines the quantity of a good that is produced and the price at which it sells. We have also seen that several variables cause demand curves to shift, and other variables cause supply curves to shift. As a result, demand and supply curves in most markets are constantly shifting, and the prices and quantities that represent equilibrium are constantly changing. In this section, we see how shifts in demand and supply curves affect equilibrium price and quantity.

The Effect of Shifts in Supply on Equilibrium

When Xerox decided to stop producing printers for the home market, the market supply curve for printers shifted to the left. Figure 3-12 shows the supply curve shifting from S_1 to S_2. This caused a shortage of printers at the original equilibrium price, P_1. The shortage was eliminated as the equilibrium price of printers rose to P_2, and the equilibrium quantity fell from Q_1 to Q_2. If new firms enter the printer market, the supply curve will shift to the right, causing the equilibrium price to fall and the equilibrium quantity to rise.

FIGURE 3-12

The Effect of a Decrease in Supply on Equilibrium

If a firm exits a market, as Xerox did from the market for home printers, the equilibrium price will rise and the equilibrium quantity will fall.

1. As Xerox exits the market for printers, a smaller quantity of printers will be supplied at every price, so the market supply curve shifts to the left from S_1 to S_2, which causes a shortage of printers at the original price, P_1.
2. The equilibrium price rises from P_1 to P_2.
3. The equilibrium quantity falls from Q_1 to Q_2.

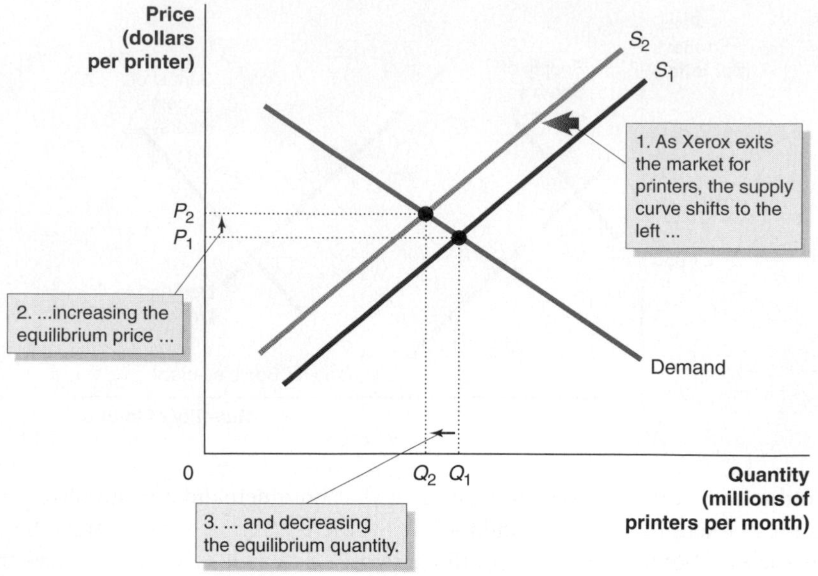

Price (dollars per printer)
S2
S1
1. As Xerox exits the market for printers, the supply curve shifts to the left ...
P2
P1
2. ...increasing the equilibrium price ...
Demand
0
Q2 Q1
Quantity (millions of printers per month)
3. ... and decreasing the equilibrium quantity.

3-4 Making the Connection

The Falling Price of Large Flat-Screen Televisions

Research on flat-screen televisions using liquid crystal displays (LCDs) began in the 1960s. However, it was surprisingly difficult to use this research to produce a television priced low enough for many consumers to purchase. One researcher noted, "In the 1960s, we used to say 'In ten years, we're going to have the TV on the wall.' We said the same thing in the seventies and then in the eighties." A key technical problem in manufacturing LCD televisions was making glass sheets large enough, thin enough, and clean enough to be used as LCD screens. Finally, in 1999, Corning, Inc., developed a process to manufacture glass less than 1 millimeter thick that was very clean because it was produced without being touched by machinery.

Corning's breakthrough led to what the *Wall Street Journal* described as a "race to build new, better factories." The firms producing the flat screens are all located in Taiwan, South Korea, and Japan. The leading firms are Korea's Samsung Electronics and LG Phillips LCD, Taiwan's AU Optronics, and Japan's Sharp Corporation. In 2004, AU Optronics opened a new factory with 2.4 million square feet of clean room in which the LCD screens are manufactured. This factory is nearly five times as large as the largest factory in which Intel makes computer chips. In all, 10 new factories manufacturing LCD screens were scheduled to come into operation between late 2004 and late 2005. The figure shows that this increase in supply was expected to drive the

LCD TV

Woo Nam-kyoon, right, president of LG Electronic Digital Display Company, poses for photographers next to the world's largest 55-inch all-in-one LCD TV during its unveiling in Seoul, Monday, September 6, 2004. It goeson sale in the domestic market Monday with the price of 19.5 million won (US $17,000).

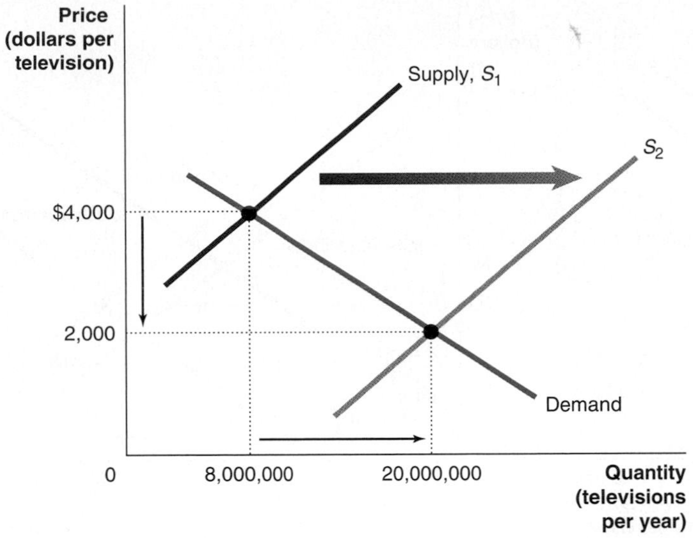

price of a typical large LCD television from $4,000 in the fall of 2004 to $2,000 in 2006, increasing the quantity demanded worldwide from 8,000,000 to 20,000,000.

Sources: Evan Ramstad, "Big Display: Once a Footnote, Flat Screens Grow into Huge Industry," *Wall Street Journal,* August 30, 2004, p. A1; and Michael Schuman, "Flat Chance: Prices on Cool TVs Are Dropping as New Factories Come on Line," *Time,* October 18, 2004, pp. 64–66.

The Effect of Shifts in Demand on Equilibrium

When population growth and income growth occur, the market demand for printers shifts to the right. Figure 3-13 shows the effect of a demand curve shifting to the right from D_1 to D_2. This shift causes a shortage at the original equilibrium price, P_1. To eliminate the shortage, the equilibrium price rises to P_2, and the equilibrium quantity rises from Q_1 to Q_2. However, if the price of a complementary good, such as personal computers, were to rise, the demand for printers would decrease. This change would cause the demand curve for printers to shift to the left, and the equilibrium price and quantity would both decrease.

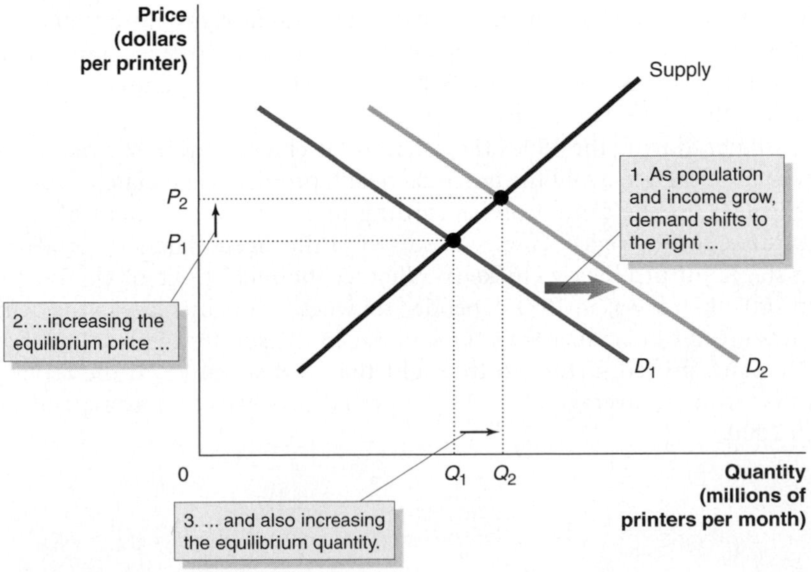

FIGURE 3-13

The Effect of an Increase in Demand on Equilibrium

Increases in income and population will cause the equilibrium price and quantity to rise.

1. As population and income grow, the quantity demanded increases at every price, and the market demand curve shifts to the right from D_1 to D_2, which causes a shortage of printers at the original price, P_1.
2. The equilibrium price rises from P_1 to P_2.
3. The equilibrium quantity rises from Q_1 to Q_2.

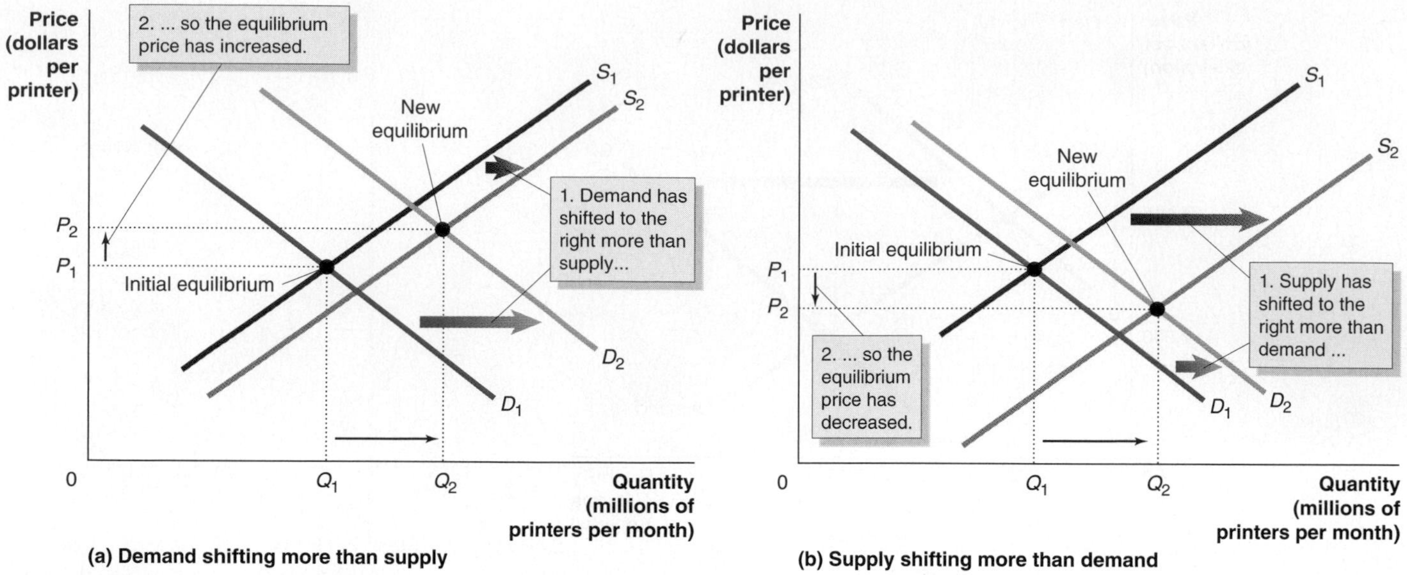

FIGURE 3-14 Shifts in Demand and Supply over Time

Whether the price of a product rises or falls over time depends on whether or not demand shifts to the right more than supply.

In panel (a), demand shifts to the right more than supply and the equilibrium price rises.

1. Demand shifts to the right more than supply.
2. Equilibrium price rises from P_1 to P_2.

In panel (b), supply shifts to the right more than demand and the equilibrium price falls.

1. Supply shifts to the right more than demand.
2. Equilibrium price falls from P_1 to P_2.

The Effect of Shifts in Demand and Supply over Time

Whenever only demand or only supply shifts, we can easily predict the effect on equilibrium price and quantity. But what happens if *both* curves shift? For instance, in many markets, the demand curve shifts to the right over time, as population and income grow. The supply curve also often shifts to the right as new firms enter the market and positive technological change occurs. Whether the equilibrium price in a market rises or falls over time usually depends on whether demand shifts to the right more than does supply. Panel (a) of Figure 3-14 shows that when demand shifts to the right more than supply, the equilibrium price rises. But, as panel (b) shows, when supply shifts to the right more than demand, the equilibrium price falls.

For instance, during the 1990s the demand for chicken increased rapidly, as many consumers attempted to avoid the potential health problems associated with eating too much red meat. At the same time, according to a U.S. Department of Agriculture report, positive technological change occurred in the "feed, hatchery, processing, and breeding stages" of producing chickens. Whether the retail price of chicken would be higher in 2000 than it was in 1991 depended on whether the increase in the demand for chicken was greater or smaller than the increase in the supply. Figure 3-15 shows that, in fact, demand shifted farther to the right than did supply, and the retail price of chicken rose from an average of $0.88 per pound in 1991 to an average of $1.07 per pound in 2000.

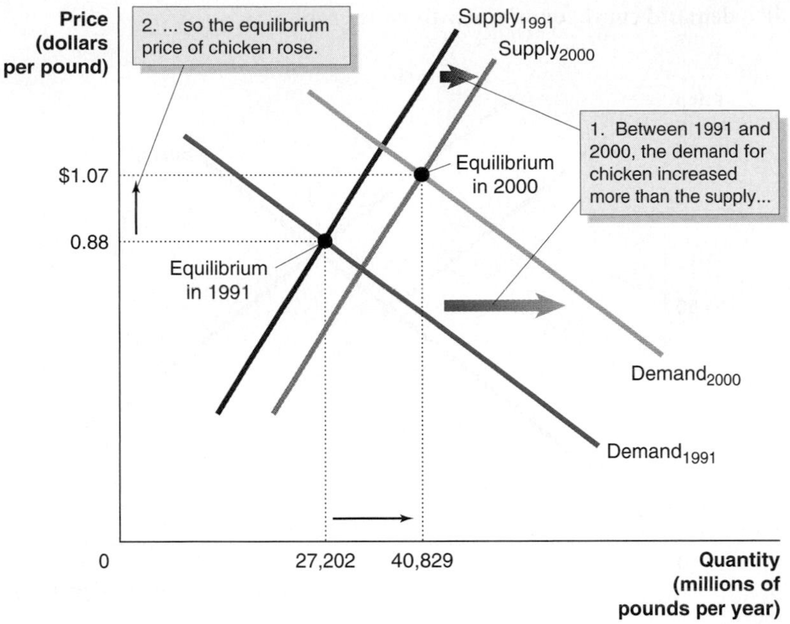

FIGURE 3-15

The Demand for Chicken Has Increased More Than the Supply

The supply of chicken increased rapidly during the 1990s, but the demand increased even faster. The result was that the equilibrium price of chicken rose. (The prices have been adjusted for the effects of inflation.)

1. Between 1991 and 2000, the demand for chicken shifted to the right more than supply.
2. The equilibrium price of chicken rose from $0.88 per pound in 1991 to $1.07 per pound in 2000.

SOLVED PROBLEM 3-2

High Demand and Low Prices in the Lobster Market?

④ LEARNING OBJECTIVE
Use demand and supply graphs to predict changes in prices and quantities.

During the spring when demand for lobster is relatively low, Maine lobster fishermen are able to sell their lobster catches for about $4.50 per pound. During the summer when demand for lobster is much higher, Maine lobster fishermen are able to sell their lobster catches for only about $3.00 per pound. It may seem strange that the market price is higher when demand is low than when demand is high. Can you resolve this paradox with the help of a demand and supply graph?

Solving the Problem:

Step 1: Review the chapter material. This problem is about how shifts in demand and supply curves affect the equilibrium price, so you may want to review the section "The Effects of Shifts in Demand and Supply over Time," which begins on page 84.

Step 2: Draw the demand and supply graph. Draw a demand and supply graph, showing the market equilibrium in the spring. Label the equilibrium price $4.50. Label both the demand and supply curves "spring."

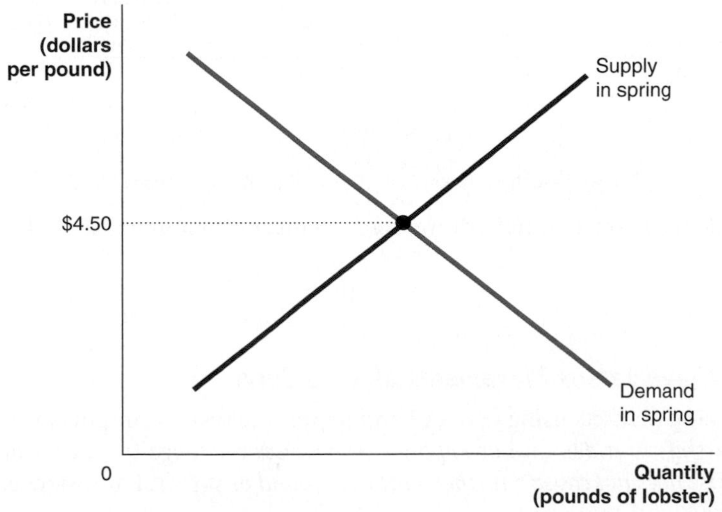

Step 3: Add a demand curve for summer to your graph.

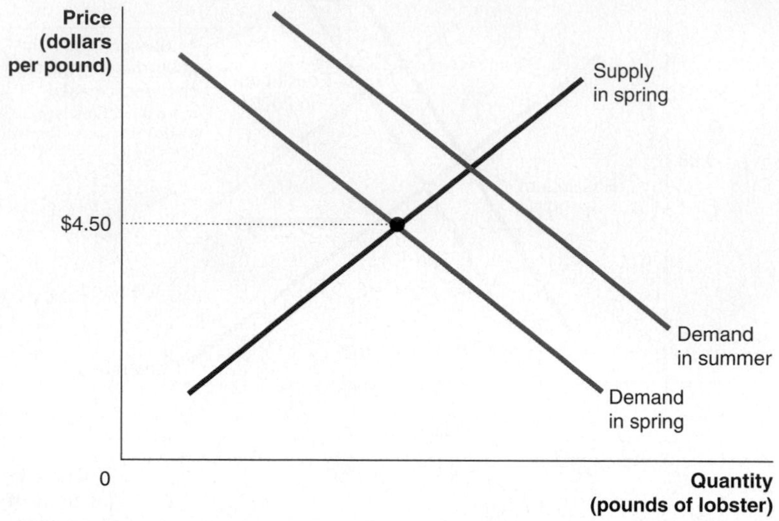

Step 4: Explain the graph. After studying the graph, it is possible to see how the equilibrium price can fall from $4.50 to $3.00 despite the increase in demand: The supply curve must have shifted to the right by enough so that the new equilibrium price is $3.00. Draw in this new supply curve, label it "summer," and label the new equilibrium price $3.00. The demand for lobster does increase in summer compared with the spring. But the increase in the supply of lobster between spring and summer is even greater. So, the equilibrium price falls.

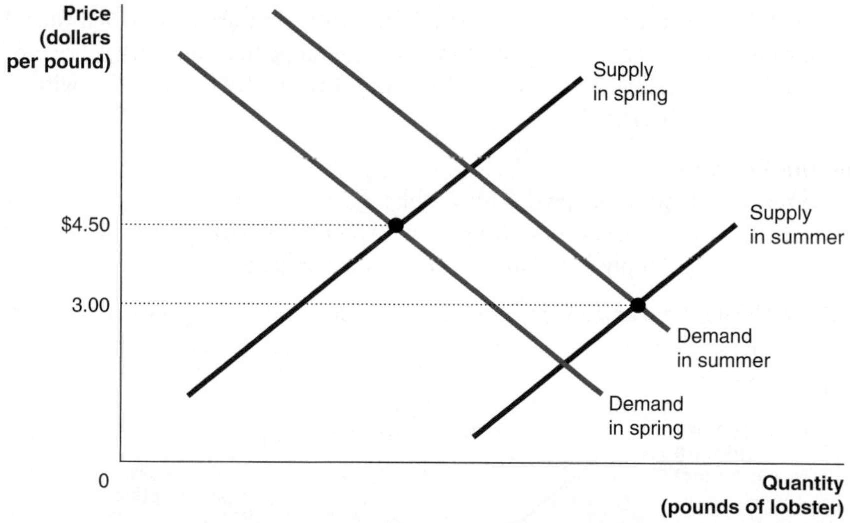

Source: Carey Goldberg, "Down East, the Lobster Hauls Are Up Big," *New York Times*, May 31, 2001.

YOUR TURN: **For more practice, do related problem 13 on page 92 at the end of this chapter.**

Shifts in a Curve versus Movements along a Curve

When analyzing markets using demand and supply curves, it is important to remember that *when a shift in a demand or supply curve causes a change in equilibrium price, the change in price does not cause a further shift in demand or supply*. For instance, suppose an

Don't Let This Happen To You!

Remember: A Change in a Good's Price Does *Not* Cause the Demand or Supply Curve to Shift.

Suppose a student is asked to draw a demand and supply graph to illustrate how an increase in the price of oranges would affect the market for apples, other things being constant. He draws the graph below and explains it as follows: "Because apples and oranges are substitutes, an increase in the price of oranges will cause an initial shift to the right in the demand curve for apples from D_1 to D_2. However, because this initial shift in the demand curve for apples results in a higher price for apples, P_2 consumers will find apples less desirable and the demand curve will shift to the left from D_2 to D_3, resulting in a final equilibrium price of P_3." Do you agree or disagree with the student's analysis?

You should disagree. The student has correctly understood that an increase in the price of oranges will cause the demand curve for apples to shift to the right. But the second demand curve shift the student describes, from D_2 to D_3, will not take place. Changes in the price of a product do not result in shifts in the product's demand curve. Changes in the price of a product result only in movements along a demand curve.

***YOUR TURN:* Test your understanding by doing related problems 6 and 23 on pages 91 and 94 at the end of this chapter.**

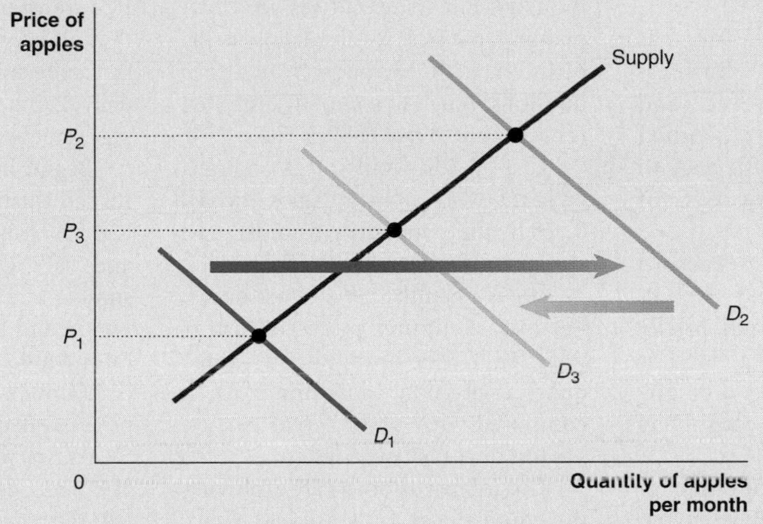

increase in supply causes the price of a good to fall, while everything else that affects the willingness of consumers to buy the good is constant. The result will be an increase in the quantity demanded, but not an increase in demand. For demand to increase, the whole curve must shift. The point is the same for supply: If the price of the good falls, but everything else that affects the willingness of sellers to supply the good is constant, the quantity supplied decreases but not the supply. For supply to decrease, the whole curve must shift.

Conclusion

The interaction of demand and supply determines market equilibrium. When many buyers and many sellers participate in the market, the result is a competitive market equilibrium. In a competitive market equilibrium, all consumers willing to pay the market price will be able to buy as much of the good as they want, and all firms willing to accept the market price will be able to sell as much of the product as they want. The model of demand and supply provides us with a powerful tool for predicting how changes in the actions of consumers and firms will cause changes in equilibrium prices and quantities. We will use the model of demand and supply in the next chapter to evaluate consumer surplus, producer surplus, price floors, and price ceilings. Before moving on, read *An Inside Look* on the next page to learn about H-P's strategy for competing with Dell.

An Inside Look Hewlett-Packard Cuts PC Prices to Sell More Printers

WALL STREET JOURNAL, MAY 12, 2004

Picking a Big Fight with Dell, H-P Cuts PC Profits Razor-Thin

In the past decade, Dell Inc. has surpassed International Business Machines Corp., Gateway Inc., and Compaq Computer Corp., riding direct sales and ruthless efficiency to become the world's largest seller of personal computers.

Two years ago, Hewlett-Packard Co. looked like the next victim. Instead, H-P is fighting back, briefly overtaking Dell in PC sales late last year, and drawing Dell into a bloody war of attrition in which consumers are the big winners.

a H-P's radical strategy for challenging Dell: selling PCs without worrying about profit.

"We think the PC business is strategic," says Chief Executive Carly Fiorina. She says she is willing to allow the company's $22 billion computer division to do little more than break even because PC sales help H-P make money on printers, consulting and consumer electronics. . . .

The result is the biggest threat yet to Dell, the PC industry's most profitable company. Having acquired Compaq in 2002, H-P is using its size to slash prices, in an attempt to undercut Dell's formula for gleaning profits in one of the nation's most competitive markets.

Still, for H-P, the strategy is a serious gamble. By cutting prices, the company earns less on each sale, leaving it with less of a cushion to absorb the inevitable shocks that roil competitive markets. H-P's profit margins in its PC division haven't exceeded 1% since the merger.

Dell continues to post solid profits; its operating profit margins of more than 8% are the widest in the industry. But its executives are complaining that H-P is subsidizing its PC business with earnings from other divisions, which to some suggests Dell is beginning to feel H-P's heat.

b The subsidies impair "the economics of the overall industry," adds Michael S. Dell, the company's founder and chairman. "It's not a healthy process."

It is healthy for customers. Personal-computer prices industry-wide fell by 9% during the first three quarters of 2003, according to Dell, compared with 4.5% a year earlier. Laptop prices fell even faster.

Corporate customers are exploiting the competition. Late last year, Getty Images, the Seattle photo distributor, asked H-P and Dell to compete for a sale of 500 desktop computers and 165 laptops. Kenneth Stringer, Getty's vice president of technical operations, specified how much he expected to pay for each computer.

"They both said, 'OK, we're ready to go there,' " Mr. Stringer says. But then H-P offered free advice for improving Getty's disaster-recovery plan and creating a digital archive of more than 70,000 film clips.

With $73 billion in annual sales, H-P offers a broader line of goods and services than Dell, with $41 billion in sales. And H-P isn't shy about tapping other parts of its empire to help sell PCs. Its credit arm offers generous financing terms. The consulting unit advises customers on how to save money on their technology operations . . .

c Only a few years ago . . . neither H-P nor Compaq could match Dell's mastery of the computer industry's central dynamic: falling prices. Most PCs are assembled from standard parts that all manufacturers buy at similar prices. Technological advances continually shrink the cost of disk drives, display screens and computer chips. . . .

Beginning in the mid-1990s, Dell turned this to its advantage. It flourished by building computers to order and selling them directly to consumers and businesses over the telephone and the Internet. Dell PCs are built only after a sale is made, with components procured at the cheapest prices available . . .

As Dell was thriving, executives from H-P and Compaq mapped out plans to take the company on, even before H-P's $19 billion acquisition of Compaq became final.

The team made plans to stop losing money in the soon-to-be-combined PC units of the two companies, agreeing to cut costs and close weak businesses as soon as the deal closed in May 2002.

Within months, H-P had shaved an average of $26 from the cost of building a PC, compared with Compaq's pre-merger costs, according to an H-P executive.

The result: H-P cut losses in the PC unit by roughly two-thirds in the fiscal year ended October 2002. . . .

In the fourth quarter of last year, H-P sold more computers than Dell . . .

But the victory would soon be reversed, as Dell retook the lead in the first quarter of 2004. . . .

Key Points in the Article

The article discusses the rivalry between Dell and Hewlett-Packard. Hewlett-Packard is willing to sell PCs for a little or no profit, because selling PCs increases demand for complementary products, such as printers. The article also notes that personal computer prices fell during 2003, as they have every year since 1981. These price declines result from positive technological change that reduces the cost of making PCs, and shifts the market supply curve to the right.

Analyzing the News

a Hewlett-Packard management sees PCs playing a strategic role in their plan to maximize profits for Hewlett-Packard as a whole. Printers, consulting provided to firms purchasing PCs, and consumer electronics are all complementary goods to PCs. We can use the economic model of demand and supply developed in this chapter to analyze this strategy.

Because PCs and printers are complementary goods, a decrease in the price of PCs will cause an increase in the demand for printers. This pattern is shown in Figure 1, where the demand curve for printers shifts from D_1 to D_2. This causes a shortage of printers at the original price, P_1. To eliminate the shortage, the equilibrium price increases from P_1 to P_2, and the equilibrium quantity increases from Q_1 to Q_2.

b Hewlett-Packard's strategy of increasing printer sales by reducing PC prices has no guarantee of success. Because Dell's own profits are made primarily from selling PCs, rather than related products, it is unlikely to pursue a strategy similar to H-P's. When Michael Dell complains that H-P's strategy is hurting "the economics of the overall industry," he means that the low prices H-P is charging for PCs hurts the profits of all PC makers. In fact, as discussed in the opener to this chapter, one of the reasons that Carly Fiorina was ousted as chief executive officer in 2005 was that H-P's board of directors became dissatisfied with the inability of the firm to earn significant profits from selling personal computers.

c Positive technological change reduces the cost of making PCs. The article notes that: "Technological advances continually shrink the cost of disk drives, display screens and computer chips." Reductions in cost make PCs more profitable to produce at every price. This causes the supply of PCs to increase, or shift to the right. This pattern is shown in Figure 2, where the supply curve for PCs shifts from S_1 to S_2. This causes a surplus of PCs at the original price, P_1. To eliminate the surplus, the equilibrium price decreases from P_1 to P_2, and the equilibrium quantity increases from Q_1 to Q_2.

Thinking Critically

1. Suppose Dell Inc., IBM, and *Gateway* Inc., simply refused to cut their prices as a result of Hewlett-Packard's strategy. What would happen to the quantity of computers sold by these companies?
2. Further suppose that one manufacturer's computers were not particularly good substitutes for another's. How would that affect your answer to the previous question?

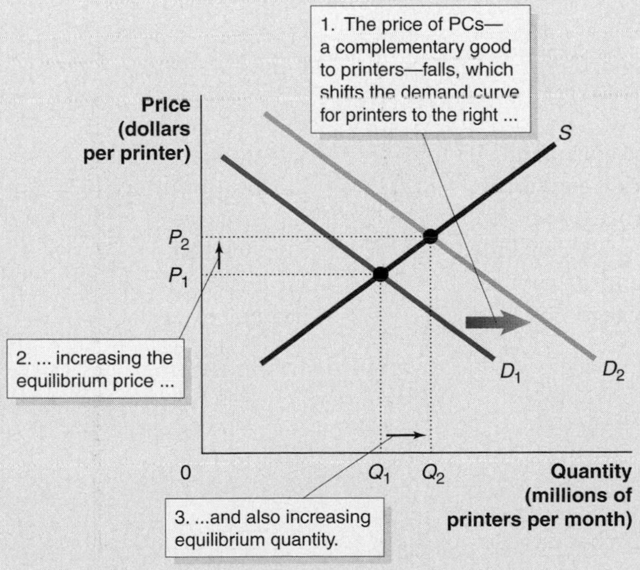

Figure 1: The fall in the price of PCs causes the demand for printers to shift to the right.

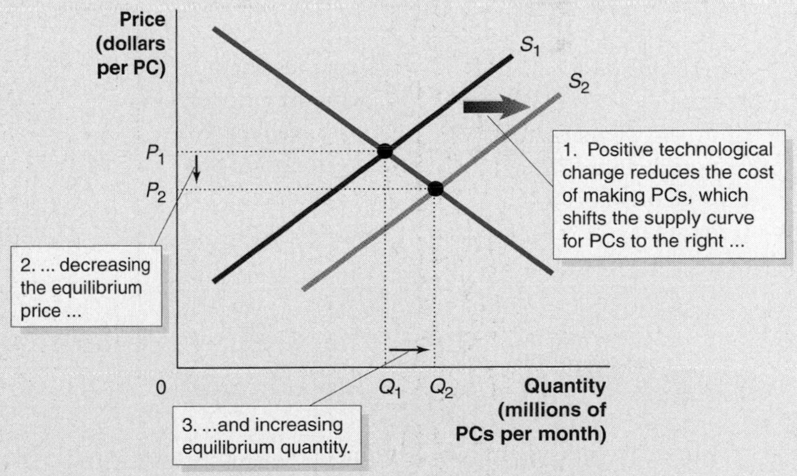

Figure 2: A fall in the cost of PCs shifts the supply curve for PCs to the right.

SUMMARY

LEARNING OBJECTIVE ① Discuss the variables that influence demand. The types and quantities of goods and services produced ultimately depend on the desires of consumers. A *demand curve* is a graph showing the relationship between the price of a good and the quantity of the good consumers are willing and able to buy over a period of time. We can find the market demand curve by adding horizontally the individual demand curves of each buyer. The *law of demand* states that *ceteris paribus*—holding everything else constant—the quantity of a product demanded increases when the price falls and decreases when the price rises. Changes in the prices of related goods, income, tastes, population and demographics, and expected future prices all cause the demand curve to shift. Demand curves always slope downward. A *change in demand* refers to a shift of the demand curve. A *change in quantity demanded* refers to a movement along the demand curve as a result of a change in the product's price.

LEARNING OBJECTIVE ② Discuss the variables that influence supply. When the price of a product rises, producing the product is more profitable and a greater amount will be supplied. The *law of supply* states that, holding everything else constant, the quantity of a product supplied increases when the price rises and decreases when the price falls. Changes in the prices of inputs, technology, the prices of substitutes in production, expected future prices, and the number of firms in a market all cause the supply curve to shift. A *change in supply* refers to a shift of the supply curve. A *change in quantity supplied* refers to a movement along the supply curve as a result of a change in the product's price.

LEARNING OBJECTIVE ③ Use a graph to illustrate market equilibrium. *Market equilibrium* occurs where the supply curve intersects the demand curve. Only at this point is the quantity supplied equal to the quantity demanded. Prices above equilibrium result in *surpluses*, which cause the market price to fall. Prices below equilibrium result in *shortages*, which cause the market price to rise.

LEARNING OBJECTIVE ④ Use demand and supply graphs to predict changes in prices and quantities. In most markets, demand and supply curves shift frequently, causing changes in equilibrium prices and quantities. Over time, if demand increases more than supply, equilibrium price will rise. If supply increases more than demand, equilibrium price will fall.

KEY TERMS

Ceteris paribus ("all else equal") 67
Competitive market equilibrium 78
Complements 68
Demand curve 64
Demand schedule 64
Demographics 70
Income effect 67
Inferior good 69
Law of demand 66
Law of supply 74
Market demand 65
Market equilibrium 78
Normal good 69
Quantity demanded 64
Quantity supplied 73
Shortage 79
Substitutes 68
Substitution effect 67
Supply curve 73
Supply schedule 73
Surplus 79
Technological change 76

REVIEW QUESTIONS

1. In a market system, who ultimately decides which goods and services will be produced?
2. What do economists mean when they use the Latin expression *ceteris paribus*?
3. What is the difference between a change in demand and a change in quantity demanded?
4. What is the law of demand? What are the main variables that will cause the demand curve to shift? Give an example of each.
5. What is the law of supply? What are the main variables that will cause a supply curve to shift? Give an example of each.
6. What do economists mean by "market equilibrium"? What will happen in a market if the current price is above the equilibrium price? What will happen if the current price is below the equilibrium price?
7. What happens to the equilibrium price in a market if the demand curve shifts to the right? Draw a demand and supply graph to illustrate your answer.

8. What happens to the equilibrium price in a market if the supply curve shifts to the left? Draw a demand and supply graph to illustrate your answer.
9. If, over time, the demand curve for a product shifts to the right more than the supply curve does, what will happen to the equilibrium price? What will happen to the equilibrium price if the supply curve shifts to the right more than the demand curve? For each case, draw a demand and supply graph to illustrate your answer.

PROBLEMS AND APPLICATIONS

Please visit **www.prenhall.com/hubbard** *for solutions to the even-numbered problems as well as multiple-choice and true or false self-assessment quizzes.*

1. Suppose the market for ice cream cones is made up of three consumers: Pedro, Curt, and Tim. Use the information in the following table to construct the market demand curve for ice cream cones. Show the information in a table and in a graph.

	PEDRO	CURT	TIM
PRICE	QUANTITY DEMANDED (CONES PER WEEK)	QUANTITY DEMANDED (CONES PER WEEK)	QUANTITY DEMANDED (CONES PER WEEK)
$1.75	2	1	0
1.50	4	3	2
1.25	6	4	3
1.00	7	6	4
0.75	9	7	5

2. For each of the following pairs of products, state which are complements, which are substitutes, and which are unrelated.
   a. Pepsi and Coke
   b. Oscar Mayer hot dogs and Wonder hot dog buns
   c. Jiffy peanut butter and Smucker's strawberry jam
   d. Hewlett-Packard printers and Texas Instruments hand calculators
3. State whether each of the following events will result in a movement along the demand curve for McDonald's Big Mac hamburgers or whether it will cause the curve to shift. If the demand curve shifts, indicate whether it will shift to the left or to the right and draw a graph to illustrate the shift.
   a. The price of Burger King's Whopper hamburger declines.
   b. McDonald's distributes coupons for $1.00 off on a purchase of a Big Mac.
   c. Because of a shortage of potatoes, the price of French fries increases.
   d. Kentucky Fried Chicken raises the price of a bucket of fried chicken.
4. Is it possible for a good to be an inferior good for one person and a normal good for another person? If it is possible, can you cite some examples?
5. Suppose the data in the following table present the price of a base model Ford Explorer sports utility vehicle and the number of Explorers sold. Do these data indicate that the demand curve for Explorers is upward sloping? Explain.

YEAR	PRICE	QUANTITY
2003	$27,865	325,265
2004	28,325	330,648
2005	28,765	352,666

6. **[Related to *Don't Let This Happen To You!*]** A student writes the following: "Increased production leads to a lower price, which in turn increases demand." Do you agree with his reasoning? Briefly explain.
7. Following are four graphs and four market scenarios, each of which would cause either a movement along the supply curve for Pepsi or a shift of the supply curve. Match each scenario with the appropriate diagram.
   a. A decrease in the supply of Coke
   b. Average household income in the United States drops from $42,000 to $41,000
   c. An improvement in soft-drink bottling technology
   d. An increase in the price of sugar

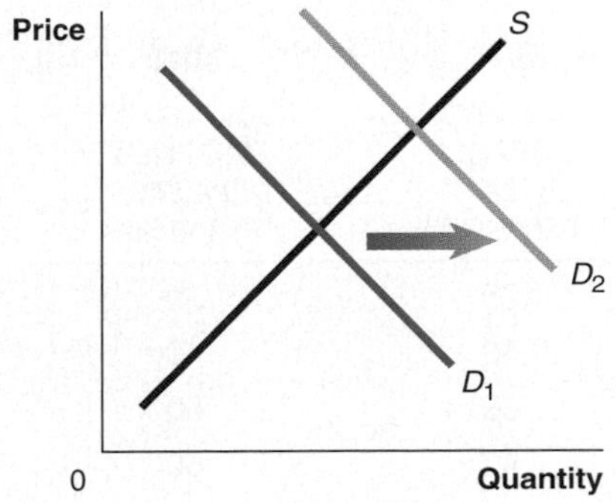

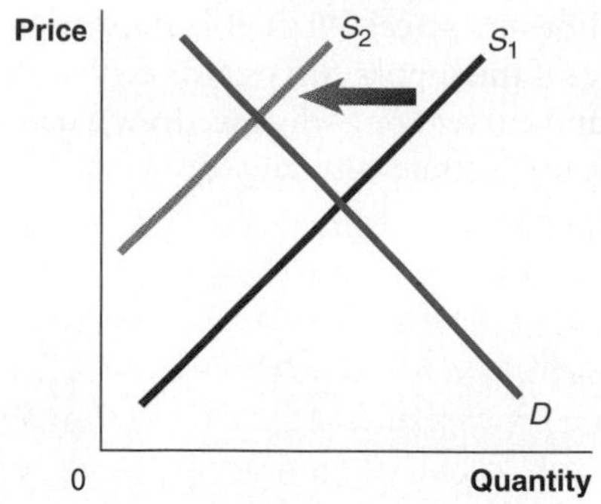

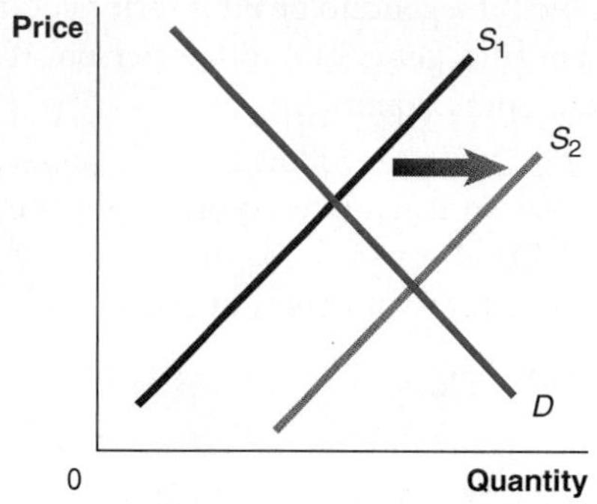

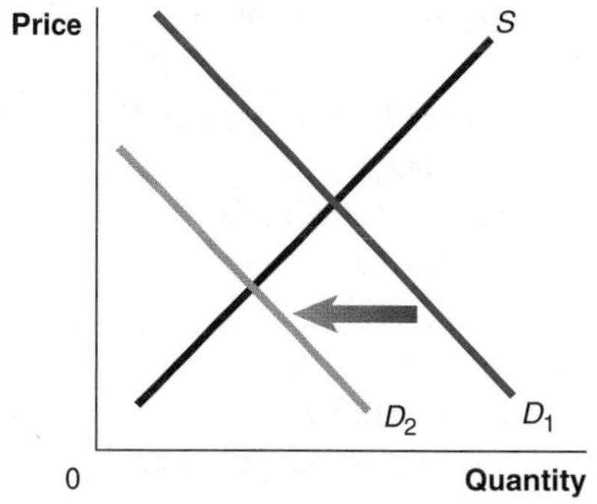

8. Suppose the pizza industry is made up of three firms: The Mark Company, Mike, Inc., and Bill Enterprises. Use the information in the following table to construct the market supply curve for pizzas. Show the information in a table and in a graph.

	MARK	MIKE	BILL
PRICE	QUANTITY SUPPLIED (PIZZAS PER WEEK)	QUANTITY SUPPLIED (PIZZAS PER WEEK)	QUANTITY SUPPLIED (PIZZAS PER WEEK)
\$5.00	25	30	20
5.50	30	40	25
5.75	35	50	30
6.00	40	60	35
6.25	45	70	40

9. **[Related to *Solved Problem 3–1*]** In *The Wealth of Nations*, Adam Smith discussed what has come to be known as the "diamond and water paradox":

> Nothing is more useful than water: but it will purchase scarce anything; scarce anything can be had in exchange for it. A diamond, on the contrary, has scarce any value in use; but a very great quantity of other goods may frequently be had in exchange for it.

Graph the market for diamonds and the market for water. Show how it is possible for the price of water to be much lower than the price of diamonds, even though the demand for water is much greater than the demand for diamonds.

10. Briefly explain under what conditions zero would be the equilibrium quantity.

11. According to an article in the *New York Times*, "Sales of DVD's in the United States have risen dramatically since the discs first went on the market in 1997, thanks in part to a drop in the price of DVD players." Draw a demand and supply graph for the DVD market and use it to show the effect on this market of a decline in the price of DVD players. Now draw a demand and supply graph for the VCR market and use it to show the effect on this market of a decline in the price of DVD players. On both graphs, make sure to indicate the equilibrium price and quantity before and after the decline in the price of DVD players.
Source: Rick Lyman, "Revolt in the Den: DVD Sends the VCR Packing to the Attic," *New York Times*, August 26, 2002.

12. A recent study indicated that "Stricter college alcohol policies, such as raising the price of alcohol, or banning alcohol on campus, decrease the number of students who use marijuana."
    a. On the basis of this information, are alcohol and marijuana substitutes or complements?
    b. Suppose that campus authorities reduce the supply of alcohol on campus. Use demand and supply graphs to illustrate the impact on the campus alcohol and marijuana markets.

Source: Jenny Williams, Rosalie Pacula, Frank Chaloupka, and Henry Wechsler, "Alcohol and Marijuana Use Among College Students: Economic Complements or Substitutes?" *Health Economics*, Volume 13, Issue 9, September 2005, pages 825–843.

13. **[Related to *Solved Problem 3-2*]** The demand for watermelons is highest during summer and lowest during winter. Yet watermelon prices are normally lower in summer than in winter. Use a demand and supply graph to demonstrate how this is possible. Be sure to carefully label the curves in your graph and to clearly indicate the equilibrium summer price and the equilibrium winter price.

14. The following appeared in the *Wall Street Journal:* "U.S. farmers are headed for the lowest corn harvest since 1997, but the soybean crop is expected to reach an all-time high. Prices for both crops are expected to rise." Draw demand and supply graphs illustrating the market for corn and the market for soybeans. Show the impact of a larger soybean crop on the equilibrium price in each market. Holding

everything else constant, what must be happening to the demand for soybeans for the equilibrium price of soybeans to rise?

15. According to an article in the *Wall Street Journal*, the price of flat-screen televisions fell between 2001 and 2004 from more than $8,000 to about $3,000. During that period Sharp, Matsushita Electric Industrial, and Samsung all began producing flat-screen televisions. Use a demand and supply graph to explain what happened to the quantity of flat-screen televisions sold during this period.
Source: Evan Ramstad and Gary McWilliams, "Flat-TV Prices Are Falling," *Wall Street Journal*, November 3, 2004, p. 81.

16. According to an article in the *New York Times*, during the summer of 2001 in San Francisco the quantity supplied of commercial real estate space—such as space in office buildings—was four million square feet more than the quantity of commercial real estate space demanded. Draw a demand and supply graph illustrating the San Francisco commercial real estate market. Predict what was likely to happen to rents for office space in San Francisco.
Source: Matt Richtel, "A City Takes a Breath after the Dot-Com Crash," *New York Times*, July 24, 2001.

17. During the late 1990s many consumers were having their vision problems corrected by laser surgery. An article in the *Wall Street Journal* in early 2001 noted two developments in the market for laser eye surgery. The first was about increasing concerns related to side effects from the surgery, including blurred vision and, occasionally, blindness. The second development was that the companies renting eye-surgery machinery to doctors had reduced their charges. One large company had cut its charge from $250 per patient to $100. Use a demand and supply graph to illustrate the effects of these two developments on the market for laser eye surgery.
Source: Laura Johannes and James Bandler, "Slowing Economy, Safety Concerns Zap Growth in Laser Eye Surgery," *Wall Street Journal*, January 8, 2001, p. B1.

18. Following the September 11, 2001, terrorist attacks, automobile companies became worried that the demand for new cars would decline. To maintain their sales, they reduced the prices of new cars. The following chart shows the effect this had on the prices of some *used* cars:

VEHICLE	PERCENTAGE CHANGE IN PRICE, JULY TO NOVEMBER
2000 Cadillac de Ville	−11.3%
1998 Lexus LS540	−12.2
1999 BMW 3231	−11.3
1999 Chevrolet Tahoe	−14.0
2000 Ford Explorer	−15.9
2000 Ford F-Series	−11.4

Explain why the prices of used cars fell in these circumstances. Use a demand and supply graph of the used car market to illustrate your answer.

19. The market for autographs, including letters or other documents signed by famous people, is subject to frequent large price changes, as are markets for most collectibles. The following table is adapted from one originally appearing in an article in the *Wall Street Journal*. It gives the 1997 price for an autograph, the 2001 price, and a brief comment by the *Wall Street Journal* reporter. Use the information contained in the Comment Column of the table to draw a demand and supply graph for each of the three autographs listed that can account for the change in its market price from 1997 to 2001.

AUTOGRAPH	1997 PRICE	2001 PRICE	COMMENT
The Beatles	$2,500	$7,475	"As boomers get rich, so do prices for pieces . . . signed by the Fab Four."
Princess Diana	14,000	2,000	"Demand rose after her death in 1997, but now the market's full of items like her signed Christmas cards."
Robert E. Lee	200,000	100,000	"The Civil War's out."

Source: Brooks Barnes, "Signature Market: Hard to Read," *Wall Street Journal*, July 13, 2001.

20. Historically, the production of many perishable foods, such as dairy products, was highly seasonal. Thus, as the supply of those products fluctuated, prices tended to fluctuate tremendously—typically by 25 to 50 percent or more—over the course of the year. One impact of mechanical refrigeration, which was commercialized on a large scale in the last decade of the nineteenth century, was that suppliers could store perishables from one season to the next. Economists have estimated that as a result of refrigerated storage, wholesale prices rose by roughly 10 percent during peak supply periods, while they fell by almost the same amount during the off season. Use a demand and supply graph for each season to illustrate how refrigeration affected the market for perishable food.
Source: Lee A. Craig, Barry Goodwin, and Thomas Grennes, "The Effect of Mechanical Refrigeration on Nutrition in the U.S.," *Social Science History*, Vol. 28, No. 2 (Summer 2004), pp. 327–328.

21. Briefly explain whether each of the following statements is true or false.
    a. If the demand and supply for a product both increase, the equilibrium quantity of the product must also increase.
    b. If the demand and supply for a product both increase, the equilibrium price of the product must also increase.

c. If the demand for a product decreases and the supply of the product increases, the equilibrium price of the product may increase or decrease, depending upon whether supply or demand has shifted by more.

22. According to an article in the *Wall Street Journal*, "Online auctioneers like eBay are having a huge impact on the price of fame. After Cal Ripken Jr. announced his retirement from baseball . . . dozens of Ripken-autographed game jerseys, baseball cards and Wheaties boxes flooded the online bazaar." Use a demand and supply graph to illustrate the impact of eBay on the equilibrium price of Cal Ripken memorabilia.

23. **[Related to *Don't Let This Happen To You!*]** A student was asked to draw a demand and supply graph to illustrate the effect on the personal computer market of a fall in the price of computer hard drives, *ceteris paribus.* She drew the graph below and explained it as follows:

> Hard drives are an input to personal computers, so a fall in the price of hard drives will cause the supply curve for personal computers to shift to the right (from S_1 to S_2). Because this shift in the supply curve results in a lower price (P_2), consumers will want to buy more personal computers and the demand curve will shift to the right (from D_1 to D_2). We know that more personal computers will be sold, but we can't be sure whether the price of personal computers will rise or fall. That depends on whether the supply curve or the demand curve has shifted farther to the right. I assume that the effect on supply is greater than the effect on demand, so I show the final equilibrium price (P_3) as being lower than the initial equilibrium price (P_1).

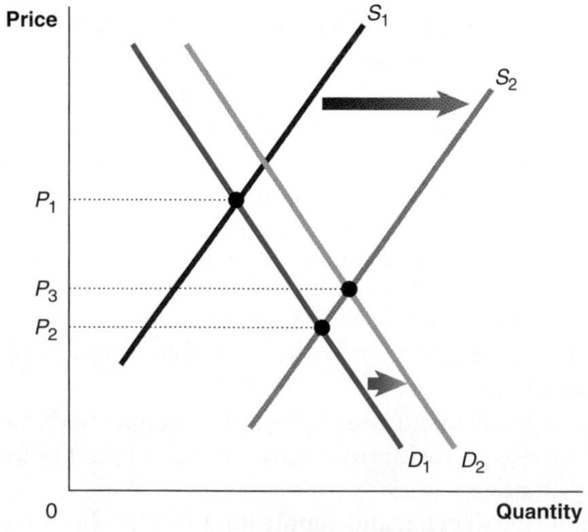

Explain whether you agree or disagree with the student's analysis. Be careful to explain exactly what—if anything—you find wrong with her analysis.

24. David Surdam, an economist at Loyola University of Chicago, makes the following observation of the world cotton market at the beginning of the Civil War:

> [A]s the supply of American-grown raw cotton decreased and the price of raw cotton increased, there would be a *movement along* the supply curve of non-American raw cotton suppliers and the quantity supplied by these producers would increase.

Illustrate this observation with one demand and supply graph for the market for American-grown cotton and another demand and supply graph for the market for non-American cotton. Make sure that your graphs clearly show: (1) the initial equilibrium before the decrease in the supply of American-grown cotton and (2) the final equilibrium. Also clearly show any shifts in the demand and supply curves for each market.

Source: David G. Surdam, "King Cotton: Monarch or Pretender? The State of the Market for Raw Cotton on the Eve of the American Civil War," *The Economic History Review*, Vol. 51, No. 1 (February 1998), p. 116.

25. Proposals have been made to increase government regulation of childcare businesses by, for instance, setting education requirements for childcare workers. Suppose that these regulations increase the quality of childcare and cause the demand for childcare services to increase. At the same time, assume that complying with the new government regulations increases the costs of childcare businesses. Draw a demand and supply graph to illustrate the effects of these changes in the market for childcare services. Briefly explain whether the total quantity of childcare services purchased will increase or decrease as a result of regulation.

26. Below are the supply and demand functions for two markets. One of the markets is for BMW automobiles, and the other is for a cancer-fighting drug, without which lung cancer patients will die. Briefly explain which diagram most likely represents which market.

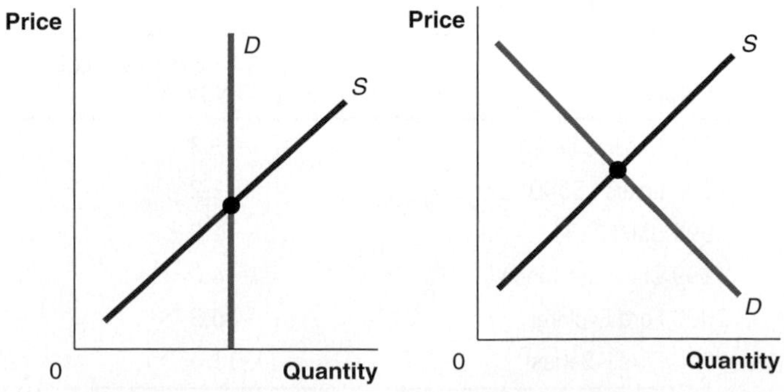

chapter four

Economic Efficiency, Government Price Setting, and Taxes

Should the Government Control Apartment Rents?

➤ Robert F. Moss owns one apartment building in New York City. He deals with more government red tape than the average businessperson. Unlike most business owners, for example, he is not free to charge the prices he would like for the service he offers. In New York, San Francisco, Los Angeles, and nearly 200 smaller cities, apartments are subject to rent control by the local government. Rent control puts a ceiling on the maximum rent that landlords can charge for an apartment.

About one million of New York City's two million apartments are subject to rent control. The other one million apartments have their rents determined in the market by the demand and supply for apartments. Mr. Moss's building includes apartments that are rent-controlled and apartments that are not. The market-determined rents are usually far above the controlled rents. The government regulations that determine what rent Mr. Moss can charge for a rent-controlled apartment are very complex. The following is Mr. Moss's description:

> [W]hen [an apartment] is vacated state rent laws entitle landlords to raise rents in three primary ways: a vacancy increase of 20 percent for a new tenant's two-year lease (a bit less for a one-year lease); one-fortieth per month of the cost of any improvements, and a "longevity bonus" for longtime residents (calculated at six-tenths of 1 percent times the tenant's last legal rent multiplied by the number of years of residency beyond eight). . . . (Apartments renting for $2,000 a month are automatically deregulated if they are vacant. Occupied apartments whose rent reaches that figure can be deregulated if the income of the tenants has been $175,000 or more for two years.)

Needless to say, a businessperson who earns a living by renting out apartments in one or two buildings in New York has to deal with much more complex government regulation of prices than a businessperson who owns, say, a McDonald's restaurant.

Larger companies also struggle with the complexity of rent control regulations. This was the case for several companies that built multiple apartment buildings in New York during the 1970s. In exchange for renting apartments to moderate- and low-income tenants at controlled rents, the companies were allowed to charge market rents after 20 years. Unfortunately for the companies, when the 20 years were over, attempts to start charging market rents were often met with lawsuits from unhappy tenants. In 2004, New York Mayor Michael Bloomberg proposed that the law be changed to keep many of these apartment buildings under rent control.

Tenants in rent-controlled apartments in New York are very reluctant to see rent control end because rents for rent-controlled apartments are much lower than rents for apartments that aren't rent-controlled. It turns out, however, that rent control actually drives up the rents of apartments that aren't rent controlled. *An Inside Look* on page 118 shows how a magazine reporter and his family ended up paying a higher rent for an apartment in New York than they would have if there had been no rent control.

Source: Robert F. Moss, "A Landlord's Lot Is Sometimes Not an Easy One," *New York Times*, August 3, 2003, Section 11, p. 1.

LEARNING OBJECTIVES

After studying this chapter, you should be able to:

① Understand the concepts of consumer surplus and producer surplus.

② Understand the concept of economic efficiency, and use a graph to illustrate how economic efficiency is reduced when a market is not in competitive equilibrium.

③ Use demand and supply graphs to analyze the economic impact of price ceilings and price floors.

④ Use demand and supply graphs to analyze the economic impact of taxes.

Price ceiling A legally determined maximum price that sellers may charge.

Price floor A legally determined minimum price that sellers may receive.

➤ We saw in Chapter 3 that, in a competitive market, the price adjusts to ensure that the quantity demanded equals the quantity supplied. Stated another way, in equilibrium, every consumer willing to pay the market price is able to buy as much of the product as the consumer wants and every firm willing to accept the market price can sell as much as it wants. Despite this, consumers would naturally prefer to pay a lower price, and sellers would prefer to receive a higher price. Normally, consumers and firms have no choice but to accept the equilibrium price if they wish to participate in the market. Occasionally, however, consumers succeed in having the government impose a **price ceiling,** which is a legally determined maximum price that sellers may charge. Rent control is an example of a price ceiling. Firms also sometimes succeed in having the government impose a **price floor,** which is a legally determined minimum price that sellers may receive. In markets for farm products such as milk, the government has been setting price floors that are above the equilibrium market price since the 1930s.

Another way in which the government intervenes in markets is by imposing taxes. The government relies on the revenue raised from taxes to finance its operations. As we will see, though, imposing taxes alters the equilibrium in a market.

Unfortunately, whenever the government imposes a price ceiling, a price floor, or a tax, there are predictable negative economic consequences. It is important for government policymakers and for voters to understand these negative consequences when evaluating the effects of these policies. Economists have developed the concepts of *consumer surplus, producer surplus*, and *economic surplus,* which we discuss in the next section. In the following sections we use them to analyze the economic effects of price ceilings, price floors, and taxes. (As we will see in later chapters, these concepts are also useful in many other contexts.)

① LEARNING OBJECTIVE
Understand the concepts of consumer surplus and producer surplus.

Consumer Surplus and Producer Surplus

We can analyze the effects of government interventions in markets, such as imposing price ceilings and price floors, using the concepts of consumer surplus, producer surplus, and economic surplus. Consumer surplus measures the dollar benefit consumers receive from buying goods or services in a particular market. Producer surplus measures the dollar benefit firms receive from selling goods or services in a particular market. Economic surplus in a market is the sum of consumer surplus plus producer surplus. As we will see, *when the government imposes a price ceiling or a price floor, the amount of economic surplus in a market is reduced*—in other words, price ceilings and price floors reduce the total benefit to consumers and firms from buying and selling in a market. To understand why this is true, we need to understand how consumer surplus and producer surplus are determined.

Consumer Surplus

Demand curves show the willingness of consumers to purchase a product at different prices. For instance, Figure 4-1 shows Joe Irvin's demand curve for chai tea. If the price is $3.00 per cup, Joe will buy 4 cups per week. If the price is $2.00 per cup, Joe will buy 5 cups per week. The fact that Joe is willing to pay $3.00 for the fourth cup means that the *marginal benefit* to him from that cup is $3.00. Similarly, the fact that Joe is willing to pay $2.00 for the fifth cup means that the marginal benefit to him from that cup is $2.00. The **marginal benefit** is the additional benefit to a consumer from consuming one more unit of a good or service. In fact, we can think of Joe's demand curve as representing his marginal benefit curve for chai tea.

Marginal benefit The additional benefit to a consumer from consuming one more unit of a good or service.

Suppose that the market price for chai tea is $2.00 per cup. In this case, for the fifth cup Joe buys in a week, his marginal benefit is equal to the price. For the other 4 cups he buys in a week, however, his marginal benefit is greater than the price he pays. In other words, for the first 4 cups of tea Joe buys in a week, he is paying less than the maximum price he would have been willing to pay, as shown by his marginal benefit. The difference between the highest price a consumer is willing to pay and the price the consumer actually pays is called **consumer surplus.**

Consumer surplus The difference between the highest price a consumer is willing to pay and the price the consumer actually pays.

Figure 4-2 shows the market demand curve for chai tea. In the figure, the quantity demanded at a price of $2.00 is 15,000 cups per week. An important point to understand is that nearly all consumers in this market receive some consumer surplus from their purchases because the marginal benefit they receive is greater than the price they pay. The only consumers who receive no consumer surplus are those who would not have purchased any chai tea if the price had been higher than $2.00. We can calculate total consumer surplus in the market by adding up the consumer surplus received on each unit purchased. Because the demand curve measures the marginal benefit received by consumers, we can draw the following important conclusion: *The total amount of consumer surplus in a market is equal to the area below the demand curve and above the market price.* Consumer surplus is shown as the blue area in Figure 4-2, and represents the benefit to consumers in excess of the price they paid to purchase the product—in this case, chai tea.

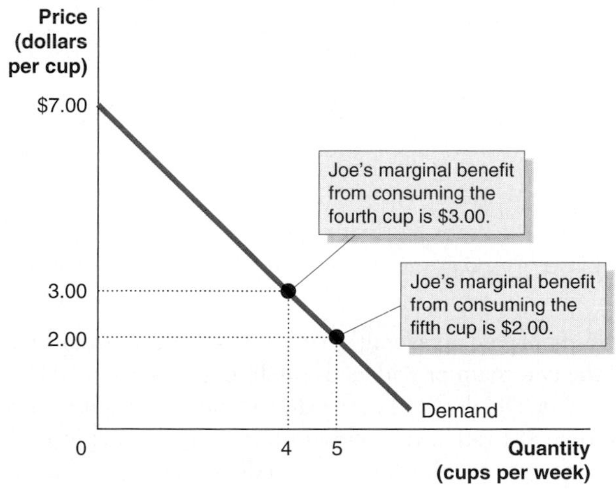

FIGURE 4-1

The Demand Curve Is Also the Marginal Benefit Curve

The demand curve shows a consumer's willingness to purchase a product at various prices. In this case, we know that Joe's willingness to pay $3.00 to purchase 4 cups of chai tea per week means that his *marginal benefit* from consuming the fourth cup is $3.00. Similarly, his willingness to pay $2.00 to purchase 5 cups of tea per week means that his marginal benefit from consuming the fifth cup is $2.00. So, the demand curve is also a marginal benefit curve.

FIGURE 4-2

Total Consumer Surplus in the Market for Chai Tea

The demand curve tells us that most buyers of chai tea would have been willing to pay more than the market price of $2.00. For each buyer, consumer surplus is equal to the difference between the highest price he or she is willing to pay and the market price actually paid. Therefore, the total amount of consumer surplus in the market for chai tea is equal to the area below the demand curve and above the market price. Consumer surplus represents the benefit to consumers in excess of the price they paid to purchase the product.

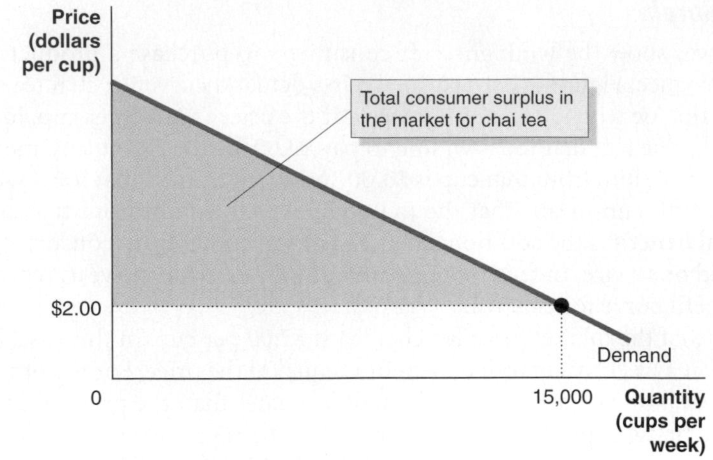

4-1 Making the Connection

The Consumer Surplus from Satellite Television

Consumer surplus allows us to measure the benefit consumers receive in excess of the price they paid to purchase the product. Recently, Austan Goolsbee and Amil Petrin, economists at the Graduate School of Business at the University of Chicago, have estimated the consumer surplus that households receive from subscribing to satellite television. To do this, they estimated the demand curve for satellite television and then computed the shaded area shown in the graph.

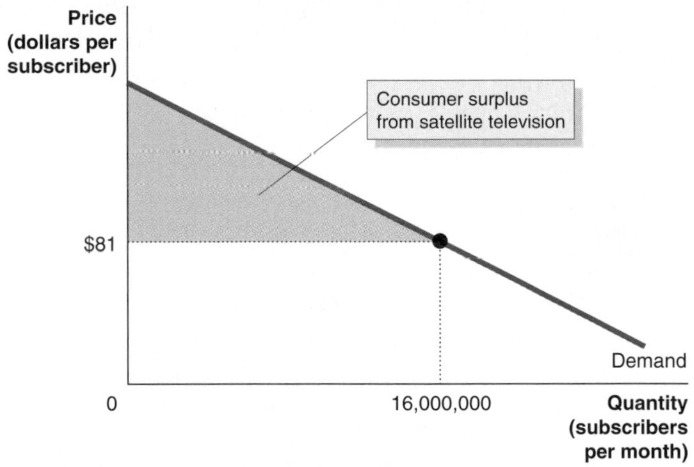

How much consumer surplus will the owner of this satellite dish receive?

Sixteen million consumers paid an average price of $81 per month to subscribe to DirectTV or DISH Network, the two main providers of satellite television in 2001, the year for which the study was conducted. The demand curve shows that many consumers would have been willing to pay more than $81 rather than do without satellite television. Goolsbee and Petrin calculated that the consumer surplus for households subscribing to satellite television averaged $127 per month, which is the difference between the price they would have paid, and the $81 they did pay. The shaded area on the graph represents the total consumer surplus in the market for satellite television. Goolsbee and Petrin estimate the value of this area is $2 billion. This is one year's benefit to the consumers who subscribe to satellite television.

Source: Austan Goolsbee and Amil Petrin, "The Consumer Gains from Direct Broadcast Satellites and the Competition with Cable TV," *Econometrica*, Vol. 72, No. 2, March 2004, pp. 351–381.

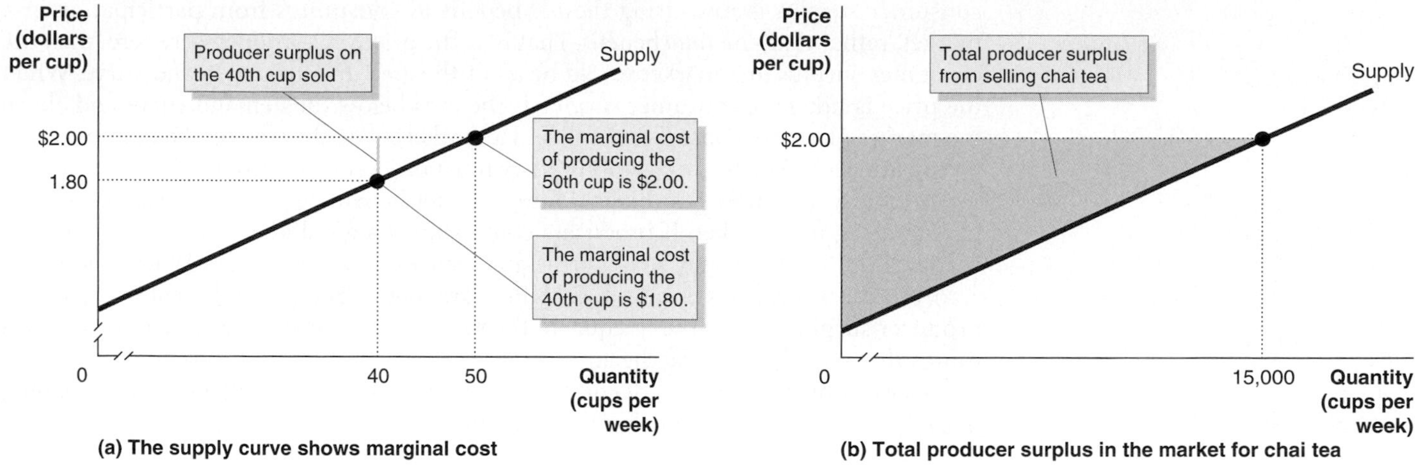

FIGURE 4-3 Producer Surplus

The supply curve shows a firm's willingness to supply a product at various prices. In panel (a), we know that Heavenly Tea's willingness to supply 40 cups of chai tea at a price of $1.80 per cup means that the *marginal cost* of producing the 40th cup is $1.80. Similarly, the firm's willingness to supply 50 cups at a price of $2.00 per cup means its marginal cost of producing the 50th cup is $2.00. Producer surplus on the 40th cup sold is the difference between the $2.00 market price of the cup and $1.80, which is the lowest price tea sellers would have been willing to accept. In panel (b), the total amount of producer surplus tea sellers receive from selling chai tea can be calculated by adding up for the entire market the producer surplus received on each cup sold. In the figure, this is equal to the area above the supply curve and below the market price, shown in red.

Producer Surplus

Supply curves show the willingness of firms to supply a product at different prices. The willingness to supply a product depends on the cost of producing it. Firms will supply an additional unit of a product only if they receive a price equal to the additional cost of producing that unit. **Marginal cost** is the additional cost to a firm of producing one more unit of a good or service. In Figure 4-3(a), we know that because Heavenly Tea is willing to supply 50 cups of chai tea at a price of $2.00 per cup, the 50th cup must have a marginal cost of $2.00. The supply curve also shows us that Heavenly Tea would be willing to supply 40 cups at a price of $1.80 per cup. So, the marginal cost of the 40th cup is $1.80. The supply curve, then, is also a marginal cost curve.

Marginal cost The additional cost to a firm of producing one more unit of a good or service.

Notice, though, that if the market price of chai tea is $2.00, Heavenly Tea is able to sell the 40th cup for $0.20 more than the lowest price—$1.80—it would have been willing to accept. This $0.20 is the *producer surplus* on that particular cup of tea. **Producer surplus** is the difference between the lowest price a firm would have been willing to accept and the price it actually receives. The supply curve shows us that Heavenly Tea receives some producer surplus on nearly every cup of chai tea supplied. The marginal cost of the 50th cup is $2.00, and Heavenly Tea receives a price of $2.00, so it receives no producer surplus on that cup. The total amount of producer surplus tea sellers receive from selling chai tea can be calculated by adding up the producer surplus received on each cup sold. Therefore, *the total amount of producer surplus in a market is equal to the area above the market supply curve and below the market price.* The total producer surplus tea sellers receive from selling chai tea is shown as the red area in Figure 4-3(b).

Producer surplus The difference between the lowest price a firm would have been willing to accept and the price it actually receives.

What Consumer Surplus and Producer Surplus Measure

We have seen that consumer surplus measures the benefit to consumers from participating in a market, and producer surplus measures the benefit to producers from participating in a market. It is important, however, to be clear what we mean by this. In a sense, consumer surplus is measuring the *net* benefit to consumers from participating in a market, rather than the *total* benefit. That is, if the price of a product were zero, then the consumer surplus in a market would be all of the area under the demand curve. When the price is not zero, consumer surplus is the area below the demand curve and above the market price. So, consumer surplus in a market is equal to the total benefit received by consumers minus the total amount they must pay to buy the good.

Similarly, producer surplus measures the net benefit received by producers from participating in a market. If producers could supply a good at zero cost, the producer surplus in a market would be all of the area below the market price. When cost is not zero, producer surplus is the area below the market price and above the supply curve. So, producer surplus in a market is equal to the total amount firms receive from consumers minus the cost of producing the good.

As we apply the concepts of consumer surplus and producer surplus in this chapter, it is important to remember what they measure.

② LEARNING OBJECTIVE

Understand the concept of economic efficiency, and use a graph to illustrate how economic efficiency is reduced when a market is not in competitive equilibrium.

The Efficiency of Competitive Markets

In Chapter 3, we defined a *competitive market* as a market with many buyers and many sellers. An important advantage of the market system is that it results in efficient economic outcomes. But what do we mean by economic efficiency? The concepts we have developed so far in this chapter give us two ways to think about the economic efficiency of competitive markets. We can think in terms of marginal benefit and marginal cost. We can also think in terms of consumer surplus and producer surplus. As we will see, these two approaches lead to the same outcome, but using both can increase our understanding of economic efficiency.

Marginal Benefit Equals Marginal Cost in Competitive Equilibrium

Figure 4-4 again shows the market for chai tea. Recall that the demand curve shows the marginal benefit received by consumers, and the supply curve shows the marginal cost of production. To achieve economic efficiency in this market, the marginal benefit from the last unit sold should equal the marginal cost of production. The figure shows that this equality occurs at competitive equilibrium where 15,000 cups per week are produced, and marginal benefit and marginal cost are both equal to $2.00. Why is this outcome economically efficient? Because every cup of chai tea has been produced where the marginal benefit to buyers is greater than or equal to the marginal cost to producers.

FIGURE 4-4

Marginal Benefit Equals Marginal Cost Only at Competitive Equilibrium

In a competitive market, equilibrium occurs at a quantity of 15,000 cups and price of $2.00 per cup, where marginal benefit equals marginal cost. This is the economically efficient level of output because every cup has been produced where the marginal benefit to buyers is greater than or equal to the marginal cost to producers.

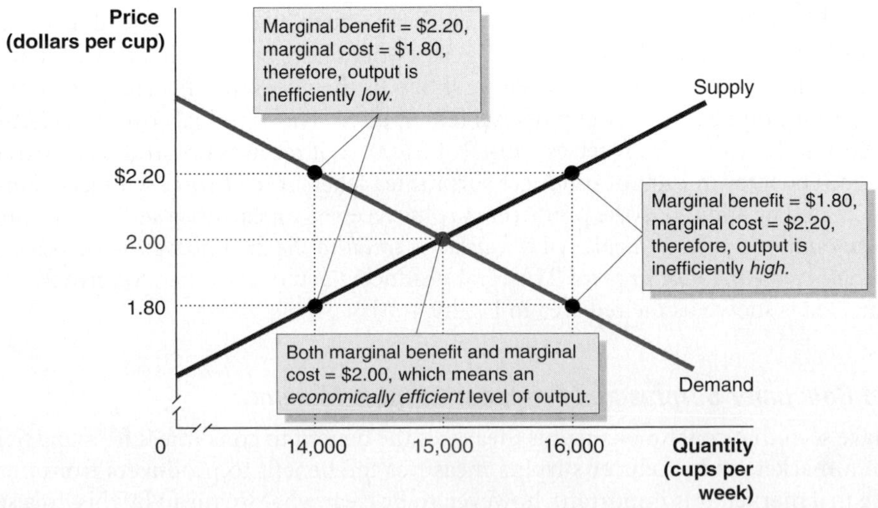

Another way to see why the level of output at competitive equilibrium is efficient is to consider what would be true if output were at a different level. For instance, suppose that output of chai tea were 14,000 cups per week. Figure 4-4 shows that at this level of output, the marginal benefit from the last cup sold is \$2.20, whereas the marginal cost is only \$1.80. This level of output is not efficient because 1,000 more cups could be produced for which the additional benefit to consumers is greater than the additional cost of production. Consumers would willingly purchase those cups, and tea sellers would willingly supply them, making both consumers and sellers better off. Similarly, if the output of chai tea were 16,000 cups per week, the marginal cost of the 16,000th cup is \$2.20, whereas the marginal benefit is only \$1.80. Tea sellers would only be willing to supply this cup at a price of \$2.20, which is \$0.40 higher than consumers would be willing to pay. In fact, consumers would not be willing to pay the price tea sellers would need to receive for any cup beyond the 15,000th.

To summarize, we can say this: *Equilibrium in a competitive market results in the economically efficient level of output, where marginal benefit equals marginal cost.*

Economic Surplus

Economic surplus in a market is the sum of consumer surplus and producer surplus. In a competitive market, with many buyers and sellers and no government restrictions, economic surplus is at a maximum when the market is in equilibrium. To see this, let's look one more time at the market for chai tea, which is shown in Figure 4-5. The consumer surplus in this market is the blue area below the demand curve and above the line indicating the equilibrium price of \$2.00. The producer surplus is the red area above the supply curve and below the price line.

Economic surplus The sum of consumer surplus and producer surplus.

Deadweight Loss

To show that economic surplus is maximized at equilibrium, consider the situation when the price of chai tea is *above* the equilibrium price, as shown in Figure 4-6. At a price of \$2.20 per cup, the number of cups consumers are willing to buy per week drops from 15,000 to 14,000. At competitive equilibrium, consumer surplus is equal to the sum of areas *A*, *B*, and *C*. At a price of \$2.20, fewer cups are sold at a higher price, so consumer surplus declines to just the area of *A*. At competitive equilibrium, producer surplus is equal to the sum of areas *D* and *E*. At the higher price of \$2.20, producer surplus changes to be equal to the sum of areas *B* and *D*. The sum of consumer and producer surplus—economic surplus—has been reduced to the sum of areas *A*, *B*, and *D*. Notice that this is less than the original economic surplus by an amount equal to areas *C* and *E*. Economic surplus has declined because at a price of \$2.20, all the cups between the 14,000th and the 15,000th, which would have been produced in competitive

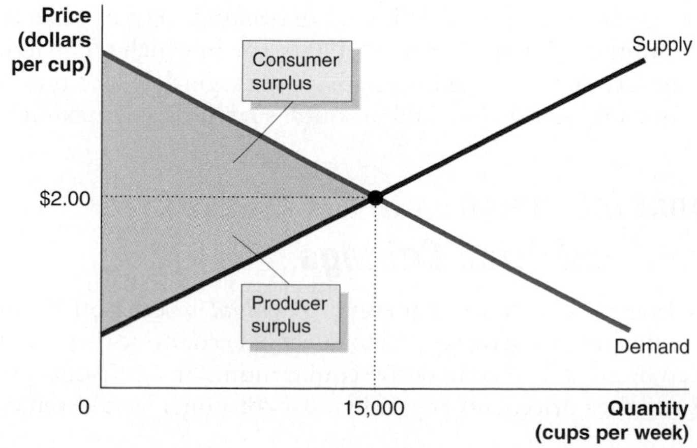

FIGURE 4-5

Economic Surplus Equals the Sum of Consumer Surplus and Producer Surplus

The economic surplus in a market is the sum of the blue area representing consumer surplus and the red area representing producer surplus.

FIGURE 4-6

When a Market Is Not in Equilibrium There Is a Deadweight Loss

Economic surplus is maximized when a market is in competitive equilibrium. When a market is not in equilibrium, there is a deadweight loss. When the price of chai tea is $2.20, instead of $2.00, consumer surplus declines from an amount equal to the sum of areas *A*, *B*, and *C*, to just area *A*. Producer surplus increases from the sum of areas *D* and *E*, to the sum of areas *B* and *D*. At competitive equilibrium, there is no deadweight loss. At a price of $2.20, there is a deadweight loss equal to the sum of areas *C* and *E*.

	At Competitive Equilibrium	At a Price of $2.20
Consumer Surplus	*A + B + C*	*A*
Producer Surplus	*D + E*	*B + D*
Deadweight Loss	None	*C + E*

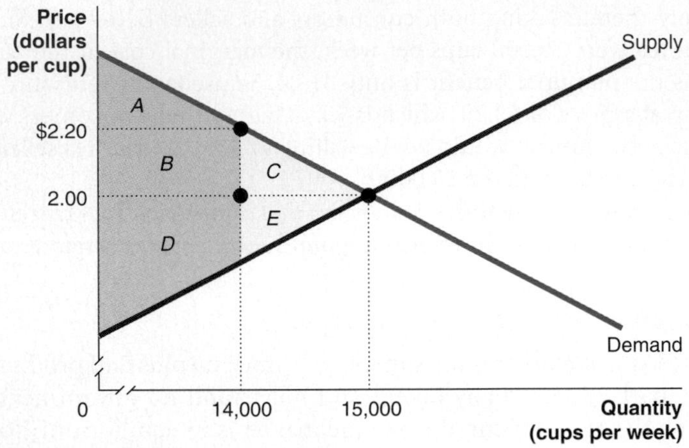

equilibrium, are not being produced. These "missing" cups are not providing any consumer or producer surplus, so economic surplus has declined. The reduction in economic surplus resulting from a market not being in competitive equilibrium is called the **deadweight loss.** In the figure, it is equal to the sum of areas *C* and *E*.

Deadweight loss The reduction in economic surplus resulting from a market not being in competitive equilibrium.

Economic Surplus and Economic Efficiency

Consumer surplus measures the benefit to consumers from buying a particular product, such as chai tea. Producer surplus measures the benefit to firms from selling a particular product. Therefore, economic surplus—which is the sum of the benefit to firms plus the benefit to consumers—is the best measure we have of the benefit to society from the production of a particular good or service. This gives us a second way of characterizing the economic efficiency of a competitive market: *Equilibrium in a competitive market results in the greatest amount of economic surplus, or total net benefit to society, from the production of a good or service.* Anything that causes the market for a good or service not to be in competitive equilibrium reduces the total benefit to society from the production of that good or service.

Now we can give a more general definition of *economic efficiency* in terms of our two approaches: **Economic efficiency** is a market outcome in which the marginal benefit to consumers of the last unit produced is equal to its marginal cost of production, and in which the sum of consumer surplus and producer surplus is at a maximum.

Economic efficiency A market outcome in which the marginal benefit to consumers of the last unit produced is equal to its marginal cost of production, and in which the sum of consumer surplus and producer surplus is at a maximum.

3 LEARNING OBJECTIVE

Use demand and supply graphs to analyze the economic impact of price ceilings and price floors.

Government Intervention in the Market: Price Floors and Price Ceilings

Notice that we have *not* concluded that every *individual* is better off if a market is at its competitive equilibrium. We have only concluded that economic surplus, or the *total* net benefit to society, is greatest at competitive equilibrium. Any individual producer would rather charge a higher price, and any individual consumer would rather pay a lower

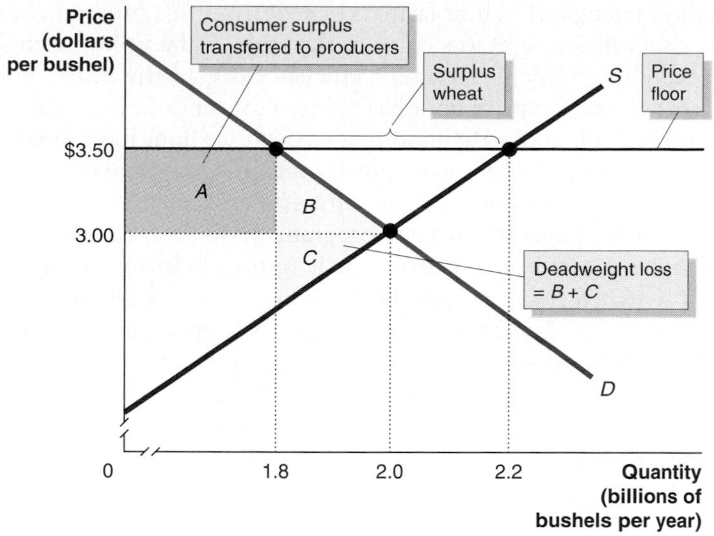

FIGURE 4-7

The Economic Effect of a Price Floor in the Wheat Market

If wheat farmers convince the government to impose a price floor of $3.50 per bushel, the amount of wheat sold will fall from 2.0 billion bushels per year to 1.8 billion. If we assume that farmers produce 1.8 billion bushels, producer surplus then increases by the red rectangle *A*—which is transferred from consumer surplus—and falls by the yellow triangle *C*. Consumer surplus declines by the red rectangle *A* plus the yellow triangle *B*. There is a deadweight loss equal to the yellow triangles *B* and *C*, representing the decline in economic efficiency due to the price floor. In reality, a price floor of $3.50 per bushel will cause farmers to expand their production from 2.0 billion to 2.2 billion bushels, resulting in a surplus of wheat.

price, but usually producers can sell and consumers can buy only at the competitive equilibrium price.

Producers or consumers who are dissatisfied with the competitive equilibrium price can lobby the government to legally require that a different price be charged. The U.S. government only occasionally overrides the market outcome by setting prices. When the government does intervene, it can either attempt to aid sellers by requiring that a price be above equilibrium—a price floor—or to aid buyers by requiring that a price be below equilibrium—a price ceiling. To affect the market outcome, a price floor must be set above the equilibrium price, and a price ceiling must be set below the equilibrium price. Otherwise, the price ceiling or price floor will not be *binding* on buyers and sellers. The preceding section demonstrates that moving away from competitive equilibrium will reduce economic efficiency. We can use the concepts of producer and consumer surplus and deadweight loss to see more clearly the economic inefficiency of binding price floors and price ceilings.

Price Floors: The Example of Agricultural Markets

The Great Depression of the 1930s was the greatest economic disaster in U.S. history, affecting every sector of the U.S. economy. Many farmers were unable to sell their products or could sell them only at very low prices. Farmers were able to convince the federal government to intervene to raise prices by setting price floors for many agricultural products. Government intervention in agriculture—often referred to as the "farm program"—has continued ever since. To see how a price floor in an agricultural market works, suppose that the equilibrium price in the wheat market is $3.00 per bushel but the government decides to set a price floor of $3.50 per bushel. As Figure 4-7 shows, the price of wheat rises from $3.00 to $3.50 and the quantity of wheat sold falls from 2.0 billion bushels per year to 1.8 billion. Suppose, initially, that production of wheat also falls to 1.8 billion bushels.

Just as we saw in the earlier example of the market for chai tea (see Figure 4-6), the producer surplus received by wheat farmers increases by an amount equal to the area of the red rectangle *A* and falls by an amount equal to the area of the yellow triangle *C*. The area of the red rectangle *A* represents a transfer from consumer surplus to producer surplus. The total fall in consumer surplus is equal to the area of the red rectangle *A* plus the area of the yellow triangle *B*. Wheat farmers benefit from this program, but consumers lose. There is also a deadweight loss equal to the areas of the yellow triangles *B* and *C*, which represents the decline in economic efficiency due to the price floor. There is a deadweight loss because the price floor has reduced the amount of economic surplus in the market for wheat. Or, looked at another way, the price floor has caused the marginal benefit of the last bushel of wheat to be greater than the marginal cost of producing it. We can conclude that a price floor reduces economic efficiency.

The actual federal government farm programs have been more complicated than just legally requiring farmers not to sell their output below a minimum price. We assumed initially that farmers reduce their production of wheat to the amount consumers are willing to buy. In fact, as Figure 4-7 shows, a price floor will cause the quantity of wheat that farmers want to supply to increase from 2.0 billion to 2.2 billion bushels. Because the higher price also reduces the amount of wheat consumers wish to buy, the result is a surplus of 0.4 billion bushels of wheat (the 2.2 billion bushels supplied minus the 1.8 billion demanded).

The federal government's farm programs often have resulted in large surpluses of wheat and other agricultural products. The government has usually either bought the surplus food or paid farmers to restrict supply by taking some land out of cultivation. Because both of these options are expensive, Congress passed the Freedom to Farm Act of 1996. The intent of the act was to phase out price floors and government purchases of surpluses and return to a free market in agriculture. To allow farmers time to adjust, the federal government began paying farmers *subsidies*, or cash payments based on the number of acres planted. Although the subsidies were originally scheduled to be phased out, Congress has continued to pay them.

4-2 Making the Connection

Price Floors in Labor Markets: The Minimum Wage

The minimum wage may be the most controversial "price floor." Supporters see the minimum wage as a way of raising the incomes of low-skilled workers. Opponents argue that it results in fewer jobs and imposes large costs on small businesses.

Congress has set a national minimum wage of $5.15 per hour for most occupations. It is illegal for an employer to pay less than this wage in those occupations. For most workers, the minimum wage is irrelevant because it is well below the wage employers are voluntarily willing to pay them. But for low-skilled workers—such as workers in fast-food restaurants—the minimum wage is above the wage they would otherwise receive. The figure shows the effect of the minimum wage on employment in the market for low-skilled labor.

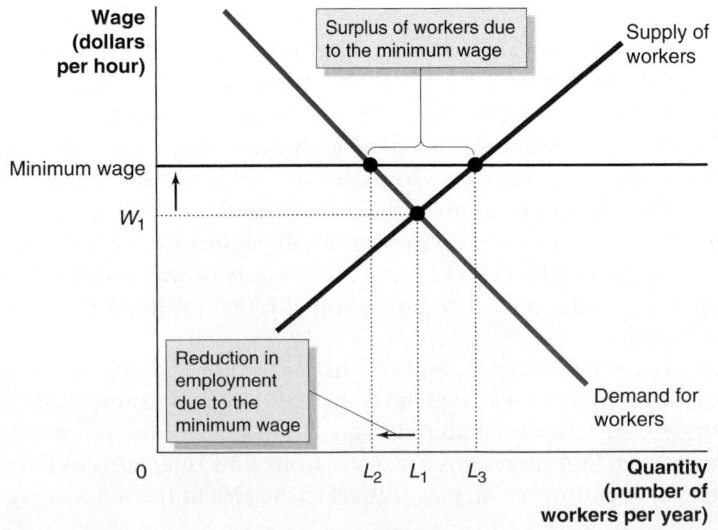

Without a minimum wage, the equilibrium wage would be W_1, and the number of workers hired would be L_1. With a minimum wage set above the equilibrium wage, the quantity of workers demanded by employers declines from L_1 to L_2 and the quantity of labor supplied increases to L_3 leading to a surplus of workers unable to find jobs equal to $L_3 - L_2$. The quantity of labor supplied increases because the higher wage attracts more people to work. For instance, some teenagers may decide that working after school is worthwhile at the minimum wage of $5.15 per hour, but would not have been worthwhile at a lower wage.

This analysis is very similar to our analysis of the wheat market in Figure 4-7. Just as a price floor in the wheat market leads to less wheat consumed, a price floor in the labor market should lead to fewer workers hired. Views differ sharply among economists, however, concerning how large a reduction in employment the minimum wage causes. For instance, David Card of the University of California, Berkeley and Alan Krueger of Princeton University conducted a study of fast-food restaurants in New Jersey and Pennsylvania that indicates the effect of minimum wage increases on employment is very small. Card and Krueger's study has been very controversial, however. Other economists have examined similar data and have come to the different conclusion that the minimum wage does lead to a significant decrease in employment.

Whatever the extent of employment losses from the minimum wage, because it is a price floor, it will cause a deadweight loss, just as a price floor in the wheat market does. Therefore, many economists favor alternative policies for attaining the goal of raising the incomes of low-skilled workers. One policy many economists support is the *earned income tax credit.* The earned income tax credit reduces the amount of tax that low-income wage earners would otherwise pay to the federal government. Workers with very low incomes who do not owe any tax receive a payment from the government. Compared with the minimum wage, the earned income tax credit can increase the incomes of low-skilled workers without reducing employment. The earned income tax credit also places a lesser burden on the small businesses that employ many low-skilled workers, and it might cause a smaller loss of economic efficiency.

Sources: David Card and Alan B. Krueger, *Myth and Measurement: The New Economics of the Minimum Wage*, Princeton, NJ: Princeton University Press, 1995; David Neumark and William Wascher, "Minimum Wages and Employment: A Case Study of the Fast-Food Industry in New Jersey and Pennsylvania: Comment," *American Economic Review*, Vol. 90, No. 5, December 2000, pp. 1,362–1,396; and David Card and Alan B. Krueger, "Minimum Wages and Employment: A Case Study of the Fast-Food Industry in New Jersey and Pennsylvania: Reply," *American Economic Review*, Vol. 90, No. 5, December 2000, pp. 1,397–1,420.

Many economists believe there are better policies than the minimum wage for raising the incomes of low-skilled workers.

Price Ceilings: The Example of Rent Controls

Support for governments setting price floors typically comes from sellers, but support for governments setting price ceilings typically comes from consumers. For example, when there is a sharp increase in gasoline prices, there will often be proposals for the government to impose a price ceiling on the market for gasoline. As we saw in the opening to this chapter, New York is one of the cities that imposes rent controls, which put a ceiling on the maximum rent that landlords can charge for an apartment. Figure 4-8 shows the market for apartments in a city that has rent controls.

Without rent control, the equilibrium rent would be $1,500 per month and 2,000,000 apartments would be rented. With a maximum legal rent of $1,000 per month, landlords reduce the quantity of apartments supplied to 1,900,000. The fall in the quantity of apartments supplied is the result of some apartments being converted to offices or sold off as condominiums, some small apartment buildings being converted to single-family homes, and, over time, some apartment buildings being abandoned. In New York City, rent control has resulted in whole city blocks being abandoned by landlords who were unable to cover their costs with the rents they were allowed to charge. In London, when rent controls were applied to rooms and apartments located in a landlord's own home, the quantity of these apartments supplied dropped by 75 percent.

FIGURE 4-8

The Economic Effect of a Rent Ceiling

Without rent control, the equilibrium rent is \$1,500 per month. At that price, 2,000,000 apartments would be rented. If the government imposes a rent ceiling of \$1,000, the quantity of apartments supplied falls to 1,900,000, while the quantity of apartments demanded increases to 2,100,000, resulting in a shortage of 200,000 apartments. Producer surplus equal to the area of the blue rectangle *A* is transferred from landlords to renters, and there is a deadweight loss equal to the areas of yellow triangles *B* and *C*.

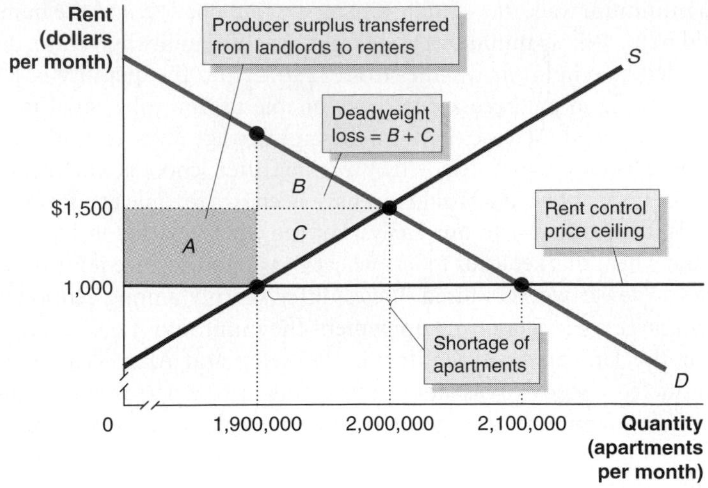

In Figure 4-8, with the rent ceiling of \$1,000, the quantity of apartments demanded rises to 2,100,000. There is a shortage of 200,000 apartments. Consumer surplus increases by rectangle *A* and falls by triangle *B*. Rectangle *A* would have been part of producer surplus if rent control were not in place. With rent control, it is part of consumer surplus. Rent control causes the producer surplus received by landlords to fall by rectangle *A* plus triangle *C*. Triangles *B* and *C* represent the deadweight loss. There is a deadweight loss because rent control has reduced the amount of economic surplus in the market for apartments. Rent control has caused the marginal benefit of the last apartment rented to be greater than the marginal cost of supplying it. We can conclude that a price ceiling, such as rent control, reduces economic efficiency. The Appendix to this chapter shows how we can make quantitative estimates of the deadweight loss, and the changes in consumer surplus and producer surplus that result from rent control.

Renters as a group benefit from rent controls—total consumer surplus is larger—but landlords lose. Because of the deadweight loss, the total loss to landlords is greater than the gain to renters. Notice also that although renters as a group benefit, the number of renters is reduced, so some renters are made worse off by rent controls because they are unable to find an apartment at the legal rent.

Don't Let This Happen To You!

Don't Confuse "Scarcity" with a "Shortage"

At first glance, the following statement seems correct: "There is a shortage of every good that is scarce." In everyday conversation, we describe a good as "scarce" if we have trouble finding it. For instance, if you are looking for a present for a child, you might call the latest hot toy "scarce" if you are willing to buy it at its listed price but can't find it online or in any store. But recall from Chapter 2 that economists have a broad definition of *scarce*. In the economic sense, almost everything—except undesirable things like garbage—is scarce. A shortage of a good occurs only if the quantity demanded is greater than the quantity supplied at the current price. Therefore, the preceding statement—"There is a shortage of every good that is scarce"—is incorrect. In fact, there is no shortage of most scarce goods.

YOUR TURN: **Test your understanding by doing related problem 10 on page 123 at the end of this chapter.**

Black Markets

To this point, our analysis of rent controls is incomplete. In practice, renters may be worse off and landlords may be better off than Figure 4-8 makes it seem. We have assumed that renters and landlords actually abide by the price ceiling, but sometimes they don't. Because rent control leads to a shortage of apartments, renters who would otherwise not be able to find apartments have an incentive to offer landlords rents above the legal maximum. When governments try to control prices by setting price ceilings or price floors, buyers and sellers often find a way around the controls. The result is a **black market** where buying and selling take place at prices that violate government price regulations.

Black market Buying and selling at prices that violate government price regulations.

In a housing market with rent controls, the total amount of consumer surplus received by renters may be reduced and the total amount of producer surplus received by landlords may be increased if apartments are being rented at prices above the legal price ceiling.

SOLVED PROBLEM 4-1

What's the Economic Effect of a "Black Market" for Apartments?

③ LEARNING OBJECTIVE
Use demand and supply graphs to analyze the economic impact of price ceilings and price floors.

In many cities with rent controls, the actual rents paid can be much higher than the legal maximum. Because rent controls cause a shortage of apartments, desperate tenants will often be willing to pay landlords rents that are higher than the law allows, perhaps by writing a check for the legally allowed rent and paying an additional amount in cash. Look again at Figure 4-8. Suppose that competition among tenants results in the black market rent rising to $2,000 per month. At this rent, tenants demand 1,900,000 apartments. Use a graph showing the market for apartments to compare this situation with the one shown in Figure 4-8. Be sure to note any differences in consumer surplus, producer surplus, and deadweight loss.

Solving the Problem:

Step 1: Review the chapter material. This problem is about price controls in the market for apartments, so you may want to review the section "Price Ceilings: The Example of Rent Controls," which begins on page 107.

Step 2: Draw a graph similar to Figure 4-8, with the addition of the black market price.

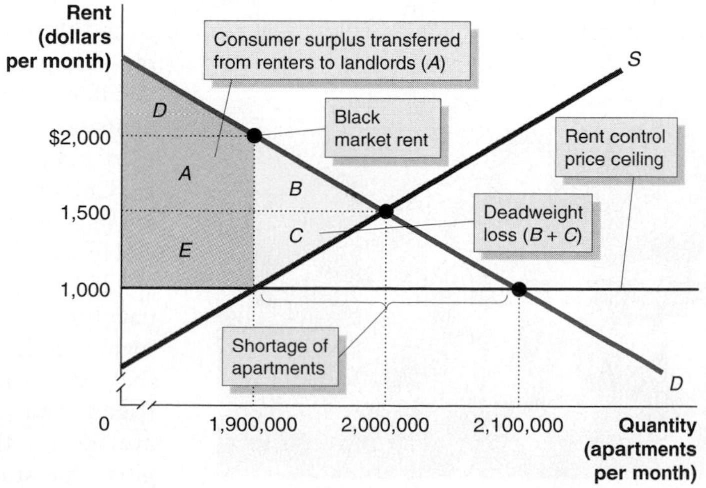

Step 3: Analyze the changes from Figure 4-8. Because the black market rent is now \$2,000—even higher than the original competitive equilibrium rent of \$1,500—compared with Figure 4-8 consumer surplus declines by an amount equal to the red rectangle *A* plus the red rectangle *E*. The remaining consumer surplus is the blue triangle *D*. Note that the rectangle *A*, which would have been part of consumer surplus without rent control, represents a transfer from renters to landlords. Compared with the situation shown in Figure 4-8, producer surplus has increased by an amount equal to rectangles *A* and *E*, and consumer surplus has declined by the same amount. Deadweight loss is equal to triangles *B* and *C*, the same as in Figure 4-8.

Extra Credit: This analysis leads to a surprising result: With an active black market in apartments, rent control may leave renters as a group worse off—with less consumer surplus—than if there were no rent control. There is one more possibility to consider, however. If enough landlords become convinced that they can get away with charging rents above the legal ceiling, the quantity of apartments supplied will increase. Eventually, the market could even end up at the competitive equilibrium with an equilibrium rent of \$1,500 and equilibrium quantity of 2,000,000 apartments. In that case the rent control price ceiling becomes nonbinding, not because it was set below the equilibrium price, but because it was not legally enforced.

YOUR TURN: **For more practice, do related problem 8 on page 122 and problem 16 on page 123 at the end of this chapter.**

Rent controls can also lead to an increase in racial and other types of discrimination. With rent controls, more renters will be looking for apartments than there are apartments to rent. Landlords can afford to indulge their prejudices by refusing to rent to people they don't like. In cities without rent controls, landlords face more competition, which makes it more difficult to turn down tenants on the basis of irrelevant characteristics, such as race.

4-3 Making the Connection

Does Holiday Gift Giving Have a Deadweight Loss?

The deadweight loss that results from rent control occurs, in part, because consumers rent fewer apartments than they would in a competitive equilibrium. Their choices are *constrained* by government. When someone receives a gift, she is also constrained because the person who gave the gift has already chosen the product. In many cases, the recipient would have chosen a different gift for herself. Economist Joel Waldfogel of the University of Pennsylvania points out that gift giving results in a deadweight loss. The amount of the deadweight loss is equal to the difference between the gift's price and the dollar value the recipient places on the gift. Waldfogel surveyed his students, asking them to list every gift they had received for Christmas, to estimate the retail price of each gift, and to state how much they would have been willing to pay for each gift. Waldfogel's students estimated that their families and friends had paid \$438 on average on the students' gifts. The students themselves, however, would have

Caution: Gift giving may lead to deadweight loss.

been willing to pay only $313 to buy the presents. If the deadweight losses experienced by Waldfogel's students were extrapolated to the whole population, the deadweight loss of Christmas gift giving could be as much as $13 billion.

If the gifts had been cash, the people receiving the gifts would not have been constrained by the gift givers' choices, and there would have been no deadweight loss. If your sister had given you cash instead of that sweater you didn't like, you could have bought whatever you wanted. Why then do people continue giving presents rather than cash? One answer is that most people receive more satisfaction from giving a present than from giving cash. If we take this satisfaction into account, the deadweight loss from gift giving will be lower than in Waldfogel's calculations.

Source: Joel Waldfogel, "The Deadweight Loss of Christmas," *American Economic Review*, Vol. 83, No. 4, December 1993, pp. 328–336.

The Results of Government Intervention: Winners, Losers, and Inefficiency

When the government imposes price floors or price ceilings, three important results occur:

- Some people win.
- Some people lose.
- There is a loss of economic efficiency.

The winners with rent control are the people who are paying less for rent because they live in rent-controlled apartments. Landlords may also gain if they break the law by charging rents above the legal maximum for their rent-controlled apartments, provided these illegal rents are higher than the competitive equilibrium rents would have been. The losers from rent control are the landlords of rent-controlled apartments who abide by the law, and renters who are unable to find apartments to rent at the controlled price. Rent control reduces economic efficiency because fewer apartments are rented than would be in a competitive market (refer again to Figure 4-8). The resulting deadweight loss measures the decrease in economic efficiency.

Positive and Normative Analysis of Price Ceilings and Price Floors

Are rent controls, government farm programs, and other price ceilings and price floors bad? As we saw in Chapter 1, questions of this type have no right or wrong answers. Economists are generally skeptical of government attempts to interfere with competitive market equilibrium. Economists know the role competitive markets have played in raising the average person's standard of living. They also know that too much government intervention has the potential to reduce the ability of the market system to produce similar increases in living standards in the future.

But recall from Chapter 1 the difference between positive and normative analysis. Positive analysis is concerned with *what is*, and normative analysis is concerned with *what should be*. Our analysis of rent control and of the federal farm programs in this chapter is positive analysis. We discussed what the economic results of these programs are. Whether these programs are desirable or undesirable is a normative question. Whether the gains to the winners more than make up for the losses to the losers and for the decline in economic efficiency is a matter of judgment and not strictly an economic question. Price ceilings and price floors continue to exist partly because they are supported by people who understand their downside but still believe they are good policies. They also persist because many people do not understand their downside, because they are unfamiliar with the economic analysis we have used in this chapter.

4 LEARNING OBJECTIVE
Use demand and supply graphs to analyze the economic impact of taxes.

The Economic Impact of Taxes

Supreme Court Justice Oliver Wendell Holmes once remarked that: "Taxes are what we pay for a civilized society." When the government taxes a good, however, it affects the market equilibrium for that good. Just as with a price ceiling or price floor, one result of a tax is a decline in economic efficiency. Analyzing taxes is an important part of the field of economics known as *public finance.* In this section, we will use the model of demand and supply, and the concepts of consumer surplus, producer surplus, and deadweight loss to analyze the economic impact of taxes.

The Effect of Taxes on Economic Efficiency

Whenever a government taxes a good or service, less of that good or service will be produced. For example, a tax on cigarettes will raise the cost of smoking and reduce the quantity of smoking that takes place. We can use a demand and supply graph to illustrate this point. Figure 4-9 shows the market for cigarettes.

Without the tax, the equilibrium price of cigarettes would be \$2.00 per pack and 4 billion packs of cigarettes would be sold per year (point *A*). If the federal government requires sellers of cigarettes to pay a \$1.00 per pack tax, then their cost of selling cigarettes will increase by \$1.00 per pack. This causes the supply curve for cigarettes to shift up by \$1.00 because sellers will now require a price that is \$1 greater to supply the same quantity of cigarettes. In Figure 4-9, for example, without the tax, sellers would be willing to supply a quantity of 3.7 billion packs of cigarettes at a price of \$1.90 per pack (point *C*). With the tax, they will supply only 3.7 billion packs of cigarettes if the price is \$2.90 per pack (point *B*). The shift in the supply curve will result in a new equilibrium price of \$2.90 and a new equilibrium quantity of 3.7 billion packs (point *B*).

The federal government will collect tax revenue equal to the tax per pack multiplied by the number of packs sold, or \$3.7 billion. The area shaded in green in Figure 4-9 represents the government's tax revenue. Consumers will pay a higher price of \$2.90 per pack. Although sellers appear to be receiving a higher price per pack, after they have paid the tax, the price they receive falls from \$2.00 per pack to \$1.90 per pack. There is a loss of consumer surplus because consumers are paying a higher price. The price producers receive falls, so there is also a loss of producer surplus. Therefore, the tax on cigarettes has reduced *both* consumer surplus and producer surplus. Some of the reduction in consumer and producer surplus becomes tax revenue for the government. The rest of the reduction in consumer and producer surplus is equal to the deadweight loss from the tax, shown by the yellow-shaded triangle in the figure.

We can conclude that the true burden of a tax is not just the amount paid to government by consumers and producers, but also includes the deadweight loss. The deadweight loss from a tax is referred to as the *excess burden* of the tax. *A tax is efficient if it imposes a small excess burden relative to the tax revenue it raises.* One contribution economists make to government tax policy is to provide advice to policymakers on which taxes are most efficient.

Tax Incidence: Who Actually Pays a Tax?

Tax incidence The actual division of the burden of a tax between buyers and sellers in a market.

The answer to the question "Who pays a tax?" seems obvious: Whoever is legally required to send a tax payment to the government pays the tax. But there can be an important difference between who is legally required to pay the tax and who actually *bears the burden* of the tax. The actual division of the burden of a tax is referred to as **tax incidence.** The federal government currently levies an excise tax of 18.4 cents per

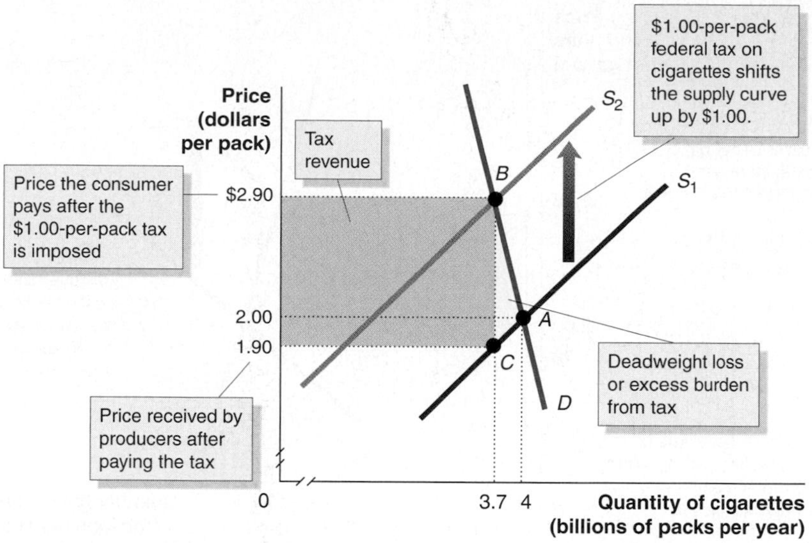

FIGURE 4-9 The Effect of a Tax on the Market for Cigarettes

Without the tax, market equilibrium occurs at point *A*. The equilibrium price of cigarettes is $2.00 per pack and 4 billion packs of cigarettes are sold per year. A $1.00-per-pack tax on cigarettes will cause the supply curve for cigarettes to shift up by $1 from S_1 to S_2. The new equilibrium occurs at point *B*. The price of cigarettes will increase by $0.90 to $2.90 per pack, and the quantity sold will fall to 3.7 billion packs. The tax on cigarettes has increased the price paid by consumers from $2.00 to $2.90 per pack. Producers receive a price of $2.90 per pack (point *B*), but after paying the $1.00 tax they are left with $1.90 (point *C*). The government will receive tax revenue equal to the green shaded box. Some consumer surplus and some producer surplus will become tax revenue for the government and some will become deadweight loss, shown by the yellow-shaded area.

gallon of gasoline sold. This tax is collected by gas station owners and forwarded to the federal government, but who actually bears the burden of the tax?

DETERMINING TAX INCIDENCE ON A DEMAND AND SUPPLY GRAPH Suppose that the retail price of gasoline—including the federal excise tax—is $2.08 per gallon, 140 billion gallons of gasoline are sold in the United States per year, and the federal excise tax is 10 cents per gallon. Figure 4-10 allows us to analyze the incidence of the tax.

First, consider the market for gasoline if there were no federal excise tax on gasoline. This equilibrium occurs at the intersection of the demand curve and supply curve S_1. The equilibrium price is $2.00 per gallon and the equilibrium quantity is 144 billion gallons. If the federal government imposes a 10-cents-per-gallon tax, the supply curve for gasoline will shift up by 10 cents per gallon. At the new equilibrium, where the demand curve intersects the supply curve S_2, the price has risen by 8 cents per gallon from $2.00 to $2.08. Notice that only in the extremely unlikely case that demand is a vertical line will the market price rise by the full amount of the tax. Consumers are paying 8 cents more per gallon. Sellers of gasoline receive a new higher price of $2.08 per gallon, but after paying the 10-cents-per-gallon tax, they are left with $1.98 per gallon, or 2 cents less than they had been receiving in the old equilibrium.

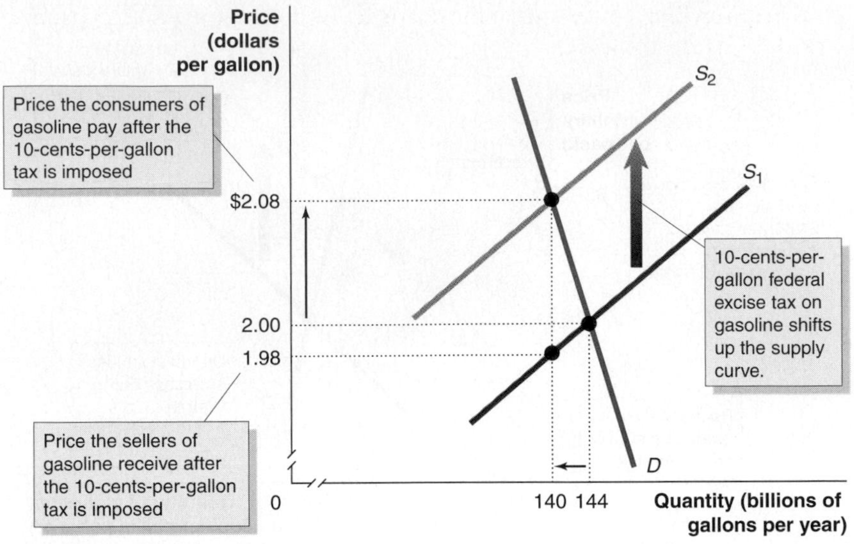

FIGURE 4-10 The Incidence of a Tax on Gasoline

With no tax on gasoline, the price would be $2.00 per gallon and 144 billion gallons of gasoline would be sold each year. A 10-cents-per-gallon excise tax shifts up the supply curve from S_1 to S_2, raises the price consumers pay from $2.00 to $2.08, and lowers the price producers receive from $2.00 to $1.98. Therefore, consumers pay 8 cents of the 10-cents-per-gallon tax on gasoline and producers pay 2 cents.

Although the sellers of gasoline are responsible for collecting the tax and sending the tax receipts to the government, they do not bear most of the burden of the tax. In this case, consumers pay 8 cents of the tax, because the market price has risen by 8 cents, and sellers pay 2 cents of the tax, because after sending the tax to the government, they are receiving 2 cents less per gallon of gasoline sold. Expressed in percentage terms, consumers pay 80 percent of the tax and sellers pay 20 percent of the tax.

SOLVED PROBLEM 4-2

(4) **LEARNING OBJECTIVE**

Use demand and supply graphs to analyze the economic impact of taxes.

When Do Consumers Pay All of a Sales Tax Increase?

Briefly explain whether you agree with the following statement: "If the federal government raises the sales tax on gasoline by $0.25, then the price of gasoline will rise by $0.25. Consumers can't get by without gasoline, so they have to pay the whole amount of any increase in the sales tax." Illustrate your answer with a graph.

Solving the Problem:

Step 1: Review the chapter material. This problem is about tax incidence, so you may want to review the section "Tax Incidence: Who Actually Pays a Tax?", which begins on page 112.

Step 2: Draw a graph like Figure 4-10 to illustrate the circumstances when consumers will pay all of an increase in a sales tax.

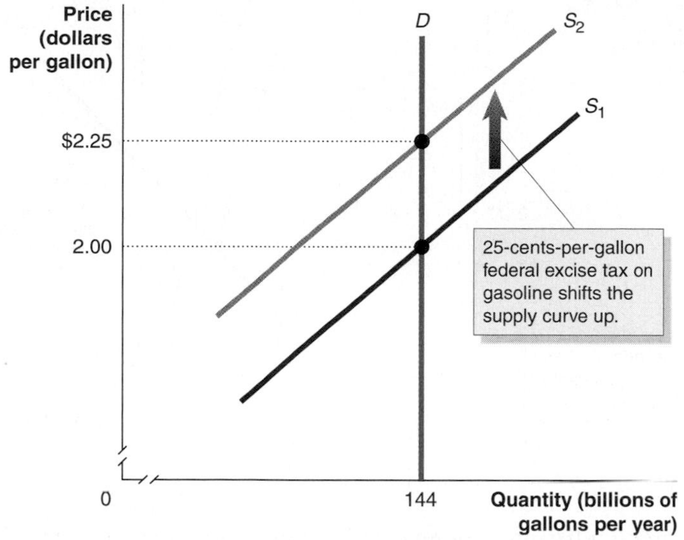

Step 3: Use the graph to evaluate the statement. The graph shows that consumers will pay all of an increase in a sales tax only if the demand curve is a vertical line. It is very unlikely that the demand for gasoline looks like this, because we expect that for every good an increase in price will cause a decrease in the quantity demanded. Because the demand curve for gasoline is not a vertical line, the statement is incorrect.

YOUR TURN: **For more practice do related problem 21 on page 124 at the end of the chapter.**

DOES IT MATTER WHETHER THE TAX IS ON BUYERS OR SELLERS? We have already seen the important distinction between the true burden of a tax and whether buyers or sellers are required legally to pay a tax. We can reinforce this point by noting explicitly that the incidence of a tax does *not* depend on whether a tax is collected from the buyers of a good or from the sellers. Figure 4-11 illustrates this point by showing the effect on equilibrium in the market for gasoline if a 10-cents-per-gallon tax is imposed on buyers, rather than on sellers. That is, we are now assuming that instead of sellers having to collect the 10-cents-per-gallon tax at the pump, buyers are responsible for keeping track of how many gallons of gasoline they purchase, and sending the tax to the government. (Of course, it would be very difficult for buyers to keep track of their purchases, or for the government to check whether they were paying all of the tax they owed. That is why the government collects the tax on gasoline from sellers.)

Figure 4-11 is similar to Figure 4-10, except that it shows the gasoline tax being imposed on buyers rather than sellers. In Figure 4-11, the supply curve does not shift because nothing has happened to change the willingness of sellers to change the quantity of gasoline they supply. The demand curve, however, has shifted because consumers now have to pay a 10 cent tax on every gallon of gasoline they buy. Therefore, at every quantity they are willing to pay a price 10 cents less than they would have without the tax. We indicate this in the figure by shifting the demand curve down by 10 cents from D_1 to D_2. Once the tax has been imposed and the demand curve has shifted down, the

FIGURE 4-11

The Incidence of a Tax on Gasoline Paid by Buyers

With no tax on gasoline, the demand curve is D_1. If a 10-cents-per-gallon tax is imposed that consumers are responsible for paying, the demand curve shifts down by the amount of the tax from D_1 to D_2. In the new equilibrium, consumers pay a price of \$2.08 per gallon, including the tax. Producers receive \$1.98 per gallon. This is the same result we saw when producers were responsible for paying the tax.

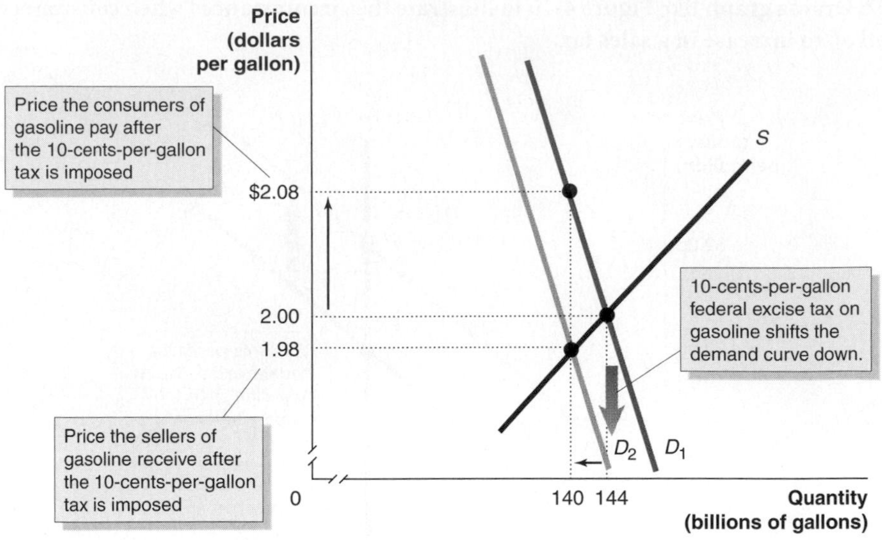

new equilibrium quantity of gasoline is 140 billion gallons, which is exactly the same as in Figure 4-10.

The new equilibrium price after the tax is imposed appears to be different in Figure 4-11 than it was in Figure 4-10, but if we include the tax, then buyers will pay and sellers will receive the same price in both figures. To see this, notice that in Figure 4-10 buyers paid sellers a price of \$2.08 per gallon. In Figure 4-11 they pay sellers only \$1.98, but they must also pay the government a tax of 10 cents per gallon. So, the total price buyers pay remains \$2.08 per gallon. In Figure 4-10, sellers receive \$2.08 per gallon from buyers, but after they pay the tax of 10 cents per gallon, they are left with \$1.98, which is the same amount they receive in Figure 4-11.

4-4 Making the Connection

How much FICA do you think this employee pays?

Is the Burden of the Social Security Tax Really Shared Equally between Workers and Firms?

Everyone who receives a paycheck has several different taxes withheld from it by their employers, who forward these taxes directly to the government. In fact, many people are shocked after getting their first job when they discover the gap between their gross pay and their net pay after taxes have been deducted. The largest tax many people of low or moderate income pay is the FICA, which stands for the Federal Insurance Contributions Act. The FICA funds the Social Security and Medicare programs, which provide income and health care to the elderly and disabled. The FICA is sometimes referred to as the payroll tax. When Congress passed the FICA, it wanted the burden of the tax to be shared equally by employers and workers. Currently, the FICA is 15.3 percent of wages, with 7.65 percent paid by workers by being withheld from their paychecks and the other 7.65 percent paid by employers.

But does requiring workers and employers to each pay half the tax mean that the burden of the tax is also shared equally? Our discussion in this chapter shows us that the answer is "No." In the labor market, employers are buyers and workers are sellers. As we saw in the example of federal taxes on gasoline, whether the tax is collected from buyers or from sellers does not affect the incidence of the tax. Most economists believe, in fact, that the burden of FICA falls almost entirely on workers. The figure on the next page, which shows the market for labor, illustrates why.

In the market for labor, the demand curve reflects the quantity of labor demanded by employers at various wages, and the supply curve reflects the quantity of labor supplied by workers at various wages. The intersection of the demand curve and the supply curve determines the equilibrium wage. In both panels the equilibrium wage without a Social Security

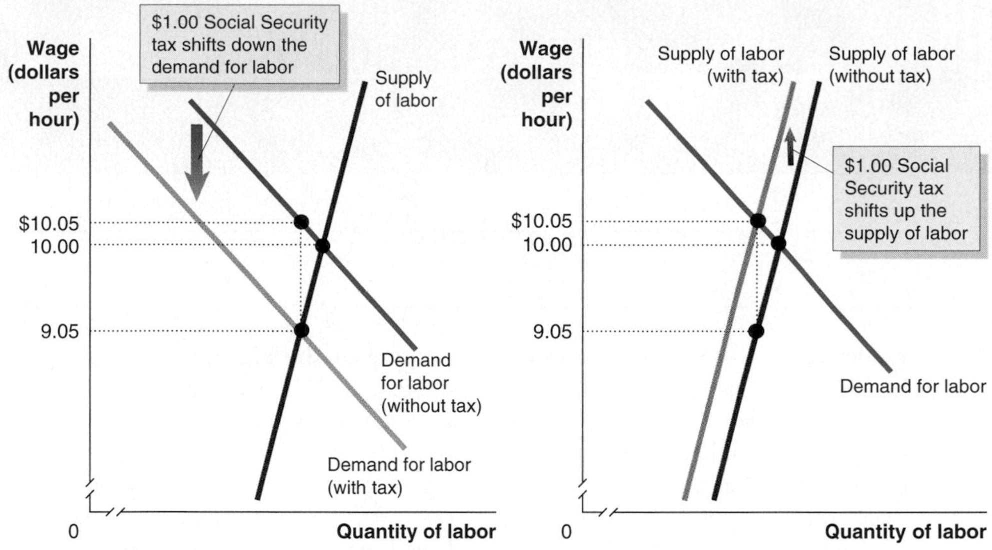

(a) The Social Security tax paid by employers **(b) The Social Security tax paid by workers**

payroll tax is $10 per hour. For simplicity, let's assume that the payroll tax equals $1 per hour of work. In panel (a) we assume that the tax must be paid by employers. Imposing the tax causes the demand for labor curve to shift down by $1 at every quantity of labor, because firms now must pay a $1 tax for every hour of labor they hire. We have drawn the supply curve for labor as being very steep to reflect the fact that most economists believe the quantity of labor supplied by workers does not change much as the wage rate changes. In panel (a), after the tax is imposed, the equilibrium wage declines from $10 per hour to $9.05 per hour. Firms are now paying a total of $10.05 for every hour of work they hire: $9.05 in wages to workers and $1 in tax to the government. In other words, workers have paid $0.95 of the $1 tax, and firms have paid only $0.05.

Panel (b) shows that this result is exactly the same if the tax is imposed on workers, rather than on firms. In this case, the tax causes the supply curve for labor to shift up by $1 at every quantity of labor, because workers must now pay a tax of $1 for every hour they work. After the tax is imposed, the equilibrium wage increases to $10.05 per hour. But workers receive only $9.05 after they have paid the $1.00 tax. Once again, workers have paid $0.95 of the $1 tax, and firms have paid only $0.05.

Although the figure presents a simplified analysis, it does reflect the conclusion of most economists who have studied the incidence of FICA: Even though Congress requires half the tax to be paid by employers and the other half to be paid by workers, in fact the burden of the tax falls almost entirely on workers. The forces of demand and supply working in the labor market, and not Congress, determine the incidence of the tax.

Conclusion

The model of demand and supply introduced in Chapter 3 showed that markets free from government intervention eliminate surpluses and shortages, and do a good job of responding to the wants of consumers. We have seen in this chapter that both consumers and firms sometimes try to use the government to change market outcomes in their favor. The concepts of consumer and producer surplus and deadweight loss allow us to measure the benefits consumers and producers receive from competitive market equilibrium. They also allow us to measure the effects of government price floors and price ceilings and the economic impact of taxes.

Read *An Inside Look* on the next page to learn how rent control affects people looking for apartments in New York City.

An Inside Look

Dealing with Rent Control

SLATE, MAY 18, 1997

The Romance of Rent Control

If you want to understand the bitter debate over rent control that now dominates social interaction in New York, you have to begin by ignoring arguments about social justice, market economics, and all appeals to principle. Instead, apply crude Marxist dogma: It's a battle of naked class interest. The catch is that the "classes" glowering at each other across the barricades aren't rich and poor. They're the New Yorkers with scandalously sweet deals vs. all those who get screwed as a result.

Recent experience has done much to reinforce my own class consciousness as a member of the latter group. **a** My wife and I were minding our own business in an unregulated apartment in the rapidly gentrifying East Village when we returned from work one day to a letter informing us that our already (to non-New Yorkers) alarming rent of $1,950 was going up $700. That's for a largish one-bedroom in a marginal neighborhood. . . . Thanks to a connection, we fell into a nice, $2,000 one-bedroom in Chelsea, without paying a finder's fee. Absent the artificial shortage created by rent regulation, we would either have a bigger place or pay much less for the one we've got.

The moral and economic arguments against rent control are pretty much unassailable. Under the present system, government intervenes in the market to protect a class of people defined to some extent by long-term residency, but to an even larger extent by luck. This massive intrusion in the real-estate market, which might be hard to justify even if it had purely beneficial consequences, has a number of obviously disastrous ones. It deters young people and new immigrants from moving to New York City; it encourages landlords to neglect their buildings; it makes them hate their tenants. . . .

b What would happen if rent regulations were really abolished? It's a pretty safe bet that in most parts of Manhattan, market rents would settle in somewhere between the $2,000 a month I pay and the $600 that others pay for nearly identical apartments in the same building. Using the estimates promoted by the Rent Stabilization Association (the newspeak name for the group representing landlords who actually wish to *end* rent stabilization), the typical one-bedroom in the Village or on the Upper West Side might go for $1,300 to $1,400 after the shakeout. A rent like that calls for a pretax income of at least $50,000. Once you figure in New York City and state taxes, a more realistic figure would be $60,000.

c The poor, who are subsidized directly, and are likely to be exempted even in the case of radical decontrol, would stay put. What Manhattan would lose is what remains of its middle class, those earning between $25,000 and, say, $75,000. This would mean a tremendous blow to the city's social variety and cultural vitality. Gone would be the used-bookstore owner, the public-school teacher, the family that's been in the same Upper West Side building for 100 years.

One of the big points made by opponents of rent control is that the present system prevents the construction of new buildings. Because rent regulations say you can't evict people when their leases are up (if they even have leases), one obstinate tenement dweller can block the creation of a 50-story high-rise. But who wants new buildings in Manhattan? What an apartment building looks like—on the outside—affects everybody, not just the landlord and the tenant. New York's old buildings are gracious and charming, even those that are rundown. Its new ones—at least those of the residential variety—are generally horrible. It is rent control that has preserved the aesthetic as well as the social fabric of the kind of variegated, low-rise neighborhoods Jane Jacobs celebrated in *The Death and Life of Great American Cities*. . . .

The goal of a rent-regulation compromise should be to diminish unfairness and mitigate perverse side effects without giving a shock to the city's social system. This argues for a fairly straightforward means test for rent control, say $100,000 a year. . . . There will be people, some of them elderly, who make more than $100,000 but still can't afford the rents their apartments could command on the free market. They will have to move. How big a tragedy is that?

Key Points in the Article

This article provides a look at the market for rental apartments in New York City. Jacob Weisberg, the author of the article, is the managing editor of *Slate*, the online magazine owned by Microsoft. Weisberg's experiences highlight key aspects of life in a city with rent control. Weisberg also presents an argument in favor of rent control, even though he has been made worse off by it financially.

Analyzing the News

We can use the concepts from this chapter to analyze the article:

a Jacob Weisberg and his wife were living in an unregulated apartment, so the rent adjusted according to movements in demand and supply. Because higher-income people were moving into the neighborhood, it was becoming more desirable, and the demand for apartments shifted to the right. This increase in demand caused the equilibrium rent to increase from $1,950 to $2,650 per month.

b The author is correct in noting that: "Absent the artificial shortage created by rent regulation, we would either have a bigger place or pay much less for the one we've got." Figure 1 (a) shows the market for apartments currently subject to rent control. For these apartments, eliminating rent control would increase the quantity of apartments rented from Q_1 to Q_2. The rent would rise from $1,000, the rent control ceiling, to $1,500, the competitive equilibrium rent. Figure 1 (b) shows the market for apartments not currently subject to rent control. The elimination of rent control would cause the demand curve for these apartments to shift to the left from D_1 to D_2, which would lower the equilibrium rent from $2,000 to $1,500 per month.

c Although the author is well aware that rent control has resulted in his paying more for his apartment than he would have in a competitive market, he is reluctant to see rent control eliminated. In other words, he understands the positive analysis that shows the economic costs of rent control, but his normative analysis leads him still to support the policy.

Thinking Critically ABOUT POLICY

1. The author of the article notes that a rent control law "encourages landlords to neglect their buildings. . . ." How does rent control do this?
2. Despite his complaints, the author supports rent control laws. He implicitly balances the cost and benefits of the policy. How might his conclusion change if he were confronted with an estimate of the deadweight loss of the policy? How large would such deadweight loss have to be before you would predict the author would change his mind? Against what measure of benefit would the deadweight loss have to be weighed?

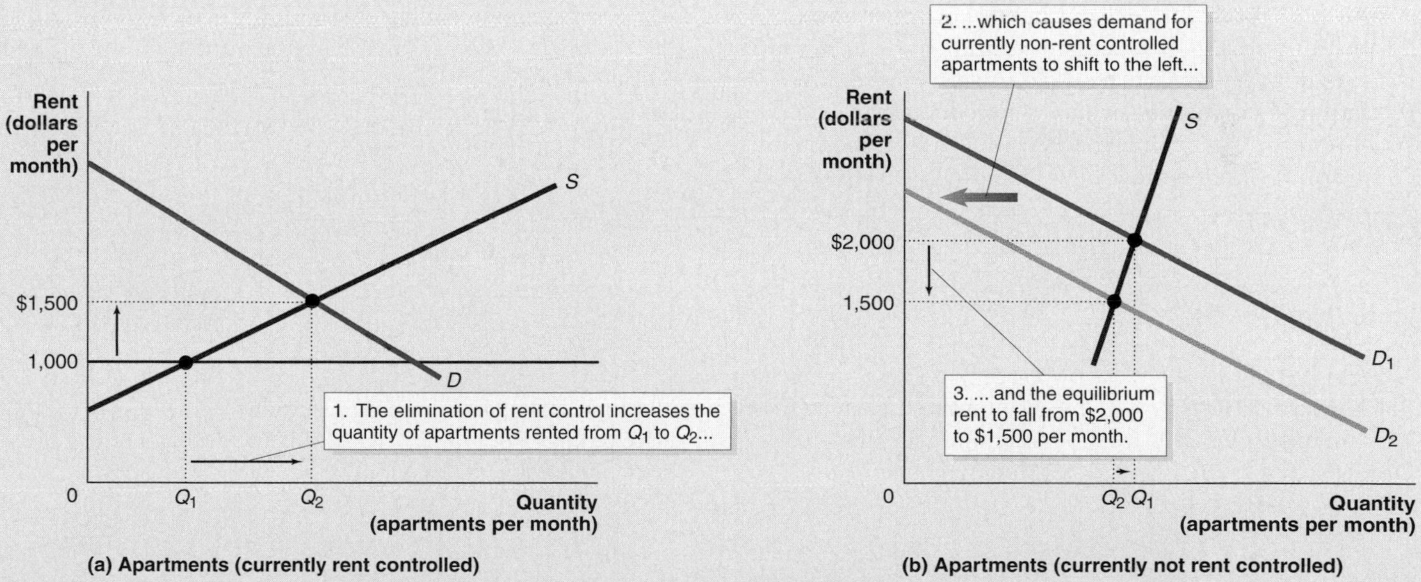

Figure 1: In (a), the elimination of rent control causes an increase from Q_1 to Q_2 in the quantity of apartments being rented. In (b) this causes the demand for currently non-rent-controlled apartments to shift to the left from D_1 to D_2. The equilibrium rent declines from $2,000 to $1,500.

SUMMARY

LEARNING OBJECTIVE ① Understand the concepts of consumer surplus and producer surplus. *Marginal benefit* is the additional benefit to a consumer from consuming one more unit of a good or service. The demand curve is also a marginal benefit curve. *Consumer surplus* is the difference between the highest price a consumer is willing to pay for a product and the price the consumer actually pays. The total amount of consumer surplus in a market is equal to the area below the demand curve and above the market price. *Marginal cost* is the additional cost to a firm of producing one more unit of a good or service. The supply curve is also a marginal cost curve. *Producer surplus* is the difference between the lowest price a firm is willing to accept and the price it actually receives. The total amount of producer surplus in a market is equal to the area above the supply curve and below the market price.

LEARNING OBJECTIVE ② Understand the concept of economic efficiency, and use a graph to illustrate how economic efficiency is reduced when a market is not in competitive equilibrium. Equilibrium in a competitive market is *economically efficient. Economic surplus* is the sum of consumer surplus and producer surplus. Economic efficiency is a market outcome in which the marginal benefit to consumers from the last unit produced is equal to the marginal cost of production, and where the sum of consumer surplus and producer surplus is at a maximum. When the market price is above or below the equilibrium price, there is a reduction in economic surplus. The reduction in economic surplus resulting from a market not being in competitive equilibrium is called the *deadweight loss.*

LEARNING OBJECTIVE ③ Use demand and supply graphs to analyze the economic impact of price ceilings and price floors. Producers or consumers who are dissatisfied with the market outcome can attempt to convince the government to impose *price floors* or *price ceilings.* Price floors usually increase producer surplus, decrease consumer surplus, and cause a deadweight loss. Price ceilings usually increase consumer surplus, reduce producer surplus, and cause a deadweight loss. The results of the government imposing price ceilings and prices floors are that some people win, some people lose, and a loss of economic efficiency occurs. Positive analysis is concerned with what is, and normative analysis is concerned with what should be. Positive analysis shows that price ceilings and price floors cause deadweight losses. Whether these policies are desirable or undesirable, though, is a normative question.

LEARNING OBJECTIVE ④ Use demand and supply graphs to analyze the economic impact of taxes. Most taxes result in a loss of consumer surplus, a loss of producer surplus, and a deadweight loss. The true burden of a tax is not just the amount paid to government by consumers and producers, but also includes the deadweight loss. The deadweight loss from a tax is the excess burden of the tax. *Tax incidence* is the actual division of the burden of a tax. In most cases, consumers and firms share the burden of a tax levied on a good or service.

KEY TERMS

Black market 109
Consumer surplus 99
Deadweight loss 104
Economic efficiency 104
Economic surplus 103
Marginal benefit 99
Marginal cost 101
Price ceiling 98
Price floor 98
Producer surplus 101
Tax incidence 112

REVIEW QUESTIONS

1. What is marginal benefit? Why is the demand curve referred to as a marginal benefit curve?
2. What is marginal cost? Why is the supply curve referred to as a marginal cost curve?
3. What is consumer surplus? How does consumer surplus change as the equilibrium price of a good rises or falls?
4. What is producer surplus? How does producer surplus change as the equilibrium price of a good rises or falls?
5. What is economic efficiency? Why do economists define efficiency in this way?
6. Why would some consumers tend to favor price controls, while others would be against them?

7. Do producers tend to favor price floors or price ceilings? Why?
8. What is a "black" market? Under what circumstances do black markets arise?
9. Can economic analysis provide a final answer to the question of whether the government should intervene in markets by imposing price ceilings and price floors? Why or why not?
10. What is meant by tax incidence? Do the people who are legally required to pay a tax always bear the burden of the tax? Briefly explain.

PROBLEMS AND APPLICATIONS

Please visit **www.prenhall.com/hubbard** *for solutions to the even-numbered problems as well as multiple-choice and true or false self-assessment quizzes.*

1. The figure below illustrates the market for apples in which the government has imposed a price floor of $10 per crate.

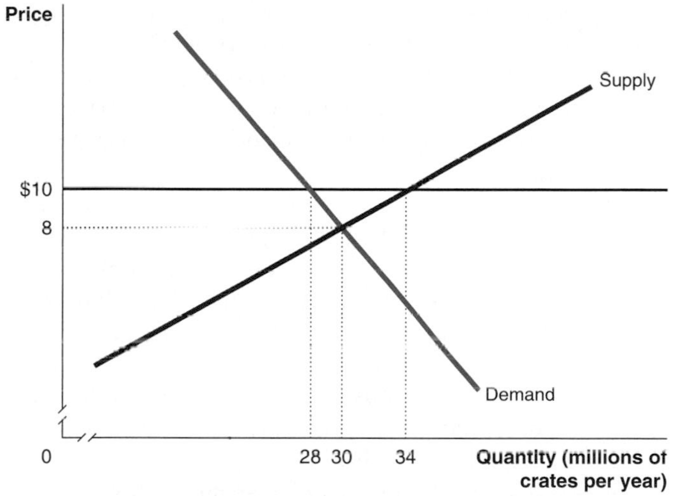

   a. How many crates of apples will be sold after the price floor has been imposed?
   b. Will there be a shortage or a surplus? If there is a shortage or a surplus, how large will it be?
   c. Will apple producers benefit from the price floor? If so, explain how they will benefit.

2. Use the information on the kumquat market in the following table to answer the questions.

PRICE (PER CRATE)	QUANTITY DEMANDED (MILLIONS OF CRATES PER YEAR)	QUANTITY SUPPLIED (MILLIONS OF CRATES PER YEAR)
$10	120	20
15	110	60
20	100	100
25	90	140
30	80	180
35	70	220

   a. What are the equilibrium price and quantity? How much revenue do kumquat producers receive when the market is in equilibrium? Draw a graph showing the market equilibrium and the area representing the revenue received by kumquat producers.
   b. Suppose the federal government decides to impose a price floor of $30 per crate. Now how many crates of kumquats will consumers purchase? How much revenue will kumquat producers receive? Assume that the government does not purchase any surplus kumquats. On your graph from question (a), show the price floor, the change in the quantity of kumquats purchased, and the revenue received by kumquat producers after the price floor is imposed.
   c. Suppose the government imposes a price floor of $30 per crate and purchases any surplus kumquats from producers. Now how much revenue will kumquat producers receive? How much will the government spend purchasing surplus kumquats? On your graph from question (a), show the area representing the amount the government spends to purchase the surplus kumquats.

3. Suppose that the government sets a price floor for milk that is above the competitive equilibrium price.
   a. Draw a graph showing this situation. Be sure that your graph shows the competitive equilibrium price, the price floor, the quantity that would be sold in competitive equilibrium, and the quantity that is sold with the price floor.
   b. Compare the economic surplus in this market when there is a price floor and when there is no price floor.

4. Suppose that the government restricts the number of dairy farmers, which results in the supply curve for milk shifting to the left. Briefly explain whether each of the following will increase or decrease.
   a. Consumer surplus
   b. Producer surplus
   c. Economic surplus

   Using a demand and supply graph, illustrate your answer in each case.

5. To drive a taxicab legally in New York City, you must have a medallion issued by the city government. Only 12,187 medallions have been issued. Let's assume this puts an absolute limit on the number of taxi rides that can be supplied in New York City on any day, because no one breaks the law by driving a taxi without a medallion. Let's also assume that each taxi can provide 6 trips per day. In that case, the supply of taxi rides is fixed at 73,122 (or 6 rides per taxi × 12,187 taxis). We show this in the following graph with a vertical line at this quantity. *Assume that there are no government controls on the prices that drivers can charge for rides.* Use the figure to answer the following questions.

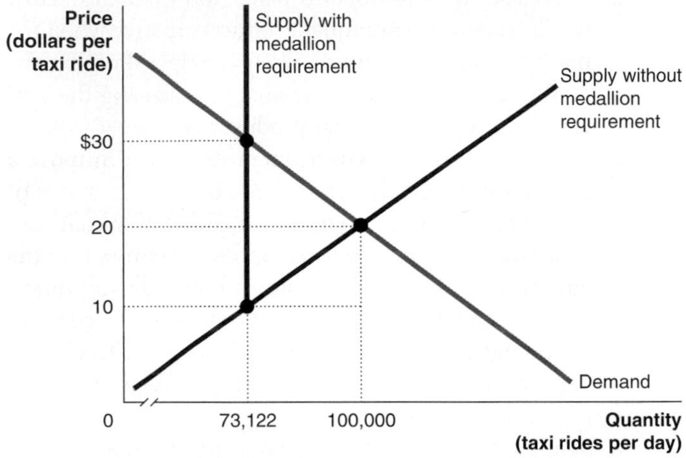

   a. What would the equilibrium price and quantity be in this market if there were no medallion requirement?
   b. What are the price and quantity with the medallion requirement?
   c. Indicate on the graph the areas representing consumer surplus and producer surplus if there were no medallion requirement.
   d. Indicate on the graph the areas representing consumer surplus, producer surplus, and deadweight loss with the medallion requirement.

6. If the goal of the federal government's farm program is to raise the incomes of poor family farmers, is the current system of price floors and subsidy payments based on the number of acres farmed a good way to reach the goal? Briefly explain. What other ways might the federal government attempt to reach its goals?

7. Suppose the competitive equilibrium rent for a standard two-bedroom apartment in Lawrence is $600. Now suppose the city council passes a rent control law imposing a price ceiling of $500. Use a demand and supply graph to illustrate the impact of the rent control law. Suppose that shortly after the law is passed, a large employer in the area announces that it will close a plant in Lawrence and lay off 5,000 workers. Show on your graph how this will affect the market for rental property in Lawrence.

8. **[Related to *Solved Problem 4–1*]** Use the information in the following table on the market for apartments in Bay City to answer the following questions.

RENT	QUANTITY DEMANDED	QUANTITY SUPPLIED
$500	375,000	225,000
600	350,000	250,000
700	325,000	275,000
800	300,000	300,000
900	275,000	325,000
1000	250,000	350,000

   a. In the absence of rent control, what is the equilibrium rent and what is the equilibrium quantity of apartments rented? Draw a demand and supply graph of the market for apartments to illustrate your answer. In equilibrium, will there be any renters who are unable to find an apartment to rent or any landlords who are unable to find a renter for an apartment?
   b. Suppose the government sets a ceiling on rents of $600 per month. What is the quantity of apartments demanded, and what is the quantity of apartments supplied?
   c. Assume that all landlords abide by the law. Use a demand and supply graph to illustrate the impact of this price ceiling on the market for apartments. Be sure to indicate on your diagram each of the following: (i) the area representing consumer surplus after the price ceiling has been imposed, (ii) the area representing producer surplus after the price ceiling has been imposed, and (iii) the area representing the deadweight loss after the ceiling has been imposed.
   d. Assume that the quantity of apartments supplied is the same as you determined in (b). But now assume that landlords ignore the law and rent this quantity of apartments for the highest rent they can get. Briefly explain what this rent will be.

9. The following is from an article in the *New York Times*:

> Imagine finding the perfect apartment, only to learn that the landlord is denying you the place because you are on a blacklist of supposedly high-risk renters. Nothing is wrong with your credit rating, but your name showed up on the list because a private screening service found it in housing court records about a dispute you had with a previous landlord—a dispute that was resolved in your favor.

Is it more likely that a "blacklist" of "high-risk" tenants will exist in a city with rent control, or one without rent control? Briefly explain.

Source: Motoko Rich, "A Blacklist of Renters," *New York Times*, April 8, 2004.

10. **[Related to *Don't Let This Happen To You!*]** Briefly explain whether you agree or disagree with the following statement: "If there is a shortage of a good it must be scarce, but there is not a shortage of every scarce good."
11. A student makes the following argument:

    > A price floor reduces the amount of a product that consumers buy, because it keeps the price above the competitive market equilibrium. A price ceiling, on the other hand, increases the amount of a product that consumers buy, because it keeps the price below the competitive market equilibrium.

    Do you agree with the student's reasoning? Use a demand and supply graph to illustrate your answer.
12. An advocate of medical care system reform makes the following argument:

    > The 15,000 kidneys that are transplanted in the United States each year are received free from organ donors. Despite this, because of hospital and doctor's fees, the average price of a kidney transplant is $250,000. As a result, only rich people or people with very good health insurance can afford these transplants. The government should put a ceiling of $100,000 on the price of kidney transplants. That way, middle-income people will be able to afford them, the demand for kidney transplants will increase, and more kidney transplants will take place.

    Do you agree with the advocate's reasoning? Use a demand and supply graph to illustrate your answer.
13. **[Related to the *Chapter Opener*]** The cities of Peabody and Woburn are five miles apart. Woburn enacts a rent control law that puts a ceiling on rents well below their competitive market value. Predict the impact of this law on the competitive equilibrium rent in Peabody, which does not have a rent control law. Illustrate your answer with a demand and supply graph.
14. **[Related to the *Chapter Opener*]** Rent controls were first imposed in New York City in the early 1940s during a housing shortage brought on by World War II. Why do you think that, once established, rent controls continued in New York City for many decades?
15. **[Related to the *Chapter Opener*]** The political commentator George Will asked the following question in a column in *Newsweek* magazine:

    > Are rent controls compassionate, or do they create a shortage of rental units and a disincentive for landlords to spend on maintenance?

    How would you answer Will's question?

    Source: George F. Will, "One Judge's Conservatism," *Newsweek*, March 3, 2003.
16. **[Related to *Solved Problem 4–1*]** Suppose that initially the gasoline market is in equilibrium at a price of $2.00 per gallon and a quantity of 45 million gallons per month. Then a war in the Middle East disrupts imports of oil into the United States, shifting the supply curve for gasoline from S_1 to S_2. The price of gasoline begins to rise and consumers protest. The federal government responds by setting a price ceiling of $2.00 per gallon. Use the graph to answer the following questions.

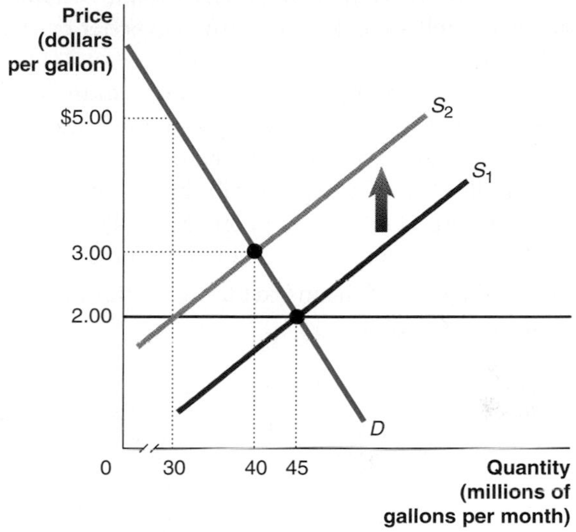

    a. If there were no price ceiling, what would be the equilibrium price of gasoline, the quantity of gasoline demanded, and the quantity of gasoline supplied? Now assume that the price ceiling is imposed and that there is no black market in gasoline. What are the price of gasoline, the quantity of gasoline demanded, and the quantity of gasoline supplied? How large is the shortage of gasoline?
    b. Assume that the price ceiling is imposed and there is no black market in gasoline. Show on the graph the areas representing consumer surplus, producer surplus, and deadweight loss.
    c. Now assume there is a black market and the price of gasoline rises to the maximum that consumers are willing to pay for the amount supplied by producers at $2.00 per gallon. Show on the graph the areas representing producer surplus, consumer surplus, and deadweight loss.
    d. Are consumers made better off by the price ceiling? Briefly explain.
17. In the United States, Amazon.com, BarnesandNoble.com, and many other retailers sell books, DVDs, and music CDs for less than the price marked on the package. In Japan, retailers are not allowed to discount prices in this way. Who benefits and who loses from this Japanese law?

18. Most family businesses in the United States receive little direct support from the federal government. However, family farms have been receiving support from the federal government since the 1930s. Why do you suppose family farms have been singled out as meriting special support from the government?

19. The competitive equilibrium rent in the city of Lowell is currently $1,000 per month. The government decides to enact rent control and to establish a price ceiling for apartments of $750 per month. Briefly explain whether rent control is likely to make you personally better or worse off if you are:
    a. someone currently renting an apartment in Lowell.
    b. someone who will be moving to Lowell next year and who intends to rent an apartment.
    c. a landlord who intends to abide by the rent control law.
    d. a landlord who intends to ignore the law and illegally charge the highest rent you can for your apartments.

20. Use this diagram of the market for cigarettes to answer the following questions.

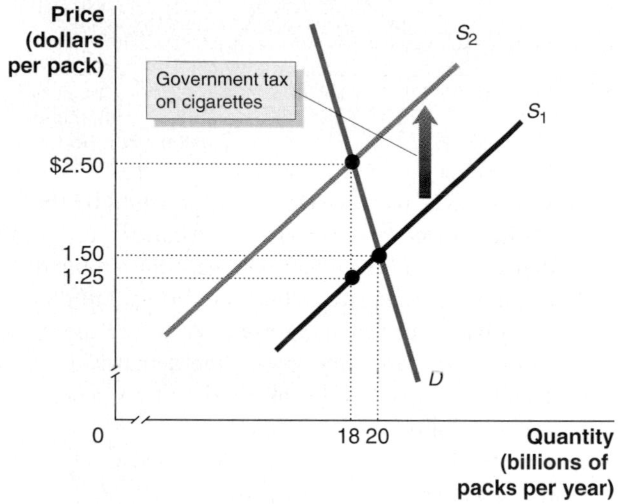

    a. According to the diagram, how much is the government tax on cigarettes?
    b. What price do producers receive after paying the tax?
    c. How much tax revenue does the government collect?

21. **[Related to *Solved Problem 4–2*]** Suppose the federal government decides to levy a sales tax on pizza of $1.00 per pie. Briefly explain whether you agree with the following statement by a representative of the pizza industry: "The pizza industry is very competitive. As a result, pizza sellers will have to pay the whole tax, because they are unable to pass any of it on to consumers in the form of higher prices. Therefore, a sales tax of $1.00 per pie will result in pizza sellers receiving $1 less on each pie sold, after paying the tax." Illustrate your answer with a graph.

22. The following figure illustrates the market for a breast-cancer-fighting drug, without which breast cancer patients cannot survive. What is the consumer surplus in this market? How does it differ from the consumer surplus in the markets you have studied up to this point?

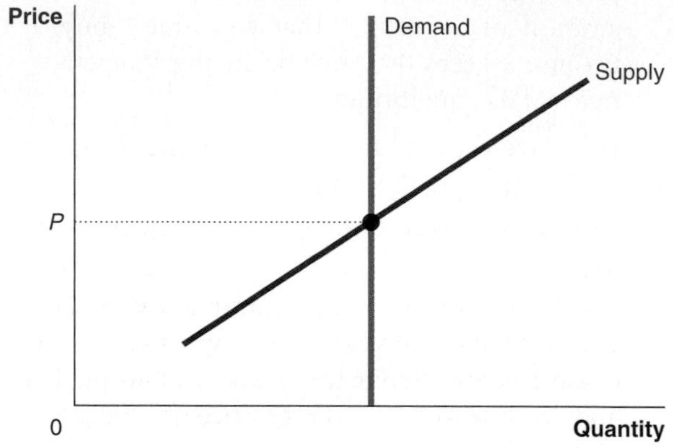

23. The diagram below illustrates the market for seats at a concert, which will be held in a local stadium that seats 15,000 people. What is the producer surplus in this market? How does it differ from the producer surplus in the markets you have studied up to this point?

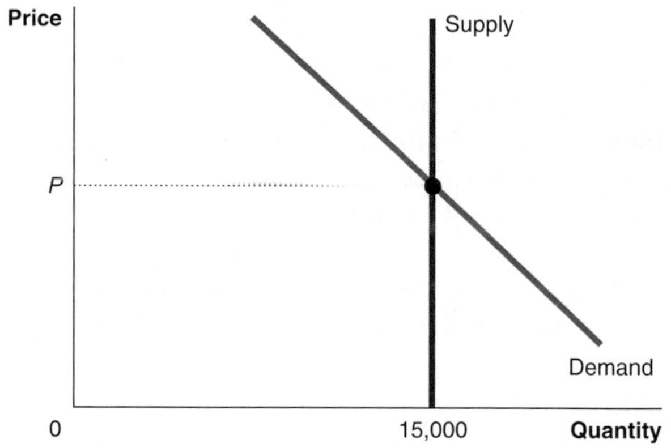

24. Suppose you were assigned the task of developing an economic indicator that measured the "wealth of a nation"—that is, come up with a single number that would allow someone to compare the economic activity in one country to that in another country or to another point in time. How might such a number be related to economic efficiency and consumer and producer surplus?

Quantitative Demand and Supply Analysis

Appendix

Graphs help us understand economic change *qualitatively*. For instance, a demand and supply graph can tell us that if household incomes rise, the demand curve for a normal good will shift to the right and its price will rise. Often, though, economists, business managers, and policymakers want to know more than the qualitative direction of change, they want a *quantitative estimate* of the size of the change.

In Chapter 4, we carried out a qualitative analysis of rent controls. We saw that imposing rent controls involves a trade-off: Renters as a group gain, but landlords lose and the market for apartments becomes less efficient, as shown by the deadweight loss. To better evaluate rent controls we need to know more than just that these gains and losses exist; we need to know how large they are. A quantitative analysis of rent controls will tell us how large the gains and losses are.

Demand and Supply Equations

The first step in a quantitative analysis is to supplement our use of demand and supply curves with demand and supply *equations*. We noted briefly in Chapter 3 that economists often statistically estimate equations for demand curves. Supply curves can also be statistically estimated. For example, suppose that economists have estimated that the demand for apartments in New York City is

$$Q^D = 3{,}000{,}000 - 1{,}000P,$$

and the supply of apartments is

$$Q^S = -450{,}000 + 1{,}300P.$$

We have used Q^D for the quantity of apartments demanded per month, Q^S for the quantity of apartments supplied per month, and P for the apartment rent in dollars per month. In reality, both the quantity of apartments demanded and the quantity of apartments supplied will depend on more than just the rental price of apartments in New York City. For instance, the demand for apartments in New York City will also depend on the average incomes of families in the New York area and on the rents of apartments in surrounding cities. For simplicity, we will ignore these other factors.

With no government intervention, we know that at competitive market equilibrium the quantity demanded must equal the quantity supplied, or

$$Q^D = Q^S.$$

We can use this equation, which is called an *equilibrium condition*, to solve for the equilibrium monthly apartment rent by setting the demand equation equal to the supply equation:

$$3{,}000{,}000 - 1{,}000P = -450{,}000 + 1{,}300P$$

$$3{,}450{,}000 = 2{,}300P$$

$$P = \frac{3{,}450{,}000}{2{,}300} = \$1{,}500$$

FIGURE 4A-1

Graphing Supply and Demand Equations

After statistically estimating supply and demand equations, we can use the equations to draw supply and demand curves. In this case, the equilibrium rent for apartments is $1,500 per month and the equilibrium quantity of apartments rented is 1,500,000. The supply equation tells us that at a rent of $346, the quantity of apartments supplied will be zero. The demand equation tells us that at a rent of $3,000, the quantity of apartments demanded will be zero. The areas representing consumer surplus and producer surplus are also indicated on the graph.

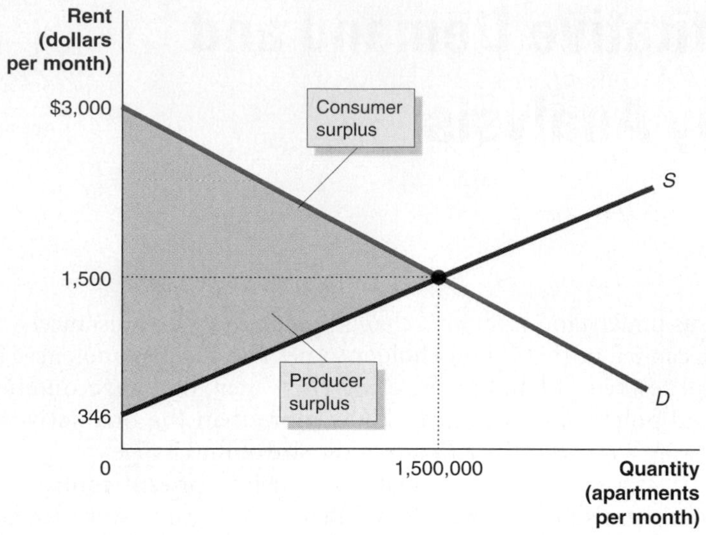

We can then substitute this price back into either the supply equation or the demand equation to find the equilibrium quantity of apartments rented:

$$Q^D = 3{,}000{,}000 - 1{,}000P = 3{,}000{,}000 - 1{,}000(1{,}500) = 1{,}500{,}000$$

$$Q^S = -450{,}000 + 1{,}300P = -450{,}000 + 1{,}300(1{,}500) = 1{,}500{,}000$$

Figure 4A-1 illustrates the information from these equations in a graph. The figure shows the values for rent when the quantity supplied is zero and when the quantity demanded is zero. These values can be calculated from the demand equation and the supply equation by setting Q^D and Q^S equal to zero and solving for price:

$$Q^D = 0 = 3{,}000{,}000 - 1{,}000P$$

$$P = \frac{3{,}000{,}000}{1{,}000} = \$3{,}000$$

and

$$Q^S = 0 = -450{,}000 + 1{,}300P$$

$$P = \frac{-450{,}000}{-1{,}300} = \$346.15.$$

Calculating Consumer Surplus and Producer Surplus

Figure 4A-1 also shows consumer surplus and producer surplus in this market. Recall that the sum of consumer surplus and producer surplus equals the net benefit that renters and landlords receive from participating in the market for apartments. We can use the values from the demand and supply equations to calculate the value of consumer surplus and producer surplus. Remember that consumer surplus is the area below the demand curve and above the line representing market price. Notice that this area forms a right triangle, because the demand curve is a straight line—it is *linear.* As we noted in the Appendix to Chapter 1, the area of a triangle is equal to ½ multiplied by the base of the triangle multiplied by the height of the triangle. In this case, the area is

$$\tfrac{1}{2} \times (1{,}500{,}000) \times (3{,}000 - 1{,}500) = \$1{,}125{,}000{,}000.$$

So, this calculation tells us that the consumer surplus in the market for rental apartments in New York City would be about $1.125 billion.

We can calculate producer surplus in a similar way. Remember that producer surplus is the area above the supply curve and below the line representing market price. Because our supply curve is also a straight line, producer surplus on the figure is equal to the area of the right triangle:

$$\tfrac{1}{2} \times (1{,}500{,}000) \times (1{,}500 - 346) = \$865{,}500{,}000.$$

This calculation tells us that the producer surplus in the market for rental apartments in New York City is about $865 million.

We can use this same type of analysis to measure the impact of rent control on consumer surplus, producer surplus, and economic efficiency. For instance, suppose the city imposes a rent ceiling of $1000 per month. Figure 4A-2 below can help guide us as we measure the impact. First, we can calculate the quantity of apartments that will actually be rented by substituting the rent ceiling of $1,000 into the supply equation:

$$Q^S = -450{,}000 + (1{,}300 \times 1{,}000) = 850{,}000.$$

We also need to know the price on the demand curve when the quantity of apartments is 850,000. We can do this by substituting in 850,000 for quantity in the demand equation and solving for price:

$$850{,}000 = 3{,}000{,}000 - 1{,}000P$$

$$P = \frac{-2{,}150{,}000}{-1{,}000} = \$2{,}150.$$

Compared with its value in competitive equilibrium, consumer surplus has been reduced by a value equal to the area of the yellow triangle *B*, but increased by a value equal to the area of the blue rectangle *A*. The area of the yellow triangle *B* is

$$\tfrac{1}{2} \times (1{,}500{,}000 - 850{,}000) \times (2{,}150 - 1{,}500) = \$211{,}250{,}000,$$

and the area of the blue rectangle *A* is base multiplied by height, or

$$(\$1{,}500 - \$1{,}000) \times (850{,}000) = \$425{,}000{,}000.$$

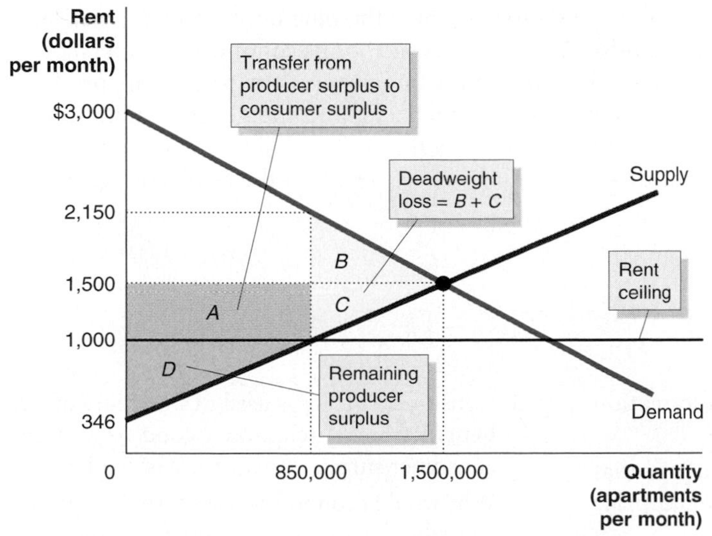

FIGURE 4A-2

Calculating the Economic Effect of Rent Controls

Once we have estimated equations for the demand and supply of rental housing, a diagram can guide our numerical estimates of the economic effects of rent control. Consumer surplus falls by an amount equal to the area of the yellow triangle *B* and increases by an amount equal to the area of the blue rectangle *A*. The difference between the values of these two areas is $213,750,000. Producer surplus falls by an amount equal to the area of the blue rectangle *A* plus the area of the yellow triangle *C*. The value of these two areas is $587,500,000. The remaining producer surplus is equal to the area of triangle *D*, or $278,000,000. Deadweight loss is equal to the area of triangle *B* plus the area of triangle *C*, or $373,750,000.

The value of consumer surplus in competitive equilibrium was $1,125,000,000. As a result of the rent ceiling it will be increased to

$$(\$1{,}125{,}000{,}000 + \$425{,}000{,}000) - \$211{,}250{,}000 = \$1{,}338{,}750{,}000.$$

Compared with its value in competitive equilibrium, producer surplus has been reduced by a value equal to the area of the yellow triangle *C* plus a value equal to the area of the blue rectangle. The area of the yellow triangle *C* is

$$\tfrac{1}{2} \times (1{,}500{,}000 - 850{,}000) \times (1{,}500 - 1{,}000) = \$162{,}500{,}000.$$

We have already calculated the area of the blue rectangle *A* as $425,000,000. The value of producer surplus in competitive equilibrium was $865,500,000. As a result of the rent ceiling it will be reduced to

$$\$865{,}500{,}000 - \$162{,}500{,}000 - \$425{,}000{,}000 = \$278{,}000{,}000.$$

The loss of economic efficiency, as measured by the deadweight loss, is equal to the value represented by the areas of the yellow triangles *B* and *C*, or

$$\$211{,}250{,}000 + \$162{,}500{,}000 = \$373{,}750{,}000.$$

The following table summarizes the results of the analysis (the values are in millions of dollars):

CONSUMER SURPLUS		PRODUCER SURPLUS		DEADWEIGHT LOSS	
COMPETITIVE EQUILIBRIUM	RENT CONTROL	COMPETITIVE EQUILIBRIUM	RENT CONTROL	COMPETITIVE EQUILIBRIUM	RENT CONTROL
$1,125	$1,338.75	$865.50	$278	$0	$373.75

Qualitatively, we know that imposing rent controls will make consumers better off, landlords worse off, and decrease economic efficiency. The advantage of the analysis that we have just gone through is that it puts dollar values on the qualitative results. We can now see how much consumers have gained, how much landlords have lost, and how great the decline in economic efficiency has been. Sometimes the quantitative results can be surprising. Notice, for instance, that after the imposition of rent control, the deadweight loss is actually greater than the remaining producer surplus.

Economists often study issues where the qualitative results of actions are apparent, even to non-economists. You don't have to be an economist to understand who wins and loses from rent control, or that if a company cuts the price of its product, its sales will increase. Business managers, policymakers, and the general public do, however, need economists to measure quantitatively the effects of different actions—including policies such as rent control—so that they can better assess the results of these actions.

REVIEW QUESTIONS

1. In a linear demand equation, what economic information is conveyed by the intercept on the price axis?
2. Suppose you were assigned the task of choosing a price that maximized economic surplus in a market. What price would you choose? Why?
3. Consumer surplus is used as a measure of a consumer's net benefit from purchasing a good or service. Explain why consumer surplus is a measure of net benefit.
4. Why would economists use a term like "deadweight loss" to describe the impact on consumer and producer surplus from a price control?

PROBLEMS AND APPLICATIONS

Please visit **www.prenhall.com/hubbard** *for solutions to the even-numbered problems as well as multiple-choice and true or false self-assessment quizzes.*

1. Suppose that you have been hired to analyze the impact on employment from the imposition of a minimum wage in the labor market. Further suppose that you estimate the supply and demand functions for labor, where L stands for the quantity of labor (measured in thousands of workers), and W stands for the wage rate (measured in dollars per hour):

   Demand: $L^D = 100 - 4W$

   Supply: $L^S = 6W$

   First, calculate the free-market equilibrium wage and quantity of labor. Now suppose the proposed minimum wage is $12. How large will the surplus of labor in this market?

2. The diagrams below illustrate the markets for two different types of labor. Suppose an identical minimum wage is imposed in both markets. In which market will the minimum wage have the largest impact on employment? Why?

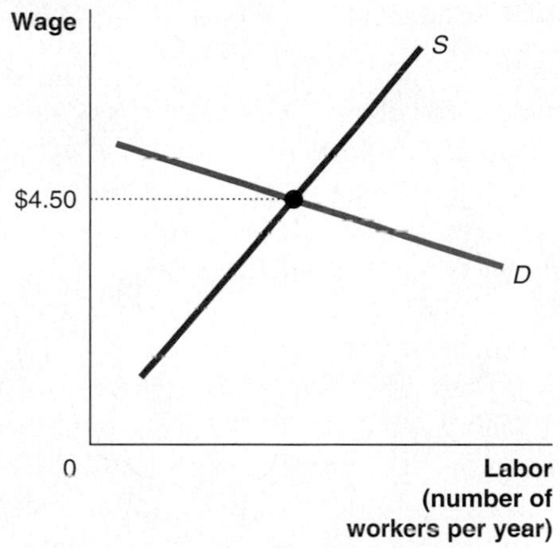

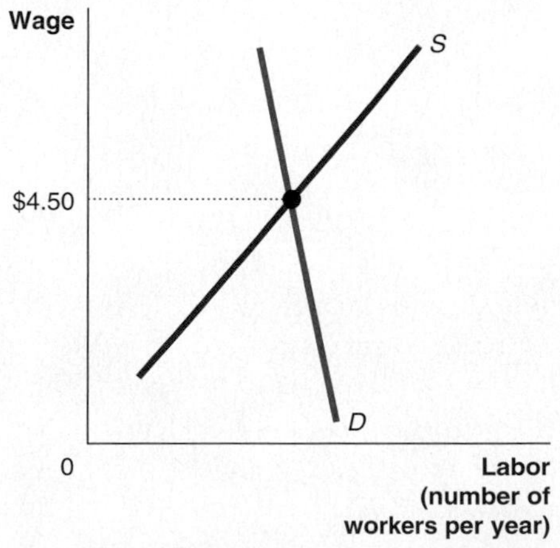

3. Suppose that you are the vice president of operations of a manufacturing firm, which sells an industrial lubricant in a competitive market. Further suppose that your economist gives you the following supply and demand functions:

   Demand: $Q^D = 45 - 2P$

   Supply: $Q^S = -15 + P$

   What is the consumer surplus in this market? What is the producer surplus?

4. The graph below shows a market in which a price floor has been imposed. Identify the following: (a) the deadweight loss; (b) the transfer of producer surplus to consumers or the transfer of consumer surplus to producers; (c) the remaining producer surplus; (d) the remaining consumer surplus.

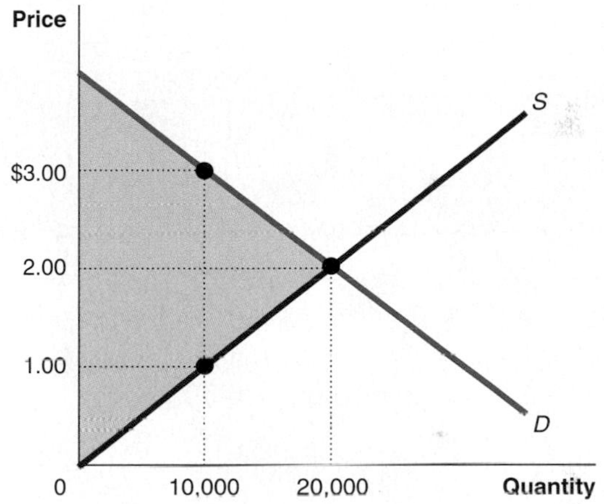

5. Construct a table like the one in this Appendix under the assumption that the rent ceiling is $1,200, rather than $1,000.

chapter five

5

Firms, the Stock Market, and Corporate Governance

Google: From Dorm Room to Wall Street

➤ There could be no question that Google was cool. The world's most widely used Internet search engine, Google had become the essence of cool as a way to research information stored on Web sites. Founded in 1998 by Larry Page and Sergey Brin, Google grew quickly. In 2005, Google employed 3,000 people and earned $3.2 billion in revenue. Google's founders had transformed the Internet search engine and brought value to users through a combination of intellect, technology, and the talents of many employees. Google's key advantage over competitors such as A9 and Ask Jeeves was its search algorithms that

most relevant to a subject. Google had other advantages as well, such as its automatic foreign-language translation. Google had become so dominant that other major Web sites, such as AOL and Yahoo, were using it as their search engine. And "Google" had even become a verb: "I couldn't remember the name of the founder of Microsoft, so I googled it." Google's huge popularity allowed it to do what most other Internet sites could not: make money selling advertising.

And Google was hot. In 2004, Google sold part of the firm to outside investors by offering stock—and partial ownership—to the pub-

Page and Sergey Brin to the ranks of the super-rich. Google's stock offering also gained significant press attention, as the firm bypassed conventional financial practice and used an automated online auction to help set the share price and determine who should receive stock. The offering's size grabbed attention, too: It was the most anticipated stock sale since the 1995 launch of Netscape, a deal that sparked the late-1990s Internet gold rush on Wall Street. *An Inside Look* on page 146 discusses movements in Google's stock price in the months following the firm's first sale of stock in August 2004.

A business like Google is more than a black box, transforming inputs into outputs. As the firm grew larger, it was less the informal organization put together by the founders and more a complex organization with greater need for management and funds to grow. Indeed, Google's offering of stock to outside investors provided the firm with a major inflow of funds for growth.

Once a firm grows very large, its owners often do not continue to manage it. The large modern corporation is owned by millions of individual investors who have purchased the firm's stock. With ownership so dispersed, the top managers who actually run the firm have the opportunity to make decisions that are in the managers' best interests, but that may not be in the best interests of the stockholders who own the firm.

Against this backdrop, Google faced significant costs associated with selling stock to the public. High-profile corporate accounting scandals in 2001 and 2002 at major U.S. firms, such as Enron, WorldCom, and Tyco, led to the passage of stronger—and more costly—securities regulation under the Sarbanes-Oxley Act, enacted by Congress in 2002. Google's growth prospects and the health of the financial system were intertwined.

LEARNING OBJECTIVES

After studying this chapter, you should be able to:

1. Categorize the major types of business in the United States.
2. Describe the typical management structure of corporations and understand the concepts of separation of ownership from control and the principal-agent problem.
3. Explain how firms obtain the funds they need to operate and expand.
4. Understand the information provided in firms' financial statements.
5. Understand the business accounting scandals of 2002, as well as the role of government in corporate governance.

In this chapter, we look at the firm: how it is organized, how it raises funds, and the information it provides to investors. As we have already discussed, in a market system, firms are responsible for organizing the factors of production to produce goods and services. Firms are the vehicles entrepreneurs use to earn profits by responding to consumer wants as expressed in the market. To succeed, entrepreneurs must meet consumer wants by producing new or better goods and services, or by finding ways of producing existing goods and services at a lower cost so they can be sold at a lower price. Entrepreneurs also need access to sufficient funds, and they must be able to efficiently organize production. As the typical firm in many industries has become larger during the past hundred years, the task of efficiently organizing production has become more difficult. The problem of successfully coordinating the activities of large firms is one of the causes of the recent business scandals in the United States. Toward the end of this chapter, we look at why these scandals occurred and at the steps businesses and the government have taken to avoid similar problems in the future.

① LEARNING OBJECTIVE

Categorize the major types of business in the United States.

Types of Firms

In studying a market economy, it is important to understand the basics of how firms operate. In the United States, there are three legal categories of firms: *sole proprietorships, partnerships,* and *corporations.* A **sole proprietorship** is a firm owned by a single individual. Although most sole proprietorships are small, some are quite large in terms of sales, number of persons employed, and profits earned. **Partnerships** are firms owned jointly by two or more—sometimes many—persons. Most law and accounting firms are partnerships. The famous Lloyd's of London insurance company is a partnership. Although some partnerships, such as Lloyd's, can be quite large, most large firms are organized as *corporations.* A **corporation** is a legal form of business that provides the owners with limited liability.

Sole proprietorship A firm owned by a single individual and not organized as a corporation.

Partnership A firm owned jointly by two or more persons and not organized as a corporation.

Corporation A legal form of business that provides the owners with limited liability.

Who Is Liable? Limited and Unlimited Liability

A key distinction among these three types of firms is that the owners of sole proprietorships and partnerships have unlimited liability. Unlimited liability means there is no legal distinction between the personal assets of the owners of the firm and the assets of the firm. An **asset** is anything of value owned by a person or a firm. If a sole proprietorship or a partnership owes a lot of money to the firm's suppliers or employees, the suppliers and employees have a legal right to sue the firm for payment, even if this requires the firm's owners to sell some of their personal assets, such as stocks or bonds. In other words, with sole proprietorships and partnerships, the owners are not legally distinct from the firms they own.

Asset Anything of value owned by a person or a firm.

It may seem only fair that the owners of a firm be responsible for a firm's debts. But early in the nineteenth century it became clear to many state legislatures in the United States that unlimited liability was a significant problem for any firm that was attempting to raise funds from large numbers of investors. An investor might be interested in making a relatively small investment in a firm but be unwilling to become a partner in the firm for fear of placing at risk all of his or her personal assets if the firm were to fail. To get around this problem, state legislatures began to pass *general incorporation laws,* which allowed firms to be organized as corporations. Under the corporate form of business, the owners of a firm have **limited liability,** which means that if the firm fails, the owners can never lose more than the amount they had invested in the firm. The personal assets of the owners of the firm are not affected by the failure of the firm. In fact, in the eyes of the law, a corporation is a legal "person" separate from its owners. Limited liabil-

Limited liability The legal provision that shields owners of a corporation from losing more than they have invested in the firm.

TABLE 5-1

Differences among Business Organizations

	SOLE PROPRIETORSHIP	PARTNERSHIP	CORPORATION
Advantages	• Control by owner	• Ability to share work	• Limited personal liability
	• No layers of management	• Ability to share risks	• Greater ability to raise funds
Disadvantages	• Unlimited personal liability	• Unlimited personal liability	• Costly to organize
	• Limited ability to raise funds	• Limited ability to raise funds	• Possible double taxation of income

ity has made it possible for corporations to raise funds by issuing shares of stock to large numbers of investors. For example, if you buy a share of Google stock, you are part owner of the firm, but even if Google were to go bankrupt, you would not be personally responsible for any of Google's debts. Therefore, you could not lose more than the amount you had paid for the stock.

Corporate organizations also have some disadvantages. In the United States, corporate profits are taxed twice—once at the corporate level and again when investors receive a share of corporate profits. Corporations, because they generally are larger than sole proprietorships and partnerships, also are more difficult to organize and harder to run. Table 5-1 reviews the advantages and disadvantages of different forms of business organization.

5-1 Making the Connection

What's in a "Name"? Lloyd's of London Learns about Unlimited Liability the Hard Way

Investors in Lloyd's of London lost billions of dollars during the 1980s and 1990s.

The world-famous insurance company Lloyd's of London got its start in Edward Lloyd's coffeehouse in London in the late 1600s. Ship owners would come to the coffeehouse looking for someone to insure (or "underwrite") their ships and cargos in exchange for a flat fee (or "premium"). The customers of the coffeehouse, themselves merchants or ship owners, who agreed to insure ships or cargos would have to make payment from their personal funds if an insured ship were lost at sea. By the late 1700s the system had become more formal: Each underwriter would recruit investors, known as "Names," and use the funds raised to back insurance policies sold to a wide variety of clients. In the twentieth century Lloyd's became famous for some of its unusual insurance policies. It issued an insurance policy on the legs of Betty Grable, a 1940s movie star. One man bought an insurance policy against seeing a ghost.

By the late 1980s, 34,000 persons around the world had invested in Lloyd's as Names. A series of disasters in the late 1980s and early 1990s—including the *Exxon Valdez* oil spill in Alaska, Hurricane Hugo in South Carolina, and an earthquake in San Francisco—resulted in huge payments on insurance policies written by Lloyd's. In 1989, Lloyd's lost \$3.85 billion. In 1990 it lost an additional \$4.4 billion. It then became clear to many of the Names that Lloyd's was not a corporation and that the Names did not have the limited liability enjoyed by corporate shareholders. On the contrary, the Names were personally responsible for paying the losses on the insurance policies. Many Names lost far more than they had invested. Some investors, such as Charles Schwab, the discount stockbroker, were wealthy enough that their losses were sustainable, but others were less fortunate. One California investor ended up living in poverty after having to sell his \$1 million house to pay his share of the losses. Another Name, Sir Richard Fitch, a British admiral, committed suicide after most of his wealth was wiped out. As many as 30 Names may have committed suicide as a result of their losses.

By 2004, only 2,500 Names—undoubtedly sadder but wiser—remained as investors in Lloyd's. New rules have allowed insurance companies to underwrite Lloyd's policies for the first time. Today, Names provide only about 20 percent of Lloyd's funds.

Sources: Charles Fleming, "The Master of Disaster Is Trying to Avoid One," *Wall Street Journal*, November 17, 2003 and "Lloyd's of London: Insuring for the Future," *Economist*, September 16, 2004.

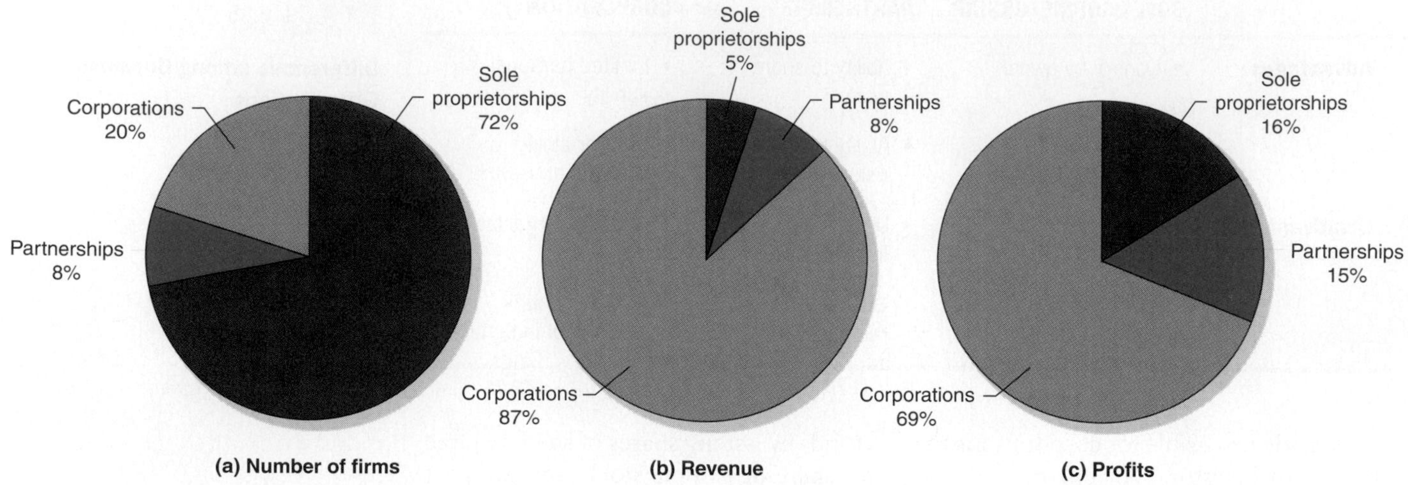

FIGURE 5-1 Business Organizations: Sole Proprietorships, Partnerships, and Corporations

The three types of firms in the United States are sole proprietorships, partnerships, and corporations. Panel (a) shows that only 20 percent of all firms are corporations. Yet, as panels (b) and (c) show, corporations account for a majority of the total revenue and profits earned by all firms.

Source: Statistical Abstract of the United States, 2004–2005.

Corporations Earn the Majority of Revenue and Profits

Figure 5-1 gives basic statistics on the three types of business organizations. Panel (a) shows that almost three-quarters of all firms are sole proprietorships. Panels (b) and (c) show that although only 20 percent of all firms are corporations, corporations account for the majority of revenue and profits earned by all firms. *Profit* is the difference between revenue and the total cost to the firm of producing the goods and services it offers for sale.

There are nearly 5 million corporations in the United States, but only 22,000 have annual revenues of more than $50 million. We can think of these 22,000 firms—including Microsoft, General Electric, and Exxon Mobil—as representing "big business." These large firms account for more than four-fifths of all U.S. corporate profits.

(2) LEARNING OBJECTIVE

Describe the typical management structure of corporations and understand the concepts of separation of ownership from control and the principal-agent problem.

Corporate governance The way in which a corporation is structured and the impact a corporation's structure has on the firm's behavior.

The Structure of Corporations and the Principal-Agent Problem

Because large corporations account for most sales and profits in the economy, it is important to know how they are managed. Most large corporations have a similar management structure. This structure can lead to problems on the scale of the 2002 business scandals, which we will discuss later. The way in which a corporation is structured and the impact a corporation's structure has on the firm's behavior is referred to as **corporate governance.**

Corporate Structure and Corporate Governance

Corporations are legally owned by their *shareholders,* the owners of the corporation's stock. Unlike founder-dominated businesses, such as family businesses, a corporation's shareholders, although they are the firm's owners, do not manage the firm directly. Instead, they elect a *board of directors* to represent their interests. The board of directors appoints a *chief executive officer* (CEO) to run the day-to-day operations of the corporation. Sometimes the board of directors will also appoint other members of *top management,* such as the *chief financial officer* (CFO). At other times the CEO appoints other members of top management. Members of top management, including the CEO and CFO, will often serve on the board of directors. Members of management serving on the board of directors are referred to as *inside directors.* Members of the board of directors who do not have a direct management role in the firm are referred to as *outside directors.* The outside directors are intended to act as checks on the decisions of top managers, but the distinction between an outside director and an inside director is not always clear. For example, the CEO of a firm that sells a good or service to a large corporation may sit on the board of directors of that corporation. Although an outside director, this person may be reluctant to displease the top managers because the top managers have the power to stop purchasing from his firm. In some instances, top managers have effectively controlled their firms' boards of directors.

Unlike founder-dominated businesses, the top management of large corporations does not generally own a large share of the firm's stock, so large corporations have a **separation of ownership from control.** Although the shareholders actually own the firm, top management controls the day-to-day operations of the firm. Because top managers do not own the entire firm, they may have an incentive to decrease the firm's profits by spending money to purchase private jets or schedule management meetings at luxurious resorts. Economists refer to the conflict between the interests of shareholders and the interests of top management as a **principal-agent problem.** This problem occurs when agents—in this case, a firm's top management—pursue their own interests rather than the interests of the principal who hired them—in this case, the shareholders of the corporation. To reduce the impact of the principal-agent problem, in the 1990s, many boards of directors began to tie the salaries of top managers to the profits of the firm or to the price of the firm's stock. They hoped this would give top managers an incentive to make the firm as profitable as possible, thereby benefiting its shareholders.

Separation of ownership from control In many large corporations the top management, rather than the shareholders, control day-to-day operations.

Principal-agent problem A problem caused by an agent pursuing his own interests rather than the interests of the principal who hired him.

SOLVED PROBLEM 5-1

Does the Principal-Agent Problem Also Apply to the Relationship between Managers and Workers?

(2) LEARNING OBJECTIVE
Describe the typical management structure of corporations and understand the concepts of separation of ownership from control and the principal-agent problem.

Briefly explain whether you agree or disagree with the following argument: "The principal-agent problem applies not just to the relationship between shareholders and top managers. It also applies to the relationship between managers and workers. Just as shareholders have trouble monitoring whether top managers are earning as much profit as possible, managers have trouble monitoring whether workers are working as hard as possible."

Solving the Problem:

Step 1: Review the chapter material. This problem concerns the principal-agent problem, so you may want to review the section "Corporate Structure and Corporate Governance," which begins on page 134.

Step 2: Evaluate the argument. You should agree with the argument. A corporation's shareholders have difficulty monitoring the activities of top managers. In practice, they attempt to do so indirectly through the corporation's board of directors. But a board of directors may be influenced heavily by—or even controlled by—the firm's top managers. Even if a board of directors is not controlled by top management, it may be difficult for the board to know whether actions taken by top managers—say, opening a branch office in Paris—will increase the profitability of the firm or just increase the enjoyment of the top managers.

To answer the problem, we must extend this analysis to the relationship between managers and workers: Managers would like workers to work as hard as possible. Workers would often rather not work hard, particularly if they do not see a direct financial reward for doing so. Managers can have trouble monitoring whether workers are working hard or goofing off. Is that worker in his cubicle diligently staring at a computer screen because he is hard at work on a report or because he is surfing the Web for sports scores or writing a long e-mail to his girlfriend? Thus, the principal-agent problem does apply to the relationship between managers and workers.

Extra Credit: Boards of directors try to reduce the principal-agent problem by designing compensation policies for top managers that give them financial incentives to increase profits. (Although, as we will see later in this chapter, these plans can sometimes backfire.) Similarly, managers try to reduce the principal-agent problem by designing compensation policies that give workers an incentive to work harder. For example, some manufacturers pay factory workers on the basis of how much they produce, rather than on the basis of how many hours they work.

YOUR TURN: **For more practice, do related problems 6 and 7 on page 149 at the end of this chapter.**

③ **LEARNING OBJECTIVE**

Explain how firms obtain the funds they need to operate and expand.

How Firms Raise Funds

Owners and managers of firms try to earn a profit. To earn a profit, a firm must raise funds to pay for its operations, including paying its employees and buying machines. Indeed, a central challenge for anyone running a firm, whether that person is a sole proprietor or a top manager of a large corporation, is raising the funds needed to operate and expand the business. Suppose you decide to open an online trading service using $100,000 you have saved in a bank. You use the $100,000 to rent a building for your firm, to buy computers, and to pay other start-up expenses. Your firm is a great success and you decide to expand by moving to a larger building and buying more computers. You can obtain the funds for this expansion in three ways:

1. If you are making a profit, you could reinvest the profits back into your firm. Profits that are reinvested in a firm, rather than taken out of a firm and paid to the firm's owners, are *retained earnings*.
2. You could also obtain funds by taking on one or more partners who would invest in the firm. This arrangement would increase the firm's *financial capital.*
3. Finally, you could borrow the funds from relatives, friends, or a bank.

Sources of External Funds

Unless firms rely on retained earnings, they have to obtain the *external funds* they need from others who have funds available to invest. It is the role of an economy's *financial system* to transfer funds from savers to borrowers—directly through financial markets or indirectly through financial intermediaries such as banks.

Firms can raise external funds in two distinct ways. The first relies on financial intermediaries such as banks and is called **indirect finance.** If you put $1,000 in a checking account or a savings account, or if you buy a $1,000 certificate of deposit (CD), the bank will loan most of those funds to borrowers. The bank will combine your funds with those of other depositors and, for example, make a $100,000 loan to a local business.

Indirect finance A flow of funds from savers to borrowers through financial intermediaries such as banks. Intermediaries raise funds from savers to lend to firms (and other borrowers).

The second way for firms to acquire external funds is through *financial markets.* Raising funds in these markets, such as the New York Stock Exchange on Wall Street in New York, is called **direct finance.** Direct finance usually takes the form of the borrower selling the lender a *financial security.* A financial security is a document—sometimes in electronic form—that states the terms under which the funds have passed from the buyer of the security—who is lending funds—to the borrower. *Bonds* and *stocks* are the two main types of financial securities.

Direct finance A flow of funds from savers to firms through financial markets.

BONDS **Bonds** are financial securities that represent promises to repay a fixed amount of funds. When General Electric (GE) sells a bond to raise funds, it promises to pay the purchaser of the bond an interest payment each year for the term of the bond, as well as a final payment of the amount of the loan, or the *principal,* at the end of the term. GE may need to raise many millions of dollars to build a factory, but each individual bond has a principal or *face value,* of $1,000, which is the amount each bond purchaser is lending GE. So, GE must sell many bonds to raise all the funds it needs. Suppose GE promises it will pay interest of $60 per year to anyone who will buy one of its bonds. The interest payments on a bond are referred to as **coupon payments.** The **interest rate** is the cost of borrowing funds, usually expressed as a percentage of the amount borrowed. If we express the coupon as a percentage of the face value of the bond, we have the interest rate on the bond, called the *coupon rate.* In this case the interest rate is

Bond A financial security that represents a promise to repay a fixed amount of funds.

Coupon payment Interest payment on a bond.

Interest rate The cost of borrowing funds, usually expressed as a percentage of the amount borrowed.

$$\frac{\$60}{\$1{,}000} = 0.06, \text{ or } 6\%.$$

Many bonds issued by corporations have terms, or *maturities,* of 30 years. If you bought a bond from GE, GE would pay you $60 per year for 30 years, and at the end of the thirtieth year GE would pay you back the $1,000 principal.

STOCKS When you buy a newly issued bond from a firm, you are lending funds to that firm. When you buy **stock** issued by a firm, you are actually buying part ownership of the firm. When a corporation sells stock, it is doing the same thing the owner of a small business does when she takes on a partner: The firm is increasing its financial capital by bringing additional owners into the firm. Any individual shareholder usually owns only a small fraction of the total shares of stock issued by a corporation. As we discussed earlier, corporations are run by their top managers who answer to the corporation's board of directors, which is elected by the shareholders. Although some individuals may own enough of a firm's stock to influence the actions of the firm, the average shareholder does not.

Stock A financial security that represents partial ownership of a firm.

A shareholder is entitled to a share of the corporation's profits, if there are any. Corporations generally keep some of their profits—known as retained earnings—to finance future expansion. The remaining profits are paid to shareholders as **dividends.** If investors expect the firm to earn economic profits on its retained earnings, the firm's share price will rise, providing a *capital gain* for investors. If a corporation is unable to make a profit, it usually will not pay a dividend. Under the law, corporations must make payments on any debt they have before making payments to their owners. That is, the corporation must make promised payments to bondholders before it may make any dividend payments to shareholders. In addition, when firms sell stock, they acquire from investors an open-ended commitment of funds to the firm. Therefore, unlike bonds, stocks do not have a maturity date, so the firm is not obliged to return the investor's funds at any particular date.

Dividends Payments by a corporation to its shareholders.

Stock and Bond Markets Provide Capital—and Information

The original purchasers of stocks and bonds may resell them to other investors. In fact, most of the buying and selling of stocks and bonds that takes place each day is investors reselling existing stocks and bonds to each other, rather than corporations selling new stocks and bonds to investors. The buyers and sellers of stocks and bonds together make up the *stock and bond markets.* There is no single place where stocks and bonds are bought and sold. Some trading of stocks and bonds takes place in buildings known as *exchanges,* such as the New York Stock Exchange or Tokyo Stock Exchange. In the United States, the stocks and bonds of the largest corporations are traded on the New York Stock Exchange. The development of computer technology has spread the trading of stocks and bonds outside of exchanges to *securities dealers* linked by computers. These

Don't Let This Happen To You!

When Google Shares Change Hands, Google Doesn't Get the Money

If Google becomes a popular investment, with shares changing hands often as views about the firm's valuation shift, that's great for Google, right? Think of all that money flowing into Google's coffers as shares change hands and the stock price goes up. *Wrong.* Google raises funds in a primary market, but shares change hands in a secondary market. Those trades don't put money into Google's hands, but they do give important information to the firm's managers. Let's see why.

Primary markets are those in which newly issued claims are sold to initial buyers by the issuer. Businesses can raise funds in a primary financial market in two ways—by borrowing or by selling shares—which result in different types of claims on the borrower's future income. Although you hear about the stock market fluctuations each night on the evening news, debt instruments actually account for more of the funds raised by borrowers. In mid-2005, the value of debt instruments in the United States was about $25 trillion compared to $12 trillion for equities.

In *secondary markets,* claims that have already been issued are sold by one investor to another. If Google sells shares to the public, it is turning to a primary market for new funds. Once Google shares are issued, investors trade the shares in the secondary market. The founders of Google do not receive any new funds when Google shares are traded on secondary markets. The initial seller of a financial instrument raises funds from a lender only in the primary market. Secondary markets convey information to firms' managers and to investors by determining the price of financial instruments. For example, a major increase in Google's stock price conveys the market's good feelings about the firm, and the firm may decide to raise funds to expand. Hence, secondary markets are valuable sources of information for corporations that are considering raising funds.

Primary and secondary markets are both important, but they play different roles. As an investor, you principally will trade financial instruments in a secondary market. As a corporate manager, you may help decide how to raise new funds to expand the firm where you work.

YOUR TURN: **Test your understanding by doing related problem 14 on page 150 at the end of this chapter.**

dealers comprise the *over-the-counter market.* The stocks of many computer and other high-technology firms—including Microsoft and Intel—are traded in the most important of the over-the-counter markets, the *National Association of Securities Dealers' Automated Quotation System,* which is referred to by its acronym, NASDAQ.

Shares of stock represent claims on the profits of the firms that issue them. Therefore, as the fortunes of the firms change and they earn more or less profit, the prices of the stock the firms have issued should also change. Similarly, bonds represent claims to receive coupon payments and one final payment of principal. Therefore, a particular bond that was issued in the past may have its price go up or down depending upon whether the coupon payments being offered on newly issued bonds are higher or lower than on existing bonds. If you hold a bond with a coupon of $80 per year and newly issued bonds have coupons of $100 per year, the price of your bond will fall because it is less attractive to investors. The price of a bond will be affected by changes in investors' perceptions of the issuing firm's ability to make the coupon payments. For example, if investors begin to believe that a firm may soon go out of business and stop making coupon payments to its bondholders, the price of the firm's bonds will fall to very low levels.

Changes in the value of a firm's stocks and bonds offer important information for a firm's managers, as well as for investors. An increase in the stock price means that investors are more optimistic about the firm's profit prospects, and the firm's managers may wish to expand the firm's operations as a result. By contrast, a decrease in the firm's stock price indicates that investors are less optimistic about the firms' profit prospects, so that management may want to shrink the firm's operations. Likewise, changes in the value of the firm's bonds imply changes in the cost of external funds to finance the firm's investment in research and development or in new factories. A higher bond price indicates a lower cost of new external funds, while a lower bond price indicates a higher cost of new external funds.

5-2 Making the Connection

Following General Electric's Stock and Bond Prices in the Financial Pages

If you read the stock and bond listings in your local paper or the *Wall Street Journal,* you will notice that newspapers manage to pack into a small space a lot of information about what happened to stocks and bonds during the previous day's trading. The following figure reproduces a section from one page of the stock quotations from the *Wall Street Journal.* Let's focus on the highlighted listing for General Electric, and examine the information in each column.

Stock and bond tables in local newspapers help investors track a firm's prospects.

- The first column (YLD %CHG) gives the percentage change in the price of the stock from the beginning of the year to date. In this case, the price of GE's stock had fallen 1.1 percent since the beginning of 2005.
- The second column (52-WEEK HI) and the third column (52-WEEK LO) give the highest price GE stock has traded for and the lowest price GE has traded for during the previous year. These numbers tell you how *volatile* the stock price is—that is, how much it fluctuates over the course of the year.
- The fourth column (STOCK (SYM)) gives a compact version of the firm's name followed by the firm's "ticker" symbol, which you may have seen scrolling along the bottom of the screen on cable financial news channels.
- The fifth column (DIV) gives the dividend expressed in dollars. In this case, .88 means that GE paid a dividend of $0.88 per share.
- The sixth column (YLD %) gives the *dividend yield,* which is calculated by dividing the dividend by the *closing price* of the stock—that is, the price at which GE stock last sold before the close of trading on the previous day.
- The seventh column (PE) gives the *P-E ratio* (or price-earnings ratio), which is calculated by dividing the price of the firm's stock by its earnings per share (remember that because firms retain some earnings, earnings per share is not necessarily the same as dividends per share). GE's P-E ratio was 22, meaning that its price per share was 22 times its earnings per share. You would have to pay $22 to buy $1 of GE earnings.
- The eighth column (VOL 100s) gives the number of shares of stock traded on the previous day (in hundreds of shares). So, 26,135,600 shares of GE stock were traded the previous day on the New York Stock Exchange.
- The ninth column (CLOSE) is the price the stock sold for the last time it was traded before the close of trading on the previous day, which in this case was $36.10.
- The tenth and final column (NET CHG) gives the amount by which the closing price changed from the closing price the day before. In this case, the price of GE's stock had fallen by $0.15 per share from its closing price the day before. Changes in GE's stock price give the firm's managers a signal that they may want to expand or contract the firm's operations.

YTD % CHG	52-WEEK HI	52-WEEK LO	STOCK (SYM)	DIV	YLD %	PE	VOL 100s	CLOSE	NET CHG
−14.9	14.10	6.79	GenlCbl BGC		...	51	2066	11.79	−0.26
0.9	109.98	90.61	GenDynam GD	1.60F	1.5	16	7304	105.57	0.06
−1.1	37.75	29.55	GenElec GE	.88	2.4	22	261356	36.10	−0.15
3.8	39.30	24.31	GenGrthProp GGP	1.44	3.8	31	21099	37.53	−0.86
11.7	53.98	17.75	GenMaritime GMR	1.77p	...	6	5522	44.64	−0.46

Now we can look at the listings for corporate bonds. As with stocks, to understand the information printed on bonds, you must understand the conventions used. Look at the highlighted Ford bond, and once again we examine the information in each column of the listing.

- The first column (COMPANY (TICKER)) gives the firm name and ticker symbol.
- The second column (COUPON) gives the coupon rate. It is always expressed as a percentage of $1,000. So, this corporate bond pays a coupon of $50.00 per year and has a coupon rate of 5.00%.

- The third column (MATURITY) gives the date on which the bond matures, when the investor will receive a payment of the face value, or principle, of $1,000.
- The fourth column (LAST PRICE) gives the price that the bond sold for the last time it was traded before the close of trading the previous day. (Because this listing is from the paper of May 4, the listed price is for May 3.) The price is expressed as a percentage of $1,000. So, the price was 101.666 percent of $1,000, or $1,016.66.
- The fifth column (LAST YIELD) shows the interest rate on the bond if an investor purchased the bond at its current price. The yield of 4.739% is lower than the coupon rate of 5.00% because the bond is currently selling for a price greater than $1,000.
- The sixth column (EST SPREAD) and seventh column (UST) allow an investor to compare the interest rate on this bond to the interest rate on a corresponding bond issued by the United States Treasury. The spread is quoted in *basis points,* with 100 basis points equal to one percentage point. The 10 under UST indicates that the spread is calculated relative to the interest rate on a 10-year Treasury note. Therefore, we know that the interest rate on the Treasury note must have been 4.739% − 0.54% = 4.199%.
- Finally, the eighth column (EST $ VOL) gives the dollar value of the bonds traded the previous day in thousands of dollars. In this case, $53,979,000 worth of these GE bonds were traded.

	COUPON	MATURITY	LAST PRICE	LAST YIELD	*EST SPREAD	UST†	EST $ VOL (000's)
Morgan Stanley	5.300	May 01, 2013	102.064	4.977	78	10	57,739
Clear Channel Communications Inc. (CCU)	4.900	May 15, 2015	89.270	6.364	220	10	55,270
General Electric (GE)	5.000	Feb 01, 2013	101.666	4.739	54	10	53,979
Clear Channel Communications Inc. (CCU)	5.500	Sep 15, 2014	94.359	6.306	214	10	53,535
May Department Stores (MAY)	5.750	Jul 15, 2014	103.837	5.218	105	10	53,200

4 LEARNING OBJECTIVE
Understand the information provided in firms' financial statements.

Using Financial Statements to Evaluate a Corporation

To raise funds, a firm's managers must persuade financial intermediaries or buyers of its bonds or stock that it will be profitable. Before a firm can sell new issues of stock or bonds, it must first provide investors and financial regulators with information about its finances. To borrow from a bank or other financial intermediary, the firm must disclose financial information to the lender as well.

In most high-income countries, government agencies set requirements for information disclosure for firms that desire to sell securities in financial markets. In the United States, the Securities and Exchange Commission requires publicly owned firms to report their performance in financial statements prepared using standard accounting methods, often referred to as *generally accepted accounting principles.* Such disclosure reduces information costs, but it doesn't eliminate them, for two reasons. First, some firms may be too young to have much information for potential investors to evaluate. Second, managers may try to present the required information in the best possible light so that investors will overvalue their securities.

Private firms also collect information on business borrowers and sell the information to lenders and investors. As long as the information-gathering firm does a good job, lenders and investors purchasing the information will be better able to judge the quality of borrowing firms. Firms specializing in information—including Moody's Investor Service, Standard & Poor's Corporation, Value Line, and Dun and Bradstreet—collect information from businesses and sell it to subscribers. Buyers include individual investors, libraries, and financial intermediaries. You can find some of these publications in your college library or through online information services.

A Bull in China's Financial Shop

5-3 Making the Connection

Prospects for Sichuan Changhong Electric Co., manufacturer of plasma televisions and liquid crystal displays, looked excellent in 2004, with rapidly growing output, employment, and profits earned from trade in the world economy. And Changhong was not alone. In the early 2000s the Chinese economy was sizzling. China's output grew by 9.5 percent during 2004, dominated by an astonishing 26 percent growth in investment in plant and equipment. The Chinese economic juggernaut caught the attention of the global business community—and charged onto the U.S. political stage, as China's growth fueled concerns about job losses in the United States.

Yet at the same time many economists and financial commentators worried that the Chinese expansion—which was fueling rising living standards in a rapidly developing economy with 1.3 billion people—would come to an end. Indeed, the debate seemed to be over whether China's boom would have a "soft landing" (with gradually declining growth) or a "hard landing" (possibly leading to an economic financial crisis).

Why? Although China's saving rate was estimated to be a very high 40 percent of GDP, the financial system was doing a poor job of allocating capital. Excessive expansion in office construction and factories was fueled less by careful financial analysis than by the directions of national and local government officials trying to encourage growth. With nonperforming loans—where the borrower cannot make promised payments to lenders—at unheard-of levels, China's banks were in financial trouble. Worse still, they continued to lend to weak, politically connected borrowers.

China's prospects for long-term economic growth depend importantly on a better developed financial system to generate information for borrowers and lenders. Many economists have urged Chinese officials to improve accounting transparency and information disclosure so that stock and bond markets can flourish. In the absence of well-functioning financial markets, banks are crucial allocators of capital. There, too, information disclosure and less government direction of lending will help oil the Chinese growth machine in the long run.

Chinese firms, like Changhong, may well play a major role on the world's economic stage. For Chinese firms to add enough value to raise the standard of living for Chinese workers over the long run, though, China's creaky financial system needs repair.

Will China's weak financial system derail economic growth?

What kind of information do investors and firm managers need? A firm must answer three basic questions: what to produce, how to produce it, and what price to charge. To answer these questions, a firm's managers need two pieces of information: The first is the firm's revenues and costs, and the second is the value of the property and other assets the firm owns and the firm's debts, or other **liabilities,** that it owes to other persons and firms. Potential investors in the firm also need this information to decide whether to buy the firm's stocks or bonds. Managers and investors find this information in the firm's *financial statements,* principally its

Liability Anything owed by a person or a firm.

income statement and balance sheet. We discuss each of these statements and then use them to understand the business scandals of 2002 we mentioned at the beginning of this chapter.

The Income Statement

Income statement A financial statement that sums up a firm's revenues, costs, and profit over a period of time.

A firm's **income statement** sums up its revenues, costs, and profit over a period of time. Corporations issue annual income statements, although the 12-month *fiscal year* covered may be different from the calendar year to reflect the seasonal pattern of the business better. We explore an income statement in greater detail in the appendix to this chapter.

GETTING TO ACCOUNTING PROFIT The income statement shows a firm's revenue, costs, and profit for the firm's fiscal year. To determine profitability, the income statement starts with the firm's revenue and subtracts its operating expenses and taxes paid. The remainder, *net income,* is the **accounting profit** of the firm.

Accounting profit A firm's net income measured by revenue less operating expenses and taxes paid.

Opportunity cost The highest-valued alternative that must be given up to engage in an activity.

Explicit cost A cost that involves spending money.

Implicit cost A nonmonetary opportunity cost.

. . . AND ECONOMIC PROFIT Accounting profit is not the ideal measure of a firm's profits because it neglects some of the firm's costs. Remember that economists always measure cost as *opportunity cost.* The **opportunity cost** of any activity is the highest-valued alternative that must be given up to engage in that activity. Costs are either *explicit* or *implicit.* When the firm spends money, an **explicit cost** results. If the firm incurs an opportunity cost but does not spend money, an **implicit cost** results. For example, firms pay explicit labor costs to employees. They have many other explicit costs as well, such as the cost of the electricity used to light their office buildings.

Some costs are implicit, however. The most important of these is the opportunity cost to investors of the funds they have invested in the firm. Economists refer to the minimum amount that investors must earn on the funds they invest in a firm, expressed as a percentage of the amount invested, as a *normal rate of return.* If a firm fails to provide investors with at least a normal rate of return, it will not be able to remain in business over the long run because investors will not continue to invest their funds in the firm. For example, Bethlehem Steel was once the second-leading producer of steel in the United States and a very profitable firm with stock that sold for more than $50 per share. By 2002, investors became convinced that the firm's uncompetitive labor costs in world markets meant that the firm would never be able to provide investors with a normal rate of return. Many investors expected the firm would eventually have to declare bankruptcy, and as a result, the price of Bethlehem Steel's stock plummeted to $1 per share. Shortly thereafter the firm declared bankruptcy, and its remaining assets were sold off to a competing steel firm. The return (in dollars) that investors require to continue investing in the firm is a true cost to the firm and should be subtracted from the firm's revenues to calculate its profits.

The necessary rate of return that investors must receive to continue investing in a firm varies from firm to firm. If the investment is risky—as would be the case with a biotechnology start-up—investors will require a high rate of return to compensate them for the risk. Investors in firms in more established industries, such as electric utilities, may require lower rates of return. With respect to any particular firm, the exact rate of return required by investors is difficult to calculate, which also makes it difficult to include in an income statement. Firms have other implicit costs besides the return required by investors that can also be difficult to calculate. As a result, the rules of accounting generally require that only explicit costs be recognized for purposes of keeping the firm's financial records and for paying taxes. *Economic costs* include both explicit costs *and* implicit costs. **Economic profit** is equal to the firm's revenues minus all of its costs, implicit and explicit. Because accounting profit excludes some implicit costs, it will be larger than economic profit.

Economic profit A firm's revenues minus all of its costs, implicit and explicit.

The Balance Sheet

A firm's **balance sheet** sums up its financial position on a particular day, usually the end of a quarter or a year. We analyze a balance sheet in detail in the appendix to this chapter. Recall that an asset is anything of value that the firm owns, and a liability is a debt or obligation owed by the firm. Subtracting the value of a firm's liabilities from the value of its assets leaves its *net worth*. We can think of the net worth as what the firm's owners would be left with if the firm were closed, its assets were sold, and its liabilities were paid off. Investors can determine a firm's net worth by inspecting its balance sheet.

Balance sheet A financial statement that sums up a firm's financial position on a particular day, usually the end of a quarter or a year.

Understanding the Business Scandals of 2002

5 LEARNING OBJECTIVE

Understand the business accounting scandals of 2002, as well as the role of government in corporate governance.

A firm's financial statements provide important information on the firm's ability to add value for investors and the economy. Accurate and easy-to-understand financial statements are inputs for decisions by the firm's managers and investors. Indeed, the information in accounting statements helps guide resource allocation in the economy.

Firms disclose financial statements in periodic filings to the federal government and in *annual reports* to shareholders. An investor is more likely to buy a firm's stock if the firm's income statement shows a large after-tax profit and if its balance sheet shows a large net worth. The top management of a firm has at least two reasons to attract investors and keep the firm's stock price high. First, a higher stock price increases the funds the firm can raise when it sells a given amount of stock. Second, to reduce the principal-agent problem, boards of directors will often tie the salaries of top managers to the firm's stock price or to the profitability of the firm.

Top managers clearly have an incentive to maximize the profits reported on the income statement and the net worth reported on the balance sheet. If top managers make good decisions, the firm's profits will be high, and the firm's assets will be large relative to its liabilities. The business scandals that came to light in 2002 revealed, however, that some top managers inflated profits and hid liabilities that should have been listed on their balance sheets.

At Enron, an energy trading firm, chief financial officer Andrew Fastow was accused of creating partnerships that were supposedly independent of Enron, but in fact were owned by the firm. He was accused of transferring large amounts of Enron's debts to these partnerships, which reduced the liabilities on Enron's balance sheet, thereby increasing the firm's net worth. Falstow's deception made Enron more attractive to investors, increasing its stock price—and Fastow's compensation. In 2001, however, Enron was forced into bankruptcy. The firm's shareholders lost billions of dollars, and many employees lost their jobs. In 2004, Fastow pleaded guilty to conspiracy and was sentenced to 10 years in federal prison.

At WorldCom, a telecommunications firm, David Myers, the firm's controller, pleaded guilty to falsifying "WorldCom's books, to reduce WorldCom's reported actual costs and therefore increase WorldCom's reported earnings." Myers's actions caused WorldCom's income statement to overstate the firm's profits by more than $10 billion. The scandals at Enron and WorldCom were the largest cases of corporate fraud in U.S. history.

How was it possible for corporations such as Enron and WorldCom to falsify their financial statements? The federal government does regulate how financial statements are prepared, but this regulation cannot by itself guarantee the accuracy of the statements. All firms that issue stock to the public have their statements *audited* by a certified public accountant. The accountant is an employee of an accounting firm, *not* of the firm being audited. The audit is intended to provide investors with an independent opinion as to whether the firm's financial statements fairly reflect the true financial condition of the firm. Unfortunately, as the Enron and WorldCom scandals revealed, top managers who are determined to deceive investors about the true financial condition of their firms also can deceive outside auditors.

The private sector's response to the corporate scandals was almost immediate. In addition to the reexamination of corporate governance practices at many corporations, the New York Stock Exchange and the NASDAQ put forth initiatives to ensure the accuracy and accessibility of information.

To guard against future scandals, new federal legislation was enacted in 2002. The landmark *Sarbanes-Oxley Act* of 2002 requires that corporate directors have a certain level of expertise with financial information and mandates that chief executive officers personally certify the accuracy of financial statements. The Sarbanes-Oxley Act also requires that financial analysts and auditors disclose whether any conflicts of interest might exist that would limit their independence in evaluating a firm's financial condition. The purpose of this provision is to ensure that analysts and auditors are acting in the best interests of shareholders. The Act promotes management accountability by specifying the responsibilities of corporate officers and by increasing penalties (including long jail sentences) for managers who do not meet their responsibilities.

Perhaps the most noticeable corporate governance reform under the Sarbanes-Oxley Act is the creation of the Public Company Accounting Oversight Board, a special national board to oversee the auditing of public companies' financial reports. The board's mission is to promote the independence of auditors to ensure they disclose accurate information. On balance, most observers acknowledge that the Sarbanes-Oxley Act brought back confidence in the U.S. corporate governance system, though questions remain for the future about whether the Act may chill legitimate business risk-taking by diverting management attention from the core business toward regulatory compliance. And the high accounting costs of implementing Sarbanes-Oxley are borne by all shareholders.

Outside the United States, the European Commission released plans in 2003 to tighten corporate governance rules, and Japan has debated such reforms as well. The challenge of ensuring the accurate reporting of firms' economic profits is a global one.

SOLVED PROBLEM 5-2

5 LEARNING OBJECTIVE
Understand the business accounting scandals of 2002, as well as the role of government in corporate governance.

What Makes a Good Board of Directors?

Business Week magazine has listed 3M Company as having one of the best boards of directors of any U.S. corporation:

> With just one insider on its nine-member board, the company gets high marks for independence. Outside directors include the CEOs of Lockheed-Martin, Allstate, and Amgen. . . . No directors have business ties to the company.

a. What is an "insider" on a board of directors?

b. Why might having too many insiders be a problem?

c. Why would having outside directors who are CEOs of large firms be a good thing?

d. Why would directors not having business ties to the firm be a good thing?

Source: "The Best Boards and the Worst Boards," *Business Week,* October 7, 2002, p. 107.

Solving the Problem:

Step 1: Review the chapter material. The context of this problem is the business scandals of 2002 and the underlying principal-agent problem that arises because of the separation of ownership from control in large corporations, so you may want to review the section "Understanding the Business Scandals of 2002," which begins on page 143.

Step 2: Answer question (a) by defining "insiders." "Insiders" are members of top management who also serve on the board of directors.

Step 3: Answer question (b) by explaining why having too many insiders on a board may be a problem. Having members of top management on the board of directors provides the board with information about the firm that only top managers possess. Having too many insiders on a board, however, means that top managers may end up controlling the board rather than the other way around. A corporation's board of directors is supposed to provide the monitoring and control of top managers that shareholders cannot provide directly.

Step 4: Answer question (c) by explaining why having directors who are CEOs of large firms may be a good thing. Members of boards of directors are sometimes retired politicians, academics, or philanthropists. Although these people may be well intentioned and hard working, some of them may lack the knowledge and experience to successfully monitor top managers. CEOs of other large corporations, on the other hand, do have the experience to judge better whether top managers are making decisions in the best interests of the firm.

Step 5: Answer question (d) by stating why directors should not have business ties to the firm. If a CEO of Firm 1 sits on the board of directors of Firm 2, she is an outside director, but if her company does a significant amount of business with Firm 2, she may be reluctant to do anything to displease the top managers because the top managers have the power to stop doing business with her firm.

***YOUR TURN:* For more practice, do related problems 16 and 17 on page 150 at the end of this chapter.**

Conclusion

In a market system, firms make independent decisions about which goods and services to produce, how to produce them, and what prices to charge. In modern high-income countries, such as the United States, large corporations account for a majority of the sales and profits earned by firms. Generally, the managers of these corporations do a good job of representing the interests of stockholders, while providing the goods and services demanded by consumers. As the business scandals of 2002 showed, however, some top managers enriched themselves at the expense of stockholders and consumers by manipulating financial statements. Legislative strengthening of financial regulation in the Sarbanes-Oxley Act of 2002 and greater financial market scrutiny of financial statements have helped restore investor and management confidence in firms' financial statements.

Read *An Inside Look* on the next page about Google's initial pubic offering (IPO) for a discussion of the role expectations of future profits play in determining stock prices.

An Inside Look

Google's Initial Public Offering

WALL STREET JOURNAL, JANUARY 3, 2005

Technology Shares Slip, But Google Passes $200

a Google shares soared past $200 Monday, with an upbeat note from Goldman Sachs buoying Web search stocks as the broader technology market fell. Goldman Sachs raised its earnings and revenue estimates for Google and Yahoo, sending Google shares up $9.92, or 5.1%, to $202.71 on the Nasdaq Stock Market. It was the company's highest close since its initial public offering, and marked the first time the search giant's shares finished above the $200 mark.

Search companies fared well last year, helped by Google's high-profile IPO in August. Since then, the company's shares have more than doubled. Goldman raised its fourth-quarter revenue estimate for Google to $592 million from $579 million. The firm also increased its earnings-per-share forecast to 76 cents from 74 cents.

The Goldman note helped push other search stocks higher. Yahoo climbed 50 cents to $38.18 on Nasdaq as Goldman increased its fourth-quarter sales estimate for the company to $773 million from $747 million.

b The note also lifted search rival Ask Jeeves $1.07, or 4%, to $27.82 on Nasdaq.

But the broader tech market didn't fare as well, with lackluster manufacturing numbers for December and the onset of jitters ahead of this month's slew of earnings news. The Nasdaq Composite Index shed 23.29, or 1.1%, to close at 2152.15 in the first session of the new year. The tech heavy index gained 8.6% last year.

Morgan Stanley's high-tech index declined 5.17 to 502.50, and the Nasdaq 100 Index of nonfinancial stocks fell 17.61 to 1603.51.

Among some individual stocks, Sun Microsystems lost 28 cents, or 5.2%, to $5.11 on Nasdaq after Sanford Bernstein cut the network giant's shares to "underperform" from "market perform." The firm says the company's calendar fourth quarter didn't experience a material acceleration, and that it doesn't see upside to its revenue expectations for the fiscal second-quarter of 2005.

Shares of Corning eased 6 cents to $11.71 on the Big Board after the technology giant announced that the Chinese Ministry of Commerce found Saturday that the company had not dumped standard single-mode optical fiber into the Chinese market.

c Nortel Networks rose 6 cents to $3.55 on the New York Stock Exchange. The telecommunications-equipment supplier said the Big Board has granted it an additional three months to file its 2003 annual report with the Securities and Exchange Commission. The exchange will allow Nortel to continue listing while the company continues to sort through accounting irregularities in 2003.

Shares of Tellabs gained 59 cents, or 6.9%, to $9.18 on Nasdaq after Robert W. Baird upgraded the maker of telecom equipment to "outperform" from "neutral." Analysts expect solid bookings due to improved international and fiber-to-the-premises business.

Key Points in the Article

The Money and Investing section (or C section) of the *Wall Street Journal* is devoted to analyzing the stock and bond markets. Because technology stocks, such as Google, have been an important part of the stock market, the *Wall Street Journal* prints an article each day called "Tech Stocks." This particular article discusses price changes in the stocks of Google, Ask Jeeves, Nortel, and several other companies. In each case, the author attempts to explain why the prices of the stocks changed as they did.

Analyzing the News

a Buying a share of stock in Google, or any other firm, means buying part ownership of the firm. As a part owner, you have a claim to your share of the firm's profits. Therefore, firms that earn large profits have high stock prices. Investors are always searching for new information on the future profitability of firms. In the instance discussed here, an analyst for Goldman Sachs, an investment firm, issued a "research note" that forecast higher profits for Google than most investors had been expecting. Apparently, enough investors believed the Goldman Sachs analyst was correct, because demand for Google's shares increased, raising the price per share by almost $10 during the day.

Google sold stock to the public for the first time on August 19, 2004. This *initial public offering*, or IPO, was unusual because the firm used an Internet auction to determine the price and who would receive the shares. Most firms use investment bankers to handle their IPOs, with the result that small investors sometimes have difficulty buying shares on the day they are first issued. Figure 1 shows movements in the price of Google's stock from the time of the IPO through mid-January 2005.

b As discussed earlier in this chapter, the stocks of many computer and other high-technology firms, including Google, are traded on NASDAQ. The NASDAQ Composite Index declined during the day discussed in the article. The NASDAQ Composite Index converts the stock prices of all the stocks that are traded on Nasdaq into a single index number. This index makes it possible for investors to gauge the overall performance of these stocks. Although the stocks of some firms, such as Google and Ask Jeeves, rose during the day, investors at that time were worried about the profitability of high-technology firms, so on average, the prices of NASDAQ stocks declined.

c In the chapter, we discussed some of the accounting problems that had plagued many firms. For a firm's stock to be traded on the New York Stock Exchange—the "Big Board"—the firm needs to meet certain requirements, including the filing of accurate financial statements with the Securities and Exchange Commission. Failure to meet these requirements can cause a firm to be "delisted," which means its stock can no longer be traded on the Big Board. Being delisted makes it extremely difficult for a firm to continue selling stock. Nortel, which is based in Ontario, Canada, and manufactures telecommunications equipment, had failed to file its 2003 annual report with the Securities and Exchange Commission because the firm had discovered accounting irregularities that resulted in its reported profits being higher than its actual profits. The firm had fired ten executives and finance officials. Several of the executives gave back $8.6 million in salary bonuses they had received on the basis of the firm's profits being overstated.

Thinking Critically ABOUT POLICY

1. According to Figure 1, on October 22, 2004, Google's stock was selling for about $150 per share, then Google reported its net profit at $52 million and the stock's price jumped to over $175 per share.
   a. Did investors as a group expect the stock to jump by over $25 per share before the company announced its net profit?
   b. Do stocks' prices always jump upward when companies announce that they've earned a profit? Explain.
2. Someone who knew that Google was about to announce a big profit—for example, someone in Google's top management—could have earned a bundle quickly by buying Google stock at $150 per share and then selling it at $175 per share a day or so later. Such "insider trading" is illegal, however. Do you think that "insider trading" should be illegal? What are the benefits associated with it? What are the problems associated with it?

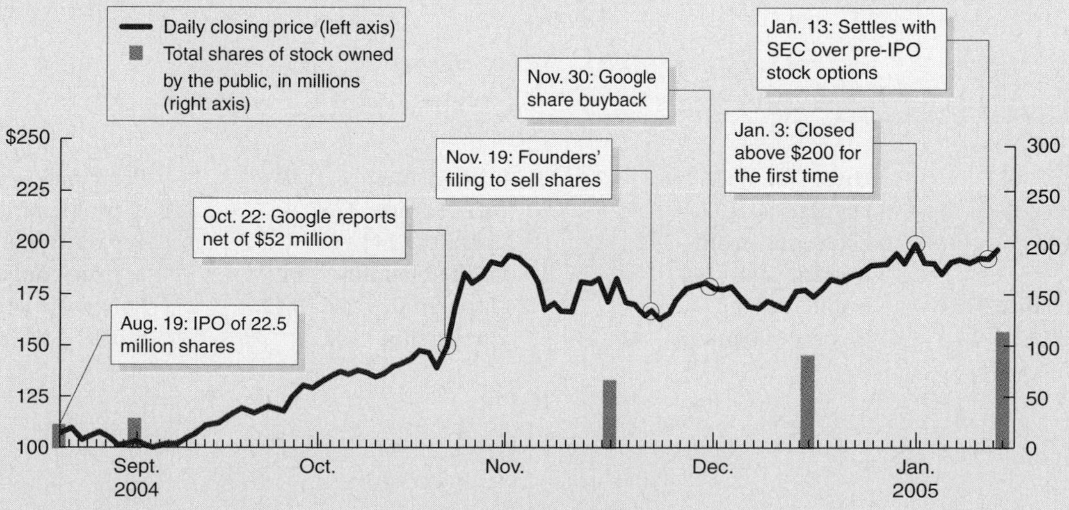

Figure 1: Movements in Google's stock price, August 2004–January 2005.

SUMMARY

LEARNING OBJECTIVE ① Categorize the major types of business in the United States. There are three types of firms: *sole proprietorships, partnerships,* and *corporations.* The owners of sole proprietorships and partners have *unlimited liability,* which means there is no legal distinction between the personal assets of the owners of the business and the assets of the business. The owners of corporations have *limited liability,* which means they can never lose more than their investment in the firm. Although only 20 percent of firms are corporations, they account for the majority of revenue and profit earned by all firms.

LEARNING OBJECTIVE ② Describe the typical management structure of corporations and understand the concepts of separation of ownership from control and the principal-agent problem. Most corporations have a similar management structure: The shareholders elect a board of directors that appoints the corporation's top managers, such as the chief executive officer. Because the top management often does not own a large fraction of the stock in the corporation, large corporations have a *separation of ownership from control.* Because top managers have less incentive to increase the corporation's profits than to increase their own salaries and their own enjoyment, corporations can suffer from a *principal-agent problem.* A principal-agent problem exists when the principals—in this case, the shareholders of the corporation—have difficulty in getting the agent—the corporation's top management—to carry out their wishes.

LEARNING OBJECTIVE ③ Explain how firms obtain the funds they need to operate and expand. Firms rely on *retained earnings*—which are profits retained by the firm and not paid out to the firm's owners—or on using the savings of households for the funds they need to operate and expand. The savings of households flow directly to businesses when investors buy stocks and bonds in financial markets. Savings flow indirectly to businesses when households deposit money in saving and checking accounts in banks and the banks lend these funds to businesses. Federal, state, and local governments also sell bonds in financial markets and households also borrow funds from banks. When a firm sells a bond, it is borrowing money from the buyer of the bond. When a firm sells stock, it is selling part ownership of the firm to the buyer of the stock. The original purchasers of stocks and bonds may resell them in stock and bond markets, such as the New York Stock Exchange.

LEARNING OBJECTIVE ④ Understand the information provided in firms' financial statements. A firm's *income statement* sums up its revenues, costs, and profit over a period of time. A firm's *balance sheet* sums up its financial position on a particular day, usually the end of a quarter or year. Firms report their *accounting profit* on their income statements. Because accounting profit excludes some implicit costs, it is larger than *economic profit.*

LEARNING OBJECTIVE ⑤ Understand the business accounting scandals of 2002, as well as the role of government in corporate governance. Because their compensation often rises with the profitability of the corporation, top managers have an incentive to overstate the profits reported on their firm's income statements. During 2002, it became clear that the top managers of several large corporations had done this, even though intentionally falsifying financial statements is illegal. The *Sarbanes-Oxley Act* of 2002 and greater scrutiny of financial statements have helped to restore investor and management confidence in firm's financial statements.

KEY TERMS

Accounting profit 142
Asset 132
Balance sheet 143
Bond 137
Corporate governance 134
Corporation 132
Coupon payment 137
Direct finance 136
Dividends 137
Economic profit 142
Explicit cost 142
Implicit cost 142
Income statement 142
Indirect finance 136
Interest rate 137
Liability 141
Limited liability 132
Opportunity cost 142
Partnership 132
Principal-agent problem 135
Separation of ownership from control 135
Sole proprietorship 132
Stock 137

REVIEW QUESTIONS

1. What are the three major types of business in the United States? Briefly discuss the most important characteristics of each type.
2. What is limited liability? Why are owners of corporations granted limited liability by the government?
3. What do we mean by the separation of ownership from control in large corporations? How is this related to the principal-agent problem?
4. What is the difference between direct finance and indirect finance? If you borrow money from a bank to buy a new car, are you using direct finance or indirect finance?
5. Why is a bond considered to be a loan but a share of stock is not? Why do corporations issue both bonds and shares of stock?
6. How do the stock and bond markets provide information to businesses? Why do stock and bond prices change over time?
7. What is the Sarbanes-Oxley Act? Why was it passed?

PROBLEMS AND APPLICATIONS

Please visit **www.prenhall.com/hubbard** *for solutions to the even-numbered problems as well as multiple-choice and true or false self-assessment quizzes.*

1. Suppose that shortly after graduating from college you decide to start your own business. Will you organize the business as a sole proprietorship, a partnership, or a corporation? Explain your reasoning.
2. In a May 10, 2003, opinion piece in the *New York Times*, sociologist Dalton Conley proposed the *elimination* of limited liability to corporate shareholders. Do you think that corporations should be granted limited liability? What are the benefits of limited liability? What is its downside? Would you be more willing to buy bonds from a company with limited liability? Would you be more willing to buy the stock of a company with limited liability?
3. Suppose that a firm in which you have invested is losing money. Would you rather own the firm's stock or the firm's bonds? Explain.
4. Suppose you originally invested in a firm when it was small and unprofitable. Now the firm has grown considerably and is large and profitable. Would you be better off if you had bought the firm's stock or the firm's bonds? Explain.
5. The principal-agent problem arises almost everywhere in the business world—but it also crops up even closer to home. Discuss the principal-agent problem that exists in the college classroom. Who is the principal? Who is the agent? What is the problem between this principal and this agent?
6. **[Related to *Solved Problem 5-1*]** Briefly explain whether you agree or disagree with the following argument: "The separation of ownership from control in large corporations and the principal-agent problem means that top managers can work short days, take long vacations, and otherwise slack off."
7. **[Related to *Solved Problem 5-1*]** An economic consultant gives the board of directors of a firm the following advice: "You can increase the profitability of the firm if you change your method of compensating top management. Instead of paying your top management a straight salary, you should pay them a salary plus give them the right to buy the firm's stock in the future at a price above the stock's current market price." Explain the consultant's reasoning. To what difficulties might this compensation scheme lead?
8. The following is from an article in the *New York Times:*

   > In theory, boards [of directors] design pay packages to attract and inspire good chief executives and to align their interests with those of shareholders. . . . But what kind of pay packages are appropriate at companies still run by the founding family?

   The article quotes one expert as arguing: "There is little or no justification for treating an owner-manager in exactly the same way as a standard CEO."

   What does the article mean by saying that pay packages should "align [chief executives'] interests with those of shareholders"? What kind of pay packages would achieve this objective? Do you agree that an "owner-manager" should have a pay package different from that of a CEO who is not a member of the family that started the firm? Briefly explain.

   Source: Diana B. Henriques, "What's Fair Pay for Running the Family Store?," *New York Times*, January 12, 2003.

9. If you deposit $20,000 in a savings account at a bank, you might earn 3 percent interest per year. Someone who borrows $20,000 from a bank to buy a new car might have to pay an interest rate of 8 percent per year on the loan. Knowing this, why don't you just lend your money directly to the car buyer, cutting out the bank?

10. **[Related to the *Chapter Opener*]** When Google's owners wanted to raise funds for expansion in 2004, they decided to sell stock in their company rather than to borrow the money. Why do some companies fund their expansion by borrowing, while others fund expansion by issuing new stock?

11. The following listing for a corporate bond issued by Sara Lee Corporation appeared in the *Wall Street Journal* on May 4, 2005:

COUPON	MATURITY	LAST PRICE	LAST YIELD	EST SPREAD	UST	EST $ VOL (000s)
3.875	June 15, 2013	91.047	5.244	108	10	84,860

   a. If you bought this bond, what is the total coupon payment you would receive during the next year (in dollars)?
   b. For what price did this bond sell at the close of trading on May 3?
   c. What was the yield on a 30-year U.S. Treasury bond on May 3?

12. Consider again the information for the Sara Lee bond in problem 11. Why weren't investors willing to pay $1,000 for this bond, which has a face value of $1,000?

13. In 2005, the French government began issuing bonds with 50-year maturities. Would this bond be purchased only by very young investors who expect to still be alive when the bond matures? Briefly explain.

14. **[Related to *Don't Let This Happen To You!*]** Briefly explain whether you agree or disagree with the following statement: "The total value of the shares of Microsoft stock traded on the NASDAQ last week was $250 million, so the firm actually received more revenue from stock sales than from selling software."

15. Loans from banks are the most important external source of funds to businesses because most businesses are too small to borrow in financial markets by issuing stocks or bonds. Most investors are reluctant to buy the stocks or bonds of small businesses because of the difficulty of gathering accurate information on the financial strength and profitability of the businesses. Nevertheless, news about the stock market is included in nearly every network news program and is often the lead story in the business section of most newspapers. Is there a contradiction here? Why is the average viewer of TV news or the average reader of a newspaper interested in the fluctuations in prices in the stock market?

16. **[Related to *Solved Problem 5-2*]** In the fall of 2002, Buford Yates, director of accounting at WorldCom, pleaded guilty to fraud. In federal court he said that top managers at WorldCom ordered him to make certain adjustments to the firm's financial statements.

    > I came to believe that the adjustments I was being directed to make in WorldCom's financial statements had no justification and contravened generally accepted accounting principles. I concluded that the purpose of these adjustments was to incorrectly inflate WorldCom's reported earnings.

    What are "generally accepted accounting principles"? How would the "adjustments" Yates was ordered to make benefit top managers at WorldCom? Would these adjustments also benefit WorldCom's stockholders? Briefly explain.

    Source: Devlin Barrett, "Ex-WorldCom Exec Pleads Guilty," Associated Press, October 8, 2002.

17. **[Related to *Solved Problem 5-2*]** In 2002, *Business Week* listed Apple Computer as having one of the worst boards of directors:

    > Founder Steve Jobs owns just two shares in the company. . . . The CEO of Micro Warehouse, which accounted for nearly 2.9% of Apple's net sales in 2001, sits on the compensation committee. . . . There is an interlocking directorship—with Gap CEO Mickey Drexler and Jobs sitting on each other's boards.

    Why might investors be concerned that a top manager like Steve Jobs owns only two shares in the firm? Why might investors be concerned if a member of the board of directors also has a business relationship with the firm? What is an "interlocking directorship"? Why is it a bad thing?

    Source: "The Best Boards and the Worst Boards," *Business Week*, October 7, 2002, p. 107.

18. The following is from a *Business Week* editorial:

    > Welcome to the revolution. After years of paying lip service to reform, Enron Corp. and the ensuing wave of business scandal has finally produced a dramatic change in corporate governance. . . . [I]nvestors are rewarding companies with good governance and punishing those without it.

    How are investors able to reward or punish firms? What impact will these rewards and punishments have on boards of directors and top managers?

    Source: "Boardrooms Are Starting to Wake Up," *Business Week*, October 7, 2002, p. 107.

19. Dane decides to give up a job earning $100,000 per year as a corporate lawyer and converts the duplex that he owns into a UFO museum. (He had been renting out the duplex for $20,000 a year.) His direct expenses include $50,000 per year paid to his assistants and $10,000 per year for utilities. Fans flock to the museum to see his collection of extraterrestrial paraphernalia, which he easily could sell on eBay for $1,000,000. Over the course of the year, the museum brings in revenues of $100,000.
   a. How much is Dane's accounting profit for the year?
   b. Is he earning an economic profit? Explain.

20. **[Related to the *Chapter Opener*]** What impact would these events be likely to have on the price of Google's stock?
   a. A competitor launches a search engine that's just as good as Google's.
   b. The corporate income tax is abolished.
   c. Google's board of directors becomes dominated by close friends and relatives of its top management.
   d. The price of wireless Internet connections unexpectedly drops, so more and more people use the Internet.
   e. Google announces a huge profit of $1 billion, but everybody anticipated that Google would earn a huge profit of $1 billion.

Appendix

Tools to Analyze Firms' Financial Information

As we saw in the chapter, modern business organizations are not just "black boxes" transforming inputs into output. Most business revenues and profits are earned by large corporations. Unlike founder-dominated firms, the typical large corporation is run by managers who generally do not own a controlling interest in the firm. Large firms raise funds from outside investors, and outside investors seek information on firms and the assurance that the managers of firms will act in the interests of the investors.

This chapter showed how corporations raise funds by issuing stocks and bonds. This appendix provides more detail to support that discussion. We begin by analyzing *present value* as a key concept in determining the prices of financial securities. We then provide greater information on *financial statements* issued by corporations, using Google as an example.

Using Present Value to Make Investment Decisions

Firms raise funds equity (stock) and debt (bonds and loans) to investors and lenders. If you own shares of stock or a bond, you will receive payments in the form of dividends or coupons over a number of years. Most people value funds they already have more highly than funds they will not receive until some time in the future. For example, you would probably not trade $1,000 you already have for $1,000 you will not receive for one year. The longer you will have to wait to receive a payment, the less value it will have for you. One thousand dollars you will not receive for two years is worth less to you than $1,000 you will receive after one year. The value you give today to money you will receive in the future is called the future payment's **present value.** The present value of $1,000 you will receive in one year will be less than $1,000.

Why is this true? Why is the $1,000 you will not receive for one year less valuable to you than the $1,000 you already have? The most important reason is that if you have $1,000 today, you can use that $1,000 today. You can buy goods and services with the money and receive enjoyment from them. The $1,000 you receive in one year does not have direct use to you now.

Also, prices likely will rise during the year you are waiting to receive your $1,000. So, when you finally do receive the $1,000 in one year you will not be able to buy as much with it as you could with $1,000 today. Finally, there is some risk that you will not receive the $1,000 in one year. The risk may be very great if an unreliable friend borrows $1,000 from you and vaguely promises to pay you back in one year. The risk may be very small when you lend money to the federal government by buying a United States Treasury bond. In either case, there is at least some risk that you will not receive the funds promised.

When someone lends money, the lender expects to be paid back both the amount of the loan and some additional interest. If you decide that to be willing to lend your $1,000 today and you must be paid back $1,100 one year from now, you are charging $100/$1,000 = 0.10 or 10 percent interest on the funds you have loaned. Economists would say that you value $1,000 today as equivalent to the $1,100 to be received one year in the future.

Present value The value in today's dollars of funds to be paid or received in the future.

Notice that \$1,100 can be written as \$1,000 (1 + 0.10). That is, the value of money received in the future is equal to the value of money in the present multiplied by 1 plus the interest rate, with the interest rate expressed as a decimal. Or,

$$\$1{,}100 = 1{,}000\,(1 + 0.10).$$

Notice, also, that if we divide both sides by (1 + 0.10), we can rewrite this formula as:

$$\$1{,}000 = \frac{\$1{,}100}{(1+0.10)}.$$

The rewritten formula states that the present value is equal to the future value to be received in one year divided by one plus the interest rate. This formula is an important one because it can be used to convert any amount to be received in one year into its present value. Writing the formula generally, we have:

$$\text{Present Value} = \frac{\text{Future Value}_1}{(1+i)}.$$

The present value of funds to be received in one year—Future Value$_1$—can be calculated by dividing the amount of those funds to be received by 1 plus the interest rate. With an interest rate of 10 percent, the present value of \$1,000,000 to be received one year from now is:

$$\frac{\$1{,}000{,}000}{(1+0.10)} = \$909{,}090.91.$$

This method is a very useful way of calculating the value today of funds that won't be received for one year. But financial securities such as stocks and bonds involve promises to pay funds over many years. Therefore, it would be even more useful if we could expand this formula to calculate the present value of funds to be received more than one year in the future.

This expansion is easy to do. Go back to the original example where we assumed you were willing to loan out your \$1,000 for one year, provided you received 10 percent interest. Suppose you are asked to lend the funds for two years and that you are promised 10 percent interest per year for each year of the loan. That is, you are lending \$1,000, which at 10 percent interest will grow to \$1,100 after one year, and you are agreeing to loan that \$1,100 out for a second year at 10 percent interest. So, after two years you will be paid back \$1,100 (1 + 0.10) or \$1,210. Or,

$$\$1{,}210 = \$1{,}000\,(1 + 0.10)(1 + 0.10)$$

or,

$$\$1{,}210 = \$1{,}000\,(1 + 0.10)^2.$$

This formula can also be rewritten as:

$$\$1{,}000 = \frac{\$1{,}210}{(1+0.10)^2}.$$

To put the formula in words, the \$1,210 you receive two years from now has a present value equal to \$1,210 divided by the quantity 1 plus the interest rate squared. If you were to agree to lend out your \$1,000 for three years at 10 percent interest, you would receive:

$$\$1{,}331 = \$1{,}000\,(1 + 0.10)^3.$$

Notice, again, that:

$$\$1{,}000 = \frac{\$1{,}331}{(1+0.10)^3}.$$

You can probably see a pattern here. We can generalize the concept to say that the present value of funds to be received n years in the future—whether n is 1, 20, or 85 does not matter—equals the amount of the funds to be received divided by the quantity 1 plus the interest rate raised to the nth power. For instance, with an interest rate of 10 percent, the value of $1,000,000 to be received 25 years in the future is:

$$\text{Present Value} = \frac{\$1{,}000{,}000}{(1+0.10)^{25}} = \$92{,}296.$$

Or, more generally:

$$\text{Present Value} = \frac{\text{Future Value}_n}{(1+i)^n},$$

where Future Value$_n$ represents funds that will be received in n years.

SOLVED PROBLEM 5A-1

How to Receive Your Contest Winnings

Suppose you win a contest and are given the choice of the following prizes:

Prize 1: $50,000 to be received right away, with four additional payments of $50,000 to be received each year for the next four years
Prize 2: $175,000 to be received right away

Explain which prize you would choose and the basis for your decision.

Solving the Problem:

Step 1: Review the material. This problem involves applying the concept of present value, so you may want to review the section "Using Present Value to Make Investment Decisions," which begins on page 152.

Step 2: Explain the basis for choosing the prize. Unless you need immediate cash, you should choose the prize with the highest present value.

Step 3: Calculate the present value of each prize. Prize 2 consists of one payment of $175,000 received right away, so its present value is $175,000. Prize 1 consists of five payments spread out over time. To find the present value of the prize, we must find the present value of each of these payments and add them together. To calculate present value we must use an interest rate. Let's assume an interest rate of 10 percent. In that case the present value of Prize 1 is:

$$\$50{,}000 + \frac{\$50{,}000}{(1+0.10)} + \frac{\$50{,}000}{(1+0.10)^2} + \frac{\$50{,}000}{(1+0.10)^3} + \frac{\$50{,}000}{(1+0.10)^4} =$$

$$\$50{,}000 + \$45{,}454.55 + \$41{,}322.31 + \$37{,}565.74 + \$34{,}150.67 = \$208{,}493.$$

Step 4: State your conclusion. Prize 1 has the greater present value, so you should choose it rather than Prize 2.

YOUR TURN: **For more practice, do related problems 1, 3, 4, and 5 on page 160 at the end of this appendix.**

Using Present Value to Calculate Bond Prices

Anyone who buys a financial asset, such as shares of stock or a bond, is really buying a promise to receive certain payments—dividends in the case of shares of stock or coupons in the case of a bond. The price investors are willing to pay for a financial asset should be equal to the value of the payments they will receive as a result of owning the asset. Because most of the coupon or dividend payments will be received in the future, it is their present value that matters. Put another way, we have the following important idea: *The price of a financial asset should be equal to the present value of the payments to be received from owning that asset.*

Let's consider an example. Suppose that in 1980 General Electric issued a bond with an \$80 coupon that will mature in 2010. It is now 2008 and that bond has been bought and sold by investors many times. You are considering buying it. If you buy the bond, you will receive two years of coupon payments plus a final payment of the bond's principal or face value of \$1,000. Suppose, once again, that you need an interest rate of 10 percent to invest your funds. If the bond has a coupon of \$80, the present value of the payments you receive from owning the bond—and, therefore, the present value of the bond—will be:

$$\text{Present Value} = \frac{\$80}{(1+0.10)} + \frac{\$80}{(1+0.10)^2} + \frac{\$1{,}000}{(1+0.10)^2} = \$965.29.$$

That is, the present value of the bond will equal the present value of the three payments you will receive during the two years you own the bond. You should, therefore, be willing to pay \$965.29 to own this bond and have the right to receive these payments from GE. This process of calculating present values of future payments is used to determine bond prices, with one qualification. The relevant interest rate used by investors in the bond market to calculate the present value and, therefore, the price of an existing bond is usually the coupon rate on comparable newly issued bonds. Therefore, the general formula for the price of a bond is:

$$\text{Bond Price} = \frac{\text{Coupon}_1}{(1+i)} + \frac{\text{Coupon}_2}{(1+i)^2} + \ldots + \frac{\text{Coupon}_n}{(1+i)^n} + \frac{\text{Face Value}}{(1+i)^n},$$

where Coupon_1 is the coupon payment to be received after one year, Coupon_2 is the coupon payment to be received after two years, up to Coupon_n, which is the coupon payment received in the year the bond matures. The ellipsis takes the place of the coupon payments—if any—received between the second year and the year the bond matures. Face Value is the face value of the bond, to be received when the bond matures. The interest rate on comparable newly issued bonds is i.

Using Present Value to Calculate Stock Prices

When you own a firm's stock, you are legally entitled to your share of the firm's profits. Remember that the profits a firm pays out to its shareholders are referred to as dividends. The price of a share of stock should be equal to the present value of the dividends investors expect to receive as a result of owning that stock. Therefore, the general formula for the price of a stock is:

$$\text{Stock Price} = \frac{\text{Dividend}_1}{(1+i)} + \frac{\text{Dividend}_2}{(1+i)^2} + \ldots$$

Notice that this formula looks very similar to the one we used to calculate the price of a bond, with a couple of important differences. First, unlike a bond, stock has no maturity date, so we have to calculate the present value of an infinite number of dividend payments. At first, it may seem that the stock's price must be infinite as well, but remember that dollars you don't receive for many years are worth very little today. For instance, a dividend payment of $10 that will be received 40 years in the future is worth only a little more than $0.20 today at a 10 percent interest rate. The second difference between the stock price formula and the bond price formula is that whereas the coupon payments you receive from owning the bond are known with certainty—they are written on the bond and cannot be changed—you don't know for sure what the dividend payments from owning a stock will be. How large a dividend payment you will receive depends upon how profitable the company will be in the future.

Although it is possible to forecast the future profitability of a company, this cannot be done with perfect accuracy. To emphasize this point, some economists rewrite the basic stock price formula by adding a superscript *e* to each Dividend term to emphasize that these are *expected* dividend payments. Because the future profitability of companies is often very difficult to forecast, it is not surprising that differences of opinion exist over what the price of a particular stock should be. Some investors will be very optimistic about the future profitability of a company and will, therefore, believe that the company's stock should have a high price. Other investors might be very pessimistic and believe that the company's stock should have a low price.

A Simple Formula for Calculating Stock Prices

It is possible to simplify the formula for determining the price of a stock, if we assume that dividends will grow at a constant rate:

$$\text{Stock Price} = \frac{\text{Dividend}}{(i - \text{Growth Rate})},$$

where Dividend is the dividend being received currently and Growth Rate is the rate at which those dividends are expected to grow. If a company currently is paying a dividend of $1 per share and Growth Rate is 10 percent, the company is expected to pay a dividend of $1.10 next year, $1.21 the year after that, and so on.

Now suppose that IBM currently is paying a dividend of $5 per share, the consensus of investors is that these dividends will increase at a rate of 5 percent per year for the indefinite future, and the interest rate is 10 percent. Then the price of IBM's stock should be:

$$\text{Stock Price} = \frac{\$5.00}{(0.10 - 0.05)} = \$100.00.$$

Particularly during the years 1999 and 2000, there was much discussion of whether the high prices of many Internet stocks—such as the stock of Amazon.com—were justified given that many of these companies had not made any profit yet and so had not paid any dividends. Is there any way that a rational investor would pay a high price for the stock of a company currently not earning profits? The formula for determining stock prices shows that it is possible, provided the investor's assumptions are optimistic enough! For example, during 1999, one stock analyst predicted that Amazon.com would soon be earning $10 per share of stock. That is, Amazon.com's total earnings divided by the number of shares of its stock outstanding would be $10. Suppose Amazon.com pays out that $10 in dividends and that the $10 will grow rapidly over the years, by, say, 7 percent per year. Then our formula indicates that the price of Amazon.com stock should be:

$$\text{Stock Price} = \frac{\$10.00}{(0.10 - 0.07)} = \$333.33.$$

If you are sufficiently optimistic about the future prospects of a company, a high stock price can be justified even if the company currently is not earning a profit. But investors in growth stocks must be careful. Suppose that investors believe that growth prospects for Amazon are only 4 percent per year instead of 7 percent because the firm turns out not to be as profitable as initially believed. Then our formula indicates that the price of Amazon.com stock should be:

$$\text{Stock Price} = \frac{\$10.00}{(0.10 - 0.04)} = \$166.67,$$

or only half the value assuming a more optimistic growth rage. Hence investors use information about firms' profitability and growth prospects to determine what the firm is worth.

Going Deeper into Financial Statements

Corporations disclose substantial information about their business operations and financial position to actual and potential investors. Some of this information meets the demands of participants in financial markets and of information-collection agencies, such as Moody's Investors Service, which develops credit ratings that help investors judge the riskiness of corporate bonds. Other information meets the requirements of the U.S. Securities and Exchange Commission.

Key sources of information about a corporation's profitability and financial position are its principal financial statements—the *income statement* and the *balance sheet.* These important information sources were first introduced in the chapter. Here we go into more detail, using recent data for Google as an example.

Analyzing Income Statements

As discussed in the chapter, a firm's income statement summarizes its revenues, costs, and profit over a period of time. Figure 5A-1 shows Google's income statement for 2004.

Revenue		$3,189	Revenue from sales
Operating expenses			
	Cost of revenue	$1,458	Categories of costs
	Research and development	$226	Categories of costs
	Sales and marketing	$246	Categories of costs
	General and administrative	$140	Categories of costs
	Other expenses	$480	
Total operating expenses		$2,549	Total cost
Operating income		$640	Operating income = revenue – operating expenses
Investment income		$10	
Income before income taxes		$650	Before-tax accounting profit
Income taxes		–$251	
Net income (accounting profit)		$399	After-tax accounting profit

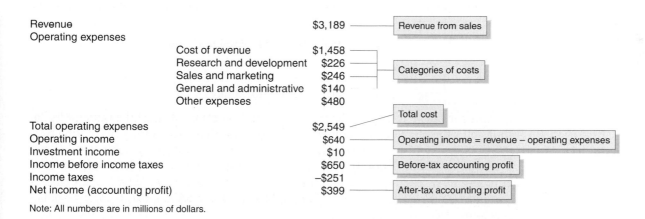

Note: All numbers are in millions of dollars.

FIGURE 5A-1

Google's Income Statement for 2004

Google's income statement shows the company's revenue, costs, and profit for 2004. The difference between its revenue ($3,189 million) and its operating expenses ($2,549 million) is its operating income ($640 million). Most corporations also have investments, such as government or corporate bonds, that generate some income for them. In this case, Google earned $10 million, giving the firm an income before taxes of $650 million. After paying taxes of $251 million, Google was left with a net income, or accounting profit, of $399 million for the year.

Source: Google's Income Statement for 2004. Google Inc. "Consolidated Statements of Income," February 1, 2005. Used with permission of Google, Inc.

Google's income statement presents the results of the company's operations during the year. Listed first are the revenues it earned, largely from selling advertising on its Web site, from January 1, 2004 to December 31, 2004: $3,189 million. Listed next are Google's operating expenses, the most important of which is its *cost of revenue*—which is commonly known as *cost of sales* or *cost of goods sold:* $1,458 million. Cost of revenue is the direct cost of producing the products sold, including in this case the salaries of the computer programmers Google hires to write the software for its Web site. Google also has substantial costs for researching and developing its products ($226 million) and for advertising and marketing them ($246 million). General and administrative expenses ($140 million) includes costs such as the salaries of top managers.

The difference between a firm's revenue and its costs is its profit. "Profit" shows up in several forms on an income statement. A firm's *operating income* is the difference between its revenue and its operating expenses. Most corporations, including Google, also have investments, such as government and corporate bonds, that normally generate some income for them. In this case, Google earned $10 million on its investments, which increased its *income before taxes* to $650 million. The federal government taxes the profits of corporations. During 2004, Google paid $251 million—or about 39 percent of its profits—in taxes. *Net income* after taxes was $399 million. The net income that firms report on their income statements is referred to as their after-tax *accounting profit.*

Analyzing Balance Sheets

As discussed in the chapter, whereas a firm's income statement reports a firm's activities for a period of time, a firm's balance sheet summarizes its financial position on a particular day, usually the end of a quarter or a year. To understand how a balance sheet is organized, first recall that an asset is anything of value that the firm owns and a liability is a debt or obligation owed by the firm. Subtracting the value of a firm's liabilities from the value of its assets leaves its *net worth.* Because a corporation's stockholders are its owners, net worth is often listed as **stockholders' equity** on a balance sheet. Using these definitions, we can state the balance sheet equation (also called the basic accounting equation) as follows:

Stockholders' equity The difference between the value of a corporation's assets and the value of its liabilities; also known as net worth.

$$\text{Assets} - \text{Liabilities} = \text{Stockholders' Equity}$$

or,

$$\text{Assets} = \text{Liabilities} + \text{Stockholders' Equity}.$$

This formula tells us that the value of a firm's assets must equal the value of its liabilities plus the value of stockholders' equity. An important accounting rule dating back to the beginning of modern bookkeeping in fifteenth-century Italy holds that balance sheets should list assets on the left side and liabilities and net worth or stockholders' equity on the right side. Notice that this means that *the value of the left side of the balance sheet must always equal the value of the right side.* Figure 5A-2 shows Google's balance sheet as of December 31, 2004.

A couple of the entries on the asset side of the balance sheet may be unfamiliar: *Current assets* are assets that the firm could convert into cash quickly, such as the balance in its checking account or its accounts receivable, which is money currently owed to the firm for products that have been delivered but not yet paid for. *Goodwill* represents the difference between the purchase price of a company and the market value of its assets. It represents the ability of a business to earn an economic profit from its assets. For example, if you buy a restaurant that is located on a busy intersec-

ASSETS		LIABILITIES AND STOCKHOLDERS' EQUITY	
Current assets	$2,693	Current liabilities	$340
Property and equipment	379	Long-term liabilities	44
Investments	71	Total liabilities	384
Goodwill	123	Stockholders' equity	2,929
Other long-term assets	47		
Total assets	3,313	Total liabilities and stockholders' equity	3,313

FIGURE 5A-2

Google's Balance Sheet as of December 31, 2004

Corporations list their assets on the left of their balance sheets and their liabilities on the right. The difference between the value of the firm's assets and the value of its liabilities equals the net worth of the firm, or stockholders' equity. Stockholders' equity is listed on the right side of the balance sheet. Therefore, the value of the left side of the balance sheet must always equal the value of the right side.

Note: All numbers are in millions of dollars.

Source: Google's Balance Sheet as of December 31, 2004, source: Google, Inc., "Consolidated Balance Sheets," February 1, 2004. Used with permission of Google, Inc.

tion and you employ a chef with a reputation for preparing delicious food, you may pay more than the market value of the tables, chairs, ovens, and other assets. This additional amount you pay will be entered on the asset side of your balance sheet as goodwill.

Current liabilities are short-term debts such as accounts payable, which is money owed to suppliers for goods received but not yet paid for, or bank loans that will be paid back in less than one year. Long-term bank loans and the value of outstanding corporate bonds are *long-term liabilities.*

KEY TERMS

Present value 153

Stockholders' equity 158

REVIEW QUESTIONS

1. Why is money you receive at some future date worth less than money you receive today? If the interest rate rises, what effect does this have on the present value of payments you receive in the future?
2. Give the formula for calculating the present value of a bond that will pay a coupon of $100 per year for 10 years and that has a face value of $1,000.
3. Compare the formula for calculating the present value of the payments you will receive from owning a bond to the formula for calculating the present value of the payments you will receive from owning a stock. What are the key similarities? What are the key differences?
4. How is operating income calculated? How does operating income differ from net income? How does net income differ from accounting profit?
5. What's the key difference between a firm's income statement and its balance sheet? What is listed on the left side of a balance sheet? What is listed on the right side?

PROBLEMS AND APPLICATIONS

Please visit **www.prenhall.com/hubbard** *for solutions to the even-numbered problems as well as multiple-choice and true or false self-assessment quizzes.*

1. **[Related to *Solved Problem 5A-1*]** If the interest rate is 10 percent, what is the present value of a bond that matures in two years, pays $85 one year from now, and pays $1,085 two years from now?
2. The following is from an Associated Press story on the contract of baseball star Carlos Beltran:

   > Beltran's contract calls for his $11 million signing bonus to be paid in four installments: $5 million upon approval and $2 million each this June 15, 2005, and on Jan. 15, 2006, and Jan. 15, 2007. He gets a $10 million salary this year, $12 million in each of the following two seasons and $18.5 million in each of the final four seasons, with $8.5 million deferred annually from 2008–11. The players' association calculated the present day value of the contract at $115,726,946, using a 6 percent discount rate (the prime rate [which is the interest rate banks charge on loans to their best customers] plus 1 percent, rounded to the nearest whole number). For purposes of baseball's luxury tax, which currently uses a 3.62 percent discount rate, the contract is valued at $116,695,898.

   Briefly explain why the present value of Beltran's contract is lower if a higher interest is used to make the calculation than if a lower interest rate is used.

   Source: "Like Pedro, Beltran Gets Suite on Road," Associated Press, January 18, 2005.
3. **[Related to *Solved Problem 5A-1*]** Before the 2005 season pitcher Armando Benitez signed a contract with the San Francisco Giants baseball team that would pay him the following amounts: $4.1 million in 2005, $6.6 million in 2006, $7.6 million in 2007, $1.6 million in 2008, and $1.6 million in 2009. Assume that he receives each payment as a lump sum at the end of the season and that he received his 2005 payment one year after he signed the contract.
   a. Some newspaper reports described Benitez as having signed a "$21.5 million contract" with the Giants. Do you agree that $21.5 million was the value of this contract? Briefly explain.
   b. What was the present value of Benitez's contract at the time he signed it (assume an interest rate of 10 percent)?
   c. If you use an interest rate of 5 percent, what was the present value of his contract?
4. **[Related to *Solved Problem 5A-1*]** A winner of the Pennsylvania Lottery was given the choice of receiving $18 million at once or $1,440,000 per year for 25 years.
   a. If the winner had opted for the 25 annual payments, how much in total would she have received?
   b. At an interest rate of 10 percent, what would be the present value of the 25 payments?
   c. At an interest rate of 5 percent, what would be the present value of the 25 payments?
   d. What interest rate would make the present value of the 25 payments equal to the one payment of $18 million? (This question is difficult and requires the use of a financial calculator or a spreadsheet. *Hint:* If you are familiar with the Excel spreadsheet program, use the RATE function. Questions b and c can be answered by using the Excel NPV—Net Present Value—function.)
5. **[Related to *Solved Problem 5A-1*]** Before the start of the 2000 baseball season, the New York Mets decided they didn't want Bobby Bonilla playing for them any longer. But Bonilla had a contract with the Mets for the 2000 season that would have obliged the Mets to pay him $5.9 million. When the Mets released Bonilla, he agreed to take the following payments in lieu of the $5.9 million the Mets would have paid him in the year 2000: He will receive 25 equal payments of $1,193,248.20 each July 1 from 2011 to 2035. If you were Bobby Bonilla, which would you rather have had, the lump sum $5.9 million or the 25 payments beginning in 2011? Explain the basis for your decision.
6. Suppose that eLake, an online auction site, is paying a dividend of $2.00 per share. You expect this dividend to grow 2 percent per year, and the interest rate is 10 percent. What is the most you would be willing to pay for a share of stock in eLake? If the interest rate is 5 percent, what is the most you would be willing to pay? When interest rates in the economy decline, would you expect stock prices in general to rise or fall? Explain.
7. Suppose you buy the bond of a large corporation at a time when the inflation rate is very low. If the inflation rate increases during the time you hold the bond, what is likely to happen to the price of the bond?

8. Use the information in the following table for calendar year 2004 to prepare the McDonald's Corporation's income statement. Be sure to include entries for operating income and net income.

Revenue from company restaurants	$14,224 million
Revenue from franchised restaurants	4,841 million
Cost of operating company-owned restaurants	12,100 million
Income taxes	924 million
Interest expense	338 million
General and administrative cost	1,980 million
Cost of restaurant leases	1,003 million
Other operating costs	441 million

Source: McDonald's Corporation, *Consolidated Statement of Income, 2004*, January 28, 2005.

9. Use the information in the following table on the financial situation of Starbucks Corporation as of October 3, 2004, to prepare the firm's balance sheet. Be sure to include an entry for stockholders' equity.

Current assets	$1,359 million
Current liabilities	774 million
Property and equipment	1,471 million
Long-term liabilities	58 million
Goodwill	69 million
Other assets	419 million

Source: Starbucks Corporation, *Annual Report, 2004*.

10. The *current ratio* is equal to a firm's current assets divided by its current liabilities. Use the information in Figure 5A-2 to calculate Google's current ratio on December 31, 2004. Investors generally prefer that a firm's current ratio is greater than 1.5. What problems might a firm encounter if the value of its current assets is low relative to the value of its current liabilities?

chapter six 6

Comparative Advantage and the Gains from International Trade

Sugar Quota Drives U.S. Candy Manufacturers Overseas

➤ Trade is, simply, the act of buying or selling. Is there a difference when trade takes place within a country or when the trade is international? Within the United States, domestic trade makes it possible for consumers in Ohio to eat salmon caught in Alaska or for consumers in Montana to drive cars built in Michigan. Similarly, international trade makes it possible for consumers in the United States to drink wine from France or use DVD players from Japan. But one significant difference between domestic trade and international trade is that international trade is more controversial. At one time, nearly all the televisions, shoes, clothing, and toys consumed in the United States were also produced in the United States. Today, these goods are produced mainly by firms in other countries. This shift has benefited U.S. consumers because foreign-made goods have lower prices than the U.S.-made goods they have replaced. But at the same time, many U.S. firms that produced these goods have gone out of business and their workers have lost their jobs. Not surprisingly, opinion polls show that many Americans favor reducing international trade because they believe this would preserve jobs in the United States.

But would it? Congress enacted a sugar quota to preserve jobs in the U.S. sugar industry by reducing the quantity of sugar allowed into the United States. Several countries around the world can produce sugar at lower costs than can U.S. sugar producers. As a result the *world price* of sugar, which is the price at which sugar can be bought on the world market, is too low for U.S. sugar companies to cover their costs. The sugar quota allows U.S. companies to sell sugar domestically for a price that is about three times as high as the world price. Without the sugar quota, competition from foreign sugar producers would drive many U.S. producers out of business. But the United States also has a large candy industry, which uses many tons of sugar. So how have U.S. candy firms and their employees been affected by high sugar prices in the United States?

Life Savers used to be called the "All-American Candy." Life Savers were invented in 1912 by Clarence Crane, who wanted to develop a candy that would not melt in the heat of the summer. Because the sinking

of the cruise liner *Titanic* had been the most publicized event of the year, Crane hit on the idea of selling a hard candy in the shape of a life preserver. Today, Life Savers is no longer advertised as the all-American candy because in 2003 it moved production from Holland, Michigan, to Montreal, Canada. The six hundred workers employed at the Michigan Life Savers plant lost their jobs. The price of sugar is about 21 cents per pound in the United States, but the world price is only about 8 cents per pound. In Canada, Life Savers can be made using sugar purchased at the world price, which saves almost $9 million per year in lower sugar costs.

Life Savers is only one of several candies no longer produced in the United States. Brach's Confections, maker of Star Brites mints, closed its factory in Illinois and moved production to Argentina. Bob's Candies, the largest manufacturer of candy canes, and the Spangler Candy Company, maker of Cherry Balls, have both moved to Mexico.

Should the United States have a sugar quota? The sugar quota creates winners—U.S. sugar companies and their employees—and losers—U.S. companies that use sugar, their employees, and U.S. consumers who must pay higher prices for goods that contain sugar. In this chapter, we will explore who wins and who loses from international trade and review the political debate over whether international trade should be restricted. *An Inside Look* on page 188 discusses a recent trade agreement between the United States and Australia.

LEARNING OBJECTIVES

After studying this chapter, you should be able to:

① Discuss the increasing importance of international trade to the United States.

② Understand the difference between comparative advantage and absolute advantage.

③ Explain how countries gain from international trade.

④ Discuss the sources of comparative advantage.

⑤ Analyze the economic effects of government policies that restrict international trade.

⑥ Evaluate the arguments for and against government policies that restrict international trade.

➤ Markets for internationally traded goods and services can be analyzed using the tools of demand and supply that we developed in Chapter 3. We saw in Chapter 2 that trade in general—whether within a country or between countries—is based on the principle of comparative advantage. In this chapter, we look more closely at how this principle is applied to international trade. We can also use the concepts of consumer surplus, producer surplus, and deadweight loss that were developed in Chapter 4 to analyze government policies, such as the sugar quota, that interfere with trade. With this background we can return to the political debate over the desirability of international trade. We begin by looking at how large a role international trade plays in the U.S. economy.

① LEARNING OBJECTIVE

Discuss the increasing importance of international trade to the United States.

An Overview of International Trade

International trade has grown tremendously over the past 50 years. The increase in trade is the result of the falling costs of shipping products around the world, the spread of cheap and reliable communications, and changes in government policies. Businesspeople today can travel to Europe or Asia using fast, cheap, and reliable air transportation. The Internet allows managers to communicate instantaneously and at a very low cost with customers and suppliers around the world. Firms can use large container ships to send their products across the oceans at low cost. These and other improvements in transportation and communication have created a global marketplace only dreamed about by earlier generations of businesspeople.

In addition, over the past 50 years many governments have changed policies to facilitate international trade. For example, tariff rates have fallen. A **tariff** is a tax imposed by a government on *imports* of a good into a country. **Imports** are goods and services bought domestically but produced in other countries. In the 1930s, the United States charged an average tariff rate above 50 percent. Today, the rate is less than 2 percent. In North America, most tariffs between Canada, Mexico, and the United States were eliminated in 1994 with passage of the North American Free Trade Agreement (NAFTA). Twenty-five countries in Europe have formed the European Union, which has eliminated all tariffs among member countries, greatly increasing both imports and **exports,** which are goods and services produced domestically, but sold to other countries.

Tariff A tax imposed by a government on imports.

Imports Goods and services bought domestically but produced in other countries.

Exports Goods and services produced domestically but sold to other countries.

The Importance of Trade to the U.S. Economy

U.S. consumers buy increasing quantities of goods and services produced in other countries. At the same time, U.S. businesses sell increasing quantities of goods and services to consumers in other countries. Figure 6-1 shows that since 1950, both exports and imports have been steadily increasing as a fraction of U.S. gross domestic product (GDP). Recall that GDP is the value of all the goods and services produced in a country during a year. In 1950, exports and imports were both about 4 percent of GDP. In 2004, exports were about 10 percent of GDP, and imports were about 15 percent.

Not all sectors of the U.S. economy are affected equally by international trade. On the one hand, it's difficult to import or export some services, such as haircuts or appendectomies. On the other hand, a large percentage of U.S. agricultural production is exported. Each year the United States exports about 50 percent of the wheat crop, 40 percent of the rice crop, and 20 percent of the corn crop.

Many U.S. manufacturing industries also depend on trade. About 20 percent of U.S. manufacturing jobs depend directly or indirectly on exports. In some industries, such as computers, the products these workers make are directly exported. In other industries, such as steel, the products are used to make other products, such as bulldoz-

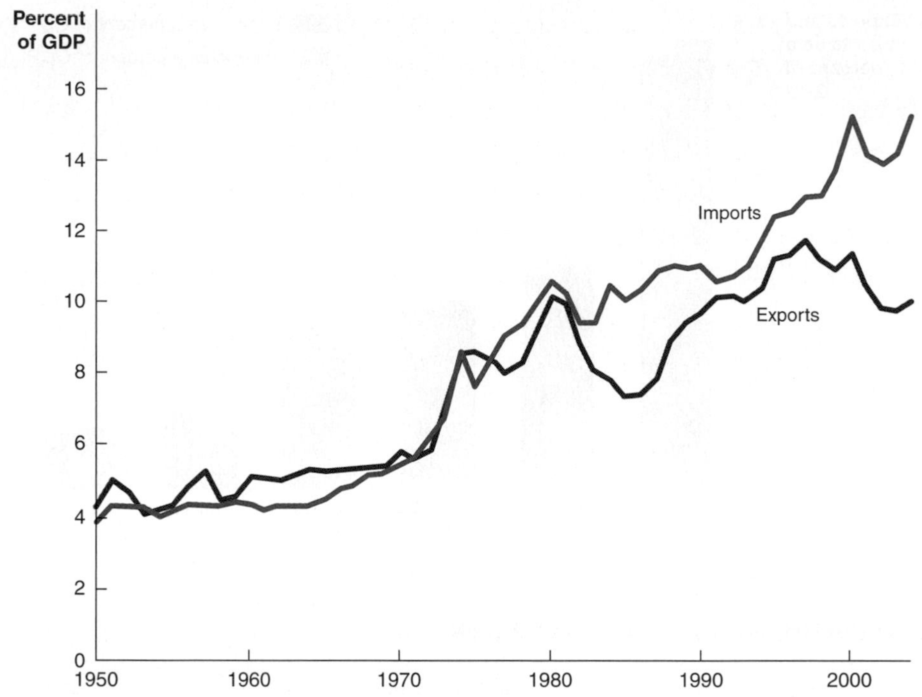

FIGURE 6-1

International Trade Is of Increasing Importance to the United States

Exports and imports of goods and services as a percentage of total production—measured by GDP—show the importance of international trade to an economy. Since 1950, both imports and exports have been steadily rising as a fraction of U.S. GDP.

Source: U.S. Department of Commerce, Bureau of Economic Analysis.

ers or machine tools, that are then exported. In all, about two-thirds of U.S. manufacturing industries depend on exports for at least 10 percent of jobs.

U.S. International Trade in a World Context

The United States is the largest exporter in the world, as Figure 6-2 illustrates. Six of the other seven leading exporting countries are also large, high-income countries. The rapid growth of the Chinese economy over the past 20 years has resulted in its becoming the fifth largest exporter.

International trade remains less important to the United States than it is to most other countries. Figure 6-3 on the next page shows that imports and exports remain smaller fractions of GDP in the United States than in other countries. In some smaller countries, like Belgium, imports and exports make up more than half of GDP. Japan is the only high-income country that is less dependent on international trade than is the United States.

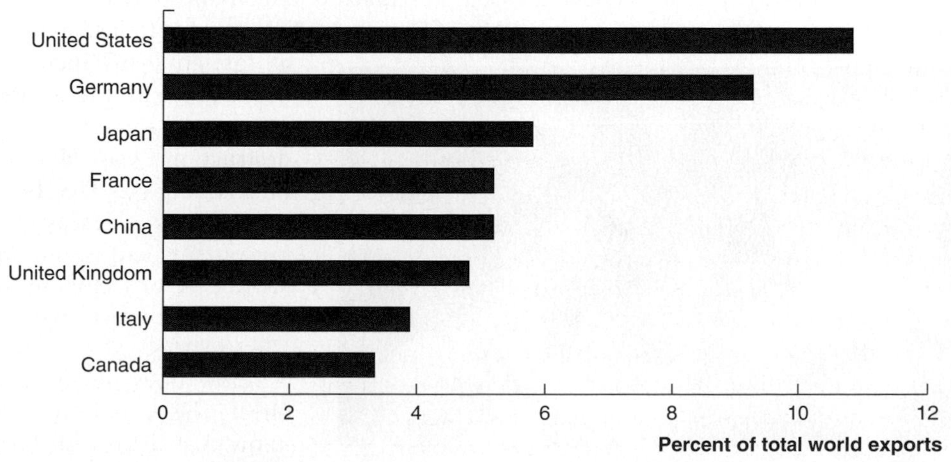

FIGURE 6-2

The Eight Leading Exporting Countries

The United States is the leading exporting country, accounting for about 11 percent of total world exports. The values are the shares of total world exports of merchandise and commercial services.

Source: World Trade Organization, *International Trade Statistics*, 2004.

FIGURE 6-3

International Trade as a Percent of GDP

International trade is still less important to the United States than to most other countries, with the significant exception of Japan.

Source: International Monetary Fund, *International Financial Statistics Yearbook*, 2004.

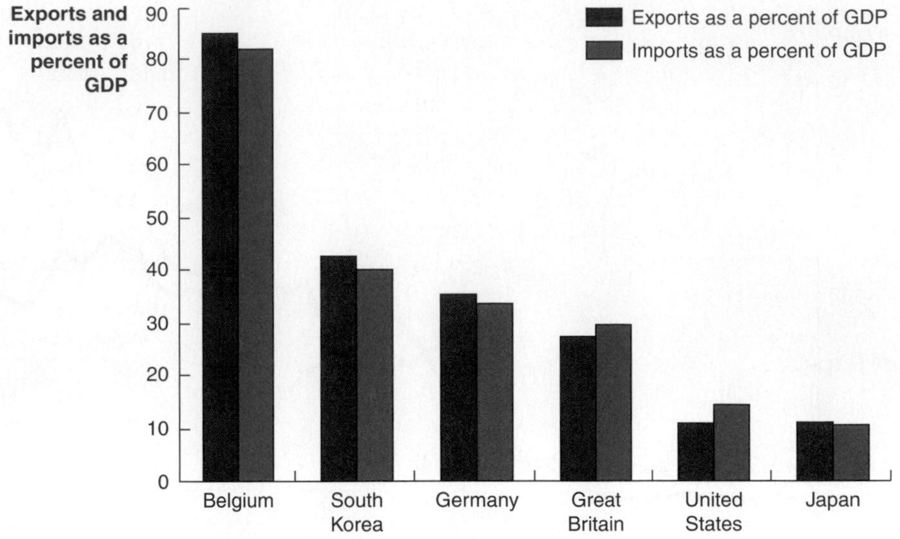

6-1 Making the Connection

Has Outsourcing Hurt the U.S. Economy?

One aspect of the increase in international trade that has been particularly controversial in recent years is *outsourcing*. Outsourcing—sometimes called "offshoring"—occurs when a domestic firm uses workers in a foreign country to produce a good or service that is then sold to domestic consumers. An example is Dell Computer using workers in Bangalore, India, to provide telephone technical support to U.S. buyers of Dell's computers. From the viewpoint of the Indian economy, this would be *insourcing*. The increase in outsourcing and insourcing reflects advances in communications and information technology that make it easier for firms to coordinate the activities of their employees in foreign countries. Outsourcing became a source of political controversy during the early 2000s as employment in the United States grew slowly following the 2001 recession. Some political commentators believed that outsourcing played a significant role in this slow employment growth.

Exact statistics are not available, but the number of jobs outsourced by U.S. companies appears to be small relative to the size of the economy. For example, a study by the U.S. Bureau of Labor Statistics indicates that during the first three months of 2003, outsourcing accounted for only 4,633 of 239,361 jobs lost at a large group of firms. The study covered only firms that employed at least 50 employees and that had eliminated at least 50 jobs, so it was not complete. It seems unlikely, however, that including smaller firms in the study would have significantly changed the results. In a market economy, new jobs are constantly being created as old jobs are destroyed. For example, during 2003, more than 30 million jobs were created and about the same number were destroyed. Some of the job creation was due to insourcing—as foreign firms increased production in the United States—and some of the job destruction was due to outsourcing—as U.S. firms moved jobs overseas. But outsourcing and insourcing are not major factors in the employment situation in the United States.

Some companies outsource technical support services to India.

How does outsourcing affect the economy? We know that firms outsource to reduce their costs. Competition among firms ensures that lower costs are passed on to consumers in the form of lower prices. In this sense, outsourcing has an effect similar to a technological change that lowers cost. The lower prices that outsourcing makes possible are spread widely among consumers, but the costs of outsourcing are concentrated among workers who lose their jobs. Although jobs that are outsourced are lost to U.S. workers, other jobs are created in the United States to take their place. The same is true of jobs lost to technological change. Over the last 20 years, the U.S. economy has created 30 million more jobs than have been destroyed due to outsourcing, technological change, and all other causes. Nevertheless, individual workers whose jobs are lost to outsourcing may have difficulty finding jobs as desirable as the ones they have lost.

Source: U.S. Bureau of Labor Statistics, "Extended Mass Layoffs Associated with Domestic and Overseas Relocations, First Quarter 2004," June 10, 2004.

Comparative Advantage: The Basis of All Trade

(2) LEARNING OBJECTIVE
Understand the difference between comparative advantage and absolute advantage.

Why have businesses around the world increasingly looked for markets in other countries? Why have consumers increasingly purchased goods and services made in other countries? People trade for one reason: Trade makes them better off. Whenever a buyer and seller agree to a sale, they must both believe they are better off—otherwise there would be no sale. This outcome must hold whether the buyer and seller live in the same city or in different countries. As we will see, governments are more likely to interfere with international trade than they are with domestic trade, but the reasons for the interference are more political than they are economic.

A Brief Review of Comparative Advantage

In Chapter 2, we discussed the key economic concept of *comparative advantage.* **Comparative advantage** is the ability of an individual, firm, or country to produce a good or service at a lower opportunity cost than other producers. Recall that **opportunity cost** is the highest-valued alternative that must be given up to engage in an activity. People specialize in those economic activities in which they have a comparative advantage. In trading, we benefit from the comparative advantage of other people (or firms or countries), and other people benefit from our comparative advantage.

Comparative advantage The ability of an individual, firm, or country to produce a good or service at a lower opportunity cost than other producers.

Opportunity cost The highest-valued alternative that must be given up to engage in an activity.

A good way to think of comparative advantage is to recall the example in Chapter 2 of you and your neighbor picking fruit. Your neighbor is better at picking both apples and cherries than you are. Why, then, doesn't your neighbor pick both types of fruit? Because the opportunity cost of picking her own apples is very high: She is a particularly skilled cherry picker, and every hour spent picking apples is an hour taken away from picking cherries. You can pick apples at a much lower opportunity cost than your neighbor, so you have a comparative advantage in picking apples. Your neighbor can pick cherries at a much lower opportunity cost than you can, so your neighbor has a comparative advantage in picking cherries. Your neighbor is better off specializing in picking cherries, and you are better off specializing in picking apples. You can then trade some of your apples for some of your neighbor's cherries and both of you will end up with more of each fruit.

Comparative Advantage in International Trade

The principle of comparative advantage can explain why people pursue different occupations. It can also explain why countries produce different goods and services. International trade involves many countries importing and exporting many different goods and services. Countries are better off if they specialize in producing the goods for which they have a comparative advantage. They can then trade for the goods for which other countries have a comparative advantage.

We can illustrate why specializing on the basis of comparative advantage makes countries better off with a simple example involving just two countries and two

TABLE 6-1

An Example of Japanese Workers Being More Productive Than American Workers

	OUTPUT PER HOUR OF WORK	
	CELL PHONES	MP3 PLAYERS
Japan	12	6
United States	2	4

products. Suppose the United States and Japan produce only cell phones and MP3 players, like Apple's iPod. Assume that each country uses only labor to produce each good, and that Japanese and U.S. cell phones and MP3 players are exactly the same. Table 6-1 shows how much each country can produce of each good with one hour of labor.

Notice that Japanese workers are more productive than U.S. workers in making both goods. In 1 hour of work, Japanese workers can make six times as many cell phones and one and one-half times as many MP3 players as U.S. workers. Japan has an *absolute advantage* over the United States in producing both goods. **Absolute advantage** is the ability to produce more of a good or service than competitors when using the same amount of resources. In this case, Japan can produce more of both goods using the same amount of labor as the United States.

Absolute advantage The ability to produce more of a good or service than competitors when using the same amount of resources.

It might seem at first that Japan has nothing to gain from trading with the United States because it has an absolute advantage in producing both goods. However, Japan should specialize and produce only cell phones and obtain the MP3 players it needs by exporting cell phones to the United States in exchange for MP3 players. The reason that Japan benefits from trade is that although it has an *absolute advantage* in the production of both goods, it has a *comparative advantage* only in the production of cell phones. The United States has a comparative advantage in the production of MP3 players.

If this seems contrary to common sense, think about the opportunity cost to each country of producing each good. If Japan wants to produce more MP3 players, it has to switch labor away from cell phone production. Every hour of labor switched from producing cell phones to producing MP3 players increases MP3 player production by 6 and reduces cell phone production by 12. Japan has to give up 12 cell phones for every 6 MP3 players it produces. Therefore, the opportunity cost to Japan of producing one more MP3 player is 12/6, or 2 cell phones.

If the United States switches 1 hour of labor from cell phones to MP3 players, production of cell phones falls by 2 and production of MP3 players rises by 4. Therefore, the opportunity cost to the United States of producing one more MP3 player is 2/4, or 0.5 cell phone. The United States has a lower opportunity cost of producing MP3 players and, therefore, has a comparative advantage in making this product. By similar reasoning, we can see that Japan has a comparative advantage in producing cell phones. Table 6-2 summarizes this result.

③ LEARNING OBJECTIVE

Explain how countries gain from international trade.

The Gains from Trade

Can Japan really gain from producing only cell phones and trading with the United States for MP3 players? To see that it can, assume at first that Japan and the United States

TABLE 6-2

The Opportunity Costs of Producing Cell Phones and MP3 Players

	OPPORTUNITY COSTS	
	CELL PHONES	MP3 PLAYERS
Japan	0.5 MP3 player	2 cell phones
United States	2 MP3 players	0.5 cell phone

TABLE 6-3

Production without Trade

	WITHOUT TRADE	
	PRODUCTION AND CONSUMPTION	
	CELL PHONES	MP3 PLAYERS
Japan	9,000	1,500
United States	1,500	1,000

do not trade with each other. A situation in which a country does not trade with other countries is called **autarky.** Assume that in autarky each country has 1,000 hours of labor available to produce the two goods, and each country produces the quantities of the two goods shown in Table 6-3. Because there is no trade, these quantities also represent consumption of the two goods in each country.

Autarky A situation in which a country does not trade with other countries.

Increasing Consumption through Trade

Suppose now that Japan and the United States begin to trade with each other. The **terms of trade** is the ratio at which a country can trade its exports for imports from other countries. As Table 6-1 on the previous page shows, it takes twice as much labor in Japan to produce one MP3 player as to produce one cell phone. In the United States, the situation is reversed: It takes twice as much labor to produce a cell phone as it does to produce an MP3 player. For simplicity, let's assume that the terms of trade end up with Japan and the United States being willing to trade one cell phone for one MP3 player.

Terms of trade The ratio at which a country can trade its exports for imports from other countries.

Once trade has begun, the United States and Japan can exchange MP3 players for cell phones or cell phones for MP3 players. For example, if Japan specializes by using all 1,000 available hours of labor to produce cell phones, it will be able to produce 12,000. It then could export 1,500 cell phones to the United States in exchange for 1,500 MP3 players (remember we are assuming the terms of trade are one cell phone for one MP3 player). Japan ends up with 10,500 cell phones and 1,500 MP3 players. Compared with the situation before trade, Japan has the same number of MP3 players, but 1,500 more cell phones. If the United States specializes in producing MP3 players, it will be able to produce 4,000. It then could export 1,500 MP3 players to Japan in exchange for 1,500 cell phones. The United States ends up with 2,500 MP3 players and 1,500 cell phones. Compared with the situation before trade, the United States has the same number of cell phones, but 1,500 more MP3 players. Trade has allowed both countries to increase the quantities of goods consumed. Table 6-4 summarizes the gains from trade for the United States and Japan.

By trading, Japan and the United States are able to consume more than they could without trade. This outcome is possible because world production of both goods increases after trade (remember, in this example, our "world" consists of just the United States and Japan):

	WORLD PRODUCTION	
	BEFORE TRADE	AFTER TRADE
Cell Phones	10,500	12,000
MP3 Players	2,500	4,000

Why does total production of cell phones and MP3 players increase when the United States specializes in producing MP3 players and Japan specializes in producing cell phones? A domestic analogy helps to answer this question: If a company shifts production from an old factory to a more efficient modern factory, its output will increase. In effect, the same thing happens in our example. Producing MP3 players in Japan and cell phones in the United States is inefficient. Shifting production to the more efficient

TABLE 6-4

The Gains from Trade for Japan and the United States

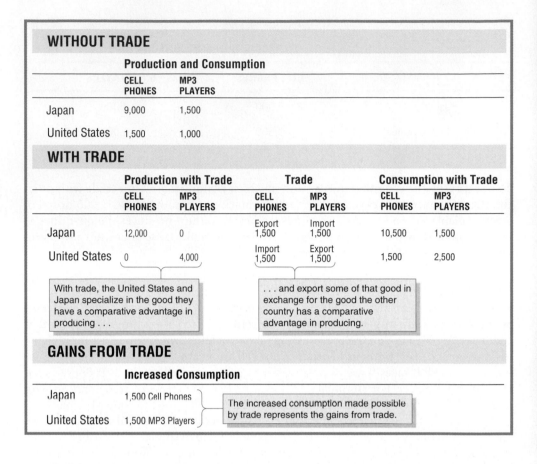

WITHOUT TRADE

	Production and Consumption	
	CELL PHONES	MP3 PLAYERS
Japan	9,000	1,500
United States	1,500	1,000

WITH TRADE

	Production with Trade		Trade		Consumption with Trade	
	CELL PHONES	MP3 PLAYERS	CELL PHONES	MP3 PLAYERS	CELL PHONES	MP3 PLAYERS
Japan	12,000	0	Export 1,500	Import 1,500	10,500	1,500
United States	0	4,000	Import 1,500	Export 1,500	1,500	2,500

With trade, the United States and Japan specialize in the good they have a comparative advantage in producing . . .

. . . and export some of that good in exchange for the good the other country has a comparative advantage in producing.

GAINS FROM TRADE

	Increased Consumption
Japan	1,500 Cell Phones
United States	1,500 MP3 Players

The increased consumption made possible by trade represents the gains from trade.

country—the one with the comparative advantage—increases total production. The key point is this: *Countries gain from specializing in producing goods in which they have a comparative advantage and trading for goods in which other countries have a comparative advantage.*

SOLVED PROBLEM 6-1

③ LEARNING OBJECTIVE

Explain how countries gain from international trade.

The Gains from Trade

The first discussion of comparative advantage appears in *On the Principles of Political Economy and Taxation,* a book written by David Ricardo in 1817. Ricardo provided a famous example of the gains from trade using wine and cloth production in Portugal and England. The following table is adapted from Ricardo's example, with cloth measured in sheets and wine measured in kegs:

	OUTPUT PER YEAR OF LABOR	
	CLOTH	WINE
Portugal	100	150
England	90	60

a. Explain which country has an absolute advantage in the production of each good.

b. Explain which country has a comparative advantage in the production of each good.

c. Suppose that Portugal and England currently do not trade with each other. Each has 1,000 years of labor to use producing cloth and wine, and the countries are currently producing the amounts of each good shown in the table:

	CLOTH	WINE
Portugal	18,000	123,000
England	63,000	18,000

Show that Portugal and England can both gain from trade. Assume that the terms of trade are that one sheet of cloth can be traded for one keg of wine.

Solving the Problem:

Step 1: Review the chapter material. This problem is about absolute and comparative advantage and the gains from trade, so you may want to review the section "Comparative Advantage: The Basis of All Trade," which begins on page 167, and the section "The Gains from Trade," which begins on page 168.

Step 2: Answer question (a) by determining which country has an absolute advantage. Remember that a country has an absolute advantage over another country when it can produce more of a good using the same resources. The table shows that Portugal can produce more cloth *and* more wine with 1 year's worth of labor than can England. Thus, Portugal has an absolute advantage in the production of both goods and, therefore, England does not have an absolute advantage in the production of either good.

Step 3: Answer question (b) by determining which country has a comparative advantage. A country has a comparative advantage when it can produce a good at a lower opportunity cost. To produce 100 sheets of cloth, Portugal must give up 150 kegs of wine. Therefore, the opportunity cost to Portugal of producing one sheet of cloth is 150/100 or 1.5 kegs of wine. England has to give up 60 kegs of wine to produce 90 sheets of cloth, so its opportunity cost of producing one sheet of cloth is 60/90 or 0.67 keg of wine. The opportunity costs of producing wine can be calculated in the same way. The following table shows the opportunity cost to Portugal and England of producing each good.

OPPORTUNITY COSTS		
	CLOTH	WINE
Portugal	1.5 kegs of wine	0.67 sheets of cloth
England	0.67 keg of wine	1.5 sheets of cloth

Portugal has a comparative advantage in wine because its opportunity cost is lower. England has a comparative advantage in cloth because its opportunity cost is lower.

Step 4: Answer question (c) by showing that both countries can benefit from trade. By now it should be clear that both countries would be better off if they specialize where they have a comparative advantage and trade for the other product. The following table is very similar to Table 6-4 and shows one example of trade making both countries better off (to test your understanding, construct another example):

WITHOUT TRADE		
	PRODUCTION AND CONSUMPTION	
	CLOTH	WINE
Portugal	18,000	123,000
England	63,000	18,000

WITH TRADE						
	PRODUCTION WITH TRADE		TRADE		CONSUMPTION WITH TRADE	
	CLOTH	WINE	CLOTH	WINE	CLOTH	WINE
Portugal	0	150,000	Import 18,000	Export 18,000	18,000	132,000
England	90,000	0	Export 18,000	Import 18,000	72,000	18,000

GAINS FROM TRADE	
	INCREASED CONSUMPTION
Portugal	9,000 wine
England	9,000 cloth

***YOUR TURN:* For more practice, do related problems 3 and 10 on pages 191 and 192 at the end of this chapter.**

Why Don't We See Complete Specialization?

In our example of two countries producing only two products, each country specializes in producing one of the goods. In the real world, many goods and services are produced in more than one country. For example, the United States and Japan both produce automobiles. We do not see complete specialization in the real world for three main reasons:

- ***Not all goods and services are traded internationally.*** Even if, for example, Japan had a comparative advantage in the production of medical services, it would be difficult for Japan to specialize in their production and export them. There is no easy way for U.S. patients in need of appendectomies to receive them from Japanese surgeons.
- ***Production of most goods involves increasing opportunity costs.*** Recall from Chapter 2 that production of most goods involves increasing opportunity costs. As a result, when the United States devotes more workers to producing MP3 players, the opportunity cost of producing more MP3 players will increase. At some point, the opportunity cost of producing MP3 players in the United States will rise to the level of the opportunity cost of producing MP3 players in Japan. Once that happens, international trade will no longer push the United States further toward complete specialization. The same will be true of Japan: Increasing opportunity cost will cause Japan to stop short of complete specialization in producing cell phones.
- ***Tastes for products differ.*** Most products are *differentiated.* Cell phones, MP3 players, cars, and televisions—to name just a few products—come with a wide variety of features. When buying automobiles, some people are looking for reliability and good gasoline mileage, others are looking for room to carry seven passengers, and still others want styling and high performance. So, some car buyers prefer Toyota Corollas, some prefer Ford minivans, and others prefer BMWs. As a result, Japan, the United States, and Germany may each have a comparative advantage in producing different types of automobiles.

Does Anyone Lose as a Result of International Trade?

In our cell phone and MP3 player example, consumption increases in both the United States and Japan as a result of trade. Everyone gains and no one loses. Or do they? In our example, we referred repeatedly to "Japan" or the "United States" producing cell phones or MP3 players. But countries do not produce goods—firms do. In a world without trade, there would be cell phone and MP3 player firms in both Japan and the

Don't Let This Happen To You!

Remember That Trade Creates Both Winners and Losers

The following statement is from a Federal Reserve publication: "Trade is a win–win situation for all countries that participate." Statements like this are sometimes taken to mean that there are no losers from international trade. But notice that the statement refers to *countries*, not individuals. When countries participate in trade, they make their consumers better off by increasing the quantity of goods and services available to them. As we have seen, however, expanding trade eliminates the jobs of workers employed at companies that are less efficient than foreign companies. Trade also creates new jobs at companies that export to foreign markets. It may be difficult, though, for workers who lose their jobs because of trade to easily find others. That is why in the United States the federal government uses the Trade Adjustment Assistance program to provide funds for workers who have lost their jobs due to international trade. These funds can be used for retraining, for searching for new jobs, or for relocating to areas where new jobs are available. This program—and similar programs in other countries—recognizes that there are losers from international trade as well as winners.

Source: Quote from Federal Reserve Bank of Dallas Web site, "International Trade and the Economy," www.dallasfed.org/educate/everyday/ev7.html.

YOUR TURN: **Test your understanding by doing related problem 24 on page 194 at the end of this chapter.**

United States. In a world with trade, there would only be Japanese cell phone firms and U.S. MP3 player firms. Japanese MP3 player firms and U.S. cell phone firms would disappear. The owners of Japanese MP3 player firms, the owners of U.S. cell phone firms, and the people who work for them are likely to do their best to convince the Japanese and U.S. governments to interfere with trade by barring imports of the competing products from the other country or by imposing high tariffs on them. Later in this chapter we will discuss government policies that restrict trade.

Where Does Comparative Advantage Come From?

④ LEARNING OBJECTIVE
Discuss the sources of comparative advantage.

Among the main sources of comparative advantage are the following:

- *Climate and natural resources.* This source of comparative advantage is the most obvious. Because of geology, Saudi Arabia has a comparative advantage in the production of oil. Because of climate and soil conditions, Costa Rica has a comparative advantage in the production of bananas, and the United States has a comparative advantage in the production of wheat.
- *Relative abundance of labor and capital.* Some countries, such as the United States, have many highly skilled workers and a great deal of machinery. Other countries, such as China, have many unskilled workers and relatively little machinery. As a result, the United States has a comparative advantage in the production of goods that require highly skilled workers or sophisticated machinery to manufacture, such as aircraft, semiconductors, and computer software. China has a comparative advantage in the production of goods that require unskilled workers and small amounts of simple machinery, such as children's toys.
- *Technology.* Broadly defined, *technology* is the process firms use to turn inputs into goods and services. At any given time, firms in different countries do not all have access to the same technologies. In part, this difference reflects past investments countries have made in supporting higher education or in providing support for research and development. Some countries are strong in *product technologies,* which involve the ability to develop new products. For example, firms in the United States have pioneered the development of such products as televisions, digital computers, airliners, and many prescription drugs. Other countries are strong in *process technologies,* which involve the ability to improve the processes used to make existing products. For example, firms in Japan, such as Toyota and Nissan, succeeded by greatly improving the processes for making automobiles.

- *External economies.* It is difficult to explain the location of some industries on the basis of climate, natural resources, the relative abundance of labor and capital, or technology. For example, why does southern California have a comparative advantage in making movies or Switzerland in making watches or New York in providing financial services? The answer is that once an industry becomes established in an area, firms that locate in that area gain advantages over firms located elsewhere. The advantages include the availability of skilled workers, the opportunity to interact with other firms in the same industry, and being close to suppliers. These advantages result in lower costs to firms located in the area. Because these lower costs result from increases in the size of the industry in an area, economists refer to them as **external economies.**

External economies Reductions in a firm's costs that result from an expansion in the size of an industry.

6-2 Making the Connection

Why Is Dalton, Georgia, the Carpet-Making Capital of the World?

Factories within a 65-mile radius of Dalton, Georgia, account for 80 percent of U.S. carpet production and more than half of world carpet production. Carpet production is highly automated and relies primarily on synthetic fibers. Dalton, a small city located in rural northwest Georgia, would not seem to have any advantages in carpet production. In fact, the location of the carpet industry in Dalton was an historical accident.

In the early 1900s, Catherine Evans Whitener started making bedspreads using a method called "tufting," in which she sewed cotton yarn through the fabric and then cut the ends of the yarn so it would fluff up. These bedspreads became very popular. By the 1930s, the process was mechanized and was then applied to carpets. In the early years, the industry used cotton grown in Georgia, but today synthetic fibers, such as nylon and olefin, have largely replaced cotton and wool in carpet manufacturing.

More than 170 carpet factories are now located in the Dalton area. Supporting the carpet industry are local yarn manufacturers, machinery suppliers, and maintenance firms. Dye plants have opened solely to supply the carpet industry. Printing shops have opened whose whole business is printing tags and labels for carpets. Box factories have opened to produce cartons designed specifically for shipping carpets. The local workforce has developed highly specialized skills for running and maintaining the carpet-making machinery.

Because Catherine Evans Whitener started making bedspreads by hand in Dalton, Georgia, a hundred years ago, a multibillion-dollar carpet industry is now located there.

A company establishing a carpet factory outside the Dalton area is unable to use the suppliers or the skilled workers available to factories in Dalton. As a result, carpet factories located outside of Dalton may have higher costs than factories located in Dalton. Although there is no particular reason why the carpet industry should have originally located in Dalton, external economies gave the area a comparative advantage in carpet making once it began to grow there.

Comparative Advantage Over Time: The Rise and Fall—and Rise—of the U.S. Consumer Electronics Industry

A country may develop a comparative advantage in the production of a good, then as time passes and circumstances change, the country may lose its comparative advantage in producing that good and develop a comparative advantage in producing other goods. For several decades, the United States had a comparative advantage in the production of consumer electronic goods, such as televisions, radios, and stereos. The comparative advantage of the United States in these products was based on having developed most of the underlying technology, having the most modern factories, and having a skilled and experienced workforce. Gradually, however, other countries, particularly Japan, gained access to the technology, built modern factories, and developed skilled workforces. As mentioned earlier, Japanese firms have excelled in process technologies, which involve the ability to improve the processes used to make existing products. By the 1970s and 1980s, Japanese firms were able to produce many consumer electronic goods more cheaply and with higher quality than could U.S. firms. Sony, Panasonic, and Pioneer replaced Magnavox, Zenith, and RCA as world leaders in consumer electronics.

By 2005, however, as the technology underlying consumer electronics evolved, comparative advantage began to shift again, and several U.S. firms surged ahead of their Japanese competitors. For example, Apple Computer developed the iPod; palmOne developed the Treo smartphone that has the capacity for e-mail, Web surfing, and picture taking; and Kodak developed digital cameras with EasyShare software that made it easy to organize, enhance, and share digital pictures. As pictures and music converted to digital data, process technologies became less important than the ability to design and develop new products. These new consumer electronics products required skills similar to those in computer design and software writing where the United States had long maintained a comparative advantage.

Once a country has lost its comparative advantage in producing a good, its income will be higher and its economy will be more efficient if it switches from producing the good to importing it, as the United States did when it switched from producing televisions to importing them. As we will see in the next section, however, there is often political pressure on governments to attempt to preserve industries that have lost their comparative advantage.

Government Policies That Restrict Trade

5 LEARNING OBJECTIVE

Analyze the economic effects of government policies that restrict international trade.

Free trade Trade between countries that is without government restrictions.

Free trade, or trade between countries that is without government restrictions, makes consumers better off. We can expand on this idea using the concepts of consumer surplus and producer surplus developed in Chapter 4. Figure 6-4 shows the market for lumber in the United States assuming autarky, where the United States does not trade with other countries. The equilibrium price of lumber is $3 per board foot and the equilibrium quantity is 1,000,000 board feet. (A board foot is a piece of lumber one inch thick and one foot wide by one foot long.) The blue area represents consumer surplus and the red area represents producer surplus.

Now suppose that the United States begins importing lumber from Canada and other countries, and that lumber is selling in these countries for $2 per board foot. Because the world market for lumber is large, we will assume that the United States can buy as much lumber as it wants to without causing the *world price* of $2 to rise. Therefore, once imports of lumber are permitted into the United States, U.S. lumber companies will not be able to sell lumber at prices higher than the world price of $2, and the U.S. price will become equal to the world price.

Figure 6-5 shows the result of allowing imports of lumber into the United States. With the price lowered from $3 to $2, U.S. consumers increase their purchases from 1,000,000 board feet to 1,200,000 board feet. Equilibrium moves from point *E* to point *F*. In the new equilibrium, U.S. producers have reduced the quantity of lumber they supply from 1,000,000 board feet to 700,000 board feet. Imports will equal 500,000 board feet, which is the difference between U.S. consumption and U.S. production.

FIGURE 6-4

The U.S. Lumber Industry under Autarky

This figure shows the market for lumber in the United States assuming autarky, where the United States does not trade with other countries. The equilibrium price of lumber is $3 per board foot and the equilibrium quantity is 1,000,000 board feet. The blue area represents consumer surplus, and the red area represents producer surplus.

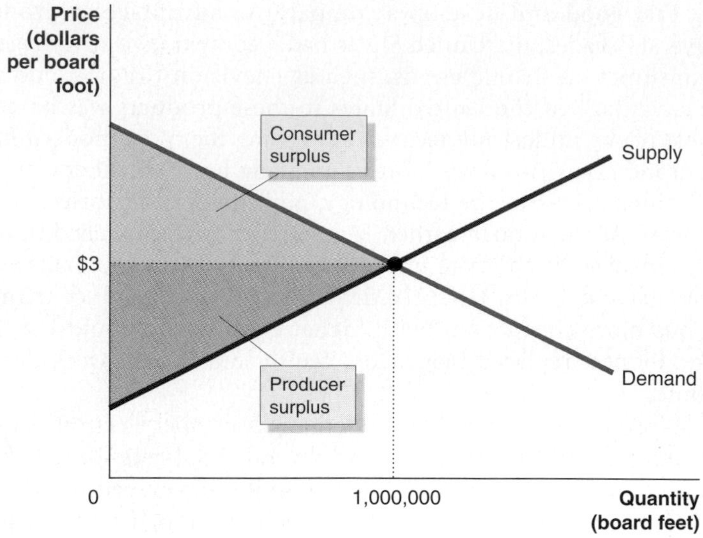

Under autarky, consumer surplus would be area *A* in Figure 6-5. With imports, the reduction in price increases consumer surplus, so it is now equal to the sum of areas *A*, *B*, *C*, and *D*. Although the lower price increases consumer surplus, it reduces producer surplus. Under autarky, producer surplus was equal to the sum of the areas *B* and *E*. With imports, producer surplus is equal to only area *E*. Recall that economic surplus equals the sum of consumer surplus and producer surplus. Moving from autarky to allowing imports increases economic surplus in the United States by an amount equal to the sum of areas *C* and *D*.

We can conclude that international trade helps consumers, but hurts firms that are less efficient than foreign competitors. As a result, these firms and their workers are

FIGURE 6-5

The Effect of Imports on the U.S. Lumber Market

When imports are allowed into the United States, the price of lumber falls from $3 to $2. U.S. consumers increase their purchases from 1,000,000 board feet to 1,200,000 board feet. Equilibrium moves from point *F* to point *G*. U.S. producers reduce the quantity of lumber they supply from 1,000,000 board feet to 700,000 board feet. Imports equal 500,000 board feet, which is the difference between U.S. consumption and U.S. production. Consumer surplus equals the areas *A*, *B*, *C*, and *D*. Producer surplus equals the area of *E*.

	Under Autarky	With Imports
Consumer Surplus	*A*	*A* + *B* + *C* + *D*
Producer Surplus	*B* + *E*	*E*
Economic Surplus	*A* + *B* + *E*	*A* + *B* + *C* + *D* + *E*

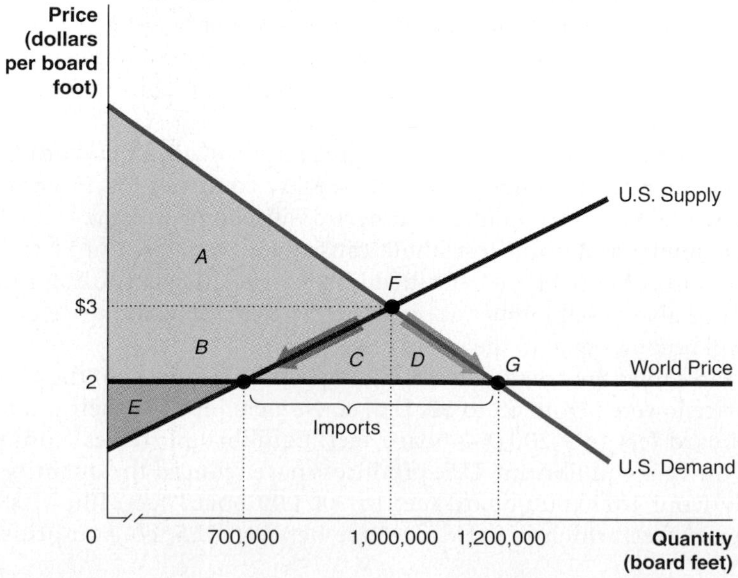

often strong supporters of government policies that restrict trade. These policies usually take one of two forms:

- Tariffs
- Quotas and voluntary export restraints

Tariffs

The most common interferences with trade are *tariffs,* which are taxes imposed by a government on goods imported into a country. Like any other tax, a tariff will increase the cost of selling a good. Figure 6-6 shows the impact of a tariff of $0.50 per board foot on lumber imports into the United States. The $0.50 tariff raises the price of lumber in the United States from the world price of $2.00 per board foot to $2.50 per board foot. At this higher price, U.S. lumber producers increase the quantity they supply from 700,000 board feet to 900,000 board feet. U.S. consumers, though, cut back their purchases of lumber from 1,200,000 board feet to 1,100,000 board feet. Imports decline from 500,000 board feet (1,200,000 − 700,000) to 200,000 board feet (1,100,000 − 900,000). Equilibrium moves from point *E* to point *F.*

By raising the price of lumber from $2.00 to $2.50, the tariff reduces consumer surplus by the sum of areas *A, B, C,* and *D.* Area *A* is the increase in producer surplus from the higher price. The government collects tariff revenue equal to the tariff of $0.50 per board feet multiplied by the 200,000 board feet imported. Area *C* represents the government's tariff revenue. Areas *B* and *D* represent losses to U.S. consumers that are not captured by anyone. They are deadweight loss and represent the decline in economic efficiency resulting from the lumber tariff. Area *B* shows the effect on U.S. consumers of being forced to buy from U.S. producers who are less efficient than foreign producers, and area *D* shows the effect of U.S. consumers buying less lumber than they would have at the world price. As a result of the tariff, economic surplus has been reduced by the

Loss of Consumer Surplus	=	Increase in Producer Surplus	+	Government Tariff Revenue	+	Deadweight Loss
A + *B* + *C* + *D*		*A*		*C*		*B* + *D*

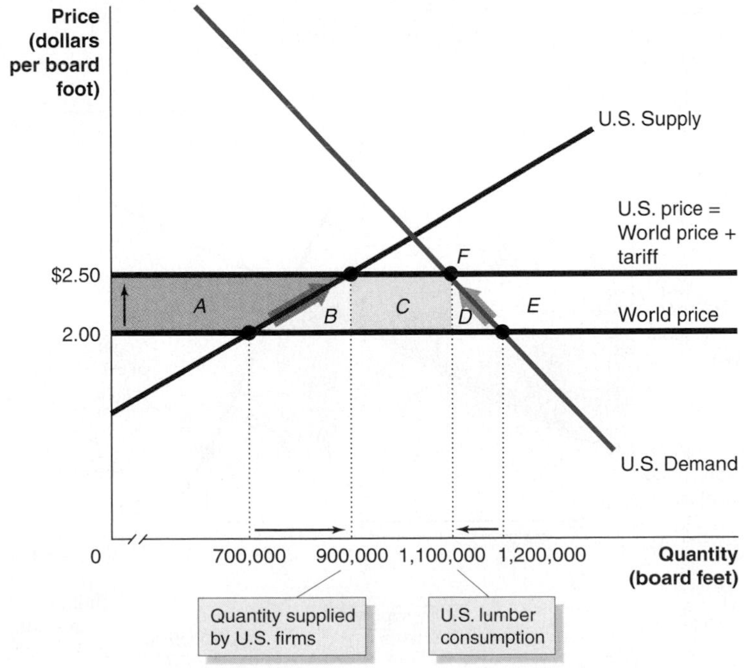

FIGURE 6-6

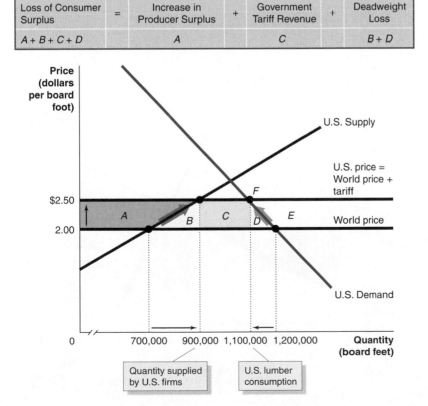

The Effects of a Tariff on Lumber

Without a tariff on lumber, U.S. lumber producers will sell 700,000 board feet of lumber, U.S. consumers will purchase 1,200,000 board feet, and imports will be 500,000 board feet. The U.S. price will equal the world price of $2.00 per board foot. The $0.50 per board foot lumber tariff raises the price of lumber in the United States to $2.50 per board foot and U.S. producers increase the quantity they supply to 900,000 board feet. U.S. consumers reduce their purchases to 1,100,000 board feet. Equilibrium moves from point *E* to point *F.* The lumber tariff causes a loss of consumer surplus equal to the area *A* + *B* + *C* + *D.* The area *A* is the increase in producer surplus due to the higher price. The area *C* is the government's tariff revenue. The areas *B* and *D* represent deadweight loss.

sum of areas *B* and *D*. Recall from Chapter 4 that deadweight loss represents a loss of economic efficiency.

We can conclude that the tariff succeeds in helping U.S. lumber producers, but hurts U.S. consumers and the efficiency of the U.S. economy.

Quotas

Quota A numerical limit imposed by the government on the quantity of a good that can be imported into a country.

Voluntary export restraint An agreement negotiated between two countries that places a numerical limit on the quantity of a good that can be imported by one country from the other country.

A **quota** is a numerical limit on the quantity of a good that can be imported, and it has an effect similar to a tariff. A quota is imposed by the government of the importing country. A **voluntary export restraint** is an agreement negotiated between two countries that places a numerical limit on the quantity of a good that can be imported by one country from the other country. In the early 1980s, the United States and Japan negotiated a voluntary export restraint that limited the quantity of automobiles the United States would import from Japan. Quotas and voluntary export restraints have similar economic effects.

The main purpose of most tariffs and quotas is to reduce the foreign competition faced by domestic firms. We saw an example of this at the beginning of this chapter when we discussed the sugar quota, which Congress imposed to protect U.S. sugar producers. Figure 6-7 shows the actual statistics for the U.S. sugar market in 2003. The effect of a quota is very similar to the effect of a tariff. By limiting imports, a quota forces the domestic price of a good above the world price. In this case, the sugar quota limits sugar imports to 3.5 billion pounds (shown by the bracket in Figure 6-7), forcing the U.S. price of sugar up to $0.21 per pound, or

FIGURE 6-7

The Effect of the U.S. Sugar Quota

Without a sugar quota, U.S. sugar producers would have sold 1.0 billion pounds of sugar, U.S. consumers would have purchased 24.3 billion pounds of sugar, and imports would have been 23.3 billion pounds. The U.S. price would have equaled the world price of $0.08 per pound. Because the sugar quota limits imports to 3.5 billion pounds (the bracket in the graph), the price of sugar in the United States rises to $0.21 per pound and U.S. producers increase the quantity of sugar they supply to 16.8 billion pounds. U.S. consumers reduce their sugar purchases to 20.3 billion pounds. Equilibrium moves from point *E* to point *F*. The price of sugar in the United States is now $0.13 per pound higher than the world price. The sugar quota causes a loss of consumer surplus equal to the area *A* + *B* + *C* + *D*. The area *A* is the gain to U.S. sugar producers. The area *C* is the gain to foreign sugar producers. The areas *B* and *D* represent deadweight loss. The total loss to U.S. consumers in 2003 was $2.91 billion.

Loss of Consumer Surplus	=	Gain by U.S. Sugar Producers	+	Gain to Foreign Sugar Producers	+	Deadweight Loss
A + *B* + *C* + *D*		*A*		*C*		*B* + *D*
$2.91 billion	=	$1.16 billion	+	$.46 billion	+	$1.29 billion

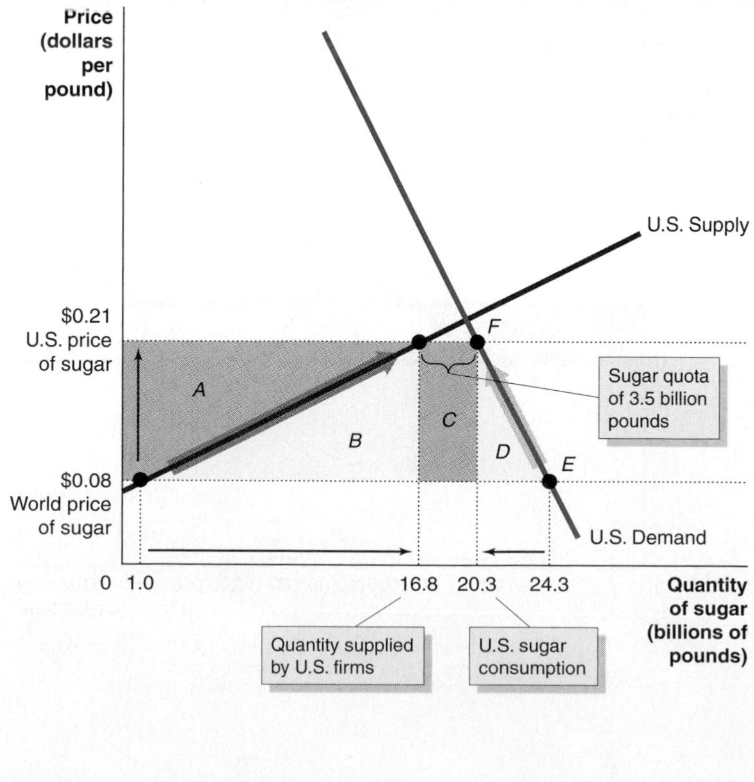

\$0.13 higher than the world price. The U.S. price is above the world price because the quota keeps foreign sugar producers from selling the additional sugar in the United States that would drive the price down to the world price. At a price of \$0.21 cents per pound, U.S. producers increased the quantity of sugar they supply from 1.0 billion pounds to 16.8 billion pounds, and U.S. consumers cut back their purchases of sugar from 24.3 billion pounds to 20.3 billion pounds. Equilibrium moves from point *E* to point *F*.

Measuring the Economic Impact of the Sugar Quota

Once again, we can use the concepts of consumer surplus, producer surplus, and deadweight loss to measure the economic impact of the sugar quota. Without a sugar quota, the world price of \$0.08 per pound would also be the U.S. price. In Figure 6-7, consumer surplus equals the area above the \$0.08 price line and below the demand curve. The sugar quota causes the U.S. price to rise to \$0.21 cents and reduces consumer surplus by the area $A + B + C + D$. Without a sugar quota, producer surplus received by U.S. sugar producers would be equal to the area below the \$0.08 price line and above the supply curve. The higher U.S. price resulting from the sugar quota increases the producer surplus of U.S. sugar producers by an amount equal to area *A*.

A license from the U.S. government is required to import sugar under the quota system. These import licenses are distributed to foreign producers. Therefore, foreign sugar producers who are lucky enough to have an import license also benefit from the quota because they are able to sell sugar on the U.S. market at \$0.21 per pound instead of \$0.08 per pound. The gain to foreign sugar producers is area *C*. Areas *A* and *C* represent transfers from U.S. consumers of sugar to U.S. and foreign producers of sugar. Areas *B* and *D* represent losses to U.S. consumers that are not captured by anyone. They are deadweight losses and represent the decline in economic efficiency resulting from the sugar quota. Area *B* shows the effect of U.S. consumers being forced to buy from U.S. producers who are less efficient than foreign producers, and area *D* shows the effect of U.S. consumers buying less sugar than they would have at the world price.

Enough information is available in the figure to calculate the dollar value of each of the four areas. The results of these calculations are shown in the table in Figure 6-7. The total loss to consumers from the sugar quota was \$2.91 billion in 2003. About 40 percent of this loss, or \$1.16 billion, was gained by U.S. sugar producers as increased producer surplus. About 16 percent, or \$0.46 billion, was gained by foreign sugar producers as increased producer surplus, and about 44 percent, or \$1.29 billion, was a deadweight loss to the U.S. economy. The U.S. International Trade Commission estimates that eliminating the sugar quota would result in the loss of about 3,000 jobs in the U.S. sugar industry. The cost to U.S. consumers of saving these jobs is equal to \$2.91 billion/3,000 or about \$970,000 per job. In fact, this cost is an underestimate because eliminating the sugar quota would result in new jobs being created, particularly in the candy industry. As we saw at the beginning of this chapter, U.S. candy companies have been moving factories to other countries to escape the impact of the sugar quota.

SOLVED PROBLEM 6-2

Measuring the Economic Effect of a Quota

(5) LEARNING OBJECTIVE

Analyze the economic effects of government policies that restrict international trade.

Suppose that the United States currently both produces apples and imports them. The U.S. government then decides to restrict international trade in apples by imposing a quota that allows imports of only four million boxes of apples into the United States each year. The figure shows the results of imposing the quota:

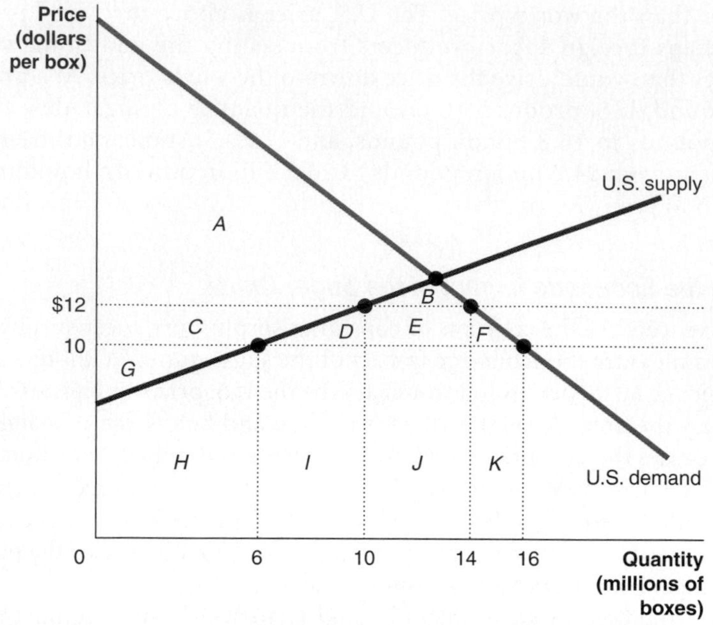

Fill in the following table using the prices, quantities, and letters in the figure:

	WITHOUT QUOTA	WITH QUOTA
World price of apples	________	________
U.S. price of apples	________	________
Quantity supplied by U.S. firms	________	________
Quantity demanded by U.S. consumers	________	________
Quantity imported	________	________
Area of consumer surplus	________	________
Area of producer surplus	________	________
Area of deadweight loss	________	________

Solving the Problem:

Step 1: Review the chapter material. This problem is about measuring the economic effects of a quota, so you may want to review the section "Quotas," which begins on page 178, and "Measuring the Economic Impact of the Sugar Quota," which begin on page 179.

Step 2: Fill in the table. After studying Figure 6-7, you should be able to fill in the table. Remember that consumer surplus is the area below the demand curve and above the market price.

	WITHOUT QUOTA	WITH QUOTA
World price of apples	$10	$10
U.S. price of apples	$10	$12
Quantity supplied by U.S. firms	6 million boxes	10 million boxes
Quantity demanded by U.S. consumers	16 million boxes	14 million boxes
Quantity imported	10 millions boxes	4 million boxes
Area of consumer surplus	A + B + C + D + E + F	A + B
Area of domestic producer surplus	G	G + C
Area of deadweight loss	No deadweight loss	D + F

YOUR TURN: **For more practice, do related problem 25 on page 194 at the end of this chapter.**

TABLE 6-5

Preserving U.S. Jobs with Tariffs and Quotas Is Expensive

PRODUCT	NUMBER OF JOBS SAVED	COST TO CONSUMERS PER YEAR FOR EACH JOB SAVED
Benzenoid chemicals	216	$1,376,435
Luggage	226	1,285,078
Softwood lumber	605	1,044,271
Dairy products	2,378	685,323
Frozen orange juice	609	635,103
Ball bearings	146	603,368
Machine tools	1,556	479,452
Women's handbags	773	263,535
Canned tuna	390	257,640

Source: Federal Reserve Bank of Dallas, *2002 Annual Report,* Exhibit 11.

The High Cost of Preserving Jobs with Tariffs and Quotas

The sugar quota is not alone in imposing a high cost on U.S. consumers to save jobs at U.S. firms. Table 6-5 shows the cost tariffs and quotas impose on U.S. consumers per year for each job saved for several other industries.

Many other countries also use tariffs and quotas to try to protect jobs. Table 6-6 shows the cost to Japanese consumers per year for each job saved as a result of tariffs and quotas in the listed industries. Note the staggering cost imposed on Japanese consumers by the Japanese government's restrictions on imports of rice.

Just as the sugar quota costs jobs in the candy industry, other tariffs and quotas cost jobs outside the industries immediately affected. For example, in 1991, the United States imposed tariffs on flat-panel displays used in laptop computers. This was good news for U.S. producers of these displays but bad news for companies producing laptop computers. Toshiba, Sharp, and Apple all closed their U.S. laptop production facilities and moved production overseas. In fact, whenever one industry receives tariff or quota protection, jobs will be lost in other domestic industries.

Gains from Unilateral Elimination of Tariffs and Quotas

Some politicians argue that eliminating U.S. tariffs and quotas will help the U.S. economy only if other countries eliminate their tariffs and quotas in exchange. It is easier to gain

TABLE 6-6

Preserving Japanese Jobs with Tariffs and Quotas Is Also Expensive

PRODUCT	COST TO CONSUMERS PER YEAR FOR EACH JOB SAVED
Rice	$51,233,000
Natural gas	27,987,000
Gasoline	6,329,000
Paper	3,813,000
Beef, pork, and poultry	1,933,000
Cosmetics	1,778,000
Radio and television sets	915,000

Source: Yoko Sazabami, Shujiro Urata, and Hiroki Kawai, "Measuring the Cost of Protection in Japan," Washington, DC: Institute for International Economics, 1995. Used with permission.

political support for reducing or eliminating a tariff or quota if it is done as part of an agreement with other countries that involves their eliminating some of their tariffs or quotas. But as the example of the sugar quota shows, *the U.S. economy would gain from the elimination of tariffs and quotas, even if other countries do not reduce their tariffs and quotas.*

Other Barriers to Trade

In addition to tariffs and quotas, governments sometimes erect other barriers to trade. For example, all governments require that imports meet certain health and safety requirements. Sometimes, however, health and safety requirements are used to shield domestic firms from foreign competition. This can be true when a government imposes stricter health and safety requirements on imported goods than on goods produced by domestic firms.

Many governments also restrict imports of certain products on national security grounds. The argument is that in time of war, a country should not be dependent on imports of critical war materials. Once again, these restrictions are sometimes used more to protect domestic companies from competition than to protect national security. For example, for years, the United States government would only buy military uniforms from U.S. manufacturers, even though uniforms are not a critical war material.

6 LEARNING OBJECTIVE
Evaluate the arguments for and against government policies that restrict international trade.

The Argument over Trade Policies and Globalization

The argument over whether the U.S. government should regulate international trade dates back to the beginning of the country. One particularly controversial attempt to restrict trade took place during the Great Depression of the 1930s. At that time the United States and other countries attempted to help domestic firms by raising tariffs on foreign imports. The United States started the process by passing the Smoot-Hawley Tariff in 1930, which raised average tariff rates to more than 50 percent. As other countries retaliated by raising their tariffs, international trade collapsed.

By the end of World War II in 1945, government officials in the United States and Europe were looking for a way to reduce tariffs and revive international trade. To help achieve this goal, they set up the General Agreement on Tariffs and Trade (GATT) in 1948. Countries that joined the GATT agreed not to impose new tariffs or import quotas. In addition, a series of *multilateral negotiations,* called *trade rounds,* took place, in which countries agreed to reduce tariffs from the very high levels of the 1930s.

In the 1940s, most international trade was in goods, and the GATT agreement covered only goods. In the following decades, trade in services and in products incorporating *intellectual property,* such as software programs and movies, grew in importance. Many GATT members pressed for a new agreement that would cover services and intellectual property, as well as goods. A new agreement was negotiated, and in January 1995 the GATT was replaced by the **World Trade Organization (WTO),** headquartered in Geneva, Switzerland. More than 130 countries are currently members of the WTO.

World Trade Organization (WTO) An international organization that enforces international trade agreements.

Why Do Some People Oppose the World Trade Organization?

During the years immediately after World War II, many low-income, or developing, countries erected high tariffs and restricted investment by foreign companies. When these policies failed to produce much economic growth, many of these countries decided during the 1980s to become more open to foreign trade and investment. This process became known as **globalization.** Most developing countries joined the WTO and began to follow its policies.

Globalization The process of countries becoming more open to foreign trade and investment.

During the 1990s, opposition to globalization began to increase. In 1999, this opposition took a violent turn at a meeting of the WTO in Seattle, Washington. The purpose of the meeting was to plan a new round of negotiations aimed at further reductions in trade barriers. A large number of protestors assembled in Seattle to meet the WTO delegates. Protests started peacefully but quickly became violent. Protesters looted stores and burned cars, and many delegates were unable to leave their hotel rooms.

Why would attempts to reduce trade barriers with the objective of increasing income around the world cause such a furious reaction? The opposition to the WTO comes from three sources. First, some opponents are specifically against the globalization process that began in the 1980s and became widespread in the 1990s. Second, other opponents have the same motivation as the supporters of tariffs in the 1930s—to erect trade barriers to protect domestic firms from foreign competition. Third, some critics of the WTO support globalization in principle but believe that the WTO favors the interests of the high-income countries at the expense of the low-income countries. Because of the importance of this issue, we will look more closely at the sources of opposition to the WTO.

ANTI-GLOBALIZATION Many of the protestors in Seattle distrust globalization. Some believe that free trade and foreign investment destroy the distinctive cultures of many countries. As developing countries began to open their economies to imports from the United States and other high-income countries, these imports of food, clothing, movies, and other goods began to replace the equivalent local products. So, a teenager in Thailand might be sitting in a McDonald's restaurant, wearing Levi's jeans and a Ralph Lauren shirt, listening to a recording by U2 on his iPod, before going to the local movie theater to watch *Spider-Man 2*. Globalization has increased the variety of products available to consumers in developing countries, but some people argue this is too high a price to pay for what they see as the damage to local cultures.

Globalization has also allowed multinational corporations to relocate factories from high-income countries to low-income countries. These new factories in Indonesia, Malaysia, Pakistan, and other countries pay much lower wages than are paid in the United States, Europe, and Japan and often do not meet the environmental or safety regulations that are imposed in high-income countries. Some factories use child labor, which is illegal in high-income countries. Some people have argued that firms with factories in developing countries should pay workers wages as high as those paid in the high-income countries. They also believe these firms should follow the health, safety, and environmental regulations that exist in the high-income countries.

The governments of most developing countries have resisted these proposals. They argue that when the currently rich countries were poor, they also lacked environmental or safety standards, and their workers were paid low wages. They argue that it is easier for rich countries to afford high wages and environmental and safety regulations than it is for poor countries. They also point out that many jobs that seem very poorly paid by high-income country standards are often better than the alternatives available to workers in low-income countries.

The Unintended Consequences of Banning Goods Made with Child Labor

6-3 Making the Connection

In many developing countries, such as Indonesia, Thailand, and Peru, children as young as seven or eight work 10 or more hours a day. Reports of very young workers laboring long hours producing goods for export have upset many people in the high-income countries. In the United States, boycotts have been organized against stores that stock goods made in developing countries with child labor. Many people assume that if child workers in developing countries weren't working in factories making clothing, toys, and other products, they would be in school, as are children in the high-income countries.

In fact, there are usually few good alternatives to work for children in developing countries. Schooling is frequently available for only a few months each year, and even children who attend school rarely do so for more than a few years. Poor families are often unable to afford even the small costs of sending their children to school. Families may even rely on the earnings of very young children to survive, as once did poor families in the the United States,

Would eliminating child labor in developing countries be a good thing?

Europe, and Japan. The United States did not outlaw child labor until 1938. In developing countries, jobs producing export goods are usually better paying and less hazardous than the alternatives.

As preparations began in France for the 1998 World Cup, there were protests that Baden Sports—the main supplier of soccer balls—was purchasing the balls from suppliers in Pakistan who used child workers. France decided to ban all use of soccer balls made by child workers. Bowing to this pressure, Baden Sports moved production from Pakistan, where the balls were hand-stitched by child workers, to China, where the balls were machine-stitched by adult workers in factories. There was some criticism of the boycott of hand-stitched soccer balls at the time. In a broad study of child labor, three economists argued:

> [O]f the array of possible employment in which impoverished children might engage, soccer ball stitching is probably one of the most benign. . . . [In Pakistan] children generally work alongside other family members in the home or in small workshops. . . . Nor are the children exposed to toxic chemicals, hazardous tools or brutal working conditions. Rather, the only serious criticism concerns the length of the typical child stitcher's work-day and the impact on formal education.

In fact, the alternatives to soccer ball stitching for child workers in Pakistan turned out to be extremely grim. According to Keith Maskus, an economist at the University of Colorado and the World Bank, a "large proportion" of the children who lost their jobs stitching soccer balls ended up begging or in prostitution.

Sources: Drusilla K. Brown, Alan V. Deardorff, and Robert M. Stern, "U.S. Trade and Other Policy Options to Deter Foreign Exploitation of Child Labor," in Magnus Blomstrom and Linda S. Goldberg, eds., *Topics in Empirical International Economics: A Festschrift in Honor of Bob Lipsey,* Chicago: University of Chicago Press, 2001; and Tomas Larsson, *The Race to the Top: The Real Story of Globalization,* 2001,p. 48.

Protectionism The use of trade barriers to shield domestic firms from foreign competition.

"OLD-FASHIONED" PROTECTIONISM The anti-globalization argument against free trade and the WTO is relatively new. Another argument against free trade is called *protectionism* and has been around for centuries. **Protectionism** is the use of trade barriers to shield domestic firms from foreign competition. For as long as international trade has existed, governments have attempted to restrict it to protect domestic firms. As we saw with the analysis of the sugar quota, protectionism causes losses to consumers and eliminates jobs in the domestic industries that use the protected product. In addition, by reducing the ability of countries to produce according to comparative advantage, protectionism reduces incomes.

Why, then, does protectionism attract support? Protectionism is usually justified on the basis of one of the following arguments:

- ***Saving jobs.*** Supporters of protectionism argue that free trade reduces employment by driving domestic firms out of business. It is true that when more-efficient foreign firms drive less-efficient domestic firms out of business, jobs are lost, but jobs are also lost when more-efficient domestic firms drive less-efficient domestic firms out of business. These job losses are rarely permanent. In the U.S. economy, jobs are being lost and new jobs are being created continually. No economic study has ever found a connection in the long run between the total number of jobs available and the level of tariff protection for domestic industries. In addition, trade restrictions destroy jobs in some industries at the same time that they preserve jobs in others. The U.S. sugar quota may have saved jobs in the U.S. sugar industry, but, as we saw at the beginning of this chapter, it also has destroyed jobs in the U.S. candy industry.

- *Protecting high wages.* Some people worry that firms in the high-income countries will have to start paying much lower wages to compete with firms in the developing countries. This fear is misplaced, however, because free trade actually raises living standards by increasing economic efficiency. When a country practices protectionism and produces goods and services it could obtain more cheaply from other countries, it reduces its standard of living. The United States could ban imports of coffee and begin growing it domestically. But this would entail a very high opportunity cost because coffee could only be grown in the U.S. in greenhouses and would require large amounts of labor and equipment. The coffee would have to sell for a very high price to cover these costs. Suppose the United States did ban coffee imports: Eliminating the ban at some future time would eliminate the jobs of U.S. coffee workers, but the standard of living in the United States would rise as coffee prices declined and labor, machinery, and other resources moved out of coffee production and into production of goods and services for which the U.S. has a comparative advantage.
- *Protecting infant industries.* It is possible that firms in a country may have a comparative advantage in producing a good, but because the country begins production of the good later than other countries, its firms initially have higher costs. In producing some goods and services, substantial "learning by doing" occurs. As workers and firms produce more of the good or service, they gain experience and become more productive. Over time, costs and prices will fall. As the firms in the "infant industry" gain experience, their costs will fall and they will be able to compete successfully with foreign producers. Under free trade, however, they may not get the chance. The established foreign producers can sell the product at a lower price and drive domestic producers out of business before they gain enough experience to compete. To economists, this is the most persuasive of the protectionist arguments. It does have a significant drawback, however. Tariffs used to protect an infant industry eliminate the need for the firms in the industry to become productive enough to compete with foreign firms. After World War II, the governments of many developing countries used the "infant industry" argument to justify high tariff rates. Unfortunately, most of their infant industries never grew up and they continued for years as inefficient drains on their economies.
- *Protecting national security.* As already discussed, a country should not rely on other countries for goods that are critical to its military defense. For example, the United States would probably not want to import all of its jet fighter engines from China. The definition of which goods are critical to military defense is a slippery one, however. In fact, it is rare for an industry to ask for protection without raising the issue of national security even if its products have mainly nonmilitary uses.

Has NAFTA Helped or Hurt the U.S. Economy?

6-4 Making the Connection

The North American Free Trade Agreement (NAFTA) was very controversial when it was being negotiated in the early 1990s. During the 1992 presidential campaign, independent candidate Ross Perot claimed to hear a "giant sucking sound" as jobs were pulled out of the United States and into Mexico. NAFTA went into effect in 1994 and eliminated most tariffs on products shipped between the United States, Canada, and Mexico. This policy change made it possible for each country to better pursue its comparative advantage. For example, before NAFTA the Mexican government had used tariffs to protect its domestic automobile industry, but the industry was much less efficient than the U.S. automobile industry. Once tariffs were removed, Mexican consumers could take advantage of the efficiency of the U.S. industry, and U.S. exports of motor vehicles to Mexico soared. Similarly, Canadian consumers could take advantage of lower-priced U.S. beef, and U.S. consumers could take advantage of lower-priced Canadian lumber. As we would expect, expanding trade increased consumption in all three countries. In the United States, consumption increased about $400 per year for a family of four as a result of NAFTA.

Contrary to Ross Perot's prediction, NAFTA did not lead to a loss of jobs in the United States. Between 1994, when NAFTA went into effect, and 2004, the number of jobs in the United States increased by more than 17 million. Some commentators argued that jobs in the United States could be preserved with NAFTA, but only if wages for U.S. workers declined to the much lower levels being paid Mexican workers. In fact, a study by Gordon Hanson of the University of California, San Diego, showed that the opposite occurred: wages for both U.S. and Mexican workers increased following NAFTA. In addition, the gap between U.S. wages and Mexican wages did not close.

Despite resistance to NAFTA, time proved that the U.S. economy gained jobs.

There were, of course, people in all three countries who were made worse off by NAFTA. Some firms in each country were no longer competitive once tariffs had been lowered. In the United States, government assistance helped workers who lost their jobs to retrain or relocate. Overall, most economists have concluded that NAFTA helped the U.S. economy become more efficient, thereby expanding the consumption of U.S. households.

Sources: Gordon H. Hanson, "What Has Happened to Wages in Mexico Since NAFTA? Implications for Hemispheric Free Trade" in Toni Estevadeordal, Dani Rodrick, Alan Taylor Andres Velasco, eds., *FTAA and Beyond: Prospects for Integration in the Americas,* Cambridge: Harvard University Press, 2004.

Dumping

Dumping Selling a product for a price below its cost of production.

In recent years, the United States has extended protection to some domestic industries by using a provision in the WTO agreement that allows governments to impose tariffs in the case of *dumping.* **Dumping** is selling a product for a price below its cost of production. Although allowable under the WTO agreement, using tariffs to offset the effects of dumping is very controversial.

In practice, it is difficult to determine if foreign companies are dumping goods because the true production costs of a good are not easy for foreign governments to calculate. As a result, the WTO allows countries to determine that dumping has occurred if a product is exported for a lower price than it sells for on the home market. There is a problem with this approach, however. Often there are good business reasons for a firm to sell a product for different prices to different consumers. For example, the airlines charge business travelers higher ticket prices than leisure travelers. Firms also use "loss leaders"—products that are sold below cost, or even given away free—when introducing a new product or, in the case of retailing, to attract customers who also will buy full-price products. For example, when Sun Microsystems attempted to establish StarOffice as a competitor to Microsoft's Office, it gave it away free on its Web site. During the Christmas season, Wal-Mart sometimes offers toys at prices below what they pay to buy them from manufacturers. It's unclear why these normal business practices should be unacceptable when used in international trade.

Positive versus Normative Analysis (Once Again)

Economists emphasize the burden on the economy imposed by tariffs, quotas, and other government restrictions on free trade. Does it follow that these interferences are bad? Remember from Chapter 1 the distinction between *positive analysis* and *normative analysis.* Positive analysis concerns what *is.* Normative analysis concerns what *ought to be.* Measuring the impact of the sugar quota on the U.S. economy is an example of positive analysis. Asserting that the sugar quota is bad public policy and should be eliminated is normative analysis. The sugar quota—like all other interferences with trade—makes some people better off, some people worse off, and reduces total income and consumption. Whether increasing the profits of U.S. sugar companies and the number of workers they employ justifies the costs imposed on consumers and the reduction in economic efficiency is a normative question.

Most economists do not support interferences with trade, such as the sugar quota. Few people become economists if they don't believe that markets should usually be as free as possible. But the opposite view is certainly intellectually respectable. It is possible for someone to understand the costs of tariffs and quotas but still believe that tariffs and quotas are a good idea, perhaps because they believe unrestricted free trade would cause too much disruption to the economy.

The success of industries in getting the government to erect barriers to foreign competition depends partly on some members of the public knowing full well the costs of trade barriers but supporting them anyway. Two other factors are also at work:

1. The costs tariffs and quotas impose on consumers are large in total but relatively small per person. For example, the sugar quota imposes a total burden of about $3 billion per year on consumers. Spread across 295 million Americans, the burden is only about $10 per person: too little for most people to worry about, even if they know the burden exists.
2. The jobs lost to foreign competition are easy to identify, but the jobs created by foreign trade are less easy to identify.

In other words, the industries that benefit from tariffs and quotas benefit a lot—the sugar quota increases the profits of U.S. sugar producers by more than $1 billion—whereas each consumer loses relatively little. This concentration of benefits and widely spread burdens makes it easy to understand why members of Congress receive strong pressure from some industries to enact tariffs and quotas and relatively little pressure from the general public to reduce them.

Conclusion

There are few issues economists agree upon more than the economic benefits of free trade. However, there are few political issues as controversial as government policy toward trade. Many people who would be reluctant to see the government interfere with domestic trade are quite willing to see it interfere with international trade. The damage high tariffs inflicted on the world economy during the 1930s shows what can happen when governments around the world abandon free trade. Whether future episodes of that type can be avoided is by no means certain.

Read *An Inside Look* on the next page to learn how eliminating tariffs on wine benefits the United States and Australia.

An Inside Look The United States and Australia Reduce Trade Barriers

SAN FRANCISCO CHRONICLE, MAY 15, 2004

U.S., Australia Commerce to Leap Forward

An already close commercial and cultural relationship will grow even closer Tuesday, when the United States **a** and Australia sign a bilateral free trade agreement that will slash tariffs, streamline investment rules and open up access to a broad spectrum of each country's markets. The free trade agreement, this country's first with a developed nation since Washington struck a free trade deal with Canada in 1988, won't take effect for months to come.

The legislatures of both nations will have to approve it before it becomes law. Australia's Parliament is expected to approve the agreement without too much fuss, while a spokesperson for the U.S. Trade Representative's office said Friday that the Bush administration plans to submit the pact to Congress "sometime this summer. We are seeing good bipartisan support for it."

Two-way trade between Washington and Canberra is already robust, with annual two-way trade of $28 billion. Australia, with a population of just 20 million, is the 13th-largest export market for the United States, while this country is Australia's top export market. Unusually, the United States, which ran a record $46 billion trade deficit with the rest of the world last month, racks up a trade surplus with Australia; the annual surplus crested at $9 billion in 2002.

California, in particular, finds an eager Aussie market for its computers, electronic gizmos, farm produce, Hollywood movies and Silicon Valley software in Australian shops and homes. The Golden State shipped out $1.9 billion worth of goods to Australia in 2002, and ranks just behind Washington State as this country's largest exporting state to Australia.

"It's hugely positive, it's a winner for both countries," said Robert Hunt, senior investment commissioner for North America at Invest Australia, an **b** Australian federal agency. The agreement, said Hunt, who is based in Invest Australia's San Francisco office, means "the virtual elimination of tariffs, except on beef, dairy and sugar. But they are very far from being the main game. It's probably the most comprehensive agreement anywhere by any two countries."

Even in this ambitious agreement, some sectors of the economy are off-**c** limits to the Aussies. Notwithstanding its free-trade rhetoric, Washington shelters beef, dairy and sugar industries from foreign competition. In line with that, the proposed agreement would allow no increase in quotas for inexpensive Australian sugar and only modest increases in Aussie beef and dairy products in the huge U.S. market.

But while the free trade agreement won't change everything, it will, if enacted, be far-reaching. The rules of the game for investors, for example, will be radically revised, according to Hunt, whose agency is charged with attracting foreign direct investment. Aussie rules barring foreigners from buying more than a $37 million stake in Australian businesses would be raised to $600 million, for example, enabling Americans to buy into Australian companies and giving Aussie firms much greater access to U.S. capital.

Companies that do businesses with Australia are broadly supportive of the trade agreement. "We have a big interest in Australia, and in general, we support free trade agreements," said Johnny Ng, a spokesman for San Ramon's Chevron Texaco. The energy company is exploring for natural gas on Australia's northwest coast, where it owns 57.1 percent of a natural gas project on the northwest shelf and has a one-sixth stake in a project in the Indian Ocean called Gorgon.

Key Points in the Article

The article discusses a new trade agreement between the United States and Australia that will reduce most restrictions on trade between the two countries. Agreements, such as this one, to expand trade between two countries are known as *bilateral agreements*. The trade agreements worked out by the World Trade Organization are *multilateral agreements*. As the article predicted, both the Australian parliament and the U.S. Congress approved the agreement later in 2004. The U.S. market is the largest in the world. As the article points out, Australia exports more to the United States than to any other country, despite the great distance that separates the two countries.

Analyzing the News

a In this chapter, we have seen that expanding trade raises living standards by increasing consumption and economic efficiency. Reducing tariffs on trade between Australia and the United States will aid consumers in both countries. Figure 1 shows the U.S. market for wine following the elimination of the tariff on Australian wine (just for simplicity, we assume that there are no remaining U.S. tariffs on wine). The price of wine in the United States falls from P_1 to P_2, and equilibrium in the U.S. wine market moves from point *E* to point *F*. U.S. consumption of wine increases from Q_3 to Q_4, the quantity of wine supplied by U.S. winemakers declines from Q_2 to Q_1, and imports increase from $Q_3 - Q_2$ to $Q_4 - Q_1$. Consumer surplus increases by the sum of areas *A*, *B*, *C*, and *D*. Area *A* represents a transfer from producer surplus under the tariff to consumer surplus. Areas *B* and *D* represent the conversion of deadwight loss to consumer surplus. Area *C* represents a conversion of government tariff revenue to consumer surplus. Eliminating the tariff reduces the cost to Australian wine producers of selling their product in the United States. U.S. consumers purchase a larger quantity of Australian wine at a lower price.

b Figure 1 shows that eliminating the tariff on wine also eliminates the revenue the U.S. government had been collecting from this tariff. In high-income countries, such as Australia and the United States, governments receive most of their revenue from taxes on personal and corporate income. For example, tariff revenue in the United States for 2004 amounted to only about 1 percent of all revenue received by the federal government, but governments in low-income countries often have difficulty collecting income taxes, so they rely heavily on tariffs for revenue. In these countries, the government's need for revenue can pose a serious barrier to expanding international trade by reducing tariffs, because governments have difficulty replacing the revenues lost from tariff reductions. This was also true in the United States early in its history. In 1800, tariffs brought in 90 percent of all federal government revenue. As late as the 1950s, tariffs accounted for 14 percent of federal revenues.

c Political factors enter into most trade negotiations. In this case, for political reasons the United States was unwilling to reduce its quotas on beef, dairy products, and sugar. In this chapter, we analyzed the sugar quota's economic effect on the United States.

Thinking Critically ABOUT POLICY

1. Import quotas on sugar, beef, and dairy products save jobs for Americans working in those industries. Do you support these quotas? Why or why not?
2. In which goods mentioned in the article does the United States have a comparative advantage? In which does Australia have a comparative advantage? Explain your reasoning.

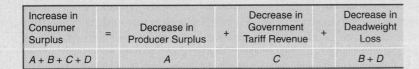

Increase in Consumer Surplus	=	Decrease in Producer Surplus	+	Decrease in Government Tariff Revenue	+	Decrease in Deadweight Loss
A + B + C + D		*A*		*C*		*B + D*

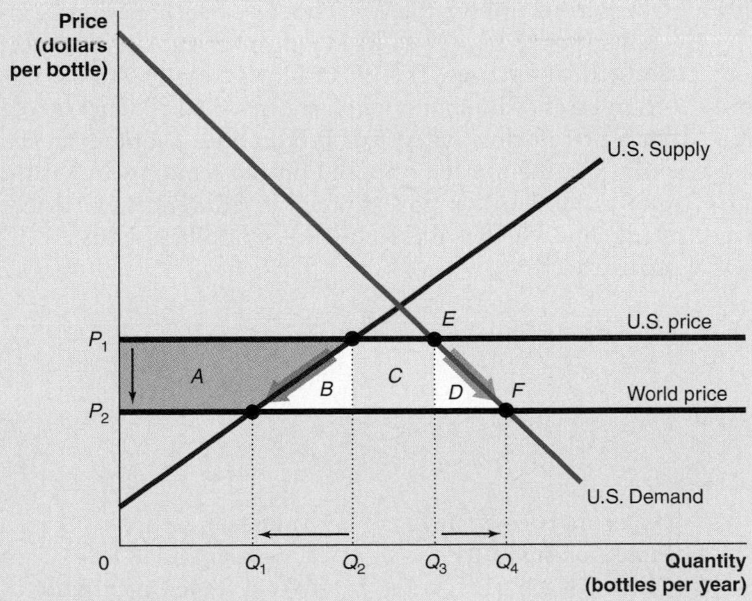

Figure 1: The market for wine in the United States after the tariff on Australian wine is eliminated.

SUMMARY

LEARNING OBJECTIVE ① Discuss the increasing importance of international trade to the United States. The quantity of goods and services the United States imports and exports has been continually increasing. Today, the United States is the leading exporting country in the world, and about 20 percent of U.S. manufacturing jobs depend upon exports.

LEARNING OBJECTIVE ② Understand the difference between comparative advantage and absolute advantage. *Comparative advantage* is the ability of an individual, business, or country to produce a good or service at the lowest opportunity cost. *Absolute advantage* is the ability to produce more of a good or service than competitors when using the same amount of resources. Countries trade on the basis of comparative advantage, not on the basis of absolute advantage.

LEARNING OBJECTIVE ③ Explain how countries gain from international trade. When a country specializes in producing goods where it has a comparative advantage and trades for the other goods it needs, the country will have a higher level of income and consumption. We do not see complete specialization in production for three reasons: Not all goods and services are traded internationally; production of most goods involves increasing opportunity costs; and tastes for products differ across countries. Although the population of a country as a whole benefits from trade, companies—and their workers—that are unable to compete with lower-cost foreign producers lose.

LEARNING OBJECTIVE ④ Discuss the sources of comparative advantage. Among the main sources of comparative advantage are these: climate and natural resources, relative abundance of labor and capital, technology, and *external economies.* A country may develop a comparative advantage in the production of a good, then as time passes and circumstances change, the country may lose its comparative advantage in producing that good and develop a comparative advantage in producing other goods.

LEARNING OBJECTIVE ⑤ Analyze the economic effects of government policies that restrict international trade. Government policies that interfere with trade usually take the form of: *tariffs, quotas,* or *voluntary export restraints.* A tariff is a tax imposed by a government on imports. A quota is a numerical limit imposed by the government on the quantity of a good that can be imported into a country. A voluntary export restraint is an agreement negotiated between two countries that places a numerical limit on the quantity of a good that can be imported by one country from the other country. The federal government's sugar quota costs U.S. consumers $2.91 billion per year, or about $970,000 per year for each job saved in the sugar industry. Saving jobs by using tariffs and quotas is often very expensive.

LEARNING OBJECTIVE ⑥ Evaluate the arguments for and against government policies that restrict international trade. The *World Trade Organization* (*WTO*) is an international organization that enforces international trade agreements. The WTO has promoted *globalization,* the process of countries becoming more open to foreign trade and investment. Some critics of the WTO argue that globalization has damaged local cultures around the world. Other critics oppose the WTO because they believe governments should be free to use tariffs and quotas to protect domestic industries. The WTO allows countries to use tariffs in cases of *dumping,* when an imported product is sold for a price below its cost of production. Economists can point out the burden imposed on the economy by tariffs, quotas, and other government interferences with free trade. But whether these policies should be used is a normative decision.

KEY TERMS

Absolute advantage 168
Autarky 169
Comparative advantage 167
Dumping 186
Exports 164
External economies 174
Free trade 175
Globalization 182
Imports 164
Opportunity cost 167
Protectionism 184
Quota 178
Tariff 164
Terms of trade 169
Voluntary export restraint 178
World Trade Organization (WTO) 182

REVIEW QUESTIONS

1. Briefly explain whether you agree or disagree with the following statement: "International trade is more important to the U.S. economy than to most other economies."
2. A World Trade Organization publication calls comparative advantage "arguably the single most powerful insight in economics." What is comparative advantage? What makes it such a powerful insight?
   Source: World Trade Organization, *Trading into the Future*, April 1999.
3. What is the difference between absolute advantage and comparative advantage? Will a country always be an exporter of a good where it has an absolute advantage in production?
4. Briefly explain how international trade increases a country's consumption.
5. What is meant by a country specializing in the production of a good? Is it typical for countries to be completely specialized? Briefly explain.
6. What are the main sources of comparative advantage?
7. What is a tariff? What is a quota? Give an example of a non-tariff barrier to trade.
8. Who gains and who loses when a country imposes a tariff or a quota on imports of a good?
9. What events led to the General Agreement on Tariffs and Trade? Why did the World Trade Organization eventually replace the GATT?
10. What is globalization? Why are some people opposed to globalization?
11. What is protectionism? Who benefits and who loses from protectionist policies? What are the main arguments people use to justify protectionism?
12. What is dumping? Who benefits and who loses from dumping? What problems arise when implementing anti-dumping laws?

PROBLEMS AND APPLICATIONS

Please visit **www.prenhall.com/hubbard** *for solutions to the even-numbered problems as well as multiple-choice and true or false self-assessment quizzes.*

1. Why do the goods that countries import and export change over time? Use the concept of comparative advantage in your answer.
2. In 1987, an economic study showed that, on average, workers in the Japanese consumer electronics industry produced less output per hour than did U.S. workers producing the same goods. Despite this fact, Japan exported large quantities of consumer electronics to the United States. Briefly explain how this is possible.
   Source: Study cited in Douglas A. Irwin, *Free Trade under Fire*, Princeton: Princeton University Press, 2002, p. 27.
3. **[Related to *Solved Problem 6-1*]** The following table shows the hourly output per worker in two industries in Chile and Argentina:

	OUTPUT PER HOUR OF WORK	
	HATS	BEER
Chile	8	6
Argentina	1	2

   a. Explain which country has an absolute advantage in the production of hats and which country has an absolute advantage in the production of beer.
   b. Explain which country has a comparative advantage in the production of hats and which country has a comparative advantage in the production of beer.
   c. Suppose that Chile and Argentina currently do not trade with each other. Each has 1,000 hours of labor to use producing hats and beer, and the countries are currently producing the amounts of each good shown in the following table:

	HATS	BEER
Chile	7,200	600
Argentina	600	800

   Using this information, give a numerical example of how Chile and Argentina can both gain from trade. Assume that after trading begins, one hat can be exchanged for one barrel of beer.
4. Demonstrate how the opportunity costs of producing cell phones and MP3 players in Japan and the United States in Table 6-2 were calculated.

5. Briefly explain whether you agree or disagree with the following statement: "Most countries exhaust their comparative advantage in producing a good or service before they reach complete specialization."

6. Patrick J. Buchanan, a former presidential candidate, argues in his book on the global economy that there is a flaw in David Ricardo's theory of comparative advantage:

   > [C]lassical free trade theory fails the test of common sense. According to Ricardo's law of comparative advantage . . . if America makes better computers and textiles than China does, but our advantage in computers is greater than our advantage in textiles, we should (1) focus on computers, (2) let China make textiles, and (3) trade U.S. computers for Chinese textiles. . . .
   >
   > The doctrine begs a question. If Americans are more efficient than Chinese in making clothes . . . why surrender the more efficient American industry? Why shift to a reliance on a Chinese textile industry that will take years to catch up to where American factories are today?

   Do you agree with Buchanan's argument? Briefly explain.
   Source: Patrick J. Buchanan, *The Great Betrayal: How American Sovereignty and Social Justice Are Being Sacrificed to the Gods of the Global Economy*, Boston: Little, Brown, 1998, p. 66.

7. Is free trade likely to benefit a large populous country more than a small country with fewer people? Briefly explain.

8. An editorial in *Business Week* argued the following:

   > [President] Bush needs to send a pure and clear signal that the U.S. supports free trade on its merits. . . . That means resisting any further protectionist demands by lawmakers. It could even mean unilaterally reducing tariffs or taking down trade barriers rather than erecting new ones. Such moves would benefit U.S. consumers while giving a needed boost to struggling economies overseas.

   What does the editorial mean by "protectionist demands"? How would the unilateral elimination of U.S. trade barriers benefit both U.S. consumers and economies overseas?
   Source: "The Threat of Protectionism," *Business Week*, June 3, 2002.

9. Political commentator B. Bruce-Biggs once wrote the following in the *Wall Street Journal:*

   > This is not to say that the case for international free trade is invalid; it is just irrelevant. It is an "if only everybody . . . " argument. . . . In the real world almost everybody sees benefits in economic nationalism.

   What do you think he means by "economic nationalism"? Do you agree that a country only benefits from free trade if every other country also practices free trade? Briefly explain.
   Source: B. Bruce-Biggs, "The Coming Overthrow of Free Trade," *Wall Street Journal*, February 24, 1983, p. 28.

10. **[Related to *Solved Problem 6-1*]** A political commentator makes the following statement:

    > The idea that international trade should be based on the comparative advantage of each country is fine for rich countries like the United States and Japan. Rich countries have educated workers and large quantities of machinery and equipment. These advantages allow them to produce every product more efficiently than poor countries can. Poor countries like Kenya and Bolivia have nothing to gain from international trade based on comparative advantage.

    Do you agree with this argument? Briefly explain.

11. Explain why there are advantages to a movie studio operating in Southern California, rather than in, say, Florida.

12. The United States produces beef and also imports beef from other countries.
    a. Draw a graph showing the supply and demand for beef in the United States. Assume that the United States can import as much as it wants at the world price of beef without causing the world price of beef to increase. Be sure to indicate on your diagram the quantity of beef imported.
    b. Now show on your graph the effect of the United States imposing a tariff on beef. Be sure to indicate on your diagram the quantity of beef sold by U.S. producers before and after the tariff is imposed, the quantity of beef imported before and after the tariff, and the price of beef in the United States before and after the tariff.
    c. Discuss who benefits and who loses when the U.S. imposes a tariff on beef.

13. The following excerpt is from a newspaper story on President Bill Clinton's proposals for changes in the World Trade Organization. The story was published just before the 1999 World Trade Organization meeting in Seattle that ended in rioting:

    > [President Clinton] suggested that a working group on labor be created within the WTO to develop core labor standards that would become "part of every trade agreement. And ultimately I would favor a system in which sanctions would come for violating any provision of a trade agreement. . . . " But the new U.S. stand is sure to meet massive resistance

> from developing countries, which make up more than 100 of the 135 countries in the WTO. They are not interested in adopting tougher U.S. labor standards.

What did President Clinton mean by "core labor standards"? Why would developing countries resist adopting these standards?

14. **[Related to the *Chapter Opener*]** Which industries are affected unfavorably by the sugar quota? Are any industries (other than the sugar industry) affected favorably by the sugar quota? (*Hint:* Think about what sugar is used for and whether substitutes exist for these uses.)

15. When Congress was considering a bill to impose quotas on imports of textiles, shoes, and other products, Milton Friedman, a Nobel Prize–winning economist, made the following comment:

> The consumer will be forced to spend several extra dollars to subsidize the producers [of these goods] by one dollar. A straight handout would be far cheaper.

Why would a quota result in consumers paying much more than domestic producers receive? Where do the other dollars go? What does Friedman mean by a "straight handout"? Why would this be cheaper than a quota?

Source: Milton Friedman, "Free Trade," *Newsweek,* August 27, 1970.

16. The European Union is an organization of more than 20 European countries. Half of the spending by the European Union consists of subsidies to farmers. These payments result in European farmers producing much more food than they otherwise would. A substantial amount of this food is exported. According to an article in the *Wall Street Journal,* Monica Shandu, a farmer in South Africa, works full-time raising sugar cane on her four-acre farm:

> Ms. Shandu was named South Africa's small-scale Cane Grower of the Year for a top-quality harvest in 2001. Yet . . . she earned only $200 after costs on that harvest. Sugar prices depressed by [European] subsidies cut her annual income by about a third.

Why would subsidies paid by European governments to European sugar farmers reduce the income of a sugar farmer in South Africa?

Source: Roger Thurow and Geoff Winestock, "Addiction to Sugar Subsidies Chokes Poor Nations' Exports," *Wall Street Journal,* September 16, 2002.

17. An economic analysis of a proposal to impose a quota on steel imports into the United States indicated that the quota would save 3,700 jobs in the steel industry but cost about 35,000 jobs in other U.S. industries. Why would a quota on steel imports cause employment to fall in other industries? Which other industries are likely to be most affected?

Source: Study cited in Douglas A. Irwin, *Free Trade Under Fire,* Princeton: Princeton University Press, 2002, p. 82.

18. A student makes the following argument: "Tariffs on imports of foreign goods into the United States will cause the foreign companies to add the amount of the tariff to the prices they charge in the United States for those goods. Instead of putting a tariff on imported goods, we should ban importing them. Banning imported goods is better than putting tariffs on them because U.S. producers benefit from the reduced competition and U.S. consumers don't have to pay the higher prices caused by tariffs." Briefly explain whether you agree with the student's reasoning.

19. Steven Landsburg, an economist at the University of Rochester, wrote the following in an article in the *New York Times:*

> Free trade is not only about the right of American consumers to buy at the cheapest possible price; it's also about the right of foreign producers to earn a living. Steelworkers in West Virginia struggle hard to make ends meet. So do steelworkers in South Korea. To protect one at the expense of the other, solely because of where they happened to be born, is a moral outrage.

How does the U.S. government protect steelworkers in West Virginia at the expense of steelworkers in South Korea? Is Landsburg making a positive or a normative statement? A few days later, Tom Redburn published an article disagreeing with Landsburg:

> It is not some evil character flaw to care more about the welfare of people nearby than about that of those far away—it's human nature. And it is morally—and economically—defensible. . . . A society that ignores the consequences of eco nomic disruption on those among its citizens who come out at the short end of the stick is not only heartless, it also undermines its own cohesion and adaptability.

Which of the two arguments do you find most convincing?

Source: Steven E. Landsburg, "Who Cares If the Playing Field Is Level?" *New York Times,* June 13, 2001; and Tom Redburn, "Economic View: Of Politics, Free Markets, and Tending to Society," *New York Times,* June 17, 2001.

20. Suppose China decides to pay large subsidies to any Chinese company that exports goods or services to the United States. As a result, these companies are able to sell products in the United States at far below their cost of production. In addition, China decides to bar all imports from the United States. The dollars that the United States pays to import Chinese goods are left in banks in China. Will this strategy raise or lower the standard of living in China? Will it raise or lower the standard of living in the United States? Briefly explain. Be sure to indicate your definition of "standard of living" in your answer.

21. A Federal Reserve publication offers the following observation: "Too many U.S. citizens associate free trade with job losses rather than opportunities and a higher standard of living." Do you agree? Briefly explain.
Source: Surya Sen and Dan Wassmann, "The Great Trade Debate: From Rhetoric to Reality," Federal Reserve Bank of Chicago, January 1999.

22. Hal Varian, an economist at the University of California, Berkeley, has made two observations about international trade:
    1. Trade allows a country "to produce more with less."
    2. There is little doubt who wins [from trade] in the long run: consumers.

    Briefly explain whether or not you agree with either or both of these observations.
    Source: Hal R. Varian, "The Mixed Bag of Productivity," *New York Times*, October 23, 2003.

23. **[Related to the *Chapter Opener*]** According to an editorial in the *New York Times*, because of the sugar quota, "Sugar growers in this country, long protected from global competition, have had a great run at the expense of just about everyone else—refineries, candy manufacturers, other food companies, individual consumers and farmers in the developing world." Briefly explain how each group mentioned in this editorial is affected by the sugar quota.
Source: "America's Sugar Daddies," *New York Times*, November 29, 2003.

24. **[Related to *Don't Let This Happen To You!*]** Briefly explain whether you agree or disagree with the following statement: "I can't believe that anyone opposes expanding international trade. After all, when international trade expands, everyone wins."

25. **[Related to *Solved Problem 6-2*]** Suppose that the United States currently both produces kumquats and imports them. The U.S. government then decides to restrict international trade in kumquats by imposing a quota that allows imports of only six million pounds of kumquats into the United States each year. The figure shows the results of imposing the quota:

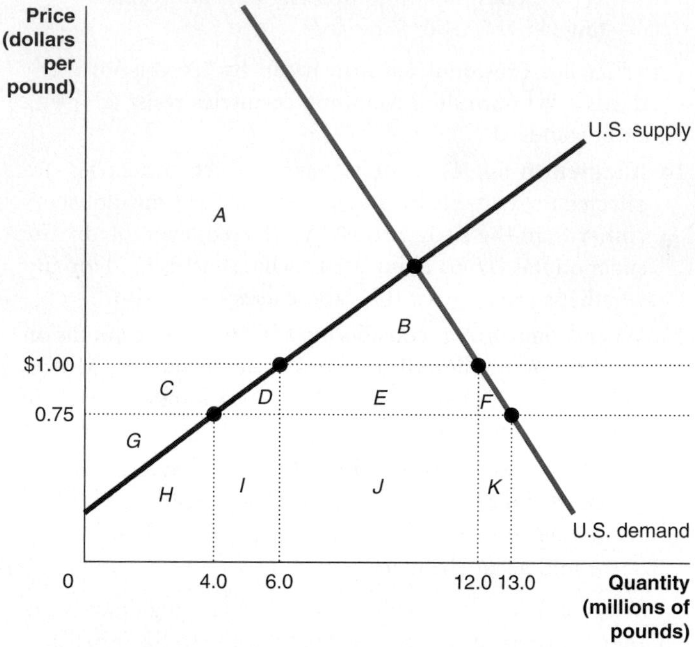

Fill in the following table using the letters in the figure:

	WITHOUT QUOTA	WITH QUOTA
World price of kumquats	______	______
U.S. price of kumquats	______	______
Quantity supplied by U.S. firms	______	______
Quantity demanded	______	______
Quantity imported	______	______
Area of consumer surplus	______	______
Area of domestic producer surplus	______	______
Area of deadweight loss	______	______

Multinational Firms

Appendix

Most large corporations are multinational. **Multinational enterprises** are firms that conduct operations in more than one country—as opposed to simply trading with other countries. For example, the U.S. firm General Electric employs nearly 300,000 people in more than one hundred countries. Toyota Motor Corporation of Japan has invested more than $10 billion in factories and other facilities in the United States and assembles more than a million cars and trucks in North American factories (almost two-thirds of the cars and trucks Toyota sells in the United States are assembled in North American factories). The Nestlé Company is headquartered in the small city of Vevey, Switzerland, but it produces and sells food products in practically every country in the world. It has more than 500 factories worldwide, employing more than 240,000 people.

Table 6A-1 shows the top 25 multinational corporations ranked by the value of their revenues in 2004. Large corporations based in the United States generally established multinational operations earlier than did firms based in other countries. Today, 5 of the top 10 multinational corporations in the world are based in the United States. The table shows that large corporations in the motor vehicle, electronics, insurance, and petroleum refining industries are most likely to have extensive multinational operations.

A Brief History of Multinational Enterprises

From at least 2500 B.C., companies have traded over long distances. Well-developed systems of long-distance trade existed in the eastern Mediterranean by 1500 B.C. By the Middle Ages, a number of multinational firms had been established in Europe. For example, the Medici bank was based in Florence, Italy, but had branches in France, Switzerland, and England. Some multinational companies founded during these years still exist. The Austrian freight forwarding firm Gerbrueder Weiss, which had offices in several countries in the fourteenth century, continues to operate today. Before the twentieth century, multinational firms were still relatively rare, however.

In the late nineteenth and early twentieth centuries, a few large U.S. corporations began to expand their operations beyond the domestic market. Two key technological innovations made it possible for these firms to coordinate operations on several continents. The first innovation was the successful completion of the transatlantic cable in 1866, which made possible instant communication by telegraph between the United States and Europe. The second innovation was the development of more efficient steam engines, which reduced the cost and increased the speed of long ocean voyages. U.S. firms such as Standard Oil, the Singer Sewing Machine Company, and the American Tobacco Company took advantage of these innovations to establish factories and distribution networks around the world. When firms build or buy facilities in foreign countries they are engaging in **foreign direct investment.** When an individual or firm buys stocks or bonds issued in another country, they are engaging in **foreign portfolio investment.** In the early twentieth century, most U.S. firms expanded abroad through foreign direct investment because the stock and bond markets in other countries were often too poorly developed to make foreign portfolio investment practical.

A - 1

op 25 Multinational orporations, 2004

RANK	CORPORATION	HOME COUNTRY	INDUSTRY
1	Wal-Mart Stores	United States	Retailing
2	BP	Great Britain	Petroleum Refining
3	Exxon Mobil	United States	Petroleum Refining
4	Royal Dutch/Shell Group	Netherlands/ United Kingdom	Petroleum Refining
5	General Motors	United States	Motor Vehicles
6	Ford Motor	United States	Motor Vehicles
7	DaimlerChrysler	Germany	Motor Vehicles
8	Toyota Motor	Japan	Motor Vehicles
9	General Electric	United States	Diversified Financials
10	Total	France	Petroleum Refining
11	Allianz	Germany	Insurance
12	ChevronTexaco	United States	Petroleum Refining
13	Axa	France	Insurance
14	ConocoPhillips	United States	Petroleum
15	Volkswagen	Germany	Motor Vehicles
16	Nippon Telephone and Telegraph	Japan	Telecommunications
17	ING Group	Netherlands	Insurance
18	Citigroup	United States	Banking
19	International Business Machines	United States	Computers
20	American International Group	United States	Insurance
21	Siemens AG	Germany	Electronics
22	Carrefour	France	Food and Drug Stores
23	Hitachi	Japan	Electronics
24	Hewlett-Packard	United States	Computers
25	Honda Motor	Japan	Motor Vehicles

Source: "Fortune Global 500," *Fortune*, July 26, 2004 ©2004 Time Inc. All rights reserved.
Note: Corporations are ranked by their revenue in 2004.

Multinational enterprise A firm that conducts operations in more than one country.

Foreign direct investment The purchase or building by a domestic firm of a facility in a foreign country.

Foreign portfolio investment The purchase by an individual or firm of stocks or bonds issued in another country.

Strategic Factors in Moving from Domestic to Foreign Markets

Today, most large U.S. corporations have established factories and other facilities overseas. Corporations expand their operations outside the United States when they expect to increase their profitability by doing so. Firms might expect to increase their profits through overseas operations for five main reasons:

- ***To avoid tariffs or the threat of tariffs.*** As we saw in this chapter, tariffs are taxes imposed by countries on imports from other countries. Sometimes firms will establish factories in other countries to avoid the need to pay tariffs. At other times, firms will establish a factory in a country to which they are exporting because they fear the other country's government will impose a tariff or some other restriction on their product. Governments often are less concerned about domestic production by foreign-owned companies than they are about imports. As we also saw in this chapter, government restrictions on imports frequently result from a fear that imports will cause job losses in domestic industries. For example, in the 1970s and 1980s many Americans feared that imports of Japanese automobiles would reduce employment in the U.S. automobile industry. Members of Congress threatened to increase tariffs or impose quotas on imports of Japanese automobiles. In fact, beginning in 1981, a voluntary export restraint did reduce imports of Japanese automobiles. In response to this political pressure, the Japanese automobile companies established assembly plants in the United States. Now that a majority of Japanese automobiles sold in the United States are also assembled in the United States by U.S. workers, the Japanese share of the U.S. automobile market is a less heated political issue than it was during the 1970s and 1980s.

- ***To gain access to raw materials.*** Some U.S. firms have expanded abroad to secure supplies of raw materials. U.S. oil firms—beginning with Standard Oil in the late nineteenth century—have had extensive overseas operations aimed at discovering, recovering, and refining crude oil. In early 2001, one of Standard Oil's successor firms, ChevronTexaco, headquartered in San Francisco, opened its largest oil field in Kazakstan, in the former Soviet Union. ChevronTexaco also constructed a 990-mile pipeline to bring the oil from this field on the Caspian Sea across Russia to a port on the Black Sea.
- ***To gain access to low-cost labor.*** In the past 20 years, some U.S. firms have located factories or other facilities in countries such as China, India, Malaysia, and El Salvador to take advantage of the lower wages paid to workers in those countries. As we saw in "Making the Connection 8-1," most economists believe that this *outsourcing* ultimately improves the efficiency of the economy and raises the consumption of U.S. households, but it also can disrupt the lives of U.S. workers who lose their jobs. For this reason outsourcing has caused political controversy.
- ***To minimize exchange-rate risk.*** The exchange rate tells us how many units of foreign currency are received in exchange for a unit of domestic currency. Fluctuations in exchange rates can reduce the profits of a firm that exports goods to other countries. The J. M. Smucker Company is headquartered in Orrville, Ohio, and ships jams, ice cream toppings, peanut butter, and other products to more than 70 countries. Suppose Smucker's has contracted to sell 200,000 cases of jam to a British importer. The British importer will be paying for the shipment in British currency, the pound (the symbol for the pound is £). The importer will pay Smucker's £21 million in 60 days. It is currently possible to exchange 1 dollar for 0.7 British pounds, so Smucker's expects to receive $30 million (£21 million/£0.70 per dollar) in 60 days. But if the value of the pound falls against the dollar during the next 60 days, the amount Smucker's receives in dollars could be significantly reduced. For example, if the value of the pound falls to 0.80 pounds per dollar, then Smucker's will only receive $26.25 million (£21 million/£0.80 per dollar).

  Firms, like Smucker's, that have extensive international operations are exposed to significant risk to their profits from fluctuations in the values of international currencies. This risk is known as *exchange-rate risk.* If Smucker's began producing jam in Britain, it would reduce its exposure to exchange-rate risk.
- ***To respond to industry competition.*** In some instances, companies expand overseas as a competitive response to an industry rival. The worldwide competition for markets between Pepsi and Coke is an example of this kind of expansion. Coke began expanding overseas before World War II and by the 1970s was earning more from its foreign sales than from its sales in the United States. It became clear to

Pepsi's management that the firm needed to compete with Coke in foreign as well as domestic markets. In 1972, Pepsi had a major success when it signed an agreement with the Soviet Union to become the first foreign product sold in that country. Coke and Pepsi continue to compete vigorously in many countries, with their shares of the market often fluctuating significantly.

6A-1 Making the Connection

Many U.S. jobs require technical training.

Have Multinational Corporations Reduced Employment and Lowered Wages in the United States?

During the 1990s, some U.S. corporations responded to the greater economic openness of many poorer countries by relocating manufacturing operations to these countries. For example, most U.S. toy firms, such as Mattel, now produce nearly all their toys in factories in China. Most U.S. clothing manufacturers now produce the bulk of their goods in factories in Central America or Asia. These firms have reduced their production costs by paying much lower wages in their overseas factories than they were paying in the United States. The workers who lost their jobs in U.S. factories have often experienced periods of unemployment and have sometimes had to accept lower wages when they find new jobs. Towns and cities where factories closed also have been hurt by losses of tax revenues to support schools and other local services.

Most economists, however, do not believe that relocating jobs abroad has reduced either total employment in the United States or the average wage paid to U.S. workers. The overall level of employment in the United States in the long run is not affected by job losses in particular industries, however painful the losses may be to those experiencing them. The U.S. economy creates more than 2 million additional new jobs during a typical year. Nearly all workers who lose jobs at one firm eventually find new ones at another firm.

Competition from low-wage foreign workers has not reduced the average wages of U.S. workers. Wages are determined by the ability of workers to produce goods and services. This ability depends in part on the workers' education and training and in part on the machinery and equipment available to them. American workers have high wages because, on average, they are well trained and because of the quantity and quality of the machinery and equipment they work with. Low-wage foreign workers are generally less well trained and work with smaller amounts of machinery and equipment than do American workers.

During the 1990s and early 2000s, the gap in the United States between the wages of skilled workers and the wages of unskilled workers increased. It has been suggested that competition from low-wage foreign workers forced unskilled U.S. workers to accept lower wages to keep their jobs. To a small extent, the increase in the wage gap in the United States may have been due to this cause. But careful economic studies have shown that most of the increase in the wage gap is due to developments within the U.S. economy—such as the increasing number of jobs that require technical training—that have resulted in higher pay to skilled workers, rather than to competition from low-wage foreign workers.

Most U.S. firms have followed similar steps in expanding their operations overseas: Newly established firms usually begin by selling only within the United States. If successful in the domestic market, they will begin to export. They initially use foreign firms to market and distribute their products. If sales are good in these foreign markets, U.S. firms will establish their own overseas marketing and distribution networks. Finally, firms will establish their own production facilities in these foreign countries. Since World War II, many U.S. firms have switched from building their own production facilities to a strategy of acquiring local firms that were already producing the good. Some firms have first licensed production to local firms, only later acquiring the firms. U.S.-based Colgate-Palmolive, for example, typically has entered a foreign market first by licensing a foreign soap manufacturer to produce its brands, while keeping control over marketing and distribution. Typically, Colgate-Palmolive eventually has acquired ownership of the foreign firm.

Challenges to U.S. Firms in Foreign Markets

It seems obvious that any successful firm will want to expand into foreign markets. After all, it is always better to have more customers than fewer customers. In fact, however, expanding into foreign markets can often be quite difficult and the additional costs incurred may end up being greater than the additional revenue gained. One problem encountered by U.S. firms is differences in tastes between U.S. and foreign consumers. Although products like Coke seem to appeal to consumers everywhere in the world, other products run into problems because of cultural differences among countries. For example, Singapore banned Janet Jackson's album *All for You* because, according to a government spokesman, its "sexually explicit lyrics" were "not acceptable to our society." In 2002, eBay closed its online auction site in Japan. Although eBay is successful selling collectibles in the United States, many Japanese consumers do not like to buy used goods.

Some U.S. companies have had difficulty adapting their employment practices to deal with the differences between U.S. and foreign labor markets. Many countries have much stronger labor unions than does the United States, and many foreign governments regulate labor markets much more than does the U.S. government. For example, government regulations in most European countries make it much more difficult than it is in the United States to lay off workers.

Competitive Advantages of U.S. Firms

Some U.S. firms have successful foreign operations because of the strength of their brand names. Many producers of soft drinks and many fast food restaurants can be found in nearly every foreign country, but Coca-Cola and McDonald's have such strong name recognition that their appeal extends around the world. Other firms have developed a significant technological edge over foreign rivals. Microsoft, the software giant, and Hewlett-Packard, the computer and printer firm, are examples. Some U.S. firms, such as Dell Computer and Boeing, have advantages over foreign manufacturers based on having developed the most efficient and low-cost way of producing a good.

A U.S. firm's global competitive advantage changes over time. This change is illustrated dramatically by the experience of U.S. semiconductor firms. The semiconductor industry originated in the United States with the invention of the transistor at Bell Telephone Laboratories in 1947. United States predominance in the industry was enhanced further in 1959 with the invention of the integrated circuit, which contains multiple transistors on a single silicon chip. Through 1980, U.S. firms held between 60 and 80 percent of the global market for semiconductors. Beginning in the 1970s, the Japanese government moved to establish a strong domestic semiconductor industry by subsidizing domestic firms and by limiting imports of semiconductors from the United States. The Japanese policy was very successful with respect to DRAM—dynamic random access memory—the most basic chip. By the mid-1980s, Japanese firms dominated the global market and nearly all U.S. chipmakers had abandoned DRAM manufacture. Many observers predicted the collapse of the U.S. semiconductor industry. Even Intel Corporation, the most successful U.S. semiconductor firm, appeared close to bankruptcy.

From this low point, U.S. semiconductor firms rebounded to regain global predominance by the 1990s. The key to the rebound of U.S. firms was the decreasing demand for simple memory chips and the increasing demand for two products: microprocessors—such as Intel's Pentium 4 chip used in personal computers—and ASICs—application-specific integrated circuits—which are used in many electronic products. In manufacturing microprocessors and ASICs, a firm's ability to rapidly design and develop new products is more important than using low-cost production processes. U.S. firms, such as Intel, have proven to be much better at designing and rapidly bringing to market advanced microprocessors and ASICs than have competing firms in Japan, South Korea, and elsewhere.

KEY TERMS

Foreign direct investment 195

Foreign portfolio investment 195

Multinational enterprise 195

REVIEW QUESTIONS

1. When did large U.S. corporations first begin to operate internationally? What key technological changes made it easier for U.S. corporations to operate overseas?
2. What is the difference between foreign direct investment and foreign portfolio investment? Is the Camry assembly plant that Toyota operates in Kentucky an example of foreign direct investment or foreign portfolio investment?
3. What are the five main reasons why firms expand their operations overseas? Which of these reasons explains why U.S.-based oil companies have extensive overseas operations?
4. What are the main reasons U.S. firms succeed overseas?

PROBLEMS AND APPLICATIONS

Please visit **www.prenhall.com/hubbard** *for solutions to the even-numbered problems as well as multiple-choice and true or false self-assessment quizzes.*

1. Suppose that in 1850 you are operating a large factory manufacturing cotton cloth. You are considering expanding your operations overseas. What technical problems are you likely to encounter in coordinating your overseas and domestic operations?
2. The Ford Motor Company and the International Harvester Company were two of the first U.S. firms to establish extensive manufacturing operations overseas. Why might a producer of automobiles and a producer of farm machinery find it particularly advantageous to manufacture their products in countries in which they had substantial sales?
3. Why might many U.S. firms that were expanding their operations overseas after World War II have been more likely to acquire an existing firm in the market they were entering rather than building new facilities there?
4. Would a firm based in the United States ever produce a good in another country if it cost less to produce it in the United States and ship it to the other country? Explain.
5. Is expanding a firm's operations internationally really any different than expanding within a nation? For example, if a firm is based in Texas, what's the difference between it expanding operations to Mexico, Canada, Singapore, or Germany rather than to North Carolina or Pennsylvania?
6. Is expanding a firm's operations internationally really any different than expanding into a new product market? For example, is Whirlpool's expansion into Europe different than Whirlpool expanding by making a new line of appliances, such as dehumidifiers?
7. If you ran a successful U.S. firm like Wal-Mart, IBM, or Hershey's, into which countries would you first expand? Why?

chapter seven

GDP: Measuring Total Production and Income

Increases in GDP Spur Hiring at Freightliner

Freightliner is the leading manufacturer of commercial vehicles in North America, producing more than 110,000 trucks and other vehicles in a typical year and exporting to more than 30 countries. The firm is owned by the DaimlerChrysler Corporation and is headquartered in Portland, Oregon. In the summer of 2004, Freightliner began hiring more workers in several of its manufacturing plants in North America. It added 700 workers at its plant near Portland, Oregon, 593 workers at its plant in Cleveland, North Carolina, 300 workers at its plant in St. Thomas, Ontario, Canada, and 165 workers at its plant in Gaffney, South Carolina. The firm's leading product is the Freightliner Class 8 heavy truck. It also manufactures American LaFrance fire trucks and emergency vehicles and Thomas Built Buses, along with other commercial vehicles.

Freightliner's increased hiring in the summer of 2004 was caused by an increase in demand for its trucks. This increase in demand was not the result of Freightliner's introducing innovative new products or starting an effective new marketing campaign. Instead, Freightliner was experiencing the effects of the *business cycle,* which refers to the alternating periods of economic expansion and recession that occur in the United States and other industrial economies. Production and employment increase during expansions and fall during recessions. In 2004, Freightliner was benefiting from the effects of an economic expansion, but just a few years earlier it had suffered from the effects of an economic recession. In fact, many of the workers hired in 2004 had previously been laid off by the firm. Rainer Schmüeckle, the president and chief executive officer (CEO) of Freightliner, explained the new hiring in terms of the business cycle: "The North American heavy-duty truck market continues its vigorous recovery and we have a positive outlook for further improvement. . . . Favorable economic conditions and customers' need to replace older equipment or expand their operations are driving a robust recovery of the North American Class 8 market."

Freightliner was not alone in experiencing an increase in demand

LEARNING OBJECTIVES

After studying this chapter, you should be able to:

① Explain how total production is measured.

② Discuss whether GDP is a good measure of economic well-being.

③ Discuss the difference between real variables and nominal variables.

④ Become familiar with other measures of total production and total income.

during 2004. *An Inside Look* on page 22[illegible] discusses the increase in demand being experienced by Canadian firms during this period. As firms benefited from the economic expansion, they increased their hiring. This was good news for college graduates searching for work. In the summer of 2004, almost 150,000 fewer college graduates were unemployed than had been unemployed the previous summer. Although the job market had improved, it was still not as strong as in the late 1990s, when even fewer workers were unemployed.

Activities at companies like Freightliner can offer important insight into whether U.S. economic activity is surging or flagging. In 2001, as fears of recession in the United States intensified, the President's Council of Economic Advisers contacted economists in the trucking, airline, retailing, and financial services industries. In so doing, the government economists were able to collect and assess information on economic conditions before official data for the economy as a whole were tabulated. Individual firms like Freightliner must pay attention to developments in the overall economy. Macroeconomists and financial market participants also study economic developments at key firms to evaluate the current pace of economic activity.

Source: Robert Guy Matthews, "U.S. Recovery in Manufacturing Gains Momentum," *Wall Street Journal*, July 9, 2004, p. A2.

Microeconomics The study of how households and firms make choices, how they interact in markets, and how the government attempts to influence their choices.

Macroeconomics The study of the economy as a whole, including topics such as inflation, unemployment, and economic growth.

Business cycle Alternating periods of economic expansion and economic recession.

Expansion The period of a business cycle during which total production and total employment are increasing.

Recession The period of a business cycle during which total production and total employment are decreasing.

Economic growth The ability of an economy to produce increasing quantities of goods and services.

Inflation rate The percentage increase in the price level from one year to the next.

➤ As we saw in Chapter 1, we can divide economics into the subfields of microeconomics and macroeconomics. **Microeconomics** is the study of how households and firms make choices, how they interact in markets, and how the government attempts to influence their choices. **Macroeconomics** is the study of the economy as a whole, including topics such as inflation, unemployment, and economic growth. In microeconomic analysis, economists generally study individual markets, such as the market for personal computers. In macroeconomic analysis, economists study factors that affect many markets at the same time. As we saw in the chapter opener, one important macroeconomic issue is the business cycle. The **business cycle** refers to the alternating periods of expansion and recession that the U.S. economy has experienced dating back at least to the early nineteenth century. A business cycle **expansion** is a period during which total production and total employment are increasing. A business cycle **recession** is a period during which total production and employment are decreasing. In the following chapters, we will discuss the causes of the business cycle and policies the government may use to reduce its effects.

Another important macroeconomic topic is **economic growth,** which refers to the ability of the economy to produce increasing quantities of goods and services. Economic growth is important because an economy that grows too slowly fails to raise living standards. In many countries in Africa, very little economic growth has occurred in the past 50 years, and many people remain in severe poverty. Macroeconomics analyzes both what determines the rate of economic growth within a country and the reasons why growth rates differ so greatly across countries.

Macroeconomics also analyzes what determines the total level of employment in an economy. As we will see, the level of employment is affected significantly by the business cycle, but other factors also help determine the level of employment in the long run. A related issue is why some economies are more successful than others in maintaining high levels of employment over time. Another important macroeconomic issue is what determines the **inflation rate,** or the percentage increase in the average level of prices from one year to the next. As with employment, inflation is affected both by the business cycle and by other long-run factors. Finally, macroeconomics is concerned with the linkages among economies: international trade and international finance.

Macroeconomic analysis provides information that consumers and firms need in order to understand current economic conditions and to help predict future conditions. A family may be reluctant to buy a house if employment in the economy is declining because some family members may be at risk of losing their jobs. Similarly, firms may be reluctant to invest in building new factories or to undertake major new expenditures on information technology if they expect that future sales may be weak. For example, in early 2003, DaimlerChrysler canceled plans to spend $1.2 billion to build a new factory in Windsor, Ontario, to manufacture Dodge pickup trucks. The decision was made because macroeconomic forecasts indicated that consumer demand for trucks and automobiles would be weak. Macroeconomic analysis can also aid the federal government in designing policies that help the U.S. economy perform more efficiently.

In this chapter and Chapter 8, we begin our study of macroeconomics by considering how best to measure key macroeconomic variables. As we will see, there are important issues involved in measuring macroeconomic variables. We start by considering measures of total production and total income in an economy.

Gross Domestic Product Measures Total Production

1 LEARNING OBJECTIVE

Explain how total production is measured.

"Second Quarter [U.S.] GDP Data Show Economic Fundamentals Solid"

"Russian Government Cuts 2005 GDP Forecast to 5.8%"

"German Government Cuts 2005 GDP Forecast to 1.7% from 1.8%"

"Key Scandinavian Data: Danish Third Quarter GDP Growth Seen Easing"

"Chile's Third Quarter GDP Surges 6.8% on Year"

These headlines are from articles that appeared during one month in the *Wall Street Journal.* Why is GDP so often the focus of news stories? In this section, we explore what GDP is and how it is measured. We also explore why knowledge of GDP is important to consumers, firms, and government policymakers.

Measuring Total Production: Gross Domestic Product

Economists measure total production by **gross domestic product** or **GDP.** GDP is the market *value* of all *final* goods and services produced in a country during a period of time. In the United States, the Bureau of Economic Analysis (BEA) in the Department of Commerce compiles the data needed to calculate GDP. The BEA issues reports on the GDP every three months. GDP is a central concept in macroeconomics, so we need to consider its definition carefully.

Gross domestic product (GDP) The market value of all final goods and services produced in a country during a period of time.

GDP IS MEASURED USING MARKET VALUES, NOT QUANTITIES The word *value* is important in the definition of GDP. In microeconomics, we measure production in quantity terms: number of iPods produced by Apple, billions of tons of wheat grown by U.S. farmers, or number of trucks produced by Freightliner. When we measure total production in the economy, we can't just add together the quantities of every good and service because the result would be a meaningless jumble. Tons of wheat would be added to gallons of milk and numbers of trucks and so on. Instead, we measure production by taking the *value* in dollar terms of all the goods and services produced.

GDP INCLUDES ONLY THE MARKET VALUE OF FINAL GOODS In measuring GDP, we include only the value of **final goods and services.** A final good or service is one that is purchased by its final user and is not included in the production of any other good or service. A hamburger purchased by a consumer or a computer purchased by a business are final goods. Some goods and services, though, are used in the production of other goods and services. For example, Freightliner does not produce tires for its heavy trucks; it buys them from tire companies, such as Goodyear and Michelin. The tires are an **intermediate good,** whereas a Freightliner truck is a final good. In calculating GDP, we include the value of the Freightliner truck but not the value of the tire. If we included the value of the tire, we would be *double counting.* The value of the tire would be counted once when it was sold to Freightliner and a second time when Freightliner sold the truck that the tire was installed on to Federal Express or some other customer.

Final good or service A good or service purchased by a final user.

Intermediate good or service A good or service that is an input into another good or service, such as a tire on a truck.

GDP INCLUDES ONLY CURRENT PRODUCTION GDP includes only production that takes place during the indicated time period. For example, GDP in 2006 includes only the goods and services produced during that year. In particular, GDP does *not* include the value of used goods. If you buy a DVD of *The War of the Worlds* from Amazon.com, the purchase is included in GDP. If six months later you resell that DVD on eBay, that transaction is not included in GDP.

SOLVED PROBLEM 7-1

① LEARNING OBJECTIVE
Explain how total production is measured.

Calculating GDP

Suppose that a very simple economy produces only the following four goods and services: eye examinations, pizzas, textbooks, and paper. Assume that all of the paper in this economy is used in the production of textbooks. Use the information in the following table to compute GDP for the year 2007.

PRODUCTION AND PRICE STATISTICS FOR 2007

(1) PRODUCT	(2) QUANTITY	(3) PRICE PER UNIT
Eye examinations	100	$50.00
Pizzas	80	10.00
Textbooks	20	100.00
Paper	2,000	0.10

Solving the Problem:
Step 1: Review the chapter material. This problem is about gross domestic product, so you may want to review the section "Measuring Total Production: Gross Domestic Product," which begins on page 205.

Step 2: Determine which goods and services listed in the table should be included in the calculation of GDP. GDP is the value of all final goods and services. Therefore, we need to calculate the value of the final goods and services listed in the table. Eye examinations, pizzas, and textbooks are final goods. Paper would also be a final good if, for instance, a consumer bought it to use in a printer. However, here we are assuming that publishers purchase all the paper to use in manufacturing textbooks, so the paper is an intermediate good and its value is not included in GDP.

Step 3: Calculate the value of the three final goods and services listed in the table. Value is equal to the quantity produced multiplied by the price per unit, so we multiply the numbers in column (1) by the numbers in column (2):

PRODUCT	(1) QUANTITY	(2) PRICE PER UNIT	(3) VALUE
Eye examinations	100	$50	$5,000
Pizzas	80	10	800
Textbooks	20	100	2,000

Step 4: Add the value for each of the three final goods and services to find GDP.
GDP = Value of eye examinations produced + value of pizzas produced + value of textbooks produced = $5,000 + $800 + $2,000 = $7,800

YOUR TURN: **For more practice, do related problem 7 on page 225 at the end of this chapter.**

Production, Income, and the Circular Flow Diagram

When we measure the value of total production in the economy by calculating GDP, we are simultaneously measuring the value of total income. To see why the value of total production is equal to the value of total income, consider what happens to the money you spend on a single product. Suppose you buy an Apple iPod for $250 at a Best Buy store. *All* of that $250 must end up as someone's income. Apple and Best Buy will receive some of the $250 as profits, workers at Apple will receive some as wages, the salesperson who sold you the iPod will receive some as salary, the firms that sell parts to Apple will receive some as profits, the workers for these firms will receive some as wages, and so on: Every penny must end up as someone's income. (Note, though, that any sales tax on the iPod will be collected by the store and sent to the government without ending up as anyone's income.) Therefore, if we add up the value of every good and service sold in the economy, we must get a total that is exactly equal to the value of all of the income in the economy.

The circular-flow diagram in Figure 7-1 (page 208) was introduced in Chapter 2 to illustrate the interaction of firms and households in markets. We use it here to illustrate the flow of spending and money in the economy. Firms sell goods and services to three groups: domestic households, foreign firms and households, and the government. Expenditures by foreign firms and households (shown as the "Rest of the World" in the diagram) on domestically produced goods and services are called *exports.* For example, Freightliner sells 30 percent of its heavy trucks outside the United States. As we note at the bottom of Figure 7-1, we can measure GDP by adding up the total expenditures of these three groups on goods and services.

Firms use the *factors of production*—labor, capital, natural resources, and entrepreneurship—to produce goods and services. Households supply the factors of production to firms in exchange for income. We divide income into four categories: wages, interest, rent, and profit. Firms pay wages to households in exchange for labor services, interest for the use of capital, and rent for natural resources such as land. Profit is the income that remains after a firm has paid wages, interest, and rent. Profit is the return to entrepreneurs for organizing the other factors of production and for bearing the risk of producing and selling goods and services. As Figure 7-1 shows, federal, state, and local governments make payments of wages and interest to households in exchange for hiring workers and other factors of production. Governments also make *transfer payments* to households. **Transfer payments** include Social Security payments to retired and disabled people and unemployment insurance payments to unemployed workers. These payments are not included in GDP because they are not received in exchange for production of a new good or service. The sum of wages, interest, rent, and profit is total income in the economy. As we note at the top of Figure 7-1, we can measure GDP as the total income received by households.

Transfer payments Payments by the government to individuals for which the government does not receive a good or service in return.

The diagram also allows us to trace the ways that households use their income. Households spend some of their income on goods and services. Some of this spending is on domestically produced goods and services, and some is on foreign produced goods and services. Spending on foreign produced goods and services is known as *imports.* Households also use some of their income to pay taxes to the government. (Note that firms also pay taxes to the government.) Some of the income earned by households is not spent on goods and services or paid in taxes but is deposited in checking or savings accounts in banks or is used to buy stocks or bonds. Banks and stock and bond markets make up the *financial system.* The flow of funds from households into the financial system makes it possible for the government and firms to borrow. As we will see, the health of the financial system is of vital importance to an economy. Without the ability to borrow funds through the financial system, firms will have difficulty expanding and adopting new technologies. In fact, as we will discuss in Chapter 9, no country without a well-developed financial system has been able to sustain high levels of economic growth.

The circular flow diagram shows that we can measure GDP either by calculating the total value of expenditures on final goods and services or by calculating the value of total income. We get the same dollar amount of GDP whichever approach we take.

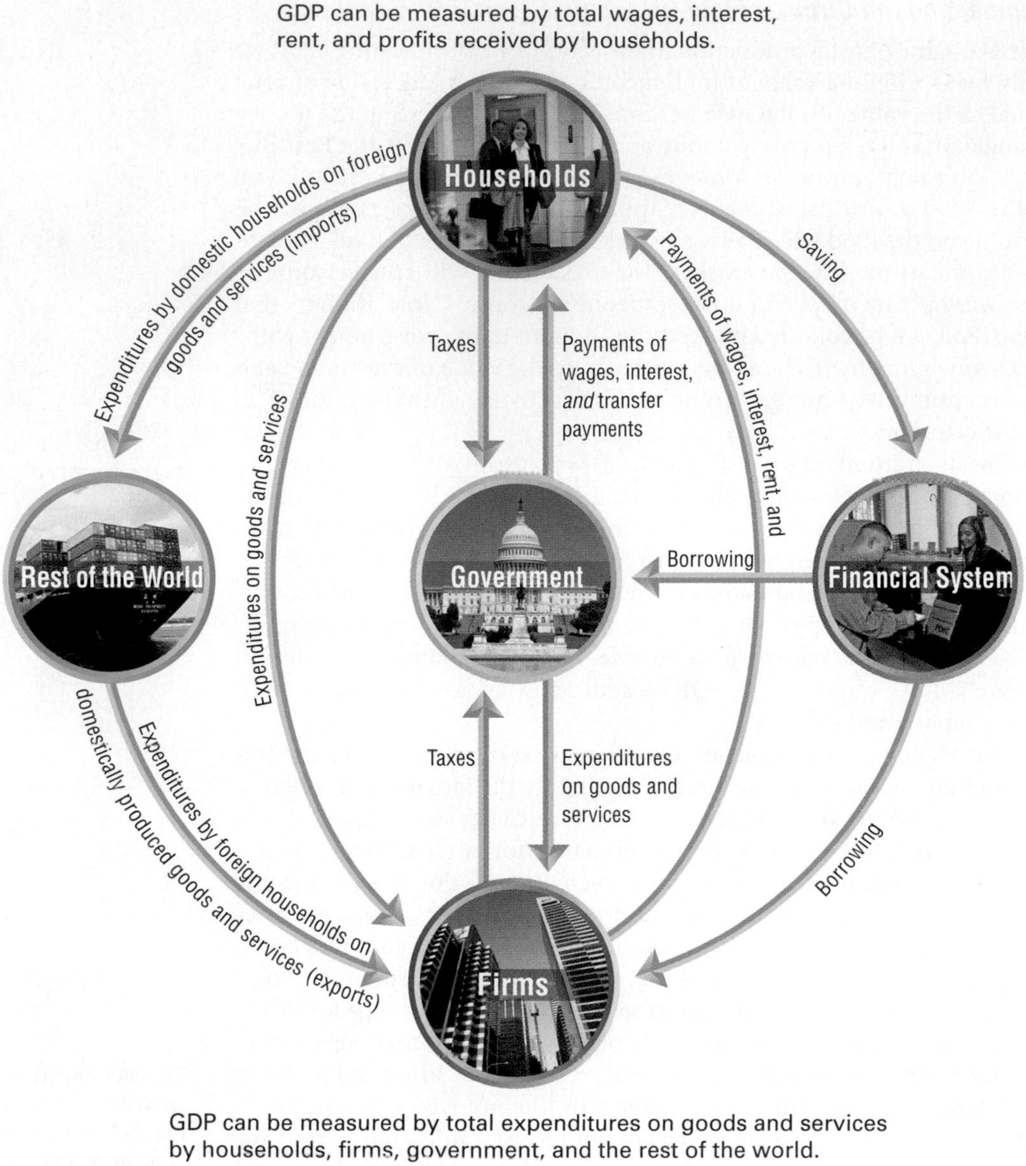

FIGURE 7-1 The Circular Flow and the Measurement of GDP

The circular-flow diagram illustrates the flow of spending and money in the economy. Firms sell goods and services to three groups: domestic households, foreign firms and households, and the government. To produce goods and services, firms use factors of production: labor, capital, natural resources, and entrepreneurship. Households supply the factors of production to firms in exchange for income in the form of wages, interest, profit, and rent. Firms make payments of wages and interest to households in exchange for hiring workers and other factors of production. The sum of wages, interest, rent, and profit is total income in the economy. We can measure GDP as the total income received by households. The diagram also shows that households use their income to purchase goods and services, pay taxes, and save. Firms and the government borrow the funds that flow from households into the financial system. We can measure GDP either by calculating the total value of expenditures on final goods and services or by calculating the value of total income.

Components of GDP

The Bureau of Economic Analysis (BEA) divides its statistics on GDP into four major categories of expenditures. Economists use these categories to understand why GDP fluctuates and to forecast future GDP.

Consumption Spending by households on goods and services, not including spending on new houses.

PERSONAL CONSUMPTION EXPENDITURES, OR "CONSUMPTION" **Consumption** expenditures are made by households and are divided into expenditures on *services,*

Don't Let This Happen To You!

Remember What Economists Mean by "Investment"

Notice that the definition of *investment* in this chapter is narrower than in everyday use. For example, people often say they are investing in the stock market or in rare coins. As we have seen, economists reserve the word *investment* for purchases of machinery, factories, and houses. Economists don't include purchases of stock or rare coins or deposits in savings accounts in the definition of investment because these activities don't result in the production of new goods. For example, a share of Microsoft stock represents part ownership of that company. When you buy a share of Microsoft stock, nothing new is produced—there is just a transfer in ownership. Similarly, buying a rare coin or putting $1,000 in a savings account does not result in an increase in production. GDP is not affected by any of these activities, so they are not included in the economic definition of investment.

YOUR TURN: **Test your understanding by doing related problem 9 on page 225 at the end of this chapter.**

such as medical care, education, and haircuts; expenditures on *nondurable goods*, such as food and clothing; and expenditures on *durable goods*, such as automobiles and furniture. The spending by households on new houses is not included in consumption. Instead, spending on new houses is included in the investment category, which we discuss next.

GROSS PRIVATE DOMESTIC INVESTMENT, OR "INVESTMENT" Spending on *gross private domestic investment*, or simply **investment** is divided into three categories: *Business fixed investment* is spending by firms on new factories, office buildings, and machinery used to produce other goods. *Residential investment* is spending by households on new housing. *Changes in business inventories* are also included in investment. Inventories are goods that have been produced, but not yet sold. If Freightliner has $200 million worth of unsold trucks at the beginning of the year and $350 million worth of unsold trucks at the end of the year, then the firm has spent $150 million on inventory investment during the year.

Investment Spending by firms on new factories, office buildings, machinery, and inventories, and spending by households on new houses.

GOVERNMENT CONSUMPTION AND GROSS INVESTMENT, OR "GOVERNMENT PURCHASES" **Government purchases** are spending by federal, state, and local governments on goods and services, such as teachers' salaries, highways, and aircraft carriers. Again, government spending on transfer payments is not included in government purchases because it does not result in the production of new goods and services.

Government purchases Spending by federal, state, and local governments on goods and services.

7-1 Making the Connection

Spending on Homeland Security

The federal government established the Department of Homeland Security after September 11, 2001, to guard against future terrorist attacks within the United States. Spending by this department is intended to increase the security of the nation's borders and transportation system, identify and arrest terrorists within the United States, and gather intelligence on potential terrorist threats.

Although the Department of Homeland Security has overall responsibility for homeland security, other federal agencies also have increased their spending on related programs. For example, the Department of Health and Human Services increased its spending on research to find new ways to combat the use of biological weapons from $300 million in 2001 to more than $4 billion in 2004. Several other federal agencies, such as the Department of Justice, the Department of Agriculture, and the Department of Transportation, increased their spending as well. In 2004, the total spending on homeland security by the Department of Homeland Security and other federal agencies was about $41.4 billion—about double the amount spent on these activities before 2001.

Government spending on homeland security more than doubled between 2001 and 2004.

Because the United States has a federal system of government, responsibility for some homeland security activities lies with state or local authorities. For example, spending to provide security for the Golden Gate Bridge is the responsibility of the state of California and the city of San Francisco. The Department of Homeland Security provides grants to help support this state and local spending. Of course, governments at all levels have limited budgets, so at some point spending more on homeland security requires them to spend less on other programs.

Sources: Congressional Budget Office, *Federal Funding for Homeland Security,* April 30, 2004; and Executive Office of the President, Office of Management and Budget, *Homeland Security.*

Net exports Exports minus imports.

NET EXPORTS OF GOODS AND SERVICES, OR "NET EXPORTS" **Net exports** is equal to *exports* minus *imports.* Exports are goods and services produced in the United States, but purchased by foreign firms, households, and governments. We add exports to our other categories of expenditures because otherwise we would not be including all spending on new goods and services produced in the United States. For example, if Freightliner sells $90 billion worth of trucks to firms in other countries, those exports are included in GDP because they represent production in the United States. Imports are goods and services produced in foreign countries, but purchased by U.S. firms, households, and governments. We subtract imports from total expenditures, because otherwise we would be including spending that does not result in production of new goods and services in the United States. For example, if U.S. consumers buy $150 billion worth of furniture manufactured in China, that spending is included in consumption expenditures. But the value of those imports is subtracted from GDP because the imports do not represent production in the United States.

An Equation for GDP and Some Actual Values

A simple equation sums up the components of GDP:

$$Y = C + I + G + NX.$$

The equation tells us that GDP (denoted as Y) equals consumption (C) plus investment (I) plus government purchases (G) plus net exports (NX). Figure 7-2 shows the values of the components of GDP for the year 2004. The graph in the figure highlights that consumption is by far the largest component of GDP. The table provides a more detailed breakdown and shows several interesting points:

- Consumer spending on services is greater than the sum of spending on durable and nondurable goods. This greater spending on services is reflected in the United States and other high-income countries by a continuing trend away from the production of goods and toward the production of services. As the populations of these countries have become, on average, both older and wealthier, their demand for services such as medical care and financial advice has increased faster than their demand for goods.

COMPONENTS OF GDP (billions of dollars)		
Consumption		$8,214
Durable Goods	$988	
Nondurable Goods	2,368	
Services	4,858	
Investment		1,928
Business Fixed Investment	1,199	
Residential Construction	674	
Change in Business Inventories	55	
Government Purchases		2,216
Federal	828	
State and Local	1,388	
Net Exports		–624
Exports	1,174	
Imports	1,798	
Total GDP		$11,734

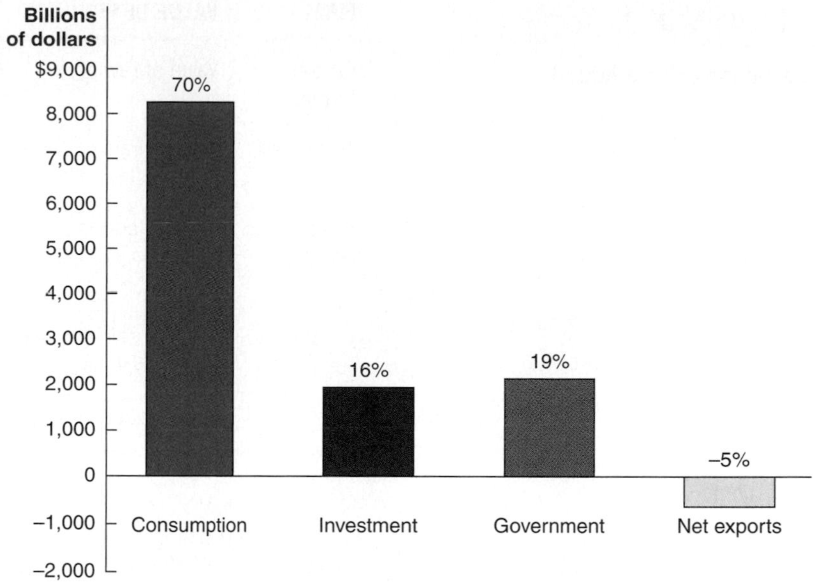

FIGURE 7-2 Components of GDP in 2004

Consumption accounts for 70 percent of GDP, far more than any of the other components. In recent years, net exports typically have been negative, which reduces GDP.

- Business fixed investment is the largest component of investment. As we will see in later chapters, spending by firms on new factories, computers, and machinery can fluctuate. For example, a decline in business fixed investment played an important role in causing the 2001 recession.
- Purchases made by state and local governments are greater than purchases made by the federal government. State and local government purchases are greater than federal government purchases because basic government activities, such as education and law enforcement, occur largely at the state and local levels.
- Imports are greater than exports, so net exports are negative. We will discuss in Chapter 17 why this pattern has been true typically for the U.S. economy.

Measuring GDP by the Value Added Method

We have seen that GDP can be calculated by adding together all expenditures on final goods and services. An alternative way of calculating GDP is the *value added method.* **Value added** refers to the additional market value a firm gives to a product and is equal to the difference between the price the firm sells a good for and the price it paid other firms for intermediate goods. Table 7-1 gives a hypothetical example of the value added by each firm involved in the production of a shirt offered for sale on L.L.Bean's Web site.

Value added The market value a firm adds to a product.

Suppose a cotton farmer sells $1.00 of raw cotton to a textile mill. If, for simplicity, we ignore any inputs the farmer may have purchased from other firms—such as cottonseed or fertilizer—then the farmer's value added is $1.00. The textile mill then weaves the raw cotton into cotton fabric, which it sells to a shirt company for $3.00. The textile mill's value added ($2.00) is the difference between the price it paid for the raw cotton ($1.00) and the price for which it can sell the cotton fabric ($3.00). Similarly, the shirt company's value added is the difference between the price it paid for the cotton fabric ($3.00) and the price it receives for the shirt from L.L.Bean ($15.00). L.L.Bean's value added is the difference between the price it pays for the shirt ($15.00) and the price it can sell the shirt for on its Web site ($35.00). Notice that *the price of the shirt on*

TABLE 7-1

Calculating Value Added

FIRM	VALUE OF PRODUCT	VALUE ADDED	
Cotton farmer	Value of raw cotton = $1.00	Value added by cotton farmer	= $1.00
Textile mill	Value of raw cotton woven into cotton fabric = $3.00	Value added by cotton textile mill = ($3.00 – $1.00)	= 2.00
Shirt company	Value of cotton fabric made into a shirt = $15.00	Value added by shirt manufacturer = ($15.00 –$3.00)	= 12.00
L.L.Bean	Value of shirt for sale on L.L. Bean's Web site = $35.00	Value added by L.L.Bean = ($35.00 – $15.00)	= 20.00
	Total Value Added		**= $35.00**

L.L.Bean's Web site is exactly equal to the sum of the value added by each firm involved in the production of the shirt. Therefore, we can calculate GDP by adding up the market value of every final good and service produced during a particular period. Or, we can arrive at the same value for GDP by adding up the value added of every firm involved in producing those final goods and services.

② LEARNING OBJECTIVE

Discuss whether GDP is a good measure of economic well-being.

Does GDP Measure What We Want It to Measure?

Economists use GDP to measure total production in the economy. For that purpose, we would like GDP to be as comprehensive as possible, not overlooking any significant production that takes place in the economy. Most economists believe that GDP does a good—but not flawless—job of measuring production. GDP is also sometimes used as a measure of well-being. Although it is generally true that the more goods and services people have, the better off they are, we will see that GDP provides only a rough measure of well-being.

Shortcomings in GDP as a Measure of Total Production

When the BEA calculates GDP, it does not include two types of production: production in the home and production in the underground economy.

HOUSEHOLD PRODUCTION With only a couple of exceptions, the U.S. Commerce Department does not attempt to estimate the value of goods and services that are not bought and sold in markets. If a carpenter makes and sells bookcases, the value of those bookcases will be counted in GDP. If the carpenter makes a bookcase for personal use, it will not be counted in GDP. *Household production* refers to goods and services people produce for themselves. The most important type of household production is the services a homemaker provides to the homemaker's family. If a person has been caring for children, cleaning house, and preparing the family meals, the value of such services is not included in GDP. If the person then decides to work outside the home, enrolls the children in day care, hires a cleaning service, and begins eating family meals in restaurants, the value of GDP will rise by the amount paid for day care, cleaning services, and restaurant meals, even though production of these services has not actually increased.

THE UNDERGROUND ECONOMY Individuals and firms sometimes conceal the buying and selling of goods and services, in which case their production won't be counted in GDP. Individuals and firms conceal what they buy and sell for three basic reasons: They are dealing in illegal goods and services, such as drugs or prostitution; they want to avoid paying taxes on the income they earn; or they want to avoid government regulations. This concealed buying and selling is referred to as the **underground economy.** Estimates of the size of the underground economy in the United States vary widely, but it may be as much as 10 percent of measured GDP, or more than $1 trillion. The underground economy in some poorer countries, such as Zimbabwe or Peru, may be more than half of measured GDP.

Underground economy Buying and selling of goods and services that is concealed from the government to avoid taxes or regulations or because the goods and services are illegal.

Is not counting household production or production in the underground economy a serious shortcoming of GDP? Most economists would answer "no" because the most important use of GDP is to measure changes in how the economy is performing over short periods of time, such as from one year to the next. For this purpose, omitting household production and production in the underground economy won't have much effect, because there is not likely to be much change in the amounts of these types of production from one year to the next.

We also use GDP statistics to measure how production of goods and services grows over fairly long periods of a decade or more. For this purpose, omitting household production and production in the underground economy may be more important. For example, beginning in the 1970s, the number of women working outside the home increased dramatically. Some of the goods and services—such as childcare and restaurant meals—produced in the following years were replacing what had been household production, rather than being true additions to total production.

How the Underground Economy Hurts Developing Countries

7-2 Making the Connection

In some developing countries, more than half the workers may be in the underground economy.

Although few economists believe the underground economy in the United States amounts to more than 10 percent of measured GDP, the underground economy in some developing countries may be more than 50 percent of measured GDP. In developing countries, the underground economy is often referred to as the *informal sector,* as opposed to the *formal sector* in which output of goods and services is measured. Although it might not seem to matter whether production of goods and services is measured and included in GDP or unmeasured, a large informal sector can be a sign of government policies that are retarding economic growth.

Because firms in the informal sector are acting illegally, they tend to be smaller and have less capital than firms acting legally. The entrepreneurs who start firms in the informal sector may be afraid their firms could someday be closed or confiscated by the government. Therefore, the entrepreneurs limit their investments in these firms. As a consequence, workers in these firms have less machinery and equipment to work with, and so can produce fewer goods and services. Entrepreneurs in the informal sector also have to pay the costs of avoiding government authorities. These costs can take the form of bribes to government officials. Construction firms operating in the informal sector in Brazil have to employ lookouts who can warn workers to hide when government inspectors come around. The informal sector is large in some developing economies because taxes are high and government regulations are extensive. For example, firms in Brazil pay 85 percent of all taxes collected, as compared with 41 percent in the United States. Not surprisingly, about half of all Brazilian workers are employed in the informal sector. In Zimbabwe and Peru, the fraction of workers in the informal sector may be as high as 60 or 70 percent.

Many economists believe taxes in developing countries are so high because these countries are attempting to pay for government sectors that are as large relative to their economies as the government sectors of industrial economies. Government spending in Brazil, for example, is 39 percent of measured GDP, compared to 31 percent in the United States. In the early twentieth century, when the United States was much poorer than it is today, government spending was only about 8 percent of GDP, so the tax burden on U.S. firms was much lower. In countries like Brazil, bringing firms into the formal sector from the informal sector may require reductions in government spending and taxes. In many developing countries, however, voters are very reluctant to see government services reduced.

Sources: Mary Anastasia O'Grady, "Why Brazil's Underground Economy Grows and Grows," *Wall Street Journal,* September 10, 2004, p. A13; and "In the Shadows," *Economist,* June 17, 2004.

Shortcomings of GDP as a Measure of Well-Being

The main purpose of GDP is to measure a country's total production. GDP is also frequently used, though, as a measure of well-being. For example, newspaper and magazine articles will show tables with levels of GDP per person in different countries, with the implication that people in the countries with higher levels of GDP are better off. Although increases in GDP often do lead to increases in the well-being of the population, it is important to be aware that GDP is not a perfect measure of well-being for several reasons.

THE VALUE OF LEISURE IS NOT INCLUDED IN GDP If an economic consultant decides to retire, GDP will decline even though the consultant may value increased leisure more than the income he or she was earning running a consulting firm. The consultant's well-being has increased, but GDP has decreased. In 1890, the typical American worked 60 hours per week. Today, the typical American works fewer than 40 hours per week. If Americans still worked 60-hour weeks, GDP would be much higher than it is, but the well-being of the typical person would be lower, because less time would be available for leisure activities.

GDP IS NOT ADJUSTED FOR POLLUTION OR OTHER NEGATIVE EFFECTS OF PRODUCTION When a dry cleaner cleans and presses clothes, the value of this service is included in GDP. If chemicals used by the dry cleaner pollute the air or water, GDP is not adjusted to compensate for the costs of the pollution. Similarly, the value of cigarettes produced is included in GDP with no adjustment made for the costs of the lung cancer that some smokers develop.

We should note, though, that increasing GDP often leads countries to devote more resources to pollution reduction. For example, in the United States between 1970 and 2004, as GDP was steadily increasing, emissions of the six main air pollutants declined by more than 50 percent. Developing countries often have higher levels of pollution than high-income countries because the lower GDPs of the developing countries make them more reluctant to spend resources on pollution reduction. Levels of pollution in China are much higher than in the United States, Japan, or the countries of Western Europe. According to the World Health Organization, seven of the ten most polluted cities in the world are in China, but as Chinese GDP continues to rise, it may devote more resources to reducing pollution.

GDP IS NOT ADJUSTED FOR CHANGES IN CRIME AND OTHER SOCIAL PROBLEMS An increase in crime will reduce well-being but may actually increase GDP if it leads to greater spending on police, security guards, and alarm systems. GDP is also not adjusted for changes in divorce rates, drug addiction, or other factors that may affect people's well-being.

To summarize, we can say that a person's well-being depends on many factors that are not taken into account in calculating GDP. Because GDP is designed to measure total production, it is perhaps not surprising that it does an imperfect job of measuring well-being.

7-3 Making the Connection

Did World War II Bring Prosperity?

The Great Depression of the 1930s was the worst economic downturn in U.S. history. GDP declined by more than 25 percent between 1929 and 1933 and did not reach its 1929 level again until 1938. The unemployment rate remained at very high levels of 10 percent or more through 1940. Then, in 1941 the United States entered World War II. The following graph shows that GDP rose dramatically during the war years of 1941 to 1945. (The graph shows values for real GDP, which as we will see in the next section, corrects measures of GDP for changes in the price level.) The unemployment rate also fell to very low levels—below 2 percent.

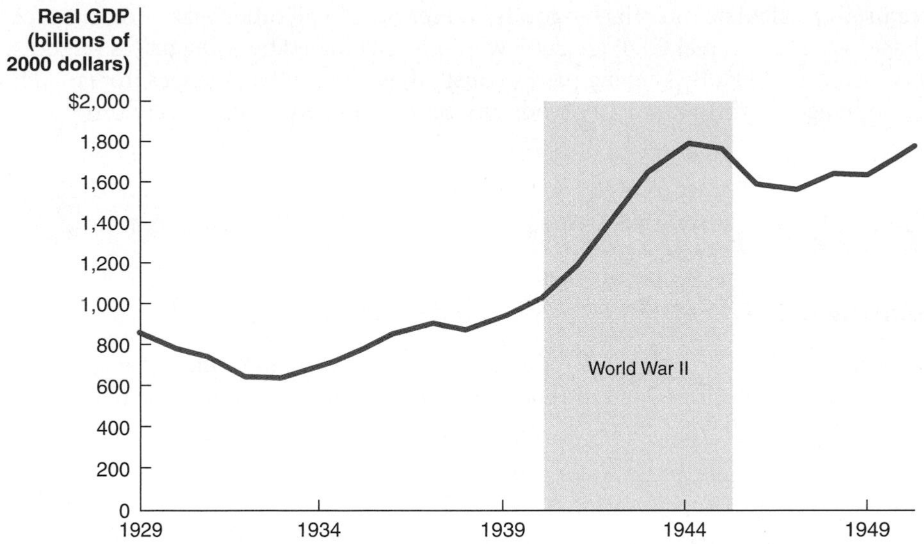

Source: Bureau of Economic Analysis.

Production of military goods soared during World War II, but production of consumption goods lagged.

Traditionally, historians have argued that World War II brought prosperity back to the U.S. economy. But did it? Economist Robert Higgs argues that if we look at the well-being of the typical person, then the World War II years were anything but prosperous. Higgs points out that increased production of tanks, ships, planes, and munitions account for most of the increase in GDP during those years. Between 1943 and 1945, more than 40 percent of the labor force was either in the military or producing war goods. As a result, between 1939 and 1944, production of consumption goods per person increased only about 2 percent, leaving the quantity of consumption goods available to the typical person in 1944 still below what it had been in 1929. With the end of the war, true prosperity did return to the U.S. economy, and by 1946 production of consumption goods per person had risen by more than 25 percent from what it had been in 1929.

World War II was a period of extraordinary sacrifice and achievement by the "greatest generation." But statistics on GDP may give a misleading indication of whether it was also a period of prosperity.

Source: Robert Higgs, "Wartime Prosperity? A Reassessment of the U.S. Economy in the 1940s," *Journal of Economic History*, Vol. 52, No. 1 (March 1992).

Real GDP versus Nominal GDP

③ LEARNING OBJECTIVE

Discuss the difference between real variables and nominal variables.

Because GDP is measured in value terms, we have to be careful about interpreting changes over time. To see why, consider interpreting an increase in the total value of heavy truck production from $40 billion in 2005 to $44 billion in 2006. Can we be sure—because $44 billion is 10 percent greater than $40 billion—that the number of trucks produced in 2006 was 10 percent greater than the number produced in 2005? We can draw this conclusion only if the average price of trucks did not change between 2005 and 2006. In fact, when GDP increases from one year to the next, the increase is due partly to increases in production of goods and services and partly to increases in prices. Because we are interested mainly in GDP as a measure of production, we need a way of separating the price changes from the quantity changes.

Calculating Real GDP

Real GDP The value of final goods and services evaluated at base year prices.

Nominal GDP The value of final goods and services evaluated at current year prices.

The Bureau of Economic Analysis separates price changes from quantity changes by calculating a measure of production called **real GDP. Nominal GDP** is calculated by summing the current values of final goods and services. Real GDP is calculated by designating a particular year as the *base year.* The prices of goods and services in the base year are used to calculate the value of goods and services in all other years. For instance, if the base year is 2000, real GDP for 2005 would be calculated by using prices of goods and services from 2000. By keeping prices constant, we know that changes in real GDP represent changes in the quantity of goods and services produced in the economy.

SOLVED PROBLEM 7-2

③ LEARNING OBJECTIVE

Discuss the difference between real variables and nominal variables.

Calculating Real GDP

Suppose that a very simple economy produces only the following three final goods and services: eye examinations, pizzas, and textbooks. Use the information in the table to compute real GDP for the year 2005. Assume the base year is 2000.

	2000		2005	
PRODUCT	QUANTITY	PRICE	QUANTITY	PRICE
Eye examinations	80	$40	100	$50
Pizzas	90	11	80	10
Textbooks	15	90	20	100

Solving the Problem:

Step 1: Review the chapter material. This problem is about calculating real GDP, so you may want to review the section "Calculating Real GDP," which begins on page 215.

Step 2: Calculate the value of the three goods and services listed in the table using the quantities for 2005 and the prices for 2000. The definition on page 215 tells us that real GDP is the value of all final goods and services, evaluated at base year prices. In this case, the base year is 2000 and we are given information on the price of each product in that year.

PRODUCT	QUANTITY	PRICE	VALUE
Eye examinations	100	$40	$4,000
Pizzas	80	11	880
Textbooks	20	90	1,800

Step 3: Add up the values for the three products to find real GDP.

Real GDP for 2005 equals the sum of:

Quantity of eye examinations in 2005 × Price of eye exams in 2000 = $4,000

+ Quantity of pizzas produced in 2005 × Price of pizzas in 2000 = $880

+ Quantity of textbooks produced in 2005 × Price of textbooks in 2000 = $1,800

or, $6,680

Extra Credit: Notice that the quantities of each good produced in 2000 were irrelevant for calculating real GDP in 2005. Notice also that the value of $6,680 for real GDP in 2005 is lower than the value of $7,800 for nominal GDP in 2005 calculated in Solved Problem 7–1.

YOUR TURN: **For more practice, do related problem 8 on page 225 at the end of this chapter.**

One drawback to calculating real GDP using base year prices is that, over time, prices may change relative to each other. For example, the price of cell phones may fall relative to the price of gasoline. Because this change is not reflected in the fixed prices from the base year, the estimate of real GDP is somewhat distorted. The further away the current year is from the base year, the worse the problem becomes. To make the calculation of real GDP more accurate, in 1996, the BEA switched to using *chain-weighted prices,* and now publishes statistics on real GDP in "chained (2000) dollars."

The details of calculating real GDP using chain-weighted prices are more complicated than we need to discuss here, but the basic idea is straightforward. Starting with the base year, the BEA takes an average of prices in that year and prices in the following year. It then uses this average to calculate real GDP in the year following the base year (currently the year 2000). For the next year—in other words, the year that is two years after the base year—the BEA calculates real GDP by taking an average of prices in that year and the previous year. In this way, prices in each year are "chained" to prices from the previous year, and the distortion from changes in relative prices is minimized.

Holding prices constant means that the *purchasing power* of a dollar remains the same from one year to the next. Ordinarily, the purchasing power of the dollar falls every year as price increases reduce the amount of goods and services that a dollar can buy.

Comparing Real GDP and Nominal GDP

Real GDP holds prices constant, which makes it a better measure than nominal GDP of changes in the production of goods and services from one year to the next. In fact, growth in the economy is almost always measured as growth in real GDP. If a headline in the *Wall Street Journal* states, "U.S. Economy Grew 4.3% Last Year," the article will report that real GDP increased by 4.3 percent during the previous year.

We describe real GDP as being measured in "base year dollars." For example, with a base year of 2000, nominal GDP in 2004 was $11,734 billion, and real GDP in 2004 was $10,756 billion in 2000 dollars. Because, on average, prices rise from one year to the next, real GDP is greater than nominal GDP in years before the base year and less than nominal GDP for years after the base year. In the base year, real GDP and nominal GDP are the same, because both are calculated for the base year using the same prices and quantities. Figure 7-3 shows movements in nominal GDP and real GDP between 1990 and 2004. In the 1990s, prices were, on average, lower than in 2000, so nominal GDP was lower than real GDP. In 2000, nominal and real GDP were equal. Since 2000, prices have been, on average, higher than in 2000, so nominal GDP is higher than real GDP.

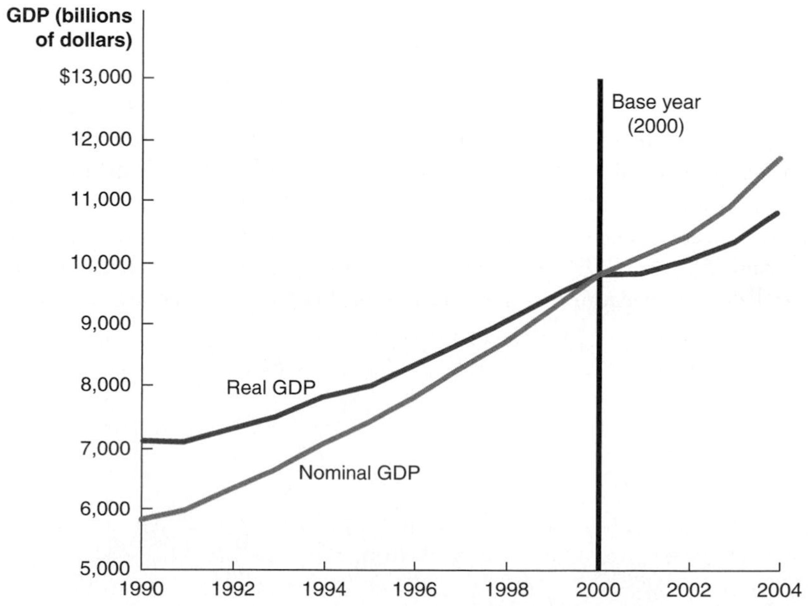

FIGURE 7-3

Nominal GDP and Real GDP, 1990–2004

Currently, the base year for calculating GDP is 2000. In the 1990s, prices were, on average, lower than in 2000, so nominal GDP was lower than real GDP. In 2000, nominal and real GDP were equal. After 2000, prices have been, on average, higher than in 2000, so nominal GDP is higher than real GDP.

Source: U.S. Bureau of Economic Analysis.

7-4 Making the Connection

Freightliner increased hiring and production in 2004 based on forecasts of GDP.

How Freightliner Uses Forecasts of GDP

As we will see in later chapters, increases and decreases in real GDP play an important role in determining the demand for the products of firms such as Freightliner that sell durable goods. Freightliner devotes significant resources to tracking and forecasting GDP because accurate forecasts of GDP help the company schedule production and decide whether or not to increase employment.

Jim Hebe, then Freightliner president and CEO, responded to the early 2001 U.S. recession by reducing sales forecasts of Class 8 trucks from 162,000 to a "disaster scenario" of 135,000. The forecast led Freightliner to lay off 1,085 workers at its Portland, Oregon, plant, reducing the number of trucks built at the plant from 74 per day to 35.

By 2002, new Freightliner president and CEO Rainer Schmüeckle was more optimistic about the economy. But he did not forecast sales increasing soon because he believed many trucking firms—his main customers—had excess capacity, meaning they had more trucks than they needed for the freight they were hauling: "Our forecast calls for gradual economic recovery in the second through the fourth quarters [of 2002], but we believe this will occur without making a major impact on the trucking business because there is still some excess capacity that needs to be worked out. Real, structural recovery will not come until the second quarter of '03."

We saw in the opening to this chapter that by 2004 managers at Freightliner were convinced that GDP would continue to increase, resulting in increased sales of heavy trucks. In early 2004, Mark Lampert, senior vice president of sales and marketing at Freightliner, predicted total sales of Class 8 trucks would rise to 245,000, an increase of more than 33 percent compared to 2003. These favorable forecasts led Freightliner to expand employment and production at its North American plants.

Sources: "Hotline," *Heavy Duty Trucking,* March 2001; Wendy Leavitt, "Freightliner's New Voice," *Fleet Owner,* March 2002; and "ITS Hosts Heavy Truck Economic Forecast," *ITS Business Daily.*

The GDP Deflator

Price level A measure of the average prices of goods and services in the economy.

GDP deflator A measure of the price level, calculated by dividing nominal GDP by real GDP, and multiplying by 100.

Economists and policymakers are interested not just in the level of total production, as measured by real GDP, but also in the *price level.* The **price level** measures the average prices of goods and services in the economy. One of the goals of economic policy is a stable price level. We can use values for nominal GDP and real GDP to compute a measure of the price level, called the *GDP deflator.* We can calculate the **GDP deflator** using this formula:

$$\text{GDP deflator} = \frac{\text{Nominal GDP}}{\text{Real GDP}} \times 100.$$

To see why the GDP deflator is a measure of the price level, think about what would happen if prices of goods and services rose while production remained the same. In that case, nominal GDP would increase, but real GDP would remain constant, so the GDP deflator would increase. In reality, both prices and production increase each year, but the more prices increase relative to the increase in production, the more nominal GDP increases relative to real GDP and the higher the value for the GDP deflator. Increases in the GDP deflator allow economists and policymakers to track increases in the price level over time.

Remember that in the base year (currently 2000) nominal GDP is equal to real GDP, so the value of the GDP price deflator will always be 100 in the base year. The following table gives the values for nominal and real GDP for 2003 and 2004:

	2003	2004
Nominal GDP	$10,971 billion	$11,734 billion
Real GDP	$10,321 billion	$10,756 billion

We can use the information from the table to calculate values for the GDP price deflator for 2003 and 2004:

FORMULA	APPLIED TO 2003	APPLIED TO 2004
$\text{GDP Deflator} = \frac{\text{Nominal GDP}}{\text{Real GDP}} \times 100$	$\left(\frac{\$10,971 \text{ billion}}{\$10,321 \text{ billion}}\right) \times 100 = 106$	$\left(\frac{\$11,734 \text{ billion}}{\$10,756 \text{ billion}}\right) \times 100 = 109$

From these values for the deflator, we can calculate that the price level increased by 2.8 percent between 2003 and 2004:

$$\left(\frac{109 - 106}{106}\right) \times 100 = 2.8\%.$$

In Chapter 8, we will see that economists and policymakers also rely on another measure of the price level, known as the consumer price index. In addition, we will discuss the strengths and weaknesses of the two measures.

Other Measures of Total Production and Total Income

(4) LEARNING OBJECTIVE

Become familiar with other measures of total production and total income.

National income accounting refers to the methods the BEA uses to keep track of total production and total income in the economy. The statistical tables containing this information are called the *National Income and Product Accounts* (NIPA). Every quarter, the BEA releases NIPA tables containing data on several measures of total production and total income. We already have discussed the most important measure of total production and total income: gross domestic product (GDP). In addition to computing GDP, the Bureau of Economic Analysis computes the following five measures of production and income.

Gross National Product (GNP)

Gross domestic product is the value of final goods and services produced within the United States. Gross national product, or GNP, is the value of final goods and services produced by residents of the United States, even if the production takes place *outside* of the United States. U.S. firms have facilities in foreign countries, and foreign firms have facilities in the United States. Ford, for example, has assembly plants in the United Kingdom, and Toyota has assembly plants in the United States. GNP includes foreign production by U.S. firms but excludes U.S. production by foreign firms. For the United

States, these two numbers are almost the same, so GNP is almost the same as GDP. For example, in 2004, GDP was $11,734 billion and GNP was $11,788 billion. This difference is less than one-half of 1 percent.

For many years GNP was the main measure of total production compiled by the government and used by economists and policymakers. However, in many countries other than the United States, a significant fraction of domestic production takes place in foreign-owned facilities. For these countries, GDP will be much larger than GNP, and is a more accurate measure of the level of production within the country's borders. As a result, many countries and international agencies had long preferred using GDP to using GNP. In 1991, the United States joined these countries in using GDP as its main measure of total production.

Net National Product (NNP)

In producing goods and services, some machinery, equipment, and buildings wear out and have to be replaced. The value of this worn-out machinery, equipment, and buildings is *depreciation*. If we subtract this value from GNP, we are left with net national product, or NNP. In the NIPA tables, depreciation is referred to as the *consumption of fixed capital*.

National Income

When a consumer pays sales tax on a product, there is a difference between the amount the consumer has paid for the product and the amount that will be received as income by the people who produced the product. For instance, suppose you buy a television that is priced at $200. If the sales tax is 6 percent, you will actually pay $212, but the $12 in tax will be sent directly to the government and never show up as anyone's income. Therefore, to calculate the total income actually received by a country's residents, the BEA has to subtract the value of sales taxes from net national product. In the NIPA tables, sales taxes are referred to as *indirect business taxes*. Previously in this chapter, we stressed that the value of total production is equal to the value of total income. This point is not strictly true if by "value of total production" we mean GDP and by "value of total income" we mean national income, because national income will always be smaller than GDP. In practice, though, this distinction does not matter for most macroeconomic issues.

Personal Income

Personal income is income received by households. To calculate personal income, we subtract the earnings that corporations retain rather than pay to shareholders in the form of dividends. We also add in the payments received by households from the government in the form of *transfer payments* or interest on government bonds.

Disposable Personal Income

Disposable personal income is equal to personal income minus personal tax payments, such as the federal personal income tax. It is the best measure of the income households actually have available to spend.

Figure 7-4 shows the values of these measures of total production and total income for the year 2004 in a table and a graph.

Measure	Billions of dollars
GDP	$11,734
GNP	11,788
NNP	10,353
National Income	10,276
Personal Income	9,713
Disposable Personal Income	8,664

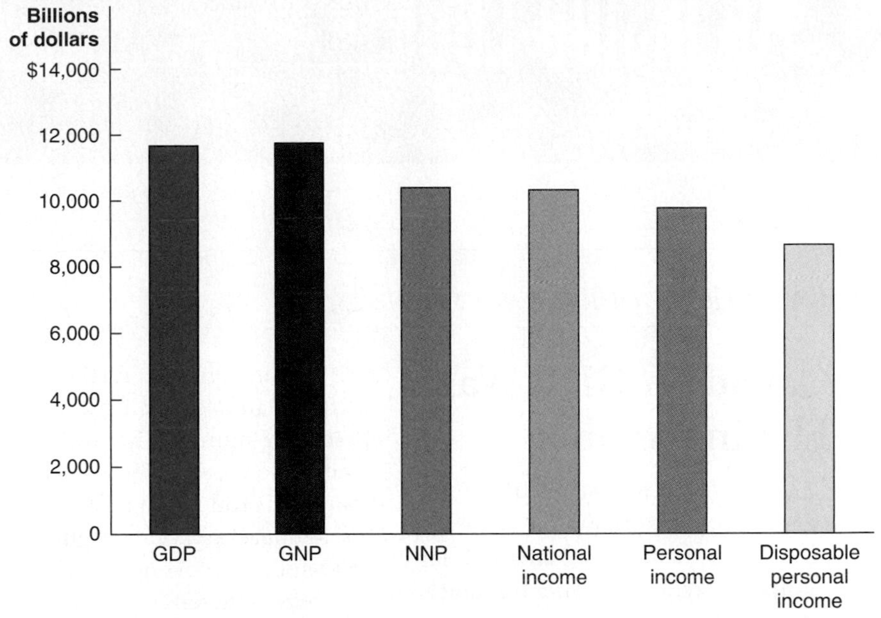

FIGURE 7-4 Measures of Total Production and Total Income, 2004

The most important measure of total production and total income is gross domestic product (GDP). As we will see in later chapters, for some purposes, the other measures of total production and total income shown in the figure turn out to be more useful than GDP. The numbers are in billions of dollars.

Conclusion

In this chapter, we have begun the study of macroeconomics by examining an important concept—how a nation's total production and income can be measured. Understanding GDP is important for understanding the business cycle and the process of long-run economic growth. In the next chapter, we discuss the issues involved in measuring two other key economic variables: the unemployment rate and the inflation rate.

Read *An Inside Look* on the next page for a discussion of fluctuations in Canadian real GDP during a recent year.

WALL STREET JOURNAL, DECEMBER 23, 2004

Canadian GDP Was Flat in October

Canada's economy began the final quarter on a softer-than-expected note as the stronger Canadian dollar crimped foreign demand for fabricated products and labor disputes in the public sector and professional sports hurt services industries.

Gross domestic product, the sum of goods and services produced in the country, was steady in October from the month before, Statistics Canada said yesterday. The mean forecast of economists surveyed by Thomson IFR Bonddata was for GDP to expand 0.1%.

"For the second month in a row, growth in the Canadian economy was at a standstill in October largely due to reduced foreign demand for fabricated products and to labor strife," the statistics agency said. . . .

Industrial production, the total output of Canada's factories, mines and utilities, shrank a further 0.2% in October, after declining 0.3% in the preceding month. This was in stark contrast to the U.S where the index of industrial production rose 0.6%.

Manufacturers cut output by 0.3% in October, following a 0.2% reduction in September.

a "Foreign demand for fabricated products was reduced in the wake of a strengthening [Canadian] dollar that gained 3.3% during the month vis-à-vis the U.S. currency, reaching its highest level in 12 months," Statistics Canada said.

The weakness was widespread as only four of the 21 major manufacturing groups increased output during the month. Production of nondurable goods shrank 0.6% while output of durable products fell 0.1%.

The utilities sector's output fell 0.3% following a 0.7% gain in September. Production in the mining sector was up 0.2% after a 1.0% decline in the previous month, driven by surging oil and gas exploration and the end of a strike in iron mines that started in July.

b The construction sector shrank 0.6% after edging up 0.1% in September. Fewer housing starts pulled down residential construction by 0.5%, while nonresidential construction fell 1.2%, the seventh straight month of declines.

Overall output of goods-producing industries was down 0.2%, following a 0.1% drop in September. The services sector expanded 0.1%, the same as in September, driven by retail trade, which rose 0.9% on the back of strong motor vehicle sales.

c Two major labor disputes held back the sector. A nationwide public sector strike cut federal public administration sector production by 1.2%.

The lockout of National Hockey League players resulted in a 2.1% decline in the output of the arts and entertainment industries, Statistics Canada said.

Key Points in the Article

This article discusses the latest announcement of GDP data by Statistics Canada. Statistics Canada plays the same role in Canada that the Bureau of Economic Analysis does in the United States. Notice that Statistics Canada calculates GDP monthly, unlike in the United States, where the BEA calculates GDP quarterly. Calculating GDP entails gathering an enormous amount of information on production. The greater size of the U.S. economy, compared with the Canadian economy, would make it very costly to attempt to calculate GDP every month. Figure 1 shows movements in real GDP in Canada from October 2002 to October 2004. During several months of these two years, real GDP declined. The real GDP numbers in the figure are measured in billions of 1997 (Canadian) dollars, because Statistics Canada uses 1997 as the base year, unlike the BEA, which currently uses 2000 as the base year.

Analyzing the News

a We saw in this chapter that net exports are one component of GDP. In later chapters, we will discuss the effect of exchange rates on net exports. Recall from Chapter 6 that the exchange rate tells us how many units of foreign currency are received in exchange for a unit of domestic currency. When the exchange rate rises, exports fall because domestic goods become more expensive to foreign consumers. In this case, the exchange rate of the Canadian dollar for the U.S. dollar had risen. The result was that prices of Canadian exports to the United States—such as lumber, trucks, and small aircraft—rose, which reduced the quantity demanded. This caused a reduction in Canadian net exports, and GDP.

b Construction spending on new houses, factories, and office buildings is part of the investment component of GDP. This article indicates that both the residential (houses) and nonresidential (factories and office buildings) segments of construction spending declined, contributing to the decline in GDP.

c Government purchases are about 22 percent of GDP in Canada, as opposed to about 19 percent in the United States. The article indicates that there was a strike of public employees, which reduced government purchases. The fall in government purchases contributed to the fall in GDP.

Thinking Critically ABOUT POLICY

1. Would policymakers in the United States benefit from having monthly GDP data available to them? If so, why doesn't the U.S. Commerce Department collect GDP data on a monthly basis?
2. Exports are 37 percent of Canadian GDP, in contrast to the United States, where exports are only about 10 percent of GDP. More than 80 percent of Canadian exports are to the United States. Use these facts to explain how forecasts of U.S. real GDP could be helpful in forecasting Canadian real GDP.

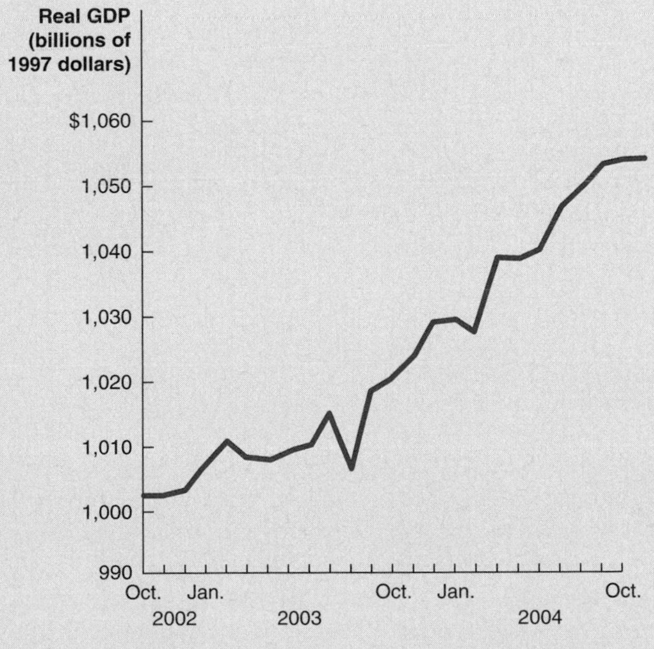

Figure 1: Monthly real GDP for Canada, October 2002 to October 2004.

Source: Statistics Canada.

SUMMARY

LEARNING OBJECTIVE ① Explain how total production is measured. Total production is measured by *gross domestic product (GDP)*, which is the value of all *final goods and services* produced in an economy during a period of time. When we measure the value of total production in the economy by calculating GDP, we are simultaneously measuring the value of total income. GDP is divided into four major categories of expenditures: consumption, investment, government purchases, and net exports. We can also calculate GDP by adding up the *value added* of every firm involved in producing final goods and services.

LEARNING OBJECTIVE ② Discuss whether GDP is a good measure of economic well-being. GDP does not include household production, which refers to goods and services people produce for themselves, nor does it include production in the *underground economy*, which consists of concealed buying and selling. The underground economy in some poorer countries may be more than half of measured GDP. GDP is not a perfect measure of well-being because it does not include the value of leisure, it is not adjusted for pollution or other negative effects of production, and it is not adjusted for changes in crime and other social problems.

LEARNING OBJECTIVE ③ Discuss the difference between real variables and nominal variables. *Nominal GDP* is the value of final goods and services evaluated at current year prices. *Real GDP* is the value of final goods and services evaluated at *base year* prices. By keeping prices constant, we know that changes in real GDP represent changes in the quantity of goods and services produced in the economy. When the price level is increasing, real GDP is greater than nominal GDP in years before the base year and less than nominal GDP for years after the base year. The *GDP deflator* is a measure of the price level, and is calculated by dividing nominal GDP by real GDP, and multiplying by 100.

LEARNING OBJECTIVE ④ Become familiar with other measures of total production and total income. The most important measure of total production and total income is gross domestic product (GDP). As we will see in later chapters, for some purposes the other measures of total production and total income shown in Figure 7-4 are actually more useful than GDP. These measures are gross national product (GNP), net national product (NNP), national income, personal income, and disposable personal income.

KEY TERMS

Business cycle 204
Consumption 208
Economic growth 204
Expansion 204
Final good or service 205
GDP deflator 218
Government purchases 209
Gross domestic product (GDP) 205
Inflation rate 204
Intermediate good of service 205
Investment 209
Macroeconomics 204
Microeconomics 204
Net exports 210
Nominal GDP 215
Price level 218
Real GDP 215
Recession 204
Transfer payments 207
Underground economy 213
Value added 211

REVIEW QUESTIONS

1. Distinguish between the topics covered by macroeconomics and the topics covered by microeconomics.
2. Why in microeconomics can we measure production in terms of quantity, but in macroeconomics we measure production in terms of market value?
3. If the U.S. Bureau of Economic Analysis added up the values of every good and service sold during the year, would the total be larger or smaller than GDP?
4. Why does the size of a country's GDP matter? How does it affect the quality of life of the country's people?
5. In the circular flow of expenditure and income, why must the value of total production in an economy equal the value of total income?
6. Describe the four major components of expenditures in GDP and write the equation used to represent the relationship between GDP and the four expenditure components.
7. Distinguish between the value of a firm's final product and the value added by the firm to the final product.
8. Why is GDP an imperfect measure of economic well-being? What types of production does GDP not measure?

Even if GDP included these types of production, why would it still be an imperfect measure of economic well-being?

9. Why does inflation make nominal GDP a poor measure of the increase in total production from one year to the next? How does the U.S. Bureau of Economic Analysis deal with the problem inflation causes with nominal GDP?
10. What is the GDP deflator and how is it calculated?
11. Under what circumstances would GDP be a better measure of total production and total income than GNP?

PROBLEMS AND APPLICATIONS

Please visit **www.prenhall.com/hubbard** *for solutions to the even-numbered problems as well as multiple-choice and true or false self-assessment quizzes.*

1. **[Related to the *Chapter Opener*]** Macroeconomic conditions affect the decisions firms and families make. Why, for example, might a college student after graduation enter the job market during an economic expansion but apply for graduate school during a recession?
2. **[Related to the *Chapter Opener*]** Recall from Chapter 3 the definitions of normal and inferior goods. During an economic expansion, would you rather be working in an industry that produces a normal good or in an industry that produces an inferior good? Why? During a recession, would you rather be working in an industry that produces a normal good or an inferior good? Why?
3. For the total value of expenditures on final goods and services to equal the total value of income generated from producing those final goods and services, all the money that a business receives from the sale of its product must be paid out as income to the owners of the factors of production. How can a business make a profit if it pays out as income all the money it receives?
4. Briefly explain whether each of the following transactions represents the purchase of a final good.
   a. The purchase of wheat from a wheat farmer by a bakery
   b. The purchase of an aircraft carrier by the federal government
   c. The purchase of French wine by a U.S. consumer
   d. The purchase of a new machine tool by the Ford Motor Company
5. Is the value of intermediate goods and services produced during the year included in GDP? For example, are computer chips produced and installed on a new PC included in GDP? Note that the question does not ask whether the computer chips are directly counted in GDP but rather whether or not their production is included in GDP.
6. Is the value of a house built in 2000 and resold in 2006 included in the GDP of 2006? Why or why not? Would the services of the real estate agent who helped sell (or buy) the house in 2006 be counted in GDP for 2006? Why or why not?
7. **[Related to *Solved Problem 7-1*]** Suppose that a simple economy produces only the following four goods and services: textbooks, hamburgers, shirts, and cotton. Assume all of the cotton is used in the production of shirts. Use the information in the following table to calculate nominal GDP for 2006.

PRODUCTION AND PRICE STATISTICS FOR 2006

PRODUCT	QUANTITY	PRICE
Textbooks	100	$60.00
Hamburgers	100	2.00
Shirts	50	25.00
Cotton	8,000	0.60

8. **[Related to *Solved Problem 7-2*]** Suppose the information in the following table is for a simple economy that produces only the following four goods and services: text books, hamburgers, shirts, and cotton. Assume all of the cotton is used in the production of shirts.

	2000 STATISTICS		2006 STATISTICS		2007 STATISTICS	
PRODUCT	QUANTITY	PRICE	QUANTITY	PRICE	QUANTITY	PRICE
Textbooks	90	$50.00	100	$60.00	100	$65.00
Hamburgers	75	2.00	100	2.00	120	2.25
Shirts	50	30.00	50	25.00	65	25.00
Cotton	10,000	0.80	8,000	0.60	12,000	0.70

   a. Use the information in the table to calculate real GDP for 2006 and 2007, assuming the base year is 2000.
   b. What was the growth rate of real GDP during 2007?
9. **[Related to *Don't Let This Happen To You!*]** Briefly explain whether you agree or disagree with the following statement: "In years when people buy many shares of stock, investment will be high and, therefore, so will GDP."
10. How does the value added of a business differ from the profits of a business?
11. It is reported that some state-owned firms in the former Soviet Union produced goods and services whose value was less than the value of the raw materials the firms used to

produce their goods and services. If so, what would have been the value added of these state-owned firms? Would such a firm be able to survive in a free-market economy?

12. An artist buys scrap metal from the local steel mill as a raw material for her metal sculptures. Last year she bought $5,000 worth of the scrap metal. During the year, she produced 10 metal sculptures that she sold for $800 each to the local art store. The local art store sold all of them to local art collectors at an average price of $1,000 each. For the 10 metal sculptures, what was the total value added of the artist and what was the total value added of the local art store?

13. What would you expect to happen to household production as unemployment rises during a recession? What would you expect to happen to household production as unemployment falls during an expansion? Would you therefore expect the fluctuation in actual production—GDP plus household production—to be greater or less than the fluctuation in measured GDP?

14. Which of the following are likely to increase measured GDP, and which are likely to reduce it?
    a. The fraction of women working outside the home increases.
    b. There is a sharp increase in the crime rate.
    c. Higher tax rates cause some people to hide more of the income they earn.

15. Does the fact that the typical American works less than 40 hours per week today and worked 60 hours per week in 1890 make the difference between the economic well-being of Americans today versus 1890 higher or lower than indicated by the difference in real GDP per capita today versus 1890? Explain.

16. A report of the World Bank, an international organization devoted to increasing economic growth in developing countries, includes the following statement:

    > Informal economic activities pose a particular measurement problem [in calculating GDP], especially in developing countries, where much economic activity may go unrecorded.

    What do they mean by "informal economic activities"? Why would these activities make it harder to measure GDP? Why might they make it harder to evaluate the standard of living in developing countries relative to the standard of living in the United States?

    Source: The World Bank, *World Development Indicators*, 2003, Washington, D.C.: The World Bank, p. 189.

17. Each year the United Nations publishes the Human Development Report, which provides information on the standard of living in nearly every country in the world. The Report includes data on real GDP per person, but also contains a broader measure of the standard of living called the Human Development Index (HDI). The HDI combines data on real GDP per person with data on life expectancy at birth, adult literacy, and school enrollment. The following table shows values for real GDP per person and the HDI for several countries. Prepare one list ranking countries from highest real GDP per person to lowest, and another list ranking countries from highest HDI to lowest. Briefly discuss possible reasons for any differences in the rankings of countries in your two lists. (All values in the table are for the year 2003.)

COUNTRY	REAL GDP PER PERSON	HDI
Australia	$29,632	0.955
China	5,003	0.755
Greece	19,954	0.912
Iran	6,995	0.736
Norway	37,670	0.963
Singapore	24,481	0.907
South Korea	17,971	0.901
United Arab Emirates	22,420	0.849
United States	37,562	0.944

Source: United Nations Development Programme, *Human Development Report, 2005*, New York: Oxford University Press, 2005.

18. Assuming inflation has occurred over time, what is the relationship between nominal GDP and real GDP in each of the following situations?
    a. Years after the base year
    b. In the base year
    c. Years before the base year

19. If the quantity of final goods and services produced decreased, could real GDP increase? Could nominal GDP increase? If so, how?

20. Use the data in the following table to calculate the GDP deflator for each year (values are in billions of dollars):

	NOMINAL GDP	REAL GDP
2000	$9,817	$9,817
2001	10,128	9,891
2002	10,470	10,049
2003	10,971	10,321
2004	11,734	10,756

    Which year from 2001 to 2004 saw the largest percentage increase in the price level as measured by the GDP deflator? Briefly explain.

21. Suppose a country has many of its citizens temporarily working in other countries and many of its firms have facilities in other countries. Furthermore, relatively few citizens of foreign countries are working in this country and relatively few foreign firms have facilities in this country. In these circumstances, which would you expect to be larger for this country, GDP or GNP? Briefly explain.

chapter eight

Unemployment and Inflation

Lucent Technologies Deals with Unemployment and Inflation

➤ When we study macroeconomics, we are looking at the big picture: total production, total employment, and the price level. Of course, the big picture is determined by the decisions of millions of individual consumers and firms. When total employment in the United States declined during 2001, Lucent Technologies was one firm that contributed to the decline. In 2000, Lucent employed 175,000 workers. It began laying off large numbers of workers during 2001. By 2005, Lucent employed only 31,500 workers.

Lucent Technologies, known as the grandfather of high-technology firms, was founded in 1869. The company, originally the Western Electric Manufacturing Company, was purchased by the American Telephone and Telegraph Company (AT&T) in 1881 and renamed Bell Laboratories. Bell Labs became independent of AT&T in 1996 and took its current name, Lucent Technologies. Over the years, the company has been involved in developing many important innovations, including equipment for adding sound to motion pictures, equipment for long-distance television transmission, the transistor, the UNIX computer operating system, and Wi-Fi wireless broadband technology. Lucent's difficulties in the early 2000s were due partly to overbuilding of telecommunications infrastructure, particularly fiber-optic cables, and partly to the business cycle. We will discuss the effects of the business cycle further in later chapters. In this chapter, we will focus on measuring changes in employment and changes in the price level, or *inflation*.

Forecasts of inflation play a role in firms' wage policies. For example, in 2004 Lucent negotiated wage contracts with workers who were members of the Communications Workers of America and the International Brotherhood of Electrical Workers unions. The contracts

resulted in these workers' wages rising by a little over 16 percent over a period of seven years. To decide on an acceptable wage, both Lucent and the unions needed to forecast the inflation rate for those seven years. A higher inflation rate would make it easier for Lucent to pay any particular wage, because a higher inflation rate would allow Lucent to charge higher prices for its telecommunications equipment. A higher inflation rate would also mean that Lucent's workers could buy fewer goods and services with their wages, because prices would be higher. The contract between Lucent and its union workers increased wages by less than the increase in prices expected by the firms and the workers. Our discussion of employment and inflation in this chapter will help us understand why the negotiation between Lucent and its workers turned out as it did. *An Inside Look* on page 254 discusses the role that expectations of inflation played in a similar contract negotiation between Boeing Company and its unionized workers.

Sources: "Two Unions Ratify Contract with Lucent," *Wall Street Journal,* December 20, 2004; and "Unix's Founding Fathers," *Economist,* June 10, 2004.

LEARNING OBJECTIVES

After studying this chapter, you should be able to:

① Define the unemployment rate and the labor force participation rate, and understand how they are computed.

② Identify the three types of unemployment.

③ Explain what factors determine the unemployment rate.

④ Define the price level and the inflation rate, and understand how they are computed.

⑤ Use price indexes to adjust for the effects of inflation.

⑥ Distinguish between the nominal interest rate and the real interest rate.

⑦ Discuss the problems caused by inflation.

➤ Unemployment and inflation are the macroeconomic problems that are most often discussed in the media and during political campaigns. For many members of the general public, the state of the economy is summarized in just two measures: the unemployment rate and the inflation rate. In the 1960s, Arthur Okun, who was chairman of the Council of Economic Advisers during President Lyndon Johnson's administration, coined the term *misery index*, which adds together the inflation rate and the unemployment rate to give a rough measure of the state of the economy. As we will see in later chapters, although inflation and unemployment are important problems, the long-run success of an economy is best judged by its ability to generate high levels of real GDP per person.

In later chapters, we will explore how the inflation rate, the unemployment rate, and the rate of growth in real GDP per person are determined. We devote this chapter to discussing how the government measures the unemployment and inflation rates. In particular, we will look closely at the statistics on unemployment and inflation the federal government issues each month.

(1) LEARNING OBJECTIVE

Define the unemployment rate and the labor force participation rate, and understand how they are computed.

Measuring the Unemployment Rate and the Labor Force Participation Rate

At 8:30 A.M. on a Friday early in each month, the U.S. Department of Labor reports its estimate of the previous month's unemployment rate. If the unemployment rate is higher or lower than expected, investors are likely to change their views on the health of the economy. The result will be seen an hour later when trading begins on the New York Stock Exchange. Good news about unemployment usually causes stock prices to rise, and bad news causes stock prices to fall. The unemployment rate can also have important political implications. In most presidential elections, the incumbent president is reelected if unemployment is falling early in the election year, but is defeated if unemployment is rising. This relationship held true in 2004, when the unemployment rate was lower during the first six months of 2004 than it had been during the last six months of 2003, and incumbent George W. Bush was reelected.

The unemployment rate is a key macroeconomic statistic. But how does the Department of Labor prepare its estimates of the unemployment rate, and how accurate are these estimates? We will explore the answers to these questions in this section.

The Household Survey

Each month the U.S. Bureau of the Census conducts the *Current Population Survey*, (often referred to as the *household survey*) to collect data needed to compute the unemployment rate. The bureau interviews adults in a sample of 60,000 households, chosen to represent the U.S. population, about the employment status of everyone in the household 16 years of age and older. The Department of Labor's Bureau of Labor Statistics (BLS) uses these data to calculate the monthly unemployment rate. People are considered *employed* if they worked during the week before the survey or if they were temporarily away from their job because they were ill, on vacation, on strike, or for other reasons. People are considered *unemployed* if they did not work in the previous week, but were available for work and had actively looked for work at some time during the previous four weeks. The **labor force** is the sum of the *employed* and the *unemployed*. The **unemployment rate** is the percentage of the labor force that is unemployed.

Labor force The sum of employed and unemployed workers in the economy.

Unemployment rate The percentage of the labor force that is unemployed.

People who do not have a job and who are not actively looking for a job are *not in the labor force*. People not in the labor force according to the BLS statistics include

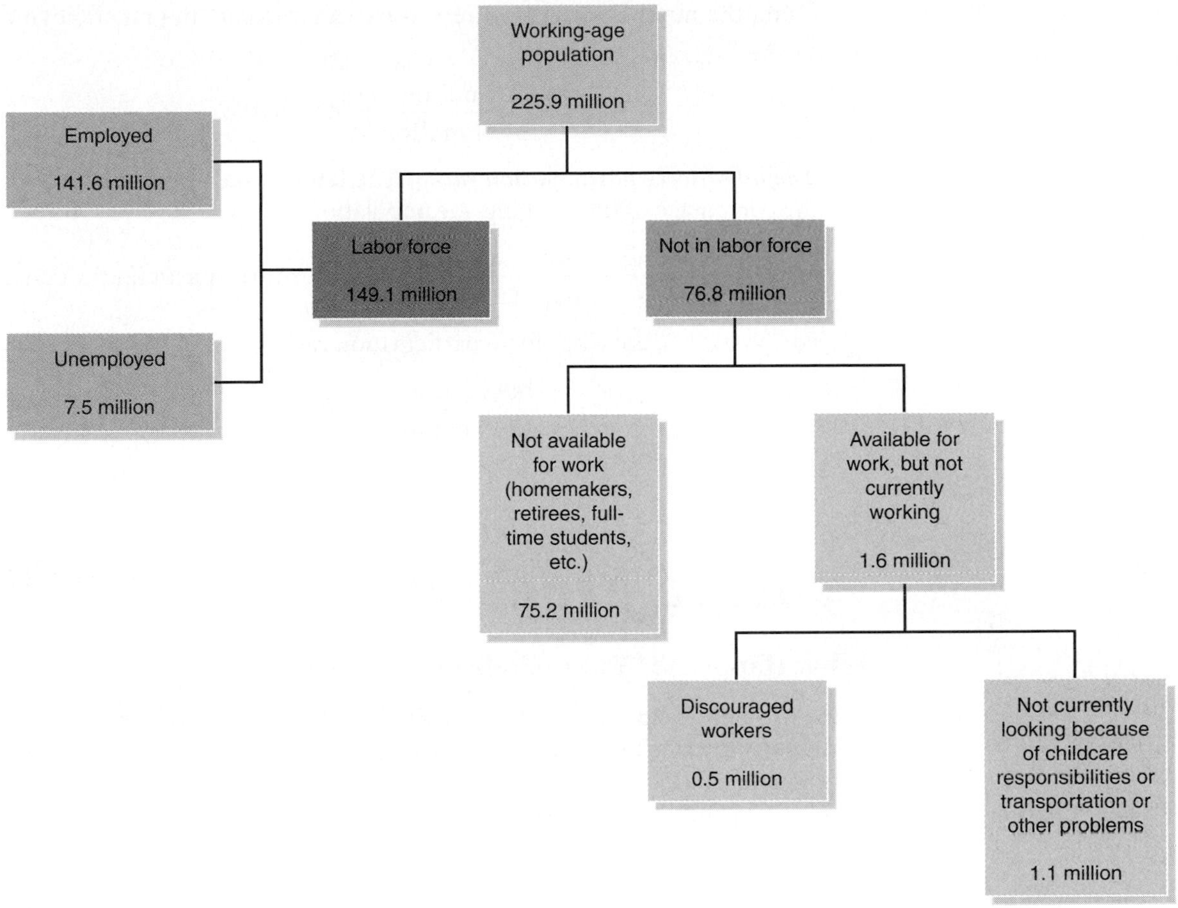

FIGURE 8-1 The Employment Status of the Civilian Working-Age Population, June 2005

In June 2005, the working-age population of the United States was 225.9 million. The working-age population is divided into those in the labor force (149.1 million) and those not in the labor force (76.8 million). The labor force is divided into the employed (141.6 million) and the unemployed (7.5 million). Those not in the labor force are divided into those not available for work (75.2 million) and those available for work (1.6 million). Finally, those available for work but not in the labor force are divided into discouraged workers (0.5 million) and those currently not working for other reasons (1.1 million).

Source: U.S. Department of Labor, "Employment Situation Summary," July 2005.

retirees, homemakers, full-time students, and people on active military service, in prison, or in mental hospitals. Also not in the labor force are people who are available for work and actively looked for a job at some point during the previous 12 months, but who have not looked during the previous four weeks. Some people have not actively looked for work lately for reasons such as transportation difficulties or child-care responsibilities. Other people who have not actively looked for work are called *discouraged workers.* **Discouraged workers** are available for work but have not looked for a job during the previous four weeks because they believe no jobs are available for them.

Discouraged workers People who are available for work but have not looked for a job during the previous four weeks because they believe no jobs are available for them.

Figure 8-1 shows the employment status of the civilian working-age population in June 2005. We can use the information in the figure to calculate two important macroeconomic indicators—the unemployment rate and the labor force participation rate.

➤ ***The unemployment rate.*** The unemployment rate measures the percentage of the labor force that is unemployed:

$$\frac{\text{Number of unemployed}}{\text{Labor force}} \times 100 = \text{Unemployment rate.}$$

Using the numbers from Figure 8-1, we can calculate the unemployment rate for June 2005:

$$\frac{7.5\text{ million}}{149.1\text{ million}} \times 100 = 5.0\%.$$

Labor force participation rate The percentage of the working-age population in the labor force.

➤ ***The labor force participation rate.*** The **labor force participation rate** measures the percentage of the working-age population that is in the labor force:

$$\frac{\text{Labor force}}{\text{Working-age population}} \times 100 = \text{Labor force participation rate.}$$

For June 2005, the labor force participation rate was:

$$\frac{149.1\text{ million}}{225.9\text{ million}} \times 100 = 66.0\%.$$

SOLVED PROBLEM 8-1

① LEARNING OBJECTIVE

Define the unemployment rate and the labor force participation rate, and understand how they are computed.

What Happens If You Include the Military?

In the BLS household survey, people on active military service are not included in the totals for employment, the labor force, or the working-age population. Suppose people in the military were included in these categories. How would the unemployment rate and the labor force participation rate change?

Solving the Problem:

Step 1: Review the chapter material. This problem is about calculating the unemployment rate and the labor force participation rate, so you may want to review the section "Measuring the Unemployment Rate and the Labor Force Participation Rate," which begins on page 230.

Step 2: Show that including the military decreases the measured unemployment rate. The unemployment rate is calculated as:

$$\frac{\text{Number of unemployed}}{\text{Labor force}} \times 100.$$

Including people in the military would increase the number of people counted as being in the labor force but would leave unchanged the number of people counted as unemployed. Therefore, the unemployment rate would decrease.

Step 3: Show that including the military increases the measured labor force participation rate. The labor force participation rate is calculated as:

$$\frac{\text{Labor force}}{\text{Working-age population}} \times 100.$$

Including people in the military would increase both the number of people in the labor force and the number of people in the working-age population by the same amount. This change would increase the labor force participation rate because adding the same number to both the numerator and the denominator of a fraction that is less than one increases the value of the fraction.

To see why this is true, consider the following simple example. Suppose that 100,000,000 people are in the working-age population and 50,000,000 are in the labor force, not counting people in the military. Suppose 1,000,000 people are in the military. Then, the labor force participation rate excluding the military is:

$$\frac{50,000,000}{100,000,000} \times 100 = 50\%,$$

and the labor force participation rate including the military is:

$$\frac{51,000,000}{101,000,000} \times 100 = 50.5\%.$$

YOUR TURN: **For more practice, do related problem 4 on page 257 at the end of this chapter.**

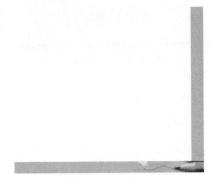

Problems with Measuring the Unemployment Rate

Although the BLS reports the unemployment rate measured to the tenth of a percentage point, it is not a perfect measure of the current state of joblessness in the economy. One problem confronting the BLS is distinguishing between the unemployed and people who are not in the labor force. During an economic recession, for example, an increase in discouraged workers usually occurs, as people who have had trouble finding a job stop actively looking. Because these workers are not counted as unemployed, the unemployment rate as measured by the BLS may significantly understate the true degree of joblessness in the economy. The BLS also counts as employed people who hold part-time jobs even though they would prefer to hold full-time jobs. Furthermore, in a recession, counting as "employed" a part-time worker who wants to work full time tends to understate the degree of joblessness in the economy and make the employment situation appear better than it is.

Not counting discouraged workers as unemployed and counting people as employed who are working part time, although they would prefer to be working full time, has a substantial effect on the measured unemployment rate. For example, in June 2005, if the BLS counted as unemployed all people who were available for work but not actively looking for a job and all people who were in part-time jobs but wanted full-time jobs, the unemployment rate would have increased from 5.0 percent to 9.0 percent.

There are other measurement problems, however, that cause the measured unemployment rate to *overstate* the true extent of joblessness. These problems arise because the Current Population Survey does not verify the responses of people included in the survey. Some people who claim to be unemployed and actively looking for work may not be actively looking. A person might claim to be actively looking for a job to remain eligible for government payments to the unemployed. In this case, a person who is actually not in the labor force is counted as unemployed. Other people might be employed but engaged in illegal activity—such as drug dealing—or might want to conceal a legitimate job to avoid paying taxes. In this case, a person who is actually employed is counted as unemployed. These inaccurate responses to the survey cause the unemployment rate as measured by the BLS to overstate the true extent of joblessness. We can conclude that, although the unemployment rate provides some useful information about the employment situation in the country, it is far from an exact measure of joblessness in the economy.

Trends in Labor Force Participation

The labor force participation rate is important because it determines the amount of labor that will be available to the economy from a given population. The higher the labor force participation rate, the more labor will be available and the higher a country's

FIGURE 8-2

Trends in the Labor Force Participation Rates of Adult Men and Women Since 1948

The labor force participation rate of adult men has declined gradually since 1948, but the labor force participation rate of adult women has increased rapidly, leaving the overall labor force participation rate higher today than it was in 1948.

Source: U.S. Bureau of Labor Statistics.

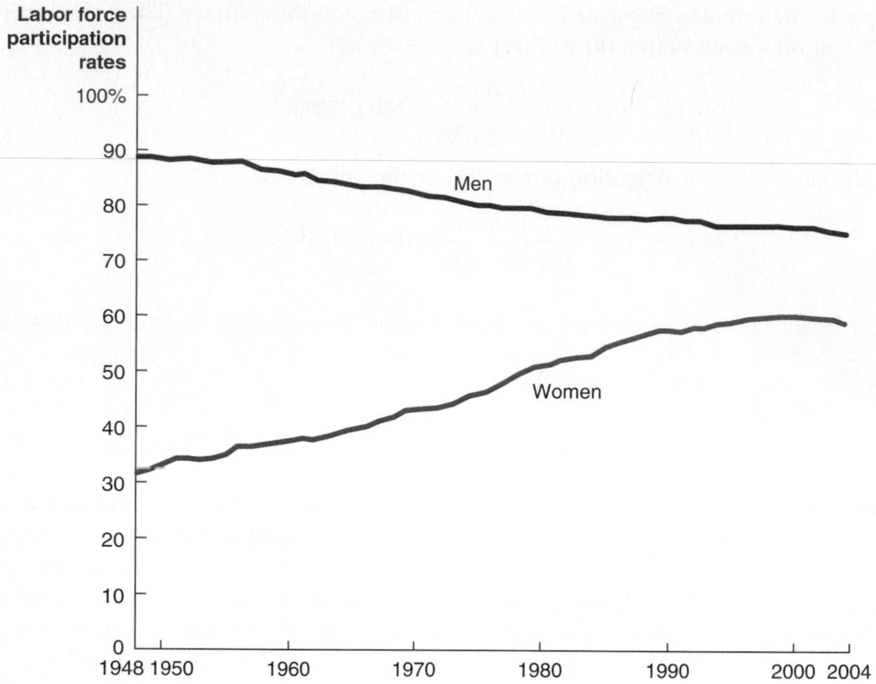

levels of GDP and GDP per person. Figure 8-2 highlights two important trends in labor force participation rates of adults aged 20 and over in the United States since 1950—the rising labor force participation rate of adult women and the falling labor force participation rate of adult men.

The labor force participation rate of adult males has fallen from 89 percent in 1948 to 76 percent in 2004. Most of this decline is due to older men retiring earlier and younger men remaining in school longer. There has also been a decline in labor force participation among males who are not in school but who are too young to retire.

8-1 Making the Connection

What Explains the Increase in "Kramers"?

Why do more men seem to be adopting Kramer's lifestyle?

Cosmo Kramer is the name of Jerry Seinfeld's next-door neighbor on the popular television comedy *Seinfeld.* One of the running jokes on the program is Kramer's ability to support himself without apparently ever holding a job. In recent years, there has been an increase in the number of men who seem to be following Kramer's lifestyle. In 1967, only 2.2 percent of men between the ages of 25 and 54 who were not in school did no paid work at all during the year. By 2002, 8 percent of men in this age category did not work. The rate of nonworking men is even higher among some groups. For example, almost 20 percent of men aged 25 to 54 who lack a high school degree do not have a job and are not looking for one.

More than half of nonworking men receive Social Security Disability Insurance. Under this program, people with disabilities receive cash payments from the federal government and receive medical benefits under the Medicaid program. In 1984, Congress passed legislation that made it easier for people with disabilities that are difficult to verify medically, such as back injuries or mental illnesses, to qualify for disability payments. In addition, the value of disability payments has increased faster than the wages of low-skilled workers. The result is that some men who in the past might have been working or actively looking for work are now being supported by disability payments and are not in the labor force.

An increasing share of nonworking men, however, are not disabled. How do nonworking men who do not receive disability payments support themselves, and how do they spend their time? Most nonworking men live with their parents, wives, or other relatives. Many of these men appear to rely on these other household members for food, clothing, and money.

A recent study by Jay Stewart of the Bureau of Labor Statistics shows that most nonworking men are not substituting nonmarket work—such as childcare or housework—for market work. Instead, nonworking men engage in leisure activities, such as sports, watching television, or sleeping during the hours freed up by not working. Stewart concludes that "the average day of a nonworking man looks very much like the average day-off of a man who works full time."

Sources: Alan Krueger, "A Growing Number of Men Are Not Working, So What Are They Doing?" *New York Times*, April 29, 2004, p. C2; and Jay Stewart, "What Do Male Nonworkers Do?" U.S. Bureau of Labor Statistics, Working Paper 371, April 2004.

The decline in labor force participation among adult men has been more than offset by a sharp increase in the labor force participation rate for adult women, which has risen from 32 percent in 1948 to 60 percent in 2004. As a result, the overall labor force participation rate has risen from 59 percent in 1948 to 68 percent in 2004. The increase in the labor force participation rate for women has several causes, including changing social attitudes due in part to the women's movement, federal legislation outlawing discrimination, increasing wages for women, and the typical family having fewer children.

Unemployment Rates for Demographic Groups

Different groups in the population can have very different unemployment rates. Figure 8-3 shows unemployment rates for different demographic groups in June 2005, when the unemployment rate for the entire population was 5.0 percent. White adults had an unemployment rate of 3.7 percent. The unemployment rate for black adults was 9.2 percent, or more than twice the rate for white adults. Teenagers have higher unemployment rates than adults. The black teenage unemployment rate of 32.4 percent was the highest for the groups shown.

How Long Are People Usually Unemployed?

The longer a person is unemployed, the greater the hardship. During the Great Depression of the 1930s, some people were unemployed for years at a time. In the modern U.S. economy, the typical unemployed person stays unemployed for a relatively brief period of time. Table 8-1 shows for June 2005 the percentage of the unemployed who had been

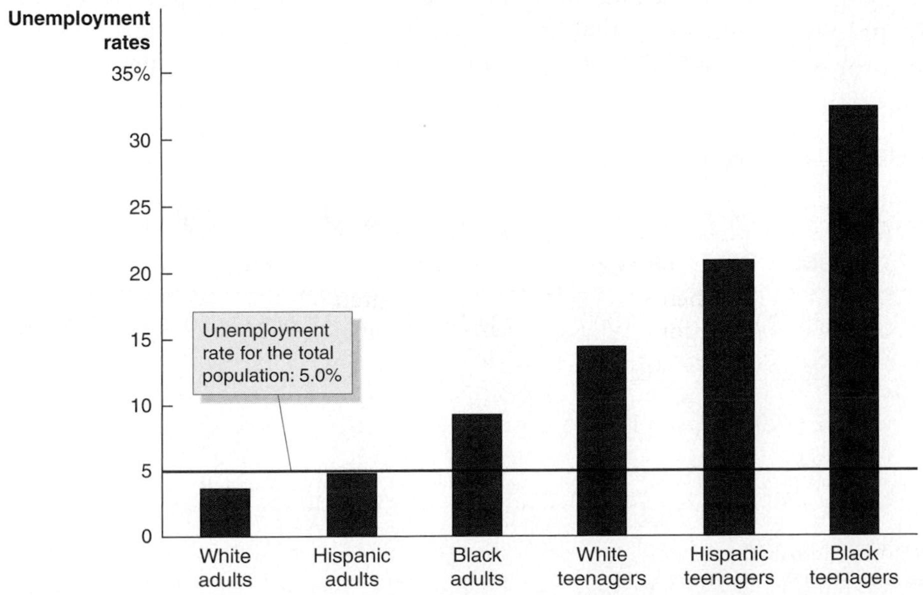

FIGURE 8-3

Unemployment Rates in the United States by Demographic Group, June 2005

The unemployment rate of black adults is more than twice that of white adults, and the unemployment rate of black teenagers is more than twice that of white teenagers. The adult unemployment rates apply to persons aged 20 and over who are in the labor force. The teenage unemployment rates apply to persons aged 16 to 19 who are in the labor force. Note that people identified as Hispanic may be of any race.

Source: U.S. Department of Labor, "Employment Situation Summary," July 2005.

TABLE 8-1

Duration of Unemployment

LENGTH OF TIME UNEMPLOYED	PERCENTAGE OF TOTAL UNEMPLOYED
Less than 5 weeks	36.2%
5 to 14 weeks	31.8
15 to 26 weeks	14.1
27 weeks or more	17.8

Source: U.S. Department of Labor, "Employment Situation Summary," July 2005.

unemployed for a given period of time. Eighty-two percent of the people unemployed in that month had been unemployed for fewer than six months. Half had been unemployed for nine weeks or less. The important conclusion is that, *except in severe recessions, the typical person who loses a job finds another one or is recalled to a previous job within a few months.*

The Establishment Survey: Another Measure of Employment

In addition to the household survey, the BLS uses the *establishment survey,* sometimes called the *payroll survey,* to measure total employment in the economy. This monthly survey samples about 300,000 business establishments. An establishment is a factory, store, or office. A small company may operate only one establishment, but large companies may operate many establishments. The establishment survey provides information on the total number of persons who are employed *and on a company payroll.* The establishment survey has three drawbacks. First, the survey does not provide information on the number of self-employed persons, because they are not on a company payroll. Second, the survey may fail to count some persons employed at newly opened firms that are not included in the survey. Third, the survey provides no information on unemployment. Despite these drawbacks, the establishment survey has the strength of being determined by actual payrolls, rather than by unverified answers, as is the case with the household survey. In recent years, some economists have come to rely more on establishment survey data than on household survey data in analyzing current labor market conditions. Some financial analysts who forecast the future state of the economy so they can better forecast stock prices have also begun to rely more on establishment survey data than on household survey data.

Table 8-2 shows household survey and establishment survey data for the months of May and June 2005. Notice that the household survey, because it includes the self-employed, gives a larger total for employment than does the establishment survey. The

TABLE 8-2 Household and Establishment Survey Data for May and June 2005

	HOUSEHOLD SURVEY			ESTABLISHMENT SURVEY		
	MAY	JUNE	CHANGE	MAY	JUNE	CHANGE
Employed	141,475,000	141,638,000	+163,000	133,391,000	133,537,000	+146,000
Unemployed	7,647,000	7,486,000	−161,000			
Labor Force	149,122,000	149,123,000	+1,000			
Unemployment Rate	5.1%	5.0%	−0.1%			

Source: U.S. Department of Labor, "Employment Situation Summary," July 2005.
Note: The sum of employed and unemployed may not equal labor force due to rounding.

TABLE 8-3

Establishments Creating and Eliminating Jobs, September–December 2004

	NUMBER OF ESTABLISHMENTS	NUMBER OF JOBS
ESTABLISHMENTS CREATING JOBS		
Existing establishments	1,530,000	6,365,000
New establishments	379,000	1,716,000
ESTABLISHMENTS ELIMINATING JOBS		
Continuing establishments	1,467,000	5,727,000
Closing establishments	320,000	1,485,000

Source: U.S. Bureau of Labor Statistics, "Business Employment Dynamics: Fourth Quarter 2004," August 18, 2005.

household survey provides information on the number of persons unemployed and on the number of persons in the labor force. This information is not available in the establishment survey. In both surveys, employment increased between May and June 2005, but the increase was greater in the household survey.

Job Creation and Job Destruction Over Time

One important fact about employment is not very well known: The U.S. economy creates and destroys millions of jobs every year. In 2004, for example, about 31.5 million jobs were created and about 29.4 million jobs were destroyed. This degree of job creation and destruction is what we would expect in a vibrant market system where new firms are constantly being started, some existing firms are expanding, some existing firms are contracting, and some firms are going out of business. The creation and destruction of jobs results from changes in consumer tastes, technological progress, and the success and failures of entrepreneurs in responding to the opportunities and challenges of shifting consumer tastes and technological change. The volume of job creation and job destruction helps explain why the typical person who loses a job is unemployed for a relatively brief period of time.

When the BLS announces each month the increases or decreases in the number of persons employed and unemployed, these are net *figures.* That is, the change in the number of persons employed is equal to the total number of jobs created minus the number of jobs eliminated. Take, for example, the months from September to December 2004. During that period, 8,081,000 jobs were created and 7,212,000 were eliminated, for a net increase of 869,000 jobs. Because the net change is so much smaller than the total job increases and decreases, the net change gives a misleading indication of how dynamic the U.S. job market really is.

The data in Table 8-3 reinforce the idea of how large the volume of job creation and job elimination is over a period as brief as three months. The table shows the number of establishments creating and eliminating jobs during the period between September and December 2004. During these three months, 14 percent of all private sector jobs were either created or destroyed. Fifty-six percent of establishments either eliminated jobs or added new jobs. About 379,000 new establishments opened, creating 1.72 million new jobs, and 320,000 establishments closed, eliminating 1.47 million jobs.

Types of Unemployment

(2) **LEARNING OBJECTIVE**
Identify the three types of unemployment.

Figure 8-4 illustrates that the unemployment rate follows the business cycle, rising during recessions and falling during expansions. Notice, though, that the unemployment

FIGURE 8-4

The Annual Unemployment Rate in the United States, 1950–2004

The unemployment rate rises during recessions and falls during expansion. Shaded areas mark recessions.

Source: U.S. Bureau of Labor Statistics.

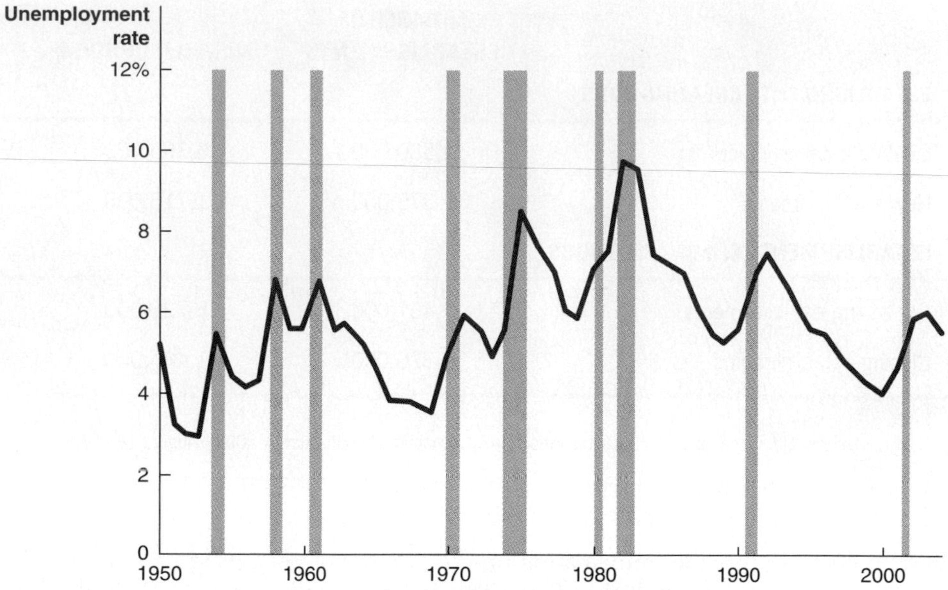

rate never falls to zero. To understand why this is true, we need to discuss the three types of unemployment:

- Frictional unemployment
- Structural unemployment
- Cyclical unemployment

Frictional Unemployment and Job Search

Frictional unemployment Short-term unemployment arising from the process of matching workers with jobs.

Workers have different skills, interests, and abilities, and jobs have different skill requirements, working conditions, and pay levels. As a result, a new worker entering the labor force or a worker who has lost a job probably will not find an acceptable job right away. Most workers spend at least some time engaging in *job search,* just as most firms spend time searching for a new person to fill a job opening. **Frictional unemployment** is short-term unemployment that arises from the process of matching workers with jobs. Some frictional unemployment is unavoidable. As we have seen, the U.S. economy creates and destroys millions of jobs each year. The process of job search takes time, so there will always be some workers who are frictionally unemployed because they are between jobs and in the process of searching for new ones.

Some unemployment is due to seasonal factors, such as weather or fluctuations in demand during different times of the year. For example, stores located in beach resort areas reduce their hiring during the winter, just as ski resorts reduce their hiring during the summer. Department stores increase their hiring in November and December, and reduce their hiring after New Year's Day. In agricultural areas, employment increases during harvest season, and declines thereafter. Construction workers experience greater unemployment during the winter than during the summer. *Seasonal unemployment* refers to unemployment due to factors such as weather, variations in tourism, and other calendar-related events. Because seasonal unemployment can make the unemployment rate seem artificially high during some months and artificially low during other months, the BLS reports two unemployment rates each month—one that is *seasonally adjusted* and one that is not seasonally adjusted. The seasonally adjusted data eliminate the effects of seasonal unemployment. Economists and policymakers rely on the seasonally adjusted data as a more accurate measure of the current state of the labor market.

Would eliminating all frictional unemployment be good for the economy? In fact, some frictional unemployment is good for the economy because it represents workers and firms taking the time necessary to ensure a good match between the attributes of workers and the characteristics of jobs. By devoting time to job search, workers end up with jobs they find satisfying and in which they can be productive. Of course, having more productive and better satisfied workers is also in the best interest of firms.

Structural Unemployment

By 2004, computer-generated three-dimensional animation, which was used in movies such as *Shrek* and *The Incredibles,* had become much more popular than traditional hand-drawn two-dimensional animation. Many people who were highly skilled in hand-drawn animation lost their jobs at Walt Disney Pictures, Dreamworks, and other movie studios. To become employed again, many of these people either became skilled in computer-generated animation or found new occupations. In the meantime, they were unemployed. Economists consider these animators *structurally unemployed.* **Structural unemployment** arises from a persistent mismatch between the job skills or attributes of workers and the requirements of jobs. While frictional unemployment is short term, structural unemployment can last for longer periods because workers need time to learn new skills. For example, employment by U.S. auto firms dropped by more than half between the early 1980s and the early 2000s as a result of competition from foreign producers and technological change that substituted machines for workers. Many autoworkers found new jobs in other industries only after lengthy periods of retraining.

Structural unemployment Unemployment arising from a persistent mismatch between the skills and characteristics of workers and the requirements of jobs.

Some workers lack even basic skills, such as literacy, or have addictions to drugs or alcohol that make it difficult for them to perform adequately the duties of almost any job. These workers may remain structurally unemployed for years.

Cyclical Unemployment

When the economy moves into recession, many firms find their sales falling and cut back on production. As production falls, they start laying off workers. Workers who lose their jobs because of a recession are experiencing **cyclical unemployment.** For example, we saw in Chapter 7 that Freightliner laid off workers from its heavy truck plants during the recession of 2001. As the economy recovered from the recession, Freightliner began rehiring these workers. These Freightliner workers had experienced cyclical unemployment.

Cyclical unemployment Unemployment caused by a business cycle recession.

Full Employment

As the economy moves through the expansion phase of the business cycle, cyclical unemployment will eventually drop to zero. The unemployment rate will not be zero, however, because of frictional and structural unemployment. As Figure 8-4 shows, the unemployment rate in the United States is rarely below 4 percent. When the only remaining unemployment is structural and frictional unemployment, the economy is said to be at *full employment.*

Economists often think of frictional and structural unemployment as being the normal underlying level of unemployment in the economy. The fluctuations around this normal level of unemployment, which we see in Figure 8-4, are mainly due to the changes in the level of cyclical unemployment. This normal level of unemployment, which is the sum of frictional and structural unemployment, is referred to as the **natural rate of unemployment.** Economists disagree on the exact value of the natural rate of unemployment, and there is good reason to believe it varies over time. Currently, most economists estimate the natural rate to be about 5 percent. The natural rate of unemployment is also sometimes called the *full-employment rate of unemployment.*

Natural rate of unemployment The normal rate of unemployment, consisting of structural unemployment plus frictional unemployment.

8-2 Making the Connection

How Should We Categorize the Unemployment at Lucent Technologies?

How can we categorize the unemployment at Lucent?

We saw at the beginning of this chapter that Lucent Technologies experienced a sharp decline in employment in the early 2000s. Was the unemployment caused by the layoffs at Lucent frictional unemployment, structural unemployment, or cyclical unemployment? In answering this question we should acknowledge that categorizing unemployment as frictional, structural, or cyclical is useful in understanding the sources of unemployment, but it can be difficult to apply these categories in a particular case. The Bureau of Labor Statistics, for instance, provides estimates of total unemployment but does not classify it as frictional, structural, or cyclical.

Despite these difficulties, we can roughly categorize the unemployment at Lucent. We begin by considering the three basic reasons the layoffs occurred: the long-lived decline in the telecommunications products Lucent sells; the recession of 2001 that reduced the demand for Lucent's products; and the failure of Lucent managers to respond to rapid technological change in the industry. Each reason corresponds to a category of unemployment. Because the demand for the telecommunications products Lucent sells—particularly products used with fiber-optic cable networks—declined for a significant period, employment at Lucent and competing firms also declined. Between late 2000 and mid-2002, employment in the telecommunications industry declined by more than 500,000. Certain categories of employees, such as optical engineers, had difficulty finding new jobs. They were structurally unemployed because they were not able to find new jobs without learning new skills. Some of the decline in Lucent's sales was due to the recession rather than to long-term problems in the telecommunications industry. So, some of the workers who lost their jobs at Lucent were cyclically unemployed. Finally, sales and employment declined more sharply at Lucent than at some competing firms because of mistakes made by Lucent's managers. Some workers who lost their jobs at Lucent were able to find new jobs at Lucent's competitors after relatively brief job searches. These workers were frictionally unemployed.

③ LEARNING OBJECTIVE
Explain what factors determine the unemployment rate.

Explaining Unemployment

We have seen that some unemployment is caused by the business cycle. In later chapters, we will explore the causes of the business cycle, which will help us understand the causes of cyclical unemployment. In this section, we will look at what determines the levels of frictional and structural unemployment.

Government Policies and the Unemployment Rate

The process of job search is primarily carried out privately. Workers search for jobs by sending out resumes, registering with Internet job sites such as Monster.com, or getting job referrals from friends and relatives. Firms fill job openings by advertising in newspapers, participating in job fairs, or recruiting on college campuses. Government policy can aid these private efforts. Governments can help reduce the level of frictional unemployment by pursuing policies that help speed up the process of matching unemployed workers with unfilled jobs. Governments can help reduce structural unemployment through policies that aid the retraining of workers. For example, the federal government's Trade Adjustment Assistance program offers training to workers whose firms laid them off as a result of competition from foreign firms.

Some government policies, however, can add to the level of frictional and structural unemployment. These government policies increase the unemployment rate either by increasing the time workers devote to searching for jobs, by providing disincentives to firms to hire workers, or by keeping wages above their market level.

UNEMPLOYMENT INSURANCE AND OTHER PAYMENTS TO THE UNEMPLOYED Suppose you have been in the labor force for a few years but have just lost your job. You could probably find a low-wage job immediately if you needed to—perhaps at Wal-Mart or McDonald's. But you might decide to search for a better, higher-paying job by sending out resumes and responding to want ads and Internet job postings. Remember from Chapter 1 that the *opportunity cost* of any activity is the highest-valued alternative that you must give up to engage in that activity. In this case, the opportunity cost of continuing to search for a job is the salary you are giving up at the job you could have taken. The longer you search, the better your chances of finding a better, higher-paying job, but the longer you search, the greater the opportunity cost of the salary you are giving up by not working.

In the United States and most other industrial countries, the unemployed are eligible for *unemployment insurance payments* from the government. In the United States, these payments are equal to about half the average wage. The unemployed spend more time searching for jobs because they receive these payments. This additional time spent searching raises the unemployment rate. Does this mean that the unemployment insurance program is a bad idea? Most economists would say no. Before the unemployment insurance program was created at the end of the 1930s, unemployed workers suffered very large declines in their incomes, which led them to greatly reduce their spending. This reduced spending contributed to the severity of recessions. Unemployment insurance helps the unemployed maintain their income and spending, which lessens the personal impact of being unemployed and also helps reduce the severity of recessions.

INTERNATIONAL COMPARISONS In the United States, typical unemployed workers are eligible to receive unemployment insurance payments equal to about half their previous wage for only six months. After that, the opportunity cost of continuing to search for a job rises. In many other high-income countries, such as Canada and most of the countries of Western Europe, workers are eligible to receive unemployment payments for a year or more, and the payments may equal 70 percent to 80 percent of their previous wage. In addition, many of these countries have generous *social insurance programs* that allow unemployed adults to receive some government payments even after their eligibility for unemployment insurance has ended. In the United States, very few government programs make payments to healthy adults, with the exception of the Temporary Assistance for Needy Families program, which allows single parents to receive payments for up to five years. Because the opportunity cost of job search is lower in Canada and Western Europe, unemployed workers in those countries search longer for jobs and, therefore, the unemployment rates in those countries tend to be higher than in the United States.

Figure 8-5 shows the average yearly unemployment rate for the ten-year period from 1995 to 2004 for the United States, Canada, Japan, and several Western European countries. The United States and Japan provide unemployment insurance payments for only a short period of time, and their average unemployment rate during these years was lower than for the other countries shown. Many European countries also have laws that make it difficult for companies to fire workers. These laws create a disincentive for firms to hire workers, which also contributes to a higher unemployment rate.

MINIMUM WAGE LAWS In 1938, the federal government enacted a national minimum wage law. At first, the lowest legal wage firms could pay workers was $0.25 per hour. Over the years, Congress gradually raised the minimum wage until it reached its current level of $5.15 per hour. Some states and cities also have minimum wage laws. For example, in 2005 California has set its minimum wage at $6.75 per hour, and the minimum wage in San Francisco is $8.50 per hour. If the minimum wage is set above the market wage determined by the demand and supply of labor, the quantity of labor supplied will be greater than the quantity of labor demanded. Some workers will be unemployed who would have been employed if there were no minimum wage. As a result, the unemployment rate will be higher than it would be without a minimum wage. Economists agree that the current minimum wage is above the market wage for some workers, but they

FIGURE 8-5

Average Unemployment Rates in the United States, Canada, Japan, and Europe, 1995–2004

The unemployment rate in the United States is usually lower than the unemployment rates in most other high-income countries, partly because the United States has tougher requirements for the unemployed to receive government payments. These requirements raise the costs of searching for a better job and lower the unemployment rate.

Source: Organization for Economic Cooperation and Development.

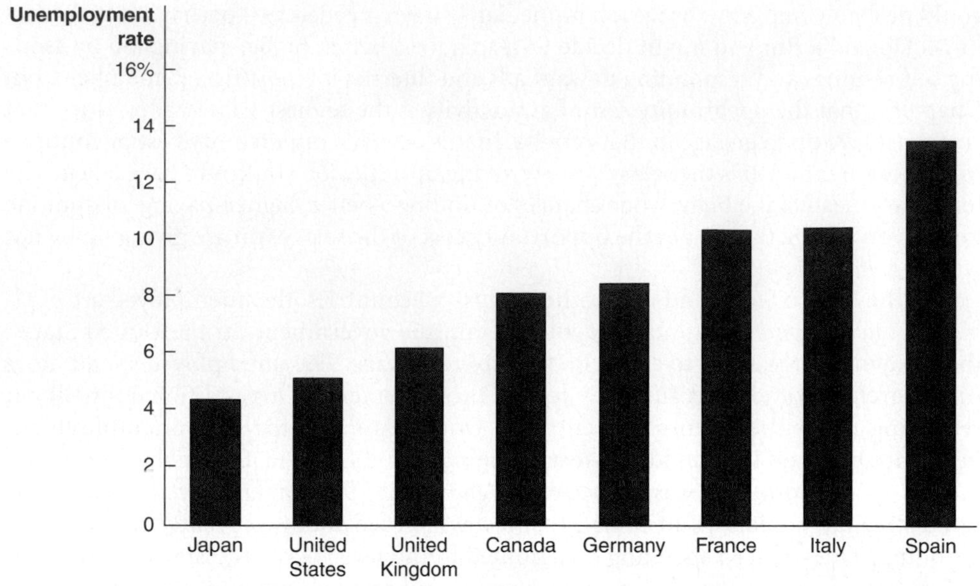

disagree on the amount of unemployment that has resulted. Because teenagers generally have relatively few job-related skills, they are the group most likely to receive the minimum wage. Studies estimate that a 10-percent increase in the minimum wage reduces teenage employment by about 2 percent. Because teenagers and others receiving the minimum wage are a relatively small part of the labor force, most economists believe that, at its present level, the effect of the minimum wage on the unemployment rate in the United States is fairly small.

Labor Unions

Labor unions are organizations of workers that bargain with employers for higher wages and better working conditions for their members. In unionized industries, the wage is usually above what otherwise would be the market wage. This above-market wage results in employers in unionized industries hiring fewer workers, but does it also increase the overall unemployment rate in the economy? Most economists would say the answer is no, because only about 9 percent of workers outside of the government sector are unionized. Although unions remain strong in a few industries, such as automobiles, steel, and telecommunications, most industries in the United States are not unionized. The result is that workers who can't find jobs in unionized industries because the wage is above its market level can find jobs in other industries.

Efficiency Wages

Efficiency wage A higher-than-market wage paid by a firm to increase worker productivity.

Many firms pay higher-than-market wages, not because the government requires them to or because they are unionized, but because they believe doing so will increase their profits. This link may seem like a paradox. Wages are the largest cost for many employers, so paying higher wages seems like a good way for firms to lower profits rather than to increase them. The key to understanding the paradox is that the level of wages can affect the level of worker productivity. Many studies have shown that workers are motivated to work harder by higher wages. An **efficiency wage** is a higher-than-market wage paid by a firm to motivate workers to be more productive. Can't firms ensure that workers work hard by supervising them? In some cases they can. For example, telemarketers can be monitored electronically to ensure they make the required number of phone calls per hour. In many business situations, however, it is much more difficult to monitor workers. Many firms must rely on workers being motivated enough to work hard. In fact, the following is the key to the efficiency wage: By paying a wage above the market wage, the firm raises the costs to workers of losing their jobs because most alternative jobs will pay only the market wage. The increase in productivity that results from paying the high wage can more than offset the cost of the wage, thereby lowering the firm's costs of production.

Because the efficiency wage is above the market wage, it results in the quantity of labor supplied being greater than the quantity of labor demanded, just as do minimum wage laws and unions. So, efficiency wages are another reason economies experience some unemployment even when cyclical unemployment is zero.

8-3 Making the Connection

Why Did Henry Ford Pay His Workers Twice as Much as Other Car Manufacturers?

In January 1914, Henry Ford announced that he would begin paying his workers \$0.625 per hour, or \$5.00 for an eight-hour day. Other automobile firms paid an average of only \$0.29 per hour. Why would Henry Ford pay his workers more than twice as much as other firms? Ford had recently installed the first moving assembly line in his factory at Highland Park, Michigan. The moving assembly line greatly increased labor productivity, but most Ford workers hated it.

Under the old assembly system, the cars remained stationary on the factory floor and each worker had several jobs to do as he moved from one car to another. With the moving assembly line, each worker remained in the same spot all day, performing the same task—sometimes just installing a bolt or tightening a nut—over and over. Many workers found this excruciatingly boring, and many quit to take less monotonous jobs at other firms. Each time a worker quit, Ford had the expense of hiring and training a new one. These expenses became very high: Of the 15,000 workers employed by the company on December 31, 1913, only 640 had worked at Ford for more than three months.

With the introduction of the \$5-dollar-a-day wage, Ford went from having difficulty keeping workers to having long lines of men at the factory gate every morning applying for work. The *New York Times* described the situation the morning Ford first began paying the new wage: "Twelve thousand men . . . [rushed] the plant which resulted in a riot and turning of a fire hose on the crowd in weather but little different from zero [degrees] . . . . As soon as the job hunters had dried or changed their clothing they came back." Ford had begun paying an efficiency wage. According to Ford's official biographer, paying \$5 per day had "improved the discipline of the workers, given them a more loyal interest in the institution, and raised their personal efficiency." Ford himself later wrote, "The payment of five dollars a day for an eight-hour day was one of the finest cost-cutting moves we ever made."

Henry Ford claimed that paying a wage twice as high as his competitors was the finest cost-cutting move he ever made.

Sources: David A. Hounshell, *From the American System to Mass Production, 1800–1932,* Baltimore: The Johns Hopkins University Press, 1984, Ch. 6; Daniel M. G. Raff and Lawrence H. Summers, "Did Henry Ford Pay Efficiency Wages?" *Journal of Labor Economics,* Vol. 5, Issue 4, Part 2, October 1987, pp. S57–S86; and Alan Nevins and Frank Ernest Hill, *Ford: The Times, the Man, the Company,* New York: Scribner's, 1954, pp. 538, 550.

Measuring Inflation

④ LEARNING OBJECTIVE

Define the price level and the inflation rate, and understand how they are computed.

One of the facts of economic life is that the prices of most goods and services rise over time. As a result, the cost of living continually rises. In 1914, Henry Ford's \$5-a-day wage seemed shockingly high. But in that year, Ford's Model T, the best-selling car in the country, sold for less than \$600, the price of a man's suit was \$15, the price of a ticket to a movie theater was \$0.15, and the price of a box of Kellogg's Corn Flakes was \$0.08. Today, when the cost of living is much higher, the minimum wage law requires firms to pay a wage of at least \$5.15 per *hour,* more than Ford's highly paid workers earned in a day.

Price level A measure of the average prices of goods and services in the economy.

Inflation rate The percentage increase in the price level from one year to the next.

Knowledge of how the government's employment and unemployment statistics are compiled is important in interpreting them. The same is true of the government's statistics on the cost of living. As we saw in Chapter 7, the **price level** measures the average prices of goods and services in the economy. The **inflation rate** is the percentage increase in the price level from one year to the next. In Chapter 7, we introduced the *GDP deflator* as a measure of the price level. The GDP deflator is the broadest measure we have of the price level because it includes the price of every final good and service. But, for some purposes, it is too broad. For example, if we want to know the impact of inflation on the typical household, the GDP price deflator may be misleading because it includes the prices of products such as large electric generators and machine tools that are included in the investment component of GDP, but are not purchased by the typical household. In this chapter, we will focus on measuring the inflation rate by changes in the *consumer price index* because changes in this index come closest to measuring changes in the cost of living as experienced by the typical household. We will also briefly discuss a third measure of inflation: the *producer price index*.

The Consumer Price Index

Consumer price index (CPI) An average of the prices of the goods and services purchased by the typical urban family of four.

To obtain prices of a representative group of goods and services, the Bureau of Labor Statistics (BLS) surveys 30,000 households nationwide on their spending habits. They use the results of this survey to construct a *market basket* of 211 types of goods and services purchased by the typical urban family of four. Figure 8-6 shows the goods and services in the market basket grouped into eight broad categories. Almost three-quarters of the market basket falls into the categories of housing, transportation, and food. Each month, hundreds of BLS employees visit 23,000 stores in 87 cities and record prices of the goods and services in the market basket. Each price in the consumer price index is given a weight equal to the fraction of the typical family's budget spent on that good or service. The **consumer price index (CPI)** is an average of the prices of the goods and services purchased by the typical family. One year is chosen as the base year, and the value of the CPI is set equal to 100 for that year. In any year other than the base year, the CPI is equal to the ratio of the dollar amount necessary to buy the market basket of goods in that year divided by the dollar amount necessary to buy the market basket of goods in the base year, multiplied by 100. Because the CPI measures the cost to the typical family to buy a representative basket of goods and services, it is sometimes referred to as the *cost-of-living index*.

FIGURE 8-6

The CPI Market Basket, December 2004

The BLS surveys 30,000 households on their spending habits. The results are used to construct a *market basket* of goods and services purchased by the typical urban family of four. The chart shows these goods and services grouped into eight broad categories. The percentages represent the expenditure shares of the categories within the market basket. The categories of housing, transportation, and food make up about three-quarters of the market basket.

Source: Bureau of Labor Statistics.

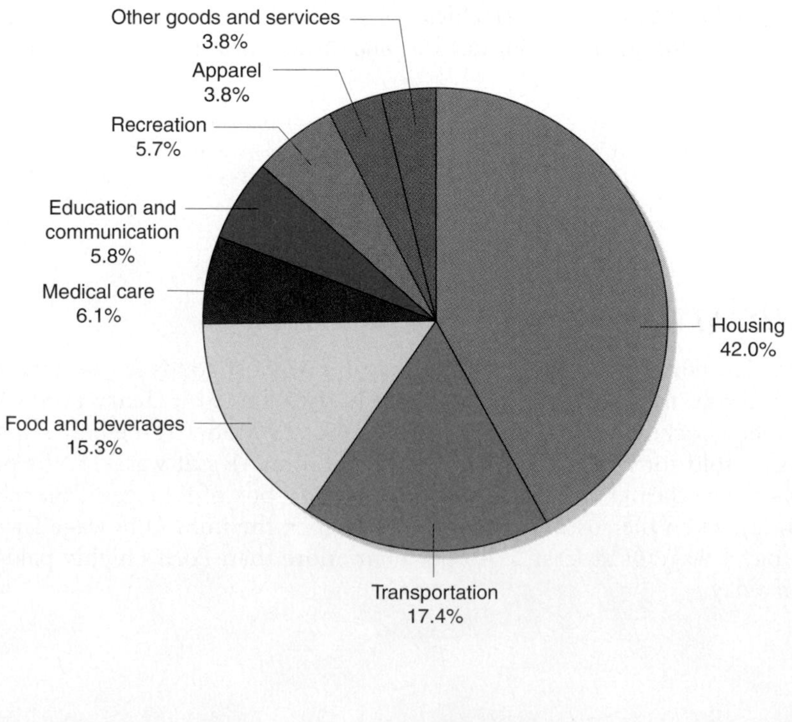

A simple example can clarify how the consumer price index is constructed. For purposes of this example, assume the market basket has only three products: eye examinations, pizzas, and books:

	BASE YEAR (1999)			2006		2007	
PRODUCT	QUANTITY	PRICE	EXPENDITURES	PRICE	EXPENDITURES (ON BASE YEAR QUANTITIES)	PRICE	EXPENDITURES (ON BASE YEAR QUANTITIES)
Eye examinations	1	$50.00	$50.00	$100.00	$100.00	$85.00	$85.00
Pizzas	20	10.00	200.00	15.00	300.00	14.00	280.00
Books	20	25.00	500.00	25.00	500.00	27.50	550.00
Total			$750.00		$900.00		$915.00

Suppose that during the base year of 1999 a survey determines that each month the typical family purchases 1 eye examination, 20 pizzas, and 20 books. At 1999 prices, the typical family must spend $750.00 to purchase this market basket of goods and services. The CPI for every year after the base year is determined by dividing the amount necessary to purchase the market basket in that year by the amount required in the base year, multiplied by 100. Notice that the quantities of the products purchased in 2006 and 2007 are irrelevant in calculating the CPI, because *we are assuming that households buy the same market basket of products each month.* Using the numbers in the table, we can calculate the CPI for 2006 and 2007:

FORMULA	APPLIED TO 2006	APPLIED TO 2007
$\text{CPI} = \dfrac{\text{Expenditures in the current year}}{\text{Expenditures in the base year}} \times 100$	$\left(\dfrac{\$900}{\$750}\right) \times 100 = 120$	$\left(\dfrac{\$915}{\$750}\right) \times 100 = 122$

How do we interpret values such as 120 and 122? The first thing to recognize is that they are *index numbers,* which means they are not measured in dollars or any other units. *The CPI is intended to measure changes in the price level over time.* We can't use the CPI to tell us in an absolute sense how high the price level is, only how much it has changed over time. We measure the inflation rate as the percentage increase in the CPI from one year to the next. For our simple example, the inflation rate in 2007 would be the percentage change in the CPI from 2006 to 2007:

$$\left(\frac{122 - 120}{120}\right) \times 100 = 1.7\%.$$

Because the CPI is designed to measure the cost of living, we can also say that the cost of living increased by 1.7 percent during 2007.

Is the CPI Accurate?

The CPI is the most widely used measure of inflation. Policymakers use the CPI to track the state of the economy. Businesses use it to help set the prices of their products and the wages and salaries of their employees. Each year the federal government increases the Social Security payments made to retired workers by a percentage equal to the increase in the CPI during the previous year. In setting alimony and child support payments in divorce cases, judges will often order the payments increase each year by the inflation rate as measured by the CPI.

It is important that the CPI be as accurate as possible, but there are four biases that make changes in the CPI overstate the true inflation rate:

Don't Let This Happen To You!

Don't Miscalculate the Inflation Rate

Suppose you are given the data in the following table and are asked to calculate the inflation rate for 2004.

YEAR	CPI
2003	184
2004	189

It is tempting to avoid any calculations and simply to report that the inflation rate in 2004 was 89 percent because 189 is an 89 percent increase from 100. But 89 percent would be the wrong answer. A value for the CPI of 189 in 2004 tells us that the price level in 2004 was 89 percent higher than in the base year, but the inflation rate is the percentage increase in the price level from the previous year, *not* the percentage increase from the base year. A correct calculation of the inflation rate for 2004 is:

$$\left(\frac{189-184}{184}\right)\times 100 = 2.7\%.$$

YOUR TURN: **Test your understanding by doing related problems 14 and 20 on pages 258 and 259 at the end of this chapter.**

- *Substitution bias.* In constructing the CPI, the Bureau of Labor Statistics assumes that each month consumers purchase the same amount of each product in the market basket. In fact, consumers are likely to buy fewer of those products that increase most in price and more of those products that increase least in price (or fall the most in price). For instance, if apple prices rise rapidly during the month while orange prices fall, consumers will reduce their apple purchases and increase their orange purchases. Therefore, the prices of the market basket consumers actually buy will rise less than the prices of the market basket the BLS uses to compute the CPI.
- *Increase in quality bias.* Over time, most products included in the CPI improve in quality: Automobiles become more durable and side air bags become standard equipment, computers become faster and have more memory, dishwashers use less water while getting dishes cleaner, and so on. Increases in the prices of these products partly reflect their improved quality and partly are pure inflation. The BLS attempts to make adjustments so that only the pure inflation part of price increases is included in the CPI. These adjustments are difficult to make, so the recorded price increases overstate the pure inflation in some products.
- *New product bias.* For many years the Bureau of Labor Statistics updated the market basket of goods used in computing the CPI only every ten years. That meant that new products introduced between updates were not included in the market basket. For example, the 1987 update took place before cell phones were introduced. Although millions of American households used cell phones by the mid-1990s, they were not included in the CPI until the 1997 update. The prices of many products, such as cell phones, DVD players, and computers, decrease in the years immediately after they are introduced. Unless the market basket is updated frequently, these price decreases will not be included in the CPI.
- *Outlet bias.* During the mid-1990s, many consumers began to increase their purchases from discount stores such as Sam's Club. By the late 1990s, the Internet began to account for a significant fraction of sales of some products. Because the BLS continued to collect price statistics from traditional full-price retail stores, the CPI was not reflecting the prices some consumers actually paid.

Most economists believe these biases cause changes in the CPI to overstate the true inflation rate by one-half of a percentage point to one percentage point. That is, if the CPI indicates that the inflation rate was 3 percent, it is probably between 2 percent and 2.5 percent. The BLS continues to take steps to reduce the size of the bias. For example, the BLS has reduced the size of the substitution and new product biases by updating the market basket every two years, rather than every 10 years. The BLS has reduced the size of the outlet bias by conducting a point-of-purchase survey to track where consumers actually make their purchases. Finally, the BLS has used statistical methods to reduce the size of the quality bias. Prior to these changes, the size of the total bias in the CPI was probably greater than 1 percent.

The Producer Price Index

In addition to the GDP deflator and the CPI, the government also computes the **producer price index (PPI).** Like the consumer price index, the producer price index tracks the prices of a market basket of goods. But, whereas the consumer price index tracks the prices of goods and services purchased by the typical household, the producer price index tracks the prices firms receive for goods and services at all stages of production. The producer price index includes the prices of intermediate goods, such as flour, cotton, yarn, steel, and lumber, and raw materials, such as raw cotton, coal, and crude petroleum. If the prices of these goods rise, the cost to firms of producing final goods and services will rise, which may lead firms to increase the prices of goods and services purchased by consumers. Changes in the producer price index therefore can give an early warning of future movements in the consumer price index.

Producer price index (PPI) An average of the prices received by producers of goods and services at all stages of the production process.

Using Price Indexes to Adjust for the Effects of Inflation

(5) LEARNING OBJECTIVE

Use price indexes to adjust for the effects of inflation.

The typical college student today is likely to receive a much higher salary than the student's parents did 25 or more years ago, but prices 25 years ago were, on average, much lower than prices today. Put another way, the purchasing power of a dollar was much higher 25 years ago because the prices of most goods and services were much lower. Price indexes, such as the CPI, give us a way of adjusting for the effects of inflation so that we can compare dollar values from different years. For example, suppose your mother received a salary of $20,000 in 1980. By using the consumer price index, we can calculate what $20,000 in 1980 is equivalent to in 2004. The consumer price index is 82 for 1980 and 189 for 2004. Because 189/82 = 2.3, we know that, on average, prices were more than twice as high in 2004 as in 1980. We can use this result to inflate a salary of $20,000 received in 1980 to its value in current purchasing power:

$$\text{Value in 2004 dollars} = \text{Value in 1980 dollars} \times \left(\frac{\text{CPI in 2004}}{\text{CPI in 1980}}\right)$$

$$= \$20{,}000 \times \left(\frac{189}{82}\right) = \$46{,}098.$$

Our calculation shows that if you are paid a salary of $46,098 today, you will be able to purchase roughly the same amount of goods and services that your mother could have purchased with a salary of $20,000 in 1980. Economic variables that are calculated in current year prices are referred to as *nominal variables.* The calculation we have just made used a price index to adjust a nominal variable—your mother's salary—for the effects of inflation.

For some purposes, we are interested in tracking changes in an economic variable over time, rather than in seeing what its value would be in today's dollars. In that case, to correct for the effects of inflation we can divide the nominal variable by a price index and multiply by 100 to obtain a *real variable.* The real variable will be measured in dollars of the base year for the price index. Currently, the base year for the CPI is the average of prices in the years 1982 to 1984.

SOLVED PROBLEM 8-2

(5) LEARNING OBJECTIVE

Use price indexes to adjust for the effects of inflation.

Calculating Real Average Hourly Earnings

In addition to data on employment, the BLS establishment survey gathers data on average hourly earnings of production workers. Production workers are all workers, except for managers and professionals. Average hourly earnings are the wages or salaries earned by these workers per hour. Economists closely follow average hourly earnings because they are a broad measure of the typical worker's income. Use the information in the following table to calculate real average hourly earnings for each year. What was the percentage change in real average hourly earnings between 2003 and 2004?

YEAR	NOMINAL AVERAGE HOURLY EARNINGS	CPI (1982–1984 = 100)
2002	$14.95	179.9
2003	15.35	184.0
2004	15.67	188.9

Solving the Problem:

Step 1: Review the chapter material. This problem is about using price indexes to correct for inflation, so you may want to review the section "Using Price Indexes to Adjust for the Effects of Inflation," which begins on page 247.

Step 2: Calculate real average hourly earnings for each year. To calculate real average hourly earnings for each year, divide nominal average hourly earnings by the CPI, and multiply by 100. For example, real average hourly earnings for 2002 are equal to:

$$\left(\frac{\$14.95}{179.9}\right) \times 100 = \$8.31.$$

The results for all the years:

YEAR	NOMINAL AVERAGE HOURLY EARNINGS	CPI (1982–1984 = 100)	REAL AVERAGE HOURLY EARNINGS (1982–1984 DOLLARS)
2002	$14.95	179.9	$8.31
2003	15.35	184.0	8.34
2004	15.67	188.9	8.30

Step 3: Calculate the percentage change in real average earnings from 2003 to 2004. This percentage change is equal to:

$$\left(\frac{\$8.30 - \$8.34}{\$8.34}\right) \times 100 = -0.5\%.$$

We can conclude that although nominal average hourly earnings increased between 2003 and 2004, real average hourly earnings declined.

Extra Credit: The values we have computed for real average hourly earnings are in 1982–1984 dollars. Because this period is more than 20 years ago, the values are somewhat difficult to interpret. We can convert the earnings to 2004 dollars by using the method we used earlier to calculate your mother's salary. But notice that, for purposes of calculating the *change* in the value of real average hourly earnings over time, the base year of the price index doesn't matter. The change from 2003 to 2004 would have still been −0.5 percent, no matter what the base year of the price index. If you don't see that this is true, test it by using the mother's salary method to calculate real average hourly earnings for 2003 and 2004 in 2004 dollars. Then calculate the percentage change. Unless you make an arithmetic error, you should find the answer is still −0.5 percent.

YOUR TURN: **For more practice, do related problems 15 and 16 on page 258 at the end of this chapter.**

Falling Real Wages at Lucent

Nominal average hourly earnings are often referred to as the *nominal wage,* and real average hourly earnings are often referred to as the *real wage.* In a multiyear wage contract, a union knows that unless it is able to negotiate increases in nominal wages that are greater than the expected inflation rate, real wages will fall. We saw at the beginning of this chapter that the contract between Lucent and its unionized workers would result in nominal wage increases of 16 percent over a period of seven years. If the inflation rate is 3 percent per year over those seven years, the price level will have risen by about 23 percent by the end of the seventh year. With nominal wages rising 16 percent and the price level rising 23 percent, Lucent's workers will have experienced falling real wages.

Both Lucent and its unions realized that the agreement they were signing was likely to lead to falling real wages. The unions accepted the agreement because employment at telecommunications firms had declined sharply. Lucent stated that it might grant further wage increases in the later years of the contract. Lucent probably made this promise because it recognized that if output and employment in the telecommunications industry revived more quickly than expected, the firm would need to pay higher wages to attract and retain good workers.

Real versus Nominal Interest Rates

(6) LEARNING OBJECTIVE

Distinguish between the nominal interest rate and the real interest rate.

The difference between nominal and real values is also important when money is being borrowed and lent. As we saw in Chapter 5, the *interest rate* is the cost of borrowing funds, expressed as a percentage of the amount borrowed. If you lend someone $1,000 for one year and charge an interest rate of 6 percent, the borrower will pay back $1,060, or 6 percent more than the amount you lent. But is $1,060 that you won't receive for one year really 6 percent more than $1,000 today? Because prices will have gone up during the year, you will not be able to buy as much with $1,060 one year from now as you could with that amount today. To calculate your true return from lending the $1,000, we need to take into account the effects of inflation.

Nominal interest rate The stated interest rate on a loan.

Real interest rate The nominal interest rate minus the inflation rate.

The stated interest rate on a loan is the **nominal interest rate.** The **real interest rate** corrects the nominal interest rate for the effect of inflation and is equal to the nominal interest rate minus the inflation rate. For example, suppose you lend $1,000 for one year at an interest rate of 6 percent. Six percent is the nominal interest rate on the loan. If the inflation rate during the year is 2 percent, your real interest rate is 6 percent − 2 percent = 4 percent. If the inflation rate during the year is 4 percent, the real interest rate will be only 2 percent. Holding the nominal interest rate constant, the higher the inflation rate, the lower the real interest rate. Notice that if the inflation rate turns out to be higher than expected, borrowers pay and lenders receive a lower real interest rate than either of them expected. For example, if both you and the person to whom you lent the $1,000 expected the inflation rate to be 2 percent, you both expected the real interest rate on the loan to be 4 percent. If inflation actually turns out to be 4 percent, the real interest rate on the loan will be 2 percent: That's bad news for you but good news for your borrower.

For the economy as a whole, we can measure the nominal interest rate as the interest rate on three-month U.S. Treasury bills. U.S. Treasury bills are short-term loans investors make to the federal government. We can use inflation as measured by changes in the CPI to calculate the real interest rate on Treasury bills. Figure 8-7 shows the nominal and real interest rates for the years 1970 to 2004. Notice that when the inflation rate is low, as it was during the 1990s, the gap between the nominal and real interest rates is small. When the inflation rate is high, as it was during the 1970s, the gap between the nominal and real interest rates becomes large. In fact, a particular nominal interest rate can be associated in different periods with very different real interest rates. For example, during late 1975 the nominal interest rate was about 5.5 percent, but because the inflation rate was 7.5 percent, the real interest rate was −2 percent. In early 1991, the nominal interest rate was also 5.5 percent, but because the inflation rate was only 2.5 percent, the real interest rate was 3 percent.

This example shows that it is impossible to know whether a particular nominal interest rate is "high" or "low." It all depends on the inflation rate. *The real interest rate provides a better measure of the true cost of borrowing and the true return to lending than does the nominal interest rate.* When a firm like Lucent Technologies is deciding whether to borrow the funds to buy an investment good, such as a new factory, it will look at the real interest rate, because the real interest rate measures the true cost to the firm of borrowing.

Deflation A decline in the price level.

You can also see in Figure 8-7 that the nominal interest rate is less than the real interest rate only when the inflation rate is negative. A negative inflation rate is referred to as **deflation** and occurs on the rare occasions when the price level falls. During the years shown in Figure 8-7, the price level as measured by the consumer price index declined during the second quarter of 1986 and the fourth quarter of 2001.

FIGURE 8-7

Nominal and Real Interest Rates, 1970–2004

The real interest rate is equal to the nominal interest rate minus the inflation rate. The real interest rate provides a better measure of the true cost of borrowing and the true return to lending than does the nominal interest rate. The nominal interest rate in the figure is the interest rate on 3-month U.S. Treasury bills. The inflation rate is measured by changes in the CPI.

Source: Federal Reserve Bank of St. Louis, http://research.stlouisfed.org/fred2/.

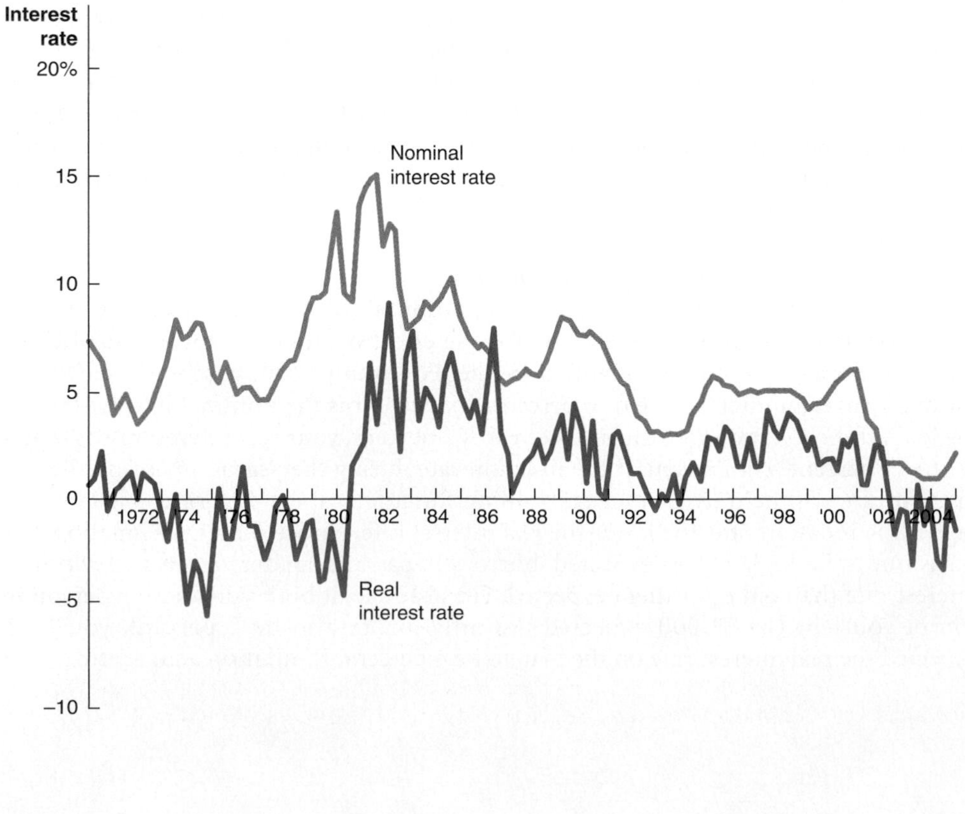

Does Inflation Impose Costs on the Economy?

(7) LEARNING OBJECTIVE

Discuss the problems caused by inflation.

Imagine waking up tomorrow morning and finding that every price in the economy has doubled. The prices of food, gasoline, televisions, and houses have all doubled. But suppose that all wages and salaries also have doubled. Will this doubling of prices and wages matter? Think about walking into Best Buy expecting to find an iPod selling for $250. Instead, you find it selling for $500. Will you turn around and walk out? Probably not, because your salary has also increased overnight from $30,000 per year to $60,000 per year. So, the purchasing power of your salary has remained the same, and you are just as likely to buy the iPod today as you were yesterday.

This hypothetical situation makes an important point: Nominal incomes generally increase with inflation. Remember from Chapter 7 that we can think of the $250 price of the iPod as representing either the value of the product or the value of all the income generated in producing the product. The two amounts are the same whether the iPod sells for $250 or $500. When the price of the iPod rises from $250 to $500, that extra $250 ends up as income that goes to the workers at Apple, the salespeople at Best Buy, or the stockholders of Apple, just as the first $250 did.

It's tempting to think that the problem with inflation is that, as prices rise, consumers can no longer afford to buy as many goods and services, but our example shows that this is a fallacy. An expected inflation rate of 10 percent will raise the average price of goods and services by 10 percent, but it will also raise average incomes by 10 percent. Goods and services will be as affordable to the average consumer as they were before the inflation.

Inflation Affects the Distribution of Income

Why, then, do people dislike inflation? One reason is that the argument in the previous section applies to the *average* person, but not to every person. Some people will find their incomes rising faster than the rate of inflation and so their purchasing power will rise. Other people will find their incomes rising slower than the rate of inflation—or not at all—and their purchasing power will fall. People on fixed incomes are particularly likely to be hurt by inflation. If a retired worker receives a pension fixed at $2,000 per month, over time inflation will reduce the purchasing power of that payment. In that way, inflation can change the distribution of income in a way that strikes many people as being unfair.

The extent to which inflation redistributes income depends in part on whether the inflation is *anticipated*—in which case consumers, workers, and firms can see it coming and can prepare for it—or *unanticipated*—in which case they do not see it coming and do not prepare for it.

The Problem with Anticipated Inflation

Like many of life's problems, inflation is easier to manage if you see it coming. Suppose that everyone knows that the inflation rate for the next ten years will be 10 percent per year. Workers know that unless their wages go up by at least 10 percent per year, the real purchasing power of their wages will fall. Businesses will be willing to increase workers' wages enough to compensate for inflation because they know that the prices of the products they sell will increase. Lenders will realize that the loans they make will be paid back with dollars that are losing 10 percent of their value each year, so they will charge a higher interest rate to compensate them for this. Borrowers will be willing to pay these higher interest rates because they also know they are paying back these loans with dollars that are losing value. So far, there don't seem to be costs to anticipated inflation.

Even when inflation is perfectly anticipated, however, some individuals will experience a cost. Inevitably, there will be a redistribution of income, as some people's incomes fall behind even an anticipated level of inflation. In addition, firms and consumers have to hold some paper money to facilitate their buying and selling. Anyone holding paper money will find its purchasing power decreasing each year by the rate of inflation. To avoid this cost, workers and firms will try to hold as little paper money as possible, but they will have to hold some. In addition, firms that print catalogs listing the prices of their products will have to reprint them more frequently. Supermarkets and other stores that mark prices on packages or on store shelves will have to devote more time and labor to changing the marked prices. The costs to firms of changing prices are called **menu costs.** Although at moderate levels of anticipated inflation menu costs are relatively small, at very high levels of inflation, such as are experienced in some developing countries, menu costs and the costs from paper money losing value can become substantial. Finally, even anticipated inflation acts to raise the taxes paid by investors and raises the cost of capital for business investment. These effects arise because investors are taxed on the nominal payments they receive, rather than on the real payments.

Menu costs The costs to firms of changing prices.

8-4 Making the Connection

A lower inflation rate is like a tax cut for investors.

Why a Lower Inflation Rate Is Like a Tax Cut for Lucent's Bondholders

Borrowers and lenders are interested in the real interest rate, rather than the nominal interest rate. Therefore, if expected inflation increases, the nominal interest rate will rise, and if expected inflation decreases, the nominal interest rate will fall. Suppose that Lucent sells bonds to investors to raise funds to purchase investment goods. Suppose also that Lucent is willing to pay, and investors are willing to receive, a real interest rate of 4 percent. If the inflation rate is expected to be 2 percent, the nominal interest rate on Lucent's bonds must be 6 percent for the real interest rate to be 4 percent. If the inflation rate is expected to be 6 percent, the nominal rate on the bond must rise to 10 percent for the real interest rate to be 4 percent. The following table summarizes this information, assuming that the bond has a principal, or face value, of $1,000 (see Chapter 5 for a review of bonds):

PRINCIPAL	REAL INTEREST RATE	INFLATION RATE	NOMINAL INTEREST RATE
$1,000	4%	6%	10%
$1,000	4%	2%	6%

With a nominal interest rate of 6 percent, the interest payment (also known as the *coupon payment*) on newly issued bonds is $60. When the nominal interest rate rises to 10 percent, the interest payment on newly issued bonds is $100. Unfortunately for investors, the government taxes the nominal payment on bonds with no adjustment for inflation. So, even though in this case the increase in the interest payment from $60 to $100 represents only compensation for inflation, the whole $100 is subject to the income tax. The following table shows the effect of inflation on an investor's real after-tax interest payment assuming a tax rate of 25 percent:

INFLATION RATE	NOMINAL INTEREST PAYMENT	TAX PAYMENT	AFTER-TAX INTEREST PAYMENT	ADJUSTMENT FOR INFLATION	REAL AFTER-TAX INTEREST PAYMENT
6%	$100	– $25	= $75	– $60	= $15
2%	$60	– $15	= $45	– $20	= $25

The table shows that reducing the inflation rate from 6 percent to 2 percent will increase the real after-tax payment received by investors who purchase a $1,000 Lucent bond from $15 to $25. By raising the after-tax reward to investors, lower inflation rates will increase the incentive for investors to lend funds to firms. The greater the flow of funds to firms, the greater the amount of investment spending that will occur.

The Problem with Unanticipated Inflation

In any high-income economy—such as the United States—households, workers, and firms routinely enter into contracts that commit them to make or receive certain payments for years in the future. As we saw in the beginning of the chapter, Lucent Technologies signed a seven-year wage contract with two of its unions during 2004. Once signed, this contract committed Lucent to paying a specified wage for the duration of the contract. When people buy homes, they usually borrow most of the amount they need from a bank. These loans, called *mortgage loans,* commit the borrower to make a fixed monthly payment for the length of the loan. Most mortgage loans are for long periods, often as much as 30 years.

To make these long-term commitments, households, workers, and firms must forecast the rate of inflation. If a firm believes the inflation rate over the next three years will be 6 percent per year, signing a three-year contract with a union that calls for wage increases of 8 percent per year may seem reasonable because the firm may be able to raise its prices by at least the rate of inflation each year. If the firm believes that the inflation rate will be only 2 percent over the next three years, paying wage increases of 8 percent may significantly reduce its profits, or even force it out of business.

When people borrow money or banks lend money, they must forecast the inflation rate so they can calculate the real rate of interest on a loan. In 1980, banks were charging interest rates of 18 percent or more on mortgage loans. This rate seems very high compared to the roughly 6 percent charged on such loans in 2005, but the inflation rate in 1980 was more than 13 percent and was expected to remain high. In fact, the inflation rate declined unexpectedly during the early 1980s. By 1983, the inflation rate was only about 3 percent. People who borrowed money for 30 years at the high interest rates of 1980 soon found that the real interest rate on their loans was much higher than they expected.

When the actual inflation rate turns out to be very different from the expected inflation rate, some people gain and other people lose. This outcome seems unfair to most people because they are either winning or losing only because something unanticipated has happened. This apparently unfair redistribution is a key reason why people dislike unanticipated inflation.

Conclusion

Inflation and unemployment are key macroeconomic problems. Presidential elections are often won or lost on the basis of which candidate is able to convince the public that he or she can best deal with these problems. Many economists, however, would argue that, in the long run, maintaining high rates of growth of real GDP per person is the most important macroeconomic concern. Only when real GDP per person is increasing will a country's standard of living increase. We turn in the next chapter to discussing this important issue of economic growth.

Read *An Inside Look* on the next page to see how expectations of inflation affected the negotiations of a union contract between Boeing and its workers.

An Inside Look Managers and Workers at Boeing Negotiate Wages

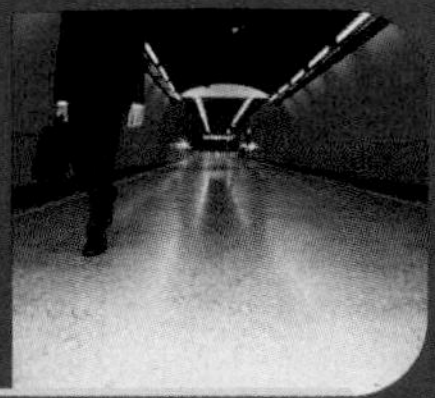

WICHITA EAGLE, MARCH 6, 2004

Boeing Offers Unionized Workers in Wichita, Kan., Wage Increases

Boeing Wichita is offering more than 3,000 union-represented technical and professional workers wage increases of 3 percent, 2 percent and 3 percent in the next three years. The company's offer, which also includes a 2 percent signing bonus, was harshly criticized Friday by a union leader.

Negotiations between Boeing Wichita and the Society of Professional Engineering Employees in Aerospace on a three-year contract for about 3,450 Wichita technical and professional employees appear to be nearing completion. Bob Brewer, SPEEA's Midwest director, said he expects Boeing to present the union with its "last, best and final offer" sometime Tuesday or Wednesday.

a As it stands now, the union could not recommend Boeing's offer to its members when they vote on a new agreement, Brewer said. Boeing's wage offer "was very insulting and disrespectful to the employees here in Wichita," Brewer said. "That doesn't even cover the market increases and inflation."

Boeing officials called the offer a fair one and in keeping with economic realities and with the Wichita market.

b The wage proposal is "taking into consideration where we are in the latest business cycle, which has been in a downturn (and) not expected to pick up until perhaps 2006," Boeing Wichita spokesman Fred Solis said. The current contract, which expired Feb. 19, has been extended until March 19. Both sides agree there is more work to be done.

"We're still negotiating," Solis said. "We will continue looking for a solution that's fair to everybody." Talks have been tense in the past few days, Brewer said, when the two sides began talking about an economic package of benefits and wages. A large gap remains between where the offer is today and where it will have to be for the membership to accept it, Brewer said.

c "They're looking at short-term cost-cutting," Brewer said. "This isn't all about cutting costs. This is also about investing in your most valuable assets, and that is your employees."

Workers in the SPEEA bargaining unit voted last month to retain the union after an effort by some Wichita employees to decertify the unit.

Key Points in the Article

This article discusses wage contract negotiations between Boeing Company, a manufacturer of commercial and military aircraft, and workers at its Wichita, Kansas, factory. The union argues that the company's wage offer is too low because it fails to "cover the market increases and inflation." A spokesman for Boeing argues that the contract offer takes into account that the aircraft industry is still in recession.

Analyzing the News

a We saw in Solved Problem 8-2 that real earnings will increase only if nominal earnings increase faster than the price level. Therefore, not surprisingly, the expected inflation rate is important in wage negotiations. Workers hope that their real wages will increase over time. The only way their real wages can increase is if the nominal wage increases they receive are greater than increases in the cost of living. Firms can grant increases in real wages without seeing their costs rise only if they can get increased production from their workers.

b Fred Holis, the spokesman for Boeing, argues that Boeing's wage offer to its workers reflected the stage of the business cycle. That is, workers could not expect larger wage increases during a recession. As we have already seen, when economists use the phrase "business cycle," they are referring to the alternating periods of economic expansion and economic recession *in the economy as a whole*. Many firms, however, think of the business cycle in terms of the sales of their own products. Figure 1 shows Boeing's annual sales of passenger aircraft from 1979 to 2004. The shaded areas represent years in which the U.S. economy was in a business cycle recession. The figure shows that the cycle in sales of Boeing's aircraft do not follow the business cycle exactly. For example, Boeing experienced dips in sales from 1992 to 1995 and in 2002 and 2003, when the economy as a whole was expanding, and increases in sales during 1990–91 and 2001, when the economy as a whole was in recession. This pattern reflects, in part, the fact that aircraft take a long time to build, so aircraft actually shipped in one year were typically ordered in an earlier year. But sales of aircraft are also dependent on such factors as the health of the airline industry, which are not as important for the economy as a whole.

c The union representative argues that, for Boeing, paying higher wages is the equivalent of "investing in your most valuable assets . . . your employees." According to the union representative, holding down wage increases would amount to "short-term cost cutting" by the company. Such arguments are, of course, in the best interests of a union that wants the largest wage increases it can obtain for its members. But our discussion of efficiency wages indicated that sometimes it is in the best interests of firms to pay wages that are above market levels. Making the Connection 8-3 discussed Henry Ford's view that paying his workers twice what his competitors paid actually lowered his costs by causing his workers to be more productive and less likely to quit.

Thinking Critically

1. If a firm grants nominal wage increases that turn out to be greater than the actual inflation rate, will the firm's profits necessarily fall? Briefly explain.
2. For which types of occupations is it likely that paying efficiency wages will be an effective strategy for a firm?

Source: Molly McMillin, "Boeing Offers Unionized Workers in Wichita, Kan., Wage Increases," *Wichita Eagle*, March 6, 2004, p. 1. Copyright 2004, Knight Ridder/Tribune Media Services Reprinted with permission.

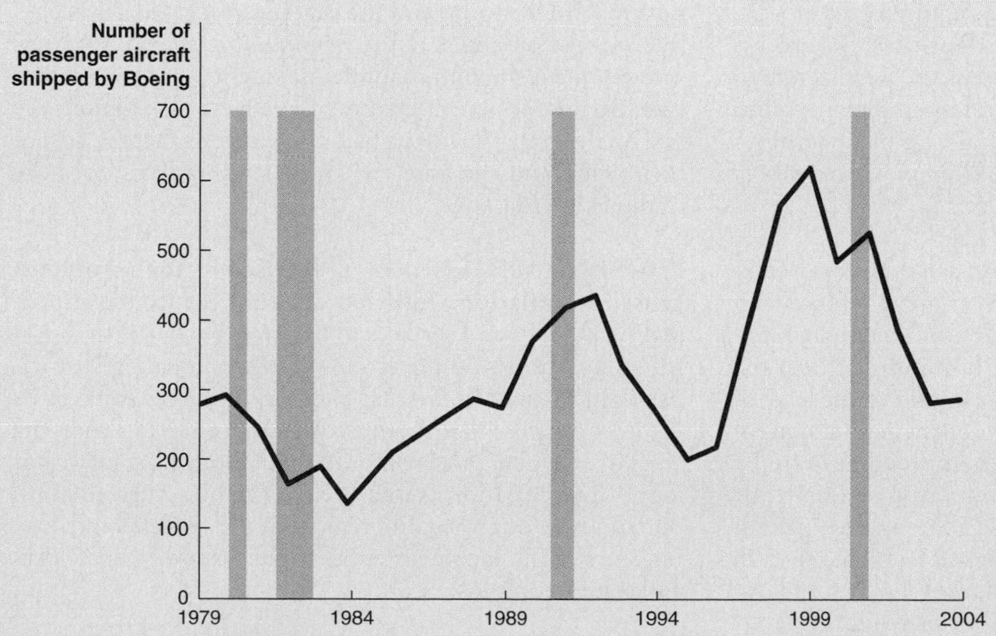

Note: The shaded areas represent years in which the U.S. economy was in a business cycle recession.

Figure 1: Cycles in Aircraft Production at Boeing.

Source: Aerospace Industries Association.

SUMMARY

LEARNING OBJECTIVE ① Define the unemployment rate and the labor force participation rate, and understand how they are computed. The U.S. Bureau of Labor Statistics uses the results of the monthly household survey to calculate the *unemployment rate* and the *labor force participation rate.* The *labor force* is the total number of people who have jobs plus the number of people who do not have jobs but are actively looking. The labor force participation rate is the percentage of the working-age population in the labor force. Since 1950, the labor force participation rate of women has been rising, while the labor force participation rate of men has been falling. White men and women have below-average unemployment rates. Teenagers and black men and women have above-average unemployment rates. The typical unemployed person finds a new job or returns to his or her previous job within a few months. Each year millions of jobs are created and destroyed in the United States.

LEARNING OBJECTIVE ② Identify the three types of unemployment. There are three types of unemployment: frictional, structural, and cyclical. *Frictional unemployment* is short-term unemployment arising from the process of matching workers with jobs. One type of frictional unemployment is *seasonal unemployment,* which refers to unemployment due to factors such as weather, variations in tourism, and other calendar-related events. *Structural unemployment* arises from a persistent mismatch between the job skills or attributes of workers and the requirements of jobs. *Cyclical unemployment* is caused by a business cycle recession. The *natural rate of unemployment* is the normal rate of unemployment, consisting of structural unemployment and frictional unemployment. The natural rate of unemployment is also sometimes called the *full-employment rate of unemployment.*

LEARNING OBJECTIVE ③ Explain what factors determine the unemployment rate. Government policies can reduce the level of frictional and structural unemployment by aiding the search for jobs and the retraining of workers. Some government policies, however, can add to the level of frictional and structural unemployment. Unemployment insurance payments can raise the unemployment rate by extending the time that unemployed workers search for jobs. Government policies have caused the unemployment rates in most other industrial countries to be higher than in the United States. Wages above market levels can also increase unemployment. Wages may be above market levels because of the minimum wage, labor unions, and *efficiency wages.*

LEARNING OBJECTIVE ④ Define the price level and the inflation rate, and understand how they are computed. The *price level* measures the average prices of goods and services. The *inflation rate* is equal to the percentage change in the price level from one year to the next. The federal government compiles statistics on three different measures of the price level: the consumer price index (CPI), the GDP price deflator, and the producer price index (PPI). The *consumer price index* is an average of the prices of goods and services purchased by the typical urban family of four. Changes in the consumer price index are the best measure of changes in the cost of living as experienced by the typical household. Biases in the construction of the CPI cause changes in it to overstate the true inflation rate by one-half of a percentage point to one percentage point. The *producer price index* is an average of prices received by producers of goods and services at all stages of production.

LEARNING OBJECTIVE ⑤ Use price indexes to adjust for the effects of inflation. Price indexes are designed to measure changes in the price level over time, not the absolute level of prices. To correct for the effects of inflation we can divide a *nominal variable* by a price index and multiply by 100 to obtain a *real variable.* The real variable will be measured in dollars of the base year for the price index.

LEARNING OBJECTIVE ⑥ Distinguish between the nominal interest rate and the real interest rate. The stated interest rate on a loan is the *nominal interest rate.* The *real interest rate* is the nominal interest rate minus the inflation rate. Because it is corrected for the effects of inflation, the real interest rate provides a better measure of the true cost of borrowing and the true return to lending than does the nominal interest rate.

LEARNING OBJECTIVE ⑦ Discuss the problems caused by inflation. Inflation does not reduce the affordability of goods and services to the average consumer, but it still imposes costs on the economy. When inflation is anticipated, its main costs are that paper money loses some of its value and firms incur menu costs. *Menu costs* include the costs of changing prices on products and printing new catalogs. When inflation is unanticipated, the actual inflation rate can turn out to be different from the expected inflation rate. As a result, income is redistributed as some people gain and some people lose.

KEY TERMS

Consumer price index (CPI) 244
Cyclical unemployment 239
Deflation 250
Discouraged workers 231
Efficiency wage 242
Frictional unemployment 238
Inflation rate 244
Labor force 230
Labor force participation rate 232
Menu costs 252
Natural rate of unemployment 239
Nominal interest rate 249
Price level 244
Producer price index (PPI) 247
Real interest rate 249
Structural unemployment 239
Unemployment rate 230

REVIEW QUESTIONS

1. How is the unemployment rate calculated? Which groups tend to have above-average unemployment rates, and which groups tend to have below-average unemployment rates?
2. How is the labor force participation rate calculated? In the years since 1950, how have the labor force participation rates of men and women changed?
3. What is the difference between the household survey and the establishment survey? Which survey do many economists prefer for measuring changes in employment? Why?
4. If employment increases during a month, is it likely that the total number of *new* jobs created is about equal to the increase in employment? Explain.
5. What is the relationship between the natural rate of unemployment and cyclical unemployment, frictional unemployment, and structural unemployment?
6. Discuss the effect on the unemployment rate of the following:
   a. The minimum wage law
   b. Labor unions
   c. Efficiency wages
7. Briefly describe the three major measures of the price level. Which measure is used most frequently?
8. What potential biases exist in calculating the consumer price index? What steps has the Bureau of Labor Statistics taken to reduce the size of the biases?
9. If you were lending your savings, which would you prefer: a nominal interest rate of 20 percent and an inflation rate of 18 percent, or a nominal interest rate of 10 percent and an inflation rate of 5 percent? If you were a borrower, would your answer change?
10. Which is a greater problem: anticipated inflation or unanticipated inflation? Why?

PROBLEMS AND APPLICATIONS

Please visit **www.prenhall.com/hubbard** *for solutions to the even-numbered problems as well as multiple-choice and true or false self-assessment quizzes.*

1. Fill in the missing values in the table of data collected in the household survey for the year of 2000.

Working-age population	
Employment	136,891,000
Unemployment	
Unemployment rate	4.0%
Labor force	
Labor force participation rate	67.1%

2. **[Related to the *Chapter Opener*]** What would be some general reasons a firm would lay off a substantial number of workers?
3. Figure 8-2 on page 234 shows that the rapid increases in the labor force participation rate of women slowed down after 1995. Why might this slowdown have occurred? Discuss whether the labor force participation rate for women eventually might be equal to the rate for men.
4. **[Related to *Solved Problem 8-1*]** Homemakers are not included in the employment or labor force totals compiled in the Bureau of Labor Statistics household survey. They are included in the working-age population totals. Suppose

that homemakers were counted as employed and included in the labor force statistics. What would be the impact on the unemployment rate and the labor force participation rate?

5. Discuss the average amount of time the typical unemployed person in the United States has been out of work. Is the average unemployed person in Europe likely to be out of work for a shorter or a longer period of time than the average unemployed person in the United States? Why?
6. What advice for finding a job would you give someone frictionally unemployed? Someone structurally unemployed? Someone cyclically unemployed?
7. When the U.S. economy is at full employment, why isn't the unemployment rate, as measured by the Bureau of Labor Statistics, equal to zero?
8. Discuss the likely impact of each of the following on the unemployment rate:
   a. The length of time workers are eligible to receive unemployment insurance payments doubles.
   b. The minimum wage is abolished.
   c. Most U.S. workers join labor unions.
   d. More companies make information on job openings easily available on Internet job sites.
9. Why do you think the minimum wage was set at only $0.25 per hour in 1938? Wouldn't this wage have been well below the equilibrium wage?
10. An economic consultant studies the labor policies of a firm where it is difficult to monitor workers and prepares a report in which she recommends that the firm raise employee wages. At a meeting of the firm's managers to discuss the report, one manager makes the following argument: "I think the wages we are paying are fine. As long as enough people are willing to work here at the wages we are currently paying, why should we raise them?" What argument can the economic consultant make to justify her advice that the firm should increase its wages?
11. In an article on the conditions in the labor market, two business reporters remarked that the unemployment rate "typically rises months after the economy rebounds." What do they mean by the phrase "the economy rebounds"? Why would the unemployment rate be rising if the economy is rebounding?
    Source: Vince Golle and Terry Barrett, "Hiring Picks Up, Factories Expand," Bloomberg News, April 1, 2002.
12. Between December 2001 and January 2002, the total number of people employed and the unemployment rate both fell. Briefly explain how this is possible.
13. The following appeared in a *Business Week* article:

    > [The household survey for January 2002] from the Bureau of Labor Statistics showed that the labor force participation rate—the percentage of people either employed or actively job-hunting—fell by 0.8 percentage points over the past year, to 66.4%. . . . The sharp decline suggests the published unemployment rate understates the damage to the labor market."

    Why would a fall in the labor force participation rate indicate that the unemployment rate is not doing a good job reflecting labor market conditions?
14. **[Related to *Don't Let This Happen to You!*]** Briefly explain whether you agree or disagree with the following statement: "I don't believe the government price statistics. The CPI for 2004 was 189, but I know that the inflation rate couldn't have been as high as 89 percent in 2004."
15. **[Related to *Solved Problem 8-2*]** Use the information in the following table to determine the percentage changes in the U.S. and French *real* minimum wages between 1956 and 2004.

	UNITED STATES		FRANCE	
YEAR	MINIMUM WAGE (DOLLARS PER HOUR)	CPI	MINIMUM WAGE (EUROS PER HOUR)	CPI
1956	$1.00	27	0.19 euros	10
2004	5.15	189	7.61 euros	110

    Does it matter for your answer that you have not been told the base year for the U.S. CPI or the French CPI? Was the percentage increase in the price level greater in the United States or in France during these years?
    Source: For 1956 French data: John M. Abowd, Francis Kramarz, Thomas Lemieux, and David N. Margolis, "Minimum Wages and Youth Employment in France and the United States," in D. Blanchflower and R. Freeman, eds., *Youth Employment and Joblessness in Advanced Countries*, Chicago: University of Chicago Press, 1999, pp. 427–472 (the value for the minimum wage is given in francs; it was converted to euros at a conversion rate of 1 euro = 6.55957 francs); for 2004 French data: Insee online data bank (www.insee.fr); and for U.S. values both years: U.S. Department of Labor and U.S. Bureau of Labor Statistics.
16. **[Related to *Solved Problem 8-2*]** The Great Depression was the worst economic disaster in U.S. history in terms of declines in real GDP and increases in the unemployment rate. Use the data in the following table to calculate the percentage decline in real GDP between 1929 and 1933:

YEAR	NOMINAL GDP (BILLIONS OF DOLLARS)	GDP PRICE DEFLATOR (2000 = 100)
1929	103.6	11.9
1933	56.4	8.9

17. Consider a simple economy that produces only three products. Use the information in the following table to calculate the inflation rate for 2006 as measured by the consumer price index:

		BASE YEAR (1999)	2005	2006
PRODUCT	QUANTITY	PRICE	PRICE	PRICE
Haircuts	2	$10.00	$11.00	$16.20
Hamburgers	10	2.00	2.45	2.40
DVDs	6	15.00	15.00	14.00

18. The following table shows the top 10 films of all time through 2004, measured by box office receipts in the United States, as well as several other films farther down the list:

RANK	FILM	TOTAL BOX OFFICE RECEIPTS	YEAR RELEASED	CPI
1	*Titanic*	$600,779,824	1997	161
2	*Star Wars*	460,935,655	1977	61
3	*Shrek 2*	436,471,036	2004	189
4	*E.T. the Extra-Terrestrial*	434,949,459	1982	97
5	*Star Wars: Episode I—The Phantom Menace*	431,065,444	1999	167
6	*Spider-Man*	403,706,375	2002	180
7	*Lord of the Rings: The Return of the King*	377,019,252	2003	184
8	*Spider-Man 2*	373,377,893	2004	189
9	*The Passion of the Christ*	370,270,943	2004	189
10	*Jurassic Park*	356,784,000	1993	145
31	*Jaws*	260,000,000	1975	54
62	*Gone with the Wind*	198,655,278	1939	14
70	*Snow White and the Seven Dwarfs*	184,208,842	1937	14
110	*The Sound of Music*	163,214,286	1965	32
129	*One Hundred and One Dalmatians*	153,000,000	1961	30

The CPI in 2004 was 189. Use this information and the data in the table to calculate the box office receipts for each film in 2004 dollars. Assume that each film generated all of its box office receipts during the year it was released. Use your results to prepare a new list of the top 10 films based on their earnings in 2004 dollars. (Some of the films, such as the first *Star Wars* film, *Gone with the Wind,* and *Snow White and the Seven Dwarfs,* were re-released several times, so their receipts were actually earned during several different years, but we will ignore that complication.)
Source: IMBd online database, **www.imdb.com**.

19. The *Wall Street Journal* publishes an index of the prices of luxury homes in various cities. Here are the indexes for January 2001 and January 2002:

CITY	JANUARY 2001	JANUARY 2002
New York	113.8	120.9
San Francisco	122.4	113.3
Detroit	104.6	108.9
Boston	118.7	121.6

a. In which city did the prices of luxury homes increase the most during this year?
b. Can you determine on the basis of these numbers which city had the most expensive luxury homes in January 2002?

20. **[Related to *Don't Let This Happen to You!*]** The following appeared in an article in the Allentown *Morning Call:*

> Inflation in the Lehigh Valley during the first quarter of [the year] was less than half the national rate. . . . So, unlike much of the nation, the fear here is deflation—when prices sink so low the CPI drops below zero.

Do you agree with the reporter's definition of deflation?

21. Describing the situation in England in 1920, the historian Robert Skidelsky wrote the following:

> Who would not borrow at 4 per cent a year, with prices going up 4 per cent a *month?*

What was the real interest rate paid by borrowers in this situation? (*Hint:* What is the annual inflation rate, if the monthly inflation rate is 4 percent?)
Source: Robert Skidelsky, *John Maynard Keynes: Volume 2, The Economist as Saviour, 1920–1937,* New York: The Penguin Press, 1992, p. 39, emphasis in original.

22. During the late nineteenth century in the United States, many farmers borrowed heavily to buy land. During most of the period between 1870 and the mid-1890s, the United States experienced mild deflation: The price level declined each year. Many farmers engaged in political protests during these years and deflation was often a subject of their protests. Explain why farmers would have felt burdened by deflation.

chapter nine

Economic Growth, the Financial System, and Business Cycles

Growth and the Business Cycle at the Ford Motor Company

➤ The Ford Motor Company is a little over 100 years old. In that time, its experiences have often mirrored those of the U.S. economy. Two key macroeconomic facts are that in the long run the U.S. economy has experienced economic growth and in the short run the economy has experienced a series of business cycles. Living standards in the United States have increased enormously because, in the long run, growth in the production of goods and services has been faster than growth in population. But the increase in living standards has been interrupted by periods of business cycle recession during which production of goods and services has declined. Ford has also experienced growth over the long run, but has been greatly affected by the business cycle.

Economic growth is produced by technological progress that makes possible the production of greater quantities of goods and services, and—even more importantly—the production of new and better goods and services. When the Ford Motor Company was established in 1903, personal transportation relied largely on electric street cars and horse-drawn carriages and trucks. Horse-drawn carriages and trucks were slow, unreliable, and uncomfortable. Cleaning up after the horses was itself a major problem in big cities. Ford's first cars were not a huge step forward because they were relatively slow, unreliable, difficult to repair, and expensive. In 1908, Ford introduced one of the most innovative products in business history—the Model T. Because the Model T used parts that were interchangeable, it was much easier to repair than any previous car. When Henry Ford began producing Model Ts on a moving assembly line, he increased the number of cars his workers could produce each day to such an extent that his costs fell dramatically, and he made a profit even after cutting the price as low as $250 per car.

The widespread use of automobiles has not been an unmixed blessing, of course, as shown by the toll of highway deaths and air pollution. But the speed, efficiency, and reliability of gasoline-powered cars and trucks dramatically improved transpor-

LEARNING OBJECTIVES

After studying this chapter, you should be able to:

① Discuss the importance of long-run economic growth.

② Discuss the role of the financial system in facilitating long-run economic growth.

③ Explain what happens during a business cycle.

tation, greatly contributing to the economic growth of the twentieth century. The personal mobility offered by automobiles improved the quality of life for millions by, among other things, making it possible to escape from crowded apartment houses in the city to single-family homes in the suburbs that had sprung up around every major city by the 1920s.

Ford remains a major force in the U.S. economy, earning the fourth-highest revenues of any U.S. firm in 2004. In 2005, however, Ford suffered losses as an increase in gasoline prices caused fewer consumers to buy SUVs. The firm also remains vulnerable to the effects of the business cycle. Early in its history, during the recession of 1920–21 and again during the Great Depression of the 1930s, Ford came close to bankruptcy as falling sales led to large losses. More recent business cycle recessions have also hurt the firm's sales. During 2000, Ford sold 7.4 million vehicles worldwide, including almost 5 million in North America. The recession that began in 2001 cut sharply into the demand for Ford's cars. By 2003, sales had declined to 6.7 million vehicles worldwide and to just over 4 million in North America. In this chapter, we will look at long-run growth and the business cycle and why they are important for individual firms and the economy as a whole. *An Inside Look* on page 286 discusses the growth of the Chinese automobile industry.

➤ A key measure of the success of any economy is its ability to increase production of goods and services faster than the growth in population. Increasing production faster than population growth is the only way that the standard of living of the average person in a country can increase. Unfortunately, many economies around the world are not growing at all, or are growing very slowly. In many countries in sub-Saharan Africa, living standards are barely higher, or in some cases lower, than they were 50 years ago. Most people in these countries live in the same grinding poverty as their ancestors. In the United States and other developed countries, however, living standards increase during most years and are much higher than they were 50 years ago. An important macroeconomic question is why some countries grow much faster than others.

As we will see, one determinant of economic growth is the ability of firms to expand their operations, buy additional equipment, train workers, and adopt new technologies. To carry out these activities, firms must acquire funds from households, either directly through financial markets—such as the stock and bond markets—or indirectly through financial intermediaries—such as banks. Financial markets and financial intermediaries together comprise the *financial system.* In this chapter, we will present an overview of the financial system and see how funds flow from households to firms through the *market for loanable funds.*

Dating back to at least the early nineteenth century, the U.S. economy has experienced periods of expanding production and employment followed by periods of recession during which production and employment decline. As we noted in Chapter 7, these alternating periods of expansion and recession are called the **business cycle.** The business cycle is not uniform: Each period of expansion is not the same length, nor is each period of recession, but every period of expansion in American history has been followed by a period of recession, and every period of recession has been followed by a period of expansion.

Business cycle Alternating periods of economic expansion and economic recession.

In this chapter, we begin the exploration of these two key aspects of macroeconomics—the long-run growth that has steadily raised living standards in the United States and the short-run fluctuations of the business cycle.

① LEARNING OBJECTIVE
Discuss the importance of long-run economic growth.

Long-Run Economic Growth Is the Key to Rising Living Standards

Most people in the United States, Western Europe, Japan, and other advanced countries expect that over time their standard of living will improve. They expect that year after year firms will introduce new and improved products, new prescription drugs and better surgical techniques will overcome more diseases, and their ability to afford these goods and services will increase. For most people, these are reasonable expectations.

In 1900, the United States was already enjoying the highest standard of living in the world. Yet in that year, only 3 percent of U.S. homes had electricity, and only 15 percent had indoor flush toilets. Diseases such as smallpox, typhus, dysentery, and cholera were

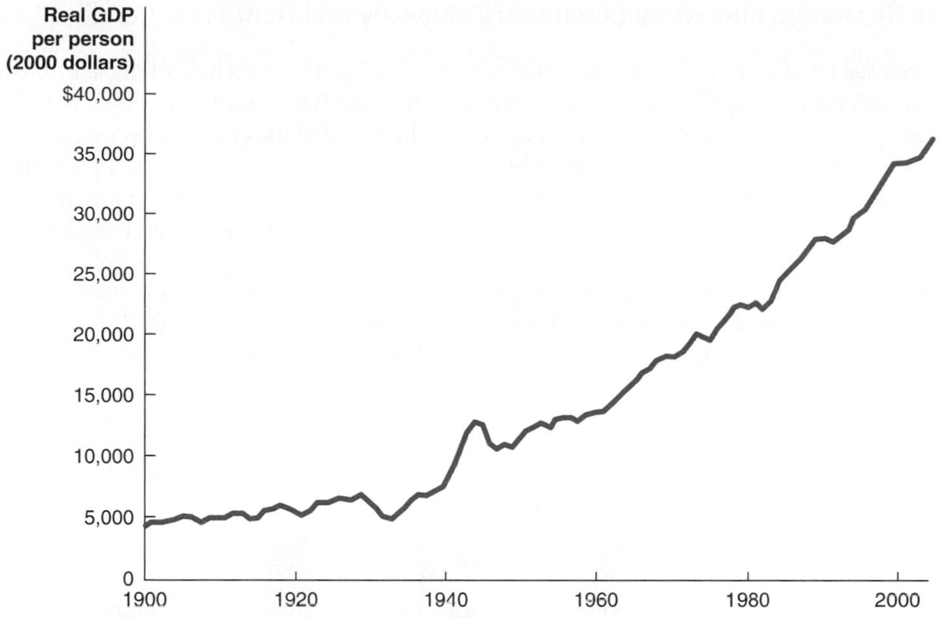

FIGURE 9-1

The Growth in Real GDP per capita, 1900–2004

Measured in 2000 dollars, real GDP per capita in the United States grew from about $4,300 in 1900 to about $37,000 in 2004. The average American in the year 2004 could buy more than eight times as many goods and services as the average American in the year 1900.

Source: Real GDP, 1900–1928: Louis Johnston and Samuel H. Williamson, "The Annual Real and Nominal GDP for the United States, 1789–Present," Economic History Services, March 2004, www.eh.net/hmit/gdp; Real GDP, 1929–2004: U.S. Bureau of Economic Analysis.

still menacing the health of Americans. In 1900, 5,000 of the 45,000 children born in Chicago died before their first birthday. In 1900, there were, of course, no televisions, radios, computers, air conditioners, or refrigerators. Many homes were heated in the winter by burning coal, which contributed to the severe pollution that fouled the air of most large cities. There were no modern appliances, so most women worked inside the home at least 80 hours per week. The typical American homemaker in 1900 baked a half ton of bread per year.

The process of **long-run economic growth** brought the typical American from the standard of living of 1900 to the standard of living of today. The best measure of the standard of living is real GDP per person, which is usually referred to as *real GDP per capita.* So, we measure long-run economic growth by increases in real GDP per capita. We use real GDP rather than nominal GDP to adjust for changes in the price level over time. Figure 9-1 shows the growth in real GDP per capita in the United States from 1900 to 2004.

Long-run economic growth The process by which rising productivity increases the average standard of living.

The values in Figure 9-1 are measured in prices of the year 2000, so they represent constant amounts of purchasing power. In 1900, real GDP per capita was about $4,300. Just over a century later, in 2004, it had risen to about $37,000, which means that the average American in 2004 could purchase more than eight times as many goods and services as the average American in 1900. Large as it is, this increase in real GDP per capita actually understates the true increase in the standard of living of Americans in 2004 compared with 1900. Many of today's goods and services were not available in 1900. For example, if you lived in 1900 and became ill with a serious infection, you would have been unable to purchase antibiotics to treat your illness no matter how high your income. You might have died from an illness for which even a very poor person in today's society could receive effective medical treatment. Of course, the quantity of goods and services that a person can buy is not a perfect measure of how happy or contented that person may be. The level of pollution, the level of crime, spiritual well-being, and many other factors ignored in calculating GDP contribute to a person's happiness. Nevertheless, economists rely heavily on comparisons of real GDP per capita because it is the best means of comparing the performance of one economy over time or the performance of different economies at any particular time.

9-1 Making the Connection

Because of technological advance, these children in India will live longer, be healthier, and work less than their parents and grandparents.

The Connection between Economic Prosperity and Health

We can see the direct impact of economic growth on living standards by looking at improvements in health in the high-income countries over the past 100 years. The research of Robert Fogel, winner of the Nobel Prize in Economics, has highlighted the close connection between economic growth, improvements in technology, and improvements in human physiology. One important measure of health is life expectancy at birth. As the following graph shows, life expectancy in 1900 was less than 50 years in the United States, the United Kingdom, and France. Today, life expectancy is nearly 80 years. Although life expectancies in the lowest-income countries remain very short, some countries that have begun to experience economic growth have seen dramatic increases in life expectancies. For example, life expectancy in India has more than doubled from 27 years in 1900 to 64 years today.

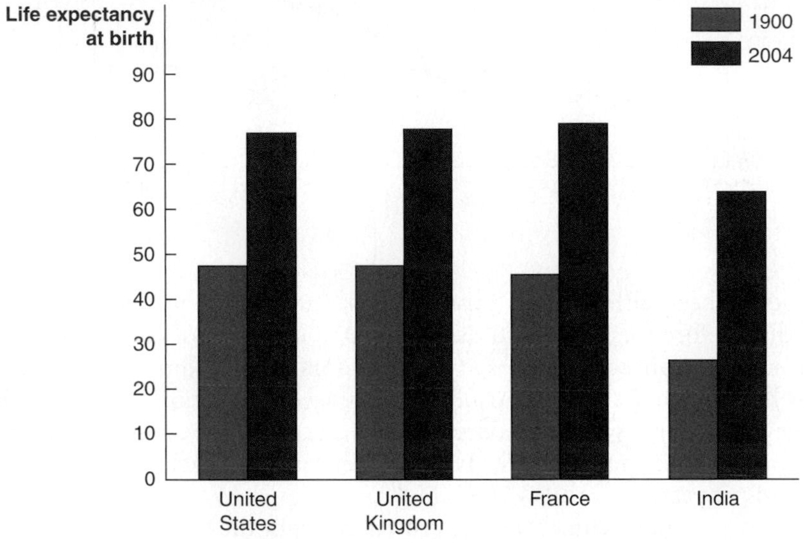

Sources: For 1900: Robert William Fogel, *The Escape from Hunger and Premature Death, 1700–2100,* New York: Cambridge University Press, 2004, p. 2; for 2004: U.S. Central Intelligence Agency, *The World Factbook 2004,* online version.

Many economists believe there is a link between health and economic growth. In the United States and Western Europe during the nineteenth century, improvements in agricultural technology and rising incomes led to dramatic improvements in the nutrition of the average person. The development of the germ theory of disease and technological progress in the purification of water in the late nineteenth century led to sharp declines in sickness from waterborne diseases. As people became taller, stronger, and less susceptible to disease, they also became more productive. Today, economists studying economic development have put increasing emphasis on the need for low-income countries to reduce disease and increase nutrition if they are to experience economic growth.

Many researchers believe that the state of human physiology will continue to improve as technology advances. In the high-income countries, life expectancy at birth is expected to rise from about 80 years today to about 90 years by the middle of the twenty-first century. Technological advance will continue to reduce the average number of hours worked per day and the number of years the average person spends in the paid workforce. Individuals spend about 10 hours per day sleeping, eating, and bathing. Their remaining "discretionary hours" are divided between paid work and leisure. The following graph is based on estimates by Robert Fogel that contrast how individuals in the United States will divide their time in 2040 compared with 1880 and 1995.

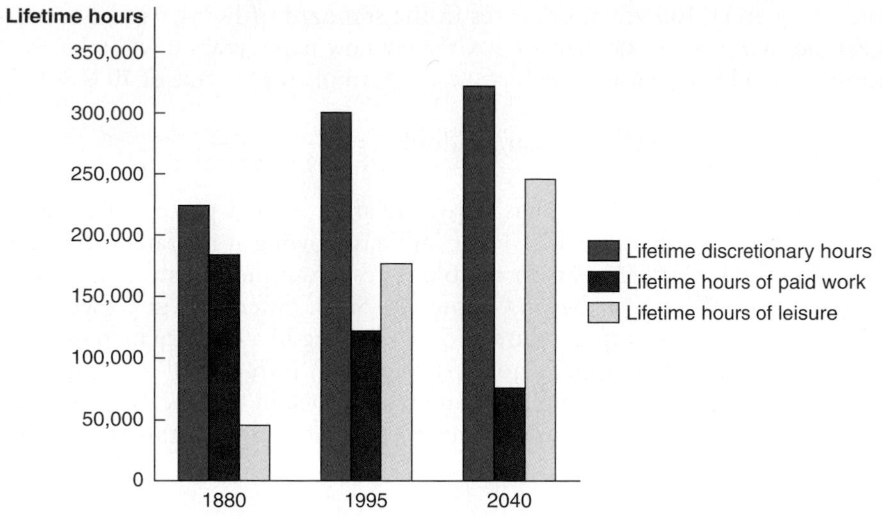

Not only will technology and economic growth allow people in the near future to live longer lives, but a much smaller fraction of those lives will need to be spent at paid work.

Source: Robert William Fogel, *The Escape from Hunger and Premature Death, 1700–2100,* New York: Cambridge University Press, 2004; second graph adapted from Table 4.2, p. 71.

Calculating Growth Rates and the Rule of 70

The growth rate of real GDP or real GDP per capita during a particular year is equal to the percentage change from the previous year. For example, measured in prices of the year 2000, real GDP equaled $10,321 billion in 2003 and rose to $10,756 billion in 2004. We calculate the growth of real GDP in 2004 as:

$$\frac{(\$10{,}756 \text{ bllion} - \$10{,}321 \text{ billion})}{\$10{,}321 \text{ billion}} \times 100 = 4.2\%.$$

For longer periods of time, we can use the *average annual growth rate.* For example, real GDP in the United States was $1,777 billion in 1950 and $10,756 billion in 2004. To find the average annual growth rate during this 54-year period, we compute the growth rate that would result in $1,777 billion growing to $10,756 billion over 54 years. In this case the growth rate is 3.4 percent. That is, if $1,777 billion grows at an average rate of 3.4 percent per year, after 54 years it will have grown to $10,756 billion.

For shorter periods of time, we get approximately the same answer by averaging the growth rate for each year. For example, real GDP in the United States grew by 1.6 percent in 2002, 2.7 percent in 2003, and 4.2 percent in 2004. So, the average annual growth rate of real GDP for the period 2002–2004 was 2.8 percent, which is the average of the three annual growth rates:

$$\frac{1.6\% + 2.7\% + 4.2\%}{3} = 2.8\%.$$

When discussing long-run economic growth, we will usually shorten "average annual growth rate" to "growth rate."

We can judge how rapidly an economic variable is growing by calculating the number of years it would take to double. For example, if real GDP per capita in a country doubles, say, every 20 years, most people in the country will experience significant increases in their standard of living over the course of their lives. If real GDP per capita doubles only every 100 years, increases in the standard of living will be too slow to notice. One easy way to calculate approximately how many years it will take real GDP per capita to double is to use the *rule of 70*. The formula for the rule of 70 is as follows:

$$\text{Number of years to double} = \frac{70}{\text{Growth rate}}.$$

For example, if real GDP per capita is growing at a rate of 5 percent per year, it will double in 70/5 = 14 years. If real GDP per capita is growing at the rate of 2 percent per year, it will take 70/2 = 35 years to double. These examples illustrate an important point that we will discuss further in Chapter 10: Small differences in growth rates can have large effects on how rapidly the standard of living in a country increases. Finally, notice that the rule of 70 applies not just to growth in real GDP per capita but to growth in any variable. For example, if you invest $1,000 in the stock market and your investment grows at an average annual rate of 7 percent, your investment will double to $2,000 in 10 years.

What Determines the Rate of Long-Run Growth?

In Chapter 10, we will explore the sources of economic growth in more detail and discuss why growth in the United States and other high-income countries has been so much faster than growth in poorer countries. For now, we will focus on the basic point that *increases in real GDP per capita depend on increases in labor productivity.* **Labor productivity** is the quantity of goods and services that can be produced by one worker or by one hour of work. In analyzing long-run growth, economists usually measure labor productivity as output per hour of work to avoid fluctuations in the length of the workday and in the fraction of the population employed. If the quantity of goods and services consumed by the average person is to increase, the quantity of goods and services produced per hour of work must also increase. Why in 2004 was the average American able to consume more than eight times as many goods and services as the average American in 1900? Because the average American worker in 2004 was more than eight times as productive as the average American worker in 1900.

Labor productivity The quantity of goods and services that can be produced by one worker or by one hour of work.

If increases in labor productivity are the key to long-run economic growth, what causes labor productivity to increase? Economists believe two key factors determine labor productivity: the quantity of capital per hour worked and the level of technology. Therefore, economic growth occurs if the quantity of capital per hour worked increases and if technological change occurs.

INCREASES IN CAPITAL PER HOUR WORKED Workers today in high-income countries such as the United States have more physical capital available than workers in low-income countries or workers in the high-income countries of a hundred years ago. Recall that **capital** refers to manufactured goods that are used to produce other goods and services. Examples of capital are computers, factory buildings, machine tools, warehouses, and trucks. The total amount of physical capital available in a country is known as the country's *capital stock*.

Capital Manufactured goods that are used to produce other goods and services.

As the capital stock per hour worked increases, worker productivity increases. A secretary with a personal computer can produce more documents per day than a secretary who has only a typewriter. A worker with a backhoe can excavate more earth than a worker who has only a shovel.

Human capital refers to the accumulated knowledge and skills workers acquire from education and training or from their life experiences. For example, workers with a college education generally have more skills and are more productive than workers who have only a high school degree. Increases in human capital are particularly important in stimulating economic growth.

Human capital The accumulated knowledge and skills workers acquire from education and training or from their life experiences.

TECHNOLOGICAL CHANGE Economic growth depends more on *technological change* than on increases in capital per hour worked. Technology refers to the processes a firm uses to turn inputs into outputs of goods and services. Technological change is an increase in the quantity of output firms can produce using a given quantity of inputs. Technological change can come from many sources. For example, a firm's managers may rearrange a factory floor or the layout of a retail store, thereby increasing production and sales. Most technological change, however, is embodied in new machinery, equipment, or software.

A very important point is that just accumulating more inputs—such as labor, capital, and natural resources—will not ensure that an economy experiences economic growth unless technological change also occurs. For example, the Soviet Union failed to maintain a high rate of economic growth, even though it continued to increase the quantity of capital available per hour worked, because it experienced very little technological change.

In implementing technological change, *entrepreneurs* are of crucial importance. Recall from Chapter 2 that an entrepreneur is someone who operates a business, bringing together the factors of production—labor, capital, and natural resources—to produce goods and services. In a market economy, entrepreneurs make the crucial decisions about whether or not to introduce new technology to produce better or lower-cost products. Entrepreneurs also decide whether to allocate the firm's resources to research and development that can result in new technologies. One of the difficulties centrally planned economies have in sustaining economic growth is that managers employed by the government are usually much slower to develop and adopt new technologies than entrepreneurs in a market system.

SOLVED PROBLEM 9-1

The Role of Technological Change in Growth

(1) LEARNING OBJECTIVE
Discuss the importance of long-run economic growth.

Between 1960 and 1995, real GDP per capita in Singapore grew at an average annual rate of 6.2 percent. This very rapid growth rate results in the level of real GDP per capita doubling about every 11.5 years. In 1995, Alywn Young of the University of Chicago published an article in which he argued that Singapore's growth depended more on increases in capital per hour worked, increases in the labor force participation rate, and the transfer of workers from agricultural to nonagricultural jobs than on technological change. If Young's analysis was correct, predict what was likely to happen to Singapore's growth rate in the years after 1995.

Solving the Problem:

Step 1: Review the chapter material. This problem is about the determinants of the rate of long-run growth, so you may want to review the section "What Determines the Rate of Long-Run Growth?" which begins on page 266.

Step 2: Predict what happened to the growth rate in Singapore after 1995. As countries begin to develop, they often experience an increase in the labor force participation rate, as workers who are not part of the paid labor force respond to rising wage rates. Many workers also leave the agricultural sector—where output per hour worked is often low—for the nonagricultural sector. These changes will increase real GDP per capita, but they are "one-shot" changes that eventually will come to an end, as the labor force participation rate and the fraction of the labor force outside of agriculture both approach the levels found in high-income countries. Similarly, as we already noted, increases in capital per hour worked cannot sustain high rates of economic growth, unless accompanied by technological change.

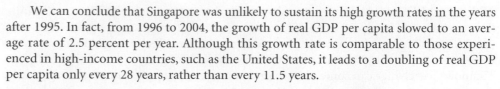

We can conclude that Singapore was unlikely to sustain its high growth rates in the years after 1995. In fact, from 1996 to 2004, the growth of real GDP per capita slowed to an average rate of 2.5 percent per year. Although this growth rate is comparable to those experienced in high-income countries, such as the United States, it leads to a doubling of real GDP per capita only every 28 years, rather than every 11.5 years.

Source: Alwyn Young, "The Tyranny of Numbers: Confronting the Statistical Realities of the East Asian Growth Experience," *Quarterly Journal of Economics*, Vol. 110, No. 3 (August 1995), pp. 641–680.

YOUR TURN: **For more practice, do related problem 8 on page 289 at the end of this chapter.**

Finally, an additional requirement for economic growth is that the government provides secure rights to private property. As we saw in Chapter 2, a market system cannot function unless rights to private property are secure. In addition, the government can help the market work and aid economic growth by establishing an independent court system that enforces contracts between private individuals. Many economists would also say the government has a role in facilitating the development of an efficient financial system, as well as systems of education, transportation, and communication. Economist Richard Sylla of New York University has argued that every country that has experienced economic growth first experienced a "financial revolution." For example, before the United States was able to experience significant economic growth in the early nineteenth century, the country's banking and monetary systems were reformed under the guidance of Alexander Hamilton, the first Secretary of the Treasury. Without supportive government policies, long-run economic growth is unlikely.

9-2 Making the Connection

Firms like the Botswana Meat Company benefit from government policies that protect private property.

What Explains Rapid Economic Growth in Botswana?

Economic growth in much of sub-Saharan Africa has been very slow. As desperately poor as most of these countries were in 1960, some are even poorer today. Growth rates in one country in this region stand out, however, as being exceptionally rapid. The graph on the facing page shows the average annual growth rate in real GDP per capita between 1960 and 2000 for Botswana and the six most populous sub-Saharan countries. Botswana's average annual growth rate over this 40-year period was almost five times as great as that of Kenya, which was the second-fastest-growing country in the group.

What explains Botswana's rapid growth rate? Several factors have been important. Botswana avoided the civil wars that plagued other African countries during these years. The country also benefited from earnings from diamond exports. But many economists believe the pro-growth policies of its government are the most important reason for the country's success. Economists Shantayanan Devarajan of the World Bank, William Easterly of New York University, and Howard Pack of the University of Pennsylvania have summarized these policies:

> The government [of Botswana] made it clear it would protect private property rights. It was a "government of cattlemen" who were attuned to commercial interests. . . . The relative political stability and relatively low corruption also made Botswana a favorable location for investment. Botswana's relatively high level of press freedom and democracy (continuing a pre-colonial tradition that held chiefs responsible to tribal members) held the government responsible for any economic policy mistakes.

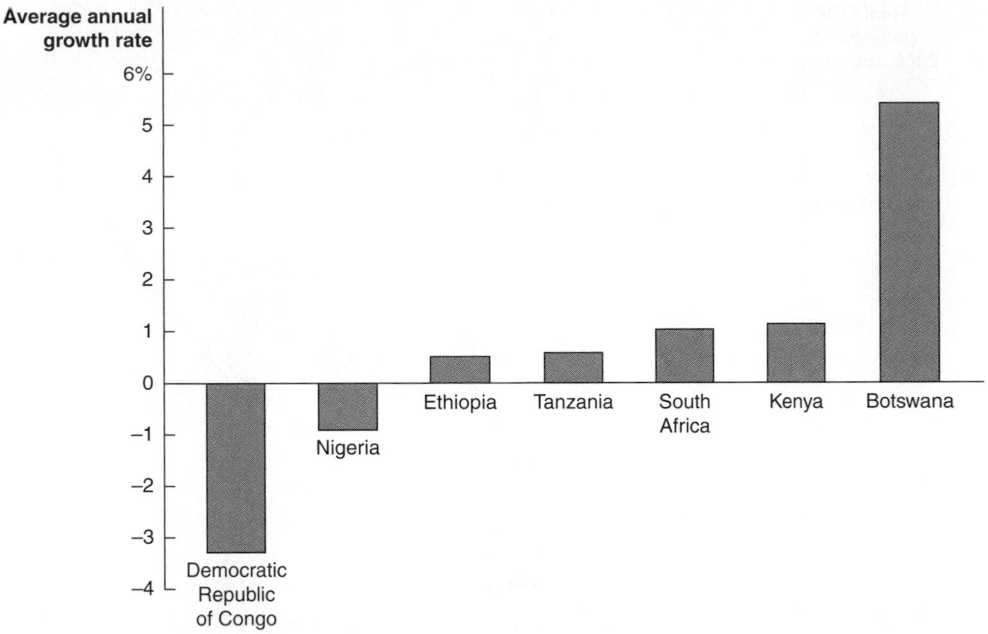

Source: Authors' calculations from data in Alan Heston, Robert Summers, and Bettina Aten, Penn World Table Version 6.1, Center for International Comparisons at the University of Pennsylvania (CICUP), October 2002.

These policies—protecting private property, avoiding political instability and corruption, and allowing press freedom and democracy—may seem a straightforward recipe for providing an environment in which economic growth can occur. As we will see in Chapter 10, however, in practice, these are policies many countries have difficulty implementing successfully.

Source: Shantayanan Devarajan, William Easterly, and Howard Pack, "Low Investment Is Not the Constraint on African Development," *Economic Development and Cultural Change*, Vol. 51, No. 3 (April 2003), pp. 547–571.

Potential Real GDP

Potential GDP The level of GDP attained when all firms are producing at capacity.

Because economists take a long-run perspective in discussing economic growth, the concept of *potential GDP* is useful. **Potential GDP** is the level of GDP attained when all firms are producing at capacity. Every firm has a certain capacity to produce goods and services. The capacity of a firm is *not* the maximum output the firm is capable of producing. A Ford assembly plant could operate 24 hours per day for 52 weeks per year and would be at its maximum production level. The plant's capacity, however, is measured by its production when operating on normal hours, using a normal workforce. If all firms in the economy were operating at capacity, the level of total production of final goods and services would equal potential GDP. As the labor force grows over time, new factories and office buildings are built, new machinery and equipment are installed, and technological change takes place, and potential GDP will increase.

Growth in potential real GDP is estimated to be about 3.5 percent per year. In other words, each year the capacity of the economy to produce final goods and services expands by 3.5 percent. The *actual* level of GDP may increase by more or less than 3.5 percent as the economy moves through the business cycle. Figure 9-2 shows movements in actual and potential real GDP for the years since 1950. The smooth light blue line represents potential real GDP and the dark blue line represents actual real GDP.

FIGURE 9-2

Actual and Potential Real GDP

Potential real GDP increases every year as the labor force and the capital stock grow and technological change occurs. The smooth light blue line represents potential real GDP and the dark blue line represents actual real GDP. Because of the business cycle, actual real GDP has sometimes been greater than potential real GDP and sometimes less.

Sources: Potential GDP: Congressional Budget Office, "Spreadsheets for Selected Estimates and Projections," January 2005; Real GDP: Bureau of Economic Analysis.

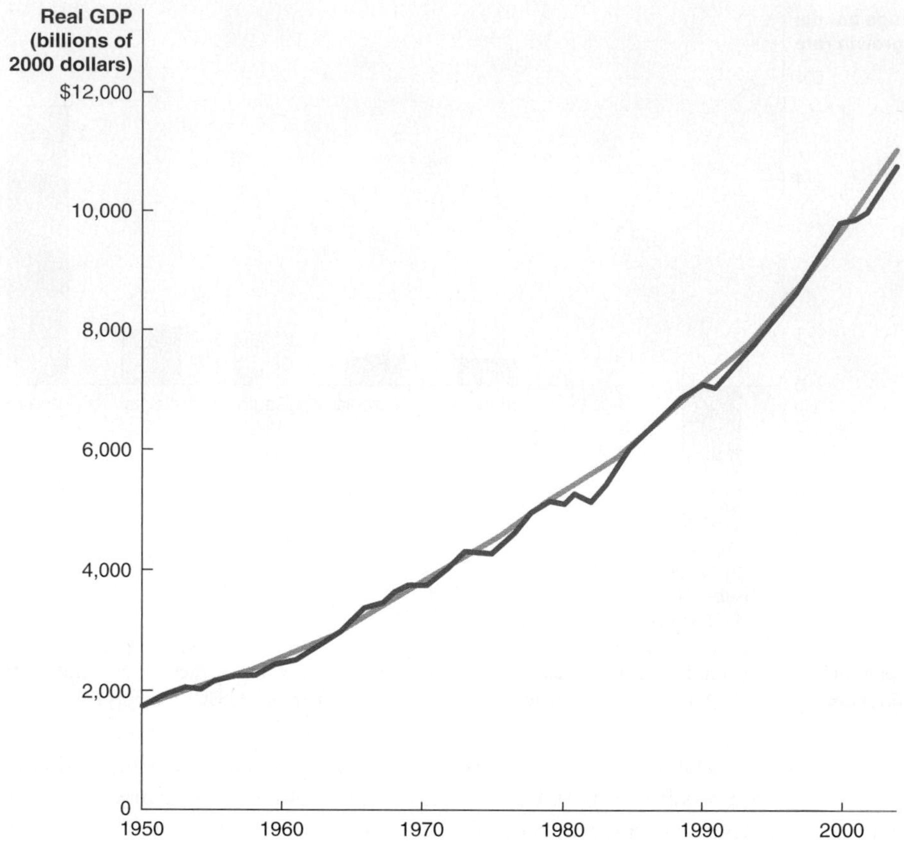

② LEARNING OBJECTIVE

Discuss the role of the financial system in facilitating long-run economic growth.

Saving, Investment, and the Financial System

The process of economic growth depends on the ability of firms to expand their operations, buy additional equipment, train workers, and adopt new technologies. Firms can finance some of these activities from *retained earnings,* which are profits that are reinvested in the firm rather than taken out of the firm and paid to the firm's owners. For many firms, retained earnings are not sufficient to finance the rapid expansion required in economies experiencing high rates of economic growth. Firms acquire funds from households, either directly through financial markets—such as the stock and bond markets—or indirectly through financial intermediaries—such as banks. Financial markets and financial intermediaries together comprise the **financial system.** Without a well-functioning financial system, economic growth is impossible because firms will be unable to expand and adopt new technologies. As we noted earlier, no country without a well-developed financial system has been able to sustain high levels of economic growth.

Financial system The system of financial markets and financial intermediaries through which firms acquire funds from households.

An Overview of the Financial System

The financial system channels funds from savers to borrowers and channels returns on the borrowed funds back to savers. Recall from Chapter 5 that in *financial markets,* such as the stock market or the bond market, firms raise funds by selling financial securities directly to savers. A financial security is a document—sometimes in electronic form—that states the terms under which funds pass from the buyer of the security—who is lending funds—to the seller. *Stocks* are financial securities that represent partial ownership of a firm. If you buy one share of stock in General Electric, you become one of millions of owners of that firm. *Bonds* are financial securities that represent promises to repay a fixed amount of funds. When General Electric sells a bond, the firm promises to pay the purchaser of the bond an interest payment each year for the term of the bond, as well as a final payment of the amount of the loan.

Financial intermediaries, such as banks, mutual funds, pension funds, and insurance companies, act as go-betweens for borrowers and lenders. When you deposit funds in your checking account, the bank may lend the funds (together with the funds of other savers) to an entrepreneur who wants to start a business. Suppose Lena wants to open a laundry. Rather than you lending money directly to Lena's Laundry, the bank acts as a go-between for you and Lena. Intermediaries pool the funds of many small savers to lend to many individual borrowers. The intermediaries pay interest to savers in exchange for the use of savers' funds and earn a profit by lending money to borrowers and charging borrowers a higher rate of interest on the loans. For example, a bank might pay you as a depositor a 3 percent rate of interest, while it lends the money to Lena's Laundry at a 6 percent rate of interest.

Banks, mutual funds, pension funds, and insurance companies also make investments in stocks and bonds on behalf of savers. For example, *mutual funds* sell shares to savers and then use the funds to buy a portfolio of stocks, bonds, mortgages, and other financial securities. Mutual funds are either closed-end or open-end funds. In closed-end mutual funds, the mutual fund company issues shares that investors may buy and sell in financial markets, like shares of stock issued by corporations. More common are open-end mutual funds, which issue shares that the mutual fund company will buy back—or redeem—at a price that reflects the underlying value of the financial securities owned by the fund. Large mutual fund companies, such as Fidelity, Vanguard, and Dreyfus, offer many alternative stock and bond funds. Some funds hold a wide range of stocks or bonds; others specialize in securities issued by a particular industry or sector, such as technology; and others invest as an index fund in a fixed market basket of securities such as shares of the Standard and Poor's 500 firms. Over the past 30 years, the role of mutual funds in the financial system has increased dramatically. By 2005, competition among hundreds of mutual fund firms gave investors thousands of funds from which to choose.

In addition to matching households that have excess funds with firms that want to borrow funds, the financial system provides three key services for savers and borrowers: risk sharing, liquidity, and information. *Risk* is the chance that the value of a financial security will change relative to what you expect. For example, you may buy a share of stock in Google at a price of $100, only to have the price fall to $20. Most individual savers are not gamblers and seek a steady return on their savings rather than erratic swings between high and low earnings. The financial system provides risk sharing by allowing savers to spread their money among many financial investments. For example, you can divide your money among a bank certificate of deposit, individual bonds, and a mutual fund.

Liquidity is the ease with which a financial security can be exchanged for money. The financial system provides the service of liquidity by providing savers with markets in which they can sell their holdings of financial securities. For example, savers can easily sell their holdings of the stocks and bonds issued by large corporations on the major stock and bond markets.

A third service that the financial system provides savers is the collection and communication of *information,* or facts about borrowers and expectations about returns on financial securities. For example, Lena's Laundry may want to borrow $10,000 from you. Finding out what Lena intends to do with the funds and how likely she is to pay you back may be costly and time-consuming. By depositing $10,000 in the bank, you are, in effect, allowing the bank to gather this information for you. Because banks specialize in gathering information on borrowers, they are able to do it faster and at a lower cost than can individual savers. The financial system plays an important role in communicating information. If you read a newspaper headline announcing that an automobile firm has invented a car with an engine that runs on water, how would you determine the effect of this discovery on the firm's profits? Financial markets do that job for you by incorporating information into the prices of stocks, bonds, and other financial securities. In this example, the expectation of higher future profits would boost the prices of the automobile firm's stock and bonds.

The Macroeconomics of Saving and Investment

As we have seen, the funds available to firms through the financial system come from saving. When firms use funds to purchase machinery, factories, and office buildings, they are engaging in investment. In this section, we explore the macroeconomics of saving and investment. A key point we will develop is that *the total value of saving in the economy must equal the total value of investment.* We saw in Chapter 7 that *national income accounting* refers to the methods the Bureau of Economic Analysis uses to keep track of total production and total income in the economy. We can use some relationships from national income accounting to understand why total saving must equal total investment.

We begin with the relationship between GDP and its components, consumption (C), investment (I), government purchases (G), and net exports (NX):

$$Y = C + I + G + NX.$$

Remember that GDP is a measure of both total production in the economy and total income.

In an *open economy*, there is interaction with other economies in terms of both trading of goods and services and borrowing and lending. All economies today are open economies, although they vary significantly in the extent of their openness. In a *closed economy*, there is no trading or borrowing and lending with other economies. For simplicity, we will develop the relationship between saving and investment for a closed economy. This allows us to focus on the most important points in a simpler framework. We will consider the case of an open economy in Chapter 17.

In a closed economy, net exports are zero, so we can rewrite the relationship between GDP and its components as:

$$Y = C + I + G.$$

If we rearrange this relationship, we have an expression for investment in terms of the other variables:

$$I = Y - C - G.$$

This expression tells us that in a closed economy investment spending is equal to total income minus consumption spending and minus government purchases.

We can also derive an expression for total saving. *Private saving* is equal to what households retain of their income after purchasing goods and services (C) and paying taxes (T). Households receive income for supplying the factors of production to firms. This portion of household income is equal to Y. Households also receive income from government in the form of transfer payments (TR). Recall that transfer payments include Social Security payments and unemployment insurance payments. We can write an expression for private saving (S_{private}):

$$S_{\text{private}} = Y + TR - C - T.$$

The government also engages in saving. *Public saving* (S_{public}) equals the amount of tax revenue the government retains after paying for government purchases and making transfer payments to households:

$$S_{\text{public}} = T - G - TR.$$

So, total saving in the economy (S) is equal to the sum of private saving and public saving:

$$S = S_{\text{private}} + S_{\text{public}},$$

or,

$$S = (Y + TR - C - T) + (T - G - TR)$$

or,

$$S = Y - C - G.$$

The right-hand side of this expression is identical to the expression we derived earlier for investment spending. So, we can conclude that total saving must equal total investment:

$$S = I.$$

When the government spends the same amount that it collects in taxes, there is a *balanced budget.* When the government spends more than it collects in taxes, there is a *budget deficit.* In the case of a deficit, T is less than $G + TR$, which means that public saving is negative. Negative saving is also known as *dissaving.* How can public saving be negative? When the federal government runs a budget deficit, the U.S. Department of the Treasury sells Treasury bonds to borrow the money necessary to fund the gap between taxes and spending. In this case, rather than adding to the total amount of saving available to be borrowed for investment spending, the government is subtracting from it. (Notice that if households borrow more than they save, the total amount of saving will also fall.) With less saving, investment must also be lower. We can conclude that, holding constant all other factors, there is a lower level of investment spending in the economy when there is a budget deficit than when there is a balanced budget.

When the government spends less than it collects in taxes, there is a *budget surplus.* A budget surplus increases public saving and the total level of saving in the economy. A higher level of saving results in a higher level of investment spending. Therefore, holding constant all other factors, there is a higher level of investment spending in the economy when there is a budget surplus than when there is a balanced budget.

The U.S. federal government has experienced dramatic swings in the state of its budget over the past 15 years. In 1992, the federal budget deficit was $297.4 billion. This figure changed to a surplus of $189.5 billion in 2000 and back to a deficit of $406.5 billion in 2004.

The Market for Loanable Funds

We have seen that value of total saving must equal the value of total investment, but we have not yet discussed how this equality actually is brought about in the financial system. We can think of the financial system as being comprised of many markets through which funds flow from lenders to borrowers: the market for certificates of deposit at banks, the market for stocks, the market for bonds, the market for mutual fund shares, and so on. For simplicity, we can combine these markets into a single market for *loanable funds.* In the model of the **market for loanable funds,** the interaction of borrowers and lenders determines the market interest rate and the quantity of loanable funds exchanged. As we will discuss in Chapter 17, firms can also borrow from savers in other countries. For the remainder of this chapter, we will assume there are no interactions between households and firms in the United States and those in other countries.

Market for loanable funds The interaction of borrowers and lenders that determines the market interest rate and the quantity of loanable funds exchanged.

DEMAND AND SUPPLY IN THE LOANABLE FUNDS MARKET The demand for loanable funds is determined by the willingness of firms to borrow money to engage in new investment projects, such as building new factories or engaging in research and development of new products. In determining whether or not to borrow funds, firms compare the return they expect to make on an investment with the interest rate they must pay to borrow the necessary funds. For example, if Home Depot is considering opening several new stores and expects to earn a return of 15 percent on its investment, the investment will be profitable if it can borrow the funds at an interest rate of 10 percent but will not be profitable if the interest rate is 20 percent. In Figure 9-3, the demand for loanable funds is downward sloping because the lower the interest rate, the more investment projects firms can profitably undertake, and the greater the quantity of loanable funds they will demand.

The supply of loanable funds is determined by the willingness of households to save and by the extent of government saving or dissaving. When households save, they reduce the amount of goods and services they can consume and enjoy today. The

FIGURE 9-3

The Market for Loanable Funds

The demand for loanable funds is determined by the willingness of firms to borrow money to engage in new investment projects. The supply of loanable funds is determined by the willingness of households to save, and by the extent of government saving or dissaving. Equilibrium in the market for loanable funds determines the real interest rate and the quantity of loanable funds exchanged.

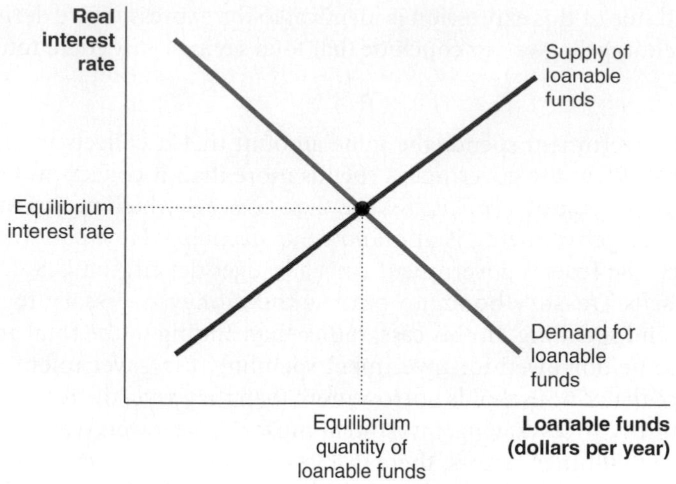

willingness of households to save rather than consume their incomes today will be determined in part by the interest rate they receive when they lend their savings. The higher the interest rate, the greater the reward to saving and the larger the amount of funds households will save. Therefore, the supply curve for loanable funds in Figure 9-3 is upward sloping to reflect the fact that the higher the interest rate, the greater the quantity of saving supplied.

In Chapter 8, we discussed the distinction between the *nominal interest rate* and the *real interest rate.* The nominal interest rate is the stated interest rate on a loan. The real interest rate corrects the nominal interest rate for the impact of inflation and is equal to the nominal interest rate minus the inflation rate. Because both borrowers and lenders are interested in the real interest rate they will receive or pay, equilibrium in the market for loanable funds determines the real interest rate rather than the nominal interest rate.

9-3 Making the Connection

Who was better for economic growth: Scrooge the saver or Scrooge the spender?

Ebenezer Scrooge: Accidental Promoter of Economic Growth?

Ebenezer Scrooge's name has become synonymous with miserliness. Before his reform at the end of Charles Dickens's *A Christmas Carol,* Scrooge is extraordinarily reluctant to spend money. Although he earns a substantial income, he lives in a cold, dark house that he refuses to heat or light properly, and he eats a meager diet of gruel because he refuses to buy more expensive food. Throughout most of the book, Dickens portrays Scrooge's behavior in an unfavorable way. Only at the end of the book, when the reformed Scrooge begins to spend lavishly on himself and others, does Dickens praise his behavior.

As economist Steven Landsburg of the University of Rochester points out, however, economically speaking it may be the pre-reform Scrooge who is more worthy of praise:

> In this whole world, there is nobody more generous than the miser—the man who *could* deplete the world's resources but chooses not to. The only difference between miserliness and philanthropy is that the philanthropist serves a favored few while the miser spreads his largess far and wide.

We can extend Landsburg's discussion to consider whether the actions of the pre-reform Scrooge or the actions of the post-reform Scrooge were more helpful to economic growth. Pre-reform Scrooge spends very little, investing most of his income in the financial markets. These funds became available for firms to borrow to build new factories and carry out research and development. Post-reform Scrooge spends much more—and saves much less. Funds that he had previously saved are now spent on food for Bob

Cratchit's family and on "making merry" at Christmas. In other words, the actions of post-reform Scrooge contributed to more consumption goods being produced and fewer investment goods. We can conclude that Scrooge's reform caused economic growth to slow down—if only by a little. The larger point is, of course, that savers provide the funds that are indispensable for the investment spending that economic growth requires, and the only way to save is to not consume.

Source: Steven E. Landsburg, "What I Like About Scrooge," *Slate,* December 9, 2004.

EXPLAINING MOVEMENTS IN SAVING, INVESTMENT, AND INTEREST RATES Equilibrium in the market for loanable funds determines the quantity of loanable funds that will flow from lenders to borrowers each period. It also determines the real interest rate that lenders will receive and that borrowers must pay. We draw the demand curve for loanable funds by holding constant all factors, other than the interest rate, that affect the willingness of borrowers to demand funds. We draw the supply curve by holding constant all factors, other than the interest rate, that affect the willingness of lenders to supply funds. A shift in either the demand curve or the supply curve will change the equilibrium interest rate and the equilibrium quantity of loanable funds.

Suppose, for example, that the profitability of new investment increases due to technological change. Firms will increase their demand for loanable funds. Figure 9-4 shows the impact of an increase in demand in the market for loanable funds. As in the markets for goods and services we studied in Chapter 3, an increase in demand in the market for loanable funds shifts the demand curve to the right. In the new equilibrium, the interest rate increases from i_1 to i_2, and the equilibrium quantity of loanable funds increases from L_1 to L_2. Notice that an increase in the quantity of loanable funds means that both the quantity of saving by households and the quantity of investment by firms have increased. Increasing investment increases the capital stock and the quantity of capital per hour worked, helping to increase economic growth.

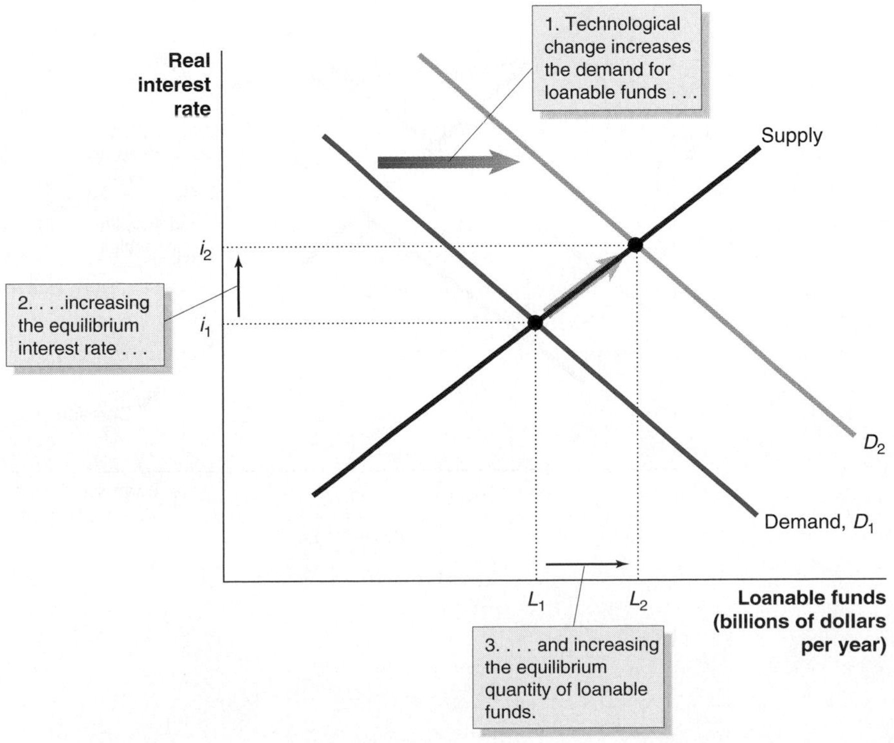

FIGURE 9-4

An Increase in the Demand for Loanable Funds

An increase in the demand for loanable funds increases the equilibrium interest rate from i_1 to i_2, and it increases the equilibrium quantity of loanable funds from L_1 to L_2. As a result, saving and investment both increase.

We can also use the market for loanable funds to examine the impact of a government budget deficit. Putting aside the effects of foreign saving—which we will consider in Chapter 17—recall that if the government begins running a budget deficit, it reduces the total amount of saving in the economy. We illustrate this in Figure 9-5 by shifting the supply of loanable funds to the left. In the new equilibrium, the interest rate is higher and the equilibrium quantity of loanable funds is lower. Running a deficit has reduced the level of total saving in the economy and, by increasing the interest rate, has also reduced the level of investment spending by firms. By borrowing to finance its budget deficit, the government will have *crowded out* some firms that would otherwise have been able to borrow to finance investment. Lower investment spending means that the capital stock and the quantity of capital per hour worked will not increase as much.

A government budget surplus would have the opposite effect to a deficit. A budget surplus increases the total amount of saving in the economy, shifting the supply of loanable funds to the right. In the new equilibrium, the interest rate will be lower and the quantity of loanable funds will be higher. We can conclude that a budget surplus increases the level of saving and investment.

In practice, however, the impact of government budget deficits and surpluses on the equilibrium interest rate is relatively small. (This finding reflects in part the importance of global saving in determining the interest rate.) For example, a recent study found that increasing government borrowing by an amount equal to 1 percent of GDP would increase the equilibrium real interest rate by only about three one-hundredths of a percentage point. However, this small effect on interest rates does not imply that we can ignore the effect of deficits on economic growth. Paying off government debt in the future may require higher taxes, which can depress economic growth.

FIGURE 9-5

The Effect of a Budget Deficit on the Market for Loanable Funds

When the government begins running a budget deficit, the supply of loanable funds shifts to the left. The equilibrium interest rate increases from i_1 to i_2, and the equilibrium quantity of loanable funds falls from L_1 to L_2. As a result, saving and investment both decline.

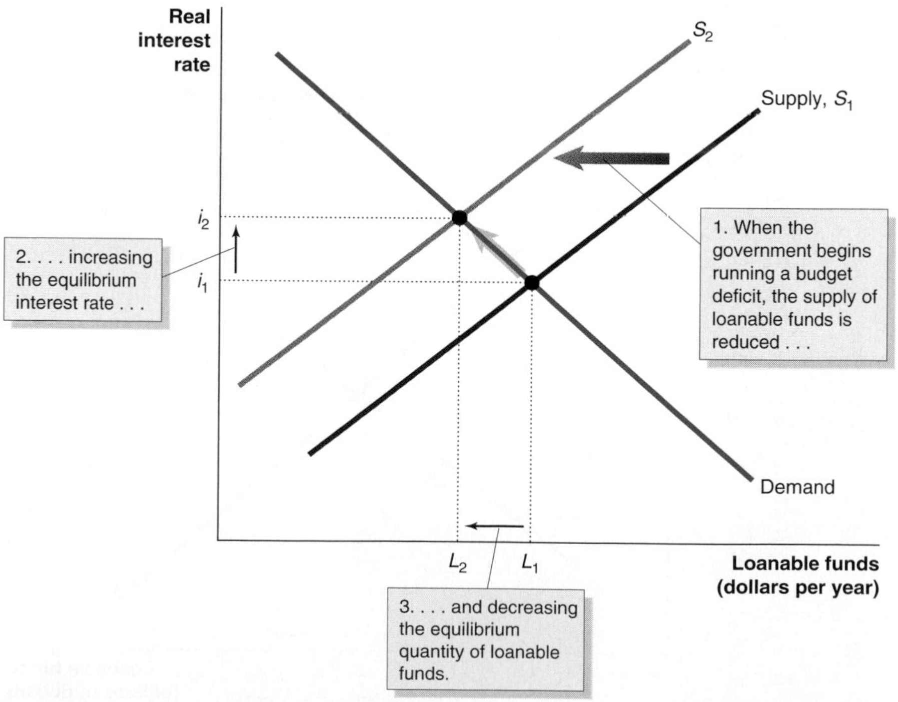

SOLVED PROBLEM 9-2

How Would a Consumption Tax Affect Saving, Investment, the Interest Rate, and Economic Growth?

(2) LEARNING OBJECTIVE

Discuss the role of the financial system in facilitating long-run economic growth.

Some economists and policymakers have suggested that the federal government shift from relying on an income tax to relying on a *consumption tax.* Under the income tax, households pay taxes on all income earned. Under a consumption tax, households pay taxes only on the income they spend. Households would pay taxes on saved income only if they spend the money at a later time. Use the market for loanable funds model to analyze the effect on saving, investment, the interest rate, and economic growth of switching from an income tax to a consumption tax.

Solving the Problem:

Step 1: Review the chapter material. This problem is about applying the market for loanable funds model, so you may want to review the section "Explaining Movements in Saving, Investment, and Interest Rates," which begins on page 275.

Step 2: Explain the effect of switching from an income tax to a consumption tax. Households are interested in the return they receive from saving after they have paid their taxes. For example, consider someone who puts his savings in a certificate of deposit at an interest rate of 4 percent and whose tax rate is 25 percent. Under an income tax, this person's after-tax return to saving is 3 percent $[4 \times (1 - 0.25)]$. Under a consumption tax, income that is saved is not taxed, so the return rises to 4 percent. We can conclude that moving from an income tax to a consumption tax would increase the return to saving, causing the supply of loanable funds to increase.

Step 3: Draw a graph of the market for loanable funds to illustrate your answer. The supply curve for loanable funds will shift to the right as the after-tax return to saving increases under the consumption tax. The equilibrium interest rate will fall, and the levels of saving and investment will both increase. Because investment increases, the capital stock and the quantity of capital per hour worked will grow and the rate of economic growth should increase. Note that the size of the fall in the interest rate and the increase in loanable funds shown in the graph are larger than the effects that most economists expect would actually result from the replacement of the income tax with a consumption tax.

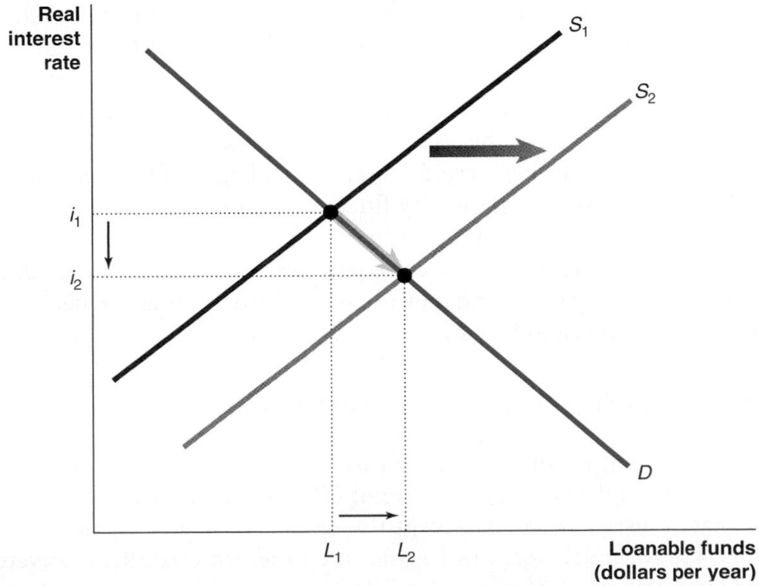

YOUR TURN: **For more practice, do related problem 18 on page 291 at the end of this chapter.**

FIGURE 9-6

Movements in Real GDP, 1998–2004

The expansion that began in 1991 continued through the late 1990s until a business cycle peak was reached in March 2001. The following recession, marked by the shaded vertical bar, was fairly short and a business cycle trough was reached in November 2001, when the next expansion began.

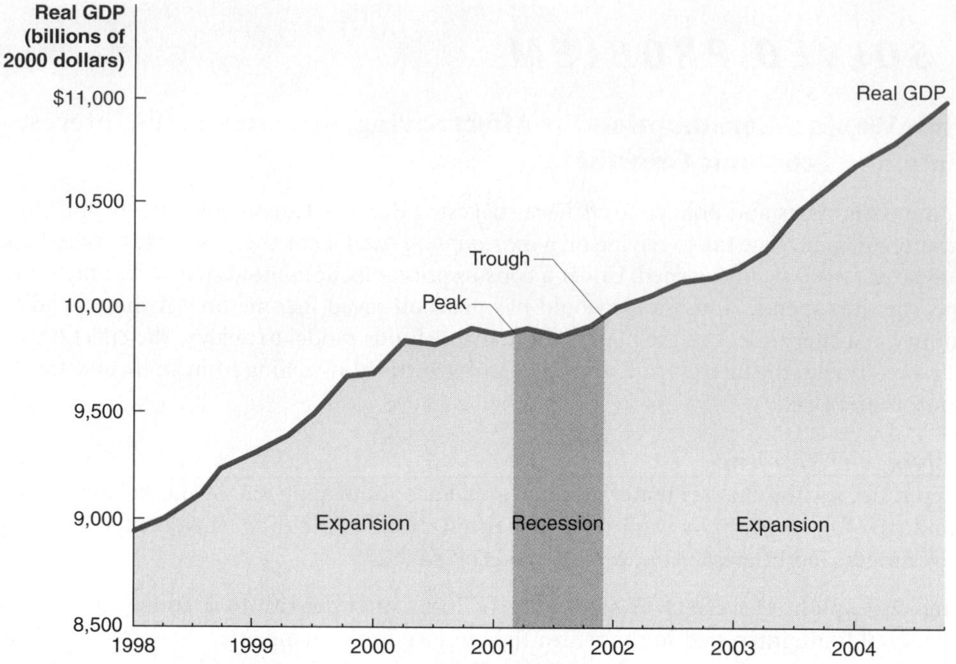

③ LEARNING OBJECTIVE

Explain what happens during a business cycle.

The Business Cycle

Figure 9-1 on page 263 showed the tremendous increase during the last century in the standard of living of the average American. But close inspection of the figure reveals that real GDP per capita did not increase every year during this century. For example, during the first half of the 1930s, real GDP per capita *fell* for several years in a row. What accounts for these fluctuations in the long-run upward trend?

Some Basic Business Cycle Definitions

The fluctuations in real GDP per capita shown in Figure 9-1 reflect the underlying fluctuations in real GDP. Dating back at least to the early nineteenth century, the U.S. economy has experienced a business cycle, consisting of alternating periods of expanding and contracting economic activity. Because real GDP is our best measure of economic activity, the business cycle is usually illustrated using movements in real GDP.

During the *expansion phase* of the business cycle, production, employment, and income are increasing. The period of expansion ends with a *business cycle peak.* Following the business cycle peak, production, employment, and income decline as the economy enters the *recession phase* of the cycle. The recession comes to an end with a *business cycle trough,* after which another period of expansion begins. Figure 9-6 illustrates the phases of the business cycle as shown by fluctuations in real GDP during the period from 1998 to 2004. The figure shows that the expansion that began in 1991 continued through the late 1990s until a business cycle peak was reached in March 2001. The following recession was fairly short and a business cycle trough was reached in November 2001, when the next expansion began.

9-4 Making the Connection

Who Decides If the Economy Is in a Recession?

The federal government produces many statistics that make it possible to monitor the economy, but the federal government does not officially decide when a recession begins or ends. Instead, most economists accept the decisions of the Business Cycle Dating Committee of the National Bureau of Economic Research (NBER), a private research group located in Cambridge, Massachusetts. Although writers for newspapers and magazines often define a recession as two consecutive quarters of declining real GDP, the

NBER has the following broader definition:

> A recession is a significant decline in activity spread across the economy, lasting more than a few months, visible in industrial production, employment, real income, and wholesale-retail trade.

The National Bureau of Economic Research determines when recessions begin and end.

The Business Cycle Dating Committee decided that the U.S. economy had reached a business cycle peak in March 2001 and a business cycle trough in November 2001.

The NBER is fairly slow in announcing business cycle dates because it takes time to gather and analyze economic statistics. Typically, the NBER will announce that the economy is in a recession only well after the recession has begun. For instance, the NBER did not announce that a recession had begun in March 2001 until nearly eight months later at the end of November. November was the same month that the NBER subsequently decided that the recession had ended, but it did not make this announcement until July 2003. Similarly, the NBER did not announce that a recession had begun in July 1990 until April 1991, one month after the recession had actually ended. Nonetheless, policymakers look to the NBER to chronicle the economy's expansions and contractions.

The following table lists the business cycle peaks and troughs identified by the NBER for the years since 1950. The length of each recession is the number of months from the peak to the following trough:

PEAK	TROUGH	LENGTH OF RECESSION
July 1953	May 1954	10 months
August 1957	April 1958	8 months
April 1960	February 1961	10 months
December 1969	November 1970	11 months
November 1973	March 1975	16 months
January 1980	July 1980	6 months
July 1981	November 1982	16 months
July 1990	March 1991	8 months
March 2001	November 2001	8 months

Source: *NBER Reporter*, Fall 2001, and NBER Web site (www.nber.org) for business cycle dates.

What Happens during a Business Cycle?

Each business cycle is different. The lengths of the expansion and recession phases and which sectors of the economy are most affected will rarely be the same in any two cycles. But most business cycles share certain characteristics, which we will discuss in this section. As the economy nears the end of an expansion, interest rates usually are rising, and the wages of workers usually are rising faster than prices. As a result of rising interest rates and rising wages, the profits of firms will be falling. Typically, toward the end of an expansion both households and firms will have substantially increased their debts. These debts are the result of the borrowing firms and households undertake to help finance their spending during the expansion.

A recession will often begin with a decline in spending by firms on capital goods, such as machinery, equipment, new factories, and new office buildings, or by households on new houses and consumer durables, such as furniture and automobiles. As spending declines, firms selling capital goods and consumer durables will find their sales declining. As sales decline, firms cut back on production and begin to lay off workers. Rising unemployment and falling profits reduce income, which leads to further declines in spending.

As the recession continues, economic conditions gradually begin to improve. The declines in spending eventually come to an end; households and firms begin to reduce their debt, thereby increasing their ability to spend; and interest rates decline, making it more likely that households and firms will borrow to finance new spending. Firms begin to increase their spending on capital goods as they anticipate the need for additional production during the next expansion. Increased spending by households on consumer durables and by businesses on capital goods will finally bring the recession to an end and begin the next expansion.

THE EFFECT OF THE BUSINESS CYCLE ON AUTOMOBILE PRODUCTION Durables are goods that are expected to last for three or more years, such as furniture, appliances, and automobiles. Consumer durables are affected more by the business cycle than are nondurables—such as food and clothing—or services—such as haircuts and medical care. During a recession, workers reduce spending if they lose their jobs, fear losing their jobs, or suffer wage cuts. Because people can often continue to use their existing furniture, appliances, or automobiles, they are more likely to postpone spending on durables than spending on other goods. Automobiles are among the most expensive products consumers buy, so consumers are very likely to postpone buying a new one during a recession.

We saw in our discussion of Ford at the beginning of this chapter that the firm's sales were significantly affected by the business cycle. Figure 9-7 shows that this is

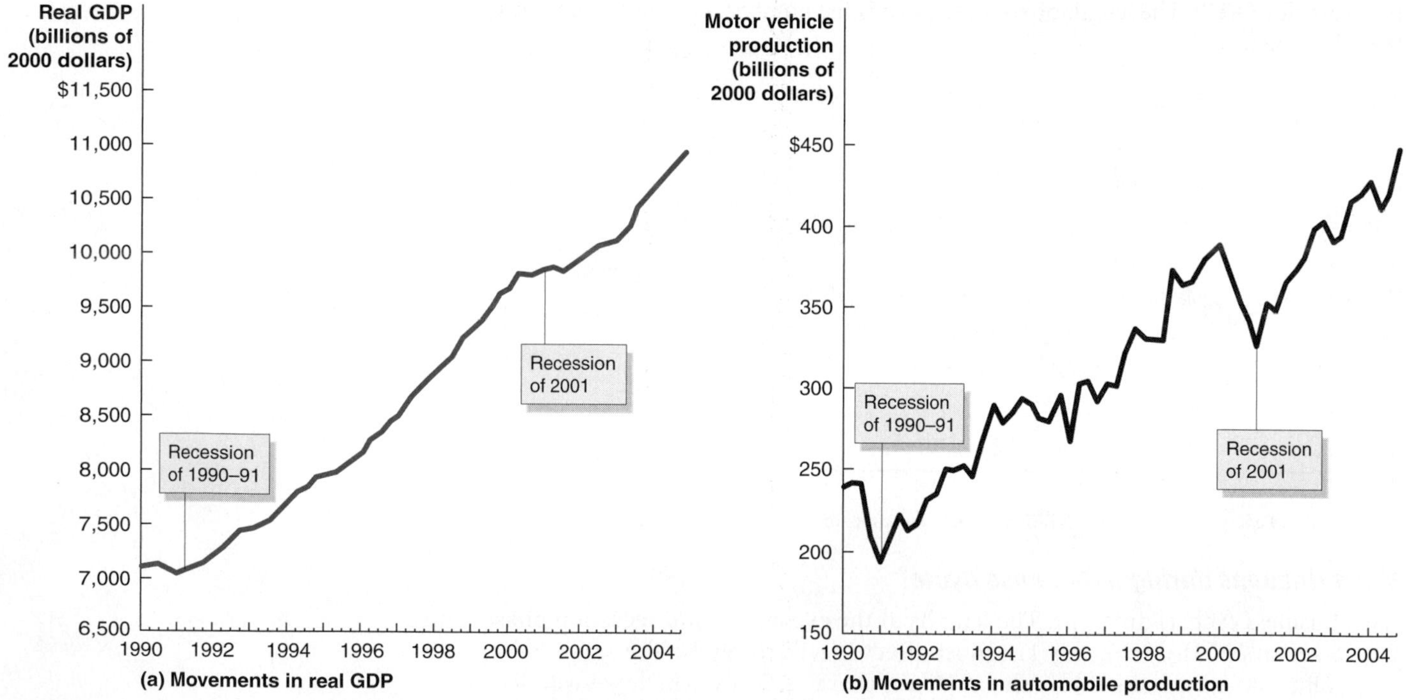

FIGURE 9-7 The Effect of the Business Cycle on Automobile Production

Panel (a) shows movements in real GDP for each quarter from the beginning of 1990 through the end of 2004. Panel (b) shows movements in the value of total motor vehicle production in the United States (in 2000 dollars) for the same period. In panel (b), the effects of the recessions are more dramatic. Real GDP declined by less than 1.5 percent during the 1990–91 recession and by less than 0.5 percent during the 2001 recession, while automobile production declined by more than 15 percent during both recessions.

Source: U.S. Bureau of Economic Analysis.

true for the automobile industry in the United States as a whole. Panel (a) shows movements in real GDP for each quarter from the beginning of 1990 through the end of 2004. We can see both the upward trend in real GDP over time and the effects of the recessions of 1990–91 and 2001. Panel (b) shows movements in the value of total motor vehicle production in the United States (in 2000 dollars) for the same period. Once again, we can see an upward trend in production over time, but now the effects of the recessions are more dramatic. Real GDP declined by less than 1.5 percent during the 1990–91 recession and by less than 0.5 percent during the 2001 recession, while automobile production declined by more than 15 percent during both recessions.

THE EFFECT OF THE BUSINESS CYCLE ON THE INFLATION RATE In Chapter 8, we saw that the *price level* measures the average prices of goods and services in the economy, and that the *inflation rate* is the percentage increase in the price level from one year to the next. An important fact about the business cycle is that during economic expansions the inflation rate usually increases, particularly near the end of the expansion, and during recessions the inflation rate usually decreases. Figure 9-8 illustrates that this was true of the recession of 2001.

As Figure 9-8 shows, toward the end of the 1991–2001 expansion, the inflation rate rose from about 1.5 percent to about 3.5 percent. The recession that began in March 2001 caused the inflation rate to fall back to below 2 percent. Figure 9-9 shows that recessions have consistently had the effect of lowering the inflation rate. In every recession since 1950, the inflation rate has been lower during the 12 months after the recession ends than it was during the 12 months before the recession began. The average decline in the inflation rate has been about 2.5 percentage points. This result is not surprising. During a business cycle expansion, spending by businesses and households is strong and producers of goods and services find it easier to raise

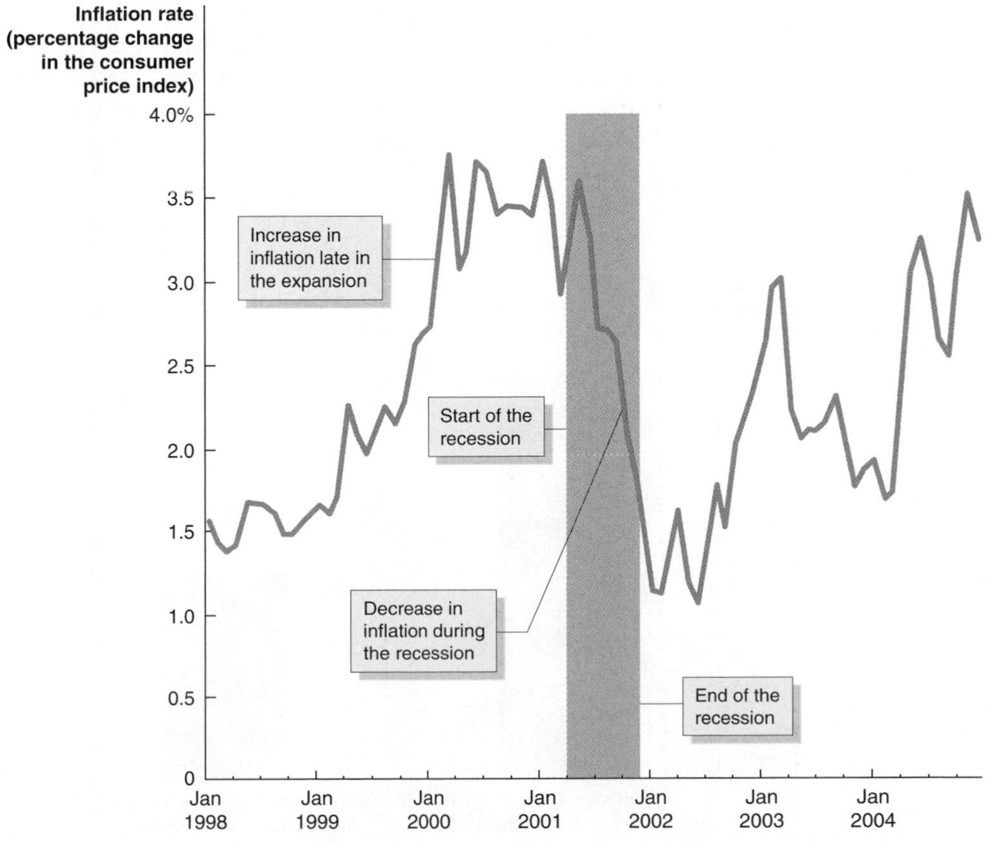

FIGURE 9-8

The Effect of the 2001 Recession on the Inflation Rate

Toward the end of the 1991–2001 expansion, the inflation rate began to rise. The recession that began in March 2001, marked by the shaded vertical bar, caused the inflation rate to fall. By the end of the recession in November 2001, the inflation rate was significantly below what it had been at the beginning of the recession.

Note: The points on the figure represent the annual inflation rate measured by the change in the CPI for the year ending in the indicated month.

Don't Let This Happen To You!

Don't Confuse the Price Level and the Inflation Rate

Do you agree with the following statement: "The consumer price index is a widely used measure of the inflation rate." The statement may sound plausible, but it is incorrect. As we saw in Chapter 8, the consumer price index is a measure of the *price level,* not of the inflation rate. We can measure the inflation rate as the *percentage change* in the consumer price index from one year to the next. In macroeconomics, it is important not to confuse the level of a variable with the change in the variable. To give another example, real GDP does not measure economic growth. Economic growth is measured by the percentage change in real GDP from one year to the next.

YOUR TURN: **Test your understanding by doing related problem 20 on page 291 at the end of this chapter.**

prices. As spending declines during a recession, firms have a more difficult time selling their goods and services and are likely to increase prices less than they otherwise might have.

THE EFFECT OF THE BUSINESS CYCLE ON THE UNEMPLOYMENT RATE Recessions cause the inflation rate to fall, but they cause the unemployment rate to increase. As firms see their sales decline, they begin to reduce production and lay off workers. Figure 9-10 shows the impact of the recession of 2001 on the unemployment rate. As the recession began in March 2001, the unemployment rate started to rise. The rate continued to rise even after the end of the recession in November 2001. This pattern is typical and is due to two factors. First, during the business cycle, discouraged workers drop out of and then return to the labor force, as we discussed in Chapter 8. When discouraged workers drop out of the labor force during a recession, they keep the measured unemployment rate from increasing as much as it would if these workers were counted as unemployed. When discouraged workers return to the labor force as the recession ends, they increase the measured unemployment rate because they are now counted as being unemployed. Second, firms continue to operate well below their capacity even after a recession has ended and production has begun to increase. As a result, at first, firms may not hire back all of the workers they have laid off and may even continue for a while to lay off more workers.

FIGURE 9-9

The Impact of Recessions on the Inflation Rate

In every recession since 1950, the inflation rate has been lower during the 12 months after the business cycle trough than it was during the 12 months before the business cycle peak. The average decline in the inflation rate has been 2.5 percentage points.

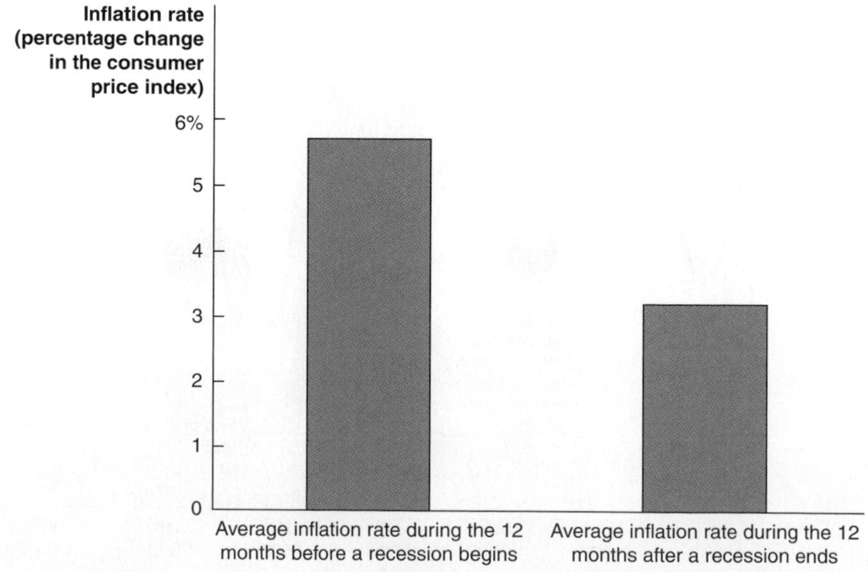

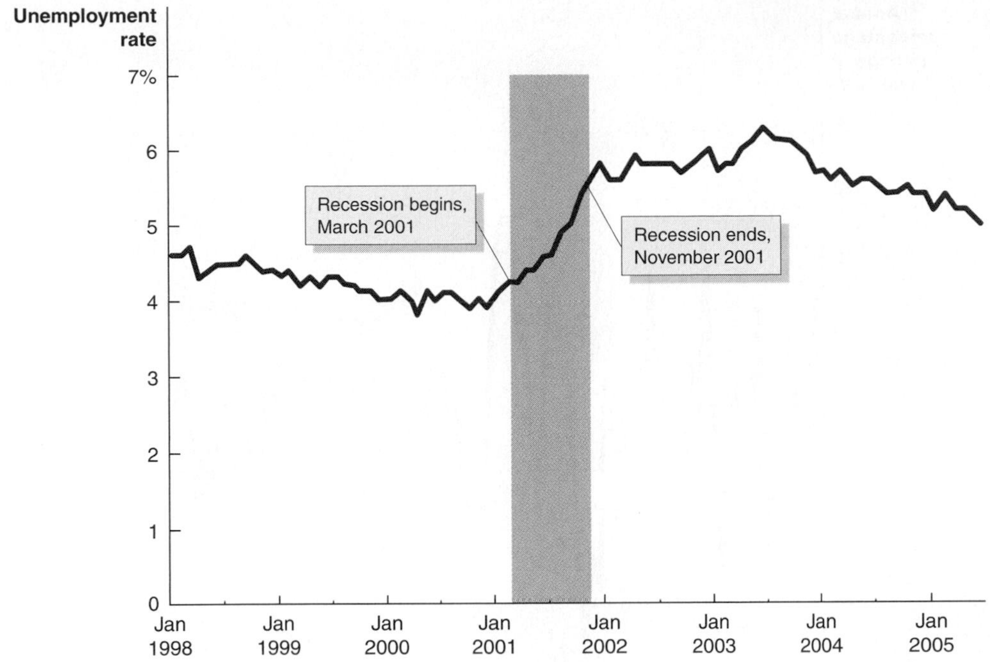

FIGURE 9-10

The Effect of the 2001 Recession of the Unemployment Rate

The reluctance of firms to hire new employees during the early stages of a recovery means that the unemployment rate usually continues to rise even after the recession has ended.

As the U.S. economy began to recover from the 2001 recession, the *Wall Street Journal* published an article giving advice to small firms on their hiring policies during the period after a recession has ended. One piece of advice was "Just because some new orders arrived, don't run out and hire a bunch of new workers." The owner of one small accounting firm suggested that during the early stages of an expansion, companies should use overtime by existing employees to meet sales, rather than hire new workers.

Figure 9-11 shows that for the recessions since 1950, the unemployment rate has risen on average by about 1.2 percentage points during the 12 months after a recession begins. So, on average, more than a million more workers have been unemployed during the 12 months after a recession begins than during the previous 12 months.

RECESSIONS HAVE BEEN MILDER AND THE ECONOMY HAS BEEN MORE STABLE SINCE 1950 Although today the U.S. economy still experiences business cycles, just as it has for at least the past 175 years, the cycles have become milder. Figure 9-12, which

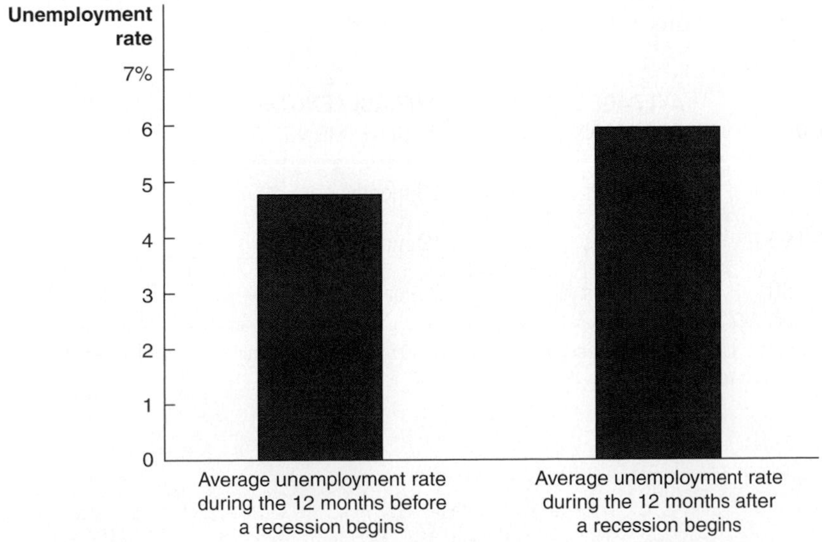

FIGURE 9-11

The Impact of Recessions on the Unemployment Rate

Unemployment rises in every recession. For the recessions since 1950, the unemployment rate rises, on average, by about 1.2 percentage points during the 12 months after a recession begins.

FIGURE 9-12

Fluctuations in Real GDP, 1900–2004

In the first half of the twentieth century, real GDP had much more severe swings than in the second half of the twentieth century.

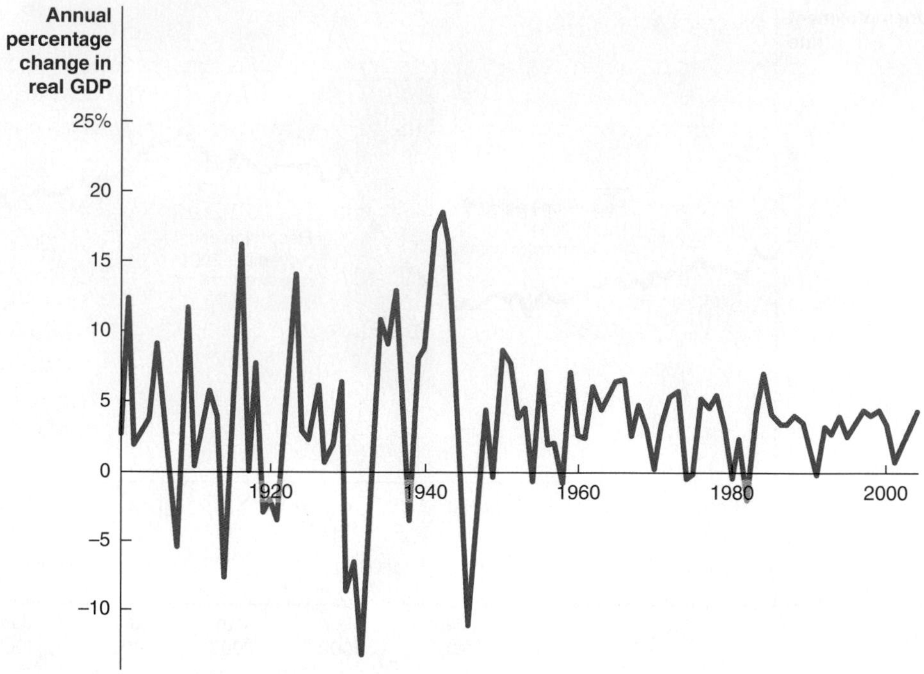

shows the year-to-year percentage changes in real GDP since 1900, illustrates a striking change in fluctuations in real GDP beginning around 1950. Before 1950, real GDP went through much greater year-to-year fluctuations than it has since that time. During the past 50 years, the U.S. economy has not experienced anything similar to the sharp fluctuations in real GDP that occurred during the early 1930s.

Another way to compare changes in the severity of business cycles over time is to look at changes in the lengths of expansions and recessions. Table 9-1 shows that in the late nineteenth century the average length of recessions was the same as the average length of expansions. During the first half of the twentieth century, the average length of expansions decreased slightly and the average length of recessions decreased significantly. As a result, expansions were about six months longer than recessions during these years. The most striking change comes after 1950, when the length of expansions has greatly increased and the length of recessions has fallen. In the second half of the twentieth century, expansions were more than five times as long as recessions. In other words, in the late nineteenth century the U.S. economy spent as much time in recession as it did in expansion. During the second half of the twentieth century, the U.S. economy experienced long expansions, interrupted by relatively short recessions.

TABLE 9-1

The Business Cycle Has Become Milder

PERIOD	AVERAGE LENGTH OF EXPANSIONS	AVERAGE LENGTH OF RECESSIONS
1870–1900	26 months	26 months
1900–1950	25 months	19 months
1950–2001	61 months	9 months

Note: The World War I and World War II periods have been omitted from the computations in the table, as has the expansion that began in November 2001.

Why Is the Economy More Stable?

Shorter recessions, longer expansions, and less severe fluctuations in real GDP have resulted in a significant improvement in the economic well-being of Americans. Economists have offered three explanations of why the economy has been more stable since 1950:

- ***The increasing importance of services and the declining importance of goods.*** As services, such as medical care or investment advice, have become a much larger fraction of GDP, there has been a corresponding decline in the production of goods. For example, at one time, manufacturing production accounted for about 40 percent of GDP, while today it accounts for about only 12 percent. Manufacturing production, particularly production of durable goods such as automobiles, fluctuates more than the production of services. Because durable goods are more expensive, during a recession households will cut back more on purchases of them than they will on purchases of services.
- ***The establishment of unemployment insurance and other government transfer programs that provide funds to the unemployed.*** Before the 1930s, programs such as unemployment insurance, which provides government payments to workers who lose their jobs, and Social Security, which provides government payments to retired and disabled workers, did not exist. These and other government programs make it possible for workers who lose their jobs during recessions to have higher incomes and, therefore, spend more than they would otherwise. This additional spending may have helped to shorten recessions.
- ***Active federal government policies to stabilize the economy.*** Before the Great Depression of the 1930s, the federal government did not attempt to end recessions or prolong expansions. Because the Great Depression was so severe, with the unemployment rate rising to more than 25 percent of the labor force and real GDP declining by almost 30 percent, public opinion began favoring attempts by the government to stabilize the economy. In the Employment Act of 1946, the federal government committed itself to "foster and promote . . . conditions under which there will be afforded useful employment to those able, willing, and seeking to work; and to promote maximum employment, production, and purchasing power." Since that time, the federal government has actively tried to end recessions and prolong expansions. Many economists believe that these government policies have played a key role in stabilizing the economy in the years since 1950. Other economists, however, argue that active policy has had little effect. This macroeconomic debate is an important one, so we will consider it further in Chapters 14 and 15 when we discuss the federal government's *monetary* and *fiscal policies.*

Conclusion

The U.S. economy remains a remarkable engine for improving the well-being of Americans. The standard of living of Americans today is much higher than it was 100 years ago. But households and firms are still subject to the ups and downs of the business cycle. In the following chapters we will continue our analysis of this basic fact of macroeconomics: Ever-increasing long-run prosperity is achieved in the context of short-run instability.

Read *An Inside Look* on the next page to learn about the growth of the Chinese automobile industry.

An Inside Look

Growth and the Chinese Automobile Industry

BUSINESSWEEK ONLINE, JUNE 6, 2005

Here Come Chinese Cars

Audacious, gutsy, and maybe a little nutty—how else to describe the push by New York auto entrepreneur Malcolm Bricklin and China's Chery Automobile Co. President Yin Tongyao to import and sell 250,000 mainland-made sport utilities, sedans, and sports coupes in the U.S. starting in 2007? After all, Chery produced only 80,000 cars in all of 2004, has near-zero brand recognition outside China, and has been sued by General Motors Corp.'s South Korean unit for allegedly ripping off the design for its best-selling QQ minicars in China—a charge Chery denies. And while Bricklin was expected to announce his first dealer on May 26, U.S. auto execs aren't exactly losing sleep over the Chery threat—not yet, anyway.

Big Three execs did take notice, however, when Honda Motor Corp. announced plans to export compact cars from China to Europe starting in June. Honda already sells about 200,000 locally built vehicles in China a year, ranging from Accord sedans to Odyssey SUVs. In April, with local partners, it began production at a new assembly plant in Guangzhou that will eventually build and export 50,000 Fit compacts a year to be sold in Europe as the Jazz. Honda won't say if it plans to send China-built cars to the U.S., but it hasn't ruled out exporting other models from China eventually.

In the global auto industry, Chery and Honda are on opposite ends of the spectrum. But they do share this: Both are betting big that the Chinese auto industry is entering a new phase that will see a shift from manufacturing only for the fast-growing local market to become an export base for the rest of the world, too. . . .

. . . China is closing the quality gap and building a base of low-cost suppliers that could eventually allow it to unleash inexpensive, well-made cars on the West. . . .

Rising Quality

a Korean cars gave Detroit fits in the late '90s by undercutting domestic small cars on price and outdoing them on quality—then moving up into other segments. Autos from China could provide more lower-cost competition for the Big Three at a time when GM and Ford Motor Co. are already reeling. . . .

How fast can the Chinese gear up? The way things are going, it won't take 20 years to match Toyota Motor Corp. quality levels, as it did for the Koreans. And with Chinese auto assembly workers earning $2 an hour—vs. $22 in Korea and nearly $60 in the U.S. for wages and benefits—it may not be long before China has the wherewithal to start selling competitively priced cars overseas. "The Chinese are probably five or six years away from being able to sell a competent low-end car," says auto analyst Maryann N. Keller.

The Chinese government is putting its heft behind the export push—subsidizing the export drive of such local players as Chery and giving the likes of Honda big incentives. Beijing also is nudging foreign auto makers to divert investment into export production so local partners can become familiar with managing foreign-exchange risk and global supply chains. . . .

b Another challenge is a bit of mind-bender: While China's labor costs are dirt cheap, the overall cost of bolting a car together there is anything but. Honda officials say the cost of making the Accord in China is still higher than in Japan or the U.S. And it costs about the same to build the Fit compact in China as it does in Japan. Honda makes money selling cars locally because prices are high. . . .

That will begin to change as higher volumes start bringing costs down. Jack Perkowski, CEO of ASMICO Technologies, which owns 13 parts factories in China, figures that will happen once the domestic market gets closer to 10 million units a year. . . .

Counter-Strategies

c For Detroit, that's a scary prospect. "Our strategy is to become competitive at the low end of the market," says GM's LaNeve. That means importing cars built by its Korean affiliate, Daewoo, to sell as Chevys, such as the $10,000 Aveo subcompact launched in fall, 2003. LaNeve wouldn't discuss GM's long-term plans. But analysts say that, under pressure from Chinese cars, the auto giant could step up exports from Korea, where quality and supplier connections are already established. Eventually, though, it might turn to its own plants in China, where it has been producing cars since 1999. . . .

In the meantime, China's auto industry is roaring into the future—building out its supplier networks and boosting quality. . . . Look out, Detroit.

Key Points in the Article

This article discusses the fast-growing Chinese automobile industry, which until recently manufactured relatively low-quality vehicles for local Chinese markets. Now the five-year-old Chinese automobile manufacturer, Chery, plans to sell 250,000 entry-level vehicles in the United States by 2007. U.S. automobile manufacturers Ford and General Motors plan to counter this credible Chinese threat with similarly priced entry-level vehicles of their own. Auto analysts predict that to keep costs low both U.S. firms will ultimately produce their vehicles in China.

Analyzing the News

a Since the late 1970s, when the Chinese government introduced market-oriented economic reforms, the Chinese economy has grown dramatically. This economic growth has spurred, in a relatively short time frame, a globally competitive Chinese automobile industry. To be sure, China remains an emerging economy, with relatively high unemployment, low labor productivity, and a low standard of living. Nonetheless, as countries develop, they tend to move from manufacturing simple goods like textiles to more complex goods like automobiles. And, in the case of China, automobile producers such as Chery have enjoyed a competitive advantage over their U.S. counterparts, because, all else equal, labor costs in China remain extremely low. This advantage is shown in Figure 1.

b Despite China's strong economic growth, the country's automobile production technologies remain relatively primitive and small-scale. Therefore, China cannot manufacture at low cost the highly sophisticated components required to produce efficient, safe, and durable automobiles. So, although labor is relatively cheap in China, the cost to manufacture an automobile is not. This competitive disadvantage will disappear in the next few years, as investment in Chinese automobile parts plants improves their efficiency and growing markets for Chinese automobiles increase the scale of parts production.

c When China does enter the U.S. automobile market, it will be at the entry or low-end level—subcompacts with a sticker price of roughly $10,000. U.S. automakers Ford and General Motors plan to counter with entry-level vehicles of their own. As the Chinese economy continues to grow, and as its network of cost-effective parts manufacturers increases, Ford and GM may determine that their least-cost option is to produce their automobiles in China. In any case, the U.S. consumer will benefit from these changes in the global automobile market, because entry-level automobile prices in the United States will fall. This pattern is shown in Figure 2, where the supply of entry-level automobiles shifts from S_1 to S_2, while the price of entry-level automobiles falls from P_1 to P_2.

Thinking Critically ABOUT POLICY

1. Suppose the Chinese government imposes restrictions on foreign direct investment in Chinese automobile parts plants. For example, suppose the Chinese government restricts U.S. firms that manufacture automobile components, from investing in and managing automobile parts plants in China. What effect would this policy have on China's automobile production costs in the next several years?
2. Suppose the U.S. government imposes an import tariff on Chinese entry-level automobiles. What effect would this policy have on the equilibrium price and quantity of entry-level automobiles sold in the United States?

Source: Brian Bremner and Kathleen Kerwin, with Dexter Roberts in Beijing, Gail Edmondson in Frankfurt, and David Kiley in New York, "Here Come Chinese Cars: Detroit Isn't Looking in the Rearview Mirror—Yet," Business Week Online, www.businessweek.com. June 6, 2005.

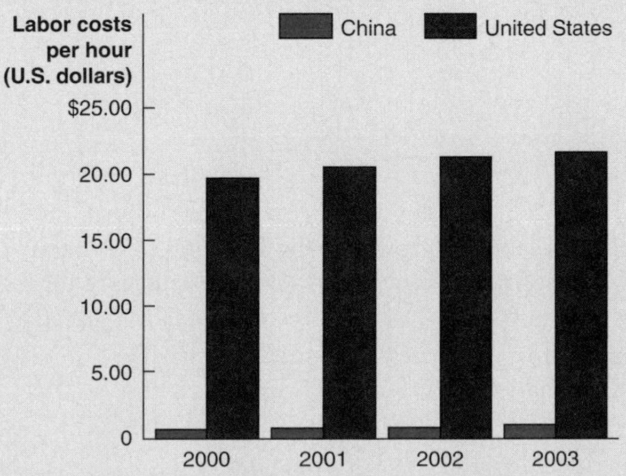

Figure 1: Labor costs per hour China v. United States
Source: The Economist Intelligence Unit.

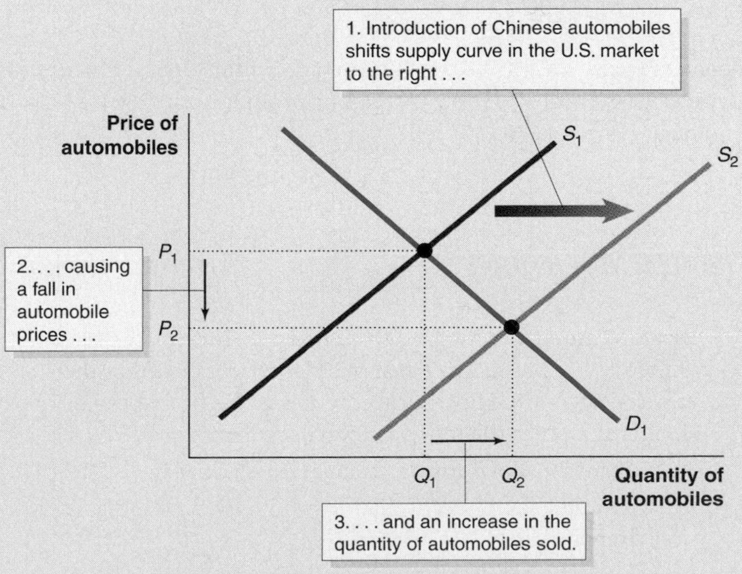

Figure 2: The introduction of Chinese automobiles causes a decrease in the price of automobiles.

SUMMARY

LEARNING OBJECTIVE ① Discuss the importance of long-run economic growth. Long-run economic growth is the process by which rising productivity increases the standard of living of the typical person. Because of economic growth, the typical American today can buy more than eight times as much as the typical American of 1900. Long-run growth is measured by increases in real GDP per capita. Increases in real GDP per capita depend on increases in *labor productivity*. Labor productivity is the quantity of goods and services that can be produced by one worker or by one hour of work. Economists believe two key factors determine labor productivity—the quantity of capital per hour worked and the level of technology. Therefore, economic growth occurs if the quantity of capital per hour worked increases and if technological change occurs.

LEARNING OBJECTIVE ② Discuss the role of the financial system in facilitating long-run economic growth. Financial markets and financial intermediaries together comprise the *financial system*. A well-functioning financial system is an important determinant of economic growth. Firms acquire funds from households, either directly through financial markets—such as the stock and bond markets—or indirectly through financial intermediaries—such as banks. The funds available to firms come from *saving*. There are two categories of saving in the economy: *private saving* by households and *public saving* by the government. The value of total saving in the economy is always equal to the value of total investment spending. In the model of the *market for loanable funds,* the interaction of borrowers and lenders determines the market interest rate and the quantity of loanable funds exchanged.

LEARNING OBJECTIVE ③ Explain what happens during a business cycle. A *business cycle* consists of alternating periods of economic expansion and contraction. During the expansion phase of a business cycle, production, employment, and income are increasing. The period of expansion ends with a business cycle peak. Following the business cycle peak, production, employment, and income decline during the recession phase of the cycle. The recession comes to an end with a business cycle trough, after which another period of expansion begins. The inflation rate usually rises near the end of a business cycle expansion and then falls during a recession. The unemployment rate declines during the later part of an expansion and increases during a recession. The unemployment rate often continues to increase even after an expansion has begun. Economists have not found a method to predict when recessions will begin and end. Recessions are difficult to predict because they have more than one cause. Recessions have been milder and the economy has been more stable since 1950.

KEY TERMS

Business cycle 262
Capital 266
Financial system 270
Human capital 266
Labor productivity 266
Long-run economic growth 263
Market for loanable funds 273
Potential GDP 269

REVIEW QUESTIONS

1. By how much did real GDP per capita increase in the United States between 1900 and 2004? Discuss whether the increase in real GDP per capita is likely to be greater or smaller than the true increase in living standards.
2. The rule of 70 allows for the calculation of what value?
3. What two key factors cause labor productivity to increase over time?
4. What supportive government policies are crucial for long-run economic growth?
5. Why is the financial system of a country important for long-run economic growth? Why is it vital for economic growth that firms have access to adequate sources of funds?
6. How does the financial system—either financial markets or financial intermediaries—provide risk sharing, liquidity, and information for savers and borrowers?
7. Briefly explain why the total value of saving in the economy must equal the total value of investment.

8. What are loanable funds? Why do businesses demand loanable funds? Why do households supply loanable funds?
9. What are the names of the following events in a business cycle?
   a. The high point of economic activity
   b. The low point of economic activity
   c. The period between the high point of economic activity and the following low point
   d. The period between the low point of economic activity and the following high point
10. Briefly describe the effect of the business cycle on the inflation rate and the unemployment rate.
11. Briefly compare the severity of recessions in the first half of the twentieth century with recessions in the second half. Do economists agree on how to explain this difference?

PROBLEMS AND APPLICATIONS

Please visit **www.prenhall.com/hubbard** *for solutions to the even-numbered problems as well as multiple-choice and true or false self-assessment quizzes.*

1. **[Related to the *Chapter Opener*]** Briefly explain whether production of each of the following goods is likely to fluctuate more or less during the business cycle than does real GDP:
   a. Ford F-150 trucks
   b. McDonald's Big Macs
   c. Kenmore refrigerators
   d. Huggies diapers
   e. Caterpillar industrial tractors
2. Briefly discuss whether you would rather live in the United States of 1900 with an income of $1,000,000 per year or the United States of 2006 with an income of $50,000 per year. Assume the incomes for both years are measured in 2000 dollars.
3. A question from Chapter 7 asked about the relationship between real GDP and the standard of living in a country. After reading about economic growth in this chapter, elaborate on the importance of growth in GDP, particularly real GDP per capita, to the quality of life of a country's citizens.
4. Use the table to answer the following questions:

YEAR	REAL GDP (BILLION OF 2000 DOLLARS)
1990	$7,113
1991	7,101
1992	7,337
1993	7,533
1994	7,836

   a. Calculate the growth rate of real GDP for each year from 1991 to 1994.
   b. Calculate the average annual growth rate of real GDP for the period from 1991 to 1994.
5. Real GDP per capita in the United States, as mentioned in the chapter, grew from about $4,300 in 1900 to about $37,000 in 2004, which represents an annual growth rate of 2.1 percent. If the United States continues to grow at this rate, how many years will it take for real GDP per capita to double?
6. The economy of China has boomed since the late 1970s, having periods of double-digit growth rates in real GDP. At a 10 percent growth rate in real GDP, how many years will it take for China's economy to double?
7. Labor productivity in the agricultural sector of the United States is more than 31 times higher than in the agricultural sector of China. What factors would cause U.S. labor productivity to be so much higher than Chinese labor productivity?
   Source: "China: Awakening Giant," Federal Reserve Bank of Dallas, *Southwest Economy*, September/October 2003, p. 2.
8. **[Related to *Solved-Problem 9-1*]** Two reasons for the rapid economic growth of China over the past two to three decades have been the massive movement of workers from agriculture to manufacturing jobs and the transformation of parts of its economy into a market system. In China, labor productivity in manufacturing substantially exceeds labor productivity in agriculture, and as many as 150 million Chinese workers will move from agriculture to manufacturing over the next decade or so. In 1978, China began to transform its economy into a market system, and today nearly 40 percent of Chinese workers are employed in private firms (up from 0 percent in 1978). In the long run, which of these two factors—movement of workers from agriculture to manufacturing or transforming the economy into a market system—will be more important for China's economic growth? Briefly explain.
   Source: "China: Awakening Giant," Federal Reserve Bank of Dallas, *Southwest Economy*, September/October 2003.
9. Suppose you can receive an interest rate of 3 percent on a certificate of deposit (CD) at a bank that is charging

borrowers 7 percent on new car loans. Why might you be unwilling to loan money directly to someone who wants to borrow from you to buy a new car, even if that person offers to pay you an interest rate higher than 3 percent?

10. Consider the following data for a closed economy:
    $Y = \$11$ trillion
    $C = \$8$ trillion
    $I = \$2$ trillion
    $TR = \$1$ trillion
    $T = \$3$ trillion

    Use the data to calculate the following:
    a. Private saving
    b. Public saving
    c. Government purchases
    d. The government budget deficit or budget surplus

11. Consider the following data for a closed economy:
    $Y = \$12$ trillion
    $C = \$8$ trillion
    $G = \$2$ trillion
    $S_{public} = -\$0.5$ trillion
    $T = \$2$ trillion

    Use the data to calculate the following:
    a. Private saving
    b. Investment spending
    c. Transfer payments
    d. The government budget deficit or budget surplus

12. In problem 11, suppose that government purchases increase from \$2 trillion to \$2.5 trillion. If the values for Y and C are unchanged, what must happen to the values of S and I? Briefly explain.

13. Use the graph to answer the following questions:

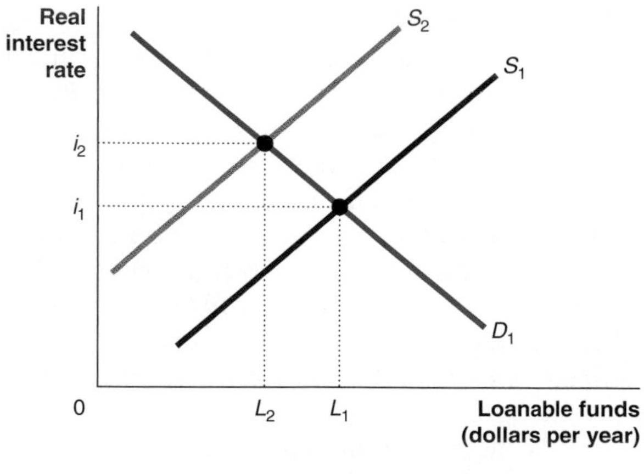

a. Does the shift from S_1 to S_2 represent an increase or decrease in the supply of loanable funds?
b. With the shift in supply, what happens to the equilibrium quantity of loanable funds?
c. With the change in the equilibrium quantity of loanable funds, what happens to the quantity of saving? What happens to the quantity of investment?

14. Use the graph to answer the following questions:

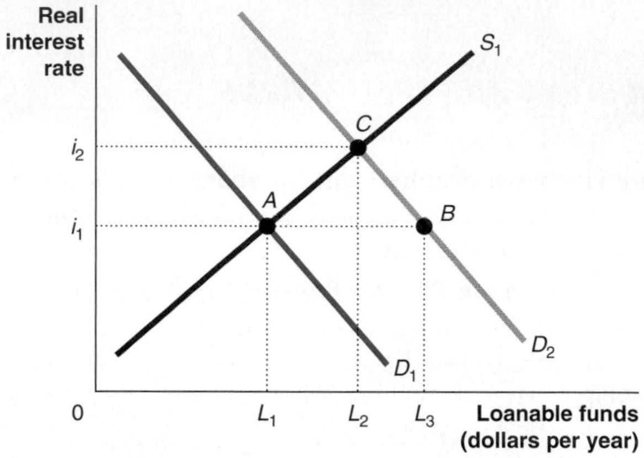

a. With the shift in the demand for loanable funds, what happens to the equilibrium real interest rate and the equilibrium quantity of loanable funds?
b. How can the equilibrium quantity of loanable funds increase when the real interest rate increases? Doesn't the quantity of loanable funds demanded decrease when the interest rate increases?
c. How much would the quantity of loanable funds demanded have increased if the interest rate had remained at i_1?
d. How much does the quantity of loanable funds supplied increase with the increase in the interest rate from i_1 to i_2?

15. Suppose the economy is currently in a recession and that economic forecasts indicate that the economy will soon enter an expansion. What is the likely effect of the expansion on the expected profitability of new investment in plant and equipment? In the market for loanable funds, graph and explain the effect of the forecast of an economic expansion, assuming borrowers and lenders believe the forecast is accurate. What happens to the equilibrium real interest rate and the quantity of loanable funds? What happens to the quantity of saving and investment?

16. Firms care about their after-tax rate of return on investment projects. In the market for loanable funds, graph and explain the effect of an increase in business taxes. (For simplicity, assume no change in the federal budget deficit or budget surplus.) What happens to the equilibrium real interest rate and the quantity of loanable funds? What will be the effect on the quantity of investment by firms and the economy's capital stock in the future?
17. Use a market for loanable funds graph to illustrate the effect of the federal budget surpluses of the late 1990s. What happens to the equilibrium real interest rate and the quantity of loanable funds? What happens to the quantity of saving and investment?
18. **[Related to *Solved Problem 9-2*]** As discussed in Chapter 8, savers are taxed on the nominal interest payments they receive rather than the real interest payments. Suppose the government shifted from taxing nominal interest payments to taxing only real interest payments. Use a market for loanable funds graph to analyze the effects of this change in tax policy. What happens to the equilibrium real interest rate and the equilibrium quantity of loanable funds? What happens to the quantity of saving and investment?
19. The National Bureau of Economic Research, a private group, is responsible for declaring when recessions begin and end. Can you think of reasons why the Bureau of Economic Analysis, part of the federal government, might not want to take on this responsibility?
20. **[Related to *Don't Let This Happen To You!*]** "GDP in 2002 was $10.4 trillion. This value is a large number. Therefore, economic growth must have been high during 2002." Briefly explain whether you agree or disagree with this statement.
21. During the later half of the 1990s, some people asserted that the business cycle was dead, meaning that we would have no more recessions. Examine this chapter's table of business cycle peaks and troughs since 1950. How many recessions has the U.S. economy experienced since the end of 1982? Since 1950, have recessions become more or less frequent? From the history of the business cycle, do you think that the U.S. economy will have another recession within the next 20 years?
22. Imagine you own a business and that during the next recession you lay off 20 percent of your workforce. Once economic activity picks up, why might you not immediately start rehiring workers?

chapter ten

Long-Run Economic Growth: Sources and Policies

The Chinese Economic Miracle

➤ Economic growth is not inevitable. For most of human history, no sustained increases in output per capita occurred and, in the words of the philosopher Thomas Hobbes, the lives of most people were "poor, nasty, brutish, and short." Sustained economic growth first began with the Industrial Revolution in England in the late eighteenth century. From there, economic growth spread to the United States, Canada, and the countries of Western Europe. Following World War II, rapid economic growth also began in Japan, but the economies of most other countries stagnated, leaving their people mired in poverty. China, the most populous country in the world, was no exception.

Throughout the first half of the twentieth century, China was wracked by revolution and war. The victory of Mao Zedong and the Communist Party in 1949 replaced the market system with a *centrally planned economy*. Mao died in 1976. Two years later, Deng Xiaoping, the new leader of the Communist Party, began moving China away from a centrally planned economy toward a more market-oriented system. Although some sectors of the economy—including the banking system—remained under the control of the government, the effect of Deng's reforms was to spur sustained economic growth for the first time in China's history.

Statistics on the Chinese economy are not considered completely reliable, particularly for the period before 1978. However, the best estimates available indicate that real GDP per capita grew at an average annual rate of 1.8 percent between 1952 and 1978. At that relatively slow rate, real GDP per capita would take about 40 years to double. Following Deng's reforms, real GDP per capita grew at a rate of 6.5 percent per year between 1979 and 1995, and at the white hot rate of 9.1 percent per year between 1996 and 2004. At the rapid growth rate of recent years, per capita GDP in China will double every eight years. These rapid growth rates have transformed the Chinese economy. Not only is real GDP per capita ten times higher than it was 50 years ago, but it is now possible for the typical family in China to aspire for the first time to own an automobile, a television set, a refrigerator, an air conditioner, and other goods that have long been taken for granted by consumers in high-income countries.

At the heart of Chinese economic growth are the entrepreneurs who were set free by the economic reforms to fulfill their role in the mar-

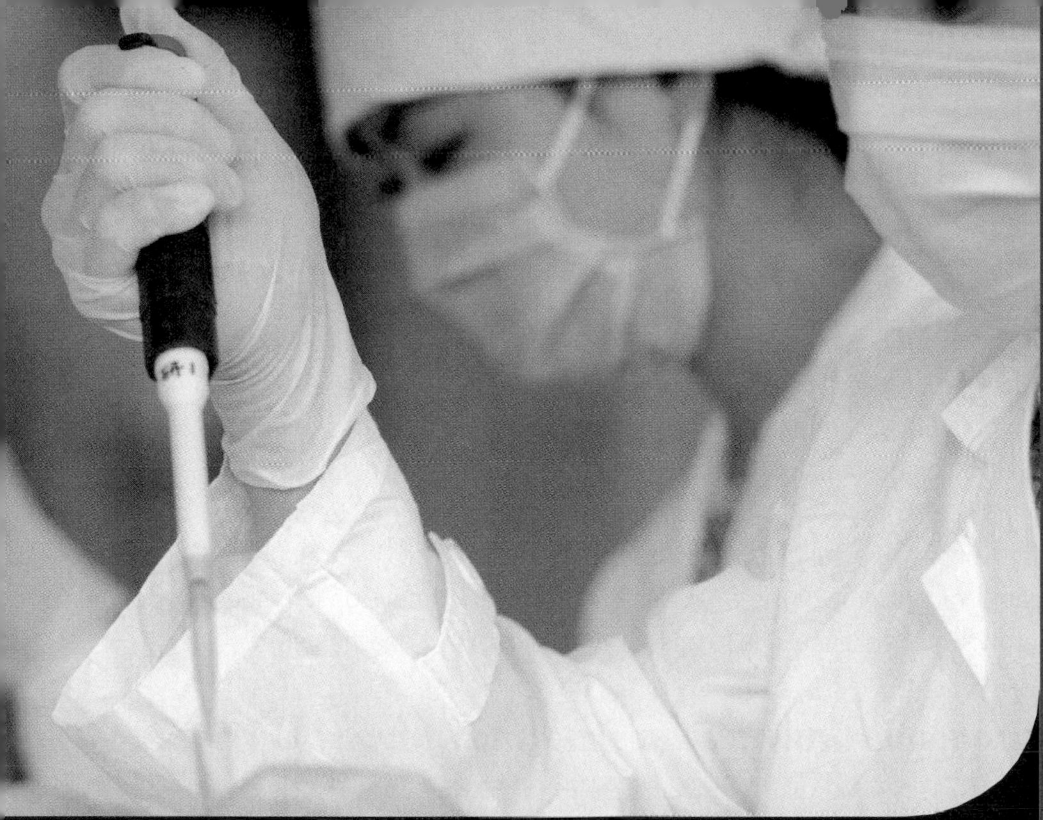

ket system: to bring together the factors of production—labor, capital, and natural resources—to produce goods and services. Guo Guangchang, the chairman of the board and president of Shanghai Fosun High Technology (Fosun), has been a particularly successful entrepreneur in the new Chinese economy. Guo was born in 1967 to a poor family in rural Zhejiang province. He received a business degree from Fudan University in Shanghai. Along with several classmates, he borrowed $4,500 from his teachers at Fudan and used the funds to develop a kit to test for hepatitis A. From there, Guo built a nationwide distribution system for pharmaceuticals, before buying several steel plants being sold by the Chinese government.

Guo Guangchang's personal net worth has been estimated to be $400 million, making him one of the wealthiest individuals in China, but the future for Guo and Fosun is not entirely unclouded. China is not a democracy, and the Chinese government still intervenes in the economy in sometimes arbitrary ways. In 2004, Fosun was set to open a new steel mill in the city of Ningbo when the government accused the firm of violating land-use regulations. The government allowed the new mill to open only after Fosun agreed to merge it with the government-owned firm, Hangzhou Steel. Whether China's economic miracle can continue without political liberalization remains to be seen. *An Inside Look* on page 322 discusses the recent increase in economic growth in India.

Source: "Some Like It Hot," *Economist*, May 17, 2005.

LEARNING OBJECTIVES

After studying this chapter, you should be able to:

① Define economic growth, calculate economic growth rates, and describe trends in economic growth.

② Use the economic growth model to explain why growth rates differ across countries.

③ Discuss fluctuations in productivity growth in the United States.

④ Explain economic catch-up, and discuss why many poor countries have not experienced rapid economic growth.

⑤ Discuss government policies that foster economic growth.

➤ Real GDP per capita is the best measure we have of a country's standard of living because GDP measures a country's total income. Economic growth occurs when real GDP per capita increases. Why have countries such as the United States and the United Kingdom, which had high standards of living at the beginning of the twentieth century, continued to grow rapidly? Why have countries such as Argentina, which at one time had relatively high standards of living, failed to keep pace? Why was the Soviet Union unable to sustain the rapid growth rates of its early years? Why are some countries that were very poor at the beginning of the twentieth century still very poor today? And why have some countries, such as South Korea and Japan, that once were very poor now become much richer? What explains China's very rapid recent growth rates? In this chapter, we will develop a *model of economic growth* that will enable us to answer these important questions.

① LEARNING OBJECTIVE

Define economic growth, calculate economic growth rates, and describe trends in economic growth.

Economic Growth Over Time and Around the World

You live in a world that is very different from the world when your grandparents were young. You can buy a DVD and watch your favorite films as many times as you want. Your grandparents could see movies only in a theater. You can pick up a cell phone or send an e-mail to someone in another city, state, or country. Your grandparents mailed letters that took days or weeks to arrive. More importantly, you have access to health care and medicines that have prolonged life and improved its quality. In many poorer countries, however, people endure grinding poverty and have only the bare necessities of life, just as their great-grandparents did.

The difference between you and people in poor countries is that you live in a country that has experienced substantial economic growth. With economic growth, an economy produces increasing quantities of goods and services and better goods and services. It is only through economic growth that living standards can increase, but through most of human history no economic growth took place. Even today, billions of people are living in countries where economic growth is extremely slow.

Economic Growth from 1,000,000 B.C. to the Present

In 1,000,000 B.C., our ancestors survived by hunting animals and gathering edible plant life. Farming was many years in the future. The production of these early humans was limited to food, clothing, shelter, and simple tools. Bradford DeLong, an economist at the University of California, Berkeley, estimates that in these primitive circumstances, GDP per capita was about $123 per year in 2004 dollars, which was the bare amount necessary to sustain life. DeLong estimates that real GDP per capita worldwide was still $123 in the year 1300 A.D. In other words, no sustained economic growth occurred between 1,000,000 B.C. and 1300 A.D.

A peasant toiling on a farm in France in the year 1300 was no better off than his ancestors thousands of years before. In fact, for most of human existence, the typical person had the bare minimum of food, clothing, and shelter necessary to sustain life. Few people survived beyond the age of forty, and most people suffered from severe tooth decay, lice, and debilitating illnesses.

Industrial Revolution The application of mechanical power to the production of goods, beginning in England around 1750.

Significant economic growth did not begin until the **Industrial Revolution,** which started in England around the year 1750. The production of cotton cloth in factories using machinery powered by steam engines marked the beginning of the Industrial Revolution. Before that time, production of goods had relied almost exclusively on human or animal power. Mechanical power spread to the production of many other goods, greatly increasing the quantity of goods each worker could produce. First England, and then other countries, such as the United States, France, and Germany, experienced *long-run economic growth,* with sustained increases in real GDP per capita that eventually raised living standards in these countries to the high levels of today.

Why Was England First?

10-1 Making the Connection

The Industrial Revolution was a key turning point in human history. Before the Industrial Revolution, economic growth was slow and halting. After the Industrial Revolution, economic growth became rapid and sustained. Historians and economists have not reached a consensus on the key question: Why did the Industrial Revolution occur where and when it did? Why the eighteenth century and not the sixteenth century or the twenty-first century? Why England and not China or India or Africa or Japan?

There is always a temptation to read history backward. We know when and where the Industrial Revolution occurred, therefore, it had to happen where it did and when it did. But what was so special about England in the eighteenth century? Douglass North, an economist at Washington University in St. Louis and winner of the Nobel Prize in Economics, has argued that institutions in England differed significantly from those in other countries in ways that greatly aided economic growth. North believes that the Glorious Revolution of 1688 was a key turning point. After that date, the British Parliament, rather than the king, controlled the government. The British court system also became independent of the king. As a result, the British government was able credibly to commit to upholding private property rights, protecting wealth, and eliminating arbitrary increases in taxes. These institutional changes gave entrepreneurs the incentive to make the investments necessary to use the important technological developments of the second half of the eighteenth century—particularly the spinning jenny and the water frame, which were used in the production of cotton textiles, and the steam engine, which was used in mining and in the manufacture of textiles and other products. Without the institutional changes, entrepreneurs would have been reluctant to risk having their property seized or their wealth confiscated by the government.

Recently, economists Carol Shiue and Wolfgang Keller of the University of Texas at Austin have provided support for North's argument. They have studied "market efficiency" in the eighteenth century in England, other European countries, and China. If the markets in a country are efficient, a product should have the same price wherever in the country it is sold, allowing for the effect of transportation costs. If prices are not the same in two areas within a country, it is possible to make profits by buying the product where its price is low and reselling it where its price is high. This trading will drive prices to equality. Trade is most likely to occur, however, if entrepreneurs feel confident that their gains will not be seized by the government and that contracts to buy and sell can be enforced in the courts. Therefore, the more efficient a country's markets were, the more its institutions would have favored long-run growth. Shuie and Keller found that in 1770 the efficiency of markets in England was significantly greater than the efficiency of markets elsewhere in Europe and in China.

Why did the Industrial Revolution occur in England?

Although not all economists accept North's specific argument about the origins of the Industrial Revolution, we will see that most economists accept the idea that economic growth is not likely to occur unless a country's government provides the type of institutional framework North describes.

Sources: Douglass C. North, *Understanding the Process of Economic Change,* Princeton: Princeton University Press, 2005; Douglass C. North and Barry R. Weingast, "Constitutions and Commitment: The Evolution of Institutions Governing Public Choice in Seventeenth-Century England," *Journal of Economic History,* Vol. 49, No. 4 (December 1989); and Carol H. Shiue and Wolfgang Keller, "Markets in China and Europe on the Eve of the Industrial Revolution," National Bureau of Economic Research, Working Paper 10778, September 2004.

Figure 10-1 shows how growth rates of real GDP per capita for the entire world have changed over long periods. Prior to 1300 A.D., there were no sustained increases in real GDP per capita. Over the next 500 years to 1800, there was very slow growth. Significant growth began in the nineteenth century as a result of the Industrial Revolution. A further acceleration in growth occurred during the twentieth century as the average annual growth rate increased from 1.3 percent per year to 2.3 percent per year.

Small Differences in Growth Rates Are Important

The difference between 1.3 percent and 2.3 percent may seem trivial but, over long periods, small differences in growth rates can have a large impact. For example, suppose you have $100 in a savings account earning an interest rate of 1.3 percent, which means you will receive an interest payment of $1.30 this year. If the interest rate on the account is 2.3 percent, you will earn $2.30. The difference of an extra $1.00 interest payment seems insignificant. But if you leave the interest as well as the original $100 in your account for another year, the difference becomes greater because now the higher interest rate is applied to a larger amount—$102.30—and the lower interest rate is applied to a smaller amount—$101.30. This process, known as *compounding,* magnifies even small differences in interest rates over long periods of time. Over a period of 50 years, your $100 would grow to $312 at an interest rate of 2.3 percent but to only $191 at an interest rate of 1.3 percent.

What applies to interest rates also applies to growth rates. For example, in 1950 real GDP per capita in Argentina was $6,430 (measured in 1996 dollars), while real GDP in France was $5,429. Over the next 50 years the economic growth rate in France averaged 2.9 percent per year, while in Argentina it was only 1.1 percent per year. Although this difference in growth rates seems small, in the year 2000 real GDP per capita in France had risen to $22,358, while real GDP per capita in Argentina was only $11,006. In other words, the standard of living of the typical person in France became considerably higher

FIGURE 10-1

Average Annual Growth Rates for the World Economy

World economic growth essentially was zero in the years before 1300, and very slow—an average of only 0.2 percent per year—before 1800. The Industrial Revolution made possible the sustained increases in real GDP per capita that have allowed some countries to attain a high standard of living.

Source: J. Bradford DeLong, "Estimating World GDP, One Million B.C.–Present," working paper, University of California, Berkeley.

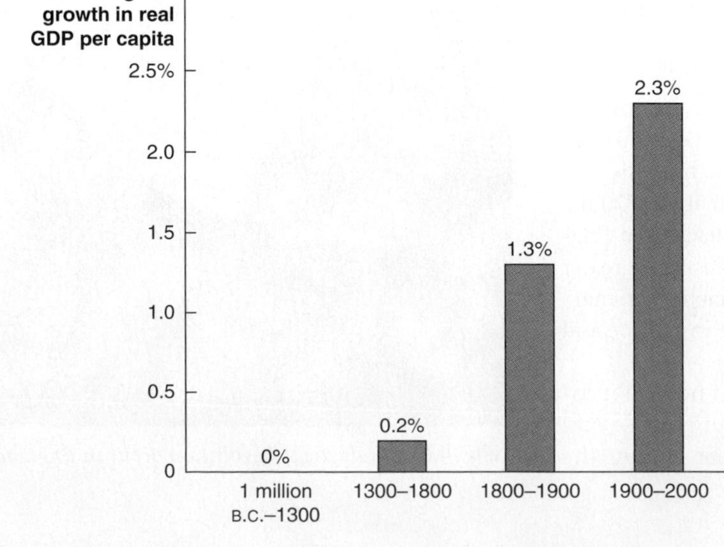

Don't Let This Happen To You!

Don't Confuse Average Annual Percentage Change with Total Percentage Change

When economists talk about growth rates over a period of more than one year, the numbers are always *average annual percentage changes* and *not* total percentage changes. For example, real GDP was $1,777 billion in 1950 and $10,756 billion in 2004. The percentage change in real GDP between these two years is:

$$\left(\frac{\$10{,}756 \text{ billion} - \$1{,}777 \text{ billion}}{\$1{,}777 \text{ billion}}\right) \times 100 = 505\%.$$

However, this is *not* the growth rate between the two years. As we discuss in Chapter 9, the growth rate between these two years is the rate at which $1,777 billion in 1950 would have to grow on average *each year* to end up as $10,842 billion in 2004, which is 3.4 percent.

YOUR TURN: **Test your understanding by doing related problem 2 on page 325 at the end of this chapter.**

n the standard of living of the typical person in Argentina because of a relatively ıll difference in the growth rates of the two economies. The important point to keep nind is this: *In the long run, small differences in economic growth rates result in big dif-·nces in living standards.*

ıy Do Growth Rates Matter?

.y should anyone care about growth rates? Growth rates matter because an economy t grows too slowly fails to raise living standards. In many countries in Africa and Asia, y little economic growth has occurred in the past 50 years, so many people remain in ere poverty. In high-income countries, only 4 out of every 1,000 babies die before the of one. In the poorest countries, more than 100 out of every 1,000 babies die before age of one, and millions of children die each year from diseases that could be avoided ıccess to clean water or cured by medicines costing only a few dollars.

Although their problems are less dramatic, countries that experience slow growth e also missed an opportunity to improve the lives of their citizens. For example, the ure of Argentina to grow as rapidly as the other countries that had similar levels of ·P per capita in 1950 has left many of its people in poverty. Life expectancy in ;entina is several years lower than in the United States and other high-income coun-s and almost three times as many babies in Argentina die before the age of one.

ɜ Benefits of an Earlier Start: Standards of Living in China and Japan

10-2 Making the Connection

noted at the beginning of this chapter that China has experienced very high growth rates ecent years. Between 1996 and 2004, real GDP per capita in China grew at an average ual rate of 9.1 percent. Japan, in contrast, grew at the much slower rate of 2.1 percent. ween 1950 and 1978, however, China had grown relatively slowly while Japan was grow-rapidly. As a result, in 2004, the standard of living in China was still well below that in ın. For example, real GDP per capita measured in U.S. dollars was $5,600 in China in 4, but $29,400—or more than five times higher—in Japan. The following table shows er measures of the standard of living for China and Japan.

	CHINA	JAPAN
expectancy at birth	71.5 years	81.9 years
t mortality (per 1,000 live births)	30	3
entage of the population surviving on less than $2 per day	47%	0%
entage of the population with access to treated water	77%	100%
entage of the population with access to improved sanitation	44%	100%

If rapid economic growth continues in China, its standard of living will begin to approach those in the United States and Japan.

In each of the measures shown in the preceding table, China continues to lag behind Japan as well as the United States and other high-income countries. If the Chinese economy can sustain the high growth rates of recent years, it will continue to close the gap with Japan in real GDP per capita and other measures of the standard of living. The moral of the story is that only by sustaining high rates of economic growth over many years will the currently low-income countries be able to attain the high standards of living enjoyed today by people in Japan, the United States, and other high-income countries.

Source: United Nations Development Programme, *Human Development Report, 2005,* New York: Oxford University Press, 2005.

"The Rich Get Richer and . . . "

We can divide the world's economies into two groups: the *high-income countries,* sometime also referred to as the industrial countries, and the poorer countries, or *developing countries.* The high-income countries include the countries of Western Europe, Japan, the United States, Canada, Australia, and New Zealand. The developing countries include most of the countries of Asia, Africa, and Latin America. In the 1980s and 1990s, a small group of countries, mostly East Asian countries such as South Korea, Taiwan, and Singapore, experienced high rates of growth and are sometimes referred to as the *newly industrializing countries.* Figure 10-2 shows the levels of GDP per capita around the world in 2004. GDP is measured in U.S. dollars, corrected for differences across countries in the cost of living. In 2004, GDP per capita ranged from a high of $58,900 in Luxembourg to a low of $600 in Sierra Leone and Somalia. To understand why the gap between rich and poor countries exists, we need to look at what causes economies to grow.

2 LEARNING OBJECTIVE

Use the economic growth model to explain why growth rates differ across countries.

What Determines How Fast Economies Grow?

To explain changes in economic growth rates over time within countries, and differences in growth rates among countries, we need to develop an *economic growth model.* An **economic growth model** explains growth rates in real GDP per capita. As we noted in Chapter 9, the average person can buy more goods and services only if the average worker produces more goods and services. Recall that **labor productivity** is the quantity of goods and services that can be produced by one worker or by one hour of work. Because of the importance of labor productivity in explaining economic growth, the economic growth model focuses on the causes of long-run increases in labor productivity.

Economic growth model A model that explains changes in real GDP per capita in the long run.

Labor productivity The quantity of goods and services that can be produced by one worker or by one hour of work.

How can a country's workers become more productive? Economists believe two key factors determine labor productivity: the quantity of capital per hour worked and the level of technology. Therefore, the economic growth model will focus on technological change and changes over time in the quantity of capital per hour worked in explaining

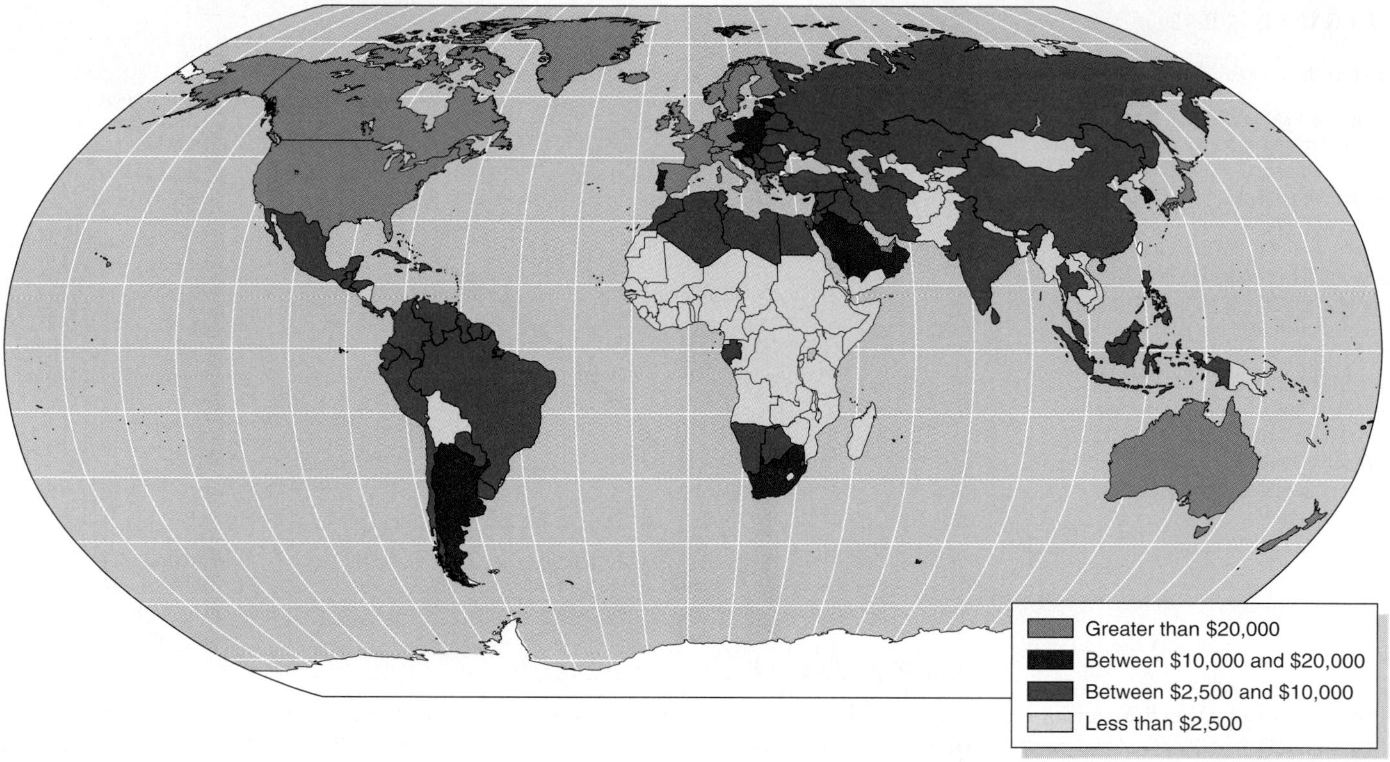

FIGURE 10-2 **GDP per Capita, 2004**

GDP per capita is measured in U.S. dollars corrected for differences across countries in the cost of living.

changes in real GDP per capita. Recall that **technological change** is an increase in the quantity of output firms can produce using a given quantity of inputs.

Technological change Change in the ability of a firm to produce a given level of output with a given quantity of inputs.

There are three main sources of technological change:

- ***Better machinery and equipment.*** Beginning with the steam engine during the Industrial Revolution, the invention of new machinery has been an important source of rising labor productivity. Today, continuing improvements in computers, factory machine tools, electric generators, and many other machines contribute to increases in labor productivity.
- ***Increases in human capital.*** Capital refers to physical capital, including computers, factory buildings, machine tools, warehouses, and trucks. The more physical capital workers have available, the more output they can produce. **Human capital** is the accumulated knowledge and skills that workers acquire from education and training or from their life experiences. As workers increase their human capital through education or on-the-job training, their productivity will also increase. The more educated workers are, the greater is their human capital.

Human capital The accumulated knowledge and skills that workers acquire from education and training or from their life experiences.

- ***Better means of organizing and managing production.*** Labor productivity will increase if managers can do a better job of organizing production. For example, the *just-in-time system,* first developed by Toyota Motor Corporation, involves assembling goods from parts that arrive at the factory at the exact time they are needed. With this system, fewer workers are needed to store and keep track of parts in the factory, so the quantity of goods produced per hour worked will increase.

To summarize, we can say an economy will have a higher standard of living the more capital it has per hour worked, the better the capital, the more human capital workers have, and the better job business managers do in organizing production.

FIGURE 10-3

The Per-Worker Production Function

The per-worker production function shows the relationship between capital per hour worked and real GDP per hour worked, holding technology constant. Increases in capital per hour worked increase output per hour worked, but at a diminishing rate. For example, an increase in capital per hour worked from $20,000 to $30,000 increases real GDP per hour worked from $200 to $350. An increase in capital per hour worked from $30,000 to $40,000 increases real GDP per hour worked only from $350 to $475. Each additional $10,000 increase in capital per hour worked results in progressively smaller increases in output per work.

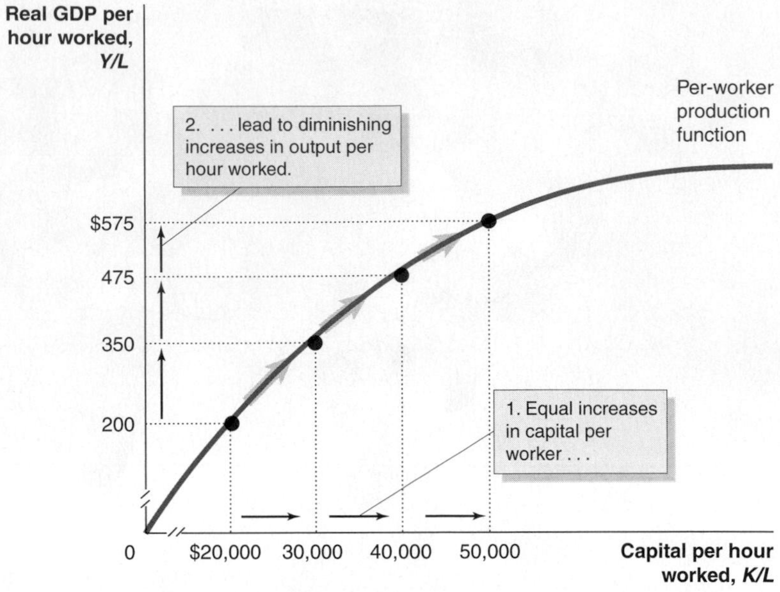

Per-worker production function The relationship between real GDP, or output, per hour worked and capital per hour worked, holding the level of technology constant.

The Per-Worker Production Function

We can illustrate the economic growth model using the **per-worker production function,** which is the relationship between real GDP, or output, per hour worked and capital per hour worked, holding the level of technology constant. Using the per-worker production function, we explore further the effects of increases in the amount of capital per hour worked and increases in technology on economic growth. In the per-worker production function graph shown in Figure 10-3, we measure capital per hour worked along the horizontal axis and real GDP per hour worked along the vertical axis. Letting K stand for capital, L stand for labor, and Y stand for real GDP, real GDP per hour worked is Y/L and capital per hour worked is K/L. Initially, we assume that the level of technology does not change.

The figure shows that increases in the quantity of capital per hour worked result in movements up the per-worker production function, increasing the quantity of output each worker produces. When *holding technology constant,* however, equal increases in the amount of capital per hour worked lead to *diminishing* increases in output per hour worked. For example, increasing capital per hour worked from $20,000 to $30,000 increases real GDP per hour worked from $200 to $350, an increase of $150. Another $10,000 increase in capital per hour worked, from $30,000 to $40,000, increases real GDP per hour worked from $350 to $475, an increase of only $125. Each additional $10,000 increase in capital per hour worked results in progressively smaller increases in real GDP per hour worked. In fact, at very high levels of capital per hour worked, further increases in capital per hour worked will not result in any increase in real GDP per hour worked. This effect results from the *law of diminishing returns,* which states that as we add more of one input—in this case, capital—to a fixed quantity of another input—in this case, labor—output increases by smaller additional amounts.

Why are there diminishing returns to capital? Consider a simple example in which you own a copy store. At first you have 10 employees, but only one copy machine, so each of your workers is able to produce relatively few copies per day. When you buy a second copy machine, your employees will be able to produce more copies. Adding additional copy machines will continue to increase your output but by increasingly smaller amounts. For example, adding a twentieth copy machine to the nineteen you already have will not increase the copies each worker is able to make by nearly as much as adding a second copy machine did. Eventually, adding additional copying machines will not increase your output at all.

Which Is More Important for Economic Growth: More Capital or Technological Change?

Technological change helps economies avoid diminishing returns to capital. Consider the following simple examples of the effects of technological change: Suppose you have 10 copy machines in your copy store. Each of the copy machines can produce 10 copies per minute. You don't believe that adding an eleventh machine, identical to the 10 you already have, will significantly increase the number of copies your employees can produce in a day. Then you find out that a new copy machine has become available that produces 20 copies per minute. If you replace your existing machines with the new machines, the productivity of your workers will increase. The replacement of existing capital with more productive capital is an example of technological change.

Or suppose you realize that the layout of your store could be improved. Maybe the paper for the machines is on shelves at the back of the store, which makes your workers waste time walking back and forth whenever the machines run out of paper. By placing the paper closer to the copy machines, you also will improve the productivity of your workers. Reorganizing how production takes place so as to increase output is also an example of technological change.

Technological Change: The Key to Sustaining Economic Growth

Figure 10-4 shows the impact of technological change on the per-worker production function. Technological change shifts up the per-worker production function and allows an economy to produce more real GDP per hour worked with the same quantity of capital per hour worked. For example, if the current level of technology puts the economy on Production function$_1$, then when capital per hour worked is \$50,000, real GDP per hour worked is \$575. Technological change that shifts the economy to Production function$_2$ makes it possible to produce \$675 in goods and services per hour worked with the same level of capital per hour worked. Further increases in technology that shift the economy to higher production functions result in further increases in real GDP per hour worked. Because of diminishing returns to capital, continuing increases in real

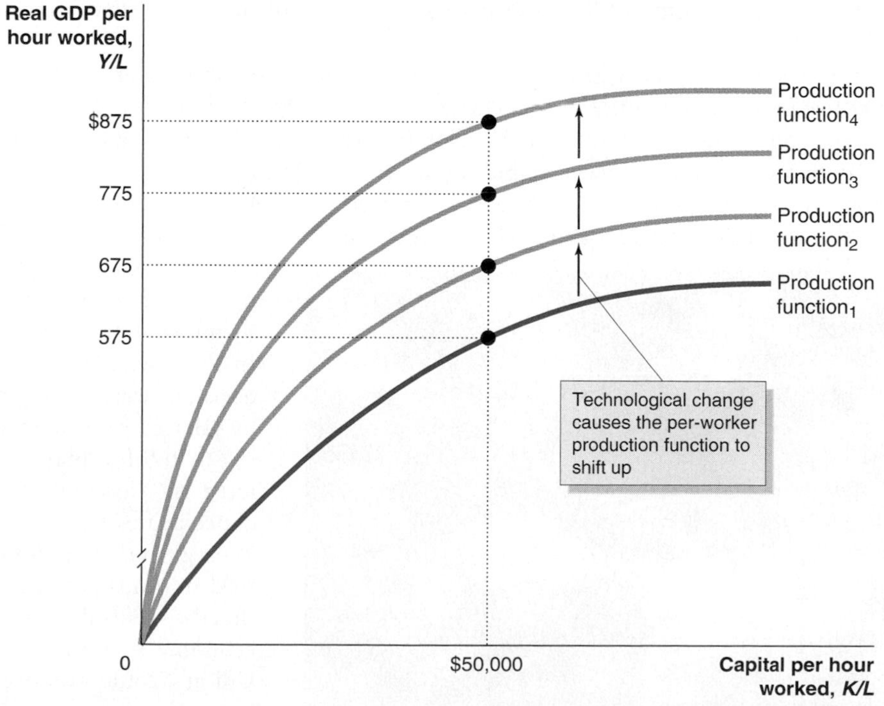

FIGURE 10-4

Technological Change Increases Output per Hour Worked

Technological change shifts up the production function and allows more output per hour worked with the same amount of capital per hour worked. For example, along Production function$_1$ with \$50,000 in capital per hour worked, the economy can produce \$575 in real GDP per hour worked. However, an increase in technology that shifts the economy to Production function$_2$ makes it possible to produce \$675 in real GDP per hour worked with the same level of capital per hour worked.

GDP per hour worked can be sustained only if there is technological change. Remember that a country will experience increases in its standard of living only if it experiences increases in real GDP per hour worked. Therefore, we can draw the following important conclusion: *In the long run, a country will experience an increasing standard of living only if it experiences continuing technological change.*

10-3 Making the Connection

Why Did the Soviet Union's Economy Fail?

The economic growth model can help explain one of the most striking events of the twentieth century: the economic collapse of the Soviet Union. The Soviet Union was formed from the old Russian Empire following the Communist revolution of 1917. Under Communism, the Soviet Union was a centrally planned economy where the government owned nearly every business and made all production and pricing decisions. In 1960, Nikita Khrushchev, the leader of the Soviet Union, addressed the United Nations in New York City. He declared to the United States and the other democracies, "We will bury you. Your grandchildren will live under Communism."

Many people at the time took Khrushchev's boast seriously. Capital per hour worked grew rapidly in the Soviet Union from 1950 through the 1980s. At first, these increases in capital per hour worked also produced rapid increases in real GDP per hour worked. Rapid increases in real GDP per hour worked during the 1950s caused some economists in the United States wrongly to predict that the Soviet Union would some day surpass the United States economically. In fact, diminishing returns to capital meant that the additional factories the Soviet Union was building resulted in smaller and smaller increases in real GDP per hour worked.

The Soviet Union did experience some technological change, but at a rate much slower than in the United States and other industrial countries. Why did the Soviet Union fail the crucial requirement for growth: implementing new technologies? The key reason is that in a centrally planned economy the persons in charge of running most businesses were government employees and not entrepreneurs or independent business people, as is the case in market economies. Soviet managers had little incentive to adopt new ways of doing things. Their pay depended on producing the quantity of output specified in the government's economic plan, not on discovering new, better, and lower-cost ways to produce goods. In addition, these managers did not have to worry about competition from either domestic or foreign firms.

Entrepreneurs and managers of firms in the United States, by contrast, are under intense competitive pressure from other firms. They must constantly search for better ways of producing the goods and services they sell. Developing and using new technologies is an important way to gain a competitive edge and higher profits. The drive for profit provides an incentive for technological change that centrally planned economies are unable to duplicate. In market economies, decisions about which investments to make and which technologies to adopt are made by entrepreneurs and managers with their own money on the line. In the Soviet system, these decisions were usually made by salaried bureaucrats trying to fulfill a plan formulated in Moscow. Nothing concentrates the mind like having your own funds at risk. In hindsight, it is clear that a centrally planned economy, such as the Soviet Union's, could not, over the long run, grow faster than a market economy. The Soviet

He did not bury us.

Union collapsed in 1991, and contemporary Russia now has a more market-oriented system, although the government continues to play a much larger role in the economy than it does in the United States.

SOLVED PROBLEM 10-1

Using the Economic Growth Model to Analyze the Failure of the Soviet Union's Economy

② LEARNING OBJECTIVE
Use the economic growth model to explain why growth rates differ across countries.

Use the economic growth model and the information in "Making the Connection 10-3: Why Did the Soviet Union's Economy Fail?" to analyze the economic problems the Soviet Union encountered.

Solving the Problem:

Step 1: Review the chapter material. This problem is about using the economic growth model to explain the failure of the Soviet economy, so you may want to review "Making the Connection 10–3, Why Did the Soviet Union's Economy Fail?" which begins on page 302.

Step 2: Draw a graph like Figure 10-3 to illustrate the economic problems of the Soviet Union. For simplicity, we can assume that the Soviet Union experienced no technological change.

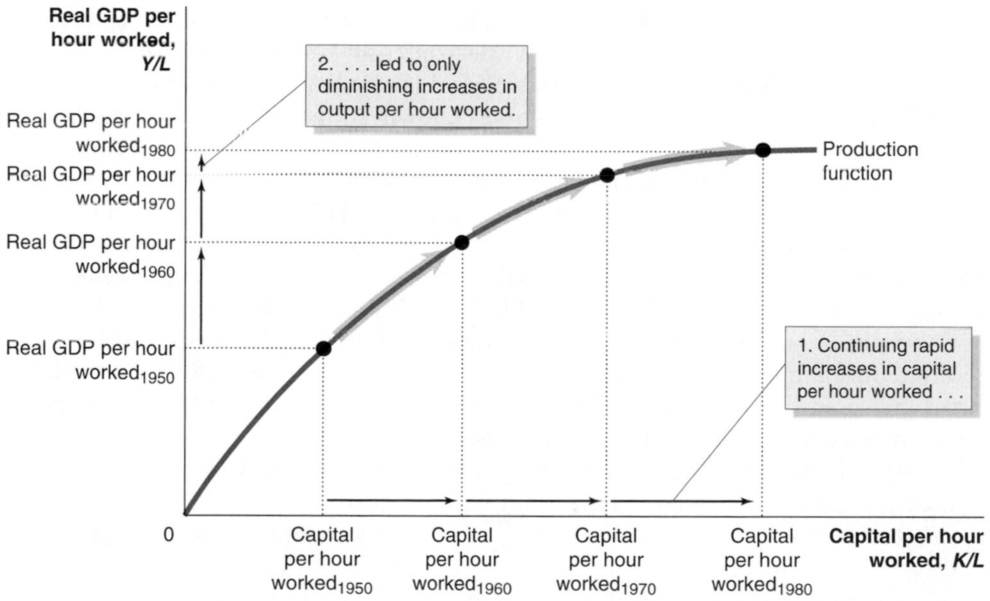

The Soviet Union experienced rapid increases in capital per hour worked from 1950 through the 1980s, but its failure to implement new technology meant that output per hour worked grew at a slower and slower rate.

Extra Credit: The Soviet Union hoped to raise the standard of living of its citizens above that enjoyed in the United States and other high-income countries. Its strategy was to make continuous increases in the quantity of capital available to its workers. The economic growth model helps us understand the flaws in this policy for achieving economic growth.

YOUR TURN: **For more practice, do related problems 5 and 6 on page 326 at the end of this chapter.**

Endogenous Growth Theory

The economic growth model we have been using was first developed in the 1950s by Robert Solow, an economist at MIT and winner of the Nobel Prize in Economics. According to this model, productivity growth is the key factor in explaining long-run growth in real GDP per capita. In recent years, some economists have become dissatisfied with this model because it does not explain the factors that determine productivity growth. **Endogenous growth theory**—sometimes called the *new growth theory*—was developed by Paul Romer, an economist at Stanford University, to provide a better explanation of the sources of productivity change. Romer argues that the rate of technological change is influenced by economic incentives, and so is *endogenous,* or determined by the working of the market system, rather than *exogenous,* or determined outside of the market system. Exogenous technological change is unexplained or attributed to factors such as chance scientific discoveries.

Endogenous growth theory A model of long-run economic growth that emphasizes that technological change is influenced by economic incentives, and so is determined by the working of the market system.

Romer argues that the accumulation of *knowledge capital* is a key determinant of economic growth. Firms contribute to an economy's stock of knowledge capital when they engage in research and development or otherwise contribute to technological change. We have seen that accumulation of physical capital is subject to diminishing returns: Increases in capital per hour worked lead to increases in real GDP per hour worked, but at a decreasing rate. Romer argues that the same is true of knowledge capital, *at the firm level.* As firms add to their stock of knowledge capital they will increase their output, but at a decreasing rate. At the level of the economy, however, Romer argues that knowledge capital is subject to *increasing returns.* This result holds true because knowledge, once discovered, becomes available to everyone. The use of physical capital, such as a computer or machine tool, is *rival* because if one firm uses it other firms cannot, and *excludable* because the firm that owns the capital can keep other firms from using it. The use of knowledge capital, such as the chemical formula for a drug that cures cancer, is nonrival, however, because one firm's using this knowledge does not prevent another firm's using it. Knowledge capital is also nonexcludable because once something like a chemical formula becomes known, it becomes widely available for other firms to use (unless, as we will discuss below, the government gives the firm that invents a new product the legal right to exclusive use of it).

Because knowledge capital is nonrival and nonexcludable, firms can *free ride* on the research and development of other firms. Firms free ride when they benefit from the results of research and development they did not pay for. For example, transistor technology was first developed at Western Electric's Bell Laboratories in the 1950s and served as the basic technology of the information revolution. Bell Laboratories, however, received only a tiny fraction of the immense profits that were eventually made by all the firms that used this technology. Romer points out that firms are unlikely to invest in research and development up to the point where the marginal cost of the research equals the marginal return from the knowledge gained because much of the marginal return will be gained by *other* firms. Therefore, there is likely to be an inefficiently small amount of research and development, slowing the accumulation of knowledge capital and economic growth.

Government policy can help increase the accumulation of knowledge capital in three ways:

- ***Protecting intellectual property with patents and copyrights.*** Governments can increase the incentive to engage in research and development by giving firms the exclusive rights to their discoveries for a period of years. The U.S. government grants patents to companies that develop new products or new ways of making existing products. A **patent** gives a firm the exclusive legal right to a new product for a period of 20 years from the date the product was invented. For example, a pharmaceutical firm that develops a drug that cures cancer can secure a patent on the drug, keeping other firms from manufacturing the drug without permission. The profits earned during the period the patent was in force would provide an incentive for undertaking the research and development. The patent system has

Patent The exclusive right to a product for a period of 20 years from the date the product was invented.

drawbacks, however. In filing for a patent, firms must disclose information about the product or process. This information enters the public record and may help competing firms develop products or processes that are similar but that do not infringe on the patent. To avoid this problem, some firms try to keep the results of their research a *trade secret*, without patenting it. A famous example of a trade secret is the formula for Coke. Tension also arises between the government's objectives of providing patent protection that give firms the incentive to engage in research and development and making sure that the knowledge gained by the research is widely disseminated for the greatest impact on the economy. Economists debate the characteristics of an ideal patent system.

Just as a new product or a new method of making a product receives patent protection, books, films, and software receive *copyright* protection. Under U.S. law, the creator of a book, film, or piece of software has the exclusive right to use the creation during the creator's lifetime. The creator's heirs retain this exclusive right for 70 years after the creator's death.

- ***Subsidizing research and development.*** The government can use subsidies to increase the quantity of research and development that takes place. In the United States, the federal government carries out some research directly. For example, the National Institutes of Health conducts medical research. The government also subsidizes research by providing grants to researchers in universities through the National Science Foundation and other agencies. Finally, the government provides tax benefits to firms that invest in research and development.
- ***Subsidizing education.*** Research and development are carried out by people with technical training. If firms are unable to capture all the profits from research and development, the wages and salaries paid to technical workers will be reduced. These lower wages and salaries reduce the incentive to workers to receive this training. If the government subsidizes education, it can increase the number of workers with technical training. In the United States, the government subsidizes education by directly providing free education from grades kindergarten through 12 and by providing support for public colleges and universities. The government also provides student loans at reduced interest rates.

These government policies can bring the accumulation of knowledge capital closer to the optimal level.

Joseph Schumpeter and Creative Destruction

Endogenous growth theory has revived interest in the ideas of Joseph Schumpeter. Schumpeter was born in Austria in 1883. He served briefly as that country's finance minister, before becoming an economics professor at Harvard in 1932. Schumpeter developed a model of growth that emphasized his view that new products unleash a "gale of creative destruction" in which older products—and, often, the firms that produced them—are driven out of the market. According to Schumpeter, the key to rising living standards is not small changes to existing products but, rather, products that meet consumer wants in qualitatively better ways. For example, in the early twentieth century, the automobile displaced the horse-drawn carriage by meeting consumer demand for personal transportation in a way that was qualitatively better. In the early twenty-first century, the DVD and the DVD player displaced the VHS tape and the VCR by better meeting consumer demand for watching films at home.

To Schumpeter, the entrepreneur is central to economic growth:

> [T]he function of entrepreneurs is to reform or revolutionize the pattern of production by exploiting an invention or, more generally, an untried technological possibility for producing new commodities or producing an old one in a new way.

The profits an entrepreneur hopes to earn provide the incentive for bringing together the factors of production—labor, capital, and natural resources—to start new firms and introduce new goods and services. Successful entrepreneurs can use their profits to finance the development of new products and are better able to attract funds from investors.

③ LEARNING OBJECTIVE
Discuss fluctuations in productivity growth in the United States.

Economic Growth in the United States

The economic growth model can also help us understand the record of growth in the United States. Figure 10-5 shows average annual growth rates in real GDP per hour worked since 1800. As the United States experienced the Industrial Revolution during the nineteenth century, U.S. firms increased the quantities of capital per hour worked. New technologies such as the steam engine, the railroad, and the telegraph also became available. Together, these factors resulted in an average annual growth rate of real GDP per worker of 1.3 percent during the century from 1800 to 1900. Real GDP per capita grew at a slower rate of 1.1 percent during this period. At this growth rate, real GDP per capita would double about every 63 years, which means that living standards were growing relatively slowly, but steadily.

By the twentieth century, technological change had been institutionalized. Many large corporations began to set up research and development facilities to improve the quality of their products and the efficiency with which they produced them. Universities also began to conduct research that had business applications. After World War II, many corporations began to provide significant funds to universities to help pay for research. In 1950, the federal government created the National Science Foundation, whose main goal was to support university researchers. The accelerating rate of technological change led to more rapid growth rates.

Economic Growth in the United States Since 1950: Fast, Then Slow, Then Fast Again

Continuing technological change allowed the U.S. economy to avoid the diminishing returns to capital that stifled growth in the Soviet economy. In fact, until the 1970s, the growth rate of the U.S. economy accelerated over time. As Figure 10-5 shows, growth in the first half of the twentieth century was faster than growth during the nineteenth cen-

FIGURE 10-5

Average Annual Growth Rates in Real GDP per Hour Worked in the United States

The growth rate in the United States increased from 1800 through the mid-1970s. Then, for more than 20 years, growth slowed before increasing again in the mid-1990s.

Note: The values for 1800–1900 are real GDP per worker. The values for 1900–2004 are real GDP per hour worked and are the authors' calculations from data in Neville Francis and Valerie A. Ramey, "The Source of Historical Economic Fluctuations: An Analysis Using Long-Run Restrictions," forthcoming in Jeffrey Frankel, Richard Clarida, and Francesco Giavazzi, eds., *International Seminar in Macroeconomics,* Chicago: University of Chicago Press, 2005; the authors thank Neville Francis for kindly providing these data.

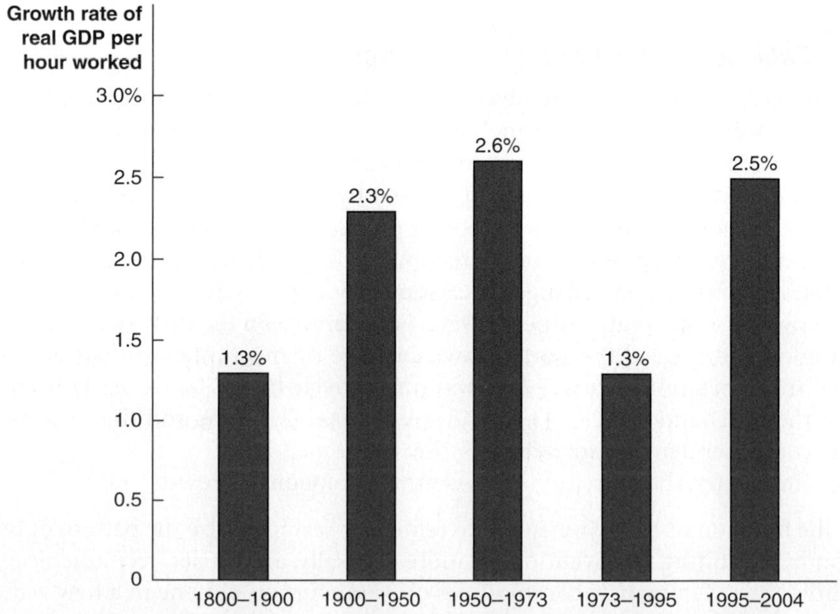

tury, and growth from 1950 to 1973 was faster yet. Then the unexpected happened: For more than 20 years, from 1973 to 1995, the growth rate of real GDP per hour worked slowed. The growth rate during these years was more than one percentage point per year lower than during the 1950–1973 period. Measured in 2000 dollars, real GDP per hour worked in the United States was $26,345 in 1973. If it had continued to grow from 1973 to 1995 at the same rate it had been growing from 1950 to 1973, it would have been about $46,000 in 1995, which is 30 percent higher than it actually was. The United States would today be a significantly richer country if the growth in the productivity of U.S. workers had not slowed down from the mid-1970s to the mid-1990s.

What Caused the Productivity Slowdown of 1973–1995?

Several explanations have been offered for the productivity slowdown of the mid-1970s to mid-1990s, but none is completely satisfying. We can briefly discuss three possible explanations for the slowdown:

- Measurement problems
- High oil prices
- A decline in labor quality

WAS IT A MEASUREMENT PROBLEM? Some economists argue that productivity really didn't slow down during these years. It only *appears* to have slowed down because of problems in measuring productivity accurately. After 1970, services—such as haircuts and financial advice—became a larger fraction of GDP, and goods—such as automobiles and hamburgers—became a smaller fraction. It is harder to measure increases in the output of services than to measure increases in the output of goods. Beginning in the 1970s, advances in information technology improved the convenience of some services without actually increasing the quantity of the services offered. For example, before banks began using automated teller machines (ATMs) in the 1980s, to withdraw money you would have to go to a bank before closing time—which was usually 3:00 P.M. Once ATMs became available, you could withdraw money at any time of the day or night at a variety of locations. This increased convenience from ATMs does not show up in GDP. If it did, measured output per hour worked would have grown more rapidly.

There may also be a measurement problem in accounting for improvements in the environment and in health and safety. The Clean Air Act, passed in 1970, was the first of several federal laws that required firms to significantly reduce pollution. Other laws passed during the 1970s were aimed at promoting health and safety. The Occupational Safety and Health Administration (OSHA) and the Consumer Products Safety Commission were also given the authority to issue guidelines that firms are legally required to obey. As a result, firms had to spend billions of dollars reducing pollution, improving workplace safety, and redesigning products to improve their safety. This spending did not result in additional output that would be included in GDP—although it may have increased overall well-being. If these increases in well-being had been included in GDP, measured output per hour worked would have grown more rapidly.

It is possible that these changes in the economy during the 1970s—increased production of services and increased spending by firms to comply with environmental, safety, and health regulations—can account for some of the slowdown in the growth rate of output per hour worked. However, most economists do not believe that the effect of these factors is large enough to be the whole explanation.

WAS IT THE EFFECT OF HIGH OIL PRICES? In 1973, the Organization of Petroleum Exporting Countries (OPEC) increased the price of a barrel of oil from less than $3 to more than $10. A second sharp increase in oil prices occurred in the late 1970s, when the price of a barrel of oil rose from about $20 to more than $35. These higher oil prices increased production costs for many firms in the United States. Some firms use oil directly in the production process. Other firms use products, such as plastics, that are made from oil. Some utilities burn oil to generate electricity, so electricity prices rose. Rising oil prices led to rising gasoline prices, which raised transportation costs for many firms. To conserve oil and use less energy, firms reorganized production in ways that reduced output per hour worked.

In the early 1980s, many economists thought the oil price increases explained the productivity slowdown, but the productivity slowdown continued after U.S. firms had fully adjusted to high oil prices. In fact, it continued into the late 1980s and early 1990s when oil prices declined.

WAS IT THE DECLINING QUALITY OF LABOR? Some economists argue that deterioration in the U.S. educational system may have contributed to the slowdown. Scores on some standardized tests began to decline in the 1970s. This decline may indicate that, on average, workers entering the labor force were less well educated and less productive than in earlier decades. A more subtle argument is that the skills required to perform many jobs increased during the 1970s and 1980s, while the preparation that workers had received in school did not keep pace. It is difficult to quantify the skill requirements of jobs and the skills of workers. So, it is difficult to estimate how much of the growth slowdown may have been due to the failure of worker skills to keep pace with the skill requirements of jobs.

THE PRODUCTIVITY SLOWDOWN AFFECTED ALL INDUSTRIAL COUNTRIES In assessing possible causes of the productivity slowdown, it is important to note that the United States was not alone in experiencing the slowdown in productivity. All the leading industrial countries experienced a growth slowdown between the mid-1970s and the mid-1990s. Therefore, explanations for the slowdown that rely on factors affecting only the United States—such as the deterioration in the quality of schooling—are not likely to be correct. Because all the industrial economies began producing more services and fewer goods and enacted stricter environmental regulations at about the same time, explanations of the productivity slowdown that emphasize measurement problems become more plausible. In the end, though, economists have not yet reached a consensus on why the productivity slowdown took place.

The Productivity Boom: Are We in a "New Economy"?

The productivity slowdown began abruptly in the mid-1970s and ended just as abruptly in the mid-1990s. As Figure 10-5 showed, productivity growth in the United States between 1995 and 2004 was almost as fast as before the growth slowdown. Some economists argue that the higher productivity growth that began in the mid-1990s reflects the development of a "New Economy" based on information technology. The spread of ever faster and ever cheaper computers has made communication and data processing easier and faster than ever before. Today, a single desktop computer has more computing power than all the mainframe computers NASA used to control the Apollo spacecrafts that landed on the moon in the late 1960s and early 1970s.

Faster data processing has a major impact on nearly every firm. Business record keeping, once done laboriously by hand, is now done more quickly and accurately by computer. The increase in Internet use during the 1990s brought changes to the ways firms sell to consumers and to each other. Cell phones, laptop computers, and wireless Internet access allow people to work away from the office, whether at home or while traveling. Many economists believe that these developments have significantly increased labor productivity. A recent study by economists at the U.S. Department of Commerce has quantified the contribution of information technology to growth in real GDP. Figure 10-6 shows that information technology industries, such as computers, semiconductors, cell phones, computer programming, and computer software, have accounted for as much as one-third of the growth in real GDP in recent years. For example, in 1997, real GDP grew by 4.5 percent. Of that increase, 1.5 percentage points—or, one-third—was due to information technology industries.

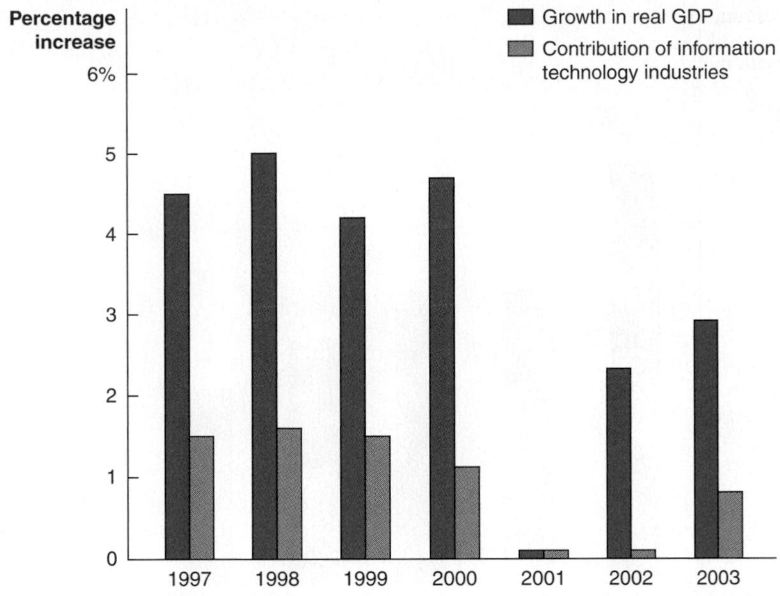

FIGURE 10-6

The Contribution of Information Technology to Growth in Real GDP

Information technology industries, such as computers, semiconductors, cell phones, computer programming, and computer software, have accounted for as much as one-third of the growth in real GDP in recent years. For example, in 1997, real GDP grew by 4.5 percent. Of that increase, 1.5 percentage points was due to information technology industries.

Source: U.S. Department of Commerce, Economics and Statistics Administration, *Digital Economy 2003*, December 2003, Table 1.1, p. 10.

Many economists are optimistic that the increases in productivity that began in the mid-1990s will continue. The use of computers, and information and communications technology generally, has increased as prices continue to fall. By 2005, well-equipped desktop computers could be purchased for less than $300. Further innovations in information and communications technology may continue to contribute to strong productivity growth. Some economists are more skeptical, however, about the ability of the economy to continue to sustain high rates of productivity growth. These economists argue that in the 1990s, innovations in information and communications technology—such as the development of the World Wide Web, Windows 95, and computerized inventory control systems—raised labor productivity by having a substantial effect on how businesses operated. By the early 2000s, these economists argue, innovations in information and communications technology were having a greater impact on consumer products, such as cell phones, than on the processes internal to firms that would lead to higher productivity. If the rapid increases in output per hour worked that began in the mid-1990s do continue, this trend will be good news for increases in living standards in the United States.

Why Has Productivity Growth Been Faster in the United States than in Other Countries?

One notable aspect of the increase in productivity after 1995 is that, unlike the earlier productivity slowdown, it has not been experienced equally by all of the leading industrial countries. Figure 10-7 shows labor productivity growth during the years from 1996 to 2004 for the leading industrial countries, known collectively as the *Group of Seven* or the *G-7* countries. Productivity growth was significantly higher in the United States than in the other six countries. The next most rapidly growing country was the United Kingdom, although its productivity growth rate was still more than 30 percent below the growth rate in the United States. The productivity growth rate was actually *slower* in Japan, France, Germany, and Italy during these years than it had been during the years from 1973 to 1995.

Why has productivity growth in the United States been more rapid than in the other industrial countries? Many economists believe there are two main explanations: the greater flexibility of U.S. labor markets and the greater efficiency of the U.S. financial system. U.S. labor markets are more flexible than labor markets in other countries for several reasons. In many European countries, government regulations make it difficult for firms to fire workers. These regulations make firms reluctant to hire workers. As a result, many younger workers have difficulty finding jobs, and once a job is found

FIGURE 10-7

Productivity Growth in the Leading Industrial Economies, 1996–2004

Productivity growth as measured by the average annual growth rate of labor productivity was more rapid in the United States than in the other leading industrial countries during the years between 1996 and 2004.

Source: Organization for Economic Cooperation and Development, *Economic Outlook, 2005,* Annex Table 12.

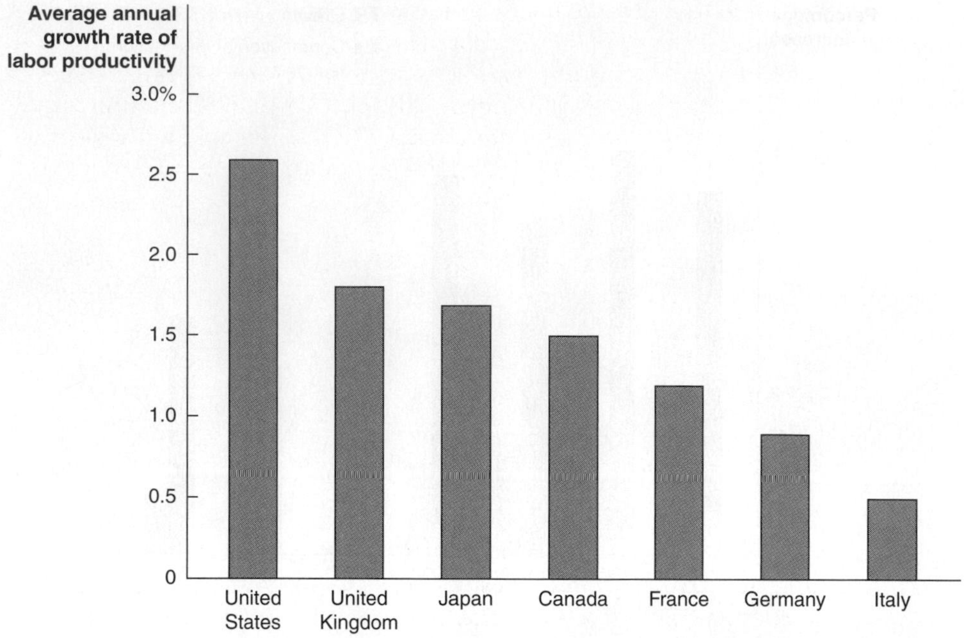

a worker tends to remain in it even if the worker's skills and preferences are not a good match for the characteristics of the job. In the United States, by contrast, government regulations are less restrictive, workers have an easier time finding jobs, and workers also change jobs fairly frequently. For example, a typical young worker in the United States will hold seven different jobs during the worker's first 10 years in the labor force. This high rate of job mobility ensures a better match between workers' skills and preferences and the characteristics of jobs, which increases labor productivity. The higher productivity translates into higher wages: One-third of the increase in wages experienced by young workers results from job changes. Workers can also build skills through being exposed to a variety of different jobs. Workers in the United States may acquire as much as half of their skills through job mobility, on-the-job learning, and workplace education.

Many European countries also have restrictive work rules that limit the flexibility of firms to implement new technologies. Some of these work rules are imposed by government regulation, others are negotiated by labor unions. Because these rules restrict the tasks workers can be asked to perform and the hours during the day they can be asked to work, they reduce the ability of firms to use new technologies that may require workers to learn new skills, perform new tasks, or work during the night or early mornings. Firms must often negotiate with workers before introducing new products or relocating facilities. The hours that retail stores may be open are regulated in most European countries. These regulations reduce the revenue firms can generate from implementing new technologies, and therefore reduce the incentives that firms have to adopt the technologies.

Workers in the United States tend to enter the labor force earlier, retire later, and experience fewer long spells of unemployment than do workers in Europe. These differences between the labor force experiences of U.S. and European workers, including the greater tendency for U.S. teenagers and college students to work at least part time, can be explained in several ways. One key difference, however, is the design of the systems of government-provided unemployment insurance. As we noted in Chapter 8, unemployed workers in the United States are usually eligible to receive unemployment insurance payments equal to about half their previous wage for only six months. After that time, the opportunity cost of continuing to search for a job rises. In many other high-income countries, such as Canada and most of the countries of Western Europe, workers are eligible to receive unemployment payments for a year or more, and the payments may equal 70 percent to 80 percent of their previous wage. Because the opportunity cost of being unemployed is lower in these other countries, the unemployment rate tends to be higher and the fraction of the labor force that is unemployed for more than one year also tends to be higher. Studies have shown that workers who are employed for longer periods tend to have higher skills, greater productivity, and higher wages. Many economists believe that the design of the U.S. unemployment insurance program has contributed to the greater flexibility of U.S. labor markets and to higher rates of growth in labor productivity.

As we have seen, technological change is essential for rapid productivity growth. To obtain the funds needed to implement new technologies, firms turn to the financial system. It is important that funds for investment be not only available but also allocated efficiently. In the Soviet Union, there was no shortage of funds available for investment, but these funds were directed by the government mainly into building additional factories that employed old technologies, rather than being directed by entrepreneurs into funding the innovations that would have raised productivity and living standards. We saw in Chapter 5 that large corporations can raise funds by selling stocks and bonds in financial markets. U.S. corporations benefit from the efficiency of U.S. financial markets. The level of legal protection of investors is relatively high in U.S. financial markets, which encourages both U.S. and foreign investors to buy stocks and bonds issued by U.S. firms. The volume of trading in U.S. financial markets also assures investors that they will be able to quickly sell the stocks and the bonds they buy. This *liquidity* also serves to attract investors to U.S. markets.

Smaller firms that are unable to issue stocks and bonds often obtain funding from banks. However, entrepreneurs founding new firms, particularly firms that are based on new technologies, often cannot rely on banks or on sales of stocks and bonds in financial markets. Investors are usually unwilling to buy the stocks and bonds of a new firm that lacks a track record of profitability. Banks are similarly reluctant to lend money to a firm whose business plan is based on introducing a new product or a new way of producing an existing product. Many firms that are established to bring new technologies to market obtain funds from *venture capital firms*. Venture capital firms raise funds from institutional investors, such as pension funds, and from wealthy individuals, to invest in start-up firms. The owners of venture capital firms closely examine the business plans of start-up firms looking for those that appear most likely to succeed. In exchange for providing funding, the venture capital firm often becomes part owner of the start-up, placing its representative on the start-up's board of directors and sometimes even playing a role in managing the firm. A successful venture capital firm is able to attract investors who would not otherwise be willing to provide funds to start-up firms because the investors would lack sufficient credible information on any start-up's prospectus. The ability of venture capital firms to finance technology-driven start-up firms may be giving the United States an advantage in bringing new products and new processes to market.

Why Isn't the Whole World Rich?

(4) LEARNING OBJECTIVE

Explain economic catch-up, and discuss why many poor countries have not experienced rapid economic growth.

The economic growth model tells us that economies grow when the quantity of capital per hour worked increases and when technological change takes place. This model seems to provide a good blueprint for developing countries to become rich: Increase the quantity of capital per hour worked and use the best available technology. There are economic incentives for both of these things to happen in poor countries. The profitability of using additional capital or better technology is generally greater in a developing country than in a high-income country. For example, replacing an existing computer with a new, faster computer will generally have a relatively small payoff for a firm in the United States. In contrast, installing a new computer in a Zambian firm where records are kept by hand is likely to have an enormous payoff.

This observation leads to the following important conclusion: *The economic growth model predicts that poor countries will grow faster than rich countries.* If this prediction is correct, we should observe poor countries catching up to the rich countries in levels of

Catch-up The prediction that the level of GDP per capita (or income per capita) in poor countries will grow faster than in rich countries.

GDP per capita (or income per capita). Has this **catch-up**—or *convergence*—actually occurred? Here we come to a paradox: The lower-income *industrial* countries have been catching up to the higher-income industrial countries, but the developing countries as a group have not been catching up to the industrial countries as a group.

Catch-up: Sometimes, But Not Always

We can construct a graph that makes it easier to see whether catch-up is happening. In Figure 10-8 the horizontal axis shows the initial level of GDP per capita and the vertical axis shows the rate at which GDP per capita is growing. We can then plot points on the graph for rich and poor countries. Each point represents the combination of a country's initial level of GDP per capita and its growth rate over the following years. Low-income countries should be in the upper-left part of the graph because they would have low initial levels of GDP per capita but fast growth rates. High-income countries should be in the lower-right part of the graph because they would have high initial levels of GDP per capita but slow growth rates.

CATCH-UP AMONG THE INDUSTRIAL COUNTRIES If we look at only the industrial countries, we can see the catch-up predicted by the economic growth model. Figure 10-9 shows that the industrial countries that had the lowest incomes in 1960, such as Ireland and Japan, grew the fastest between 1960 and 2000. Countries that had the highest incomes in 1960, such as Switzerland and the United States, grew the slowest.

ARE THE DEVELOPING COUNTRIES CATCHING UP TO THE INDUSTRIAL COUNTRIES? If we expand the analysis to include every country for which statistics are available, it becomes more difficult to find the catch-up predicted by the economic growth model. Figure 10-10 does not show a consistent relationship between the level of real GDP in 1960 and growth from 1960 to 2000. Some countries, such as Niger or the Central African Republic, that had low levels of real GDP per capita in 1960 actually experienced *negative* economic growth: They had *lower* levels of real GDP per capita in 2000 than in 1960. Other countries, such as Malaysia and South Korea, that started with low levels of real GDP per capita grew rapidly. Some middle-income countries in 1960, such as Argentina, hardly grew between 1960 and 2000, while others, such as Israel, experienced significant growth.

FIGURE 10-8

The Catch-up Predicted by the Economic Growth Model

According to the economic growth model, countries that start with lower levels of GDP per capita should grow faster (points near the top of the line) than countries that start with higher levels of GDP per capita (points near the bottom of the line).

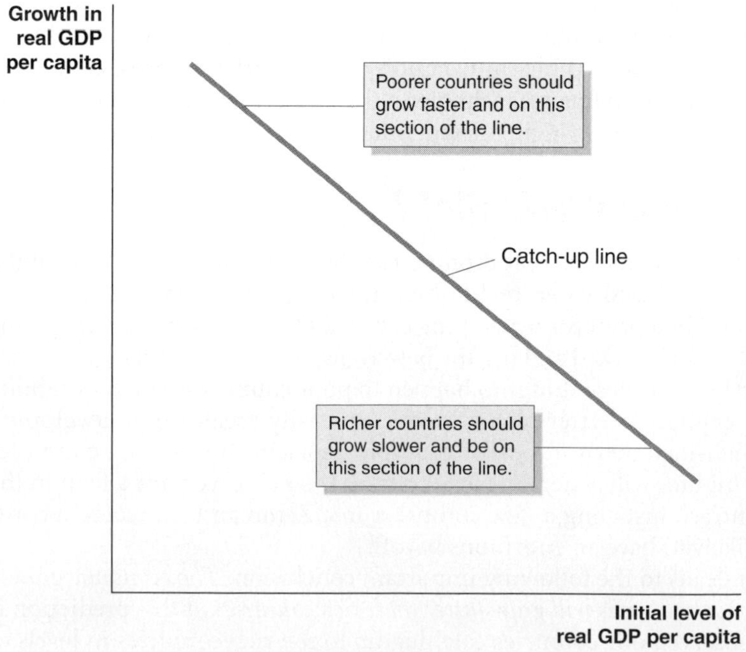

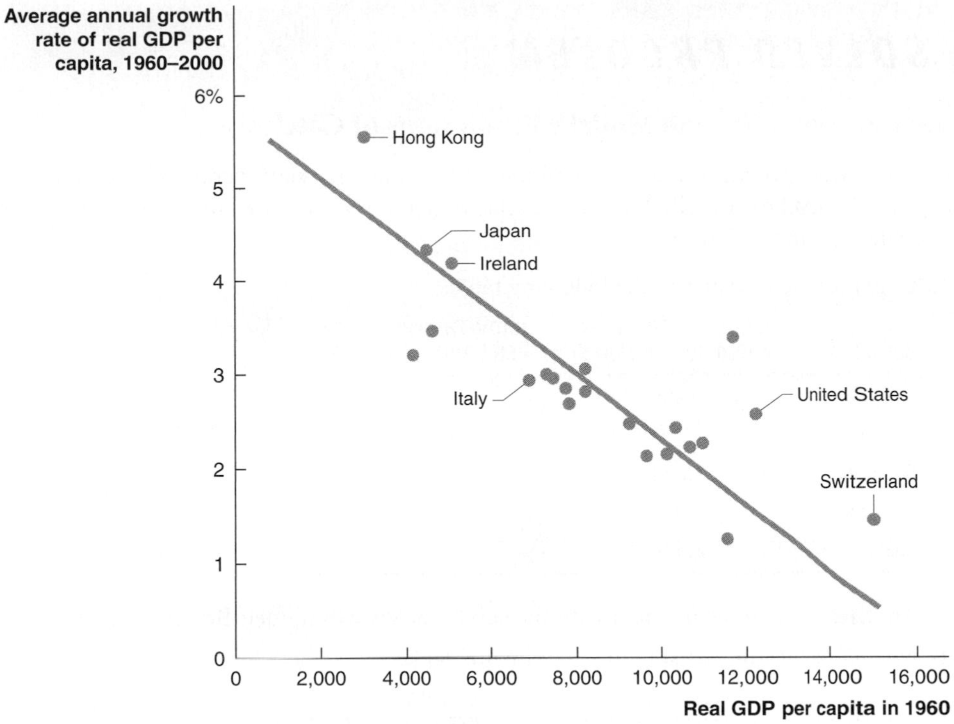

FIGURE 10-9

There Has Been Catch-up among Industrial Countries

The industrial countries such as Ireland and Japan that had the lowest incomes in 1960 grew the fastest between 1960 and 2000. Countries like Switzerland and the United States that had the highest incomes in 1960 grew the slowest. Data are real GDP per capita in 1996 dollars. Each point in the figure represents an industrial country.

Source: Authors' calculations from data in Alan Heston, Robert Summers, and Bettina Aten, Penn World Table, Version 6.0, Center for International Comparisons at the University of Pennsylvania (CICUP), December 2001.

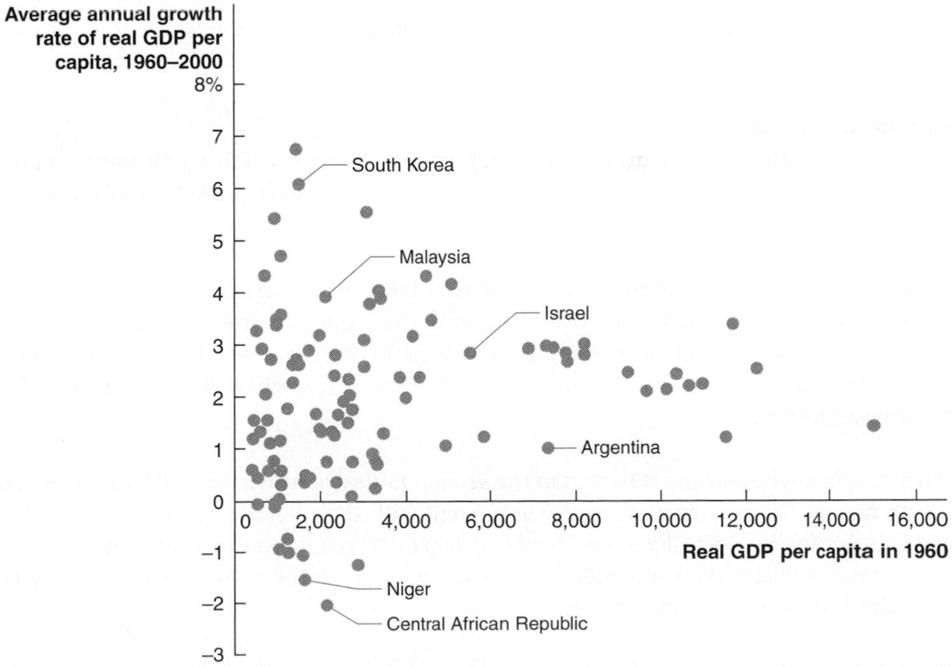

FIGURE 10-10

Most of the World Hasn't Been Catching Up

Looking at all countries for which statistics are available does not show the catch-up predicted by the economic growth model. Some countries, such as Niger or the Central African Republic, that had low levels of real GDP per capita in 1960 actually experienced *negative* economic growth. Other countries, such as Malaysia and South Korea, that started with low levels of real GDP per capita grew rapidly. Some middle-income countries in 1960, such as Argentina, hardly grew between 1960 and 2000, while others, such as Israel, experienced significant growth.

Note: Data are real GDP per capita in 1996 dollars. Each point in the figure represents a country.

Source: Authors' calculations from data in Alan Heston, Robert Summers, and Bettina Aten, Penn World Table, Version 6.0, Center for International Comparisons at the University of Pennsylvania (CICUP), December 2001.

SOLVED PROBLEM 10-2

④ LEARNING OBJECTIVE
Explain economic catch-up, and discuss why many poor countries have not experienced rapid economic growth.

The Economic Growth Model's Predictions of Catch-up

The economic growth model makes predictions about the relationship between an economy's initial level of real GDP per capita relative to other economies and how fast the economy will grow in the future.

a. Consider the statistics in the following table:

COUNTRY	REAL GDP PER CAPITA IN 1960 (1996 DOLLARS)	GROWTH IN REAL GDP PER CAPITA, 1960–2000
Botswana	$958	5.29%
Thailand	1,091	4.70
Sri Lanka	1,333	2.29
Ecuador	2,003	1.38
Guatemala	2,344	1.29

Are these statistics consistent with the economic growth model? Briefly explain.

b. Now consider the statistics in the following table:

COUNTRY	REAL GDP PER CAPITA IN 1960 (1996 DOLLARS)	GROWTH IN REAL GDP PER CAPITA, 1960–2000
Japan	$4,544	4.32%
Norway	8,240	3.00
The Netherlands	9,245	2.45
United Kingdom	9,674	2.10

Are these statistics consistent with the economic growth model? Briefly explain.

c. Construct a new table that lists all nine countries, from lowest real GDP per capita in 1960 to highest. Are the statistics in your new table consistent with the economic growth model?

Solving the Problem:

Step 1: Review the chapter material. This problem is about catch-up in the economic growth model, so you may want to review the section "Why Isn't the Whole World Rich?" which begins on page 311.

Step 2: Explain whether the statistics in the first table are consistent with the economic growth model. These statistics are consistent with the economic growth model. The countries with the lowest levels of real GDP per capita in 1960 had the fastest growth rates between 1960 and 2000, and the countries with the highest levels of real GDP per capita had the slowest growth rates.

Step 3: Explain whether the statistics in the second table are consistent with the economic growth model. These statistics are also consistent with the economic growth model. Once again, the countries with the lowest levels of real GDP per capita in 1960 had the fastest growth rates between 1960 and 2000, and the countries with the highest levels of real GDP per capita had the slowest growth rates.

Step 4: Construct a table that includes all nine countries from the tables in questions (a) and (b) and discuss the results.

COUNTRY	REAL GDP PER CAPITA IN 1960 (1996 DOLLARS)	GROWTH IN REAL GDP PER CAPITA, 1960–2000
Botswana	$958	5.29%
Thailand	1,091	4.70
Sri Lanka	1,333	2.29
Ecuador	2,003	1.38
Guatemala	2,344	1.29
Japan	4,544	4.32
Norway	8,240	3.00
The Netherlands	9,245	2.45
United Kingdom	9,674	2.10

The statistics in the new table are not consistent with the predictions of the economic growth model. For example, Japan and Norway had much higher levels of real GDP per capita in 1960 than did Sri Lanka, Ecuador, and Guatemala. The economic growth model predicts Japan and Norway would, therefore, have grown more slowly than Sri Lanka, Ecuador, and Guatemala. The data in the table show, however, that they grew faster.

Extra Credit: The statistics in these tables confirm what we saw in Figures 10-9 and 10-10: There has been catch-up among the industrial countries, but there has not been catch-up if we include all of the countries of the world in the analysis.

YOUR TURN: **For more practice, do problems 8 and 9 on page 326 at the end of this chapter.**

Why Don't More Low-Income Countries Experience Rapid Growth?

The economic growth model predicts that the countries that were very poor in 1960 should have grown rapidly over the next 40 years. As we have just seen, a few did, but most did not. Why are many low-income countries growing so slowly? There is no one answer, but most economists point to four key factors:

- Failure to enforce the rule of law
- Wars and revolutions
- Poor public education and health
- Low rates of saving and investment

FAILURE TO ENFORCE THE RULE OF LAW In the years since 1960, increasing numbers of developing countries, including China, have abandoned centrally planned economies in favor of more market-oriented economies. For entrepreneurs in a market economy to succeed, the government must guarantee private property rights and enforce contracts. Unless entrepreneurs feel secure in their property, they will not risk starting a business. It is also very difficult for businesses to operate successfully in a market economy unless they can use an independent court system to enforce contracts.

Consider, for example, the production of shoes in a developing country. Suppose the owner of a shoe factory signs a contract with a leather supplier to deliver a specific quantity of leather on a particular date for a particular price. On the basis of this contract, the owner of the shoe factory signs a contract to deliver a specific quantity of shoes to a shoe wholesaler. Once again, the contract will specify the quantity of shoes to be delivered, the quality of the shoes, the delivery date, and the price. The owner of the tannery that produces the leather will use the contract with the shoe factory to enter into a contract with cattle growers for the delivery of hides. The shoe wholesaler will enter into contracts to deliver shoes to retail stores where they are sold to consumers. For the flow of goods from cattle growers to shoe customers to operate efficiently, each business must carry out the terms of the contract it has signed. In developed countries, such as the United States, businesses know that if they fail to carry out a contract, they may be sued in court and forced to compensate the other party for any economic damages.

Many developing countries do not have a functioning, independent court system. Even if a court system does exist, a case may not be heard for many years. In some countries, bribery of judges and political favoritism in court rulings are common. If firms cannot enforce contracts through the court system, they will insist on carrying out only face-to-face cash transactions. For example, the shoe manufacturer will wait until the leather producer brings the hides to the factory and will then buy them for cash. The wholesaler will wait until the shoes have been produced before making plans for sales to retail stores. Production still takes place, but it is carried out more slowly and inefficiently. In these circumstances, firms have difficulty finding investors willing to provide them with the funds they need to expand.

Rule of law The ability of a government to enforce the laws of the country, particularly with respect to protecting private property and enforcing contracts.

The **rule of law** refers to the ability of a government to enforce the laws of the country, particularly with respect to protecting private property and enforcing contracts. The World Bank is an agency of the United Nations whose role is to provide financial aid and policy advice to low-income countries. Economists at the World Bank have ranked 118 developing countries on the basis of how well their governments enforce the rule of law. Figure 10-11 shows the difference in average annual growth rates between the 20 developing countries that do the best job of enforcing the rule of law, such as the Czech Republic and Israel, and the 20 countries that do the worst job, such as the Congo and Albania. Real GDP per capita in the 20 countries with the strongest rule of law grew more than six times faster during the 1990s than in the 20 countries with the weakest rule of law.

WARS AND REVOLUTIONS Many of the countries that were very poor in 1960 have experienced extended periods of war or violent changes of government during the years since. These wars made it impossible for countries such as Afghanistan, Angola, Ethiopia, the Central African Republic, and the Congo to accumulate capital or adopt new technologies. In fact, conducting any kind of business was very difficult. The positive effect on growth of ending war was shown in Mozambique, which suffered through almost two decades of civil war and declining real GDP per capita. With the end of civil war, Mozambique experienced a strong annual growth rate of 4.5 percent in real GDP per capita from 1990 to 2002.

FIGURE 10-11

The Rule of Law and Growth

The 20 developing countries that have the strongest rule of law, such as the Czech Republic and Israel, grew more than six times faster during the 1990s than the 20 developing countries that have the weakest rule of law, such as the Congo and Albania.

Source: Authors' calculation from data in David Dollar and Aart Kraay, "Property Rights, Political Rights, and the Development of Poor Countries in the Post-Colonial Period," World Bank Development Research Group Working Paper, October 2000.

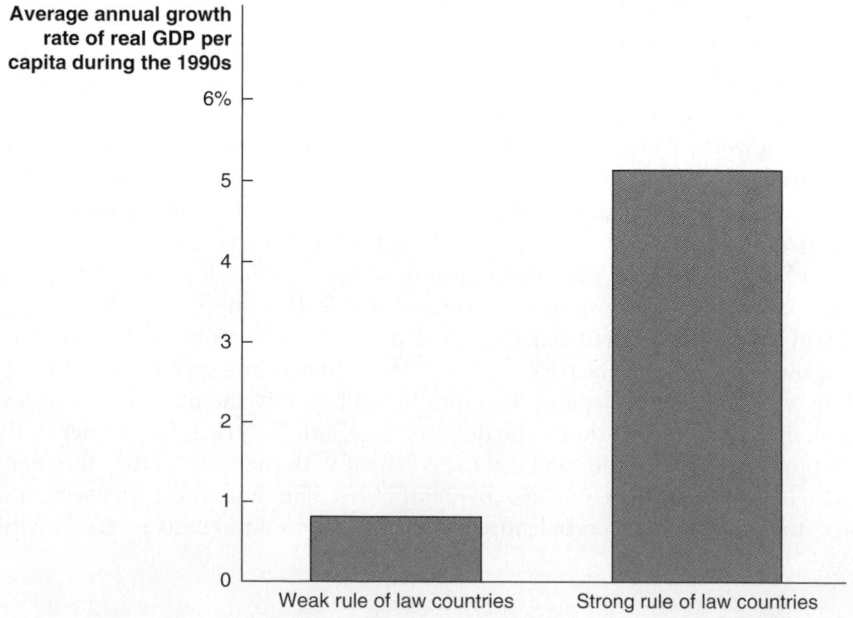

POOR PUBLIC EDUCATION AND HEALTH We have seen that human capital is one of the determinants of labor productivity. Many low-income countries have weak public school systems, so many workers are unable to read and write. Few workers acquire the skills necessary to use the latest technology.

Many low-income countries suffer from diseases that are either nonexistent or treated readily in high-income countries. For example, few people in the developed countries suffer from malaria, but more than a million Africans die from it each year. Treatments for AIDS have greatly reduced deaths from this disease in the United States and Europe. But millions of people in low-income countries continue to die from AIDS. Low-income countries often lack the resources, and their governments are often too ineffective to provide even routine medical care, such as childhood vaccinations.

People who are sick work less and are less productive when they do work. Poor nutrition or exposure to certain diseases in childhood can leave people permanently weakened and can affect their intelligence as adults. Poor health has a significant negative impact on the human capital of workers in developing countries.

LOW RATES OF SAVING AND INVESTMENT To invest in factories, machinery, and computers, firms need funds. Some of the funds can come from the owners of the firm and from their friends and family, but as we noted in Chapter 9, firms in high-income countries raise most of their funds from bank loans and selling stocks and bonds in financial markets. In most developing countries, stock and bond markets do not exist and often the banking system is very weak. In high-income countries, the funds that banks lend to businesses come from the savings of households. In high-income countries, many households are able to save a significant fraction of their income. In developing countries, many households barely survive on their incomes and, therefore, have little or no savings.

The low savings rates in developing countries contribute to a *vicious cycle* of poverty. Because households have low incomes, they save very little. Because households save very little, few funds are available for firms to borrow. Lacking funds, firms do not invest in the new factories, machinery, and equipment needed for economic growth. Because the economy does not grow, household incomes remain low, as do their savings, and so on.

The Benefits of Globalization

One way for a developing country to break out of the vicious cycle of low saving and investment and low growth is through foreign investment. **Foreign direct investment (FDI)** occurs when corporations build or purchase facilities in foreign countries. **Foreign portfolio investment** occurs when an individual or firm buys stock or bonds issued in another country. Foreign direct investment and foreign portfolio investment can give a low-income country access to funds and technology that otherwise would not be available. Until recently, many developing countries were reluctant to take advantage of this opportunity.

Foreign direct investment (FDI) The purchase or building by a corporation of a facility in a foreign country.

Foreign portfolio investment The purchase by an individual or firm of stock or bonds issued in another country.

From the 1940s through the 1970s, many developing countries sealed themselves off from the global economy. They did this for several reasons. During the 1930s and early 1940s, the global trading and financial system collapsed as a result of the Great Depression and World War II. Developing countries that relied on exporting to the industrial countries were hurt economically. The example of the Soviet Union indicated that it might be possible to achieve rapid growth without participating in the global economy. Also, many countries in Africa and Asia achieved independence from the colonial powers of Europe during the 1950s and 1960s and were afraid of being dominated by them economically. As a result, many developing countries imposed high tariffs on foreign imports and strongly discouraged or even prohibited foreign investment. This made it difficult to break out of the vicious cycle of poverty.

The policies of high tariff barriers and avoiding foreign investment failed to produce much growth, so by the 1980s many developing countries began to change policies.

FIGURE 10-12

Globalization and Growth

Countries that were more open to foreign trade and investment grew much faster during the 1990s than countries that were less open.

Source: "David Dollar, "Globalization, Inequality, and Poverty Since 1980," WPS3333, World Bank, June 2004.

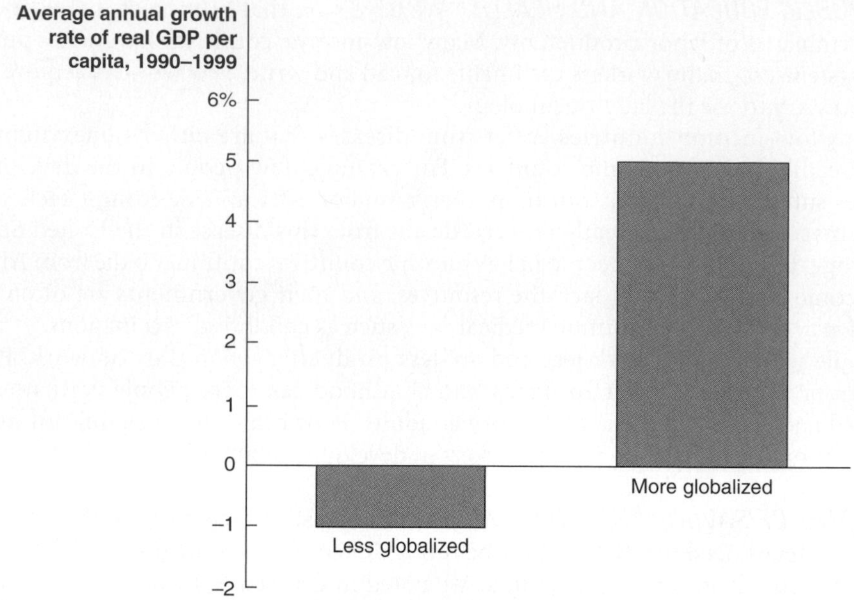

Globalization The process of countries becoming more open to foreign trade and investment.

The result was *globalization.* **Globalization** refers to the process of countries becoming more open to foreign trade and investment.

If we measure globalization by the fraction of a country's GDP accounted for by exports, we see that globalization and growth are strongly positively associated. Figure 10-12 shows that developing countries that were more globalized grew faster during the 1990s than developing countries that were less globalized. Globalization has benefited developing countries by making it easier for them to get investment funds and technology.

10-4 Making the Connection

Globalization and the Spread of Technology in Bangladesh

Today, Bangladesh exports more than $2 billion worth of shirts and other clothing. But the manufacture of clothing in factories only began in Bangladesh in 1980 when a local entrepreneur, Noorul Quader, started Desh Garments Ltd. This firm had just one shirt factory that employed 40 workers and produced only $55,550 worth of shirts its first year. Initially, Quader relied on an agreement with Daewoo Corporation of South Korea. Daewoo could export only limited amounts of shirts from Korea to the United States and Europe because the U.S. and European governments placed restrictions on clothing imports from Korea in an effort to protect domestic clothing producers. These restrictions did not apply to imports from Bangladesh.

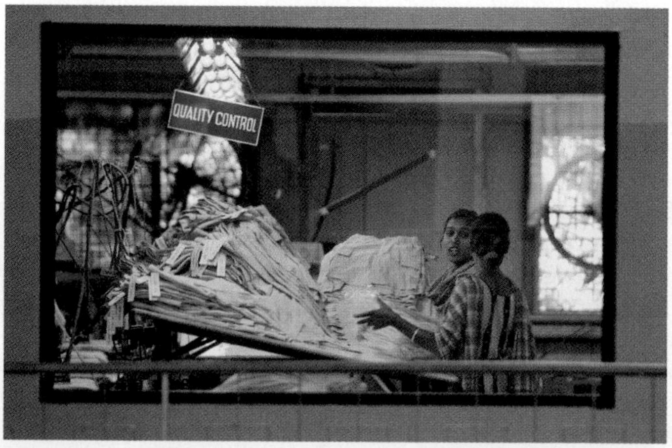

The spread of technology spurred Bangladesh's booming clothing industry.

Under the agreement with Daewoo, Quader was responsible for setting up and running the clothing factory. Daewoo would provide the most critical ingredient: training for 130 Desh workers at one of Daewoo's plants in Korea. In return, Quader would pay Daewoo an 8-percent royalty on each shirt sold. The business was a tremendous success for Quader, with production soaring from 43,000 shirts in 1980 to 2.3 million in 1987. It was an even greater success for Bangladesh. Almost all the 130 Desh workers trained in Korea eventually left Desh to set up their own firms. In addition to making shirts, these new firms began producing coats, pants, and other clothing. The Desh workers, trained by Daewoo in garment-making technology, became the basis of Bangladesh's booming clothing industry.

This story illustrates not only how globalization can aid the spread of technology to the developing world, but also the important difference between capital and technology: Although there are diminishing returns to capital, there actually may be increasing returns to technology. The investment Daewoo made in developing the best way to manufacture clothing and export it to the high-income countries provided a return not only to Daewoo, but also to Desh, and then to the other companies in Bangladesh founded by workers who left Desh. Unlike a piece of machinery, there is no limit to the number of people who can use knowledge about the best way to produce a good. As we discussed previously, the idea that there may be increasing returns to technology has been an important part of recent developments in the theory of economic growth. From this perspective, technological advance is not just a matter of new scientific discoveries, but also depends upon the incentives given to entrepreneurs to find new and better ways of producing goods and services.

Source: The story of Noorul Quader is from William Easterly, *The Elusive Quest for Growth: Economists' Adventures and Misadventures in the Tropics*, Cambridge, MA: MIT Press, 2001, pp. 146–150.

Growth Policies

(5) LEARNING OBJECTIVE

Discuss government policies that foster economic growth.

What can governments do to promote long-run economic growth? We have seen that even small differences in growth rates compounded over the years can lead to major differences in standards of living. Therefore, there is potentially a very high payoff to government policies that increase growth rates. We have already discussed some of these policies in this chapter. In this section, we explore additional policies.

Enhancing Property Rights and the Rule of Law

We have seen that a market system cannot work well unless property rights are enforced. Entrepreneurs are unlikely to risk their own funds, and investors are unlikely to lend their funds to entrepreneurs, unless property is safe from being arbitrarily seized. In many developing countries, the rule of law and property rights are undermined by *corruption*. With corruption, government officials may require bribes to carry out their obligations or steal government property and resources. For example, in some developing countries, it is impossible for an entrepreneur to obtain a permit to start a business without paying bribes, often to several different officials. In some countries, tax revenues and foreign aid also frequently end up in the pockets of government officials. Research has shown that countries where corruption is most widespread grow much more slowly than countries where corruption is less of a problem.

Although today the United States ranks among the least corrupt countries, recent research by economists Edward Glaeser and Claudia Goldin of Harvard University has shown that in the late nineteenth and early twentieth centuries corruption was a significant problem in the United States. The fact that political reform movements and crusading newspapers helped to reduce corruption in the United States to relatively low levels by the 1920s provides some hope for reform movements that aim to reduce corruption in developing countries today.

Property rights are unlikely to be secure in countries that are afflicted by wars and civil strife. For a number of countries, increased political stability is a necessary prerequisite to economic growth.

Improving Health and Education

Recently, many economists have become convinced that poor health is a major impediment to growth in some countries. As we saw in Chapter 9, the research of Nobel laureate Robert Fogel has emphasized the important interaction between health and economic growth. As people's health improves and they became taller, stronger, and less susceptible to disease, they also became more productive. Recent initiatives in developing countries to increase vaccinations against infectious diseases and to improve access to treated water and to improved sanitation have begun to reduce rates of illness and death.

We discussed earlier in this chapter Paul Romer's argument that there are increasing returns to knowledge capital. Robert Lucas, an economist at the University of Chicago and winner of the Nobel Prize in Economics, has made a similar argument that there are increasing returns to human capital. Lucas argues that productivity increases as the total stock of human capital increases, but that these productivity increases are not completely captured by individuals as they decide how much education to purchase. Therefore, the market may produce an inefficiently low level of education and training, unless education is supported by the government. Some researchers have been unable to find evidence of increasing returns to human capital, but many economists believe that government subsidies to education have played an important role in promoting economic growth.

The rising incomes that result from economic growth can help developing countries deal with the *brain drain.* The brain drain refers to highly educated and successful individuals leaving developing countries for high-income countries. This migration occurs when successful individuals believe that economic opportunities are very limited in the domestic economy. Rapid economic growth in India and China in recent years has resulted in more entrepreneurs, engineers, and scientists deciding to remain in those countries rather than leave for the United States or other high-income countries.

Policies with Respect to Technology

One of the lessons from the economic growth model is that technological change is more important than increases in capital in explaining long-run growth. Government policies that facilitate access to technology are crucial for low-income countries. The easiest way for developing countries to gain access to technology is through foreign direct investment in which foreign firms are allowed to build new facilities or to buy domestic firms. Recent economic growth in India has been greatly aided by the Indian government's relaxation of regulations on foreign investment. Relaxing these regulations made it possible for India to have access to the technology of Dell, Microsoft, and other multinational corporations.

In the high-income countries, government policies can aid the growth of technology by subsidizing research and development. As we noted previously, in the United States, the federal government conducts some research and development on its own and also provides grants to researchers in universities. Tax breaks to firms undertaking research and development also facilitate technological change.

Policies with Respect to Saving and Investment

We noted in Chapter 9 that firms turn to the loanable funds market to finance expansion and research and development. Policies that increase the incentives to save and invest will increase the equilibrium level of loanable funds and may increase the level of real GDP per capita. As we also discussed in Chapter 9, tax incentives can lead to increased savings. In the United States, many workers are able to save for retirement by placing funds in 401k or 403b plans or in Individual Retirement Accounts (IRAs). Income placed in these accounts is not taxed until it is withdrawn during retirement. Because the funds are allowed to accumulate tax-free, the return is increased, which raises the incentive to save.

Governments also increase incentives for firms to engage in investment in physical capital by using *investment tax credits.* Investment tax credits allow firms to deduct from their taxes some fraction of the funds they have spent on investment. Reductions in the taxes firms pay on their profits also increase the after-tax return on investments.

Is Economic Growth Good or Bad?

Although we didn't state so explicitly, in this chapter we have assumed that economic growth is desirable and that governments should undertake policies that will increase growth rates. It seems undeniable that increasing the growth rates of very low-income countries would help relieve the daily suffering that many people in these countries must endure. But some people are unconvinced that, at least in the high-income countries, further economic growth is desirable.

The arguments against further economic growth tend to be motivated either by concern about the effects of growth on the environment or by concern about the effects of the globalization process that has accompanied economic growth in recent years. In 1973, the Club of Rome published a controversial book titled *The Limits to Growth,* which predicted that economic growth would likely grind to a halt in the United States and other high-income countries because of increasing pollution and the depletion of natural resources, such as oil. Although these dire predictions have not yet come to pass, many remain concerned that economic growth may be contributing to global warming, deforestation, and other environmental problems.

In Chapter 6, we discussed the opposition to globalization. We noted that some people believe that globalization has undermined the distinctive cultures of many countries, as imports of food, clothing, movies, and other goods displace domestically produced goods. We have seen that allowing foreign direct investment is an important way in which low-income countries can gain access to the latest technology. Some people, however, see multinational firms that locate in low-income countries as paying very low wages and as failing to follow the same safety and environmental regulations they are required to follow in the high-income countries.

As with many other normative questions, economic analysis can contribute to the ongoing political debate over the consequences of economic growth, but it cannot settle the issue.

Conclusion

For much of human history, most people have had to struggle to survive. Even today, two-thirds of the world's population lives in extreme poverty. The differences in living standards among countries today are the result of many decades of sharply different rates of economic growth. According to the economic growth model, increases in the quantity of capital per hour worked and increases in technology determine how rapidly real GDP per hour worked and a country's standard of living will increase. The keys to higher living standards seem straightforward enough: Establish the rule of law, provide basic education and healthcare for the population, increase the amount of capital per hour worked, adopt the best technology, and participate in the global economy. However, for many countries these policies have proved very difficult to implement.

Having discussed what determines the growth rate of economies, we will turn in the following chapters to the question of why economies experience short-run fluctuations in output, employment, and inflation. First, read An *Inside Look* on the next page for a discussion of recent economic growth in India.

An Inside Look

India Achieves Growth through Efficiency and Globalization

WALL STREET JOURNAL, JUNE 6, 2005

India Comes of Age, As Focus on Returns Lures Foreign Capital

MUMBAI, India—When New York investment firm Blackstone Group LP announced last month that its first foray in Asia would be a $1 billion fund targeted at India, the decision seemed to ratify the country's slow—and sometimes painful—approach to economic development. Unlike China, where transformation has been captured by daily headlines of rapid growth on the macroeconomic level, India's conversion occurred quietly on the corporate level.

Now, after decades of relative isolation, corporate India has become a showcase for the benefits of globalization, the free flow of capital across borders and competition.

a India hasn't managed to replicate China's astounding record of sustained annual economic growth. But then, corporate India hasn't had many of the advantages of China, notably cheap capital and supportive government policies. Fears that India would be marginalized by China instead have proved a catalyst for India's private-sector awakening. The enthusiasm for India reflects the country's strong management culture. "Indian companies are very return-focused," says Jim Walker, chief economist for Credit Lyonnais Securities Asia in Hong Kong. "By contrast, China is just market-share driven."

What the world is discovering is that India's handicap of high-cost capital has become a blessing; it has forced companies to become efficient. Indian companies "couldn't waste money," says Chip Kaye, co-president of Warburg Pincus LLC, one of the earliest U.S. private-equity funds to invest in Idnia. "They became good at managing because of the bad years." Warburg has deployed nearly $1 billion in India and has taken more than it has invested in profit, with another $1 billion in value that hasn't yet been realized.

The case of textile maker Welspun India Ltd. demonstrates how far Indian companies have come. Textiles were one of the more highly regulated sectors in India, reserved for so-called small-scale industry. Now, textile companies are expanding, frequently with the help of foreign capital. A few years ago, Welspun was a second-rate producer without any economies of scale. The company now is moving upmarket to higher-profit-margin areas and looking to expand internationally. Last year, a unit of Singapore's Temasek Holdings Pte. Ltd., an investment fund, bought a 14% stake in the company.

b Now, Welspun makes towels, bedsheets and bathrobes and is positioning itself not as a low-cost maker of a commodity product but the high-end maker of a fashion. It produces for such brands as Nautica and Tommy Hilfiger. Moreover, with the Temasek name and money behind it, Welspun is looking to acquire distressed U.S. textile companies that it can turn around. "We would keep their branding and distribution and move a lot of the production to India," says Welspun Vice Chairman B.K. Goenka. "In a few years, we will be a multinational, too."

Mahindra & Mahindra Ltd., which started life as a tractor maker and now is a conglomerate making everything from cars to consumer loans, also is a testament to the newfound confidence of Indian executives. Its Scorpio sport-utility vehicle competes successfully with a comparable SUV from Toyota Motor Corp. in India. It recently formed a $165 million venture with Renault SA to make sedans. . . .

c Change is coming even to India's inadequate infrastructure, particularly at India's ports, thanks to a policy shift that has opened ports to private-sector and foreign competition.

A decade ago, India was so uncompetitive that the conveyor belts in the port of Mumbai (formerly called Bombay) went one way—to unload goods from ships. Those conveyor belts came to symbolize all that was wrong with India: The lack of roads, the congested railways, the paucity of runways at even major airports.

The difficulty of exporting didn't matter much because there was little India had to export anyhow. Today, the conveyor belts go both ways, and there are more exports leaving the port than imports arriving at it.

Key Points in the Article

This article discusses foreign investors' growing interest in India, whose economic growth depends in large part on technological innovations because of the relatively high cost of capital there. In the past decade, the Indian government has moved its economy closer to market capitalism: It has reduced private-sector subsidies for the purchase of capital, embraced foreign investment, and welcomed globalization.

Analyzing the News

a The cost of capital in India is relatively high. To make the most of its capital stock, India's private sector has improved the means of organizing and managing production. These improvements represent technological innovations that have shifted India's macroeconomic production function up, as shown by panel (a) in Figure 1. These shifts have enabled India to increase output per hour worked without increasing capital per hour worked. In panel (a), capital per hour worked remains $(K/L)_1$, while output per hour worked increases from $(Y/L)_1$ at point *A* to $(Y/L)_2$ at point *B*. By comparison, the cost of capital in China is relatively low, so the Chinese economy has employed relatively more of it. That is, China has moved up its macroeconomic production function. This movement along the production function has also enabled China to increase output per hour worked, but at a decreasing rate due to the law of diminishing returns. In panel (b) of Figure 1 output per hour worked in China increases from $(Y/L)_1$ to $(Y/L)_2$ as capital per hour worked increases from $(K/L)_1$ to $(K/L)_2$.

b Because Indian firms have improved the means of organizing and managing production, the return to capital is relatively high there. High returns attract foreign investment, which the Indian government, in recent years, has welcomed. Therefore, economic growth in India has not relied exclusively on Indians' savings. Rather, foreign savings in the forms of direct and portfolio investment have given India access to funds and technology that otherwise would not be available. This inflow of foreign investment has enabled firms such as textile maker Welspun India Ltd. to expand its product line and service the global fashion industry.

c Because India has embraced globalization, it has opened its economy to foreign competition. This competition has introduced opportunities and incentives to Indian entrepreneurs, who have contributed to an increase in Indian exports and fueled the development of India's export infrastructure, including roads, railways, ports, and airports.

Thinking Critically ABOUT POLICY

1. Suppose that the Indian government, in an attempt to increase household disposable income, taxes returns on foreign portfolio investment and then transfers this tax revenue to Indian households, which use the funds to purchase consumer goods. What effect would this policy have on India's long-run economic growth?
2. Suppose the Indian government's policy of welcoming foreign direct and portfolio investment is perceived, by the foreign investment community, as weak. For example, assume that the foreign investment community does not believe that the Indian government has the political will to maintain this policy should voters want the government to do otherwise. What effect would this perception have on India's long-run economic growth?

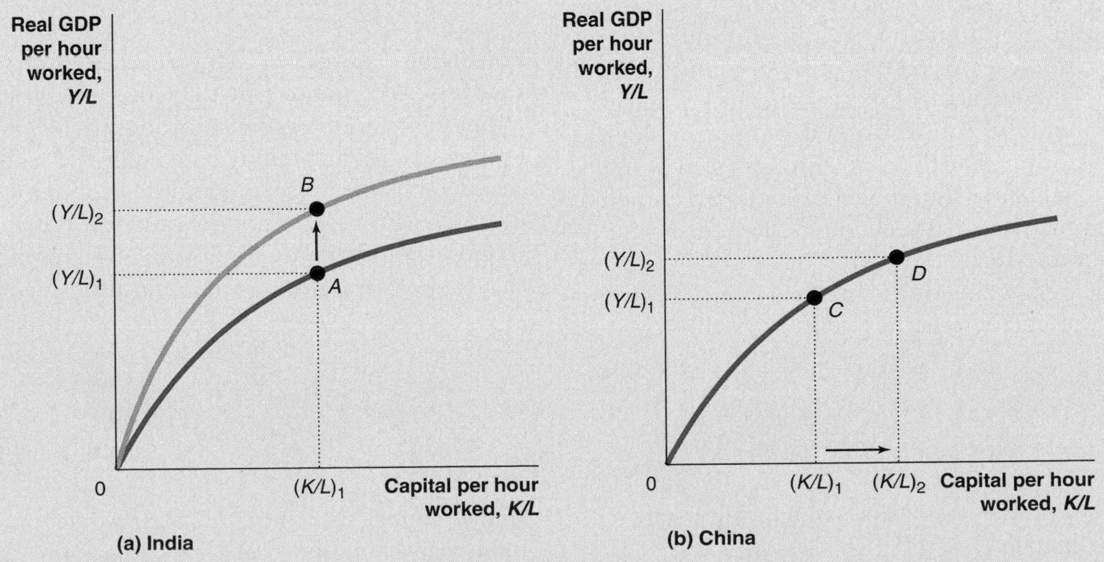

Figure 1: To increase output per worker, Indian firms have improved their management techniques; Chinese firms have increased their use of capital.

SUMMARY

LEARNING OBJECTIVE ① Define economic growth, calculate economic growth rates, and describe trends in economic growth. Until around the year 1300 A.D., most people survived with barely enough food. Living standards began to rise significantly only after the Industrial Revolution began in England in the 1700s. The best measure of a country's standard of living is its level of real GDP per capita. Economic growth occurs when real GDP per capita increases, thereby increasing the country's standard of living.

LEARNING OBJECTIVE ② Use the economic growth model to explain why growth rates differ across countries. *Labor productivity* is the quantity of goods and services that can be produced by one worker or by one hour of work. Economic growth depends on increases in labor productivity. Labor productivity will increase if there is an increase in the amount of *capital* available to each worker or if there is an improvement in *technology.* There are three main sources of improvements in technology: better machinery and equipment, increases in human capital, and better means of organizing and managing production. To summarize, we can say this: An economy will have a higher standard of living the more capital it has per hour worked, the more human capital its workers have, the better its capital, and the better the job its business managers do in organizing production. The *per-worker production function* shows the relationship between capital per hour worked and output per hour worked, holding technology constant. *Diminishing returns to capital* mean that increases in the quantity of capital per hour worked will result in diminishing increases in output per hour worked. *Technological change* shifts up the per-worker production function, resulting in more output per hour worked at every level of capital per hour worked. The *economic growth model* stresses the importance of changes in capital per hour worked and technological change in explaining growth in output per hour worked. *Endogenous growth theory* is a model of long-run economic growth that emphasizes that technological change is influenced by economic incentives, and so is endogenous, or determined by the working of the market system. To Joseph Schumpeter, the entrepreneur is central to the "creative destruction" by which the standard of living increases as qualitatively better products replace existing products.

LEARNING OBJECTIVE ③ Discuss fluctuations in productivity growth in the United States. Productivity in the United States grew rapidly from the end of World War II until the mid-1970s. Growth then slowed down for 20 years, before increasing again after 1995. Economists continue to debate the reasons for the growth slowdown of the mid-1970s to mid-1990s. Leading explanations for the productivity slowdown are measurement problems, high oil prices, and a decline in labor quality. Because Western Europe and Japan experienced a productivity slowdown at the same time as the United States, explanations that focus on factors affecting only the United States are unlikely to be correct. Some economists argue that the faster growth in productivity beginning in the mid-1990s reflects the development of a "New Economy" based on information technology.

LEARNING OBJECTIVE ④ Explain economic catch-up, and discuss why many poor countries have not experienced rapid economic growth. The economic growth model predicts that poor countries will grow faster than rich countries, resulting in *catch-up.* In recent decades, some poor countries have grown faster than rich countries, but many have not. Some poor countries do not experience rapid growth for four main reasons: wars and revolutions, poor public education and health, failure to enforce the rule of law, and low rates of saving and investment. *Globalization* has aided countries that have opened their economies to foreign trade and investment.

LEARNING OBJECTIVE ⑤ Discuss government policies that foster economic growth. Governments can attempt to increase economic growth through policies that enhance property rights and the rule of law, improve health and education, subsidize research and development, and provide incentives for savings and investment. Whether continued economic growth is desirable or not is a normative question that cannot be settled by economic analysis.

KEY TERMS

Catch-up 312
Economic growth model 298
Endogenous growth theory 304
Foreign direct investment (FDI) 317
Foreign portfolio investment 317
Globalization 318
Human capital 299
Industrial Revolution 294
Labor productivity 298
Patent 304
Per-worker production function 299
Rule of law 316
Technological change 299

REVIEW QUESTIONS

1. Explain the difference between the total percentage increase in real GDP between 1997 and 2004 and the average annual growth rate in real GDP between the same years.
2. What is the relationship between increases in labor productivity and increases in real GDP per capita? Which two factors are most important in determining the level of labor productivity?
3. Using the per-worker production function, show the effect on real GDP per hour worked of an increase in capital per hour worked, holding technology constant. Now, using the per-worker production function, show the effect on real GDP per hour worked of an increase in technology, holding the quantity of capital per hour worked constant.
4. What are the consequences for growth of diminishing returns to capital? How are some economies able to maintain high growth rates despite diminishing returns to capital?
5. Why did some economists in the 1950s predict that the Soviet Union would continue to grow faster than the United States for decades to come? Why did this prediction turn out to be wrong?
6. Why are firms likely to underinvest in research and development, which slows the accumulation of knowledge capital, slowing economic growth? Briefly discuss three ways in which government policy can increase the accumulation of knowledge capital.
7. Describe the record of productivity growth in the United States from 1800 to the present. What explains the slowdown in productivity growth from the mid-1970s to the mid-1990s? Why did productivity growth increase beginning in 1995?
8. Why does the economic growth model predict that poor countries should catch up to rich countries in income per capita? Have poor countries been catching up to rich countries?
9. What are the main reasons many poor countries have experienced slow growth?
10. What does globalization mean? How have developing countries benefited from globalization?

PROBLEMS AND APPLICATIONS

Please visit **www.prenhall.com/hubbard** *for solutions to the even-numbered problems as well as multiple-choice and true or false self-assessment quizzes.*

1. Andover Bank and Lowell Bank each sell one-year certificates of deposit (CDs). The interest rates on these CDs are given in the following table for a three-year period:

BANK	2005	2006	2007
Andover Bank	2%	9%	10%
Lowell Bank	7	7	7

Suppose you deposit $1,000 in a CD in each bank at the beginning of 2005. At the end of 2005, you take your $1,000 and any interest earned and invest it in a CD for the following year. You do this again at the end of 2006. At the end of 2007, will you have earned more on your Andover Bank CDs or on your Lowell Bank CDs? Briefly explain.

2. **[Related to *Don't Let This Happen To You!*]** Use the data in the following table to calculate: (a) the percentage increase in real GDP per capita between 1997 and 2000 and (b) the average annual growth rate in real GDP per capita between 1997 and 2000. (Remember from the previous chapter that the average annual growth rate for relatively short periods can be approximated by averaging the growth rate for each year.)

YEAR	REAL GDP PER CAPITA (2000 PRICES)
1996	$31,403
1997	32,502
1998	33,550
1999	34,729
2000	34,788

3. According to a study by an economist at the Federal Reserve Bank of Minneapolis, during the middle 1980s managers at iron mines in Canada and the United States increased output per hour worked by 100 percent through changes in work rules that increased workers' effort per hour worked and increased the efficiency of workers' effort. Briefly explain whether this increase in output per hour worked is an example of an improvement in technology.
Source: James A. Schmitz, Jr., "What Determines Labor Productivity? Lessons from the Dramatic Recovery of the U.S. and Canadian Iron-Ore Industries Following Their Early 1980s Crisis," Federal Reserve Bank of Minneapolis Research Department Staff Report 286, February 2005.

4. Which of the following will result in a movement along Japan's per-worker production function, and which will result in a shift of Japan's per-worker production function? Briefly explain.
   a. Capital per hour worked increases from ¥5 million per hour worked to ¥6 million per hour worked.
   b. The Japanese government doubles its spending on support of university research.
   c. A reform of the Japanese school system results in more highly trained Japanese workers.
5. **[Related to *Solved Problem 10-1*]** Use the following graph to answer the questions:

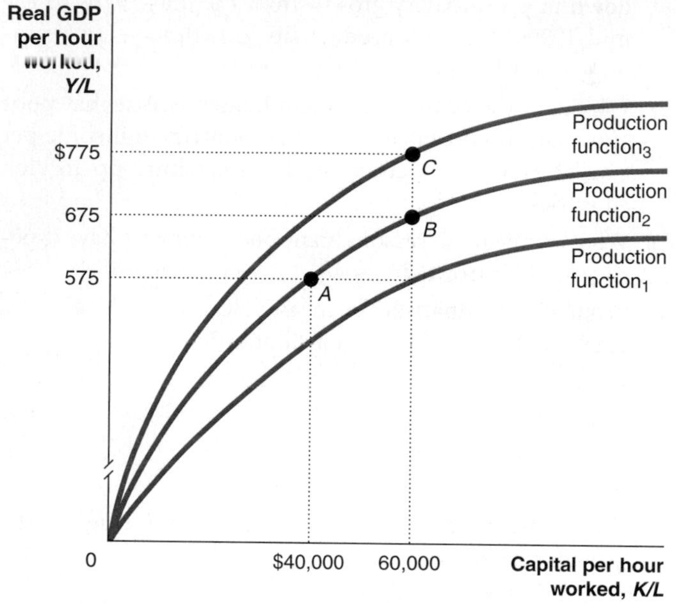

   a. True or False: The movement from point *A* to point *B* shows the effects of technological change.
   b. True or False: The economy can move from point *B* to point *C* only if there are no diminishing returns to capital.
   c. True or False: To move from point *A* to point *C*, the economy must increase the amount of capital per hour worked and experience technological change.
6. **[Related to *Solved Problem 10-1*]** Shortly before the fall of the Soviet Union, the economist Gur Ofer of the Hebrew University of Jerusalem, wrote this:

   > The most outstanding characteristic of Soviet growth strategy is its consistent policy of very high rates of investment, leading to a rapid growth rate of [the] capital stock.

   Explain why this turned out to be a very poor growth strategy.

   Source: Gur Ofer, "Soviet Economic Growth, 1928-1985," *Journal of Economic Literature*, December 1987, p. 1,784.
7. Briefly explain which of the following policies are likely to increase the rate of economic growth in the United States:
   a. Congress passes an investment tax credit, which reduces a firm's taxes if it installs new machinery and equipment.
   b. Congress passes a law that allows taxpayers to reduce their income taxes by the amount of state sales taxes they pay.
   c. Congress provides more funds for low-interest loans to college students.
8. **[Related to *Solved Problem 10-2*]** Briefly explain whether the statistics in the following table are consistent with the economic growth model's predictions of catch-up.

COUNTRY	REAL GDP PER CAPITA IN 1960	GROWTH IN REAL GDP PER CAPITA, 1960–2000
Ethiopia	$526	0.47%
China	681	4.35
Madagascar	1,239	−1.00
Ireland	5,136	4.18
United States	12,272	2.53

9. **[Related to *Solved Problem 10-2*]** In the figure below, each dot represents a country with its initial real GDP per capita and its growth rate of real GDP per capita.

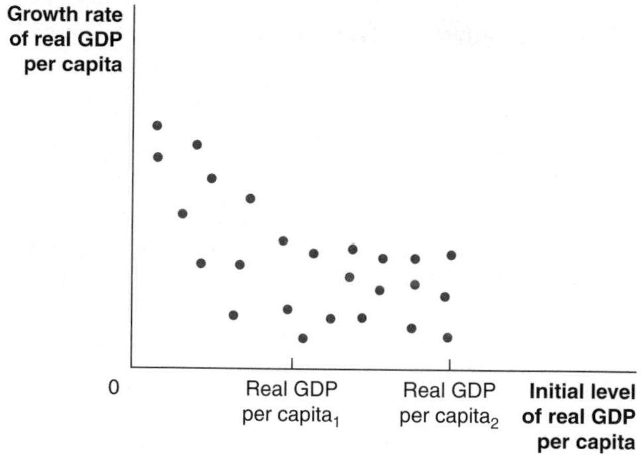

   a. For the range of initial GDP per capita from 0 to Real GDP per capita$_2$, does the figure support the economic growth model's prediction of catch-up? Why or why not?
   b. For the range of initial GDP per capita from 0 to Real GDP per capita$_1$, does the figure support the catch-up prediction? Why or why not?
   c. For the range from initial Real GDP per capita$_1$ to Real GDP per capita$_2$, does the figure support the catch-up prediction? Why or why not?

10. In 2003, then U.S. Secretary of State Colin Powell urged Argentina to take steps to correct:

    [I]nstitutional flaws that encourage excess public sector borrowing, corruption, [and] politicized judicial systems. . . .

    Briefly discuss how each of the three problems cited by Secretary Powell would contribute to reducing Argentina's economic growth rate.

    Source: Matt Moffett, "One Tough Mayor Shows Argentina How to Clean House," *Wall Street Journal,* July 1, 2003.

11. Why does the role of the entrepreneur become much more important in the new growth theory—the endogenous growth model—than in the traditional economic growth model?

12. This chapter argues that a key difference between market economies and centrally planned economies, like the former Soviet Union, is that "In market economies, decisions on which investments to make and which technologies to adopt are made by entrepreneurs and managers with their own money on the line. In the Soviet system, these decisions were usually made by salaried bureaucrats trying to fulfill a plan formulated in Moscow." But in large corporations, investment decisions are often made by salaried managers who do not, in fact, have their own money on the line. These managers are spending the money of the firm's shareholders, rather than their own money. Why then do the investment decisions of salaried managers in the United States tend to be better for the long-term growth of the economy than were the decisions of salaried bureaucrats in the Soviet Union?

13. The chapter argues that a key problem for the Soviet economy was that: "The Soviet managers' pay depended on filling [production] goals, not on discovering new and better means of producing goods." How might a centrally planned economy get around the problem of managers lacking incentives to discover and make use of new technologies? What are the main obstacles to solving this problem?

14. Figure 10-7 shows the annual growth rate of labor productivity in the leading industrial economies for 1996 to 2004. Using the Rule of 70 from the previous chapter, indicate why the countries of Western Europe, for example Germany, should be concerned about their current growth rates.

15. An opinion column in the *Economist* argued, "[G]lobalisation, far from being the greatest cause of poverty, is its only feasible cure." What does globalization have to do with reducing poverty?

    Source: Clive Crook, "Globalisation and Its Critics," *Economist,* September 27, 2001.

16. How might multinational corporations that establish facilities in developing countries help break the vicious cycle of poverty in those countries?

17. An opinion column by Hernando De Soto in the *New York Times* argued, "Those who favor the market [have] forgotten that the only way capitalism can help the poor prosper is by bringing them into the capitalist system. But that has not happened. . . . The poor in the vast majority of nations cannot yet take advantage of legal structures that are central to the production of wealth." What does De Soto mean by "legal structures"? Why would they have anything to do with the production of wealth?

    Source: Hernando De Soto, "The Constituency of Terror," *New York Times,* October 15, 2001.

18. A columnist in the *New York Times* argues that "[I]f you really want to reduce world poverty, you should be cheering on those guys in pinstripe suits at the free-trade negotiations and those investors jetting around the world." What do free-trade negotiations and investors jetting around the world have to do with reducing poverty?

    Source: David Brooks, "Good News About Poverty," *New York Times,* November 27, 2004.

19. The Roman Empire lasted from 27 B.C. to 476 A.D. The empire was wealthy enough to build such monuments as the Roman Coliseum. Roman engineering skill was at a level high enough that aqueducts built during the empire to carry water long distances remained in use for hundreds of years. Yet the growth rate of income per capita during the empire was very low, perhaps zero. Why was the Roman Empire unable to bring about modern economic growth? What would the world be like today if it had? (There are no definite answers to this question; it is intended to get you to think about the pre-conditions for economic growth.)

20. Economist George Ayittey, in an interview on PBS about economic development in Africa, states that of the 54 African countries, only eight have a free press. For Africa's economic development, Ayittey argues strongly for the establishment of a free press. Why would a free press be vital for the enhancing of property rights and the rule of law? How could a free press help reduce corruption?

    Source: George Ayittey, "Border Jumpers," Anchor Interview Transcript, WideAngle, PBS.org, July 24, 2005.

chapter eleven

Output and Expenditure in the Short Run

Demand Forecasts Backfire at Cisco Systems

In the spring of 2001, Cisco Systems, Inc., the leading seller of hardware for computer networks, announced it would cut production, sell hardware it had already manufactured at deeply discounted prices, and lay off 6,000 of its 44,000 employees. Less than one year earlier, Cisco had rapidly expanded its workforce, purchased large amounts of hardware components, and even loaned $600 million to its suppliers to encourage them to speed up production. What had happened? Cisco had sold much less than it had forecast. As a result, Cisco had hired more people than it needed and produced more computer hardware than it could sell.

Cisco was founded in 1984 by Sandra Lerner and Len Bosack, who were members of the computer support staff at Stanford University. The firm's early success was tied to the growth of the Internet. Cisco's software engineers helped pioneer the networking technologies based on the Internet Protocol (IP) that became the foundation for the Internet and the World Wide Web. Cisco manufactured the routers and switches used by many firms as the Internet rapidly expanded in the 1990s. In 2000, Cisco was supplying 80 percent of the routers used on the Internet.

During the Internet boom of the late 1990s, many new start-up firms were able to attract funds from investors to open Web sites selling a variety of products. Many existing firms also spent heavily to establish a presence on the Internet. Firms also increased spending on information technology to deal with the "Y2K" problem, the likelihood that existing computers and software would be unable to process dates for the years 2000 and later. In addition, telecommunications firms laid more than 39 million miles of fiber-optic cable, anticipating that the volume of high-speed Internet traffic would increase rapidly. Unfortunately, for Cisco and other firms, the Internet bubble popped in late 2000. Many of the Internet start-ups went out of business without ever earning a profit. Although some forecasters believed Internet traffic would dou-

ble every three or four months, between 1995 and 2001 Internet traffic doubled only about once per year. Applications requiring high-speed, broadband connections—so-called "killer apps"—were slow to develop, leaving many consumers satisfied with slower, dial-up connections to the Internet. The slower than expected growth of the Internet was bad news for Cisco, and its sales in the first three months of 2001 were 30 percent below what they had been during the last three months of 2000.

However, something beyond the Internet bust was happening to the U.S. economy during the spring of 2001. Firms far removed from the Internet and telecommunications were also experiencing problems. Sales at General Motors and Ford dropped 15 percent from the spring of 2000 to the spring of 2001. Delivery of two- and three-day packages at Federal Express was down about 10 percent. These firms were all experiencing the effects of a slowdown in the total amount of spending, or *aggregate expenditure*, in the economy. This slowdown caused the U.S. economy to move into recession. In this chapter, we will explore the reasons for fluctuations in total spending in the economy. *An Inside Look* on page 362 discusses the effect of an increase in aggregate expenditure on the Japanese economy at the beginning of 2005.

LEARNING OBJECTIVES

After studying this chapter, you should be able to:

① Understand how macroeconomic equilibrium is determined in the aggregate expenditure model.

② Discuss the determinants of the four components of aggregate expenditure and define the marginal propensity to consume and the marginal propensity to save.

③ Use a 45°-line diagram to illustrate macroeconomic equilibrium.

④ Calculate a numerical example of macroeconomic equilibrium.

⑤ Define the multiplier effect and use it to calculate changes in equilibrium GDP.

⑥ Understand the relationship between the aggregate demand curve and aggregate expenditure.

➤ In Chapter 10, we analyzed the determinants of long-run growth in the economy. As we saw in Chapter 9, in the short run the economy also experiences a business cycle around the long-run upward trend in real GDP. In this chapter, we begin exploring the causes of the business cycle by examining the effect of fluctuations in total spending on real GDP.

Aggregate expenditure (*AE*) The total amount of spending in the economy: the sum of consumption, planned investment, government purchases, and net exports.

During some years, total spending in the economy, or **aggregate expenditure (*AE*),** increases about as much as does the production of goods and services. If this happens, most firms will sell about what they expected to sell and they probably will not increase or decrease production or the number of workers hired. During other years, total spending in the economy increases more than the production of goods and services. In these years, firms will increase production and hire more workers. But in the spring of 2001, total spending did not increase as much as total production. As a result, firms cut back on production and laid off workers. In this chapter, we will explore why fluctuations in total spending play such an important role in the economy.

① LEARNING OBJECTIVE
Understand how macroeconomic equilibrium is determined in the aggregate expenditure model.

The Aggregate Expenditure Model

Aggregate expenditure model A macroeconomic model that focuses on the relationship between total spending and real GDP, assuming the price level is constant.

The business cycle involves the interaction of many economic variables. To understand the relationships among some of the most important of these variables, we begin our study of the business cycle in this chapter with a simple model called the *aggregate expenditure model.* Recall from Chapter 7 that gross domestic product (GDP) is the value of all the final goods and services produced in an economy during the year. Real GDP corrects nominal GDP for the effects of inflation. The **aggregate expenditure model** focuses on the relationship between total spending and real GDP in the short run. An important assumption of the model is that the price level is constant. In Chapter 12, we will develop a more complete model of the business cycle that relaxes the assumption of constant prices.

The key idea of the aggregate expenditure model is that *in any particular year, the level of gross domestic product (GDP) is determined mainly by the level of aggregate expenditure.* To understand the relationship between aggregate expenditure and real GDP, we need to look more closely at the components of aggregate expenditure.

Aggregate Expenditure

Economists first began to study the relationship between fluctuations in aggregate expenditure and fluctuations in GDP during the Great Depression of the 1930s. The United States, the United Kingdom, and other industrial countries suffered declines in real GDP of 25 percent or more during the early 1930s. In 1936, the English economist John Maynard Keynes published a book, *The General Theory of Employment, Interest, and Money,* that systematically analyzed the relationship between fluctuations in aggregate expenditure and fluctuations in GDP. Keynes identified four categories of aggregate expenditure that together equal GDP (these are the same four categories we discussed in Chapter 7):

- *Consumption (C):* Spending by households on goods and services, such as automobiles and haircuts.
- *Planned Investment (I):* Planned spending by firms on capital goods, such as factories, office buildings, and machine tools, and by households on new homes.
- *Government Purchases (G):* Spending by local, state, and federal governments on goods and services, such as aircraft carriers, bridges, and the salaries of FBI agents.

- *Net Exports (NX):* Spending by foreign firms and households on goods and services produced in the United States minus spending by U.S. firms and households on goods and services produced in other countries.

So, we can write:

Aggregate expenditure = Consumption + Planned investment + Government purchases + Net exports

or,

$$AE = C + I + G + NX.$$

Governments around the world gather statistics on aggregate expenditure on the basis of these four categories. Economists and business analysts usually explain fluctuations in GDP in terms of fluctuations in these four categories of spending.

The Difference between Planned Investment and Actual Investment

Before considering further the relationship between aggregate expenditure and GDP, we need to consider an important distinction: Notice that it is *planned* investment spending, rather than actual investment spending, that is a component of aggregate expenditure. You might wonder how the amount that businesses plan to spend on investment can be different from the amount they actually spend. We can begin resolving this puzzle by remembering that goods that have been produced, but not yet sold, are referred to as **inventories.** Changes in inventories are included as part of investment spending along with spending on machinery, equipment, office buildings, and factories. We assume that businesses always spend the amount they planned on machinery and office buildings, but the amount businesses plan to spend on inventories may be different from the amount they actually spend.

Inventories Goods that have been produced but not yet sold.

For example, Doubleday may print 1.5 million copies of the latest John Grisham novel expecting to sell them all. If Doubleday does sell all 1.5 million, its inventories will be unchanged, but if it sells only 1.2 million it will have an unplanned increase in inventories. In other words, changes in inventories depend on sales of goods, which firms cannot always forecast with perfect accuracy.

For the economy as a whole, we can say that actual investment spending will be greater than planned investment spending when there is an unplanned increase in inventories. Actual investment spending will be less than planned investment spending when there is an unplanned decrease in inventories. *Therefore, actual investment will equal planned investment only when there is no unplanned change in inventories.*

Macroeconomic Equilibrium

Macroeconomic equilibrium is similar to microeconomic equilibrium. In microeconomics, equilibrium in the apple market occurs at the point at which the demand for apples equals the supply of apples. When we have equilibrium in the apple market, the quantity of apples produced and sold will not change unless the demand for apples or the supply of apples changes. For the economy as a whole, macroeconomic equilibrium occurs where total spending, or aggregate expenditure, equals total production, or GDP:

Aggregate expenditure = GDP.

As we saw in Chapter 10, over the long run, real GDP in the United States grows and the standard of living rises. In this chapter, we are interested in understanding why GDP fluctuates in the short run. To simplify the analysis of macroeconomic equilibrium, we assume that the economy is not growing. In the next chapter, we discuss the more realistic case of macroeconomic equilibrium in a growing economy. If we assume that the economy is not growing, then equilibrium GDP will not change unless aggregate expenditure changes.

Adjustments to Macroeconomic Equilibrium

The apple market isn't always in equilibrium because sometimes the quantity of apples demanded is greater than the quantity supplied, and sometimes the quantity supplied is greater than the quantity demanded. The same outcome holds for the economy as a whole. Sometimes the economy is in macroeconomic equilibrium and sometimes it isn't. When aggregate expenditure is greater than GDP, the total amount of spending in the economy is greater than the total amount of production. In this situation, many businesses will sell more goods and services than they had expected. For example, the manager of a Home Depot store might like to keep 50 refrigerators in stock to give customers the opportunity to see a variety of different sizes and models. If sales are unexpectedly high, the store may end up with only 20 refrigerators. In that case, the store will have an unplanned decrease in inventories: Its inventory of refrigerators has declined by 30.

How will the store manager react when more refrigerators are sold than expected? The manager is likely to order more refrigerators. If other stores selling refrigerators are experiencing similar sales increases and are also increasing their orders, then General Electric, Whirlpool, and other refrigerator manufacturers will significantly increase their production. These manufacturers may also increase the number of workers they hire. If the increase in sales is affecting not just refrigerators but also other appliances, automobiles, furniture, computers, and other goods and services, then GDP and total employment will begin to increase. In summary: *When aggregate expenditure is greater than GDP, inventories will decline and GDP and total employment will increase.*

Now suppose that aggregate expenditure is less than GDP. In this situation, many businesses will sell fewer goods and services than they had expected, so their inventories will increase. For example, the manager of the Home Depot store who wants 50 refrigerators in stock may find that because of slow sales the store has 75 refrigerators, so the store manager will cut back on orders for new refrigerators. If other stores also cut back on their orders, General Electric and Whirlpool will reduce production and lay off workers.

If the decrease in sales is affecting not just refrigerators but also many different goods and services, GDP and total employment will begin to decrease. These events happened at many firms during the spring of 2001. In summary: *When aggregate expenditure is less than GDP, inventories will increase and GDP and total employment will decrease.*

Only when aggregate expenditure equals GDP will firms sell what they expected to sell. In that case, their inventories will be unchanged and they will not have an incentive to increase or decrease production. The economy will be in macroeconomic equilibrium. Table 11-1 summarizes the relationship between aggregate expenditure and GDP.

Increases and decreases in aggregate expenditure cause the year-to-year fluctuations in GDP. Economists devote considerable time and energy to forecasting what will happen to each component of aggregate expenditure. If economists forecast that aggregate expenditure will decline in the future, that is equivalent to forecasting that GDP will decline and that the economy will enter a recession. Individuals and firms closely watch these forecasts because fluctuations in GDP can have dramatic consequences. When GDP is increasing, so are wages, profits, and job opportunities. Declining GDP can be bad news for wages, profits, and job seekers.

TABLE 11-1

The Relationship between Aggregate Expenditure and GDP

IF...	THEN...	AND...
Aggregate expenditure is **equal** to GDP	inventories are **unchanged**	the economy is in **macroeconomic equilibrium.**
Aggregate expenditure is **less** than GDP	inventories **rise**	GDP and employment **decrease.**
Aggregate expenditure is **greater** than GDP	inventories **fall**	GDP and employment **increase.**

When economists forecast that aggregate expenditure is likely to decline and that the economy is headed for a recession, the federal government may implement *macroeconomic policies* in an attempt to head off the fall in expenditure and keep the economy from falling into recession. We discuss these macroeconomic polices in Chapters 14 and 15.

Determining the Level of Aggregate Expenditure in the Economy

(2) LEARNING OBJECTIVE

Discuss the determinants of the four components of aggregate expenditure and define the marginal propensity to consume and the marginal propensity to save.

To better understand how macroeconomic equilibrium is determined in the aggregate expenditure model, we look more closely at the components of aggregate expenditure. Table 11-2 lists the four components of aggregate expenditure for the year 2004. Each component is measured in *real* terms, meaning that it is corrected for inflation by being measured in billions of 2000 dollars. Consumption is clearly the largest component of aggregate expenditure. Investment and government purchases are of roughly similar size. Net exports are negative, reflecting the fact that in 2004, as in most years since the early 1970s, the United States imported more goods and services than it exported. Next, we consider the variables that determine each of the four components of aggregate expenditure.

Consumption

Figure 11-1 on page 334 shows movements in real consumption for the years 1979 to 2004. Notice that consumption follows a smooth, upward trend. Only during periods of recession does the growth in consumption slow or decline.

The following are the five most important variables that determine the level of consumption:

- Current disposable income
- Household wealth
- Expected future income
- The price level
- The interest rate

We can discuss how changes in each of these variables affect consumption.

CURRENT DISPOSABLE INCOME The most important determinant of consumption is the current disposable income of households. Recall from Chapter 7 that disposable income is the income remaining to households after they have paid the personal income tax and received government *transfer payments,* such as Social Security payments. For most households, the higher their disposable income, the more they spend, and the lower their income, the less they spend. Macroeconomic consumption is the total of all

TABLE 11-2

Components of Aggregate Expenditure, 2004

EXPENDITURE CATEGORY	EXPENDITURE (BILLIONS OF 2000 DOLLARS)
Consumption	$7,589
Investment	1,810
Government	1,952
Net exports	−601

Source: Bureau of Economic Analysis.

FIGURE 11-1

Real Consumption, 1979–2004

Consumption follows a smooth, upward trend, interrupted only infrequently by brief recessions.

Note: The values are seasonally adjusted at an annual rate.

Source: Bureau of Economic Analysis.

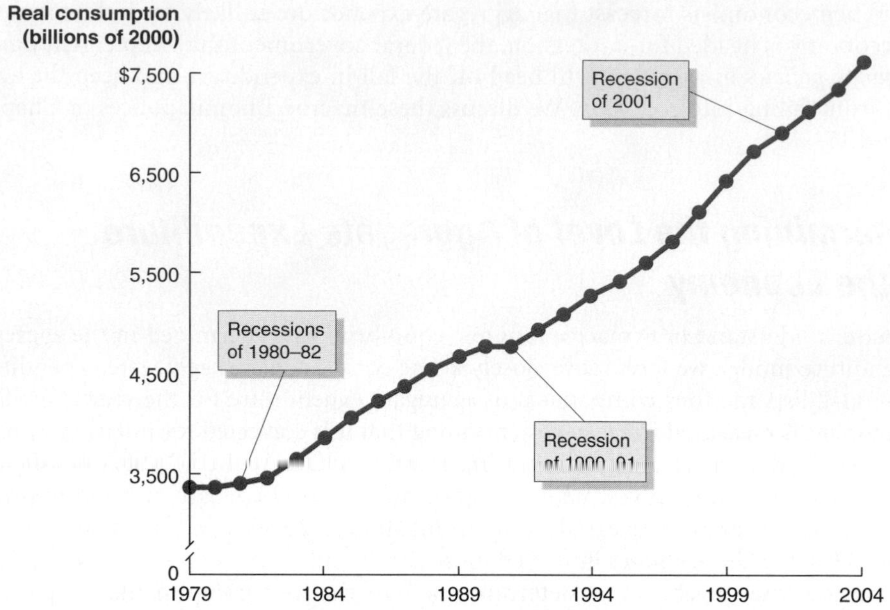

the consumption of U.S. households. So, we would expect consumption to increase when the current disposable income of households increases and to decrease when the current disposable income of households decreases. As we discussed in Chapter 7, total income in the United States expands during most years. Only during recessions, which happen infrequently, does total income decline. The main reason for the general upward trend in consumption shown in Figure 11-1 is that disposable income has followed a similar upward trend.

HOUSEHOLD WEALTH Consumption also depends on the wealth of households. A household's *wealth* is the value of its *assets* minus the value of its *liabilities.* Recall from Chapter 5 that an asset is anything of value owned by a person or a firm, and a liability is anything owed by a person or a firm. A household's assets include its home, stock and bond holdings, and bank accounts. A household's liabilities include any loans that it owes. A household with $10 million in wealth is likely to spend more than a household with $10,000 in wealth, even if both households have the same disposable income. Therefore, when the wealth of households increases, consumption should increase, and when the wealth of households decreases, consumption should decrease. Shares of stock are an important category of household wealth. When stock prices increase, household wealth will increase, and so should consumption. For example, a family whose stock holdings increase in value from $50,000 to $100,000 may be willing to spend a larger fraction of its income because it is less concerned with adding to its savings. A decline in stock prices should lead to a decline in consumption. Economists who have studied the determinants of consumption have concluded that permanent increases in wealth have a larger impact than temporary increases. A recent estimate of the effect of changes in wealth on consumption spending indicates that, for every permanent one-dollar increase in household wealth, consumption spending will increase by between four and five cents per year.

EXPECTED FUTURE INCOME Consumption also depends on expected future income. Most people prefer to keep their consumption fairly stable from year to year, even if their income fluctuates significantly. Real estate brokers, for example, earn most of their income from commissions (fixed percentages of the sale price) on houses they sell. Real estate brokers might have very high incomes some years and much lower incomes in other years. Most brokers will keep their consumption steady and not increase it during good years and then drastically cut back during the slower years. If we looked just at a broker's current income, we might have difficulty estimating the broker's current consumption. Instead, we need to take into account the broker's expected future income. We can conclude that current income explains current consumption well, *but only when current income is not unusually high or unusually low compared with expected future income.*

THE PRICE LEVEL Recall from Chapter 8 that the *price level* measures the average prices of goods and services in the economy. Consumption is affected by changes in the price level. It is tempting to think that an increase in prices will reduce consumption by making goods and services less affordable. In fact, the effect of an increase in the price of *one* product on the quantity demanded of that product is different from the effect of an increase in the price level on *total* spending by households on goods and services. Changes in the price level affect consumption mainly through their effect on household wealth. An increase in the price level will result in a decrease in the *real* value of household wealth. For example, if you have $2,000 in a checking account, the higher the price level, the fewer goods and services you can buy with your money. If the price level falls, the real value of your $2,000 would increase. Therefore, as the price level rises, the real value of your wealth declines and so will your consumption, at least a little. Conversely, as the price level falls, your consumption will increase.

THE INTEREST RATE Finally, consumption also depends on the interest rate. When the interest rate is high, the reward to saving is increased and households are likely to save more and spend less. In Chapter 8, we discussed the distinction between the *nominal interest rate* and the *real interest rate.* The nominal interest rate is the stated interest rate on a loan or a financial investment such as a bond. The real interest rate corrects the nominal interest rate for the impact of inflation and is equal to the nominal interest rate minus the inflation rate. Because households are concerned with the payments they will make or receive after the effects of inflation are taken into account, consumption spending depends on the real interest rate.

We saw in Chapter 7 that consumption spending is divided into three categories: spending on *services,* such as medical care, education, and haircuts; spending on *non-durable goods,* such as food and clothing; and spending on *durable goods,* such as automobiles and furniture. Spending on durable goods is most likely to be affected by changes in the interest rate because a high real interest rate increases the cost of spending financed by borrowing. The monthly payment on a four-year car loan will be higher if the real interest rate on the loan is 4 percent than if the real interest rate is 2 percent.

THE CONSUMPTION FUNCTION Panel (a) in Figure 11-2 illustrates the relationship between consumption and disposable income during the years 1960–2004. In panel (b), we draw a straight line through the points representing consumption and disposable income. The fact that most of the points lie almost on the line shows the close relationship between consumption and disposable income. Because changes in consumption depend on changes in disposable income, we can say that *consumption is a function of disposable income.* The relationship between consumption spending and disposable income illustrated in panel (b) of Figure 11-2 is called the **consumption function.**

Consumption function The relationship between consumption spending and disposable income.

The slope of the consumption function is equal to the change in consumption divided by the change in disposable income and is referred to as the **marginal propensity to consume** or ***MPC.*** Using the Greek letter delta, Δ, to represent "change in," *C* to represent consumption spending, and *YD* to represent disposable income, we can write the expression for the *MPC* as follows:

Marginal propensity to consume (*MPC*) The slope of the consumption function: The amount by which consumption spending increases when disposable income increases.

$$MPC = \frac{\text{Change in consumption}}{\text{Change in disposable income}} = \frac{\Delta C}{\Delta YD}.$$

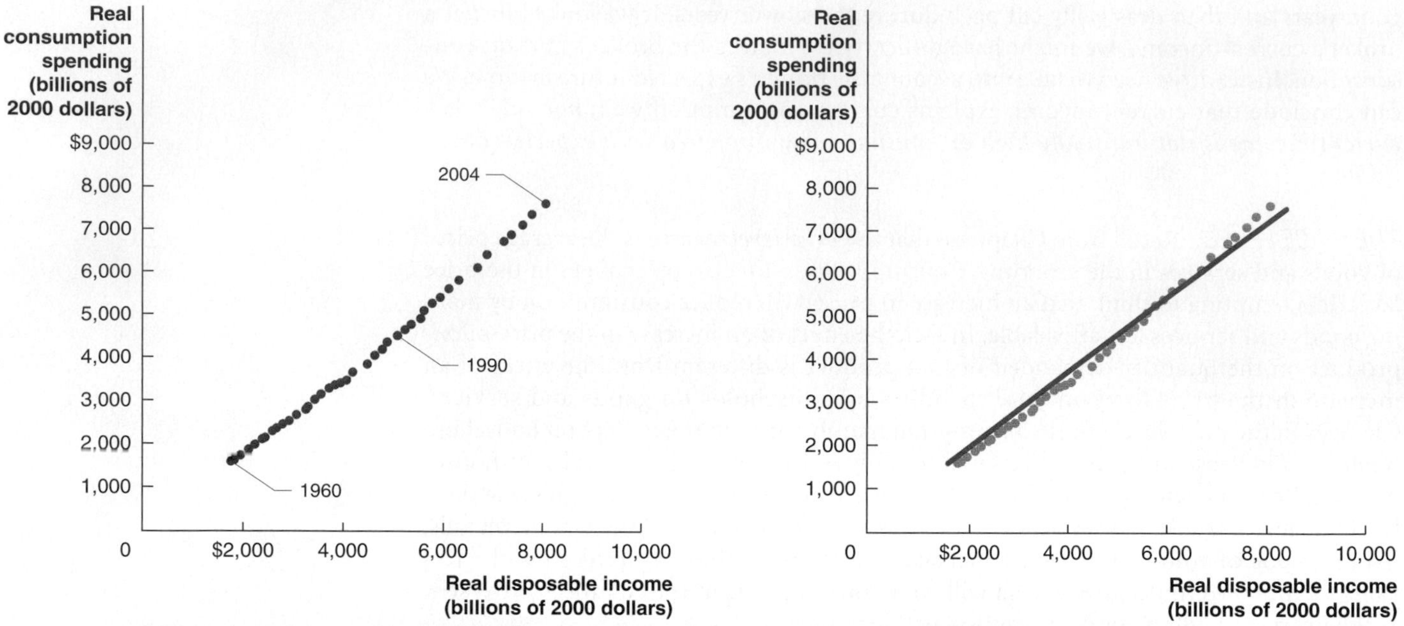

(a) Consumption and income, 1960–2004

(b) The consumption function

FIGURE 11-2 The Relationship between Consumption and Income, 1960–2004

Panel (a) shows the relationship between consumption and income. The points represent combinations of real consumption spending and real disposable income for the years between 1960 and 2004. In panel (b), we draw a straight line through the points from panel (a). The line represents the relationship between consumption and disposable income and is called the *consumption function*. The slope of the consumption function is the marginal propensity to consume.

For example, between 2003 and 2004, consumption spending increased by $277 billion, while disposable income increased by $285 billion. The marginal propensity to consume was therefore:

$$\frac{\Delta C}{\Delta YD} = \frac{\$277 \text{ billion}}{\$285 \text{ billion}} - 0.97.$$

The value for the *MPC* tells us that households in 2004 spent 97 percent of the increase in their household income.

We can also use the *MPC* to tell us how much consumption will change as income changes. To see this relationship, rewrite the expression for the *MPC*:

$$MPC = \frac{\text{Change in consumption}}{\text{Change in disposable income}}, \text{or}$$

$$\text{Change in consumption} = \text{change in disposable income} \times MPC.$$

For example, with an *MPC* of 0.97, a $10 billion increase in disposable income will increase consumption by $10 billion × 0.97, or $9.7 billion.

The Relationship between Consumption and National Income

We have seen that consumption spending by households depends on disposable income. We now shift our focus slightly to the similar relationship that exists between consumption spending and GDP. We make this shift because we are interested in using the aggregate expenditure model to explain fluctuations in real GDP, rather than fluctuations in disposable income. The first step in examining the relationship between consumption and GDP is to recall from Chapter 7 that the differences between GDP and national income are small and can be ignored without affecting our analysis. In fact, in this and the following chapters we will use the terms *GDP* and *national income* interchangeably.

Also recall that disposable income is equal to national income plus government transfer payments minus taxes. Taxes minus government transfer payments are referred to as *net taxes.* So, we can write the following:

Disposable income = National income − Net taxes.

Rearranging the equation:

National income = GDP = Disposable income + Net taxes.

The table in Figure 11-3 shows hypothetical values for national income (or GDP), net taxes, disposable income, and consumption spending. Notice that national income and disposable income differ by a constant amount, which is equal to net taxes of $1,000 billion. In fact, net taxes are not a constant amount because they are affected by changes in income. As income rises, net taxes rise because some taxes, such as the personal income tax, increase and some government transfer payments, such as government payments to unemployed workers, fall. Nothing important is affected in our analysis, however, by our simplifying assumption that net taxes are constant. The graph in Figure 11-3 shows a line representing the relationship between consumption and national income. The line is very similar to the consumption function shown in panel (b) of Figure 11-2. We defined the marginal propensity to consume (*MPC*) as the change in consumption divided by the change in disposable income, which is the slope of the consumption function. In fact, notice that if we calculate the slope of the line in Figure 11-3 between points *A* and *B*, we get a result that will not change whether we use the values for

National Income or GDP (billions of dollars)	Net Taxes (billions of dollars)	Disposable Income (billions of dollars)	Consumption (billions of dollars)	Change in National Income (billions of dollars)	Change in Disposable Income (billions of dollars)
$1,000	$1,000	$0	$750	—	—
3,000	1,000	2,000	2,250	2,000	2,000
5,000	1,000	4,000	3,750	2,000	2,000
7,000	1,000	6,000	5,250	2,000	2,000
9,000	1,000	8,000	6,750	2,000	2,000
11,000	1,000	10,000	8,250	2,000	2,000
13,000	1,000	12,000	9,750	2,000	2,000

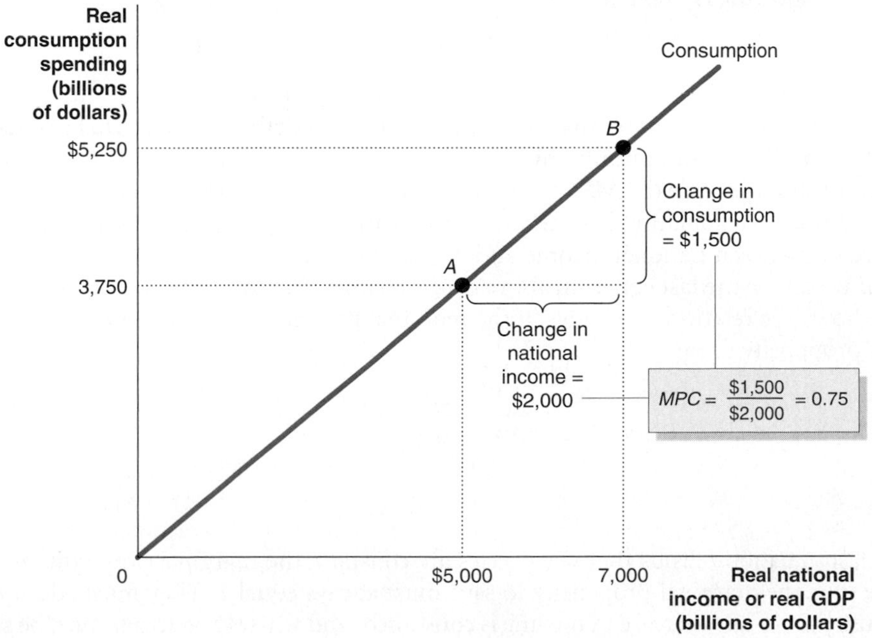

FIGURE 11-3

The Relationship between Consumption and National Income

Because national income differs from disposable income only by net taxes—which, for simplicity, we assume are constant—we can graph the consumption function using national income, rather than disposable income. We can also calculate the *MPC,* which is the slope of the consumption function, using either the change in national income or the change in disposable income and always get the same value. The slope of the consumption function between point *A* and point *B* is equal to the change in consumption—$1,500 billion—divided by the change in national income—$2,000 billion—or 0.75.

national income or the values for disposable income. Using the values for national income:

$$\frac{\Delta C}{\Delta Y} = \frac{\$5{,}250 \text{ billion} - \$3{,}750 \text{ billion}}{\$7{,}000 \text{ billion} - \$5{,}000 \text{ billion}} = 0.75.$$

Using the corresponding values for disposable income from the table:

$$\frac{\Delta C}{\Delta YD} = \frac{\$5{,}250 \text{ billion} - \$3{,}750 \text{ billion}}{\$6{,}000 \text{ billion} - \$4{,}000 \text{ billion}} = 0.75.$$

It should not be surprising that we get the same result in either case. National income and disposable income differ by a constant amount, so changes in the two numbers always give us the same value, as is shown by the last two columns of the table in Figure 11-3. Therefore, we can graph the consumption function using national income, rather than using disposable income. We can also calculate the *MPC* using either the change in national income or the change in disposable income and always get the same value.

Income, Consumption, and Saving

To complete our discussion of consumption, we can look briefly at the relationships among income, consumption, and saving. Households either spend their income, save it, or use it to pay taxes. For the economy as a whole, we can write the following:

National income = Consumption + Saving + Taxes.

When national income increases, there must be some combination of an increase in consumption, an increase in saving, or an increase in taxes:

Change in national income = Change in consumption + Change in saving + Change in taxes.

Using symbols, where Y represents national income (and GDP), C represents consumption, S represents saving, and T represents taxes, we can write the following:

$$Y = C + S + T$$

and,

$$\Delta Y = \Delta C + \Delta S + \Delta T.$$

To simplify, we can assume that taxes are always a constant amount, in which case $\Delta T = 0$, so the following is also true:

$$\Delta Y = \Delta C + \Delta S.$$

Marginal propensity to save (*MPS*) The change in saving divided by the change in disposable income.

We have already seen that the marginal propensity to consume equals the change in consumption divided by the change in income. We can define the **marginal propensity to save (*MPS*)** as the amount by which saving increases when disposable income increases, and measure the *MPS* as the change in saving divided by the change in disposable income. In calculating the *MPS*, as in calculating the *MPC*, we can safely ignore the difference between national income and disposable income.

If we divide the last equation above by the change in income, ΔY, we get an equation that shows the relationship between the marginal propensity to consume and the marginal propensity to save:

$$\frac{\Delta Y}{\Delta Y} = \frac{\Delta C}{\Delta Y} + \frac{\Delta S}{\Delta Y}$$

or,

$$1 = MPC + MPS.$$

This last equation tells us that when taxes are constant, the marginal propensity to consume plus the marginal propensity to save must always equal 1. They must add up to 1 because part of any increase in income is consumed, and whatever remains must be saved.

SOLVED PROBLEM 11-1

Calculating the Marginal Propensity to Consume and the Marginal Propensity to Save

② LEARNING OBJECTIVE

Discuss the determinants of the four components of aggregate expenditure and define the marginal propensity to consume and the marginal propensity to save.

Fill in the blanks in the following table. For simplicity, assume that taxes are zero. Show that the *MPC* plus the *MPS* equals 1.

NATIONAL INCOME AND REAL GDP (*Y*)	CONSUMPTION (*C*)	SAVING (*S*)	MARGINAL PROPENSITY TO CONSUME (*MPC*)	MARGINAL PROPENSITY TO SAVE (*MPS*)
$9,000	$8,000		—	—
10,000	8,600			
11,000	9,200			
12,000	9,800			
13,000	10,400			

Solving the Problem:

Step 1: Review the chapter material. This problem is about the relationship among income, consumption, and saving, so you may want to review the section "Income, Consumption, and Saving," which begins on page 338.

Step 2: Fill in the table. We know that $Y = C + S + T$. With taxes equal to zero, this equation becomes $Y = C + S$. We can use this equation to fill in the "Saving" column. We can use the expressions for the *MPC* and the *MPS* to fill in the other two columns:

$$MPC = \frac{\Delta C}{\Delta Y}$$

$$MPS = \frac{\Delta S}{\Delta Y}.$$

For example, to calculate the value of the *MPC* in the second row we have:

$$MPC = \frac{\Delta C}{\Delta Y} = \frac{\$8{,}600 - \$8{,}000}{\$10{,}000 - \$9{,}000} = \frac{\$600}{\$1{,}000} = 0.6.$$

To calculate the value of the *MPS* in the second row, we have:

$$MPS = \frac{\Delta S}{\Delta Y} = \frac{\$1{,}400 - \$1{,}000}{\$10{,}000 - \$9{,}000} = \frac{\$400}{\$1{,}000} = 0.4.$$

NATIONAL INCOME AND REAL GDP (*Y*)	CONSUMPTION (*C*)	SAVING (*S*)	MARGINAL PROPENSITY TO CONSUME (*MPC*)	MARGINAL PROPENSITY TO SAVE (*MPS*)
$9,000	$8,000	$1,000	—	—
10,000	8,600	1,400	0.6	0.4
11,000	9,200	1,800	0.6	0.4
12,000	9,800	2,200	0.6	0.4
13,000	10,400	2,600	0.6	0.4

Step 3: Show that the *MPC* plus the *MPS* equals 1. At every level of national income, the *MPC* is 0.6 and the *MPS* is 0.4. Therefore, the *MPC* plus the *MPS* is always equal to 1.

YOUR TURN: **For more practice, do related problem 9 on page 366 at the end of this chapter.**

Planned Investment

Figure 11-4 shows movements in real investment spending for the years 1979–2004. Notice that, unlike consumption, investment does not follow a smooth, upward trend. Investment declined significantly during the recessions of 1980, 1981–82, 1990–91, and 2001. Following the recovery from the 1981–82 recession, real investment increased only slowly, so that in 1992 it was at about the same level as in 1984. But during the mid- to late 1990s, investment increased very rapidly, led by increases in spending on computers and other information technology, partly as a result of the growth of the Internet. In 2000, real investment spending had risen to nearly twice its 1992 level, before declining by 10 percent between 2000 and 2002. Real investment spending increased by more than 18 percent between 2002 and 2004, as the economy recovered from the 2001 recession.

The four most important variables that determine the level of investment are:

- Expectations of future profitability
- The interest rate
- Taxes
- Cash flow

EXPECTATIONS OF FUTURE PROFITABILITY Investment goods, such as factories, office buildings, and machinery and equipment, are long-lived. A firm is unlikely to build a new factory unless it is optimistic that the demand for its product will remain strong for a period of at least several years. When the economy moves into a recession, many firms will postpone buying investment goods even if the demand for their own product is strong because they are afraid that the recession may become worse. The reverse may be true during an expansion. In the late 1990s, many firms increased their investment spending in the expectation that capital goods that embodied new information and telecommunication technologies would prove very profitable. The key point is this: *The optimism or pessimism of firms is an important determinant of investment spending.*

THE INTEREST RATE A significant fraction of business investment is financed by borrowing. This borrowing takes the form of issuing corporate bonds or borrowing from banks. Households also borrow to finance most of their spending on new homes. The

FIGURE 11-4

Real Investment, 1979–2004

Investment is subject to more fluctuations than is consumption. Investment declined significantly during the recessions of 1980, 1981–82, 1990–91, and 2001. Following the recovery from the 1981–82 recession, investment increased only slowly, so that in 1992 it was at about the same level as in 1984. But during the mid-to-late 1990s, investment increased very strongly, led by increases in spending on computers and other information technology, partly as a result of the growth of the Internet. In 2000, real investment had risen to more than twice its 1992 level, before declining by more than 10 percent in 2001.

Note: The values are seasonally adjusted at an annual rate.

Source: Bureau of Economic Analysis.

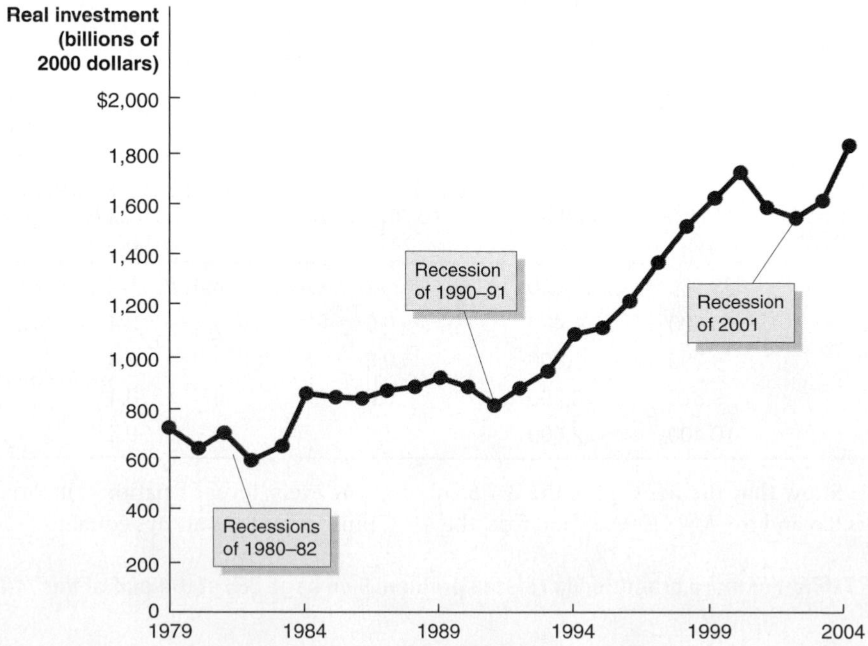

higher the interest rate, the more expensive it becomes for firms and households to borrow. Because households and firms are interested in the cost of borrowing after taking into account the effects of inflation, investment spending will depend on the real interest rate. Therefore, holding the other factors that affect investment spending constant, there is an inverse relationship between the real interest rate and investment spending: *A higher real interest rate results in less investment spending, and a lower real interest rate results in more investment spending.*

TAXES The level of investment spending is also affected by taxes. Firms focus on the profits that remain after they have paid taxes. The federal government imposes a *corporate income tax* on the profits corporations earn, including profits from the new buildings, equipment, and other investment goods they purchase. A reduction in the corporate income tax increases the after-tax profitability of investment spending. An increase in the corporate income tax decreases the after-tax profitability of investment spending. *Investment tax incentives* also increase investment spending. An investment tax incentive provides firms with a tax reduction when they spend on new investment goods. For example, in 2002, Congress enacted an investment tax incentive for new investment in equipment and software. This incentive expired at the end of 2004. Partially as a result of this incentive, spending on equipment and software increased from $801 billion at an annual rate in the first quarter of 2002 to $996 billion in the fourth quarter of 2004.

CASH FLOW Most firms do not borrow to finance spending on new factories, machinery, and equipment. Instead, they use their own funds. **Cash flow** is the difference between the cash revenues received by the firm and the cash spending by the firm. Non-cash receipts or noncash spending would not be included in cash flow. For example, tax laws allow firms to count as a cost an annual amount for depreciation to replace worn out or obsolete machinery and equipment even if new machinery and equipment have not actually been purchased. Because this is noncash spending, it would not be included when calculating cash flow. The largest contributor to cash flow is profit. The more profitable a firm is, the greater its cash flow and the greater its ability to finance investment. During periods of recession, many firms experience reduced profits, which in turn reduces their ability to finance spending on new factories or machinery and equipment.

Cash flow The difference between the cash revenues received by the firm and the cash spending by the firm.

11-1 Making the Connection

Cisco Rides the Roller Coaster of Information Technology Spending

We saw in the beginning of this chapter that Cisco Systems was taken by surprise by the decline in demand for its routers, switches, and other equipment during the first quarter of 2001. In fact, the Internet and telecommunications busts of 2001 were unusual in their severity. The graph on page 342 shows that spending on information processing equipment and software followed a fairly smooth, upward trend from the beginning of 1990 to the end of 2000. Measured in 2000 dollars, real spending on information processing equipment and software increased from $101 billion at an annual rate in the first quarter of 1990 to $488 billion in the fourth quarter of 2000. Spending then declined sharply and did not regain the level of the fourth quarter of 2000 until almost three years later in the third quarter of 2003.

Cisco benefited greatly from the increased spending on information technology in the 1990s. By the end of 2000, Cisco was second to only Microsoft in the total value of its shares of stock. In early 2000, John Chambers, Cisco's chief executive officer, predicted that by 2004 the firm's annual revenues would rise from $12.2 billion to $50 billion and that the total value of its stock would rise from $454 billion to $1 trillion. Unfortunately, the Internet and telecommunications busts made these goals impossible to attain. Cisco made an accounting profit of $2.1 billion in 2000, but by 2002 this profit had turned into a $1 billion loss as revenues declined. By 2004, Cisco's revenues had risen back to $22 billion, and the firm made a $3.6 billion accounting profit.

Cisco Systems has survived the wild Internet boom and bust.

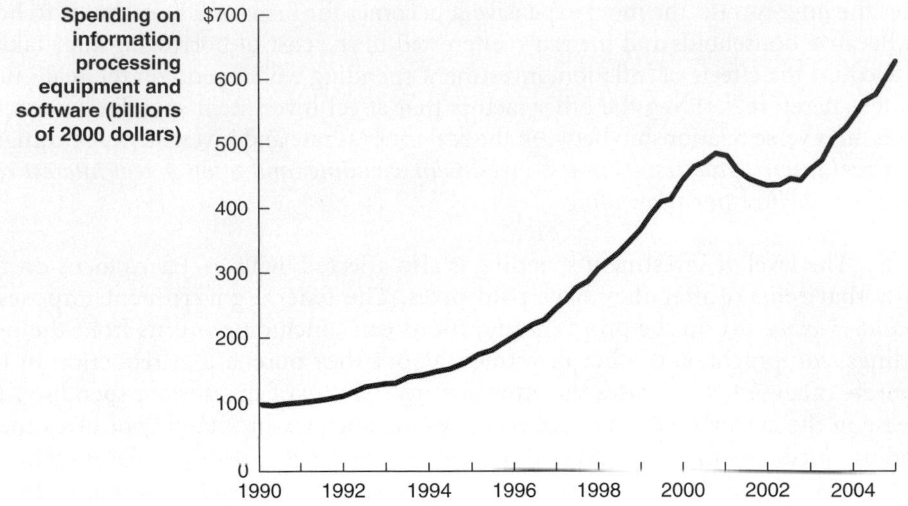

Note: The values are seasonally adjusted at an annual rate.

Source: Bureau of Economic Analysis.

What explains Cisco's roller-coaster ride? As we have seen, a key determinant of investment spending is firms' expectations of the future profitability of their purchases of investment goods. In the 1990s, many firms investing in equipment to establish Web sites or to use the fiber optic cable networks being built, overestimated how profitable their investments in this equipment would be. When forecasts of future profitability were adjusted sharply downward in 2001, spending on information technology plummeted. By 2005, however, the spread of high-speed Internet access led industry analysts to forecast that Internet traffic would be increasing by 70 percent or more per year. Cisco was still selling 70 percent to 85 percent of all network switches and routers, which left the firm well positioned to profit from this future growth.

Source: "Growing Pains of the Cisco Kid," *Economist,* November 11, 2004.

Government Purchases

Total government purchases include all spending by federal, local, and state governments for goods and services. Recall from Chapter 7 that government purchases do not include transfer payments, such as Social Security payments by the federal government or pension payments by local governments to retired police officers and firefighters, because the government does not receive a good or service in return.

Figure 11-5 shows levels of real government purchases during the years 1979–2004. Government purchases grew steadily for most of this period, with the exception of the mid-1990s when concern that spending by the federal government was growing much faster than tax receipts led Congress and Presidents George H. W. Bush and Bill Clinton to sign a series of spending reductions. As a result, real government purchases declined for three years, beginning in 1992. Contributing to the slow growth of government purchases during the 1990s was the end of the Cold War between the United States and the Soviet Union in 1989. Real federal government spending on national defense declined from $479 billion in 1990 to $365 billion in 1998, before rising again to $481 billion in 2004 in response to the war on terrorism and the war in Iraq.

Net Exports

Net exports equal exports minus imports. We can calculate net exports by taking the value of spending by foreign firms and households on goods and services produced in

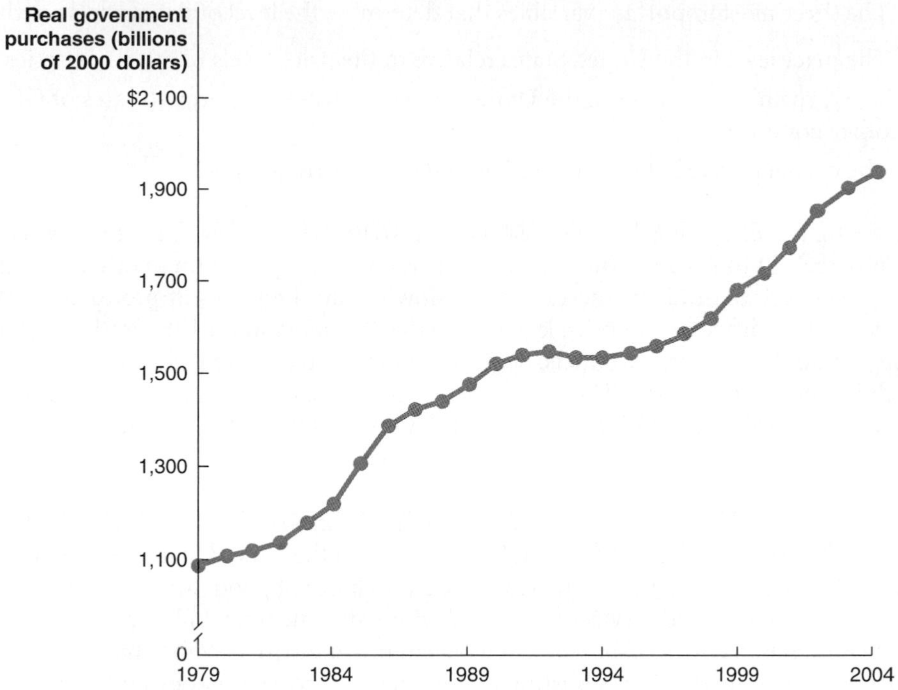

FIGURE 11-5

Real Government Purchases, 1979–2004

Government purchases grew steadily for most of the 1979–2004 period, with the exception of the mid-1990s when concern about the federal budget deficit caused real government purchases to fall for three years, beginning in 1992.

Note: The values are seasonally adjusted at an annual rate.

Source: Bureau of Economic Analysis.

the United States and *subtracting* the value of spending by U.S. firms and households on goods and services produced in other countries. Figure 11-6 illustrates movements in real net exports during the years 1979–2004. During nearly all these years, the United States has imported more goods and services than it has exported, so net exports have been negative. Net exports usually increase when the U.S. economy is in recession—although this did not happen during the 2001 recession—and fall when the U.S. economy is expanding. We will explore further the behavior of net exports in Chapter 17.

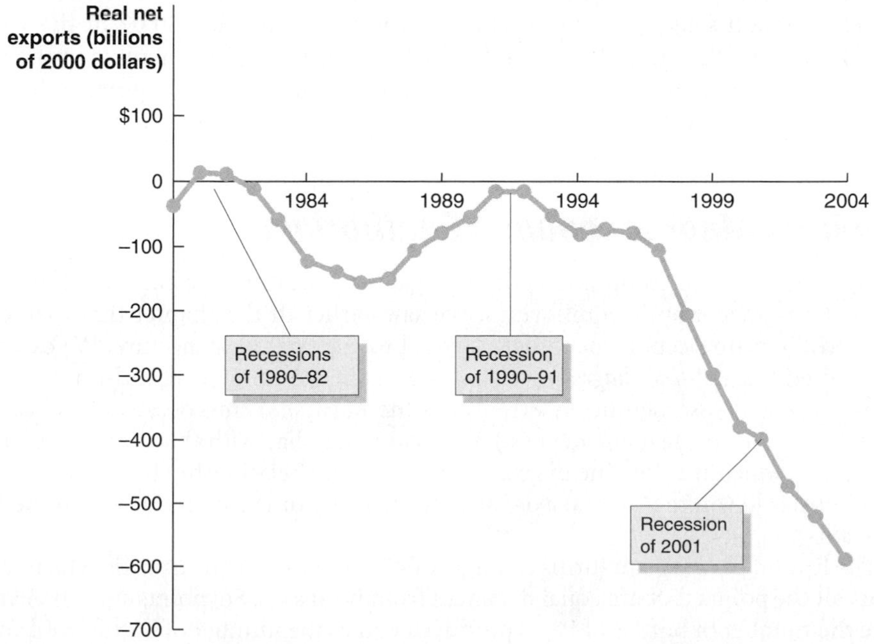

FIGURE 11-6

Real Net Exports, 1979–2004

Net exports have been negative in most years between 1979 and 2004. Net exports have usually increased when the U.S. economy is in recession and decreased when the U.S. economy is expanding, although they fell during the 2001 recession.

Note: The values are seasonally adjusted at an annual rate.

Source: Bureau of Economic Analysis.

The three most important variables that determine the level of net exports are these:

- The price level in the United States relative to the price levels in other countries
- The growth rate of GDP in the United States relative to the growth rates of GDP in other countries
- The exchange rate between the dollar and other currencies

THE PRICE LEVEL IN THE UNITED STATES RELATIVE TO THE PRICE LEVELS IN OTHER COUNTRIES If inflation in the United States is lower than inflation in other countries, then prices of U.S. products increase more slowly than the prices of products of other countries. This difference in price levels increases the demand for U.S. products relative to the demand for foreign products. So, U.S. exports increase and U.S. imports decrease, which increases net exports. The reverse will happen during periods when the inflation rate in the United States is higher than the inflation rates in other countries: U.S. exports decrease and U.S. imports increase, which decreases net exports.

THE GROWTH RATE OF GDP IN THE UNITED STATES RELATIVE TO THE GROWTH RATES OF GDP IN OTHER COUNTRIES As GDP increases in the United States, the incomes of households rise, leading them to increase their purchases of goods and services. Some of the additional goods and services purchased with rising incomes will be produced in the United States, but some will be imported. When incomes rise faster in the United States than in other countries, U.S. consumers' purchases of foreign goods and services will increase faster than foreign consumers' purchases of U.S. goods and services. As a result, net exports will fall. When incomes in the United States rise more slowly than incomes in other countries, net exports will rise.

THE EXCHANGE RATE BETWEEN THE DOLLAR AND OTHER CURRENCIES As the value of the U.S. dollar rises, the foreign currency price of U.S. products sold in other countries rises, and the dollar price of foreign products sold in the United States falls. For example, suppose that the exchange rate between the Japanese yen and the U.S. dollar is ¥100 = $1. Leaving aside transportation costs, a U.S. product that sells for $1 in the United States will sell for ¥100 in Japan, and a Japanese product that sells for ¥100 in Japan will sell for $1 in the United States. If the exchange rate rises to ¥150 = $1, then the U.S. product that still sells for $1 in the United States will now sell for ¥150 in Japan, reducing the quantity demanded by Japanese consumers. The Japanese product that still sells for ¥100 in Japan will now sell for only $0.67 in the United States, increasing the quantity demanded by U.S. consumers. An increase in the value of the dollar will reduce exports and increase imports, so net exports will fall. A decrease in the value of the dollar will increase exports and reduce imports, so net exports will rise.

③ **LEARNING OBJECTIVE**

Use a 45°-line diagram to illustrate macroeconomic equilibrium.

Graphing Macroeconomic Equilibrium

Having examined the components of aggregate expenditure, we can now look more closely at macroeconomic equilibrium. We saw earlier in the chapter that macroeconomic equilibrium occurs when GDP is equal to aggregate expenditure. We can use a graph called the *45°-line diagram* to illustrate macroeconomic equilibrium. (The 45°-line diagram is also sometimes referred to as the *Keynesian cross* because it is based on the analysis of John Maynard Keynes.) To become familiar with this diagram, consider Figure 11-7, which is a 45°-line diagram that shows the relationship between the quantity of Pepsi sold (on the vertical axis) and the quantity of Pepsi produced (on the horizontal axis).

The line on the diagram forms an angle of 45° with the horizontal axis. The line represents all the points that are equal distances from both axes. So, points such as *A* and *B*, where the number of bottles of Pepsi produced equals the number of bottles sold, are on the 45° line. Points such as *C*, where the quantity sold is greater than the quantity pro-

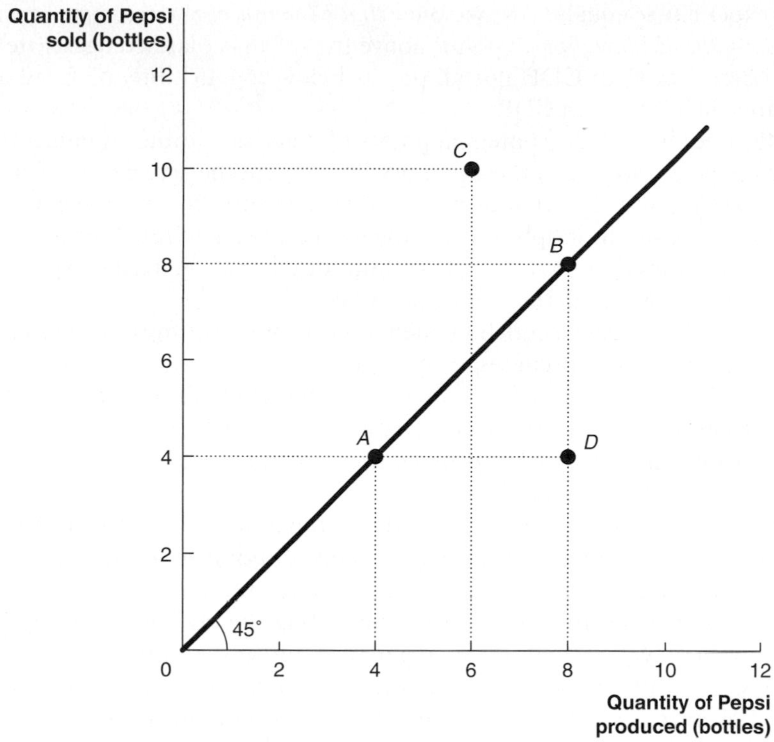

FIGURE 11-7

An Example of a 45°-Line Diagram

The 45° line shows all the points that are equal distances from both axes. Points such as *A* and *B*, at which the quantity produced equals the quantity sold, are on the 45° line. Points such as *C*, at which the quantity sold is greater than the quantity produced, lie above the line. Points such as *D*, at which the quantity sold is less than the quantity produced, lie below the line.

duced, lie above the line. Points such as *D*, where the quantity sold is less than the quantity produced, lie below the line.

Figure 11-8 is very similar to Figure 11-7, except now we are measuring real national income or real GDP (*Y*) on the horizontal axis and planned real aggregate expenditure (*AE*) on the vertical axis. Because macroeconomic equilibrium occurs where planned

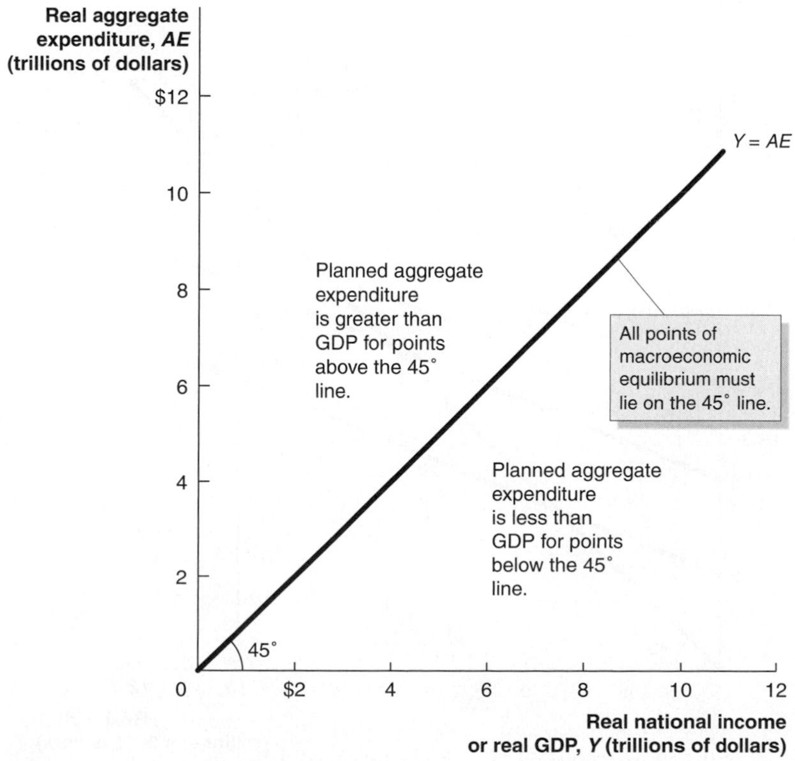

FIGURE 11-8

The Relationship between Planned Aggregate Expenditure and GDP on a 45°-Line Diagram

Every point of macroeconomic equilibrium is on the 45° line, where planned expenditure equals GDP. At points above the line, planned aggregate expenditure is greater than GDP. At points below the line, planned aggregate expenditure is less than GDP.

aggregate expenditure equals GDP, we *know that all points of macroeconomic equilibrium must lie along the 45° line.* For all points above the 45° line, planned aggregate expenditure will be greater than GDP. For all points below the 45° line, planned aggregate expenditure will be less than GDP.

The 45° line shows many potential points of macroeconomic equilibrium. During any particular year, only one of these points will represent the actual level of equilibrium real GDP, given the actual level of planned real expenditure. To determine this point, we need to draw a line on the graph showing the *aggregate expenditure function.* The aggregate expenditure function shows us the amount of planned aggregate expenditure that will occur at every level of national income or GDP.

Changes in GDP have a much greater impact on consumption than on planned investment, government purchases, or net exports. We assume for simplicity that the variables that determine planned investment, government purchases, and net exports all remain constant, as do the variables other than GDP that affect consumption. For example, we will assume a firm's level of planned investment at the beginning of the year will not change during the year, even if the level of GDP changes.

Figure 11-9 shows the aggregate expenditure function on the 45°-line diagram. The lowest upward-sloping line, *C*, represents the consumption function, just as shown in Figure 11-2 on page 336. The quantities of planned investment, government purchases, and net exports are constant because we assumed that the variables they depend on are constant. So, the level of planned aggregate expenditure at any level of GDP is the amount of consumption spending at that level of GDP plus the sum of the constant amounts of planned investment, government purchases, and net exports. In Figure 11-9 we add each component of spending successively to the consumption function line to arrive at the line representing planned aggregate expenditure (*AE*). The $C + I$ line is higher than the *C* line by the constant amount of planned investment; the $C + I + G$

FIGURE 11-9

Macroeconomic Equilibrium on the 45°-Line Diagram

Macroeconomic equilibrium occurs where the aggregate expenditure line (*AE*) crosses the 45° line. The lowest upward-sloping line, *C*, represents the consumption function. The quantities of planned investment, government purchases, and net exports are constant because we assumed that the variables they depend on are constant. So, the total of planned aggregate expenditure at any level of GDP is just the amount of consumption at that level of GDP plus the sum of the constant amounts of planned investment, government purchases, and net exports. We successively add each component of spending to the consumption function line to arrive at the line representing aggregate expenditure.

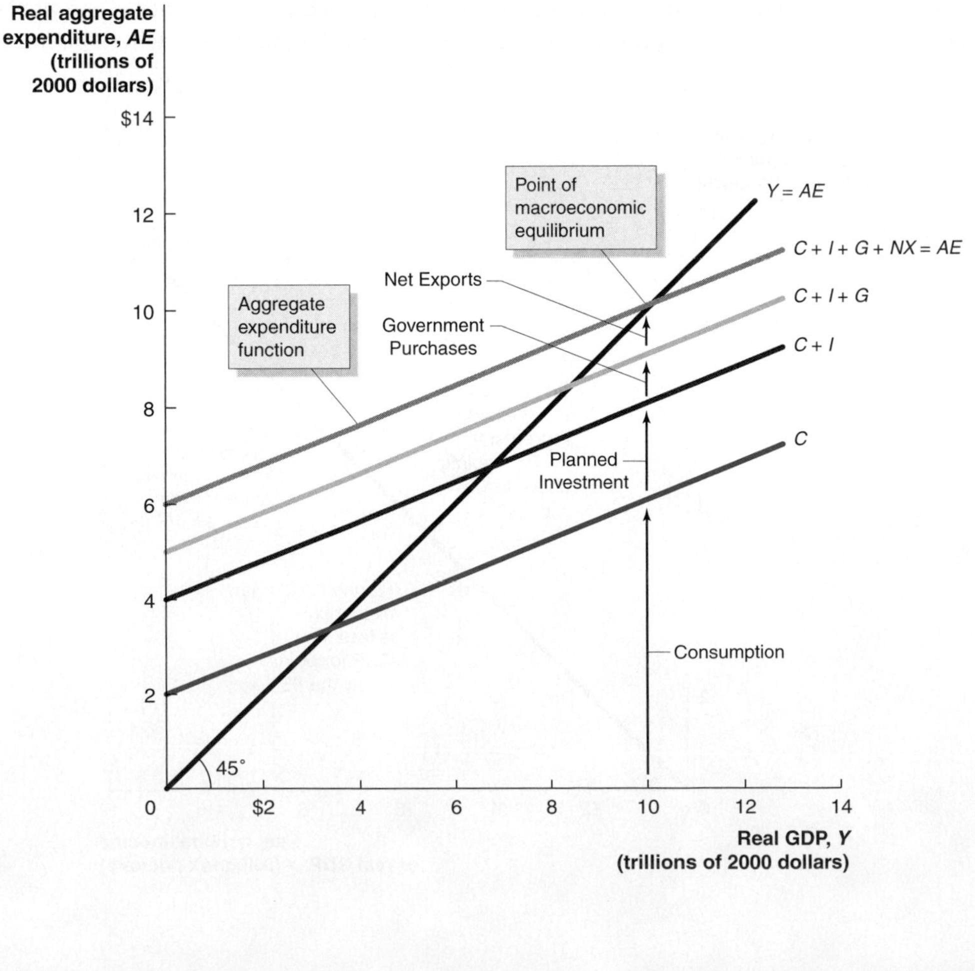

line is higher than the $C + I$ line by the constant amount of government purchases; and the $C + I + G + NX$ line is higher than the $C + I + G$ line by the constant amount of NX. (Notice that in many years NX is negative, which would cause the $C + I + G + NX$ line to be *below* the $C + I + G$ line.) The $C + I + G + NX$ line shows all four components of expenditure and is the aggregate expenditure (AE) function. At the point where the AE line crosses the 45° line, planned aggregate expenditure is equal to GDP and the economy is in macroeconomic equilibrium.

Figure 11-10 makes the relationship between planned aggregate expenditure and GDP clearer by showing only the 45° line and the AE line. The figure shows that the AE line intersects the 45° line at a level of real GDP of $10 trillion. Therefore, $10 trillion represents the equilibrium level of real GDP. To see why this is true, consider the situation if real GDP were only $8 trillion. By moving vertically from $8 trillion on the horizontal axis up to the AE line, we can see that planned aggregate expenditure will be greater than $8 trillion at this level of real GDP. Whenever total spending is greater than total production, firms' inventories will fall. The fall in inventories is equal to the vertical distance between the AE line, which shows the level of total spending, and the 45° line, which shows the $8 trillion of total production. Unplanned declines in inventories lead firms to increase their production. As real GDP increases from $8 trillion, so will total income and, therefore, consumption. The economy will move up the AE line as consumption increases. The gap between total spending and total production will fall, but as long as the AE line is above the 45° line, inventories will continue to decline and firms will continue to expand production. When real GDP rises to $10 trillion, inventories stop falling and the economy will be in macroeconomic equilibrium.

As Figure 11-10 shows, if GDP initially is $12 trillion, planned aggregate expenditure will be less than GDP and firms will experience an unplanned increase in inventories. Rising inventories lead firms to decrease production. As GDP falls from $12 trillion,

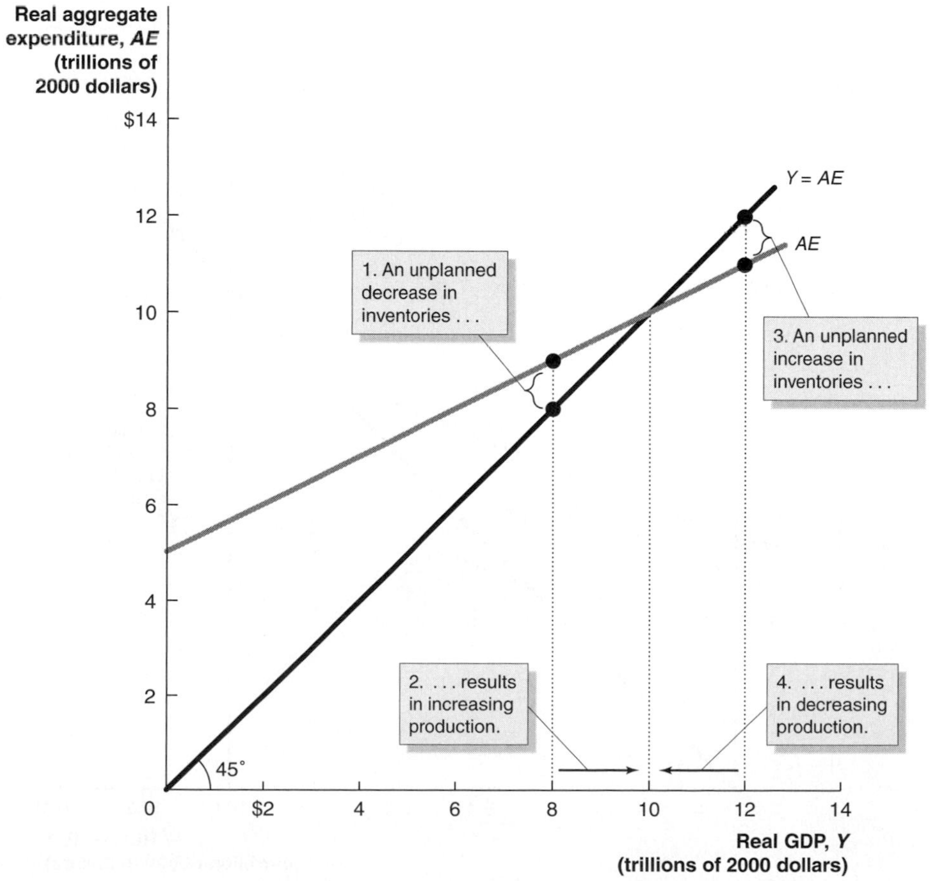

FIGURE 11-10

Macroeconomic Equilibrium

Macroeconomic equilibrium occurs where the *AE* line crosses the 45° line. In this case, that occurs at GDP of $10 trillion. If GDP is less than $10 trillion, the corresponding point on the *AE* line is above the 45° line, planned aggregate expenditure is greater than total production, firms will experience an unplanned decrease in inventories, and GDP will increase. If GDP is greater than $10 trillion, the corresponding point on the *AE* line is below the 45° line, planned aggregate expenditure is less than total production, firms will experience an unplanned increase in inventories, and GDP will decrease.

so will consumption, which causes the economy to move down the *AE* line. The gap between planned aggregate expenditure and GDP will fall, but as long as the *AE* line is below the 45° line, inventories will continue to rise and firms will continue to cut production. When GDP falls to $10 trillion, inventories will stop rising, and the economy will be in macroeconomic equilibrium.

Showing a Recession on the 45°-Line Diagram

Notice that *macroeconomic equilibrium can occur at any point on the 45° line.* Ideally, we would like equilibrium to occur at *potential real GDP.* At potential real GDP, firms will be operating at their normal level of capacity and the economy will be at the *natural rate of unemployment.* As we saw in Chapter 8, at the natural rate of unemployment, the economy will be at *full employment:* Everyone in the labor force who wants a job will have one, except the structurally and frictionally unemployed. However, for equilibrium to occur at the level of potential real GDP, planned aggregate expenditure must be high enough. As Figure 11-11 shows, if there is insufficient total spending, equilibrium will occur at a lower level of real GDP. Many firms will be operating below their normal capacity, and the unemployment rate will be above the natural rate of unemployment.

Suppose that the level of potential real GDP is $10 trillion. As Figure 11-11 shows, when GDP is $10 trillion, planned aggregate expenditure is below $10 trillion, perhaps because business firms have become pessimistic about their future profitability and have reduced their investment spending. The shortfall in planned aggregate expenditure that leads to the recession can be measured as the vertical distance between the *AE* line and the 45° line at the level of potential real GDP. The shortfall in planned aggregate expenditure is exactly equal to the unplanned increase in inventories that would occur if the economy were initially at a level of GDP of $10 trillion. The unplanned increase in

FIGURE 11-11

Showing a Recession on the 45°-Line Diagram

When the aggregate expenditure line intersects the 45° line at a level of GDP below potential real GDP, the economy is in recession. The figure shows potential real GDP is $10 trillion, but because planned aggregate expenditure is too low, the equilibrium level of GDP is only $9.8 trillion, where the *AE* line intersects the 45° line. As a result, some firms will be operating below their normal capacity and unemployment will be above the natural rate of unemployment. We can measure the shortfall in planned aggregate expenditure as the vertical distance between the *AE* line and the 45° line at the level of potential real GDP.

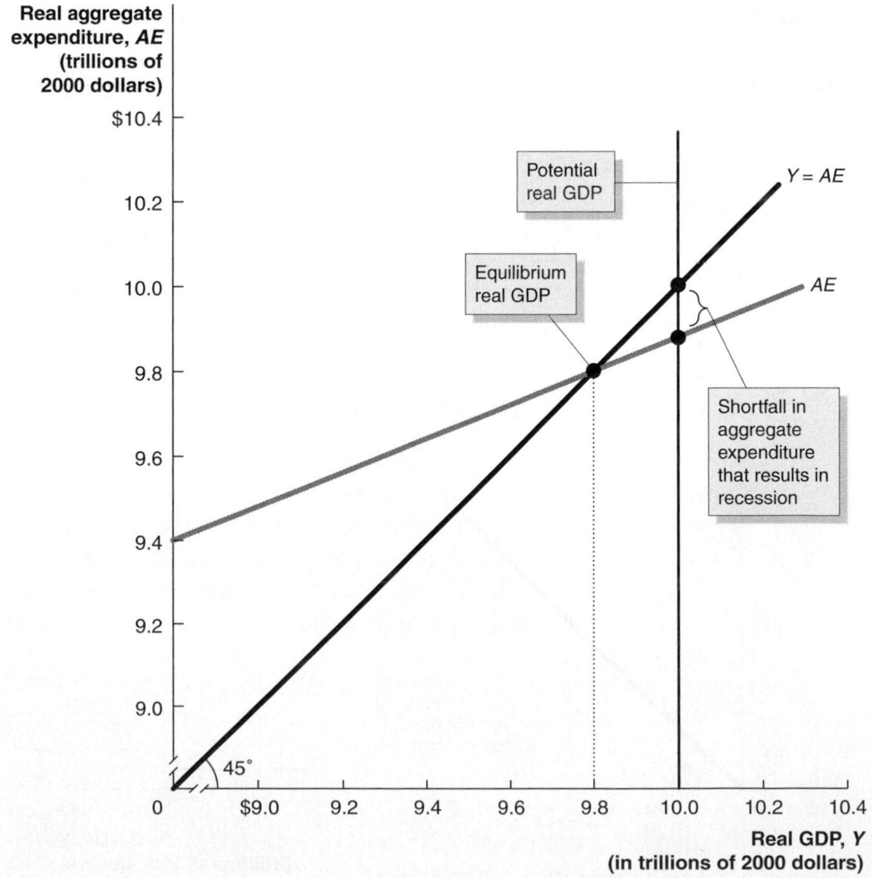

inventories measures the amount by which current planned aggregate expenditure is too low for the current level of production to be the equilibrium level. Or, put another way, if any of the four components of aggregate expenditure increased by this amount, the *AE* line would shift upward and intersect the 45° line at GDP of $10 trillion and the economy would be in macroeconomic equilibrium at full employment.

Figure 11-11 shows that macroeconomic equilibrium will occur when real GDP is $9.8 trillion. Because this is 2 percent below the potential level of real GDP of $10 trillion, many firms will be operating below their normal capacity and the unemployment rate will be well above the natural rate of unemployment. The economy will remain at this level of real GDP until there is an increase in one or more of the components of aggregate expenditure.

The Important Role of Inventories

Whenever planned aggregate expenditure is less than real GDP, some firms will experience an unplanned increase in inventories. If firms do not cut back their production promptly when spending declines, they will accumulate inventories. If firms accumulate excess inventories, then even if spending quickly returns to its normal levels, firms will have to sell these excess inventories before they can return to producing at normal levels. The possibility that firms will accumulate excess inventories explains why a brief decline in spending can result in a fairly long recession. In the early twentieth century, the inability of many firms to control their inventories contributed to the length and severity of recessions. By the 1980s and 1990s, many firms used improved systems of inventory control, which helped make recessions shorter and less severe.

Business Attempts to Control Inventories, Then . . . and Now

11-2 Making the Connection

Dell Computer uses supply chain management to keep its inventories low.

A failure to control inventories can cause a firm to suffer losses or even drive it into bankruptcy. For example, early in the twentieth century, excessive accumulation of inventories was a serious problem for the automobile industry. In his memoirs, Alfred Sloan, president of General Motors during the 1920s, described checking on inventory by traveling around the country by train and literally counting the number of unsold cars on dealers' lots. Not too surprisingly, this weak method of inventory control caused General Motors to suffer severe financial losses in 1920 and again in 1924. Eventually, automobile firms improved their inventory control methods, although not before a number of firms, including United States Motors, the predecessor of Chrysler Corporation, had been driven into bankruptcy.

Modern computer firms, such as Dell and Hewlett-Packard, can also suffer significant losses if they accumulate large inventories of computer components, because the prices of the components they buy from their suppliers can decline significantly, even from one week to the next. A firm that has large inventories of components may find that its costs of assembling computers are significantly greater than the costs of competitors who hold smaller inventories.

Dell Computer has pioneered in reducing costs by controlling inventories. Dell does not begin to assemble a new computer until it receives an order from a customer by telephone or over the Internet. As a result, Dell holds no inventories of finished computers. Dell still must hold some inventories of computer components, most of which are purchased from outside suppliers. Dell developed a system of *supply chain management* by which it quickly communicates orders to its suppliers and closely monitors their ability to fill its orders promptly. By the mid-1990s, Dell's suppliers could provide Dell with computer components in only two or three days. Dissatisfied with even this strong performance, in 1999 Dell set up valuechain.dell.com, an Internet site that allows Dell's suppliers to monitor Dell's need for components minute by minute and to track the suppliers' components as they move through Dell's computer assembly process. As a result, the amount of time suppliers take to provide Dell with components has dropped to only six hours. When Dell assembles a computer, suppliers will have manufactured many of the components only a few hours earlier. The inventory control techniques that allow Dell to be a low-cost seller of computers also help the firm to respond quickly to sales declines without a significant buildup of inventories.

At the beginning of this chapter we discussed Cisco's difficulties during 2001. Unlike Dell, Cisco failed to track demand well or to monitor its supply chain closely. The result was that Cisco was stuck during 2001 with large amounts of unsold inventories and had to trim production and lay off workers.

4 LEARNING OBJECTIVE
Calculate a numerical example of macroeconomic equilibrium.

A Numerical Example of Macroeconomic Equilibrium

In forecasting real GDP, economists rely on quantitative models of the economy. We can increase our understanding of the causes of fluctuations in real GDP by considering a simple numerical example of macroeconomic equilibrium. Although simplified, this example captures some of the key features contained in the quantitative models used by economic forecasters. Table 11-3 shows several hypothetical combinations of real GDP and planned aggregate expenditure. The first column lists real GDP. The next four columns list levels of planned aggregate expenditure that occur at the corresponding level of real GDP. We assume that planned investment, government purchases, and net exports do not change as GDP changes. Because consumption depends on GDP, it increases as GDP increases.

In the first row, GDP of $8,000 billion (or $8 trillion) results in consumption of $6,200 billion. Adding consumption, planned investment, government purchases, and net exports across the row gives planned aggregate expenditure of $8,700 billion. Because planned aggregate expenditure is greater than GDP, inventories will fall by $700 billion. This unplanned decline in inventories will lead firms to increase production, and GDP will increase. GDP will continue to increase until it reaches $10,000 billion. At that level of GDP, planned aggregate expenditure is also $10,000 billion, unplanned changes in inventories are zero, and the economy is in macroeconomic equilibrium.

In the last row of Table 11-3, GDP of $12,000 billion results in consumption of $8,800 billion and planned aggregate expenditure of $11,300 billion. Because planned aggregate expenditure is less than GDP, inventories will increase by $700 billion. This unplanned increase in inventories will lead firms to decrease production, and GDP will decrease. GDP will continue to decrease until it reaches $10,000 billion, unplanned changes in inventories are zero, and the economy is in macroeconomic equilibrium.

Only when real GDP equals $10,000 billion will the economy be in macroeconomic equilibrium. At other levels of real GDP, planned aggregate expenditure will be higher or lower than GDP and the economy will be expanding or contracting.

TABLE 11-3 Macroeconomic Equilibrium

REAL GDP (*Y*)	CONSUMPTION (*C*)	PLANNED INVESTMENT (*I*)	GOVERNMENT PURCHASES (*G*)	NET EXPORTS (*NX*)	PLANNED AGGREGATE EXPENDITURE (*AE*)	UNPLANNED CHANGE IN INVENTORIES	REAL GDP WILL...
$8,000	$6,200	$1,500	$1,500	−$500	$8,700	−$700	increase
9,000	6,850	1,500	1,500	−500	9,350	−350	increase
10,000	7,500	1,500	1,500	−500	10,000	0	be in equilibrium
11,000	8,150	1,500	1,500	−500	10,650	+350	decrease
12,000	8,800	1,500	1,500	−500	11,300	+700	decrease

Note: The values are in billions of 2000 dollars.

Don't Let This Happen To You!

Don't Confuse Aggregate Expenditure with Consumption Spending

Macroeconomic equilibrium occurs where planned aggregate expenditure equals GDP. But, remember that planned aggregate expenditure equals the sum of consumption spending, planned investment spending, government purchases, and net exports, *not* consumption spending by itself. If GDP were equal to consumption, the economy would not be in equilibrium. Planned investment plus government purchases plus net exports will always be a positive number. Therefore, if consumption were equal to GDP, aggregate expenditure would have to be greater than GDP. In that case, inventories would be decreasing and GDP would be *increasing;* GDP would not be in equilibrium.

Test your understanding of macroeconomic equilibrium with this problem:

Question: Do you agree with the following argument? "The chapter says macroeconomic equilibrium occurs where planned aggregate expenditure equals GDP. GDP is equal to national income. So, at equilibrium planned aggregate expenditure must equal national income. But, we know that consumers do not spend all of their income: They save at least some and use some to pay taxes. Therefore, aggregate expenditure will never equal national income and the basic macro story is incorrect."

Answer: As was discussed in Chapter 7, national income does equal GDP (disregarding, as we have throughout this chapter, depreciation and indirect business taxes). So, it is correct to say that in macroeconomic equilibrium planned aggregate expenditure must equal national income. But the last sentence of the argument is incorrect because it assumes that aggregate expenditure is the same as consumption spending. Because of saving and taxes, consumption spending is always much less than national income, but in equilibrium the sum of consumption spending, planned investment spending, government purchases, and net exports do, in fact, equal GDP and national income. So, the argument is incorrect because it has confused consumption spending with aggregate expenditure.

***YOUR TURN:* Test your understanding by doing related problem 10 on page 366 at the end of this chapter.**

SOLVED PROBLEM 11-2

Determining Macroeconomic Equilibrium

(4) LEARNING OBJECTIVE

Calculate a numerical example of macroeconomic equilibrium.

Fill in the blanks in the following table and determine the equilibrium level of real GDP. All values are in billions of 2000 dollars.

REAL GDP (*Y*)	CONSUMPTION (*C*)	PLANNED INVESTMENT (*I*)	GOVERNMENT PURCHASES (*G*)	NET EXPORTS (*NX*)	PLANNED AGGREGATE EXPENDITURE (*AE*)	UNPLANNED CHANGE IN INVENTORIES
$8,000	$6,200	$1,675	$1,675	−$500		
9,000	6,850	1,675	1,675	−500		
10,000	7,500	1,675	1,675	−500		
11,000	8,150	1,675	1,675	−500		
12,000	8,800	1,675	1,675	−500		

Solving the Problem:

Step 1: Review the chapter material. This problem is about determining macroeconomic equilibrium, so you may want to review the section "A Numerical Example of Macroeconomic Equilibrium," which begins on page 350.

Step 2: Fill in the missing values in the table. We can calculate the missing values in the last two columns by using two equations:

(1) Planned aggregate expenditure (AE) = Consumption (C) + Planned investment (I) + Government (G) + Net exports (NX).

(2) Unplanned change in inventories = Real GDP (Y) − Planned aggregate expenditure (AE).

For example, to fill in the first row, we have AE = \$6,200 billion + \$1,675 billion + \$1,675 billion + (−\$500 billion) = \$9,050 billion; and Unplanned Change in Inventories = \$8,000 billion − \$9,050 billion = −\$1,050 billion.

REAL GDP (*Y*)	CONSUMPTION (*C*)	PLANNED INVESTMENT (*I*)	GOVERNMENT PURCHASES (*G*)	NET EXPORTS (*NX*)	PLANNED AGGREGATE EXPENDITURE (*AE*)	UNPLANNED CHANGE IN INVENTORIES
\$8,000	\$6,200	\$1,675	\$1,675	−\$500	\$9,050	−\$1,050
9,000	6,850	1,675	1,675	−500	9,700	−700
10,000	7,500	1,675	1,675	−500	10,350	−350
11,000	8,150	1,675	1,675	−500	11,000	0
12,000	8,800	1,675	1,675	−500	11,650	350

Step 3: Determine the equilibrium level of real GDP. Once you fill in the table, you should see that equilibrium real GDP must be \$11,000 billion, because only at that level is real GDP equal to planned aggregate expenditure.

***YOUR TURN:* For more practice, do related problem 8 on page 366 at the end of this chapter.**

⑤ LEARNING OBJECTIVE

Define the multiplier effect and use it to calculate changes in equilibrium GDP.

The Multiplier Effect

At this point, we have seen that aggregate expenditure determines real GDP in the short run, and how the economy adjusts if it is not in equilibrium. We have also seen that whenever aggregate expenditure changes, there will be a new level of equilibrium real GDP. In this section, we look more closely at the effects of a change in aggregate expenditure on equilibrium real GDP. We begin the discussion with Figure 11-12, which illustrates the effects of an increase in planned investment spending. We assume the economy starts in equilibrium at point *A*, at which real GDP is \$9.6 trillion. Firms then become more optimistic about their future profitability and increase spending on factories, machinery, and equipment by \$100 billion. This increase in investment spending shifts the *AE* line up by \$100 billion, from the dark gray line (AE_1) to the light gray line (AE_2). The new equilibrium occurs at point *B*, at which real GDP is \$10.0 trillion, which equals potential real GDP.

Notice that the initial \$100 billion increase in planned investment spending results in a \$400 billion increase in equilibrium real GDP. The increase in planned investment spending has had a *multiplied effect* on equilibrium real GDP. It is not only investment spending that will have this multiplied effect; any increase in **autonomous expenditure** will shift up the aggregate expenditure function and lead to a multiplied increase in equilibrium GDP. Autonomous expenditure does not depend on the level of GDP. In the aggregate expenditure model that we have been using, planned investment spending, government spending, and net exports are all autonomous expenditures. Consumption actually has both an autonomous component, which does not depend on the level of GDP, and a nonautonomous—or *induced*—component that does depend on the level of GDP. For example, if households decide to spend more of their incomes—and save less—at every level of income there will be an autonomous increase in consumption spending and the aggregate expenditure function will shift up. If, however, real GDP increases and households increase their consumption spending as indicated by the consumption function, the economy will move up the aggregate expenditure function and the increase in consumption spending will be nonautonomous.

Autonomous expenditure Expenditure that does not depend on the level of GDP.

The ratio of the increase in equilibrium real GDP to the increase in autonomous expenditure is called the **multiplier.** The series of induced increases in consumption spending that results from an initial increase in autonomus expenditures is called the **multiplier effect**.

Multiplier The increase in equilibrium real GDP divided by the increase in autonomous expenditure.

Multiplier effect The series of induced increases in consumption spending that results from an initial increase in autonomous expenditures.

We can now look more closely at the multiplier effect in Figure 11-12. Suppose the whole \$100 billion increase in investment spending consists of firms buying additional factories and office buildings. Initially, this additional spending will cause the construc-

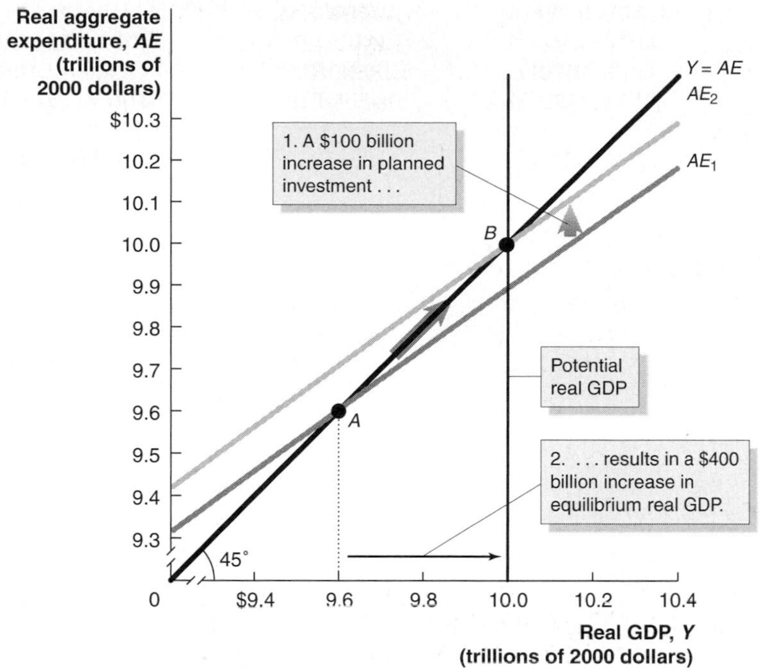

FIGURE 11-12

The Multiplier Effect

The economy begins at point *A,* at which equilibrium real GDP is $9.6 trillion. A $100 billion increase in planned investment shifts up aggregate expenditure from AE_1 to AE_2. The new equilibrium is at point *B,* where real GDP is $10.0 trillion, which is potential real GDP. Because of the multiplier effect, a $100 billion increase in investment results in a $400 billion increase in equilibrium real GDP.

tion of factories and office buildings to increase by $100 billion, so GDP will also increase by $100 billion. Remember that increases in production result in equal increases in national income. So, this increase in real GDP of $100 billion is also an increase in national income of $100 billion. In this example, the income is received as wages and salaries by the employees of the construction firms, as profits by the owners of the firms, and so on. After receiving this additional income, these workers, managers, and owners will increase their consumption of cars, televisions, DVD players, and many other products. If the marginal propensity to consume (*MPC*) is 0.75, we know this increase in consumption spending will be $75 billion. This additional $75 billion in spending will cause the firms making the cars, televisions, and other products to increase production by $75 billion, so GDP will rise by $75 billion. This increase in GDP means national income has also increased by another $75 billion. This increased income will be received by the owners and employees of the firms producing the cars, televisions, and other products. These workers, managers, and owners in turn will increase their consumption spending, and the process of increasing production, income, and consumption will continue.

Eventually the total increase in consumption will be $300 billion (we will soon show how we know this is true). This $300 billion increase in consumption combined with the initial $100 billion increase in investment spending will result in a total change in equilibrium GDP of $400 billion. Table 11-4 summarizes how changes in GDP and spending caused by the initial $100 billion increase in investment will result in equilibrium GDP rising by $400 billion. We can think of the multiplier effect occurring in rounds of spending. In round 1, there is an increase of $100 billion in autonomous expenditure—the $100 billion in planned investment spending in our example—which causes GDP to rise by $100 billion. In round 2, induced expenditure rises by $75 billion (which equals

TABLE 11-4

The Multiplier Effect in Action

	ADDITIONAL AUTONOMOUS EXPENDITURE (INVESTMENT)	ADDITIONAL INDUCED EXPENDITURE (CONSUMPTION)	TOTAL ADDITIONAL EXPENDITURE = TOTAL ADDITIONAL GDP
Round 1	$100 billion	$0	$100 billion
Round 2	0	75 billion	175 billion
Round 3	0	56 billion	231 billion
Round 4	0	42 billion	273 billion
Round 5	0	32 billion	305 billion
⋮	⋮	⋮	⋮
Round 10	0	8 billion	377 billion
⋮	⋮	⋮	⋮
Round 15	0	2 billion	395 billion
⋮	⋮	⋮	⋮
Round 19	0	1 billion	398 billion
⋮	⋮	⋮	⋮
n	0	0	$400 billion

the $100 billion increase in real GDP in round 1 multiplied by the *MPC*). The $75 billion in induced expenditure in round 2 causes a $75 billion increase in real GDP, which leads to a $56 billion increase in induced expenditure in round 3, and so on. The final column sums up the total increases in expenditure, which equal the total increase in GDP. In each round, the additional induced expenditure becomes smaller because the *MPC* is less than 1. By round 10, additional induced expenditure is only $8 billion and the total increase in GDP is $377 billion. By round 19, the process is almost complete: Additional induced expenditure is only $1 billion, and the total increase in GDP is $398 billion. Eventually, the process will be complete, although we cannot say precisely how many spending rounds it will take, so we simply label the last round "*n*," rather than giving it a specific number.

We can calculate the value of the multiplier in our example by dividing the increase in equilibrium real GDP by the increase in autonomous expenditure:

$$\frac{\Delta Y}{\Delta I} = \frac{\text{Change in real GDP}}{\text{Change in investment spending}} = \frac{\$400 \text{ billion}}{\$100 \text{ billion}} = 4.$$

With a multiplier of 4, each increase in autonomous expenditure of $1 will result in a change in equilibrium GDP of $4.

11-3 Making the Connection

The Multiplier in Reverse: The Great Depression of the 1930s

An increase in autonomous expenditure causes an increase in equilibrium real GDP, but the reverse is also true: A decrease in autonomous expenditure causes a decrease in real GDP. Many Americans became aware of this fact in the 1930s when reductions in autonomous expenditure were magnified by the multiplier into the largest decline in real GDP in U.S. history.

In August 1929, the economy reached a business cycle peak, and a downturn in production began. In October, the stock market crashed, destroying billions of dollars of wealth and increasing pessimism among households and firms. Both consumption spending and planned investment spending declined. The passage by the U.S. Congress of the Smoot–Hawley Tariff in June 1930 helped set off a trade war that reduced net exports. A series of banking crises that began in the fall of 1930 limited the ability of households and firms to finance consumption and investment. As aggregate expenditure declined, many firms experienced declining sales and began to lay off workers. Falling levels of production and income induced further declines in consumption spending, which led to further cutbacks in production and employment, leading to further declines in income and so on, in a downward spiral. The following table shows the severity of the economic downturn by contrasting the business cycle peak of 1929 with the business cycle trough of 1933 (the values are in 2000 dollars).

The multiplier effect contributed to the very high levels of unemployment during the Great Depression.

YEAR	CONSUMPTION	INVESTMENT	NET EXPORTS	REAL GDP	UNEMPLOYMENT RATE
1929	\$661 billion	\$91.3 billion	−\$9.4 billion	\$865 billion	3.2%
1933	\$541 billion	\$17.0 billion	−\$10.2 billion	\$636 billion	24.9%

Sources: Bureau of Economic Analysis and Bureau of Labor Statistics.

We can use a 45°-line diagram to illustrate the multiplier effect working in reverse during these years. The economy was at potential real GDP in 1929 before the declines in aggregate expenditure began. Declining consumption, planned investment, and net exports shifted the aggregate expenditure function down from AE_{1929} to AE_{1933}, reducing equilibrium real GDP from \$865 billion in 1929 to \$636 billion in 1933. The depth and length of this economic downturn led to its being labeled the Great Depression.

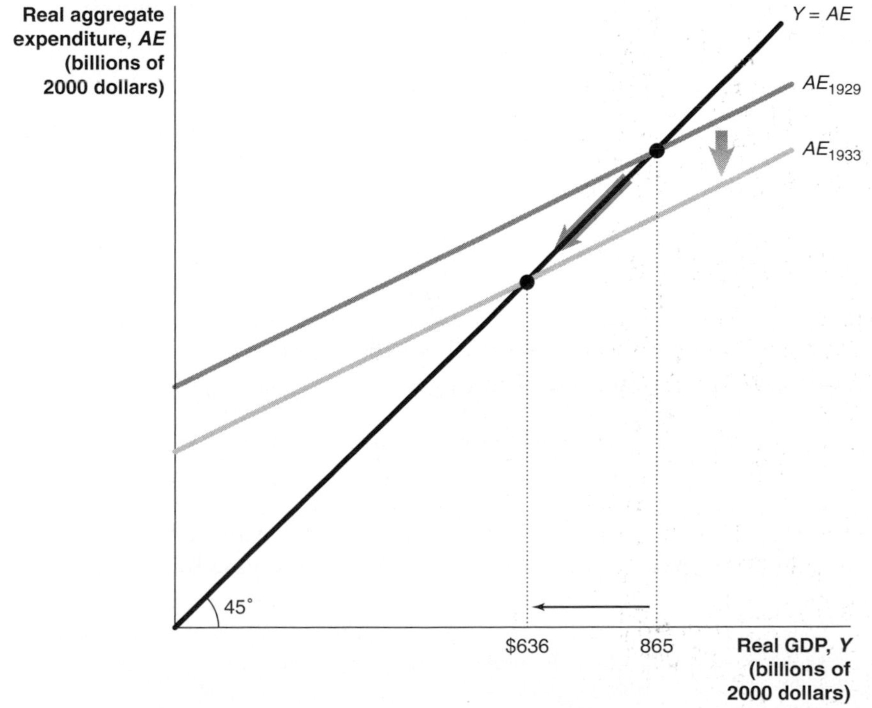

The severity of the Depression meant bankruptcy for thousands of firms. Even firms that survived experienced sharp declines in sales. By 1933, production at U.S. Steel had declined by 90 percent and production at General Motors had declined by more than 75 percent. High rates of unemployment forced many families into poverty and a daily struggle for survival. Recovery from the business cycle trough in 1933 was slow. Real GDP did not regain its 1929 level until 1936, and a growing labor force meant that the unemployment rate did not fall below 10 percent until the United States entered World War II in 1941.

A Formula for the Multiplier

Table 11-4 shows that during the multiplier process each round of increases in consumption is smaller than in the previous round, so eventually the increases will come to an end and we will have a new macroeconomic equilibrium. But how do we know that when we add all the increases in GDP the total will be $400 billion? We can show this is true by first writing out the total change in equilibrium GDP:

The total change in equilibrium real GDP equals the initial increase in planned investment spending

$$= \$100 \text{ billion}$$

Plus the first induced increase in consumption

$$= MPC \times \$100 \text{ billion}$$

Plus the second induced increase in consumption

$$= MPC \times (MPC \times \$100 \text{ billion}) = MPC^2 \times \$100 \text{ billion}$$

Plus the third induced increase in consumption

$$= MPC \times (MPC^2 \times \$100 \text{ billion}) = MPC^3 \times \$100 \text{ billion}$$

Plus the fourth induced increase in consumption

$$= MPC \times (MPC^3 \times \$100 \text{ billion}) = MPC^4 \times \$100 \text{ billion}$$

And so on . . .

Or,

$$\text{The total change in GDP} = \$100 \text{ billion} + MPC \times \$100 \text{ billion} + MPC^2 \times \$100 \text{ billion} + MPC^3 \times \$100 \text{ billion} + MPC^4 \times \$100 \text{ billion} + \ldots$$

where the ellipsis (. . .) indicates that the expression contains an infinite number of similar terms.

If we factor out the $100 billion from each expression we have:

$$\text{Total change in GDP} = \$100 \text{ billion} \times (1 + MPC + MPC^2 + MPC^3 + MPC^4 + \ldots)$$

Mathematicians have shown that an expression like the one in the parenthesis sums to:

$$\frac{1}{1 - MPC}.$$

In this case, the *MPC* is equal to 0.75. So, we can now calculate that the change in equilibrium GDP = $1 billion × [1/(1 − 0.75)] = $100 billion × 4 = $400 billion. We have also derived a general formula for the multiplier:

$$\text{Multiplier} = \frac{\text{Change in equilibrium real GDP}}{\text{Change in autonomous expenditure}} = \frac{1}{1 - MPC}.$$

In this case the multiplier is 1(1 − 0.75) or 4, which means that for each additional $1 of autonomous spending, equilibrium GDP will increase by $4. A $100 billion increase in planned investment spending results in a \$400 billion increase in equilibrium GDP. Notice that the value of the multiplier depends on the value of the *MPC*. In particular, the larger the value of the *MPC*, the larger the value of the multiplier. For example, if the *MPC* were 0.9, instead of 0.75, the value of the multiplier would increase from 4 to $1(1 - 0.9) = 10$.

Summarizing the Multiplier Effect

You should note four key points about the multiplier effect:

1. The multiplier effect occurs both when autonomous expenditure increases and when it decreases. For example, with an *MPC* of 0.75, a *decrease* in planned investment of \$100 billion will lead to a *decrease* in equilibrium income of \$400 billion.
2. The multiplier effect makes the economy more sensitive to changes in autonomous expenditure than it would otherwise be. When firms decided to cut back their spending on information technology, following the Internet and telecommunications busts of 2001, the decision did not only affect firms such as Cisco that made computer and telecommunications equipment. Because the initial decline in investment spending set off a series of declines in production, income, and spending, firms such as automobile dealerships and furniture stores, which are far removed from the computer and telecommunications industries, also experienced sales declines.
3. The larger the *MPC*, the larger the value of the multiplier. With an *MPC* of 0.75, the multiplier is 4, but with an *MPC* of 0.50, the multiplier is only 2. This inverse relationship between the value of the *MPC* and the value of the multiplier holds true because the larger the *MPC*, the more additional consumption takes place after each rise in income during the multiplier process.
4. The formula for the multiplier, $1(1 - MPC)$, is oversimplified because it ignores some real-world complications, such as the effect that an increasing GDP can have on imports, inflation, and interest rates. These effects combine to cause our simple formula to overstate the true value of the multiplier. Beginning in Chapter 12, we will start to take into account these real-world complications.

SOLVED PROBLEM 11-3

Using the Multiplier Formula

(5) LEARNING OBJECTIVE

Define the multiplier effect and use it to calculate changes in equilibrium GDP.

Use the information in the table to answer the following questions:

REAL GDP (*Y*)	CONSUMPTION (*C*)	PLANNED INVESTMENT (*I*)	GOVERNMENT PURCHASES (*G*)	NET EXPORTS (*NX*)
\$8,000	\$6,900	\$1,000	\$1,000	−\$500
9,000	7,700	1,000	1,000	−500
10,000	8,500	1,000	1,000	−500
11,000	9,300	1,000	1,000	−500
12,000	10,100	1,000	1,000	−500

a. What is the equilibrium level of real GDP?

b. What is the *MPC*?

c. Suppose government purchases increase by $200 billion. What will be the new equilibrium level of real GDP? Use the multiplier formula to determine your answer.

Solving the Problem:

Step 1: Review the chapter material. This problem is about the multiplier process, so you may want to review the section "The Multiplier Effect," which begins on page 352.

Step 2: Determine equilibrium real GDP. Just as in Solved Problem 11-2 on page 351, we can find macroeconomic equilibrium by calculating the level of planned aggregate expenditure for each level of real GDP:

REAL GDP (*Y*)	CONSUMPTION (*C*)	PLANNED INVESTMENT (*I*)	GOVERNMENT PURCHASES (*G*)	NET EXPORTS (*NX*)	PLANNED AGGREGATE EXPENDITURE (*AE*)
$8,000	$6,900	$1,000	$1,000	−$500	$8,400
9,000	7,700	1,000	1,000	−500	9,200
10,000	8,500	1,000	1,000	−500	10,000
11,000	9,300	1,000	1,000	−500	10,800
12,000	10,100	1,000	1,000	−500	11,600

We can see that macroeconomic equilibrium will occur when real GDP equals $10,000 billion.

Step 3: Calculate *MPC*.

$$MPC = \frac{\Delta C}{\Delta Y}.$$

In this case,

$$MPC = \frac{\$800 \text{ billion}}{\$1{,}000 \text{ billion}} = 0.8.$$

Step 4: Use the multiplier formula to calculate the new equilibrium level of real GDP. We could find the new level of equilibrium real GDP by constructing a new table with government purchases increased from $1,000 to $1,200. But the multiplier allows us to calculate the answer directly. In this case:

$$\text{Multiplier} = \frac{1}{1 - MPC} = \frac{1}{1 - 0.8} = 5.$$

So,

$$\text{Change in equilibrium real GDP} = \text{Change in autonomous expenditure} \times 5.$$

Or,

$$\text{Change in equilibrium real GDP} = \$200 \text{ billion} \times 5 = \$1{,}000 \text{ billion}.$$

Therefore,

The new level of equilibrium GDP = $10,000 billion + $1,000 billion = $11,000 billion.

YOUR TURN: **For more practice, do related problem 17 on page 367 at the end of this chapter.**

The Aggregate Demand Curve

(6) LEARNING OBJECTIVE

Understand the relationship between the aggregate demand curve and aggregate expenditure.

When demand for a product increases, firms will usually respond by increasing production, but they are also likely to increase prices. Similarly, when demand falls, production will fall, but often prices will also fall. We would expect then, that an increase or decrease in aggregate expenditure would affect not just real GDP but also the *price level.* So far, we haven't taken into account the effect of changes in the price level on the components of aggregate expenditure. In fact, as we will see, increases in the price level will cause aggregate expenditure to fall and decreases in the price level will cause aggregate expenditure to rise. There are three main reasons for this inverse relationship between changes in the price level and changes in aggregate expenditure. We discussed the first two reasons earlier in this chapter when considering the factors that determine consumption and net exports:

- A rising price level decreases consumption by decreasing the real value of household wealth; a falling price level has the reverse effect.
- If the price level in the United States rises relative to the price levels in other countries, U.S. exports will become relatively more expensive and foreign imports will become relatively less expensive, causing net exports to fall. A falling price level in the United States has the reverse effect.
- When prices rise, firms and households need more money to finance buying and selling. If the central bank (the Federal Reserve in the United States) does not increase the money supply, the result will be an increase in the interest rate. We will analyze in more detail why this happens in Chapter 13. As we discussed earlier in this chapter, at a higher interest rate investment spending falls as firms borrow less money to build new factories or to install new machinery and equipment and households borrow less money to buy new houses. A falling price level has the reverse effect. Other things equal, interest rates will fall and investment spending will rise.

We can now incorporate the effect of a change in the price level into the basic aggregate expenditure model in which equilibrium real GDP is determined by the intersection of the aggregate expenditure (*AE*) line and the 45° line. Remember that we measure the price level as an index number with a value of 100 in the base year. If the price level rises from, say, 100 to 103, consumption, planned investment, and net exports will all fall, causing the *AE* line to shift down on the 45°-line diagram. The *AE* line shifts down because with higher prices less spending will occur in the economy at every level of GDP. Panel (a) of Figure 11-13 shows that the downward shift of the *AE* line results in a lower level of equilibrium real GDP.

If the price level falls from, say, 100 to 97, then investment, consumption, and net exports would all rise. As panel (b) of Figure 11-13 shows, the *AE* line would shift up, which would cause equilibrium real GDP to increase.

Figure 11-14 summarizes the effect of changes in the price level on real GDP. The table shows the combinations of price level and real GDP from Figures 11-13. The figure plots the numbers from the table. In the figure, the price level is measured on the vertical axis and real GDP is measured on the horizontal axis. The relation shown in Figure 11-14 between the price level and the level of planned aggregate expenditure is known as the **aggregate demand curve (*AD*).**

Aggregate demand curve (*AD*) A curve showing the relationship between the price level and the level of planned aggregate expenditure in the economy, holding constant all other factors that affect aggregate expenditure.

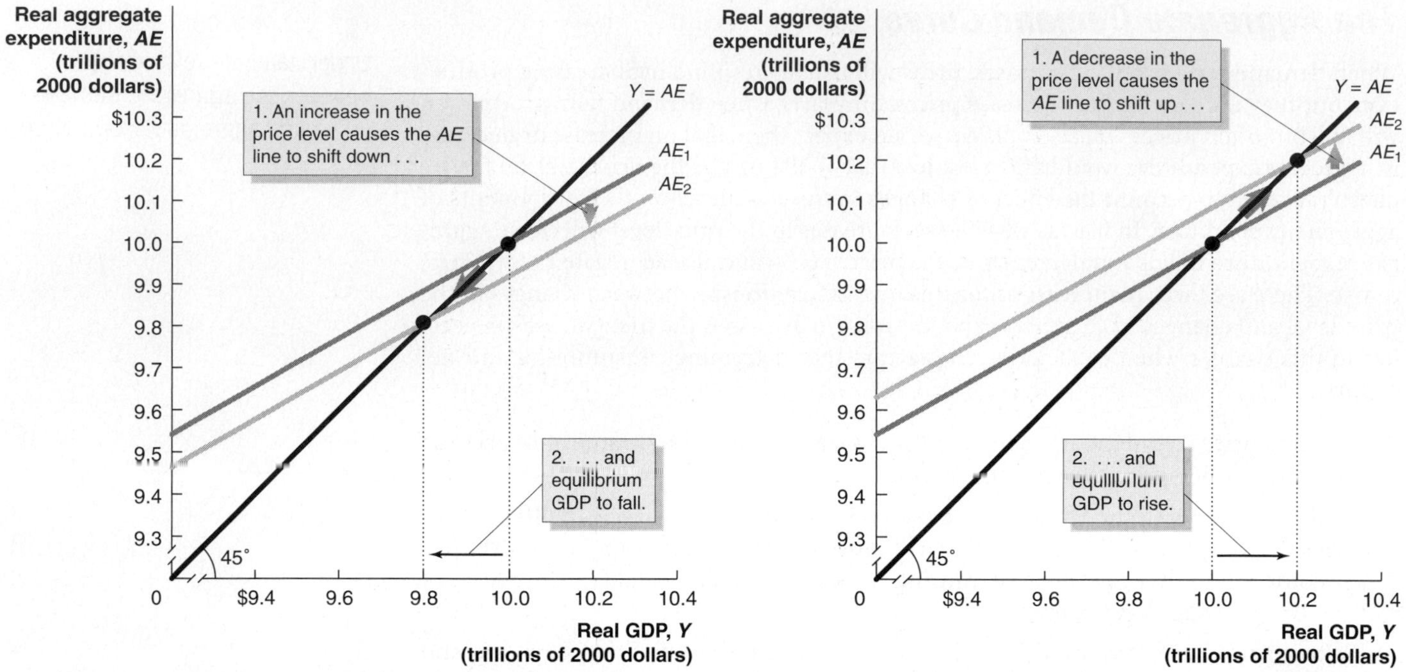

(a) The effect of a higher price level on real GDP

(b) The effect of a lower price level on real GDP

FIGURE 11-13 The Effect of a Change in the Price Level on Real GDP

In panel (a), an increase in the price level results in declining consumption, planned investment, and net exports and causes the aggregate expenditure line to shift down from AE_1 to AE_2. As a result, equilibrium real GDP declines from \$10.0 trillion to \$9.8 trillion. In panel (b), a decrease in the price level results in rising consumption, planned investment, and net exports and causes the aggregate expenditure line to shift up from AE_1 to AE_2. As a result, equilibrium real GDP increases from \$10.0 trillion to \$10.2 trillion.

FIGURE 11-14

The Aggregate Demand Curve

The aggregate demand curve (*AD*) shows the relation between the price level and the level of planned aggregate expenditure in the economy. When the price level is 97, real GDP is \$10.2 trillion. An increase in the price level to 100 causes consumption, investment, and net exports to fall, which reduces real GDP to \$10.0 trillion.

Prive Level	Equilibrium Real GDP
97	$10.2 trillion
100	10.0 trillion
103	9.8 trillion

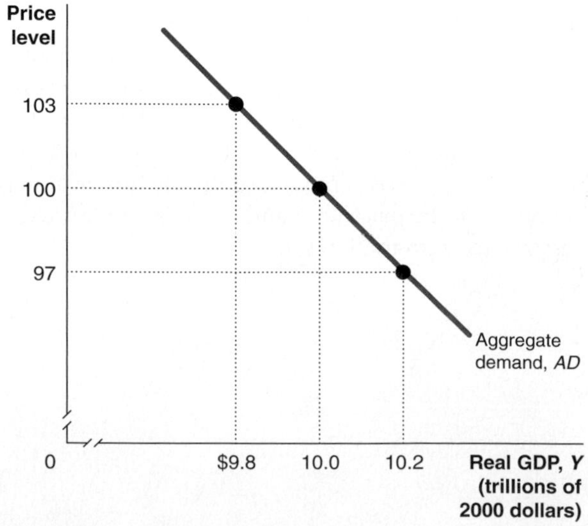

Conclusion

In this chapter, we learned a key macroeconomic idea: In the short run, the level of GDP is determined mainly by the level of aggregate expenditure. When economists forecast changes in GDP, they do so by forecasting changes in the four components of aggregate expenditure. We constructed an aggregate demand curve by taking into account the effect on aggregate expenditure of changes in the price level.

But our story is incomplete. In the next chapter, we will analyze the *aggregate supply curve*. Then, we will use the aggregate demand curve and the aggregate supply curve to show how equilibrium real GDP *and* the equilibrium price level are simultaneously determined.

We also need to discuss the role the financial system and government policy play in determining real GDP and the price level in the short run. We will cover these important topics in the next three chapters. Before moving on, read *An Inside Look* on the next page to learn about the effect of an increase in aggregate expenditure on the Japanese economy at the beginning of 2005.

An Inside Look

Expenditure in Japan Soars, Nudging Up GDP

WALL STREET JOURNAL, MAY 18, 2005

Japan's Consumers Show Signs of Life

TOKYO—Japan's economy grew at a robust annualized pace of 5.3% in the three months ended March 31, as strong consumption jolted the world's second-largest economy out of three quarters of stagnation.

Gross domestic product, the broadest measure of economic activity, expanded 1.3% in price-adjusted terms from the previous quarter. Economists said the strength was a sign that the economy could be on track for better longer-term growth. But they also said the January–March expansion was in large part a reaction to weakness in the previous quarter, and that growth likely would slow in the current quarter.

a Domestic private consumption, which accounts for more than half of Japan's GDP, rose 1.2% from the previous quarter, compared with a drop of 0.4% in the October–December quarter. During that October–December period, a series of typhoons and deadly earthquakes depressed spending. That left consumers with money that they appear to have spent in the following three months. Similarly, capital investment was far stronger, increasing 2% in the latest quarter after falling 0.2% in the October–December period.

"The underlying growth is rather less impressive" than the headline numbers, said Peter Morgan, senior economist at HSBC Securities. He said that averaging growth from the past two quarters would provide a better picture of the underlying trends: about 0.4% quarter-on-quarter growth in personal consumption, and about 0.9% growth in capital investment.

b In addition, about a third of the January–March growth came from inventories, as manufacturers increased their stocks of finished products. That could mean less production in coming months. Another big reason that economists remained skeptical was recent data showing that household incomes are flat or declining slightly, giving consumers less money to spend.

Still, other indicators point to possible future improvement in household income. The latest jobs data showed that unemployment fell to 4.5% in March—equaling the lowest level in more than three years—and companies are hiring more full-time workers.

"Clearly encouraging things are going on in the economy," said Ryo Hino, economist at J.P. Morgan Chase's Tokyo office. "Yes, there is mild positive growth, in the 2% range [of annualized growth]—and that's a positive message."

c Another surprise was in exports data. Normally Japan's most reliable driver of growth, exports fell 0.2% in the latest quarter, marking the first drop since October–December 2001. Exports were hurt by weak demand in Asia for shipbuilding materials and telecommunication equipment. Whether or not they recover will depend heavily on demand for Japanese products in China.

Key Points in the Article

After three consecutive quarters of stagnation in 2004, Japan's GDP grew at an annual rate of 5.3 percent in the first quarter of 2005. These fluctuations in GDP over the past four quarters were driven largely by aggregate expenditure. During the fourth quarter of 2004, private consumption, *C*, and capital investment expenditure, *I*, which together comprise over 50 percent of Japan's GDP, decreased. Economists suspect that natural disasters—typhoons and earthquakes—were largely responsible. Then, in the first quarter of 2005, aggregate expenditure reversed course: Private consumption and capital investment grew by 1.2 percent and 2.0 percent, respectively.

Analyzing the News

The fall in aggregate spending in the fourth quarter of 2004 created an unplanned increase in inventories. In Figure 1, the economy begins in equilibrium at point *E* and then aggregate expenditure falls from AE_1 to AE_2. Because planned aggregate expenditure is now less than GDP_1 (point *A*) unplanned inventories increase. In response, Japanese firms decrease production and employment until the economy reaches an aggregate expenditure equilibrium at point *B*.

Likewise, the rise in aggregate spending in the first quarter of 2005 created an unplanned decrease in inventories. This pattern is shown in Figure 2, where the economy begins at point *B* and aggregate expenditure rises from AE_2 to AE_1. This time, because planned aggregate expenditure is now greater than GDP_2 (point *C*), unplanned inventories decrease. In response, Japanese firms increase production and employment until the economy reaches an aggregate expenditure equilibrium at point *E*.

b Roughly a third of Japan's first-quarter-2005 growth in GDP was created by an increase in *planned* inventories, which manufacturers accumulated deliberately in anticipation of an increase in consumer spending. Recall that *planned* inventory expenditure is included in planned aggregate expenditure.

Nonetheless, many economists remain skeptical about the long-term prospects for Japan's GDP growth, because consumer incomes either have remained the same or fallen in recent months. This problem arises because the most important determinant of consumption is the current disposable income of households.

c Japan's first-quarter-2005 growth in GDP was hampered by an unexpected fall in exports of shipbuilding and telecommunications equipment. Because Japanese exports are determined, in part, by the relative growth rates of GDP in Japan versus its major trading partners, future demand for Japanese exports will depend in large part on growth of its trading partners' economies, especially China's.

Thinking Critically ABOUT POLICY

1. Suppose the Japanese government reduced income taxes to stimulate consumption and increase GDP. Compare and contrast the relative effectiveness of this policy when Japan's marginal propensity to consume (*MPC*) is close to 1, versus when Japan's *MPC* is close to 0.
2. Suppose the Chinese government lifts the price ceiling that it has imposed on its currency, the yuan, so that the yuan can appreciate in value relative to the Japanese yen. What effect would this change in China's exchange-rate policy have on Japan's aggregate expenditure?

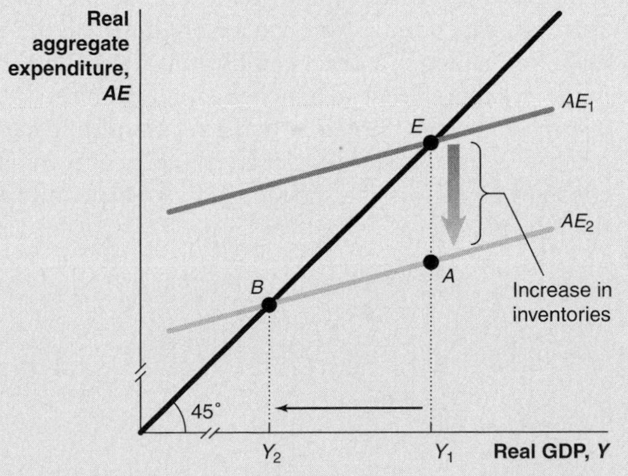

Figure 1: A decrease in aggregate expenditure causes a decrease in GDP.

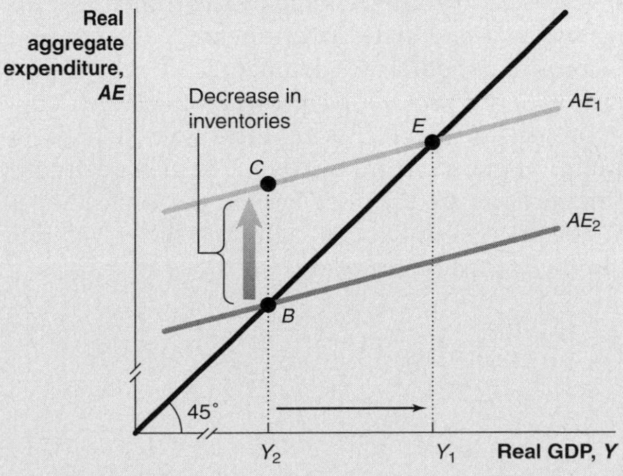

Figure 2: An increase in aggregate expenditure causes an increase in GDP.

SUMMARY

LEARNING OBJECTIVE ① Understand how macroeconomic equilibrium is determined in the aggregate expenditure model. The *aggregate expenditure model* focuses on the relationship between total spending and real GDP in the short run, assuming the price level is constant. In any particular year, the level of GDP is determined by the level of total spending, or aggregate expenditure, in the economy. The four components of aggregate expenditure are consumption (C), planned investment (I), government purchases (G), and net exports (NX). When aggregate expenditure is greater than GDP, there is an unplanned decrease in *inventories,* and GDP and total employment will increase. When aggregate expenditure is less than GDP, there is an unplanned increase in inventories, and GDP and total employment will decline. When aggregate expenditure is equal to GDP, firms will sell what they expected to sell, production and employment will be unchanged, and the economy will be in macroeconomic equilibrium.

LEARNING OBJECTIVE ② Discuss the determinants of the four components of aggregate expenditure and define the marginal propensity to consume and the marginal propensity to save. The five determinants of consumption are current disposable income, household wealth, expected future income, the price level, and the interest rate. The *consumption function* is the relationship between consumption and disposable income. The *marginal propensity to consume* (*MPC*) is the change in consumption divided by the change in disposable income. The *marginal propensity to save* is the change in saving divided by the change in disposable income. The determinants of planned investment are expectations of future profitability, the real interest rate, taxes, and *cash flow,* which is the difference between the cash revenues received by the firm and the cash spending by the firm. Government purchases include spending by the federal government and by local and state governments for goods and services. Government purchases do not include *transfer payments,* such as Social Security payments by the federal government or pension payments by local governments to retired police officers and firefighters. The three determinants of net exports are the price level in the United States relative to the price levels in other countries, the growth rate of GDP in the United States relative to the growth rates of GDP in other countries, and the exchange rate between the dollar and other currencies.

LEARNING OBJECTIVE ③ Use a 45°-line diagram to illustrate macroeconomic equilibrium. The 45°-line diagram shows all the points where aggregate expenditure equals real GDP. On the 45°-line diagram, macroeconomic equilibrium occurs where the line representing the aggregate expenditure function crosses the 45° line.

LEARNING OBJECTIVE ④ Calculate a numerical example of macroeconomic equilibrium. Numerically, macroeconomic equilibrium occurs when:

$$\text{Consumption} + \text{Planned investment} + \text{Government purchases} + \text{Net exports} = \text{GDP}.$$

LEARNING OBJECTIVE ⑤ Define the multiplier effect and use it to calculate changes in equilibrium GDP. An *autonomous change* is a change in expenditure not caused by a change in income. An *induced change* is a change in aggregate expenditure caused by a change in income. An autonomous change in expenditure will cause rounds of induced changes in expenditure. Therefore, an autonomous change in expenditure will have a multiplier effect on equilibrium GDP. The multiplier is the ratio of the change in equilibrium GDP to the change in autonomous expenditure. The formula for the multiplier is:

$$\frac{1}{1 - MPC}.$$

LEARNING OBJECTIVE ⑥ Understand the relationship between the aggregate demand curve and aggregate expenditure. Increases in the price level cause a reduction in consumption, investment, and net exports. This causes the aggregate expenditure function to shift down on the 45°-line diagram, leading to a lower equilibrium real GDP. A decrease in the price level leads to a higher equilibrium real GDP. The *aggregate demand curve* shows the relationship between the price level and the level of aggregate expenditure, holding constant all factors that affect aggregate expenditure other than the price level.

KEY TERMS

Aggregate demand curve (*AD*) 359
Aggregate expenditure (*AE*) 330
Aggregate expenditure model 330
Autonomous expenditure 352
Cash flow 341
Consumption function 335
Inventories 331
Marginal propensity to consume (*MPC*) 335
Marginal propensity to save (*MPS*) 338
Multiplier 352
Multiplier effect 352

REVIEW QUESTIONS

1. What is the main reason for fluctuations in GDP in the short run?
2. What are the four categories of aggregate expenditure? Give an example of each.
3. What are inventories? What usually happens to inventories at the beginning of a recession? At the beginning of an expansion?
4. What are the five main determinants of consumption spending? Which of these is the most important?
5. Compare what happened to real investment between 1979 and 2004 with what happened to real consumption.
6. Use a 45°-line diagram to illustrate macroeconomic equilibrium. Make sure that your diagram shows the aggregate expenditure function and the level of equilibrium real GDP and that your axes are properly labeled.
7. What is the macroeconomic consequence if firms accumulate large amounts of unplanned inventory at the beginning of a recession?
8. What is the multiplier effect? Use a 45°-line diagram to illustrate the multiplier effect of a decrease in government purchases.
9. What is the formula for the multiplier? Explain why this formula is considered to be too simple.
10. Briefly explain the difference between aggregate expenditure and aggregate demand.

PROBLEMS AND APPLICATIONS

Please visit **www.prenhall.com/hubbard** *for solutions to the even-numbered problems as well as multiple-choice and true or false self-assessment quizzes.*

1. **[Related to the *Chapter Opener*]** How would the demand forecast for a major U.S. furniture manufacturer be affected by each of the following?
   a. A decrease in consumer spending in the economy
   b. An increase in real interest rates
   c. An increase in the exchange rate value of the U.S. dollar
   d. A decrease in planned investment spending in the economy
2. Many people have difficulty borrowing as much money as they would like, even if they are confident that their incomes in the future will be high enough to pay it back easily. For example, many students in medical school will earn high incomes after they graduate and become physicians. If they could, they would probably borrow now in order to live more comfortably while in medical school and pay the loans back out of their higher future income. Unfortunately, banks are usually reluctant to make loans to people who currently have low incomes, even if there is a good chance their incomes will be much higher in the future. If people could always borrow as much as they would like, would you expect consumption to become more or less sensitive to current income? Why?
3. An economics student raises the following objection: "The textbook said that a higher interest rate lowers investment, but this doesn't make sense. I know that if I can get a higher interest rate I am certainly going to invest more in my savings account." Do you agree with this reasoning?
4. During recessions, unemployed workers receive unemployment insurance payments from the government. Does the existence of unemployment insurance make it likely that consumption will fluctuate more or fluctuate less over the business cycle than it would in the absence of unemployment insurance? Briefly explain.

5. Explain whether you agree or disagree with the following argument: "Transfer payments should be counted as part of government purchases when we calculate aggregate expenditure. After all, spending is spending. Why does it matter whether the spending is for an aircraft carrier or for a Social Security payment to a retired person?"
6. Suppose we drop the assumption that net exports do not depend on real GDP. Draw a graph with the value of net exports on the vertical axis and the value of real GDP on the horizontal axis. Now, add a line representing the relationship between net exports and real GDP. Briefly explain why you drew the graph the way you did.
7. At point *A* in the following graph, is planned aggregate expenditure greater than, equal to, or less than GDP? At point *B*? At point *C*? For points *A* and *C*, indicate the vertical distance that measures the unintended change in inventories.

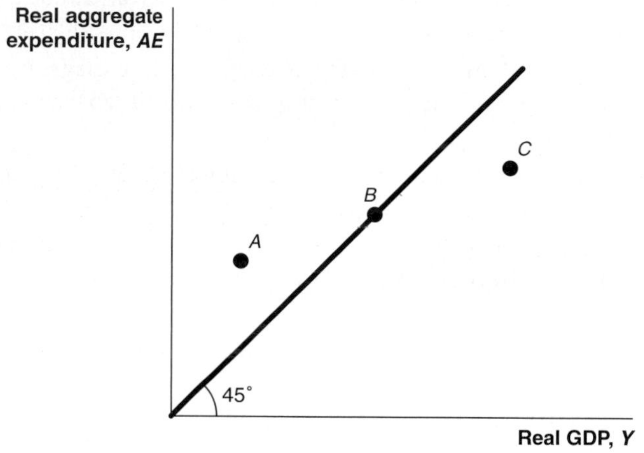

8. **[Related to *Solved Problem 11-2*]** Fill in the missing values in the following table. Assume that the value of the *MPC* does not change as real GDP changes.

REAL GDP (*Y*)	CONSUMPTION (*C*)	PLANNED INVESTMENT (*I*)	GOVERNMENT PURCHASES (*G*)	NET EXPORTS (*NX*)	PLANNED AGGREGATE EXPENDITURE (*AE*)	UNPLANNED CHANGE IN INVENTORIES
$9,000	$7,600	$1,200	$1,200	−$400		
10,000	8,400	1,200	1,200	−400		
11,000		1,200	1,200	−400		
12,000		1,200	1,200	−400		
13,000		1,200	1,200	−400		

a. What is the value of the *MPC*?
b. What is the value of equilibrium real GDP?

9. **[Related to *Solved Problem 11-1*]** Fill in the blanks in the following table. Assume for simplicity that taxes are zero.

NATIONAL INCOME AND REAL GDP (*Y*)	CONSUMPTION (*C*)	SAVING (*S*)	MARGINAL PROPENSITY TO CONSUME (*MPC*)	MARGINAL PROPENSITY TO SAVE (*MPS*)
$9,000	$8,000		—	—
10,000	8,750			
11,000	9,500			
12,000	10,250			
13,000	11,000			

10. **[Related to *Don't Let This Happen To You!*]** Briefly explain whether or not you agree with the following argument: "The equilibrium level of GDP is determined by the level of aggregate expenditure. Therefore, GDP will decline only if households decide to spend less on goods and services."
11. Is it possible for the economy to be in macroeconomic equilibrium at a level of real GDP that is greater than the potential level of real GDP? Illustrate using a 45°-line diagram.
12. In the second quarter of 2005, business inventories declined by $10 billion. What does this information tell us about the relationship between aggregate expenditure and GDP during the second quarter of 2005?
13. Suppose you read that business inventories increased dramatically last month. What does this tell you about the state of the economy? Would your answer be affected by whether the increase in inventories was taking place at the end of a recession or the end of an expansion? Briefly explain.

14. In a Federal Reserve Board publication, the following observation was made: "The impact of inventory increases on the business cycle depends upon whether they are planned or unplanned." Do you agree? Briefly explain.

15. An article in *Business Week* observes the following: "A further ebbing in the inventory drawdown is probably adding to GDP growth this quarter." What does the article mean by "inventory drawdown"? What component of aggregate expenditure would be affected by an inventory drawdown? Why would this add to GDP growth?
Source: James C. Cooper and Kathleen Madigan, "Forward Spin from a Backward Glance at GDP," *Business Week*, April 29, 2002.

16. In each of the following situations, indicate what happens to the firm's inventories and whether the firm will be likely to increase or decrease its production in the future.
    a. General Electric expected to sell 120,000 microwaves during the current month but actually sold 100,000.
    b. Ford expected to sell 80,000 Explorers during the current month but actually sold 90,000.

17. **[Related to *Solved Problem 11-3*]** Use the information in the table to answer the following questions:

REAL GDP (*Y*)	CONSUMPTION (*C*)	PLANNED INVESTMENT (*I*)	GOVERNMENT PURCHASES (*G*)	NET EXPORTS (*NX*)
$8,000	$7,300	$1,000	$1,000	−$500
9,000	7,900	1,000	1,000	−500
10,000	8,500	1,000	1,000	−500
11,000	9,100	1,000	1,000	−500
12,000	9,700	1,000	1,000	−500

    a. What is the equilibrium level of real GDP?
    b. What is the *MPC*?
    c. Suppose net exports increase by $400 billion. What will be the new equilibrium level of real GDP? Use the multiplier formula to determine your answer.

18. Explain whether you agree or disagree with the following statement: "Many economists claim that the recession of 2001 was caused by a decline in investment. This can't be true. If there had just been a decline in investment, the only firms hurt would have been construction firms, computer firms, and other firms selling investment goods. In fact, many firms experienced falling sales during that recession, including automobile firms and furniture firms."

19. Suppose a booming economy in Europe causes net exports to rise by $75 billion in the United States. If the *MPC* is 0.8, what will be the change in equilibrium GDP?

20. Would a larger multiplier lead to longer and more severe recessions or shorter and less severe recessions? Briefly explain.

21. Use the following graph to answer the questions.

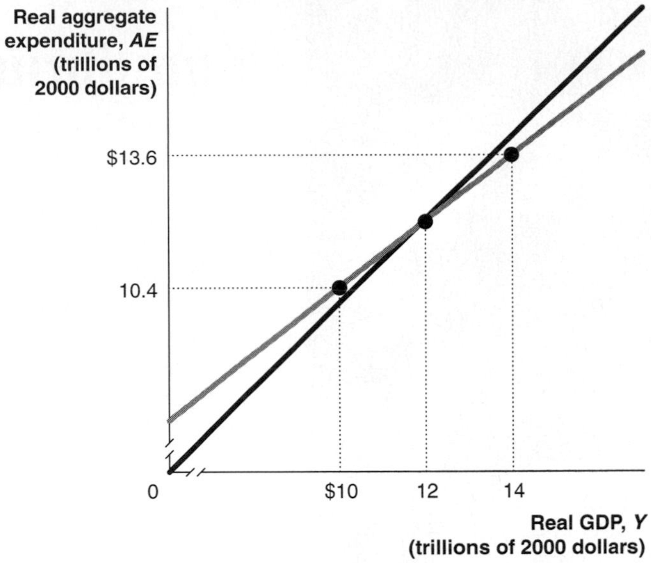

    a. What is the value of equilibrium real GDP?
    b. What is the value of the *MPC?*
    c. What is the value of the multiplier?
    d. What is the value of unplanned changes in inventories when real GDP has each of the following values?
        - $10 trillion
        - $12 trillion
        - $14 trillion

22. An article in the *New York Times* makes the following observation:

> [B]usiness spending is a powerful force. It can lift an economy when companies invest in machinery, software, office buildings, factories, trucks, aircraft and all the other tools used in the production of goods and services—or sink an economy when companies cut back.

What does the article mean by "business spending"? How can business spending "lift an economy" or "sink" it? Use a 45°-line diagram to illustrate your answer.
Source: Louis Uchitelle and Jennifer Bayot, "Business Spending Helps to Offset Lag in Refinancing," *New York Times*, August 9, 2003.

Appendix

The Algebra of Macroeconomic Equilibrium

In this chapter, we relied primarily on graphs and tables to illustrate the aggregate expenditure model of short-run real GDP. Graphs help us understand economic change *qualitatively.* When we write down an economic model using equations, we make it easier to make *quantitative estimates.* When economists forecast future movements in GDP, they often rely on *econometric models.* An econometric model is an economic model written in the form of equations, where each equation has been statistically estimated, using methods similar to the methods used in estimating demand curves that we briefly described in Chapter 3. We can use equations to represent the aggregate expenditure model described in this chapter.

The following equations are based on the example shown in Table 11-3 on page 350. Y stands for real GDP and the numbers (with the exception of the *MPC*) represent billions of dollars.

1. $C = 1{,}000 + 0.65Y$	Consumption function
2. $I = 1{,}500$	Planned investment function
3. $G = 1{,}500$	Government spending function
4. $NX = -500$	Net export function
5. $Y = C + I + G + NX$	Equilibrium condition

The first equation is the consumption function. The *MPC* is 0.65 and 1,000 is autonomous consumption, which is the level of consumption that does not depend on income. If we think of the consumption function as a line on the 45°-line diagram, 1,000 would be the intercept and 0.65 would be the slope. The "functions" for the other three components of planned aggregate expenditure are very simple because we have assumed that these components are not affected by GDP and, therefore, are constant. Economists who use this type of model to forecast GDP would, of course, use more realistic investment, government, and net export functions. The *parameters* of the functions—such as the value of autonomous consumption and the value of the *MPC* in the consumption function—would be estimated statistically using data on the values of each variable over a period of years.

In this model, equilibrium GDP occurs where GDP is equal to planned aggregate expenditure. Equation 5—the equilibrium condition—shows us how to calculate equilibrium in the model: To calculate equilibrium, we substitute equations 1 through 4 into equation 5. This gives us the following:

$$Y = 1{,}000 + 0.65Y + 1{,}500 + 1{,}500 - 500.$$

We need to solve this expression for Y to find equilibrium *GDP.* The first step is to subtract $0.65Y$ from both sides of the equation:

$$Y - 0.65Y = 1{,}000 + 1{,}500 + 1{,}500 - 500.$$

Then, we solve for Y:

$$0.35Y = 3{,}500.$$

Or,

$$Y = \frac{3{,}500}{0.35} = 10{,}000.$$

To make this result more general, we can replace particular values with general values represented by letters:

1. $C = \overline{C} + MPC(Y)$	Consumption function
2. $I = \overline{I}$	Planned investment function
3. $G = \overline{G}$	Government spending function
4. $NX = \overline{NX}$	Net export function
5. $Y = C + I + G + NX$	Equilibrium condition

The letters with "bars" represent fixed or autonomous values. So, $\overline{C}$ represents autonomous consumption, which had a value of 1,000 in our original example. Now, solving for equilibrium we get:

$$Y = \overline{C} + MPC(Y) + \overline{I} + \overline{G} + \overline{NX},$$

or,

$$Y - MPC(Y) = \overline{C} + \overline{I} + \overline{G} + \overline{NX},$$

or,

$$Y(1 - MPC) = \overline{C} + \overline{I} + \overline{G} + \overline{NX},$$

or,

$$Y = \frac{\overline{C} + \overline{I} + \overline{G} + \overline{NX}}{1 - MPC}.$$

Remember that $1/(1 - MPC)$ is the multiplier, and all four variables in the numerator of the equation represent autonomous expenditure. Therefore an alternative expression for equilibrium GDP is:

Equilibrium GDP = Autonomous expenditure × multiplier.

PROBLEMS AND APPLICATIONS

Please visit **www.prenhall.com/hubbard** *for solutions to the even-numbered problems as well as multiple-choice and true or false self-assessment quizzes.*

1. Write a general expression for the aggregate expenditure function. If you think of the aggregate expenditure function as a line on the 45°-line diagram, what would be the intercept and what would be the slope, using the general values represented by letters?
2. Find equilibrium GDP using the following macroeconomic model (rhe numbers with exception of *MPC*, represent billions of dollars):

a. $C = 1{,}500 + 0.75Y$	Consumption function
b. $I = 1{,}250$	Planned investment function
c. $G = 1{,}250$	Government spending function
d. $NX = -500$	Net export function
e. $Y = C + I + G + NX$	Equilibrium condition

3. For the macroeconomic model in problem 2, write the aggregate expenditure function. For GDP of \$16,000, what is the value of aggregate expenditure, and what is the value of unintended change in inventories? For GDP of \$12,000, what is the value of aggregate expenditure, and what is the value of the unintended change in inventories?
4. Suppose that autonomous consumption is 500, government purchases are 1,000, planned investment spending is 1,250, net exports is −250, and the *MPC* is 0.8. What is equilibrium GDP?

chapter twelve

Aggregate Demand and Aggregate Supply Analysis

Caterpillar Recovers Slowly from the 2001 Recession

➤ Caterpillar Inc., headquartered in Peoria, Illinois, manufactures more construction and mining equipment than any company in the world. The firm has worldwide revenue of more than $30 billion, about half of which comes from sales outside of North America. About half of its 80,000 employees work outside the United States. As these figures indicate, Caterpillar competes for business around the world. In fact, Caterpillar's main competitor is the Japanese company, Komatsu, Ltd.

Caterpillar is a multinational corporation, so its sales are affected by factors that are unimportant for firms that sell only in the domestic market. Included among these factors are exchange rates, tariffs, and changing attitudes of foreign governments toward multinational corporations. In earlier chapters, we saw that the U.S. economy has experienced a business cycle, with alternating periods of expansion and recession, since at least the early nineteenth century. We also saw that recessions often will begin with a decline in investment spending as firms purchase less machinery and equipment and fewer new factories and office buildings. As investment spending declines, firms like Caterpillar that sell capital goods will find their sales declining.

In the fall of 2000, even before the recession had formally begun, Caterpillar experienced a decline in sales. The firm responded to the recession by reducing production, laying off some workers, cutting the compensation of other workers, and lowering prices. These are the typical responses of a capital goods firm to a recession. (Caterpillar was hurt less by the recession than some other capital goods firms because during the late 1990s it had diversified into areas, such as renting equipment and providing financing for equipment purchases, that are less vulnerable to the effects of a recession.) What was not typical about this recession for Caterpillar was how slow sales were to revive. Not until late in 2003—nearly two years after the recession ended—did the company experience a significant increase in sales. By the end of 2003, the number of workers Caterpillar employed in the United States was still 10 percent below what it had been at the beginning of

2001. During this period, Caterpillar's sales of construction equipment suffered from a decline in spending by state governments on highway construction. Caterpillar also suffered from a decline in construction spending in several of its important overseas markets, as well as a longer-run decline in the worldwide mining business.

The slow recovery from the 2001 recession was not unique to Caterpillar. The manufacturing sector as a whole recovered more slowly from the 2001 recession than from any recession since World War II. Just as Caterpillar was slow to increase employment even as its sales began to revive, the level of employment in the economy as a whole was slow to regain its pre-recession level. *An Inside Look,* on page 396 discusses the recovery of the Japanese economy and its effect on Komatsu, Caterpillar's Japanese rival.

The recession of 2001 illustrates an important point about macroeconomics: All recessions share certain characteristics, but no two recessions are identical. In this chapter, we use the aggregate demand and aggregate supply model to analyze what happens during the business cycle and to understand why Caterpillar and many other U.S. companies recovered so slowly from the recession of 2001. In later chapters, we use the model to understand how the federal government can use fiscal and monetary policy to reduce the severity of the business cycle.

LEARNING OBJECTIVES

After studying this chapter, you should be able to:

① Discuss the determinants of aggregate demand, and distinguish between a movement along the aggregate demand curve and a shift of the curve.

② Discuss the determinants of aggregate supply, and distinguish between a movement along the short-run aggregate supply curve and a shift of the curve.

③ Use the aggregate demand and aggregate supply model to illustrate the difference between short-run and long-run macroeconomic equilibrium.

④ Use the dynamic aggregate demand and aggregate supply model to analyze macroeconomic conditions.

➤ We saw in Chapter 9 that the U.S. economy has experienced a long-run upward trend in real gross domestic product (GDP). This upward trend has resulted in the standard of living in the United States being much higher today than it was 50 years ago. In the short run, however, real GDP fluctuates around this long-run upward trend because of the business cycle. Fluctuations in GDP lead to fluctuations in employment. These fluctuations in real GDP and employment are the most visible and dramatic part of the business cycle. During recessions, for example, we see factories close, small businesses declare bankruptcy, and workers lose their jobs. During expansions, we see new businesses open and new jobs created. In addition to these changes in output and employment, the business cycle causes changes in wages and prices. Some firms react to a decline in sales by cutting back on production, but they may also cut the prices they charge and the wages they pay, which, as we have just seen, is what Caterpillar did during the 2001 recession. Even more firms respond to a recession by raising prices and workers' wages by less than they would have otherwise. During 2002 and 2003, even though the U.S. economy was in the expansion phase of the business cycle, some firms still experienced sluggish sales and unemployment remained relatively high. By 2005, real GDP was approaching its potential level as the economy experienced sustained increases in employment.

In this chapter, we expand our story of the business cycle by developing the aggregate demand and aggregate supply model. This model will help us analyze the effects of recessions and expansions on production, employment, and prices.

① LEARNING OBJECTIVE

Discuss the determinants of aggregate demand, and distinguish between a movement along the aggregate demand curve and a shift of the curve.

Aggregate Demand

To understand what happens during the business cycle, we need an explanation of why real GDP, the unemployment rate, and the inflation rate fluctuate. We already have seen that fluctuations in the unemployment rate are caused mainly by fluctuations in real GDP. In this chapter, we use the **aggregate demand and aggregate supply model** to explain fluctuations in real GDP and the price level. As Figure 12-1 shows, real GDP and the price level in this model are determined in the short run by the intersection of the *aggregate demand curve* and the *aggregate supply curve*. Fluctuations in real GDP and the price level are caused by shifts in the aggregate demand curve or in the aggregate supply curve.

Aggregate demand and aggregate supply model A model that explains short-run fluctuations in real GDP and the price level.

Aggregate demand curve (*AD*) A curve showing the relationship between the price level and the quantity of real GDP demanded by households, firms, and the government.

Short-run aggregate supply curve (*SRAS*) A curve showing the relationship in the short run between the price level and the quantity of real GDP supplied by firms.

The **aggregate demand curve (*AD*)** shows the relationship between the price level and the quantity of real GDP demanded by households, firms, and the government. The **short-run aggregate supply curve (*SRAS*)** shows the relationship in the short run between the price level and the quantity of real GDP supplied by firms. The aggregate demand and short-run aggregate supply curves in Figure 12-1 look similar to the individual market demand and supply curves we studied in Chapter 3. However, because these curves apply to the whole economy, rather than to just a single market, the aggregate demand and aggregate supply model is very different from the model of demand and supply in individual markets. Because we are dealing with the economy as a whole, we need *macroeconomic* explanations of why the aggregate demand curve is downward sloping, why the short-run aggregate supply curve is upward sloping, and why the curves shift. We begin by explaining why the aggregate demand curve is downward sloping.

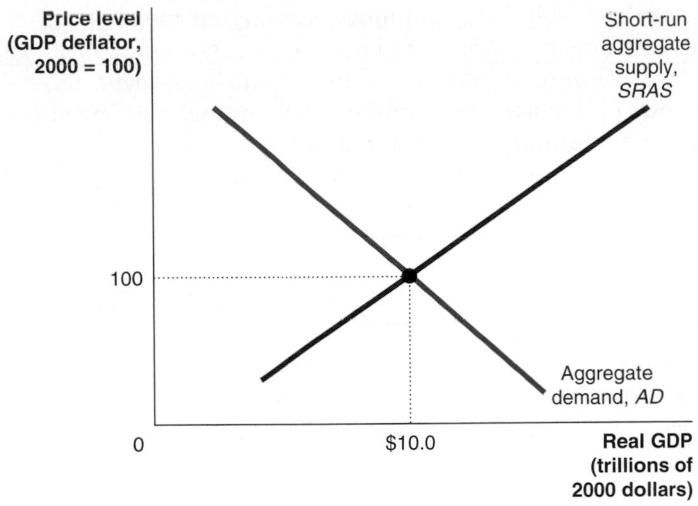

FIGURE 12-1

Aggregate Demand and Aggregate Supply

In the short run, real GDP and the price level are determined by the intersection of the aggregate demand curve and the short-run aggregate supply curve. In the figure, real GDP is measured on the horizontal axis, and the price level is measured on the vertical axis by the GDP deflator. In this example, equilibrium real GDP is $10.0 trillion and the equilibrium price level is 100.

Why Is the Aggregate Demand Curve Downward Sloping?

We saw in Chapter 7 that GDP has four components: consumption *(C)*, investment *(I)*, government purchases *(G)*, and net exports *(NX)*. If we let *Y* stand for GDP, we can write the following:

$$Y = C + I + G + NX.$$

The aggregate demand curve is downward sloping because a fall in the price level increases the quantity of real GDP demanded. To understand why this is true, we need to look at how changes in the price level affect each of the components of aggregate demand. We begin with the assumption that government purchases are determined by the policy decisions of lawmakers and are not affected by changes in the price level. We then can consider the effect of changes in the price level on each of the other three components: consumption, investment, and net exports.

THE WEALTH EFFECT: HOW A CHANGE IN THE PRICE LEVEL AFFECTS CONSUMPTION Current income is the most important variable determining the consumption of households. As income rises, consumption will rise, and as income falls, consumption will fall. But consumption also depends on household wealth. A household's wealth is the difference between the value of its assets and the value of its debts. Consider two households, both with incomes of $80,000 per year. The first household has wealth of $5 million, whereas the second household has wealth of $50,000. The first household is likely to spend more of its income than the second household. So, as total household wealth rises, consumption will rise. Some household wealth is held in cash or other *nominal assets* that lose value as the price level rises and gain value as the price level falls. For instance, if you have $10,000 in cash, a 10 percent increase in the price level will reduce the purchasing power of that cash by 10 percent. When the price level rises, the *real value* of household wealth declines, and so will consumption. When the price level falls, the real value of household wealth rises, and so will consumption. This impact of the price level on consumption is called the *wealth effect.*

THE INTEREST-RATE EFFECT: HOW A CHANGE IN THE PRICE LEVEL AFFECTS INVESTMENT When prices rise, households and firms need more money to finance buying and selling. Therefore, when the price level rises households and firms try to increase the amount of money they hold by withdrawing funds from banks, borrowing from banks, or selling financial assets, such as bonds. These actions tend to drive up the interest rate charged on bank loans and the interest rate on bonds. (In Chapter 14, we analyze in more detail the relationship between money and interest rates.) A higher interest rate raises the cost of borrowing for firms and households. As a result, firms will borrow less to build new factories or to install new machinery and equipment, and households will borrow less to buy new houses. To a smaller extent, households will also borrow less to finance spending on automobiles, furniture, and other durable goods. Consumption will therefore be reduced. A lower price level will have the reverse effect, leading to an increase in investment and—to a lesser extent—consumption. This impact of the price level on investment is known as the *interest-rate effect.*

THE INTERNATIONAL-TRADE EFFECT: HOW A CHANGE IN THE PRICE LEVEL AFFECTS NET EXPORTS *Net exports* equal spending by foreign households and firms on goods and services produced in the United States minus spending by U.S. households and firms on goods and services produced in other countries. If the price level in the United States rises relative to the price levels in other countries, U.S. exports will become relatively more expensive and foreign imports will become relatively less expensive. Some consumers in foreign countries will shift from buying U.S. products to buying domestic products, and some U.S. consumers will also shift from buying U.S. products to buying imported products. U.S. exports will fall and U.S. imports will rise, causing net exports to fall. A lower price level in the United States has the reverse effect, causing net exports to rise. This impact of the price level on net exports is known as the *international-trade effect.*

Shifts of the Aggregate Demand Curve versus Movements Along It

An important point to remember is that the aggregate demand curve tells us the relationship between the price level and the quantity of real GDP demanded, *holding everything else constant.* If the price level changes, but other variables that affect the willingness of households, firms, and the government to spend are unchanged, the economy will move up or down a stationary aggregate demand curve. If any variable changes other than the price level, the aggregate demand curve will shift. For example, if government purchases increase and the price level remains unchanged, the aggregate demand curve will shift to the right at every price level. Or, if firms become pessimistic about the future profitability of investment and cut back spending on factories and machinery, the aggregate demand curve will shift to the left.

Don't Let This Happen To You!

Be Clear Why the Aggregate Demand Curve Is Downward Sloping

The aggregate demand curve and the demand curve for a single product are both downward sloping—but for different reasons. When we draw a demand curve for a single product, such as apples, we know that it will slope downward because as the price of apples rises, apples becomes more expensive relative to other products—like oranges—and consumers buy fewer apples and more of the other products. In other words, consumers substitute other products for apples. When the overall price level rises, the prices of all domestically-produced goods and services are rising, so consumers have no other domestic products to which they can switch. The aggregate demand curve slopes downward for the reasons given on pages 373–374: A lower price level raises the real value of household wealth (which increases consumption), lowers interest rates (which increases investment and consumption), and makes U.S. exports less expensive and foreign imports more expensive (which increases net exports).

***YOUR TURN:* Test your understanding by doing related problem 4 on page 399 at the end of this chapter.**

The Variables That Shift the Aggregate Demand Curve

The variables that cause the aggregate demand curve to shift fall into three categories:

- Changes in government policies
- Changes in the expectations of households and firms
- Changes in foreign variables

CHANGES IN GOVERNMENT POLICIES As we will discuss further in Chapters 14 and 15, the federal government uses monetary policy and fiscal policy to shift the aggregate demand curve. Monetary policy involves changes in interest rates, and fiscal policy involves changes in government purchases and taxes. Lower interest rates lower the cost to firms and households of borrowing. Lower borrowing costs increase consumption and investment spending, which shifts the aggregate demand curve to the right. Higher interest rates shift the aggregate demand curve to the left. Because government purchases are one component of aggregate demand, an increase in government purchases shifts the aggregate demand curve to the right, and a decrease in government purchases shifts the aggregate demand curve to the left. An increase in personal income taxes reduces the amount of spendable income available to households. Higher personal income taxes reduce consumption spending and shift the aggregate demand curve to the left. Lower personal income taxes shift the aggregate demand curve to the right. Increases in business taxes reduce the profitability of investment spending and shift the aggregate demand curve to the left. Decreases in business taxes shift the aggregate demand curve to the right.

CHANGES IN THE EXPECTATIONS OF HOUSEHOLDS AND FIRMS If households become more optimistic about their future incomes, they are likely to increase their current consumption. This increased consumption will shift the aggregate demand curve to the right. If households become more pessimistic about their future incomes, the aggregate demand curve will shift to the left. Similarly, if firms become more optimistic about the future profitability of investment spending, the aggregate demand curve will shift to the right. If firms become more pessimistic, the aggregate demand curve will shift to the left.

CHANGES IN FOREIGN VARIABLES If firms and households in other countries buy fewer U.S. goods or if firms and households in the United States buy more foreign goods, net exports will fall and the aggregate demand curve will shift to the left. As we saw in Chapter 7, when real GDP increases, so does the income available for consumers to spend. If real GDP in the United States increases faster than real GDP in other countries, U.S. imports will increase faster than U.S. exports, and net exports will fall. This pattern occurred in the late 1990s and early 2000s. Net exports will also fall if the *exchange rate* between the dollar and foreign currencies rises, because the price in foreign currency of U.S. products sold in other countries will rise, and the dollar price of foreign products sold in the United States will fall. An increase in net exports at every price level will shift the aggregate demand curve to the right. Net exports will increase if real GDP grows more slowly in the United States than in other countries or if the value of the dollar falls against other currencies. A change in net exports that results from a change in the price level in the United States will *not* cause the aggregate demand curve to shift.

12-1 Making the Connection

The Effect of Exchange Rates on Caterpillar's Sales

As we saw at the beginning of this chapter, Caterpillar sells more than half its construction equipment and engines outside of North America. As a result, its sales are significantly affected by changes in the exchange rate between the dollar and foreign currencies. For instance, about 30 percent of Caterpillar's sales are to Europe, so changes in the exchange rate between the dollar and the euro (€)—the common currency of many European economies—can have a significant effect on sales. The following chart shows changes in the exchange rate between the dollar and the euro—expressed as the number of euros necessary to purchase one dollar—from 1999 to mid-2005.

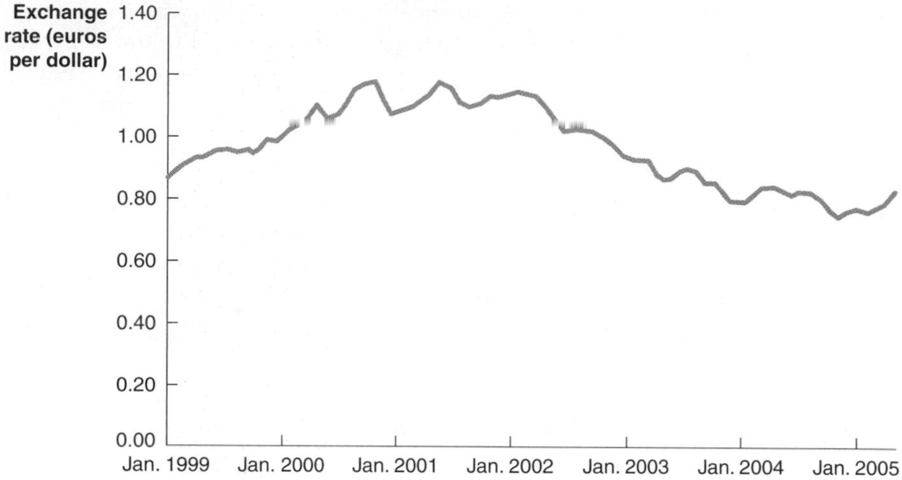

The more euros it takes to buy one dollar, the higher the euro price of Caterpillar's equipment. For example, consider a bulldozer that had a price of $100,000 in the United States. If the exchange rate was €0.86 = $1, as it was in January 1999, the equivalent price of the bulldozer in Europe would be €86,000 (= $100,000 × 0.86 euros per dollar). At the exchange rate of €1.17 = $1 in June 2001, the euro price of the bulldozer would be €117,000, or more than 35 percent higher than it had been in 1999. Not surprisingly, the rising value of the dollar during 2000 and 2001 combined with the effects of the recession to depress Caterpillar's sales. The falling value of the dollar from 2002 to 2004 combined with the economic expansion to increase Caterpillar's sales.

Because the value of the dollar rose against most currencies during 2000 and 2001, and fell against most currencies from 2002 to 2004, most U.S. exporters had experiences similar to Caterpillar's during those years.

The falling value of the dollar against the euro helped increase Caterpillar's sales from 2002 to 2004.

SOLVED PROBLEM 12-1

Movements along the Aggregate Demand Curve versus Shifts of the Aggregate Demand Curve

1 LEARNING OBJECTIVE

Discuss the determinants of aggregate demand, and distinguish between a movement along the aggregate demand curve and a shift of the curve.

Suppose the current price level is 110 and the current level of real GDP is $11.2 trillion. Illustrate each of the following situations on a graph:

a. The price level rises to 115, while all other variables remain constant.

b. Firms become pessimistic and reduce their investment. Assume the price level remains constant.

Solving the Problem:

Step 1: Review the chapter material. This problem is about understanding the difference between movements along an aggregate demand curve and shifts of an aggregate demand curve, so you may want to review the section "Shifts of the Aggregate Demand Curve versus Movements Along It," which begins on page 374.

Step 2: To answer question (a), draw a graph showing a movement along the aggregate demand curve. Because there will be a movement along the aggregate demand curve, but no shift of the aggregate demand curve, your graph should look like this:

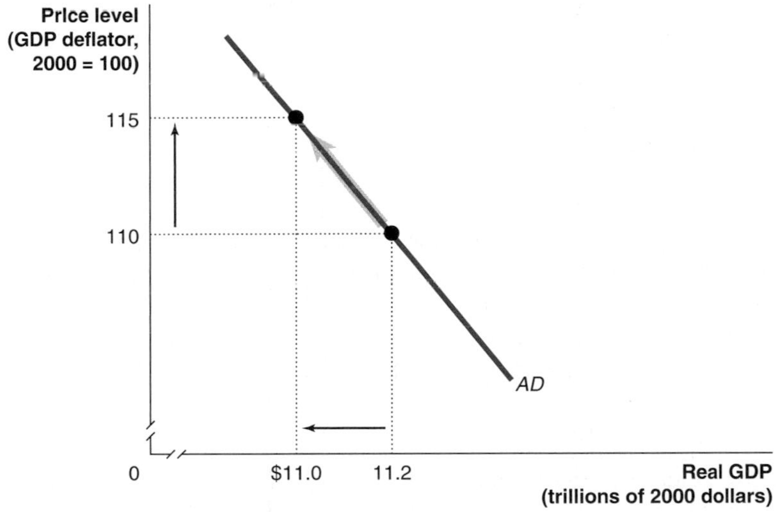

We don't have enough information to be certain what the new level of real GDP will be. We only know that it will be less than the initial level of $11.2 trillion—the graph shows the value as $11.0 trillion.

Step 3: To answer question (b), draw a graph showing a shift of the aggregate demand curve. We know that the aggregate demand curve will shift to the left, but we don't have enough information to know how far to the left it will shift. Let's assume the shift is $300 billion (or $0.3 trillion). In that case, your graph should look like this:

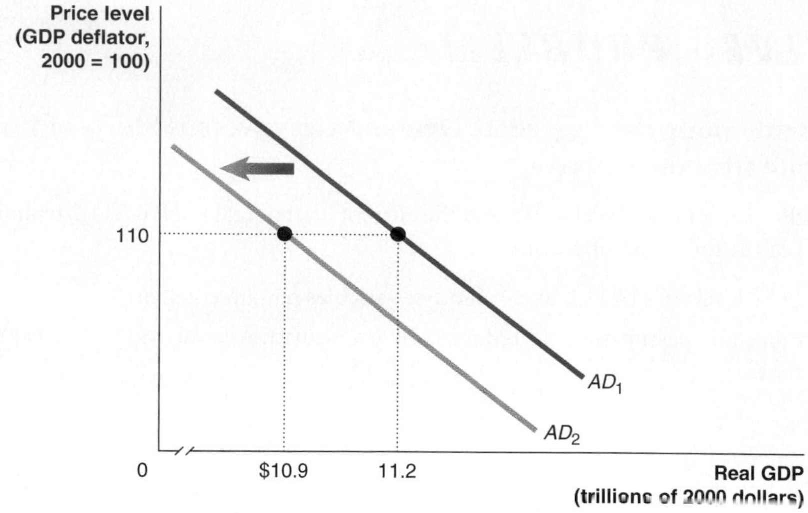

The graph shows a parallel shift in the aggregate demand curve, so that at every price level the quantity of real GDP demanded declines by $300 billion. For example, at a price level of 110, the quantity of real GDP demanded declines from $11.2 trillion to $10.9 trillion.

YOUR TURN: **For more practice, do related problem 5 on page 400 at the end of this chapter.**

Table 12-1 summarizes the most important variables that cause the aggregate demand curve to shift. It is important to notice that the table shows the shift in the aggregate demand curve that results from an increase in each of the variables. A *decrease* in these variables would cause the aggregate demand curve to shift in the opposite direction.

2 LEARNING OBJECTIVE

Discuss the determinants of aggregate supply, and distinguish between a movement along the short-run aggregate supply curve and a shift of the curve.

Aggregate Supply

We just discussed the aggregate demand curve, which is one component of the aggregate demand and aggregate supply model. Now we turn to aggregate supply, which shows the effect of changes in the price level on the quantity of goods and services that firms are willing and able to supply. Because the effect of changes in the price level is very different in the short run than in the long run, we use two aggregate supply curves: one for the short run and one for the long run. We start by considering the *long-run aggregate supply curve.*

The Long-Run Aggregate Supply Curve

In Chapter 10, we saw that in the long run the level of real GDP is determined by the number of workers, the *capital stock*—including factories, office buildings, and machinery and equipment—and the available technology. Because changes in the price level do not affect the number of workers, the capital stock, or technology, *in the long run, changes in the price level do not affect the level of real GDP.* Remember that the level of real GDP in the long run is called *potential GDP* or *full-employment GDP.* At potential GDP, firms will operate at their normal level of capacity and everyone who wants a job will have one, except the structurally and frictionally unemployed. There is no reason for this normal level of capacity to change just because the price level has changed. The **long-run aggregate supply curve (*LRAS*)** is a curve showing the relationship in the long run between the price level and the quantity of real GDP supplied. As Figure 12-2 on page 380 shows, the price level was 108 in 2004 and potential real GDP was $11.0 trillion. If the price level had been 95, or if it had been 112, long-run aggregate supply would still have been a constant $11.0 trillion. Therefore, the *LRAS* is a vertical line.

Long-run aggregate supply curve (*LRAS*) A curve showing the relationship in the long run between the price level and the quantity of real GDP supplied.

TABLE 12-1

Variables That Shift the Aggregate Demand Curve

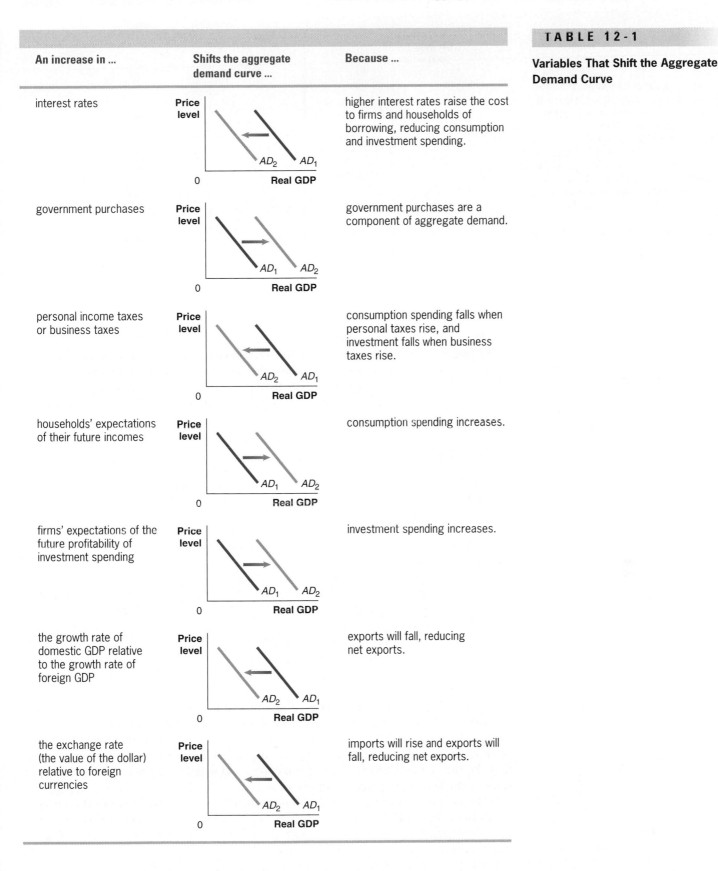

<table>
<tr><th>An increase in ...</th><th>Shifts the aggregate demand curve ...</th><th>Because ...</th></tr>
<tr><td>interest rates</td><td>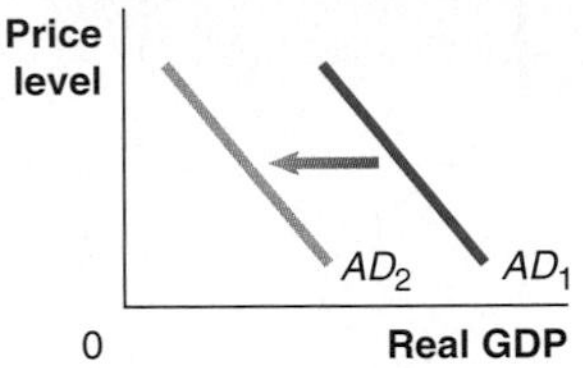
</td><td>higher interest rates raise the cost to firms and households of borrowing, reducing consumption and investment spending.</td></tr>
<tr><td>government purchases</td><td>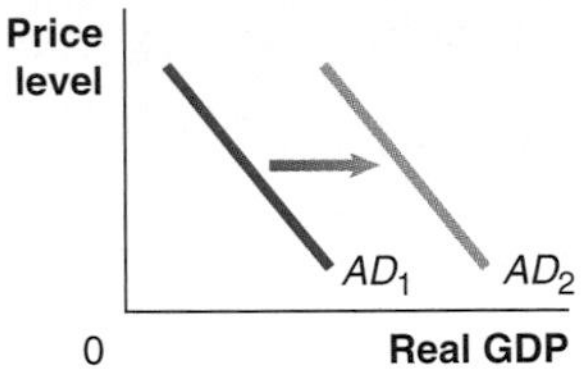
</td><td>government purchases are a component of aggregate demand.</td></tr>
<tr><td>personal income taxes or business taxes</td><td>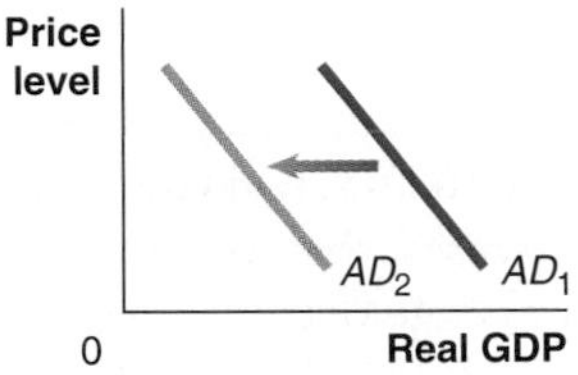
</td><td>consumption spending falls when personal taxes rise, and investment falls when business taxes rise.</td></tr>
<tr><td>households' expectations of their future incomes</td><td>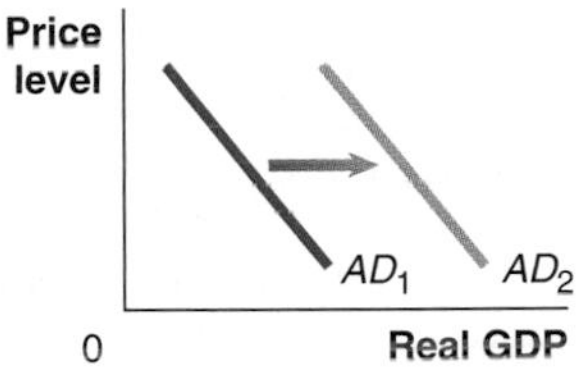
</td><td>consumption spending increases.</td></tr>
<tr><td>firms' expectations of the future profitability of investment spending</td><td>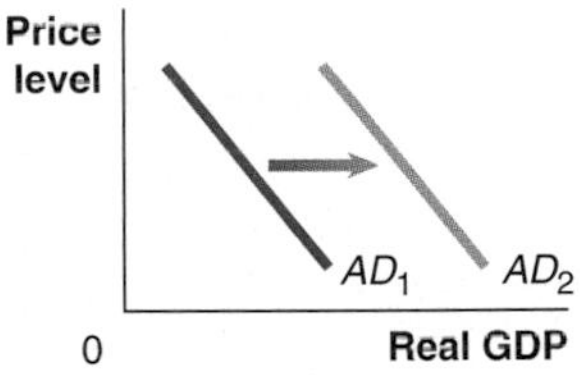
</td><td>investment spending increases.</td></tr>
<tr><td>the growth rate of domestic GDP relative to the growth rate of foreign GDP</td><td>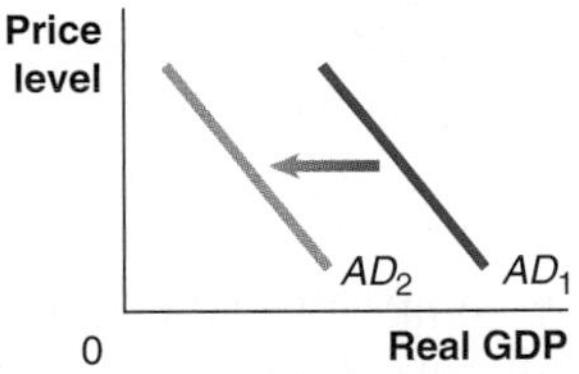
</td><td>exports will fall, reducing net exports.</td></tr>
<tr><td>the exchange rate (the value of the dollar) relative to foreign currencies</td><td>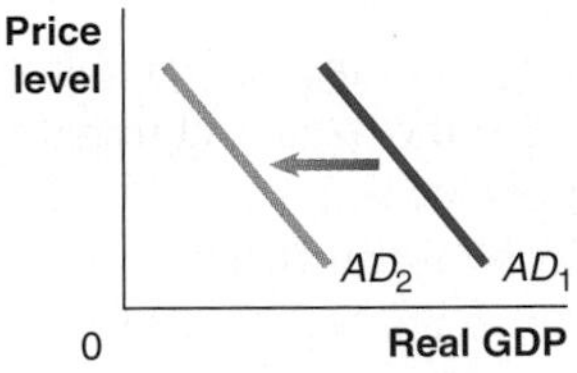
</td><td>imports will rise and exports will fall, reducing net exports.</td></tr>
</table>

FIGURE 12-2

The Long-Run Aggregate Supply Curve

Changes in the price level do not affect the level of aggregate supply in the long run. Therefore, the long-run aggregate supply curve *(LRAS)* is a vertical line at the potential level of real GDP. For instance, the price level was 108 in 2004 and potential real GDP was $11.0 trillion. If the price level had been 95, or if it had been 112, long-run aggregate supply would still have been a constant $11.0 trillion. Each year the long-run aggregate supply curve shifts to the right as the number of workers in the economy increases, more machinery and equipment are accumulated, and technological change occurs.

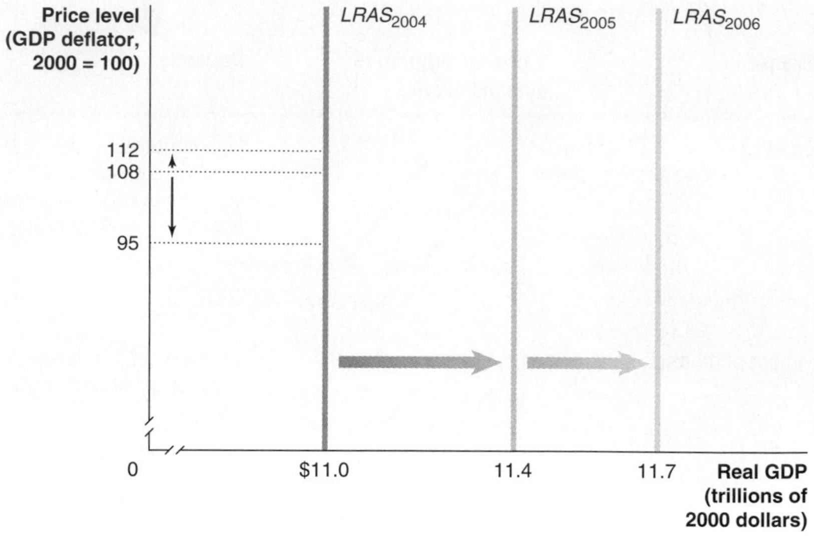

Figure 12-2 also shows that the long-run aggregate supply curve shifts to the right every year. This shift occurs because potential real GDP increases each year, as the number of workers in the economy increases, the economy accumulates more machinery and equipment, and technological change occurs. As Figure 12-2 shows, potential real GDP increased from $11.0 trillion in 2004 to $11.4 trillion in 2005 and to $11.7 trillion in 2006.

The Short-Run Aggregate Supply Curve

Although the *LRAS* is vertical, the short-run aggregate supply curve *(SRAS)* is upward sloping. The *SRAS* is upward sloping because, over the short run, as the price level increases, the quantity of goods and services firms are willing to supply will increase. The main reason firms are willing to supply more goods and services as the price level rises is that, *as prices of final goods and services rise, prices of inputs—such as the wages of workers or the price of natural resources—rise more slowly.* Profits rise when the prices of the goods and services firms sell rise more rapidly than the prices they pay for inputs. Therefore, a higher price level leads to higher profits and increases the willingness of firms to supply more goods and services. A secondary reason the *SRAS* curve slopes upward is that, as the price level rises or falls, some firms are slow to adjust their prices. A firm that is slow to raise its prices when the price level is increasing may find its sales increasing and, therefore, will increase production. A firm that is slow to reduce its prices when the price level is decreasing may find its sales falling and, therefore, will decrease production.

Why do some firms adjust prices more slowly than others, and why might the wages of workers and the prices of other inputs change more slowly than the prices of final goods and services? Most economists believe the explanation is that *some firms and workers fail to predict accurately changes in the price level.* If firms and workers could predict the future price level exactly, the short-run aggregate supply curve would be the same as the long-run aggregate supply curve.

But how does the failure of workers and firms to predict the price level accurately result in an upward-sloping short-run aggregate supply curve? Economists are not in complete agreement on this point, but we can briefly discuss the three most common explanations:

1. Contracts make some wages and prices "sticky."
2. Firms are often slow to adjust wages.
3. Menu costs make some prices sticky.

CONTRACTS MAKE SOME WAGES AND PRICES "STICKY" Prices or wages are said to be "sticky" when they do not respond quickly to changes in demand or supply. Contracts can make wages or prices sticky. For example, suppose the Ford Motor Company negotiates a three-year contract with the United Automobile Workers union at a time when demand for cars is increasing slowly. Suppose that after the contract is signed, the demand for cars starts to increase rapidly and prices of cars rise. Ford will find that producing more cars will be profitable, because it can increase car prices, while the wages it pays its workers are fixed by contract. Or a steel mill might have signed a multi-year contract to buy coal, which is used in making steel, at a time when the demand for steel is stagnant. If steel demand and steel prices begin to rise rapidly, producing additional steel will be profitable, because coal prices will remain fixed by contract. In both of these cases, rising prices lead to higher output. If these examples are representative of enough firms in the economy, a rising price level should lead to a greater quantity of goods and services supplied. In other words, the short-run aggregate supply curve will be upward sloping.

Notice, though, that if the workers at Ford or the managers of the coal companies had accurately predicted what would happen to prices, this prediction would have been reflected in the contracts, and Ford and the steel mill would not have earned greater profits when prices rose. In that case, rising prices would not have led to higher output.

FIRMS ARE OFTEN SLOW TO ADJUST WAGES We just noted that the wages of many union workers remain fixed by contract for several years. Many nonunion workers also have their wages or salaries adjusted only once a year. For instance, suppose you accept a job at a management consulting firm in June at a salary of $45,000 per year. The firm probably will not adjust your salary until the following June, even if the prices it can charge for its services later in the year are higher or lower than the firm had expected them to be when you were first hired. If firms adjust wages only slowly, a rise in the price level will increase the profitability of hiring more workers and producing more output. A fall in the price level will decrease the profitability of hiring more workers and producing more output. Once again, we have an explanation for why the short-run aggregate supply curve slopes upward.

It is worth noting that firms are often slower to *cut* wages than to increase them. Cutting wages can have a negative effect on the morale and productivity of workers and can also cause some of the firm's best workers to quit and look for jobs elsewhere.

MENU COSTS MAKE SOME PRICES STICKY Firms base their prices today partly on what they expect future prices to be. For instance, a restaurant has to decide ahead of time the prices it will charge for meals before printing menus. Many firms print catalogs that list the prices of their products. If demand for their products is higher or lower than the firms had expected, they may want to charge prices that are different from the ones printed in their menus or catalogs. Changing prices would be costly, however, because it would involve printing new menus or catalogs. The costs to firms of changing prices are called **menu costs**. To see why menu costs can lead to an upward-sloping short-run aggregate supply curve, consider the effect of an unexpected increase in the price level. In this case, firms will want to increase the prices they charge. Some firms, however, may not be willing to increase prices because of menu costs. Because of their relatively low prices, these firms will find their sales increasing, which will cause them to increase output. Once again, we have an explanation for a higher price level leading to a larger quantity of goods and services supplied.

Menu costs The costs to firms of changing prices.

Shifts of the Short-Run Aggregate Supply Curve versus Movements Along It

It is always important to remember the difference between a shift in a curve and a movement along a curve. The short-run aggregate supply curve tells us the short-run relationship between the price level and the quantity of goods and services firms are willing to supply, *holding constant all other variables that affect the willingness of firms to supply goods and services*. If the price level changes but other variables are unchanged, the economy will move up or down a stationary aggregate supply curve. If any variable other than the price level changes, the aggregate supply curve will shift.

Variables That Shift the Short-Run Aggregate Supply Curve

We now briefly discuss the five most important variables that cause the short-run aggregate supply curve to shift.

INCREASES IN THE LABOR FORCE AND IN THE CAPITAL STOCK A firm will supply more output at every price if it has more workers and more physical capital. The same is true of the economy as a whole. So, as the labor force and the capital stock grow, firms will supply more output at every price level, and the short-run aggregate supply curve will shift to the right. In Japan, the population is aging and the labor force is decreasing. Holding other variables constant, this decrease in the labor force causes the short-run aggregate supply curve in Japan to shift to the left.

TECHNOLOGICAL CHANGE As technological change takes place, the *productivity* of workers and machinery increases, which means firms can produce more goods and services with the same amount of labor and machinery. This improvement reduces the firms' costs of production and, therefore, allows them to produce more output at every price level. As a result, the short-run aggregate supply curve shifts to the right.

EXPECTED CHANGES IN THE FUTURE PRICE LEVEL If workers and firms believe that the price level is going to increase by 3 percent during the next year, they will try to adjust their wages and prices accordingly. For instance, if the United Automobile Workers union believes there will be 3 percent inflation next year, it knows that wages must rise 3 percent to preserve the purchasing power of those wages. Similar adjustments by other workers and firms will result in costs increasing throughout the economy by 3 percent. The result, shown in Figure 12-3, is that the short-run aggregate supply curve will shift to the left, so that any level of real GDP is now associated with a price level that is 3 percent higher. In general, *if workers and firms expect the price level to increase by a certain percentage, the* SRAS *curve will shift by an equivalent amount,* holding constant all other variables that affect the *SRAS* curve.

ADJUSTMENTS OF WORKERS AND FIRMS TO ERRORS IN PAST EXPECTATIONS ABOUT THE PRICE LEVEL Workers and firms sometimes make wrong predictions about the price level. As time passes, they will attempt to compensate for these errors. Suppose, for example, that the United Automobile Workers union signs a contract with Ford that contains only small wage increases because the company and the union expect only small increases in the price level. If increases in the price level turn out to be unexpectedly large, the union will take this into account when negotiating the next contract. The higher wages Ford's workers receive under the new contract will increase Ford's costs and result in Ford's needing to receive higher prices to produce the same level of output. If workers and firms across the economy are adjusting to the price level being higher than expected, the short-run aggregate supply curve will shift to the left. If they are adjusting to the price level being lower than expected, the short-run aggregate supply curve will shift to the right.

UNEXPECTED CHANGES IN THE PRICE OF AN IMPORTANT NATURAL RESOURCE An unexpected increase or decrease in the price of an important natural resource can cause firms' costs to be different from what they had expected. Oil prices can be particularly volatile. Some firms use oil in the production process. Other firms use products, such as plastics, that are made from oil. If oil prices rise unexpectedly, the costs of production will rise for these firms. Some utilities also burn oil to generate electricity, so electricity prices will rise. Rising oil prices lead to rising gasoline prices, which raise trans-

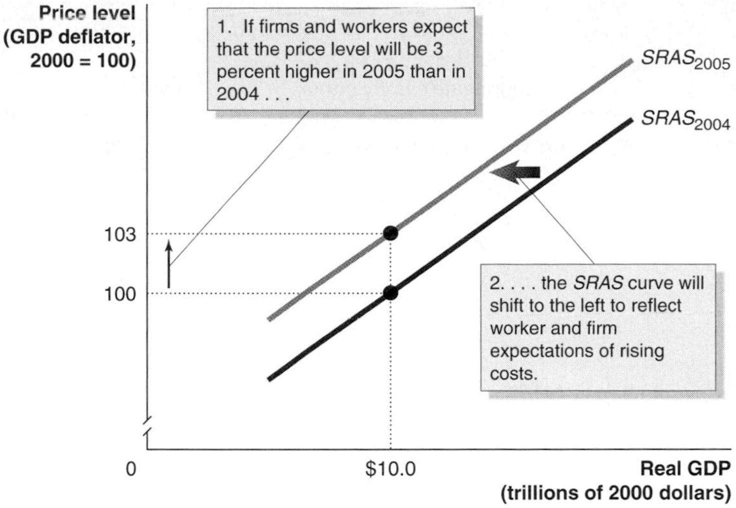

FIGURE 12-3

How Expectations of the Future Price Level Affect the Short-Run Aggregate Supply

The *SRAS* curve shifts to reflect worker and firm expectations of future prices.

1. If workers and firms expect the price level will rise by 3 percent from 100 to 103, they will adjust their wages and prices by that amount.
2. Holding constant all other variables that affect aggregate supply, the short-run aggregate supply curve will shift to the left.

If workers and firms expect the price level will be lower in the future, the short-run aggregate supply curve will shift to the right.

portation costs for many firms. Because firms face rising costs, they will only supply the same level of output at higher prices, and the short-run aggregate supply curve will shift to the left. An unexpected event that causes the short-run aggregate supply curve to shift is known as a **supply shock**. Supply shocks are often caused by an unexpected increase or decrease in the price of an important natural resource. In September 2005, the U.S. economy was hit with a different type of supply shock when hurricane Katrina slammed into the Gulf Coast region. Many people were killed, the city of New Orleans had to be evacuated, and as many as one million people in the region were forced to relocate. The Congressional Budget Office estimated that up to 400,000 jobs were temporarily lost because of the hurricane. About one-quarter of U.S. oil and natural gas output comes from the Gulf Coast, and about half of this output was disrupted by Katrina. The fall in oil production caused prices to soar, with the price of gasoline rising above $3.00 per gallon.

Supply shock An unexpected event that causes the short-run aggregate supply curve to shift.

Because the U.S. economy has experienced inflation every year since the 1930s, workers and firms always expect next year's price level to be higher than this year's price level. Holding everything else constant, this will cause the short-run aggregate supply curve to shift to the left. But everything else is not constant, because every year the U.S. labor force and the U.S. capital stock expand and changes in technology occur, which cause the short-run aggregate supply curve to shift to the right. Whether in any particular year the short-run aggregate supply curve shifts to the left or to the right depends on which of these variables has the largest impact during that year.

Table 12-2 on page 384 summarizes the most important variables that cause the short-run aggregate supply curve to shift. It is important to notice that the table shows the shift in the short-run aggregate supply curve that results from an *increase* in each of the variables. A *decrease* in these variables would cause the short-run aggregate supply curve to shift in the opposite direction.

Macroeconomic Equilibrium in the Long Run and the Short Run

(3) LEARNING OBJECTIVE

Use the aggregate demand and aggregate supply model to illustrate the difference between short-run and long-run macroeconomic equilibrium.

Now that we have discussed the components of the aggregate demand and aggregate supply model, we can use it to analyze changes in real GDP and the price level. In Figure 12-4 on page 385, we bring the aggregate demand curve, the short-run aggregate supply curve, and the long-run aggregate supply curve together in one graph, to show the *long-run macroeconomic equilibrium* for the economy. In the figure, equilibrium occurs at real GDP of $10.0 trillion and a price level of 100. Notice that in long-run equilibrium, the

TABLE 12-2

Variables That Shift the Short-Run Aggregate Supply Curve

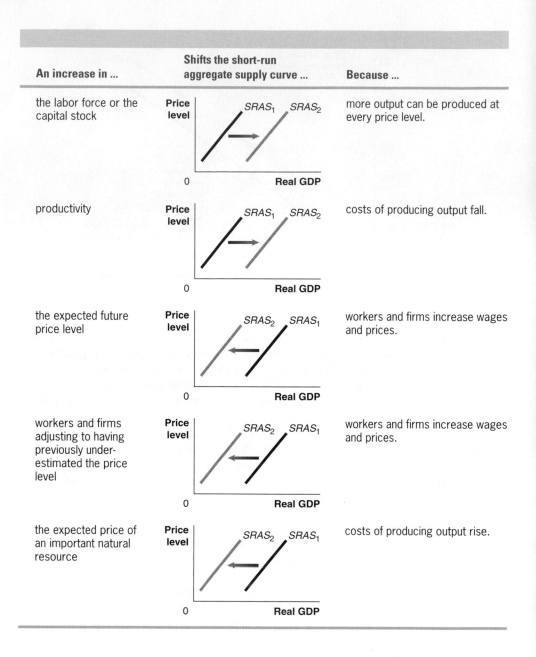

An increase in ...	Shifts the short-run aggregate supply curve ...	Because ...
the labor force or the capital stock	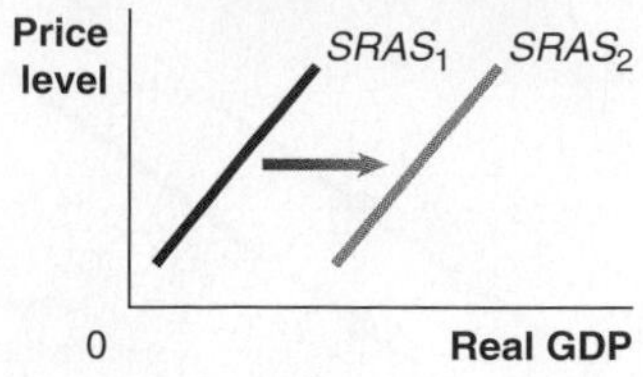	more output can be produced at every price level.
productivity	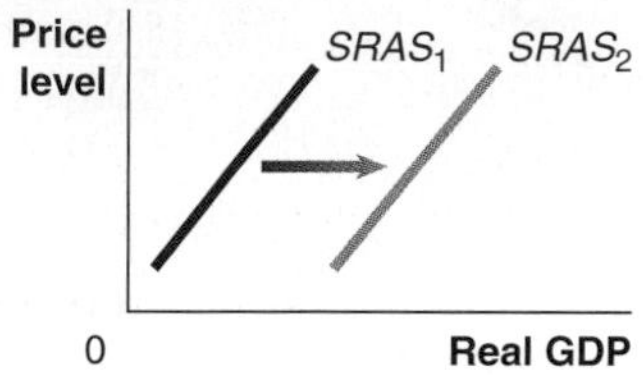	costs of producing output fall.
the expected future price level	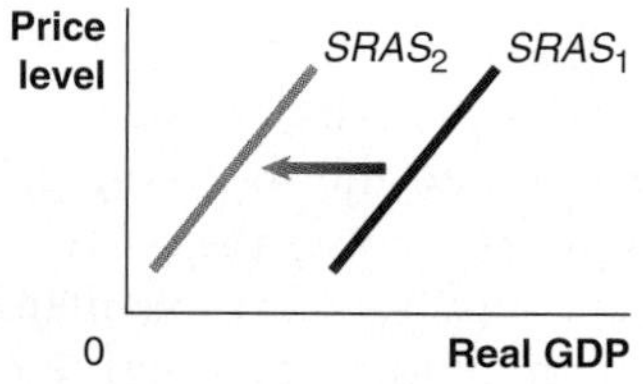	workers and firms increase wages and prices.
workers and firms adjusting to having previously underestimated the price level	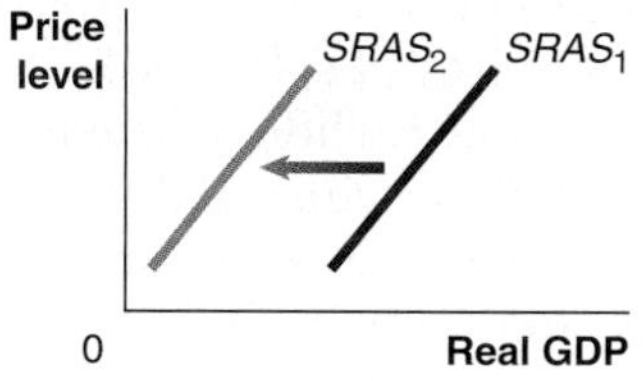	workers and firms increase wages and prices.
the expected price of an important natural resource	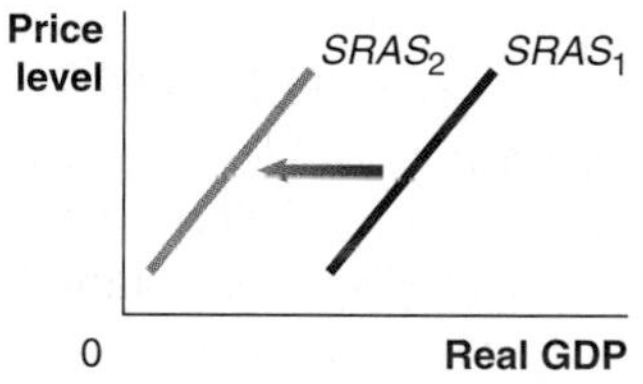	costs of producing output rise.

short-run aggregate supply curve and the aggregate demand curve intersect at a point on the long-run aggregate supply curve. Because equilibrium occurs at a point along the long-run aggregate supply curve, we know the economy is at potential real GDP: Firms will be operating at their normal level of capacity, and everyone who wants a job will have one, except the structurally and frictionally unemployed. We know, however, that the economy is often not in long-run macroeconomic equilibrium. In the following section, we discuss the economic forces that can push the economy away from long-run equilibrium.

Recessions, Expansions, and Supply Shocks

Because the full analysis of the aggregate demand and aggregate supply model can be complicated, we begin with a simplified case, using two assumptions:

1. The economy has not been experiencing any inflation. The price level is currently 100, and workers and firms expect it to remain at 100 in the future.
2. The economy is not experiencing any long-run growth. Potential real GDP is \$10.0 trillion and will remain at that level in the future.

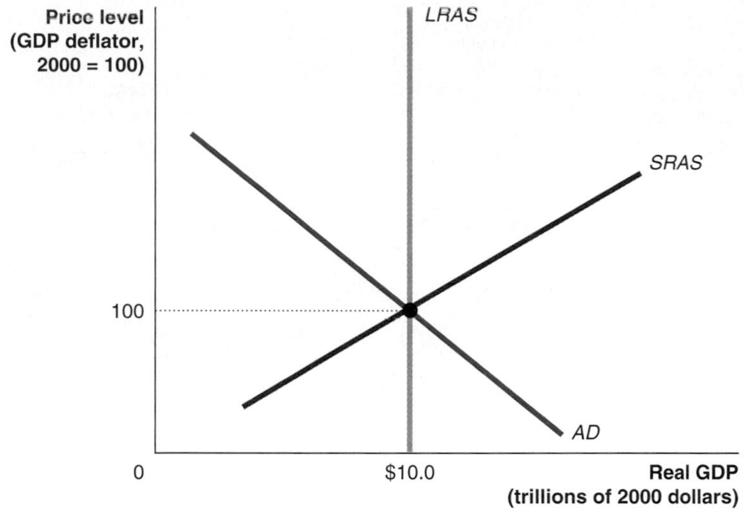

FIGURE 12-4

Long-Run Macroeconomic Equilibrium

In long-run macroeconomic equilibrium, the *AD* and *SRAS* curves intersect at a point on the *LRAS* curve. In this case, equilibrium occurs at real GDP of $10.0 trillion and a price level of 100.

These assumptions are simplifications because in reality the U.S. economy has experienced at least some inflation every year since the 1930s, and the potential real GDP also increases every year. However, the assumptions allow us to understand more easily the key ideas of the aggregate demand and aggregate supply model. In this section, we examine the short-run and long-run effects of recessions, expansions, and supply shocks.

RECESSION

The short-run effect of a decline in aggregate demand. Suppose that an outbreak of fighting in the Middle East causes firms to become pessimistic about the future profitability of new spending on factories and equipment. The decline in investment that results will shift the aggregate demand curve to the left, from AD_1 to AD_2, as shown in Figure 12-5 on page 386. The economy moves from point *A* to a new *short-run macroeconomic equilibrium* where the AD_2 curve intersects the *SRAS* curve at point *B*. In the new short-run equilibrium, real GDP has declined from $10.0 trillion to $9.8 trillion and is below its potential level. This lower level of GDP will result in declining profitability for many firms and layoffs for some workers: The economy will be in recession.

Adjustment back to potential GDP in the long run. We know that the recession will eventually end because there are forces at work that push the economy back to potential GDP in the long run. Figure 12-5 also shows how the economy moves from recession back to potential GDP. The shift from AD_1 to AD_2 initially leads to a short-run equilibrium with the price level having fallen from 100 to 98 (point *B*). Workers and firms will begin to adjust to the price level being lower than they had expected it to be. Workers will be willing to accept lower wages—because each dollar of wages is able to buy more goods and services—and firms will be willing to accept lower prices. In addition, the unemployment resulting from the recession will make workers more willing to accept lower wages, and the decline in demand will make firms more willing to accept lower prices. As a result, the *SRAS* curve will shift to the right from $SRAS_1$ to $SRAS_2$. At this point the economy will be back in long-run equilibrium (point *C*). The shift from $SRAS_1$ to $SRAS_2$ will not happen instantly. It may take the economy several years to return to potential GDP. The important conclusion is that a decline in aggregate demand causes a recession in the short run, but in the long run it causes only a decline in the price level.

Economists refer to the process of adjustment back to potential GDP just described as an *automatic mechanism* because it occurs without any actions by the government. An alternative to waiting for the automatic mechanism to end the recession is for the government to use monetary and fiscal policy to shift the *AD* curve to the right and restore potential GDP more quickly. We will discuss monetary and fiscal policy in Chapters 15 and 16. Economists debate whether or not we should wait for the automatic mechanism to end recessions, or whether it would be better to use monetary and fiscal policy.

FIGURE 12-5

The Short-Run and Long-Run Effects of Decrease in Aggregate Demand

In the short run, a decrease in aggregate demand causes a recession. In the long run, it causes only a decrease in the price level.

1. The decline in investment shifts aggregate demand from AD_1 to AD_2. Short-run equilibrium moves from potential GDP at point *A*, to recession at point *B*.
2. The price level of 98 at point *B* is lower than the price level of 100 that workers and firms had expected. As workers and firms adjust to the lower price level, prices and wages fall, and the short-run aggregate supply curve shifts from $SRAS_1$ to $SRAS_2$.
3. Equilibrium moves from point *B* back to potential GDP at point *C*, with a lower price level of 96.

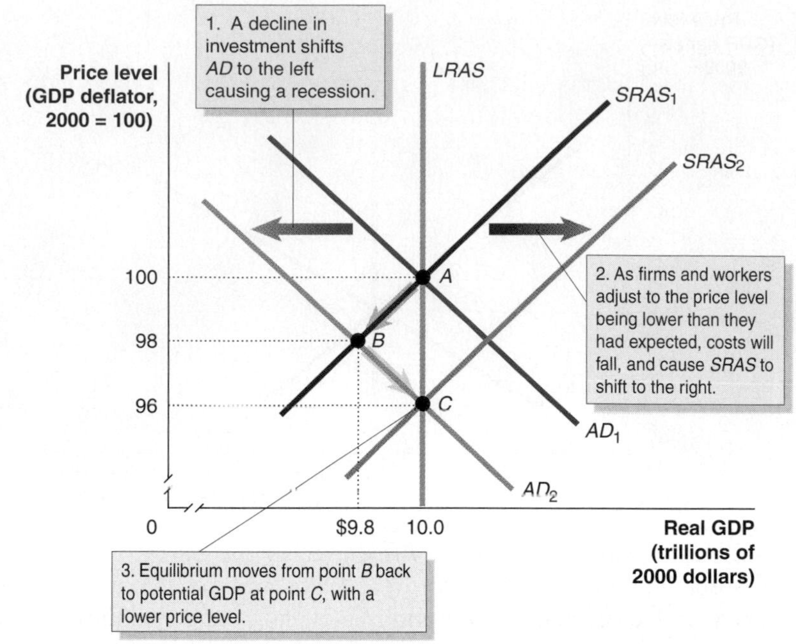

EXPANSION

The short-run effect of an increase in aggregate demand. Suppose that instead of becoming pessimistic, many firms become optimistic about the future profitability of new investment, as happened during the information technology and telecommunications booms of the late 1990s. The resulting increase in investment will shift the *AD* curve to the right, as is shown in Figure 12-6. Equilibrium moves from point *A* to point *B*. Real GDP rises from $10.0 trillion to $10.3 trillion, and the price level rises from 100 to 103. The economy will be above potential real GDP: Firms are operating beyond their

FIGURE 12-6

The Short-Run and Long-Run Effects of an Increase in Aggregate Demand

In the short run, an increase in aggregate demand causes an increase in real GDP. In the long run, it causes only an increase in the price level.

1. The increase in investment shifts aggregate demand from AD_1 to AD_2. Short-run equilibrium moves from potential GDP at point *A*, to beyond potential GDP at point *B*.
2. The price level of 103 at point *B* is higher than the price level of 100 that workers and firms had expected. As workers and firms adjust to the higher price level, prices and wages rise, and the short-run aggregate supply curve shifts from $SRAS_1$ to $SRAS_2$.
3. Equilibrium moves from point *B* back to potential GDP at point *C*, with a higher price level of 106.

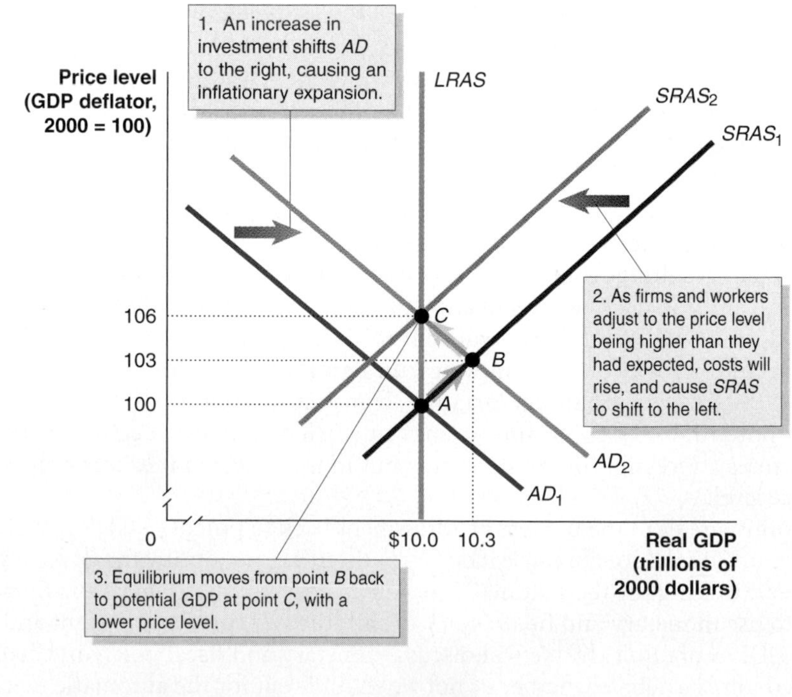

normal level of capacity, and some workers are employed who ordinarily would be structurally or frictionally unemployed, or who would not be in the labor force.

Adjustment back to potential GDP in the long run. Just as an automatic mechanism brings the economy back to potential GDP from a recession, an automatic mechanism brings the economy back from a short-run equilibrium beyond potential GDP. Figure 12-6 illustrates this mechanism. The shift from AD_1 to AD_2 initially leads to a short-run equilibrium with the price level rising from 100 to 103 (point *B*). Workers and firms will begin to adjust to the price level being higher than they had expected. Workers will push for higher wages—because each dollar of wages is able to buy fewer goods and services—and firms will charge higher prices. In addition, the low levels of unemployment resulting from the expansion will make it easier for workers to negotiate for higher wages, and the increase in demand will make it easier for firms to receive higher prices. As a result, the *SRAS* curve will shift to the left from $SRAS_1$ to $SRAS_2$. At this point, the economy will be back in long-run equilibrium. Once again, the shift from $SRAS_1$ to $SRAS_2$ will not happen instantly. The process of returning to potential GDP may stretch out for more than a year.

SUPPLY SHOCK

The short-run effect of a supply shock. Suppose oil prices increase substantially. This supply shock will increase many firms' costs and cause the *SRAS* curve to shift to the left, as is shown in panel (a) of Figure 12-7. Notice that the price level is higher in the

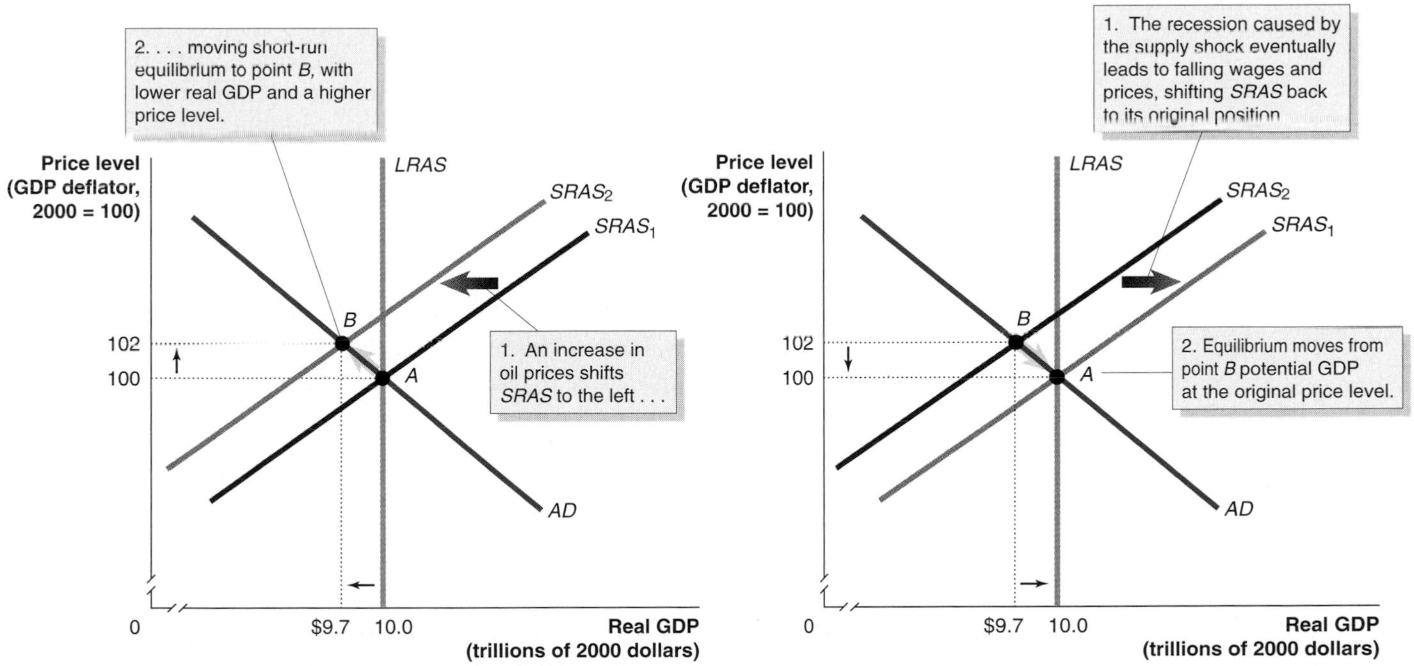

(a) A recession with a rising price level the short-run effect of a supply shock

(b) Adjustment back to potential GDP the long-run effect of a supply shock

FIGURE 12-7 The Short-Run and Long-Run Effects of a Supply Shock

Panel (a) shows that a supply shock, such as a large increase in oil prices, will cause a recession and a higher price level in the short run. The recession caused by the supply shock increases unemployment and reduces output. In panel *B*, rising unemployment and falling output result in workers being willing to accept lower wages and firms being willing to accept lower prices. The short-run aggregate supply curve shifts from $SRAS_2$ to $SRAS_1$. Equilibrium moves from point *B* back to potential GDP and the original price level at point *A*.

Stagflation A combination of inflation and recession, usually resulting from a supply shock.

new short-run equilibrium (102 rather than 100) but real GDP is lower ($9.7 trillion rather than $10 trillion). This unpleasant combination of inflation and recession is called **stagflation**.

Adjustment back to potential GDP in the long run. The recession caused by the supply shock increases unemployment and reduces output. This eventually results in workers being willing to accept lower wages and firms being willing to accept lower prices. In panel (b) of Figure 12-7, the short-run aggregate supply curve shifts from $SRAS_2$ to $SRAS_1$, moving the economy from point *B* back to point *A*. Potential GDP is regained at the original price level. It may take several years for this process to be completed. An alternative would be to use monetary and fiscal policy to shift the aggregate demand to the right. Using policy in this way would bring the economy back to potential GDP more quickly but would result in a permanently higher price level.

④ LEARNING OBJECTIVE

Use the dynamic aggregate demand and aggregate supply model to analyze macroeconomic conditions.

A Dynamic Aggregate Demand and Aggregate Supply Model

The basic aggregate demand and aggregate supply model used so far in this chapter gives us important insights into how short-run macroeconomic equilibrium is determined. Unfortunately, the model also gives us some misleading results. For instance, it incorrectly predicts that a recession caused by the aggregate demand curve shifting to the left will cause the price level to fall, which has not happened for an entire year since the 1930s. The difficulty with the basic model arises from the two assumptions we made when using it: (1) that the economy does not experience continuing inflation and (2) that the economy does not experience long-run growth. We can develop a more useful aggregate demand and aggregate supply model by dropping these assumptions. The result will be a model that takes into account that the economy is not *static*, with an unchanging level of potential real GDP and no continuing inflation, but *dynamic*, with potential real GDP that grows over time and inflation that continues every year. We can create a *dynamic aggregate demand and aggregate supply model* by making three changes to the basic model:

- Potential real GDP increases continually, shifting the long-run aggregate supply curve *(LRAS)* to the right.
- During most years, the aggregate demand curve *(AD)* will be shifting to the right.
- Except during periods when workers and firms expect high rates of inflation, the short-run aggregate supply curve *(SRAS)* will be shifting to the right.

The long-run aggregate supply curve continually shifts to the right, because over time the U.S. labor force and the U.S. capital stock will increase. Technological progress will also occur. Figure 12-8 shows the resulting increase in potential real GDP, which we illustrate by a shift to the right in the long-run aggregate supply curve from $LRAS_1$ to $LRAS_2$. The figure also shows that the short-run aggregate supply curve shifts from $SRAS_1$ to $SRAS_2$. This shift occurs because the same variables that cause the long-run aggregate supply to shift to the right, will also increase the quantity of goods and services that firms are willing to supply in the short run.

In Figure 12-8, potential real GDP increases over the course of a year from $10.0 trillion to $10.5 trillion. Assuming that no other variables that affect the *SRAS* curve have changed, the *LRAS* and *SRAS* curves will shift to the right by the same amount. But keep in mind that the *SRAS* curve is also affected by workers' and firms' expectations of future changes in the price level and by supply shocks. These variables can partially, or completely, offset the normal tendency of the *SRAS* curve to shift to the right over the course of a year.

The aggregate demand curve will usually be shifting to the right for several reasons: As population grows and incomes rise, consumption will increase over time. As the

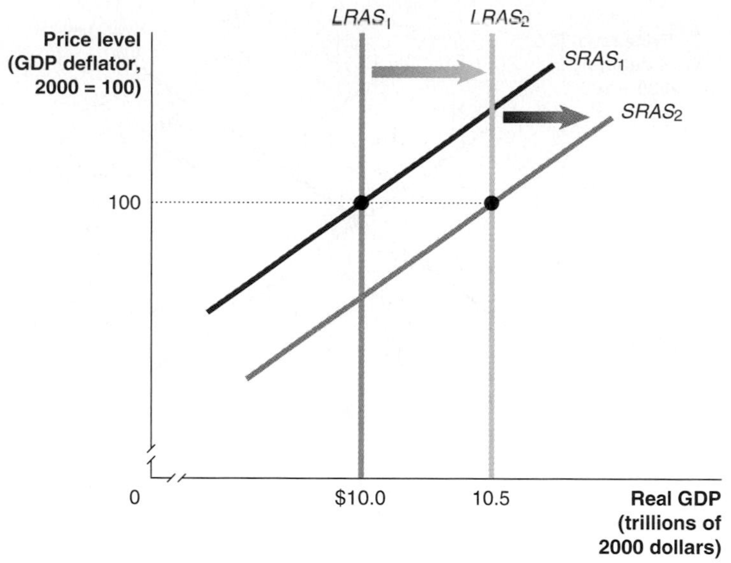

FIGURE 12-8

An Increase in Potential Real GDP

Increases in the labor force and the capital stock and technological change cause long-run aggregate supply to shift over the course of a year from $LRAS_1$ to $LRAS_2$, and cause short-run aggregate supply to shift from $SRAS_1$ to $SRAS_2$. If no other variables that affect the *SRAS* curve have changed, the *LRAS* and *SRAS* curves will shift to the right by the same amount.

economy grows, firms will expand capacity and new firms will be formed, increasing investment. An expanding population and an expanding economy require increased government services, such as more police officers and teachers, so government purchases will increase. Of course, we know that sometimes consumers, firms, and the government may cut back their expenditures. This reduced spending will result in the aggregate demand curve shifting to the right less than it normally would or, possibly, shifting to the left. As we will see, the aggregate demand curve shifting to the left will push the economy into recession, just as in the basic aggregate demand and aggregate supply model.

What Is the Usual Cause of Inflation?

The dynamic aggregate demand and aggregate supply model provides a more accurate explanation than the basic model of the source of most inflation. If total spending in the economy grows faster than total production, prices rise. Figure 12-9 illustrates this point by showing that if the *AD* curve shifts to the right by more than the *LRAS* curve, inflation results because equilibrium occurs at a higher price level, point *B*. In the new equilibrium, point *B*, the *SRAS* curve has shifted to the right by less than the *LRAS* curve because the anticipated increase in prices offsets some of the technological change and increases in the labor force and capital stock that occur during the year. Although inflation is generally the result of total spending growing faster than total production, a shift to the left of the short-run aggregate supply curve can also cause an increase in the price level, as we saw earlier in the discussion of supply shocks.

If aggregate demand increases by the same amount as short-run and long-run aggregate supply, the price level will not change. In this case, the economy experiences economic growth without inflation.

The Slow Recovery from the Recession of 2001

We can use the dynamic aggregate demand and aggregate supply model to analyze the slow recovery from the recession of 2001. The long economic expansion that began in March 1991 ended in March 2001, when a recession began. The recession was caused by a decline in aggregate demand. Several factors contributed to this decline:

- ***The end of the stock market "bubble."*** In the late 1990s, stock prices increased rapidly. Higher stock prices partly reflected higher corporate profits, but as we saw

FIGURE 12-9

Using Dynamic Aggregate Demand and Aggregate Supply to Understand Inflation

The most common cause of inflation is total spending increasing faster than total production.

1. The economy begins at point *A*, with real GDP of $10.0 trillion and a price level of 100. An increase in full-employment real GDP from $10.0 trillion to $10.5 trillion causes long-run aggregate supply to shift from $LRAS_1$ to $LRAS_2$. Aggregate demand shifts from AD_1 to AD_2.
2. Because *AD* shifts to the right by more than the *LRAS* curve, the price level in the new equilibrium rises from 100 to 104.

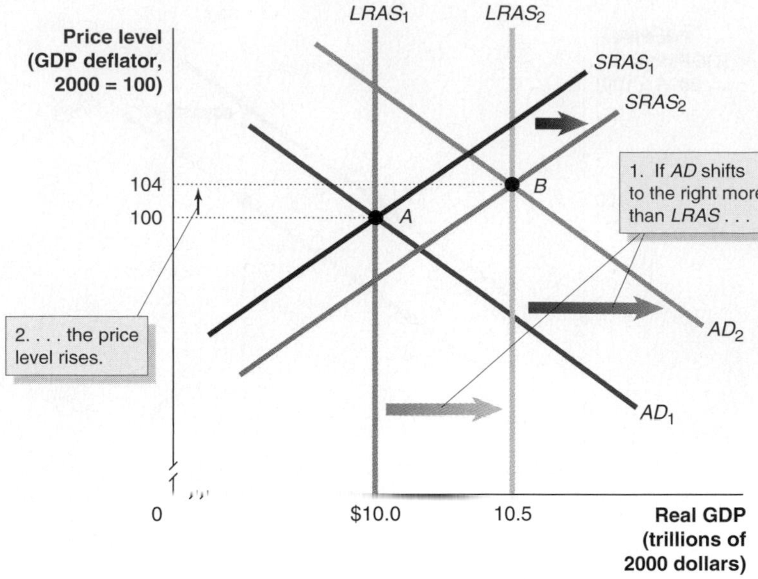

in Chapter 1, they also reflected the excessive optimism of investors about the future of dot-com companies. The increase in stock prices between 1995 and 2000 increased the wealth of U.S. households by $9 trillion. Stock prices began to fall in the spring of 2000 and eventually fell almost as far as they had risen. By 2002, the total value of stocks had declined by $7 trillion from their peak of two years before. The fall in stock prices reduced spending by households and firms. Firms that had financed investment spending by issuing new stock now had a more difficult time raising funds.

- ***Excessive investment in information technology.*** During the late 1990s, many firms overestimated the future profitability of investment in information technology. For example, telecommunications firms laid many more miles of fiber-optic cable than there was demand in the short run. Some firms also invested in computers and software in anticipation of the year 2000 (Y2K) problem. This problem arose from the technical difficulty many older computers had in correctly interpreting dates in years after 1999. Once older software and computers had been replaced, spending declined. Similarly, many firms had invested heavily to establish a presence on the Internet. When their Internet sales proved disappointing, the companies had more computers than they needed. For these reasons, by the spring of 2001, many companies had sharply cut back on their investment spending.
- ***The terrorist attacks of September 11, 2001.*** The terrorist attacks on New York and Washington, D.C., increased the level of uncertainty in the economy. Many feared further attacks would occur, and they were uncertain how the economy would respond. When firms and households face uncertainty, they often postpone spending until the uncertainty is resolved.
- ***The corporate accounting scandals.*** As we saw in Chapter 5, the top managers of some corporations, such as WorldCom, Tyco, and Enron, manipulated their financial statements during the stock market boom to make their corporations appear more profitable than they actually were. When these accounting manipulations were finally brought to light, some investors lost faith in the accuracy of corporate financial statements, which helped depress stock prices and added to the uncertainty in the economy.

Few economists were surprised that the long expansion of the 1990s eventually ended in recession. Although forecasting the exact date the recession would begin was

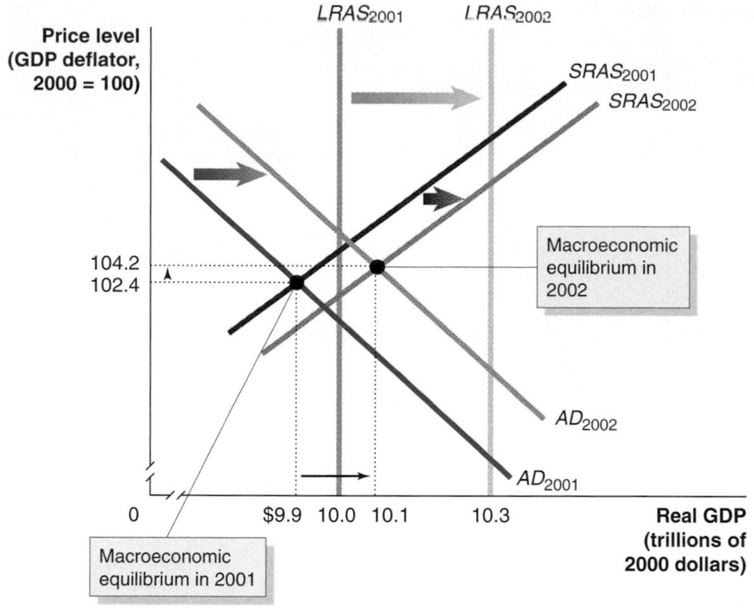

FIGURE 12-10

Using Dynamic Aggregate Demand and Aggregate Supply to Understand the Recovery from the 2001 Recession

Between 2001 and 2002, *AD* shifted to the right but not by nearly enough to offset the shift to the right of *LRAS,* which reflected the increase in potential real GDP from \$10.0 trillion to \$10.3 trillion. Although real GDP increased from \$9.9 trillion in 2001 to \$10.1 trillion in 2002, this still was far below the potential real GDP, shown by $LRAS_{2002}$. As a result, the unemployment rate rose from 4.7 percent in 2001 to 5.8 percent in 2002. Because the increase in aggregate demand was small, the price level increased only from 102.4 in 2001 to 104.2 in 2002, so the inflation rate for 2002 was only 1.8 percent.

very difficult, it was inevitable that the expansion would end, just as all previous expansions had. Some economists were surprised, however, at the weakness of the expansion that began when the recession ended in November 2001. Figure 12-10 illustrates the changes in the economy from 2001 to 2002 and shows that the economy remained well below potential GDP during 2002.

In Figure 12-10, the *AD* curve shifts to the right much less than does the *LRAS* curve. As a result, the price level increases only from 102.4 in 2001 to 104.2 in 2002, for a very low inflation rate of 1.8 percent. Real GDP increases only from \$9.9 trillion to \$10.1 trillion, which is below the potential level of \$10.3 trillion, shown by $LRAS_{2002}$. Not surprisingly, the unemployment rate actually rose from 4.7 percent in 2001 to 5.8 percent in 2002.

The increase in aggregate demand during 2002 was weak because the factors that had caused the recession continued to weigh on the economy. Stock prices did not begin to rise significantly until 2003. Many firms still did not feel the need to increase investment spending, particularly on information technology, on which they had spent heavily during the late 1990s. Uncertainty remained high as the federal government continued the war on terrorism and prepared for the invasion of Iraq. Finally, each week during 2002 seemed to bring the revelation of a new corporate accounting scandal. It is not surprising, as we saw at the beginning of this chapter, that Caterpillar and other firms were still experiencing slow sales during 2002.

12-2 Making the Connection

Does Rising Productivity Growth Reduce Employment?

We saw in Chapter 10 that growth in output per worker—labor productivity—is the key to rising living standards over the long run. But if firms can produce more output with the same number of workers, are they less likely to hire additional workers? Some observers argued that this was happening during 2002 and 2003 as productivity and real GDP rose, yet employment grew very little. The following two charts show that productivity—measured as total output of all nonfarm businesses produced per hour worked—did in fact grow very rapidly during 2002 and 2003, and that employment as measured by the Bureau of Labor Statistics' establishment survey declined.

In 2002–2003, companies like Harley-Davidson expanded output without expanding employment.

Productivity Growth, 1994–2004

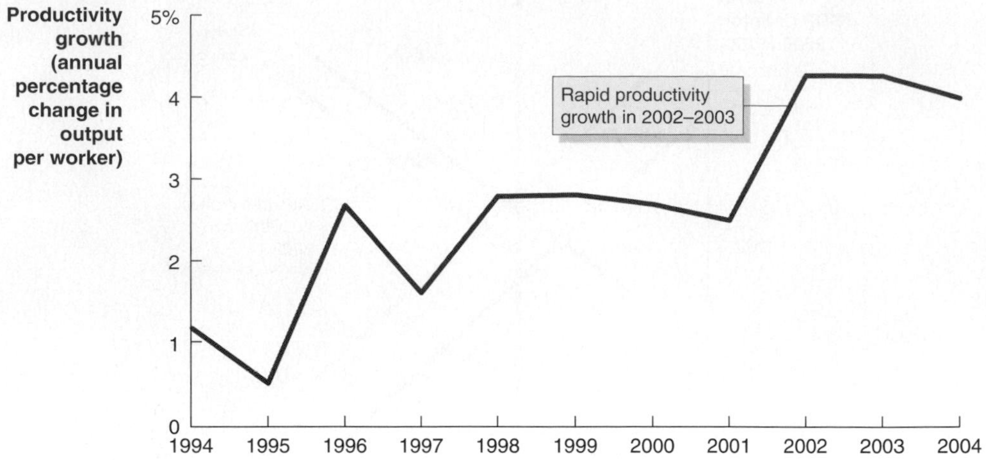

Employment, January 1994–December 2004

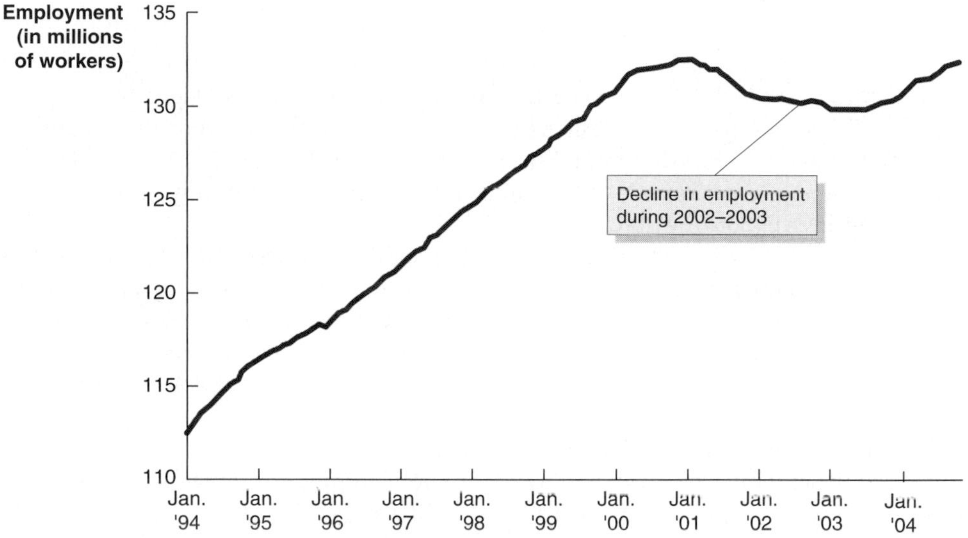

Source (both charts): Bureau of Labor Statistics; employment data from the establishment survey.

In the dynamic aggregate demand and aggregate supply model, the higher the growth of productivity during a year, the further to the right the *LRAS* and *SRAS* curves will shift. But rising productivity also leads to rising incomes, in part because rising output per worker makes it possible for firms to pay higher wages. These rising incomes raise consumption spending and allow the *AD* curve to shift to the right by enough to maintain GDP at its potential level. In 2002–2003, however, the economy was still operating below potential GDP and many firms appeared reluctant to expand employment as rapidly as typically happens during an economic recovery. In these circumstances, rising productivity made it possible for at least some firms to expand output without expanding employment. Most economists agree that rapid productivity growth probably played some role in the slow employment growth of 2002 and 2003, but the effect was only temporary. We know that over the long run, the level of employment is determined by population growth and by factors—such as the level of retirement benefits and government unemployment insurance payments—that affect the fraction of the population in the labor force. The level of employment is not determined in the long run by the rate of productivity growth. In fact, a report from the Federal Reserve Bank of Dallas noted that between 1979 and 2003 the level of productivity in the U.S. economy increased by 67 percent, while during the same period 40 million new jobs were created. That the effect of productivity growth on employment is only temporary was demonstrated in 2004, as productivity growth remained high, but employment began to increase more rapidly.

Source: Federal Reserve Bank of Dallas, *2003 Annual Report.*

The More Rapid Recovery of 2003–2004

The recovery from the recession of 2001 accelerated in the second half of 2003 and through 2004. For several reasons, aggregate demand increased more rapidly than it had during 2002 and early 2003. Low interest rates spurred spending on new houses and helped increase investment spending by firms. Tax cuts increased both consumption and investment spending. Rising stock prices contributed to increased consumption and investment spending. Finally, the value of the dollar declined against most foreign currencies, which helped exports.

Figure 12-11 shows the results of the more rapid increase in aggregate demand during 2004. In 2003, real GDP was 3.7 percent below its potential level, while the unemployment rate was 6.0 percent. The figure shows that the large shift in aggregate demand during 2004 led to an increase in real GDP from \$10.3 trillion to \$10.8 trillion. This level was still below potential real GDP of \$11.0 trillion, but the gap had narrowed to 1.8 percent. As a result, the unemployment rate fell from 6.0 percent to 5.2 percent. The rapid increase in aggregate demand caused a rise in the inflation rate. The price level increased from 106.3 in 2003 to 109.1 in 2004, for an inflation rate of 2.6 percent. This was higher than the inflation rate of 2.0 percent during 2003.

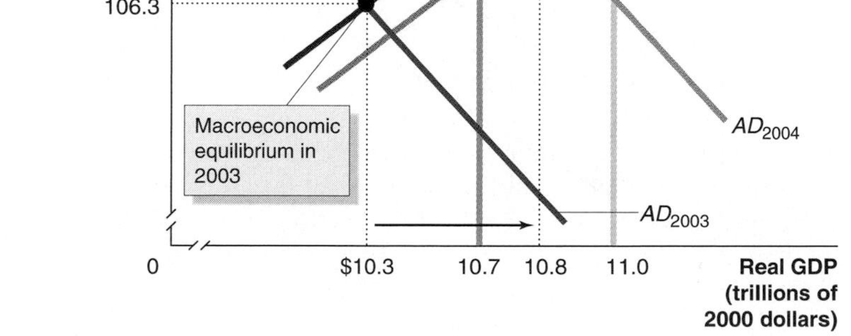

FIGURE 12-11

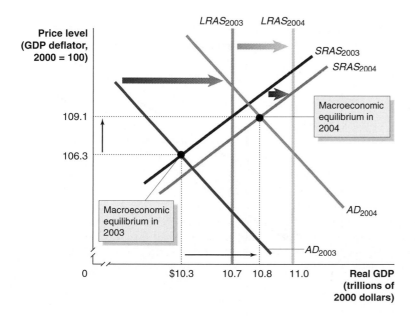

Using Dynamic Aggregate Demand and Aggregate Supply to Understand the More Rapid Recovery of 2003–2004

The figure shows that the large shift in aggregate demand during 2004 led to an increase in real GDP from \$10.3 trillion to \$10.8 trillion. This was still below the potential real GDP of \$11.0 trillion, but the gap had narrowed to 1.8 percent. As a result, the unemployment rate fell from 6.0 percent to 5.2 percent. The rapid increase in aggregate demand did cause a rise in the inflation rate. The price level increased from 106.3 in 2003 to 109.1 in 2004, for an inflation rate of 2.6 percent.

SOLVED PROBLEM 12-2

④ LEARNING OBJECTIVE

Use the dynamic aggregate demand and aggregate supply model to analyze macroeconomic conditions.

Showing the Oil Shock of 1974–1975 on a Dynamic Aggregate Demand and Aggregate Supply Graph

The 1974–1975 recession clearly illustrates how a supply shock affects the economy. Following the Arab–Israeli War of 1973, the Organization of Petroleum Exporting Countries (OPEC) increased the price of a barrel of oil from less than $3 to more than $10. Use this information and the statistics in the following table to draw a dynamic aggregate demand and aggregate supply graph showing macroeconomic equilibrium for 1974 and 1975. Assume that the aggregate demand curve did not shift between 1974 and 1975. Provide a brief explanation of your graph.

	ACTUAL REAL GDP	POTENTIAL REAL GDP	PRICE LEVEL
1974	$4.32 trillion	$4.35 trillion	34.7
1975	$4.31 trillion	$4.50 trillion	38.0

Source: U.S. Department of Commerce, Bureau of Economic Analysis.

Solving the Problem:

Step 1: Review the chapter material. This problem is about using the dynamic aggregate demand and aggregate supply model, so you may want to review the section "A Dynamic Aggregate Demand and Aggregate Supply Model," which begins on page 388.

Step 2: Use the information in the table to draw the graph. We need to draw five curves: *AD*, *SRAS*, and *LRAS* for both 1974 and 1975 (the *AD* curve will be the same for both years). We know that the two *LRAS* curves will be vertical lines at the values given for potential GDP in the table. Because of the large supply shock, we know that the *SRAS* curve shifted to the left. We are instructed to assume that the *AD* curve did not shift. Your graph should look like this:

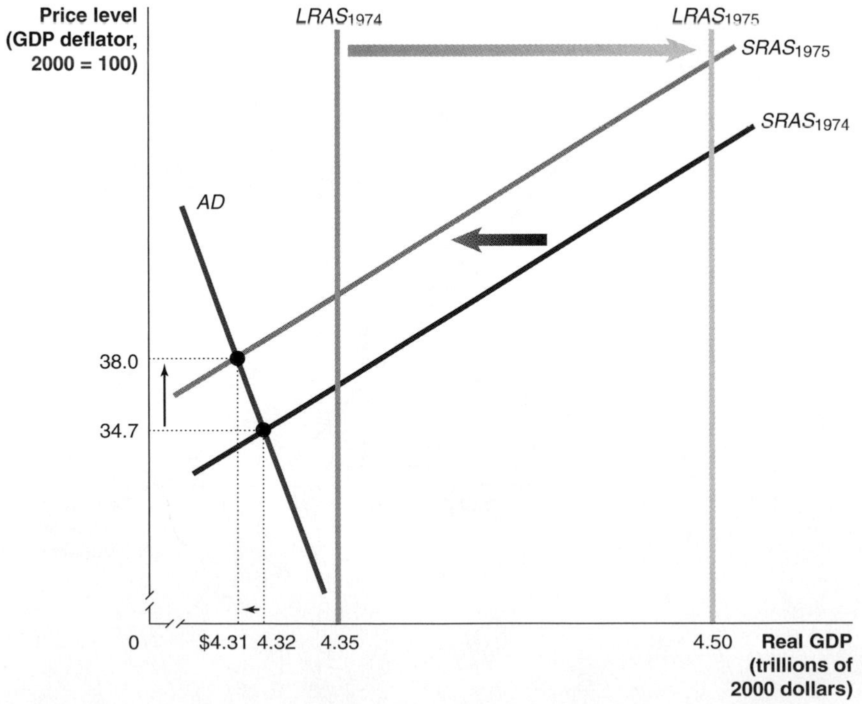

Step 3: Explain your graph. $LRAS_{1974}$ and $LRAS_{1975}$ are at the levels of potential real GDP for each year. Macroeconomic equilibrium for 1974 occurs where the *AD* curve intersects the $SRAS_{1974}$ curve, with real GDP of $4.32 trillion and a price level of 34.7. Macroeconomic equilibrium for 1975 occurs where the *AD* curve intersects the $SRAS_{1975}$ curve, with real GDP of $4.31 trillion and a price level of 38.0.

Extra Credit: As a result of the supply shock, the economy moved from an equilibrium output just below potential GDP in 1974 (the recession actually began right at the end of 1973) to an equilibrium well below potential GDP in 1975. With real GDP in 1975 about 4.2 percent below its potential level, the unemployment rate soared from 5.6 percent in 1974 to 8.5 percent in 1975.

YOUR TURN: **For more practice, do related problems 13 and 15 on pages 400–401 at the end of this chapter.**

Conclusion

Chapter 3 demonstrated the power of the microeconomic model of demand and supply in explaining how the prices and quantities of individual products are determined. This chapter showed that we need a different model to explain the behavior of the whole economy. We saw that the macroeconomic model of aggregate demand and aggregate supply explains fluctuations in real GDP and the price level.

One of the great disagreements among economists and political leaders is whether the federal government should intervene to try to reduce fluctuations in real GDP and keep the unemployment and inflation rates low. We explore this important issue in Chapters 14 and 15, but first, in the next chapter we consider the role money plays in the economy.

Read *An Inside Look* on the next page to learn how real GDP in Japan responded to increases in net exports.

An Inside Look Construction Company Komatsu Benefits from Exports to China

FINANCIAL TIMES, MARCH 2, 2004

The Recovery Is Still Fragile

a . . . Anyone would think Japan had become the world's latest tiger economy. According to official figures, gross domestic product rose 7 percent in real, deflation-adjusted terms in the fourth quarter–a rate of growth not seen since the intoxicating 1980s. The January trade surplus, swollen by shipments to China, rose almost fivefold from last year as exporters brushed aside the effects of a strengthening yen.

Moreover, the benefits of an export-led recovery are beginning to filter into the job market. Unemployment has fallen from a postwar peak of 5.5 percent in January last year to 4.9 percent in December. Corporate profits have surged, while wages have stabilized after years of decline. . . .

The Nikkei stock average, which has clawed its way back to 11,300, is 50 percent above last April's post-bubble lows. . . . Last year's talk of spiralling deflation, or an imminent collapse of the financial system under the weight of non-performing loans, now seems like absurd scaremongering. . . .

Indeed, with many reasons for caution it would be foolish to take recent headline growth figures at face value. But some things really do seem different this time around.

For a start, unlike the recoveries of the 1990s, this one has not been started by lavish government spending. Although the annual budget deficit is still running at a worrying 8 percent of GDP, the government has been paring discretionary spending and raising taxes to pay for non-discretionary items such as social security.

In the absence of government-led stimulation, companies have been taking matters into their own hands. Masamoto Yashiro, chairman of Shinsei, a rescued bank whose successful initial public offering in Tokyo last month has become symbolic of corporate revitalization, says many Japanese companies have spent several years quietly getting back into shape.

b According to Mr Yashiro, years after the bubble burst most businesses were still postponing tough decisions, convinced that asset prices would recover and that their problems would float away. Since the late 1990s, he says, prodded by the need to compete with China and by the realization that Japan's years of easy growth were over, they had been disposing of non-core businesses, shifting production abroad and paying down borrowings. Merrill Lynch estimates that, at this rate, corporate debt will be back to pre-bubble levels within two years.

. . . Japan's recovery, like those before it, leans heavily on exports. It is true about two-thirds of recent growth has been accounted for by private investment. But most economists say this is almost overwhelmingly due to capital investment by export-oriented companies.

ING calculates that as much as 80 percent of the export improvement is thanks to China, which has surpassed the US as Japan's biggest trading partner. Some of those shipments may be supplying Japanese factories in China and therefore ultimately destined for the US. In any case, Japan remains extremely vulnerable to an external shock, whether it be a slowdown in the US or in China itself. . . .

Three times a year, Komatsu, the world's second largest construction equipment maker, holds an auction for used machinery in the Japanese ports of Yokohama, Kobe and Nagoya . . .

c Komatsu's used machines–remnants from Japan's heady bubble-era building days–account for nearly half of its machines in use in China, which has a voracious appetite for goods related to infrastructure. By 2005, Komatsu's sales to China are expected to reach ¥107bn (Dollars 980m, Pounds 530m, Euros 790m), more than double the ¥45.2bn achieved in 2002.

Throughout Japan, industries including construction machinery, steel and shipbuilding, which until recently had been sitting on idle capacity, are suddenly worried that they will not be able to meet China's seemingly endless demand.

The value of Japanese goods exported to China rose 33.8 percent in January compared with the same period a year ago, while shipments to the US, until recently Japan's biggest trading partner, fell 5.4 percent. . . .

Key Points in the Article

This article discusses the strong performance of the Japanese economy at the end of 2003. It highlights the effect of increasing exports on aggregate demand. It also mentions that capital spending, or investment spending, which is another component of aggregate demand, has been increasing in Japan.

Analyzing the News

a Japanese economic growth from the late 1940s through the 1980s had been very rapid. This rapid growth had allowed Japan to make the transition to becoming an industrialized, high-income country. But during the 1990s, the growth rate of the Japanese economy slowed, and real GDP in Japan was below its potential GDP level for most of the 1990s and early 2000s. We will discuss further in Chapters 14 and 15 why this happened. A large part of the rapid growth Japan experienced during 2003 occurred due to increases in the net export component of aggregate demand. Net exports rose despite the fact that the yen was increasing in value. As we saw in Chapter 8, an increasing exchange rate will usually cause net exports to fall. In this case, however, the Chinese economy was growing so rapidly that demand for Japanese products grew despite the rising value of the yen.

b Although Japan was experiencing an "export-led recovery," investment spending was also increasing. During the 1990s and early 2000s, investment spending had grown slowly. Many corporations had borrowed heavily to finance expansion during the 1980s, and had been unwilling to consider additional investment until their debt had been reduced.

We can use the aggregate demand and aggregate supply model to analyze what happened to the Japanese economy during 2002 and 2003. Information from the article and from Japanese government statistics is used in Figure 1. The figure shows that in 2002 the economy was in short-run macroeconomic equilibrium with real GDP (measured in Japanese yen) of ¥533 trillion and a price level of 93.5. During 2003, aggregate demand, short-run aggregate supply, and long-run aggregate supply all shifted to the right. Equilibrium real GDP rose to ¥547 trillion. At the same time, the price level actually fell to 91.1. So, during 2003 the Japanese economy experienced growth in real GDP of 2.6 percent, but *deflation* of 2.6 percent. Because deflation continued several years, wages and other costs fell, which caused aggregate supply to shift to the right by more than it would have had workers and firms expected a constant price level.

c Komatsu is the second-largest manufacturer of construction equipment in the world, behind Caterpillar. Komatsu is expected to more than double its sales to China by 2005, compared with 2002. Construction companies, such as Komatsu and Caterpillar, usually do well in rapidly growing economies, particularly if economic growth is accompanied by population growth. The very slow growth of the Japanese population has been a disadvantage for Komatsu, but has been at least partially offset by the firm's access to the Chinese economy.

Thinking Critically ABOUT POLICY

1. Briefly explain whether investment spending is likely to increase more rapidly in a country with a rapidly growing population, or in a country with a slowly growing population. Does your answer depend on whether the country is a high-income industrial country or a low-income developing country?
2. In 2004, the value of the dollar was fixed against the Chinese yuan at a constant rate of about 8.3 yuan to the dollar. Suppose that the government of China decided to stop fixing the value of the yuan versus the dollar, and that as a result the value of the yuan rose against the dollar. Would this be good news or bad news for Caterpillar? For Komatsu?

Source: David Pilling and Mariko Sanchanta, "The Recovery Is Still Fragile," *Financial Times*, March 2, 2004. Used with permission of Financial Times.

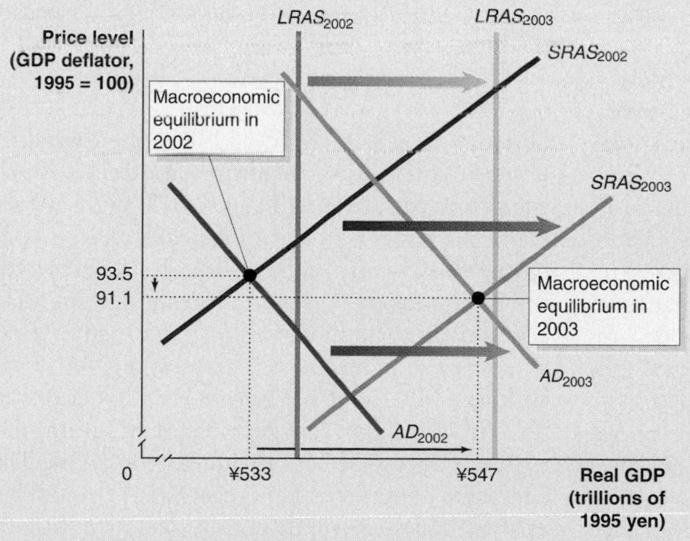

Figure 1: Japanese economic expansion during 2003.

SUMMARY

LEARNING OBJECTIVE ① Discuss the determinants of aggregate demand, and distinguish between a movement along the aggregate demand curve and a shift of the curve. The *aggregate demand and aggregate supply model* enables us to explain short-run fluctuations in real GDP and the price level. The *aggregate demand curve (AD)* shows the relationship between the price level and the quantity of real GDP demanded by households, firms, and the government. The *short-run aggregate supply curve (SRAS)* shows the relationship in the short run between the price level and the quantity of real GDP supplied by firms. The *long-run aggregate supply curve* shows the relationship in the long run between the price level and the quantity of real GDP supplied. The four components of aggregate demand are consumption *(C)*, investment *(I)*, government purchases *(G)*, and net exports *(NX)*. The aggregate demand curve is downward sloping because a decline in the price level causes consumption, investment, and net exports to increase. If the price level changes but all else remains constant, the economy will move up or down a stationary aggregate demand curve. If any variable other than the price level changes, the aggregate demand curve will shift. The variables that cause the aggregate demand curve to shift are divided into three categories: changes in government policies, changes in the expectations of households and firms, and changes in foreign variables.

LEARNING OBJECTIVE ② Discuss the determinants of aggregate supply, and distinguish between a movement along the short-run aggregate supply curve and a shift of the curve. The long-run aggregate supply curve is a vertical line because in the long run real GDP is always at its potential level and is unaffected by the price level. The short-run aggregate supply curve slopes upward because workers and firms fail to predict accurately the future price level. The three main explanations of why this failure results in an upward-sloping aggregate supply curve are: (1) contracts make wages and prices "sticky," (2) businesses often adjust wages slowly, and (3) menu costs make some prices sticky. If the price level changes but all else remains constant, the economy will move up or down a stationary aggregate supply curve. If any variable other than the price level changes, the aggregate supply curve will shift. The aggregate supply curve shifts as a result of increases in the labor force and the capital stock, technological change, expected increases or decreases in the future price level, adjustments of workers and firms to errors in past expectations about the price level, and unexpected increases or decreases in the price of an important raw material.

LEARNING OBJECTIVE ③ Use the aggregate demand and aggregate supply model to illustrate the difference between short-run and long-run macroeconomic equilibrium. In long-run macroeconomic equilibrium, the aggregate demand and short-run aggregate supply curves intersect at a point *on* the long-run aggregate supply curve. In short-run macroeconomic equilibrium, the aggregate demand and short-run aggregate supply curves often intersect at a point *off* the long-run aggregate supply curve. An automatic mechanism drives the economy to long-run equilibrium. If short-run equilibrium occurs at a point below potential real GDP, wages and prices will fall and the short-run aggregate supply curve will shift to the right until potential GDP is restored. If short-run equilibrium occurs at a point beyond potential real GDP, wages and prices will rise and the short-run aggregate supply curve will shift to the left until potential GDP is restored. Real GDP can be temporarily above or below its potential level, either because of shifts in the aggregate demand curve or because supply shocks lead to shifts in the aggregate supply curve.

LEARNING OBJECTIVE ④ Use the dynamic aggregate demand and aggregate supply model to analyze macroeconomic conditions. To make the aggregate demand and aggregate supply model more realistic, we need to make it *dynamic* by incorporating three facts that were left out of the basic model: (1) Potential real GDP increases continually, shifting the long-run aggregate supply curve to the right. (2) During most years, aggregate demand will be shifting to the right. (3) Except during periods when workers and firms expect high rates of inflation, the aggregate supply curve will be shifting to the right. The dynamic aggregate demand and aggregate supply model allows us to analyze macroeconomic conditions, including the recovery from the 2001 recession.

KEY TERMS

Aggregate demand and aggregate supply model 372
Aggregate demand curve (*AD*) 372
Long-run aggregate supply curve (*LRAS*) 378
Menu costs 381
Short-run aggregate supply curve (*SRAS*) 372
Stagflation 388
Supply shock 383

REVIEW QUESTIONS

1. Explain the three reasons the aggregate demand curve (*AD*) slopes downward.
2. What are the differences between the *AD* curve and the demand curve for an individual product, such as apples?
3. What are the variables that cause the *AD* curve to shift? For each variable, identify whether an increase in that variable will cause the *AD* curve to shift to the right or to the left.
4. Explain why the long-run aggregate supply curve (*LRAS*) is vertical.
5. What variables cause the long-run aggregate supply curve to shift? For each variable, identify whether an increase in that variable will cause the *LRAS* to shift to the right or to the left.
6. Why does the short-run aggregate supply curve (*SRAS*) slope upward?
7. What variables cause the *SRAS* curve to shift? For each variable, identify whether an increase in that variable will cause the *SRAS* curve to shift to the right or to the left.
8. What are menu costs? What is their macroeconomic significance?
9. What is a supply shock? Why might a supply shock lead to stagflation?
10. Why are the long-run effects of an increase in aggregate demand on price and output different from the short-run effects?
11. What are the key differences between the basic aggregate demand and aggregate supply model and the dynamic aggregate demand and aggregate supply model?
12. In the dynamic aggregate demand and aggregate supply model, what is the result of aggregate demand increasing faster than potential real GDP? What is the result of aggregate demand increasing slower than potential GDP?

PROBLEMS AND APPLICATIONS

Please visit **www.prenhall.com/hubbard** *for solutions to the even-numbered problems as well as multiple-choice and true or false self-assessment quizzes.*

1. Explain how each of the following events would affect the aggregate demand curve.
   a. An increase in the price level
   b. An increase in government purchases
   c. Higher state income taxes
   d. Higher interest rates
   e. Faster income growth in other countries
2. Explain how each of the following events would affect the long-run aggregate supply curve.
   a. A higher price level
   b. An increase in the labor force
   c. An increase in the quantity of capital goods
   d. Technological change occurs
3. Explain how each of the following events would affect the short-run aggregate supply curve.
   a. A higher price level
   b. An increase in what the price level is expected to be in the future
   c. The price level is currently higher than expected
   d. An unexpected increase in the price of an important raw material
   e. An increase in the labor force
4. **[Related to *Don't Let This Happen To You!*]** A student was asked to draw an aggregate demand and aggregate supply graph to illustrate the effect of an increase in aggregate supply. The student drew the following graph:

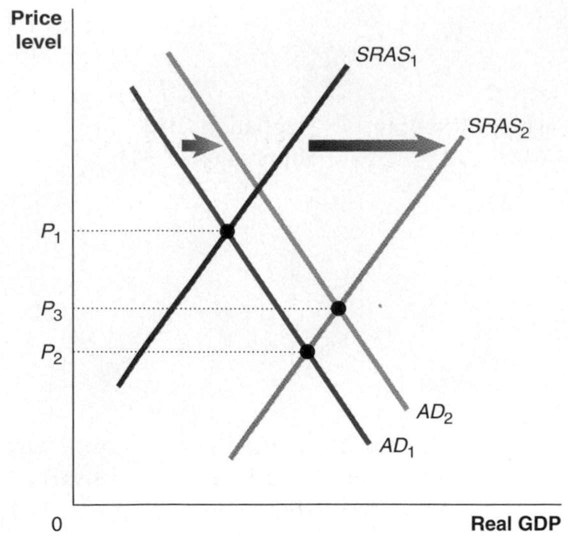

The student explained the graph as follows:

> An increase in aggregate supply causes a shift from $SRAS_1$ to $SRAS_2$. Because this shift in the aggregate supply curve results in a lower price level, consumption, investment, and net exports will increase. This change causes the aggregate demand curve to shift to the right from AD_1 to AD_2. We know that real GDP will increase, but we can't be sure whether the price level will rise or fall because that depends on whether the aggregate supply curve or the aggregate demand curve has shifted farther to the right. I assume that aggregate supply shifts out farther than aggregate demand, so I show the final price level, P_3, as being lower than the initial price level, P_1.

Explain whether you agree or disagree with the student's analysis. Be careful to explain exactly what—if anything—you find wrong with this analysis.

5. **[Related to *Solved Problem 12-1*]** Explain whether each of the following will cause a shift of the *AD* curve or a movement along the *AD* curve.
   a. Firms become more optimistic and increase their spending on machinery and equipment.
   b. The federal government increases taxes in an attempt to reduce a budget deficit.
   c. The U.S. economy experiences 4-percent inflation.
6. Suppose that workers and firms could always predict next year's price level with perfect accuracy. Briefly explain whether in these circumstances the *SRAS* curve still slopes upward.
7. Workers and firms often enter into contracts that fix prices or wages, sometimes for years at a time. If the price level turns out to be higher or lower than was expected when the contract was signed, one party to the contract will lose out. Briefly explain why, despite knowing this, workers and firms still sign long-term contracts.
8. A newspaper article published in 2004 noted, "About 50 percent of U.S. Steel's domestic production is tied up right now in long-term contracts pegged below market value price."
   a. Why would U.S. Steel have entered into contracts to sell steel below the market price? (Hint: Is it likely that these contracts were negotiated before 2004?)
   b. What impact is U.S. Steel selling steel below the current market price likely to have on its production and on the production of companies that buy its steel?

   Source: Charles Sheehan, "Happy Days Are Here Again for U.S. Steel Corp.," (Allentown, PA) *Morning Call*, November 28, 2004.
9. Suppose the price of a barrel of oil increases from \$50 to \$70. Use a basic aggregate demand and aggregate supply diagram to show the short-run and long-run effects on the economy.
10. Draw a basic aggregate demand and aggregate supply graph (with *LRAS* constant) showing the economy in long-run equilibrium.
    a. Now assume that there is an increase in aggregate demand. Show the resulting short-run equilibrium on your diagram. Explain how the economy adjusts back to long-run equilibrium.
    b. Now assume that there is an unexpected increase in the price of an important raw material. Show the resulting short-run equilibrium on your diagram. Explain how the economy adjusts back to long-run equilibrium.
11. Many economists believe that some wages and prices are "sticky downward," meaning that these wages and prices increase quickly when demand is increasing but decrease slowly, if at all, when demand is decreasing. Discuss the consequences of this for the automatic mechanism that brings the economy back to potential GDP after an increase in aggregate demand. Would your answer change if aggregate demand decreased rather than increased? Explain.
12. Draw a dynamic aggregate demand and aggregate supply graph showing the economy moving from potential GDP in 2006 to potential GDP in 2007, with no inflation. Your graph should contain the *AD, SRAS,* and *LRAS* curves for both 2006 and 2007 and should indicate the short-run macroeconomic equilibrium for each year and the directions in which the curves have shifted. Identify what must happen to have growth during 2007 without inflation.
13. **[Related to *Solved Problem 12-2*]** Consider the information in the following table for the first two years of the Great Depression (the values for real GDP are in 2000 dollars):

YEAR	ACTUAL REAL GDP	POTENTIAL REAL GDP	PRICE LEVEL
1929	$865.2 billion	$865.2 billion	12.0
1930	$790.7 billion	$895.7 billion	11.5

Source: U.S. Department of Commerce, Bureau of Economic Analysis.

a. What information in the table is different from what we would expect to happen during a recession in the past 50 years?

b. Draw a dynamic aggregate demand and aggregate supply graph to illustrate what happened during these years. Your graph should contain the *AD*, *SRAS*, and *LRAS* curves for both 1929 and 1930 and should indicate the short-run macroeconomic equilibrium for each year and the directions in which the curves have shifted.

14. Consider the data in the following table for the years 1969 and 1970 (the values for real GDP are in 2000 dollars):

YEAR	ACTUAL REAL GDP	POTENTIAL REAL GDP	UNEMPLOYMENT RATE
1969	$3.77 trillion	$3.67 trillion	3.5%
1970	$3.77 trillion	$3.80 trillion	4.9%

Source: U.S. Department of Commerce, Bureau of Economic Analysis.

a. In 1969, actual real GDP was greater than potential real GDP. Explain how this is possible.

b. Even though real GDP in 1970 was the same as real GDP in 1969, the unemployment rate increased substantially from 1969 to 1970. Why did this increase in unemployment occur?

c. Was the inflation rate in 1970 likely to have been higher or lower than the inflation rate in 1969? Does your answer depend on whether the recession was caused by a change in a component of aggregate demand or by a supply shock?

15. **[Related to *Solved Problem 12-2*]** Look again at Solved Problem 12-2 on the supply shock of 1974–1975 on pages 394–395. In the table, the price level for 1974 is given as 34.7 and the price level for 1975 is given as 38.0. The values for the price level are well below 100. Does this indicate that inflation must have been low during these years? Briefly explain.

16. Use the following graph to answer the questions:

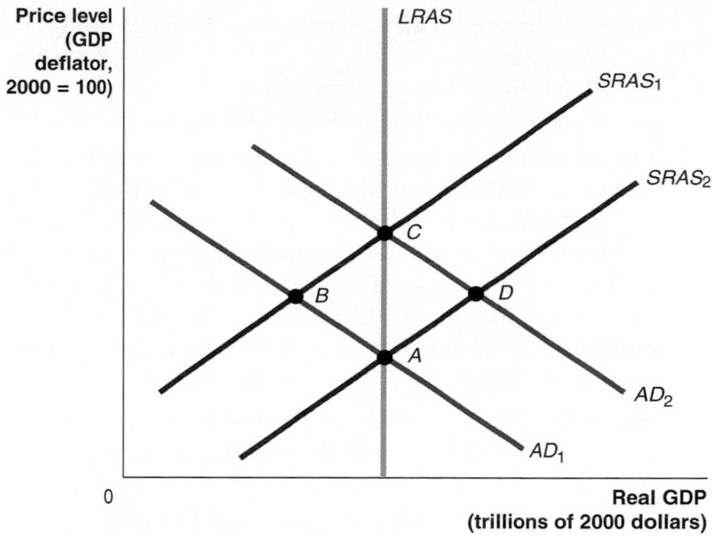

a. Which of points *A*, *B*, *C*, or *D* can represent a long-run equilibrium?

b. Suppose initially the economy is at point *A*. If aggregate demand increases from AD_1 to AD_2, which point represents the economy's short-run equilibrium? Which point represents the eventual long-run equilibrium? Briefly explain how the economy adjusts from the short-run equilibrium to the long-run equilibrium.

17. Suppose the economy moves from point *A* in year 1 to point *B* in year 2. Using the following graph, briefly explain your answers to each of the questions.

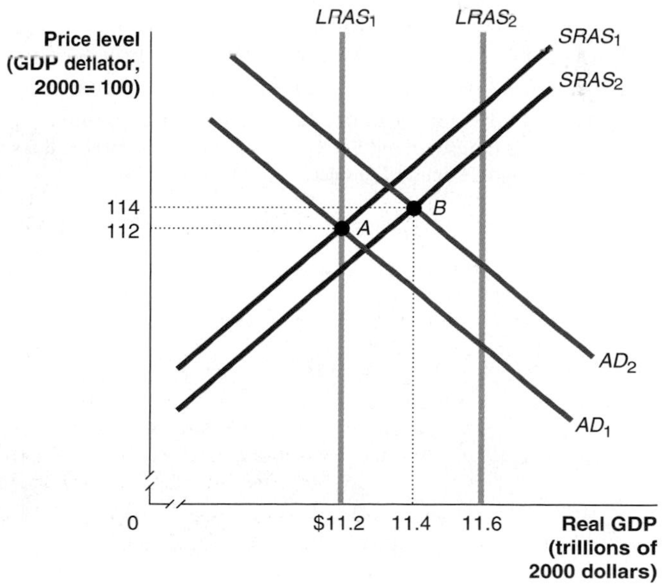

a. What is the growth rate in potential real GDP from year 1 to year 2?
b. Is the unemployment rate in year 2 higher or lower than in year 1?
c. What is the inflation rate in year 2?
d. What is the growth rate of real GDP in year 2?

18. Explain whether you agree or disagree with the following statement: "The dynamic aggregate demand and aggregate supply model predicts that a recession caused by a decline in *AD* will cause the inflation rate to fall. I know that the 2001 recession was caused by a fall in *AD*, but the inflation rate was not lower after the recession. The prices of most products were definitely higher in 2002 than they were in 2001, so the inflation rate could not have fallen."

19. An economist at the Federal Reserve Bank of St. Louis wrote the following about the recovery from the 2001 recession:

> [Since the end of the recession] real business fixed investment (BFI)—expenditures on structures, equipment and software—has declined at a 2.2 percent annual rate. By contrast, in the first four quarters of the typical recovery, real BFI *increases* a little more than 8 percent.

Why didn't investment spending increase as much as it normally does in the year following the end of the 2001 recession?
Source: Kevin L. Kliesen, "Waiting for the Investment Boom? It Might Be a While," Federal Reserve Bank of St. Louis, *National Economic Trends*, May 2003.

20. According to an article published in *Business Week* in October 2002, "The stock market plunge is weighing heavily on both businesses and consumers." Why would a decline in stock prices "weigh heavily" on businesses and consumers? What were the consequences of this for the economy?
Source: James C. Cooper and Kathleen Madigan, "Consumers: Still Some Pluses among the Minuses," *Business Week*, October 21, 2002.

21. An article in the *New York Times* in August 2003 stated the following:

> [A] cutback in business spending when the Internet and stock market bubbles burst brought on the recession of 2001 and the prolonged weakness that has existed since then.

a. What does the article mean by "business spending"?
b. What does it mean by the "Internet and stock market bubbles"?
c. Why would the bursting of these bubbles affect business spending?

Source: Louis Uchitelle and Jennifer Bayot, "Business Spending Helps to Offset Lag in Refinancing," *New York Times*, August 9, 2003.

22. The following excerpt is from an article in the *New York Times:*

> The number of Americans living below the poverty line increased by more than 1.3 million [during 2002], even though the economy technically edged out of recession during the same period.

Briefly discuss why poverty increased during 2002 even though the economy was in the expansion phase of the business cycle.
Source: Lynette Clemetson, "Census Shows Ranks of Poor Rose by 1.3 Million," *New York Times*, September 3, 2003.

23. **[Related to the *Chapter Opener*]** In the opening to this chapter, we saw that at the end of 2003, employment at Caterpillar was still 10 percent below what it had been at the beginning of 2001. Some of the employment reduction was caused by a reduction in Caterpillar's sales. But Caterpillar had also implemented new technologies that increased productivity and required fewer workers. Briefly discuss why firms might be likely to implement new technologies during a period when demand is falling, or only increasing slowly.

Macroeconomic Schools of Thought

Appendix

Macroeconomics as a separate field of economics began with the publication in 1936 of John Maynard Keynes's book, *The General Theory of Employment, Interest, and Money.* Keynes, an economist at the University of Cambridge in England, was attempting to explain the devastating Great Depression of the 1930s. As we discussed in Chapter 11, real GDP in the United States declined by more than 25 percent between 1929 and 1933 and did not return to its potential level until the United States entered World War II in 1941. The unemployment rate soared to 25 percent by 1933 and did not return to its 1929 level until 1942. Keynes developed the aggregate demand and aggregate supply model to explain these facts. The widespread acceptance during the 1930s and 1940s of Keynes's model became known as the **Keynesian revolution.**

In fact, the aggregate demand and aggregate supply model remains the most widely accepted approach to analyzing macroeconomic issues. Because the model has been modified significantly from Keynes's day, many economists who use the model today refer to themselves as *new Keynesians.* The new Keynesians emphasize the importance of the stickiness of wages and prices in explaining fluctuations in real GDP. A significant number of economists, however, dispute whether the aggregate demand and aggregate supply model, as we have discussed it in this chapter, is the best way to analyze macroeconomic issues. These alternative *schools of thought* use models that differ significantly from the standard aggregate demand and aggregate supply model. We can briefly consider each of the three major alternative models:

1. The monetarist model
2. The new classical model
3. The real business cycle model

The Monetarist Model

The monetarist model—also known as the neo-Quantity Theory of Money model—was developed beginning in the 1940s by Milton Friedman, an economist at the University of Chicago who was awarded the Nobel Prize in Economics in 1976. Friedman argued that the Keynesian approach overstates the amount of macroeconomic instability in the economy. In particular, he argued that the economy will ordinarily be at potential real GDP. In the book *A Monetary History of the United States: 1867–1960,* written with Anna Schwartz, Friedman argued that most fluctuations in real output were caused by fluctuations in the money supply, rather than by fluctuations in consumption spending or investment spending. Friedman and Schwartz argued that the severity of the Great Depression was caused by the Federal Reserve's allowing the quantity of money in the economy to fall by more than 25 percent between 1929 and 1933.

In the United States, the Federal Reserve is responsible for managing the quantity of money. As we will discuss further in Chapter 14, the Federal Reserve has typically focused more on controlling interest rates than on controlling the money supply. Friedman has argued that the Federal Reserve should change its practices and adopt a **monetary growth rule,** which is a plan for increasing the quantity of money at a fixed rate. Friedman believed that adopting a monetary growth rule would reduce fluctuations in real GDP, employment, and inflation.

Friedman's ideas, which are referred to as **monetarism,** attracted significant support during the 1970s and early 1980s, when the economy experienced high rates of unemployment and inflation. The support for monetarism declined during the late

Keynesian revolution The name given to the widespread acceptance during the 1930s and 1940s of John Maynard Keynes's macroeconomic model.

Monetary growth rule A plan for increasing the quantity of money at a fixed rate that does not respond to changes in economic conditions.

Monetarism The macroeconomic theories of Milton Friedman and his followers; particularly the idea that the quantity of money should be increased at a constant rate.

1980s and 1990s, when the unemployment and inflation rates were relatively low. We will discuss the Quantity Theory of Money, which underlies the monetarist model, in Chapter 13.

The New Classical Model

The new classical model was developed in the mid-1970s by a group of economists including Robert Lucas of the University of Chicago, Thomas Sargent of Stanford University, and Robert Barro of Harvard University. Lucas was awarded the Nobel Prize in Economics in 1995. Some of the views held by the new classical macroeconomists are similar to those held by economists before the Great Depression. Keynes referred to the economists before the Great Depression as "classical economists." Like the classical economists, the new classical macroeconomists believe that the economy normally will be at potential real GDP. They also believe that wages and prices adjust quickly to changes in demand and supply. Put another way, they believe the stickiness in wages and prices emphasized by the new Keynesians is unimportant.

Lucas argued that workers and firms have *rational expectations*, meaning that they form their expectations of the future values of economic variables, like the inflation rate, making use of all available information, including information on variables—such as changes in the quantity of money—that might affect aggregate demand. If the actual inflation rate is lower than the expected inflation rate, the actual real wage will be higher than the expected real wage. These higher real wages will lead to a recession because they will cause firms to hire fewer workers and cut back on production. As workers and firms adjust their expectations to the lower inflation rate, the real wage will decline and employment and production will expand, bringing the economy out of recession. The ideas of Lucas and his followers are referred to as the **new classical macroeconomics.** Supporters of the new classical model agree with supporters of the monetarist model that the Federal Reserve should adopt a monetary growth rule. They argue that a monetary growth rule will make it easier for workers and firms to accurately forecast the price level, thereby reducing fluctuations in real GDP.

New classical macroeconomics The macroeconomic theories of Robert Lucas and others, particularly the idea that workers and firms have rational expectations.

The Real Business Cycle Model

Beginning in the 1980s, some economists, including Finn Kydland of Carnegie Mellon University and Edward Prescott of Arizona State University (who shared the Nobel Prize in Economics in 2004), argued that Lucas was correct in assuming that workers and firms formed their expectations rationally and that wages and prices adjust quickly to supply and demand but wrong about the source of fluctuations in real GDP. They argued that fluctuations in real GDP are caused by temporary shocks to productivity. These shocks can be negative, such as a decline in the availability of oil or other raw materials, or positive, such as technological change that makes it possible to produce more output with the same quantity of inputs.

According to this school of thought, shifts in the aggregate demand curve have no impact on real GDP because the short-run aggregate supply curve is vertical. Other schools of thought all believe that the short-run aggregate supply curve is upward sloping and that only the *long-run* aggregate supply curve is vertical. Fluctuations in real GDP occur when a negative productivity shock causes the short-run aggregate supply curve to shift to the left—reducing real GDP—or a positive productivity shock causes the short-run aggregate supply curve to shift to the right—increasing real GDP. Because this model focuses on "real" factors—productivity shocks—rather than changes in the quantity of money to explain fluctuations in real GDP, it is known as the **real business cycle model.**

Real business cycle model A macroeconomic model that focuses on real, rather than monetary, causes of the business cycle.

Karl Marx: Capitalism's Severest Critic

12A-1 Making the Connection

The schools of macroeconomic thought we have discussed in this appendix are considered part of mainstream economic theory because of their acceptance of the market system as the best means of raising living standards in the long run. One quite influential critic of mainstream economic theory was Karl Marx. Marx was born in Trier, Germany, in 1818. After graduating from the University of Berlin in 1841, he began a career as a political journalist and agitator. His political activities caused him to be expelled first from Germany and then from France and Belgium. In 1849 he moved to London, where he spent the remainder of his life.

In 1867, he published the first volume of his greatest work, *Das Kapital.* Marx read closely the most prominent mainstream economists, including Adam Smith, David Ricardo, and John Stuart Mill. But Marx believed that he understood how market systems would evolve in the long run much better than those earlier authors. Marx argued that the market system would eventually be replaced by a Communist economy in which the workers would control production. He believed in the *labor theory of value,* which attributed all of the value of a good or service to the labor that was embodied in it. According to Marx, the owners of businesses—capitalists—did not earn profits by contributing anything of value to the production of goods or services. Instead, capitalists earned profits because their "monopoly of the means of production"—their ownership of factories and machinery—allowed them to exploit workers by paying them wages that were much less than the value of workers' contribution to production.

Karl Marx predicted that a final economic crisis would lead to the collapse of the market system.

Marx argued that wages of workers would be driven to levels that allowed only bare survival. He also argued that small firms would be driven out of business by larger firms, forcing owners of small firms into the working class. Eventually, control of production would be concentrated in the hands of a few firms. These few remaining firms would have difficulty selling the goods they produced to the impoverished masses. A final economic crisis would lead the working classes to rise up, seize control of the economy, and establish Communism. Marx died in 1883 without providing a detailed explanation of how the Communist economy would operate.

Marx had relatively little influence on mainstream thinking in the United States, but several political parties in Europe were guided by his ideas. In 1917, the Bolshevik party seized control of Russia and established the Soviet Union, the first Communist state. Although the Soviet Union was a vicious dictatorship under Vladimir Lenin and his successor, Joseph Stalin, its prestige rose when it avoided the macroeconomic difficulties that plagued the market economies during the 1930s. By the late 1940s, Communist parties also came to power in China, and the countries of Eastern Europe. Eventually, poor economic performance led to the collapse of the Soviet Union and its replacement by a market system. Although the Communist Party remains in power in China, the economy is evolving toward a market system. Today, only North Korea and Cuba have economies that claim to be based on the ideas of Karl Marx.

KEY TERMS

Keynesian Revolution 403
Monetarism 403
Monetary growth rule 403
New classical macroeconomics 404
Real business cycle model 404

chapter thirteen

Money, Banks, and the Federal Reserve System

McDonald's Money Problems in Argentina

➤ The McDonald's Big Mac is one of the most widely available products in the world. McDonald's 30,000 restaurants in 119 countries serve 50 million customers per day. Although some McDonald's restaurants are owned by the firm, many are franchises. A *franchise* is a business with the legal right to sell a good or service in a particular area. When a firm uses franchises, local entrepreneurs are able to buy and run the stores in their area. As McDonald's began expanding to other countries in the late 1960s, it relied on the franchise system. Franchisees in other countries were able to adapt the restaurants to the tastes of [redacted] customers. For example, although all 200 McDonald's restaurants in Argentina offer Big Macs and French fries, they also offer gourmet coffees and other foods not available in the U.S. McDonald's restaurants.

In 2001, McDonald's restaurants in Argentina began to suffer from the macroeconomic problems plaguing that country. Argentina's woes centered on "money." Households and firms had begun to lose faith in the Argentine peso, the country's official money. They believed that the peso would rapidly lose its value, reducing their ability to buy goods and services. Many people converged on banks and tried to withdraw their money so they could either immediately buy goods and services or exchange [redacted]ntine pesos for U.S. dollars. T[redacted]op the outflow of money from the banking system, the government limited the amount of Argentine currency that could be withdrawn to $1,000 per account per month. This action further weakened the economy by reducing the funds households and firms had available to spend. In addition, banks became cautious about making loans, which in turn led to additional reductions in spending. An Argentine doctor was quoted as saying, "Now there's a lack of cash. . . . None of my patients can pay." Another person observed, "The chain of payments has been broken. There are millions of people forced to resort to bartering—an old sweater, anything, for goods just to survive." A cell phone dealer said, "These days, if customers want to pay us in tomatoes, I'll consider making a deal."

During the currency crisis, one Argentine province decided to issue

its own currency, which it called the *patacone*. Because the patacone was not part of Argentina's official currency, there were doubts as to how widely it would be accepted by local firms. McDonald's restaurants in the province decided to accept the new currency as payment for a meal they labeled the "Patacombo": two cheeseburgers, an order of French fries, and a soft drink.

Although the crisis in Argentina eventually passed, confidence in money remains vitally important. When you buy a DVD from a store, you get something of value. You give the store clerk dollar bills, or you might write a check with your name and the name of a bank on it or use a debit card linked to your checking account. These pieces of paper have no value in and of themselves. You and the DVD store owner consider them valuable because others consider them valuable. This confidence and trust are hallmarks of money.

Confidence and trust cannot be taken for granted. As this example from Argentina shows, when households and firms lose faith in an official money, it can harm trade and economic activity in an economy. *An Inside Look* on page 432 discusses how several Latin American countries have moved away from fixing the value of their currencies against the dollar.

Sources: Tony Smith, "Freeze Has Argentines Crying All the Way to the Bank," Associated Press, December 11, 2001, and Matt Moffett, "Unfunny Money," *Wall Street Journal*, August 21, 2001.

LEARNING OBJECTIVES

After studying this chapter, you should be able to:

① Define money and discuss its four functions.

② Discuss the definitions of the money supply used in the United States today.

③ Explain how banks create checking account deposits.

④ Discuss the three policy tools the Federal Reserve uses to manage the money supply.

⑤ Explain the quantity theory of money and use it to explain how high rates of inflation occur.

➤ In this chapter, we will explore the role of money in the economy. We will see how the banking system creates money and what policy tools the Federal Reserve uses to manage the quantity of money. At the end of the chapter, we will explore the link between changes in the quantity of money and changes in the price level. What you learn in this chapter will serve as an important foundation to understanding monetary policy and fiscal policy, which we study in the next three chapters.

① LEARNING OBJECTIVE
Define money and discuss its four functions.

What Is Money and Why Do We Need It?

Money Assets that people are generally willing to accept in exchange for goods and services or for payment of debts.

Asset Anything of value owned by a person or a firm.

Could an economy function without money? We know the answer to this is yes, because there are many historical examples of economies where people traded goods for other goods, rather than using money. For example, a family operating a farm on the American frontier during colonial times might trade a cow for a plow. Most economies, though, use money. What is money? The economic definition of **money** is any asset that people are generally willing to accept in exchange for goods and services or for payment of debts. Recall from Chapter 5 that an **asset** is anything of value owned by a person or a firm. There are many possible kinds of money: In West Africa, at one time cowrie shells served as money. During World War II, prisoners of war used cigarettes as money.

Barter and the Invention of Money

To understand the importance of money, let's consider further the situation in economies that do not use money. These economies, where goods and services are traded directly for other goods and services, are called *barter economies.* Barter economies have a major shortcoming. To illustrate this shortcoming, consider a farmer on the American frontier in colonial days. Suppose the farmer needs another cow and proposes to trade a spare plow to a neighbor for one of the neighbor's cows. If the neighbor does not want the plow, the trade will not happen. For a barter trade to take place between two people, each person must want what the other one has. Economists refer to this requirement as a *double coincidence of wants.* The farmer who wants the cow might eventually be able to obtain one if he first trades with some other neighbor for something the neighbor with the cow wants. However, it may take several trades before the farmer is ultimately able to trade for what the neighbor with the cow wants. Locating several trading partners and making several intermediate trades can take considerable time and energy.

Commodity money A good used as money that also has value independent of its use as money.

The problems with barter provide an incentive to identify a product that most people will accept in exchange for what they have to trade. For example, in colonial times animal skins were very useful in making clothing. The first governor of Tennessee actually received a salary of 1,000 deerskins per year, and the secretary of the treasury received 450 otter skins per year. A good used as money that also has value independent of its use as money is called a **commodity money.** Historically, once a good became widely accepted as money, people who did not have an immediate use for it would be willing to accept it. A colonial farmer—or the governor of Tennessee—might not want a deerskin, but as long as he knew he could use the deerskin to buy other goods and services, he would be willing to accept it in exchange for what he had to sell.

For hundreds of years, the cowrie shell, found on the shores of the Indian and Pacific Oceans, was widely used as money throughout Africa, Asia, and the islands of the South Pacific. The symbol representing the cowrie was adopted as the word for money in ancient China. Cowries continued to be used as money in remote areas of Asia and Africa until the mid-twentieth century.

Trading goods and services is much easier once money becomes available. People only need to sell what they have for money and then use the money to buy what they want. If the colonial family can find someone to buy their plow, they can use the money to buy the cow they want. The family with the cow will accept the money because they know they can use it to buy what they want. Families will be less likely to produce everything or nearly everything they need themselves and more likely to specialize.

Most people in modern economies are highly specialized. They do only one thing—work as a nurse, an accountant, or an engineer—and use the money they earn to buy everything else they need. As we discussed in Chapter 2, people become much more productive by specializing because they can pursue their *comparative advantage.* The high income levels in modern economies are based on the specialization that money makes possible. We can now answer the question, "Why do we need money?" *By making exchange easier, money allows for specialization and higher productivity.*

Money in a World War II Prisoner-of-War Camp

13-1 Making the Connection

R. A. Radford has described his experiences as a captured British soldier in a German prisoner-of-war camp during World War II. At first, the prisoners traded the goods they received in packages from the Red Cross or from relatives at home on a barter basis, but the usual inefficiencies of barter led the prisoners to begin using cigarettes as money. Cigarettes were included in the Red Cross packages. According to Radford, "Everyone, including non-smokers, was willing to sell for cigarettes, using them to buy at another time and place. Cigarettes became the normal currency." Even a labor market developed: "Laundrymen advertised at two cigarettes a garment. Battle-dress [uniform] was scrubbed and pressed and a pair of trousers lent for the interim period for twelve. . . . Odd tailoring and other jobs similarly had their prices."

Prisoners set up small businesses in the camp, using cigarettes for money: "There was a coffee stall owner who sold tea, coffee or cocoa at two cigarettes a cup, buying his raw materials at market prices and hiring labour to gather fuel and to stoke; he actually enjoyed the services of a chartered accountant at one stage." Even a restaurant was organized "where food and hot drinks were sold while a band . . . performed."

In January 1945, near the end of the war, the Red Cross ration of cigarettes was eliminated. Given that some of the prisoners were heavy smokers, most of the rest of the cigarette money disappeared from circulation—a disadvantage of this particular commodity money!—and the camp went back to barter trading until it was liberated by the U.S. 30th Infantry Division in April 1945.

Source: R. A. Radford, "The Economic Organization of a P.O.W. Camp," *Economica,* Vol. 12, November 1945, pp. 189–201.

During World War II, cigarettes were used as money in some prisoner-of-war camps.

The Functions of Money

Anything used as money—whether a deerskin, a cowrie seashell, or a dollar bill—should fulfill the following four functions:

- Medium of exchange
- Unit of account
- Store of value
- Standard of deferred payment

MEDIUM OF EXCHANGE Money serves as a medium of exchange when sellers are willing to accept it in exchange for goods or services. When the local supermarket accepts your $5 bill in exchange for bread and milk, the $5 bill is serving as a medium of exchange. To go back to our earlier example, with a medium of exchange, the farmer with the extra plow does not have to want a cow, and the farmer with the extra cow does not have to want a plow. Both can exchange their products for money and use the money to buy what they want. An economy is more efficient when a single good is recognized as a medium of exchange.

UNIT OF ACCOUNT In a barter system, each good has many prices. A cow may be worth two plows, 20 bushels of wheat, or six axes. Using a good as a medium of exchange confers another benefit: It reduces the need to quote many different prices in trade. Instead of having to quote the price of a single good in terms of many other goods, each good has a single price quoted in terms of the medium of exchange. This function of money gives buyers and sellers a *unit of account,* a way of measuring value in the economy in terms of money. Because the U.S. economy uses dollars as money, each good has a price in terms of dollars.

STORE OF VALUE Money allows value to be stored easily: If you do not use all your accumulated dollars to buy goods and services today, you can hold the rest to use in the future. In fact, a fisherman and a farmer would be better off holding money rather than inventories of their perishable goods. The acceptability of money in future transactions depends on its not losing value over time. Money is not the only store of value. Any asset—shares of Google stock, Treasury bonds, real estate, or Renoir paintings, for example—represents a store of value. Indeed, financial assets offer an important benefit relative to holding money because they generally pay a higher rate of interest or offer the prospect of gains in value. Other assets also have advantages relative to money because they provide services. A house, for example, offers you a place to sleep.

Why, then, would you bother to hold any money? The answer has to do with *liquidity,* or the ease with which a given asset can be converted into the medium of exchange. When money is the medium of exchange, it is the most liquid asset. You incur costs when you exchange other assets for money. When you sell bonds or shares of stock to buy a car, for example, you pay a commission to your broker. If you have to sell your house on short notice to finance an unexpected major medical expense, you pay a commission to a real estate agent and probably have to accept a lower price to exchange the house for money quickly. To avoid such costs, people are willing to hold some of their wealth in the form of money, even though other assets offer a greater return as a store of value.

STANDARD OF DEFERRED PAYMENT Money is also useful because it can serve as a standard of deferred payment in borrowing and lending. Money can facilitate exchange at a *given point in time* by providing a medium of exchange and unit of account. It can facilitate exchange *over time* by providing a store of value and a standard of deferred payment. For example, a furniture maker may be willing to sell a chair to a boat builder now in exchange for money in the future.

How important is it that money be a reliable store of value and standard of deferred payment? People care about how much food, clothing, and other goods and services their dollars will buy. The value of money depends on its purchasing power, which refers to its ability to buy goods and services. Inflation causes a decline in purchasing power because rising prices cause a given amount of money to purchase fewer goods and services. With deflation, the value of money increases because prices are falling.

You have probably heard relatives or friends exclaim, "A dollar doesn't buy what it used to!" They really mean that the purchasing power of a dollar has fallen, that a given amount of money will buy a smaller quantity of the same goods and services in the economy than it once did.

What Can Serve as Money?

Having a medium of exchange helps to make transactions easier, allowing the economy to work more smoothly. The next logical question is this: What can serve as money? That is, which assets should be used as the medium of exchange? We saw earlier that an asset must, at a minimum, be generally accepted as payment to serve as money. In practical terms, however, it must be even more.

There are five criteria that make a good suitable to use as a medium of exchange:

1. The good must be *acceptable* to (that is, usable by) most traders.
2. It should be of *standardized quality* so that any two units are identical.

3. It should be *durable* so that value is not lost by spoilage.
4. It should be *valuable* relative to its weight so that amounts large enough to be useful in trade can be easily transported.
5. The medium of exchange should be *divisible* because different goods are valued differently.

Dollar bills meet all these criteria. What determines the acceptability of dollar bills as a medium of exchange? Basically, it is through self-fulfilling expectations: You value something as money only if you believe that others will accept it from you as payment. A society's willingness to use green paper dollars as money makes them an acceptable medium of exchange. This property of acceptability is not unique to money. Your personal computer has the same keyboard organization of letters as other computer keyboards because manufacturers agreed on a standard layout. You learned to speak English because it is probably the language that most people around you speak.

COMMODITY MONEY Commodity money meets the criteria for a medium of exchange. Gold, for example, was a common form of money in the nineteenth century because it was a medium of exchange, a unit of account, a store of value, and a standard of deferred payment. But commodity money has a significant problem: Its value depends on its purity. Therefore, someone who wanted to cheat could mix impure metals with a precious metal. Unless traders trusted each other completely, they needed to check the weight and purity of the metal at each trade. In the Middle Ages, respected merchants, who were the predecessors of modern bankers, solved this problem by assaying metals and stamping them with a mark certifying weight and purity and earned a commission in the process. Unstamped (uncertified) commodity money was acceptable only at a discount. Another problem with using gold as money was that the money supply was difficult to control, because it depended partly on unpredictable discoveries of new gold fields.

FIAT MONEY It can be inefficient for an economy to rely on only gold or other precious metals for its money supply. What if you had to transport bars of gold to settle your transactions? Not only would doing so be difficult and costly, but you would also run the risk of being robbed. To get around this problem, private institutions or governments began to store gold and issue paper certificates that could be redeemed for gold. In modern economies, paper currency is generally issued by a *central bank,* which is an agency of the government, like the Federal Reserve in the United States, that regulates the money supply. Today, no government in the world issues paper currency that can be redeemed for gold. Paper currency has no value unless it is used as money and is therefore not a commodity money. Instead, paper currency is a **fiat money,** which has no value except as money. If paper currency has no value except as money, why do consumers and firms use it?

Fiat money Money, such as paper currency, that is authorized by a central bank or governmental body and that does not have to be exchanged by the central bank for gold or some other commodity money.

If you look at a the top of a U.S. dollar bill, you will see that it is actually a *Federal Reserve Note,* issued by the Federal Reserve, which is the central bank in the United States. Because U.S. dollars are fiat money, the Federal Reserve is not required to give you gold or silver for your dollar bills. Federal Reserve currency is *legal tender* in the United States, which means the federal government requires that it be accepted in payment of debts and requires that cash or checks denominated in dollars be used in payment of taxes. Despite being legal tender, without everyone's acceptance dollar bills would not be a good medium of exchange and could not serve as money. In practice, you, along with everyone else, agree to accept Federal Reserve currency as money. The key to this acceptance is that *households and firms have confidence that if they accept paper dollars in exchange for goods and services, the dollars will not lose much value during the time they hold them.* Without this confidence, dollar bills would not serve as a medium of exchange.

13-2 Making the Connection

Money without a Government? The Strange Case of the Iraqi Dinar

The value of the Iraqi dinar was rising against the U.S. dollar. This result may not seem surprising. We saw in Chapter 12 that the exchange rate, or the value of one currency in exchange for another currency, fluctuates—but this was May 2003. The Iraqi government of Saddam Hussein had collapsed the month before, following an invasion by U.S. and British forces. No new Iraqi government had been formed yet, but Iraqi paper currency with pictures of Saddam on it continued to be used in Iraq for buying and selling.

U.S. officials in Iraq had expected that once the war was over and Saddam had been forced from power, the currency with his picture on it would lose all of its value. This result had seemed inevitable once the United States had begun paying Iraqi officials in U.S. dollars. However, many Iraqis continued to use the dinar because they were familiar with that currency. As one Iraqi put it, "People trust the dinar more than the dollar. It's Iraqi." In fact, for some weeks after the invasion, increasing demand for the dinar caused its value to rise against the dollar. In early April, when U.S. troops first entered Baghdad, it took about 4,000 dinar to buy one U.S. dollar. Six weeks later, in mid-May, it took only 1,500 dinar.

Eventually, a new Iraqi government was formed, and the government ordered that dinars with Saddam's picture be replaced by a new dinar. The new dinar was printed in factories around the world, and 27 Boeing 747s filled with paper dinars were flown to Baghdad. By January 2004, two billion paper dinars in varying denominations had been distributed to banks throughout Iraq and the old Saddam dinars disappeared from circulation. That dinars issued by Saddam's government actually increased in value for a period after his government had collapsed illustrates an important fact about money: *Anything can be used as money as long as people are willing to accept it in exchange for goods and services,* even paper currency issued by a government that no longer exists.

Many Iraqis continued to use currency with Saddam's picture on it, even after he was forced from power.

Sources: Edmund L. Andrews, "His Face Still Gives Fits as Saddam Dinar Soars," *New York Times,* May 18, 2003; Yaroslav Trofimov, "Saddam Hussein Is Scarce, but Not the Saddam Dinar," *Wall Street Journal,* April 24, 2003; and "A Tricky Operation," *Economist,* June 24, 2004.

② LEARNING OBJECTIVE

Discuss the definitions of the money supply used in the United States today.

How Do We Measure Money Today?

The definition of money as a medium of exchange depends on beliefs about whether others will use the medium in trade now and in the future. This definition offers guidance for measuring money in an economy. Interpreted literally, this definition says that money should include only those assets that obviously function as a medium of exchange: currency, checking account deposits, and traveler's checks. These assets can easily be used to buy goods and services, and thus act as a medium of exchange.

This strict interpretation is too narrow, however, as a measure of the money supply in the real world. Many other assets can be used as a medium of exchange, but they are not as liquid as a checking account deposit or cash. For example, you can convert your savings account at a bank to cash. Likewise, if you have an account at a brokerage firm, you can write checks against the value of the stocks and bonds the firm holds for you. Although these assets have restrictions on their use and there may be costs to converting them into cash, they can be considered part of the medium of exchange.

Economists have developed several different definitions of the money supply. Each definition includes a different group of assets. The definitions range from narrow to broad and are based on how liquid the assets are. The most narrow measure of money is cash. Broader measures include other assets that can be easily converted to cash, such as your checking account or savings account. In the United States, the Federal Reserve has conducted several studies of the appropriate definition of money. The job of defining the money supply has become more difficult during the past two decades as innovation in financial markets and institutions has created new substitutes for the traditional measures of the medium of exchange. During the 1980s, the Fed changed its definitions of money in response to financial innovation. Outside the United States, other central banks use similar measures. Now we will look more closely at the Fed's definitions of the money supply.

M1: The Narrowest Definition of the Money Supply

Figure 13-1 illustrates the definitions of the money supply. The narrowest definition of the money supply is called **M1.** It includes:

M1 The narrowest definition of the money supply: The sum of currency in circulation, checking account balances in banks, and holdings of traveler's checks.

1. all the paper money and coins that are in circulation—meaning what is not held by banks or the government.
2. the value of all checking account balances at banks.
3. the value of traveler's checks.

The sum of paper money and coins is called *currency.* The value of checking account balances is roughly equal to the value of currency. Holdings of traveler's checks are much smaller than currency, amounting to less than $8 billion in May 2005.

Although currency and checking account balances are roughly equal in value, checking account balances are used much more often than currency to make payments. More than 80 percent of all expenditures on goods and services are made with a check, rather than with currency. In fact, the total amount of currency in circulation—$715 billion in September 2005—is a misleading number. This amount is more than $2,300

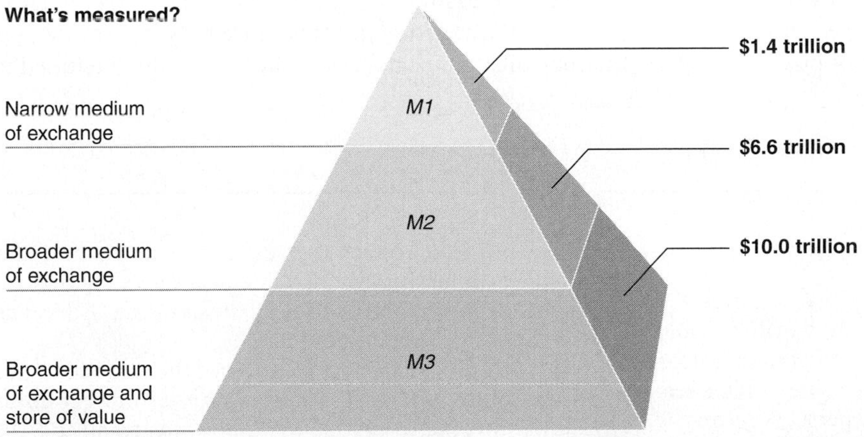

What's included?

M1	*M2*	*M3*
• Currency • Checking account balances • Traveler's checks	*M1* + • Savings account balances • Small-denomination time deposits • Money market deposit accounts in banks • Nonistitutional money market fund shares	*M2* + • Large-denomination time deposits • Institutional money market fund shares

FIGURE 13-1

Measuring the Money Supply, September 2005

The Federal Reserve uses several different measures of the money supply. In the pyramid, each measure includes the assets of the measure above it, as well as additional assets.

Source: Board of Governors of the Federal Reserve System, "Federal Reserve Statistical Release, H6," October 20, 2005.

for every man, woman, and child in the United States. If this sounds like an unrealistically large amount of currency to be held per person, it is. Economists estimate that about 60 percent of U.S. currency is actually outside the borders of the United States.

Who holds these dollars outside the United States? Foreign banks and foreign governments hold some dollars, but most are held by households and firms in countries where there is not much confidence in the local currency. When inflation rates are very high, many households and firms do not want to hold their domestic currency because it is losing its value too rapidly. The value of the U.S. dollar will be much more stable. If enough people are willing to accept dollars as well as—or instead of—domestic currency, then dollars become a second currency for the country. In some countries, such as Russia and many Latin American countries, large numbers of U.S. dollars are in circulation.

M2: A Broader Definition of Money

Before 1980, U.S. law prohibited banks from paying interest on checking account deposits. Households and firms held checking account deposits primarily to buy goods and services. M1 was, therefore, very close to the function of money as a medium of exchange. Almost all currency, checking account deposits, and traveler's checks were held with the intention of buying and selling, not to store value. People could store value and receive interest by placing funds in savings accounts in banks or by buying other financial assets, such as stocks and bonds. In 1980, the law was changed to allow banks to pay interest on certain types of checking accounts. This change reduced the difference between checking accounts and savings accounts, although people are still not allowed to write checks against their savings account balances.

M2 A broader definition of the money supply: M1 plus savings account balances, small-denomination time deposits, balances in money market deposit accounts in banks, and noninstitutional money market fund shares.

Economists began to pay closer attention to a broader definition of the money supply, **M2.** M2 includes everything that is in M1, plus savings account balances, small-denomination time deposits, such as certificates of deposit (CDs), balances in money market deposit accounts in banks, and noninstitutional money market fund shares. Small-denomination time deposits are similar to savings accounts, but the deposits are for a fixed period of time—usually from six months to several years—and withdrawals before that time are subject to a penalty. Mutual fund companies sell shares to investors and use the funds raised to buy financial assets such as stocks and bonds. Some of these mutual funds, such as Vanguard's Treasury Money Market Fund or Fidelity's Cash Reserves Fund, are called *money market mutual funds* because they invest in very short-term bonds, such as U.S. Treasury bills. The balances in these funds are included in M2.

Don't Let This Happen To You!

Don't Confuse Money with Income or Wealth

According to *Forbes* magazine, Bill Gates's wealth of $46.5 billion made him the richest person in the world in 2005. He also has a very large income, but how much money does he have? A person's *wealth* is equal to the value of his assets minus the value of any debts he has. A person's *income* is equal to his earnings during the year. Bill Gates's earnings as chairman of Microsoft and from his investments are very large. But his *money* is just equal to what he has in currency and in checking accounts. Only a small proportion of Gates's $46.5 billion in wealth is likely to be in currency or checking accounts. Most of his wealth is invested in stocks and bonds and other financial assets that are not included in the definition of money.

In everyday conversation, we often describe someone who is wealthy or who has a high income as "having a lot of money." But when economists use the word "money," they are usually referring to currency plus checking account deposits. It is important to keep straight the differences between wealth, income, and money.

Just as money and income are not the same for a person, they are not the same for the whole economy. National income in the United States was equal to $10.3 trillion in 2004. The money supply in 2004 was $1.4 trillion (using the M1 measure). There is no reason national income in a country should be equal to the country's money supply, nor will an increase in a country's money supply necessarily increase the country's national income.

YOUR TURN: **Test your understanding by doing related problem 9 on page 436 at the end of this chapter.**

There is also an M3 definition of the money supply that includes even more financial assets, including large-denomination time deposits and institutional money market mutual fund balances. Because of its relative simplicity and because it corresponds most closely to money as a medium of exchange, for the remainder of this book we will use the M1 definition of the money supply.

There are two key points about the money supply to keep in mind:

1. The money supply consists of *both* currency and balances in checking accounts and traveler's checks.
2. Because balances in checking accounts are included in the money supply, banks play an important role in the process by which the money supply increases and decreases. We will discuss this second point further in the next section.

SOLVED PROBLEM 13-1

The Definitions of M1 and M2

② LEARNING OBJECTIVE
Discuss the definitions of the money supply used in the United States today.

Suppose you decide to withdraw $2,000 from your checking account and use the money to buy a bank certificate of deposit (CD). Briefly explain how this will affect M1 and M2.

Solving the Problem:

Step 1: Review the chapter material. This problem is about the definitions of the money supply, so you may want to review the section "How Do We Measure Money Today?" which begins on page 412.

Step 2: Use the definitions of M1 and M2 to answer the problem. Funds in checking accounts are included in both M1 and M2. Funds in certificates of deposit are included in only M2. It is tempting to answer this problem by saying that shifting $2,000 from a checking account to a certificate of deposit reduces M1 by $2,000 and increases M2 by $2,000, but the $2,000 in your checking account was already counted in M2. So, the correct answer is that your action reduces M1 by $2,000 but leaves M2 unchanged.

YOUR TURN: **For more practice, do related problem 4 on page 436 at the end of this chapter.**

What about Credit Cards and Debit Cards?

Many people buy goods and services with credit cards, yet credit cards are not included in definitions of the money supply. The reason is that when you buy something with a credit card, you are in effect taking out a loan from the bank that issued the credit card. Only when you pay your credit card bill at the end of the month—usually with a check—is the transaction complete. In contrast, with a debit card the funds to make the purchase are taken directly from your checking account. In either case, the cards themselves do not represent money.

How Do Banks Create Money?

③ LEARNING OBJECTIVE
Explain how banks create checking account deposits.

We have seen that the most important component of the money supply is checking accounts in banks. To understand the role money plays in the economy, we need to look more closely at how banks operate. Banks are profit-making private businesses, just like bookstores and supermarkets. Some banks are quite small, with just a few branches, and they do business in a limited area. Others are among the largest corporations in the United States, with hundreds of branches spread across many states. The key role that banks play in the economy is to accept deposits and make loans. By doing this, they create checking account deposits.

FIGURE 13-2

Balance Sheet for Wachovia Bank, December 31, 2004

The items on a bank's balance sheet of greatest economic importance are its reserves, loans, and deposits. Notice that the difference between the value of Wachovia's total assets and its total liabilities is equal to its stockholders' equity. As a consequence, the left side of the balance sheet always equals the right side.

Note: Some entries have been combined to simplify the balance sheet.

Source: Wachovia Corporation and Subsidiaries Consolidated Balance Sheets from Wachovia Corporation, *Annual Report*, 2004.

ASSETS (IN MILLIONS)		LIABILITIES AND STOCKHOLDERS' EQUITY (IN MILLIONS)	
Reserves	$34,150	Deposits	$295,053
Loans	221,083	Short-term borrowing	64,161
Deposits with other banks	4,441	Long-term debt	46,750
Securities	110,597	Other liabilities	37,216
Buildings and equipment	5,628	Total liabilities	$443,189
Other assets	117,425		
		Stockholders' equity	50,135
Total assets	$493,324	Total liabilities and stockholders' equity	$493,324

Bank Balance Sheets

To understand how banks create money, we need to briefly examine a typical bank balance sheet. Recall from Chapter 5 that on a balance sheet, a firm's assets are listed on the left and its liabilities and stockholders' equity are listed on the right. Assets are the value of anything owned by the firm, liabilities are the value of anything the firm owes, and stockholders' equity is the difference between the total value of assets and the total value of liabilities. Stockholders' equity represents the value of the firm if it had to be closed, all of its assets were sold, and all of its liabilities were paid off. A corporation's stockholders' equity is also referred to as its *net worth.*

Figure 13-2 shows the balance sheet of Wachovia Bank, which is based in Charlotte, North Carolina, and in 2005 had branches in 15 states. The key assets on a bank's balance sheet are its **reserves,** loans, and holdings of securities, such as U.S. Treasury bills. Reserves are deposits that a bank has retained, rather than loaned out or invested by, for instance, buying a U.S. Treasury bill. Banks keep reserves either physically within the bank, as *vault cash,* or on deposit with the Federal Reserve. Banks are required by law to keep as reserves 10 percent of their checking account deposits above a threshold level, which in 2005 was $47.6 million. (In 2005, the required reserve ratio was zero on a bank's first $7 million in checking account deposits, 3 percent on deposits between $7 million and $47.6 million, and 10 percent on deposits above $47.6 million.) These reserves are called **required reserves.** The minimum fraction of deposits that banks are required to keep as reserves—currently 10 percent—is called the **required reserve ratio.** We can abbreviate the required reserve ratio as *RR.* Any reserves banks hold over and above the legal requirement are called **excess reserves.** The balance sheet in Figure 13-2 shows that loans are Wachovia's largest asset, which is true of most banks.

Reserves Deposits that a bank keeps as cash in its vault or on deposit with the Federal Reserve.

Required reserves Reserves that a bank is legally required to hold, based on its checking account deposits.

Required reserve ratio The minimum fraction of deposits banks are required by law to keep as reserves.

Excess reserves Reserves that banks hold over and above the legal requirement.

Banks make *consumer loans* to households and *commercial loans* to businesses. A loan is an asset to a bank because it represents a promise by the person taking out the loan to make certain specified payments to the bank. A bank's reserves and its holdings of securities are also assets because they are things of value owned by the bank.

Don't Let This Happen To You!

Know When a Checking Account Is an Asset and When It Is a Liability

Consider the following reasoning: "How can checking account deposits be a liability to a bank? After all, they are something of value that is in the bank. Therefore, checking account deposits should be counted as a bank *asset,* rather than as a bank liability."

This statement is incorrect. The balance in a checking account represents something the bank *owes* to the owner of the account. Therefore, it is a liability to the bank, although it is an asset to the owner of the account. Similarly, your car loan is a liability to you—because it is a debt you owe to the bank—but it is an asset to the bank.

***YOUR TURN:* Test your understanding by doing related problem 17 on page 437 at the end of this chapter.**

As with most banks, Wachovia's largest liability is its deposits. Deposits include checking accounts, savings accounts, and certificates of deposit. Deposits are liabilities to banks because they are owed to the households or firms that have deposited the funds. If you deposit $100 in your checking account, the bank owes you the $100 and you can ask for it back at any time.

Using T-Accounts to Show How a Bank Can Create Money

It is easier to show how banks create money using a T-account rather than a balance sheet. A T-account is a stripped-down version of a balance sheet that shows only how a transaction *changes* a bank's balance sheet. For example, suppose you deposit $1,000 in currency into an account at Wachovia Bank. This transaction raises the total deposits at Wachovia by $1,000 and also raises Wachovia's reserves by $1,000. We can show this on the following T-account:

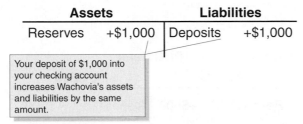

Assets		Liabilities	
Reserves	+$1,000	Deposits	+$1,000

Your deposit of $1,000 into your checking account increases Wachovia's assets and liabilities by the same amount.

Remember that because the total value of all the entries on the right side of a balance sheet must always be equal to the total value of all the entries on the left side of a balance sheet, any transaction that increases (or decreases) one side of the balance sheet must also increase (or decrease) the other side of the balance sheet. In this case, the T-account shows that we increased both sides of the balance sheet by $1,000.

Initially, this transaction does not increase the money supply. The currency component of the money supply declines by $1,000 because the $1,000 you deposited is no longer in circulation and, therefore, is not counted in the money supply. But the decrease in currency is offset by a $1,000 increase in the checking account deposit component of the money supply.

This initial change is not the end of the story, however. Banks are required to keep 10 percent of deposits as reserves. Because banks do not earn interest on reserves, they have an incentive to loan out or buy securities with the other 90 percent. In this case, Wachovia can keep $100 as required reserves and loan out the other $900, which represents excess reserves. Suppose Wachovia loans out the $900 to someone to buy an inexpensive used car. Wachovia could give the $900 to the borrower in currency, but usually banks make loans by increasing the borrower's checking account. We can show this with another T-account:

Assets		Liabilities	
Reserves	+$1,000	Deposits	+$1,000
Loans	+$900	Deposits	+$900

1. By loaning out $900 in excess reserves. . .

2. . . .Wachovia has increased the money supply by $900.

A key point to recognize is that *by making this $900 loan, Wachovia has increased the money supply by $900.* The initial $1,000 in currency you deposited into your checking account has been turned into $1,900 in checking account deposits—a net increase in the money supply of $900.

But the story does not end here. The person who took out the $900 loan did so to buy a used car. To keep things simple, let's suppose he buys the car for exactly $900 and pays by writing a check on his account at Wachovia. The owner of the used car will now deposit the check in her bank. That bank may also be a branch of Wachovia, but in most cities there are many banks, so let's assume that the seller of the car has her account at a branch of PNC Bank. Once she deposits the check, PNC Bank will send it to Wachovia Bank to *clear* the check and collect the $900. We can show the result using T-accounts:

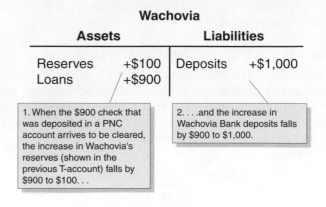

Wachovia

Assets		Liabilities	
Reserves	+$100	Deposits	+$1,000
Loans	+$900		

1. When the $900 check that was deposited in a PNC account arrives to be cleared, the increase in Wachovia's reserves (shown in the previous T-account) falls by $900 to $100. . .

2. . . .and the increase in Wachovia Bank deposits falls by $900 to $1,000.

PNC Bank

Assets		Liabilities	
Reserves	+$900	Deposits	+$900

1. After the check drawn on the account at Wachovia clears, PNC's reserves and deposits both increase by $900.

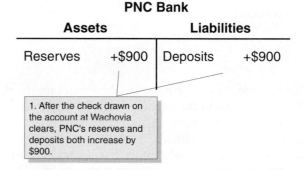

Once the car buyer's check has cleared, Wachovia has lost $900 in deposits—the amount loaned to the car buyer—and $900 in reserves—the amount it had to pay PNC when PNC sent it the car buyer's check. PNC has an increase in checking account deposits of $900—the deposit of the car seller—and an increase in reserves of $900—the amount it received from Wachovia.

PNC has 100 percent reserves against this new $900 deposit, when it only needs 10 percent reserves. It has an incentive to keep $90 as reserves and to loan out the other $810, which are excess reserves. If PNC does this, we can show the change in its balance sheet using another T-account.

PNC Bank

Assets		Liabilities	
Reserves	+$900	Deposits	+$900
Loans	+$810	Deposits	+$810

By making an $810 loan, PNC has increased both its loans and its deposits by $810.

In loaning out the $810 in excess reserves, PNC creates a new checking account deposit of $810. The initial deposit of $1,000 in currency into Wachovia Bank has now resulted in the creation of $1,000 + $900 + $810 = $2,710 in checking account deposits. The money supply has increased by $2,710 − $1,000 = $1,710.

The process is still not finished. The person who borrows the $810 will spend it by writing a check against his account. Whoever receives the $810 will deposit it in his bank, which could be a Wachovia branch or a PNC branch or a branch of some other bank. That new bank—if it's not PNC—will send the check to PNC and will receive $810 in new reserves. That new bank will have an incentive to loan out 90 percent of these reserves—keeping 10 percent to meet the legal requirement—and the process will go on. At each stage, the additional loans being made and the additional deposits being created are shrinking by 10 percent, as each bank has to withhold that amount as required reserves. We can show the total increase in checking account deposits set off by your initial deposit of $1,000:

BANK	INCREASE IN CHECKING ACCOUNT DEPOSITS	
Wachovia	$1,000	
PNC	900	(= 0.9 × $1,000)
Third Bank	810	(= 0.9 × $900)
Fourth Bank	729	(= 0.9 × $810)
•	•	
•	•	
•	•	
Total Change in Checking Account Deposits	$10,000	

The Simple Deposit Multiplier

Your initial deposit of $1,000 increased the reserves of the banking system by $1,000 and led to a total increase in checking account deposits of $10,000. The ratio of the amount of deposits created by banks to the amount of new reserves is called the **simple deposit multiplier.** In this case, the simple deposit multiplier is equal to $10,000/$1,000 = 10. Why 10? How do we know that your initial $1,000 deposit ultimately leads to a total increase in deposits of $10,000?

Simple deposit multiplier The ratio of the amount of deposits created by banks to the amount of new reserves.

There are two ways to answer this question. First, each bank in the process is keeping reserves equal to 10 percent of its deposits. For the banking system as a whole, the total increase in reserves is $1,000—the amount of your original currency deposit. Therefore, the system as a whole will end up with $10,000 in deposits, because $1,000 is 10 percent of $10,000.

A second way to answer the question is by deriving an expression for the simple deposit multiplier using the method we used with the expenditure multiplier in Chapter 11. The total increase in deposits equals:

$$\$1{,}000 + 0.9 \times \$1{,}000 + (0.9 \times 0.9) \times \$1{,}000 + (0.9 \times 0.9 \times 0.9) \times \$1{,}000 + \ldots$$

Or,

$$\$1{,}000 + 0.9 \times \$1{,}000 + 0.9^2 \times \$1{,}000 + 0.9^3 \times \$1{,}000 + \ldots$$

Or,

$$\$1{,}000 \times (1 + 0.9 + 0.9^2 + 0.9^3 + \ldots).$$

An expression like the one in the parentheses sums to:

$$\frac{1}{1-0.9}.$$

Simplifying further we have:

$$\frac{1}{0.10} = 10.$$

So,

$$\text{The total increase in deposits} = \$1{,}000 \times 10 = \$10{,}000.$$

Note that 10 is equal to 1 divided by the required reserve ratio, *RR*, which in this case is 10 percent or 0.10. This gives us another way of expressing the simple deposit multiplier:

$$\text{Simple deposit multiplier} = \frac{1}{RR}.$$

This formula makes it clear that the higher the required reserve ratio, the smaller the simple deposit multiplier. With a required reserve ratio of 10 percent, the simple deposit multiplier is 10. If the required reserve ratio were 20 percent, the simple deposit multiplier would fall to 1/0.20, or 5. We can use this formula to calculate the total increase in checking account deposits from an increase in bank reserves due to, for instance, currency being deposited in a bank:

$$\text{Change in checking account deposits} = \text{Change in bank reserves} \times \frac{1}{RR}.$$

For example, if $100,000 in currency is deposited in a bank and the required reserve ratio is 10 percent, then:

$$\text{Change in checking account deposits} = \$100{,}000 \times \frac{1}{0.10} = \$100{,}000 \times 10 = \$1{,}000{,}000.$$

SOLVED PROBLEM 13-2

③ LEARNING OBJECTIVE

Explain how banks create checking account deposits.

Showing How Banks Create Money

Suppose you deposit $5,000 in currency into your checking account at a branch of PNC Bank, which we will assume has no excess reserves at the time you make your deposit. Also assume that the required reserve ratio is 0.10.

a. Use a T-account to show the initial effect of this transaction on PNC's balance sheet.

b. Suppose that PNC makes the maximum loan they can from the funds you deposited. Use a T-account to show the initial effect on PNC's balance sheet from granting the loan. Also include in this T-account the transaction from question (a).

c. Now suppose that whoever took out the loan in question (b) writes a check for this amount and that the person receiving the check deposits it in Wachovia Bank. Show the effect of these transactions on the balance sheets of PNC Bank and Wachovia Bank, *after the check has been cleared.* On the T-account for PNC Bank, include the transactions from questions (a) and (b).

d. What is the maximum increase in checking account deposits that can result from your $5,000 deposit? What is the maximum increase in the money supply? Explain.

Solving the Problem:

Step 1: Review the chapter material. This problem is about how banks create checking account deposits, so you may want to review the section "Using T-Accounts to Show How a Bank Can Create Money," which begins on page 417.

Step 2: Answer question (a) by using a T-account to show the impact of the deposit. Keeping in mind that T-accounts show only the changes in a balance sheet that result from the relevant transaction and that assets are on the left side of the account and liabilities are on the right side, we have:

PNC Bank

Assets		Liabilities	
Reserves	+$5,000	Deposits	+$5,000

Because the bank now has your $5,000 in currency in its vault, its reserves (and, therefore, its assets) have risen by $5,000. But this transaction also increases your checking account balance by $5,000. Because the bank owes you this money, the bank's liabilities have also risen by $5,000.

Step 3: Answer question (b) by using a T-account to show the impact of the loan. The problem tells you to assume that PNC Bank currently has no excess reserves and that the required reserve ratio is 10 percent. This requirement means that if the bank's checking account deposits go up by $5,000, they must keep $500 as reserves and can loan out the remaining $4,500. Remembering that new loans usually take the form of setting up, or increasing, a checking account for the borrower, we have:

PNC Bank

Assets		Liabilities	
Reserves	+$5,000	Deposits	+$5,000
Loans	+$4,500	Deposits	+$4,500

The first line of the T-account shows the transaction from question (a). The second line shows that PNC has loaned out $4,500 by increasing the checking account of the borrower by $4,500. The loan is an asset to PNC because it represents a promise by the borrower to make certain payments spelled out in the loan agreement.

Step 4: Answer question (c) by using T-accounts for PNC and Wachovia to show the impact of the check clearing. We now show the effect of the borrower having spent the $4,500 he received as a loan from PNC. The person who received the $4,500 check deposits it in her account at Wachovia. We need two T-accounts to show this:

PNC Bank

Assets		Liabilities	
Reserves	+$500	Deposits	+$5,000
Loans	+$4,500		

Wachovia Bank

Assets		Liabilities	
Reserves	+$4,500	Deposits	+$4,500

Look first at the T-account for PNC. Once Wachovia sends the check written by the borrower to PNC, PNC loses $4,500 in reserves and Wachovia gains $4,500 in reserves. The $4,500 is also deducted from the account of the borrower. PNC is now satisfied with the result. It received a $5,000 deposit in currency from you. When that money was sitting in the bank vault, it wasn't earning any interest for PNC. Now $4,500 of the $5,000 has been loaned out and is earning interest. These interest payments allow PNC to cover its costs and earn a profit, which it has to do to remain in business.

Wachovia now has an increase in deposits of $4,500, resulting from the check deposited by the contractor, and an increase in reserves of $4,500. Wachovia is in the same situation as

PNC was in question (a): It has excess reserves as a result of this transaction and a strong incentive to lend them out in order to earn some interest.

Step 5: Answer question (d) by using the simple deposit multiplier formula to calculate the maximum increase in checking account deposits and the maximum increase in the money supply. The simple deposit multiplier expression is (remember that *RR* is the required reserve ratio):

$$\text{Change in checking account deposits} = \text{Change in bank reserves} \times \frac{1}{RR}.$$

In this case, bank reserves rose by \$5,000 as a result of your initial deposit and the required reserve ratio is 0.10, so

$$\text{Change in checking account deposits} = \$5{,}000 \times \frac{1}{0.10} = \$5{,}000 \times 10 = \$50{,}000.$$

Because checking account deposits are part of the money supply, it is tempting to say that the money supply has also increased by \$50,000. Remember, though, that your \$5,000 in currency was counted as part of the money supply while you had it, but it is not included when it is sitting in a bank vault. Therefore,

$$\text{Change in the money supply} = \text{Increase in checking account deposits} - \text{Decline in currency in circulation} = \$50{,}000 - \$5{,}000 = \$45{,}000.$$

YOUR TURN: **For more practice, do related problem 12 on page 436 at the end of the chapter.**

The story we have told about the way an increase in reserves in the banking system leads to the creation of new deposits and, therefore, an increase in the money supply has been simplified in two ways. First, we assumed that banks do not keep any excess reserves. That is, we assumed that when you deposited \$1,000 in currency into your checking account at Wachovia Bank, Wachovia loaned out \$900, keeping only the \$100 in required reserves. In fact, banks often keep at least some excess reserves to guard against the possibility that many depositors may simultaneously make withdrawals from their accounts. The more excess reserves banks keep, the smaller the deposit multiplier. Imagine an extreme case where Wachovia keeps your entire \$1,000 as reserves. If Wachovia does not loan out any of your deposit, the process described earlier of loans leading to the creation of new deposits, leading to the making of additional loans, and so on, will not take place. The \$1,000 increase in reserves will lead to a total increase of \$1,000 in deposits, and the deposit multiplier will be only 1, not 10.

Second, we assumed that the whole amount of every check is deposited in a bank; no one takes any of it out as currency. In reality, households and firms keep roughly constant the amount of currency they hold relative to the value of their checking account balances. So, we would expect to see people increasing the amount of currency they hold as the balances in their checking accounts rise. Once again, think of the extreme case. Suppose that when Wachovia makes the initial \$900 loan to the borrower who wants to buy a used car, the seller of the car cashes the check instead of depositing it. In that case, PNC does not receive any new reserves and does not make any new loans. Once again, the \$1,000 increase in your checking account at Wachovia is the only increase in deposits, and the deposit multiplier is 1.

The effect of these two factors is to reduce the real-world deposit multiplier to about 2.5. That means that a \$1 increase in the reserves of the banking system results in about a \$2.50 increase in deposits.

Although the story of the deposit multiplier can be complicated, the key point to bear in mind is that the most important part of the money supply is the checking account balance component. When banks make loans, they increase checking account balances, and the money supply expands. Banks make new loans whenever they gain reserves. The whole process can also work in reverse. If banks lose reserves, they reduce their outstanding loans and deposits, and the money supply contracts.

We can summarize these important conclusions:

1. Whenever banks gain reserves, they make new loans and the money supply expands.
2. Whenever banks lose reserves, they reduce their loans and the money supply contracts.

The Federal Reserve System

(4) LEARNING OBJECTIVE

Discuss the three policy tools the Federal Reserve uses to manage the money supply.

Many people are surprised to learn that banks do not keep in their vaults all of the funds that are deposited into checking accounts. In fact, in September 2005 the total amount of checking account balances in all banks in the United States was $641 billion, while total reserves were only $46 billion. The United States, like nearly all other countries, has a **fractional reserve banking system.** In a fractional reserve banking system, banks keep less than 100 percent of deposits as reserves. When people deposit money in a bank, the bank loans most of the money to someone else. What happens, though, if depositors want their money back? This would seem to be a problem because banks have loaned out most of the money and can't get it back easily.

Fractional reserve banking system A banking system in which banks keep less than 100 percent of deposits as reserves.

In practice, though, withdrawals are usually not a problem for banks. On a typical day, about as much money is deposited as is withdrawn. If a small amount more is withdrawn than deposited, banks can cover the difference from their excess reserves or by borrowing from other banks. Sometimes depositors lose confidence in a bank when they question the value of the bank's underlying assets, particularly its loans. Often, the reason for a loss of confidence is bad news, whether true or false. When many depositors simultaneously decide to withdraw their money from a bank, there is a **bank run.** If many banks experience runs at the same time, the result is a **bank panic.** It is possible for one bank to handle a run by borrowing from other banks, but if many banks simultaneously experience runs, the banking system may be in trouble.

Bank run Many depositors simultaneously decide to withdraw money from a bank.

Bank panic Many banks experiencing runs at the same time.

A *central bank*, like the Federal Reserve in the United States, can help stop a bank panic by acting as a *lender of last resort.* In acting like a lender of last resort, a central bank makes loans to banks that cannot borrow funds elsewhere. The bank can use these loans to pay off depositors. When the panic ends and the depositors put their money back in their accounts, the bank can repay the loan to the central bank.

The 2001 Bank Panic in Argentina

13-3 Making the Connection

We saw at the beginning of this chapter that Argentina suffered a bank panic in 2001. Some unusual aspects of the Argentine banking system made it very difficult for the Argentine central bank to act as a lender of last resort. As an alternative policy to stop the banking panic, the Argentine government limited the amount of Argentine currency that depositors could withdraw to $1,000 per account per month. Consumers cut back on their spending because much of the money in their bank accounts could not be withdrawn. Firms like McDonald's experienced declining sales as the country's recession worsened.

The inability of the Argentine central bank to act as a lender of last resort resulted from a decision made by the Argentine government in 1991 to fix the value of the Argentine peso relative to the U.S. dollar at one to one. This policy was meant to restore public faith in the ability of the Argentine currency to retain its value. Argentina had suffered through several periods of high inflation. In 1990, the inflation rate had been a staggering 2,300 percent. These inflationary episodes had caused the purchasing power of the currency to decline rapidly. Although the policy of fixing the value of the peso against the dollar was successful in greatly reducing inflation, it ultimately placed the banking system in an awkward situation. After 1991, Argentine banks were encouraged to take in U.S. dollar deposits and to make U.S. dollar loans, and U.S. dollars were legally recognized as a means of payment within Argentina. By 1994, 60 percent of time deposits and 50 percent of loans were in U.S. dollars.

The Argentine central bank was unable to stop the bank panic of 2001.

The Argentine central bank was allowed to issue pesos only in exchange for dollars, which limited its ability to provide pesos to banks experiencing a bank run.

By 2000, many observers had begun to doubt the ability of the Argentine government to maintain the one-to-one exchange rate. As a result, Argentine households and firms, as well as foreign investors, began moving funds out of pesos and into dollars. By late 2001, fully 80 percent of time deposits in Argentine banks were in dollars rather than in pesos. In addition, many depositors began withdrawing money from their accounts. Forty-seven of the top 50 Argentine banks experienced major withdrawals by December 2001. In January 2002, the crisis was ended when the government abandoned its commitment to the one-to-one exchange rate between the peso and the dollar and decreed that dollar deposits in banks would be converted to peso deposits at a rate of 1.4 pesos to the dollar. Although some financial stability was restored, the damage to the banking system from the crisis contributed to a decline in real GDP of 11.5 percent during 2002.

Source: Kathryn M. E. Dominguez and Linda Tesar, "International Borrowing and Macroeconomic Performance in Argentina," National Bureau of Economic Research, Working Paper 11353, May 2005.

The Organization of the Federal Reserve System

Federal Reserve System The central bank of the United States.

Bank panics lead to severe disruptions in business activity because neither households nor firms can gain access to their accounts. Not surprisingly, in the United States each banking panic in the late nineteenth and early twentieth centuries was accompanied by a recession. With the intention of putting an end to banking panics, in 1913 Congress passed the Federal Reserve Act setting up the **Federal Reserve System.** The system began operation in 1914. The Federal Reserve—often referred to as the "Fed"—is the central bank of the United States. The Fed acts as a lender of last resort to banks and as a bankers' bank, providing services such as check clearing to banks. The Fed also takes actions to control the money supply.

To aid the Fed in carrying out these functions, Congress divided the country into 12 Federal Reserve districts, as shown in Figure 13-3. Each district has its own Federal Reserve bank, which provides services to banks in that district. The real power of the Fed, however, lies in Washington, D.C., with the Board of Governors. There are seven members of the Board of Governors, all of whom are appointed by the President of the United States to 14-year, nonrenewable terms. Board members come from banking, business, and academic backgrounds. One of the seven board members is appointed chairman for a four-year, renewable term. Chairmen of the Board of Governors since World War II have come from various backgrounds, including Wall Street (William McChesney Martin), academia (Arthur Burns and Ben Bernanke), business (G. William Miller), public service (Paul Volcker), and economic forecasting (Alan Greenspan).

How the Federal Reserve Manages the Money Supply

Although Congress established the Fed to stop banking panics by acting as a lender of last resort, today an important activity for the Fed is managing the money supply. As we

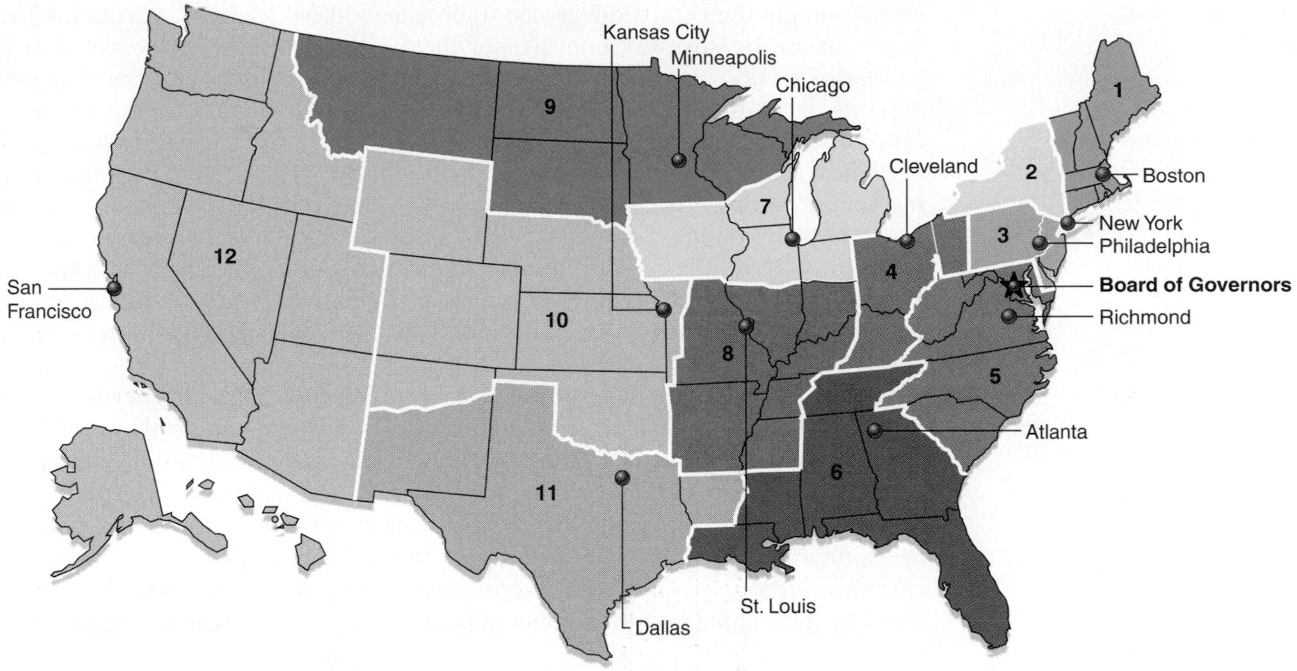

FIGURE 13-3 **Federal Reserve Districts**

The United States is divided into 12 Federal Reserve districts, each of which has a Federal Reserve bank. The real power within the Federal Reserve System, however, lies in Washington, D.C., with the Board of Governors.

Source: Board of Governors of the Federal Reserve System.

will discuss in more detail in Chapter 14, managing the money supply is part of **monetary policy,** which the Fed undertakes to pursue economic objectives.

Monetary policy The actions the Federal Reserve takes to manage the money supply and interest rates to pursue economic objectives.

To manage the money supply, the Fed uses three *monetary policy tools:*

1. Open market operations
2. Discount policy
3. Reserve requirements

Remember that the most important component of the money supply is checking account balances. Not surprisingly, all three of the Fed's policy tools are aimed at affecting the reserves of banks as a means of changing the volume of checking account balances.

OPEN MARKET OPERATIONS Eight times per year the **Federal Open Market Committee (FOMC)** meets in Washington, D.C., to discuss monetary policy. The committee has 12 members: the seven members of the Federal Reserve's Board of Governors, the president of the Federal Reserve Bank of New York, and four presidents from the other 11 Federal Reserve banks. These four presidents serve one-year rotating terms on the FOMC.

Federal Open Market Committee (FOMC) The Federal Reserve committee responsible for open market operations and managing the money supply.

The U.S. Treasury borrows money by selling bills, notes, and bonds. Remember that the *maturity* of a financial asset is the period of time until the purchaser receives payment of the face value or principal. Usually, bonds have face values of $1,000. Treasury bills have maturities of 1 year or less, Treasury notes have maturities of 2 years to 10 years, and Treasury bonds have maturities of 30 years. To increase the money supply, the FOMC directs the *trading desk,* located at the Federal Reserve Bank of New York to *buy* U.S. Treasury securities—most frequently bills but sometimes notes or bonds—from the public. When the sellers of the Treasury securities deposit the funds in their banks, the reserves of banks will rise. This increase in reserves will start the process of increasing loans and checking account deposits that increases the money supply. To decrease the money supply, the FOMC directs the trading desk to *sell* Treasury securities. When the buyers of the Treasury securities pay for them with checks, the reserves of their banks will fall. This decrease in reserves starts a contraction of loans and checking account deposits that reduces the money supply. The buying and selling of Treasury securities is called **open market operations.**

Open market operations The buying and selling of Treasury securities by the Federal Reserve in order to control the money supply.

There are three reasons the Fed conducts monetary policy principally through open market operations. First, because the Fed initiates open market operations, it completely controls their volume. Second, the Fed can make both large and small open market operations. Third, the Fed can implement its open market operations quickly, with no administrative delay or required changes in regulations. Many other central banks, including the European Central Bank and the Bank of Japan, also use open market operations in conducting monetary policy.

The Federal Reserve is responsible for printing the paper currency of the United States. Recall that if you look at the top of a dollar bill, you will see the words "Federal Reserve Note." When the Fed takes actions to increase the money supply, commentators will sometimes say that it is "printing more money." The main way the Fed increases the money supply, however, is not by printing more money but by buying Treasury securities. Similarly, to reduce the money supply, the Fed does not set fire to stacks of paper currency. Instead, it sells Treasury securities. We will spend more time discussing how and why the Fed manages the money supply in Chapter 14, when we discuss monetary policy.

Discount loans Loans the Federal Reserve makes to banks.

Discount rate The interest rate the Federal Reserve charges on discount loans.

DISCOUNT POLICY The loans the Fed makes to banks are called **discount loans,** and the interest rate it charges on the loans is called the **discount rate.** When a bank receives a loan from the Fed, its reserves increase by the amount of the loan. By lowering the discount rate, the Fed can encourage banks to take additional loans and thereby to increase their reserves. With more reserves, banks will make more loans to households and firms, which will increase checking account deposits and the money supply. Raising the discount rate will have the reverse effect.

The Fed doesn't control discount policy as completely as it controls open market operations, and changing discount policy is much more difficult than changing open market operations because banks must decide whether to accept discount loans. The volume of discount loans is generally small except when the Fed is actively acting as a lender of last resort, as it did, for example, in the aftermath of the U.S. stock market crash of October 1987 and the September 11, 2001, terrorist attacks. In practice, the Fed prefers to limit discount loans to helping banks that experience temporary problems with deposit withdrawals, rather than to use them to increase or decrease the money supply. Outside the United States, central banks such as the European Central Bank and the Bank of Japan use discount lending both as a monetary policy tool and as a means of mitigating financial crises.

The Fed is not called on to use discount policy to stop bank panics because of the existence of *deposit insurance.* Congress in 1933 set up the Federal Deposit Insurance Corporation (FDIC) to insure deposits in banks. Today, nearly all banks are members of FDIC, and in 2005 each deposit in these banks was insured to a limit of $100,000. Deposit insurance has largely stopped bank panics because it has reassured depositors that their deposits are safe even if their bank goes out of business.

RESERVE REQUIREMENTS When the Fed reduces the required reserve ratio, it converts required reserves into excess reserves. For example, suppose a bank has $100 million in checking account deposits and the required reserve ratio is 10 percent. The bank will be required to hold $10 million as reserves. If the Fed reduces the required reserve ratio to 8 percent, the bank will need to hold only $8 million as reserves. The Fed has converted $2 million worth of reserves from required to excess. This $2 million is now available for the bank to lend out. If the Fed *raises* the required reserve ratio from 10 percent to 12 percent, it would have the reverse effect.

The Fed changes reserve requirements much more rarely than it conducts open market operations or changes the discount rate. Because changes in reserve requirements require significant alterations in banks' holdings of loans and securities, frequent changes would be disruptive. Also, because reserves earn no interest, the use of reserve requirements to manage the money supply effectively places a tax on banks' deposit-taking and lending activities, which can be costly for the economy.

Putting It All Together: Decisions of the Nonbank Public, Banks, and the Fed

Using its three tools—open market operations, the discount rate, and reserve requirements—the Fed has substantial influence over the money supply, but that influence is not absolute. Two other actors—the nonbank public and banks—also influence the money supply in practice.

The nonbank public—households and firms—must decide how much money to hold as deposits in banks. The larger the money holdings in deposits, the greater are the reserves of banks and the more money the banking system can create. The smaller the money holdings in deposits, the lower are the reserves of banks and the less money the banking system can create. In addition, the Fed does not have absolute control over the amount bankers decide to lend. Banks create money only if they lend their reserves. If bankers retain excess reserves, they make a smaller volume of loans and create less money.

The roles of the nonbank public and banks in the money supply process do not mean that the Fed lacks meaningful control of the money supply. The Fed's staff monitors information on banks' reserves and deposits every week, and the Fed can respond quickly to shifts in behavior by depositors or banks. The Fed can therefore steer the money supply close to the level it desires.

The Quantity Theory of Money

(5) LEARNING OBJECTIVE

Explain the quantity theory of money and use it to explain how high rates of inflation occur.

People have been aware of the connection between increases in the money supply and inflation for centuries. In the sixteenth century, the Spanish conquered Mexico and Peru and shipped large quantities of gold and silver back to Spain. The gold and silver were minted into coins and spent across Europe to further the political ambitions of the Spanish kings. Prices in Europe rose steadily during these years, and many observers discussed the relationship between this inflation and the flow of gold and silver into Europe from the Americas.

Connecting Money and Prices: The Quantity Equation

In the early twentieth century, Irving Fisher, an economist at Yale, formalized the connection between money and prices using the *quantity equation:*

$$M \times V = P \times Y.$$

The equation states that the money supply (M) multiplied by the **velocity of money** (V) equals the price level (P) multiplied by real output (Y). Fisher defined the velocity of money, often referred to simply as "velocity," as the average number of times each dollar of the money supply is used to purchase goods and services included in GDP. Rewriting the original equation by dividing both sides by M, we have the equation for velocity:

Velocity of money The average number of times each dollar in the money supply is used to purchase goods and services included in GDP.

$$V = \frac{P \times Y}{M}.$$

We can use M1 to measure the money supply, the GDP price deflator to measure the price level, and real GDP to measure real output. Then the value for velocity for 2004 was:

$$V = \frac{1.082 \times \$10{,}842 \text{ billion}}{\$1{,}363 \text{ billion}} = 8.6.$$

This result tells us that, on average during 2004, each dollar of M1 was spent about nine times on goods or services included in GDP.

Because velocity is *defined* to be equal to $(P \times Y)/M$, we know that the quantity equation must always hold true: The left side *must* be equal to the right side. A theory is a statement about the world that might possibly be false. Therefore, the quantity equation is not a theory. Irving Fisher turned the quantity equation into the **quantity theory of money** by asserting that velocity was constant. He argued that the average number of times a dollar is spent depends on how often people get paid, how often they do their grocery shopping, how often businesses mail bills, and other factors that do not change very often. Because this assertion may be true or false, the quantity theory of money is, in fact, a theory.

Quantity theory of money A theory of the connection between money and prices that assumes that the velocity of money is constant.

The Quantity Theory Explanation of Inflation

The quantity equation gives us a way of showing the relationship between changes in the money supply and changes in the price level, or inflation. To see this relationship more clearly, we can use a handy mathematical rule that states that an equation where variables are multiplied together is equal to an equation where the *growth rates* of these variables are *added* together. So, we can transform the quantity equation from:

$$M \times V = P \times Y$$

to:

Growth rate of the money supply + Growth rate of velocity =
Growth rate of the price level (or inflation rate) + Growth rate of real output.

This way of writing the quantity equation is more useful for investigating the effect of changes in the money supply on the inflation rate. Remember that the growth rate for any variable is just the percentage change in the variable from one year to the next. The growth rate of the price level is just the inflation rate, so we can rewrite the quantity equation to help us understand the factors that determine inflation:

Inflation rate = Growth rate of the money supply +
Growth rate of velocity – Growth rate of real output.

If Irving Fisher was correct that velocity is constant, then the growth rate of velocity will be zero. That is, if velocity is, say, always 8.6, then its percentage change from one year to the next will always be zero. This assumption allows us to rewrite the equation one last time:

Inflation rate = Growth rate of the money supply – Growth rate of real output.

This equation leads to the following predictions:

1. If the money supply grows at a faster rate than real GDP, there will be inflation.
2. If the money supply grows at a slower rate than real GDP, there will be deflation. (Recall that *deflation* is a decline in the price level.)
3. If the money supply grows at the same rate as real GDP, the price level will be stable, and there will be neither inflation nor deflation.

It turns out that Irving Fisher was wrong in asserting that the velocity of money is constant. From year to year there can be significant fluctuations in velocity. As a result, the predictions of the quantity theory of money do not hold every year, but most economists agree that the quantity theory provides a useful insight into the long-run relationship between the money supply and inflation: *In the long run, inflation results from the money supply growing at a faster rate than real GDP.*

High Rates of Inflation

Why do governments allow high rates of inflation? The quantity theory can help us to understand the reasons for high rates of inflation, such as that experienced in Argentina during the 1980s. Very high rates of inflation—in excess of hundreds or thousands of percentage points per year—are known as *hyperinflation.* Hyperinflation is caused by central banks increasing the money supply at a rate far in excess of the growth rate of real GDP. A high rate of inflation causes money to lose its value so rapidly that households and firms avoid holding it. If the inflation becomes severe enough, people stop using paper currency, so it no longer serves the important functions of money discussed previously in this chapter. Economies suffering from high inflation usually also suffer from very slow growth, if not severe recession.

Given the dire consequences that follow from high inflation, why do governments allow it by expanding the money supply so rapidly? The main reason is that governments often want to spend more than they are able to raise through taxes. Developed countries, such as the United States, can usually bridge gaps between spending and taxes by borrowing through selling bonds to the public. Developing countries often have difficulty selling bonds because the public is skeptical of their ability to pay back the money. If they are unable to sell bonds to the public, governments in developing countries will force their central banks to purchase them. As we discussed previously, when a central bank buys bonds, the money supply will increase.

High Inflation in Argentina

The link between rapid money growth and high inflation was evident in the experience of Argentina during the 1980s. Panel (a) of Figure 13-4 shows rates of growth of the money supply and the inflation rate in Argentina in the years from 1981 to 1991. Both the average annual growth rate of the money supply and the average annual inflation rate from 1981 to 1990 were greater than 750 percent. With prices rising so quickly, Argentine currency could not fulfill the normal functions of money. Not surprisingly, the Argentine economy struggled during these years, with real GDP in 1990 ending up 6 percent lower than it had been in 1981.

This weak economic performance was particularly frustrating to many people in Argentina because early in the twentieth century the country had had one of the highest standards of living in the world. In 1910, only the United States and Great Britain had higher levels of real GDP per capita. In U.S.-made films of the 1920s and 1930s, the rich foreigner was often from Argentina.

It was clear to policymakers in Argentina that the only way to bring inflation under control was to limit increases in the money supply. As we saw in Making the Connection 13-3, in 1991 the Argentine government enacted a new policy that fixed the exchange rate of the peso versus the U.S. dollar at one to one. In addition, the Argentine central bank was allowed to issue pesos only in exchange for dollars. As panel (b) in Figure 13-4 shows, the new policy greatly reduced increases in the money supply and the inflation rate (notice that the scale of panel (b) is different from the scale of panel (a), which partly disguises the fall in money growth and inflation). Economic growth also revived, with real GDP increasing at an average annual rate of almost 6 percent from 1991 to 1998. Unfortunately, though, Argentina had not come to grips with several underlying economic problems, perhaps the most important of which was the continuing gap between government expenditures and tax receipts.

By 2000, many observers expected that the Argentine government would not be able to maintain the one-to-one exchange rate between the peso and the U.S. dollar. As Argentine firms and households, along with foreign investors, began exchanging pesos

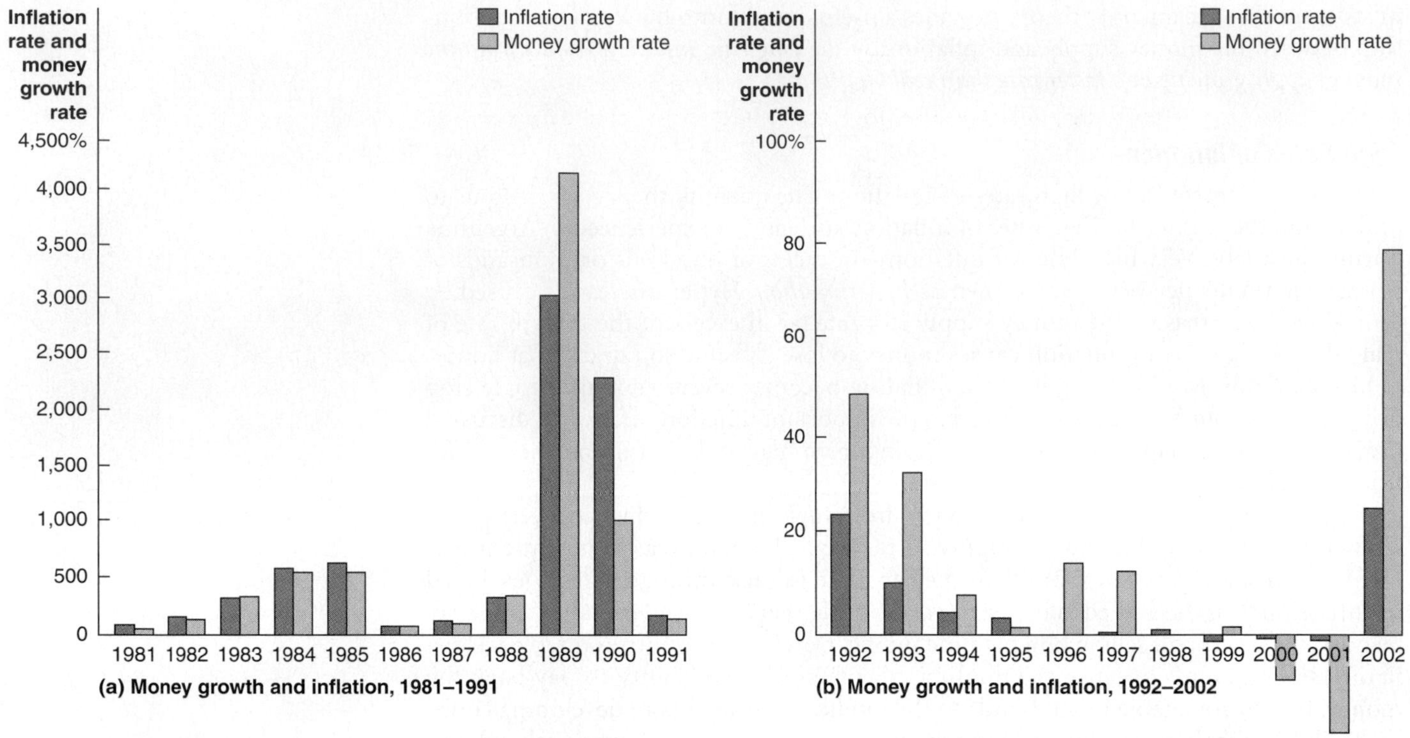

FIGURE 13-4 Money Growth and Inflation in Argentina

Panel (a) shows rates of growth of the money supply and the inflation rate in Argentina in the years from 1981 to 1991. Both the average annual growth rate of the money supply and the average annual inflation rate from 1981 to 1990 were greater than 750 percent. In 1991, the Argentine government enacted a new policy that fixed the exchange rate of the peso versus the U.S. dollar at one to one. As panel (b) shows, the new policy greatly reduced increases in the money supply and the inflation rate (notice that the scale of panel (b) is different from the scale of panel (a), which partly disguises the fall in money growth and inflation).

Source: International Monetary Fund.

for dollars, the Argentine money supply declined. The money supply declined by 9 percent in 2000 and by an additional 20 percent in 2001. Argentina experienced falling prices, or deflation, during both years, along with falling real GDP. Finally, in January 2002, the Argentine government abandoned its commitment to the one-to-one exchange rate between the peso and the dollar, and the money supply increased rapidly. During 2002, the money supply increased by nearly 80 percent and deflation was transformed to an inflation rate of 25 percent. Although the inflation rate declined over the next few years, Argentina continues to struggle to keep its money supply from growing at rates likely to result in high inflation.

13-4 Making the Connection

The German Hyperinflation of the Early 1920s

When Germany lost World War I, a revolution broke out that overthrew Kaiser Wilhelm II and installed a new government known as the Weimar Republic. In the peace treaty of 1919, the Allies—the United States, Great Britain, France, and Italy—imposed payments called *reparations* on the new German government. The reparations were meant as compensation to the Allies for the damage Germany had caused during the war. It was very difficult for the German government to use tax revenue to cover both its normal spending and the reparations.

The German government decided to pay for the difference between its spending and its tax revenues by selling bonds to the central bank, the Reichsbank. After a few years, the German government fell far behind in its reparations payment. In January 1923, the French government sent troops into the German industrial area known as the Ruhr to try to collect the payments directly. German workers in the Ruhr went on strike, and the German government decided to support them by paying their salaries. Raising the funds to do so was financed by an inflationary monetary policy—the German government sold bonds to the Reichsbank, thereby increasing the money supply.

The inflationary increase in the money supply was very large: The total number of marks—the German currency—in circulation rose from 115 million in January 1922 to 1.3 billion in January 1923 and then to 497 billion *billion* or 497,000,000,000,000,000,000 in December 1923. Just as the quantity theory predicts, the result was a staggeringly high rate of inflation. The German price index that stood at 100 in 1914 and 1,440 in January 1922 had risen to 126,160,000,000,000 in December 1923. The German mark became worthless. The German government ended the hyperinflation by (1) negotiating a new agreement with the Allies that reduced its reparations payments, (2) reducing other government expenditures and raising taxes to balance its budget, and (3) replacing the existing mark with a new mark. Each new mark was worth 1 trillion old marks. The German central bank was also limited to issuing a total of 3.2 billion new marks.

These steps were enough to bring the hyperinflation to an end—but not before the savings of anyone holding the old marks had been wiped out. Most middle-income Germans were extremely resentful of this outcome. Many historians believe that the hyperinflation greatly reduced the allegiance of many Germans to the Weimar Republic and may have helped pave the way for Hitler and the Nazis to seize power 10 years later.

Source: Thomas Sargent, "The End of Four Big Hyperinflations," in *Rational Expectations and Inflation*, New York: Harper and Row, 1986.

During the hyperinflation of the 1920s, people in Germany used paper currency to light their stoves.

Conclusion

Money plays a key role in the functioning of an economy by facilitating trade in goods and services and by making specialization possible. Without specialization, no advanced economy can prosper. Households and firms, banks, and the central bank (the Federal Reserve in the United States) are participants in the process of creating the money supply. In the next chapter, we will explore how the Federal Reserve uses monetary policy to promote its economic objectives.

An Inside Look on the next page discusses how several Latin American countries have moved away from fixing the value of their currencies against the dollar.

An Inside Look Does Using the Dollar Destabilize Latin American Countries?

WALL STREET JOURNAL, MAY 12, 2004

Latin Governments Try to Unseat the Dollar

a Once considered the bedrock of monetary stability, the U.S. dollar is losing fans among Latin American officials eager to promote their own domestic currencies. Yet recent government attempts to limit the role of the dollar contrast with the behavior of consumers who remain partial to the dollar as a dependable medium of exchange and store of value. Before governments can expect consumers to voluntarily switch allegiances, they will have to build credibility in their own currencies.

It wasn't long ago that governments saw the U.S. Federal Reserve as a legitimate and effective substitute for homegrown monetary institutions. Beginning in the late 1980s and well into the 1990s several countries set the value of their currencies at a fixed rate against the dollar.

The plan helped bring inflation under control, but a lack of accompanying structural economic policy adjustments consistent with stable money brought about the collapse of most fixed exchange rate regimes. Those countries that adopted the dollar as legal tender—Ecuador, EI Salvador and Panama—have so far avoided devastating monetary crises.

b Argentina abandoned its currency peg known as "convertibility" in 2002, a painful episode that marked the end of the latest chapter in fixed exchange schemes. By then, several other countries had already adopted explicit inflation targeting as an alternative way to try to keep prices in check. Now that nine nations in the region rely on inflation targeting and the value of most currencies fluctuates in the foreign exchange market, these governments are becoming more wary of the dollar, particularly dollar borrowing on bank balance sheets.

For consumers and companies however, the dollar remains popular. Because of the trust it inspires among both borrowers and lenders, rates for commercial loans in dollars where they are available are more attractive than those on local currency lending.

The continued reliance on dollar borrowing worries officials who fret about the danger of instability if local currencies were to suddenly lose value versus the dollar. In Peru, where the dollar is widely circulated in parallel to the Peruvian sol, the government has engaged in a vocal campaign to reduce the amount of dollars in circulation.

The results have been mildly effective: During the first quarter of this year, Peru's central bank reported the amount of dollars in the banking system had dropped to 54% in 2004 from as high as 70% in 2000. . . .

c In a recent release titled "The Importance of The De-dollarization of the Banking Credit Sector," Peru's central bank states that having 74% of all bank loans denominated in dollars creates a potential currency imbalance for consumers as well as companies since most receive income denominated in soles rather than in dollars.

"The mismatch implies a currency exchange risk: if the exchange rate weakens, foreign currency liabilities rise while income doesn't. In this manner, the dollarization of the bank credit sector makes the economy vulnerable," argues the central bank. For anyone following the painful and ongoing debt cleanup of billions of dollars borrowed by Argentina's consumers and companies when the local currency was valued at parity with the dollar, the warning seems merited.

Besides Peru, other Latin American countries have conducted campaigns over the years to reduce the dollar dependency of its citizens and raise the profile of local currencies.

Mexico developed a futures market in pesos following its devaluation and financial crisis in the mid 1990s. Chile avoided the dollarization of its financial sector with the introduction of local currency deposits indexed to inflation, a measure that failed in other countries. Colombia and Uruguay have successfully issued international bonds denominated in domestic currencies.

The development of new financial instruments and markets has had an impact in some sectors, as the figures from Peru suggest. Changing the ingrained habits of individual consumers and local companies that are still partial to the U.S. currency will be a slow process. . . .

Key Points in the Article

In many Latin American countries today, businesses and households accept U.S. dollars—or Federal Reserve notes—in exchange for goods and services. The dollar's popularity in Latin America dates to the 1980s and 1990s, when local monetary policies fueled hyperinflation. Local currencies failed as mediums of exchange and stores of value, and Latin American governments had no choice but to allow their citizens to exchange goods for U.S. dollars. Today, many Latin American governments want to eliminate the U.S. dollar from local circulation because they believe these dollars threaten the stability of the region's economies.

Analyzing the News

a Fiat money is useful as long as all businesses and households accept it in exchange for goods and services. This acceptance occurs only if everyone in the economy is confident that money will not lose value over time. That is, fiat money exists because it provides two fundamental functions: it serves as a medium of exchange and a store of value. The U.S. dollar provides both of these functions in many Latin American countries. In the 1980s and 1990s, many Latin American governments accepted U.S. dollars as legal tender. They did so in response to monetary crises that occurred throughout the region. Today, Latin American governments would like businesses and households to accept only local currencies in exchange for goods and services.

b In 2002, Argentina abandoned its currency peg, which set the value of one peso equal to the value of one U.S. dollar. The result of this decision is shown in Figure 1. The value of the Argentine peso fell to roughly one third the value of a U.S. dollar. And, as the purchasing power of the peso fell, consumer price inflation in Argentina rose. This pattern is shown in Figure 2. Today, the values of many Latin American currencies are determined by demand and supply in the foreign exchange market, and Latin American central banks have low inflation rate targets to ensure that their currencies provide the functions of money described in this chapter. Inflation targeting is a monetary policy that requires a central bank to announce publicly an inflation target, and then to increase or decrease its money supply in order to hit that target. If Latin America's households and firms are confident that their central banks will have a low inflation rate target, local currencies will become the primary medium of exchange.

c In a "dollarized" economy, the value of the local currency is fixed to the value of the U.S. dollar and both currencies circulate as legal tender. Peru's central bank is concerned about the consequences of its dollarized economy. On the one hand, dollarization strengthens Peru's economy because the U.S. dollar is an excellent medium of exchange and store of value in Peru. On the other hand, dollarization threatens Peru's economy because most of Peru's businesses and households earn *soles* but owe *dollars*. If dollarization were to fail, the sol's value would fall relative to the dollar and Peru's dollar-denominated debt burden would increase in terms of soles. This currency imbalance is what caused Argentina's economy to collapse in 2002. Peru's central bankers are worried that the same could happen there.

Thinking Critically ABOUT POLICY

1. Suppose Peru's central bank announces that it will target an inflation rate of 3 percent. Now suppose Peru's economy enters a recession. Should Peru's central bank abandon its inflation target and increase the money supply to stimulate economic activity in the short run? Why or why not?
2. Why would Latin American economies tie the value of their currencies to the dollar rather than, say, the euro or the yen?

Source: *Wall Street Journal*, Online [Only Staff-Produced Materials May Be Used] by Eduardo Kaplan.

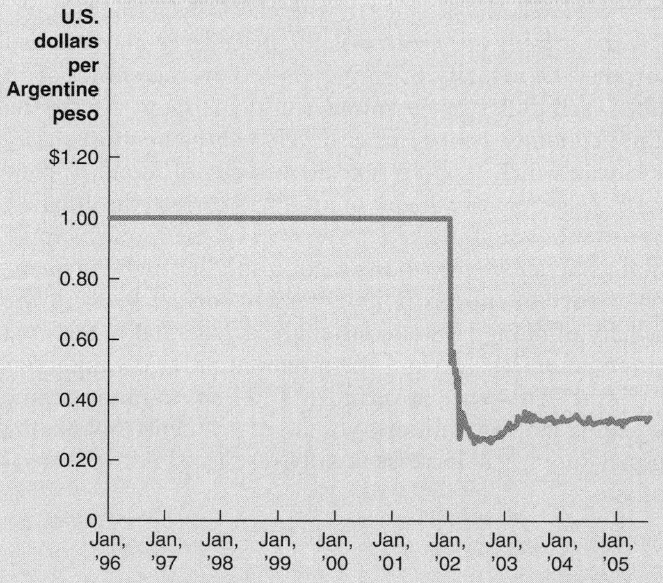

Figure 1: U.S. dollar/Argentine peso exchange rate, January 1996 to July 2005.

Source: OANDA.com.

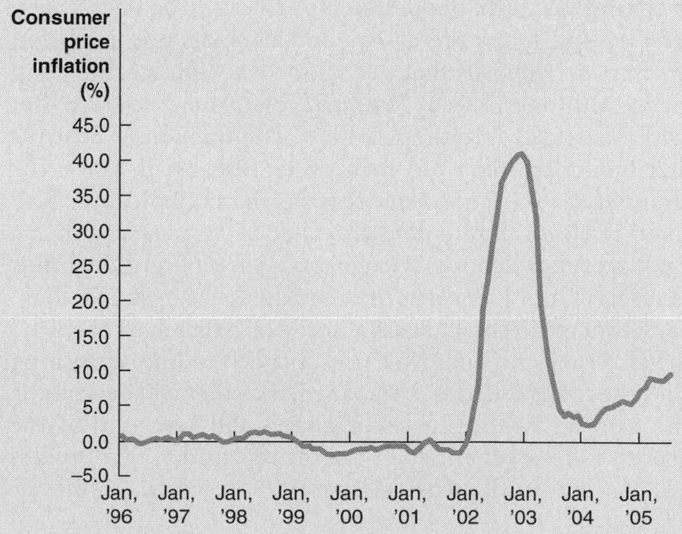

Figure 2: Greater Buenos Aires consumer price inflation, January 1996 to July 2005.

Source: National Institute of Statistics and Census, Argentina.

SUMMARY

LEARNING OBJECTIVE ① Define money and discuss its four functions. A *barter economy* is an economy that does not use money and in which people trade goods and services directly for other goods and services. Barter trade occurs only if there is a *double coincidence of wants,* where both parties to the trade want what the other one has. Because barter is inefficient, there is strong incentive to use *money,* which is anything that people are generally willing to accept in exchange for goods or services or in payment of debts. Money has four functions: a medium of exchange, a unit of account, a store of value, and a standard of deferred payment. The *gold standard* was a monetary system under which the government produced gold coins and paper currency convertible into gold. The gold standard collapsed in the early 1930s. Today no government in the world issues paper currency that can be redeemed for gold. Instead, paper currency is *fiat money,* which has no value except as money.

LEARNING OBJECTIVE ② Discuss the definitions of the money supply used in the United States today. The narrowest definition of the money supply in the United States today is M1, which includes currency, checking account balances, and traveler's checks. A broader definition of the money supply is M2, which includes everything that is in M1, plus savings accounts, small-denomination time deposits [such as certificates of deposit (CDs)], money market deposit accounts in banks, and noninstitutional money market fund shares.

LEARNING OBJECTIVE ③ Explain how banks create checking account deposits. On a bank's balance sheet, *reserves* and loans are assets, and deposits are liabilities. Reserves are deposits that the bank has retained, rather than loaned out or invested. *Required reserves* are reserves that banks are legally required to hold. The fraction of deposits that banks are required to keep as reserves is called the *required reserve ratio.* Any reserves banks hold over and above the legal requirement are called *excess reserves.* When a bank accepts a deposit, it keeps only a fraction of the funds as reserves and loans out the remainder. In making a loan, banks increase the checking account balance of the borrower. When the borrower uses a check to buy something with the funds the bank has loaned, the seller will deposit the check in his bank. The seller's bank will keep part of the deposit as reserves and loan out the remainder. This process will continue until no banks have excess reserves. In this way, the process of banks making new loans increases the volume of checking account balances and the money supply. This money creation process can be illustrated with T-accounts, which are stripped-down versions of balance sheets that show only how a transaction changes a bank's balance sheet. The *simple deposit multiplier* is the ratio of the amount of deposits created by banks to the amount of new reserves. An expression for the simple deposit multiplier is $1/RR$.

LEARNING OBJECTIVE ④ Discuss the three policy tools the Federal Reserve uses to manage the money supply. The Federal Reserve System (the "Fed") is the central bank of the United States. It was originally established in 1914 to stop banking panics, but today its main role is to control the money supply. *Monetary policy* refers to the actions the Federal Reserve takes to manage the money supply and interest rates to pursue economic objectives. The Fed's three monetary policy tools are open market operations, discount policy, and reserve requirements. *Open market operations* are the buying and selling of Treasury securities by the Federal Reserve. The loans the Fed makes to banks are called *discount loans,* and the interest rate the Fed charges on discount loans is the *discount rate.* The *Federal Open Market Committee* (FOMC) meets in Washington, D.C., eight times per year to discuss monetary policy.

LEARNING OBJECTIVE ⑤ Explain the quantity theory of money and use it to explain how high rates of inflation occur. The *quantity equation* relates the money supply to the price level: $M \times V = P \times Y$, where M is the money supply, V is the *velocity of money,* P is the price level, and Y is real output. The velocity of money is the average number of times each dollar in the money supply is spent during the year. Economist Irving Fisher developed the *quantity theory of money,* which assumes that the velocity of money is constant. If the quantity theory of money is correct, the inflation rate should equal the rate of growth of the money supply minus the rate of growth of real output. Although the quantity theory of money is not literally correct because the velocity of money is not constant, it is true that in the long run inflation results from the money supply growing faster than real GDP. When governments attempt to raise revenue by selling large quantities of bonds to the central bank, the money supply will increase rapidly, resulting in a high rate of inflation.

KEY TERMS

Asset 408
Bank panic 423
Bank run 423
Commodity money 408
Discount loans 426
Discount rate 426
Excess reserves 416
Federal Open Market Committee (FOMC) 425
Federal Reserve System 424
Fiat money 411
Fractional reserve banking system 423
M1 413
M2 414
Monetary policy 425
Money 408
Open market operations 426
Quantity theory of money 428
Required reserve ratio 416
Required reserves 416
Reserves 416
Simple deposit multiplier 419
Velocity of money 427

REVIEW QUESTIONS

1. Glyn Davies, an economist at the University of Wales, wrote: "In pure barter if the owner of an orchard, having a surplus of apples, required boots he would need to find not simply a cobbler but a cobbler who wanted to purchase apples." What do economists call the problem Davies is describing?
   Source: Glyn Davies, *A History of Money: From Ancient Times to the Present*, Cardiff: University of Wales Press, 1994.
2. What is the difference between commodity money and fiat money?
3. What are the four functions of money? Can something be considered money if it does not fulfill all four functions?
4. What is the main difference between the M1 and M2 definitions of the money supply?
5. What are the largest asset and the largest liability of the typical bank?
6. Suppose you decide to withdraw $100 in cash from your checking account. Draw a T-account showing the effect of this transaction on your bank's balance sheet.
7. Give the formula for the simple deposit multiplier. If the required reserve ratio is 20 percent, what is the maximum increase in checking account deposits that will result from an increase in bank reserves of $20,000?
8. Why did Congress decide to set up the Federal Reserve System in 1914? Today, what is the most important role of the Federal Reserve in the U.S. economy?
9. What are the policy tools the Fed uses to control the money supply? Which tool is the most important?
10. What is the quantity theory of money? How does the quantity theory explain why inflation occurs?
11. What is hyperinflation? Why do governments sometimes allow it to occur?

PROBLEMS AND APPLICATIONS

Please visit **www.prenhall.com/hubbard** *for solutions to the even-numbered problems as well as multiple-choice and true-false self-assessment quizzes.*

1. The English economist Stanley Jevons described a world tour during the 1880s by a French singer, Mademoiselle Zélie. One stop on the tour was a theater in the Society Islands, part of French Polynesia in the South Pacific. She performed for her usual fee, which was one-third of the receipts. This turned out to be three pigs, 23 turkeys, 44 chickens, 5,000 coconuts, and "considerable quantities of bananas, lemons, and oranges." She estimated that all of this would have had a value in France of 4,000 francs. According to Jevons, "as Mademoiselle could not consume any considerable portion of the receipts herself, it became necessary in the meantime to feed the pigs and poultry with the fruit." Do the goods Mademoiselle Zélie received as payment fulfill the four functions of money described in the chapter? Why or why not?
   Source: W. Stanley Jevons, *Money and the Mechanism of Exchange*, New York: D. Appleton and Company, 1889, pp. 1–2.
2. In the late 1940s, the Communists under Mao Zedong were defeating the government of China in a civil war. The paper currency issued by the Chinese government was losing much of its value and most businesses refused to accept it. At the same time, there was a paper shortage in Japan. During these years, Japan was still under military occupation by the United States, following its defeat in World War II. Some of the U.S. troops in Japan realized that they could

use dollars to buy up vast amounts of paper currency in China, ship it to Japan to be recycled into paper, and make a substantial profit. Under these circumstances, was the Chinese paper currency a commodity money or a fiat money? Briefly explain.

3. Briefly explain whether each of the following is counted in M1.
   a. The coins in your pocket
   b. The funds in your checking account
   c. The funds in your savings account
   d. The traveler's check that you have left over from a trip
   e. Your Citibank Platinum MasterCard
4. **[Related to *Solved Problem 13-1*]** Suppose you have $2,000 in currency in a shoebox in your closet. One day you decide to deposit the money in a checking account. Briefly explain how this will affect M1 and M2.
5. The paper currency of the United States is technically called "Federal Reserve Notes." The following excerpt is from the Federal Reserve Act:

   > Federal reserve notes . . . shall be redeemed in lawful money on demand at the Treasury Department of the United States, in the city of Washington, District of Columbia, or at any Federal Reserve bank.

   If you took a $20 bill to the Treasury Department or a Federal Reserve bank, with what type of "lawful money" is the government likely to redeem it?
6. The following is from a newspaper story on local, or community, banks: "Community banks . . . are awash in liabilities these days, and they couldn't be happier about it." To which "liabilities" does the story refer? Why would these banks be happy about being "awash" in these liabilities?
   Source: Christian Millman, "Bank Deposits on the Rise as People Flee the Stock Market," (Allentown, PA) *Morning Call*, August 11, 2002, pp. D1, D4.
7. The president of a local bank described deposits this way: "That's the fuel we use to be able to go out and make loans and mortgages." Briefly explain what he means.
   Source: Christian Millman, "Bank Deposits on the Rise as People Flee the Stock Market," (Allentown, PA) *Morning Call*, August 11, 2002, pp. D1, D4.
8. Suppose you decide to withdraw $100 in currency from your checking account. What is the effect on M1? Ignore any actions the bank may take as a result of your having withdrawn the $100.
9. **[Related to *Don't Let This Happen To You!*]** Briefly explain whether you agree or disagree with the following statement: "I recently read that more than half of the money issued by the government is actually held by people in foreign countries. If that's true, then the United States is less than half as wealthy as government statistics indicate."
10. "Most of the money supply of the United States is created by banks making loans." Briefly explain whether you agree or disagree with this statement.
11. Would a series of bank runs in a country decrease the total quantity of M1? Wouldn't a bank run simply move funds in a checking account to currency in circulation? How could that movement of funds decrease the quantity of money?
12. **[Related to *Solved Problem 13-2*]** Suppose you deposit $2,000 in currency into your checking account at a branch of Bank of America, which we will assume has no excess reserves at the time you make your deposit. Also assume that the required reserve ratio is 0.20.
    a. Use a T-account to show the initial impact of this transaction on Bank of America's balance sheet.
    b. Suppose that Bank of America makes the maximum loan they can from the funds you deposited. Using a T-account, show the initial impact of granting the loan on Fleet's balance sheet. Also include on this T-account the transaction from (a).
    c. Now suppose that whoever took out the loan in (b) writes a check for this amount and that the person receiving the check deposits it in a branch of Citibank. Show the effect of these transactions on the balance sheets of Bank of America and Citibank Bank, *after the check has been cleared.* [On the T-account for Bank of America, include the transactions from (a) and (b).]
    d. What is the maximum increase in checking account deposits that can result from your $2,000 deposit? What is the maximum increase in the money supply? Explain.
13. Consider the following simplified balance sheet for a bank:

Assets		Liabilities	
Reserves	$10,000	Deposits	$70,000
Loans	$66,000	Stockholders' equity	$6,000

    a. If the required reserve ratio is 10 percent, how much in excess reserves does the bank hold?
    b. What is the maximum amount by which the bank can expand its loans?
    c. If the bank makes the loans in (b), show the *immediate* impact on the bank's balance sheet.
14. Suppose that the Federal Reserve makes a $10 million discount loan to the First National Bank by increasing FNB's account at the Fed.
    a. Use a T-account to show the impact of this transaction on FNB's balance sheet. Remember that the funds a bank has on deposit at the Fed count as part of its reserves.

b. Assume that before receiving the discount loan, FNB has no excess reserves. What is the maximum amount of this $10 million that FNB can lend out?
c. What is the maximum total increase in the money supply that can result from the Fed's discount loan? Assume the required reserve ratio is 10 percent.

15. If the money supply is growing at a rate of 6 percent per year, real GDP is growing at a rate of 3 percent per year, and velocity is constant, what will the inflation rate be? If velocity is increasing 1 percent per year instead of remaining constant, what will the inflation rate be?

16. The following is from an article in the *Wall Street Journal*: Japan's "money supply is surging. If that doesn't curtail Japan's debilitating price deflation, a lot of economics textbooks may need to be rewritten."
    a. What is "price deflation"?
    b. If rapid increases in the money supply don't stop deflation, why will economics textbooks need to be rewritten?
    c. (This is a more difficult question.) Why might price deflation in Japan be "debilitating"? *Hint:* What reaction might consumers have to price deflation?

    Source: Peter Landers, "Japan Shows Vague Signs of Recovery," *Wall Street Journal*, March 5, 2002.

17. **[Related to *Don't Let This Happen To You!*]** Briefly explain whether you agree or disagree with the following statement: "Assets are things of value that people own. Liabilities are debts. Therefore, a bank will always consider a checking account deposit to be an asset, and a car loan to be a liability."

18. "Banks don't really create money, do they?" was the challenge that a retired professor of economics was known to have used in his upper division American economic history course to ascertain what his students remembered from introductory macroeconomics about the creation of money. He reported that few students were confident enough or remembered enough to reply correctly to his question. How would you reply?

19. In the 1970s, it was reported that a leader of a country proclaimed that he intended to do away with money in his country because money represents the decadence of the West (Western Europe and the United States). Historically, did money only exist in the West? What effect would the elimination of money have on the economy?

20. **[Related to the *Chapter Opener*]** During the Civil War, the Confederate States of America printed lots of its own currency—Confederate dollars—to fund the war. By the end of the war, nearly 1.5 billion paper dollars had been printed by the Confederate government. How would such a large quantity of Confederate dollars have affected the value of the Confederate currency? With the war drawing to an end, would Southerners have been as willing to use and accept Confederate dollars? How else could they have made exchanges?

    Source: Textual Transcript of Confederate Currency, Federal Reserve Bank of Richmond.

chapter fourteen

Monetary Policy

Why Did Homebuilder Toll Brothers, Inc., Prosper during the 2001 Recession?

In March 2001, the U.S. economy moved into recession. During a typical recession, sales of new homes decline sharply as unemployment increases and incomes fall. Homebuilders are usually among the businesses hit hardest during recessions. For example, during the recession of 1974–75, spending on residential construction declined by more than 30 percent. Homebuilders fared even worse during the recessions of 1980–82, when spending on residential construction plummeted by more than 40 percent. The situation was very different during the recession of 2001, however, when spending on residential construction actually rose by 5 percent.

Founded in 1967 by Bruce and Robert Toll, Toll Brothers, Inc., is a homebuilder headquartered in Huntingdon Valley, Pennsylvania. Toll Brothers started small; on the firm's first project, Robert Toll would spend time walking around the construction site collecting discarded nails and pieces of lumber to be reused the next day. Toll Brothers expanded by buying inexpensive land and learning how to quickly obtain the approvals of local governments to build on the land. Toll Brothers specializes in building luxury homes but uses many of the techniques employed by builders of low-cost starter homes. In two factories in Pennsylvania and one in Virginia, Toll Brothers manufactures the trusses that support the roofs and the panels that form the walls of the homes it constructs. The firm employs computer-controlled machines in its factories to cut spaces for doors and windows. These practices give Toll Brothers lower costs than other builders of luxury homes, who often use carpenters and other skilled workers at construction sites to assemble wall panels and cut out doors and windows. Today, Toll Brothers builds homes in 21 states and has revenues of $6 billion, which place it among the 500 largest firms in the United States.

Still, despite its success, Toll Brothers should have experienced a

decline in sales during the recession of 2001. But look at the following excerpt from their report to shareholders for the third quarter of 2001:

> Amid continuing sluggishness in the U.S. economy, Toll Brothers once again posted record results. Thanks to hard work and efficient planning and the [housing] market's ability to weather the downturn, we have just completed the best third quarter and first nine months in our history.

The success of Toll Brothers during 2001 was not the result of good luck but rather of a policy decision made by the Federal Reserve's Federal Open Market Committee (FOMC). In early 2001, the members of the FOMC concluded that a recession was about to begin and implemented an expansionary monetary policy to keep the recession as short and mild as possible. By driving down interest rates, the Fed succeeded in heading off what some economists had predicted would be a prolonged and severe recession. *An Inside Look* on page 466 considers whether the actions taken by the Fed to stimulate spending on residential construction may have led to a "bubble" in housing prices.

Source: Shawn Tully, "Toll Brothers: The New King of the Real Estate Boom," *Fortune*, April 5, 2005.

LEARNING OBJECTIVES

After studying this chapter, you should be able to:

① Define monetary policy and describe the Federal Reserve's monetary policy goals.

② Describe the Federal Reserve's monetary policy targets, and explain how expansionary and contractionary monetary policies affect the interest rate.

③ Use aggregate demand and aggregate supply graphs to show the effects of monetary policy on real GDP and the price level.

④ Discuss the Fed's setting of monetary policy targets.

⑤ Assess the arguments for and against the independence of the Federal Reserve.

➤ In Chapter 13, we saw that banks play an important role in creating the money supply. We also saw that the Fed manages the money supply to achieve its policy goals. As we will see in this chapter, the Fed has four policy goals: (1) price stability, (2) high employment, (3) economic growth, and (4) stability of financial markets and institutions. In this chapter, we will explore how the Federal Reserve decides which *monetary policy* actions to take to achieve its goals.

① LEARNING OBJECTIVE
Define monetary policy and describe the Federal Reserve's monetary policy goals.

What Is Monetary Policy?

When Congress created the Federal Reserve System (the "Fed") in 1914, its main responsibility was to make discount loans to banks suffering from large withdrawals by depositors. As a result of the Great Depression of the 1930s, Congress amended the Federal Reserve Act to give the Federal Reserve's Board of Governors broader responsibility to act "so as to promote effectively the goals of maximum employment, stable prices, and moderate long-term interest rates."

Monetary policy The actions the Federal Reserve takes to manage the money supply and interest rates to pursue its economic objectives.

Since World War II, the Federal Reserve has carried out an active **monetary policy.** Monetary policy refers to the actions the Fed takes to manage the money supply and interests rates to pursue its economic objectives.

The Goals of Monetary Policy

The Fed has set four *monetary policy goals* that are intended to promote a well-functioning economy:

1. Price stability
2. High employment
3. Economic growth
4. Stability of financial markets and institutions

We briefly consider each of these goals.

PRICE STABILITY As we have seen in previous chapters, rising prices erode the value of money as a medium of exchange and a store of value. Especially after inflation rose dramatically and unexpectedly during the 1970s, policymakers in most industrial countries have set price stability as a policy goal. Figure 14-1 shows that from the early 1950s until 1968, the inflation rate remained below 4 percent per year. Inflation was above 4 percent for most of the 1970s. In early 1979, the inflation rate increased to more than 10 percent, where it remained until late 1981, when it began to rapidly fall back to the 4-percent range. Since 1992, the inflation rate has been below 4 percent. In 2004 inflation was 2.7 percent and, in the view of most economists, inflationary pressures were well contained.

The inflation rates during the years 1979–1981 were the highest the United States has ever experienced during peacetime. When Paul Volcker became chairman of the Federal Reserve's Board of Governors in August 1979, he made fighting inflation his top policy goal. Alan Greenspan, who succeeded Volcker in August 1987, and Ben Bernanke, who succeeded Greenspan in January 2006, continued to focus on inflation. Volcker, Greenspan, and Bernanke argued that if inflation is low over the long run, the Fed will have the flexibility it needs to lessen the impact of recessions. And many economists agree.

HIGH EMPLOYMENT High employment, or a low rate of unemployment, is another monetary policy goal. Unemployed workers and underused factories and office buildings reduce GDP below its potential level. Unemployment causes financial distress and decreases self-esteem for workers who lack jobs. The goal of high employment extends beyond the Fed to other branches of the federal government. At the end of World War II,

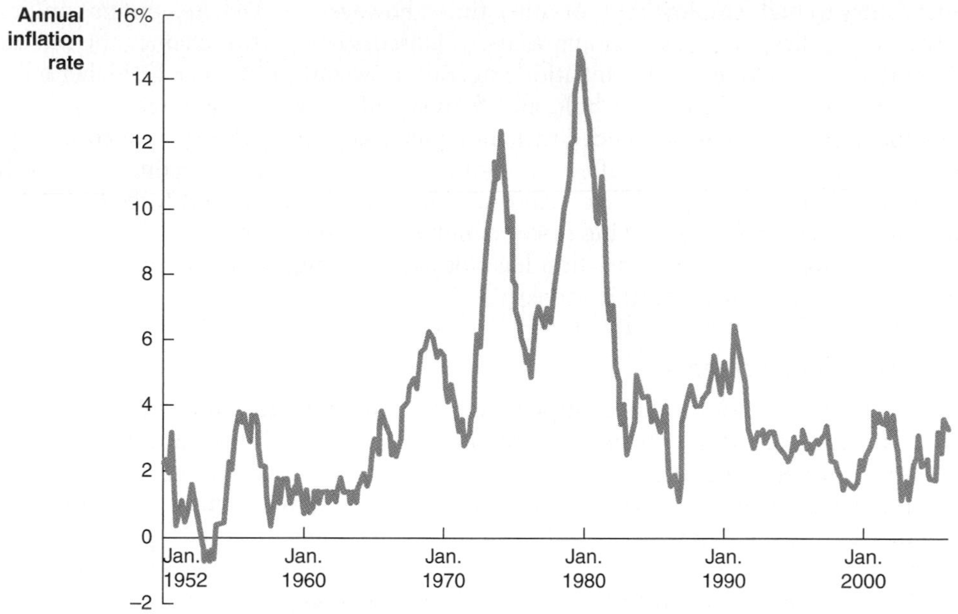

FIGURE 14-1

The Inflation Rate, 1952–2004

For most of the 1950s and 1960s, the inflation rate in the United States was 4 percent or less. During the 1970s, the inflation rate increased, peaking during 1979–1981, when it averaged more than 10 percent. Since 1992, the inflation rate has been less than 4 percent.

Note: The inflation rate is measured as the percentage increase in the consumer price index (CPI) from the same month in the previous year.

Source: Bureau of Labor Statistics.

Congress passed the Employment Act of 1946, which stated that it was the "responsibility of the Federal Government . . . to foster and promote . . . conditions under which there will be afforded useful employment, for those able, willing, and seeking to work, and to promote maximum employment, production, and purchasing power."

ECONOMIC GROWTH We discussed in Chapters 9 and 10 the importance of economic growth to raising living standards. Policy can spur economic growth by providing incentives for saving to ensure a large pool of investment funds, as well as by providing direct incentives for business investment. Policymakers aim to encourage *stable* economic growth because stable growth allows households and firms to plan accurately and encourages the long-run investment that is needed to sustain growth.

STABILITY OF FINANCIAL MARKETS AND INSTITUTIONS When financial markets and institutions are not efficient in matching savers and borrowers, resources are lost. Firms with the potential to produce goods and services valued by consumers cannot obtain the financing they need to design, develop, and market these products. Savers waste resources looking for satisfactory investments. The Fed promotes the stability of financial markets and institutions so that an efficient flow of funds from savers to borrowers will occur. The Fed's response to problems in financial markets has averted financial panics. For example, following the stock market crash of 1987 and the terrorist attacks of September 11, 2001, the Fed's willingness to rapidly increase the volume of discount loans reassured financial markets and promoted financial stability.

In the next section, we will look at how the Fed attempts to attain its monetary policy goals. Although the Fed has multiple monetary policy goals, during most periods the most important goals of monetary policy have been price stability and high employment. In the remainder of this chapter we will focus on these two goals.

The Money Market and the Fed's Choice of Targets

(2) LEARNING OBJECTIVE

Describe the Federal Reserve's monetary policy targets, and explain how expansionary and contractionary monetary policies affect the interest rate.

The Fed's objective in setting monetary policy is to use its policy tools to achieve its monetary policy goals. Recall from Chapter 13 that the Fed's policy tools are open market operations, discount policy, and reserve requirements. Sometimes the Fed can be successful in pursuing multiple goals at the same time. For example, it can take actions that increase both employment and economic growth because steady economic growth contributes to high employment. At other times, however, the Fed encounters conflicts between its policy goals. For example, as we will discuss later in this chapter, the Fed can raise interest rates to reduce the inflation rate. But, as we saw in Chapter 12, higher interest rates typically reduce household and firm spending, which may result in slower growth. So, a policy that is intended to achieve one monetary policy goal, such as lower inflation, may have an adverse effect on another policy goal, such as economic growth. Some members of Congress have introduced legislation that would force the Fed to focus almost entirely on achieving price stability, and many economists support such a focus. Although so far this legislation has not passed Congress, the debate has gained momentum within the Federal Reserve.

Monetary Policy Targets

The Fed tries to keep both the unemployment and inflation rates low, but it can't affect either of these economic variables directly. The Fed cannot tell firms how many people to employ or what prices to charge for their products. Instead, the Fed uses variables, called *monetary policy targets,* that it can affect directly and that, in turn, affect variables that are closely related to the Fed's policy goals, such as real GDP and the price level. The two main monetary policy targets are the money supply and the interest rate. As we will see, the Fed typically uses the interest rate as its policy target.

The Demand for Money

The Fed's two monetary policy targets are related in an important way. To see this relationship, we first need to examine the demand and supply for money. Figure 14-2 shows the demand curve for money. The interest rate is on the vertical axis, and the quantity of money is on the horizontal axis. Here we are using the M1 definition of money, which equals currency in circulation plus checking account balances. Notice that the demand curve for money is downward sloping.

To understand why the demand curve for money is downward sloping, consider that households and firms have a choice between holding money or other financial assets, such as U.S. Treasury bills. Money has one very desirable characteristic: You can use it to buy goods, services, or financial assets. Money also has one undesirable characteristic: It earns either no interest or a very low rate of interest. The currency in your wallet earns no interest, and the money in your checking account earns either no interest or very little interest. Alternatives to money, such as U.S. Treasury bills, pay interest but have to be sold if you want to use the funds to buy something. When interest rates rise on financial assets such as U.S. Treasury bills, the amount of interest that households

FIGURE 14-2

The Demand for Money

The money demand curve slopes downward because lower interest rates cause households and firms to switch from financial assets like U.S. Treasury bills to money. All other things being equal, a fall in the interest rate from 4 percent to 3 percent will increase the quantity of money demanded from $900 billion to $950 billion: An increase in the interest rate will decrease the quantity of money demanded.

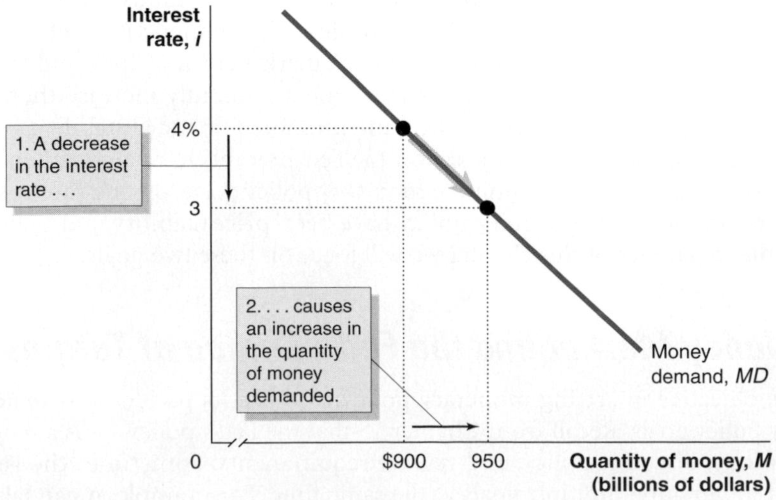

and firms lose by holding money increases. When interest rates fall, the amount of interest households and firms lose by holding money decreases. Remember that *opportunity cost* is what you have to forgo to engage in an activity. The interest rate is the opportunity cost of holding money.

We now have an explanation for why the demand curve for money slopes downward: When interest rates on Treasury bills and other financial assets are low, the opportunity cost of holding money is low, so the quantity of money demanded by households and firms will be high; when interest rates are high, the opportunity cost of holding money will be high, so the quantity of money demanded will be low. In Figure 14-2, a decrease in interest rates from 4 percent to 3 percent causes the quantity of money demanded by households and firms to rise from $900 billion to $950 billion.

Shifts in the Money Demand Curve

We saw in Chapter 3 that the demand curve for a good is drawn holding constant all variables, other than the price, that affect the willingness of consumers to buy the good. Changes in variables other than the price cause the demand curve to shift. Similarly, the demand curve for money is drawn holding constant all variables, other than the interest rate, that affect the willingness of households and firms to hold money. Changes in variables other than the interest rate cause the demand curve to shift. The two most important variables that cause the money demand curve to shift are real GDP and the price level.

An increase in real GDP means that the amount of buying and selling of goods and services will increase. This additional buying and selling increases the demand for money as a medium of exchange, so the quantity of money households and firms want to hold increases at each interest rate. Therefore, the money demand curve will shift to the right. A decrease in real GDP decreases the quantity of money demanded at each interest rate, shifting the money demand curve to the left. A higher price level increases the quantity of money required for a given amount of buying and selling. Eighty years ago, for example, when a new car could be purchased for $500 and a salary of $30 per week was considered middle-income earnings, the quantity of money demanded by households and firms was much lower than today, even adjusting for the effect of the lower real GDP and smaller population of those years. An increase in the price level increases the quantity of money demanded at each interest rate, shifting the money demand curve to the right. A decrease in the price level decreases the quantity of money demanded at each interest rate, shifting the money demand curve to the left. Figure 14-3 illustrates shifts in the money demand curve.

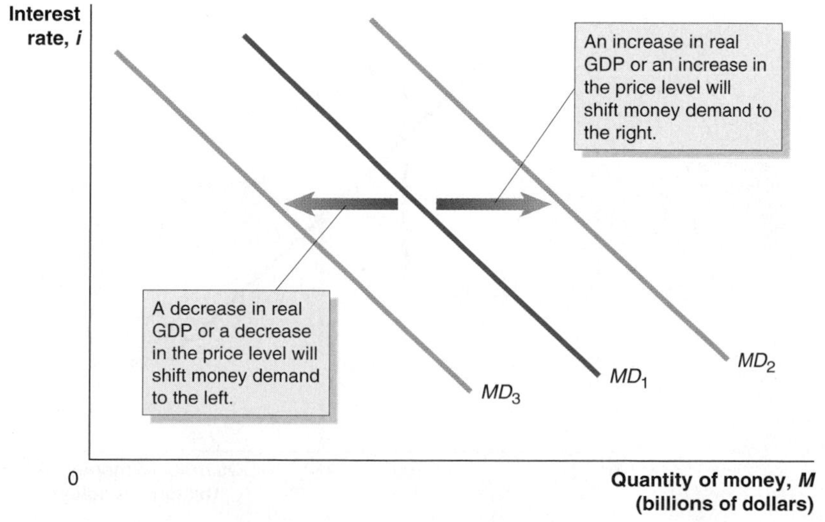

FIGURE 14-3

Shifts in the Money Demand Curve

Changes in real GDP or the price level cause the money demand curve to shift. An increase in real GDP or an increase in the price level will cause the money demand curve to shift from MD_1 to MD_2. A decrease in real GDP or a decrease in the price level will cause the money demand curve to shift from MD_1 to MD_3.

How the Fed Manages the Money Supply: A Quick Review

Having discussed money demand, we now turn to money supply. In Chapter 13, we discussed how the Federal Reserve manages the money supply. Eight times per year, the FOMC meets in Washington, D.C. If the FOMC decides to increase the money supply, it orders the trading desk at the Federal Reserve Bank of New York to purchase U.S. Treasury securities. The sellers of these Treasury securities deposit the funds they receive from the Fed in banks, which increases the banks' reserves. The banks loan out most of these reserves, which creates new checking account deposits and expands the money supply. If the FOMC decides to decrease the money supply, it orders the trading desk to sell Treasury securities, which decreases banks' reserves and contracts the money supply.

Equilibrium in the Money Market

In Figure 14-4, we include both the money demand and money supply curves. We can use this figure to see how the Fed affects both the money supply *and the interest rate.* For simplicity, we assume that the Federal Reserve is able to completely fix the money supply (although, in fact, the behavior of the public and banks can also affect the money supply). Therefore, the money supply curve is a vertical line, and changes in the interest rate have no effect on the quantity of money supplied. Just as with other markets, equilibrium in the *money market* occurs where the money demand curve crosses the money supply curve. If the Fed increases the money supply, the money supply curve will shift to the right and the equilibrium interest rate will fall. In Figure 14-4, when the Fed increases the money supply from $900 billion to $950 billion, the money supply curve shifts from MS_1 to MS_2 and the equilibrium interest rate falls from 4 percent to 3 percent.

In the money market, the adjustment from one equilibrium to another equilibrium is a little different from the adjustment in the market for a good. In Figure 14-4, the money market is initially in equilibrium with an interest rate of 4 percent and a money supply of $900 billion. When the Fed increases the money supply by $50 billion, initially households and firms will have more money than they want to hold at an interest rate of 4 percent. What do households and firms do with the extra $50 billion? They are most likely to use the money to buy short-term financial assets, such as Treasury bills. Short-term financial assets have maturities—the date when the last payment by the seller is

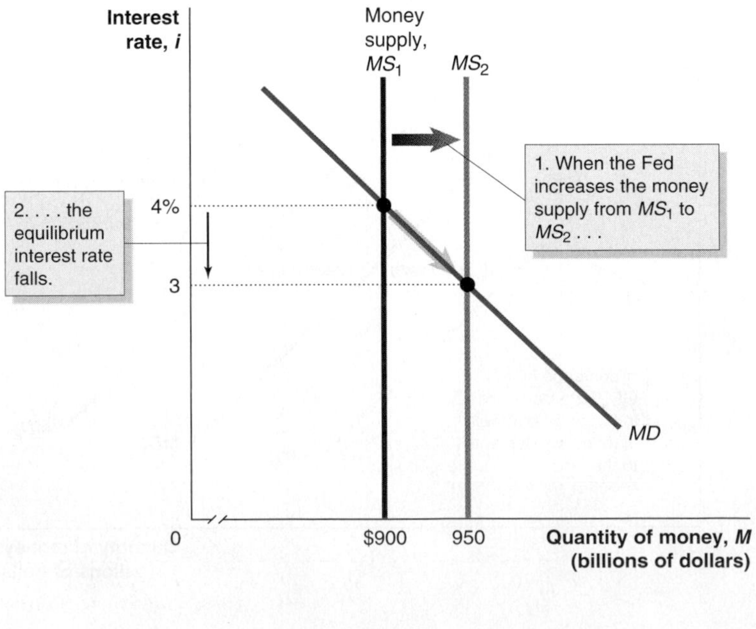

FIGURE 14-4

The Impact on the Interest Rate When the Fed Increases the Money Supply

When the Fed increases the money supply, households and firms will initially hold more money than they want, relative to other financial assets. Households and firms buy Treasury bills and other financial assets with the money they don't want to hold. This increase in demand drives up the prices of these assets and drives down their interest rates. Eventually, interest rates will fall enough that households and firms will be willing to hold the additional money the Fed has created. In the figure, an increase in the money supply from $900 billion to $950 billion causes the money supply curve to shift to the right from MS_1 to MS_2 and causes the equilibrium interest rate to fall from 4 percent to 3 percent.

made—of one year or less. By buying short-term assets, households and firms drive up their prices and drive down their interest rates.

To see why an increasing demand for Treasury bills will lower their interest rate, recall from Chapter 5 that *the prices of financial assets and their interest rates move in opposite directions.* Suppose you buy a U.S. Treasury bill today for \$962 that matures in one year, at which time the Treasury will pay you \$1,000. (Remember that Treasury bills are sold by the government at a price below their face value of \$1,000. The difference between the price of the bill and its \$1,000 face value represents the return to investors for lending their money to the Treasury.) You will earn \$38 in interest on your investment of \$962. The interest rate on the Treasury bill is:

$$\left(\frac{\$38}{\$962}\right) \times 100 = 4\%.$$

Now suppose that many households and firms increase their demand for Treasury bills. This increase in demand will have the same effect on Treasury bills that an increase in the demand for apples has on apples: The price will rise. Suppose the price of Treasury bills rises from \$962 to \$971. Now if you buy a Treasury bill you will receive only \$29 in interest on your investment of \$971. The interest rate on the Treasury bill is now:

$$\left(\frac{\$29}{\$971}\right) \times 100 = 3\%.$$

An increase in the price of Treasury bills has lowered the interest rate on Treasury bills.

As the interest rates on financial assets fall, the opportunity cost of holding money also falls. Households and firms move down the money demand curve. Eventually the interest rate will have fallen enough that households and firms are willing to hold the additional \$50 billion worth of money the Fed has created and the money market will be back in equilibrium. To summarize: *When the Fed increases the money supply, the short-term interest rate must fall until it reaches a level at which households and firms are willing to hold the additional money.*

Figure 14-5 shows what happens when the Fed decreases the money supply. The money market is initially in equilibrium at an interest rate of 4 percent and a money supply of \$900 billion. If the Fed decreases the money supply to \$850 billion, households and firms will be holding less money than they would like—relative to other financial assets—at an interest rate of 4 percent. To increase their money holdings, they

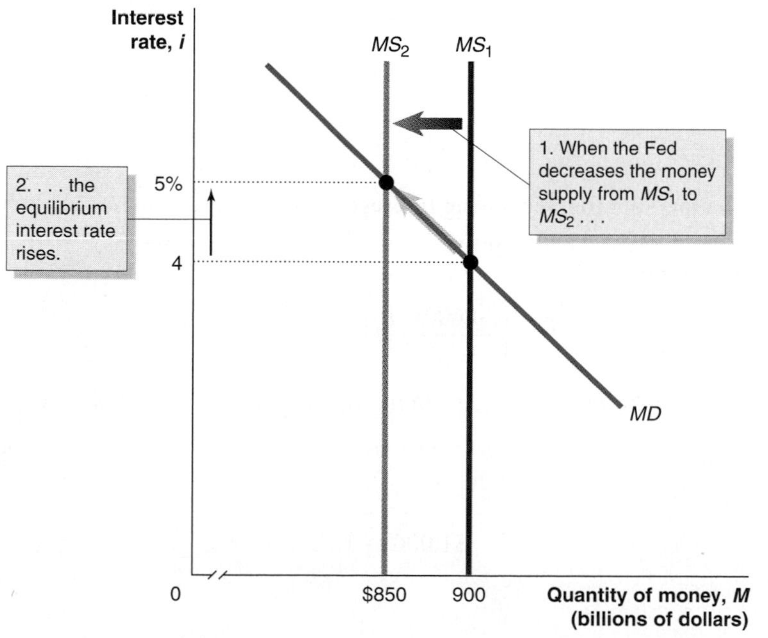

FIGURE 14-5

The Impact on Interest Rates When the Fed Decreases the Money Supply

When the Fed decreases the money supply, households and firms will initially hold less money than they want, relative to other financial assets. Households and firms will sell Treasury bills and other financial assets, reducing their prices and increasing their interest rates. Eventually, interest rates will rise to the point at which households and firms will be willing to hold the smaller amount of money that results from the Fed's actions. In the figure, a reduction in money supply from \$900 billion to \$850 billion causes the money supply curve to shift to the left from MS_1 to MS_2 and causes the equilibrium interest rate to rise from 4 percent to 5 percent.

will sell Treasury bills and other financial assets. The increased supply of Treasury bills for sale will decrease their prices and increase their interest rates. Rising short-term interest rates increase the opportunity cost of holding money, causing households and firms to move up the money demand curve. Equilibrium is finally restored at an interest rate of 5 percent.

SOLVED PROBLEM 14-1

(2) LEARNING OBJECTIVE

Describe the Federal Reserve's monetary policy targets, and explain how expansionary and contractionary monetary policies affect the interest rate.

The Relationship between Treasury Bill Prices and Their Interest Rates

What is the price of a Treasury bill that pays $1,000 in one year, if its interest rate is 4 percent? What is the price of the Treasury bill if its interest rate is 5 percent?

Solving the Problem:

Step 1: Review the chapter material. This problem is about the relationship between Treasury bill prices and interest rates, so you may want to review the section "Equilibrium in the Money Market," which begins on page 444.

Step 2: Use the formula for calculating interest rates to determine the Treasury bill price when the interest rate is 4 percent. In this situation, the interest rate will be equal to the percentage increase from the initial purchase price of the bill to the $1,000 buyers will receive in one year. We can set up the problem like this, where P is the purchase price of the Treasury bill:

$$\left(\frac{\$1{,}000 - P}{P}\right) \times 100 = 4.$$

Dividing both sides by 100 and multiplying both sides by P, we get:

$$\$1{,}000 - P = 0.04P,$$

or,

$$\$1{,}000 = 1.04P,$$

or,

$$\frac{\$1{,}000}{1.04} = P,$$

or, rounding to the nearest dollar,

$$P = \$962.$$

Step 3: Use the formula for calculating interest rates to determine the Treasury bill price when the interest rate is 5 percent. We can apply the same formula to find the price when the interest rate is 5 percent:

$$\left(\frac{\$1{,}000 - P}{P}\right) \times 100 = 5.$$

Once again, dividing both sides by 100 and multiplying both sides by P we get:

$$\$1{,}000 - P = 0.05P,$$

or,

$$\$1{,}000 = 1.05P,$$

or,

$$\frac{\$1{,}000}{1.05} = P,$$

or,

$$P = \$952.$$

Extra Credit: The interest rate on a Treasury bill or other financial asset is also called its *yield.* It's important to remember that prices of financial assets and their yields move in opposite directions. Consider this excerpt from the credit market column in the *Wall Street Journal:*

> The [price of the] 10-year [Treasury] note was up . . . $0.9375 per $1,000 face value. Its yield fell to 4.563% Friday, as yields move inversely to prices.

A similar reminder that the yield moves inversely to the price appears in this newspaper column every day. Any fact the *Wall Street Journal* feels is important enough to remind its readers of every day is probably worth remembering!

Source: *Wall Street Journal,* November 1, 2005, p. C1.

YOUR TURN: **For more practice, do problem 5 on page 469 at the end of this chapter.**

A Tale of Two Interest Rates

In Chapter 9, we discussed the loanable funds model of the interest rate. In that model, the equilibrium interest rate was determined by the supply and demand for loanable funds. Why do we need two models of the interest rate? The answer is that the loanable funds model is concerned with the *long-term real rate of interest,* and the money-market model is concerned with the *short-term nominal rate of interest.* The long-term real rate of interest is the interest rate that is most relevant when savers consider purchasing a long-term financial investment such as a corporate bond. It is also the rate of interest that is most relevant to firms who are borrowing to finance long-term investment projects such as new factories or office buildings, or to households who are taking out a mortgage loan to buy a new home.

When conducting monetary policy, however, the short-term nominal interest rate is the most relevant interest rate because it is the interest rate most affected by increases and decreases in the money supply. Often—but not always—there is a close connection between movements in the short-term nominal interest rate and movements in the long-term real interest rate. So, when the Fed takes actions to increase the short-term nominal interest, usually the long-term real interest rate will also increase. In other words, as we will discuss in the next section, when the interest rate on Treasury bills rises, the real interest rate on mortgage loans will also usually rise, although sometimes only after a delay.

Choosing a Monetary Policy Target

As we have seen, the Fed uses monetary policy targets to affect economic variables such as real GDP or the price level, which are closely related to the Fed's policy goals. The Fed chooses the money supply or the interest rate as its monetary policy target. As Figure 14-5 shows, the Fed is capable of affecting both. The Fed has generally focused more on the interest rate than on the money supply. After 1980, deregulation and financial innovations, including paying interest on checking accounts and the introduction of money market mutual funds, have made M1 less relevant as a measure of the medium of exchange. These developments led the Fed to rely for a time on M2, a broader measure of the money supply that had a more stable historical relationship to economic growth.

Even this relationship broke down in the early 1990s. In July 1993, then Fed Chairman Alan Greenspan informed the U.S. Congress that the Fed would cease using M1 or M2 targets to guide the conduct of monetary policy. The Fed has correspondingly increased its reliance on interest rate targets.

There are many different interest rates in the economy. For purposes of monetary policy, the Fed has targeted the interest rate known as the *federal funds rate.* In the next section, we discuss the federal funds rate before examining how targeting the interest rate can help the Fed achieve its monetary policy goals.

The Importance of the Federal Funds Rate

Recall from Chapter 13 that every bank must keep 10 percent of its checking account deposits above a certain threshold as reserves, either as currency held in the bank or as deposits with the Fed. Banks receive no interest on their reserves, so they have an incentive to invest reserves above the 10-percent minimum. Banks that need additional reserves can borrow in the *federal funds market* from banks that have reserves available. The **federal funds rate** is the interest rate banks charge on loans in the federal funds market. The loans in the federal funds market are usually very short term, often just overnight.

Federal funds rate The interest rate banks charge each other for overnight loans.

Despite the name, the federal funds rate is not set administratively by the Fed. Instead, the rate is determined by the supply of reserves relative to the demand for them. Because the Fed can increase and decrease bank reserves through open market operations, it can set a target for the federal funds rate and come very close to hitting it. The FOMC announces a target for the federal funds rate after each meeting. In Figure 14-6, the orange line shows the Fed's targets for the federal funds rate since 1995. The jagged green line represents the actual federal funds rate on a weekly basis.

The federal funds rate is not directly relevant for households and firms. No households or firms, except banks, can borrow or lend in the federal funds market. However, changes in the federal funds rate usually will result in changes in both interest rates on other short-term financial assets, such as Treasury bills, and interest rates on long-term financial assets, such as corporate bonds and mortgages. The effect of a change in the federal funds rate on long-term interest rates is usually smaller than it is on short-term interest rates and the effect may occur only after a lag in time. Although a majority of

FIGURE 14-6

Federal Funds Rate Targeting, January 1995–July 2005

The Fed does not set the federal funds rate, but its ability to increase or decrease bank reserves quickly through open market operations keeps the actual federal funds rate close to the Fed's target rate. The orange line is the Fed's target for the federal funds rate and the jagged green line represents the actual value for the federal funds rate on a weekly basis.

Source: Board of Governors of the Federal Reserve System.

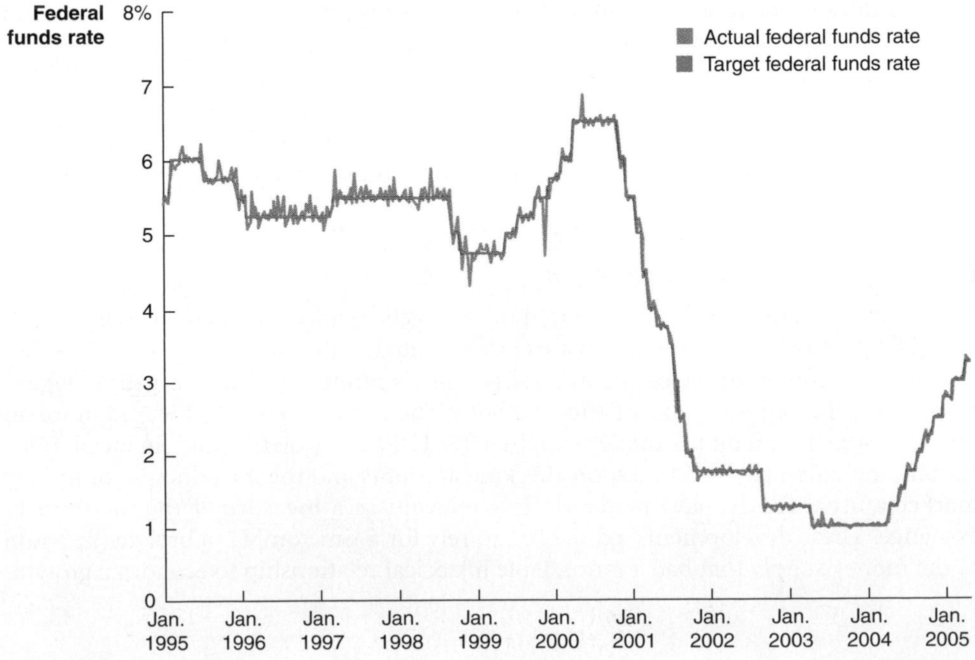

economists support the Fed's choice of the interest rate as its monetary policy target, some economists believe the Fed should concentrate on the money supply instead. We will discuss the views of these economists later in this chapter.

Monetary Policy and Economic Activity

③ **LEARNING OBJECTIVE**
Use aggregate demand and aggregate supply graphs to show the effects of monetary policy on real GDP and the price level.

Remember that the Fed uses the federal funds rate as a monetary policy target because it has good control of the federal funds rate through open market operations and because it believes that changes in the federal funds rate will ultimately affect economic variables that are related to its monetary policy goals. Here it is important to consider again the distinction between the nominal interest rate and the real interest rate. Recall that we calculate the real interest rate by subtracting the inflation rate from the nominal interest rate. Ultimately, the ability of the Fed to use monetary policy to affect economic variables such as real GDP depends upon its ability to affect real interest rates, such as the real interest rates on mortgages and corporate bonds. Because the federal funds rate is a short-term nominal interest rate, the Fed sometimes has difficulty affecting long-term real interest rates. Nevertheless, for purposes of the following discussion we will assume that the Fed is able to use open market operations to affect long-term real interest rates.

How Interest Rates Affect Aggregate Demand

Changes in interest rates affect *aggregate demand,* which is the total level of spending in the economy. Recall from Chapter 13 that aggregate demand has four components: consumption, investment, government purchases, and net exports. Changes in interest rates will not affect government purchases, but they will affect the other three components of aggregate demand in the following ways:

- *Consumption.* Many households finance purchases of consumer durables, such as automobiles and furniture, by borrowing. Lower interest rates cause increased spending on durables because they lower the total cost of these goods to consumers by lowering the interest payments on loans. Higher interest rates raise the cost of these consumer durables, and households will buy fewer of them.
- *Investment.* Firms finance most of their spending on machinery, equipment, and factories out of their profits or by borrowing. Firms borrow either from the financial markets by issuing corporate bonds or from banks. Higher interest rates on corporate bonds or on bank loans make it more expensive for firms to borrow, so they will undertake fewer investment projects. Lower interest rates make it less expensive for firms to borrow, so they will undertake more investment projects. Lower interest rates can also increase investment through their impact on stock prices. As interest rates decline, stocks become a more attractive investment relative to bonds. The increase in demand for stocks raises their price. An increase in stock prices sends a signal to firms that the future profitability of investment projects has increased. By issuing additional shares of stocks, firms can acquire the funds they need to buy new factories and equipment, thereby increasing investment.

  Finally, spending by households on new homes is also part of investment. When interest rates on mortgage loans rise, the cost of buying new homes rises, and fewer new homes will be purchased. When interest rates on mortgage loans fall, more new homes will be purchased.
- *Net exports.* Recall that net exports are equal to spending by foreign households and firms on goods and services produced in the United States minus spending by U.S. households and firms on goods and services produced in other countries. The value of net exports depends partly on the exchange rate between the dollar and foreign currencies. When the value of the dollar rises, households and firms in other countries must pay more for goods and services produced in the United States, but U.S. households and firms will pay less for goods and services produced in other countries. As a result, the United States will export less and import more, so net

exports fall. When the value of the dollar falls, net exports rise. If interest rates in the United States rise relative to interest rates in other countries, investing in U.S. financial assets becomes more desirable, causing foreign investors to increase their demand for dollars, which increases the value of the dollar. As the value of the dollar increases, net exports will fall. If interest rates in the United States decline relative to interest rates in other countries, the value of the dollar will fall and net exports will rise.

14-1 Making the Connection

Was there a "bubble" in housing prices in the early 2000s?

Was There a Housing Market "Bubble" in the Early 2000s?

We have seen that low interest rates helped boost demand for housing during the 2001 recession and for several years thereafter. Lower interest rates can have a dramatic effect on the affordability of housing. For example, in 2000 the average interest rate on a new home mortgage was 7.5 percent. In 2005, the average rate was only 5.75 percent. Suppose you buy a home and need a $150,000 mortgage loan. On a 30-year mortgage with an interest rate of 7.5 percent, your monthly payment on the loan would be about $1,050. With an interest rate of 5.75 percent, your monthly payment would fall to about $875. So, it is not surprising that as interest rates fell after 2000, sales of new houses increased.

Some observers have argued that more was going on than just the normal increase in the quantity of new homes demanded due to lower interest rates; they argued that a "bubble" had formed in the housing market. As we discussed in Chapter 5, the price of any asset reflects the returns received by the owner of the asset. For example, the price of a share of stock reflects the profitability of the firm issuing the stock because the owner of a share of stock has a claim on the firm's profits and its assets. Many economists believe, however, that sometimes a stock market "bubble" can form when the prices of stocks rise above levels that can be justified by the profitability of the firms issuing the stock. This appears to have been true of many Internet stocks in the late 1990s. Bubbles end when enough investors decide stocks are overvalued and begin to sell. The resulting fall in prices can be very steep, as when the total value of stocks traded on the New York Stock Exchange declined by several trillion dollars between 2000 and 2002. Why would an investor be willing to pay more for a share of stock than would be justified by its underlying value? There are two main explanations: The investor may be caught up in the enthusiasm of the moment and, by failing to gather sufficient information, may overestimate the true value of the stock; or the investor may expect to profit from buying stock at inflated prices if the investor can sell the stock at an even higher price before the bubble bursts.

By 2004, some economists believed that a bubble was occurring in housing prices. The price of a house should reflect the value of the housing services the house provides. A measure of the value of these housing services is the rent charged for comparable houses in the area. Some economists argued that in certain housing markets the prices of houses had risen so much that monthly mortgage payments were far above the monthly rent on comparable houses. In addition, in some markets there was an increase in the number of buyers who did not intend to live in the houses they purchased but were using them as investments. Like stock investors during a stock market bubble, these housing investors were expecting to make a profit by selling houses at a higher price than they had paid for them, and they were not concerned about whether the prices of the houses were above the value of the housing services provided.

Other economists were skeptical that a bubble in housing prices actually was occurring. These economists argued that rising incomes, falling interest rates, and high rates of family formation, due in part to high levels of immigration, were sufficient to explain the increase in housing prices, and they were skeptical that investors interested in buying houses and quickly reselling them were playing an important role in the market. Unlike stocks, houses are expensive to buy and sell, which makes it difficult to make an economic profit from buying houses and quickly reselling them.

At the beginning of this chapter, we discussed the success of Robert Toll and his home building firm, Toll Brothers. Robert Toll was also skeptical that rising house prices represented a bubble. Instead, he argued that higher house prices reflected restrictions imposed by local governments on building new houses. He argued that the restrictions resulted from "NIMBY"— "Not in My Back Yard"—politics. Many existing homeowners are reluctant to see nearby farms and undeveloped land turned into new housing developments. As a result, according to Toll, "Towns don't want anything built."

In the fall of 2005, it was still unclear whether the housing price increases of the early 2000s could be sustained.

Source: Quote from Robert Toll from Shawn Tully, "Toll Brothers: The New King of the Real Estate Boom," *Fortune*, April 5, 2005.

The Effects of Monetary Policy on Real GDP and the Price Level

Figure 14-7 uses the dynamic aggregate demand and aggregate supply (*AD-AS*) model developed in Chapter 12 to illustrate how monetary policy affects real GDP and the price level. Recall from Chapter 12 that over time the U.S. labor force and U.S. capital stock will increase. Technological progress will also occur. The result will be an increase in potential real GDP, which we show by the long-run aggregate supply curve (*LRAS*) shifting to the right. These factors will also result in firms supplying more goods and services at any given price level in the short run, which we show by the short-run aggregate supply curve (*SRAS*) shifting to the right. During most years, the aggregate demand curve (*AD*) will also shift to the right, indicating that aggregate expenditure will be higher at every price level. There are several reasons why aggregate expenditure usually increase: As population grows and incomes rise, consumption will increase over time. Also, as the economy grows, firms expand capacity and new firms are established, increasing investment spending. Finally, an expanding population and an expanding economy require increased government services, such as more police officers and teachers, so government purchases will expand.

During certain periods, however, *AD* does not increase enough during the year to keep the economy at potential GDP. This slow growth in aggregate demand may be due to households and firms becoming pessimistic about the future state of the economy, leading them to cut back their spending on consumer durables, houses, and factories. Other possibilities exist, as well: The federal government might decide to balance the budget by cutting back its purchases, or recessions in other countries might cause a

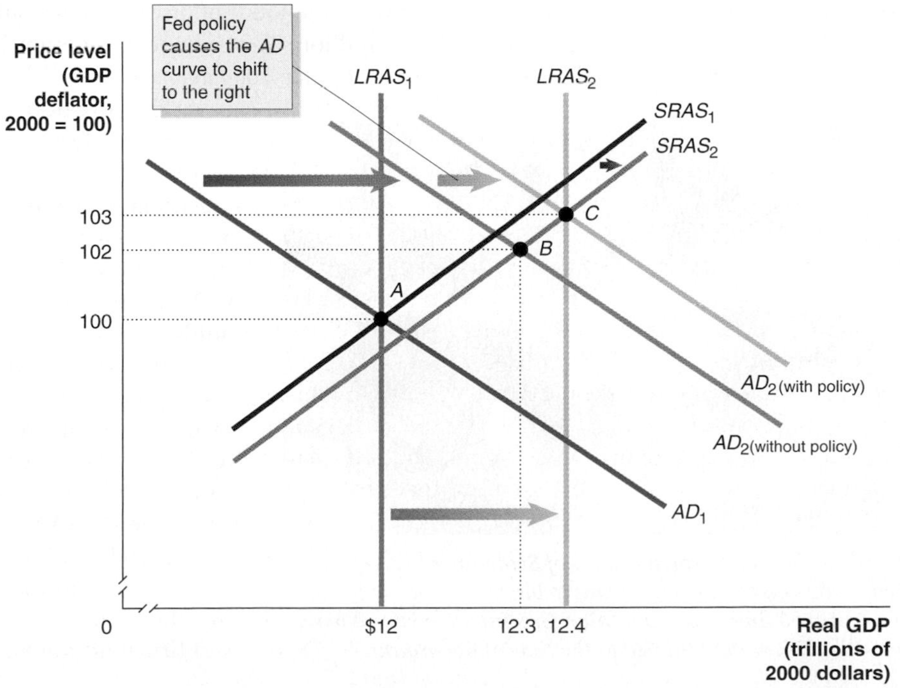

FIGURE 14-7

An Expansionary Monetary Policy

The economy begins in equilibrium at point *A*, with real GDP of $12 trillion and a price level of 100. Without monetary policy, aggregate demand will shift from AD_1 to $AD_{2(\text{without policy})}$, which is not enough to keep the economy at full employment because long-run aggregate supply has shifted from $LRAS_1$ to $LRAS_2$. The economy will be in short-run equilibrium at point *B*, with real GDP of $12.3 trillion and a price level of 102. By lowering interest rates, the Fed increases investment, consumption, and net exports sufficiently to shift aggregate demand to $AD_{2(\text{with policy})}$. The economy will be in equilibrium at point *C* with real GDP of $12.4 trillion, which is its full-employment level, and a price level of 103. The price level is higher than it would have been if the Fed had not acted to increase spending in the economy.

decline in U.S. exports. In Figure 14-7, in the first year the economy is in equilibrium at potential real GDP of $12 trillion and a price level of 100 (point *A*). In the second year *LRAS* increases to $12.4 trillion, but *AD* increases only to AD_2(without policy), which is not enough to keep the economy in macroeconomic equilibrium at potential GDP. Without the Fed intervening, the short-run equilibrium will occur at $12.3 trillion (point *B*). The $100 billion gap between this level of real GDP and potential real GDP at $LRAS_2$ means that some firms are operating at less than their normal capacity. Incomes and profits will fall, firms will begin to lay off workers, and the unemployment rate will rise.

The economists at the Federal Reserve closely monitor the economy and continually update forecasts of future levels of real GDP and prices. When these economists anticipate that aggregate demand is not growing fast enough to allow the economy to remain at full employment, they present their findings to the Federal Open Market Committee, which decides whether circumstances require a change in monetary policy. For example, suppose that the FOMC meets and considers a forecast from the staff indicating that during the following year a gap of $100 billion will open between equilibrium real GDP and potential real GDP. In other words, the situation shown in Figure 14-7 will occur. The FOMC may then decide to take action to lower interest rates to stimulate aggregate demand. The figure shows the results of a successful attempt to do this: *AD* has shifted to the right and equilibrium occurs at potential GDP (point *C*). The Fed will have successfully headed off the falling incomes and rising unemployment that otherwise would have occurred.

Expansionary monetary policy The Federal Reserve's increasing the money supply and decreasing interest rates to increase real GDP.

When the Fed increases the money supply and decreases interest rates to increase real GDP, it is engaging in **expansionary monetary policy.** Notice that in Figure 14-7 the expansionary monetary policy caused the inflation rate to be higher than it would have been. Without the expansionary policy, the price level would have risen from 100 to 102, so the inflation rate for the year would have been 2 percent. By shifting the aggregate demand curve, the expansionary policy caused the price level to increase from 102 to 103, raising the inflation rate from 2 percent to 3 percent.

14-2 Making the Connection

The Fed Responds to the Terrorist Attacks of September 11, 2001

When the Fed was founded, its main purpose was to make discount loans to banks suffering from deposit withdrawals. Today, discount loans have become relatively less important in the operations of the Fed. For example, the average weekly amount of discount loans outstanding in 2001 through September 11 was only $34 million. This volume of discount loans is very small compared with total bank reserves of more than $66 *billion.*

The day after the terrorist attacks of September 11, 2001, the Fed made massive discount loans to banks and succeeded in preventing a financial panic. Alan Greenspan, pictured here, was the chairman of the Fed at the time of the attacks.

Still, discount loans remain an effective way for the Fed to make funds quickly available to banks in an emergency. The banks can use these funds to provide cash or loans to households and firms. The day after the terrorist attacks of September 11, 2001, the Fed made massive discount loans to banks. Discount loans rose from $99 million on September 5 to $45.5 *billion* on September 12, or to 500 times their normal level. In the end, households and firms did not withdraw excessive amounts from their bank accounts following the attack, and the volume of discount loans returned to normal levels very quickly. By September 19, discount loans had fallen to $2.6 billion and by September 26, they had fallen to only $20 million. The Fed had also relied on discount loans to cushion the banking and financial systems from potential instability during the stock market crash of 1987 and the Y2K difficulties of late 1999.

Although the modern Fed concentrates on its objectives for inflation and economic growth, which it implements through open market operations, it still retains its original purpose of dealing with potential financial panics. For this purpose, discount loans are an effective tool.

Source: Federal Reserve Board of Governors, Statistical Release H.4.1, various weekly issues.

Can the Fed Eliminate Recessions?

Figure 14-7 shows an expansionary monetary policy that performs so well that no recession actually takes place. The Fed manages to shift the *AD* curve to keep the economy continually at potential GDP. In fact, however, this ideal is very difficult for the Fed to achieve. Keeping recessions shorter and milder than they would otherwise be is usually the best the Fed can do. The recession of 2001 shows the Fed performing about as well as it can in the real world. Let's review the events leading up to the 2001 recession and the actions the Fed took in response.

In the spring of 2000, stock prices began to decline. Hardest hit were the dot.coms, because online retailing failed to grow as rapidly as many Wall Street analysts had predicted. As we saw in Chapter 12, when stock prices fall, the wealth of households declines and, as a result, consumption falls. At the same time, many firms began to cut their expenditure on information technology.

On December 19, 2000, at the last FOMC meeting of the year, the committee left the target for the federal funds rate unchanged, although committee members believed the risk of recession had increased. Within a few days, increasing evidence indicated that the growth of aggregate demand was slowing, and the committee held a telephone conference meeting on January 3, 2001, four weeks before its regularly scheduled meeting. During the telephone conference, the committee decided to reduce the target for the federal funds rate from 6.5 percent to 6 percent. The committee continued to reduce the federal funds target at subsequent meetings. By December 2001, it had reduced the rate to 1.75 percent. Further decreases brought the federal funds rate to 1 percent in June 2003, the lowest it had been in more than 40 years.

Falling interest rates were not enough to head off a recession, which began in March 2001. The recession was milder than many economists had expected, despite the impact of the September 11, 2001, terrorist attacks. Real GDP declined only during two quarters in 2001, and GDP was actually higher for 2001 as a whole than it had been during 2000. We saw in Chapter 12 that the recovery from the recession was weaker than had been expected. The unemployment rate rose from 4.3 percent at the beginning of the recession to 5.6 percent at the end of the recession and to a peak of 6.3 percent in June 2003. Even at its peak, though, this was a relatively low unemployment rate compared to the more severe recessions of the post-World War II period, such as the 1981–82 recession when the unemployment rate was above 10 percent. Household purchases of consumer durables and new homes remained strong during 2001, keeping real GDP from falling too far below its potential level. Many homebuilders, like Toll Brothers, enjoyed a surprisingly good year in 2001. Although home building is usually hit hard during recessions, new home construction increased by more than 2 percent, from less than 1.57 million units in 2000 to more than 1.60 million units in 2001.

Although the Fed was able to use expansionary monetary policy successfully to reduce the severity of the 2001 recession, it was unable to entirely eliminate it. In fact, the Fed has no realistic hope of "fine-tuning" the economy to eliminate the business cycle and achieve absolute price stability.

14-3 Making the Connection

Why Was Monetary Policy Ineffective in Japan?

Spending on housing and other types of investment has not been high enough to bring the Japanese economy back to potential GDP.

Because the Japanese economy had been an amazing success story since the end of World War II, few economists predicted that it would perform as poorly as it did beginning in the early 1990s. Between 1950 and 1990, real GDP in Japan grew at an average annual rate of 6.9 percent, compared with an average annual rate of 3.5 percent in the United States. This rapid growth made the Japanese economy the second largest in the world, behind only the United States.

When the Japanese economy entered recession in 1992, most economists assumed that it would quickly recover and resume its rapid growth rate. In fact, the Japanese economy has experienced only sluggish growth since 1992. From 1992 to 2004, real GDP in Japan grew at an average annual rate of only 1.4 percent. Real GDP declined in both 1998 and 2002. During this same period, real GDP in the United States grew at an average annual rate of 3.2 percent. Since the early 1990s, Japan has also experienced significant periods of deflation—or a falling price level. Deflation can contribute to slow growth by raising real interest rates, increasing the real value of debts, and causing consumers to postpone purchases in the hope of experiencing even lower prices in the future. In the United States, the price level has not fallen for an entire year since the 1930s.

During the 1990s, the Japanese central bank, the Bank of Japan, used expansionary monetary policy to spur the economy, but the policy was unsuccessful even though interest rates were driven to very low levels. By 1999, the interest rate on overnight bank loans—the equivalent of the U.S. federal funds rate—was reduced to zero. Other interest rates were also very low. For example, the interest rate on three-month certificates of deposit in banks was only 0.2 percent. Even with these low interest rates, aggregate demand increased very slowly.

Monetary policy worked well in the United States to keep the recession of 2001 from being as severe as some economists had feared it might be. Why hasn't it worked as well in Japan? Having driven short-term interest rates to zero, it would seem that expansionary monetary policy in Japan could not go any further, but this is not quite true. Recall that the *nominal interest rate* is the stated interest rate on a loan, whereas the *real interest rate* is equal to the nominal interest rate minus the inflation rate. Although the nominal interest rate cannot go below zero, the real interest rate can be negative if the inflation rate is greater than the nominal interest rate. Some economists have argued that if the Bank of Japan increased the money supply by enough to cause a significant level of inflation, the negative real interest rate that would result might cause a substantial increase in investment spending. Furthermore, replacing deflation with inflation is likely to increase spending by reducing the real value of debts and by reducing the incentive households have to postpone spending. These sources of increased spending might be sufficient to bring the economy back to potential GDP.

The Bank of Japan, however, has been unwilling to try this approach. The leadership of the Bank of Japan believed that the Japanese economy had overheated in the late 1980s and early 1990s. The leadership believed that the deflation Japan has experienced may in fact have been beneficial in reversing previous inflationary excesses, particularly in real estate and stock prices. Although real GDP in Japan increased by more than 4 percent in 2004, consumer prices continued to decline. It was unclear in 2005 whether Japan's prolonged economic slowdown was yet over.

Using Monetary Policy to Fight Inflation

In addition to using monetary policy to reduce the severity of recessions, the Fed can also use monetary policy to keep aggregate demand from expanding so rapidly that the inflation rate begins to increase. Figure 14-8 shows the situation during 1999 and 2000, when the Fed faced this possibility. During 1999, the economy was at equilibrium beyond potential GDP, although the inflation rate for the entire year was only about 1.5 percent. By December, Alan Greenspan and other members of the FOMC were worried that aggregate demand was increasing so rapidly that the inflation rate would begin to accelerate. In fact, during the last three months of 1999, inflation had

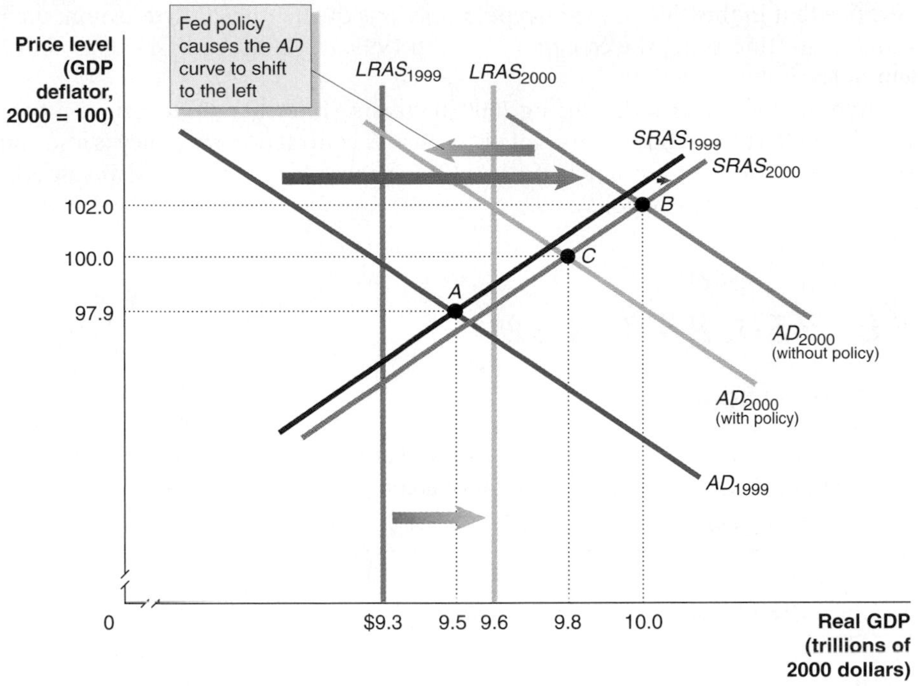

FIGURE 14-8

A Contractionary Monetary Policy in 2000

The economy began 1999 in equilibrium at point *A*, with real GDP of $9.5 trillion and a price level of 97.9. From 1999 to 2000, potential real GDP increased from $9.3 trillion to $9.6 trillion, as long-run aggregate supply increased from $LRAS_{1999}$ to $LRAS_{2000}$. The Fed raised interest rates because it believed aggregate demand was increasing too rapidly. Without the increase in interest rates, aggregate demand would have shifted from AD_{1999} to $AD_{2000\text{(without policy)}}$, and the new short-run equilibrium would have occurred at point *B*. Real GDP would have been $10.0 trillion—$200 billion higher than it actually was—and the price level would have been 102.0. The increase in interest rates resulted in aggregate demand increasing only to $AD_{2000\text{(with policy)}}$. Equilibrium occurred at point *C*, with real GDP of $9.8 trillion and the price level rising only to 100.0.

increased to an annual rate of about 2.5 percent. The FOMC issues a statement after each meeting that summarizes the committee's views on the current state of the economy and gives some indication of how monetary policy might change in the near future. After its meeting on December 21, 1999, the FOMC included the following remarks in its statement:

> [T]he Committee remains concerned with the possibility that over time increases in demand will continue to exceed the growth in potential supply. . . . Such trends could foster inflationary imbalances that would undermine the economy's exemplary performance. . . . At its next meeting the Committee will assess available information on the likely balance of supply and demand, conditions in financial markets, and the possible need for adjustment in the stance of policy to contain inflationary pressures.

At its next meeting on February 2, 2000, the committee raised the target for the federal funds rate from 5.5 percent to 5.75 percent. According to the minutes of the meeting:

> The Committee's decision . . . was intended to help bring the growth of aggregate demand into better alignment with the expansion of sustainable aggregate supply in an effort to avert rising inflationary pressures in the economy.

The committee raised the target for the federal funds rate twice more in following meetings until it reached 6.5 percent in May, where it remained for the rest of 2000. Although it is impossible to know exactly what would have happened during 2000 without the Fed's policy change, Figure 14-8 presents a plausible scenario. The figure shows that without the Fed's actions to increase interest rates, aggregate demand would have shifted farther to the right and equilibrium would have occurred at a level of real GDP that was even farther beyond the potential level. The price level would have risen from 97.9 in 1999 to 102.0 in 2000, meaning that the inflation rate would have been above 4 percent. Because the Fed kept aggregate demand from increasing as much as it otherwise would have, equilibrium occurred closer to potential real GDP and the price level in 2000 rose to only 100.0, keeping the inflation rate to a little over 2 percent.

Notice that in this case, as with its policy actions during the 2001 recession, the Fed was unable to "fine-tune" the economy: In both 1999 and 2000, real GDP was above its potential level.

Contractionary monetary policy The Fed's adjusting the money supply to increase interest rates to reduce inflation.

When the Fed acts as it did during 2000, increasing interest rates to reduce inflation, it is engaging in **contractionary monetary policy.** A contractionary policy is also sometimes known as a *tight* monetary policy. An expansionary policy is also sometimes known as a *loose* monetary policy.

SOLVED PROBLEM 14-2

③ LEARNING OBJECTIVE

Use aggregate demand and aggregate supply graphs to show the effects of monetary policy on real GDP and the price level.

The Effects of Monetary Policy

The hypothetical information in the table shows what the values for real GDP and the price level will be in 2011 if the Fed does *not* use monetary policy:

YEAR	POTENTIAL REAL GDP	REAL GDP	PRICE LEVEL
2010	$13.3 trillion	$13.3 trillion	140
2011	$13.7 trillion	$13.6 trillion	142

a. If the Fed wants to keep real GDP at its potential level in 2011, should it use an expansionary policy or a contractionary policy? Should the trading desk buy Treasury bills or sell them?

b. Suppose the Fed's policy is successful in keeping real GDP at its potential level in 2011. State whether each of the following will be higher or lower than if the Fed had taken no action:

   i. Real GDP
   ii. Potential real GDP
   iii. The inflation rate
   iv. The unemployment rate

c. Draw an aggregate demand and aggregate supply graph to illustrate your answer. Be sure that your graph contains *LRAS* curves for 2010 and 2011; *SRAS* curves for 2010 and 2011; *AD* curve for 2010 and for 2011, with and without monetary policy action; and equilibrium real GDP and the price level in 2011, with and without policy.

Solving the Problem:

Step 1: Review the chapter material. This problem is about the effects of monetary policy on real GDP and the price level, so you may want to review the section "The Effects of Monetary Policy on Real GDP and the Price Level," which begins on page 451.

Step 2: Answer question (a) by explaining how the Fed can keep real GDP at its potential level. The information in the table tells us that without monetary policy, the economy will be below potential real GDP in 2011. To keep real GDP at its potential level, the Fed must undertake an expansionary policy. To implement an expansionary policy, the trading desk needs to buy Treasury bills. Buying Treasury bills will increase reserves in the banking system. Banks will increase their loans, which will increase the money supply and lower the interest rate.

Step 3: Answer question (b) by explaining the effect of the Fed's policy. If the policy is successful, real GDP in 2011 will increase from the level given in the table of $13.3 trillion to its potential level of $13.7 trillion. Potential real GDP is not affected by monetary policy, so its value will not change. Because the level of real GDP will be higher, the unemployment rate will be lower than it would have been without policy. The expansionary monetary policy shifts the *AD* curve to the right, so short-run equilibrium will move up the short-run aggregate supply curve (*SRAS*) and the price level will be higher.

Step 4: Answer question (c) by drawing the graph. Your graph should look similar to Figure 14-7.

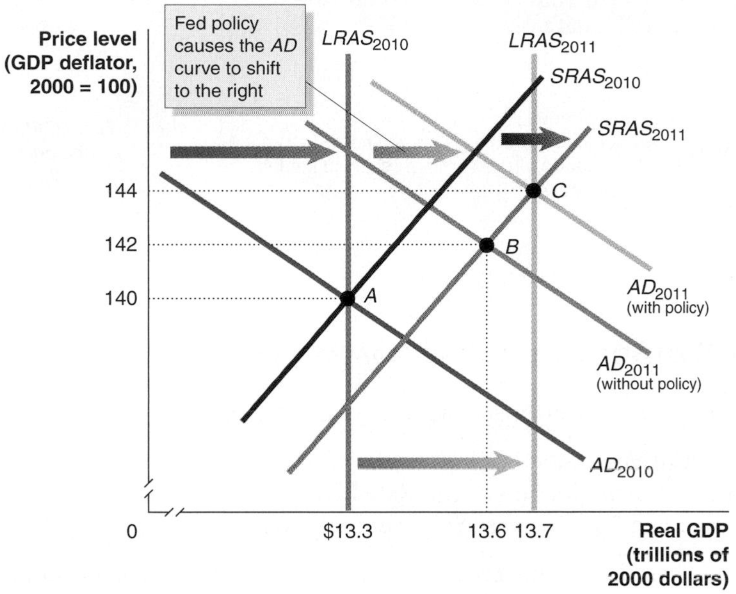

The economy starts in equilibrium in 2010 at point *A*, with the *AD* and *SRAS* curves intersecting along the *LRAS* curve. Real GDP is at its potential level of \$13.3 trillion and the price level is 140. Without monetary policy, the *AD* curve shifts to AD_{2011}(without policy) and the economy is in short-run equilibrium at point *B*. Because potential real GDP has increased from \$13.3 trillion to \$13.7 trillion, short-run equilibrium real GDP of \$13.6 trillion is below the potential level. The price level has increased from 140 to 142. With policy, the *AD* curve shifts to AD_{2011}(with policy) and the economy is in equilibrium at point *C*. Real GDP is at its potential level of \$13.7 trillion. We don't have enough information to be sure of the new equilibrium price level. We do know that it will be higher than 142. The graph shows the price level rising to 144. Therefore, without policy, the inflation rate in 2011 would have been about 1.4 percent. With policy, it will be about 2.9 percent.

Extra Credit: It's important to bear in mind that in reality the Fed is unable to use monetary policy to keep real GDP exactly at its potential level, as this problem suggests. In a later section, we will discuss some of the difficulties the Fed encounters in conducting monetary policy.

YOUR TURN: **For more practice, do problem 14 on page 470 at the end of this chapter.**

A Summary of How Monetary Policy Works

Table 14-1 compares the steps involved in expansionary and contractionary monetary policies. We need to add a very important qualification to this summary. At every point we should add the phrase "relative to what would have happened without the policy." Figure 14-9 is isolating the impact of monetary policy, *holding constant all other factors affecting the variables involved.* In other words, we are invoking the *ceteris paribus condition,* discussed in Chapter 3. This point is important because, for example, a contractionary monetary policy does not cause the price level to fall. As Figure 14-8 showed, a contractionary monetary policy causes the price level *to rise by less than it would have without the policy.*

TABLE 14-1 Expansionary and Contractionary Monetary Policy

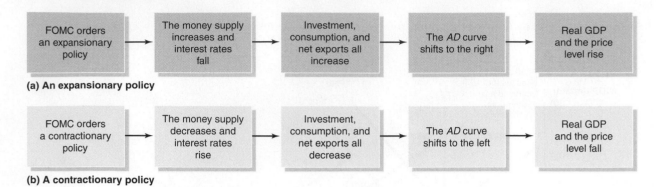

FOMC orders an expansionary policy →	The money supply increases and interest rates fall →	Investment, consumption, and net exports all increase →	The *AD* curve shifts to the right →	Real GDP and the price level rise

(a) An expansionary policy

FOMC orders a contractionary policy →	The money supply decreases and interest rates rise →	Investment, consumption, and net exports all decrease →	The *AD* curve shifts to the left →	Real GDP and the price level fall

(b) A contractionary policy

14-4 Making the Connection

Why Does Wall Street Care about Monetary Policy?

You have probably seen newspaper headlines similar to these:

> "Fed Rate Cut Fuels Stock Gains"
> "Stocks Fall in Anticipation of Fed Rate Increase"
> "Worries of Fed Rate Increase Send Stocks Lower"

Before most meetings of the Federal Open Market Committee, newspapers report stock traders' predictions of possible Fed actions and whether those actions will cause stock prices to increase or decrease. Some Wall Street analysts are known as *Fed watchers* because they study the Fed and attempt to forecast future changes in the target for the federal funds rate. Why do changes in the federal funds rate affect the stock market? There are two main explanations. In thinking about both explanations, remember that changes in the federal funds rate usually cause changes in other interest rates.

The first reason that stock prices react to the Fed raising or lowering interest rates is because changes in interest rates affect the economy. As we have seen, lower interest rates usually result in increases in real GDP. Fundamentally, the value of a share of stock depends on the profitability of the firm that issued the stock. When real GDP is increasing, the profitability of many firms will also be increasing. Stock prices tend to rise when investors expect that the Fed will be lowering interest rates to stimulate the economy. When investors expect that the Fed will be raising interest rates to slow down an economy at risk of rising inflation, stock prices tend to fall.

The second reason that stock prices react to changes in interest rates is that changes in interest rates make it more or less attractive for people to invest in stock rather than in other financial assets. Investors look for the highest return possible on their investments, holding constant the riskiness of the investments. If the interest rates on Treasury bills, bank certificates of deposit, and corporate bonds are all low, an investment in stocks will be more attractive. When interest rates are high, an investment in stocks will be less attractive.

The stock market reacts when the Fed either raises or lowers interest rates.

Don't Let This Happen To You!

Remember That with Monetary Policy It's the Interest Rates—Not the Money—that Counts

It is tempting to think of monetary policy working like this: If the Fed wants more spending in the economy, it increases the money supply and people spend more because they now have more money. If the Fed wants less spending in the economy, it decreases the money supply and people spend less because they now have less money. In fact, that is *not* how monetary policy works. Remember the important difference between money and income: The Fed increases the money supply by buying Treasury bills. The sellers of the Treasury bills have just exchanged one asset—Treasury bills—for another asset—a check from the Fed; they have *not* increased their income. Even though the money supply is now larger, no one's income has increased, so no one's spending should be affected.

It is only when this increase in the money supply results in lower interest rates that spending is affected. When interest rates are lower, households are more likely to buy new homes and automobiles and businesses are more likely to buy new factories and computers. Lower interest rates also lead to a lower value of the dollar, which lowers the prices of exports and raises the prices of imports, thereby increasing net exports. It isn't the increase in the money supply that has brought about this additional spending; *it's the lower interest rates*. To understand how monetary policy works, and to interpret news reports about the Fed's actions, it is necessary to remember that it is the change in interest rates, not the change in the money supply, that is most important.

***YOUR TURN:* Test your understanding by doing related problem 16 on page 471 at the end of this chapter.**

Can the Fed Get the Timing Right?

The Fed's ability to quickly recognize the need for a change in monetary policy is a key to its success. If the Fed is late recognizing that a recession has begun or that the inflation rate is increasing, it may not be able to implement a new policy soon enough to do much good. In fact, if the Fed implements a policy too late, it may actually destabilize the economy. To see how this can happen, consider Figure 14-9. The straight line represents the long-run growth trend in real GDP in the United States. On average, real GDP grows about 3.5 percent per year. The actual path of real GDP differs from the underlying trend because of the business cycle, which is shown by the red curving line. As we saw in Chapter 8, the actual business cycle is more irregular than the stylized cycle shown here.

Suppose that a recession begins in August 2008. Because it takes months for economic statistics to be gathered by the Commerce Department, the Census Bureau, the Bureau of Labor Statistics, and by the Fed itself, there is often a *lag*, or delay, before the Fed recognizes that a recession has begun. Then it takes time for the Fed's economists to

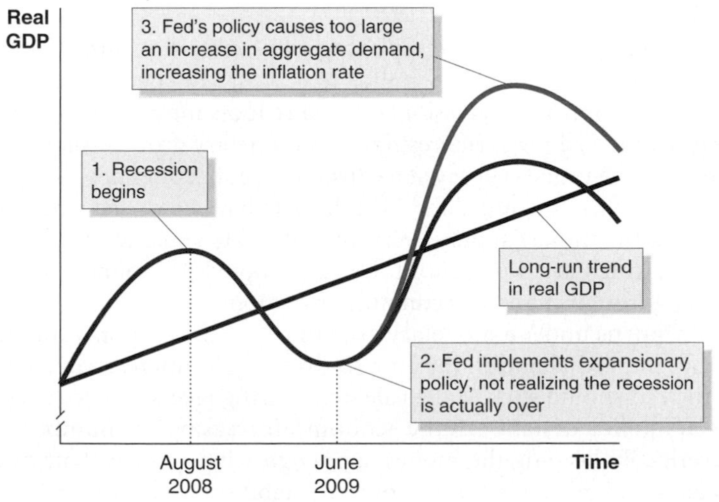

FIGURE 14-9

The Effect of a Poorly Timed Monetary Policy on the Economy

The upward-sloping straight line represents the long-run growth trend in real GDP. The red curving line represents the path real GDP takes because of the business cycle. If the Fed implements a change in monetary policy too late, real GDP will follow the blue curving line. The Fed's expansionary monetary policy has resulted in too great an increase in aggregate demand during the next expansion, which causes an increase in the inflation rate.

analyze the data. Finally, in June 2009, the FOMC concludes that the economy is in recession and begins an expansionary monetary policy. As it turns out, June 2009 is actually the trough of the recession, meaning that the recession has already ended and an expansion has begun. In these circumstances, the Fed's expansionary policy is not needed to end the recession. The increase in aggregate demand caused by the Fed's lowering interest rates is likely to push the economy beyond potential real GDP and cause a significant acceleration in inflation. Real GDP ends up following the path indicated by the curving blue line. The Fed has inadvertently engaged in a *procyclical policy.* A procyclical policy is one that increases the severity of the business cycle, as opposed to a *countercyclical policy*, which is meant to reduce the severity of the business cycle, and which is what the Fed intends to use.

It is not unusual for employment or manufacturing production to decline for a month or two in the middle of an expansion. Distinguishing these minor ups and downs from the beginning of a recession is difficult. The National Bureau of Economic Research (NBER) announces dates for the beginning and ending of recessions that are generally accepted by most economists. An indication of how difficult it is to determine when recessions begin and end is that the NBER generally makes its announcements only after a considerable delay. The NBER did not announce that a recession had begun in March 2001 until November 2001, which is the same month it later determined the recession had ended. It did not announce that a recession had begun in July 1990 until April 1991, which was one month *after* it later determined the recession had ended. Failing to react until well after a recession has begun (or ended) can be a serious problem for the Fed.

(4) LEARNING OBJECTIVE

Discuss the Fed's setting of monetary policy targets.

A Closer Look at the Fed's Setting of Monetary Policy Targets

We have seen that the Fed, in carrying out monetary policy, changes its target for the federal funds rate depending on the state of the economy. Is using the federal funds rate as a target the best way to conduct monetary policy? If the Fed targets the federal funds rate, how should it decide what the target level should be? In this section, we consider some important issues concerning the Fed's targeting policy.

Should the Fed Target the Money Supply?

Some economists have argued that rather than using an interest rate as its monetary policy target, the Fed should use the money supply. Many of the economists who make this argument belong to a school of thought known as *monetarism.* The leader of the monetarist school is Milton Friedman, who was awarded the Nobel Prize in Economics in 1976 and who has long been critical of the Fed's ability to correctly time changes in monetary policy.

Friedman and his followers favor replacing *monetary policy* with a *monetary growth rule.* Ordinarily, we expect monetary policy to respond to changing economic conditions: When the economy is in recession, the Fed reduces interest rates, and when inflation is increasing, the Fed raises interest rates. A monetary growth rule, in contrast, is a plan for increasing the money supply at a constant rate that does not change in response to economic conditions. Friedman and his followers have proposed a monetary growth rule of increasing the money supply every year at a rate equal to the long-run growth rate of real GDP, which is 3.5 percent. If the Fed adopted this monetary growth rule, it would stick to it through changing economic conditions.

But what happens under a monetary growth rule if the economy moves into recession? Shouldn't the Fed abandon the rule to drive down interest rates? Friedman has argued that the Fed should stick to the rule even during recessions because, he believes, active monetary policy destabilizes the economy, increasing the number of recessions and their severity. By keeping the money supply growing at a constant rate, Friedman argues, the Fed would greatly increase economic stability.

Although during the 1970s some economists and politicians pressured the Federal Reserve to adopt a monetary growth rule, most of that pressure has disappeared in recent years. A key reason is that the fairly close relationship between movements in the money supply and movements in real GDP and the price level that existed before 1980 has become much weaker. Since 1980, the growth rate of M1 has been unstable. In some years it has grown more than 10 percent, while in other years it has actually fallen. Yet despite these wide fluctuations in the growth of M1, growth in real GDP has been fairly stable and inflation has remained low.

Why Doesn't the Fed Target Both the Money Supply and the Interest Rate?

Most economists believe that an interest rate is the best monetary policy target, but, as we have just seen, other economists believe the Fed should target the money supply. Why doesn't the Fed satisfy both groups by targeting both the money supply and an interest rate? The simple answer to this question is that the Fed can't target both at the same time. To see why, look at Figure 14-10, which shows the money market.

Remember that the Fed controls the money supply, but it does not control money demand. Money demand is determined by decisions of households and firms as they weigh the trade-off between the convenience of money and its low interest rate compared with other financial assets. Suppose the Fed is targeting the interest rate and decides, given conditions in the economy, that the interest rate should be 5 percent. Or, suppose the Fed is targeting the money supply and decides that the money supply should be $900 billion. Figure 14-10 shows that the Fed can bring about an interest rate of 5 percent, or a money supply of $900 billion, but it can't bring about both. The point representing an interest rate of 5 percent and a money supply of $900 billion is not on the money demand curve, so it can't represent an equilibrium in the money market. Only combinations of the interest rate and the money supply that represent equilibrium in the money market are possible.

The Fed has to choose between targeting an interest rate and targeting the money supply. For most of the period since World War II, the Fed has chosen an interest rate target.

The Taylor Rule

How does the Fed choose a target for the federal funds rate? The discussions at the meetings of the FOMC can be complex and take into account many economic variables. John Taylor of Stanford University has analyzed the factors involved in Fed decision making and developed the **Taylor rule** for federal funds rate targeting. The Taylor rule begins with an estimate of the value of the equilibrium real federal funds rate, which is the federal funds rate—adjusted for inflation—that would be consistent with real GDP being

Taylor rule A rule developed by John Taylor that links the Fed's target for the federal funds rate to economic variables.

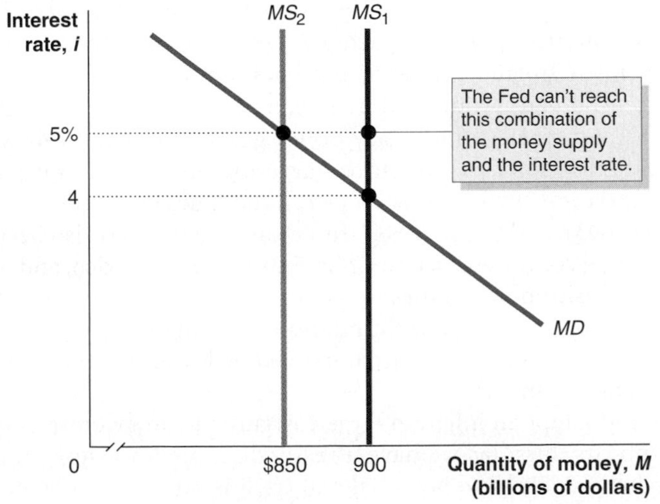

FIGURE 14-10

The Fed Can't Target Both the Money Supply and the Interest Rate

The Fed is forced to choose between using either an interest rate or the money supply as its monetary policy target. In this figure, the Fed can set a target of a money supply of $900 billion or a target of an interest rate of 5 percent, but it can't have both because only combinations of the interest rate and the money supply that represent equilibrium in the money market are possible.

equal to potential real GDP in the long run. According to the Taylor rule, the Fed should set the target for the federal funds rate so that it is equal to the sum of the inflation rate, the equilibrium real federal funds rate, and two additional terms. The first of these additional terms is the *inflation gap*—the difference between current inflation and a target rate; the second is the *output gap*—the percentage difference between real GDP and potential real GDP. The inflation gap and output gap are each given "weights" that reflect their influence on the federal funds target rate. With weights of 1/2 for both gaps, we have the following Taylor rule:

$$\text{Federal funds target rate} = \text{Current inflation rate} + \text{Real equilibrium federal funds rate} + (1/2) \times \text{Inflation gap} + (1/2) \times \text{Output gap}.$$

The presence in the Taylor rule of expressions for the inflation gap and the output gap reflect the fact that the Fed is concerned about both inflation and fluctuations in real GDP. Taylor demonstrated that if the equilibrium real federal funds rate is 2 percent, and the target rate of inflation is 2 percent, the preceding expression does a good job of explaining changes in the Fed's target for the federal funds rate. Consider an example where the inflation rate is 1 percent and real GDP is 1 percent below potential real GDP. In that case, the inflation gap is 1 percent $-$ 2 percent $= -1$ percent, and the output gap is also -1 percent. Inserting these values in the Taylor rule we can calculate the predicted value for the federal funds target rate:

$$\text{Federal funds target rate} = 1\% + 2\% + ((1/2) \times -1\%) + ((1/2) \times -1\%) = 2\%.$$

The Taylor rule has accurately predicted changes in the federal funds target during the period of Alan Greenspan's leadership of the Federal Reserve. For the period of the late 1970s and early 1980s when Paul Volcker was chairman of the Federal Reserve, the Taylor rule predicts a federal funds rate target *lower* than the actual target used by the Fed. This indicates that Chairman Volcker kept the federal funds rate at an unusually high level to bring down the very high inflation rates plaguing the economy in the late 1970s and early 1980s. In contrast, using data from the chairmanship of Arthur Burns from 1970 to 1978, the Taylor rule predicts a federal funds rate target *higher* than the actual target. This indicates that Chairman Burns kept the federal funds rate at an unusually low level during these years, which can help explain why the inflation rate grew worse.

Although the Taylor rule does not account for changes in the target inflation rate or the equilibrium interest rate, many economists view the rule as a convenient way to analyze the federal funds target.

Should the Fed Target Inflation?

Inflation targeting Conducting monetary policy so as to commit the central bank to achieving a publicly announced level of inflation.

Over the past decade, many economists and central bankers, including the current Fed Chairman Ben Bernanke, have expressed significant interest in using *inflation targeting* as a framework for carrying out monetary policy. With **inflation targeting,** the central bank commits to conducting policy to achieve a publicly announced inflation target of, for example, 2 percent. Inflation targeting need not impose an inflexible rule on the central bank. The central bank would still be free, for example, to take action in case of a severe recession. Nevertheless, monetary policy goals and operations would focus on inflation and inflation forecasts. Inflation targeting has been adopted by the central banks of New Zealand (1990), Canada (1991), the United Kingdom (1992), Finland (1993), Sweden (1993), and Spain (1994). Inflation targeting has also been used in some newly industrializing countries, such as Chile, South Korea, Mexico, and South Africa, as well as in some transition economies in Eastern Europe, such as the Czech Republic, Hungary, and Poland. Experience with inflation targeting has varied, but typically the move to inflation targeting has been accompanied by lower inflation (sometimes at the cost of higher unemployment).

Should the Fed adopt an inflation target? Arguments in favor of inflation targeting focus on four points. First, as we have already discussed, in the long run real GDP returns to its potential level and potential real GDP is not affected by monetary policy.

Therefore, in the long run, the Fed can have an impact on inflation but not on real GDP. Having an explicit inflation target would draw the public's attention to this fact. Second, by announcing an inflation target, the Fed would make it easier for households and firms to form accurate expectations of future inflation, improving their planning and the efficiency of the economy. Third, an announced inflation target would help institutionalize good U.S. monetary policy. It would be less likely that abrupt changes in policy would occur as members join and leave the FOMC. Finally, an inflation target would promote accountability for the Fed by providing a yardstick against which its performance could be measured.

Inflation targeting also has opponents, who typically raise three points. First, a numerical target for inflation reduces the flexibility of monetary policy to address other policy goals. Second, inflation targeting assumes the Fed can accurately forecast future inflation rates, which is not always the case. And, finally, holding the Fed accountable only for an inflation goal may make it less likely that the Fed will achieve other important policy goals.

The Fed's performance in the 1980s, 1990s, and early 2000s has generally received high marks from economists, even without formal inflation targeting. The 1990s, for example, saw low inflation and a substantial economic expansion. Although not stated explicitly, the Fed's strategy has been to keep inflation low and stable in the long run. In addition, in recent years the Fed has acted to head off the threat of future inflation before it can become established. The Fed's strategy has much to recommend it. The Fed has been successful at building public support for the idea that low inflation is important to the efficient performance of the economy. The Fed's preemptive attacks on threatening inflation are likely to be more successful than waiting to act until actual inflation is rising. The Fed's strategy is not without risk, however. The Fed's prestige during the past two decades has been dependent on public trust in the effectiveness of Fed leadership in containing inflation, while maintaining economic growth. However, Fed leadership changes over time, which highlights what may be a need for more formal procedures to reassure both the public and elected officials about the continuity of policy. As Ben Bernanke assumed the chairmanship of the Fed in early 2006, his support for inflation targeting increased the chances the Fed would adopt such a policy.

Is the Independence of the Federal Reserve a Good Idea?

(5) **LEARNING OBJECTIVE**

Assess the arguments for and against the independence of the Federal Reserve.

In our discussion of monetary policy, we have made no mention of Congress or the president. In fact, the Fed conducts monetary policy independently of them. The seven members of the Board of Governors are nominated by the president and confirmed by the Senate. Because members serve 14-year terms, they are insulated from political pressure. The seven members of the Board of Governors, along with five presidents of the Federal Reserve banks, make up the membership of the Federal Open Market Committee. The FOMC determines the monetary policy of the United States without the input of Congress or the president.

The Fed's political independence is reinforced by its financial independence. As we have discussed, when the FOMC wants to increase the money supply and decrease interest rates, it buys Treasury securities. To decrease the money supply and increase interest rates, it sells Treasury securities. Because a growing economy requires increases in the money supply, the Fed buys more Treasury securities than it sells. Currently the Fed owns more than $700 billion worth of Treasury securities. The interest it receives from these Treasury securities means that, unlike any other agency of the federal government, it does not have to ask Congress for the funds it needs to operate.

The Fed does not, however, have absolute independence. The U.S. Constitution contains no provision for a central bank. The authority of the Fed comes from legislation passed by Congress and signed by the president. Congress and the president are free at any time to pass new legislation to reorganize the Fed or even to abolish it. So, it is unlikely that the Fed would pursue a monetary policy that was strongly opposed by the president and a large majority in Congress. In addition, most Fed chairmen have attempted to remain in regular contact with other members of the government.

Nevertheless, the Fed is able to formulate monetary policy without taking into account the wishes of Congress and the president, unless it chooses to. Since the founding of the Fed in 1914, debate has occurred about whether or not the independence of the Fed is a good idea.

The Case for Fed Independence

The main reason to keep the Fed—or any country's central bank—independent of the rest of the government is to avoid inflation. Whenever a government is spending more than it is collecting in taxes, it must borrow the difference by selling bonds. The governments of many developing countries have difficulty finding anyone other than their central bank to buy their bonds. The more bonds the central bank buys, the faster the money supply grows and the higher the inflation rate will be. Even in developed countries, governments that control their central banks will be tempted to sell bonds to the central bank, rather than to the public.

Another fear is that if the government controls the central bank it may use that control to further its political interests. It is difficult in any democratic country for a government to be reelected at a time of high unemployment. If the government controls the central bank, it may be tempted just before an election to increase the money supply and drive down interest rates to increase production and employment. In the United States, for example, a president who had direct control over the Fed might be tempted to increase the money supply just before running for reelection, even if this led in the long run to higher inflation and accompanying economic costs.

We might expect that the more independent a country's central bank is, the lower the inflation rate in the country, and the less independent a country's central bank, the higher the inflation rate. Alberto Alesina and Lawrence Summers, economists at Harvard University, tested this idea by comparing the degree of central bank independence and the inflation rate for 16 high-income countries during the years 1955–1988. Figure 14-11 shows the results.

FIGURE 14-11

The More Independent the Central Bank, the Lower the Inflation Rate

For 16 high-income countries, the greater the degree of central bank independence from the rest of the government, the lower the inflation rate. Central bank independence is measured by an index ranging from 1 (minimum independence) to 4 (maximum independence). During these years, Germany had a high index of independence of 4 and a low average inflation rate of just over 3 percent. New Zealand had a low index of independence of 1 and a high average inflation rate of over 7 percent.

Source: Alberto Alesina and Lawrence H. Summers, "Central Bank Independence and Macroeconomic Performance: Some Comparative Evidence," *Journal of Money, Credit and Banking,* Vol. 25, No. 2, May 1993, pp. 151–162.

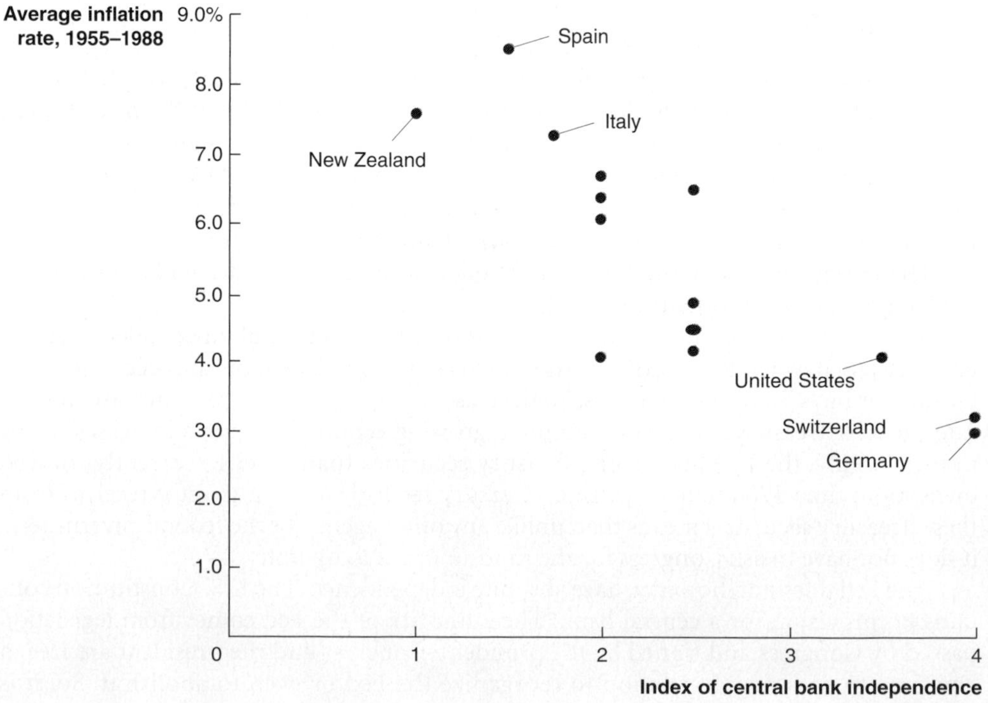

Countries with highly independent central banks, such as the United States, Switzerland, and Germany, had lower inflation rates than countries whose central banks had little independence, such New Zealand, Italy, and Spain. In the last few years, New Zealand and Canada have granted their banks more independence, at least partly to better fight inflation.

The Case against Fed Independence

In democracies, elected representatives usually decide important policy matters. In the United States, however, monetary policy is not decided by elected officials. Instead, it is decided by the unelected Federal Open Market Committee. Only rarely has anyone served on the FOMC who has ever held any elected office. The members are usually academic economists or people with careers in banking, finance, or other areas of business. Because those deciding monetary policy do not have to run for election, they are not accountable for their actions to the ultimate authorities in a democracy: the voters.

Some economists and politicians argue that the Fed should operate like other parts of the executive branch of government. Under this proposal, the members of the Board of Governors would serve only as long as the president wanted them to, as members of the president's cabinet do today. That way, if the president didn't like the current monetary policy, he would have the authority to dismiss the members of the Board of Governors and appoint others in their place. When the president ran for reelection, the voters would have an opportunity to express their approval or disapproval of his monetary policy.

The Fed's independence from the rest of the government, coupled with the Fed's decision-making process, has concentrated power in the hands of the chairman. The chairman has only 1 vote in 7 on the Board of Governors and only 1 vote in 12 on the FOMC. Nevertheless, the very strong tradition at the Fed is that the chairman plays an outsized role in setting policy.

The Fed has never set out any specific guidelines regarding when it will adopt a particular monetary policy. The Fed adopts an expansionary policy when the chairman and the FOMC decide that the economy is in danger of moving into recession. The chairman's recommendations for a policy change are based on his own experience, on the analysis prepared by the Fed's economists, and on discussions with other members of the FOMC. The Fed adopts a contractionary policy when the chairman and FOMC decide that there is a threat of rising inflation. In either case, the decision to change policy depends in part on the personal judgment of the chairman. Most economists would say that monetary policy has been successful during the years since 1979, but some economists suggest that greater transparency about the Fed's objectives would help lock in future good performance.

In periods like the 1970s, when the performance of the U.S. economy was poor, proposals to reduce the independence of the Fed gained support. On balance, though, the U.S. economy has performed well during the past 25 years, which has greatly reduced discontent with the Fed's structure. At this point, it appears unlikely that Congress would consider legislation to reduce the independence of the Fed.

Conclusion

Monetary policy is one way governments pursue goals for inflation, economic growth, and financial stability. Many journalists and politicians refer to the chairman of the Federal Reserve as second only to the president of the United States in his ability to affect the U.S. economy. Congress and the president, however, also use their power over spending and taxes to try to stabilize the economy. In the next chapter, we discuss how *fiscal policy*—changes in government spending and taxes—affect the economy.

Read *An Inside Look* on the next page for a discussion of whether the actions taken by the Fed to stimulate spending on residential construction may have led to a "bubble" in housing prices.

An Inside Look

Monetary Policy Spurs Housing Boom

WALL STREET JOURNAL, JUNE 9, 2005

In Treating U.S. After Bubble, Fed Helped Create New Threats

By many yardsticks, the Federal Reserve's response to the bursting of the stock and tech-spending bubbles in 2000 has been a remarkable success. The 2001 recession was mild and economic growth since has been brisk. **b** Employment is up and inflation remains within the Fed's hallowed zone of price stability.

But five years after the stock market's peak, the economy faces other threatening imbalances: a potential housing bubble, rock-bottom personal saving rates and a gargantuan trade deficit. And the Fed's post-bubble prescription bears some responsibility for all three. Fed officials acknowledge as much but say the alternatives were worse.

a By slashing short-term interest rates to 45-year lows, the Fed encouraged Americans to borrow more, gave them little reward for saving and helped ignite a surge in housing prices. President Bush and Congress joined in with steep tax cuts that boosted household purchasing power. All that spending contributed to a growing U.S. economy, a steady increase in imports and—given that Americans are so eager to borrow and foreigners so eager to lend—a mountain of foreign debt.

This is pleasant for Americans as long as it lasts. But Fed officials, international financial watchdogs and private economists say it can't. At some point, American consumers must spend less, save more and rely less on foreigners' savings.

How that will happen puts the nation in uncharted territory: After treating a bubble, how does the Fed manage the side effects of its medicine?

Faced with an asset bubble, a central bank has two choices: Prick it early or wait for it to burst and try to contain the damage. The Fed in 1929 and the Bank of Japan in 1989 tried the first route, raising interest rates in response to rapidly rising asset prices. The result in the U.S. in the 1930s was depression and deflation. In Japan it was stagnation and deflation that continues today.

In the 1990s, Mr. Greenspan chose the second route. As long as the prices of goods and services were stable, he would leave the stock market alone. When the stock bubble finally burst, the Fed cut short-term rates aggressively beginning in 2001 and then held them at a 45-year low of 1% through early 2004 until the Fed was sure the threat of deflation had receded.

Mr. Greenspan knew his strategy carried risks. But he saw far greater ones in responding timidly as the collapse of the biggest asset bubble in history wiped out more than $5 trillion in shareholder value, and terrorist attacks, war and corporate scandal rattled confidence. The economic expansion to date suggests he was right . . . The Fed is conducting a "crucial experiment" in post-bubble monetary policy, says Edward Chancellor, a financial historian. "We don't know what the outcome is yet."

c Lower interest rates normally operate through several channels. They encourage consumers to buy things on credit today instead of saving to buy the items later. They boost stock and home prices, which makes the owners of those assets wealthier and more willing to spend. They encourage businesses to borrow and invest. And they depress the dollar, boosting exports.

But after 2001, some of these channels were blocked. Businesses, burdened with a glut of unused equipment from the bubble years and cowed by geopolitical and regulatory uncertainty, didn't borrow to invest. And the dollar didn't fall initially, but rose because foreign economies were in even worse shape than the U.S.'s. This meant the economy relied disproportionately on the one channel that did respond: consumers. They bought record numbers of houses and cars, mostly on credit. They also borrowed against their houses' appreciated values, allowing them to spend more still. . . .

Key Points in the Article

When the so-called tech-spending bubble burst in 2000, the Federal Reserve responded with an expansionary monetary policy. The 2001 recession that followed was short-lived, with a relatively small decline in real gross domestic product and no deflation. Generally speaking, central banks can either prick asset price bubbles early or wait for them to burst. Economists believe that the Federal Reserve's decision to wait for the bubble to burst in 2000 has had at least three unintended consequences: a housing bubble, a low saving rate, and a large trade deficit. This is because from 2001 to 2004, as interest rates fell, households saved less, borrowed more, and purchased houses and consumer durables, many of which were imports.

Analyzing the News

a When the tech-spending bubble burst in 2000, the U.S. government resonded with both monetary and fiscal policies to increase aggregate demand. The Federal Reserve engaged in an expansionary monetary policy. As a result, the money supply increased and interest rates fell. Figure 1 illustrates the effect of the policy in the money market, where the money supply curve shifts from MS_1 to MS_2 and the interest rate falls from i_1 to i_2. The fall in the interest rate increased aggregate spending, particularly consumer durables and housing, and hence aggregate demand. Figure 2 shows that the aggregate demand curve shifted from AD_2 to AD_3. AD_2 is the economy's aggregate demand curve without an expansionary monetary policy. (For simplicity, we are ignoring the effect of an increase in real GDP on the demand for money.)

Finally, President Bush and Congress engaged in an expansionary fiscal policy. They cut taxes to increase household disposable income and hence aggregate demand.

b A central bank can either prick an asset price bubble early or wait for it to burst. Two examples of pricking a bubble are the Federal Reserve's actions just prior to the Great Depression and the Bank of Japan's actions just prior to its current decade-long recession. Although the two central banks were not entirely responsible for the severe recessions that followed their attempts to prick asset price bubbles, in both cases deflation resulted from their actions.

c Typically, a change in the interest rate affects three components of aggregate spending: consumption, investment, and net exports. However, in 2001—as interest rates fell, households saved less, borrowed more, and purchased consumer durables, many of which were imports, and houses. Indeed, many households fell further into debt as they borrowed against the rising values of their homes. By comparison, because firms had invested so heavily during the tech-spending bubble, investment spending did not increase when interest rates fell. Because foreign economies were performing less well than the U.S. economy, the dollar's exchange value did not fall very much when interest rates fell, and therefore exports did not rise.

Thinking Critically ABOUT POLICY

1. The Federal Reserve can choose either the interest rate or the money supply as its monetary policy target. Suppose business cycle fluctuations are fueled by aggregate demand shocks, only. All else equal, which of these two targeting strategies will more effectively dampen business cycle fluctuations?
2. Suppose households and firms are extremely interest rate sensitive with respect to their demand for money: For example, a very small fall in the interest rate causes households and firms to increase dramatically their quantities of money demanded; put differently, suppose the money demand curve is nearly horizontal. What does this extreme interest rate sensitivity imply about the relative effectiveness of an expansionary monetary policy?

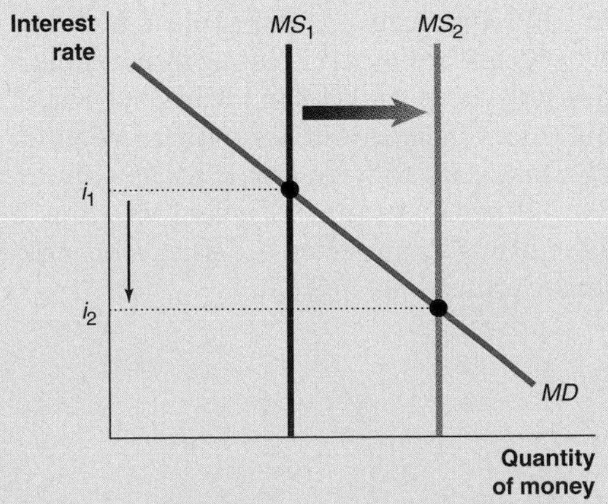

Figure 1: An increase in the money supply causes a decrease in the interest rate.

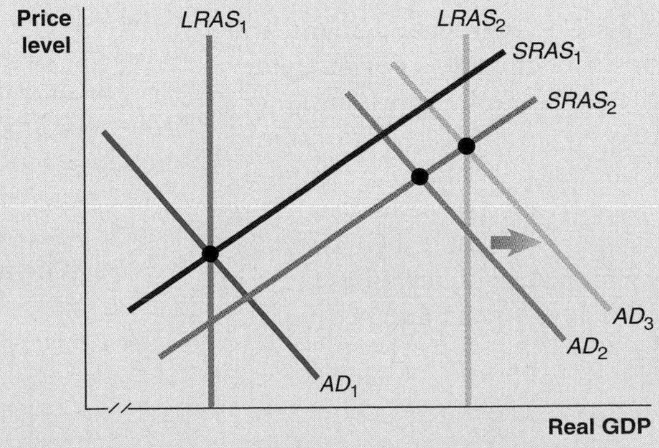

Figure 2: A decrease in the interest rate causes an increase in aggregate demand.

SUMMARY

LEARNING OBJECTIVE ① Define monetary policy and describe the Federal Reserve's monetary policy goals. *Monetary policy* is the actions the Federal Reserve takes to manage the money supply and interest rates to pursue its economic objectives. The Fed has set four *monetary policy goals* that are intended to promote a well-functioning economy: price stability, high employment, economic growth, and stability of financial markets and institutions.

LEARNING OBJECTIVE ② Describe the Federal Reserve's monetary policy targets, and explain how expansionary and contractionary monetary policies affect the interest rate. The Fed's *monetary policy targets* are economic variables that it can affect directly and that in turn affect variables such as real GDP and the price level that are closely related to the Fed's policy goals. The two main monetary policy targets are the money supply and the interest rate. The Fed has most often chosen to use the interest rate as its monetary policy target. The Federal Open Market Committee announces a target for the *federal funds rate* after each meeting. The federal funds rate is the interest rate banks charge each other for overnight loans. To fight a recession, the Fed conducts an *expansionary policy* by increasing the money supply. The increase in the money supply lowers the interest rate. To reduce the inflation rate, the Fed conducts a *contractionary policy* by adjusting the money supply to increase the interest rate. In a graphical analysis of the money market, an expansionary policy shifts the money supply curve to the right, causing a movement down the money demand curve and a new equilibrium at a lower interest rate. A contractionary policy shifts the money supply curve to the left, causing a movement up the money demand curve and a new equilibrium at a higher interest rate.

LEARNING OBJECTIVE ③ Use aggregate demand and aggregate supply graphs to show the effects of monetary policy on real GDP and the price level. An expansionary monetary policy lowers interest rates to increase consumption, investment, and net exports. This increased spending causes the aggregate demand curve (*AD*) to shift out more than it otherwise would, raising the level of real GDP and the price level. A contractionary monetary policy raises interest rates to decrease consumption, investment, and net exports. This decreased spending causes the aggregate demand curve to shift out less than it otherwise would, reducing both the level of real GDP and the inflation rate below what they would be in the absence of policy.

LEARNING OBJECTIVE ④ Discuss the Fed's setting of monetary policy targets. Some economists have argued that the Fed should use the money supply as its monetary target, rather than an interest rate. Milton Friedman and other monetarists argue that the Fed should adopt a monetary growth rule of increasing the money supply every year at a fixed rate. Support for this proposal declined after 1980 because the relationship between movements in the money supply and movements in real GDP and the price level has weakened. John Taylor has analyzed the factors involved in Fed decision making and developed the *Taylor rule* for federal funds targeting. The Taylor rule links the Fed's target for the federal funds rate to economic variables. Over the past decade, many economists and central bankers have expressed significant interest in using *inflation targeting.* Under inflation targeting, monetary policy is conducted to commit the central bank to achieving a publicly announced inflation target. A number of foreign central banks have adopted inflation targeting, but the Fed has not. The Fed's performance in the 1980s, 1990s, and early 2000s generally received high marks from economists, even without formal inflation targeting.

LEARNING OBJECTIVE ⑤ Assess the arguments for and against the independence of the Federal Reserve. The Fed conducts monetary policy without input from Congress or the president. It uses the interest it earns from purchasing U.S. Treasury bills to avoid asking Congress for the funds it needs to operate. However, the Fed's independence is not absolute because Congress and the president can pass legislation at any time to reorganize, or even abolish, it. Advocates of Fed independence argue that isolating it from political pressure allows it to choose policies in the best interest of the economy. Internationally, countries with more independent central banks tend to have lower inflation rates. Opponents of Fed independence argue that concentrating so much power in the hands of unelected officials is inconsistent with democratic principles.

KEY TERMS

Contractionary monetary policy 456
Expansionary monetary policy 452
Federal funds rate 448
Inflation targeting 462
Monetary policy 440
Taylor rule 461

REVIEW QUESTIONS

1. When Congress established the Fed in 1914, what was its main responsibility? What is its most important responsibility today? Why did this change take place?
2. What is a monetary policy target? Why does the Fed use policy targets?
3. Draw a demand and supply graph showing equilibrium in the money market. Suppose the Fed wants to lower the equilibrium interest rate. Show on the graph how the Fed would accomplish this objective.
4. Explain the effect an open market purchase has on the equilibrium interest rate.
5. What is the federal funds rate? What role does it play in monetary policy?
6. How does an increase in interest rates affect aggregate demand? Briefly discuss how each component of aggregate demand is affected.
7. If the Fed believes the economy is about to fall into recession, what actions should it take? If the Fed believes that the inflation rate is about to increase, what actions should it take?
8. What is a monetary rule, as opposed to a monetary policy? What monetary rule would Milton Friedman like the Fed to follow? Why has support for a monetary rule of the kind advocated by Friedman declined since 1980?
9. For more than 20 years, the Fed has used the federal funds rate as its monetary policy target. Why doesn't it target the money supply at the same time?
10. In what ways is the Federal Reserve more independent of the executive branch of the federal government than other agencies, like, for instance, the Environmental Protection Agency? Why did the Federal Reserve Act of 1913 give so much independence to the Fed? What arguments do economists make in favor of reducing the independence of the Fed?

PROBLEMS AND APPLICATIONS

Please visit **www.prenhall.com/hubbard** *for solutions to the even-numbered problems as well as multiple-choice and true or false self-assessment quizzes.*

1. A newspaper headline in early 2002 read, "Companies Invest as Interest Rates Are at a 40-Year Low." Explain the connection between this headline and the monetary policy pursued by the Federal Reserve during that time.
   Source: Brendan Murray, "Companies Invest as Interest Rates Are at a 40-Year Low," Bloomberg News, March 28, 2002.
2. **[Related to the *Chapter Opener*]** In an article in the *Wall Street Journal* in March 2002, Lawrence Yun, senior economist for the National Association of Realtors was quoted as saying, "In the current [2001] brief recession, the housing-market indicators were in record territories." Economists normally expect that during a recession the housing market does badly because of rising unemployment and falling incomes. Why did the housing market do so well during the 2001 recession?
   Source: Erin Schulte, "Housing's Strength Raises Another Bubble Concern," *Wall Street Journal,* March 29, 2002.
3. **[Related to the *Chapter Opener*]** An article in the *New York Times* in March 2002 reported that the housing market had been surprisingly strong during the previous year. According to the article, "In trying to explain the resilience of the housing market in the face of rising unemployment, shrinking stock portfolios and a soft economy, economists start with the Federal Reserve." Why start with the Federal Reserve in trying to explain the strength of the housing market during a recession?
   Source: Daniel Altman, "Economy's Rock: Homes, Homes, Homes," *New York Times,* March 30, 2002.
4. A "basis point" is one one-hundredth of a percentage point. If an interest rate increases by 50 basis points, it has gone up by 1/2 of a percentage point. "Monetary aggregates" are measures of the money supply, such as M1 and M2. A Federal Reserve publication from February 2002, made the following observation:

   > As the economy slipped into recession last year, the FOMC reduced its target level for the overnight federal funds rate by 475 basis points to 1.75 percent. Also during the year, growth of the monetary aggregates jumped sharply.

   a. If the target for the federal funds rate was reduced by 475 basis points to 1.75 percent, what was its original level?
   b. Is there a connection between the federal funds rate falling and the money supply increasing? Briefly explain.

   Source: Richard G. Anderson, "Interpreting Monetary Growth," *Monetary Trends,* Federal Reserve Bank of St. Louis, February 2002.
5. **[Related to *Solved Problem 14-1*]** Suppose the interest rate is 2 percent on a Treasury bill that will pay its owner $1,000 when it matures in one year.

a. What is the price of the Treasury bill?
b. Suppose that the Fed engages in open market sales resulting in the interest rate on one-year Treasury bills rising to 3 percent. What will the price of these bills be now?

6. In this chapter we depict the money supply curve as a vertical line. Is there any reason to believe the money supply curve might actually be upward sloping? (*Hint:* Think about the role of banks in the process of creating the money supply.) Draw a money demand and money supply diagram with an upward-sloping money supply curve. Suppose that households and firms decide they want to hold more money at every interest rate. Show the result on your diagram. What is the impact on the size of M1? How does this differ from the impact if the money supply curve had been a vertical line?
7. If the Federal Reserve purchases $100 million worth of U.S. Treasury bills from the public, predict what will happen to the money supply. Explain your reasoning.
8. An editorial in the *New York Times* in 2004 made the following observation about the federal funds rate:

> The Federal Reserve Board announced yesterday that it would keep its overnight interest rate where it has been for nine months—at 1 percent, its lowest level since 1958. Factor in inflation, and Alan Greenspan is essentially lending money at a loss.

What is another name for the "overnight interest rate" mentioned in this editorial? Do you agree with the author of this editorial that the Federal Reserve lends money at this interest rate? Briefly explain.
Source: "The Cost of Cheap Money," *New York Times,* March 17, 2004.

9. In December 2001, some Fed officials were worried that the U.S. economy might make only a slow recovery from the 2001 recession. An article in the *New York Times* quoted the views of these officials as follows:

> The main force inhibiting a strong comeback, Fed officials say, is the perception among businesses that the rates of return available to them from investing in new equipment remain too low given the uncertainty about demand for their products, the overall health of the economy and the risks associated with the campaign against terrorism.

How might firms' expectations that the rates of return on new investments are too low make monetary policy less effective in ending a recession?
Source: Richard W. Stevenson and Louis Uchitelle, "Fed Now Says '02 Recovery to Be Gradual," *New York Times,* December 4, 2001.

10. According to an article in the *New York Times,* an official at the Bank of Japan had the following explanation of why monetary policy was not pulling the country out of recession:

> Despite recent major increases in the money supply, he said, the money stays in banks.

Explain what the official meant by the phrase "the money stays in banks." Where does the money go if an expansionary monetary policy is successful? Why wasn't that happening in Japan?
Source: James Brooke, "Critics Say Koizumi's Economic Medicine Is a Weak Tea," *New York Times,* February 27, 2002.

11. In March 2002, an article in the *New York Times* quoted Japanese Prime Minister Junichiro Koizumi:

> I really wonder why the Japanese economy is not becoming more revitalized, why we are not seeing more economic recovery. We have been doing everything to the limit in . . . monetary policy.

Had the Bank of Japan actually been doing everything to bring the Japanese economy out of recession? (*Hint:* Review Making the Connection 14-3 on monetary policy in Japan on page 454).
Source: James Brooke, "Japan's Premier Muses on a Recovery-Proof Economy," *New York Times,* March 29, 2002.

12. Most of the countries of Western Europe use a common currency, the euro, and have a common monetary policy determined by the European Central Bank. An article in the *Economist* magazine in late 2002 argued that the European Central Bank was not pursuing an appropriate monetary policy. According to the article, when the European Central Bank was founded in the early 1990s it was:

> intended to bear down upon an inflationary threat that no longer exists. In today's Europe, the enemies are more likely to be sluggish to non-existent growth in many countries . . . [and] high unemployment.

How will the policies of a central bank differ if the main economic problem it faces is inflation rather than slow growth and unemployment?
Source: "A Hard Sell," *Economist,* October 19, 2002, p. 54.

13. William McChesney Martin, who was Federal Reserve chairman from 1951 to 1970, was once quoted as saying, "The role of the Federal Reserve is to remove the punchbowl just as the party gets going." What did he mean?
14. **[Related to *Solved Problem 14-2*]** Use the graph on the next page to answer the questions:
    a. If the Fed does not take any policy action, what will be the level of real GDP and the price level in 2008?
    b. If the Fed wants to keep real GDP at its potential level in 2008, should it use an expansionary policy or a contractionary policy? Should the trading desk be buying Treasury bills or selling them?

c. If the Fed takes no policy action, what will be the inflation rate in 2008? If the Fed uses monetary policy to keep real GDP at its full-employment level, what will be the inflation rate in 2008?

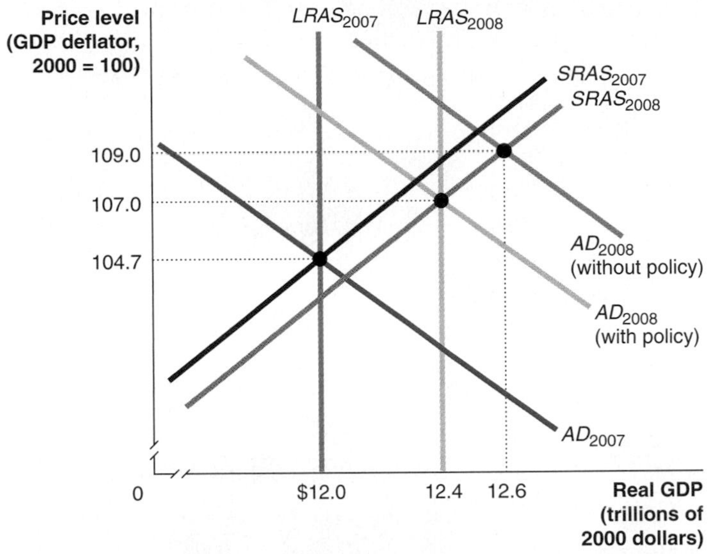

15. **[Related to *Solved Problem 14-2*]** The hypothetical information in the following table shows what the situation will be in 2011 if the Fed does *not* use monetary policy:

YEAR	POTENTIAL REAL GDP	REAL GDP	PRICE LEVEL
2010	$12.8 trillion	$12.8 trillion	140
2011	$13.3 trillion	$13.4 trillion	147

a. If the Fed wants to keep real GDP at its potential level in 2011, should it use an expansionary policy or a contractionary policy? Should the trading desk be buying T-bills or selling them?

b. If the Fed's policy is successful in keeping real GDP at its potential level in 2011, state whether each of the following will be higher, lower, or the same as it would have been if the Fed had taken no action:
   i. Real GDP
   ii. Potential real GDP
   iii. The inflation rate
   iv. The unemployment rate

c. Draw an aggregate demand and aggregate supply graph to illustrate your answer. Be sure that your graph contains *LRAS* curves for 2010 and 2011; *SRAS* curves for 2010 and 2011; *AD* curves for 2010 and for 2011, with and without monetary policy action; and equilibrium real GDP and the price level in 2011, with and without policy.

16. **[Related to *Don't Let This Happen To You!*]** Briefly explain whether you agree or disagree with the following statement: "The Fed has an easy job. Say it wants to increase real GDP by $200 billion. All it has to do is increase the money supply by that amount."

17. Some businesspeople believe that the active monetary policy of the Fed makes the economy less stable, rather than more stable. Writing in the *New York Times,* T. J. Rodgers, chief executive of Cypress Semiconductor, argued:

> There is a fundamental flaw in the Fed's operational assumption that it can know enough about the future to fine-tune the economy without continually making mistakes. Events likely to alter the economy—wars, severe winters, technology breakthroughs and so on—are not predictable. . . . Fed action is just as likely to exacerbate an economic problem as it is to mitigate it.

Do you agree with Mr. Rodgers's argument? Explain.
Source: T. J. Rodgers, "A Computer Would Do Better than the Fed," *New York Times,* April 7, 2001.

18. The following appears in a Federal Reserve publication:

> In practice, monetary policymakers do not have up-to-the-minute, reliable information about the state of the economy and prices. Information is limited because of lags in the publication of data. Also, policymakers have less-than-perfect understanding of the way the economy works, including the knowledge of when and to what extent policy actions will affect aggregate demand. The operation of the economy changes over time, and with it the response of the economy to policy measures. These limitations add to uncertainties in the policy process and make determining the appropriate setting of monetary policy . . . more difficult.

If the Fed itself admits that there are many obstacles in the way of effective monetary policy, why does it still engage in active monetary policy rather than using a monetary growth rule, as suggested by Milton Friedman and his followers?
Source: Board of Governors of the Federal Reserve System, *The Federal Reserve System: Purposes and Functions,* Washington, D.C., 1994.

19. The president of the United States appoints the comptroller of the currency and the secretary of the treasury. Until passage of the Banking Act of 1935, these officials were both members of the Board of Governors of the Federal Reserve System. How would having these two presidential appointees on the board be likely to affect monetary policy? Would it be a good idea if they were still on the board?

20. In 1975, Ronald Reagan stated that inflation "has one cause and one cause alone: government spending more than government takes in." Briefly explain whether you agree.
Source: Edward Nelson, "Budget Deficits and Interest Rates," *Monetary Trends,* Federal Reserve Bank of St. Louis, March 2004.

chapter fifteen

Fiscal Policy

A Boon for H&R Block

➤ The offices of H&R Block were very busy in the spring of 2002 because millions of taxpayers were having a more difficult time than usual completing their federal income tax forms, due by April 15. Congress and the president had used the *discretionary fiscal policy* of cutting income taxes to increase household spending. Their goal was to help pull the economy out of recession. Because most taxpayers would not see the money from the tax cut until they filed their tax returns in early 2002, the federal government decided to mail out checks during the summer of 2001 for the amount each taxpayer would receive. Single taxpayers received a check for $300, and married taxpayers received a check for $600.

A new line on the tax form was meant to give taxpayers an opportunity to claim their tax cut if they had not received it the previous summer. Many taxpayers found the instructions confusing and either incorrectly claimed an additional $300 or $600 or decided they needed the help of a professional tax preparer, such as H&R Block.

In 1946, Henry Bloch started the United Business Company, which provided accounting services to small businesses. When the local office of the United States Internal Revenue Service (IRS) announced in 1955 that it would no longer provide free preparation of individual income tax forms, Henry and his brother Richard recognized an entrepreneurial opportunity. They founded a new firm, H&R Block, dedicated to preparing individual income tax returns. When the IRS announced that it would stop offering tax preparation services at its New York City offices in 1956, the Blochs decided to expand to that city by opening seven offices close to existing IRS offices. By 2005, the firm employed more than 80,000 tax preparers to prepare more than 17 million tax returns a year and earned revenue of $4.5 billion.

The tax laws have become increasingly complicated. In 1955

when H&R Block was founded, the 1040 individual income tax form had 16 pages of instructions. In 2005, there were 191 pages of instructions. Individual tax payers in 1955 were potentially eligible for 14 credits and deductions that would reduce their tax payments. In 2005, there were 74 credits and deductions. Taxes on businesses also have become more complex over the years. In 1955, there were no business tax credits. In 2005, there were 25 business tax credits. Even Albert Einstein supposedly remarked, "The hardest thing in the world to understand is the income tax." It is not surprising that millions of Americans have given up filling out their own income tax forms, or have to rely on software such as Intuit's TurboTax or H&R Block's TaxCut.

The tax laws are complicated because Congress and the president change them repeatedly to achieve economic and social policy goals. As we will see, some changes in tax law are the result of discretionary fiscal policy and are intended to achieve macroeconomic goals of high employment, economic growth, and price stability. Other changes in tax law are intended to achieve goals such as energy conservation. *An Inside Look* on page 502 discusses the federal government's budget deficit.

LEARNING OBJECTIVES

After studying this chapter, you should be able to:

① Define fiscal policy.

② Explain how fiscal policy affects aggregate demand and how the government can use fiscal policy to stabilize the economy.

③ Explain how the multiplier process works with respect to fiscal policy.

④ Discuss the difficulties that can arise in implementing fiscal policy.

⑤ Explain how the federal budget can serve as an automatic stabilizer.

⑥ Discuss the long-run effects of fiscal policy.

In Chapter 14, we discussed how the Federal Reserve uses monetary policy to pursue macroeconomic policy goals, including price stability and high employment. In this chapter, we will explore how the government uses *fiscal policy,* which involves changes in taxes and government purchases, to achieve similar policy goals. As we have seen, the price level and the levels of real GDP and total employment in the economy depend in the short run on aggregate demand and short-run aggregate supply. The government can affect the levels of both aggregate demand and aggregate supply through fiscal policy. We will explore how Congress and the president decide which fiscal policy actions to take to achieve their goals. We will also discuss the disagreements among economists and policymakers over the effectiveness of fiscal policy.

① LEARNING OBJECTIVE
Define fiscal policy.

Fiscal Policy

Since the end of World War II, the federal government has been committed to intervening in the economy "to promote maximum employment, production, and purchasing power." As we saw in Chapter 14, the Federal Reserve closely monitors the economy and the Federal Open Market Committee meets eight times per year to decide whether to change monetary policy. Less frequently, Congress and the president also make changes in taxes and government purchases to achieve macroeconomic policy objectives, such as high employment, price stability, and high rates of economic growth. Changes in federal taxes and spending that are intended to achieve macroeconomic policy objectives are called **fiscal policy.**

Fiscal policy Changes in federal taxes and purchases that are intended to achieve macroeconomic policy objectives, such as high employment, price stability, and high rates of economic growth.

What Fiscal Policy Is and What It Isn't

In the United States, the federal, state, and local governments all have responsibility for taxing and spending. Economists restrict the term *fiscal policy* to refer only to the actions of the federal government. State and local governments will sometimes change their taxing and spending policies to aid their local economies, but these are not fiscal policy actions because they are not intended to affect the national economy. The federal government makes many decisions about taxes and spending, but not all of these decisions are fiscal policy actions because they are not intended to achieve macroeconomic policy goals. For example, a decision to cut the taxes of people who buy hybrid cars is an environmental policy action, not a fiscal policy action. Similarly, the defense and homeland security spending increases in the years after 2001 to fund the war on terrorism and the wars in Iraq and Afghanistan were part of defense and homeland security policy, not fiscal policy.

Automatic Stabilizers versus Discretionary Fiscal Policy

There is an important distinction between *automatic stabilizers* and *discretionary fiscal policy.* Some types of government spending and taxes, which automatically increase and decrease along with the business cycle, are referred to as **automatic stabilizers.** The word *automatic* refers to the fact that changes in these types of spending and taxes happen without actions by the government. For example, when the economy is expanding and employment is increasing, government spending on unemployment insurance payments to workers who have lost their jobs will automatically decrease. During a recession, as employment declines, this type of spending will automatically increase. Similarly, when the economy is expanding and incomes are rising, the amount the government collects in taxes will increase as people pay additional taxes on their higher incomes. When the economy is in recession, the amount the government collects in taxes will fall.

Automatic stabilizers Government spending and taxes that automatically increase or decrease along with the business cycle.

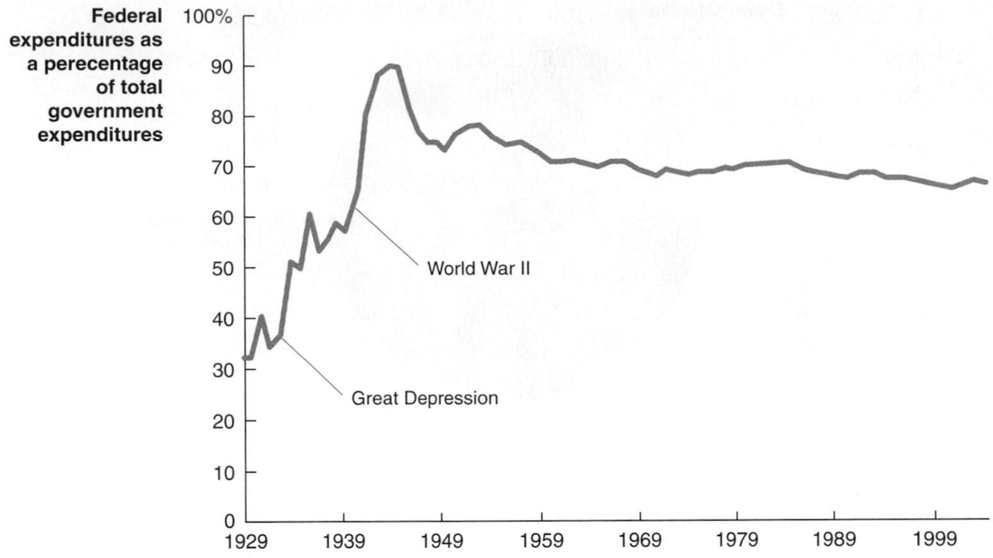

FIGURE 15-1

The Federal Government's Share of Total Government Expenditures, 1929–2004

Until the Great Depression of the 1930s, the majority of government spending in the United States was done at the state and local levels. Since World War II, the federal government's share of total government expenditures has been between two-thirds and three-quarters.

Source: Bureau of Economic Analysis.

With discretionary fiscal policy, the government is taking actions to change spending or taxes. The tax cuts passed by Congress in 2001 are an example of a discretionary fiscal policy action.

An Overview of Government Spending and Taxes

To provide a context for understanding fiscal policy, it is important to understand the big picture of government taxing and spending. Before the Great Depression of the 1930s, the majority of government spending took place at the state and local levels. As Figure 15-1 shows, the size of the federal government expanded significantly during the crisis of the Great Depression. Since World War II, the federal government's share of total government expenditures has been between two-thirds and three-quarters.

Economists often measure government spending relative to GDP. Remember that there is a difference between federal government *purchases* and federal government *expenditures.* When the federal government purchases an aircraft carrier or the services of an FBI agent, it receives a good or service in return. Federal government expenditures include purchases plus all other federal government spending. As Figure 15-2 shows,

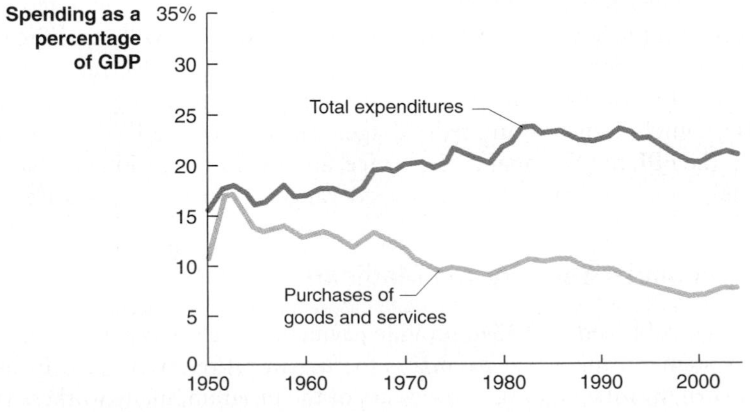

FIGURE 15-2

Federal Purchases and Federal Expenditures as a Percentage of GDP, 1950–2004

As a fraction of GDP, the federal government's *purchases* of goods and services have been declining since the Korean War in the early 1950s. Total *expenditures* by the federal government—including transfer payments—slowly rose from 1950 through the early 1990s, fell from 1992 to 2001, before rising again.

Source: Bureau of Economic Analysis.

FIGURE 15-3

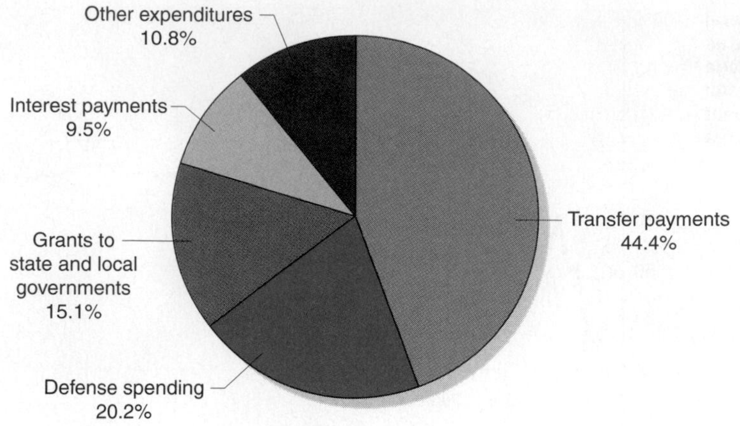

Federal Government Expenditures, 2004

Federal government *purchases* can be divided into defense spending—which makes up about 20 percent of the federal budget—and spending on everything else the federal government does—from paying the salaries of FBI agents, to operating the national parks, to supporting scientific research—which makes up less than 11 percent of the budget. In addition to purchases, there are three other categories of federal government *expenditures:* interest on the national debt, grants to state and local governments, and transfer payments. Transfer payments have risen from about 25 percent of federal government expenditures in the 1960s to almost 45 percent in 2004.

Source: Bureau of Economic Analysis.

federal government *purchases* as a percentage of GDP actually have been falling since the end of the Korean War in the early 1950s. Total federal *expenditures* as a percentage of GDP rose from 1950 to the early 1990s and fell from 1992 to 2001, before rising again. The decline in expenditures between 1992 and 2001 was partly the result of the end of the Cold War between the Soviet Union and the United States, which allowed for a substantial reduction in defense spending. Real federal government spending on national defense declined from $479 billion in 1990 to $365 billion in 1998, before rising again to $485 billion in 2004 in response to the war on terrorism and the wars in Iraq and Afghanistan.

In addition to purchases, there are three other categories of federal government expenditures: *interest on the national debt, grants to state and local governments,* and *transfer payments.* Interest on the national debt represents payments to holders of the bonds the federal government has issued to borrow money. Grants to state and local governments are payments made by the federal government to support government activity at the state and local levels. For example, to help reduce crime, Congress and the Clinton administration implemented a program of grants to local governments to hire more police officers. The largest and fastest-growing category of federal expenditures is transfer payments. Some of these programs, such as Social Security and unemployment insurance, began in the 1930s. Others, such as Medicare, which provides health care to the elderly, or the Food Stamps and Temporary Assistance for Needy Families programs, which are intended to aid the poor, began in the 1960s or later.

Figure 15-3 shows that in 2004, transfer payments were almost 45 percent of federal government expenditures. In the 1960s, transfer payments had been only about 25 percent of federal government expenditures. As the U.S. population ages, federal government spending on the Social Security and Medicare programs will continue to increase, causing transfer payments to rise above 50 percent of federal government expenditures by 2010. Figure 15-3 shows that spending on most of the federal government's day-to-day activities—including running federal agencies such as the Environmental Protection Agency, the FBI, the National Park Service, and the Immigration and Naturalization Service—makes up less than 11 percent of federal government expenditures.

15-1 Making the Connection

The Future of Social Security and Medicare

Social Security, established in 1935 to provide payments to retired workers, began as a "pay-as-you-go" system, meaning that payments to current retirees were paid from taxes collected from current workers. In the early years of the program, many workers were paying into the system and there were relatively few retirees. For example, in 1940, more than 35 million workers were paying into the system, and only 222,000 were receiving benefits—a ratio of more than 150 workers to each beneficiary. In those early years, most retirees received far more in benefits than they had paid in taxes. For example, the first beneficiary was a legal secretary named Ida May Fuller. She worked for three years while the program was in place and paid total taxes of only $24.75. During her retirement, she collected $22,888.92 in benefits.

The Social Security and Medicare programs have been a great success in reducing poverty among elderly Americans, but in recent years the ability of the federal government to finance current promises has been called into doubt. After World War II, the United States experienced a "baby boom" as birth rates rose and remained high through the early 1960s. Falling birth rates after 1965 have meant long-run problems for the Social Security system, as the number of workers per retiree has continually declined. Currently there are only about three workers per retiree, and that ratio will probably decline to two workers per retiree in the coming decades. Congress has attempted to deal with this problem by raising the age to receive full benefits from 65 to 67 and by increasing payroll taxes. In 1940, the combined payroll tax paid by workers and firms was 2 percent; in 2005, it was 15.3 percent.

Will the federal government be able to keep the promises made by the Social Security and Medicare programs?

Under the Medicare program, which was established in 1965, the federal government provides health-care coverage to people age 65 and over. The long-term financial situation for Medicare is also a cause for concern. As Americans live longer and as new—and expensive—medical procedures are developed, the projected expenditures under the Medicare program will eventually far outstrip projected tax revenues. The federal government also faces increasing expenditures under the Medicaid program, which is administered by state governments and provides healthcare coverage to low-income people. In 2005, federal spending on Social Security, Medicare, and Medicaid was 8.4 percent of GDP. Forecasts by the Congressional Budget Office show spending on these three programs rising to 14.3 percent of GDP in 2030 and 17.7 percent of GDP by 2050. Over the coming decades, the gap between the benefits projected to be paid under the Social Security and Medicare programs and projected tax revenues is a staggering $72 *trillion*.

A lively political debate has taken place over the future of the Social Security and Medicare programs. Some economists and policymakers have proposed increasing taxes to fund future benefit payments. The tax increases needed, however, could be as much as 50 percent higher than current rates, and tax increases of that magnitude could discourage work effort, entrepreneurship, and investment, thereby slowing economic growth. There also have been proposals to slow the rate of growth of future benefits, while guaranteeing benefits to current recipients. While this strategy would avoid the need to raise taxes significantly, it would also require younger workers to save more for their retirement. Some economists and policymakers have argued for slower benefit growth for higher-income workers, while leaving future benefits unchanged for lower-income workers.

Whatever changes are ultimately made, for young people the debate over Social Security and Medicare is among the most important policy issues.

Sources: "The 2005 Annual Report of the Board of Trustees of the Federal Old-Age and Survivors Insurance and Disability Insurance Trust Funds," 109th Congress, 1st Session, House Document 109-18, April 5, 2005; Congressional Budget Office, *The Long-Term Budget Outlook*, December 2003; and the Social Security Administration Web site (www.ssa.gov).

Figure 15-4 shows that in 2004 the federal government raised about 40 percent of its revenue from the individual income tax. Payroll taxes to fund the Social Security and Medicare programs raised 41 percent of federal revenues. The tax on corporate profits raised about 11 percent of federal revenues. The remaining 8 percent of federal revenues were raised from sales taxes on certain products, such as cigarettes and gasoline, from tariffs on products imported from other countries, and from other sources, such as payments by companies that cut timber on federal lands.

FIGURE 15-4

Federal Government Revenue, 2004

In 2004, the individual income tax raised about 40 percent of the federal government's revenues. The corporate income tax raised about 11 percent of revenue. Payroll taxes to fund the Social Security and Medicare programs have risen from less than 10 percent of federal government revenues in 1950 to more than 41 percent in 2004. The remaining 8 percent of revenues were raised from sales taxes, tariffs on imports, and other fees.

Note: The sales and other taxes category includes a small amount of other revenue received by the federal government.

Source: Bureau of Economic Analysis.

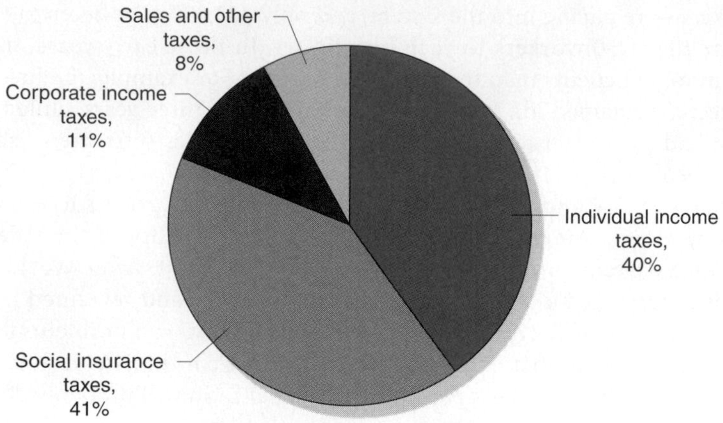

② LEARNING OBJECTIVE

Explain how fiscal policy affects aggregate demand and how the government can use fiscal policy to stabilize the economy.

Using Fiscal Policy to Influence Aggregate Demand

The federal government uses stabilization policy to offset the effects of the business cycle on the economy. We saw in Chapter 14 that the Federal Reserve carries out stabilization policy through changes in the money supply and interest rates. The government—Congress and the president—can also carry out stabilization policy through changes in government purchases and taxes. Because changes in government purchases and taxes lead to changes in aggregate demand, they can affect the level of real GDP, employment, and the price level. When the economy is in a recession, *increases* in government purchases or *decreases* in taxes will increase aggregate demand. As we have seen in Chapter 12, the inflation rate may increase when aggregate demand is increasing faster than aggregate supply. Decreasing government purchases or raising taxes can slow the growth of aggregate demand and reduce the inflation rate.

Expansionary Fiscal Policy

Expansionary fiscal policy involves increasing government purchases or decreasing taxes. An increase in government purchases will increase aggregate demand directly because government expenditures are a component of aggregate demand. A cut in taxes has an indirect effect on aggregate demand. Remember from Chapter 7 that the income households have available to spend after they have paid their taxes is called *disposable income.* If the individual income tax is cut, household disposable income will rise, and so should consumption spending. Tax cuts on business income can increase aggregate demand by increasing business investment.

Figure 15-5 shows the results of an expansionary fiscal policy. Notice that this figure is very similar to Figure 14-8 on page 455, which showed the effects of an expansionary monetary policy. The goal of both expansionary monetary policy and expansionary fiscal policy is to increase aggregate demand relative to what it would have been without the policy.

In the hypothetical situation shown in Figure 15-5, the economy begins in equilibrium at potential real GDP of $12 trillion and a price level of 100 (point *A*). In the second year *LRAS* increases to $12.4 trillion, but *AD* increases only to AD_2(without policy), which is not enough to keep the economy in macroeconomic equilibrium at potential GDP. Let's assume that the Fed does not react to the situation with an expansionary monetary policy. In that case, without an expansionary fiscal policy of spending increases or tax reductions, the short-run equilibrium will occur at $12.3 trillion (point *B*). The $100 billion gap between this level of real GDP and the potential level means that some firms are operating at less than their full capacity. Incomes

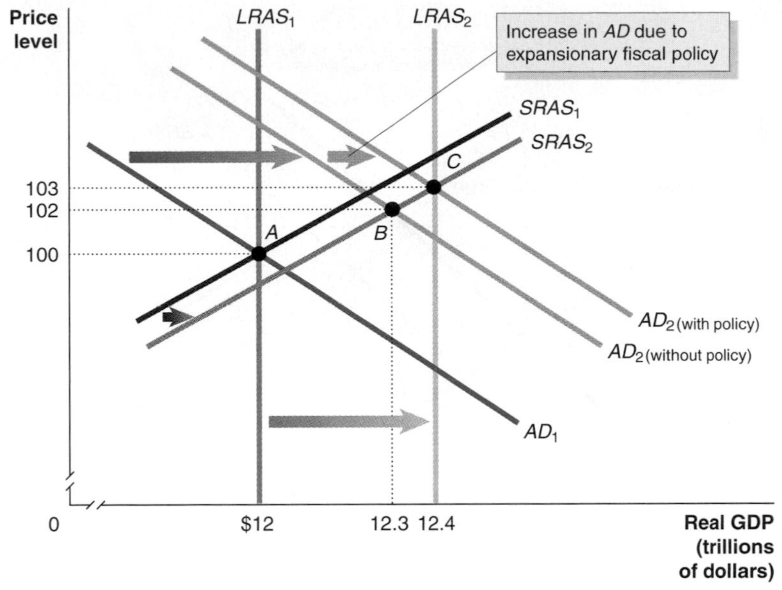

FIGURE 15-5

An Expansionary Fiscal Policy

The economy begins in equilibrium at point *A*, at potential real GDP of $12 trillion and a price level of 100. Without an expansionary policy, aggregate demand will shift from AD_1 to $AD_{2(\text{without policy})}$, which is not enough to keep the economy at potential GDP because long-run aggregate supply has shifted from $LRAS_1$ to $LRAS_2$. The economy will be in short-run equilibrium at point *B*, with real GDP of $12.3 trillion and a price level of 102. Increasing government purchases or cutting taxes will shift aggregate demand to $AD_{2(\text{with policy})}$. The economy will be in equilibrium at point *C* with real GDP of $12.4 trillion, which is its potential level, and a price level of 103. The price level is higher than it would have been if expansionary fiscal policy had not been used.

and profits will be falling, firms will begin to lay off workers, and the unemployment rate will rise.

Increasing government purchases or cutting taxes can shift aggregate demand to AD_2(with policy). The economy will be in equilibrium at point *C* with real GDP of $12.4 trillion, which is its potential level, and a price level of 103. The price level is higher than it would have been if expansionary fiscal policy had not been used.

Contractionary Fiscal Policy

Contractionary fiscal policy involves decreasing government purchases or increasing taxes. Policymakers use contractionary fiscal policy to reduce increases in aggregate demand that seem likely to lead to inflation. In Figure 15-6, the economy again begins at potential real GDP of $12 trillion and a price level of 100 (point *A*). Once again, *LRAS* increases to $12.4 trillion in the second year. In this scenario, the shift in aggregate to demand to AD_2(without policy) results in a short-run macroeconomic equilibrium beyond potential GDP (point *B*). If we assume, once again, that the Fed does not respond to the situation with a contractionary monetary policy, the economy will experience a rising inflation rate. Decreasing government purchases or increasing taxes can keep real GDP from moving beyond its potential level. The result, shown in Figure 15-6, is that in the new equilibrium at point *C*, the inflation rate is 3 percent, rather than 5 percent.

A Summary of How Fiscal Policy Affects Aggregate Demand

Table 15-1 summarizes how fiscal policy affects aggregate demand. Just as we did with monetary policy, we must add a very important qualification to this summary of fiscal

TABLE 15-1

Countercyclical Fiscal Policy

PROBLEM	TYPE OF POLICY	ACTIONS BY CONGRESS AND THE PRESIDENT	RESULT
Recession	Expansionary	Increase government spending or cut taxes	Real GDP and the price level rise
Rising inflation	Contractionary	Decrease government spending or raise taxes	Real GDP and the price level fall

FIGURE 15-6

A Contractionary Fiscal Policy

The economy begins in equilibrium at point *A*, with real GDP of \$12 trillion and a price level of 100. Without a contractionary policy, aggregate demand will shift from AD_1 to $AD_{2(\text{without policy})}$, which results in a short-run equilibrium beyond potential GDP at point *B*, with real GDP of \$12.5 trillion and a price level of 105. Decreasing government purchases or increasing taxes can shift aggregate demand to $AD_{2(\text{with policy})}$. The economy will be in equilibrium at point *C* with real GDP of \$12.4 trillion, which is its potential level, and a price level of 103. The inflation rate will be 3 percent as opposed to the 5 percent it would have been without the contractionary fiscal policy.

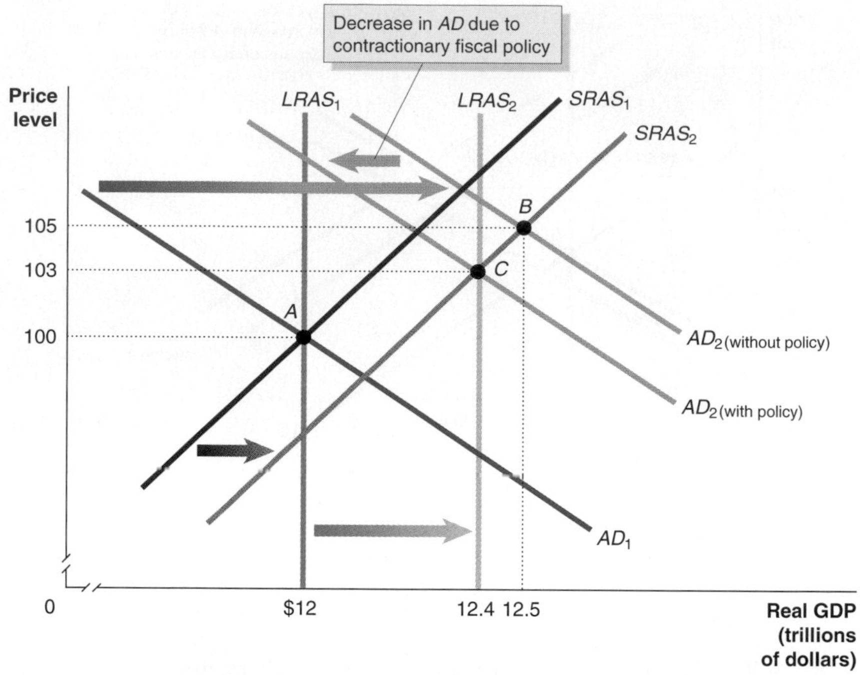

policy: The table isolates the impact of fiscal policy *by holding constant monetary policy and all other factors affecting the variables involved.* In other words, we are again invoking the *ceteris paribus* condition we discussed in Chapter 3. This point is important because, for example, a contractionary fiscal policy does not cause the price level to fall. A contractionary fiscal policy causes the price level *to rise by less than it would have without the policy,* which is the situation shown in Figure 15-6.

Don't Let This Happen To You!

Don't Confuse Fiscal Policy and Monetary Policy

If you keep in mind the definitions of *money, income,* and *spending,* the difference between monetary policy and fiscal policy will be clearer. A common mistake is to think of monetary policy as the Fed fighting recessions by increasing the money supply so people will have more money to spend, and to think of fiscal policy as Congress and the president fighting recessions by spending more money. In this view, the only difference between fiscal policy and monetary policy would be the source of the money.

To understand what's wrong with the descriptions of fiscal policy and monetary policy just given, first remember that the problem during a recession is not that there is too little *money*—currency plus checking account balances—but too little *spending.* There may be too little spending for a number of reasons. For example, households may cut back on their spending on cars and houses because they are pessimistic about the future. Firms may cut back their spending because they have lowered their estimates of the future profitability of new machinery and factories. Or the major trading partners of the United States—such as Japan and Canada—may be suffering from recessions, which cause households and firms in those countries to cut back their spending on U.S. products.

The purpose of expansionary monetary policy is to lower interest rates, which in turn increases aggregate demand. When interest rates fall, households and firms are willing to borrow more to buy cars, houses, and factories. The purpose of expansionary fiscal policy is to increase aggregate demand by either having the government directly increase its own purchases or by cutting taxes to increase household disposable income and, therefore, consumption spending.

Just as increasing or decreasing the money supply does not have any direct effect on government spending or taxes, increasing or decreasing government spending or taxes will not have any direct effect on the money supply. Fiscal policy and monetary policy have the same goals, but they have different effects on the economy.

YOUR TURN: **Test your understanding by doing related problem 6 on page 506 at the end of this chapter.**

The Government Purchases and Tax Multipliers

3 LEARNING OBJECTIVE

Explain how the multiplier process works with respect to fiscal policy.

Suppose that during a recession the government decides to use discretionary fiscal policy to increase aggregate demand by spending $100 billion more on constructing subway systems in several cities. How much will equilibrium real GDP increase as a result of this increase in government purchases? We know that the answer is greater than $100 billion because we know the initial increase in aggregate demand will lead to additional increases in income and spending. To build the subways, the government hires private construction firms. These firms will hire more workers to carry out the new construction projects. Newly hired workers will increase their spending on cars, furniture, appliances, and other products. Sellers of these products will increase their production and hire more workers. At each step, real GDP and income will rise, thereby increasing consumption spending and aggregate demand.

Economists refer to the initial increase in government purchases as *autonomous* because it does not depend on the level of real GDP. The increases in consumption spending are *induced* by the initial increase in autonomous spending. Economists refer to the series of induced increases in consumption spending that results from an initial increase in autonomous expenditures as the **multiplier effect.**

Multiplier effect The series of induced increases in consumption spending that results from an initial increase in autonomous expenditures.

Figure 15-7 illustrates how an increase in government purchases affects the aggregate demand curve. The initial increase in government purchases causes the aggregate demand to shift to the right because total spending in the economy is now higher at every price level. The shift to the right from AD_1 to AD_2 represents the impact of the initial increase of $100 billion in government purchases. Because this initial increase in government purchases raises incomes and leads to further increases in consumption spending, the aggregate demand curve will ultimately shift further to the right to AD_3.

To understand the multiplier effect, let's start with a simplified analysis in which we assume that the price level is constant. In other words, initially we will ignore the effect of an upward-sloping *SRAS*. Figure 15-8 shows how spending and real GDP increase over a number of periods beginning with the initial increase in government purchases in the first period, holding the price level constant. The initial spending in the first period raises real GDP and total income in the economy by $100 billion. How much additional consumption spending will result from $100 billion in additional income? We know that in addition to increasing their consumption spending on domestically produced goods, households will save some of the increase in income, use some to pay income taxes, and use some to purchase imported goods, which will have no direct effect on spending and

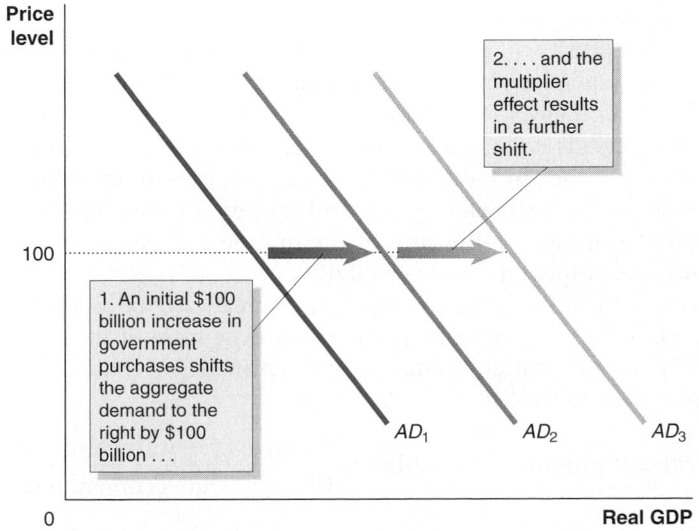

FIGURE 15-7

The Multiplier Effect and Aggregate Demand

An initial increase in government purchases of $100 billion causes the aggregate demand curve to shift to the right from AD_1 to AD_2 and represents the impact of the initial increase of $100 billion in government purchases. Because this initial increase raises incomes and leads to further increases in consumption spending, the aggregate demand curve will shift further to the right to AD_3.

Period	Additional Spending This Period	Cumulative Increase in Spending and Real GDP
1	$100 billion in government purchases	$100 billion
2	$50 billion in consumption spending	$150 billion
3	$25 billion in consumption spending	$175 billion
4	$12.5 billion in consumption spending	$187.5 billion
5	$6.25 billion in consumption spending	$193.75 billion
6	$3.125 billion in consumption spending	$196.875 billion
·	·	·
n	0	$200 billion

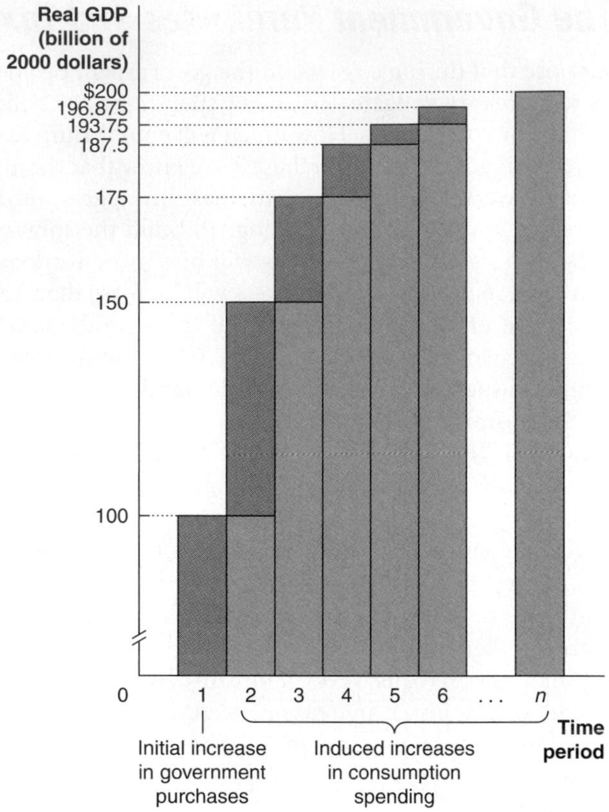

FIGURE 15-8 The Multiplier Effect of an Increase in Government Purchases

Following an initial increase in government purchases, spending and real GDP increase over a number of periods due to the multiplier effect. The new spending and increased real GDP in each period is shown in green, the level of spending from the previous period is shown in orange, so the sum of the orange and green areas represents the cumulative increase in spending and real GDP. In total, equilibrium real GDP will increase by $200 billion as a result of an initial increase of $100 billion in government purchases.

production in the U.S. economy. In Figure 15-8, we assume that in the second period households increase their consumption spending by one-half of the increase in income from the first period—or by $50 billion. This second period spending will, in turn, increase real GDP and income by an additional $50 billion. In the third period, consumption spending will increase by $25 billion, or one-half of the $50 billion increase in income from the second period.

The multiplier effect will continue through a number of periods, with the additional consumption spending in each period being half of the income increase from the previous period. Eventually, the process will be complete, although we cannot say precisely how many periods it will take, so we simply label the final period *n*, rather than giving it a specific number. In the graph in Figure 15-8, the new spending and increased real GDP in each period is shown in green, and the level of spending from the previous period is shown in orange, so the sum of the orange and green areas represents the cumulative increase in spending and real GDP.

How large will the total increase in equilibrium real GDP be as a result of the initial increase of $100 billion in government purchases? The ratio of the change in equilibrium real GDP to the initial change in government purchases is known as the *government purchases multiplier:*

$$\text{Government purchases multiplier} = \frac{\text{Change in equilibrium real GDP}}{\text{Change in government purchases}}.$$

Economists have estimated that the government purchases multiplier has a value of about 2. Therefore, an increase in government purchases of $100 billion should increase equilibrium real GDP by 2 × $100 billion = $200 billion. We show this in Figure 15-8 by having the cumulative increase in real GDP equal $200 billion.

Tax cuts also have a multiplier effect. Cutting taxes increases the disposable income of households. When household disposable income rises, so will consumption spending. These increases in consumption spending will set off further increases in real GDP and income, just as increases in government purchases do. Suppose we consider a change in taxes of a specific amount—say, a tax cut of $100 billion—with the tax *rate* remaining unchanged. The expression for this tax multiplier is:

$$\text{Tax multiplier} = \frac{\text{Change in equilibrium real GDP}}{\text{Change in taxes}}.$$

The tax multiplier is a negative number because changes in taxes and changes in real GDP move in opposite directions: An increase in taxes reduces disposable income, consumption, and real GDP, and a decrease in taxes raises disposable income, consumption, and real GDP. For example, if the tax multiplier is –1.6, a $100 billion *cut* in taxes will increase real GDP by –1.6 × –$100 billion = $160 billion. We would expect the tax multiplier to be smaller in absolute value than the government purchases multiplier. To see why, think about the difference between a $100 billion increase in government purchases and a $100 billion decrease in taxes. The whole of the $100 billion in government purchases results in an increase in aggregate demand. But some portion of a $100 billion decrease in taxes will be saved by households and not spent, and some portion will be spent on imported goods. The fraction of the tax cut that is saved or spent on imports will not increase aggregate demand. Therefore, the first period of the multiplier process will see a smaller increase in aggregate demand than occurs when there is an increase in government purchases, and the total increase in equilibrium real GDP will be smaller.

The Effect of Changes in Tax Rates

A change in tax *rates* has a more complicated effect on equilibrium real GDP than does a tax cut of a fixed amount. To begin, the value of the tax rate affects the size of the multiplier effect. The higher the tax rate, the smaller the multiplier effect. To see why, think about the size of the additional spending increases that take place in each period following an increase in government purchases. The higher the tax rate, the smaller the amount of any increase in income households have available to spend, which reduces the size of the multiplier effect. So, a cut in tax rates effects equilibrium real GDP through two channels: (1) A cut in tax rates increases the disposable income of households, which leads them to increase their consumption spending, and (2) a cut in tax rates increases the size of the multiplier effect.

Taking Into Account the Effects of Aggregate Supply

To this point, we have discussed the multiplier effect assuming that the price level was constant. We know, though, that when the *SRAS* curve is upward sloping, as the *AD* shifts to the right, the price level will rise. As a result of the rise in the price level, equilibrium real GDP will not increase by the full amount the multiplier effect indicates. Figure 15-9 illustrates how an upward-sloping *SRAS* curve affects the size of the multiplier. To keep the graph relatively simple, assume that the *SRAS* and *LRAS* curves do not shift. The economy starts at point *A*, with real GDP below its potential level. An increase in government purchases shifts the aggregate demand curve from AD_1 to AD_2. Just as in Figure 15-7, the multiplier effect causes a further shift in aggregate demand to AD_3. If the price level remained constant, real GDP would increase from $11.0 trillion at point *A* to $12.2 trillion at point *B*. However, because the *SRAS* curve is upward sloping,

FIGURE 15-9

The Multiplier Effect and Aggregate Supply

The economy is initially at point *A*. An increase in government purchases causes the aggregate demand to shift to the right from AD_1 to AD_2. The multiplier effect, results in the aggregate demand curve shifting further to the right to AD_3 (point *B*). Because of the upward-sloping supply curve, the shift in aggregate demand results in a higher price level. In the new equilibrium at point *C*, both real GDP and the price level have increased. The increase in real GDP is less than indicated by the multiplier effect with a constant price level.

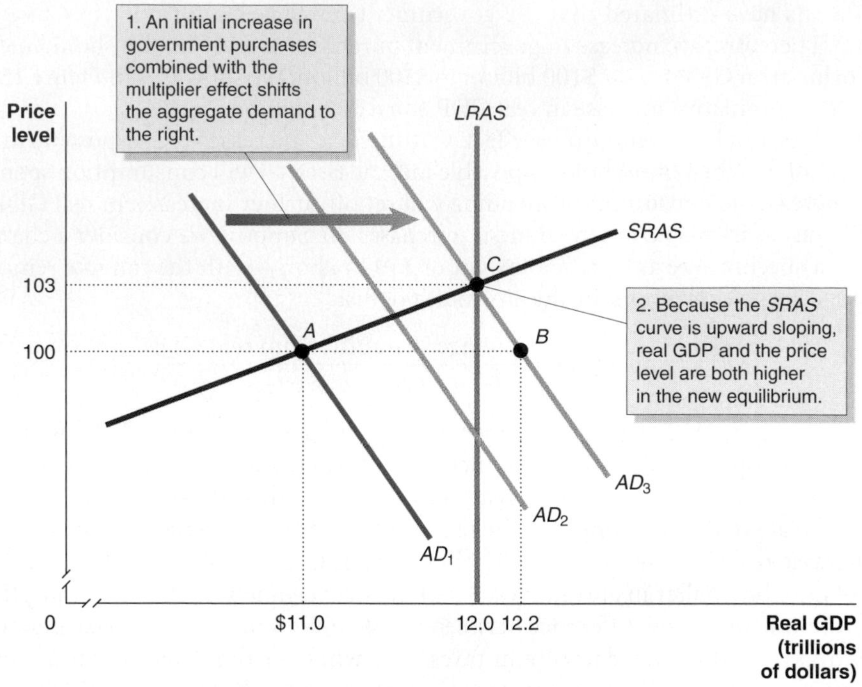
1. An initial increase in government purchases combined with the multiplier effect shifts the aggregate demand to the right.
Price level
LRAS
SRAS
C
103
A
B
100
2. Because the SRAS curve is upward sloping, real GDP and the price level are both higher in the new equilibrium.
AD3
AD2
AD1
0
$11.0
12.0 12.2
Real GDP (trillions of dollars)

the price level rises from 100 to 103, reducing the total quantity of goods and services demanded in the economy. The new equilibrium occurs at point *C* with real GDP having risen to $12.0 trillion, or by $200 billion less than if the price level had remained unchanged. We can conclude that the actual change in real GDP resulting from an increase in government purchases or a cut in taxes will be less than indicated by the simple multiplier effect with a constant price level.

The Multipliers Work in Both Directions

Increases in government purchases and cuts in taxes have a positive multiplier effect on equilibrium real GDP. Decreases in government purchases and increases in taxes also have a multiplier effect on equilibrium real GDP, only in this case the effect is negative. For example, an increase in taxes will reduce household disposable income and consumption spending. As households buy fewer cars, furniture, refrigerators, and other products, the firms that sell these products will cut back on production and begin laying off workers. Falling incomes will lead to further reductions in consumption spending. A reduction in government spending on defense would set off a similar process of decreases in real GDP and income. The cutback would be felt first by defense contractors selling directly to the government, but then it would spread to other firms.

We look more closely at the government purchases multiplier and the tax multiplier in the Appendix to this chapter.

SOLVED PROBLEM 15-1

③ LEARNING OBJECTIVE

Explain how the multiplier process works with respect to fiscal policy.

Fiscal Policy Multipliers

Briefly explain whether you agree or disagree with the following statement: "Real GDP is currently $12.2 trillion, and potential real GDP is $12.5 trillion. If Congress and the president would increase government purchases by $300 billion or cut taxes by $300 billion, the economy could be brought to equilibrium at potential GDP."

Solving the Problem:

Step 1: Review the chapter material. This problem is about the multiplier process, so you may want to review the section "The Government Purchases and Tax Multipliers," which begins on page 481.

Step 2: Explain how the necessary increase in purchases or cut in taxes is less than $300 billion because of the multiplier effect. The statement is incorrect because it neglects the multiplier effect. Because of the multiplier effect, an increase in government purchases or a decrease in taxes of less than $300 billion is necessary to increase equilibrium real GDP by $300 billion. For instance, assume that the government purchases multiplier is 2 and the tax multiplier is –1.6. We can then calculate the necessary increase in government purchases as follows:

$$\text{Government purchases multiplier} = \frac{\text{Change in equilibrium real GDP}}{\text{Change in government purchases}}$$

$$2 = \frac{\$300\text{ billion}}{\text{Change in government purchases}}$$

$$\text{Change in government purchases} = \frac{\$300\text{ billion}}{2} = \$150\text{ billion.}$$

And the necessary change in taxes:

$$\text{Tax multiplier} = \frac{\text{Change in equilibrium real GDP}}{\text{Change in taxes}}$$

$$-1.6 = \frac{\$300\text{ billion}}{\text{Change in taxes}}$$

$$\text{Change in taxes} = \frac{\$300\text{ billion}}{-1.6} = -\$187.5\text{ billion.}$$

YOUR TURN: **For more practice, do related problem 3 on page 506 at the end of this chapter.**

The Limits of Using Fiscal Policy to Stabilize the Economy

4 LEARNING OBJECTIVE

Discuss the difficulties that can arise in implementing fiscal policy.

Poorly timed fiscal policy, like poorly timed monetary policy, can do more harm than good. As we discussed in Chapter 14, it takes time for policymakers to collect statistics and identify changes in the economy. If the government decides to increase spending or cut taxes to fight a recession that is about to end, the effect may be to increase the inflation rate. Similarly, cutting spending or raising taxes to slow down an economy that has actually already moved into recession can make the recession longer and deeper.

Getting the timing right can be more difficult with fiscal policy than with monetary policy for two main reasons. Control over monetary policy is concentrated in the hands of the Federal Open Market Committee, which can change monetary policy at any of its meetings. By contrast, the president and a majority of the 535 members of Congress have to agree on changes in fiscal policy. Usually, the president initiates a change in fiscal policy by asking a member of Congress to introduce a *bill*, a proposed change in the law, that would increase or decrease spending or taxes. Figure 15-10 shows the many steps involved before a bill can become law.

The delays caused by the legislative process can be very long. For example, in 1962 President John F. Kennedy concluded the U.S. economy was operating below potential GDP and proposed a tax cut to stimulate aggregate demand. Congress eventually agreed to the tax cut—but not until 1964.

Once a change in fiscal policy has been approved, it takes time to implement the policy. Suppose Congress and the president agree to increase aggregate demand by

FIGURE 15-10

How a Bill Becomes Law

Fiscal policy actions require passing new laws. But the process of passing a new law can be very long and complicated, as this figure shows.

Source: *We the People: An Introduction to American Politics,* Third Edition by Benjamin Ginsberg, Theodore J. Lowi & Margaret Weir. Copyright © 2001, 1999, 1997 by W. W. Norton & Company, Inc. Used by permission of W. W. Norton & Company, Inc.

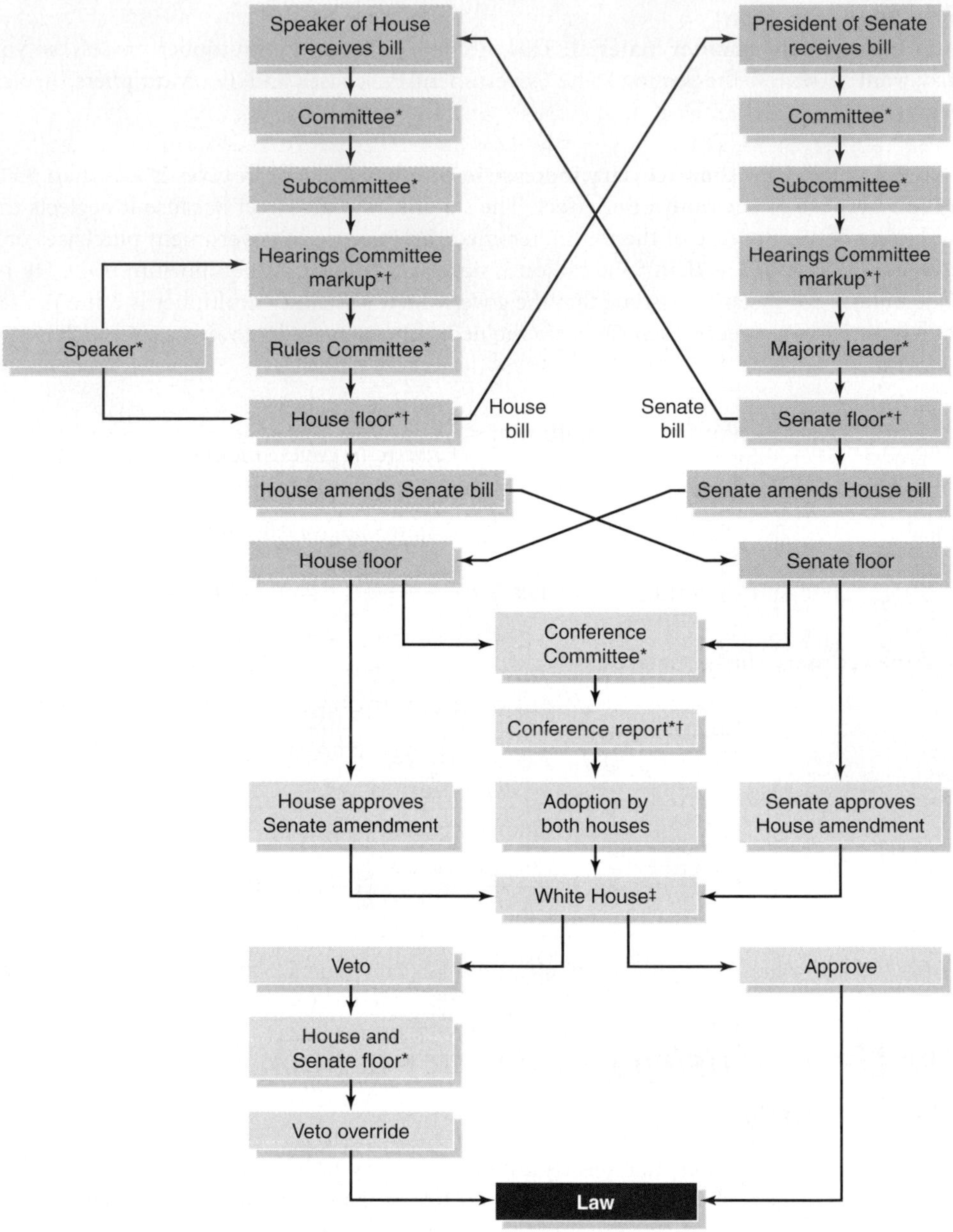

*Points at which a bill can be amended.
†Points at which a bill can die.
‡If the president neither signs nor vetoes a bill within ten days, it automatically becomes law.

spending $30 billion more on constructing subway systems in several cities. It will probably take at least several months to prepare detailed plans for the construction. Local governments will then ask for bids from private construction companies. Once the winning bidders have been selected, they will usually need several months to begin the project. Only then will significant amounts of spending actually take place. This delay may push the spending beyond the end of the recession that the spending was intended to fight.

The events of 2001 showed that it is possible to change fiscal policy in a timely manner. When President George W. Bush came into office in January 2001, he immediately proposed a tax cut. Congress passed the tax cut and the president signed it into law in early June 2001. As mentioned at the beginning of this chapter, the federal government put the tax cut into effect by mailing checks to taxpayers during the summer of 2001.

This increase in household disposable income helped increase consumption spending and contributed in part to the 2001 recession being short and relatively mild. The 2002 and 2003 tax cuts proposed by President Bush were also approved quickly. But Congress and the president use fiscal policy relatively infrequently because they are well aware of the timing problem. The Fed plays a larger role in stabilizing the economy because it can quickly change monetary policy in response to changing economic conditions.

Does Government Spending Reduce Private Spending?

In addition to the timing problem, using increases in government purchases to increase aggregate demand presents another potential problem. We have been assuming that when the federal government increases its purchases by $30 billion, the multiplier effect will cause the increase in aggregate demand to be greater than $30 billion. However, the size of the multiplier effect may be limited if the increase in government purchases causes one of the nongovernment, or private, components of aggregate expenditures—consumption, investment, or net exports—to fall. A decline in private expenditures as a result of an increase in government purchases is called **crowding out.**

Crowding out A decline in private expenditures as a result of an increase in government purchases.

Crowding Out in the Short Run

First, consider the case of a temporary increase in government purchases. Suppose the federal government decides to fight a recession by spending $30 billion more this year on subway construction. Once the $30 billion has been spent, the program will end and government spending will drop back to its previous level. As the spending takes place, income and real GDP will increase. These increases in income and real GDP will cause households and firms to increase their demand for currency and checking account balances to accommodate the increased buying and selling. Figure 15-11 shows the result, using the money market diagram introduced in Chapter 14.

At higher levels of real GDP and income, households and firms demand more money at every level of the interest rate. When the demand for money increases, the equilibrium interest rate will rise. Higher interest rates will result in a decline in each component of private expenditures. Consumption spending and investment spending will decline because households will borrow less to buy cars, furniture, and appliances, and firms will borrow less to buy factories, computers, and machine tools. Net exports will also decline because higher interest rates in the United States will attract

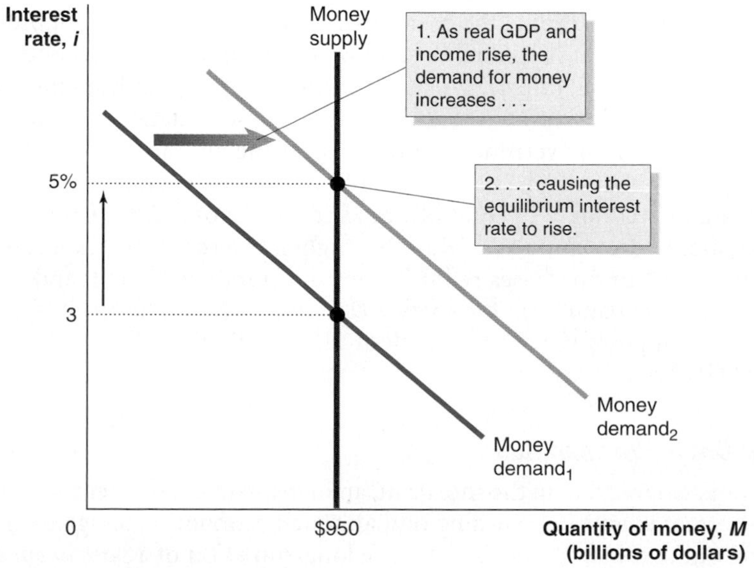

FIGURE 15-11

An Expansionary Fiscal Policy Increases Interest Rates

If the federal government increases spending, the demand for money will increase from Money demand$_1$ to Money demand$_2$ as real GDP and income rise. With the supply of money constant at $950 billion, the result is an increase in the equilibrium interest rate from 3 percent to 5 percent, which crowds out some consumption, investment, and net exports.

FIGURE 15-12

The Effect of Crowding Out in the Short Run

The economy begins at potential real GDP of $12 trillion (point *A*). In the second year, *LRAS* increases to $12.4 trillion, but *AD* fails to increase by enough to keep the economy in macroeconomic equilibrium at potential GDP. In the absence of crowding out, an increase in government purchases would shift aggregate demand to AD_2 (no crowding out) and bring the economy to equilibrium at potential real GDP of $12.4 trillion (point *B*). But the higher interest rate resulting from the increased government purchases reduces consumption, investment, and net exports, causing aggregate demand to shift only to AD_2 (crowding out). The result is a new short-run equilibrium at point *C*, with real GDP of $12.3 trillion, which is $100 billion short of potential real GDP.

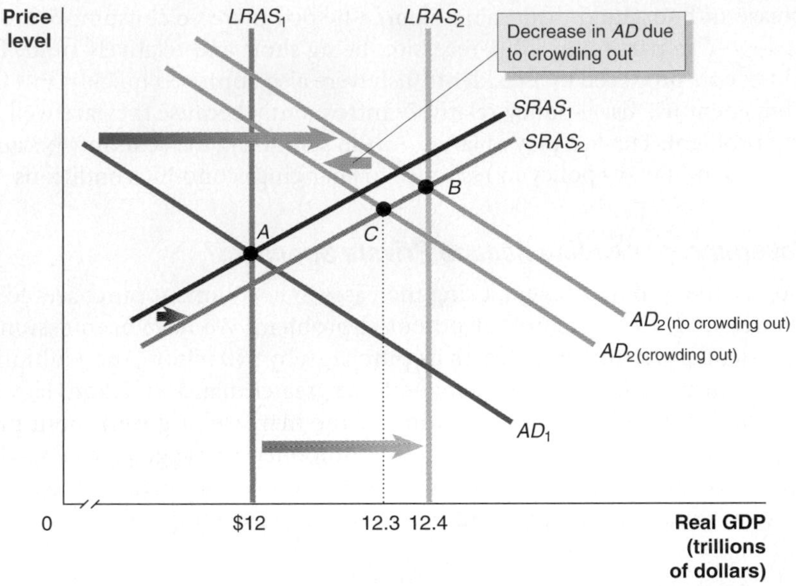

foreign investors. German, Japanese, and Canadian investors will want to exchange the currencies of their countries for U.S. dollars to invest in U.S. Treasury bills and other U.S. financial assets. This increased demand for U.S. dollars will cause an increase in the exchange rate between the dollar and other currencies. When the dollar increases in value, the prices of U.S. products in foreign countries rise—causing a reduction in U.S. exports—and the prices of foreign products in the United States fall—causing an increase in U.S. imports. Falling exports and rising imports mean that net exports are falling.

The greater the sensitivity of consumption, investment, and net exports to changes in interest rates, the more crowding out will occur. In a deep recession, many firms may be so pessimistic about the future and have so much excess capacity that investment spending falls to very low levels and is unlikely to fall much further even if interest rates rise. In this case, crowding out is unlikely to be a problem. If the economy is close to potential GDP, however, and firms are optimistic about the future, then an increase in interest rates may result in a significant decline in investment spending.

Figure 15-12 shows that crowding out may prevent an expansionary fiscal policy from meeting its goal of keeping the economy at potential GDP. The economy begins at point *A* with real GDP at its potential level of $12 trillion. In the second year, *LRAS* increases to $12.4 trillion, but *AD* fails to increase by enough to keep the economy in macroeconomic equilibrium at potential GDP. Suppose that Congress and the president decide to increase government purchases. In the absence of crowding out, the increase in government purchases would shift aggregate demand to AD_2(no crowding out) and bring the economy to equilibrium at real GDP of $12.4 trillion, which is the full-employment level (point *B*). But the higher interest rate resulting from the increased government purchases reduces consumption, investment, and net exports, causing aggregate demand to shift only to AD_2(crowding out). The result is a new short-run equilibrium at point *C*, with real GDP of $12.3 trillion, which is $100 billion short of potential GDP.

Crowding Out in the Long Run

Most economists agree that in the short run, an increase in government spending results in partial, but not complete, crowding out, although economists disagree on the extent of crowding out in the short run. What is the long-run effect of a *permanent* increase in government spending? In this case, most economists agree that the result is complete crowding out. In the long run, the decline in investment, consumption, and net exports exactly offsets the increase in government purchases, and aggregate demand remains unchanged. To understand crowding out in the long run, recall from Chapter 12 that *in the long run the economy returns to potential GDP.* Suppose that the economy is currently at potential GDP and that government purchases are 35 percent of GDP. In that case, private expenditures—the sum of consumption, investment, and net exports—will make up the other 65 percent of GDP. If government purchases are increased permanently to 37 percent of GDP, in the long run private expenditures must fall to 63 percent of GDP. There has been complete crowding out: Private expenditures have fallen by the same amount that government purchases have increased. If government spending is taking a larger share of GDP, then private spending must take a smaller share.

An expansionary fiscal policy does not have to cause complete crowding out in the short run. If the economy is below potential real GDP, it is possible for both government purchases and private expenditures to increase. But in the long run, any permanent increase in government purchases must come at the expense of private expenditures. Keep in mind, however, that it may take several, possibly many, years to arrive at this long-run outcome.

Limits to Fiscal Policy: Japan in the Late 1990s

15-2 Making the Connection

As we saw in Chapter 14, the Japanese economy did not perform well in the 1990s. From 1950 to 1990, real GDP in Japan grew at an average annual rate of 6.9 percent, but from 1992 to 2004 it grew at a rate of only 1.4 percent. Even after the Bank of Japan drove the overnight bank lending rate to 0 percent, investment spending did not increase enough to bring the Japanese economy back to potential GDP.

The Japanese government has also used fiscal policy in an attempt to stimulate the economy. Government expenditures increased from about 30 percent of GDP in 1991 to about 40 percent in 2001. Tax revenues fell from about 34 percent of GDP to about 31 percent. Many of the new spending projects involved building new bridges, roads, and airports, but some unusual spending programs were financed by grants from the central government to local governments. Kumamoto prefecture (a prefecture is similar to a U.S. state) in southern Japan hired unemployed workers to collect deer droppings, which researchers used to estimate the size of the local deer population. Shiga prefecture sent unemployed workers to mark dirty city streets on a map in its "Program to Investigate the True Condition of Litter." Together these spending increases and tax cuts resulted in large budget deficits. By the end of 2005, Japan's government debt was 160 percent of its GDP, the highest of any industrial country.

Yet fiscal policy seemed unable to bring the Japanese economy back to potential GDP. There is disagreement among economists as to why fiscal policy appears to have been ineffective in Japan. Some economists argue that fiscal policy was more effective than it seemed because without an expansionary fiscal policy, Japan would have plunged into deep recession, rather than just slow growth. During the late 1980s and early 1990s,

Fiscal policy in Japan has not been effective in expanding real GDP and reducing unemployment.

prices of many assets, particularly real estate and stocks, soared to unsustainable levels. The collapse of asset prices in the early 1990s led to reductions in consumption and investment spending that were partly offset by expansionary fiscal policy. In that sense, these economists argue, fiscal policy was at least a partial success.

Other economists argue that severe problems in the Japanese banking system made it difficult for households and firms to secure the loans necessary to finance spending. They argue that fiscal policy needed to be accompanied by reform of the banking system. Still other economists have argued that the level of investment spending in Japan is so low relative to what is needed to ensure that the economy is at potential GDP that even a very expansionary fiscal policy has not been enough to fill the gap. Finally, some economists have emphasized the wasteful nature of much of the government spending. They believe that a better-designed fiscal policy would have been more effective.

Sources: Yumiko Ono, "Japan's New Deal," *Wall Street Journal,* March 19, 2002; James Brooke, "Japan's Premier Muses on a Recovery-Proof Economy," *New York Times,* March 29, 2002; Robert H. Raashe and Daniel L. Thornton, "The Monetary/Fiscal Policy Debate: A Controlled Experiment," *Monetary Trends,* October 2001; "The Incredible Shrinking Country," *Economist,* November 11, 2004; and "Japan's Economy," *Economist,* August 22, 2005.

5 LEARNING OBJECTIVE

Explain how the federal budget can serve as an automatic stabilizer.

Deficits, Surpluses, and Federal Government Debt

Budget deficit The situation in which the government's spending is greater than its tax revenue.

Budget surplus The situation in which the government's expenditures are less than its tax revenue.

The federal government's budget shows the relationship between its expenditures and its tax revenue. If the federal government's expenditures are greater than its revenue, a **budget deficit** results. If the federal government's expenditures are less than its tax revenue, a **budget surplus** results. As with many macroeconomic variables, it is useful to consider the size of the surplus or deficit relative to the size of the overall economy. Figure 15-13 shows that, as a percentage of GDP, the largest deficits of the twentieth century came during World Wars I and II. During major wars, massive increases in government spending are only partially offset by higher taxes, leaving large budget deficits. Figure 15-13 also shows large deficits during recessions. Government spending increases during recessions and tax revenues fall, increasing the budget deficit. The federal government entered into a long period of continuous budget deficits in 1970. From 1970 through 1997, the federal government's budget was in deficit every year. From 1998 through 2001, there were four years of budget surpluses. The recession of 2001, tax cuts, and increased government spending on homeland security and the wars in Iraq and Afghanistan all helped keep the budget in deficit in the years after 2001.

How the Federal Budget Can Serve as an Automatic Stabilizer

The federal budget deficit sometimes increases during recessions because of discretionary fiscal policy actions. Discretionary increases in spending or cuts in taxes to increase aggregate demand during a recession will increase the budget deficit. For example, the decision to cut taxes during 2001 reduced federal revenues, holding constant other factors that affect the budget. As we saw earlier, in many recessions no significant fiscal policy actions are taken. In fact, most of the increase in the federal budget deficit during recessions takes place without Congress and the president taking any action because of the effects of the *automatic stabilizers* we briefly mentioned earlier in this chapter.

Deficits occur automatically during recessions for two reasons: First, during a recession, wages and profits fall, causing government tax revenues to fall. Second, the government automatically increases its spending on transfer payments when the economy moves into recession. The government's contribution to the unemployment insurance program will increase as unemployment rises. Spending will also increase on programs to aid poor people, such as the Food Stamp, Temporary Assistance for Needy Families, and Medicaid programs. These spending increases take place without Congress and the president taking any action. Existing laws already specify who is eligible for unemploy-

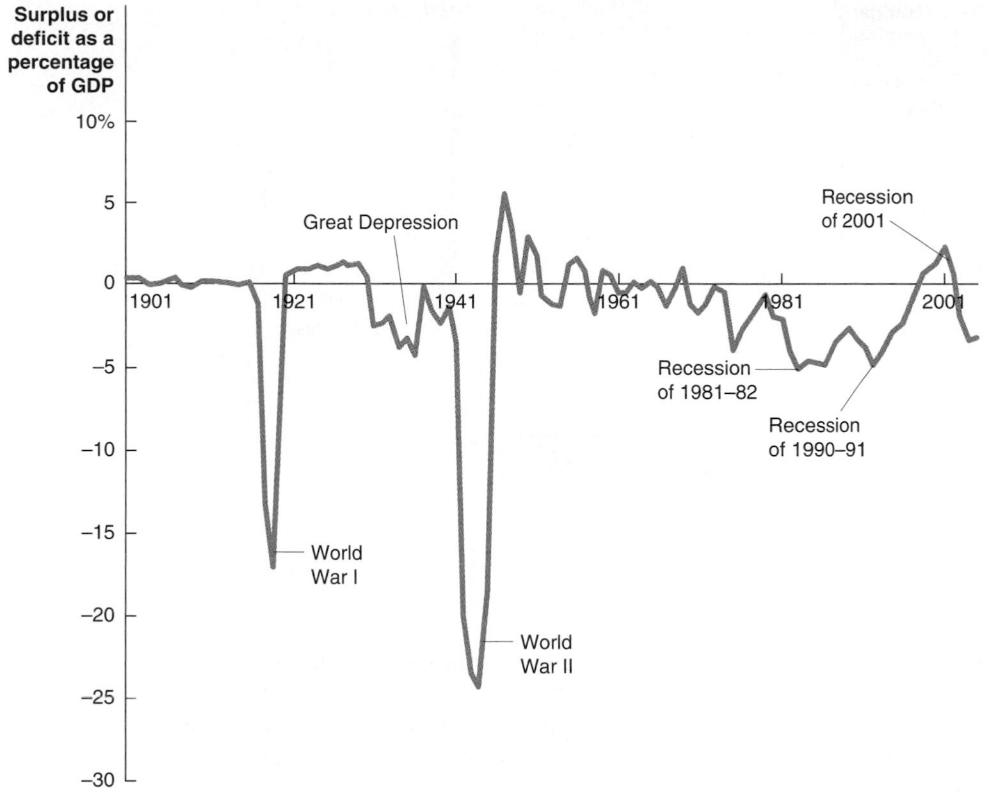

FIGURE 15-13

The Federal Budget Deficit, 1901–2004

During wars, government spending increases far more than tax revenues, increasing the budget deficit. The budget deficit also increases during recessions, as government spending increases and tax revenues fall.

Sources: *Budget of the United States Government, Fiscal Year 2003, Historical Tables,* Washington, D.C.: U.S. Government Printing Office, 2002: and Bureau of Economic Analysis.

ment insurance and these other programs. As the number of eligible persons increases during a recession, so does government spending on these programs.

Because budget deficits automatically increase during recessions and decrease during expansions, economists often look at the **cyclically adjusted budget deficit or surplus,** which can provide a more accurate measure of the effects on the economy of the government's spending and tax policies than the actual budget deficit or surplus. The cyclically adjusted budget deficit or surplus measures what the deficit or surplus would be if the economy were at potential GDP.

Cyclically adjusted budget deficit or surplus The deficit or surplus in the federal government's budget if the economy were at potential GDP.

In Figure 15-14, the federal budget is balanced at potential GDP, but it moves into surplus when GDP is above its potential level and into deficit when GDP is below its potential level. Suppose the tax code and levels of government expenditures are such that the federal budget is balanced when GDP is at its potential level of $12 trillion. If GDP is greater than $12 trillion, the increased tax revenue and the decreased transfer payments will result in a budget surplus. If GDP is less than $12 trillion, the reduced tax revenue and the increased transfer payments will result in a budget deficit.

These automatic budget surpluses and deficits can help to stabilize the economy. When the economy moves into a recession, wages and profits fall, which reduces the taxes that households and firms owe the government. In effect, households and firms have received an automatic tax cut, which keeps their spending higher than it otherwise would have been. In a recession, workers who have been laid off receive unemployment insurance payments, and households whose incomes have dropped below a certain level become eligible for food stamps and other government transfer programs. As a result of receiving this extra income, these households will spend more than they otherwise would have spent. This extra spending helps reduce the length and severity of the recession. Many economists argue that lack of an unemployment insurance system or other government transfer programs contributed to the severity of the Great Depression. During the Great Depression, workers who lost their jobs saw their wage incomes drop to zero and had to rely on their savings, what they could borrow, or what they received

FIGURE 15-14

How the Level of GDP Affects the Cyclically Adjusted Budget Deficit

Suppose the federal budget is balanced at potential real GDP of $12 trillion. If GDP is above $12 trillion, there will be a budget surplus. If GDP is below $12 trillion, there will be a budget deficit.

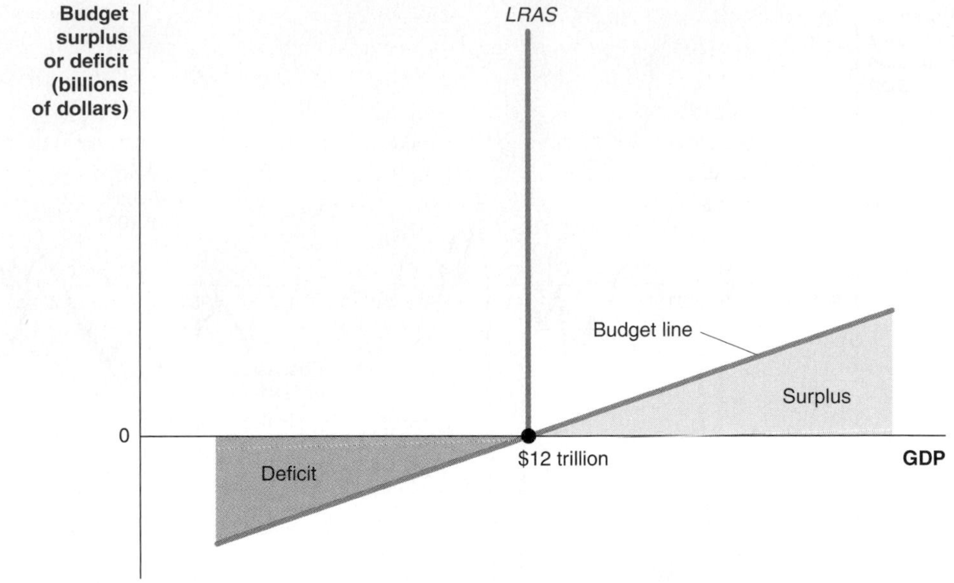

from private charities. As a result, many cut back drastically on their spending, which made the downturn worse.

When GDP increases above its potential level, households and firms have to pay more taxes to the federal government and the federal government makes fewer transfer payments. Higher taxes and lower transfer payments cause total spending to rise by less than it otherwise would have, which helps reduce the chance that the economy will experience higher inflation.

15-3 Making the Connection

Did Fiscal Policy Fail during the Great Depression?

Modern macroeconomics began during the 1930s with publication of *The General Theory of Employment, Interest, and Money* by John Maynard Keynes. One conclusion many economists drew from Keynes's book was that an expansionary fiscal policy would be necessary to pull the United States out of the Great Depression. When Franklin D. Roosevelt became president in 1933, federal government expenditures increased and there was a federal budget deficit each remaining year of the decade, except for 1937. The U.S. economy recovered very slowly, however, and did not reach potential real GDP again until the outbreak of World War II in 1941.

Although government spending increased during the Great Depression, the cyclically adjusted budget was in surplus most years.

Some economists and policymakers at the time argued that because the economy recovered slowly despite increases in government spending, fiscal policy had been ineffective. In separate studies, economists E. Cary Brown of MIT and Larry Peppers of Washington and Lee University argued that, in fact, fiscal policy had not been expansionary during the 1930s. The following table provides the data supporting the arguments of Brown and Peppers (all variables in the table are nominal, rather than real). The first column shows federal government expenditures increasing from 1933 to 1936, falling in 1937, and then increasing in 1938 and 1939. The second column shows a similar pattern, with the federal budget being in deficit each year after 1933, with the exception of 1937. The third column, though, shows that in each year after 1933 the federal government ran a cyclically adjusted budget *surplus*. Because the level of income was so low and the unemployment rate was so high during these years, tax collections were far below what they would have been if the economy had been at potential GDP. As the fourth column shows, in 1933 and again in the years 1937 to 1939, the cyclically adjusted surpluses were quite large relative to GDP.

	FEDERAL GOVERNMENT EXPENDITURES (BILLIONS OF DOLLARS)	ACTUAL FEDERAL BUDGET DEFICIT OR SURPLUS (BILLIONS OF DOLLARS)	CYCLICALLY ADJUSTED BUDGET DEFICIT OR SURPLUS (BILLIONS OF DOLLARS)	CYCLICALLY ADJUSTED BUDGET DEFICIT OR SURPLUS AS A PERCENTAGE OF GDP
1929	$2.6	$1.0	$1.24	1.20%
1930	2.7	0.2	0.81	0.89
1931	4.0	–2.1	–0.41	–0.54
1932	3.0	–1.3	0.50	0.85
1933	3.4	–0.9	1.06	1.88
1934	5.5	–2.2	0.09	0.14
1935	5.6	–1.9	0.54	0.74
1936	7.8	–3.2	0.47	0.56
1937	6.4	0.2	2.55	2.77
1938	7.3	–1.3	2.47	2.87
1939	8.4	–2.1	2.00	2.17

Although President Roosevelt did propose many new government spending programs, he had also promised during the 1932 presidential election campaign to balance the federal budget. Although he achieved a balanced budget only in 1937, his reluctance to allow the actual budget deficit to grow too large helps explain why the cyclically adjusted budget remained in surplus. Many economists today would agree with E. Cary Brown's conclusion: "Fiscal policy, then, seems to have been an unsuccessful recovery device in the 'thirties—not because it did not work, but because it was not tried."

Sources: E. Cary Brown, "Fiscal Policy in the 'Thirties: A Reappraisal," *American Economic Review*, Vol. 46, No. 5, December 1956, pp. 857–879; Larry Peppers, "Full Employment Surplus Analysis and Structural Changes," *Explorations in Economic History*, Vol. 10, Winter 1973, pp. 197–210; and Bureau of Economic Analysis.

SOLVED PROBLEM 15-2

The Effect of Economic Fluctuations on the Budget Deficit

(5) LEARNING OBJECTIVE
Explain how the federal budget can serve as an automatic stabilizer.

The federal government's budget deficit was $207.8 billion in 1983 and $185.4 billion in 1984. Someone comments, "The government must have acted during 1984 to raise taxes or cut spending or both." Do you agree? Briefly explain.

Solving the Problem:

Step 1: Review the chapter material. This problem is about the federal budget as an automatic stabilizer, so you may want to review the section "How the Federal Budget Can Serve as an Automatic Stabilizer," which begins on page 490.

Step 2: Explain how changes in the budget deficit can occur without Congress and the president acting. If Congress and the president take action to raise taxes or cut spending, the federal budget deficit will decline. But the deficit will also decline automatically when GDP increases, even if the government takes no action. When GDP increases, rising household incomes and firm profits result in higher tax revenues. Increasing GDP also usually means falling unemployment, which reduces government spending on unemployment insurance and other transfer payments. So, you should disagree with the comment. A falling deficit does not mean that the government *must* have acted to raise taxes or cut spending.

Extra Credit: Although you don't have to know it to answer the question, GDP did increase from $3.5 trillion in 1983 to $3.9 trillion in 1984.

YOUR TURN: **For more practice, do related problem 11 on page 506 at the end of this chapter.**

Should the Federal Budget Always Be Balanced?

Although many economists believe that it is a good idea for the federal government to have a balanced budget when the economy is at potential GDP, few economists believe that the federal government should attempt to balance its budget every year. To see why economists take this view, consider what the government would have to do to keep the budget balanced during a recession, when the federal budget automatically moves into deficit. To bring the budget back into balance, the government would have to raise taxes or cut spending, but these actions would reduce aggregate demand, thereby making the recession worse. Similarly, when GDP increases above its potential level, the budget automatically moves into surplus. To eliminate this surplus, the government would have to cut taxes or increase government spending. But these actions would increase aggregate demand, thereby increasing GDP further beyond potential GDP and raising the risk of higher inflation. To balance the budget every year, the government might have to take actions that would destabilize the economy.

Some economists argue that the federal government should normally run a deficit even at potential GDP. When the federal budget is in deficit, the U.S. Treasury sells bonds to investors to raise the funds necessary to pay the government's bills. Borrowing to pay the bills is a bad policy for a household, firm, or government when the bills are for current expenses, but it is not a bad policy if the bills are for long-lived capital goods. For instance, most families pay for a new home by taking out a 15- to 30-year mortgage. Because houses last many years, it makes sense to pay for the house out of the income the family makes over a long period of time, rather than out of the income received in the year the house is bought. Businesses often borrow the funds to buy machinery, equipment, and factories by selling 30-year corporate bonds. Because these capital goods generate profits for the businesses over many years, it makes sense to pay for them over a period of years as well. By similar reasoning, when the federal government contributes to the building of a new highway, bridge, or subway, it may want to borrow funds by selling Treasury bonds. The alternative is to pay for these long-lived capital goods out of the tax revenues received in the year the goods were purchased. But that means that the taxpayers in that year have to bear the whole burden of paying for the projects even though taxpayers for many years in the future will be enjoying the benefits.

The Federal Government Debt

Every time the federal government runs a budget deficit, the Treasury must borrow funds from investors by selling Treasury securities. For simplicity, we will refer to all Treasury securities as "bonds." When the federal government runs a budget surplus, the

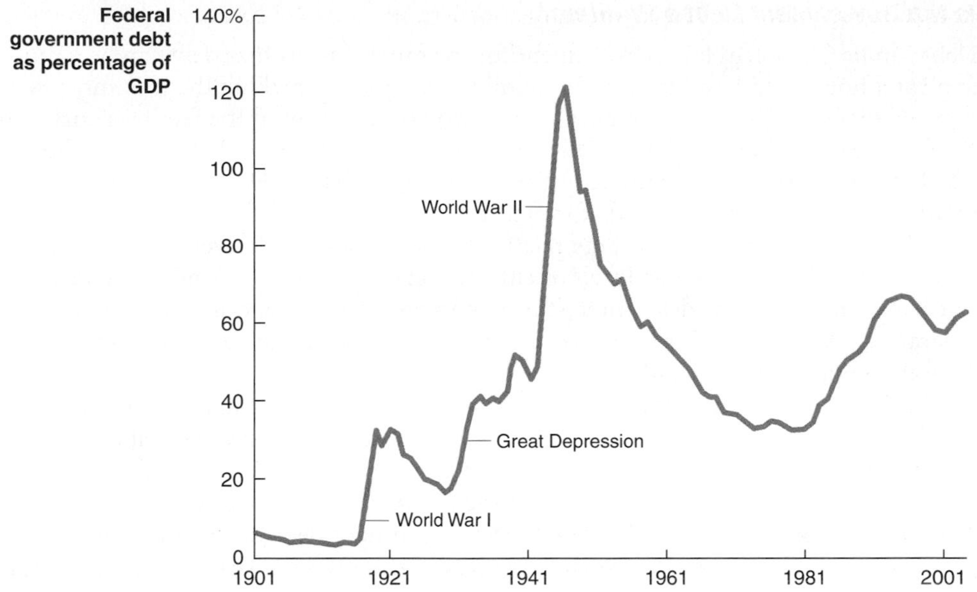

FIGURE 15-15 The Federal Government Debt, 1901–2004

The federal government debt increases whenever the federal government runs a budget deficit. The large deficits incurred during World Wars I and II, the Great Depression, and the 1980s and early 1990s increased the ratio of debt to GDP.

Sources: *Historical Statistics of the United States; Budget of the United States Government, Fiscal Year 2003, Historical Tables;* and Federal Reserve Bank of St. Louis, *National Economic Trends,* July 2005.

Treasury pays off some existing bonds. Figure 15-13 shows that there are many more years of federal budget deficits than years of federal budget surpluses. As a result, the total number of Treasury bonds has grown over the years. The total value of U.S. Treasury bonds outstanding is referred to as the *federal government debt* or, sometimes, as the *national debt.* Each year the federal budget is in deficit, the federal government debt grows. Each year the federal budget is in surplus, the debt shrinks.

Figure 15-15 shows federal government debt as a percentage of GDP over the last 100 years. The ratio of debt to GDP increased during World Wars I and II and the Great Depression, reflecting the large government budget deficits of those years. After the end of World War II, GDP grew faster than the debt until the early 1980s, which caused the ratio of debt to GDP to fall. The large budget deficits of the 1980s and early 1990s sent the debt-to-GDP ratio climbing. The budget surpluses of 1997 to 2001 caused the debt-to-GDP ratio to fall, but it rose again with the return of deficits beginning in 2002.

At the end of June 2005, the federal government debt was $7.9 trillion, but more than half of this debt was actually held by agencies of the federal government, including the Federal Reserve. In effect, the Treasury had borrowed more than half the debt from other agencies of the federal government. It may seem strange that other agencies of the federal government have purchased more than half of the bonds, or debt, issued by the Treasury. This has happened for two reasons. First, as discussed in Chapter 13, the Federal Reserve increases the money supply by buying Treasury bonds. As the economy grows, the Fed provides additional money to households and firms by adding more and more Treasury bonds to its holdings. By the end of June 2005, the Fed had accumulated about $725 billion worth of Treasury bonds. Second, the impact of the baby boom on the Social Security and Medicare systems has led the *Social Security and Medicare trust fund* to acquire more than $3.5 trillion worth of Treasury debt. Once the baby boomers retire, these bonds will be redeemed.

Is the Government Debt a Problem?

Debt can be a problem for a government for the same reasons that debt can be a problem for a household or a business. If a family has difficulty making the monthly mortgage payment, it will have to cut back spending on other things. If the family is unable to make the payments, it will have to *default* on the loan and will probably lose its house. The federal government is in no danger of defaulting on its debt. Ultimately, the government can raise the funds it needs through taxes to make the interest payments on the debt. If the debt becomes very large relative to the economy, however, the government may have to raise taxes to high levels or cut back on other types of spending to make the interest payments on the debt. Interest payments are currently about 10 percent of total federal expenditures. At this level, tax increases or significant cutbacks in other types of federal spending are not required.

In the long run, a debt that increases in size relative to GDP can pose a problem. As we discussed previously, crowding out of investment spending may occur if an increasing debt drives up interest rates. Lower investment spending means a lower capital stock in the long run and a reduced capacity of the economy to produce goods and services. This effect is somewhat offset if some of the government debt was incurred to finance improvements in *infrastructure,* such as bridges, highways, and ports, to finance education, or to finance research and development. Improvements in infrastructure, a better educated labor force, and additional research and development can add to the productive capacity of the economy.

(6) LEARNING OBJECTIVE

Discuss the long-run effects of fiscal policy.

The Effects of Fiscal Policy in the Long Run

Some fiscal policy actions are intended to meet short-run goals of stabilizing the economy. Other fiscal policy actions are intended to have long-run effects by expanding the productive capacity of the economy and increasing the rate of economic growth. Because these policy actions primarily affect aggregate supply rather than aggregate demand, they are sometimes referred to as *supply-side economics.* Most fiscal policy actions that attempt to increase aggregate supply do so by changing taxes to increase the incentives to work, save, invest, and start a business.

The Long-Run Effects of Tax Policy

Tax wedge The difference between the pre-tax and post-tax return to an economic activity.

The difference between the pre-tax and post-tax return to an economic activity is known as the **tax wedge.** The tax wedge applies to the *marginal tax rate,* which is the fraction of each additional dollar of income that must be paid in taxes. For example, in 2005, the U.S. federal income tax has several tax brackets, which are the income ranges within which a tax rate applies. For a single taxpayer, the tax rate is 10 percent on the first $7,300 earned during a year. The tax rate rises for higher income brackets, until it reaches 35 percent on income earned above $326,450. Suppose you are paid a wage of $20 per hour. If your marginal income tax rate is 25 percent, then your after-tax wage is $15, and the tax wedge is $5. When discussing the model of demand and supply in Chapter 3, we saw that increasing the price of a good or service increases the quantity supplied. So, we would expect that reducing the tax wedge by cutting the marginal tax rate on income would result in a larger quantity of labor supplied because the after-tax wage would be higher. Similarly, we saw in Chapter 9 that a reduction in the income tax would increase the after-tax return to saving, causing an increase in the supply of loanable funds, a lower equilibrium interest rate, and an increase in investment spending. In general, economists believe that the smaller the tax wedge for any economic activity—such as working, saving, investing, or starting a business—the more of that economic activity that will occur.

We can look briefly at the effects on aggregate supply of cutting each of the following taxes:

- *Individual income tax.* As we have seen, reducing the marginal tax rates on individual income will reduce the tax wedge faced by workers, thereby increasing the quantity of labor supplied. Many small businesses are *sole proprietorships,* whose profits are taxed at the individual income tax rates. Therefore, cutting the individual income tax rates also raises the return to entrepreneurship, encouraging the opening of new businesses. Most households are also taxed on their returns from saving at the individual income tax rates. Reducing marginal income tax rates, therefore, also increases the return to saving.
- *Corporate income tax.* The federal government taxes the profits earned by corporations under the corporate income tax. In 2005, most corporations faced a marginal corporate tax rate of 35 percent. Cutting the marginal corporate income tax rate would encourage investment spending by increasing the return corporations receive from new investments in equipment, factories, and office buildings. Because innovations are often embodied in new investment goods, cutting the corporate income tax potentially can increase the pace of technological change.
- *Taxes on dividends and capital gains.* Corporations distribute some of their profits to shareholders in the form of payments known as *dividends.* Shareholders also may benefit from higher corporate profits by receiving *capital gains.* A capital gain is the change in the price of an asset, such as a share of stock. Rising profits usually result in rising stock prices, and capital gains to shareholders. Individuals pay taxes on both dividends and capital gains (although the tax on capital gains can be postponed if the stock is not sold). As a result, the same earnings are, in effect, taxed twice: once when corporations pay the corporate income tax on their profits, and again when the profits are received by individual investors in the form of dividends or capital gains. Economists debate the costs and benefits of a separate tax on corporate profits. With the corporate income tax remaining in place, one way to reduce the "double taxation" problem is to reduce the taxes on dividends and capital gains. These taxes were, in fact, reduced in 2003, and currently the marginal tax rates on dividends and capital gains are well below the top marginal tax rate on individual income. Lowering the tax rates on dividends and capital gains increases the supply of loanable funds from household to firms, increasing saving and investment and lowering the equilibrium real interest rate.

Tax Simplification

In addition to the potential gains from cutting individual taxes, there are also gains from tax simplification. As we saw at the beginning of the chapter, the complexity of the tax code has created a whole industry of tax preparation services, such as H&R Block. The tax code is extremely complex and is almost 3,000 pages long. The Internal Revenue Service estimates that taxpayers spend more than 6 billion hours each year filling out their tax forms. Households and firms have to deal with more than 480 tax forms to file their federal taxes. It is not surprising that there are more H&R Block offices around the country than Starbucks coffeehouses.

If the tax code were greatly simplified, the economic resources currently used by the tax preparation industry would be available to produce other goods and services. In addition to wasting resources, the complexity of the tax code may also distort the decisions taken by households and firms. For example, the tax rate on dividends has clearly affected whether corporations pay dividends. When Congress passed a reduction in the tax on dividends in 2003, many firms—including Microsoft—began paying a dividend for the first time. A simplified tax code would increase economic efficiency by reducing the number of decisions made by households and firms solely to reduce their tax payments.

15-4 Making the Connection

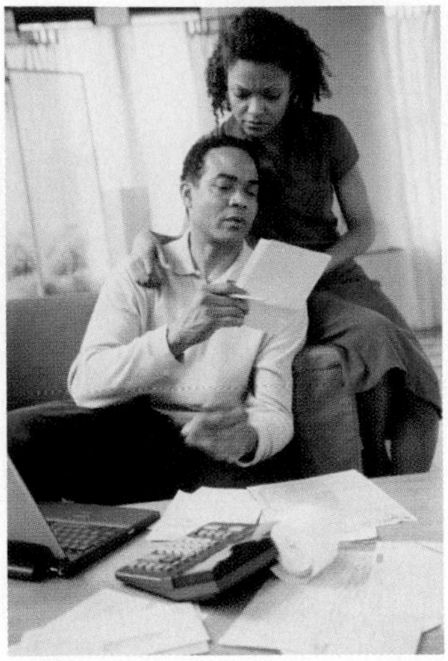

Should the United States simplify the tax code by moving to a flat tax?

Should the United States Adopt the "Flat Tax"?

In thinking about fundamental tax reform, some economists and policymakers have advocated simplifying the individual income tax by adopting a "flat tax." A flat tax would replace the current individual income tax system, with its many tax brackets, exemptions, and deductions, with a new system containing few, or perhaps no, deductions and exemptions and a single tax rate.

The proposal received publicity in the United States during the 2000 presidential election campaign when candidate Steve Forbes proposed the tax system be changed so that a family of four would pay no taxes on the first $36,000 of income and be taxed at a flat rate of 17 percent on income above that level. Under Forbes's proposal, corporate profits would also be taxed at a flat rate of 17 percent. The marginal tax rate of 17 percent is well below the top marginal tax rates on individual and corporate income. During the campaign Forbes declared, "The flat tax would be so simple, you could fill out your tax return on a postcard."

In 1994, Estonia became the first country to adopt a flat tax when it began imposing a single tax rate of 26 percent on individual income. As the table shows, a number of other countries in Eastern Europe have followed Estonia's lead. Although all these countries have a flat tax rate on income, they vary in the amount of annual income they allow to be exempt from the tax and on which income is taxable. For example, Estonia does not tax corporate profits directly, although it does tax dividends paid by corporations to shareholders.

COUNTRY	FLAT TAX RATE	YEAR FLAT TAX WAS INTRODUCED
Estonia	26%	1994
Lithuania	33	1994
Latvia	25	1995
Russia	13	2001
Serbia	14	2003
Ukraine	13	2004
Slovakia	19	2004
Georgia	12	2005
Romania	16	2005

Governments in Eastern Europe are attracted by the simplicity of the flat tax. It is easy for taxpayers to understand and easy for the government to administer. The result has been greater compliance with the tax code. A study of the effects of Russia's moving to a flat tax found that, before tax reform, Russians whose incomes had placed them in the two highest tax brackets had on average been reporting only 52 percent of their income to the government. In 2001, with the new single 13-percent tax bracket in place, these high-income groups on average reported 68 percent of their income to the government.

In the United States and Western Europe, proponents of the flat tax have focused on the reduction in paperwork and compliance cost and the potential increases in labor supply, saving, and investment that would result from a lower marginal tax rate. Opponents of the flat tax believe it has two key weaknesses. First, they point out that many of the provisions that make the current tax code so complex were enacted for good reasons. For example, currently taxpayers are allowed to deduct from their taxable income the interest they pay on mortgage loans. For many people, this provision of the tax code reduces the after-tax cost of owning a home, thereby aiding the government's goal of increasing home ownership. Similarly, the limited deduction for educational expenses increases the ability of many people to further their or their children's educations. The tax deduction of $2,000 in 2004 and 2005 for the purchase of hybrid cars that combine an electric motor with a gasoline-powered engine were intended to further the goal of reducing air pollution and oil consumption. These and other deductions would be eliminated under most flat tax proposals, thereby reducing the ability of the government to pursue some policy goals.

Second, opponents of the flat tax believe that it would make the distribution of income more unequal by reducing the marginal tax rate on high-income taxpayers. Because high-income taxpayers now can sometimes use the intricacies of the tax code to shelter a large fraction of their income from taxes, it is unclear whether the amount of taxes paid by high-income people actually would decrease under a flat tax.

Sources: "The Case for Flat Taxes," *Economist*, April 14, 2005; and Juan Carlos Conesa and Dirk Krueger, "On the Optimal Progressivity of the Income Tax Code," National Bureau of Economic Research, Working Paper 11044, January 2005.

The Economic Effect of Tax Reform

We can analyze the economic effects of tax reduction and simplification using the aggregate demand and aggregate supply model. Figure 15-16 shows that without tax changes the long-run aggregate supply curve will shift from $LRAS_1$ to $LRAS_2$. This shift reflects the increases in the labor force and the capital stock and the technological change that would occur even without tax reduction and simplification. As we know from our discussion of the *AD-AS* model in Chapter 12, during any year the aggregate demand and short-run aggregate supply curves will also shift. To focus on the impact of tax changes on aggregate supply, we will ignore the short-run aggregate supply curve and we will assume that the aggregate demand remains unchanged at AD_1. In this case, equilibrium moves from point *A* to point *B*, with real GDP increasing from Y_1 to Y_2, and the price level decreasing from P_1 to P_2.

If tax reduction and simplification is effective, the economy will experience increases in labor supply, saving, investment, and the formation of new firms. Economic efficiency will also be improved. Together these factors will result in an increase in the quantity of real GDP supplied at every price level. We show the effects of the tax changes in Figure 15-16 by a shift in long-run aggregate supply to $LRAS_3$. With aggregate demand remaining unchanged, the equilibrium in the economy moves from point *A* to point *C* (rather than to point *B*, which is the equilibrium without tax changes), with real GDP increasing from Y_1 to Y_3, and the price level decreasing from P_1 to P_3. An important point to notice is that compared with the equilibrium without tax changes (point *B*) the equilibrium with tax changes (point *C*) occurs at a lower price level and a higher level of real GDP. We can conclude that the tax changes have benefited the economy by increasing output and employment, while at the same time reducing the price level.

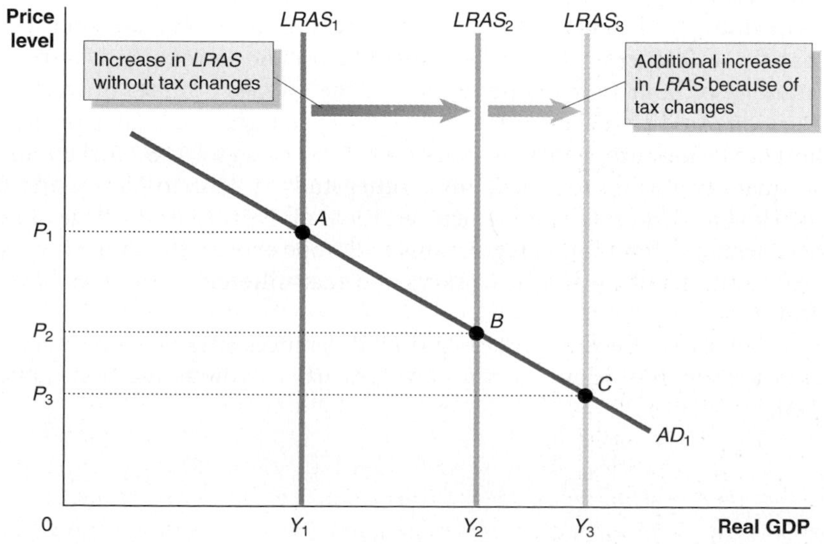

FIGURE 15-16

The Supply-Side Effects of a Tax Change

The economy's initial equilibrium is at point *A*. With no tax change, long-run aggregate supply shifts to the right from $LRAS_1$ to $LRAS_2$. Equilibrium moves to point *B*, with the price level falling from P_1 to P_2 and real GDP increasing from Y_1 to Y_2. With tax reductions and simplifications, long-run aggregate supply shifts further to the right to $LRAS_3$ and equilibrium moves to point *C*, with the price level falling to P_3 and real GDP increasing to Y_3.

Clearly our analysis is unrealistic because we ignored the changes in aggregate demand and short-run aggregate supply that will actually occur. How would a more realistic analysis differ from the simplified one in Figure 15-16? The change in real GDP would be the same because in the long run real GDP is equal to its potential level, which is represented by the long-run aggregate supply curve. The results for the price level would be different, however, because we would expect both aggregate demand and short-run aggregate supply to shift to the right. The likeliest case is that the price level would end up higher in the new equilibrium than in the original equilibrium. However, because the position of the long-run aggregate supply curve is further to the right as a result of the tax changes, the increase in the price level will be smaller—that is, the price level at point *C* is likely to be lower than at point *B*, even if it is higher than at point *A*, although—as we will discuss in the next section—not all economists would agree with this conclusion. We can conclude that a successful policy of tax reductions and simplifications will benefit the economy by increasing output and employment and, at the same time, may result in smaller increases in the price level.

How Large Are Supply-Side Effects?

Most economists would agree that there are supply-side effects to reducing taxes: Decreasing marginal income tax rates will increase the quantity of labor supplied, cutting the corporate income tax will increase investment spending, and so on. The magnitude of the effects is subject to considerable debate, however. For example, some economists argue that the increase in the quantity of labor supplied following a tax cut will be limited because many people work a number of hours set by their employers and lack the opportunity to work additional hours. Similarly, some economists believe that tax changes have only a small effect on saving and investment. In this view, saving and investment are affected much more by changes in income or changes in expectations of the future profitability of new investment due to technological change or improving macroeconomic conditions than they are by tax changes.

Economists who are skeptical of the magnitude of supply-side effects believe that tax cuts have their greatest impact on aggregate demand, rather than on aggregate supply. In their view, focusing on the impact of tax cuts on aggregate demand, while ignoring any impact on aggregate supply, yields accurate forecasts of future movements in real GDP and the price level, which indicates that the supply-side effects must be small. If tax changes have only small effects on aggregate supply, it is unlikely that they will reduce the size of price increases, as they did in the analysis in Figure 15-16.

Ultimately, the size of the supply-side effects of tax policy can be resolved only by careful studies of the effects of differences in tax rates on labor supply and saving and investment decisions. Here again, economists are not always in agreement. For example, a recent study by Nobel laureate Edward Prescott of Arizona State University concludes that the differences between the United States and Europe with respect to the average number of hours worked per week and the average number of weeks worked per year are due to differences in taxes. The lower marginal tax rates in the United States compared with Europe increase the return to working for U.S. workers and result in a larger quantity of labor supplied. But another study by Alberto Alesina and Edward Glaeser of Harvard University and Bruce Sacerdote of Dartmouth College argues that the more restrictive labor market regulations in Europe explain the shorter work weeks and longer vacations of European workers and that differences in taxes have only a small effect.

As in other areas of economics, over time differences among economists in their estimates of the supply-side effects of tax changes may narrow as additional studies are undertaken.

Conclusion

In this chapter, we have seen how the federal government uses changes in government purchases and taxes to achieve its economic policy goals. We have seen that economists debate the effectiveness of discretionary fiscal policy actions intended to stabilize the economy. Congress and the president share responsibility for economic policy with the Federal Reserve. In the next chapter, we discuss further some of the challenges facing the Federal Reserve as it carries out monetary policy. In Chapters 17 and 18, we will look more closely at the international economy, including how monetary and fiscal policy are affected by the linkages between economies.

Read *An Inside Look* on the next page for a discussion of changes in the federal budget deficit.

An Inside Look

Tax Receipts Increase in 2005, but Deficit Still Looms Large

THE ECONOMIST GLOBAL AGENDA, AUGUST 16, 2005

The Not-So-Incredible Shrinking Deficit

A new forecast from the Congressional Budget Office shows America's budget deficit once again coming in lower than expected. Republicans, unsurprisingly, are rushing to claim credit for sound economic management. But the long-term outlook is still soaked in red ink. . . .

Analysts were aghast when the Bush administration's Office of Management and Budget (OMB) projected that the fiscal year to September 2005 would bring bigger deficits still: $427 billion, according to numbers released in February. . . . Figures released by the Congressional Budget Office (CBO) in March projected a deficit of only $365 billion.

. . . In its Budget and Economic Outlook, released on Monday August 15th, the CBO's projections moved roughly into line with the administration's, forecasting a shortfall of $331 billion, or roughly 2.7% of GDP.

a Tom DeLay, the majority leader of the House of Representatives, said that the brighter budget picture "should come as no surprise" to anyone familiar with the Republican platform of cutting taxes to spur economic growth. Many voters are also prepared to give Mr. Bush the benefit of the doubt. The economy, after all, seems to be chugging along nicely. Real GDP grew at a solid 3.4% in the second quarter of 2005, an annual rate envied by most European countries. Even America's budget deficit doesn't look so bad when compared with the likes of Italy and Germany.

Democrats, of course, pooh-pooed the notion that a mere third of a trillion dollars-worth of new debt was anything to smile about. More significantly, Douglas Holtz-Eakin, the CBO's director, gave a warning that the improvement, while welcome, seemed to be largely temporary. The CBO's report attributes most of the decrease to an unexpected surge in corporate income tax receipts, thanks to double-digit growth in corporate profits since the end of the 2001 slowdown. But the boom in profits cannot be sustained over the long term, especially since much of the increase seems to stem from short-lived changes to the tax code.

Further out into the forecast period, the CBO says its outlook is largely unchanged. The deficit will shrink slowly until 2010, then drop sharply as Mr. Bush's tax cuts expire. . . .

All of this is, of course, more art than science. The CBO itself notes that even if there are no legislative changes in levels of taxation or spending, the vagaries of economic forecasting mean that there is a 25% chance that the budget will be in balance, or show a surplus, in 2010—and a 10% chance that that year will see a budget deficit greater than 5.9% of GDP. . . .

b But there's one prediction it is making with a high degree of confidence: Social Security and Medicare, America's old-age programs, will eat up an increasing share of federal spending and thus spell big trouble for the budget. The first "baby boomers" will be eligible for early retirement in 2008. . . .

The CBO's forecasting period does not stretch far enough to cover the biggest shocks to come. It is not until 2017 that Social Security's outflows will begin to exceed its inflows, forcing the government to tap general tax revenues to pay benefits. Excess Social Security contributions have been masking a large portion of the budget deficit for years; without those "off-budget" surpluses, Bill Clinton would have struggled to close the deficit in his last two years in office, and last year's shortfall would have been well over half a trillion dollars.

c As they run up the national charge account, legislators can at least take comfort that the latest round of downward revisions to forecasts seems to cast further doubt on the "twin-deficit hypothesis," which argues that Mr. Bush's spendthrift ways are driving up the current-account deficit and putting the country in danger of a catastrophic revaluation of the dollar. Trade deficits have continued to soar even as budget deficits have come down, which tends to support a theory advanced by Ben Bernanke, the chairman of Mr. Bush's Council of Economic Advisers. He has suggested that a global savings glut is flooding America with cheap money, and that the government deficits may in large part have been mopping up surplus capital that would otherwise have been borrowed by America's already debt-ridden consumers. . . .

Key Points in the Article

The U.S. federal government budget deficit for fiscal year 2005 was lower than most economists had anticipated, thanks to higher-than-expected tax receipts. Republicans attributed the higher tax receipts to President Bush's expansionary fiscal policy of 2001. Meanwhile, Democrats attributed it to a change in the corporate tax code that temporarily increased corporate profits. Nevertheless, both sides agree that the real threat to the federal budget comes shortly after 2015, when Social Security, Medicare, and Medicaid will account for over 50 percent of federal spending and tax revenues dedicated to funding these programs will no longer exceed payouts. Finally, like the federal government, the U.S. economy is also spending beyond its means; however, unlike the federal government deficit, the current account deficit continues to rise.

Analyzing the News

a Republicans and Democrats have very different views on why the federal budget deficit for fiscal year 2005 was less than most forecasters had expected, though both parties agree that higher-than-expected tax receipts had something to do with it. Republicans credit the Bush administration's tax cut of 2001. In particular, they reason that this expansionary fiscal policy increased aggregate demand and real GDP. This pattern is shown in Figure 1, where the aggregate demand curve shifts from AD_1 to AD_2; AD_1 is the economy's aggregate demand curve without an expansionary fiscal policy. Because real GDP represents income, including personal income and corporate profits, as income increases so do tax receipts.

Democrats tend to side on this issue with the Congressional Budget Office (CBO). The CBO attributes much of the decline to a one-time rise in corporate tax receipts, fueled by a change in the corporate tax code that temporarily increased corporate profits.

b Politicians and economists agree that as the U.S. population ages, Social Security, Medicare, and Medicaid will account for an increasing share of federal government expenditures. The CBO estimates that these three programs together will account for over 50 percent of federal spending by 2015. Nevertheless, Social Security and Medicare tax revenues will exceed payouts until about 2017, by which time a large portion of baby boomers will have retired. Ironically, in the meantime net revenues from these programs will add to budget surpluses and reduce budget deficits.

c The *twin-deficit hypothesis* says that federal government deficits and current account deficits are closely related: As the federal government spends beyond its means, so too does the overall economy. The recent behavior of the U.S. economy does not support this hypothesis because, while the federal budget deficit has fallen, the current account deficit has risen. According to Ben Bernanke, then chairman of the Council of Economic Advisers, the large U.S. current account deficits of the last few years were driven, in part, by foreigners' desire to save their wealth—by buying securities and opening bank accounts—in the United States. This so-called savings glut has kept U.S. interest rates low and, hence, has increased the quantity of loanable funds demanded by both the federal government and consumers.

Thinking Critically ABOUT POLICY

1. Suppose that for the U.S. economy actual real GDP is \$500 billion less than potential real GDP. To eliminate this gap, the federal government conducts an expansionary fiscal policy; in particular, it increases purchases of goods and services by \$200 billion. The government assumes that inflation will remain at zero for the foreseeable future and that the expenditure multiplier is 2.5. Determine the relative effectiveness of this expansionary fiscal policy if, to the surprise of the government, inflation increases as the economy approaches potential GDP.
2. Now suppose actual real GDP is \$500 billion greater than potential real GDP. To eliminate this gap, the federal government conducts a contractionary fiscal policy; in particular, it increases income taxes and announces that it will lower income taxes to their original levels in one year. Assess the relative effectiveness of this contractionary fiscal policy.

Source: "The Not-So-Incredible Shrinking Deficit," *The Economist Global Agenda*, August 16, 2005. www.economist.com.

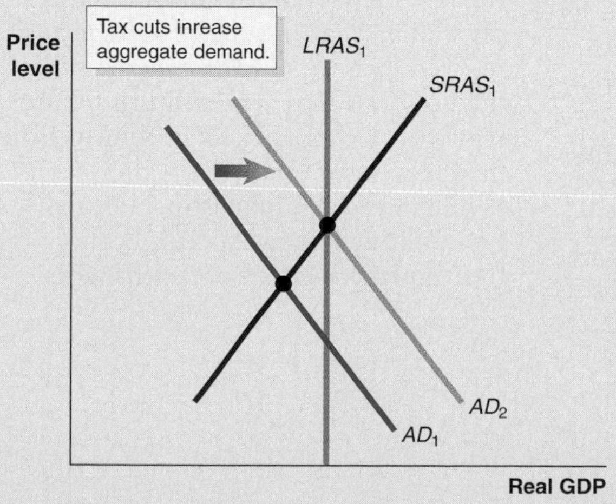

Figure 1: A decrease in taxes causes an increase in aggregate demand and real GDP.

SUMMARY

LEARNING OBJECTIVE ① Define fiscal policy. *Fiscal policy* involves changes in federal taxes and purchases that are intended to achieve macroeconomic policy objectives. Since World War II, the federal government's share of total government expenditures has been between two-thirds and three-quarters. Federal government *expenditures* as a percentage of GDP rose from 1950 to the early 1990s and fell between 1992 and 2001, before rising again. Federal government *purchases* have declined as a percentage of GDP since the end of the Korean War in the early 1950s. The largest component of federal expenditures is transfer payments. The largest source of federal government revenue is social insurance taxes, which are used to fund the Social Security and Medicare systems.

LEARNING OBJECTIVE ② Explain how fiscal policy affects aggregate demand and how the government can use fiscal policy to stabilize the economy. To fight recessions, Congress and the president can increase government purchases or cut taxes. This expansionary policy causes the aggregate demand curve *(AD)* to shift out more than it otherwise would, raising the level of real GDP and the price level. To fight rising inflation, Congress and the president can decrease government purchases or raise taxes. This contractionary policy causes the aggregate demand curve to shift out less than it otherwise would, reducing the increase in real GDP and the price level.

LEARNING OBJECTIVE ③ Explain how the multiplier process works with respect to fiscal policy. Because of the *multiplier effect,* an increase in government purchases or a cut in taxes will have a multiplied effect on equilibrium real GDP. The *government purchases multiplier* is equal to the change in equilibrium real GDP divided by the change in government purchases. The *tax multiplier* is equal to the change in equilibrium real GDP divided by the change in taxes. Increases in government purchases and cuts in taxes have a positive multiplier effect on equilibrium real GDP. Decreases in government purchases and increases in taxes have a negative multiplier effect on equilibrium real GDP.

LEARNING OBJECTIVE ④ Discuss the difficulties that can arise in implementing fiscal policy. Poorly timed fiscal policy can do more harm than good. Getting the timing right with fiscal policy can be difficult because obtaining approval from Congress for a new fiscal policy can be a very long process and because it can take months for an increase in authorized spending to actually take place. Because an increase in government purchases may lead to a higher interest rate, it may result in a decline in consumption, investment, and net exports. A decline in private expenditures as a result of an increase in government purchases is called *crowding out.* Crowding out may cause an expansionary fiscal policy to fail to meet its goal of keeping the economy at potential GDP.

LEARNING OBJECTIVE ⑤ Explain how the federal budget can serve as an automatic stabilizer. A *budget deficit* occurs when the federal government's expenditures are greater than its tax revenues. A *budget surplus* occurs when the federal government's expenditures are less than its tax revenues. The budget deficit automatically increases during recessions and decreases during expansions. The automatic movements in the federal budget help to stabilize the economy by cushioning the fall in spending during recessions and restraining the increase in spending during expansions. The federal government debt is the value of outstanding bonds issued by the U.S. Treasury. More than half of the national debt is actually owned by other federal agencies. The national debt is a problem if interest payments on it require taxes to be raised substantially or other federal expenditures to be cut.

LEARNING OBJECTIVE ⑥ Discuss the long-run effects of fiscal policy. Some fiscal policy actions are intended to have long-run effects by expanding the productive capacity of the economy and increasing the rate of economic growth. Because these policy actions primarily affect aggregate supply rather than aggregate demand, they are sometimes referred to as *supply-side economics.* The difference between the pre-tax and post-tax return to an economic activity is known as the *tax wedge.* Economists believe that the smaller the tax wedge for any economic activity—such as working, saving, investing, or starting a business—the more of that economic activity will occur. Economists debate the size of the supply-side effects of tax changes.

KEY TERMS

Automatic stabilizers 474
Budget deficit 490
Budget surplus 490
Crowding out 487
Cyclically adjusted budget deficit or surplus 491
Fiscal policy 474
Multiplier effect 481
Tax wedge 496

REVIEW QUESTIONS

1. What is fiscal policy? Who is responsible for fiscal policy?
2. What is the difference between fiscal policy and monetary policy?
3. What is the difference between federal purchases and federal expenditures? Are federal purchases higher today than they were in 1960? Are federal expenditures higher today than they were in 1960?
4. If Congress and the president decide an expansionary fiscal policy is necessary, what changes should they make in government spending or taxes? What changes should they make if they decide a contractionary fiscal policy is necessary?
5. Why does a $1 increase in government purchases lead to more than a $1 increase in income and spending?
6. Which can be changed more quickly: monetary policy or fiscal policy? Briefly explain.
7. What is meant by crowding out? Explain the difference between crowding out in the short run and in the long run.
8. In what ways does the federal budget serve as an automatic stabilizer for the economy?
9. What is the cyclically adjusted budget deficit or surplus? Suppose that the economy is currently at potential GDP and the federal budget is balanced. If the economy moves into recession, what will happen to the federal budget?
10. Why do most economists argue that it would not be a good idea to balance the federal budget every year?
11. What is the difference between the federal budget deficit and federal government debt?
12. In the United States, why is more than half of federal government debt actually owned by the federal government?
13. What is meant by supply-side economics?

PROBLEMS AND APPLICATIONS

Please visit **www.prenhall.com/hubbard** *for solutions to the even-numbered problems as well as multiple-choice and true or false self-assessment quizzes.*

1. Identify each of the following as (i) part of an expansionary fiscal policy, (ii) part of a contractionary fiscal policy, or (iii) not part of fiscal policy:
   a. The corporate income tax rate is increased.
   b. Defense spending is increased.
   c. Families are allowed to deduct all their expenses for day care from their federal income taxes.
   d. The individual income tax rate is decreased.
   e. The State of New Jersey builds a new highway in an attempt to expand employment in the state.
2. In *The General Theory of Employment, Interest, and Money,* John Maynard Keynes wrote this:

   > If the Treasury were to fill old bottles with banknotes, bury them at suitable depths in disused coal mines which are then filled up to the surface with town rubbish, and leave it to private enterprise . . . to dig the notes up again . . . there need be no more unemployment and, with the help of the repercussions, the real income of the community . . . would probably become a good deal greater than it is.

   Which important macroeconomic effect is Keynes discussing here? What does he mean by "repercussions"? Why does he appear unconcerned if government spending is wasteful?

3. **[Related to *Solved Problem 15-1*]** Briefly explain whether you agree or disagree with the following statement: "Real GDP is currently $12.7 trillion and full-employment real GDP is $12.5 trillion. If Congress and the president would decrease government purchases by $200 billion or increase taxes by $200 billion, the economy could be brought to equilibrium at potential GDP."
4. The following is from a message by President Hoover to Congress, dated May 5, 1932:

   > I need not recount that the revenues of the Government as estimated for the next fiscal year show a decrease of about $1,700,000,000 below the fiscal year 1929, and inexorably require a broader basis of taxation and a drastic reduction of expenditures in order to balance the Budget. Nothing is more necessary at this time than balancing the Budget.

   Do you think President Hoover was correct in saying that, in 1932, nothing was more necessary than balancing the federal government's budget? Explain.
5. In a column published in the *Wall Street Journal* on July 19, 2001, David Wessel wrote, "Most economic forecasters don't foresee recession this year or next." In fact, a recession had already begun in March of that year. Does this tell us anything about the difficulty of Congress and the president implementing a fiscal policy that stabilizes rather than destabilizes the economy?
   Source: David Wessel, "Economic Forecasting in Three Steps," *Wall Street Journal*, July 19, 2001, p. A1.
6. **[Related to *Don't Let This Happen To You!*]** Briefly explain whether you agree with the following remark: "Real GDP is $250 billion below its full-employment level. With a multiplier of 2, if Congress and the president increase government purchases by $125 billion or the Fed increases the money supply by $125 billion, real GDP can be brought back to its full-employment level."
7. Use the graph at the top of the next column to answer the following questions:
   a. If the government does not take any policy actions, what will be the values of real GDP and the price level in 2012?
   b. If the government purchases multiplier is 2, how much will government purchases have to be increased to bring real GDP to its potential level in 2012? (Assume the multiplier value takes into account the impact of a rising price level on the multiplier effect.)
   c. If the tax multiplier is –1.6, how much will taxes have to be cut to bring real GDP to its potential level in 2012? (Again, assume the multiplier value takes into account the impact of a rising price level.)
   d. If the government takes no policy actions, what will be the inflation rate in 2012? If the government uses fiscal policy to keep real GDP at its potential level, what will be the inflation rate in 2012?

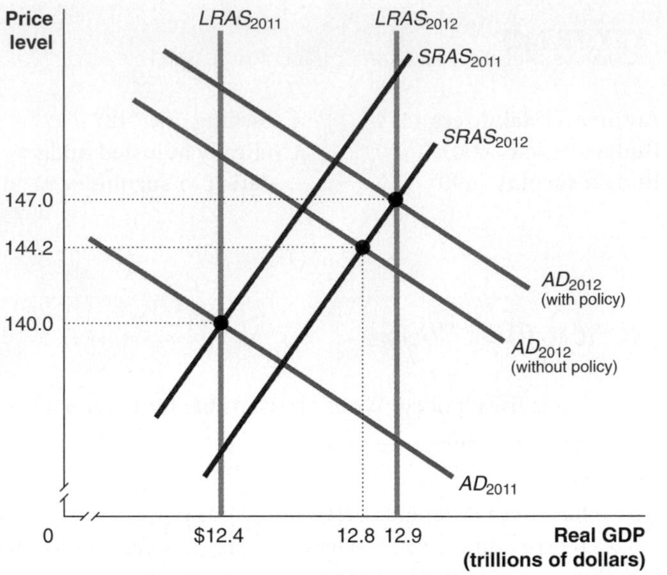

8. Figure 15-11 shows the equilibrium interest rate rising as the demand for money increases. Describe what must be happening in the market for Treasury bills.
9. Some economists argue that because increases in government spending crowd out private spending, increased government spending will reduce the long-run growth rate of real GDP.
   a. Is this most likely to happen if the private spending being crowded out is consumption spending, investment spending, or net exports? Briefly explain.
   b. In terms of its effect on the long-run growth rate of real GDP, would it matter if the additional government spending involves (i) increased spending on highways and bridges, or (ii) increased spending on the national parks? Briefly explain.
10. In his column in the *Wall Street Journal,* David Wessel wrote:

    > Global financial markets, politicians, corporate executives and ordinary Americans have confidence in [the Federal Reserve Chairman's] ability to steer the U.S. economy, particularly during times of crisis.

    But isn't it Congress and the president, and not the chairman of the Fed, who steer the U.S. economy? Discuss.
    Source: David Wessel, "Four Hard-to-Predict Factors that Will Shape the Economy," *Wall Street Journal,* April 4, 2002.
11. **[Related to *Solved Problem 15-2*]** The federal government's budget deficit was $221.4 billion in 1990 and $269.2 billion in 1991. What does this information tell us about fiscal policy actions taken by Congress and the president during these years?

12. The following is from an article in the *Wall Street Journal:*

> The Treasury Department said it expected to borrow a net $1 billion during the April-to-June quarter—not repay a net $89 billion, as it said it would earlier this year.

Why does the Treasury Department borrow? When the Treasury "repays," who is it repaying? Why would the Treasury say it was going to repay debt and then end up borrowing?

Source: Rebecca Christie and Deborah Lagomarsino, "U.S. Debt Is Set to Rise in Quarter as Tax Receipts Come Up Short," *Wall Street Journal*, April 30, 2002.

13. The federal government calculates its budget on a fiscal year that begins each year on October 1 and ends on the following September 30. At the beginning of the 1997 fiscal year, the Congressional Budget Office (CBO) forecast that the federal budget deficit would be $127.7 billion. The actual budget deficit for fiscal 1997 was only $21.9 billion. Federal expenditures were $30.3 billion less than the CBO had forecast, and federal revenue was $75.5 billion more than the CBO had forecast.
    a. Is it likely that the economy grew faster or slower during fiscal 1997 than the CBO had expected? Explain your reasoning.
    b. Suppose that Congress and the president were committed to balancing the budget each year. Does what happened during 1997 provide any insight into difficulties they might run into in trying to balance the budget every year?

14. Paul Samuelson, an economist at MIT and a Nobel Prize winner, argued that:

> It was harmful to let a large budget surplus develop in the weak 1959–60 revival and thereby help to choke off that recovery.

Why would a large budget surplus "choke off" a recovery from economic recession? What could the federal government have done to have kept a large budget surplus from developing?

Source: Paul A. Samuelson, "Economic Policy for 1962," *American Economic Review*, Vol. 44, No. 1 (February 1962), p. 6.

15. In testifying before Congress in 2003, then Federal Reserve Chairman Alan Greenspan observed, "There is no question that if you run substantial and excessive deficits over time you are draining savings from the private sector." What did Greenspan mean by "draining savings from the private sector"? How might this be bad for the economy?

Source: Martin Crutsinger, "Greenspan Warns of Rising Deficits," *Associated Press*, July 17, 2003.

16. The following is from an article in *Business Week:*

> Although the final returns from the April tax season aren't in yet, the results so far suggest that this fiscal year's budget deficit could be as much as double the roughly $50 billion last projected by the Congressional Budget Office. But there is a silver lining: The lower tax receipts mean U.S. consumers have more money to spend.

What is likely to be happening in the economy when a CBO forecast of the federal budget deficit turns out to be too low? What effect will the "silver lining" have on the economy?

17. During 2003, China ran large government budget deficits to stimulate its economy. The *Wall Street Journal* quoted an official in China's ministry of finance as saying, "The proactive fiscal policy has brought some negative effects because it has squeezed out the private investor." What did the official mean by a "proactive fiscal policy"? Why would such a policy "squeeze out" the private investor? Does that mean the policy should not have been used?

Source: Karby Leggett and Kathy Chen, "China's Rising Debt Raises Questions about the Future," *Wall Street Journal*, January 20, 2003.

18. The following was written by a political columnist:

> Today . . . the main purpose [of government's issuing bonds] is to let craven politicians launch projects they know the public, at the moment, would rather not fully finance. The tab for these projects will not come due, probably, until after the politicians have long since departed for greener (excuse the expression) pastures.

Do you agree with this commentator's explanation for why some government spending is financed from tax receipts and other government spending is financed through borrowing, by issuing bonds? Briefly explain.

Source: Paul Carpenter, "The Bond Issue Won't Be Repaid by Park Tolls," (Allentown, PA) *Morning Call*, May 26, 2002, p. B1.

19. **[Related to the *Chapter Opener*]** It would seem that both households and businesses would benefit if the federal income tax were simpler and tax forms were easier to fill out. Why then have the tax laws become increasingly complicated?

20. Suppose a political candidate hired you to develop two arguments in favor of a flat tax. What two arguments would you advance? Alternatively, if you were hired to develop two arguments against the flat tax, what two arguments would you advance?

21. Suppose that an increase in marginal tax rates on individual income affects both aggregate demand and aggregate supply. Briefly describe the effect of the tax increase on equilibrium real GDP and the equilibrium price level. Will the changes in equilibrium real GDP and the price level be larger or smaller than they would be if the tax increase affected only aggregate demand? Briefly explain.

Appendix

A Closer Look at the Multiplier

In this chapter, we saw that changes in government purchases and changes in taxes have a multiplied effect on equilibrium real GDP. In this appendix, we will build a simple economic model of the multiplier effect. When economists forecast the effect of a change in spending or taxes, they often rely on *econometric models.* As we saw in the Appendix to Chapter 11, an econometric model is an economic model written in the form of equations, where each equation has been statistically estimated, using methods similar to those methods used in estimating demand curves as briefly described in Chapter 3. In this appendix, we will start with a model similar to the one we used in the appendix to Chapter 11.

An Expression for Equilibrium Real GDP

We can write a set of equations that includes the key macroeconomic relationships we have studied in this and previous chapters. It is important to note that in this model we will be assuming that the price level is constant. We know that this is unrealistic because an upward-sloping *SRAS* curve means that when the aggregate demand curve shifts the price level will change. Nevertheless, our model will be approximately correct when changes in the price level are small. It also serves as an introduction to more complicated models that take into account changes in the price level. For simplicity, we also start out by assuming that taxes, T, do not depend on the level of real GDP, Y. We also assume that there are no government transfer payments to households. Finally, we assume that we have a closed economy, with no imports or exports. The numbers (with the exception of the *MPC*) represent billions of dollars.

(1) $C = 1{,}000 + 0.75(Y - T)$	Consumption function
(2) $I = 1{,}500$	Planned investment function
(3) $G = 1{,}500$	Government purchases function
(4) $T = 1{,}000$	Tax function
(5) $Y = C + I + G$	Equilibrium condition

The first equation is the consumption function. The marginal propensity to consume, or *MPC,* is 0.75, and 1,000 is the level of autonomous consumption, which is the level of consumption that does not depend on income. We assume that consumption depends on disposable income, which is $Y - T$. The functions for planned investment spending, government spending, and taxes are very simple because we have assumed that these variables are not affected by GDP and, therefore, are constant. Economists who use this type of model to forecast GDP would, of course, use more realistic planned investment, government purchases, and tax functions.

Equation (5)—the equilibrium condition—states that equilibrium GDP equals the sum of consumption spending, planned investment spending, and government purchases. To calculate a value for equilibrium real GDP, we need to substitute equations (1) through (4) into equation (5). This substitution gives us the following:

$$\begin{aligned} Y &= 1{,}000 + 0.75(Y - 1{,}000) + 1{,}500 + 1{,}500 \\ &= 1{,}000 + 0.75Y - 750 + 1{,}500 + 1{,}500. \end{aligned}$$

We need to solve this equation for Y to find equilibrium GDP. The first step is to subtract $0.75Y$ from both sides of the equation:

$$Y - 0.75Y = 1{,}000 - 750 + 1{,}500 + 1{,}500.$$

Then, we solve for Y:

$$0.25Y = 3{,}250$$

or,

$$Y = \frac{3{,}250}{0.25} = 13{,}000.$$

To make this result more general, we can replace particular values with general values represented by letters:

(1) $C = \bar{C} + MPC(Y - T)$	Consumption function
(2) $I = \bar{I}$	Planned investment function
(3) $G = \bar{G}$	Government purchases function
(4) $T = \bar{T}$	Tax function
(5) $Y = C + I + G$	Equilibrium condition

The letters with "bars" represent fixed or *autonomous* values that do not depend on the values of other variables. So, $\bar{C}$ represents autonomous consumption, which had a value of 1,000 in our original example. Now, solving for equilibrium we get:

$$Y = \bar{C} + MPC(Y - \bar{T}) + \bar{I} + \bar{G}$$

or,

$$Y - MPC(Y) = \bar{C} - (MPC \times \bar{T}) + \bar{I} + \bar{G}$$

or,

$$Y(1 - MPC) = \bar{C} - (MPC \times \bar{T}) + I + \bar{G}$$

or,

$$Y = \frac{\bar{C} - (MPC \times \bar{T}) + \bar{I} + \bar{G}}{1 - MPC}.$$

A Formula for the Government Purchases Multiplier

To find a formula for the government purchases multiplier, we need to rewrite the last equation for changes in each variable, rather than levels. Letting Δ stand for the change in a variable, we have:

$$\Delta Y = \frac{\Delta\bar{C} - (MPC \times \Delta\bar{T}) + \Delta\bar{I} + \Delta\bar{G}}{1 - MPC}.$$

If we hold constant changes in autonomous consumption spending, planned investment spending, and taxes, we can find a formula for the government purchases multiplier, which is the ratio of the change in equilibrium real GDP to the change in government purchases:

$$\Delta Y = \frac{\Delta G}{1 - MPC}$$

or,

$$\text{The government purchases multiplier} = \frac{\Delta Y}{\Delta G} = \frac{1}{1 - MPC}.$$

For an *MPC* of 0.75, the government purchases multiplier will be:

$$\frac{1}{1 - 0.75} = 4.$$

A government purchases multiplier of 4 means that an increase in government spending of \$10 billion will increase equilibrium real GDP by $4 \times \$10$ billion = \$40 billion.

A Formula for the Tax Multiplier

We can also find a formula for the tax multiplier. We start again with this equation:

$$\Delta Y = \frac{\Delta\bar{C} - (MPC \times \Delta\bar{T}) + \Delta\bar{I} + \Delta\bar{G}}{1 - MPC}.$$

Now we hold constant the values of autonomous consumption spending, planned investment spending, and government purchases, but we allow the value of taxes to change:

$$\Delta Y = \frac{-MPC \times \Delta T}{1 - MPC}.$$

Or,

$$\text{The tax multiplier} = \frac{\Delta Y}{\Delta T} = \frac{-MPC}{1 - MPC}.$$

For an *MPC* of 0.75, the tax multiplier will be:

$$\frac{-0.75}{1 - 0.75} = -3.$$

The tax multiplier is a negative number because an increase in taxes causes a decrease in equilibrium real GDP and a decrease in taxes causes an increase in equilibrium real GDP. A tax multiplier of –3 means that a decrease in taxes of \$10 billion will increase equilibrium real GDP by $-3 \times -\$10$ billion = \$30 billion. In this chapter, we discussed the economic reasons for the tax multiplier being smaller than the government spending multiplier.

The "Balanced Budget" Multiplier

What will be the effect of equal increases (or decreases) in government purchases and taxes on equilibrium real GDP? At first, it might appear that the tax increase would exactly offset the government purchases increase, leaving real GDP unchanged. But we have just seen that the government purchases multiplier is larger (in absolute value) than the tax multiplier. We can use our formulas for the government purchases multiplier and the tax multiplier to calculate the net effect of increasing government purchases by \$10 billion at the same time that taxes are increased by \$10 billion:

$$\text{Increase in real GDP from the increase in government purchases} = \$10 \text{ billion} \times \frac{1}{1 - MPC}$$

$$\text{Decrease in real GDP from the increase in taxes} = \$10 \text{ billion} \times \frac{-MPC}{1 - MPC}$$

So, the combined effect equals:

$$\$10 \text{ billion} \times \left[\left(\frac{1}{1-MPC}\right)+\left(\frac{-MPC}{1-MPC}\right)\right]$$

or,

$$\$10 \text{ billion} \times \left(\frac{1-MPC}{1-MPC}\right) = \$10 \text{ billion}.$$

The balanced budget multiplier is, therefore, equal to (1 − *MPC*)/(1 − *MPC*), or 1. Equal dollar increases and decreases in government purchases and in taxes lead to the same dollar increase in real GDP in the short run.

The Effects of Changes in Tax Rates on the Multiplier

We now consider the effect of a change in the tax *rate,* as opposed to a change in a fixed amount of taxes. Changing the tax rate actually changes the value of the multiplier. To see this, suppose the tax rate is 20 percent, or 0.2. In that case, an increase in household income of $10 billion will increase *disposable income* by only $8 billion [or, $10 billion × (1 − 0.2)]. In general, an increase in income can be multiplied by (1 − t) to find the increase in disposable income, where t is the tax rate. So, we can rewrite the consumption function as:

$$C = \overline{C} + MPC(1-t)Y.$$

We can use this expression for the consumption function to find an expression for the government purchases multiplier using the same method as we did previously:

$$\text{Government purchases multiplier} = \frac{\Delta Y}{\Delta G} = \frac{1}{1-MPC(1-t)}.$$

We can see the effect of changing the tax rate on the size of the multiplier by trying some values. First, assume that the *MPC* = 0.75 and $t = 0.2$. Then,

$$\text{Government purchases multiplier} = \frac{\Delta Y}{\Delta G} = \frac{1}{1-0.75(1-0.2)} = \frac{1}{1-0.6} = 2.5.$$

This value is smaller than the multiplier of 4 that we calculated by assuming that there was only a fixed amount of taxes (which is the same as assuming the marginal tax *rate* was zero). This multiplier is smaller because spending in each period is now reduced by the amount of taxes households must pay on any additional income they earn. We can calculate the multiplier for an *MPC* of 0.75 and a lower tax rate of 0.1:

$$\text{Government purchases multiplier} = \frac{\Delta Y}{\Delta G} = \frac{1}{1-0.75(1-0.1)} = \frac{1}{1-0.675} = 3.1.$$

Cutting the tax rate from 20 percent to 10 percent increased the value of the multiplier from 2.5 to 3.1.

The Multiplier in an Open Economy

Up to now, we have assumed that the economy is closed, with no imports or exports. We can consider the case of an open economy by including net exports in our analysis. Recall that net exports equal exports minus imports. Exports are determined primarily by factors, such as the exchange value of the dollar and the levels of real GDP in other countries, that we do not include in our model. So, we will assume that exports are fixed, or autonomous:

$$\text{Exports} = \overline{\textit{Exports}}$$

Imports will increase as real GDP increases because households will spend some portion of an increase in income on imports. We can define the *marginal propensity to import* (*MPI*) as the fraction of an increase in income that is spent on imports. So, our expression for imports is:

$$\text{Imports} = MPI \times Y.$$

We can substitute our expressions for exports and imports into the expression we derived earlier for equilibrium real GDP:

$$Y = \overline{C} + MPC(1-t)Y + \overline{I} + \overline{G} + (\overline{Exports} - MPI \times Y),$$

where the expression $\overline{Exports} - MPI \times Y$ represents net exports. We can now find an expression for the government purchases multiplier using the same method as we did previously:

$$\text{Government purchases multiplier} = \frac{\Delta Y}{\Delta G} = \frac{1}{1-[MPC(1-t)-MPI]}.$$

We can see the effect of changing the value of the marginal propensity to import on the size of the multiplier by trying some values of key variables. First, assume $MPC = 0.75$, $t = 0.2$, and $MPI = 0.1$. Then,

$$\text{Government purchases multiplier} = \frac{\Delta Y}{\Delta G} = \frac{1}{1-(0.75(1-0.2)-0.1)} = \frac{1}{1-0.5} = 2.$$

This value is smaller than the multiplier of 2.5 that we calculated by assuming that there were no exports or imports (which is the same as assuming the marginal propensity to import was zero). This multiplier is smaller because spending in each period is now reduced by the amount of imports households buy with any additional income they earn. We can calculate the multiplier with $MPC = 0.75$, $t = 0.20$, and a higher *MPI* of 0.2:

$$\text{Government purchases multiplier} = \frac{\Delta Y}{\Delta G} = \frac{1}{1-(0.75(1-0.2)-0.2)} = \frac{1}{1-0.4} = 1.7.$$

Increasing the marginal propensity to import from 0.1 to 0.2 decreased the value of the multiplier from 2 to 1.7. We can conclude that countries with a higher marginal propensity to import will have smaller multipliers than countries with a lower marginal propensity to import.

It is always important to bear in mind that the multiplier is a short-run effect that assumes that the economy is below the level of potential real GDP. In the long run, the economy is at potential real GDP, so an increase in government purchases causes a decline in the nongovernment components of real GDP, but it leaves the level of real GDP unchanged.

The analysis in this appendix is simplified compared to what would be carried out by an economist forecasting the effects of changes in government purchases or changes in taxes on equilibrium real GDP in the short run. In particular, our assumption that the price level is constant is unrealistic. However, looking more closely at the determinants of the multiplier has helped us see more clearly some important macroeconomic relationships.

PROBLEMS AND APPLICATIONS

Please visit **www.prenhall.com/hubbard** *for solutions to the even-numbered problems as well as multiple-choice and true or false self-assessment quizzes.*

1. Assuming a fixed amount of taxes and a closed economy, calculate the value of the government purchases multiplier, the tax multiplier, and the balanced budget multiplier if the marginal propensity to consume equals 0.6.
2. Calculate the value of the government purchases multiplier if the marginal propensity to consume equals 0.8, the tax rate equals 0.25, and the marginal propensity to import equals 0.2.
3. Show on a graph the change in the aggregate demand curve resulting from an increase in government purchases if the government purchases multiplier equals 2. Now, on the same graph, show the change in the aggregate demand curve resulting from an increase in government purchases if the government purchases multiplier equals 4.
4. From an understanding of the multiplier process, explain why an increase in the tax rate would decrease the size of the government purchases multiplier. Similarly, explain why a decrease in the marginal propensity to import would increase the size of the government purchases multiplier.

chapter sixteen

Inflation, Unemployment, and Federal Reserve Policy

Why Does Whirlpool Care about Monetary Policy?

➤ How does inflation affect monetary policy, and how does monetary policy affect inflation? Testifying before Congress in July 2005, then Federal Reserve Chairman Alan Greenspan said the following:

> [C]ore inflation had moved higher again through the first quarter [of 2005]. The rising prices of energy and other commodities continued to place upward pressures on costs, and reports of greater pricing power of firms indicated that they might be more able to pass those higher costs on to their customers. . . . Slack in labor and product markets has continued to decline. In light of these developments, the FOMC raised the federal funds rate at its June meeting to further reduce monetary policy accommodation. That action brought the cumulative increase in the funds rate over the past year to 2-1/4 percentage points.

We saw in Chapter 3 when introducing the model of demand and supply that the ability of firms to increase prices is determined partly by microeconomic factors. This statement by Chairman Greenspan indicates that macroeconomic factors, including monetary policy, also play a role.

For example, during the 2001 recession, Whirlpool Corporation, the leading manufacturer of home appliances in the world made the following statement in its annual report: "We . . . improved our average selling price by almost 2 percent in a market environment where most competitors had significant price declines." In 2005, with the economy growing more rapidly, Whirlpool was able to increase the prices of its products from 5 percent to 10 percent.

Whirlpool, headquartered in Benton Harbor, Michigan, has 68,000 employees and $13 billion in annual sales. The firm was founded in 1911 by brothers Louis, Frederick, and Emory Upton. The young firm received a major boost when Sears, Roebuck and Company agreed to sell the firm's appliances. This relationship continues with Sears selling Whirlpool appliances under the Kenmore brand. Today, the firm manufactures appliances in 12 countries and sells them in more than 170 countries. In recent years, Whirlpool has gained market share from its competitors both domestically and internationally. Some of its international success has come from an ability to adapt its products to the needs of local markets. For

example, in Brazil, where the typical home is significantly smaller than in the United States, the firm sells a compact dishwasher that fits on a kitchen countertop. Whirlpool has also promoted an image of durability and reliability, which the firm's managers believe has increased customer loyalty and has made their products less susceptible to price competition.

In 2001 and the following years, Whirlpool clearly benefited from the effects of monetary policy. The market for home appliances, such as washers, dryers, refrigerators, freezers, and dishwashers, is significantly affected by housing sales. Most new homes contain new built-in appliances, and many buyers of existing homes also buy at least some new appliances. As we saw in Chapter 14, expansionary monetary policy in 2001 and several years thereafter resulted in low real interest rates on home mortgage loans, which led to increased residential housing construction. As Chairman Greenspan's testimony indicates, however, by 2005 the Fed had embarked on a policy of raising interest rates to ensure that the expanding economy did not lead to worsening inflation.

An Inside Look on page 538 discusses the relationship between wage increases and price increases during 2005.

Sources: "Testimony of Chairman Alan Greenspan: Federal Reserve Board's Semiannual Monetary Policy Report to the Congress Before the Committee on Financial Services," U.S. House of Representatives, July 20, 2005, www.federalreserve.gov/boarddocs/hh/2005/july/testimony.htm. and Whirlpool Corporation, 2001 Summary Annual Report, media.corporate-ir.net/media_files/nys/whr/2001ar/whr_01final.pdf.

LEARNING OBJECTIVES

After studying this chapter, you should be able to:

① Describe the Phillips curve and the nature of the short-run trade-off between inflation and unemployment.

② Explain the relationship between the short-run and long-run Phillips curves.

③ Discuss how expectations of the inflation rate affect monetary policy.

④ Use a Phillips curve graph to show how the Federal Reserve can permanently lower the inflation rate.

➤ As we saw in Chapter 14, two of the Federal Reserve's monetary policy goals are price stability and high employment. These goals can sometimes be in conflict, however. Then Chairman Greenspan's testimony indicates that in 2005 the Fed was concerned that the expansionary policy that had led to increased employment following the 2001 recession was now threatening price stability. An important consideration for the Fed is that in the short run there can be a trade-off between unemployment and inflation: Lower unemployment rates can result in higher inflation rates. In the long run, however, this trade-off disappears and the unemployment rate is independent of the inflation rate. In this chapter, we will explore the relationship between inflation and unemployment in both the short run and the long run and we will discuss what this relationship means for monetary policy.

① LEARNING OBJECTIVE
Describe the Phillips curve and the nature of the short-run trade-off between inflation and unemployment.

The Discovery of the Short-Run Trade-off between Unemployment and Inflation

Unemployment and inflation are the two great macroeconomic problems the Fed must deal with in the short run. As we saw in Chapter 12, when aggregate demand increases, unemployment will usually fall and inflation will rise. When aggregate demand decreases, unemployment will usually rise and inflation will fall. As a result, there is a *short-run trade-off* between unemployment and inflation: Higher unemployment is usually accompanied by lower inflation, and lower unemployment is usually accompanied by higher inflation. As we will see later in this chapter, this trade-off exists in the short run—a period that may be as long as several years—but disappears in the long run.

Although today the short-run trade-off between unemployment and inflation plays a role in the Fed's monetary policy decisions, this trade-off was not widely recognized until the late 1950s. In 1957, New Zealand economist A. W. Phillips plotted data on the unemployment rate and the inflation rate in Great Britain and drew a curve showing their average relationship. Since that time, a graph showing the short-run relationship between the unemployment rate and the inflation rate has been called a **Phillips curve**. (Phillips actually measured inflation by the percentage change in wages, rather than by the percentage change in prices. Because wages and prices usually move together, this difference is not important to our discussion.) Figure 16-1 shows a graph similar to the one Phillips prepared. Each point on the Phillips curve represents a possible combination of the unemployment rate and the inflation rate that might be observed in a given year. Point *A* represents a year in which the inflation rate is 4 percent and the unemployment rate is 5 percent, and point *B* represents a different year in which the inflation rate is 2 percent and the unemployment rate is 6 percent. Phillips documented that there is usually an *inverse relationship* between unemployment and inflation. During years when the unemployment rate is low, the inflation rate tends to be high, and during years when the unemployment rate is high, the inflation rate tends to below.

Phillips curve A curve showing the short-run relationship between the unemployment rate and the inflation rate.

Explaining the Phillips Curve with Aggregate Demand and Aggregate Supply Curves

The inverse relationship between unemployment and inflation that Phillips discovered is consistent with the aggregate demand and aggregate supply analysis we developed in Chapter 12. Figure 16-2 shows the factors that cause this inverse relationship.

Panel (a) shows the aggregate demand and aggregate supply *(AD-AS)* model from Chapter 12, and panel (b) shows the Phillips curve. Remember that because of growth in the labor force, increases in the stock of machinery and equipment, and technological change, the long-run aggregate supply *(LRAS)* and the short-run aggregate supply

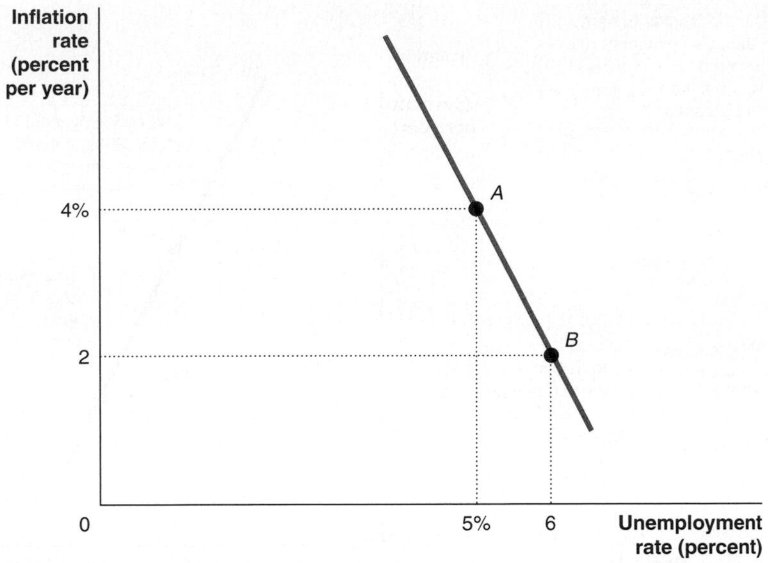

FIGURE 16-1

The Phillips Curve

A. W. Phillips was the first economist to show there is usually an inverse relationship between unemployment and inflation. Here we can see this relationship at work: In the year represented by point *A*, the inflation rate is 4 percent and the unemployment rate is 5 percent. In the year represented by point *B*, the inflation rate is 2 percent and the unemployment rate is 6 percent.

(SRAS) curves usually shift to the right each year. If aggregate demand *(AD)* shifts to the right by the same amount, the economy can remain in macroeconomic equilibrium at potential GDP. The inflation rate is determined by the increase in the price level from one year to the next. If aggregate demand does not increase by as much as long-run aggregate supply, short-run macroeconomic equilibrium will occur at a level of real GDP below the potential level. The unemployment rate will rise, but the price level will rise by less than it would have, meaning that the inflation rate will fall.

Figure 16-2 shows hypothetical data for the years 2008 and 2009. Suppose that initially, in 2008, the economy is in short-run macroeconomic equilibrium at potential real GDP of $14 trillion. Assume the unemployment rate is 5 percent and the inflation rate is 4 percent. In panel (a), we show this equilibrium as point *A* at the intersection of the 2008 *AD, SRAS,* and *LRAS* on the aggregate demand and aggregate supply graph. In panel (b), we show the same equilibrium as the corresponding point *A* on the Phillips curve, with an unemployment rate of 5 percent and an inflation rate of 4 percent. In 2009, if the *AD* curve shifts to the right by the same amount as the *LRAS* curve, then macroeconomic equilibrium occurs at real GDP of $14.5 trillion, which is the new higher level of potential real GDP (point *B*). The price level rises from 100 to 104, so the inflation rate remains 4 percent. Point *B* on the Phillips curve is the same as point *A* because the inflation and unemployment rates haven't changed.

If growth in aggregate demand is weak—perhaps because firms reduce their spending on plant and equipment or consumers reduce their spending on goods and services following a drop in stock prices—macroeconomic equilibrium occurs at $14.3 trillion (point *C*), which is below potential GDP. We know that when real GDP drops below its potential level, firms begin to lay off workers and the unemployment rate rises. In this case, the unemployment rate rises from 5 percent to 6 percent. At the same time, the price level rises only from 100 to 102 (rather than 104), so the inflation rate has fallen to 2 percent from 4 percent during the previous year. In panel (b), the short-run equilibrium has moved down the Phillips curve from point *A*, with 5 percent unemployment and 4 percent inflation, to point *C*, with 6 percent unemployment and 2 percent inflation.

To summarize, the *AD-AS* model indicates that slow growth in aggregate demand leads to both higher unemployment and lower inflation. This relationship explains why there is a short-run trade-off between unemployment and inflation, as shown by the downward-sloping Phillips curve. The *AD-AS* model and the Phillips curve are different ways of illustrating the same macroeconomic events. The Phillips curve has an advantage over the *AD-AS* model, however, when we want to analyze explicitly changes in the inflation and unemployment rates.

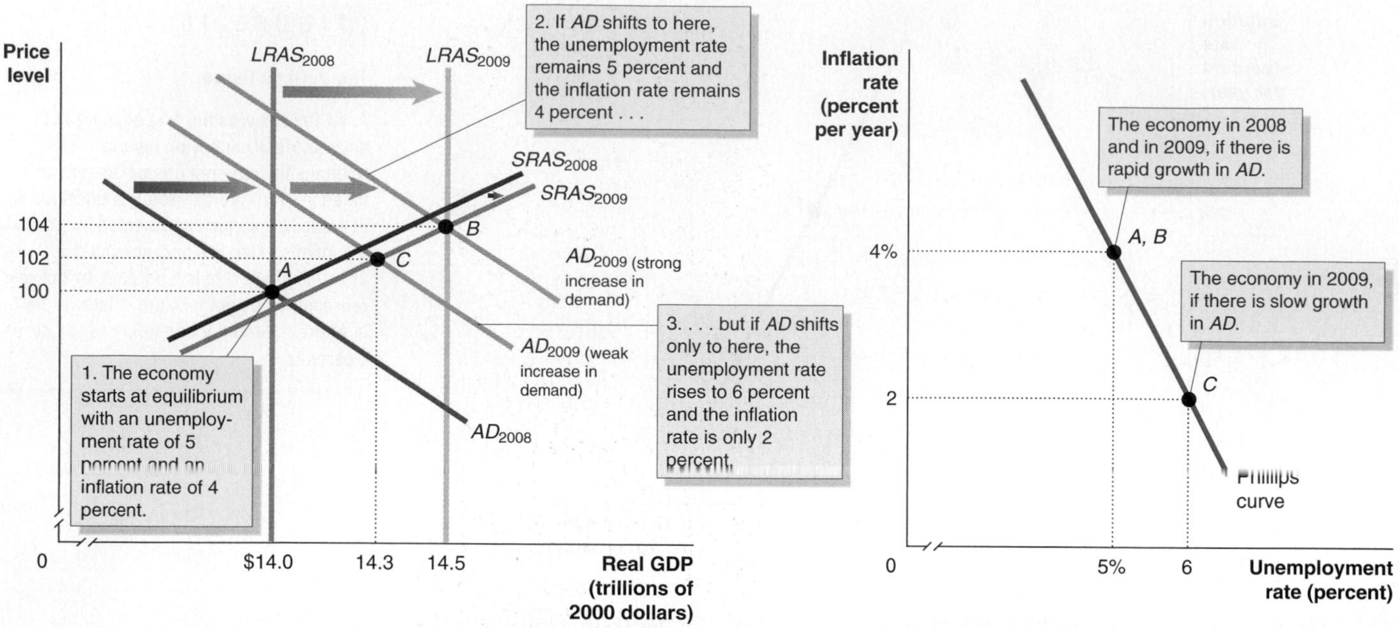

(a) The aggregate demand and aggregate supply (*AD–AS*) model.

(b) The Phillips curve.

FIGURE 16-2 Using Aggregate Demand and Aggregate Supply to Explain the Phillips Curve

The economy in 2008 is in macroeconomic equilibrium at potential real GDP of $14 trillion. The unemployment rate for the year is 5 percent and the inflation rate is 4 percent. In panel (a), point *A* at the intersection of *AD, SRAS,* and *LRAS* marks this initial equilibrium. In panel (b), the corresponding point *A* shows the same equilibrium. Suppose that in 2009 the *AD* curve shifts right by the same amount as the *LRAS* curve. In panel (a), macroeconomic equilibrium occurs at real GDP of $14.5 trillion, which is the new higher level of full-employment real GDP (point *B*). The price level rises from 100 to 104, so the inflation rate remains 4 percent. Point *B* on the Phillips curve is the same as point *A* because the inflation and unemployment rates have not changed. If growth in aggregate demand is weak, however, macroeconomic equilibrium in panel (a) occurs at $14.3 trillion, point *C,* which is below potential GDP. The unemployment rate rises from 5 percent to 6 percent. At the same time, the price level rises only from 100 to 102, so the inflation rate has fallen from 4 percent in the previous year to 2 percent. The short-run equilibrium has moved down the Phillips curve from point *A,* with an unemployment rate of 5 percent and an inflation rate of 4 percent, to point *C,* with an unemployment rate of 6 percent and an inflation rate of 2 percent.

Is the Phillips Curve a Policy Menu?

Structural relationship A relationship that depends on the basic behavior of consumers and firms and remains unchanged over long periods.

During the 1960s, some economists argued that the Phillips curve represented a **structural relationship** in the economy. A structural relationship depends on the basic behavior of consumers and firms and remains unchanged over long periods. Structural relationships are useful in formulating economic policy because policymakers can anticipate that these relationships are constant—that is, the relationships will not change as a result of changes in policy.

If the Phillips curve were a structural relationship, it would present policymakers with a reliable menu of combinations of unemployment and inflation. Potentially, policymakers could use expansionary monetary and fiscal policies to choose a point on the curve that had lower unemployment and higher inflation. They also could use contractionary monetary and fiscal policies to choose a point that had lower inflation and higher unemployment. Because many economists and policymakers in the 1960s viewed the Phillips curve as a structural relationship, they believed it represented a *permanent trade-off between unemployment and inflation.* As long as policymakers were willing to accept a permanently higher inflation rate, they would be able to keep the unemployment rate permanently lower. Similarly, a permanently lower inflation rate could be attained at the cost of a permanently higher unemployment rate. As we discuss in the next section, however, economists came to realize that the Phillips curve did *not,* in fact, represent a permanent trade-off between unemployment and inflation.

SOLVED PROBLEM 16-1

The Policy Menu View of the Phillips Curve

① LEARNING OBJECTIVE
Describe the Phillips curve and the nature of the short-run trade-off between inflation and unemployment.

In 1960, Paul Samuelson and Robert Solow wrote the first article to use the Phillips curve model to explain the relationship between unemployment and inflation in the United States. They concluded that:

> [P]rice stability is seen to involve about 5 1/2 percent unemployment; whereas . . . 3 percent unemployment is seen to involve a price rise of about 4 1/2 percent per annum. We rather expect that the tug of war of politics will end us up in the next few years somewhere in between these selected points.

What did Samuelson and Solow mean by "price stability"? What does the "tug of war of politics" have to do with what happens to the unemployment and inflation rates?

Source: Paul A. Samuelson and Robert M. Solow, "Analytical Aspects of Anti-Inflation Policy," *American Economic Review*, Vol. 50, No. 2 (May 1960), pp. 192–193.

Solving the Problem:

Step 1: Review the chapter material. This problem is about how the Phillips curve was understood in the 1960s, so you may want to review the section "Is the Phillips Curve a Policy Menu?" which begins on page 518.

Step 2: Explain what is meant by "price stability." When prices are stable, the price level does not change. So, price stability is another term for zero inflation.

Step 3: Explain how the "tug of war of politics" affects the unemployment and inflation rates. By the "tug of war of politics," Samuelson and Solow were referring to the policy menu view of the Phillips curve. Some politicians would prefer expansionary policies that would result in very low unemployment at the cost of higher inflation. Others would prefer low inflation at the cost of higher unemployment. Political compromise would result in the economy ending up somewhere in between.

Extra Credit: As we are about to discuss, although the policy menu view of the Phillips curve was popular among economists and policymakers during the 1960s, it ultimately turned out to be mistaken.

YOUR TURN: **For more practice, do related problem 5 on page 542 at the end of this chapter.**

Is the Short-Run Phillips Curve Stable?

During the 1960s, the basic Phillips curve relationship seemed to hold because a stable trade-off appeared to exist between unemployment and inflation. In the early 1960s, the inflation rate was low, while the unemployment rate was high. In the late 1960s, the unemployment rate had declined, while the inflation rate had increased. Then in 1968, in his presidential address to the American Economic Association, Milton Friedman of the University of Chicago (who would go on to win the Nobel Prize in Economics) argued that the Phillips curve did *not* represent a *permanent* trade-off between unemployment and inflation. At almost the same time, Edmund Phelps of Columbia University published an academic paper making a similar argument. Friedman and Phelps noted that economists had come to agree that the long-run aggregate supply curve was vertical (a point we discussed in Chapter 12). If this observation were true, the Phillips curve could not be downward sloping in the long run. A critical inconsistency existed between a vertical long-run aggregate supply curve and a long-run Phillips curve that is downward sloping. Friedman and Phelps argued, in essence, that there is no trade-off between unemployment and inflation in the long run.

The Long-Run Phillips Curve

To understand the argument that there is no permanent trade-off between unemployment and inflation, recall, first, that the level of real GDP in the long run is also referred to as potential real GDP. At potential real GDP, firms will operate at their normal level of capacity and everyone who wants a job will have one, except the structurally and frictionally unemployed. Friedman defined the **natural rate of unemployment** as the unemployment rate that exists when the economy is at potential GDP. The actual unemployment rate will fluctuate in the short run but will always come back to the natural rate in the long run. In the same way, the actual level of real GDP will fluctuate in the short run but will always come back to its potential level in the long run.

Natural rate of unemployment The unemployment rate that exists when the economy is at potential GDP.

In the long run, a higher or lower price level has no effect on real GDP because real GDP is always at its potential level in the long run. In the same way, in the long run a higher or lower inflation rate will have no effect on the unemployment rate because the unemployment rate is always equal to the natural rate in the long run. Figure 16-3 illustrates Friedman's conclusion that the long-run aggregate supply curve is a vertical line at the potential real GDP, and *the long-run Phillips curve is a vertical line at the natural rate of unemployment.*

The Role of Expectations of Future Inflation

If the long-run Phillips curve is a vertical line, *no trade-off exists between unemployment and inflation in the long run.* This conclusion seemed to contradict the experience of the 1950s and 1960s, which showed a stable trade-off between unemployment and inflation. Friedman argued that the statistics from those years actually showed only a short-run trade-off between inflation and unemployment.

The short-run trade-off existed, but only because workers and firms sometimes expected the inflation rate to be either higher or lower than it turned out to be. Differences between the expected inflation rate and the actual inflation rate could lead the unemployment rate to rise above or dip below the natural rate. To see why, consider a simple case of the Ford Motor Company negotiating a wage contract with the United

FIGURE 16-3

A Vertical Long-Run Aggregate Supply Curve Means a Vertical Long-Run Phillips Curve

Milton Friedman and Edmund Phelps argued that there is no trade-off between unemployment and inflation in the long run. If real GDP automatically returns to its potential level in the long run, the unemployment rate must return to the natural rate of unemployment in the long run. In this figure, we assume potential real GDP is $14 trillion and the natural rate of unemployment is 5 percent.

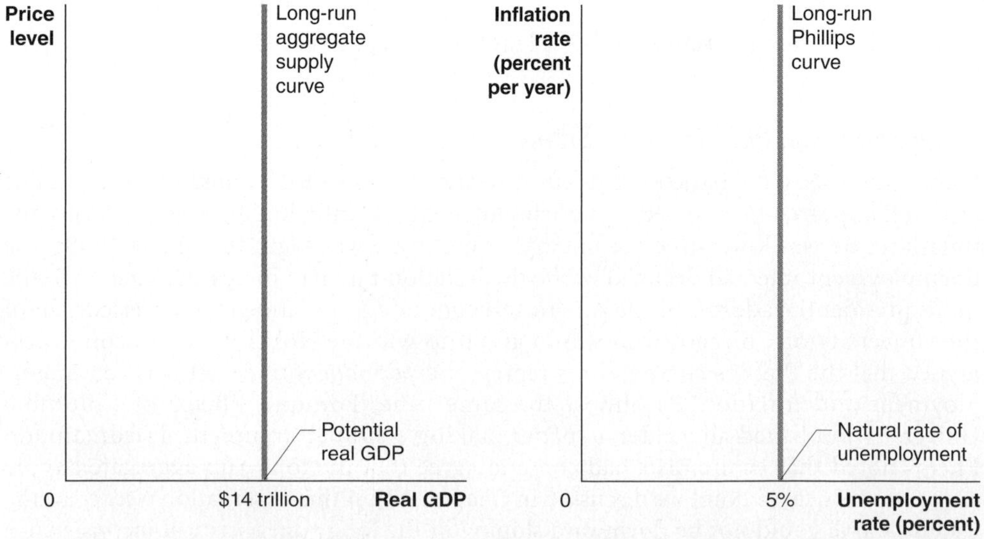

TABLE 16-1

The Impact of Unexpected Price Level Changes on the Real Wage

NOMINAL WAGE	EXPECTED REAL WAGE	ACTUAL REAL WAGE	
	Expected $P_{2009} = 105$	Actual $P_{2009} = 102$	Actual $P_{2009} = 108$
	Expected inflation = 5%	Actual inflation = 2%	Actual inflation = 8%
\$31.50	$\frac{\$31.50}{105} \times 100 = \$30$	$\frac{\$31.50}{102} \times 100 = \$30.88$	$\frac{\$31.50}{108} \times 100 = \$29.17$

Automobile Workers (UAW) union. Remember that both Ford and the UAW are interested in the real wage, which is the nominal wage corrected for inflation. Suppose, for example, that Ford and the UAW agree on a wage of \$31.50 per hour to be paid during 2009. Both Ford and the UAW expect that the price level will increase from 100 in 2008 to 105 in 2009, so the inflation rate will be 5 percent. We can calculate the real wage Ford expects to pay and the UAW expects to receive as follows:

$$\text{Real wage} = \frac{\text{Nominal wage}}{\text{Price level}} \times 100 = \frac{\$31.50}{105} \times 100 = \$30.$$

But suppose that the actual inflation rate turns out to be higher or lower than the expected inflation rate of 5 percent. Table 16-1 shows the effect on the actual real wage. If the price level rises only to 102 during 2009, the inflation rate will be 2 percent, and the actual real wage will be \$30.88, which is higher than Ford and the UAW had expected. With a higher real wage, Ford will hire fewer workers than it had planned to at the expected real wage of \$30. If the inflation rate is 8 percent, the actual real wage will be \$29.17, and Ford will hire more workers than it had planned. If Ford and the UAW expected a higher or lower inflation rate than actually occurred, other firms and workers probably made the same mistake.

If actual inflation is higher than expected inflation, actual real wages in the economy will be lower than expected real wages and many firms will hire more workers than they had planned. Therefore, the unemployment rate will fall. If actual inflation is lower than expected inflation, actual real wages will be higher than expected and many firms will hire fewer workers than they had planned, and the unemployment rate will rise. Table 16-2 summarizes this argument.

Friedman and Phelps concluded that *an increase in the inflation rate increases employment (and decreases unemployment) only if the increase in the inflation rate is unexpected.* Friedman argued that in 1968 the unemployment rate was 3.6 percent, rather than 5 percent, only because the inflation rate of 4 percent was above the 1 percent to 2 percent inflation that workers and firms had expected:

> [T]here is always a temporary trade-off between inflation and unemployment; there is no permanent trade-off. The temporary trade-off comes not from inflation per se, but from unanticipated inflation.

TABLE 16-2

The Basis for the Short-Run Phillips Curve

IF ...	THEN ...	AND ...
actual inflation is greater than expected inflation,	the actual real wage is less than the expected real wage,	the unemployment rate falls.
actual inflation is less than expected inflation,	the actual real wage is greater than the expected real wage,	the unemployment rate rises.

16-1 Making the Connection

Will her wage increases keep up with inflation?

Do Workers Understand Inflation?

A higher inflation rate can lead to lower unemployment if *both* workers and firms mistakenly expect the inflation rate to be lower than it turns out to be. But this same result might be due to firms forecasting inflation more accurately than workers do, or to firms understanding better the effects of inflation. Some large firms employ economists to help them gather and analyze information that is useful in forecasting inflation. Many firms also have human resources or employee compensation departments that gather data on wages paid at competing firms and analyze trends in compensation.

Workers generally rely on much less systematic information about wages and prices. Workers also often fail to realize a fact we discussed in Chapter 8: *Expected inflation increases the value of total production and the value of total income by the same amount.* Therefore, although not all wages will rise as prices rise, inflation will increase the average wage in the economy at the same time that it increases the average price.

Robert Shiller, an economist at Yale University, conducted a survey on inflation and discovered that, although most economists believe an increase in inflation will lead quickly to an increase in wages, a majority of the general public thinks otherwise. In one question, Shiller asked how "the effect of general inflation on wages or salary relates to your own experience and your own job." The most popular response was: "The price increase will create extra profits for my employer who can now sell output for more; there will be no effect on my pay. My employer will see no reason to raise my pay."

Shiller also asked the following question:

> Imagine that next year the inflation rate unexpectedly doubles. How long would it probably take, in these times, before your income is increased enough so that you can afford the same things as you do today? In other words, how long will it be before a full inflation correction in your income has taken place?

Eighty-one percent of the public answered either that it would take several years for the purchasing power of their income to be restored or that it would never be restored.

If workers fail to understand that rising inflation leads over time to comparable increases in wages, then when inflation increases, in the short run firms can increase wages by less than inflation without needing to worry about workers quitting or their morale falling. Once again, we have a higher inflation rate leading in the short run to lower real wages and lower unemployment. In other words, we have another explanation for a downward-sloping short-run Phillips curve.

Source: Robert J. Shiller, "Why Do People Dislike Inflation?" in *Reducing Inflation: Motivation and Strategy*, Christina D. Romer and David H. Romer, eds., Chicago: University of Chicago Press, 1997.

② LEARNING OBJECTIVE

Explain the relationship between the short-run and long-run Phillips curves.

The Short-Run and Long-Run Phillips Curves

If there is both a short-run Phillips curve and a long-run Phillips curve, how are the two curves related? We can begin answering this question with the help of Figure 16-4, which reflects macroeconomic conditions in the United States during the 1960s. In the late 1960s, workers and firms were still expecting the inflation rate to be about 1.5 percent, as it had been from 1960 to 1965. Expansionary monetary and fiscal policies, however, had moved the short-run equilibrium up the short-run Phillips curve to an inflation rate of 4.5 percent and an unemployment rate of 3.5 percent. This very low unemployment rate was only possible because the real wage rate was unexpectedly low.

Once workers and firms began to expect that the inflation rate would continue to be about 4.5 percent, they changed their behavior. Firms knew that only nominal wage increases of more than 4.5 percent would increase real wages. Workers realized that unless they received a nominal wage increase of at least 4.5 percent, their real wage would be falling. Higher expected inflation rates had an impact throughout the economy. For example, as we saw in Chapter 13, when banks make loans they are interested in the *real interest rate* on the loan. The real interest rate is the nominal interest rate

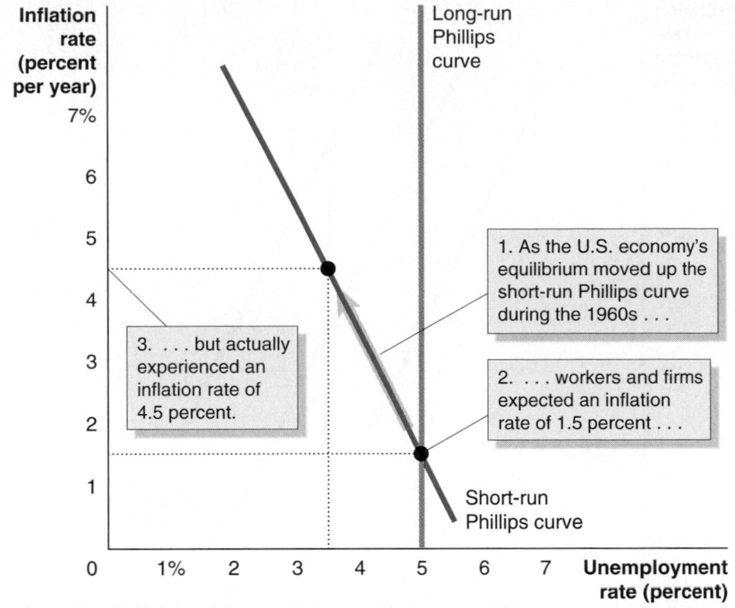

FIGURE 16-4

The Short-Run Phillips Curve of the 1960s and the Long-Run Phillips Curve

In the late 1960s, U.S. workers and firms were expecting the 1.5 percent inflation rates of the recent past to continue. However, expansionary monetary and fiscal policies moved the short-run equilibrium up the short-run Phillips curve to an inflation rate of 4.5 percent and an unemployment rate of 3.5 percent.

minus the expected inflation rate. If banks need to receive a real interest rate of 3 percent on home mortgage loans, they will charge a nominal interest rate of 5.5 percent if they expect the inflation rate to be 2.5 percent. If they revise their expectations of the inflation rate to 4.5 percent, they will increase the nominal interest rate they charge on mortgage loans to 7.5 percent.

Shifts in the Short-Run Phillips Curve

The new, higher expected inflation rate can become *embedded* in the economy, meaning that workers, firms, consumers, and the government all take the inflation rate into account when making decisions. The short-run trade-off between unemployment and inflation now takes place from this higher, less favorable level, as shown in Figure 16-5.

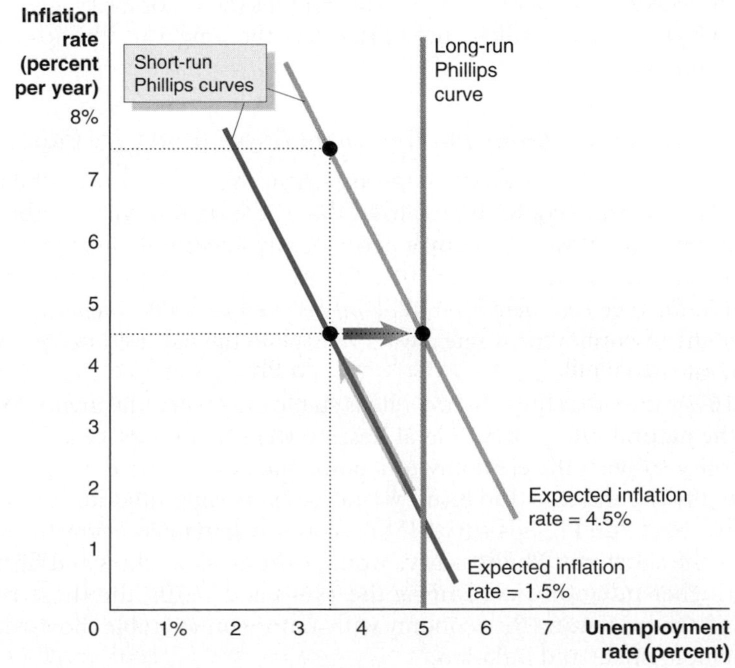

FIGURE 16-5

Expectations and the Short-Run Phillips Curve

By the end of the 1960s, workers and firms had revised their expectations of inflation from 1.5 percent to 4.5 percent. As a result, the short-run Phillips curve shifted up, which made the short-run trade-off between unemployment and inflation worse.

FIGURE 16-6

A Short-Run Phillips Curve for Every Expected Inflation Rate

There is a different short-run Phillips curve for every expected inflation rate. Each short-run Phillips curve intersects the long-run Phillips curve at the expected inflation rate.

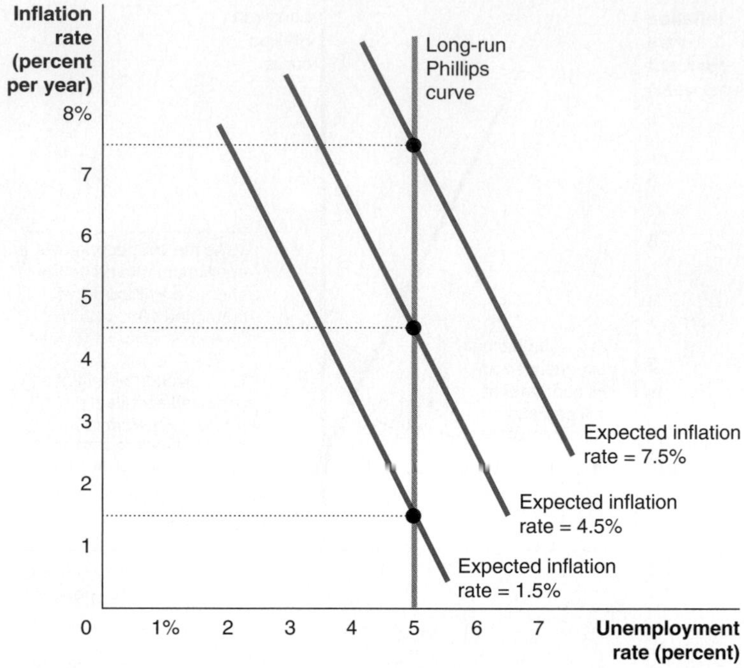

As long as workers and firms expected the inflation rate to be 1.5 percent, the short-run trade-off between unemployment and inflation was the more favorable one shown by the lower Phillips curve. Along this Phillips curve, an inflation rate of 4.5 percent was enough to drive down the unemployment rate to 3.5 percent. Once workers and firms adjusted their expectations to an inflation rate of 4.5 percent, the short-run trade-off deteriorated to the one shown by the higher Phillips curve. The economy's equilibrium returned to the natural rate of unemployment of 5 percent, but now with an inflation rate of 4.5 percent rather than 1.5 percent. On the higher short-run Phillips curve, an inflation rate of 7.5 percent would be necessary to reduce the unemployment rate to 3.5 percent. An inflation rate of 7.5 percent would keep the unemployment rate at 3.5 percent only until workers and firms revised their expectations of inflation up to 7.5 percent. In the long run, the economy's equilibrium would return to the 5 percent natural rate of unemployment.

As Figure 16-6 shows, there is a short-run Phillips curve for every level of expected inflation. Each short-run Phillips curve intersects the long-run Phillips curve at the expected inflation rate.

How Does a Vertical Long-Run Phillips Curve Affect Monetary Policy?

By the 1970s, most economists accepted the argument that the long-run Phillips curve is vertical. In other words, economists realized that the common view of the 1960s had been wrong: It was *not* possible to buy a permanently lower unemployment rate at the cost of a permanently higher inflation rate. The moral of the vertical long-run Phillips curve is that *in the long run there is no trade-off between unemployment and inflation.* In the long run, the unemployment rate always returns to the natural rate, no matter what the inflation rate is.

Figure 16-7 shows that the inflation rate is stable only when the unemployment rate is equal to the natural rate. If the Federal Reserve were to attempt to use expansionary monetary policy to push the economy to a point such as *A*, where the unemployment rate is below the natural rate, the result would be increasing inflation as the economy moved up the short-run Phillips curve. If the economy remained below the natural rate long enough, the short-run Phillips curve would shift up as workers and firms adjusted to the new, higher inflation rate. During the 1960s and 1970s, the short-run Phillips curve did shift up, presenting the economy with a more unfavorable short-run trade-off between unemployment and inflation.

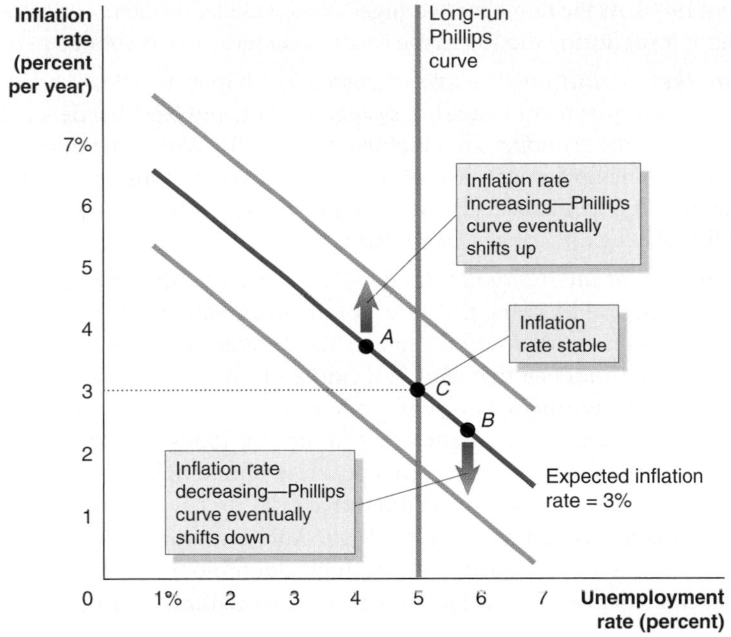

FIGURE 16-7

The Inflation Rate and the Natural Rate of Unemployment in the Long Run

The inflation rate is stable only if the unemployment rate equals the natural rate of unemployment (point *C*). If the unemployment rate is below the natural rate (point *A*), the inflation rate increases and, eventually, the short-run Phillips curve shifts up. If the unemployment rate is above the natural rate (point *B*), the inflation decreases, and, eventually, the short-run Phillips curve shifts down.

If the Federal Reserve used contractionary policy to push the economy to a point such as *B*, where the unemployment rate is above the natural rate, the inflation rate would decrease. If the economy remained above the natural rate long enough, the short-run Phillips curve would shift down as workers and firms adjusted to the new, lower inflation rate. Only at a point such as *C*, where the unemployment rate is equal to the natural rate, will the inflation rate be stable. As a result, the natural rate of unemployment is sometimes called the *nonaccelerating inflation rate of unemployment* or *NAIRU*. We can conclude this: *In the long run, the Federal Reserve can affect the inflation rate, but not the unemployment rate.*

Does the Natural Rate of Unemployment Ever Change?

16-2 Making the Connection

Life would be easier for the Federal Reserve if it knew exactly what the natural rate of unemployment was and if that rate never changed. Unfortunately for the Fed, the natural rate does change over time. Remember that at the natural rate of unemployment, only frictional and structural unemployment remains. Frictional or structural unemployment can change—thereby changing the natural rate—for several reasons:

- ***Demographic changes.*** Younger and less skilled workers have higher unemployment rates, on average, than do older and more skilled workers. Because of the baby boom, the United States had an unusually large number of younger and less skilled workers during the 1970s and 1980s. As a result, the natural rate of unemployment rose from about 5 percent in the 1960s to about 6 percent in the

What makes the natural rate of unemployment increase or decrease?

1970s and 1980s. As the number of younger and less skilled workers declined as a fraction of the labor force during the 1990s, the natural rate returned to about 5 percent.

- ***Labor market institutions.*** As we discussed in Chapter 8, labor market institutions such as the unemployment insurance system, unions, and legal barriers to firing workers can increase the economy's unemployment rate. Because many European countries have generous unemployment insurance systems, strong unions, and restrictive policies on firing workers, the natural rate of unemployment in most Europeans countries has been well above the rate in the United States.
- ***Past high rates of unemployment.*** Evidence indicates that if high unemployment persists for a period of years, the natural rate of unemployment may increase. After workers have been unemployed for longer than a year or two, their skills deteriorate, they may lose confidence that they can find and hold a job, and they may become dependent on government payments to survive. Robert Gordon, an economist at Northwestern University, has argued that in the late 1930s so many U.S. workers had been out of work for so long that the natural rate of unemployment may have risen to more than 15 percent. He has pointed out that even though the unemployment rate in the United States was 17 percent in 1939, the inflation rate did not change. Similarly, many economists have argued that the high unemployment rates experienced by European countries during the 1970s increased their natural rates of unemployment.

SOLVED PROBLEM 16-2

② LEARNING OBJECTIVE
Explain the relationship between the short-run and long-run Phillips curves.

Changing Views of the Phillips Curve

Writing in a Federal Reserve publication, Bennett McCallum, an economist at Carnegie Mellon University, argues that during the 1970s the Fed was "acting under the influence of 1960s academic ideas that posited the existence of a long-run and exploitable Phillips-type tradeoff between inflation and unemployment rates." What does he mean by a "long-run and exploitable Phillips-type tradeoff"? How would the Fed have attempted to exploit this long-run trade-off? What would be the consequences for the inflation rate?

Source: Bennett T. McCallum, "Recent Developments in Monetary Policy Analysis: The Roles of Theory and Evidence," Federal Reserve Bank of Richmond, *Economic Quarterly,* Winter 2002, p. 73.

Solving the Problem:

Step 1: Review the chapter material. This problem is about the relationship between the short-run and long-run Phillips curves, so you may want to review the section "The Short-Run and Long-Run Phillips Curves," which begins on page 522.

Step 2: Explain what a "long-run exploitable Phillips-type tradeoff" means. A "long-run exploitable Phillips-type tradeoff" means a Phillips curve that in the long run is downward sloping, rather than vertical. An "exploitable" trade-off is one that the Fed could take advantage of to *permanently* reduce unemployment at the expense of higher inflation, or to permanently reduce inflation at the expense of higher unemployment.

Step 3: Explain how the inflation rate will accelerate if the Fed tries to exploit a long-run trade-off between unemployment and inflation. As we have seen, during the 1960s the Fed conducted expansionary monetary policies to move up what they thought was a stationary short-run Phillips curve. By the late 1960s, these policies resulted in very low unemployment rates. In the long run, there is no stable trade-off between unemployment and inflation. Attempting to permanently keep the unemployment rate at very low levels leads to a rising inflation rate, which is what happened in the late 1960s and early 1970s.

YOUR TURN: **For more practice, do related problem 15 on page 543 at the end of this chapter.**

Expectations of the Inflation Rate

③ LEARNING OBJECTIVE

Discuss how expectations of the inflation rate affect monetary policy.

How long can the economy remain on the short-run Phillips curve? It depends on how quickly workers and firms adjust their expectations of future inflation to changes in current inflation. The experience in the United States over the past 50 years indicates that how workers and firms adjust their expectations of inflation depends on how high the inflation rate is. There are three possibilities:

- ***Low inflation.*** When the inflation rate is low, as it was during most of the 1950s, the early 1960s, the 1990s, and the early 2000s, workers and firms tend to ignore it. For example, if the inflation rate is low, a restaurant may not want to pay for printing new menus that would show slightly higher prices.
- ***Moderate, but stable inflation.*** For the four-year period from 1968 to 1971, the inflation rate in the United States stayed in the narrow range between 4 percent and 5 percent. This rate was high enough that workers and firms could not ignore it without seeing their real wages and profits decline. It was also likely that the next year's inflation rate would be very close to the current year's inflation rate. In fact, workers and firms during the 1960s acted as if they expected changes in the inflation rate during one year to continue into the following year. People are said to have *adaptive expectations* of inflation if they assume that future rates of inflation will follow the pattern of rates of inflation in the recent past.
- ***High and unstable inflation.*** Inflation rates above 5 percent during peacetime have been rare in U.S. history, but the inflation rate was above 5 percent every year from 1973 through 1982. Not only was the inflation rate high during these years, it was also unstable—rising from 6 percent in 1973 to 11 percent in 1974, before falling below 6 percent in 1976 and rising again to 13.5 percent in 1980. In the mid-1970s, Robert Lucas of the University of Chicago (who went on to win the Nobel Prize in Economics) and Thomas Sargent of New York University argued that the gains to forecasting inflation accurately had dramatically increased. Workers and firms that failed to correctly anticipate the fluctuations in inflation during these years could experience substantial declines in real wages and profits. Therefore, Lucas and Sargent argued, people should use all available information when forming their expectations of future inflation. Expectations formed by using all available information about an economic variable are called **rational expectations.**

Rational expectations Expectations formed by using all available information about an economic variable.

The Effect of Rational Expectations on Monetary Policy

Lucas and Sargent pointed out an important consequence of rational expectations: An expansionary monetary policy would not work. In other words, there might not be a trade-off between unemployment and inflation, even in the short run. By the mid-1970s, most economists had accepted the idea that an expansionary monetary policy could cause the actual inflation rate to be higher than the expected inflation rate. This gap between actual and expected inflation would cause the actual real wage to fall below the expected real wage, and the unemployment rate would be pushed below the natural rate. The economy's short-run equilibrium would move up the short-run Phillips curve.

Lucas and Sargent argued that this explanation of the Phillips curve assumed that workers and firms either ignored inflation or used adaptive expectations in making their forecasts of inflation. If workers and firms used rational expectations, they would make use of all available information, *including knowledge of the policy being used by the Federal Reserve.* If workers and firms know that an expansionary monetary policy would raise the inflation rate, they then should use this information in their forecasts of inflation. If they do, an expansionary monetary policy will not cause the actual inflation rate to be above the expected inflation rate. Instead, the actual inflation rate will equal the expected inflation rate, the actual real wage will equal the expected real wage, and the unemployment rate will not fall below the natural rate.

FIGURE 16-8

Rational Expectations and the Phillips Curve

If workers and firms ignore inflation, or if they have adaptive expectations, an expansionary monetary policy will cause the short-run equilibrium to move from point *A* on the short-run Phillips curve to point *B;* inflation will rise and unemployment will fall. If workers and firms have rational expectations, an expansionary monetary policy will cause the short-run equilibrium to move up the long-run Phillips curve from point *A* to point *C.* Inflation will still rise, but there will be no change in unemployment.

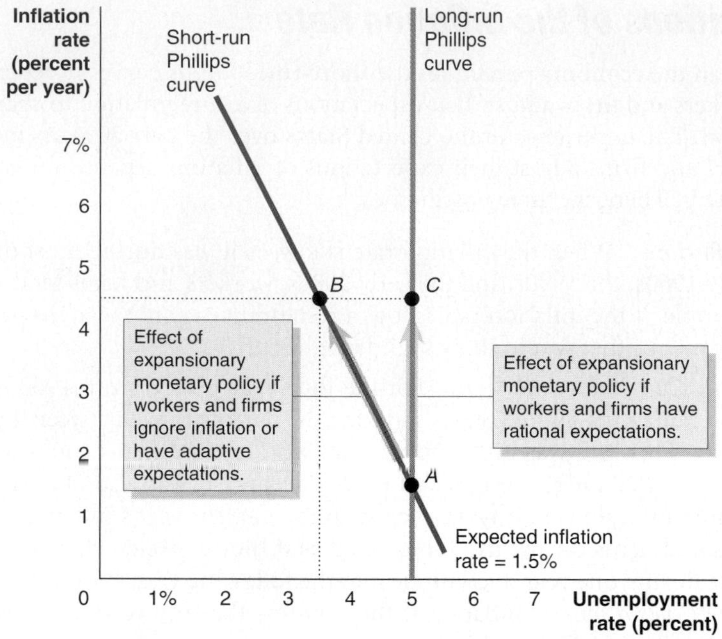

Figure 16-8 illustrates this argument. Suppose the economy begins at point *A* where the short-run Phillips curve intersects the long-run Phillips curve. The actual and expected inflation rates are both equal to 1.5 percent, and the unemployment rate equals the natural rate of 5 percent. Then suppose the Fed engages in an expansionary monetary policy. If workers ignore inflation or if they form their expectations adaptively, the expansionary monetary policy will cause the actual inflation rate to be higher than the expected inflation rate and the short-run equilibrium will move from point *A* on the short-run Phillips curve to point *B.* The inflation rate will rise to 4.5 percent and the unemployment rate will fall to 3.5 percent. The decline in unemployment is only temporary, however. Eventually, workers and firms will adjust to the fact that the actual inflation rate is 4.5 percent, not the 1.5 percent they had expected. The short-run Phillips curve will shift up, and the unemployment rate will return to 5 percent at point *C.*

Lucas and Sargent argued that if workers and firms have rational expectations, they will realize that the result of the Fed's expansionary policy will be an inflation rate of 4.5 percent. Therefore, as soon as the new policy is announced, they should adjust their expectations of inflation from 1.5 percent to 4.5 percent. As a result, the short-run equilibrium will move from point *A* to point *C* on the long-run Phillips curve. The unemployment rate will never drop below 5 percent, and the *short-run* Phillips curve will be vertical.

Is the Short-Run Phillips Curve Really Vertical?

The claim by Lucas and Sargent that the short-run Phillips curve was vertical and that an expansionary monetary policy could not reduce the unemployment rate below the natural rate surprised many economists. An obvious objection to the argument of Lucas and Sargent was that the record of the 1950s and 1960s seemed to show that there was a short-run trade-off between unemployment and inflation and that, therefore, the short-run Phillips curve was downward sloping, and not vertical. Lucas and Sargent argued that the apparent short-run trade-off was actually the result of *unexpected* changes in monetary policy. During those years, the Fed did not announce changes in policy, so workers, firms, and financial markets had to *guess* when the Fed had begun using a new policy. In that case, an expansionary monetary policy might cause the unemployment rate to fall because workers and firms would be taken by surprise and their expectations of inflation would be too low. Lucas and Sargent argued that a policy that was announced ahead of time would not cause a change in unemployment.

Many economists have remained skeptical of the argument that the short-run Phillips curve is vertical. The two main objections raised are that: (1) workers and firms actually may not have rational expectations, and (2) the rapid adjustment of wages and prices needed for the short-run Phillips curve to be vertical will not actually take place. Many economists doubt that people are able to use information on the Fed's monetary policy to make a reliable forecast of the inflation rate. If workers and firms do not know what impact an expansionary monetary policy will have on the inflation rate, the actual real wage may still end up being lower than the expected real wage. Also, firms may have contracts with their workers and suppliers that keep wages and prices from adjusting quickly. If wages and prices adjust slowly, then even if workers and firms have rational expectations, an expansionary monetary policy may still be able to reduce the unemployment rate in the short run.

Real Business Cycle Models

During the 1980s, some economists, including Finn Kydland of Carnegie Mellon University and Edward Prescott of Arizona State University, argued that Robert Lucas was correct in assuming that workers and firms formed their expectations rationally and that wages and prices adjust quickly, but that he was wrong in assuming that fluctuations in real GDP are caused by unexpected changes in the money supply. Instead, they argued that fluctuations in "real" factors, particularly *technology shocks,* explained deviations of real GDP from its potential level. Technology shocks are changes to the economy that make it possible to produce either more output—a positive shock—or less output—a negative shock—with the same amount of workers, machines, and other inputs. Real GDP will be above its previous potential level following a positive technology shock and below its previous potential level following a negative technology shock. Because these models focus on real factors—rather than on changes in the money supply—to explain fluctuations in real GDP, they are known as **real business cycle models.**

Real business cycle models Models that focus on real rather than monetary explanations of fluctuations in real GDP.

The approach of Lucas and Sargent and the real business cycle models are sometimes grouped together under the label the *new classical macroeconomics* because these approaches share the assumptions that people have rational expectations and that wages and prices adjust rapidly. Some of the assumptions of the new classical macroeconomics are similar to those held by economists before the Great Depression of the 1930s. John Maynard Keynes, in his 1936 book, *The General Theory of Employment, Interest, and Money,* referred to these earlier economists as "classical economists." Like the classical economists, the new classical macroeconomists believe that the economy will normally be at its potential level.

Economists who find the assumptions of rational expectations and rapid adjustment of wages and prices appealing have been more likely to accept the real business cycle model approach. Other economists are skeptical of these models because they explain recessions as being caused by negative technology shocks. Negative technology shocks are uncommon and, apart from the oil price increases of the 1970s, real business cycle theorists have had difficulty identifying shocks that would have been large enough to cause recessions. Some economists have begun to develop real business cycle models that allow for the possibility that changes in the money supply may affect the level of real GDP. If real business cycle models continue to develop along these lines, they may eventually converge with the approaches used by the Fed.

(4) LEARNING OBJECTIVE

Use a Phillips curve graph to show how the Federal Reserve can permanently lower the inflation rate.

How the Fed Fights Inflation

We have already seen that the high inflation rates of the late 1960s and early 1970s were due in part to an attempt by the Federal Reserve to keep the unemployment rate below the natural rate. By the mid-1970s, the Fed also had to deal with the inflationary impact of the OPEC oil price increases. By the late 1970s, as the Fed attempted to deal with the problem of high and worsening inflation rates, it received conflicting policy advice. Many economists argued that the inflation rate could be reduced only at the cost of a temporary increase in the unemployment rate. Followers of the Lucas–Sargent rational expectations approach, however, argued that a painless reduction in the inflation rate was possible. Before analyzing the actual policies used by the Fed, we can look at why the oil price increases of the mid-1970s made the inflation rate worse.

The Effect of a Supply Shock on the Phillips Curve

As we saw in Chapter 12, the increases in oil prices in 1974 resulting from actions by the Organization of Petroleum Exporting Countries (OPEC) caused the short-run aggregate supply curve to shift to the left. This shift is shown in panel (a) of Figure 16-9. (For simplicity, in this panel we use the basic rather than dynamic *AD-AS* model.) The result was a higher price level and a lower level of real GDP. On a Phillips curve graph—panel (b) of Figure 16-9—we can shift the short-run Phillips curve up to show that the inflation rate and unemployment rate both increased.

As the Phillips curve shifted up, the United States moved from an unemployment rate of about 5 percent and an inflation rate of about 5.5 percent in 1973 to an unemployment rate of 8.5 percent and an inflation rate of about 9.5 percent in 1975. This combination of rising unemployment and rising inflation placed the Federal Reserve in

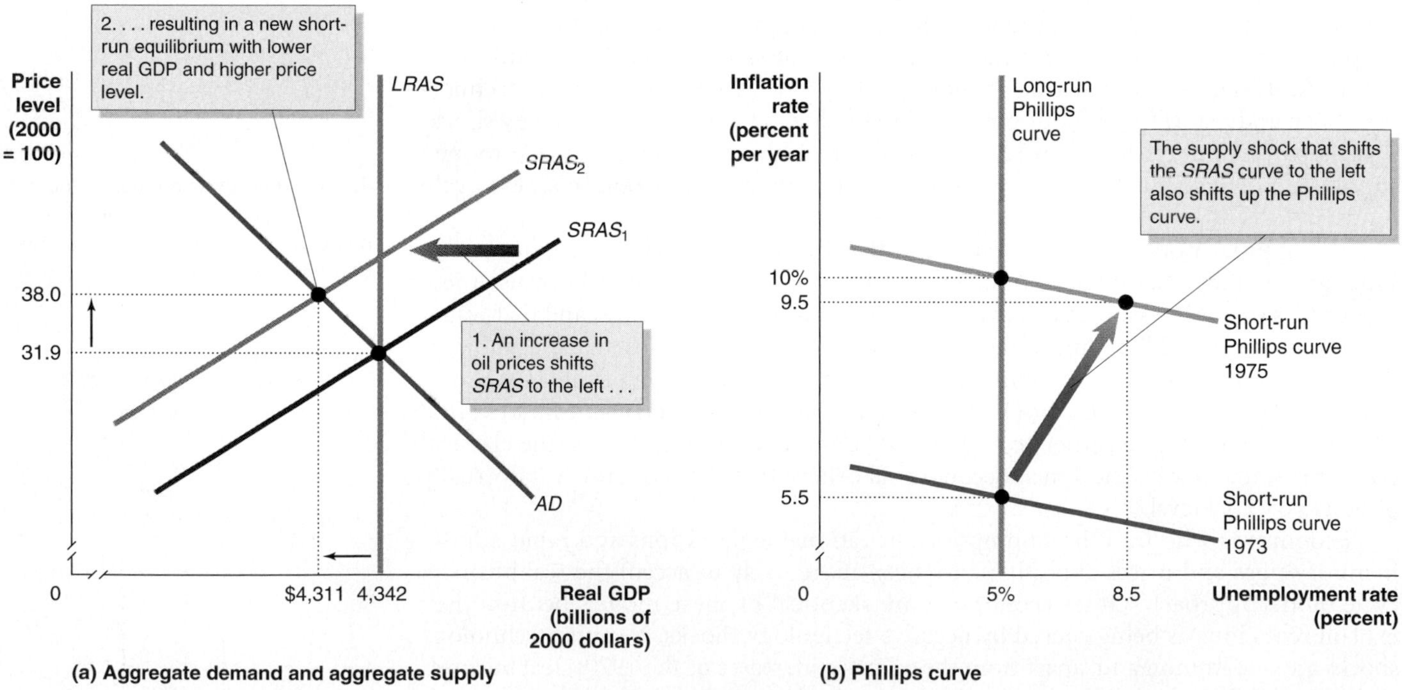

FIGURE 16-9 **A Supply Shock Shifts the *SRAS* and the Short-Run Phillips Curve**

When OPEC increased the price of a barrel of oil from less than $3 to more than $10, in panel (a) the *SRAS* curve shifted to the left. Between 1973 and 1975, real GDP declined from $4,342 billion to $4,311 billion and the price level rose from 31.9 to 38.0. Panel (b) shows that the supply shock shifted up the Phillips curve. In 1973, the U.S. economy had an inflation rate of about 5.5 percent and an unemployment rate of about 5 percent. By 1975, the inflation rate had risen to about 9.5 percent and the unemployment rate to about 8.5 percent.

a difficult position. If the Fed used an expansionary monetary policy to fight the high unemployment rate, the *AD* curve would shift to the right and the economy's equilibrium would move up the short-run Phillips curve. Real GDP would increase and the unemployment rate would fall—but at the cost of higher inflation. If the Fed used a contractionary monetary policy to fight the high inflation rate, the *AD* curve would shift to the left and the economy's equilibrium would move down the short-run Phillips curve. As a result, real GDP would fall and the inflation rate would be reduced—but at the cost of higher unemployment. In the end, the Fed chose to fight high unemployment with an expansionary monetary policy, even though this decision worsened the inflation rate.

Paul Volcker and Disinflation

By the late 1970s, the Federal Reserve had gone through a two-decade period of continually increasing the rate of growth of the money supply. In August 1979, President Jimmy Carter appointed Paul Volcker as Chairman of the Board of Governors of the Federal Reserve System. Along with most economists, Volcker was convinced that high inflation rates were inflicting significant damage on the economy and should be reduced. To reduce inflation, he decided to reduce the annual growth rate of the money supply. This contractionary monetary policy raised interest rates, causing a decline in aggregate demand. Figure 16-10 uses the Phillips curve model to analyze the movements in unemployment and inflation from 1979 to 1989.

The Fed's contractionary monetary policy shifted the economy's short-run equilibrium down the short-run Phillips curve, lowering the inflation rate from 11 percent in 1979 to 6 percent in 1982—but at a cost of raising the unemployment rate from 6 percent to 10 percent. As workers and firms lowered their expectations of future inflation, the short run Phillips curve shifted down, improving the short-run trade-off between unemployment and inflation. This adjustment in expectations allowed the Fed to switch to an expansionary monetary policy. By 1987, the economy was back to the natural rate of unemployment, which during these years was about 6 percent.

Under Volcker's leadership, the Fed had reduced the inflation rate from more than 10 percent to less than 5 percent. The inflation rate has generally remained below 5 percent ever since. A significant reduction in the inflation rate is called **disinflation.** In fact, this episode is often referred to as the "Volcker disinflation." The disinflation had come at a very high price, however. From September 1982 through June 1983, the

Disinflation A significant reduction in the inflation rate.

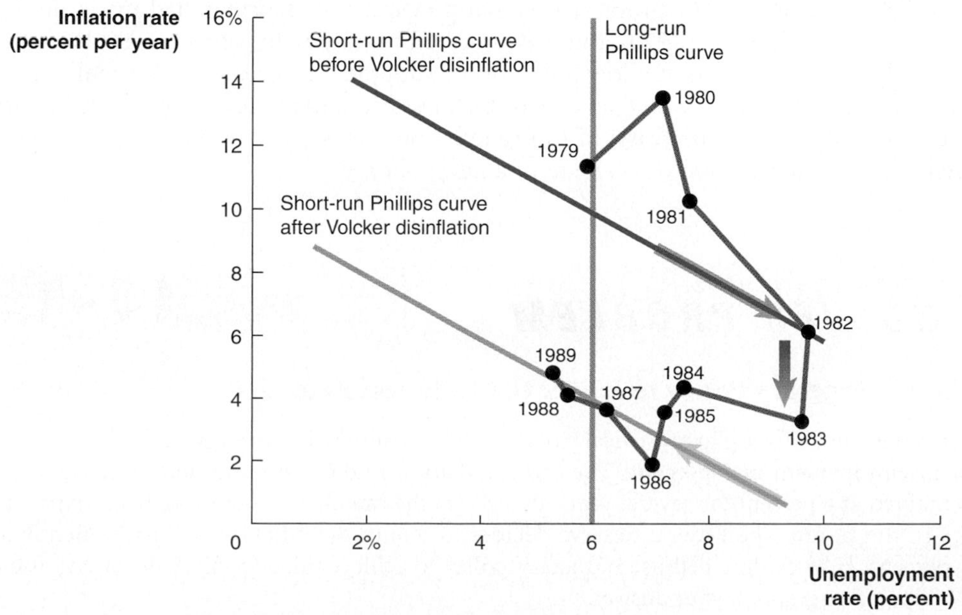

FIGURE 16-10

The Fed Tames Inflation, 1979–1989

The Fed, under Chairman Paul Volcker, began fighting inflation in 1979 by reducing the growth of the money supply, thereby raising interest rates. By 1982, the unemployment rate had risen to 10 percent and the inflation rate had fallen to 6 percent. As workers and firms lowered their expectations of future inflation, the short-run Phillips curve shifted down, improving the short-run trade-off between unemployment and inflation. This adjustment in expectations allowed the Fed to switch to an expansionary monetary policy, which by 1987 brought the economy back to the natural rate of unemployment with an inflation rate of about 4 percent. Note that during these years the natural rate of unemployment was estimated to be about 6 percent.

Don't Let This Happen To You!

Don't Confuse Disinflation with Deflation

Disinflation refers to a decline in the *inflation rate*. *Deflation* refers to a decline in the *price level*. Paul Volcker and the Federal Reserve brought about a substantial disinflation in the United States during the years between 1979 and 1983. The inflation rate fell from over 11 percent in 1979 to below 5 percent in 1984. Yet even in 1984, there was no deflation: The price level was still rising—but at a slower rate.

The last period of significant deflation in the United States was in the early 1930s during the Great Depression. The following table shows the consumer price index for those years:

YEAR	CONSUMER PRICE INDEX	DEFLATION RATE
1929	17.1	—
1930	16.7	–2.3%
1931	15.2	–9.0
1932	13.7	–9.9
1933	13.0	–5.1

Because the price level fell each year from 1929 to 1933, there was deflation.

YOUR TURN: **Test your understanding by doing related problem 13 on page 543 at the end of this chapter.**

unemployment rate was above 10 percent. This period is the only one since the end of the Great Depression of the 1930s when unemployment has been above 10 percent in the United States.

Some economists argue that the Volcker disinflation provided evidence against the view that workers and firms have rational expectations. Volcker's announcement in October 1979 that he planned to use a contractionary monetary policy to bring down the inflation rate was widely publicized. If workers and firms had had rational expectations, we might have expected them to have quickly reduced their expectations of future inflation. The economy should have moved smoothly down the long-run Phillips curve. As we have seen, however, the economy moved down the existing short-run Phillips curve, and only after several years of high unemployment did the Phillips curve shift down. Apparently, workers and firms had adaptive expectations—only changing their expectations of future inflation after the current inflation rate had fallen.

Robert Lucas and Thomas Sargent argue, however, that a less painful disinflation would have occurred if workers and firms had *believed* Volcker's announcement that he was fighting inflation. The problem was that previous Fed chairmen had made similar promises throughout the 1970s, but inflation had continued to get worse. By 1979, the credibility of the Fed was at a low point. Some support for Lucas's and Sargent's argument comes from the fact that surveys of business economists at the time showed that they also reduced their forecasts of future inflation only slowly, even though they were well aware of Volcker's announcement of a new policy.

SOLVED PROBLEM 16-3

④ **LEARNING OBJECTIVE**

Use a Phillips curve graph to show how the Federal Reserve can permanently lower the inflation rate.

Using Monetary Policy to Lower the Inflation Rate

Consider the following hypothetical situation: The economy is currently at the natural rate of unemployment of 5 percent. The actual inflation rate is 6 percent and, because it has remained at 6 percent for several years, this is also the rate that workers and firms expect to see in the future. The Federal Reserve decides to reduce the inflation rate permanently to 2 percent. How can the Fed use monetary policy to achieve this objective? Be sure to use a Phillips curve graph in your answer.

Solving the Problem:

Step 1: Review the chapter material. This problem is about using a Phillips curve graph to show how the Fed can fight inflation, so you may want to review the section "Paul Volcker and Disinflation," which begins on page 531.

Step 2: Explain how the Fed can use monetary policy to reduce the inflation rate. To reduce the inflation rate significantly, the Fed will have to raise the target for the federal funds rate. Higher interest rates will reduce aggregate demand, raise unemployment, and move the economy's equilibrium down the short-run Phillips curve.

Step 3: Illustrate your argument with a Phillips curve graph. How much the unemployment rate would have to rise to drive down the inflation rate from 6 percent to 2 percent depends on the steepness of the short-run Phillips curve. Here we have assumed the unemployment rate would have to rise from 5 percent to 7 percent.

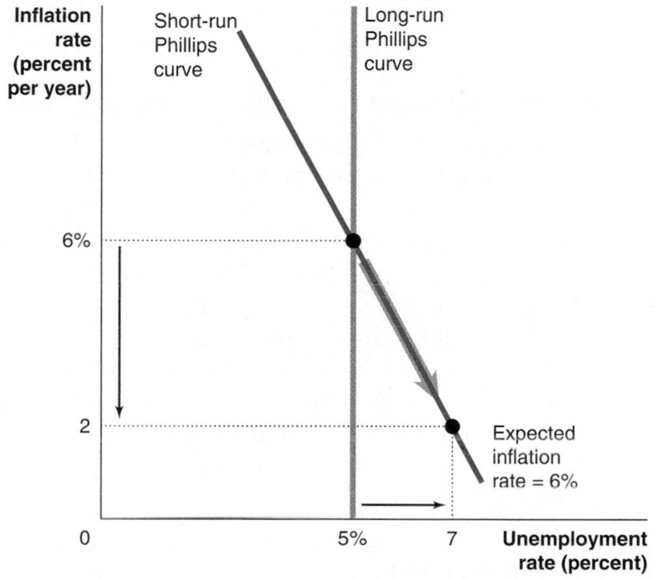

Step 4: Show on your graph the reduction in the inflation rate from 6 percent to 2 percent. For the decline in the inflation rate to be permanent, the expected inflation rate has to decline from 6 percent to 2 percent. We can show this on our graph:

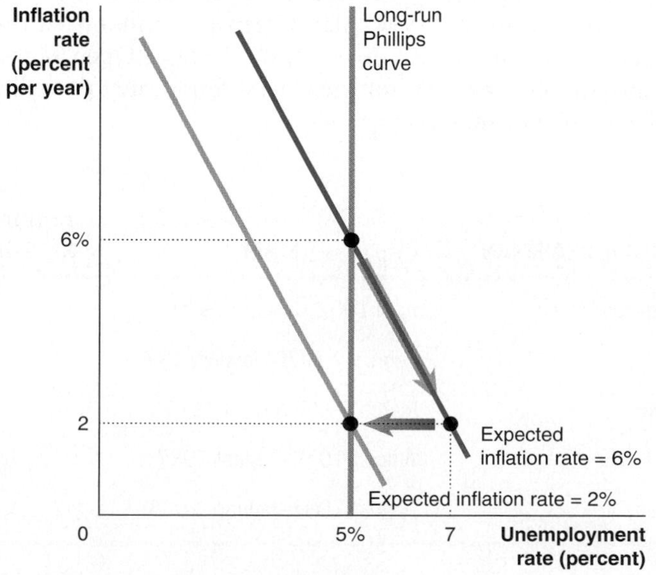

Once the short-run Phillips curve has shifted down, the Fed can push the economy back to the natural rate of unemployment with an expansionary monetary policy. This policy is similar to the one carried out by the Fed after Paul Volcker became chairman in 1979. The downside to these policies of disinflation is that they lead to significant increases in unemployment.

Extra Credit: A follower of the new classical macroeconomics approach would have a more optimistic view of the consequences of using monetary policy to lower the inflation rate from 6 percent to 2 percent. According to this approach, the Fed's policy announcement should cause people to immediately revise downward their expectations of future inflation from 6 percent to 2 percent. The economy's short-run equilibrium would move directly down the long-run Phillips curve from an inflation rate 6 percent to an inflation rate of 2 percent, while keeping the unemployment rate constant at 5 percent. For reasons discussed in this chapter, many economists are skeptical that disinflation can be brought about that painlessly.

YOUR TURN: **For more practice, do related problems 17 and 18 on page 543 at the end of this chapter.**

Alan Greenspan and the Importance of a Credible Monetary Policy

President Ronald Reagan appointed Alan Greenspan to succeed Paul Volcker as Fed chairman in 1987. Like Volcker, Greenspan was determined to keep the inflation rate low. Table 16-3 shows that the average annual inflation rate was lower during Greenspan's term than it was during the terms of his three most immediate predecessors. Under Greenspan's leadership of the Fed, inflation was reduced nearly to the low levels experienced during the term of Chairman William McChesney Martin in the 1950s and 1960s. As we discussed in Chapter 10, beginning in the mid-1990s, the U.S. economy experienced an increase in the growth of labor productivity. By increasing the capacity of the economy, productivity growth caused a more rapid increase in potential GDP. The greater capacity of the economy to produce goods and services at every price level contributed to the low rates of inflation experienced in the United States during the late 1990 and early 2000s.

De-emphasizing the Money Supply

We saw in Chapter 13 that, during the 1980s and 1990s, the close relationship between growth in the money supply and inflation broke down. Before 1987, the Fed would announce annual targets for how much M1 and M2 would increase during the year. In February 1987, near the end of Paul Volcker's term, the Fed announced that it would no longer set targets for M1. In July 1993, Alan Greenspan announced that the Fed also would no longer set targets for M2. Instead, the Federal Open Market Committee (FOMC) has relied on setting targets for the federal funds rate to meet its goals of price stability and high employment.

TABLE 16-3

The Record of Fed Chairmen and Inflation

FEDERAL RESERVE CHAIRMAN	TERM	AVERAGE ANNUAL INFLATION RATE DURING TERM
William McChesney Martin	April 1952–January 1970	2.0%
Arthur Burns	February 1970–January 1978	6.5
G. William Miller	March 1978–August 1979	9.2
Paul Volcker	August 1979–August 1987	6.2
Alan Greenspan	August 1987–January 2006	3.1

Note: Data for Greenspan are through September 2005.

The Importance of Fed Credibility

The Fed learned an important lesson during the 1970s: Workers, firms, and investors in stock and bond markets have to view Fed announcements as credible if monetary policy is to be effective. As inflation worsened throughout the late 1960s and 1970s, the Fed announced repeatedly that it would take actions to reduce inflation. In fact, inflation rose. These repeated failures to follow through on announced policies had greatly reduced the Fed's credibility by the time Paul Volcker took office in August 1979. The contractionary monetary policy that the Fed announced in October 1979 had less impact on the expectations of workers, firms, and investors than it would have had if the Fed's credibility was greater. It took a severe recession to convince people that this time the inflation rate really was coming down. Only then were workers willing to accept lower nominal wage increases, banks willing to accept lower interest rates on mortgage loans, and investors willing to accept lower interest rates on bonds.

Over the past two decades, the Fed has taken steps to enhance its credibility. Most importantly, whenever a change in Fed policy has been announced, the change has actually taken place. In addition, Greenspan revised the previous Fed policy of keeping secret the target for the federal funds rate. Since February 1994, any change in the target rate is announced at the conclusion of the FOMC meeting at which the change is made. In addition, the minutes of the FOMC meetings are now made public after a brief delay. Finally, in February 2000, the Fed helped make its intentions for future policy clearer by announcing at the end of each FOMC meeting whether it considered the economy in the future to be at greater risk of higher inflation or of recession.

During Greenspan's terms as Fed chairman, the U.S. economy experienced only two brief recessions and no periods of high inflation. The greatest challenge of his tenure resulted from the slow recovery from the recession of 2001. As we saw in Chapter 14, despite lowering the target for the federal funds rate to 1 percent, economic growth during 2002 and the early months of 2003 was disappointingly slow.

Monetary Policy Credibility after Greenspan

Even now, debate continues over policies to increase the Fed's credibility. Some economists and policymakers believe that central banks are more credible if they adopt and follow rules. A *rules strategy* for monetary policy involves the central bank's following specific and publicly announced guidelines for policy. When the central bank chooses a rule, this strategy requires that it follow the rule, whatever the state of the economy. For example, the Fed might commit to increasing the money supply 5 percent each year, regardless of whether the economy enters a recession or suffers a financial crisis. (Note that support among economists for a monetary growth rule of this type has declined over the past 25 years.) The rule adopted by the Fed should apply to variables that are significantly controllable by the Fed. For example, a rule stating that the Fed was committed to maintaining the growth rate of real GDP at 4 percent per year would not be useful because the Fed has no direct control over GDP.

Economists and policymakers who oppose the rules strategy support a *discretion strategy* for monetary policy. With a discretion strategy, the central bank should adjust monetary policy as it sees fit to achieve its policy goals, such as price stability and high employment. This approach differs from the rules strategy in that it allows the Fed to adjust its policy based on changes in the economy. In practice, the Fed has generally followed a discretion strategy.

Many economists believe a middle course between a rules strategy and a discretion strategy is desirable. In this view, the central bank should be free to make adjustments in policy as long as the adjustments are stated as part of the rules. The *Taylor rule,* which we discussed in Chapter 14, is an example of a modified rule of this type, although it has never been adopted explicitly by the Fed. According to the Taylor rule, the Fed should set the target for the federal funds rate according to an equation that includes the inflation rate, the equilibrium real federal funds rate, the "inflation gap," and the "output gap." Even a modified rule isn't foolproof. Rules are credible because they reduce central bank flexibility, thereby giving firms, workers, and investors more confidence that the central bank will actually do what it says it will do. But the same lack of flexibility that can make a rule credible can also limit the central bank's ability to respond during a financial crisis, such as a stock market crash.

Most economists believe the best way to achieve commitment to rules is to remove political pressures on the central bank. When the central bank is free of political pressures, the public is more likely to believe the central bank's announcements. In the early 2000s, many economists also suggested that the Federal Reserve should be more transparent about its objectives for inflation, a call embraced by Greenspan's successor, Ben Bernanke.

A Failure of Credibility at the Bank of Japan

Is it possible for the inflation rate to be too *low?* The answer is yes, particularly if inflation becomes deflation. We saw in Chapter 13 that the Japanese economy has been plagued by slow growth and significant periods of *deflation*—or a falling price level—since the early 1990s. Deflation can contribute to slow growth by raising real interest rates, increasing the real value of debts, and causing consumers to postpone purchases in the hope of experiencing even lower prices in the future. The Bank of Japan attempted to end deflation and spur economic growth by using expansionary monetary policy to drive down interest rates and stop deflation.

By 1999, the Bank of Japan had reduced the target interest rate on overnight bank loans—the equivalent of the U.S. federal funds rate—to zero. Because Japan was experiencing deflation, however, the *real* interest rate on these loans was greater than zero. The real interest rate on mortgages and long-term bonds also remained too high to stimulate the increase in investment spending needed to bring the Japanese economy back to potential GDP. Why was the Bank of Japan unable to end deflation and reduce real interest rates? Some economists argue the key problem was that the Bank of Japan's policies lacked credibility. Because firms, workers, and participants in financial markets doubted the Bank of Japan's willingness to continue an expansionary monetary policy long enough to end the deflation, the price level continued to fall and real interest rates remained high. In fact, this view was reinforced when the Bank of Japan raised the target interest rate on overnight bank loans in August 2000, even though deflation continued. The lack of credibility also may have stemmed in part from the unwillingness of the Bank of Japan to state an explicit target for inflation. An explicit inflation rate target of, say, 2 percent may have caused firms, workers, and investors to raise their expectations of inflation, which could have brought the deflation to an end. Some officials at the Bank of Japan also appeared reluctant to pursue too aggressive an expansionary policy for fear of reigniting the inflation in stock prices and real estate prices that Japan had experienced in the 1980s.

Although deflation was not the only reason economic growth in Japan was so weak, failing to end deflation made other problems, such as reform of the banking system, harder to manage. The Bank of Japan's failure of credibility helps to explain its weak performance compared with the performance of the Federal Reserve during the same period.

Federal Reserve Policy and Whirlpool's "Pricing Power"

We saw in the opening to this chapter that Whirlpool had much more success raising the prices of their appliances in 2005 than in 2001. Even in 2001, however, Whirlpool had managed to impose modest price increases at a time its competitors were cutting prices. This episode shows that a firm's ability to raise prices is generally determined both by the desirability of its products relative to those sold by its rivals and by macroeconomic conditions. The strength of Whirlpool's competitive position in the home appliance market was shown in 2005 by the firm's attempts to acquire rival appliance maker Maytag.

Whirlpool also benefited from the effects of expansionary monetary policy. As a seller of durable goods, Whirlpool is exposed to the potentially negative effects of the business cycle. As we discussed in Chapter 9, during a business cycle recession, consumers often reduce expenditures on new homes and on durable goods, such as household appliances. Whirlpool has a double exposure to recession because it may lose direct sales to consumers buying new or replacement appliances and also sales to builders buying appliances to be included in new home construction. In 2001 and the following years, expansionary monetary policy lessened the effects of recession by lowering interest rates. As we saw in Chapter 14, spending on new housing actually increased during 2001, as did Whirlpool's sales. Whirlpool acknowledged the importance of monetary policy to its performance in its 2004 annual report: "Consumer demand remained strong throughout 2004 as low interest rates in the United States helped maintain the momentum of new housing starts."

The dilemma for the Fed in 2005 was how quickly and how far to raise interest rates so that the rapid economic recovery brought about by low interest rates did not reignite inflation.

Conclusion

The workings of the contemporary economy are complex. The attempts by the Federal Reserve to keep the U.S. economy near the natural rate of unemployment with a low rate of inflation have not always been successful. Economists continue to debate the best way for the Fed to proceed.

An Inside Look on the next page discusses the relationship between wage increases and price increases during 2005.

An Inside Look

Wage Rates for Hourly Workers Stagnate

WALL STREET JOURNAL, JULY 19, 2005

Keeping Up Is Hard to Do

LOWER BURREL, Pa.—Mark and Donna Bellini don't need economists to tell them that wages for many workers have not kept pace with inflation.

Mr. Bellini, a 51-year-old line technician for Comcast Corp., hasn't received a pay increase in three years, since 2002. His wages have been stuck at $19.10 an hour while overall consumer prices have risen 8%. Since then, however, the cost of many necessities has soared well beyond the averages. As of June, for example, the price of gasoline had risen 55%, and bread and meat rose 10% and 18%, respectively. Milk prices jumped 14% and electricity 11%.

a Despite an economy growing at roughly 4%, healthy corporate profits and low unemployment levels, annual wages of workers in nonmanagerial positions—representing about 80% of the U.S. work force—rose 2.7% in June from a year ago, according to the Bureau of Labor Statistics. But adjusted for inflation, which cooled in June as gasoline prices declined, those wages were unchanged from a year ago. Annual wage growth hasn't outpaced inflation for 14 months.

For families like the Bellinis, the day-to-day reality behind the data is stark and far-reaching. At roughly $60,000, their annual income hovers just below the $62,400 U.S. median for married couples. And yet the family is living far less comfortably than that benchmark used to imply.

A two-room addition to their small house, begun while Mr. Bellini was still counting regular wage increases, is still unfinished. To help pay for clothes and save for a used car, the couple's 14-year-old son took a $5.15 an hour job as a dishwasher at a local restaurant. Mr. Bellini himself wears a worn pair of five-year-old sneakers. Perhaps most worrisome, the couple counts almost no savings, and they haven't, as once planned, been able to start a college fund for their two teenage sons. "The sense of security is gone," Mrs. Bellini says.

b The Bellinis, like most Americans, have managed to see some income growth. But in contrast to many employees—who received bonuses in 2004 or realized stock gains—the family has stretched itself with sweat equity. Last fall, Mr. Bellini's wife, Donna, 47, increased the hours she works as a secretary in an eye doctor's office from 24 to roughly 38 hours a week at $10 an hour, receiving vision care as well. That has boosted the family's take home pay to about $3,200 a month—money that's come in handy to offset rising property taxes. Utility, mortgage, food and life insurance bills total $2,000 a month. Other bills for gasoline, clothing, sports related expenses for the two boys, and extraordinary costs like furnace repairs, quickly consume the rest. . . .

Mr. Bellini's employer, Comcast, has fared relatively well, thanks to strong subscriber growth for its broadband Internet services. The company says its employees received wage increases averaging 2% to 4% in each of the last three years and blames Mr. Bellini's lack of a raise on unresolved union contract negotiations. "Mr. Bellini's situation is not reflective of our 59,000 cable employees," says D'Arcy Rudnay, a company spokeswoman. . . .

c At this point, companies are not hiring enough workers to tighten the labor market—a scenario that would compel increased wages. Some say rising health-care-benefit costs are consuming much of the windfall that would have gone to wage increases. Still, some economists say it's only a matter of time before wages pick up. Productivity has grown over the past three years at its fastest rate since the early 1950s, which should eventually allow companies to boost real wages beyond consumer prices.

In spite of the couple's thrift, bills mount, spurring arguments. When the delicate subject of credit-card balances creeps into a conversation, Mrs. Bellini instructs her husband, "Close your ears," and admits the balance has grown to $6,000. . . .

The couple worries about the future. They invest only 1% of Mr. Bellini's salary into his 401(k) retirement plan, down from 6% when he was getting regular wage increases, and withdrew $5,000 to pay for bills. The plan, worth $38,000 in 2000, is now worth $24,000 because of the deductions and lower stock prices. A separate IRA account is worth about $33,000, having declined from $46,000 after Sept. 11, 2001. "That's nothing," says Mr. Bellini. "What's $60,000 going to get you in retirement?"

Key Points in the Article

Despite strong U.S. economic growth, low unemployment, and high corporate profits, real wages for much of the U.S. workforce have either stagnated or fallen in the last few years. Unless nominal wages rise faster than inflation, the main way for households to increase their real incomes is to supply more labor, and hence enjoy less leisure. This tendency for nominal wages to adjust sluggishly, or not at all, to inflation is precisely why short-run Phillips curves exist. Most economists agree that workers in 2005 had difficulty in negotiating for higher wages because the labor market had not tightened sufficiently. Meanwhile, health-care benefit costs absorbed corporate profits that otherwise might have been paid to workers in the form of higher wages.

Analyzing the News

a In the summer of 2005, U.S. real GDP grew at an annual rate of roughly 4 percent. The nation's unemployment rate was 5 percent, and corporate profits were high. Nonetheless, this positive economic news masked a significant concern for 80 percent of the U.S. workforce: While nominal wages had grown by 2.7 percent from a year earlier, so too did the average price level; hence, real wages remained unchanged. Indeed, for workers like Mark Bellini, who hadn't received a wage increase since 2002, real wages had actually fallen in the last three years. This nominal wage rigidity—the tendency for nominal wages to adjust sluggishly to inflation—is why short-run Phillips curves, such as the ones depicted in Figure 1, exist. A rise in inflation causes the real wage and hence unemployment to fall, if only in the short run. This pattern is shown in Figure 1, where the inflation rate rises from 2 percent to 3 percent, and the unemployment rate falls from its (hypothetical) natural rate of 5 percent to 4 percent. In the long run, wages adjust to the inflation rate, the Phillips curve shifts up, and the unemployment rate returns to its natural rate.

b Like most Americans, the Bellinis' household expenditures depend almost entirely on their wage income because the family earns almost no capital gains or bonus-related incomes. Unless nominal wages rise faster than inflation, the only way these households can increase their real incomes is to supply more labor. For example, Donna Bellini increased her labor supply by 58 percent, from 24 hours per week to 38 hours per week. Of course, this increase in the Bellinis' household real income cost Donna 14 hours per week of leisure time.

c The short-run Phillips curve trade-off between inflation and unemployment exists because nominal wages adjust sluggishly to inflation. This nominal wage rigidity occurs either because workers do not have rational expectations—expectations formed by using all available information about an economic variable—or workers cannot negotiate for a higher wage. In the context of the current U.S. economy, most economists support the latter explanation for two reasons. First, although the unemployment rate is low, in most labor markets firms have not had to offer higher wages to attract or keep labor; that is, most labor markets have not tightened sufficiently. Second, recently strong corporate profits have gone to labor indirectly, in the form of health-care benefits instead of wages.

Thinking Critically ABOUT POLICY

1. Suppose the U.S. labor force has adaptive expectations of inflation, so that workers' expectations of the next period's inflation rate are based on last period's inflation rate. In this case, what effect does a disinflationary monetary policy have on the real wage, unemployment, and real GDP?
2. Suppose that lenders have adaptive expectations of inflation. In this case, what effect does a monetary policy that results in a significant rise in the inflation rate have on the actual real cost of borrowing, investment expenditures, unemployment, and real GDP?

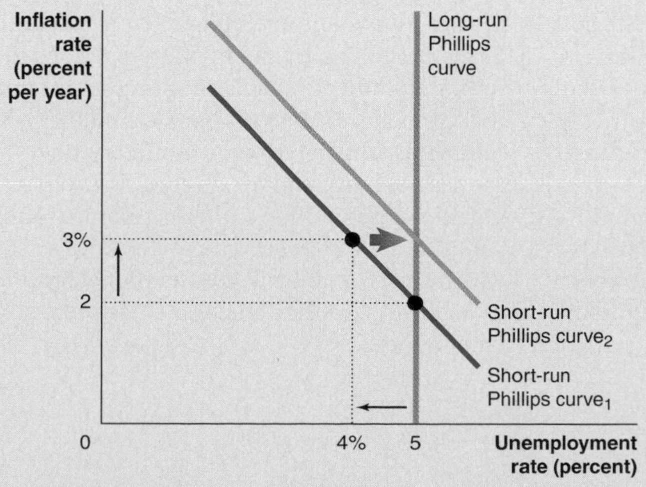

Figure 1: A rise in the inflation rate causes a fall in the unemployment rate in the short run. In the long run, nominal wages adjust to the rate of inflation and unemployment returns to its natural level.

SUMMARY

LEARNING OBJECTIVE ① Describe the Phillips curve and the nature of the short-run trade-off between inflation and unemployment. The *Phillips curve* illustrates the short-run trade-off between the unemployment rate and the inflation rate. The inverse relationship between unemployment and inflation shown by the Phillips curve is consistent with the aggregate demand and aggregate supply analysis developed in Chapter 11. The *AD-AS* model indicates that slow growth in aggregate demand leads to both higher unemployment and lower inflation, and rapid growth in aggregate demand leads to both lower unemployment and higher inflation. This relationship explains why there is a short-run trade-off between unemployment and inflation. Many economists initially believed that the Phillips curve was a *structural relationship* that depended on the basic behavior of consumers and firms and that remained unchanged over time. If the Phillips curve were a stable relationship, it would present policymakers with a menu of combinations of unemployment and inflation from which they could choose.

LEARNING OBJECTIVE ② Explain the relationship between the short-run and long-run Phillips curves. Nobel laureate Milton Friedman has argued that there is a *natural rate of unemployment* to which the economy always returns. As a result, there is no trade-off between unemployment and inflation in the long run, and the long-run Phillips curve is a vertical line at the natural rate of unemployment. There is a short-run trade-off between unemployment and inflation only if the actual inflation rate differs from the inflation rate that had been expected by workers and firms. There is a different short-run Phillips curve for every expected inflation rate. Each short-run Phillips curve intersects the long-run Phillips curve at the expected inflation rate. With a vertical long-run Phillips curve, it is not possible to buy a permanently lower unemployment rate at the cost of a permanently higher inflation rate. If the Federal Reserve attempts to keep the economy below the natural rate of unemployment, the inflation rate will increase. Eventually, the expected inflation rate will also increase, which causes the short-run Phillips curve to shift up and pushes the economy back to the natural rate of unemployment. The reverse happens if the Fed attempts to keep the economy above the natural rate of unemployment. In the long run, the Federal Reserve can affect the inflation rate but not the unemployment rate.

LEARNING OBJECTIVE ③ Discuss how expectations of the inflation rate affect monetary policy. When the inflation rate is moderate and stable, workers and firms tend to have *adaptive expectations.* That is, they form their expectations under the assumption that future inflation rates will follow the pattern of inflation rates in the recent past. During the high and unstable inflation rates of the mid- to late 1970s, Robert Lucas and Thomas Sargent argued that workers and firms would have *rational expectations.* Rational expectations are formed by using of all available information about an economic variable, including the effect of the policy being used by the Federal Reserve. Lucas and Sargent argued that if people have rational expectations, expansionary monetary policy will not work. If workers and firms know that an expansionary monetary policy is going to raise the inflation rate, the actual inflation rate will be the same as the expected inflation rate. Therefore, the unemployment rate won't fall. Many economists remain skeptical of Lucas and Sargent's argument in its strictest form. Real business cycle models focus on "real" factors—technology shocks—rather than changes in the money supply to explain fluctuations in real GDP.

LEARNING OBJECTIVE ④ Use a Phillips curve graph to show how the Federal Reserve can permanently lower the inflation rate. Inflation worsened through the 1970s. Paul Volcker became Fed chairman in 1979 and, under his leadership, the Fed used contractionary monetary policy to reduce inflation. This contractionary monetary policy pushed the economy down the short-run Phillips curve. As workers and firms lowered their expectations of future inflation, the short-run Phillips curve shifted down, improving the short-run trade-off between unemployment and inflation. This change in expectations allowed the Fed to switch to an expansionary monetary policy to bring the economy back to the natural rate of unemployment. During Alan Greenspan's terms as Fed chairman, inflation remained low and the credibility of the Fed increased. Some economists and policymakers believe a central bank's credibility is increased if it follows a *rules strategy* for monetary policy, which involves the central bank's following specific and publicly announced guidelines for policy. Other economists and policymakers support a *discretion strategy* for monetary policy, under which the central bank adjusts monetary policy as it sees fit to achieve its policy goals, such as price stability and high employment.

KEY TERMS

Disinflation 531
Natural rate of unemployment 520
Phillips curve 516
Rational expectations 527
Real business cycle models 529
Structural relationship 518

REVIEW QUESTIONS

1. What is the Phillips curve? Draw a graph of a short-run Phillips curve.
2. What actions should the Fed take if it wants to move from a point on the short-run Phillips curve representing high unemployment and low inflation to a point representing lower unemployment and higher inflation?
3. Why did economists during the early 1960s think of the Phillips curve as a "policy menu"? Were they correct to think of it in this way? Briefly explain.
4. Why did Milton Friedman argue that the Phillips curve did not represent a permanent trade-off between unemployment and inflation? In your answer, be sure to explain what Friedman meant by the "natural rate of unemployment."
5. What is the relationship between the short-run Phillips curve and the long-run Phillips curve? Why is it inconsistent to believe that the long-run aggregate supply curve is vertical and the long-run Phillips curve is downward sloping?
6. Why do workers, firms, banks, and investors in financial markets care about the future rate of inflation? How do they form their expectations of future inflation? Do current conditions in the economy have any bearing on how they form their expectations?
7. What does it mean to say that workers and firms have rational expectations?
8. Why did Robert Lucas and Thomas Sargent argue that the Phillips curve might be vertical in the short run? What difference would it make for monetary policy if they were right?
9. What was the "Volcker disinflation"? What happened to the unemployment rate during the period of the Volcker disinflation?
10. Why did Alan Greenspan believe that the credibility of the Fed's policy announcements was particularly important?

PROBLEMS AND APPLICATIONS

Please visit **www.prenhall.com/hubbard** *for solutions to the even-numbered problems as well as multiple-choice and true or false self-assessment quizzes.*

1. In the fall of 2003, the economy had not yet returned to the natural rate of unemployment following the end of the recession of 2001. An article in the *Wall Street Journal* noted the following:

   > Perhaps the best cure for [unemployed workers'] woes would be a return to the unusually strong economy of the late 1990s, when unemployment fell so low that employers couldn't be picky. President Bush and Federal Reserve Chairman Alan Greenspan are working on that, [using] tax cuts and interest-rate cuts.

   a. Which of these two actions is fiscal policy and which is monetary policy?
   b. Briefly explain how tax cuts and interest-rate cuts reduce unemployment.

   Source: David Wessel, "Clues to the Cure for Unemployment Begin to Emerge," *Wall Street Journal*, October 13, 2003.

2. Use the graphs to answer the following questions. Assume that the natural rate of unemployment is 5 percent and that the inflation rate in the first year is 2 percent.

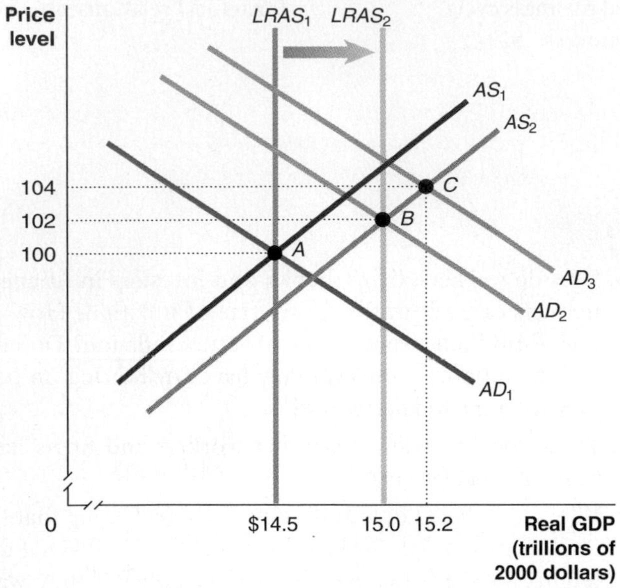

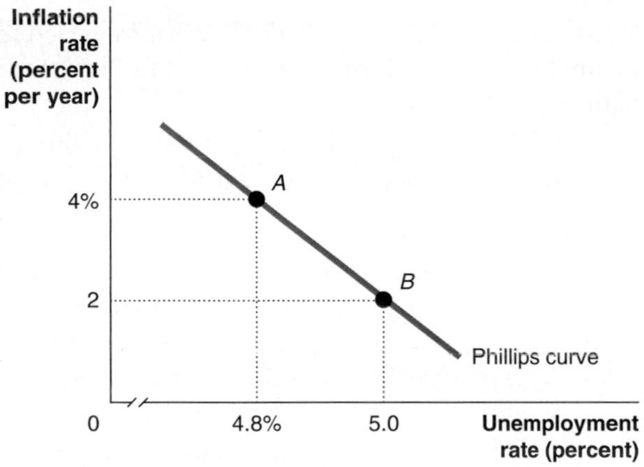

a. Briefly explain which point on the Phillips curve graph represents the same economic situation as point *A* on the aggregate demand and aggregate supply graph.

b. Briefly explain which point on the Phillips curve graph represents the same economic situation as point *B* on the aggregate demand and aggregate supply graph.

c. Briefly explain which point on the Phillips curve graph represents the same economic situation as point *C* on the aggregate demand and aggregate supply graph.

3. Given that the Phillips curve is derived from the aggregate demand and aggregate supply model, why use the Phillips curve analysis? What benefits does the Phillips curve analysis offer compared to the *AD-AS* model?

4. In macroeconomics courses in the 1960s and early 1970s, some professors taught that one of the U.S. political parties was willing to have higher unemployment in order to achieve lower inflation, and that the other major political party was willing to have higher inflation in order to achieve lower unemployment. Why might such views of the trade-off between inflation and unemployment have existed in the 1960s? Why are such views rare today?

5. **[Related to *Solved Problem 16-1*]** In 1968, Herbert Stein, who later served on President Nixon's Council of Economic Advisers, wrote, "Some who would opt for avoiding inflation would say that in the long run such a policy would cost little, if any, additional unemployment." Was Stein correct? Did most economists in 1968 agree with him? Briefly explain.
Source: Herbert Stein, *The Fiscal Revolution in America,* Chicago: University of Chicago Press, 1969, p. 382.

6. Use the following information to draw a graph showing the short-run and long-run Phillips curves:
Natural rate of unemployment = 5 percent
Current rate of unemployment = 4 percent
Expected inflation rate = 4 percent
Current inflation rate = 6 percent
Be sure your graph shows the point where the short-run and long-run Phillips curves intersect.

7. General Juan Perón, the former dictator of Argentina, once said of the labor market in his country, "Prices have gone up the elevator, and wages have had to use the stairs." In this situation, what was happening to real wages in Argentina? Was unemployment likely to have been relatively high or relatively low?
Source: Perón quote from Robert J. Shiller, "Why Do People Dislike Inflation?" in *Reducing Inflation: Motivation and Strategy,* Christina D. Romer and David H. Romer, eds., Chicago: University of Chicago Press, 1997.

8. In testifying before Congress, Alan Greenspan remarked, "The challenge of monetary policy is to interpret data on the economy and financial markets with an eye to anticipating future inflationary forces and to countering them by taking action in advance." Why should the Fed take action in anticipation of inflation's becoming worse? Why not just wait until the increase in the inflation rate has occurred?
Source: Quoted in Nicoletta Batini and Andrew G. Haldane, "Forward-Looking Rules for Monetary Policy," in John B. Taylor, ed., *Monetary Policy Rules,* Chicago: University of Chicago Press, 1999, p. 157.

9. This chapter argues that if the price level increases, over time the average wage should increase by the same amount. Why is this true?

10. Robert Shiller asked a sample of the general public and a sample of economists the following question: "Do you agree that preventing high inflation is an important

national priority, as important as preventing drug abuse or preventing deterioration in the quality of our schools?" Fifty-two percent of the general public, but only 18 percent of economists, fully agreed. Why does the general public believe inflation is a bigger problem than economists do?

11. When Shiller asked a sample of the general public what they thought caused inflation, the most frequent answer he received was "greed." Do you agree that greed causes inflation? Briefly explain.

12. According to an article in *Business Week*, many workers who retired in the year 2000 expected to live off the interest they would receive from bank certificates of deposit or money market mutual funds. "Then came disinflation—and a steep fall in interest rates." What is disinflation and why should it lead to a fall in interest rates?
Source: Peter Coy, "The Surprise Threat to Nest Eggs," *Business Week*, July 28, 2003.

13. **[Related to *Don't Let This Happen To You!*]** Look again at the chart on prices during the early 1930s in the Don't Let This Happen To You! box on page 532. Was there disinflation during 1933? Briefly explain.

14. Briefly explain whether you agree or disagree with the following statement: "Any economic relationship that changes as economic policy changes is not a structural relationship."

15. **[Related to *Solved Problem 16-2*]** In a speech in September 1975, then Fed chairman Arthur Burns said the following:

> [T]here is no longer a meaningful trade-off between unemployment and inflation. In the current environment, a rapidly rising level of consumer prices will not lead to the creation of new jobs. . . . [H]ighly expansionary monetary and fiscal policies might, for a short time, provide some additional thrust to economic activity. But inflation would inevitably accelerate—a development that would create even more difficult economic problems than we have encountered over the past year.

How do Burns's views in this speech compare with the views at the Fed in the late 1960s? Why do you think he specifically says "in the current environment" there is no trade-off between unemployment and inflation?
Source: Arthur F. Burns, "The Real Issues of Inflation and Unemployment," September 1975 in Federal Reserve Bank of New York, *Federal Reserve Readings on Inflation*, February 1979.

16. Suppose the current inflation rate and the expected inflation rate are both 4 percent. The current unemployment rate and the natural rate of unemployment are both 5 percent. Use a Phillips curve graph to show the effect on the economy of a severe supply shock. If the Federal Reserve keeps monetary policy unchanged, what will happen eventually to the unemployment rate? Show this on your Phillips curve graph.

17. **[Related to *Solved Problem 16-3*]** Suppose the inflation rate has been 15 percent for the last four years. The unemployment rate is currently at the natural rate of unemployment of 5 percent. The Federal Reserve decides that it wants to permanently reduce the inflation rate to 5 percent. How can the Fed use monetary policy to achieve this objective? Be sure to use a Phillips curve graph in your answer.

18. **[Related to *Solved Problem 16-3*]** In 1995, some economists argued that the natural rate of unemployment was 6 percent. Then Fed chairman Alan Greenspan was convinced that the natural rate was actually about 5 percent. If Greenspan had accepted the view that the natural rate was 6 percent, how might monetary policy have been different during the late 1990s?

19. **[Related to the *Chapter Opener*]** Why would Whirlpool Corporation pay more attention than most other firms to the Federal Reserve raising or lowering interest rates? In other words, why do interest rates particularly affect Whirlpool?

20. Would a rules strategy for monetary policy be more important to increasing the credibility of the Federal Reserve during the 1970s or today? Briefly explain.

chapter seventeen

Macroeconomics in an Open Economy

Chinese Towels Invade Japan

➤ Motoki Hirabayashi owns Orim Company, a firm that makes towels in the Japanese city of Imabari. Orim primarily produces high-quality towels used by hotels and other firms, rather than bath towels for household use. For years, Mr. Hirabayashi considered other Japanese textile firms to be his most important competition. Recently, though, his strongest competitors have been Chinese firms. Chinese firms have the advantage of paying their workers the equivalent of $65 per month, while Japanese firms pay their workers at least 25 times as much. Japanese firms had been able to overcome this large difference in wages by using computer-controlled machinery, while Chinese firms used older textile machinery that did not consistently produce high-quality output. By the early 2000s, however, Chinese firms had begun to use the same computer-controlled machinery used by Orim. According to Mr. Hirabayashi, "The quality of the Chinese towels is getting better and better all the time, and when it comes to price, we don't stand a chance. We just can't compete." Like many other towel manufacturers in Imabari, Mr. Hirabayashi is upset that competition from towel manufacturers in China has caused his sales to decline: He argues that the Japanese government should restrict imports of Chinese towels to give the Japanese industry a chance to recover.

Producing textile products, such as towels, and exporting them around the world was the basis of Japan's industrialization in the early twentieth century. Even Toyota began as a producer of textile-making machinery, before branching into automobile production. In recent years, maintaining a high level of net exports has been particularly important for the Japanese economy because, as we discussed in Chapters 13 and 14, the Japanese economy has experienced low levels of investment spending.

Both China and Japan have discovered that maintaining high levels of net exports can cause political problems with their trading partners. Some trading partners, including the

United States, have claimed that the Japanese government has taken unfair steps to promote exports and discourage imports. The Chinese government has found that high levels of textile exports have led to political problems not only with Japan but also with the United States and the European Union. As we will see in this chapter, any country that has a high level of net exports must also have a high level of *net foreign investment*. When the foreign investment takes the form of buying foreign stocks and bonds, relatively little political friction usually results. But when the foreign investment takes the form of purchasing foreign firms, it can result in political difficulties. For example, in 2005, Chinese firms attempted to buy the U.S. oil company Unocal Corporation and the U.S. appliance maker Maytag. Ultimately neither purchase was successful, and Cnooc, the Chinese oil company that failed to buy Unocal, blamed the political environment in the United States and "the unprecedented political opposition." *An Inside Look* on pages 564 discusses potential problems caused by imbalances in the international financial system.

Sources: Eric Weiner's story on NPR's *Morning Edition*, March 28, 2002; Eric Weiner, "Flight Risk," *The New Republic*, July 22, 2002; and Matt Pottinger, Russell Gold, Michael M. Phillips, and Kate Linebaugh, "Cnooc Drops Offer for Unocal, Exposing U.S.–Chinese Tensions," *Wall Street Journal*, August 3, 2005, p. 1.

LEARNING OBJECTIVES

After studying this chapter, you should be able to:

① Explain how the balance of payments is calculated.

② Explain how exchange rates are determined and how changes in exchange rates affect the prices of imports and exports.

③ Explain the saving and investment equation.

④ Explain the effect of a government budget deficit on investment in an open economy.

⑤ Discuss the difference between the effectiveness of monetary and fiscal policy in an open economy and in a closed economy.

➤ In Chapter 6, we looked at the basics of international trade. In this chapter, we look more closely at the linkages among countries at the macroeconomic level. Countries are linked by trade in goods and services and by flows of financial investment. We will see how policymakers in all countries take these linkages into account when conducting monetary and fiscal policy.

① LEARNING OBJECTIVE
Explain how the balance of payments is calculated.

The Balance of Payments: Linking the United States to the International Economy

Today, consumers, firms, and investors routinely interact with consumers, firms, and investors in other economies. A consumer in France may use a computer produced in the United States, listen to music on a CD player made in Japan, and wear a sweater made in Italy. A firm in the United States may sell its products in dozens of countries around the world. An investor in London may sell a U.S. Treasury bill to an investor in Mexico City. Nearly all economies are **open economies** and have extensive interactions in trade or finance with other countries. Open economies interact by trading goods and services and by making investments in each other's economies. A **closed economy** has no interactions in trade or finance with other countries. No economy today is completely closed. A few countries, such as North Korea, have very limited economic interactions with other countries.

Open economy An economy that has interactions in trade or finance with other economies.

Closed economy An economy that has no interactions in trade or finance with other economies.

Balance of payments The record of a country's trade with other countries in goods, services, and assets.

The best way to understand the interactions between one economy and other economies is through the *balance of payments.* The **balance of payments** is a record of a country's trade with other countries in goods, services, and assets. Just as the U.S. Department of Commerce is responsible for collecting data on the GDP, it is also responsible for collecting data on the balance of payments. Table 17-1 shows the balance of payments for the United States in 2004. Notice that it contains three "accounts": the *current account,* the *financial account,* and the *capital account.*

The Current Account

Current account The part of the balance of payments that records a country's net exports, net investment income, and net transfers.

The **current account** records *current,* or short-term, flows of funds into and out of a country. The current account for the United States includes imports and exports of goods and services *(net exports),* income received by U.S. residents from investments in other countries, income paid on investments in the United States owned by residents of other countries *(net investment income),* and the difference between transfers made to residents of other countries and transfers received by U.S. residents from other countries *(net transfers).* If you make a donation to a charity caring for orphans in Afghanistan, it would be included in net transfers. Any payments received by U.S. residents are positive numbers in the current account, and any payments made by U.S. residents are negative numbers in the current account.

Balance of trade The difference between the value of the goods a country exports and the value of the goods a country imports.

THE BALANCE OF TRADE Part of the current account is the **balance of trade,** which is the difference between the value of the goods a country exports and the value of the goods a country imports. The balance of trade is the largest item in the current account and is therefore a topic that the media and politicians often discuss. If a country exports more than it imports, it has a *trade surplus.* If it exports less than it imports, it has a *trade deficit.* In 2004, the United States had a trade deficit of $665 billion. In the same year, Japan had a trade surplus of about $111 billion, and China had a trade surplus of about $32 billion. Figure 17-1 on page 548 shows imports and exports of goods between the United States and its trading partners and between Japan and its trading partners. The data show that the United States ran a trade deficit in 2004 with all of its major trading partners and with every region of the world. Japan ran trade deficits with China and the Near East and trade surpluses with other regions. (Note that exports from the United States to Japan in panel (a) of Figure 17-1 should equal imports by Japan from the

TABLE 17-1

The Balance of Payments of the United States, 2004 (billions of dollars)

CURRENT ACCOUNT		
Exports of Goods	$808	
Imports of Goods	−1,473	
Balance of Trade		−666
Exports of Services	344	
Imports of Services	−296	
Balance of Services		48
Income Received on Investments	380	
Income Payments on Investments	−349	
Net Income on Investments		31
Net Transfers		−81
Balance on Current Account		−668
FINANCIAL ACCOUNT		
Increase in foreign holdings of assets in the United States	1,440	
Increase in U.S. holdings of assets in foreign countries	−856	
Balance on Financial Account		584
BALANCE ON CAPITAL ACCOUNT		**−1**
Statistical Discrepancy		85
Balance of Payments		0

Source: U.S. Department of Commerce, *Survey of Current Business*, August 2005.

United States in panel (b). The fact that the two numbers are different is an indication that international trade statistics are not measured exactly.)

NET EXPORTS EQUALS THE SUM OF THE BALANCE OF TRADE AND THE BALANCE OF SERVICES In previous chapters, we saw that *net exports* is a component of aggregate expenditures. Net exports is not explicitly shown in Table 17-1, but we can calculate it by adding together the balance of trade and the balance of services. The *balance of services* is the difference between the value of the services a country exports and the value of the services a country imports. Notice that, technically, net exports is *not* equal to the current account balance because the current account balance also includes net investment income and net transfers. But these other two items are relatively small, so it is often a convenient simplification to think of net exports as equal to the current account balance, as we will see later in this chapter.

The Financial Account

The **financial account** records purchases of assets a country has made abroad and foreign purchases of assets in the country. The financial account records long-term flows of funds into and out of a country. There is a *capital outflow* from the United States when an investor in the United States buys a bond issued by a foreign company or government or when a U.S. firm builds a factory in another country. There is a *capital inflow* into the United States when a foreign investor buys a bond issued by a U.S. firm

Financial account The part of the balance of payments that records purchases of assets a country has made abroad and foreign purchases of assets in the country.

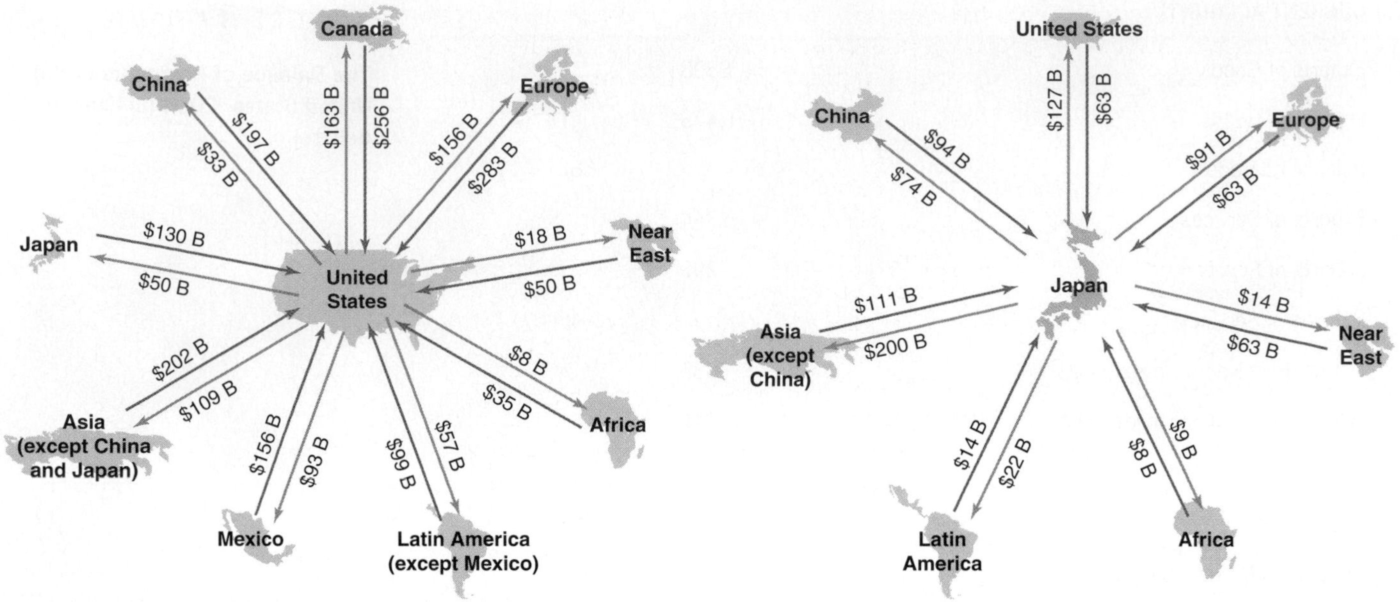

(a) Trade flows for the United States (in billions of dollars) (b) Trade flows for Japan (in billions of dollars)

FIGURE 17-1 **Trade Flows for the United States and Japan, 2004**

Panel (a) shows that in 2004, the United States ran a trade deficit with all of its major trading partners and with every region of the world. Panel (b) shows that Japan ran trade deficits with China and the Near East and trade surpluses with other regions.

Sources: U.S. data are from U.S. International Trade Commission; Japanese data are from Japanese Ministry of Finance. (Japanese data are converted from yen to dollars at the average 2004 exchange rate of 108.15 yen per dollar.)

or by the government or when a foreign firm builds a factory in the United States. Notice that we are using the word "capital" here to apply not just to physical assets, such as factories, but also to financial assets, such as shares of stock. When firms build or buy facilities in foreign countries, they are engaging in *foreign direct investment.* When investors buy stock or bonds issued in another country, they are engaging in *foreign portfolio investment.*

Net foreign investment The difference between capital outflows from a country and capital inflows, also equal to net foreign direct investment plus net foreign portfolio investment.

Another way of thinking of the balance on the financial account is as a measure of *net capital flows,* or the difference between capital inflows and capital outflows. (Here we are omitting a few transactions included in the capital account, as discussed in the next section.) A closely related concept to net capital flows is **net foreign investment,** which is equal to capital outflows minus capital inflows. Net capital flows and net foreign investment are always equal but have opposite signs: When net capital flows are positive, net foreign investment is negative, and when net capital flows are negative, net foreign investment is positive. Net foreign investment is also equal to net foreign direct investment plus net foreign portfolio investment. Later in this chapter, we will use the relationship between the balance on the financial account and net foreign investment to understand an important aspect of the international economic system.

The Capital Account

Capital account The part of the balance of payments that records relatively minor transactions, such as migrants' transfers, and sales and purchases of nonproduced, nonfinancial assets.

A third, less important, part of the balance of payments is called the *capital account.* The **capital account** records relatively minor transactions, such as migrants' transfers—which consist of goods and financial assets people take with them when they leave or enter a country—and sales and purchases of nonproduced, nonfinancial assets. A nonproduced, nonfinancial asset is a copyright, patent, trademark, or right to natural resources. The definitions of the financial account and the capital account are often misunderstood because the capital account prior to 1999 recorded all the transactions included now in both the financial account and the capital account. In other words, capital account transactions went from being a very important part of the balance of payments to being a relatively unimportant part. Because the balance on what is now called the capital account is so small, for simplicity we will ignore it in the remainder of this chapter.

Why Is the Balance of Payments Always Zero?

The sum of the current account balance, the financial account balance, and the capital account balance equals the balance of payments. Table 17-1 shows that the balance of payments for the United States in 2004 was zero. It's not just by chance that this balance was zero; *the balance of payments is always zero.* Notice that the current account balance in 2004 was –$668 billion. This value is not quite equal (with opposite sign) to the balance on the financial account, which was $584 billion. To make the balance on the current account equal the balance on the financial account, the balance of payments includes an entry called the *statistical discrepancy.* (Remember that we are ignoring the balance on the capital account. If we included the balance on the capital account, we would say the statistical discrepancy takes on a value equal to the difference between the current account balance and the sum of the balance on the financial account and the balance on the capital account.)

Why does the U.S. Department of Commerce include the statistical discrepancy entry to force the balance of payments to equal zero? It includes the statistical discrepancy because it knows that the sum of the current account balance and the financial account balance must equal zero. If it does not equal zero, a measurement error must have occurred. Some imports or exports of goods and services or some capital inflows or capital outflows must not have been measured accurately.

To understand why the balance of payments must equal zero every year, consider the following: In 2004, the United States spent $668 billion more on goods, services, and other items in the current account than it received. What happened to that $668 billion? We know that every dollar of that $668 billion was used by foreign individuals or firms to invest in the United States or was added to foreign holdings of dollars. We know this because logically there is nowhere else for the dollars to go: If the dollars weren't spent on U.S. goods and services—and we know they weren't because in that case they would have shown up in the current account—they must have been spent on investments in the United States or not spent at all. In the latter case, they would have been added to foreign holdings of dollars. Changes in foreign holdings of dollars are known as *official reserve transactions.* Foreign investment in the United States or additions to foreign holdings of dollars both show up as positive entries in the U.S. financial account. Therefore, a current account deficit must be exactly offset by a financial account surplus, leaving the balance of payments equal to zero. Similarly, a country that runs a current account surplus, such as China or Japan, must run a financial account deficit of exactly the same size. If a country's current account surplus is not exactly equal to its financial account deficit, or if a country's current account deficit is not exactly equal to its financial account surplus, some transactions must not have been accounted for. The statistical discrepancy is included in the balance of payments to compensate for these uncounted transactions.

SOLVED PROBLEM 17-1

Understanding the Arithmetic of Open Economies

① LEARNING OBJECTIVE

Explain how the balance of payments is calculated.

Test your understanding of the relationship between the current account and the financial account by evaluating the following assertion by a political commentator: "The industrial countries are committing economic suicide. Every year, they invest more and more in developing countries. Every year, more U.S., Japanese, and European manufacturing firms move their factories to developing countries. With extensive new factories and low wages, developing countries now export far more to the industrial countries than they import."

Solving the Problem:

Step 1: Review the chapter material. This problem is about the relationship between the current account and the capital account, so you may want to review the section "Why Is the Balance of Payments Always Zero?" which begins on page 549.

Step 2: Explain the errors in the commentator's argument. The argument sounds plausible. It would not be difficult to find almost identical statements to this one in books and articles published during the past few years by well-known political commentators. But the argument contains an important error. The commentator has failed to understand the relationship between the current account and the financial account. The commentator asserts that developing countries are receiving large capital inflows from industrial countries. In other words, developing countries are running financial account surpluses. The commentator also asserts that developing countries are exporting more than they are importing. In other words, they are running current account surpluses. As we have seen in this section, it is impossible to run a current surplus *and* a financial account surplus simultaneously. A country that runs a current account surplus *must* run a financial account deficit, and vice versa.

Extra Credit: Most emerging economies that have received large inflows of foreign investment during the past decade, such as South Korea, Thailand, and Malaysia, have run current account deficits—they import more goods and services than they export. Emerging economies, such as Singapore, that run current account surpluses also run financial account deficits—they invest more abroad than other countries invest in them.

The point here is not obvious—otherwise so many intelligent politicians, journalists, and political commentators wouldn't be confused about it—but unless you understand the relationship between the current account and the financial account you won't be able to understand a key aspect of the international economy.

***YOUR TURN:* For more practice, do related problems 4, 5, and 6 on page 568 at the end of this chapter.**

Don't Let This Happen To You!

Don't Confuse the Balance of Trade, the Current Account Balance, and the Balance of Payments

The terminology of international economics can be tricky. Remember that the *balance of trade* includes only trade in goods; it does not include services. This observation is important because the United States, for example, usually imports more *goods* than it exports, but it usually exports more *services* than it imports. As a result, the U.S. trade deficit is almost always larger than the current account deficit. The *current account balance* includes the balance of trade, the balance of services, net investment income, and net transfers. Net investment income and net transfers are much smaller than the balance of trade and the balance of services.

Even though the *balance of payments* is equal to the sum of the current account balance and the financial account balance—and must equal zero—you may sometimes see references to a balance of payments "surplus" or "deficit." These references have two explanations. The first is that the person making the reference has confused the balance of payments with either the balance of trade or the current account balance. This is a very common mistake. The second explanation is that the person is not including official reserve transactions in the capital account. If we separate changes in U.S. holdings of foreign currencies and changes in foreign holdings of U.S. dollars from other financial account entries, then the current account balance and the financial account balance do not have to sum to zero and there can be a balance of payments surplus or deficit. If this sounds complicated, it is! But don't worry. How official reserve transactions are accounted for is not crucial to understanding the basic ideas behind the balance of payments.

***YOUR TURN:* Test your understanding by doing related problem 3 on page 568 at the end of this chapter.**

The Foreign Exchange Market and Exchange Rates

② LEARNING OBJECTIVE

Explain how exchange rates are determined and how changes in exchange rates affect the prices of imports and exports.

A firm that operates entirely within the United States will price its products in dollars and will use dollars to pay suppliers, workers, interest to bondholders, and dividends to shareholders. A multinational corporation, in contrast, may sell its product in many different countries and receive payment in many different currencies. Its suppliers and workers may also be spread around the world and may have to be paid in local currencies. Corporations may also use the international financial system to borrow in a foreign currency. During the 1990s, for example, many large firms located in East Asian countries, such as Thailand and South Korea, received dollar loans from foreign banks. When firms make extensive use of foreign currencies, they must deal with fluctuations in the exchange rate.

The **nominal exchange rate** is the value of one country's currency in terms of another country's currency. Economists also calculate the *real exchange rate,* which corrects the nominal exchange rate for changes in prices of goods and services. We discuss the real exchange rate later in this chapter. The nominal exchange rate determines how many units of a foreign currency you can purchase with one dollar. For example, the exchange rate between the U.S. dollar and the Japanese yen can be expressed as ¥100 = $1. (This exchange rate can also be expressed as how many U.S. dollars are required to buy one Japanese yen: $0.01 = ¥1.) The market for foreign exchange is very active. Every day the equivalent of more than $1 trillion worth of currency is traded in the foreign exchange market. The exchange rates that result from this trading are reported each day in the business or financial sections of most newspapers.

Nominal exchange rate The value of one country's currency in terms of another country's currency.

Banks and other financial institutions around the world employ currency traders, who are linked together by computer. Rather than exchanging large amounts of paper currency, they buy and sell deposits in banks. A bank buying or selling dollars will actually be buying or selling dollar bank deposits. Dollar bank deposits exist not just in banks in the United States but also in banks around the world. Suppose that the Credit Lyonnais bank in France wishes to sell U.S. dollars and buy Japanese yen. It may exchange U.S. dollar deposits that it owns for Japanese yen deposits owned by the Deutsche Bank in Germany. Businesses and individuals usually obtain foreign currency from banks in their own country.

Exchange Rates in the Financial Pages

17-1 Making the Connection

The financial pages of most newspapers provide information on exchange rates.

The business pages of most newspapers list the exchange rate between the dollar and other important currencies. The rates in the following table are for August 26, 2005. Note that the euro is the common currency used by twelve European countries, including France, Germany, and Italy.

EXCHANGE RATE BETWEEN THE DOLLAR AND THE INDICATED CURRENCY

	UNITS OF FOREIGN CURRENCY PER U.S. DOLLAR	U.S. DOLLARS PER UNIT OF FOREIGN CURRENCY
Canadian dollar	1.199	0.834
Japanese yen	110.200	0.009
Mexican peso	10.841	0.092
British pound	0.555	1.801
Euro	0.814	1.228

Notice that the expression for the exchange rate stated as units of foreign currency per U.S. dollar is the *reciprocal* of the exchange rate stated as U.S. dollars per unit of foreign currency. So, the exchange rate between the U.S. dollar and the Canadian dollar can be stated as either 1.199 Canadian dollars per U.S. dollar or 1/1.199 = 0.834 U.S. dollars per Canadian dollar.

Banks are the most active participants in the market for foreign exchange. Typically, banks buy currency for slightly less than the amount for which they sell it. This spread between the buying and selling prices allows banks to cover their expenses from currency trading and to make a profit. Therefore, when most businesses and individuals buy foreign currency from a bank, they receive fewer units of foreign currency per dollar than would be indicated by the exchange rate printed in the newspaper.

Source: *Wall Street Journal,* August 29, 2005.

The market exchange rate is determined by the interaction of demand and supply, just as other prices are. Let's consider the demand for U.S. dollars in exchange for Japanese yen. There are three sources of foreign currency demand for the U.S. dollar:

1. Foreign firms and consumers who want to buy goods and services produced in the United States.
2. Foreign firms and consumers who want to invest in the United States either through foreign direct investment—buying or building factories or other facilities in the United States—or through foreign portfolio investment—buying stocks and bonds issued in the United States.
3. Currency traders who believe that the value of the dollar in the future will be greater than its value today.

Equilibrium in the Market for Foreign Exchange

Figure 17-2 shows the demand and supply of U.S. dollars for Japanese yen. Notice that as we move up the vertical axis in Figure 17-2 the value of the dollar increases relative to the value of the yen. When the exchange rate is ¥150 = $1, the dollar is worth one and a half times as much relative to the yen as when the exchange rate is ¥100 = $1. Consider, first, the demand curve for dollars in exchange for yen. The demand curve has the normal downward slope. When the value of the dollar is high, the quantity of dollars demanded will be low. A Japanese investor will be more likely to buy a $1,000 bond issued by the U.S. Treasury when the exchange rate is ¥100 = $1 and the investor pays only ¥100,000 to buy $1,000 than when the exchange rate is ¥150 = $1 and the investor must pay ¥150,000. Similarly, a Japanese firm is more likely to buy $150,000,000 worth of microchips from the Intel Corporation when the exchange rate is ¥100 = $1 and the microchips can be purchased for ¥15 billion than when the exchange rate is ¥150 = $1 and the microchips will cost ¥22.5 billion.

Consider, now, the supply curve of dollars in exchange for yen. The supply curve has the normal upward slope. When the value of the dollar is high, the quantity of dollars

FIGURE 17-2

Equilibrium in the Foreign Exchange Market

When the exchange rate is ¥150 to the dollar, it is above its equilibrium level, and there will be a surplus of dollars. When the exchange rate is ¥100 to the dollar, it is below its equilibrium level, and there will be a shortage of dollars. At an exchange rate of ¥120 to the dollar, the foreign exchange market is in equilibrium.

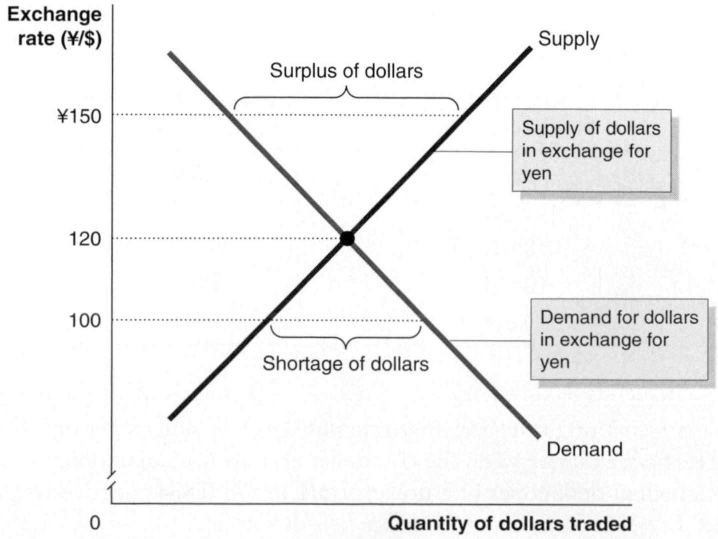

Don't Let This Happen To You!

Don't Confuse What Happens When a Currency Appreciates with What Happens When It Depreciates

One of the more confusing aspects of exchange rates is that they can be expressed in two ways. We can express the exchange rate between the dollar and the yen either as how many yen can be purchased with one dollar or as how many dollars can be purchased with one yen. That is, we can express the exchange rate as ¥100 = $1 or as $0.01 = ¥1. When a currency appreciates, it increases in value relative to another currency. When it depreciates, it decreases in value relative to another currency.

If the exchange rate changes from ¥100 = $1 to ¥120 = $1, the dollar has appreciated and the yen has depreciated because it now takes more yen to buy one dollar. If the exchange rate changes from $0.01 = ¥1 to $0.015 = ¥1, however, the dollar has depreciated and the yen has appreciated because it now takes more dollars to buy one yen. This situation can appear somewhat confusing because the exchange rate seems to have "increased" in both cases. To determine which currency has appreciated and which has depreciated, it is important to remember that an appreciation of the domestic currency means that it now takes *more* units of the foreign currency to buy one unit of the domestic currency. A depreciation of the domestic currency means it takes *fewer* units of the foreign currency to buy one unit of the domestic currency. This observation holds no matter which way we express the exchange rate.

YOUR TURN: **Test your understanding by doing related problem 9 on page 568 at the end of the chapter.**

supplied in exchange for yen will be high. A U.S. investor will be more likely to buy a ¥200,000 bond issued by the Japanese government when the exchange rate is ¥200 = $1 and he needs to pay only $1,000 to buy ¥200,000, than when the exchange rate is ¥100 = $1 and he must pay $2,000. The owner of a U.S. electronics store is more likely to buy ¥20,000,000 worth of television sets from the Sony Corporation when the exchange rate is ¥200 = $1 and she only needs to pay $100,000 to purchase the televisions, than when the exchange rate is ¥100 = $1 and she must pay $200,000.

As in any other market, equilibrium occurs in the foreign exchange market where the quantity supplied equals the quantity demanded. In Figure 17-2, ¥120 = $1 is the equilibrium exchange rate. At exchange rates above ¥120 = $1, there will be a surplus of dollars and downward pressure on the exchange rate. The surplus and the downward pressure will not be eliminated until the exchange rate falls to ¥120 = $1. If the exchange rate is below ¥120 = $1, there will be a shortage of dollars and upward pressure on the exchange rate. The shortage and the upward pressure will not be eliminated until the exchange rate rises to ¥120 = $1. Surpluses and shortages in the foreign exchange market are eliminated very quickly because the volume of trading in major currencies such as the dollar and the yen is very large and currency traders are linked together by computer.

Currency appreciation occurs when the market value of a country's currency rises relative to the value of another country's currency. **Currency depreciation** occurs when the market value of a country's currency declines relative to the value of another country's currency.

Currency appreciation Occurs when the market value of a currency rises relative to another currency.

Currency depreciation Occurs when the market value of a currency falls relative to another currency.

How Do Shifts in Demand and Supply Affect the Exchange Rate?

Shifts in the demand and supply curves cause the equilibrium exchange rate to change. Three main factors cause the demand and supply curves in the foreign exchange market to shift:

1. Changes in the demand for U.S.-produced goods and services and changes in the demand for foreign-produced goods and services.
2. Changes in the desire to invest in the United States and changes in the desire to invest in foreign countries.
3. Changes in the expectations of currency traders about the likely future value of the dollar and the likely future value of foreign currencies.

SHIFTS IN THE DEMAND FOR FOREIGN EXCHANGE Consider first how the three factors listed above will affect the demand for U.S. dollars in exchange for Japanese yen. During an economic expansion in Japan, the incomes of Japanese households will rise and the demand by Japanese consumers and firms for U.S. goods will increase. At any given exchange rate, the demand for U.S. dollars will increase and the demand curve will shift to the right. Similarly, if interest rates in the United States rise, the desirability of investing in U.S. financial assets will increase, and the demand curve for dollars will also shift to the right. Some buyers and sellers in the foreign exchange market are **speculators.** Speculators buy and sell foreign exchange in an attempt to profit from changes in exchange rates. If a speculator becomes convinced that the value of the dollar is going to rise relative to the value of the yen, the speculator will sell yen and buy dollars. If the current exchange rate is ¥120 = $1 and the speculator is convinced that it will soon rise to ¥140 = $1, the speculator could sell ¥600,000,000 and receive $5,000,000 (¥600,000,000/¥120) in return. If the speculator is correct and the value of the dollar rises against the yen to ¥140 = $1, the speculator will be able to exchange $5,000,000 for ¥700,000,000 ($5,000,000 × ¥140), leaving a profit of ¥100,000,000.

Speculators Currency traders who buy and sell foreign exchange in an attempt to profit by changes in exchange rates.

To summarize, the demand curve for dollars shifts to the right when incomes in Japan rise, when interest rates in the United States rise, or when speculators decide that the value of the dollar will rise relative to the value of the yen.

During a recession in Japan, Japanese incomes will fall, reducing the demand for U.S.-produced goods and services, and shifting the demand curve for dollars to the left. Similarly, if interest rates in the United States fall, the desirability of investing in U.S. financial assets will decrease, and the demand curve for dollars will shift to the left. Finally, if speculators become convinced that the future value of the dollar will be lower than its current value, the demand for dollars will fall and the demand curve will shift to the left.

SHIFTS IN THE SUPPLY OF FOREIGN EXCHANGE The factors affecting the supply curve for dollars are similar to those affecting the demand curve for dollars. An economic expansion in the United States increases the incomes of Americans and increases their demand for goods and services, including goods and services made in Japan. As U.S. consumers and firms increase their spending on Japanese products, they must supply dollars in exchange for yen, which causes the supply curve for dollars to shift to the right. Similarly, an increase in interest rates in Japan will make financial investments in Japan more attractive to U.S. investors. These higher Japanese interest rates will cause the supply of dollars to shift to the right, as U.S. investors exchange dollars for yen. Finally, if speculators become convinced that the future value of the yen will be higher relative to the dollar than it is today, the supply curve of dollars will shift to the right as traders attempt to exchange dollars for yen.

A recession in the United States will decrease the demand for Japanese products and cause the supply curve for dollars to shift to the left. Similarly, a decrease in interest rates in Japan will make financial investments in Japan less attractive and cause the supply curve of dollars to shift to the left. If traders become convinced that the future value of the yen will be lower relative to the dollar, the supply curve will also shift to the left.

ADJUSTMENT TO A NEW EQUILIBRIUM The factors that affect the supply and demand for currencies are constantly changing. Whether the exchange rate increases or decreases depends on the direction and size of the shifts in the demand curve and supply curve. For example, as Figure 17-3 shows, if the demand curve for dollars in exchange for Japanese yen shifts to the right by more than the supply curve does, the equilibrium exchange rate will increase.

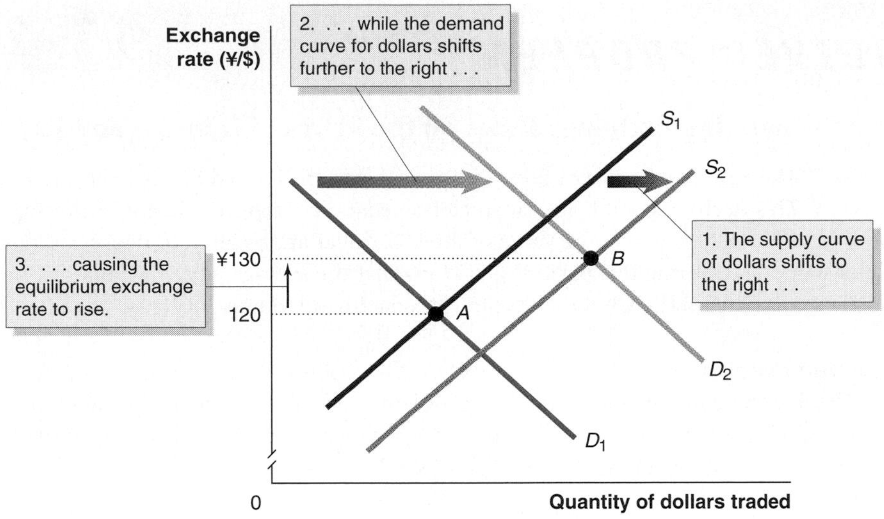

FIGURE 17-3

Shifts in the Demand and Supply Curve Resulting in a Higher Exchange Rate

An increase in the supply of dollars will decrease the equilibrium exchange rate. An increase in the demand for dollars will increase the equilibrium exchange rate, holding other factors constant. In the case shown in this figure, the demand curve and the supply curve have both shifted to the right. Because the demand curve has shifted to the right by more than the supply curve, the equilibrium exchange rate has increased from ¥120 to the dollar at point *A* to ¥130 to the dollar at point *B*.

Some Exchange Rates Are Not Determined by the Market

To this point, we have assumed that exchange rates are determined in the market. This assumption is a good one for many currencies, including the U.S. dollar, the euro, the Japanese yen, and the British pound. Some currencies, however, have *fixed exchange rates* that do not change over long periods. For example, for more than 10 years, the value of the Chinese yuan was fixed against the U.S. dollar at a rate of 8.28 yuan to the dollar. As we will discuss in more detail in Chapter 18, a country's central bank has to intervene in the foreign exchange market to buy and sell its currency to keep the exchange rate fixed.

How Movements in the Exchange Rate Affect Exports and Imports

When the market value of the dollar increases, the foreign currency price of U.S. exports rises and the dollar price of foreign imports falls. For example, suppose initially the market exchange rate between the U.S. dollar and the euro is $1 = €1. In that case, an Apple iPod Nano that has a price of $200 in the United States will have a price of €200 in France. A bottle of French wine that has a price of €50 in France will have a price of $50 in the United States. Now suppose the market exchange rate between the U.S. dollar and the euro changes to $1.20 = €1. Because it now takes more dollars to buy a euro, the dollar has *depreciated* against the euro and the euro has *appreciated* against the dollar.

The depreciation of the dollar has decreased the euro price of the iPod from €200 to $200/(1.20 dollars/euro) = €167. The dollar price of the French wine has risen from $50 to €50 × 1.20 dollars/euro = $60. As a result, we would expect more iPods to be sold in France and less French wine to be sold in the United States. To generalize, we can conclude that a depreciation in the domestic currency will increase exports and decrease imports, thereby increasing net exports. As we saw in previous chapters, net exports is a component of aggregate demand. If the economy is currently below potential GDP, then, holding all other factors constant, a depreciation in the domestic currency should increase net exports, aggregate demand, and real GDP.

An appreciation in the domestic currency should have the opposite effect: Exports should fall and imports should rise, which will reduce net exports, aggregate demand, and real GDP.

SOLVED PROBLEM 17-2

② LEARNING OBJECTIVE

Explain how exchange rates are determined and how changes in the exchange rates affect the prices of imports and exports.

Effect of Changing Exchange Rates on the Prices of Imports and Exports

In March 2001, the average price of goods imported into the United States from Canada fell 3.3 percent. This decline was the largest since the federal government began gathering such statistics in 1992. Is it likely that the value of the U.S. dollar appreciated or depreciated versus the Canadian dollar during this period? Is it likely that the average price in Canadian dollars of goods exported from the United States to Canada during March 2001 rose or fell?

Solving the Problem:

Step 1: Review the chapter material. This problem is about changes in the value of a currency, so you may want to review the section "How Movements in the Exchange Rate Affect Exports and Imports," which begins on page 555.

Step 2: Explain whether the value of the U.S. dollar appreciated or depreciated against the Canadian dollar. We know that if the U.S. dollar appreciates against the Canadian dollar, it will take more Canadian dollars to purchase one U.S. dollar. Equivalently, fewer U.S. dollars will be required to purchase one Canadian dollar. A Canadian consumer or business will need to pay more Canadian dollars to buy products imported from the United States: A good or service that had been selling for 100 Canadian dollars will now sell for more than 100 Canadian dollars. A U.S. consumer or business will have to pay fewer U.S. dollars to buy products imported from Canada: A good or service that had been selling for 100 U.S. dollars will now sell for fewer than 100 U.S. dollars. We can conclude that if the price of goods imported into the United States from Canada fell, the value of the U.S. dollar must have appreciated versus the Canadian dollar.

Step 3: Explain what happened to the average price in Canadian dollars of goods exported from the United States to Canada. If the U.S. dollar appreciated relative to the Canadian dollar, the average price in Canadian dollars of goods exported from the United States to Canada will have risen.

YOUR TURN: **For more practice, do related problem 14 on page 569 at the end of this chapter.**

The Real Exchange Rate

Real exchange rate The price of domestic goods in terms of foreign goods.

We have seen that an important factor in determining the level of a country's exports to and imports from another country is the relative prices of each country's goods. The relative prices of two countries' goods are determined by two factors: the relative price levels in the two countries and the nominal exchange rate between the two countries' currencies. Economists combine these two factors in the *real exchange rate.* The **real exchange rate** is the price of domestic goods in terms of foreign goods. Recall that the price level is a measure of the average prices of goods and services in an economy. We can calculate the real exchange rate between two currencies as:

$$\text{Real exchange rate} = \text{Nominal exchange rate} \times \left(\frac{\text{Domestic price level}}{\text{Foreign price level}}\right).$$

Notice that changes in the real exchange rate reflect both changes in the nominal exchange rate and changes in the relative price levels. For example, suppose that the exchange rate between the U.S. dollar and the British pound is \$1 = £1, the price level in the United States is 100, and the price level in the United Kingdom is also 100. Then the real exchange rate between the dollar and the pound is:

$$\text{Real exchange rate} = 1 \text{ pound / dollar} \times \left(\frac{100}{100}\right) = 1.00.$$

Now suppose the nominal exchange rate increases to 1.1 pounds per dollar, while the price level in the United States rises to 105 and the price level in the United Kingdom remains 100, then the real exchange rate will be:

$$\text{Real exchange rate} = 1.1 \text{ pound / dollar} \times \left(\frac{105}{100}\right) = 1.15.$$

The increase in the real exchange rate from 1.00 to 1.15 tells us that the prices of U.S. goods and services are now 15 percent higher than they were relative to British goods and services.

Real exchange rates are reported as index numbers with one year chosen as the base year. Like the consumer price index, the real exchange rate's main value is in tracking changes over time—in this case, changes in the relative prices of domestic goods in terms of foreign goods.

The International Sector and National Saving and Investment

(3) LEARNING OBJECTIVE

Explain the saving and investment equation.

Having studied what determines the exchange rate, we are now ready to explore further the linkages between the U.S. economy and foreign economies. Until 1970, U.S. imports and exports were usually 4 percent to 5 percent of GDP. As Figure 17-4 shows, imports and exports are now more than twice as large a fraction of U.S. GDP. The figure also shows that since 1975, imports have consistently been larger than exports, meaning that net exports have been negative.

Net Exports Equal Net Foreign Investment

If your spending is greater than your income, what can you do? You can sell some assets—maybe those 20 shares of stock in the Walt Disney Company your grandparents gave you—or you can borrow money. A firm can be in the same situation: If a firm's costs are greater than its revenues, it has to make up the difference by selling assets or by borrowing. A country is in the same situation when it imports more than it exports. The country must finance the difference by selling assets—such as land, office buildings, or factories—or by borrowing.

In other words, for any country, a current account deficit must be exactly offset by a financial account surplus. When a country sells more assets to foreigners than it buys assets from foreigners, or borrows more from foreigners than it lends to foreigners—as

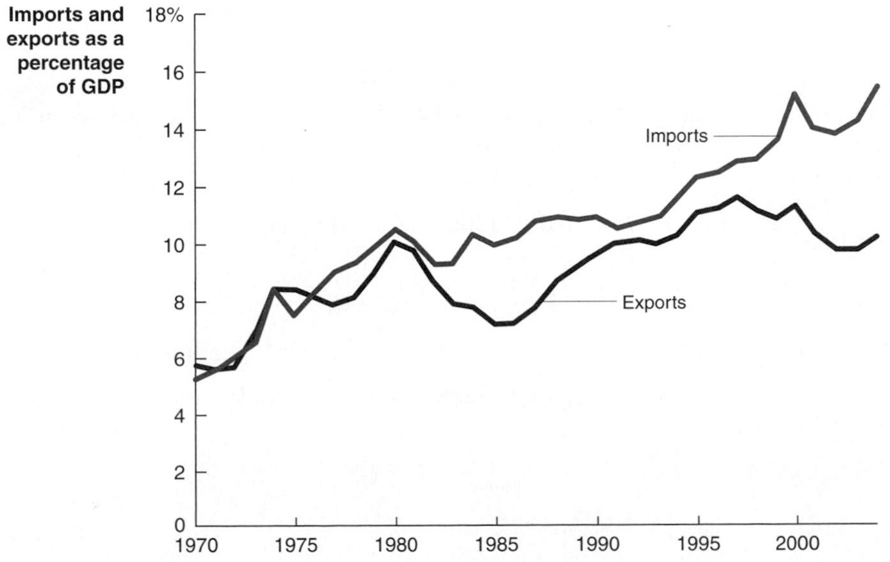

FIGURE 17-4

U.S. Imports and Exports, 1970–2004

Imports and exports are much larger fractions of GDP today than they were before 1970. Imports have increased faster than exports, which has made net exports negative every year since 1975.

Source: Bureau of Economic Analysis.

it must if it is running a current account deficit—the country experiences a net capital inflow and a financial account surplus. Remember that net exports is roughly equal to the current account balance. Remember also that the financial account balance is roughly equal to net capital flows, which are in turn equal to net foreign investment, but with the opposite sign. To review these two points, look again at Table 17-1, which shows that the current account balance is determined mainly by the balance of trade and the balance of services, and the financial account is equal to net capital flows. Also, remember the definition of net foreign investment.

When imports are greater than exports, net exports are negative and there will be a net capital inflow as people in the United States sell assets and borrow to pay for the surplus of imports over exports. Therefore, net capital flows will be equal to net exports (but with the opposite sign), and net foreign investment will also be equal to net exports (and with the same sign). Because net exports are usually negative for the United States, in most years, the United States must be a net borrower from abroad and U.S. net foreign investment will be negative.

We can summarize this discussion with the following equations:

$$\text{Current account balance} + \text{Financial account balance} = 0$$

or,

$$\text{Current account balance} = -\text{Financial account balance}$$

or,

$$\text{Net exports} = \text{Net foreign investment.}$$

This equation tells us, once again, that countries such as the United States, that import more than they export, must borrow more from abroad than they lend abroad: If net exports are negative, net foreign investment will also be negative by the same amount. Countries, such as Japan and China, that export more than they import, must lend abroad more than they borrow from abroad: If net exports are positive, net foreign investment will also be positive by the same amount.

Domestic Saving, Domestic Investment, and Net Foreign Investment

As we saw in Chapter 9, the total saving in any economy is equal to saving by the private sector plus saving by the government sector, which we called *public saving*. When the government runs a budget surplus by spending less than it receives in taxes, it is saving. When the government runs a budget deficit, public saving is negative. Negative saving is also known as *dissaving*. We can write the following expression for the level of saving in the economy:

$$\text{National saving} = \text{Private saving} + \text{Public saving}$$

or,

$$S = S_{\text{private}} + S_{\text{public}}.$$

Private saving is equal to what households have left of their income after spending on consumption goods and paying taxes (for simplicity, we assume that transfer payments are zero):

$$\text{Private saving} = \text{National income} - \text{Consumption} - \text{Taxes}$$

or,

$$S_{\text{private}} = Y - C - T.$$

Public saving is equal to the difference between government spending and taxes:

$$\text{Government saving} = \text{Taxes} - \text{Government spending}$$

or,

$$S_{\text{public}} = T - G.$$

Finally, remember the basic macroeconomic equation for GDP or national income:

$$Y = C + I + G + NX.$$

We can use this equation, our definitions of private and public saving, and the fact that net exports equal net foreign investment to arrive at an important relationship, known as the **saving and investment equation.**

Saving and investment equation An equation showing that national saving is equal to domestic investment plus net foreign investment.

$$\text{National saving} = \text{Domestic investment} + \text{Net foreign investment}$$

or,

$$S = I + NFI.$$

This equation is an *identity* because it must always be true, given the definitions we have used.

The saving and investment equation tells us that a country's saving will be invested either domestically or overseas. If you save $1,000 and use the funds to buy a bond issued by General Motors, GM may use the $1,000 to renovate a factory in the United States *(I)* or to build a factory in China *(NFI)* as a joint venture with a Chinese firm.

SOLVED PROBLEM 17-3

Arriving at the Saving and Investment Equation

(3) LEARNING OBJECTIVE

Explain the saving and investment equation.

Use the definitions of private and public saving, the equation for GDP or national income, and the fact that net exports must equal net foreign investment to arrive at the saving and investment equation.

Solving the Problem:

Step 1: Review the chapter material. This problem is about the saving and investment equation, so you may want to review the section "Domestic Saving, Domestic Investment, and Net Foreign Investment," which begins on page 558.

Step 2: Derive an expression for national saving *(S)* in terms of national income *(Y)*, consumption *(C)*, and government purchases *(G)*. We can bring together the four equations we need to use:

1. $S_{private} = Y - C - T$
2. $S_{public} = T - G$
3. $Y = C + I + G + NX$
4. $NX = NFI$

Because national saving *(S)* appears in the saving and investment equation, we need to find an equation for it in terms of the other variables. Adding equation 1 plus equation 2 yields national saving:

$$S = S_{private} + S_{public} = (Y - C - T) + (T - G) = Y - C - G.$$

Step 3: Use the result from Step 2 to derive an expression for national saving in terms of investment *(I)* and net exports *(NX)*. Because GDP *(Y)* does not appear in the saving and investment equation, we need to substitute the expression for it given in equation 3:

$$S = (C + I + G + NX) - C - G$$

and simplify:

$$S = I + NX.$$

Step 4: Use the results of Steps 2 and 3 to derive the saving and investment equation. Finally, substitute net foreign investment for net exports:

$$S = I + NFI.$$

YOUR TURN: **For more practice, do related problem 16 on page 569 at the end of this chapter.**

A country such as the United States that has negative net foreign investment must be saving less than it is investing domestically. To see this, rewrite the saving and investment equation by moving domestic investment to the left-hand side:

$$S - I = NFI.$$

If net foreign investment is negative—as it is for the United States nearly every year—domestic investment *(I)* must be greater than national saving *(S)*.

As we saw in Chapter 14, the level of saving in Japan has been well above domestic investment. The result has been high levels of Japanese net foreign investment. For example, Japanese automobile companies Toyota, Honda, and Nissan have all constructed factories in the United States. Sony purchased the Columbia Pictures film studio. Japanese investors are also estimated to hold more than $200 billion worth of U.S. Treasury bonds. Japan has made many similar investments in countries around the world, which has sometimes caused resentment in these countries. There were some protests in the United States in the 1980s, for example, when Japanese investors purchased the Pebble Beach golf course in California and the Rockefeller Center complex in New York City.

Japan needs a high level of net exports to help offset a low level of domestic investment. When exports of a product begin to decline and imports begin to increase, governments are very tempted to impose tariffs or quotas to reduce imports. (See Chapter 6 to review tariffs and quotas and their negative effects on the economy.) This intervention is what Motoki Hirabayashi, the Japanese towel manufacturer we met at the beginning of this chapter, was urging the Japanese government to do.

(4) **LEARNING OBJECTIVE**

Explain the effect of a government budget deficit on investment in an open economy.

The Effect of a Government Budget Deficit on Investment

The link we have just developed among saving, investment, and net foreign investment can help us understand some of the effects of changes in a government's budget deficit. When the government runs a budget deficit, national saving will decline unless private saving increases by the amount of the budget deficit, which is unlikely. As the saving and investment equation—$S = I + NFI$—shows, the result of a decline in national saving must be a decline in either domestic investment or net foreign investment. Why, though, does an increase in the government budget deficit cause a fall in domestic investment or net foreign investment?

To understand the answer to this question, first, remember that if the federal government runs a budget deficit, the U.S. Treasury must raise an amount equal to the deficit by selling bonds. To attract investors, the Treasury may have to raise the interest rates on its bonds. As interest rates on Treasury bonds rise, other interest rates, including those on corporate bonds and bank loans, will also rise. Higher interest rates will discourage some businesses from borrowing funds to build new factories or to buy new equipment or computers. Higher interest rates on financial assets in the United States will attract foreign investors. Investors in the United Kingdom, Canada, or Japan will have to buy U.S. dollars to be able to purchase bonds in the United States. This greater demand for dollars will increase their value relative to foreign currencies. As the value of the dollar rises, exports from the United States will fall and imports to the United States will rise. Net exports and, therefore, net foreign investment will fall.

When a government budget deficit leads to a decline in net exports, the result is sometimes referred to as the *twin deficits,* which refers to the possibility that a govern-

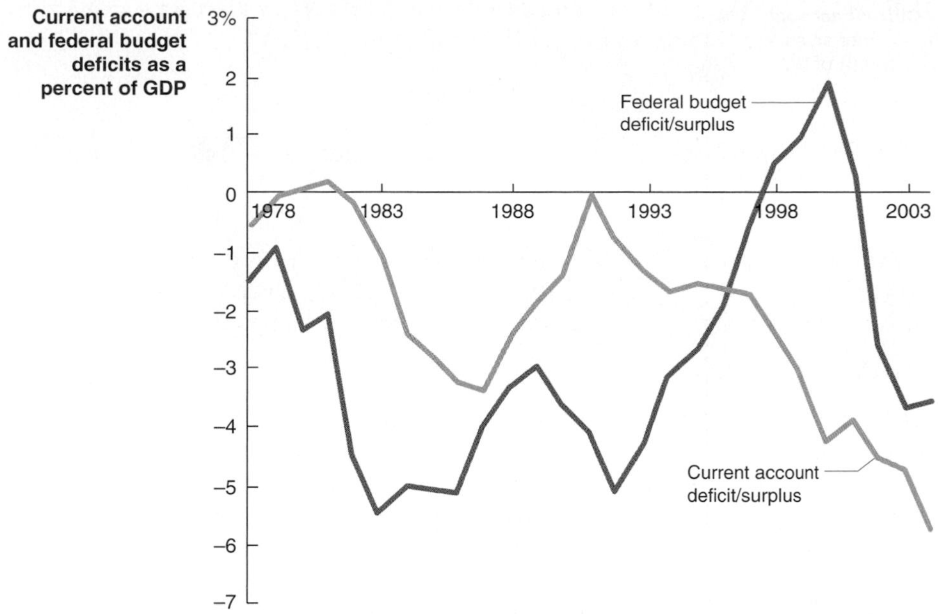

FIGURE 17-5

The Twin Deficits, 1978–2004

During the early 1980s, large federal budget deficits occurred at the same time as large current account deficits, but twin deficits did not occur in the 1990s.

Source: Bureau of Economic Analysis.

ment budget deficit will also lead to a current account deficit. The twin deficits idea first became widely discussed in the United States during the early 1980s when the federal government ran a large budget deficit that resulted in high interest rates, a high exchange value of the dollar, and a large current account deficit.

Figure 17-5 shows that in the early 1980s the United States had large federal budget deficits and large current account deficits. The figure also shows, however, that the twin deficits idea does not match the experience of the United States after 1990. The large federal budget deficits of the early 1990s occurred at a time of relatively small current account deficits, and the budget surpluses of the late 1990s occurred at a time of then record current account deficits.

The experience of other countries also shows only mixed support for the twin deficits idea. Germany ran large budget deficits and large current account deficits during the early 1990s, but both Canada and Italy ran large budget deficits during the 1980s without running current account deficits. The saving and investment equation shows that an increase in the government budget deficit will not lead to an increase in the current account deficit, provided either private saving increases or domestic investment declines. According to the twin deficits idea, when the federal government ran budget surpluses in the late 1990s the current account should also have been in surplus, or at least the current account deficit should have been small. In fact, the increase in national saving due to the budget surpluses was more than offset by a sharp decline in private saving, and the United States ran very large current account deficits.

Why Is the United States Called the "World's Largest Debtor"?

17-2 Making the Connection

The following graph shows the current account balance as a percent of GDP for the United States for the period 1950–2004. The United States has had a current account deficit every year since 1982, with the exception of 1991. Between 1950 and 1975, the United States ran a current account deficit in only five years. Many economists believe that the current account deficits of the 1980s were closely related to the federal budget deficits of those years. High interest rates attracted foreign investors to U.S. bonds, which raised the exchange rate between the dollar and foreign currencies. The high exchange rate reduced U.S. exports and increased imports, leading to current account deficits.

As the federal budget deficit narrowed in the mid-1990s and disappeared in the late 1990s, the foreign exchange value of the dollar remained high—and large current account deficits

Large current account deficits have resulted in foreign investors purchasing large amounts of U.S. assets.

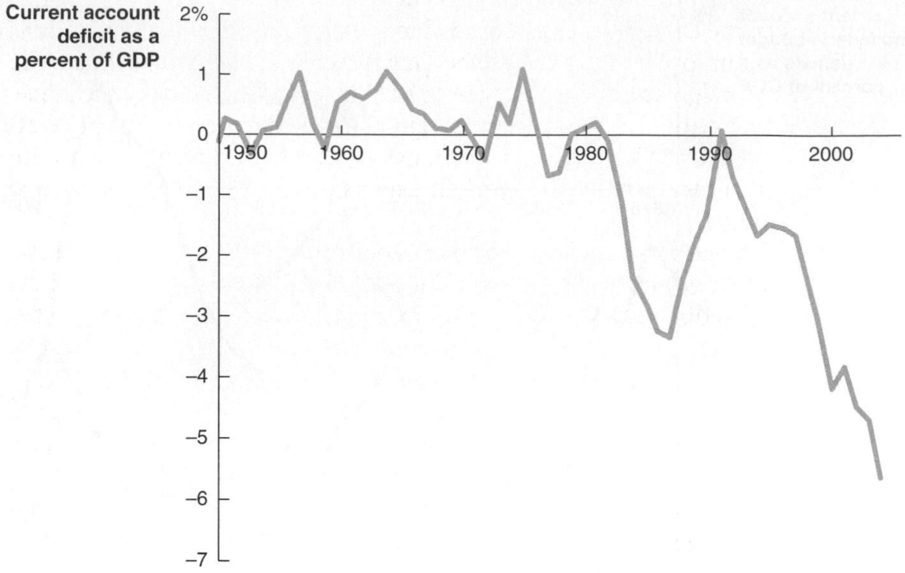

Source: Bureau of Economic Analysis.

continued—because foreign investors persisted in investing in the United States despite low interest rates. In the late 1990s, a number of countries around the world, such as South Korea, Indonesia, Brazil, and Russia, suffered severe economic problems. In a process known as a *flight to quality,* many investors sold their investments in those countries and bought investments in the United States. In addition, the strong performance of the U.S. stock market through the spring of 2000 attracted many investors. Finally, the sharp decline in private saving in the United States during the late 1990s also contributed to the U.S. current account deficit.

Do persistent current account deficits represent a problem for the United States? Current account deficits result in U.S. net foreign investment being negative. Each year, foreign investors accumulate many more U.S. assets than U.S. investors accumulate foreign assets. At the end of 2004, foreign investors owned about $2.5 trillion more of U.S. assets—such as stocks, bonds, and factories—than U.S. investors owned of foreign assets, which is why the United States is sometimes called "the world's largest debtor." But, the continued willingness of foreign investors to buy U.S. stocks and bonds and foreign companies to build factories in the United States can be seen as a vote of confidence in the strength of the U.S. economy and the buying power of U.S. consumers. With private saving rates having declined in the United States to historically low levels, only the continued flow of funds from foreign investors has made it possible for the United States to maintain the high levels of domestic investment required for economic growth.

(5) LEARNING OBJECTIVE

Discuss the difference between the effectiveness of monetary and fiscal policy in an open economy and in a closed economy.

Monetary Policy and Fiscal Policy in an Open Economy

When we discussed monetary and fiscal policy in Chapters 14 and 15, we did not emphasize that the United States is an open economy. Now that we have explored some of the links between economies, we can look at the difference between how monetary and fiscal policy work in an open economy as opposed to a closed economy. Economists refer to the ways in which monetary and fiscal policy affect the domestic economy as *policy channels.* An open economy has more policy channels than does a closed economy.

Monetary Policy in an Open Economy

When the Federal Reserve engages in an expansionary monetary policy, it buys Treasury securities to lower interest rates and stimulate aggregate demand. In a closed economy, the main effect of lower interest rates is on domestic investment spending and purchases of consumer durables. In an open economy, lower interest rates will also affect the exchange rate between the dollar and foreign currencies. Lower interest rates will cause some investors in the United States and abroad to switch from investing in U.S. financial assets to investing in foreign financial assets. This switch will lower the demand for the dollar relative to foreign currencies and cause its value to decline. A lower exchange rate will decrease the price of U.S. products in foreign markets and increase the price of foreign products in the United States. As a result, net exports will increase. This additional policy channel will increase the ability of an expansionary monetary policy to affect aggregate demand.

When the Fed wants to reduce the rate of economic growth to reduce inflation, it engages in contractionary monetary policy. The Fed sells Treasury securities to increase interest rates and reduce aggregate demand. In a closed economy, the main effect is once again on domestic investment spending and purchases of consumer durables. In an open economy, higher interest rates will lead to a higher foreign exchange value of the dollar. The prices of U.S. products in foreign markets will increase and the prices of foreign products in the U.S. will fall. As a result, net exports will fall. The contractionary policy will have a larger impact on aggregate demand, and therefore it will be more effective in slowing down the growth in economic activity. To summarize: *Monetary policy has a greater impact on aggregate demand in an open economy than in a closed economy.*

Fiscal Policy in an Open Economy

To engage in an expansionary fiscal policy, the federal government increases its purchases or cuts taxes. Increases in government purchases directly increase aggregate demand. Tax cuts increase aggregate demand by increasing household disposable income and business income, which results in increased consumption spending and investment spending. An expansionary fiscal policy may result in higher interest rates. In a closed economy, the main effect of higher interest rates is to reduce domestic investment spending and purchases of consumer durables. In an open economy, higher interest rates will also lead to an increase in the foreign exchange value of the dollar and a decrease in net exports. Therefore, in an open economy an expansionary fiscal policy may be less effective because the *crowding out effect* may be larger. In a closed economy, only consumption and investment are crowded out by an expansionary fiscal policy. In an open economy, net exports may also be crowded out.

The government can fight inflation by using a contractionary fiscal policy to slow the rate of economic growth. A contractionary fiscal policy cuts government purchases or raises taxes to reduce household disposable income and consumption spending. It also reduces the federal budget deficit (or increases the budget surplus), which may lower interest rates. Lower interest rates will increase domestic investment and purchases of consumer durables, thereby offsetting some of the reduction in government spending and increases in taxes. In an open economy, lower interest rates will also reduce the foreign exchange value of the dollar and increase net exports. Therefore, in an open economy a contractionary fiscal policy will have a smaller impact on aggregate demand, and therefore will be less effective in slowing down an economy. In summary: *Fiscal policy has a smaller impact on aggregate demand in an open economy than in a closed economy.*

Conclusion

At one time U.S. policymakers—and economics textbooks—ignored the linkages between the United States and other economies. In the modern world, these linkages have become increasingly important, and economists and policymakers must take them into account when analyzing the economy. In the next chapter, we will study more about how the international financial system operates.

Read *An Inside Look* on the next page for a further discussion of the consequences of persistent current account deficits and surpluses.

An Inside Look

Distorted Price Signals Nurture U.S. Current-Account Deficit

ECONOMIST, AUGUST 18, 2005

Traffic Lights on the Blink?

The world currently displays an alarming number of large economic and financial imbalances. America's current-account deficit is forecast to widen to over $800 billion this year, while Germany, Japan, and China look set to run record surpluses. Total government debt in rich economies has risen to a new high as a percentage of GDP, and in many countries households are sliding ever further into debt. Meanwhile, the growth rates of America and other rich economies have diverged to an unusual degree.

Many economists try to explain these trends in terms of underlying structural factors, such as differences in demographic trends or productivity growth. An alternative, more worrying, explanation is that the price signals that are supposed to bring the world economy back into balance have become distorted.

a Start with the most obvious example: America's current account. In theory, a rapidly rising current-account deficit should cause investors to demand higher interest rates to compensate them for the increased risk of currency depreciation. Dearer money then helps to dampen domestic spending and thus trim the external deficit. This is what happened when America's current-account deficit exploded in the first half of the 1980s. Real bond yields rose, cooling domestic demand. Along with a cheaper dollar, this helped to reduce the deficit.

b This time, however, the adjustment mechanism has jammed: real American bond yields have fallen not risen over the past few years, partly because Asian central banks have been eager to buy US Treasury bonds to prevent their currencies rising. So long as low yields continue to support America's housing bubble and hence strong consumer spending, they will block any significant reduction in the country's current-account deficit. . . .

Europe's single monetary policy has also severed the link between short-term interest rates and economic performance in the euro area . . . Because all member states share the same nominal interest rate, slow-growing economies with lower inflation, such as Germany and Italy, have higher real interest rates than fast growers, such as Spain and Greece. This is the exact opposite of what is needed, exacerbating the divergence in growth rates. . . .

Euro-area interest rates are giving the wrong signals to governments as well as to consumers. Yields on government bonds barely differ, despite differences in countries' fiscal health. In the early 1990s, yields on ten-year government bonds were 450 basis points higher in Italy than in Germany. Today Italy pays a penalty of only around 20 basis points, even though its ratio of public debt to GDP is almost twice Germany's. Such thin interest-rate spreads give governments little incentive to trim their deficits. The convergence in yields reflects mainly the removal of exchange-rate risk since the creation of the single currency, but that still leaves default risk. The Maastricht Treaty explicitly forbids the European Central Bank to bail out any member country, but the markets clearly reckon that there is little chance that a government would be allowed to go bust.

c Interest rates and bond yields are the traffic lights of the global economy: they tell economies when to go and when to stop. When traffic lights break down in the ways discussed above, there is a risk that the global economy can get snarled up or even crash.

In the early 1990s, James Carville, Bill Clinton's campaign manager, said: "I used to think if there was reincarnation I wanted to come back as the president or the pope . . . but now I want to come back as the bond market. You can intimidate everybody." The liberalisation of international capital flows has undoubtedly increased the power of global capital markets. Combined with new technology and financial innovation, this should have made markets more efficient at disciplining economic performance. The market would punish economies where governments or households borrow recklessly with higher bond yields, prompting them to tighten their belts. Prudent economies would be rewarded with lower real rates. So what has gone wrong? . . .

The inevitable correction, when it comes, is likely to be all the more painful. When financial conditions tighten, investors are sure to become more discriminating. Sooner or later, the traffic lights will turn red.

Key Points in the Article

The U.S. current account deficit was projected to rise to $800 billion in 2005. Foreigners will use these dollars to fund direct and portfolio investments in the United States. We might expect that foreign demand for U.S. assets should raise U.S. interest rates and higher interest rates should slow the growth of the U.S. current account deficit. Nonetheless, interest rates in the United States remain relatively low. Therefore, many economists are concerned that the U.S. current account deficit will continue to grow and that this increasing deficit could have negative economic consequences.

Analyzing the News

a The U.S. current account deficit's rise to $800 billion in 2005 is a record. This means that there will be roughly a $800 billion capital inflow into the United States by the end of 2005. Foreigners will have used dollars acquired as a result of the U.S. current account deficit to buy buildings, factories, and other facilities in the United States (direct investment) or stocks and bonds issued in the United States (portfolio investment). However, as foreigners' dollar-denominated assets increase, so too does their exposure to a sudden and significant depreciation of the U.S. dollar. Because of this risk, foreigners should demand higher returns, including higher interest rates, on their U.S. dollar-denominated assets. All else equal, higher U.S. interest rates slow U.S. expenditures on foreign goods and services and help to reduce the U.S. current account deficit.

b Interest rates in the United States remain relatively low, in part because Asian central banks do not permit their currencies to appreciate relative to the U.S. dollar. For example, China's central bank sells yuan for U.S. dollars when it wants the value of its currency to fall relative to the dollar. This pattern is shown in Figure 1, where the supply of yuan increases from S_1 to S_2, and the dollar value of the yuan decreases from $0.12 to $0.10. This exchange rate policy keeps Asian exports competitive in the global marketplace, but it also causes Asian central banks to accumulate U.S. dollars, with which they purchase U.S. Treasury bonds. This strong demand for U.S. Treasury bonds keeps U.S. interest rates relatively low. All else equal, low U.S. interest rates fuel U.S. expenditures on foreign goods and services, and help to increase the U.S. current account deficit.

c The large U.S. current account deficit concerns economists because it grows seemingly unchecked by rising interest rates. Interest rates direct capital flows to their most productive uses, much as traffic lights direct traffic. But if interest rates do not increase gradually in response to the growing U.S. current account deficit, this imbalance will correct itself some other way; for example, the exchange value of the dollar could fall suddenly and significantly.

Thinking Critically ABOUT POLICY

1. How might the central bank intervention discussed alter the relative effectiveness of a U.S. contractionary monetary policy?
2. How might the central bank intervention discussed alter the relative effectiveness of a U.S. expansionary fiscal policy?

Source: "Traffic Lights on the Blink?" *Economist*, August 18, 2005. www.economist.com.

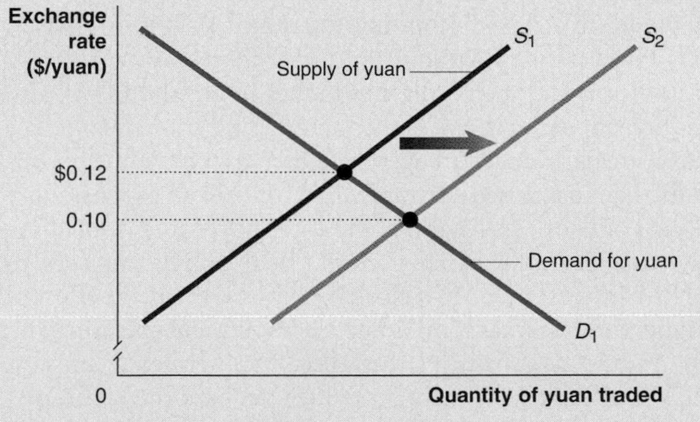

Figure 1: An increase in the supply of yuan causes a decrease in the U.S. dollar value of the yuan.

SUMMARY

LEARNING OBJECTIVE ① Explain how the balance of payments is calculated. Nearly all economies are *open economies* that trade with and invest in other economies. The *balance of payments* is the record of a country's trade with other countries in goods, services, and assets. The *current account* records a country's net exports, net investment income, and net transfers. The *financial account* shows investments a country has made abroad and foreign investments received by the country. The *balance of trade* is the difference between the value of the goods a country exports and the value of the goods a country imports. Apart from measurement errors, the sum of the current account and the financial account must equal zero. Therefore, the balance of payments must also equal zero.

LEARNING OBJECTIVE ② Explain how exchange rates are determined and how changes in exchange rates affect the prices of imports and exports. The *nominal exchange rate* is the value of one country's currency in terms of another country's currency. The exchange rate is determined in the foreign exchange market by the demand and supply of a country's currency. Changes in the exchange rate are caused by shifts in demand or supply. The three main sets of factors that cause the supply and demand curves in the foreign exchange market to shift are changes in the demand for U.S.-produced goods and services and change in the demand for foreign-produced goods and services; changes in the desire to invest in the United States and changes in the desire to invest in foreign countries; and changes in the expectations of currency traders—particularly *speculators*—concerning the likely future values of the dollar and the likely future values of foreign currencies. A currency *appreciates* when its market value rises relative to another currency. A currency *depreciates* when its market value falls relative to another currency. The *real exchange rate* is the price of domestic goods in terms of foreign goods. The real exchange rate is calculated by multiplying the nominal exchange rate by the ratio of the domestic price level to the foreign price level.

LEARNING OBJECTIVE ③ Explain the saving and investment equation. A current account deficit must be exactly offset by a financial account surplus. The financial account is equal to net capital flows, which is equal to net foreign investment but with the opposite sign. Because the current account balance is roughly equal to net exports, we can conclude that net exports will equal net foreign investment. National saving is equal to private saving plus government saving. Private saving is equal to national income minus consumption and minus taxes. Government saving is the difference between taxes and government spending. As we saw in previous chapters, GDP (or national income) is equal to the sum of investment, consumption, government spending, and net exports. We can use this fact, our definitions of private and government saving, and the fact that net exports equal net foreign investment, to arrive at an important relationship known as the *saving and investment equation:* $S = I + NFI$.

LEARNING OBJECTIVE ④ Explain the effect of a government budget deficit on investment in an open economy. When the government runs a budget deficit, national saving will decline unless private saving increases by the full amount of the budget deficit, which is unlikely. As the saving and investment equation—$S = I + NFI$—shows, the result of a decline in national saving must be a decline in either domestic investment or net foreign investment.

LEARNING OBJECTIVE ⑤ Discuss the difference between the effectiveness of monetary and fiscal policy in an open economy and in a closed economy. When the Federal Reserve engages in an expansionary monetary policy, it buys government bonds to lower interest rates and increase aggregate demand. In a closed economy, the main effect of lower interest rates is on domestic investment spending and purchases of consumer durables. In an open economy, lower interest rates will also cause an increase in net exports. When the Fed wants to slow the rate of economic growth to reduce inflation, it engages in a contractionary monetary policy. With a contractionary policy, the Fed sells government bonds to increase interest rates and reduce aggregate demand. In a closed economy, the main effect is once again on domestic investment and purchases of consumer durables. In an open economy, higher interest rates will also reduce net exports. We can conclude that monetary policy has a greater impact on aggregate demand in an open economy than in a closed economy. To engage in an expansionary fiscal policy, the government increases government spending or cuts taxes. An expansionary fiscal policy can lead to higher interest rates. In a closed economy, the main effect of higher interest rates is on domestic investment spending and spending on consumer durables. In an open economy, higher interest rates will also reduce net exports. A contractionary fiscal policy will reduce the budget deficit and may lower interest rates. In a closed economy, lower interest rates increase domestic investment and spending on consumer durables. In an open economy, lower interest rates also increase net exports. We can conclude that fiscal policy has a smaller impact on aggregate demand in an open economy than in a closed economy.

KEY TERMS

Balance of payments 546
Balance of trade 546
Capital account 548
Closed economy 546
Currency appreciation 553
Currency depreciation 553
Current account 546
Financial account 547
Net foreign investment 548
Nominal exchange rate 551
Open economy 546
Real exchange rate 556
Saving and investment equation 559
Speculators 554

REVIEW QUESTIONS

1. What is the relationship among the current account, the financial account, and the balance of payments?
2. What is the difference between net exports and the current account balance?
3. Explain why you agree or disagree with the following statement: "The United States has run a balance of payments deficit every year since 1982."
4. If the exchange rate between the Japanese yen and the U.S. dollar expressed in terms of yen per dollar is ¥110 = $1, what is the exchange rate when expressed in terms of dollars per yen?
5. Suppose that the current exchange rate between the dollar and the euro is 1.1 euros per dollar. If the exchange rate changes to 1.2 euros per dollar, did the euro appreciate or depreciate against the dollar?
6. What are the three main sets of factors that cause the supply and demand curves in the foreign exchange market to shift?
7. Explain the relationship between net exports and net foreign investment.
8. What is the saving and investment equation? If national saving declines, what will happen to domestic investment and net foreign investment?
9. If a country saves more than it invests domestically, what must be true of its net foreign investment?
10. What happens to national saving when the government runs a budget surplus? What is the twin deficits idea? Did it hold for the United States in the 1990s? Briefly explain.
11. Why were the early and mid-1980s particularly difficult times for U.S. exporters?
12. Why does monetary policy have a greater effect on aggregate demand in an open economy than in a closed economy, but fiscal policy has a smaller impact in an open economy than in a closed economy?

PROBLEMS AND APPLICATIONS

Please visit **www.prenhall.com/hubbard** *for solutions to the even-numbered problems as well as multiple-choice and true or false self-assessment quizzes.*

1. In 1999, France had a financial account deficit of $40 billion. Did France experience a net capital outflow or a net capital inflow in 1999? Briefly explain.
2. Use the information in the following table to prepare a balance of payments account, like the one shown in Table 17-1. Assume the balance on the capital account is zero.

Increase in foreign holdings of assets in the United States	$1,181
Exports of goods	856
Imports of services	–256
Statistical discrepancy	?
Net transfers	–60
Exports of services	325
Income received on investments	392
Imports of goods	–1,108
Increase in U.S. holdings of assets in foreign countries	–1,040
Income payments on investments	–315

3. **[Related to *Don't Let This Happen To You!*]** In 1999, Germany had a trade surplus of $71 billion. Which was larger in that year: Germany's exports of goods or its imports of goods? In 1999, Germany had a current account deficit of $21 billion. Explain how it was possible for Germany to have a trade surplus and a current account deficit in the same year.
4. **[Related to *Solved Problem 17-1*]** Is it possible for a country to run a trade deficit and a financial account deficit simultaneously? Briefly explain.
5. **[Related to *Solved Problem 17-1*]** Suppose we know that a country has been receiving large inflows of foreign investment. What can we say about its current account balance?
6. **[Related to *Solved Problem 17-1*]** The United States ran a current account surplus every year during the 1960s. What must have been true about the U.S. financial account balance during those years?
7. The only year since 1982 that the United States has run a current account surplus was 1991. In that year, Japan made a large payment to the United States to help pay for the Gulf War. Explain the connection between these two facts. (*Hint:* Where would Japan's payment to the United States appear in the balance of payments?)
8. According to this chapter, the U.S. trade deficit is almost always larger than the U.S. current account deficit. Why is this true?
9. **[Related to *Don't Let This Happen To You!*]** If we know the exchange rate between Country A's currency and Country B's currency, and we know the exchange rate between Country B's currency and Country C's currency, then we can compute the exchange rate between Country A's currency and Country C's currency.
   a. Suppose the exchange rate between the Japanese yen and the U.S. dollar is currently ¥120 = $1 and the exchange rate between the British pound and the U.S. dollar is £0.60 = $1. What is the exchange rate between the yen and the pound?
   b. Suppose the exchange rate between the yen and dollar changes to ¥130 = $1 and the exchange rate between the pound and dollar changes to £0.50 = $1. Has the dollar appreciated or depreciated against the yen? Has the dollar appreciated or depreciated against the pound? Has the yen appreciated or depreciated against the pound?
10. Graph the demand and supply of U.S. dollars for euros and label each axis. Show graphically and explain the effect of an increase in interest rates in Europe by the European Central Bank (ECB) on the demand and supply of dollars and the resulting change in the exchange rate of euros for U.S. dollars.
11. Graph the demand and supply of U.S. dollars for euros and label each axis. Show graphically and explain the effect of an increase in U.S. government budget deficits that increase U.S. interest rates on the demand and supply of dollars and the resulting change in the exchange rate of euros for U.S. dollars. Why might the change in the exchange rate lead to a current account deficit?
12. Use the graph to answer the following questions:

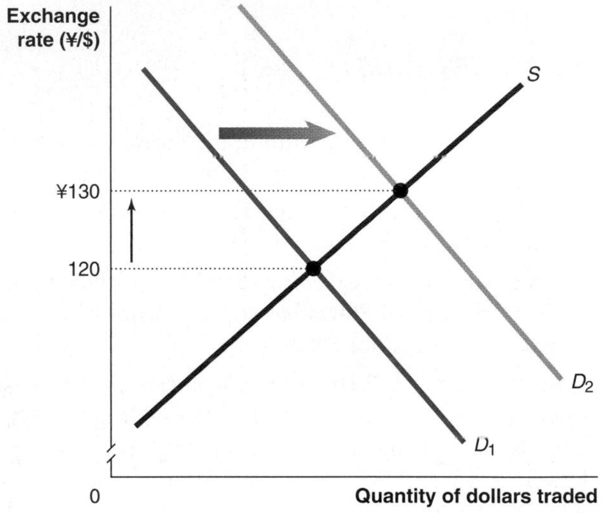

   a. Briefly explain whether the dollar appreciated or depreciated against the yen.
   b. Which of the following events could have caused the shift in demand shown in the graph?
      i. Interest rates in the United States have declined.
      ii. Income rises in Japan.
      iii. Speculators begin to believe the value of the dollar will be higher in the future.
13. Beginning January 1, 2002, 12 of the 15 member countries of the European Union eliminated their own individual currencies and began using a new common currency, the euro. For a three-year period from January 1, 1999, through December 31, 2001, these 12 countries priced goods and services in terms of both their own currencies and the euro. During this period, the value of their currencies was fixed against each other and against the euro. So during this time the dollar had an exchange rate against each of these currencies and against the euro. The information in the following table shows the fixed exchange rate of four European currencies against the euro and their exchange rates against the U.S. dollar on March 2, 2001. Use this information to calculate the exchange rate between the dollar and the euro (in euros per dollar) on March 2, 2001.

CURRENCY	UNITS PER EURO (FIXED)	UNITS PER U.S. DOLLAR (AS OF MARCH 2, 2001)
German mark	1.9558	2.0938
French franc	6.5596	7.0223
Italian lira	1,936.2700	2,072.8700
Portuguese escudo	200.4820	214.6300

14. **[*Related to Solved Problem 17-2*]** When a country's currency appreciates, is this generally good news or bad news for the country's consumers? Is it generally good news or bad news for the country's businesses? Explain your reasoning.

15. Writing in the *Wall Street Journal,* David Wessel makes the following observation:

    > Trend one: The U.S. has been buying more than $1 billion a day more from the rest of the world than it has been selling. . . . Trend two: Foreigners have been investing more than $1 billion a day of their savings in U.S. stocks, bonds, office towers, factories, and companies.

    Is it coincidence that both of his "trends" involve $1 billion per day? Briefly explain.

    Source: David Wessel, "Pain from the Dollar's Decline Will Mostly Be Felt Overseas," *Wall Street Journal,* June 13, 2002.

16. **[Related to *Solved Problem 17-3*]** Look again at how we arrived at the equation $S = I + NX$. Suppose that we define national income to be equal to $Y + TR$, where TR equals government transfer payments, and we define government spending to be equal to $G + TR$. Show that we end up with the same equation.

17. Use the saving and investment equation to explain why the United States experienced large current account deficits in the late 1990s.

18. According to an article in *Business Week*: "[T]he U.S. is depending on an ever-rising influx of foreign funds to pay for all the imported automobiles, TVs, and clothing that U.S. consumers crave." Convert this sentence into a statement about changes in the U.S. current account and the U.S. financial account.

    Source: Rich Miller and David Fairlamb, "The Greenback's Setback: Cause for Concern?" *Business Week,* May 20, 2002, p. 44.

19. Former Congressman and presidential candidate Richard Gephardt once proposed that tariffs be imposed on imports from countries with which the United States has a trade deficit. If this proposal were enacted and if it were to succeed in reducing the United States current account deficit to zero, what would be the likely effect on domestic investment spending within the United States? Assume that no other federal government economic policy is changed. (*Hint:* Use the saving and investment equation to answer this question.)

20. **[Related to the *Chapter Opener*]** Suppose that the Japanese government takes the advice of Mr. Hirabayashi, as described at the beginning of this chapter, and restricts imports of Chinese towels. Discuss the impact on the following:
    a. Japanese towel producers
    b. Chinese towel producers
    c. Japanese consumers
    d. Japanese net exports
    e. Japanese net foreign investment

21. Writing in the April 1997 issue of *International Economic Trends,* published by the Federal Reserve Bank of St. Louis, economist Michael Pakko observed the following:

    > The current account . . . reached a deficit of $165 billion in 1996, second only to the deficit of $167 billion in 1987. . . . [T]he evidence suggests that strong investment demand underlies the current economic expansion. Since the recession of 1990–91, real fixed investment spending has been growing at a rate of 6.9 percent . . . compared to 2.6 percent growth of GDP. . . . Only time will tell what the payoff to these investments will be, but they do give some reason to interpret the U.S. current account deficit with less apprehension.

    Why should the fact that investment spending in the United States has been strong reduce apprehension about the size of the current account deficit? What does the current account deficit have to do with investment spending?

22. From an article in *Business Week:* "[I]n the past year, foreign purchases of stocks and bonds are down 24%, and foreign direct investment is off 63%.. . . And a key victim is the dollar, down 12% vs. the euro and 10% vs. the yen. . . ." From the U.S. point of view, do the changes mentioned in the first sentence represent an increase or a decrease in net foreign investment? Why would this change in net foreign investment cause the exchange value of the dollar to decline?

    Source: James C. Cooper and Kathleen Madigan, "The Twin Deficits Are Back—and as Dangerous as Ever," *Business Week,* July 8, 2002, pp. 29–30.

23. Lee Morgan, chairman of Caterpillar, was quoted in 1985 as saying this of his company's difficulties in exporting: "We believe that there should be a 25% to 30% improvement in the exchange rate with the Japanese yen, because U.S. manufacturers are finding themselves disadvantaged by that amount." When Morgan talked about an "improvement" in the exchange rate between the dollar and the yen, did he want the dollar to exchange for more yen or for fewer yen? Why was the exchange value of the dollar particularly high during the mid-1980s?

24. An economist remarks, "In the 1960s, fiscal policy would have been a better way to stabilize the economy, but now I believe that monetary policy is better." What has changed about the U.S. economy that might have led the economist to this conclusion?

25. Phil Treadway, president and owner of Erie Molded Plastics, Inc., which is located in Erie, Pennsylvania, and makes electrical connectors and plastic bottle caps, was quoted in the *New York Times*:

> Our customers have a market without borders, and we know that. We can compete against China's low labor costs. . . . But we cannot compete with them if they have a 20 percent to 40 percent currency advantage.

What does Treadway mean by a "currency advantage"? How would a currency advantage make it hard for his firm to compete with Chinese firms?

Source: Elizabeth Becker and Edmund L. Andrews, "Currency of China Is Emerging as Tough Business Issue in U.S.," *New York Times*, August 26, 2003.

26. The following headline appeared on an article in the *Wall Street Journal:* "Nintendo Says Strong Yen Will Cause 1st-Half Loss."
    a. What does the reporter mean by a "strong yen"?
    b. Why would the yen being strong cause a Japanese company to lose money?

Source: Dow Jones Newswires, "Nintendo Says Strong Yen Will Cause 1st-Half Loss," *Wall Street Journal*, October 3, 2003.

chapter eighteen

The International Financial System

Fluctuating Exchange Rates Push Molson Breweries to Sell the Canadiens

➤ Molson Breweries, a Canadian firm, purchased the Montreal Canadiens hockey team in 1957. In 2001, Molson sold the team to George Gillett, Jr., a U.S. citizen and owner of Booth Creek Resorts, which operates ski resorts in several U.S. states. The declining exchange rate of the Canadian dollar against the U.S. dollar was a key reason Molson sold the team.

The Canadiens are members of the National Hockey League (NHL), which is the primary professional hockey league in North America. Currently, the NHL has 6 teams based in Canada and 24 based in the United States. The NHL was formed in 1917 from the National Hockey Association, which consisted entirely of Canadian teams. Hockey is the national sport of Canada. As the *Economist* magazine explained, "Along with the health service, hockey is a cornerstone of Canadian identity." Unfortunately for hockey fans, the economic foundation of the NHL is shakier than that of other North American sports leagues, such as the National Football League, Major League Baseball, and the National Basketball Association—the last two of which also have Canadian teams. Modern professional sports leagues depend heavily on television contracts as a source of revenue. Unlike the other sports leagues, the NHL earns relatively little money from television and has for many years been without a contract to have its games regularly carried by one of the U.S. broadcast television networks. The NHL's financial difficulties led to disputes between teams and players that resulted in the cancellation of the 2004–2005 season.

In addition to the general financial difficulties facing the NHL, during the time Molson owned the Canadiens it also had to deal with a problem posed by a provision in the labor agreement between the NHL and its players. This agreement required Molson to pay the Canadiens players in U.S. dollars,

LEARNING OBJECTIVES

After studying this chapter, you should be able to:

① Understand how different exchange rate systems operate.

② Discuss the three key aspects of the current exchange rate system.

③ Discuss the growth of international capital markets.

rather than in Canadian dollars. Because many of the Canadiens games are played in the United States, many of the team's other expenses also had to be paid in U.S. dollars. Most of the team's revenues from ticket sales and local television and radio broadcasts, however, were received in Canadian dollars.

Unfortunately for Molson, the value of the Canadian dollar declined by more than 25 percent against the U.S. dollar during the last 10 years it owned the Canadiens. In 1991, one Canadian dollar exchanged for $0.87. By 2001, one Canadian dollar exchanged for only $0.65. In U.S. dollars, the total salary payroll for Canadiens players rose from $10 million in 1991 to $38 million in 2001. If the exchange rate between the Canadian and U.S. dollars remained the same in 2001 as it had been in 1991, the Canadiens payroll would have cost Molson 43.7 million Canadian dollars. Because of the decline in the value of the Canadian dollar, Molson actually had to pay 58.5 million to meet the Canadiens payroll. *An Inside Look* on page 590 discusses the effect of a rising exchange value of the euro on the profitability of European firms.

Source: "Lessons from a Lockout," *Economist*, July 21, 2005.

➤ A key fact about the international economy is that the exchange rates among the major currencies fluctuate. These fluctuations have important consequences for firms, consumers, and governments. In Chapter 17, we discussed the basics of how exchange rates are determined. We also looked at the relationship between a country's imports and exports, and at capital flows into and out of a country. In this chapter, we look further at the international financial system and at the role central banks play in the system.

① LEARNING OBJECTIVE

Understand how different exchange rate systems operate.

Exchange Rate Systems

A country's exchange rate can be determined in several ways. Some countries simply allow the exchange rate to be determined by demand and supply, just as other prices arc. A country that allows demand and supply to determine the value of its currency is said to have a **floating currency.** Some countries attempt to keep the exchange rate between their currency and another currency constant. For example, China kept the exchange rate constant between its currency, the yuan, and the U.S. dollar, until 2005 when it announced it would allow greater exchange-rate flexibility. When countries can agree on how exchange rates should be determined, economists say that there is an **exchange rate system.** Currently, many countries, including the United States, allow their currencies to float most of the time, although they will occasionally intervene to buy and sell their currency or other currencies to affect exchange rates. In other words, many countries attempt to *manage* the float of their currencies. As a result, the current exchange rate system is a **managed float exchange rate system.**

Floating currency The outcome of a country allowing its currency's exchange rate to be determined by demand and supply.

Exchange rate system An agreement among countries on how exchange rates should be determined.

Managed float exchange rate system The current exchange rate system under which the value of most currencies is determined by demand and supply, with occasional government intervention.

Fixed exchange rate system A system under which countries agree to keep the exchange rates among their currencies fixed.

Historically, the two most important alternatives to the managed float exchange rate system were the *gold standard* and the *Bretton Woods System.* These were both **fixed exchange rate systems** where exchange rates remained constant for long periods. Under the gold standard, a country's currency consisted of gold coins and paper currency that the government was committed to redeem for gold. When countries agree to keep the value of their currencies constant, there is a fixed exchange rate system. The gold standard was a fixed exchange rate system that lasted from the nineteenth century until the 1930s.

Under the gold standard, exchange rates were determined by the relative amounts of gold in each country's currency, and the size of a country's money supply was determined by the amount of gold available. To rapidly expand its money supply during a war or an economic depression, a country would need to abandon the gold standard. Because of the Great Depression, by the mid-1930s, most countries, including the United States, had abandoned the gold standard. Although during the following decades there were occasional discussions about restoring the gold standard, no serious attempt to do so occurred.

A conference held in Bretton Woods, New Hampshire, in 1944 set up an exchange rate system in which the United States pledged to buy or sell gold at a fixed price of $35 per ounce. The central banks of all other members of the new *Bretton Woods System* pledged to buy and sell their currencies at a fixed rate against the dollar. By fixing their exchange rates against the dollar, these countries were fixing the exchange rates among their currencies as well. Unlike under the gold standard, neither the United States, nor any other country, was willing to redeem its paper currency for gold domestically. The United States would redeem dollars for gold only if they were presented by a foreign central bank. Fixed exchange rate regimes can run into difficulties because exchange rates are not free to adjust quickly to changes in demand and supply for currencies. As we will see in the next section, central banks will often encounter difficulty if they are required to keep an exchange fixed over a period of years. By the early 1970s, the difficulty of keeping exchange rates fixed led to the end of the Bretton Woods System. The Appendix to this chapter contains additional discussion of the gold standard and the Bretton Woods System.

Don't Let This Happen To You!

Remember That Modern Currencies Are Fiat Money

Although the United States has not been on the gold standard since 1933, many people still believe that somehow gold continues to "back" U.S. currency. The U.S. Department of the Treasury still owns billions of dollars worth of gold bars, most of which are stored at the Fort Knox Bullion Depository in Kentucky. (Even more gold is stored in a basement of the Federal Reserve Bank of New York, which holds about one-quarter of the world's gold supply—almost 10 percent of all the gold ever mined. This gold, however, is entirely owned by foreign governments and international agencies.) The gold in Fort Knox no longer has any connection to the amount of paper money issued by the Federal Reserve. As we saw in Chapter 13, U.S. currency—like the currencies of other countries—is fiat money, which means it has no value except as money. The link between gold and money that existed for centuries has been broken in the modern economy.

***YOUR TURN:* Test your understanding by doing related problem 1 on page 593 at the end of this chapter.**

The Current Exchange Rate System

② LEARNING OBJECTIVE

Discuss the three key aspects of the current exchange rate system.

The current exchange rate system has three important aspects:

1. The United States allows the dollar to float against other major currencies.
2. Most countries in Western Europe have adopted a single currency, the **euro.**
3. Some developing countries have attempted to keep their currencies' exchange rates fixed against the dollar or another major currency.

Euro The common currency of many European countries.

We begin by looking at the changing value of the dollar over time. In discussing the value of the dollar, we can look further at what determines exchanges rates in the short run and in the long run.

The Floating Dollar

Since 1973, the value of the U.S. dollar has fluctuated widely against other major currencies. Panel (a) of Figure 18-1 shows the exchange rate between the U.S. dollar and the

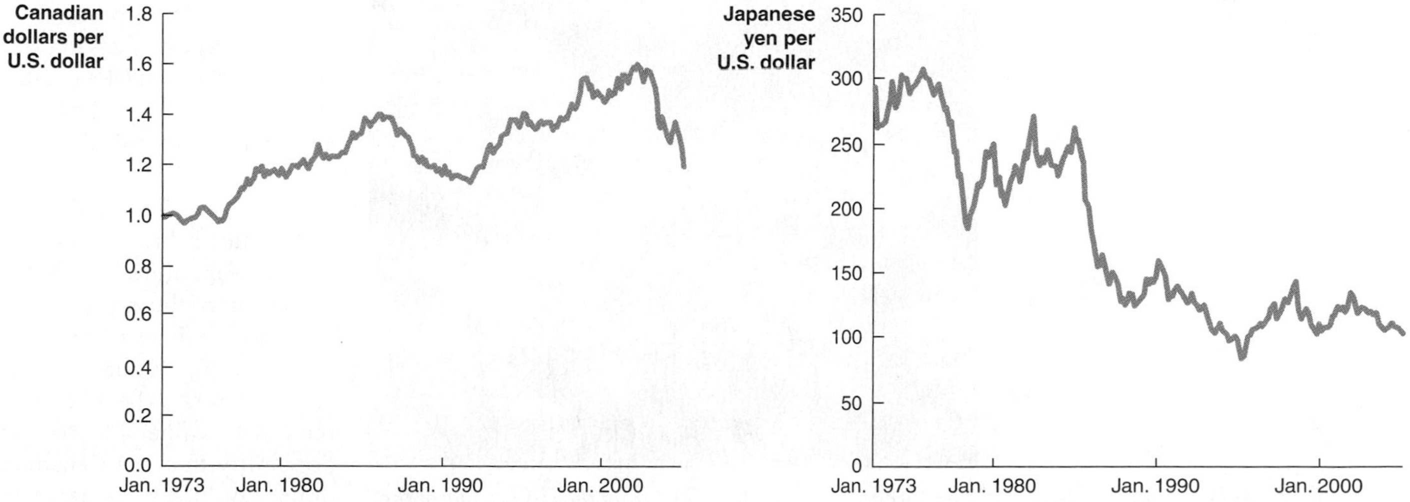

(a) The exchange rate between the Canadian dollar and the U.S. dollar

(b) The exchange rate between the Japanese yen and the U.S. dollar

FIGURE 18-1 U.S. Dollar–Canadian Dollar and U.S. Dollar–Yen Exchange Rates,1973–2004

Panel (a) shows that since the end of the Bretton Woods System in 1973, the U.S. dollar has gained value against the Canadian dollar. Panel (b) shows that during the same period the U.S. dollar has lost value against the Japanese yen.

Source: Federal Reserve data.

Canadian dollar between 1973 and 2004, and panel (b) shows the exchange rate between the U.S. dollar and the Japanese yen for the same years. Remember that the dollar increases in value when it takes more units of foreign currency to buy one dollar and falls in value when it takes fewer units of foreign currency to buy one dollar. From the beginning of 1973 to the end of 2004, the U.S. dollar lost about 65 percent in value against the yen, while increasing about 20 percent in value against the Canadian dollar.

18-1 Making the Connection

The Toronto Blue Jays Gain from the Rising Value of the Canadian Dollar

In December 2000, the Canadian firm Rogers Communications, Inc., purchased the Toronto Blue Jays baseball team from Interbrew, a Canadian beer company. Rogers is based in Toronto and is the largest provider of cable television in Canada. We saw at the beginning of this chapter that Molson Breweries was hurt as the value of the Canadian dollar declined against the U.S. dollar for most of the period from 1991 to 2001 during which Molson owned the Montreal Canadiens ice hockey team. A close look at panel (a) of Figure 18-1 shows that Rogers was in a much better situation than Molson because after 2000 the number of Canadian dollars necessary to buy one U.S. dollar was declining—that is, the value of the Canadian dollar was rising. When Rogers bought the Blue Jays in December 2000, one Canadian dollar exchanged for $0.66. By July 2005, one Canadian dollar exchanged for $0.81, an increase of more than 20 percent.

Like the Canadiens, the Blue Jays have to pay their players in U.S. dollars and, because all of the other major league baseball teams play in the United States, most of the Blue Jays' expenses for travel and lodging for their players also must be paid in dollars. In 2005, the total salary payroll for Blue Jays players was $45 million. If the exchange rate between the Canadian and U.S. dollars had remained what it had been in December 2000, the Blue Jays payroll would have cost Rogers 68.2 million Canadian dollars. Because the Canadian dollar had risen in value against the U.S. dollar, Rogers actually only had to pay 55.6 million Canadian dollars. Rogers' other U.S. dollar expenses for the Blue Jays were correspondingly lower, and the firm benefited from the rise in the value of the Canadian dollar in other ways as well. The Blue Jays play spring training games in Dunedin, Florida. The high value of the Canadian dollar led many more Canadians to travel to Florida and buy tickets to these games. Between 2004 and 2005 alone, ticket sales rose by nearly 33 percent. Overall, the Blue Jays improved from losing 71 million Canadian dollars in 2001 to nearly breaking even in 2005. A team official attributed 70 percent of the improvement in the team's financial situation to the stronger Canadian dollar. Of course, the Blue Jays remained vulnerable to the possibility that the Canadian dollar could decline again in value.

The Toronto Blue Jays benefited from the rising value of the Canadian dollar.

Sources: Rob Neyer, "Good Young Pitchers in Toronto's System," ESPN.com, August 8, 2005; and Alan Snel, "Spring-ing Back," *Tampa Tribune*, March 14, 2005.

What Determines Exchange Rates in the Long Run?

Over the past 30 years, why did the value of the U.S. dollar fall against the Japanese yen but rise against the Canadian dollar? In the short run, the two most important causes of exchange rate movements are changes in interest rates—which cause investors to change their views of which countries' financial investments will yield the highest returns—and changes in investors' expectations about the future values of currencies. Over the long run, other factors are important in explaining movements in exchange rates.

THE THEORY OF PURCHASING POWER PARITY It seems reasonable that, in the long run, exchange rates should be at a level that makes it possible to buy the same amount of goods and services with the equivalent amount of any country's currency. In other words, the purchasing power of every country's currency should be the same. The idea that in the long run exchange rates move to equalize the purchasing power of different currencies is referred to as the theory of **purchasing power parity.**

Purchasing power parity The theory that in the long run exchange rates move to equalize the purchasing power of different currencies.

To make the theory of purchasing power parity clearer, consider a simple example. Suppose that a Hershey's candy bar has a price of \$1 in the United States and £1 in the United Kingdom and that the exchange rate is one dollar per pound. In that case, at least with respect to candy bars, the dollar and the pound have equivalent purchasing power. If the price of a Hershey bar increases to £2 in the United Kingdom but stays at \$1 in the United States, the exchange rate will have to change to two pounds per dollar in order for the pound to maintain its relative purchasing power. As long as this happens, it will be possible to buy a Hershey bar for \$1 in the United States or to exchange \$1 for £2 and buy the candy bar in the United Kingdom.

If exchange rates are not at the values indicated by purchasing power parity, it appears that there are opportunities to make profits. For example, suppose a Hershey's candy bar sells for £2 in the United Kingdom and \$1 in the United States, and the exchange rate between the dollar and the pound is £1 = \$1. In this case, it would be possible to exchange one million pounds for one million dollars and use the dollars to buy one million Hershey bars in the United States. The Hershey bars could then be shipped to the United Kingdom where they could be sold for two million pounds. The result of these transactions would be a profit of one million pounds. In fact, if the dollar-pound exchange rate does not reflect the purchasing power for many products—not just Hershey bars—this process could be repeated until extremely large profits were made. In practice, though, as people attempted to make these profits by exchanging pounds for dollars they would bid up the value of the dollar until it reached the purchasing power exchange rate of £2 = \$1. Once the exchange rate reflected the purchasing power of the two currencies, there would be no further opportunities for profit.

Three real-world complications keep purchasing power parity from being a complete explanation of exchange rates, even in the long run:

- ***Not all products can be traded internationally.*** Where goods are traded internationally, profits can be made whenever exchange rates do not reflect their purchasing power parity values. However, more than half of all goods and services produced in the United States and most other countries are not traded internationally. When goods are not traded internationally, their prices will not be the same in every country. For instance, suppose that the exchange rate is one pound for one dollar but the price for having a tooth filled by a dentist is twice as high in the United States as it is in the United Kingdom. In this case, there is no way to buy up the low-priced British service and resell it in the United States. Because many goods and services are not traded internationally, exchange rates will not reflect exactly the relative purchasing powers of currencies.
- ***Products and consumer preferences are different across countries.*** We expect the same product to sell for the same price around the world, but if a product is similar but not identical to another product, their prices might be different. For example, a three-ounce Hershey's candy bar may sell for a different price than a three-ounce

Cadbury's candy bar. Prices of the same product may also differ across countries if consumer preferences differ. If consumers in Britain like candy bars more than consumers in the United States do, a Hershey's candy bar may sell for more in Britain than in the United States.

➤ ***Countries impose barriers to trade.*** Most countries, including the United States, impose **tariffs** and **quotas** on imported goods. A quota is a limit on the quantity of a good that can be imported. For example, the United States has a quota on imports of sugar. As a result, the price of sugar in the United States is much higher than the price of sugar in other countries. Because of the quota, there is no way to buy up the cheap foreign sugar and resell it in the United States.

Tariff A tax imposed by a government on imports.

Quota A limit on the quantity of a good that can be imported.

18-2 Making the Connection

The Big Mac Theory of Exchange Rates

In a lighthearted attempt to test the accuracy of the theory of purchasing power parity, the *Economist* magazine regularly compares the prices of Big Macs in different countries. If purchasing power parity holds, you should be able to take the dollars required to buy a Big Mac in the United States and exchange them for exactly the amount of foreign currency needed to buy a Big Mac in any other country. The following table is for June 2005, when Big Macs were selling for an average of $3.06 in the United States. The implied exchange rate shows what the exchange rate would be if purchasing power parity held for Big Macs. For example, a Big Mac sold for ¥250 in Japan and $3.06 in the United States, so for purchasing power parity to hold the exchange rate should have been ¥250/$3.06, or ¥82 = $1. The actual exchange rate in June 2005 was ¥107 = $1. So, on Big Mac purchasing power parity grounds, the yen was *undervalued* against the dollar by 23 percent (((¥107—¥82)/¥107) × 100 = 23 percent). That is, if Big Mac purchasing power parity held, it would have taken 23 percent fewer yen to buy a dollar than it actually did.

Could you take advantage of this difference between the purchasing power parity exchange rate and the actual exchange rate to become fabulously wealthy by buying up low-priced Big Macs in Tokyo and reselling them at a higher price in San Francisco? Unfortunately, the low-priced Japanese Big Macs would be a soggy mess by the time you got them to San Francisco. The fact that Big Mac prices are not the same around the world illustrates one reason why purchasing power parity does not hold exactly.

Is the price of a Big Mac in Finland the same as the price of a Big Mac in Chicago?

COUNTRY	BIG MAC PRICE	IMPLIED EXCHANGE RATE	ACTUAL EXCHANGE RATE
Argentina	4.74 pesos	1.55 pesos per dollar	2.89 pesos per dollar
Japan	250 yen	82 yen per dollar	107 yen per dollar
Britain	1.88 pounds	0.61 pound per dollar	0.55 pound per dollar
Switzerland	6.30 Swiss francs	2.06 Swiss francs per dollar	1.25 Swiss francs per dollar
Indonesia	14,599 rupiahs	4,771 rupiahs per dollar	9,542 rupiahs per dollar
Canada	3.27 Canadian dollars	1.07 Canadian dollars per U.S. dollar	1.24 Canadian dollars per U.S. dollar

Source: Authors' calculations from "The Economist's Big Mac Index," *Economist*, June 9, 2005.

SOLVED PROBLEM 18-1

Calculating Purchasing Power Parity Exchange Rates Using Big Macs

② LEARNING OBJECTIVE

Discuss the three key aspects of the current exchange rate system.

Fill in the missing values in the following table. Remember that the implied exchange rate shows what the exchange rate would be if purchasing power parity held for Big Macs. Assume that the Big Mac is selling for $3.06 in the United States. Explain whether the U.S. dollar is overvalued or undervalued relative to each currency and predict what will happen in the future to each exchange rate. Finally, calculate the implied exchange rate between the Polish zloty and the Brazilian real and explain which currency is overvalued in terms of Big Mac purchasing power parity.

COUNTRY	BIG MAC PRICE	IMPLIED EXCHANGE RATE	ACTUAL EXCHANGE RATE
Brazil	5.91 reals		2.47 reals per dollar
Poland	6.49 zlotys		3.31 zlotys per dollar
South Korea	2,500 won		1,004 won per dollar
Czech Republic	56.30 korunas		24.5 korunas per dollar

Solving the Problem:

Step 1: Review the chapter material. This problem is about the theory of purchasing power parity as illustrated by prices of Big Macs, so you may want to review the sections "The Theory of Purchasing Power Parity," which begins on page 577, and Making the Connection 18-2, "The Big Mac Theory of Exchange Rates," which begins on page 578.

Step 2: Fill in the table. To calculate the purchasing power exchange rate, divide the foreign currency price of a Big Mac by the U.S. price. For example, the implied exchange rate between the Brazilian real and the U.S. dollar is 5.91 reals/$3.06 or 1.93 reals per dollar.

COUNTRY	BIG MAC PRICE	IMPLIED EXCHANGE RATE	ACTUAL EXCHANGE RATE
Brazil	5.91 reals	1.93 reals per dollar	2.47 reals per dollar
Poland	6.49 zlotys	2.12 zlotys per dollar	3.31 zlotys per dollar
South Korea	2,500 won	817 won per dollar	1,004 won per dollar
Czech Republic	56.30 korunas	18.4 korunas per dollar	24.5 korunas per dollar

Step 3: Explain whether the U.S. dollar is overvalued or undervalued against the other currencies. The dollar is overvalued if the actual exchange rate is greater than the implied exchange rate. In this case, the dollar is overvalued against all four of these currencies. This overvaluation would lead us to predict that the value of the dollar should fall in the future.

Step 4: Calculate the implied exchange rate between the zloty and the real. The implied exchange rate between the zloty and the real is 6.49 zlotys/5.91 reals, or 1.10 zlotys per real. We can calculate the actual exchange rate by taking the ratio of zlotys per dollar to reals per dollar: 3.31 zlotys/2.47 reals, or 1.34 zlotys per real. The zloty is undervalued relative to the real.

Extra Credit: Because the Big Mac is a nontraded good, it's not surprising that prices differ from country to country. Nevertheless, the fact that comparing Big Mac prices indicates that the dollar was overvalued relative to the currencies of most countries is at least a small piece of evidence that the dollar was likely to decline in the period after June 2005.

Source: Authors' calculations from "The Economist's Big Mac Index," *Economist,* June 9, 2005.

YOUR TURN: **For more practice, do related problem 7 on page 593 at the end of this chapter.**

THE FOUR DETERMINANTS OF EXCHANGE RATES IN THE LONG RUN We can take into account the shortcomings of the theory of purchasing power parity to develop a more complete explanation of how exchange rates are determined in the long run. There are four main determinants of exchange rates in the long run:

- *Relative price levels.* The purchasing power parity theory is correct in arguing that in the long run the most important determinant of exchange rates between two countries' currencies is their relative price levels. If prices of goods and services rise faster in Canada than in the United States, the value of the Canadian dollar has to decline to maintain demand for Canadian products. Over the past 30 years, prices in Canada have risen faster on average than prices in the United States, while prices in Japan have risen more slowly. This difference in inflation rates is a key reason the U.S. dollar has gained value against the Canadian dollar while losing value against the Japanese yen.
- *Relative rates of productivity growth.* When the productivity of a firm increases, it is able to produce more goods and services using fewer workers, machines, or other inputs. The firm's costs of production fall, and usually so will the price of its product. If the average productivity of Japanese firms increases faster than the average productivity of U.S. firms, Japanese products will have relatively lower prices than U.S. products, which increases the quantity demanded of Japanese products relative to U.S. products. As a result, the value of the yen should rise against the dollar. For most of the period from the early 1970s to the early 1990s, Japanese productivity increased faster than U.S. productivity, which contributed to the fall in the value of the dollar versus the yen. However, between 1992 and 2005, U.S. productivity increased faster than Japanese productivity.
- *Preferences for domestic and foreign goods.* If consumers in Canada increase their preferences for U.S. products, the demand for U.S. dollars will increase relative to the demand for Canadian dollars, and the U.S. dollar will increase in value relative to the Canadian dollar. During the 1970s and 1980s, many U.S. consumers increased their preferences for Japanese products, particularly automobiles and consumer electronics. This greater preference for Japanese products helped to increase the value of the yen relative to the dollar.
- *Tariffs and quotas.* The U.S. sugar quota forces firms like Hershey Foods Corporation to buy expensive U.S. sugar rather than less expensive foreign sugar. The quota increases the demand for dollars relative to the currencies of foreign sugar producers and, therefore, leads to a higher exchange rate. Changes in tariffs and quotas have not been a significant factor in explaining trends in the U.S. dollar–Canadian dollar or U.S. dollar–yen exchange rates.

Because these four factors change over time, one country's currency can increase or decrease by substantial amounts in the long run. These changes in exchange rates can create problems for firms. A decline in the value of a country's currency lowers the foreign currency prices of the country's exports and increases the prices of imports. An increase in the value of a country's currency has the reverse effect. However, the effect of exchange rate fluctuations on a firm can be complex. For example, the decline in the value of the Canadian dollar against the U.S. dollar has helped Molson Breweries in exporting beer to the United States. But, as we saw at the beginning of this chapter, the declining value of the Canadian dollar also reduced the profitability of the Montreal Canadiens hockey team that Molson owned.

The Euro

A second key aspect of the current exchange rate system is that most Western European countries have adopted a single currency. After World War II, many of the countries of

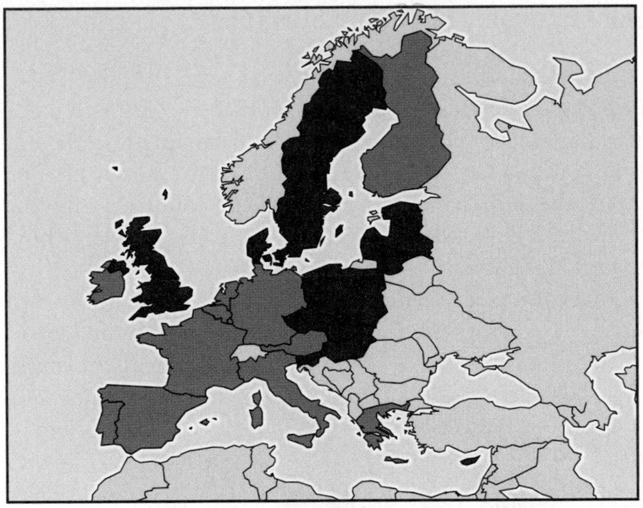

FIGURE 18-2

Countries Adopting the Euro

The 12 member countries of the European Union that have adopted the euro as their common currency as of 2005 are shaded in blue. The members of the EU that have not adopted the euro are shaded in red.

Western Europe wanted to more closely integrate their economies. In 1957, Belgium, France, West Germany, Italy, Luxembourg, and the Netherlands signed the Treaty of Rome, which established the European Economic Community, often referred to as the European Common Market. Tariffs and quotas on products being shipped within the Common Market were greatly reduced. Over the years, Britain, Sweden, Denmark, Finland, Austria, Greece, Ireland, Spain, and Portugal joined the European Economic Community, which was renamed the European Union (EU) in 1991. By 2005, 25 countries were members of the EU.

EU members decided to move to a common currency by 1999. Three of the 15 countries that were then members of the EU—the United Kingdom, Denmark, and Sweden—decided to retain their domestic currencies. The move to a common currency took place in several stages. On January 1, 1999, the exchange rates of the 12 participating countries were permanently fixed against each other and against the common currency, the *euro*. At first the euro was a pure *unit of account*. Although firms began quoting prices in both domestic currency and euros, no euro currency was actually in circulation. On January 1, 2002, euro coins and paper currency were introduced, and on June 1, 2002, the old domestic currencies were withdrawn from circulation. Figure 18-2 shows the countries in the EU that have adopted the euro.

A new European Central Bank (ECB) was also established. Although the central banks of the member countries continue to exist, the ECB has assumed responsibility for monetary policy and for issuing currency. The ECB is run by a governing council that consists of a six-member executive board—appointed by the participating governments—and the 12 governors of the central banks of the member countries that have adopted the euro. The ECB represents a unique experiment in allowing a multinational organization to control the domestic monetary policies of independent countries.

Economists are divided over whether the creation of the euro will help growth in the EU countries. Having a common currency makes it easier for consumers and firms to buy and sell across borders. It is no longer necessary for someone in France to exchange francs for marks in order to do business in Germany. This change should reduce costs and increase competition. However, the participating countries are no longer able to run independent monetary policies. In addition, with fixed exchange rates, the value of one country's currency cannot fall during a recession, thereby expanding net exports to help revive aggregate demand. The experiences of the countries using the euro will provide economists with additional information on the costs and benefits to countries from using the same currency.

18-3 Making the Connection

The Underground Economy in Europe Surfaces

In Europe, as elsewhere around the world, people who are engaged in illegal activities or who want to avoid paying taxes prefer to use cash, rather than checks or credit cards. This type of activity is known as the *underground economy.* Some participants in the underground economy accumulate huge amounts of cash. The adoption of the euro caused problems for these people. By June 2002, the domestic currencies of the 12 countries adopting the euro would no longer be accepted by legitimate firms. As a result, people with large holdings of currency rushed to redeem them for euros.

The German government estimated that as much as 30 billion deutsche marks (or about $14 billion) surfaced from the underground economy to be redeemed. Because the deutsche mark had been widely used outside of Germany, particularly in central Europe and Turkey, German customs agents discovered many stashes of currency during routine customs checks at the German border. Failing to declare that you were bringing currency into Germany could result in a fine of 50 percent of the currency. Despite this, many people were caught smuggling currency. Apparently, they preferred to run the risk of being fined rather than reveal how they had obtained the currency.

Smugglers rushed to exchange national currencies for euros before the June 2002 deadline.

Source: Edmund L. Andrews, "Euro's Entry Is Forcing Europe's Hidden Hoards to Surface," *New York Times,* September 6, 2001.

Pegging against the Dollar

A final key aspect of the current exchange rate system is that some developing countries have attempted to keep their exchange rates fixed against the dollar or another major currency. Having a fixed exchange rate can provide important advantages for a country that has extensive trade with another country. When the exchange rate is fixed, business planning becomes much easier. For instance, if the South Korean won increases in value relative to the dollar, Hyundai, the Korean car manufacturer, may have to raise the dollar price of cars it exports to the United States, thereby reducing sales. If the exchange rate between the Korean won and the dollar is fixed, Hyundai's planning is much easier.

In the 1980s and 1990s, an additional reason for having fixed exchange rates developed. During those decades the flow of foreign investment funds to developing countries, particularly those in East Asia, increased substantially. It became possible for firms in countries such as Korea, Thailand, Malaysia, and Indonesia to borrow dollars directly from foreign investors or indirectly from foreign banks. For example, a Thai firm might borrow U.S. dollars from a Japanese bank. If the Thai firm wants to build a new factory in Thailand with the borrowed dollars, it has to exchange the dollars for the equivalent amount of Thai currency, the baht. Once the factory opens and production begins, the Thai firm will be earning the additional baht it needs to exchange for dollars to make the interest payments on the loan. A problem arises if the value of the baht falls against the dollar. Suppose that the exchange rate is 25 baht per dollar when the loan is taken out. A Thai firm making an interest payment of $100,000 dollars per month on a dollar loan could buy the necessary dollars for 2.5 million baht. But if the value of the baht declines to 50 baht to the dollar, it would take 5 million baht to buy the dollars necessary to make the interest payment. These increased payments might be a crushing burden for the Thai firm. The government of Thailand would have a strong incentive to avoid this problem by keeping the exchange rate between the baht and the dollar fixed.

Finally, some countries feared the inflationary consequences of a floating exchange rate. When the value of a currency falls, the prices of imports rise. If imports are a significant fraction of the goods consumers buy, a fall in the value of the currency may significantly increase the inflation rate. During the 1990s, an important part of Brazil's and Argentina's anti-inflation policies was a fixed exchange rate against the dollar. (As we will see, though, there are difficulties with following a fixed exchange rate policy, and, ultimately, both Brazil and Argentina abandoned fixed exchange rates.)

THE EAST ASIAN EXCHANGE RATE CRISIS OF THE LATE 1990s When a country keeps its currency's exchange rate fixed against another country's currency, it is **pegging** its currency. It is not necessary for both countries involved in a peg to agree to it. When a developing country has pegged the value of its currency against the dollar, the responsibility for maintaining the peg has been entirely with the developing country.

Pegging The decision by a country to keep the exchange rate fixed between its currency and another currency.

Countries attempting to maintain a peg can run into problems, however. We saw in Chapter 4 that when the government fixes the price of a good or service, the result can be persistent surpluses or shortages. Figure 18-3 shows the exchange rate between the dollar and the Thai baht. The figure is drawn from the Thai point of view, so we measure the exchange rate on the vertical axis as dollars per baht. The figure represents the situation in the 1990s when the government of Thailand pegged the exchange rate between the dollar and the baht above the equilibrium exchange rate as determined by demand and supply. A currency pegged at a value above the market equilibrium exchange rate is said to be *overvalued.* A currency pegged at a value below the market equilibrium exchange rate is said to be *undervalued.*

Pegging made it easier for Thai firms to export products to the United States and protected Thai firms that had taken out dollar loans. The pegged exchange rate was 25.19 baht to the dollar, or about $0.04 to the baht. By 1997, this exchange rate was well above the market equilibrium exchange rate of 35 baht to the dollar, or about $0.03 to the baht. The result was a surplus of baht on the foreign exchange market. To keep the exchange rate at the pegged level, the Thai central bank, the Bank of Thailand, had to buy these baht with dollars. In buying baht with dollars, the Bank of Thailand gradually used up its dollar reserves. To continue supporting the pegged exchange rate, the Bank of Thailand borrowed additional dollar reserves from the International Monetary Fund

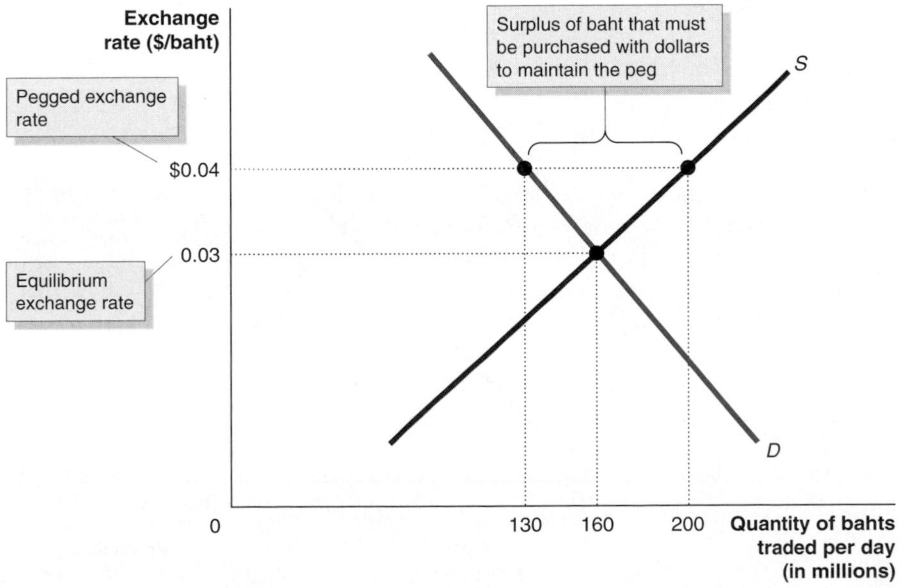

FIGURE 18-3

By 1997 the Thai Baht Was Overvalued against the Dollar

The government of Thailand pegged the value of the baht against the dollar to make it easier for Thai firms to export to the United States and to protect Thai firms that had taken out dollar loans. The pegged exchange rate of $0.04 per baht was well above the equilibrium exchange rate of $0.03 per baht. In the example in this figure, the overvalued exchange rate created a surplus of 70 million baht, which had to be purchased with dollars by the Thai central bank.

(IMF). It also raised interest rates to attract more foreign investors to investments in Thailand, thereby increasing the demand for the baht.

Although higher domestic interest rates helped attract foreign investors, they made it more difficult for Thai firms and households to borrow the funds they needed to finance their spending. As a consequence, domestic investment and consumption declined, pushing the Thai economy into recession. International investors realized that there were limits to how high the Bank of Thailand would be willing to push interest rates and how many dollar loans the IMF would be willing to extend to Thailand. They began to speculate against the baht by exchanging baht for dollars at the official, pegged exchange rate. If, as they expected, Thailand was forced to abandon the peg, they would be able to buy back the baht at a much lower exchange rate, making a substantial profit. Because these actions by investors make it more difficult to maintain a fixed exchange rate, they are referred to as *destabilizing speculation*. Figure 18-4 shows the results of this destabilizing speculation. The decreased demand for baht shifted the demand curve for baht from D_1 to D_2, increasing the quantity of baht the Bank of Thailand needed to buy in exchange for dollars.

Foreign investors also began to sell off their investments in Thailand and exchange the baht they received for dollars. This *capital flight* forced the Bank of Thailand to quickly run through its dollar reserves. Dollar loans from the IMF temporarily allowed Thailand to defend the pegged exchange rate. Finally, on July 2, 1997, Thailand abandoned its pegged exchange rate against the dollar and allowed the baht to float. Thai firms that had borrowed dollars were now faced with interest payments that were much higher than they had planned. Many firms were forced into bankruptcy, and the Thai economy plunged into a deep recession.

Many currency traders became convinced that other East Asian countries, such as South Korea, Indonesia, and Malaysia, would have to follow Thailand and abandon their pegged exchange rates. The result was a wave of speculative selling of these countries' currencies. These waves of selling—sometimes referred to as *speculative attacks*—were difficult for countries to fight off. Even if a country's currency was not initially overvalued at the pegged exchange rate, the speculative attacks would cause a large reduction in the demand for its currency. The demand curve for its currency would shift to the left, which would force the country's central bank to quickly run through its dollar reserves. Within the space of a few months, South Korea, Indonesia, the Philippines, and Malaysia abandoned their pegged currencies. All these countries also plunged into recession.

FIGURE 18-4

Destabilizing Speculation against the Thai Baht

In 1997, the pegged exchange rate of \$0.04 = 1 baht was above the equilibrium exchange rate of \$0.03 = 1 baht. As investors became convinced that Thailand would have to abandon its pegged exchange against the dollar and allow the value of the baht to fall, they decreased their demand for baht from D_1 to D_2. The new equilibrium exchange rate became \$0.02 = 1 baht. This increased the quantity of baht the Bank of Thailand had to purchase in exchange for dollars from 70 million per day to 140 million to defend the pegged exchange rate. The *destabilizing speculation* by investors caused Thailand to abandon its pegged exchange rate in July 1997.

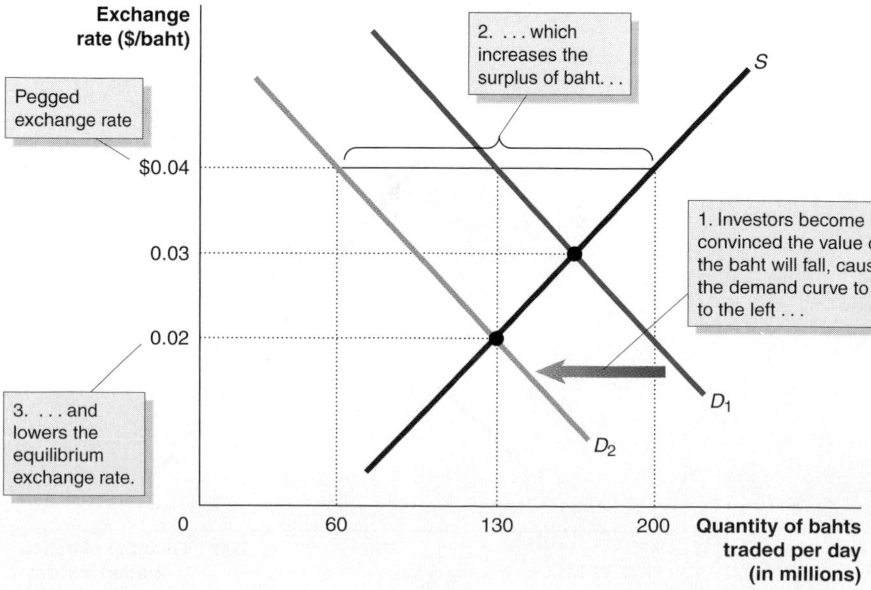

THE DECLINE IN PEGGING Following the disastrous events experienced by the East Asian countries, the number of countries with pegged exchange rates declined sharply. Most countries that continue to use pegged exchange rates are small and trade primarily with one other much larger country. So, for instance, several Caribbean countries continue to peg against the dollar, and several former French colonies in Africa that formerly pegged against the French franc now peg against the euro. Overall, the trend has been toward replacing pegged exchange rates with managed floating exchange rates.

THE CHINESE EXPERIENCE WITH PEGGING As we discussed in Chapter 10, in 1978, China began to move away from central planning and toward a market system. The result was a sharp acceleration in economic growth. Real GDP per capita grew at a rate of 6.5 percent per year between 1979 and 1995, and at the very rapid rate of 9.1 percent per year between 1996 and 2004. An important part of Chinese economic policy was the decision in 1994 to peg the value of the Chinese currency, the yuan, to the dollar at a fixed rate of 8.28 yuan to the dollar. Pegging against the dollar ensured that Chinese exporters would face stable dollar prices for the goods they sold in the United States. By the early 2000s, many economists argued that the yuan was undervalued against the dollar, possibly significantly so.

To support the undervalued exchange rate, the Chinese central bank had to buy large amounts of dollars with yuan. By 2005, the Chinese government had accumulated more than $700 billion, most of which it had used to buy U.S. Treasury bonds. In addition, China was coming under pressure from its trading partners to allow the yuan to increase in value. As we saw in Chapter 17, Chinese exports of textile products were driving some textile producers out of business in Japan, the United States, and Europe. China has also begun to export more sophisticated products, including televisions, personal computers, and cell phones. Politicians in other countries were anxious to protect their domestic industries from Chinese competition, even if the result was higher prices for domestic consumers. The Chinese government was reluctant to revalue the yuan, however, because it believed high levels of exports were needed to maintain rapid economic growth. The Chinese economy needs to create as many as 20 million new nonagricultural jobs per year to keep up with population growth and the shift of workers from rural areas to cities. Because of China's large holdings of dollars, it will also incur significant losses if the yuan increases in value.

By July 2005, the pressure on China to revalue the yuan had become too great. The government announced that it would switch from pegging the yuan against the dollar to linking the value of the yuan to the average value of a basket of currencies that would include the dollar, the Japanese yen, the euro, the Korean won, and several other currencies. The immediate effect was a fairly small increase in the value of the yuan from 8.28 to the dollar to 8.11 to the dollar. The Chinese central bank declared that it had switched from a peg to a managed floating exchange rate. Some economists and policymakers were skeptical, however, that much had actually changed because the initial increase in the value of yuan had been small and because the Chinese central bank did not explain the details of how the yuan would be linked to the basket of other currencies. It remained to be seen whether in practice the value of the yuan would be more responsive to changes in demand and supply in the foreign exchange markets.

Crisis and Recovery in South Korea

18-4 Making the Connection

Korea spent the first part of the twentieth century as a colony of Japan. In 1945, at the end of World War II, Korea was divided into Communist North Korea and democratic South Korea. North Korea's invasion of South Korea in June 1950 set off the Korean War, which devastated South Korea, before ending in 1953. Despite these difficult beginnings, by the 1960s the South Korean economy was growing rapidly. As one of the *newly industrializing countries,* South Korea was a model for other developing countries.

To make it easier for firms like Hyundai to export to the United States and to protect firms that had taken out dollar loans, the South Korean government pegged the value of its currency, the won, to the U.S. dollar. Following Thailand's decision in July 1997 to abandon its peg, large-scale destabilizing speculation took place against the won. Foreign investors scrambled to sell their investments in Korea and to convert their won into dollars. South Korea was unable to defend the peg and allowed the won to float in October 1997.

Like other countries that underwent an exchange-rate crisis, South Korea had attempted to maintain the value of the won by raising domestic interest rates. The result was a sharp decline in aggregate demand and a severe recession. However, unlike other East Asian countries—particularly Thailand and Indonesia—that made only slow progress in recovering from exchange-rate crises, South Korea bounced back rapidly. The figure shows that after experiencing falling real GDP through 1999, South Korea quickly returned to high rates of growth.

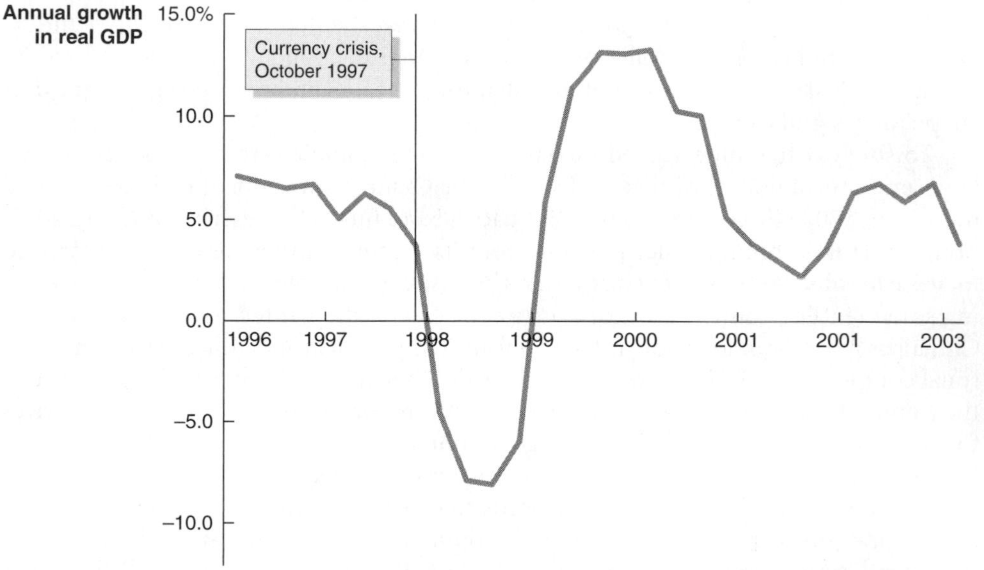

Sources: Data in figure from Korea National Statistical Office, and Jahyeong Koo and Sherry L. Kiser, "Recovery from a Financial Crisis: The Case of South Korea," Federal Reserve Bank of Dallas *Economic and Financial Review,* Fourth Quarter 2001.

Why was the performance of South Korea so much better than that of other East Asian countries? Jahyeong Koo and Sherry L. Kiser, economists at the Federal Reserve Bank of Dallas, cite several factors:

- South Korea benefited from a $21 billion loan from the IMF in December 1997. This loan helped stabilize the value of the won.
- Even though South Korean banks were badly hurt in the crisis and cut back their

The South Korean economy was able to rapidly recover from the late 1990s currency crisis.

loans, South Korean firms were able to obtain financing for investment projects from the stock and bond markets.

- The South Korean labor market was flexible enough to allow wage reductions, which offset some of the negative impact of the crisis on corporate profits.

South Korean firms remain saddled with large debts, and the Korean banking system has yet to fully recover. But South Korea was able to emerge from its exchange rate crisis without suffering the political and social upheavals that occurred in countries such as Indonesia.

SOLVED PROBLEM 18-2

Coping with Fluctuations in the Value of the U.S. Dollar

(2) LEARNING OBJECTIVE
Discuss the three key aspects of the current exchange rate system.

Analyze the following excerpt from an article in the *New York Times:*

> Some economists say that if the flow of capital into the United States dries up, the dollar could fall sharply in value, reigniting the threat of inflation and putting pressure on the Fed to raise interest rates.

Use a foreign exchange market graph in your analysis and be sure to explain what the value of the dollar has to do with the U.S. inflation rate, as well as why a falling value of the dollar puts pressure on the Fed to raise interest rates.

Solving the Problem:
Step 1: Review the chapter material. This problem is about the determinants of exchange rates, so you may want to review the section "The Current Exchange Rate System," which begins on page 575.

Step 2: Draw the graph. Begin by drawing a diagram to show the effect of a decline in the flow of capital into the United States. "Flow of capital into the United States" refers to foreign investors engaging in portfolio investment—buying U.S. stocks and bonds—or direct investment—building factories in the United States. To invest in the United States, foreign investors must exchange their currencies for dollars. If they decide to cut back on investing in the United States, their demand for dollars will fall. This reduction is shown in the following figure by the shift from D_1 to D_2. The equilibrium exchange falls from ¥130 = $1 to ¥120 = $1.

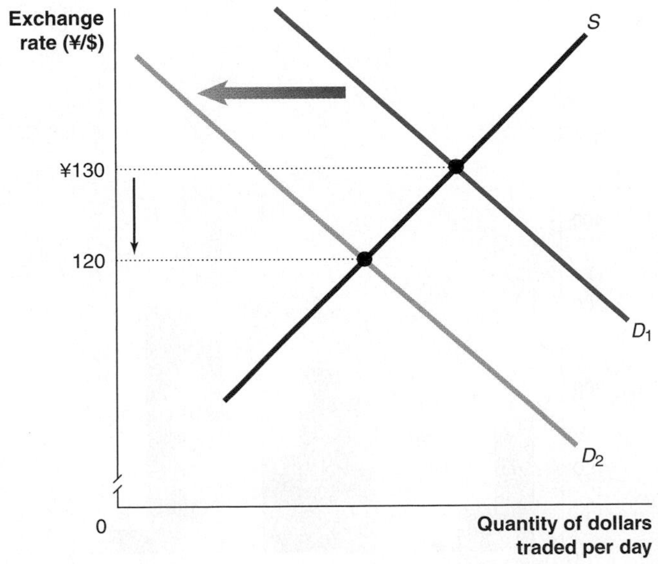

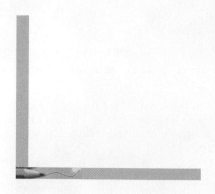

Step 3: Explain why a falling value of the dollar puts pressure on the Fed to raise interest rates. If the value of the dollar falls, the prices of imports will rise. Rising import prices add to the inflation rate. If the Fed wants to increase the value of the dollar (or keep it from falling further), it would raise interest rates to make U.S. financial investments more attractive to foreign investors. In the graph, this would result in shifting the demand for dollars back to the right.

Source: Excerpt from Richard W. Stevenson, "Dollar Falls as Top Official Casts Doubts on Intervention," *New York Times,* May 2, 2002.

YOUR TURN: **For more practice, do related problem 20 on page 594 at the end of this chapter.**

③ LEARNING OBJECTIVE

Discuss the growth of international capital markets.

International Capital Markets

One important reason exchange rates fluctuate is that investors seek out the best investments they can find anywhere in the world. For instance, if Chinese investors increase their demand for U.S. Treasury bills, the demand for dollars will increase, and the value of the dollar will rise. But if interest rates in the United States decline, foreign investors may sell U.S. investments and the value of the dollar will fall.

Shares of stock and long-term debt, including corporate and government bonds and bank loans, are bought and sold on *capital markets.* Before 1980, most U.S. corporations raised funds only in U.S. stock and bond markets or from U.S. banks. U.S. investors rarely invested in foreign capital markets. In the 1980s and 1990s, European governments removed many restrictions on foreign investments in financial markets. It became possible for U.S. and other foreign investors to freely invest in Europe and for European investors to freely invest in foreign markets. Improvements in communications and computer technology made it possible for U.S. investors to receive better and more timely information about foreign firms and for foreign investors to receive better information about U.S. firms. The growth in economies around the world also made more savings available to be invested.

Although at one time the U.S. capital market was larger than all other capital markets combined, this is no longer true. Today there are large capital markets in Europe

FIGURE 18-5

Growth of Foreign Portfolio Investment in the United States

Since 1995, a large rise has occurred in foreign purchases of bonds issued by U.S. corporations and by the federal government. Even though falling stock prices in the United States caused a fall in foreign ownership of corporate stocks between 2001 and 2004, foreign investment in these securities was still more than twice as great as it was in 1995.

Sources: 1995 data from International Monetary Fund, *International Capital Markets,* August 2001; 2001 and 2004 data from U.S. Department of the Treasury, *Treasury Bulletin,* June 2005.

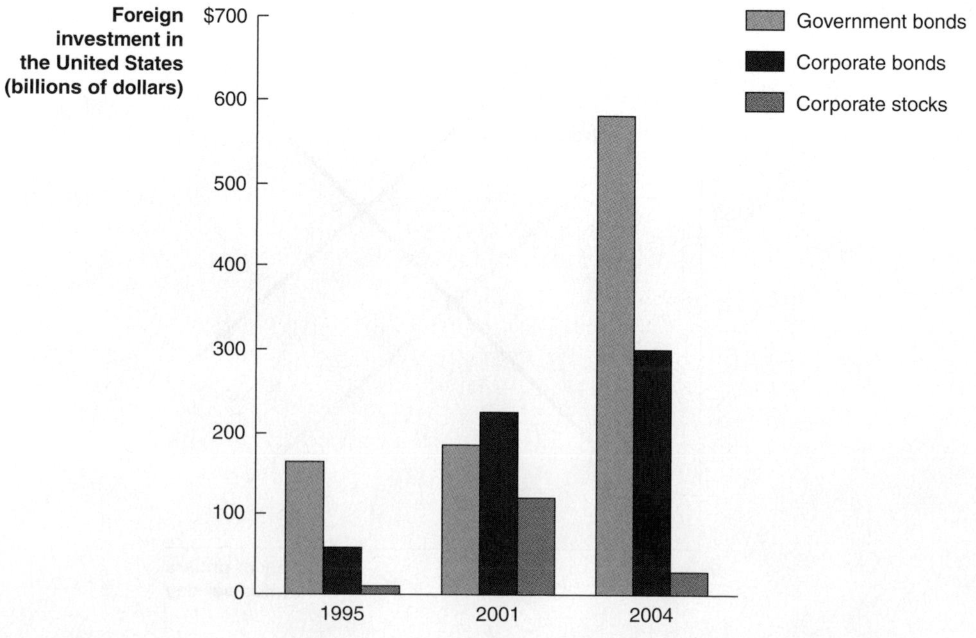

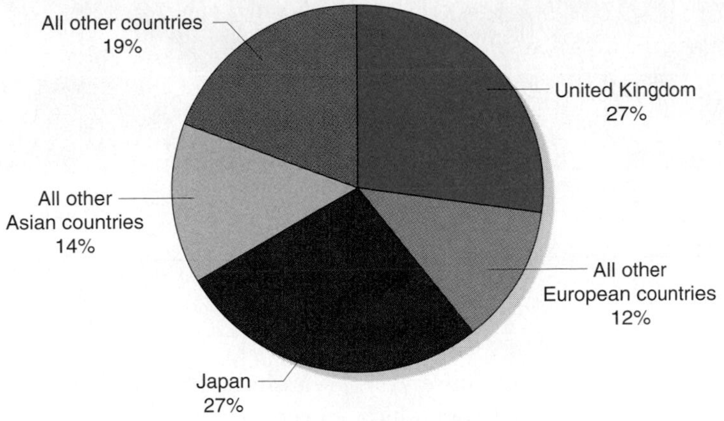

FIGURE 18-6

The Distribution of Foreign Purchases of U.S. Stocks and Bonds by Country, 2004

Investors in the United Kingdom and Japan each accounted for more than one-quarter of all foreign purchases of U.S. stocks and bonds.

Source: U.S. Department of the Treasury, *Treasury Bulletin*, June 2005.

and Japan, and smaller markets in Latin America and East Asia. The three most important international financial centers today are New York, London, and Tokyo. Each day the front page of the online version of the *Wall Street Journal* displays not just the Dow Jones Industrial Average and the Standard and Poor's 500 stock indexes of U.S. stocks, but also the Nikkei 225 average of Japanese stocks and the Euro STOXX 50 index of European stocks. By 2005, corporations, banks, and governments raised more than $1 trillion in funds on global financial markets.

During the 1990s, the flow of foreign funds into U.S. stocks and bonds—or *portfolio investments*—increased dramatically. As Figure 18-5 shows, a dramatic increase in foreign purchases of bonds issued by corporations and by the federal government has occurred since 1995. Even though falling stock prices in the United States caused a fall in foreign ownership of corporate stocks between 2001 and 2004, foreign investment in these securities was still more than twice as great as it had been in 1995.

Figure 18-6 shows the distribution of foreign portfolio investment in the United States by country. Investors in the United Kingdom and Japan each accounted for more than one-quarter of all foreign purchases of U.S. stocks and bonds. Investors in China and other Asian countries accounted for another 14 percent.

The globalization of financial markets has helped increase growth and efficiency in the world economy. Now it is possible for the savings of households around the world to be channeled to the best investments available. It also possible for firms in nearly every country to tap the savings of foreign households to gain the funds needed for expansion. No longer are firms forced to rely only on the savings of domestic households to finance investment.

Conclusion

Fluctuations in exchange rates continue to cause difficulties for firms and governments. From the gold standard to the Bretton Woods System to currency pegging, governments have attempted to find a workable system of fixed exchange rates. Fixing exchange rates runs into the same problems as fixing any price: As demand and supply shift, surpluses and shortages will occur unless the price adjusts. Most of the countries of Western Europe are attempting to avoid this problem by using a single currency. Economists are looking closely at the results of that experiment. Read *An Inside Look* on the next page for a discussion of the effect of a rising exchange value of the euro on the profitability of European firms.

An Inside Look

Strong Euro Slashes Profits at Some EU Firms

WALL STREET JOURNAL, JUNE 21, 2005

Strong Euro Bedevils EU Firms

Despite the euro's 8.2% drop against the dollar since mid-March, European companies continue to grapple with the currency's overall strength.

a STMicroelectronics NV is a case in point. Carlo Bozotti, chief executive of the Geneva-based chip maker, says the euro is among his biggest headaches. As growth slows in the chip industry and his bankers forecast that the euro, despite its recent slip, will remain relatively high for a while, Mr. Bozotti says he can't afford to wait any longer to take tough steps to boost competitiveness and profitability.

Mr. Bozotti is shifting costly, less productive European manufacturing to Asia. As part of these efforts, STMicroelectronics recently announced it would cut 2,300 jobs in Europe. Mr. Bozotti also wants to move all the manufacturing of what he calls "more mature," or commodity-type, chip products to Asia over the next five years.

STMicroelectronics' predicament shows that the still strong euro—it remains 48% higher against the dollar than it was in late 2000—is a big handicap for companies that may only now be taking steps to restructure their businesses in the face of low growth and rising competition. Reasons for this delayed response vary, including European labor laws, which make restructuring difficult and, in some cases, management that simply didn't confront the combination of the market and currency downturn with enough rigor.

b "The outside world is bored of blaming everything on the euro-dollar, but it is a huge problem. A huge problem," says Wolfgang Ziebart, the CEO of German chip maker Infineon AG, which recently displaced STMicroelectronics as Europe's largest semiconductor company by revenue. An Infineon spokeswoman said that the chip maker isn't making specific business changes as a result of the strong euro but that the company does engage in hedging strategies to help offset the impact. . . .

In March, Mr. Bozotti took the helm of STMicroelectronics, the world's sixth-largest chip maker by revenue, when he succeeded the company's long-serving CEO, Pasquale Pistorio, and he has been scrambling to restore the company's competitiveness. STMicroelectronics makes chips for mobile phones, printers and cars, among other things. It counts Nokia Corp., the world's largest maker of handsets, among its customers. . . .

c To be sure, the euro is just one of several factors affecting Mr. Bozotti's business. The semiconductor industry generally is wrestling with overcapacity. STMicroelectronics has suffered criticism for a behind-the-curve culture when it comes to technology and a management that has preferred stability for its work force at the expense of growth for investors, repeatedly issuing profit warnings and missing targets. The company also is facing stiff pricing competition from Asia and the U.S., particularly with its memory chips, which store data on phones and cameras.

In a recent interview, the 53-year-old executive said moving plants and manufacturing to Asia and other initiatives should reduce STMicroelectronics' costs by more than $500 million annually. He said he is also refocusing research-and-development resources and is betting that a new generation of chips designed to power new gadgets, such as high-definition televisions and video-enabled cellphones, will help drive growth. . . .

Mr. Bozotti says the euro isn't the company's only issue. "We clearly have challenges," he told investors at the recent conference in New York, citing industry overcapacity and falling memory prices. Addressing high costs, including the euro, is key to his strategy, he said.

Key Points in the Article

At the time this article was published, the euro was roughly 50 percent stronger against the U.S. dollar than it was in late 2000. This appreciation reduced the profits of European chip makers STMicroelectronics (STM) and Infineon because computer chips are priced throughout the world in U.S. dollars. To counter this reduction in profits, STM shifted some of its manufacturing to Asia, whereas Infineon hedged its revenues in the currency futures markets. Of course, the strong euro is not the only challenge that the industry faces. Firms such as STM and Infineon continue to deal with the legacy of the late 1990s dot.com bubble, which effectively created a glut of computer-chip production capacity and hence lowered computer-chip prices.

Analyzing the News

a The appreciation of the euro in the last five years is shown in Figure 1, where the unit of measure on the vertical axis is dollars per euro. An appreciation of the euro reduces the profits of firms like Geneva-based chip maker STM. This is because computer chips are priced throughout the world in U.S. dollars, but 70 percent of STM's costs are priced in euros. Therefore, when the exchange value of the euro increases, the euro value of the firm's dollar-denominated revenues fall but its euro-denominated costs are unchanged. To counter this fall in profits, STM's management shifted its more costly manufacturing to Asia, where the euro's strength effectively lowers production costs.

b Like STM, Germany-based chip maker Infineon AG takes steps to counter the rise in the value of the euro. However, rather than shifting manufacturing to Asia, Infineon uses the currency futures markets to hedge its revenue position. For example, suppose the date is May 1 and Infineon will receive revenues of $1,000 on June 1. Assume the current exchange rate is $1 = €0.75, so the current euro value of Infineon's June revenues is €750. To protect, or hedge, these revenues, Infineon enters into a currency futures contract with another party; that is, Infineon agrees to sell $1,000 on June 1 for a price of €750. Now, suppose that on June 1 the exchange rate is $1 = €0.50. The euro has appreciated against the dollar, so the euro value of Infineon's $1,000 is now only €500. However, the firm's futures contract allows it to sell, to the counterparty of the contract, $1,000 for €750. Hence, Infineon has hedged in the futures market to offset the impact of the rise in the euro.

c The European semiconductor industry's challenges go beyond the exchange value of the euro. The dot.com bubble in the late 1990s effectively channeled too many investment dollars into the industry. This overinvestment has created a glut of production capacity in Europe, as well as in Asia. This glut has lowered computer chip prices and hence revenues for firms like STM and Infineon.

Thinking Critically ABOUT POLICY

1. How might an expansionary monetary policy by the European Central Bank (ECB) affect the euro value of Germany-based Infineon's revenues?
2. In response to the relatively strong euro, STM shifts its more costly manufacturing to Asia, where the euro's strength effectively lowers production costs. Have Asian central banks' policy decisions to maintain undervalued currencies fueled or tempered European firms' decisions to move production to Asian countries?

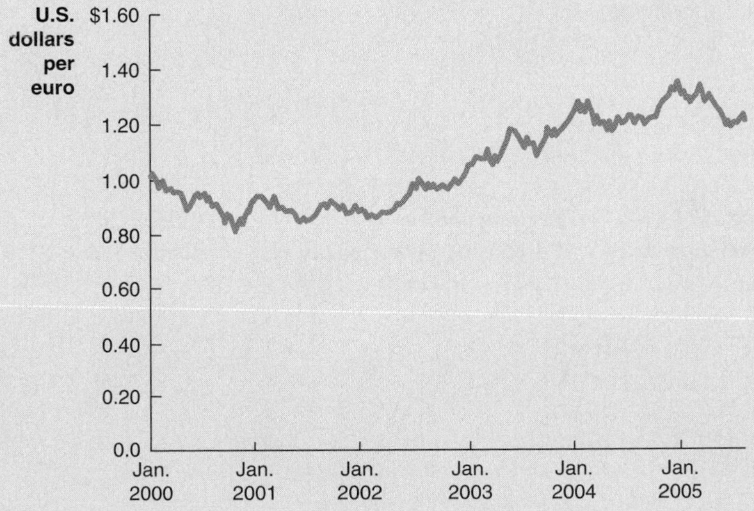

Figure 1: U.S. Dollar/Euro Exchange Rate, January 2000 to August 2005.

Source: U.S. Federal Reserve System.

SUMMARY

LEARNING OBJECTIVE ① Understand how different exchange rate systems operate. When countries agree on how exchange rates should be determined, economists say that there is an *exchange rate system*. A currency *floats* when its exchange rate is determined by demand and supply. The current exchange rate system is a *managed float exchange rate system* under which the value of most currencies is determined by demand and supply, with occasional government intervention. A *fixed exchange rate system* is a system under which countries agree to keep the exchange rates among their currencies fixed. Under the gold standard, the exchange rate between two currencies was automatically determined by the quantity of gold in each currency. By the end of the Great Depression of the 1930s, every country had abandoned the gold standard. Under the Bretton Woods System, which was in place between 1944 and the early 1970s, the United States agreed to exchange dollars for gold at a price of $35 per ounce. The central banks of all other members of the system pledged to buy and sell their currencies at a fixed rate against the dollar.

LEARNING OBJECTIVE ② Discuss the three key aspects of the current exchange rate system. The three key aspects of the current exchange rate system are: (1) the U.S. dollar floats against other major currencies; (2) most countries in Western Europe have adopted a common currency; and (3) some developing countries have fixed their currencies' exchange rates against the dollar or against another major currency. Since 1973, the value of the U.S. dollar has fluctuated widely against other major currencies. The theory of *purchasing power parity* states that in the long run exchange rates move to equalize the purchasing power of different currencies. This theory helps to explain some of the long-run movements in the value of the U.S. dollar relative to other currencies. In 2002, 12 countries of the European Union decided to adopt a common currency, known as the *euro*. The experience of the countries using the euro will provide economists with information on the costs and benefits to countries from using the same currency. When a country keeps its currency's exchange rate fixed against another country's currency, it is *pegging* its currency. Pegging can result in problems similar to the problems countries encountered with fixed exchange rates under the Bretton Woods System. If investors become convinced that a country pegging its exchange rate will eventually allow the exchange rate to decline to a lower level, the demand curve for the currency will shift to the left. This illustrates the difficulty of maintaining a fixed exchange rate in the face of destabilizing speculation.

LEARNING OBJECTIVE ③ Discuss the growth of international capital markets. A key reason that exchange rates fluctuate is that investors seek out the best investments they can find anywhere in the world. Since 1980, the markets for stocks and bonds have become global. Foreign purchases of U.S. corporate bonds and stocks and U.S. government bonds have increased greatly just in the period since 1995. As a result, firms around the world are no longer forced to rely for funds on only the savings of domestic households.

KEY TERMS

Euro 575
Exchange rate system 574
Fixed exchange rate system 574
Floating currency 574
Managed float exchange rate system 574
Pegging 583
Purchasing power parity 577
Quota 578
Tariff 578

REVIEW QUESTIONS

1. What is an exchange rate system? What is the difference between a fixed exchange rate system and a managed float exchange rate system?
2. What is the theory of purchasing power parity? Does it give a complete explanation for movements in exchange rates in the long run? Briefly explain.
3. Briefly describe the four determinants of exchange rates in the long run.
4. Which European countries currently use the euro as their currency? Why did these countries agree to replace their previous currency with the euro?

5. What does it mean when one currency is "pegged" against another currency? Why do countries peg their currencies? What problems can result from pegging?
6. If you owned a firm in Indonesia and wanted to export your product to the United States, would you like the Indonesian government to peg the value of the rupiah against the dollar? Briefly explain.
7. Briefly describe the Chinese experience with pegging the yuan.
8. What were the main factors behind the globalization of capital markets in the 1980s and 1990s?

PROBLEMS AND APPLICATIONS

Please visit **www.prenhall.com/hubbard** *for solutions to the even-numbered problems as well as multiple-choice and true or false self-assessment quizzes.*

1. **[Related to *Don't Let This Happen To You!*]** Briefly explain whether you agree with the following statement: "The Federal Reserve is limited in its ability to issue paper currency by the amount of gold the federal government has in Fort Knox. To issue more paper currency, the government first has to buy more gold."
2. Consider this newspaper report: "DuPont said that soft currencies overseas, particularly in Europe and Asia, had dragged down its sales 2 percent worldwide, ultimately costing it $35 million in net income." What is a "soft currency"? Why would soft currencies overseas hurt DuPont's sales?
   Source: Danny Hakim and Greg Winter, "G.M. Official Says Dollar Is Too Strong," *New York Times*, August 9, 2001.
3. Consider this statement: "It usually takes more than 100 yen to buy 1 U.S. dollar and more than 1.5 dollars to buy 1 British pound. These values show that the United States must be a much wealthier country than Japan and that the United Kingdom must be wealthier than the United States." Do you agree with this reasoning? Briefly explain.
4. Consider this newspaper report: "One factor contributing to [Toyota's] healthy earnings for the latest fiscal year was the favorable exchange rate, which added 410 billion yen ($3.2 billion) to earnings."
   a. What was the exchange rate between the yen and the dollar (expressed in dollars per yen) when this newspaper article was written?
   b. Would it be a "favorable exchange rate" from Toyota's point of view if the yen exchanged for more dollars or for fewer dollars? Briefly explain.

   Source: Yuri Kageyama, "Toyota's Net Profits Increased 30 Percent Last Year," Associated Press, May 14, 2002.
5. An article in the *Wall Street Journal* is headlined "Pain from the Dollar's Decline Will Mostly Be Felt Overseas." Briefly explain the reasoning behind this headline.
   Source: David Wessel, "Pain from the Dollar's Decline Will Mostly Be Felt Overseas," *Wall Street Journal*, June 13, 2002.
6. According to the theory of purchasing power parity, if the inflation rate in Australia is higher than the inflation rate in New Zealand, what should happen to the exchange rate between the Australian dollar and the New Zealand dollar? Briefly explain.
7. **[Related to *Solved Problem 18-1*]** Look again at Making the Connection 18-2 about the prices of Big Macs. Indicate which countries listed in the table have undervalued currencies versus the U.S. dollar and which have overvalued currencies.
8. Britain decided not to join with other European Union countries and use the euro as its currency. One British opponent of adopting the euro argued, "It comes down to economics. We just don't believe that it's possible to manage the entire economy of Europe with just one interest rate policy. How do you alleviate recession in Germany and curb inflation in Ireland?" What interest-rate policy would be used to alleviate recession in Germany? What interest-rate policy would be used to curb inflation in Ireland? What does adopting the euro have to do with interest-rate policy?
   Source: Alan Cowell, "Nuanced Conflict Over Euro in Britain," *New York Times*, June 22, 2001.
9. When the euro was introduced in January 1999, the exchange rate was $1.19 per euro. In early 2005, the exchange rate was $1.35 per euro. Was this change in the euro–dollar exchange rate good news or bad news for U.S. firms exporting goods and services to Europe? Briefly explain.
10. Construct a numerical example showing how an investor could have made a profit by selling Thai baht for dollars in 1997.
11. The following statement is from an article in the *New York Times:* "[G]overnment action to support [its] currency cannot be effective in the long run if it runs counter to the collective judgment of the financial markets." What does it mean to say a government is taking action to "support" its currency? Do you agree with the conclusion that these

actions are not effective in the long run if they run counter to the judgment of financial markets? Briefly explain.
Source: Richard W. Stevenson, "Dollar Falls as Top Official Casts Doubts on Intervention," *New York Times,* May 2, 2002.

12. Use the graph to answer the following questions.

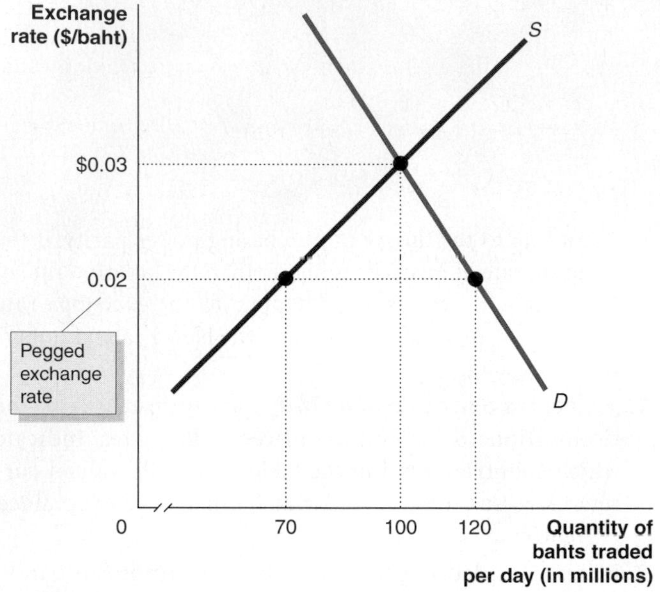

   a. According to the graph, is there a surplus or a shortage of baht in exchange for U.S. dollars? Briefly explain.
   b. To maintain the pegged exchange rate, will the Thai central bank need to buy baht in exchange for dollars or sell baht in exchange for dollars? How many baht will the Thai central bank need to buy or sell?

13. For many years, Argentina suffered from high rates of inflation. As part of its program to fight inflation, in the 1990s the Argentine government pegged the value of the Argentine peso to the U.S. dollar at a rate of one peso per dollar. In January 2002, the government decided to abandon the peg and allow the peso to float. Just before the peg was abandoned, firms in Buenos Aires posted signs urging customers to come in and shop and take advantage of the "Last 72 Hours of One to One." What was likely to happen to the exchange rate between the dollar and the peso, once Argentina abandoned the peg? Why would customers find it better to shop before the peg ended than after?
Source: Larry Rohter, "Argentina Unlinks Peso from Dollar, Bracing for Devaluation," *New York Times,* January 7, 2002.

14. The *Economist* magazine observed the following: "[I]n Argentina, many loans were taken out in dollars: this had catastrophic consequences for borrowers once the peg collapsed." What does it mean that Argentina's "peg collapsed"? Why was this catastrophic for borrowers in Argentina who had taken out dollar loans?
Source: "Spoilt for Choice," *Economist,* June 3, 2002.

15. According to the *Economist* magazine, during the period in which Argentina pegged the value of its currency to the dollar, "Argentina's monetary policy was, in effect, made in Washington and was often inappropriate for Argentina's needs . . . ." Explain the sense in which Argentina's monetary policy was made in Washington during those years.
Source: "Spoilt for Choice," *Economist,* June 3, 2002.

16. A newspaper story discussing the effects of a decline in the exchange value of the dollar contained the following two observations:
   a. "The weaker dollar will also mean higher inflation in this country."
   b. "The biggest danger in coming months is that a declining dollar will make foreigners less willing to invest in the United States . . . ."

   Explain whether you agree or disagree with these two observations.
   Source: Martin Crutsinger, "Mighty Dollar Fading," Associated Press, May 30, 2002.

17. Suppose a developing country pegs the value of its currency against the U.S. dollar. Suppose that the exchange rate between the dollar and the yen and between the dollar and the euro increases. What will be the impact on the ability of the developing country to exports goods and services to Japan and Europe? Briefly explain.

18. Graph the demand and supply of Chinese yuan for U.S. dollars and label each axis. To maintain its pegged exchange rate, the Chinese central bank bought large quantities of U.S. dollars with yuan. Indicate whether the pegged exchange rate was above or below the market equilibrium exchange rate and show on the graph the quantity of yuan the Chinese central bank would have to supply each trading period.

19. According to a newspaper story "China's critics contend that the yuan's exchange rate of slightly more than 8 yuan per dollar . . . . is far out of line with market forces and gives Chinese manufacturers a big advantage against foreign firms, adding to the enormous U.S. trade deficit and China's burgeoning trade surplus." What does it mean to say the yuan's exchange rate was "far out of line with market forces"? Why would the yuan exchange rate give Chinese manufacturers a "big advantage against foreign firms"? How does the yuan exchange rate affect the balance of trade in the United States and China?
Paul Blustein, "U.S. Urges IMF Crackdown on Currency," *Washington Post,* September 24, 2005.

20. **[Related to *Solved Problem 18-2*]** An article in the *Wall Street Journal* stated the following:

   > Romania's central bank vowed to intervene to defend the country's currency, the leu. . . . But traders said authorities will have to work

> quickly to maintain confidence in the currency. . . . With reserves at just $1.59 billion . . . the central bank's arsenal for staving off further speculation is limited.

Is it likely that the Romanian central bank was trying to defend an exchange rate that is above or below the exchange rate that would prevail in the absence of intervention? Draw a graph to illustrate your answer. Briefly explain what traders would have to gain by speculating against the leu and what the Romanian central bank's dollar reserves have to do with its ability to defend the value of the Romanian currency.

Source: John Reed, "Romania Vows to Defend Currency if Necessary," *Wall Street Journal,* March 19, 1999.

21. **[Related to the *Chapter Opener*]** For 35 years, the Montreal Expos played major league baseball in the French-speaking Canadian province of Quebec, before relocating in 2005 to Washington, D.C. All but one of the other 29 major league baseball teams were based in cities in the United States. Before they moved to Washington (and became the Nationals), an analysis of the Expos contained the following observation: "Numerous factors, from the language barrier to the floating Canadian dollar, conspire to make baseball in Quebec a difficult proposition." What is meant by a "floating" Canadian dollar? Why would a floating Canadian dollar make it difficult to operate a major league baseball team in Montreal?

    Source: Jeff Bower, et al., *Baseball Prospectus, 2002,* Washington, D.C.: Brassey, 2002, p. 358.

22. **[Related to the *Chapter Opener*]** As discussed at the beginning of this chapter, Molson Breweries, a Canadian firm, sold the Montreal Canadiens ice hockey team to George Gillett, Jr., a U.S. ski resort operator. What was a key problem that Molson encountered in operating the Canadiens? Would Gillett, as a U.S. citizen, be better able to deal with this problem? Briefly explain.

Appendix

The Gold Standard and the Bretton Woods System

It is easier to understand the current exchange rate system by considering further two earlier systems: the gold standard and the Bretton Woods System, which together lasted from the early nineteenth century through the early 1970s.

The Gold Standard

As we saw in this chapter, under the gold standard, the currency of a country consisted of gold coins and paper currency that could be redeemed in gold. Great Britain adopted the gold standard in 1816, but as late as 1870 only a few nations had followed. In the late nineteenth century, however, Great Britain's share of world trade increased as did its overseas investments. The dominant position of Great Britain in the world economy motivated other countries to adopt the gold standard. By 1913, every country in Europe, except Spain and Bulgaria, and most countries in the Western Hemisphere had adopted the gold standard.

Under the gold standard, the exchange rate between two currencies was automatically determined by the quantity of gold in each currency. If there was one-fifth of an ounce of gold in a U.S. dollar and one ounce of gold in a British pound, the price of gold in the United States would be \$5 per ounce and the price of gold in Britain would be £1 per ounce. The exchange rate would be \$5 = £1.

The End of the Gold Standard

From a modern point of view, the greatest drawback to the gold standard was that the central bank lacked control of the money supply. The size of a country's money supply depended on its gold supply, which could be greatly affected by chance discoveries of gold or by technological change in gold mining. For example, the gold discoveries in California in 1849 and Alaska in the 1890s caused rapid increases in the U.S. money supply. Because the central bank cannot determine how much gold will be discovered, it lacks the control of the money supply necessary to pursue an active monetary policy. During wartime, countries usually went off the gold standard to allow their central banks to expand the money supply as rapidly as was necessary to pay for the war. Britain abandoned the gold standard at the beginning of World War I in 1914 and did not resume redeeming its paper currency for gold until 1925.

When the Great Depression began in 1929, governments came under pressure to abandon the gold standard to allow their central banks to pursue active monetary policies. In 1931, Great Britain became the first major country to abandon the gold standard. A number of other countries also went off the gold standard that year. The United States remained on the gold standard until 1933, and a few countries, including France, Italy, and Belgium, stayed on even longer. By the late 1930s, the gold standard had collapsed.

The earlier a country abandoned the gold standard, the easier time it had fighting the Depression with expansionary monetary policies. The countries that abandoned the gold standard by 1932 suffered an average decline in production of only 3 percent between 1929 and 1934. The countries that stayed on the gold standard until 1933 or later suffered an average decline of more than 30 percent. The devastating economic performance of the countries that stayed on the gold standard the longest during the 1930s is the key reason no attempt was made to bring back the gold standard in later years.

The Bretton Woods System

In addition to the collapse of the gold standard, the global economy had suffered during the 1930s from tariff wars. The United States had started the tariff wars in June 1930 by enacting the Smoot-Hawley Tariff, which raised the average U.S. tariff rate to more than 50 percent. Many other countries raised tariffs during the next few years, leading to a collapse in world trade.

As World War II was coming to an end, economists and government officials in the United States and Europe concluded that they had to restore the international economic system to avoid another depression. In 1947, the United States and most other major countries, apart from the Soviet Union, began participating in the General Agreement on Tariffs and Trade (GATT), under which they worked to reduce trade barriers. The GATT was very successful in sponsoring rounds of negotiations among countries, which led to sharp declines in tariffs. U.S. tariffs dropped from an average rate of more than 50 percent in the early 1930s to an average rate of less than 2 percent today. In 1995, the GATT was replaced by the World Trade Organization (WTO), which has similar objectives.

The effort to develop a new exchange rate system to replace the gold standard was more complicated than establishing the GATT. A conference held in Bretton Woods, New Hampshire, in 1944 set up a system in which the United States pledged to buy or sell gold at a fixed price of $35 per ounce. The central banks of all other members of the new **Bretton Woods System** pledged to buy and sell their currencies at a fixed rate against the dollar. By fixing their exchange rates against the dollar, these countries were fixing the exchange rates among their currencies as well. Unlike under the gold standard, neither the United States, nor any other country, was willing to redeem its paper currency for gold domestically. The United States would only redeem dollars for gold if they were presented by a foreign central bank. The United States continued the prohibition, first enacted in the early 1930s, against private citizens owning gold, unless they were jewelers or rare coin collectors. The prohibition was not lifted until the 1970s, when it again became possible for Americans to own gold as an investment.

Bretton Woods System An exchange rate system that lasted from 1944 to 1971, under which countries pledged to buy and sell their currencies at a fixed rate against the dollar.

Under the Bretton Woods System central banks were committed to selling dollars in exchange for their own currencies. This commitment required them to hold *dollar reserves.* If a central bank ran out of dollar reserves, it could borrow them from the newly created **International Monetary Fund (IMF).** In addition to providing loans to central banks that were short of dollar reserves, the IMF would oversee the operation of the system and approve adjustments to the agreed-on fixed exchange rates.

International Monetary Fund (IMF) An international organization that provides foreign currency loans to central banks and oversees the operation of the international monetary system.

Under the Bretton Woods System, a fixed exchange rate was known as a *par exchange rate.* If the par exchange rate was not the same as the exchange rate that would have been determined in the market, the result would be a surplus or a shortage. For example, Figure 18A-1 shows the exchange rate between the dollar and the British pound. The figure is drawn from the British point of view, so we measure the exchange rate on the vertical axis as dollars per pound. In this case, the par exchange rate between the dollar and the pound is above the equilibrium exchange rate as determined by supply and demand.

In this example, at the par exchange rate of $4 per pound, the quantity of pounds demanded by people wanting to buy British goods and services or wanting to invest in British assets is smaller than the quantity of pounds supplied by people who would like to exchange them for dollars. As a result, the Bank of England must use dollars to buy the surplus of £1 million per day. Only at an exchange rate of $2.80 per pound would the

FIGURE 18A-1

A Fixed Exchange Rate Above Equilibrium Results in a Surplus of Pounds

Under the Bretton Woods System, central banks were obligated to defend par exchange rates by buying and selling their countries' currencies at fixed rates against the dollar. If the par exchange rate was above equilibrium, the result would be a surplus of domestic currency in the foreign exchange market. If the par exchange rate was below equilibrium, the result would be a shortage of domestic currency. In the figure, the par exchange rate between the pound and the dollar was \$4 = £1, whereas the equilibrium exchange rate was \$2.80 = £1. This gap forced the Bank of England to buy £1 million per day in exchange for dollars.

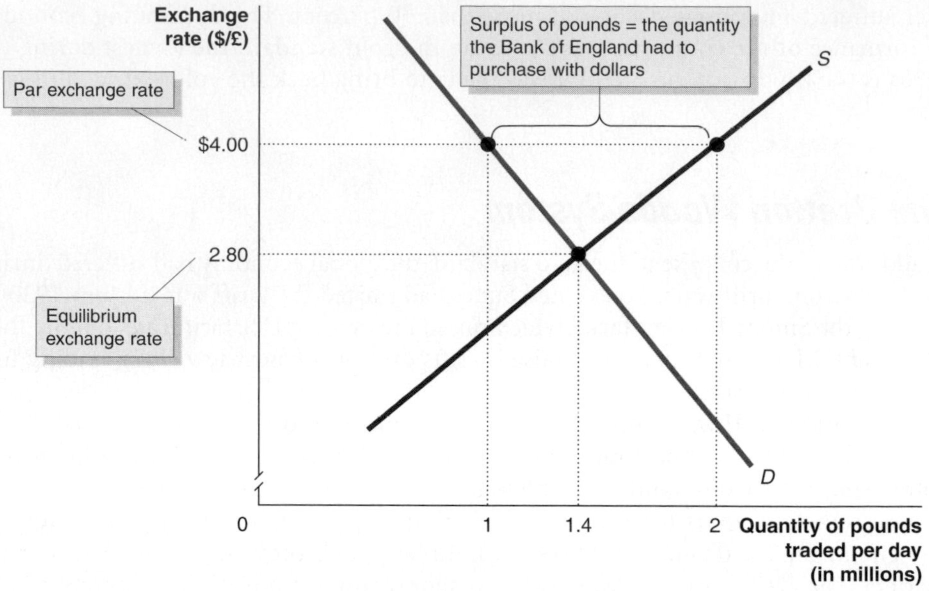

surplus be eliminated. If the par exchange rate were below the equilibrium exchange rate, there would be a shortage of domestic currency in the foreign exchange market.

A persistent shortage or surplus of a currency under the Bretton Woods System was seen as evidence of a *fundamental disequilibrium* in a country's exchange rate. After consulting with the IMF, countries in this position were allowed to adjust their exchange rates. In the early years of the Bretton Woods System, many countries found that their currencies were *overvalued* versus the dollar, meaning that their par exchange rates were too high. A reduction of a fixed exchange rate is a **devaluation.** An increase in a fixed exchange rate is a **revaluation.** In 1949, there was a devaluation of several currencies, including the British pound, reflecting the fact that those currencies had been overvalued against the dollar.

Devaluation A reduction in a fixed exchange rate.

Revaluation An increase in a fixed exchange rate.

The Collapse of the Bretton Woods System

By the late 1960s, the Bretton Woods System faced two severe problems. The first was that after 1963 the total number of dollars held by foreign central banks was larger than the gold reserves of the United States. In practice, most central banks—the Bank of France was the main exception—rarely redeemed dollars for gold. But the basis of the system was a credible promise by the United States to redeem dollars for gold if called upon to do so. By the late 1960s, as the gap between the dollars held by foreign central banks and the gold reserves of the United States grew larger and larger, the credibility of the U.S. promise to redeem dollars for gold was called into question.

The second problem faced by the Bretton Woods System was that some countries with undervalued currencies, particularly West Germany, were unwilling to revalue their currencies. Governments resisted revaluation because it would have increased the prices of their countries' exports. Many German firms, such as Volkswagen, put pressure on the government not to endanger their sales in the U.S. market by raising the exchange rate of the deutsche mark against the dollar. Figure 18A-2 shows the situation faced by the German government in 1971. The figure takes the German point of view, so the exchange rate is expressed in terms of dollars per deutsche mark.

Under the Bretton Woods System, the Bundesbank, the German central bank, was required to buy and sell deutsche marks for dollars at a rate of \$0.27 per deutsche mark. The equilibrium that would have prevailed in the foreign exchange market if the Bundesbank did not intervene was about \$0.35 per deutsche mark. Because the par exchange

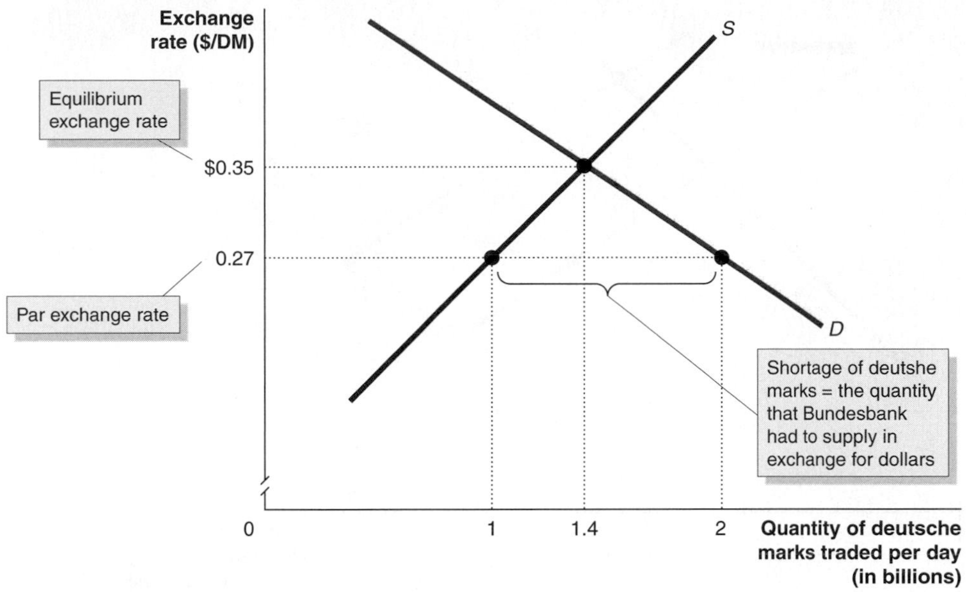

FIGURE 18A-2

West Germany's Undervalued Exchange Rate

The Bundesbank, the German central bank, was committed under the Bretton Woods System to defending a par exchange rate of $0.27 per deutsche mark (DM). Because this exchange rate was lower than what the equilibrium market exchange rate would have been, there was a shortage of deutsche marks in the foreign exchange market. The Bundesbank had to supply deutsche marks equal to the shortage in exchange for dollars. The shortage in the figure is equal to DM 1 billion per day.

rate was below the equilibrium exchange rate, the quantity of deutsche marks demanded by people wanting to buy German goods and services or wanting to invest in German assets was greater than the quantity of deutsche marks supplied by people who wanted to exchange them for dollars. To maintain the exchange rate at $0.27 per deutsche mark, the Bundesbank had to buy dollars and sell deutsche marks. The amount of deutsche marks supplied by the Bundesbank was equal to the shortage of deutsche marks at the par exchange rate.

By selling deutsche marks and buying dollars to defend the par exchange rate, the Bundesbank was increasing the West German money supply, risking an increase in the inflation rate. Because Germany had suffered a devastating hyperinflation during the 1920s, the fear of inflation was greater in Germany than in any other industrial country. No German government could survive politically if it allowed a significant increase in inflation. Knowing this fact, many investors in Germany and elsewhere became convinced that eventually the German government would have to allow a revaluation of the mark.

During the 1960s, most European countries, including Germany, relaxed their **capital controls.** Capital controls are limits on the flow of foreign exchange and financial investment across countries. The loosening of capital controls made it easier for investors to *speculate* on changes in exchange rates. For instance, an investor in the United States could sell $1 million and receive about DM 3.7 million at the par exchange rate of $0.27 per deutsche mark. If the exchange rate rose to $0.35 per deutsche mark, the investor could then exchange deutsche marks for dollars, receiving $1.3 million at the new exchange rate: a return of 30 percent on an initial $1 million investment. The more convinced investors became that Germany would have to allow a revaluation, the more dollars they exchanged for deutsche marks. Figure 18A-3 shows the results.

Capital controls Limits on the flow of foreign exchange and financial investment across countries.

The increased demand for deutsche marks by investors hoping to make a profit from the expected revaluation of the mark shifted the demand curve for marks to the right from D_1 to D_2. Because of this expectation, the Bundesbank had to increase the marks it supplied in exchange for dollars, raising further the risk of inflation in Germany. As we saw in the chapter, because these actions by investors make it more difficult to maintain a fixed exchange rate, they are referred to as *destabilizing speculation.* By May 1971, the Bundesbank had to buy more than $1 billion per day to support the fixed exchange rate against the dollar. Finally, on May 5, the West German government decided to allow the mark to float. In August, President Richard Nixon decided to abandon the U.S. commitment to redeem dollars for gold. Attempts were made over the next two years to reach a compromise that would restore a fixed exchange rate system, but, by 1973, the Bretton Woods System was effectively dead.

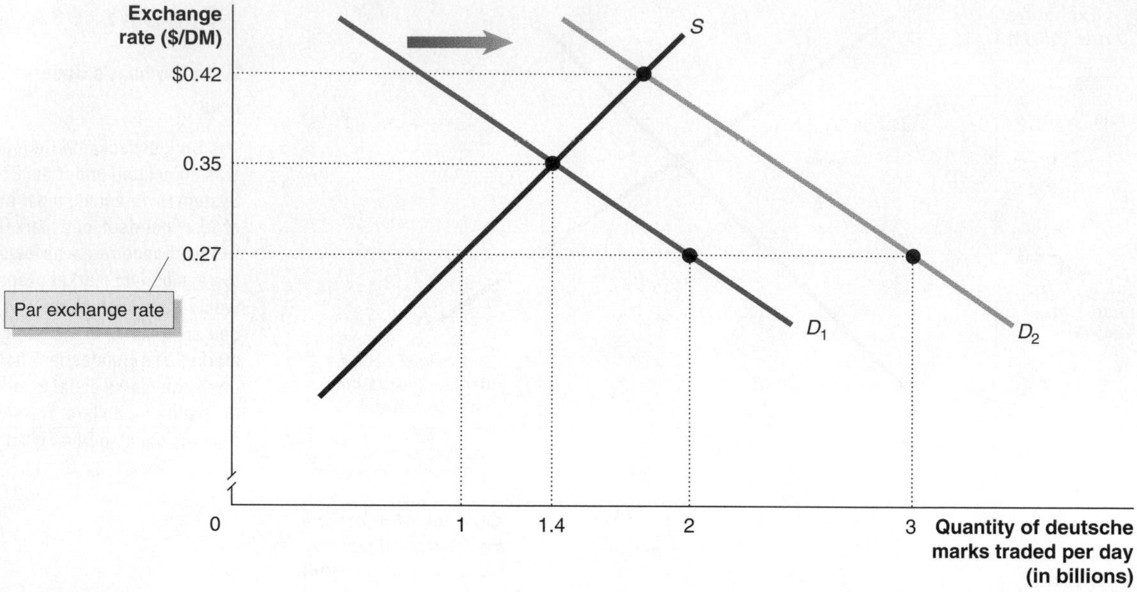

FIGURE 18A-3 Destabilizing Speculation Against the Deutsche Mark, 1971

In 1971, the par exchange rate of \$0.27 = DM1 was below the equilibrium exchange rate of \$0.35 = DM1. As investors became convinced that West Germany would have to revalue the deutsche mark, they increased their demand for marks from D_1 to D_2. The new equilibrium exchange rate became \$0.42 = DM1. This increase in demand raised the quantity of marks the Bundesbank had to supply in exchange for dollars to defend the par exchange rate from DM1 billion to DM2 billion per day.

KEY TERMS

Bretton Woods System 597
Capital controls 599
Devaluation 598
International Monetary Fund (IMF) 597
Revaluation 598

REVIEW QUESTIONS

1. What determined the exchange rates among currencies under the gold standard? Why did the gold standard collapse?
2. Briefly describe how the Bretton Woods System operated.
3. What is the difference between a devaluation and a revaluation?
4. What are capital controls?
5. What role did the International Monetary Fund play in the Bretton Woods System?
6. What is destabilizing speculation? What role did it play in the collapse of the Bretton Woods System?

PROBLEMS AND APPLICATIONS

Please visit **www.prenhall.com/hubbard** *for solutions to the even-numbered problems as well as multiple-choice and true or false self-assessment quizzes.*

1. Suppose that under the gold standard there was one-fifth of an ounce of gold in a U.S. dollar and one ounce of gold in a British pound. Demonstrate that if the exchange rate between the dollar and the pound was $4 = £1, rather than $5 = £1, you could make unlimited profits by buying gold in one country and selling it in the other. If the exchange rate was $6 = £1, how would your strategy change? For simplicity, assume there was no cost to shipping gold from one country to the other.
2. An article in the *Economist* observes that "Enthusiasm for the gold standard evaporated in the 1930s, when it made dreadful conditions worse." How did the gold standard make dreadful conditions worse during the 1930s?
   Source: "Heading for a Fall, by Fiat?" *Economist*, February 26, 2004.
3. According to an article in the *Economist,* when most countries left the gold standard in the 1930s, in South Africa "the mining industry flourished." Briefly explain why the end of the gold standard might be good news for the owners of gold mines.
   Source: "Johannesburg," *Economist*, August 18, 2004.
4. By the mid-1960s, the price of gold on the London market had increased to more than $35 per ounce. (Remember that it was not legal during these years for investors in the United States to own gold.) Would this have happened if foreign investors had believed that the U.S. commitment to buy and sell gold at $35 per ounce under the Bretton Woods System would continue indefinitely? Briefly explain.
5. One economist has argued that the East Asian exchange-rate crisis of the late 1990s was due to "the simple failure of governments to remember the lessons from the breakdown of the Bretton Woods System." What are the lessons from the breakdown of the Bretton Woods System? In what sense did the East Asian governments fail to learn these lessons?
   Source: Thomas D. Willett, "Crying for Argentina," *Milken Institute Review*, Second Quarter 2002, p. 54.
6. An article in the *Wall Street Journal* argues that "The Bretton Woods system ran into trouble in the 1960s, in part because U.S. trade deficits mounted. . . ." Why would increases in the U.S. trade deficit cause problems for the Bretton Woods System?
   Source: Jon E. Hilsenrath and Mary Kissel, "Currency Decision Marks Small Shift Toward Flexibility," *Wall Street Journal*, July 22, 2005.
7. Thomas Mayer, an economist at the German bank, Deutsche Bank, wrote that ". . . following the breakup of the Bretton Woods system that had kept the mark tied to the U.S. dollar, the Bundesbank adopted a monetary policy strategy that allowed it to keep its eyes on ensuring price stability in the long run." Why might keeping the mark tied to the value of the dollar have made it difficult for the Bundesbank to pursue a policy of price stability?
   Source: Thomas Mayer, "Euro Down," *Wall Street Journal*, July 21, 2005.

GLOSSARY

A

Absolute advantage The ability of an individual, firm, or country to produce more of a good or service than competitors using the same amount of resources.

Accounting profit A firm's net income measured by revenue less operating expenses and taxes paid.

Aggregate demand and aggregate supply model A model that explains short-run fluctuations in real GDP and the price level.

Aggregate demand curve *(AD)* A curve showing the relationship between the price level and the quantity of real GDP demanded by households, firms, and the government.

Aggregate expenditure *(AE)* The total amount of spending in the economy: the sum of consumption, planned investment, government purchases, and net exports.

Aggregate expenditure model A macroeconomic model that focuses on the relationship between total spending and real GDP, assuming the price level is constant.

Allocative efficiency A state of the economy in which production reflects consumer preferences; in particular, every good or service is produced up to the point where the last unit provides a marginal benefit to consumers equal to the marginal cost of producing it.

Asset Anything of value owned by a person or a firm.

Autarky A situation in which a country does not trade with other countries.

Automatic stabilizers Government spending and taxes that automatically increase or decrease along with the business cycle.

Autonomous expenditure Expenditure that does not depend on the level of GDP.

B

Balance of payments The record of a country's trade with other countries in goods, services, and assets.

Balance of trade The difference between the value of the goods a country exports and the value of the goods a country imports.

Balance sheet A financial statement that sums up a firm's financial position on a particular day, usually the end of a quarter or a year.

Bank panic Many banks experiencing runs at the same time.

Bank run Many depositors decide simultaneously to withdraw money from a bank.

Black market Buying and selling at prices that violate government price regulations.

Bond A financial security that represents a promise to repay a fixed amount of funds.

Bretton Woods System An exchange-rate system that lasted from 1944 to 1971, under which countries pledged to buy and sell their currencies at a fixed rate against the dollar.

Budget deficit The situation in which the government's spending is greater than its tax revenue.

Budget surplus The situation in which the government's expenditures are less than its tax revenue.

Business cycle Alternating periods of economic expansion and economic recession.

C

Capital Manufactured goods that are used to produce other goods and services.

Capital account The part of the balance of payments that records relatively minor transactions, such as migrants' transfers, and sales and purchases of nonproduced, nonfinancial assets.

Capital controls Limits on the flow of foreign exchange and financial investment across countries.

Cash flow The difference between the cash revenues received by the firm and the cash spending by the firm.

Catch-up The prediction that the level of GDP per capita (or income per capita) in poor countries will grow faster than in rich countries.

Centrally planned economy An economy in which the government decides how economic resources will be allocated.

***Ceteris paribus* ("all else equal")** The requirement that when analyzing the relationship between two variables—such as price and quantity demanded—other variables must be held constant.

Circular-flow diagram A model that illustrates how participants in markets are linked.

Closed economy An economy that has no interactions in trade or finance with other economies.

Commodity money A good used as money that also has value independent of its use as money.

Comparative advantage The ability of an individual, firm, or country to produce a good or service at a lower opportunity cost than other producers.

Competitive market equilibrium A market equilibrium with many buyers and many sellers.

Complements Goods that are used together.

Consumer price index (CPI) An average of the prices of the goods and services purchased by the typical urban family of four.

Consumer surplus The difference between the highest price a consumer is willing to pay and the price the consumer actually pays.

Consumption Spending by households on goods and services, not including spending on new houses.

Consumption function The relationship between consumption spending and disposable income.

Contractionary monetary policy The Fed's adjusting the money supply and increasing of interest rates to reduce inflation.

Corporate governance The way in which a corporation is structured and the impact a corporation's structure has on the firm's behavior.

Corporation A legal form of business that provides the owners with limited liability.

Coupon payment Interest payment on a bond.

Crowding out A decline in private expenditures as a result of an increase in government purchases.

Currency appreciation When the market value of a currency rises relative to another currency.

Currency depreciation When the market value of a currency falls relative to another currency.

Current account The part of the balance of payments that records a country's net exports, net investment income, and net transfers.

Cyclical unemployment Unemployment caused by a business cycle recession.

Cyclically adjusted budget deficit or surplus The deficit or surplus in the federal government's budget if the economy were at potential GDP.

D

Deadweight loss The reduction in economic surplus resulting from a market not being in competitive equilibrium.

Deflation A decline in the price level.

Demand curve A curve that shows the relationship between the price of a product and the quantity of the product demanded.

Demand schedule A table showing the relationship between the price of a product and the quantity of the product demanded.

Demographics The characteristics of a population with respect to age, race, and gender.

Devaluation A reduction in a fixed exchange rate.

Direct finance A flow of funds from savers to firms through financial markets.

Discount loans Loans the Federal Reserve makes to banks.

Discount rate The interest rate the Federal Reserve charges on discount loans.

Discouraged workers People who are available for work but have not looked for a job during the previous four weeks because they believe no jobs are available for them.

Disinflation A significant reduction in the inflation rate.

Dividends Payments by a corporation to its shareholders.

Dumping Selling a product for a price below its cost of production.

E

Economic efficiency A market outcome in which the marginal benefit to consumers of the last unit produced is equal to its marginal cost of production, and in which the sum of consumer surplus and producer surplus is at a maximum.

Economic growth The ability of an economy to produce increasing quantities of goods and services.

Economic growth model A model that explains changes in real GDP per capita in the long run.

Economic model Simplified versions of reality used to analyze real-world economic situations.

Economic profit A firm's revenues minus all of its costs, implicit and explicit.

Economic surplus The sum of consumer surplus and producer surplus.

Economic variable Something measurable that can have different values, such as the wages of software programmers.

Economics The study of the choices people make to attain their goals, given their scarce resources.

Efficiency wage A higher-than-market wage paid by a firm to increase worker productivity.

Endogenous growth theory A model of long-run economic growth that emphasizes that technological change is influenced by economic incentives, and so is determined by the working of the market system.

Entrepreneur Someone who operates a business, bringing together the factors of production—labor, capital, and natural resources—to produce goods and services.

Equity The fair distribution of economic benefits.

Euro The common currency of many European countries.

Excess reserves Reserves that banks hold over and above the legal requirement.

Exchange-rate system An agreement among countries on how exchange rates should be determined.

Expansion The period of a business cycle during which total production and total employment are increasing.

Expansionary monetary policy The Federal Reserve's increasing the money supply and decreasing interest rates to increase real GDP.

Explicit cost A cost that involves spending money.

Exports Goods and services produced domestically but sold to other countries.

External economies Reductions in a firm's costs that result from an expansion in the size of an industry.

F

Factor markets Markets for the factors of production, such as labor, capital, natural resources, and entrepreneurial ability.

Federal funds rate The interest rate banks charge each other for overnight loans.

Federal Open Market Committee The Federal Reserve committee responsible for open market operations and managing the money supply.

Federal Reserve System The central bank of the United States.

Fiat money Money, such as paper currency, that is authorized by a central bank or governmental body and that does not have to be exchanged by the central bank for gold or some other commodity money.

Final good or service A good or service purchased by a final user.

Financial account The part of the balance of payments that records purchases of assets a country has made abroad and foreign purchases of assets in the country.

Financial system The system of financial markets and financial intermediaries through which firms acquire funds from households.

Fiscal policy Changes in federal taxes and purchases that are intended to achieve macroeconomic policy objectives, such as high employment, price stability, and high rates of economic growth.

Fixed exchange rate system A system under which countries agree to keep the exchange rates among their currencies fixed.

Floating currency The outcome of a country allowing its currency's exchange rate to be determined by demand and supply.

Foreign direct investment The purchase or building by a corporation of a facility in a foreign country.

Foreign portfolio investment The purchase by an individual or firm of stocks or bonds issued in another country.

Fractional reserve banking system A banking system in which banks keep less than 100 percent of deposits as reserves.

Free market A market with few government restrictions on how a good or service can be produced or sold, or on how a factor of production can be employed.

Free trade Trade between countries that is without government restrictions.

Frictional unemployment Short-term unemployment arising from the process of matching workers with jobs.

G

GDP deflator A measure of the price level, calculated by dividing nominal GDP by real GDP, and multiplying by 100.

Globalization The process of countries becoming more open to foreign trade and investment.

Government purchases Spending by federal, state, and local governments on goods and services.

Gross domestic product (GDP) The market value of all final goods and services produced in a country during a period of time.

H

Human capital The accumulated knowledge and skills that workers acquire from education and training or from their life experiences.

I

Implicit cost A nonmonetary opportunity cost.

Imports Goods and services bought domestically but produced in other countries.

Income effect The change in the quantity demanded of a good that results from the effect of a change in the good's price on consumer purchasing power.

Income statement A financial statement that sums up a firm's revenues, costs, and profit over a period of time.

Indirect finance A flow of funds from savers to borrowers through financial intermediaries such as banks. Intermediaries raise funds from savers to lend to firms (and other borrowers).

Industrial Revolution The application of mechanical power to the production of goods, beginning in England in the years around 1750.

Inferior good A good for which the demand increases as income falls, and decreases as income rises.

Inflation rate The percentage increase in the price level from one year to the next.

Inflation targeting Conducting monetary policy so as to commit the central bank to achieving a publicly announced level of inflation.

Interest rate The cost of borrowing funds, usually expressed as a percentage of the amount borrowed.

Intermediate good or service A good or service that is an input into another good or service, such as a tire on a truck.

International Monetary Fund (IMF) An international organization that provides foreign currency loans to central banks and oversees the operation of the international monetary system.

Inventories Goods that have been produced but not yet sold.

Investment Spending by firms on new factories, office buildings, machinery, and inventories, and spending by households on new houses; often referred to simply as "investment."

K

Keynesian Revolution The name given to the widespread acceptance during the 1930s and 1940s of John Maynard Keynes's macroeconomic model.

L

Labor force The sum of employed and unemployed workers in the economy.

Labor force participation rate The percentage of the working-age population in the labor force.

Labor productivity The quantity of goods and services that can be produced by one worker or by one hour of work.

Law of demand Holding everything else constant, when the price of a product falls, the quantity demanded of the product will increase, and when the price of a product rises, the quantity demanded of the product will decrease.

Law of supply Holding everything else constant, increases in price cause increases in the quantity supplied, and decreases in price cause decreases in the quantity supplied.

Liability Anything owed by a person or a firm.

Limited liability The legal provision that shields owners of a corporation from losing more than they have invested in the firm.

Long-run aggregate supply curve *(LRAS)* A curve showing the relationship in the long run between the price level and the quantity of real GDP supplied.

Long-run economic growth The process by which rising productivity increases the average standard of living.

M

M1 The narrowest definition of the money supply: The sum of currency in circulation, checking account balances in banks, and holdings of traveler's checks.

M2 A broader definition of the money supply: M1 plus savings account balances, small-denomination time deposits, balances in money market deposit accounts in banks, and noninstitutional money market fund shares.

Macroeconomics The study of the economy as a whole, including topics such as inflation, unemployment, and economic growth.

Managed float exchange rate system The current exchange rate system under which the value of most currencies is determined by demand and supply, with occasional government intervention.

Marginal analysis Analysis that involves comparing marginal benefits and marginal costs.

Marginal benefit The additional benefit to a consumer from consuming one more unit of a good or service.

Marginal cost The additional cost to a firm of producing one more unit of a good or service.

Marginal propensity to consume *(MPC)* The slope of the consumption function: The amount by which consumption spending increases when disposable income increases.

Marginal propensity to save *(MPS)* The change in saving divided by the change in disposable income.

Market A group of buyers and sellers of a good or service and the institution or arrangement by which they come together to trade.

Market demand The demand by all the consumers of a given good or service.

Market economy An economy in which the decisions of households and firms interacting in markets allocate economic resources.

Market equilibrium A situation in which quantity demanded equals quantity supplied.

Market for loanable funds The interaction of borrowers and lenders that determines the market interest rate and the quantity of loanable funds exchanged.

Menu costs The costs to firms of changing prices.

Microeconomics The study of how households and firms make choices, how they interact in markets, and how the government attempts to influence their choices.

Mixed economy An economy in which most economic decisions result from the interaction of buyers and sellers in markets, but in which the government plays a significant role in the allocation of resources.

Monetarism The macroeconomic theories of Milton Friedman and his followers; particularly the idea that the quantity of money should be increased at a constant rate.

Monetary growth rule A plan for increasing the quantity of money at a fixed rate that does not respond to changes in economic conditions.

Monetary policy The actions the Federal Reserve takes to manage the money supply and interest rates to pursue its economic objectives.

Money Assets that people are generally willing to accept in exchange for goods and services or for payment of debts.

Multinational enterprise A firm that conducts operations in more than one country.

Multiplier The increase in equilibrium real GDP divided by the increase in autonomous expenditure.

Multiplier effect The series of induced increases in consumption spending that result from an initial increase in autonomous expenditures.

N

Natural rate of unemployment The normal rate of unemployment, consisting of structural unemployment plus frictional unemployment.

Net exports Exports minus imports.

Net foreign investment The difference between capital outflows from a country and capital inflows, also equal to net foreign direct investment plus net foreign portfolio investment.

New classical macroeconomics The macroeconomic theories of Robert Lucas and others, particularly the idea that workers and firms have rational expectations.

Nominal exchange rate The value of one country's currency in terms of another country's currency.

Nominal GDP The value of final goods and services evaluated at current year prices.

Nominal interest rate The stated interest rate on a loan.

Normal good A good for which the demand increases as income rises and decreases as income falls.

Normative analysis Analysis concerned with what ought to be.

O

Open economy An economy that has interactions in trade or finance with other economies.

Open market operations The buying and selling of Treasury securities by the Federal Reserve in order to control the money supply.

Opportunity cost The highest-valued alternative that must be given up to engage in an activity.

P

Partnership A firm owned jointly by two or more persons and not organized as a corporation.

Pegging The decision by a country to keep the exchange rate fixed between its currency and another currency.

Per-worker production function The relationship between real GDP, or output, per hour worked and capital per hour worked, holding the level of technology constant.

Phillips curve A curve showing the short-run relationship between the unemployment rate and the inflation rate.

Positive analysis Analysis concerned with what is.

Potential GDP The level of GDP attained when all firms are producing at capacity.

Present value The value in today's dollars of funds to be paid or received in the future.

Price ceiling A legally determined maximum price that sellers may charge.

Price floor A legally determined minimum price that sellers may receive.

Price level A measure of the average prices of goods and services in the economy.

Principal-agent problem A problem caused by an agent pursuing his own interests rather than the interests of the principal who hired him.

Producer price index (PPI) An average of the prices received by producers of goods and services at all stages of the production process.

Producer surplus The difference between the lowest price a firm would have been willing to accept and the price it actually receives.

Product markets Markets for goods—such as computers—and services—such as medical treatment.

Production possibilities frontier A curve showing the maximum attainable combinations of two products that may be produced with available resources.

Productive efficiency The situation in which a good or service is produced at the lowest possible cost.

Property rights The rights individuals or firms have to the exclusive use of their property, including the right to buy or sell it.

Protectionism The use of trade barriers to shield domestic firms from foreign competition.

Purchasing power parity The theory that, in the long run, exchange rates move to equalize the purchasing power of different currencies.

Q

Quantity demanded The amount of a good or service that a consumer is willing and able to purchase at a given price.

Quantity supplied The amount of a good or service that a firm is willing and able to supply at a given price.

Quantity theory of money A theory of the connection between money and prices that assumes that the velocity of money is constant.

Quota A numerical limit imposed by the government on the quantity of a good that can be imported into a country.

R

Rational expectations Expectations formed by using all available information about an economic variable.

Real business cycle model A macroeconomic model that focus on real, rather than monetary, causes of the business cycle.

Real exchange rate The price of domestic goods in terms of foreign goods.

Real GDP The value of final goods and services evaluated at base year prices.

Real interest rate The nominal interest rate minus the inflation rate.

Recession The period of a business cycle during which total production and total employment are decreasing.

Required reserve ratio The minimum fraction of deposits banks are required by law to keep as reserves.

Required reserves Reserves that a bank is legally required to hold, based on its checking account deposits.

Reserves Deposits that a bank keeps as cash in its vault or on deposit with the Federal Reserve.

Revaluation An increase in a fixed exchange rate.

Rule of law The ability of a government to enforce the laws of the country, particularly with respect to protecting private property and enforcing contracts.

S

Saving and investment equation An equation showing that national saving is equal to domestic investment plus net foreign investment.

Scarcity The situation in which unlimited wants exceed the limited resources available to fulfill those wants.

Separation of ownership from control In many large corporations the top management, rather than the shareholders, control day-to-day operations.

Shortage A situation in which the quantity demanded is greater than the quantity supplied.

Short-run aggregate supply curve *(SRAS)* A curve showing the relationship in the short run between the price level and the quantity of real GDP supplied by firms.

Simple deposit multiplier The ratio of the amount of deposits created by banks to the amount of new reserves.

Sole proprietorship A firm owned by a single individual and not organized as a corporation.

Speculators Currency traders who buy and sell foreign exchange in an attempt to profit by changes in exchange rates.

Stagflation A combination of inflation and recession, usually resulting from a supply shock.

Stock A financial security that represents partial ownership of a firm.

Stockholders' equity The difference between the value of a corporation's assets and the value of its liabilities; also known as net worth.

Structural relationship A relationship that depends on the basic behavior of consumers and firms and that remains unchanged over long periods.

Structural unemployment Unemployment arising from a persistent mismatch between the skills and characteristics of workers and the requirements of jobs.

Substitutes Goods and services that can be used for the same purpose.

Substitution effect The change in the quantity demanded of a good that results from a change in price making the good more or less expensive relative to other goods that are substitutes.

Supply curve A curve that shows the relationship between the price of a product and the quantity of the product supplied.

Supply schedule A table that shows the relationship between the price of a product and the quantity of the product supplied.

Supply shock An unexpected event that causes the short-run aggregate supply curve to shift.

Surplus A situation in which the quantity supplied is greater than the quantity demanded.

T

Tariff A tax imposed by a government on imports.

Tax incidence The actual division of the burden of a tax between buyers and sellers in a market.

Tax wedge The difference between the pre-tax and post-tax return to an economic activity.

Taylor rule A rule developed by John Taylor that links the Fed's target for the federal funds rate to economic variables.

Technological change Change in the ability of a firm to produce a given level of output with a given quantity of inputs.

Terms of trade The ratio at which a country can trade its exports for imports from other countries.

Trade The act of buying or selling.

Trade-off The idea that because of scarcity, producing more of one good or service means producing less of another good or service.

Transfer payments Payments by the government to individuals for which the government does not receive a good or service in return.

U

Underground economy Buying and selling of goods and services that is concealed from the government to avoid taxes or regulations or because the goods and services are illegal.

Unemployment rate The percentage of the labor force that is unemployed.

V

Value added The market value a firm adds to a product.

Velocity of money The average number of times each dollar in the money supply is used to purchase goods and services included in GDP.

Voluntary exchange The situation that occurs in markets when both the buyer and seller of a product are made better off by the transaction.

Voluntary export restraint An agreement negotiated between two countries that places a numerical limit on the quantity of a good that can be imported by one country from the other country.

W

World Trade Organization (WTO) An international organization that enforces international trade agreements.

COMPANY INDEX

3Com Corporation, 2
3M Company, 144

Allstate, 144
Amazon.com, 123, 156, 157
American International Group, 196
American LaFrance, 202
American Telephone and Telegraph Company (AT&T), 228
American Tobacco Company, 195
Amgen, 144
Andover Bank, 325
AOL, 130
Apple Computer, 6, 7, 26, 52, 150, 168, 175, 181, 205, 207, 251
Ask Jeeves, 130, 146, 147
ASMICO Technologies, 286
AU Optronics, 82
Audi, 32
Axa, 196

Baden Sports, 184
Bank of America, 436
BarnesandNoble.com, 123
Bavarian Motor Works, 32
Bayerische Motoren Werke, 32, 54
Bell Telephone Laboratories, 199, 228, 229
Best Buy, 251
Bethlehem Steel, 142
Blackstone Group LP, 322
Blockbuster Video, 70
BMW, 32, 33, 34, 35, 53, 54, 55, 57, 94, 172
Bob's Candies, 163
Boeing, 254, 255, 412
Booth Creek Resorts, 572
BP, 196
Brach's Confections, 163
Burger King, 91

Carrefour, 196
Caterpillar Inc., 289, 370, 371, 372, 376, 397, 402, 569
Charles Schwab, 133
Chery Automobile Co., 286, 287
Chevron Texaco, 196, 197
Chrysler Corporation, 349
Cisco Systems, 2, 328, 329, 341, 342, 350, 357
Citibank, 436
Citigroup, 196
Cnooc, 545
Coca-Cola, 91, 197, 198, 199, 305
Colgate-Palmolive, 198
3Com Corporation, 2
Comcast Corp., 538
Commerce Bank, 19
Compaq Computer Corporation, 62, 88
ConocoPhillips, 196
Corning, Inc., 82, 146
Credit Lyonnais, 322, 551
Cypress Semiconductor, 471

Daewoo Corporation, 286, 318, 319
DaimlerChrysler, 22, 54, 196, 202, 204
Dell Computer, 19, 87, 88, 89, 166, 320, 349, 350
Desh Garments, Ltd., 318
DirectTV, 100
DISH Network, 100
Doubleday, 331
Douglas Aircraft, 14
Dreamworks, 239
Dreyfus, 271
Dun & Bradstreet (D&B), 2, 3, 140
DuPont, 593

eBay, 199
Eberhard Faber Pencil Company of California, 49, 50
Enron, 131, 143, 150, 390
Epson, 74
Exxon Mobil, 134, 196

Fidelity, 271, 414
First National Bank, 436
Fleet, 436
Ford Motor Company, 22, 23, 70, 91, 172, 196, 243, 260, 261, 286, 287, 289, 329, 381, 520, 521
Freightliner, 202, 203, 205, 218

Gap, 150
Gateway Inc., 88, 89
General Electric, 134, 137, 139, 155, 195, 196, 270, 332
General Motors, 22, 196, 286, 287, 329, 349
Gerbrueder Weiss, 195
Getty Images, 88
Goldman Sachs, 146, 147
Goodyear, 205
Google, 130, 131, 133, 138, 145, 146, 147, 150, 151, 152, 157, 158, 159, 161, 271, 410

Harley-Davidson, 392
Heavenly Tea, 101
Hershey, 577
Hewlett-Packard (HP), 62, 63, 68, 72, 73, 74, 75, 76, 87, 88, 89, 91, 196, 349
Hitachi, 196
Home Depot, 70, 273, 332
Honda Motor Corp., 196, 286, 560
H&R Block, 472, 473, 497
HSBC Securities, 362
Huggies, 289
Hyundai, 582, 586

IBM, 14, 88, 89, 156, 196
Infineon AG, 590
ING Group, 196
Interbrew, 576
Intuit, 473

Jiffy, 91
J.M. SmuckerCompany, 197
J.P. Morgan Chase, 362

Kazaa, 51, 52
Kenmore, 289, 514
Kentucky Fried Chicken, 91
Kmart, 70
Kodak, 175
Komatsu, Ltd., 370, 371, 396, 397

Levi's, 183
LG Phillips LCD, 82
Life Savers, 162, 163
L.L. Bean, 211, 212
Lloyd's of London, 132, 133
Lockheed-Martin, 144
Lowell Bank, 325
Lucent Technologies, 228, 229, 240, 249, 252, 253

3M Company, 144
Magnavox, 175
Mahindra & Mahindra Ltd., 322
Matsushita Electric Industrial, 93
Mattel, 198
Maybach, 54
Maytag, 545
McDonald's, 91, 96, 161, 183, 199, 241, 289, 406, 407, 423
Medici Bank, 195
Mercedes, 54
Merrill Lynch, 396
Michelin, 205
Micro Warehouse, 150
Microsoft, 5, 51, 52, 119, 134, 150, 186, 199, 209, 320, 341, 414, 496
Molson Breweries, 572, 576, 580, 595
Monster.com, 240
Montreal Expos, 595
Moody's Investor Service, 140, 157
Napster, 51
Nautica, 322
NCR Corporation, 62
Nestlé Company, 195
Netscape, 130
Nintendo, 570
Nippon Telephone and Telegraph, 196
Nissan, 173, 560
Nokia Corp., 590
Nortel Networks, 146, 147

Orim Company, 544
Oscar Meyer, 91

palmOne, 175
Panasonic, 175
Pepsi, 28, 29, 30, 91, 197, 198, 344
Pioneer, 175
PNC Bank, 417, 418, 420–421, 422
Prudential Insurance Company, 64, 65

Ralph Lauren, 183
RCA, 175
R.M Smythe and Co., 80
Rogers Communications, Inc., 576
Royal Dutch/Shell Group, 196

Sam's Club, 246
Samsung Electronics, 82, 93
Sanford Bernstein, 146
Sara Lee Corporation, 150
Sears, 514
Shanghai Fosun High Technology, 293
Sharp, 93, 181
Shinsei, 396
Sichuan Changhong Electric Co., 141
Siemens AG, 196
Singer Sewing Machine Company, 195
Smart, 54
Sony, 52, 175
Spangler Candy Company, 163
Standard & Poor's Corporation, 140
Standard Oil, 195, 197
Star Brites, 163
Starbucks, 5, 161
STMicroelectronics NV, 590, 591
Sun Microsystems, 146, 186

Tellabs, 146
Temasek Holdings Pte. Ltd., 322
Texas Instruments, 91
Thomas Built Buses, 202
Thomson IFR Bonddata, 222
Toll Brothers, Inc., 438, 439, 450, 453
Tommy Hilfiger, 322
Toronto Blue Jays, 576

Toshiba, 181
Total, 196
Toyota Motor Company, 50, 172, 173, 195, 196, 286, 299, 322, 560, 593
Tyco, 131, 390

Unocal Corporation, 545
U.S. Steel, 400

Value Line, 140
Vanguard, 271, 414
Volkswagen, 32, 196, 598

Wachovia Bank, 416, 417, 418, 420, 421, 422
Wal-Mart, 68, 186, 196, 241
Walt Disney Company, 239, 557
Warburg Pincus LLC, 322
Welspun India Ltd., 322
Western Electric Bell Laboratories, 304
Western Electric Manufacturing Company, 228
Whirlpool Corporation, 332, 514, 515, 536, 543
Wonder, 91
WorldCom, 131, 143, 150, 390

Yahoo, 130, 146

Zenith, 175

SUBJECT INDEX

Key Terms and the page number on which they are defined appear in **boldface.**

45°-line diagram, 344, 345, 346, 347, 348–349, 365

a9, 130
Abowd, John M., 258
Absolute advantage, 42, 43, 44, 56, **168,** 190,
Accounting profit, 15, 142, 148, 158
Actual investment, 331
Actual real GDP, 269, 270
Adaptive expectations, 527, 540
Aggregate demand and aggregate supply model, 372, 386, 388–389, 391, 393, 398
Aggregate demand curve (AD), 358–360, 364, 397, 398, 518
  application, 372
  downward slope, 373, 374
  expectations of households, and changes in, 375
  foreign variables, and changes in, 375
  government polices, and changes in, 375
  interest-rate effect, 373–374
  international-trade effect, 374
  shifts *versus movements along the aggregate demand curve, 374–375, 377–378*
  variables, shift, 375–376, 379
  wealth effect, and the, 373
Aggregate expenditure (ae), 329, 330, 346, 351, 363
  consumption, 333–335
  consumption function, 335–336
  current disposable income, 333–334
  determining the level in the economy, 333–339
  expected future income, 334–335
  and GDP, 332
  government purchases, 342, 343
  household wealth, 334
  income, consumption, and saving, 338–339
  interest rates, and, 335
  inventories, and, 349
  and national income, 336–338
  net exports, 342–343, 344
  planned investment, 340–341
  price level, and, 335
Aggregate expenditure model, 330–333, 364
Aggregate spending, 363
Aggregate supply, 518
  application, 378
  capital stock, 378
  long-run aggregate supply curve *(LRAS), 378, 380*
  menu costs, 381
  shifts in the aggregate supply curve *versus movements along it, 381–382*
  short-run aggregate supply curve, 380–381, 383, 384
  sticky wages and prices, 381
  supply shock, 383
  variables, shift, 382–383
Alesina, Alberto, 464, 500
Allocative efficiency, 9, 18
American Bar Association, 20
Anderson, Richard G., 469
Annual percentage change, 297
Annual reports, 143
Annual unemployment rate, U.S., 238
Anticipated inflation, 251–252
Argentina
  average annual growth rate of real GDP, 313
  currency crisis,406–407, 424
  growth rates, 296
  inflation, 429–430
  monetary policy, 432, 433
Asian exchange rate crisis, 583
Asset, 132, 158
Aten, Bettina, 269, 313
Auditing, 143
Australia
  bilateral agreements, 188–189
  exports to China, 17
  real GDP per person, 226
Autarky, 169, 176
Automatic mechanism, 385
Automatic stabilizers, 474
Autonomous change, 364
Autonomous expenditure, 352, 603
Autonomous values, 509
Average annual growth rate, 265
Ayittey, George, 327

Balance of payments, 546, 547, 549, 550, 566
Balance of services, 547
Balance of trade, 546, 550, 566
Balance sheet, 143, 148, 157, 158–159
Balanced budget, 273
Balanced budget multiplier, 510–511
Balassa, Bela, 59
Bangaladesh
  globalization, 318–319
Bank balance sheets, 416
Bank of England, 597
Bank of Japan, 454, 466, 467, 535–536
Bank of Thailand, 583, 584
Bank panic, 423
Bank panic in Argentina, 2001, 423–424
Bank run, 423
Bar graphs, 22
Barriers to trade, 182, 187
Barro, Robert, 404
Barter economies, 408, 434
Base year, 215, 224
Basic accounting equation, 158
Basis points, 140
Batini, Nicoletta, 542
Baum, L. Frank, 58
Behavioral assumptions, 10
Belgium
  exports and imports as a percentage of GDP, 166
Bellini, Donna, 538, 539
Bellini, Mark, 538, 539
Beltran, Carlos, 160
Benitez, Armando, 160
Bernanke, Ben, 424, 440, 462, 502, 503
Bhagwati, Jagdish, 12, 17
Bilateral free trade agreement, 188, 189
Bill becomes a law, how a, 486
Black markets, 109, 110
Blancflower, D., 258
Bloch, Henry, 472
Blomstrom, Magnus, 184
Bloomberg, Michael, 97
Board of directors, 134
Bonds, 136, **137,** 138, 139, 148, 150, 155, 270
Bonilla, Bobby, 160
Bosack, Len, 328
Botswana
  average annual growth rate, 26
  economic growth, 268–269
Botswana, economic growth in, 268
Bower, Jeff, 595
Bozotti, Carl, 590
Brain drain, 320
Bretton Woods System, 589, 592, 596, **597–598,** 598–599
Brewer, Bob, 254
Bricklin, Malcolm, 286
Brin, Sergey, 130, 131
Brooks, David, 327
Brown, Drusilla K., 184
Brown, E. Cary, 492, 493
Bruce-Biggs, B., 192
Buchanan, Patrick J., 192
Buddress, Lee, 72–73
Budget deficit, 273, **490,** 491, 492, 503, 504, 560–561, 562, 565
Budget surplus, 273, **490,** 504
Bundesbank, 598, 599, 601
Burns, Arthur, 424, 462, 534, 543
Burruss, Jim, 72–73
Bush, George W., 188, 192, 230, 342, 466, 467, 486, 487, 502, 503, 541
Business, 14
  Business cycle, 202, **204,** 255, 261, 262, 288
  automobile production, effect on, 280–281
  business cycle trough, 278
  expansion phase, 278, 279–280
  inflation rate, effect on, 281–282
  phases of, 279–280
  recession phase, 278, 279–280
  recessions on the inflation rate, effect of, 282
  recessions on unemployment rate, effect of, 283
  stability of, 284, 285
unemployment rate, effect on, 282
Business fixed investment, 211
Business inventories, changes in, 209, 211
Canada
  comparative advantage and gains from trade, 44–45, 46
  freemarket, gains from, 48
  gross domestic product, 222–223
  inflation targeting, 463
  international trade, role of, 165
  market economy, 8
  NAFTA, 185–186
  unemployment programs, 241
  unemployment rates, 243
Capital, 15, **266,** 288, 324
Capital account, 548–549
Capital controls, 599
Capital flight, 584
Capital gain, 137, 496
Capital inflow, 547
Capital markets, 588
Capital outflow, 547
Capital stock, 266, 378
Card, David, 107
Carter, Jimmy, 531
Carville, James, 564
Cash flow, 341, 603
Catch-up, 312, 313, 314, 324
Causal relationship, 11
Central bank, 411, 423
Centrally planned economy, 8, 20, 292
Ceteris paribus, 94
Chain-weighted prices, 217
Chaloupka, 92
Chambers, John, 341
Chancellor, Edward, 466
Chief executive officer (CEO), 134
Chief financial officer (CFO), 134
Child labor, 183, 184
Chile
  inflation targeting, 463
  monetary policy, 432
China
  automobile industry, 286–287
  economic growth, 16–17, 141, 292–293,396–397
  foreign investment, 322, 323
  international trade, role of, 165
  mixed economy, transition to, 9
  outsourcing, 2–3
  real GDP per person, 226
  standards of living, 297–298
Chong, Juin-Kuan, 69
Circular-flow diagram, 47, 48, 207, 208
Clarida, Richard, 306
Classical economists, 529
Clean air act, 58, 307
Clinton, William, 192, 193, 342, 502, 564
Closed economy, 272, **54**
Closing price, 139
Club of Rome, 321
Colombia
  monetary policy, 432
Commercial loans, 416
Commodity money, 408, 411
Company, 14

Comparative advantage, 43, 44, 45, 56, 167–168, 173, 174–175, 185, 190
Competitive advantage, 199
Competitive equilibrium, 102, 103, 104, 110, 111, 119, 124, 128
Competitive market equilibrium, 78
Competitive markets, 78, 102
Complementary goods, 89
Complements, 68, 69
Conesa, Juan Carlos, 498
Conley, Dalton, 149
Consumer loans, 416
Consumer price index (CPI), 244, 245, 256
Consumer surplus, 98, **99,** 100, 101, 102, 103, 105, 108, 110, 112, 120, 126, 127, 128, 179
Consumption (C), 208, 330, 333–335, 336, 449
Consumption function, 335–336
Consumption of fixed capital, 220
Consumption spending, 26, 351
Consumption tax, 277
Contractionary fiscal policy, 479, 480
Contractionary monetary policy, 455–456, 458, 468
Contracts, enforcement of, 52
Convergence, 312
Copyright protection, 51, 305
Corporate governance, 134, 144, 148
Corporate income tax, 341
Corporate structure, 134
Corporations, 132, 133, 134, 135, 140, 141, 148
Corruption, 319
Cost of goods sold, 158
Cost-of-living index, 244
Cost of revenue, 158
Cost of sales, 158
Countercyclical fiscal policy, 479
Countercyclical policy, 460
Coupon payments, 137, 138, 156, 252
Coupon rate, 137, 139
Craig, Lee A., 93
Crane, Clarence, 162, 163
Crook, Clive, 327
Crowding out, 487–489, 504, 563
Cuba
  centrally planned economy, 8
  free market, rejection of the, 48
Culbertson, Scott, 72–73
Currency, 413
Currency appreciation, 553, 603
Currency depreciation, 553, 603
Current account, 546, 566
Current account balance, 550
Current assets, 158
Current disposable income, 333–334
Current exchange rate system, 575, 582–583, 587, 592
Current liabilities, 159
Current population survey, 230
Cyclical unemployment, 239, 256
Cyclically adjusted budget deficit or surplus, 491, 604
Czech Republic
  inflation targeting, 463
  rule of law, 316

Das Kapital, 405
Davis, Glyn, 435
De Soto, Hernando, 60, 327
Deadweight loss, 103, 104, 106, 108, 110, 111, 112, 113, 120, 177, 178
Deardorff, Alan V., 184
Deflation, 250, 532, 535
Delay, Tom, 502
Delisted, 147
Dell, Michael, 89
DeLong, Bradford, 294, 296
Demand
  ceteris paribus condition, 67
  change in demand *versus change in quantity demanded, 72, 90*
  complements, 68, 69
  demand curve, 64, 65, 90
  demand schedules, 64, 65
  demand side of the market, 64
  demographics, impact of, 70
  expected future prices, and, 70
  graphing equations, 125–126
  income effect, 66, 67
  individual buyer, demand of, 64, 65
  inferior good, 69
  law of demand, 66, 90
  market demand, 65
  normal good, 69
  population, impact of, 70
  price-quantity combination, plotting, 65
  prices of related goods, 68
  quantity demanded, 64
  shifting the demand curve, 68, 71
  shifts in a curve versus movements along a curve, 86–87
  shifts in demand over time, 84
  substitutes, 68, 69
  substitution effect, 66, 67
  tastes, consumer, 70
  variables, 90
Demand curve, 23, 25, **64,** 65, 90, 99
Demand for money, 442–443
Demand schedules, 64, 65
Democratic Republic of Congo
  average annual growth rate, 269
Demographics, impact of, 70, 604
Deposit insurance, 426
Depreciation, 220
Destabilizing speculation, 584, 599, 600
Devaluation, 598, 604
Devarajan, Shantayanan, 268, 269
Developing countries, 298
Dickens, Charles, 274
Differentiated products, 172
Diminishing returns to capital, 324
Dinar, 412
Direct finance, 136, 604
Discount loans, 426, 434
Discount policy, 426
Discount rate, 426, 434
Discouraged workers, 231, 233
Discretion strategy, 535, 540
Discretionary fiscal policy, 472, 474
Disinflation, 531, 532
Disposable personal income, 26, 220,478
Dissaving, 273, 558
Dividend yield, 139, 156
Dividends, 137, 497
Dollar, David, 316
Dollar, fluctuations in the, 587–588
Dollar reserves, 597
Domestic industries, 186, 196–197
Domestic trade, 162
Dominguez, Kathryn M.E., 424
Double coincidence of wants, 408, 434
Double counting, 205
Drexler, Mickey, 150
Dumping, 186, 190
Durable goods, 209, 211
Dynamic aggregate demand and aggregate supply model, 388–390, 398

Earned income tax credit, 107
Easterly, William, 268, 269, 319
Econometric models, 368, 508
Econometrics, 72
Economic analysis, 18
Economic costs, 142
Economic efficiency, 104, 105, 108, 111, 120, 128, 178
Economic fluctuations and the budget deficit, 493–494
Economic growth, 39–40, 204, 260, 262, 264, 265, 292, 294–295, 302, 303, 441
  from B.C. to the present, 294
  health and education, improving, 320
  long-run economic growth, 262–263
  polices of, 319–321
  property rights, enhancing, 319
  rule of law, 319
  savings and investment policies, 320
  and technological change, 301–302
  technology, policies related to, 320
  in the united states, 306, 307–308
Economic growth model, 298, 306, 312, 314, 315, 324
Economic models, 4, 17, 18
  assumptions, role of, 10
  development of, 10
  economic variable, 10
  hypotheses, forming and testing, 10–11
  use of, 10
Economic profit, 15, **142,** 148
Economic resources, 15
Economic surplus, 98, 103, 104, 106, 120
Economic variable, 10, 604
Economics, 4, 604
Economist, 578
Efficiency wages, 242, 243, 256
Einstein, Albert, 473
Employed, 230
Employment act of 1946, 285
Endogenous growth theory, 304–305, 324
England
  gains from trade, 172
  Industrial Revolution, 294–295
Entrepreneur, 14, **50,** 267
Equations, 125
Equilibrium, 92
  effect of shifts in supply, 81–82
  effects of shifts in demand, 83
  in the foreign exchange market, 552–553
Equilibrium condition, 125
Equilibrium market price, 98
Equilibrium price, 78, 89
Equilibrium quantity, 78
Equilibrium real federal funds rate,535
Equilibrium real GDP, 508–509
Equilibrium wage, 107
Equity, 9, 18, 152
Establishment survey, 236
Estonia
  flat tax, adoption of, 498
  free market, gains from, 48
Ethiopia
  average annual growth rate, 269
Euro, 575, 580–581, 592
European Central Bank, 564, 568, 581
Excess reserves, 416, 434
Exchange rate, 223, 344, 375, 376, 551, 552, 553, 555, 556, 577, 580
  shifts in demand and supply, effects in, 553–554, 555
Exchange rate risk, 197
Exchange rate system, 574, 592
Exchanges, 137
Excise tax, 112–113
Expansion, 204, 386–387
Expansionary fiscal policy, 478–479, 487, 503
Expansionary monetary policy, 451, **452,** 458, 467, 468, 590
Expectations of future inflation, 520–521
Expected future income, 334–335
Expected future prices, 70
Expenditures, 504
Explicit cost, 142, 604
Export-led recovery, 397
Exports, 164, 165, 190, 207, 211, 555, 556, 558
External economies, 174, 190
External funds, 136
Exxon Valdez, 133

Face value, 137
Factor markets, 46
Factors of production, 15, 34, 46, 207, 208
Farm program, 105, 106, 111, 122, 124
Fastow, Andrew, 143
Fed targets, 460–461, 462
Fed watchers, 458–459
Federal budget as an automatic stabilizer, 490–491
Federal funds rate, 448, 468
Federal government debt, 494–496
Federal Insurance Contributions Act (FICA), 116, 117
Federal Open Market Committee (FOMC), 425, 434, 439
Federal reserve, 534, 535
Federal Reserve Act, 424, 469
Federal reserve bank, 19, 569
Federal reserve districts, 425
Federal reserve note, 411
Federal Reserve System, 423, **424,** 604
Fiat money, 411, 433, 434, 575
Final goods and services, 205, 224, 604
Financial account, 547, 566
Financial capital, 15, 136
Financial intermediaries, 271
Financial markets, 136, 270
Financial security, 136
Financial statements, 140, 141, 143, 148, 152, 157–158
Financial system, 48, 136, 207, 262, **270,** 288
Finland
  inflation targeting, 463
Fiorina, Carly, 62, 63, 88, 89
Firm, 14, 47
  challenges to, 199
Firms, types of, 132
Fiscal policy
  aggregate demand, and, 479
  aggregate supply, and, 483–484
  automatic stabilizers, 474
  balancing the federal budget, 494
  budget deficit, 490, 491, 492, 504
  budget surplus, 490, 504
  contractionary fiscal policy, 479, 480
Fiscal year, 142
Fisher, Irving, 428–429
Fitch, Sir Richard, 133
Fixed exchange-rate system, 592, 598
Fixed-lump-of-trade fallacy, 17
Fixed exchange rate systems, 574, 604
Flat tax, 496–497
Fleming, Charles, 133
Flight to quality, 562
Floating currency, 574, 604
Floating dollar, 575
Floats, 592
Fogel, Robert, 264, 265, 320
Forbes, Steve, 496
Ford, Henry, 50, 243, 255
Foreign direct investment (FDI), 195, **196,** 317, 548

Foreign exchange market, 551
Foreign markets, 196–197, 199
Foreign portfolio investment, 195, **196,** 317, 548, 588
Formal sector, 213
Formulas
 areas of rectangles and a triangle, 28, 29
 percentage change, 28
Fractional reserve banking system, 423, **423,** 604
France
 economic prosperity and health, relationship of, 264
 international trade, role of, 165
 multinational corporations, 196
 unemployment rates, 242
Franchise, 406
Francis, Neville, 306
Frankel, Jeffrey, 306
Free market, 48, 604
Free ride, 304
Free trade, 175, 188, 189
Freeman, R., 258
Frictional unemployment, 238–239, 256
Friedman, Milton, 193, 403, 460, 468, 469, 519, 520, 521, 540
Fudan University, 293
Full employment, 239, 348
Full-employment GDP, 378
Full-employment rate of unemployment, 239, 256
Fuller, Ida May, 477
Fundamental disequilibrium, 598
Funds, raising, 136–137
Future inflation, expectations of, 520–521
Future profitability, expectations of, 340
Future value, 153, 154

Gates, Bill, 4, 19, 414
GDP. *See* gross domestic product (GDP)
GDP deflator, 218–219, 224, 244, 256
GDP per capita, 299
General Agreement on Tariffs and Trade (GATT), 182, 597
General Incorporation Laws, 132
General Motors, 22, 196, 286, 287, 329, 349
General Theory of Employment, Interest, and Money, 330, 403, 492, 505, 529
Generally accepted accounting principles, 140, 150
Georgia
 flat tax adoption of, 496
Germany
 automobile industry, 32–33, 54–55
 exports and imports as a percentage of GDP, 166
 exports to China, 17
 hyperinflation, 430
 inflation rate, 464
 international trade, role of, 165
 multinational corporations, 196
 unemployment rates, 242
Giavazzi, Francesco, 306
Gillett, Jr., George, 572, 595
Ginsberg, Benjamin, 486
Glaeser, Edward, 319, 500
Globalization, 182, 183, 190, 317–**318,** 323, 327
Gold, Russell, 545
Gold Standard, 434, 596, 601
Goldberg, Linda S., 184
Goldin, Claudia, 319
Goods, 14
Goodwill, 158
Goodwin, Barry, 93
Goolsbee, Austan, 100
Gordon, Robert, 526
Government budget deficit, 560–561, 562, 565
Government constraints, 110, 175, 177
Government consumption, 209
Government intervention, 104–105, 105, 106, 107, 111, 124
Government purchases, 209, 211, 330, 342, 343
Government purchases multiplier, 482–483, 504, 509–510
Government spending, overview of, 475–476
Graphs
 bar graphs, 22
 demand curve, 25, 26
 more than two variables, 24
 nonlinear curves, slope of, 26–27
 one variable, 22
 pie chart, 22
 plotting price and quantity, 24
 positive and negative relationships, 26
 slope of lines, 23, 25
 tangent line, 27
 three variables, 25
 time-series graph, 22, 23
 two variables, 23
Great Britain
 exports to China, 17
 multinational corporations, 196
Great Depression, 105, 214, 215, 261, 285, 317, 354–355, 403, 467, 475, 491, 492, 529, 531, 574, 596
Greece
 real GDP per person, 226
Greenspan, Alan, 424, 440, 448, 452, 454, 462, 466, 470, 507, 514, 515, 534, 540, 541, 542, 543
Grennes, Thomas, 93
Grisham, John, 331
Gross, Daniel, 38
Gross domestic product (GDP), 22, 28, 164, **205,** 222, 224, 362, 372
 calculating, 206, 265
 circular-flow diagram, and, 208
 components of, 208, 211
 consumption, 208
 equation for, 210
 GDP deflator, 218–219
 government consumption, 209
 gross private domestic investment, 209
 growth in real GDP, 263
 net exports of goods and services, 210
 real GDP *versus nominal GDP, 215–218*
 total production, as a measure of, 212–213
 value added method, measurement by, 211–212
 well-being, as a measurement of, 214
Gross National Product (GNP), 219–220
Gross private domestic investment, 209
Group of seven, 309
Growth rate, 156, 265, 297, 298
Guangchang, Guo, 293
Guild System, 48

Haldane, Andrew G., 542
Halo effect, 16, 17
Hamilton, Alexander, 268
Hanson, Gordon H., 186
Hard landing, 141
Hayek, Salma, 70
Heavenly Tea, 101
Hebe, Jim, 218
Hershey, 577
Heston, Alan, 269
Heston, Lan, 313
Higgs, Robert, 215
High-income countries, 298
Hill, Frank Ernest, 243
Hino, Ryo, 362
Hirabayashi, Motoki, 544, 560, 569
Ho, Teck-Hua, 69
Hobbes, Thomas, 292
Holding technology constant, 300
Holis, Fred, 255
Holmes, Oliver Wendell, 112
Holtz-Eakin, Douglas, 502
Homeland Security, 209, 210
Hong Kong
 average annual growth rate of real GDP, 313
 free market, gains from, 48
Hoover, Herbert, 506
Hounshell, David A., 243
Hourly earnings, calculating, 248, 249
Household, 15, 46
Household production, 212
Household survey, 230, 236
Household wealth, 334
Human capital, 15, **266,** 299, 317
Hungary
 inflation targeting, 463
Hunt, Robert, 188
Hurd, Mark, 62
Hurricane Katrina, impact of, 383
Hussein, Saddam, 412
Hyperinflation, 429, 430, 431

Implicit cost, 142, 605
Imports, 164, 176, 207, 211, 555, 556, 557, 558
Incentives, 4, 5, 6, 18
Income, circular flow of, 46
Income before taxes, 158
Income effect, 66, **67,** 605
Income statement, 142, 148, 157, 158
Index numbers, 245
India
 economic prosperity and health, relationship of, 264
 foreign investment, growth of, 322–323
Indirect business taxes, 220
Indirect finance, 136
Individual buyer, demand of, 64, 65
Indonesia
 child labor, 184
 Tsunami, effects of the, 38
Induced change, 364
Industrial Revolution, 292, **294,** 295, 296
Infant industries, 185
Inferior good, 69, 605
Inflation, 228, 389, 522, 529–530, 531
 anticipated inflation, 251–252
 costs on the economy, and, 251–252
 distribution of income, and, 251
 measuring, 243–244
 unanticipated inflation, 253
Inflation gap, 462, 535
Inflation rate, 204, **244,** 256, 281, 282, 441, 525, 526–527, 532–533, 535
 calculating, 246
Inflation targeting, 462–463, 468
Informal economic activities, 226
Informal sector, 213
Information, 271
Initial Public Offering (IPO), 145, 146, 147
Innovation, 14
Inside directors, 135, 145
Insider trading, 147
Insourcing, 166
Intellectual property, 304
Intellectual property rights, 51, 182
Interest rate, 137, 249, 340–341
Interest-rate effect, 373–374
Interest rates and aggregate demand, role of, 449–450
Intermediate good, 205, 605
International capital markets, 588–589, 592
International Monetary Fund (IMF), 597, 605
International trade, 162, 164, 165, 166, 172, 182, 190
International-trade effect, 374
Internet Protocol (IP), 328
Inventories, 331, 349, 364
Inverse relationship, 516
Investment, 209, 211, 449
Investment tax credits, 321
Investment tax incentives, 341
iPods, 6, 7, 19, 26, 27
Iran
 real GDP per person, 226
Iraq
 devaluation of the Dinar, 412
Ireland
 average annual growth, rate of real GDP, 313
Irwin, Douglas A., 191, 193
Israel
 average annual growth rate of real GDP, 313
 rule of law, 316
Italy
 average annual growth rate of real GDP, 313
 inflation rate, 464
 international trade, role of, 165
 unemployment rates, 242

Jacobs, Jane, 118
Japan
 average annual growth rate of real GDP, 313
 comparative advantage, 168, 169, 170, 174–175
 economic growth, 362–363, 396–397
 exports and imports as a percentage of GDP, 166
 exports to China, 17
 fiscal policy, 489–490
 inflation targeting, 536
 international trade, role of, 165
 market economy, 8
 monetary policy, 454
 multinational corporations, 196
 outsourcing,2–3
 standards of living, 297–298
 tariffs and quotas, effects of, 181
 unemployment rates, 242
Jevons, Stanley, 435
Job creation, 237
Job destruction, 237
Job search, 238
Jobs, Steve, 150
Johnson, Lyndon, 230
Johnston, Louis, 263
Just-in-time system, 299

Kawai, Hiroki, 181
Kaye, Chip, 322
Keeton, Ann, 22
Keller, Maryann N., 286
Keller, Wolfgang, 295, 296
Kennedy, John F., 485
Kenya
 average annual growth rate, 269

Keynes, John Maynard, 330, 344, 403, 492, 505, 529
Keynesian Cross, 344
Keynesian revolution, 403
Khrushchev, Nikita, 302
Kiser, Sherry L., 586
Kliesen, Kevin L., 402
Knowledge capital, 304
Koizumi, Junichiro, 470
Komatsu, Ltd., 370, 371, 396, 397
Koo, Jahyeong, 586
Kraay, Aart, 316
Kramarz, Francis, 258
Kramer, Cosmo, 234
Krueger, Alan B., 60, 107, 235
Krueger, Dirk, 498
Kydland, Finn, 404, 529

Labor force, 230, 256
Labor force participation rate, 232, 233, 234, 256
Labor productivity, 266, 288, **298,** 324, 391, 392
Labor theory of value, 405
Labor unions, 242
Lampert, Mark, 218
Landers, Peter, 437
Landsburg, Steven E., 193, 274, 275
Laneve, 286
Larsson, Tomas, 184
Latvia
flat tax, adoption of, 498
Law of demand, 66, 90
Law of Diminishing Return, 300
Law of supply, 74, 90
Legal environment, 50
Lemieux, Thomas, 258
Lender of last resort, 423
Lenin, V.I., 8
Lerner, Sandra, 328
Lewis, Michael, 60
Liabilities, 132, **141,** 158, 334
Limitations of, 489–490
Limited liability, 132, 148
Limits to growth, 321
Liquidity, 271, 311, 410
Lithuania
flat tax, adoption of, 498
Lloyd, Edward, 133
Loanable funds, market ror, 273, 274, 276, 277
Long run, effects of fiscal policy in the, 496–500
Long-run aggregate supply, 516
Long-run aggregate supply curve (*LRAS*), 378, 380, 398
Long-run economic growth, 263, 266, 288
Long-run macroeconomic equilibrium, 383
Long-run Phillips curve, 520, 523, 524, 527
Long-term liabilities, 159
Loose monetary policy, 456
Lowi, Theodore J., 486
Lucas, Robert, 320, 404, 527, 528, 529, 532, 540
Luthra, Hemant, 322

M1, 413–414, 415, 434, 534
M2, 414–415, 434, 534
M3, 415
Maastricht Treaty, 564
Macroeconomic equilibrium, 331–332, 344–345, 346–348, 350–351, 365, 368–369
automatic mechanism, 385
expansion, 386–387
long-run macroeconomic equilibrium, 383
recessions, 384–385
short-run effect, 387
short-run macroeconomic equilibrium, 385
stagflation, 388
supply shock, 387–388
Macroeconomic policies, 333
Macroeconomics, 13, **14,** 18, 204, 605
Malaysia
average annual growth rate of real GDP, 313
Managed float exchange rate system, 574, 592
Margin, decisions at the, 5, 18
Marginal, 6
Marginal analysis, 6, 605
Marginal benefit (MB), 6, **99,** 102, 120
Marginal cost (MC), 6, **101,** 102, 120
Marginal opportunity cost, 38–39
Marginal propensity to consume (MPC), 335, 339, 363, 364
Marginal propensity to save (MPS), 338, 339, 365
Margolis, David N., 258
Market, 46, 56
Market basket, 244
Market demand, 65, 605
Market economy, 8, 605
Market equilibrium, 77–78, 90
Market for loanable funds, 262, **273,** 274, 276, 277, 288
Market mechanism, 48–49
Market price, 98
Market supply curve, 74
Market system, 46, 49, 50, 145
Market values, 205
Markets, 5, 605
Martin, William McChesney, 424, 470, 534
Marx, Karl, 405
Maskus, Keith, 184
Maturities, 137, 140, 150
Maybach, 54
Mayer, Thomas, 601
MB. *See* marginal benefit (MB)
MC. *See* marginal cost (MC)
McCallum, Bennett T., 526
McTeer, Jr., Robert, 19, 59
Medicaid, 503
Medicare, 476–477, 502, 503
Menu costs, 252, 256, 381, 695
Metallica, 51
Mexico
inflation targeting, 463
monetary policy, 432
NAFTA,185–186
Microeconomics, 13, 18, 204
Mill, John Stuart, 405
Miller, G. William, 424, 534
Minimum wage, 106, 107, 129, 241
Misery index, 230
Mixed economy, 8, 9, 605
Molson breweries, 572, 576, 580, 595
Monetarism, 403, 460
Monetarist model, 403
Monetary growth rule, 403, 460, 461
Monetary History of the United States, A, 403
Monetary policy, 425
in an open economy, 562–563
ceteris paribus condition, 457
contractionary monetary policy, 455–456, 458, 468
countercyclical policy, 460
demand for money, 442–443
economic activity, and, 449–457
economic growth, 441
effects of, 456–457
equilibrium in the money market, 444–446
expansionary monetary policy, 451, 452, 458, 467, 468
fed targets, 460–461, 462
fed watchers, 458–459
federal funds rate, 448, 448, 468
federal reserve, independence of the, 463–465, 468
fed's management of the money supply, 444
fed's targets, 441–442
goals of, 440, 468
high employment, 440–441
inflation, role in fighting, 454–455
inflation gap, 462
inflation targeting, 462–463, 468
interest rates and aggregate demand, role of, 449–450
japanese monetary policy, 454
long-term real rate of interest, 447
loose monetary policy, 456
monetarism, and, 460
monetary growth rule, 460, 461
monetary policy target, 447–448
output gap, 462
policy targets, 442, 468
price stability, 440
procyclical policy, 460
real GDP and the price level, effects of, 451–452
recessions, 453–454
recognizing the need for changing the monetary policy, 459–460
shifts in the money demand curve, 443
short-term nominal rate of interest, 447
stability of financial markets and institutions, 441
taylor rule, 461–462, 468
tight monetary policy, 456
treasury bills and their interest rates, 446–447
Monetary policy target, 447–448
Money, 408
bank balance sheets, 416
bank panic, 423
bank run, 423
barter economies, 408, 434
central bank, 423
commodity money, 408, 411
creation of, 415–416, 420–421
credit cards and debit cards, 415
criteria, 410–411
currency, 413
deferred payment, as standard of, 410
definition of, 408, 413
deposit insurance, 426
devaluation, 432
discount loans, 426, 434
discount policy, 426
discount rate, 426, 434
double coincidence of wants, 408, 434
excess reserves, 416, 434
Federal Open Market Committee (FOMC), 425, 434
federal reserve act, 424
federal reserve districts, 425
federal reserve note, 411
Federal Reserve System, 423, 424
fiat money, 411, 433, 434
Fractional reserve banking system, 423
functions of, 409–410
gold standard, 434
hyperinflation, 429, 430, 431
legal tender, 411
lender of last resort, 423
m1, 413–414, 415, 434
m2, 414–415, 434
m3, 415
managing the money supply, 424–425
maturity of a financial asset, 425
measurement of, 412–413
medium of exchange, as, 409
monetary policy, 425, 434
net worth, 416
nonbank public, 427
open market operations, 425–426
Money supply, ee-emphasizing the, 534
Morgan, Lee, 569
Morgan, Peter, 362
Mortgage Loans, 253
Moss, Robert F., 96, 97
Multilateral negotiations, 182
Multinational enterprises, 195, **196,** 198
Multiplier, 352, 605
Multiplier effect, 352–357, 364, 481–482, 504, 511
Mutual funds, 271
Myers, David, 143

National Association of Securities Dealers' Automated Quotation System (NASDAQ), 138, 144, 146, 147, 150
National Bureau of Economic Research (NBER), 278–279
National Hockey League, 222, 572
National income, 220, 336–337
National income accounting, 219, 272
National Income And Product Accounts (NIPA), 219
National saving, 558
Natural rate of unemployment, 239, 256, 520, 525, 540, 606
Nelson, Edward, 471
Neo-quantity theory of money model, 403
Net benefit, 102, 104
Net capital flows, 548
Net exports (NX), 210, 331, 342–343, 344, 449, 546, 547, 557–558, 606
Net exports of goods and services, 210
Net foreign investment, 545, **548,** 557–558, 606
Net income, 142, 158
Net investment Account, 546
Net National Product (NNP), 220
Net taxes, 336
Netherlands
multinational corporations, 196
Nettransfers, 546
Net worth, 143, 158, 416
Neumark, David, 107
Nevins, Alan, 243
New classical macroeconomics, 404, 529, 606
New classical model, 404
"New Economy," 308, 324
New growth theory, 304
New Keynesians, 403
New product bias, 246
New York Stock Exchange, 137, 144, 148
New Zealand
inflation rate, 464
inflation targeting, 463
Newly industrializing countries, 298, 585–586
Neyer, Rob, 576
Ng, Johnny, 188

Nigeria
average annual growth rate, 269
Nixon, President, 542, 599
Nominal assets, 373
Nominal exchange rate, 551, 566, 606
Nominal GDP, 215, 224, 606
Nominal interest rate, 249, 250, 256, 274, 335, 454, 522–523, 606
Nominal variables, 247, 256
Nominal wage, 249
Nonaccelerating Inflation Rate of Unemployment (NAIRU), 525
Nonbank public, 427
Nondurable goods, 209, 211, 335
Nonlinear curves, slope of, 26–27
Normal good, 69, 606
Normal rate of return, 142
Normative analysis, 12, **13,** 20, 111, 120, 187, 606
North, Douglass C., 295, 296
North American Free Trade Agreement (NAFTA), 164, 185–186
North Korea
centrally planned economy, 8
free market, rejection of the, 48
Norway
real GDP per person, 226

Occupational Safety And Health Administration, 307
Ofer, Gur, 326
Off-shoring, 2, 166, 167
Official reserve transactions, 549
Oil shock of 1974-1975, 394
Okun, Arthur, 230
Open economies, 546, 549–550, 566, 606
Open economy, 272, 562–563, 606
Open market operations, 425–426, 434, 606
Operating income, 158
Opportunity cost, 15, **35,** 43, 56, 142, 167, 168, 172, 241, 443, 606
Optimal decisions, 4, 5, 6, 18
Organization of Petroleum Exporting Countries (OPEC), 307, 308, 530
Outlet bias, 246
Output gap, 462, 535
Outside directors, 135
Outsourcing, 2, 3, 11, 12, 17, 166, 167, 197
Over-the-counter market, 138

P-E ratio, 139
Pack, Howard, 268, 269
Pacula, Rosalie, 92
Page, Larry, 130, 131
Pakistan
child labor, 185
Pakko, Michael, 569
Panagariya, Arvind, 12
Panke, Helmut, 54
Par exchange rate, 597
Partnerships, 132, 133, 134, 148, 606
Patacone, 407
Patent, 51, **304,** 305, 606
Payroll survey, 236
Pegging, 583, 584, 585, 592, 594, 606
Peppers, Larry, 492, 493
Per-worker production function, 300, 324, 606
Percentage change, 282
Perkowski, Jack, 286
Permanent trade-off between unemployment and inflation, 518
Perón, General Juan, 542
Perot, Ross, 185, 186
Personal income, 220
Peru
child labor, 184
monetary policy, 432, 433
Petrin, Amil, 100
Phelps, Edmund, 519, 520, 521
Phillips, A.W., 516, 517
Phillips curve, 516–517, 518–520, 526, 530, 532–533, 540, 606
Physical capital, 15
Pie chart, 22
Pistorio, Pasquale, 590
Planned inventories, 363
Planned investment (*I*), 330, 331, 340–341
Poland
inflation targeting, 463
Policy channels, 562
Policy targets, 442, 468
Portfolio investments, 589
Portugal
gains from trade, 172
Positive analysis, 12, **13,** 20, 111, 120, 187, 606
Positive and negative relationships, 26
Potential GDP, 269, 270, 378, 606
Potential real GDP, 348, 389
PPF. *See* production possibilities frontier
Prescott, Edward, 404, 500, 529
Present value, 152, **153,** 154, 155, 606
Price ceiling, 98, 105, 107, 109, 120, 122, 123, 606
Price floor, 98, 105, 106, 107, 109, 120, 606
Price level, 218, 244, 256, 281, 282, 358, 606
Price stability, 440
Primary markets, 138
Principal, 137
Principal-agent problem, 135, 136, 148, 149, 606
Private property, protection of, 50–51
Private saving, 272, 288, 558
Process technologies, 173
Procyclical policy, 460
Producer price index (PPI), 244, **247,** 256, 606
Producer surplus, 98, **101,** 102, 103, 108, 112, 120, 126, 127, 177, 606
Product markets, 46, 56
Product technologies, 173
Production function, 301
Production possibilities frontier, 34, 35, 36, 37, 40, 41, 46, 55, 56, 57, 58 606
Production without trade, 169
Productive efficiency, 9, 18, 606
Productivity, 309–311, 324, 382, 391
Productivity boom, 308–309
Productivity slowdown, 1973-1995, 307–308
Profit, 15, 134, 158
Property rights, 51, 52, 56 606
Protectionism, 184, 185, 192, 606
Public finance, 112
Public saving, 272, 288, 558
Public company accounting oversight board, 144
Purchasing power, 217
Purchasing power parity, 577, 578, 579, 592

Quader, Noorul, 318, 319
Quality bias, 246
Quantitiative analysis, 125–126
Quantititative estimate, 125, 368
Quantity demanded, 64, 606
Quantity equation, 427, 434
Quantity supplied, 73, 606
Quantity theory explanation of inflation, 428–429, 606
Quantity theory of money, 427–428, 434
Quotas, 178–179, 180, 181–182, 187, 190, **578, 606**

Raab, Michael, 54
Raashe, Robert H., 490
Radford, R.A., 409
Raff, Daniel M.G., 243
Ramey, Valerie A., 306
Rational, 5, 6, 18
Rational expectations, 404, 527, 528, 540, 606
Reagan, Ronald, 471, 534
Real business cycle model, 404–405, 529, 606
Real consumption, 334
Real exchange rate, 551, **556**–557, 566, 606
Real GDP, 215, 224, 606
calculating, 265, 266
fluctuations in, 284
movements in, 278
and the price level, effects of, 451–452
Real GDP per capita, 263, 294, 296, 299, 307, 314, 324
Real GDP *versus* nominal GDP, 215–218
Real interest rate, 249, 250, 256, 274, 335, 454, 522, 606
Real investment, 340
Real value, 373
Real variable, 247, 256
Real wage, 249
Recession, 204, 348–349, 384–385, 453–454, 606
Recession of 2001, 389–390, 393, 398, 438
Redburn, Tom, 193
Red Cross, 409
Reichsbank, 430
Rent ceiling, 108
Rent control, 96, 97, 107, 108, 109, 110, 111, 118, 119, 122, 123, 124, 125, 127, 128
Rent Stabilization Association, 118
Reparations, 430
Required reserve ratio, 416, 434
Required reserves, 416
Research and development, 305
Reserve requirements, 426–427
Reserves, 416, 434
Residential investment, 209
Retained earnings, 136, 148, 270
Revaluation, 598, 606
Revenue, 6, 14
Ricardo, David, 170, 192, 405
Ripken, Jr., Cal, 94
Risk, 271
Rodgers, T.J., 471
Romania
flat tax, adoption of, 498
Romer, Paul, 304, 320
Roosevelt, Franklin D., 492, 493
Rudnay, D'arcy, 538
Rule of 70, 266
Rule of law, 316, 319, 606
Rules strategy, 535, 540
Ryard, Thomas, 54

Samuelson, Paul A., 11, 12, 17, 66, 507, 519
Sarbanes-Oxley Act, 131, 144, 145, 148, 149
Sargent, Thomas, 404, 431, 527, 528, 532, 540
Saving and investment equation, 559, 560, 566, 606
Sazxabami, Yoko, 181
Scarcity, 4, 7, 34, 108, 606
Schmitz, Jr., James A., 325
Schmüeckle, Rainer, 202
Schulte, Eric, 469
Schumpeter, Joseph, 305
Schwartz, Anna, 403
Scientific method, 11
Scrooge, Ebenezer, 274
Seasonal unemployment, 238, 256
Secondary markets, 138
Securities and Exchange Commission, 147
Securities dealers, 137
Seinfeld, Jerry, 234
Sen, Surya, 194
Separation of ownership from control, 135, 148, 606
September 11, 2001, 93, 452
Serbia
flat tax, adoption of, 498
Services, 14, 209, 211
Shandu, Monica, 193
Shareholders, 134
Shiller, Robert J., 522, 542, 543
Shiue, Carol, 295, 296
Short-run aggregate supply, 516
Short-run aggregate supply curve (*SRAS*), 372, 380–381, 383, 384, 398, 607
Short-run effect, 387
Short-run macroeconomic equilibrium, 385
Short-run Phillips curve, 521, 523, 524, 527, 528–529
Short-run trade-off between unemployment and inflation, 516–522
Short-term nominal rate of interest, 447
Shortages, 78–79, 90, 108, 123, 607
Simple deposit multiplier, 419–420, 422, 434, 607
Singapore
free market, gains from, 48
real GDP per person, 226
Skidelsky, Robert, 259
Slaughter, Matthew, 16
Sloan, Alfred, 349
Slope of lines, 23, 25
Slovakia
flat tax, adoption of, 498
Smith, Adam, 48, 49, 56, 59, 60, 92, 405
Smoot-Hawley Tariff, 182, 354, 597
Social insurance programs, 241
Social Security, 476–477, 502, 503
Social Security Tax, impact of, 116–117
Soft landing, 141
Sole proprietorships, 132, 133, 134, 148, 607
Solis, Fred, 254
Solow, Robert, 304, 519
Sony, 52, 175
South Africa
average annual growth rate, 269
inflation targeting, 463
South Korea
average annual growth rate of real GDP, 313
exports and imports as a percentage of GDP, 166
exports to China, 17
inflation targeting, 463
real GDP per person, 226
Soviet Union
centrally planned economy, 8
economic collapse, 302, 303
flat tax, adoption of, 498
Sowell, Thomas, 20
Spain
inflation rate, 464
inflation targeting, 463
unemployment rates, 242
Specialization, 172

Speculative attacks, 584
Speculators, 554, 566
Sri Lanka
  Tsunami, effects of the, 38
Srinivasan, T.N., 12
Stabilizing the economy, role in, 485–487
Stagflation, 388, 607
Stagnation, 363
Stalin, Joseph, 405
Statistical discrepancy, 549
Statistics Canada, 222, 223
Stein, Herbert, 542
Stern, Robert M., 184
Stewart, Jay, 235
Sticky wages and prices, 381
Stock and bond markets, 137, 148, 288
Stock prices, 156
Stockholders' equity, 158, 607
Stocks, 136, 137, 139, 152, 155, 270
Store of value, as, 410
Stringer, Kenneth, 88
Structural relationship, 518, 540
Structural unemployment, 239, 256
Subsidies, 106
Substitutes, 68, 69
Substitutes of production, 76
Substitution bias, 246
Substitution effect, 67, 607
Sugar quota, 164, 178, 179, 181, 184, 185, 187, 193
Summers, Lawrence, 58, 243, 464
Summers, Robert, 269, 313
Supply
  change in supply *versus change in quantity supplied, 76–77, 90*
  expected future prices, 76
  graphing equations, 125–126
  individual supply, 74
  inputs, price of, 75–76
  Law of supply, 74, 90
  market supply curve, 74
  prices of substitutes, role of, 76
  quantity of firms in the market, 76
  Quantity supplied, 73
  role of, 73
  shifting the supply curve, 75, 77
  shifts in supply over time, 84
  shifts in a curve versus movements along a curve, 86–87
  substitutes of production, 76
  Supply Curve, 73
  supply schedule, 73
  Technological change, 76
Supply chain management, 349
Supply curve, 73, 607
Supply schedule, 73
Supply shock, 383, 387–388
Supply-side economics, 496, 498–499, 500, 504
Surdam, David G., 94
Surpluses, 78–79, 90
Sweden
  inflation targeting, 463
Switzerland
  average annual growth rate of real GDP, 313
  inflation rate, 464
Sylla, Richard, 268

T-Account, 417–419, 421
Taiwan
  exports to China, 17
Tang, Christopher S., 69
Tangent line, 27
Tanzania
  average annual growth rate, 269
Tariffs, 164, 177–178, 181–182, 185, 187, 189, 190, 197, 578
Tax incidence, 112–113, 114, 116, 120
Tax multiplier, 483, 504, 510
Tax rates, effect of changes in, 483
Tax reform, economic effect of, 498–499
Tax simplification, 497
Tax wedge, 496, 504
Taxes
  buyers *versus sellers, 115–116*
  economic impact of, 112, 120
  effect on economic efficiency, 112, 114–115
  excess burden of the tax, 112
  social security tax, impact of, 116–117
  tax incidence, 112–113, 114, 116, 120
Taylor, John, 461, 468
Taylor Rule, 461–462, 468, 535
Technological change, 76, 267, 299, 301, 306–307, 309, 324
Technology, 14, 173, 324
Technology shocks, 529
Temporary assistance for needy families, 241
Terms of trade, 169, 607
Tesar, Linda, 424
Thailand
  child labor, 184
  exports to China, 17
  Tsunami, effects ofthe, 38
Thalia, 70
Thornton, Daniel L., 490
Ticker symbol, 139
Tight monetary policy, 456
Time-series graph, 22, 23
Tokoyo Stock Exchange, 137
Toll, Bruce, 438
Toll, Robert, 438, 450
Tongyao, Yin, 286
Top management, 134, 145, 148
Total benefit, 102
Total percentage change, 297
Total production, measures of, 221
Total revenue, 28
Toyoda, Sakichi, 50
Trade, 40–41, 42, 43, 162, 168–169, 170–172, 173
Trade Adjustment Assistance Program, 173
Trade flows, 548
Trade-offs, 7, 10, 34, 38, 56
Trade rounds, 182
Trade secret, 305
Trade surplus, 546
Trading desk, 425
Transfer payments, 207, 220, 333, 365
Treadway, Phil, 570
Treasury bills and their interest rates, 446–447
Twin-deficit hypothesis, 503, 560–561

Ukraine
  flat tax, adoption of, 498
Unanticipated inflation, 253
Underground economy, 212, **213,** 224, 582
Unemployment
  cyclical unemployment, 239
  frictional unemployment, 238–239
  full employment, 239
  full-employment rate of unemployment, 239
  natural rate of unemployment, 239
  seasonal unemployment, 238
  structural unemployment, 239
Unemployment insurance, 240
Unemployment insurance payments, 241
Unemployment rate, 230, 231, 232, 256, 539
  annual unemployment rate, u.s., 238
  average rates, 1995–2004, 242
  calculation, 231–232
  challenges to measurement, 233
  demographic groups, for, 235
  government policies, 240–241
  international comparisons, 241
  length of unemployment, 235, 236
  social insurance programs, 241
  unemployment insurance, 240
  unemployment insurance payments, 241
Unilateral elimination of tariffs and quotas, 181–182
United Automobile Workers, 381, 382, 520, 521
United Kingdom
  economic prosperity and health, relationship of, 264
  inflation targeting, 463
  international trade, role of, 165
  multinational corporations, 196
  unemployment rates, 242
United States
  agricultural markets and price floors, 105, 106
  autarky, 176
  average annual growth rate of real GDP, 313
  bilateral agreements, 188–189
  China's economic growth, effect of, 16–17
  Chinese automobile industry, 286–287
  comparative advantage, 44–45, 46, 162–163, 168, 169, 170, 174–175
  components in GDP, 211
  consumer price index, 244
  consumption and income, 336
  dumping, 186
  economic growth, 306–307
  economic prosperity and health, relationship of, 264
  economic recovery 2003–2004, 393
  employment rates, 392
  employment status, 231
  exports and imports as a percentage of GDP, 166
  federal budget deficit, 491, 495, 502–503
  federal funds rate targeting, 449
  federal reserve districts, 425
  firms, types of, 132, 134
  fiscal policy, 492–493
  flat tax, adoption of, 497–498
  free market, gains from, 48
  free trade, 175
  General Agreement on Tariffs and Trade, 182
  government expencitures, 475, 476
  government purchases, 342–343
  government revenue, 478
  housing "bubble", 450–451
  infltion rate, 441, 464
  inflation targeting, 463
  intellectual property rights, 51
  labor force participaton rates, 234
  market economy, 8
  mixed economy, 8–9
  monetary policy, 455, 466–467, 531
  money supply, 413
  multinational corporations, 196
  NAFTA, 185–186
  nominal and real interest rates, 250
  outsourcing, 166–167
  productivity growth, 309–310, 392
  productivity slowdown, 307–308
  quotas, effects of, 178
  real consumption, 334
  real GDP per capita, growth in, 263, 278, 284
  real GDP per person, 226
  real investment, 340
  recession of 2001, effect of 281, 283, 389–390, 391
  September 11, 2001 terrorits attacks, 452–453
  total production and total income, 221
  trade, role of, 165
  Tsunami, effects of the, 38
  unemployment rates, 235, 238, 242
  World War II, economic effects of, 214–215
Unit of account, 410, 581
Unlimited liability, 132, 148
Upton, Emory, 514
Upton, Frederick, 514
Upton, Louis, 514
Urata, Shujiro, 181
Uruguay
  monetary policy, 432
U.S. Army, 20
U.S. Department of Agriculture, 84
U.S. Department of Commerce, 401
U.S. Department of Labor, 230

Value added, 211, 224
Variables, 90
Varian, Hal R., 194
Velocity of money (*V*), 427, 434
Venture capital firms, 311
Volatility, 139
Volcker, Paul, 424, 440, 462, 530–531, 532, 534, 540
Voluntary exchange, 9, 17
Voluntary export restraint, 178, 190

Waldfogel, Joel, 110, 111
Walker, Jim, 322
Wascher, William, 107
Wassman, Dan, 194
Wealth, 334
Wealth effect, 373
Wechsler, Henry, 92
Weingast, Barry R., 296
Weir, Margaret, 486
Weisberg, Jacob, 118, 119
Wessel, David, 58, 506, 541, 569, 593
Whiterner, Catherine Evans, 174
Wilhelm Ii, Kaiser, 430
Will, George F., 123
Willett, Thomas D., 601
Williams, Jenny, 92
Williamson, Samuel H., 263
World Bank, 316
World price, 175, 177
World Trade Organization (WTO), 182, 183, 186, 190, 192, 597
Wright Brothers, 14

Xioping, Deng, 292

Yates, Buford, 150
Young, Alwyn, 268
Yun, Lawrence, 469

Zedong, Mao, 9, 292, 434
Zélie, Mademoiselle, 435
Ziebart, Wolfgang, 590

CREDITS

Photo

Chapter 1, *page 3,* Michel Setboun, Corbis/Bettmann; *page 12,* Sherwin Castro/Reuters, Landov LLC.

Chapter 2, *page 33,* BMW of North America, LLC; *page 38,* AP Wide World Photos; *page 47,* Corbis/Bettmann; *page 50,* SuperStock, Inc.; *page 52,* S.I.N., Corbis/Bettmann.

Chapter 3, *page 63,* AP Wide World Photos; *page 69,* David Young-Wolff, PhotoEdit; *page 70,* Michael Newman, PhotoEdit; *page 73,* Kathleen Olson; *page 82,* AFP, Getty Images, Inc.-Agence France Presse.

Chapter 4, *page 97,* Rudi Von Briel, PhotoEdit; *page 100,* AP Wide World Photos; *page 107,* Laima Druskis, Pearson Education/PH College; *page 110,* Zefa/N. Guegan, Masterfile Corporation; *page 117,* Bill Aron, PhotoEdit.

Chapter 5, *page 131,* Kim Kulish, Corbis/Bettmann; *page 133,* Ed Pritchard, Getty Images Inc.-Stone Allstock; *page 139,* Jeffrey Brown, Aurora & Quanta Productions Inc.; *page 141,* David McIntyre, Black Star.

Chapter 6, *page 163,* Burke/Triolo, Getty Images, Inc–Brand X Pictures; *page 166,* Corbis/Bettmann; *page 174,* Ron Sherman, Ron Sherman, Photographer; *page 184,* Pallava Bagla, Corbis/Sygma; *page 186,* AP Wide World Photos; *page 198,* The Image Works.

Chapter 7, *page 203,* Gary Moon; *page 210,* Diane Bondareff / Bloomberg News/Landov LLC; *page 213,* John Maier, Jr./The Image Works; *page 215,* Getty Images Inc.-Hulton Archive Photos; *page 218,* Chris Salvo/Getty Images, Inc.-Taxi.

Chapter 8, *page 229,* Tim Boyle/ Getty Images, Inc. Liaison; *page 234,* NBC TV/Picture Desk, Inc./ Kobal Collection; *page 240,* Tannen Maury/The Image Works; *page 243,* Image Works/ Mary Evans Picture Library Ltd; *page 252,* Tom McCarthy/ PhotoEdit.

Chapter 9, *page 261,* Jim West/The Image Works; *page 264,* Earl & Nazima Kowall/CORBIS-NY; *page 268,* David Reed/Panos Pictures; *page 274,* Getty Images Inc.–Hulton Archive Photos; *page 279,* AP Wide World Photos.

Chapter 10, *page 293,* Xin Lei/Imaginechina /ZUMA Press/NewsCom; *page 295,* Styal Quarry Bank Mill/Dennis Gilbert/The National Trust Photolibrary; *page 298,* AP Wide World Photos; *page 302,* Corbis/Bettmann; *page 319,* AP Wide World Photos.

Chapter 11, *page 329,* AP Wide World Photos; *page 341,* Neema Frederic/Corbis/Sygma; *page 349,* Ed Kashi/CORBIS- NY: *page 355,* Minnesota Historical Society/Corbis.

Chapter 12, *page 371,* Caterpillar Inc.; *page 376,* Tony Freeman/ PhotoEdit; *page 392,* Catherine Karnow/Woodfin Camp & Associates; *page 405,* Corbis/ Bettmann.

Chapter 13, *page 407,* Larry Luxner/Luxner News, Inc.; *page 409,* Reg Speller/Getty Images Inc.–Hulton Archive Photos; *page 412,* Reuters/Russell Boyce/ Corbis/Reuters America LLC; *page 424,* Alejandro Kaminetzky/ Reuters/Corbis/Reuters America LLC; *page 431,* Corbis/Bettmann.

Chapter 14, *page 439,* Corbis Royalty Free; *page 450,* Corbis Royalty Free; *page 452,* Reuters/Larry Downing/Corbis/Reuters America LLC; *page 454,* Tom Wagner/Corbis/SABA Press Photos, Inc.; *page 459,* AP Wide World Photos.

Chapter 15, *page 473,* Joe Raedle/ Getty Images, Inc. Liaison; *page 477,* Paddy Eckersley/ImageState/ International Stock Photography Ltd.; *page 489,* Tom Wagner/ Corbis/SABA Press Photos, Inc.; *page 492,* AP Wide World Photos; *page 498,* JLP/Jose L. Pelaez/ CORBIS-NY.

Chapter 16, *page 515,* AP Wide World Photos; *page 522,* Photonica/Getty Images; *page 525,* Richard Lord/The Image Works.

Chapter 17, *page 545,* Kyodo News; *page 551,* Helen King/ CORBIS- NY; *page 562,* AP Wide World Photos.

Chapter 18, *page 573,* AP Wide World Photos; *page 576,* AP Wide World Photos; *page 578,* Suan Van Etten/PhotoEdit; *page 582,* Fabrizio Bensch/Reuters/Corbis/ Reuters America LLC; *page 586,* Tom Wagner/Corbis/SABA Press Photos, Inc.

Text

Chapter 3, *page 84:* Steve W. Martinez, "Vertical Coordination in the Pork and Broiler Industries: Implications for Pork and Chicken Products," Agricultural Economics Report No. 777, April 1999.

Chapter 4, *page 107:* Thomas Sowell, *Applied Economics: Thinking Beyond Stage One*, New York: Basic Books, 2004, page 114.

Chapter 9, *page 264*: Stanley Lebergott, *The Americans: An Economic Record*, New York: W.W. Norton, 1984; Stanley Lebergott, *Pursuing Happiness: American Consumers in the Twentieth Century*, Princeton: Princeton University Press, 1993; page 268: Richard Sylla, "Financial Systems and Economic Modernization," *Journal of Economic History*, Vol. 62, No. 2, June 2002, pp. 277–292; *page 283*: Jeff Bailey, "Small Companies Prepare for the Good Times to Roll Again," *Wall Street Journal*, January 22, 2002.

Chapter 10, *pages 296–97*: Authors' calculations from data in Alan Heston, Robert Summers, and Bettina Aten, Penn World Table Version 6.1, Center for International Comparisons at the University of Pennsylvania (CICUP), October 2002; *page 297*: United Nations Development Programme, Human Development Report, 2005, New York: Oxford University Press, 2005; *page 305*: Joseph A. Schumpeter, *Capitalism, Socialism, and Democracy*, New York: Harper and Row, 1942, p. 132; *page 309*: Robert J. Gordon, "Five Puzzles in the Behavior of Productivity, Investment, and Innovation," in Augusto Lopez-Claros and Xavier Sala-i-Martin, eds., *The Global Competitiveness Report 2003–04*, New York and Oxford: Oxford University Press, 2004, pp. 117–135; *page 310*: Executive Office of the President, *Economic Report of the President, 2003*, Washington, DC: USGPO, 2003, Chapter 3; *page 319*: Edward L. Glaeser and Claudia Goldin, eds., *Corruption and Reform: Lessons from American History*, Chicago: University of Chicago Press, 2006.

Chapter 11, *page 334*: Martin Lettau and Sydney Ludvigson, "Understanding Trend and Cycle in Asset Values: Reevaluating the Wealth Effect on Consumption," *American Economic Review*, Vol. 94, No. 1, March 2004, p. 277.

Chapter 13, *page 408*: Jeremy Atack and Peter Passell, *A New Economic View of American History from Colonial Times to 1940*, 2nd ed., New York: W.W. Norton, 1994, pp. 81–82.

Chapter 15, *page 500*: Edward Prescott, "Why Do Americans Work So Much More Than Europeans?" Federal Reserve Bank of Minneapolis *Quarterly Review*, Vol. 28, No. 1, July 2004, pp. 2–13, and Alberto Alesina, Edward Glaeser, and Bruce Sacerdote, "Work and Leisure in the U.S. and Europe: Why So Different?" National Bureau of Economic Research, Working Paper 11278, April 2005.

Chapter 16, *page 521*: Milton Friedman, "The Role of Monetary Policy," *American Economic Review*, Vol. 58, No. 1 (March 1968), 1–17.

Chapter Title	Chapter Opener	Making the Connection	An Inside Look
CHAPTER 1			
Economics: Foundations and Models	What Happens When U.S. Firms Move to China?	When Economists Disagree: A Debate over Outsourcing	How Does Economic Growth in China Affect Other Countries? Source: Economist
CHAPTER 2			
Trade-offs, Comparative Advantage, and the Market System	Managers Making Choices at BMW	Trade-offs and Tsunami Relief • Story of the Market System in Action, "I, Pencil" • Property Rights in Cyberspace: Napster, Kazaa, and iTunes	Choosing the Production Mix at BMW Source: WSJ
CHAPTER 3			
Where Prices Come From: The Interaction of Demand and Supply	How Hewlett-Packard Manages the Demand for Printers	Why Supermarkets Need to Understand Substitutes and Complements • Companies Respond to a Growing Hispanic Population • Estimating the Demand for Printers at Hewlett-Packard • The Falling Price of Large Flat-Screen Televisions	Hewlett-Packard Cuts PC Prices to Sell More Printers Source: WSJ
CHAPTER 4			
Economic Efficiency, Government Price Setting, and Taxes	Should the Government Control Apartment Rents?	The Consumer Surplus from Satellite Television • Price Floors in Labor Markets: The Minimum Wage • Does Holiday Gift Giving Have a Deadweight Loss? • Is the Burden of the Social Security Tax Really Shared Equally between Workers and Firms?	Dealing with Rent Control Source: Slate
CHAPTER 5			
Firms, the Stock Market, and Corporate Governance	Google: From Dorm Room to Wall Street	What's in a "Name"? Lloyd's of London Learns about Unlimited Liability the Hard Way • Following Ford's Stock and Bond Prices in the Financial Pages • A Bull in China's Financial Shop	Google's Initial Public Offering Source: WSJ
CHAPTER 6			
Comparative Advantage and the Gains from International Trade	Sugar Quota Drives U.S. Candy Manufacturers Overseas	Has Outsourcing Hurt the U.S. Economy? • Why Is Dalton, Georgia, the Carpet-Making Capital of the World? • The Unintended Consequences of Banning Goods Made with Child Labor • Has NAFTA Helped or Hurt the U.S. Economy?	The United States and Australia Reduce Trade Barriers Source: San Francisco Chronicle